Inn & Travel™

Published to promote the wide array of European-style B&B Inn lodging properties in the USA and Canada.

Bed & Breakfast Guest Houses & Inns of America®, the largest association of B&B Inns with over 15,000 innkeeper-members since 1986.

Cover Photograph Credits:

Cover: *Baywood Inn Bed & Breakfast, Ba*ywood Park, California by permission of Trisha Chasse' and photographer John Swain, Sain Photography

The information contained in this publication is prepared as accurately as possible from material provided by the innkeepers for the most part and is subject to change. Therefore, it is necessary to contact each property listed to confirm all of the information before making a reservation. All references to ratings or approvals of the properties by any agency is based upon information provided by the innkeeper and is not guaranteed by the author and publisher.

The responsibility for making a reservation rests solely between the guest or agent and innkeeper in terms agreeable to all parties regardless of any and all representations made in this publication. We declare and disclaim any liability for errors or omissions and our liability for any loss or damage to any party that might occur through the use of this publication.

© 1997 Marie Baiunco-Brindza, Editor/Publisher
All rights reserved. No part of this book may be reproduced or utilized in any manner whatsoever in either from or by any means, electronic or mechanical, including photocopying, recording, or by any information storage and retrieval system without written permission of the author other than brief excerpts for review purposes.

Eleventh Edition, 1997
Published since 1986

Published by:

BED & BREAKFAST
Guest Houses & Inns of America®

PO Box 38929 Memphis Tennessee 38183-0929
Tel 800-431-8258 901-755-9613 Fax: 901-758-0816
email: marieb@innandtravel.com
Internet Site: http://www.innandtravel.com

ISSN: 1056-8069   ISBN: 0-9629885-6-1 2995   SAN: 279-4436

This is a special edition, dedicated to the memory of a most loyal member of our staff and family, Tuffy, who passed away this year.

For the last seventeen years, Tuffy was an important member of our company.

He didn't miss one night of burning the midnight oil with us - ready to help and always on the alert. Nary a sound passed him by except in his declining years.

He greeted every visitor and guest as a family member and long remembered acquaintance.

And like all of us, his needs were few . . .

. . . just a few treats and pats on the head made his day.

While working diligently, he made time for our children, who grew up knowing him. He taught them to be considerate, thoughtful and compassionate - lessons they hold dear and practice today and hopefully will pass onto their children. The years of companionship and loyalty will be well-remembered by all.

CONTENTS

PREFACE . . . . I - IV
INTRODUCTION . . . . V - VIII

NEW ENGLAND - SECTION ONE

Innkeeper Articles 1-1

Descriptive Listings

    Connecticut 1-5

    Maine 1-11

    Massachusetts 1-35

    New Hampshire 1-75

    Rhode Island 1-94

    Vermont 1-102

Index Section . . . . 1-124 to 1-159

MID AMERICA - SECTION TWO

Innkeeper Articles 2-1

Descriptive Listings
- Delaware 2-7
- District of Columbia 2-9
- Illinois 2-10
- Indiana 2-16
- Iowa 2-20
- Kansas 2-23
- Kentucky 2-25
- Maryland 2-30
- Michigan 2-39
- Minnesota 2-51
- Missouri 2-54
- Nebraska 2-59
- New Jersey 2-59
- New York 2-66
- Ohio 2-83
- Pennsylvania 2-87
- West Virginia 2-112
- Wisconsin 2-114

Index . . . . 2-121 to 2-193

SOUTH - SECTION THREE

Innkeeper Articles 3-1

Descriptive Listings
    Alabama 3-6

    Arkansas 3-6

    Florida 3-14

    Georgia 3-34

    Louisiana 3-44

    Mississippi 3-54

    North Carolina 3-61

    Oklahoma 3-86

    South Carolina 3-87

    Tennessee 3-95

    Texas 3-104

    Virginia 3-119

Index . . . . 3-145 to 3-185

WEST COAST - SECTION FOUR

Innkeeper Articles 4-1

Descriptive Listings
- Alaska 4-11
- Arizona 4-14
- California 4-23
- Colorado 4-82
- Hawaii 4-100
- Idaho 4-102
- Montana 4-104
- Nevada 4-107
- New Mexico 4-109
- Oregon 4-119
- Utah 4-127
- Washington 4-130
- Wyoming 4-140

Index . . . . 4-142 to 4-197

CANADA - SECTION FIVE

Descriptive & Index Listings . . . . 5-1 to 5-9

CARIBBEAN - SECTION SIX

Descriptive & Index Listings 6-1

Display Ad Section . . . . End

PREFACE

Bed & Breakfast accommodations are thriving in the United States more than ever .... as American travelers discover the excitement of European-style Bed and Breakfasts, Guest Houses and Country Inns, right in their own backyard!! Long the ***accommodation of choice*** for Europeans, Bed and Breakfast accommodations are experiencing a phenomenal growth in the United States - beginning in the late 1980's and continuing today - offering travelers exciting lodging choices at every stop.

If you're unfamiliar with Bed & Breakfast accommodations - you have a whole new experience awaiting you by selecting a different inn on each trip if you like, whether your trip is for business, a family vacation or a nearby weekend get-away or for that *special occasion!* B&Bs are smaller and more intimate compared to commercial hotels. Guests feel like they're staying at a friend's or relative's home -rather than a motel. The typical property listed in this publication is small enough which means you truly become a family member - from the moment you arrive until you return. You'll meet all of the guests and the innkeepers, who jealously see to your every comfort. After-all, they are truly people who enjoy meeting each guest, swapping tales, exchanging stories and trading ideas. They are well-travelled too and understand the meaning of comfort while traveling. So a Bed & Breakfast is not just the warmth of a cozy evening fireplace in a friend's home or a complimentary sherry upon arrival ... but a feel of being home at every stop during your trip.

And what a variety of homes, castles, tepees and entire private islands from which to choose!! Bed and Breakfasts are generally a home with one or two "extra" bedrooms located anywhere from traditional suburban neighborhoods to rural farms. Guest Houses would be similar to "tourist homes" offering five to nine guest rooms and generally more extensively furnished and decorated, including more guest amenities, while a Country Inn, for our purposes, provides more personalized service in an intimate setting with fewer than thirty guest rooms. Boutique hotels have been added with this edition. Boutique hotels are larger in room size and are superbly staffed for attending to the guests every need and interest - the true meaning of innkeeping.

Just as each family is unique - so is each Bed and Breakfast - which is looked after with the loving attention of the owner/innkeeper - insuring each guest feels at home. Each innkeepers' interests are reflected in their Bed & Breakfast and you might meet a former olympic skier, politician, artists, dancers, sailing enthusiasts, antique buffs who will lead you to the "best buys", authors, writers, well-known photographers, museum curators ... along with doctors, lawyers and Indian chiefs .... and even Clint Eastwood, if he's in, at the *Eastwood Ranch* in Carmel California - a Bed & Breakfast. Each property represents a new adventure - as close as around the corner. Travelers can choose from an endless array of accommodations - allowing their imagination to run rampant. Spend a night in a tepee on a true Indian Reservation (offering a honeymoon special), all of San Francisco's night lights are outside your windows in a Francisco Bay lighthouse or choose the bedroom where celebrities such as Clark Gable and Carole Lombard and Jack and Jackie Kennedy honeymooned. Choose a luxury 100 foot yacht for a night or your own island off the Georgia Coast! For the adventuresome, a frontier cabin in Alaska without running water, phone or

©*Inn & Travel Memphis, Tennessee*

electricity - to the world's only underwater lodge off Key West Florida offering four guest rooms twenty fathoms below the sea - are ready for guests! Today, travelers can spend the night in the estates of famous families such as Bigelow, Palmolive, Stanley (Stanley steamer auto fame), William Wrigley and Barnum of the famous Barnum and Bailey Circus fame. If you're looking for a romantic oceanfront with candlelight dining - there are many along with TV and movie sets of leading programs and/or movies such as *On Golden Pond* (Holderness, New Hampshire listings), Alan Alda's *Four Seasons* (Edson Hill Manor, Stowe, Vermont), *Matlock* (Tranquil House, Maneto, North Carolina), *Knotts Landing* (The Cotten House in California) - or a great adventure for an exciting family vacation - new adventures await within this edition.

The Mansions (Barbara Streisand's a frequent guest) in San Francisco offers it's own certified ghost, a night of magic before dining and a five million dollar art and sculpture collection - to an Inn in Santa Fe, New Mexico called *Lightening Fields*, where guests spend the night in the center of a desert field surrounded with steel rods, designed to attract lightening strikes - providing an enlightening experience! For **"kids of all ages"**, *The Hugging Bear Bed & Breakfast* offers over four thousand teddy bears throughout the Inn. You'll find over 15,000 choices and innkeepers anxious to greet you .... providing years of enjoyable memories and adventures to share with friends.

One of the B's in Bed and Breakfast represents the guest rooms where innkeepers make every effort to see to your comfort. Canopy beds abound, four posters, brilliant brass, wicker and gorgeous antique heirlooms appear almost everywhere - while fitted with a handmade quilt or down comforters. In addition, many inns offer jacuzzi, evening turn-down service, complimentary evening sherry at bedside and a late night chocolate upon your pillow.

The second B in Bed and Breakfast is important to travelers too - and that represents breakfast, normally included in your room rate. Breakfast ranges from a continental or light breakfast to a sumptuous gourmet, four course meal featuring local specialties of grits in the South, fresh-picked strawberries or blue berries for your cereal or maple syrup you made the day before. You can frequently choose to have "breakfast in bed", before a winter's fire or on the veranda in spring and summer - often overlooking a flowering patio garden or a lush rolling meadow. And if you find a particular recipe to your liking -- your innkeeper will be thrilled to share it.

You'll find **best-selling cookbook author** Julee Rosso-Miller (*The Silver Palate, The Silver Palate Good Times Cookbook*) selecting and perhaps preparing your breakfast at the *Wickwood Country Inn* in Saugatuck, Michigan while in the beautiful Northwestern Montana mountains at *Huckleberry Hanna's Montana Bed and* Why are Bed and Breakfast's increasing in popularity? Because they are economical - an important factor to every traveler today. As commercial hotel room rates soar, travelers are learning B&Bs offer the **best value today** - especially during the midweek period. Business travelers save the most because Bed and Breakfast's offer weekday discounts or additional amenities - just when business travelers need the savings and "extras." If you travel midweek - you'll find B&B Inns a 20-50% better value for your lodging dollar.

Who should consider a Bed and Breakfast for their lodging needs? Easily everyone who travels! More than fifty percent of all Europeans stay only at Bed and Breakfasts for a good reason. Business travelers tired of the **same old hotel room** and suffering with the *same old hotel blues*. Even the *Wall Street Journal* in 1989 reported the trend of business travelers changing to Bed and Breakfast accommodations. Family vacationers can choose a waterfront, mountain top wooded log cabin or a farm with all the animals where their children can feed the chickens, geese and other animals while gathering fresh eggs for their breakfast; women traveling alone love the security and comfort B&Bs offer; honeymooners, family relocations, retirees, antique collectors, the parents of college-bound children .... just about every traveler will find a lodging to meet their needs in this guide .

Once you've decided to try a Bed and Breakfast ... you face the most difficult portion of the trip ... that of finding "just the right one". Since B&Bs have small advertising budgets they are not easily found and frequently their names are *highly guarded secrets passed on only to the best of acquaintances*. Therefore, guidebooks have developed into the leading source of information on B&Bs and probably offer the only means of maintaining your sanity during your search. Your choice of guidebooks is not easy since there are literally thousands of choices. Since you chose this guide, we'll be the first to let you know you have the most comprehensive, complete and accurate guide available. We can easily say that because our primary subscribers for years have been travel agents. Published since 1986, our publications have earned the reputation as the ***most complete reference available"*** from subscribers and book reviewers alike. This means you have the largest reference available of Bed and Breakfasts - with over 15,000 listings in the Index Section, compared to other national guides with two hundred to a several thousands listings. Secondly, you will find more extensive descriptions .... **so you'll know all of the details even before contacting the Bed and Breakfast** to make your reservation. Phone numbers change, fax numbers are added, 800 numbers become available --- continuous changes you need to have to make finding *just the right Bed & Breakfast* and enjoyable part of your trip ... or job if you're a travel agent.

This edition includes changes to help you enjoy your Bed and Breakfast experiences even more. More photographs and line drawings are included. New features include *Quality Assured (QA) Properties*. Properties noted with a QA symbol have been visited by company representatives who verified the accuracy of the descriptive information. The QA symbol is your assurance the innkeeper's concern. The *Inn & Travel Club*, a frequent travel club for guests is introduced with this edition. Now guests reveice points when staying at member B&Bs which can be redeemed for thousands of travel, personal or home gifts. Choose a cruise from Carnival Cruise Lines - free lodging - free dining - free gifts - all top end from companies such as Waterford Crystal to Jacuzzi - to Zenith and Sony - and even hot tubs from Cal Spa. You'll earn points fast since meals are included too - the only frequent travel club to include awards for dining. An application and information is included at the end of this book for travelers interested in joining.

This edition continues the tradition of meeting innkeepers across the United States through their travel articles, located at the beginning of each regional section. The

©*Inn & Travel Memphis, Tennessee*

articles offer ideas, suggestions and points of interest for travelers. Just as each Bed and Breakfast and town is different .... you'll find thousands of innkeepers with a common thread of hospitality, goodwill and a sincere interest in welcoming travelers to their communities. We know you will enjoy their articles and we hope you will stop and personally meet them.

One comment pertaining to a travel industry issue regarding descriptive information on properties appearing in Bed and Breakfast and other lodging publications. Member-innkeepers prepare their own listing descriptions in our publications for a number of reasons. Due to the large number of properties, it's impossible to visit and review each property and still produce quality publications. Secondly, innkeepers know their Bed & Breakfast, nearby activities and sights and their town better than anyone else - therefore, they have the best knowledge. How objective are they going to be? We have found them to be very objective - after all, unlike a reviewer or rating organization, they face each guest upon arrival and have to justify their glowing description if it is not deserved. Even professional travel writers and reviewers are subject to over and/or under statement - but they depart the next day and won't face arriving guests to justify their review. This publication contains a listing of accommodations following traditional European Bed & Breakfast-style properties across the United States and Canada. This information, we feel, benefits travelers by learning about the thousands of wonderful and beautiful Bed & Breakfasts overlooked by many publications that review properties.

Thank you for using this guide as a reference source for your many new adventures, acquaintances and friendships that develop during your travels. If you are pleased with the book, we would appreciate your telling friends and innkeepers you visit about us. It helps innkeepers to know which books are used by guests and travel agents. More importantly, it helps you too because more Bed and Breakfasts will include descriptions in future editions providing travelers a wider choice of lodgings for their next trip. If you know of a Bed & Breakfast, Guest House or Country Inn that is not included in this guide, we would appreciate your letting us know about them or letting the innkeeper know. Perhaps you'll find your favorite Bed and Breakfast listed in future editions, allowing other travelers to experience the same enjoyment they'll treasure in the years to come and share with others.

One added note our "plugged-in" readers. A CD-Rom version of this publication is available as well as an Internet Site. Electronic publications have the advantage of easily searching for and presenting properties in color and multimedia (sound and music). If you are interested in either of these two electronic publications, more information is available at the end of this book.

INTRODUCTION

The purpose of this guide is to provide travelers and travel agents with the most comprehensive, single reference source of current, accurate and complete information on Bed and Breakfast-type of accommodations throughout the United States, Canada and the Caribbean and to promote Bed and Breakfast accommodations to the traveling public. Over 3,000 new listings have been added to this edition, bringing the total to over 15,000. In addition, boutique hotels are now included, beginning with this edition.

The properties listed meet a criteria of the traditional European style B&Bs and Country Inns, that are host-owner operated, provide period, unique, antique, unusual or non-commercial decor and furnishings, and are licensed and insured. This guide had been prepared exclusively for travel agents since 1986 and provides complete information, adequate to determine if the particular property will meet your needs and interests - even before calling. Because this publication has been prepared for professional travel agents, information not found in other books is included, such as *toll-free 800 numbers, discount periods, money-saving packages, airport distances, reservation and cancellation policies* and much more.

Making a reservation at a Bed and Breakfast is the same as any hotel, the difference is that ***each property is different***, so a full understanding and description of the property is essential to assure a pleasant and enjoyable trip. Reputable innkeepers are just as interested as the guest in making sure there aren't any misunderstandings and that the Bed and Breakfast will exceed the guests' expectations. For the sake of clarity and a common understanding, the terms utilized are listed below.

BED & BREAKFAST RESERVATIONS

It just takes a few minutes to find ***"just the right B&B"*** anywhere in the USA by following a few steps. Since each Bed & Breakfast is unique, a complete description and understanding of the property is essential and time permitting when you call to make your reservation, we suggest your requesting the innkeeper to provide you with brochures for you to review before arriving. The brochures are beautifully prepared and the innkeepers are pleased to send one to you.

1. First, look into the ***Index Section*** which is an alphabetical list by state, city and Bed & Breakfast names.

2. If the B&B's name is **bolded**, look in the **Descriptive Section** for the Bed & Breakfast's name. This section is arranged alphabetically by state, city and Bed & Breakfast name.

3. Call the Bed and Breakfast you select to confirm the information listed and to make your reservation. Request that a brochure and reservation confirmation is sent to you.

4. You will find some listings without descriptions and the notation *"Refer to the same listing name under_____ city for a complete description."* **Cross-City Listings** indicate B&Bs in nearby towns.

One last note about reservations .... ***MAKE THEM EARLY!*** You've taken an excellent step in preparing yourself for your Bed and Breakfast travels by purchasing a guide book. Don't miss an opportunity to stay at your favorite Bed and Breakfast or in a favorite room by not planing ahead. Innkeepers are booked weeks, months and even years in advance for traditional holidays, weekends, vacation periods. Weekday periods are less hectic and you'll find better availability on shorter notice. But ... that may not be the case. Since you've taken the first step in planning your trip - book early.

INTERPRETING THE DESCRIPTIVE LISTINGS

RES TIME
This is the best time to call for making a reservation. When a time is not listed you can't go wrong calling between 8am and 8 pm.

SEASONAL
This indicates any period when the B&B is closed to guests. If NO is listed, this usually means guests are accepted year round. Some listings indicate RATES VARY which means the room rates vary by season and it is necessary to obtain more information from the innkeeper regarding their seasonal period rates.

ROOMS
The number of private and shared bath guest rooms are listed here. Listed beneath each category are the Single and Double occupancy rates for that room type. Usually a range of rates are quoted and the type of room and the appropriate rate needs to be confirmed with the innkeeper. The room rate will depend upon the amenities, size, decor and location of the room. So if you're looking for a pool side or ocean front room with a canopy bed, jacuzzi and fire place and so forth, the room will be priced accordingly.

PHONES/FAX
Phone numbers are listed (including 800's when available) along with fax numbers

PAYMENT
Cash, check, travelers check and specific credit cards accepted; confirm what credit cards are accepted since this frequently changes.

MEALS
The second "B" in B&B is breakfast which is usually (but not always) included in your room rate. Information concerning breakfast is included in the descriptive information. This information should be confirmed as well since innkeepers change the type and style of breakfast served. The definition of the various meals are understood to be:

Breakfast
Continental: Juice, hot beverage and pastry or breads
Continental Plus: The same as above but also includes choices of several breads, pastries and cold cereals
Full: The same as above plus eggs, meats, pancakes, waffles or other main entree
Gourmet: An unusual or different means of preparing a food dish, often a specialty of the innkeeper

EP European Plan indicates **NO** meals are included
MAP Modified European Plan includes breakfast and dinner
AP American Plan includes all three meals
FAM Family Style Dining Service pertains to how meals are served

DESCRIPTIVE SECTION

The listings in this section have been prepared by the innkeeper to describe their property, furnishings, decor, proximity to points of interest, local activities, their background, complimentary breakfast description and is intended to provide you with a flavor of the Bed and Breakfast. All B&Bs are not museums filled with antique furnishings and not all travelers are interested in staying in museums. Hopefully the descriptions will convey the uniqueness of each Bed & Breakfast.

Permitted
Children, pets, smoking and drinking have been listed *when they are permitted* by your hosts. When one of the categories is not listed, it means the hosts do not permit that activity. Staying at a Bed and Breakfast is like staying at a friend's home .... so you should always ask the host if they permit the particular activity if you're not sure.

Reservations
Check the reservation requirements before calling and confirm them with the innkeeper when calling because they are subject to change. Ask for a **written confirmation from the innkeeper** to eliminate possible errors.

Airport
The name and distance/s to nearby airports is listed for guest's convenience.

Packages
Types of packages available are listed when available and provide excellent savings for travelers.

Discounts
Since each Bed and Breakfast has their own discount policies, check when calling.

Brochure
Each innkeeper has brochures, write-ups, news articles, maps and other material they gladly provide guests. Request a brochure when making your reservation.

©Inn & Travel Memphis, Tennessee

Quality Assurance

Each property noted with a QA symbol indicates the property's description has been verified as accurate by a company representative visiting the property. A QAR notation indicates that a quality assurance visit has been requested by the innkeeper but at the time of publication, a company representative has not yet visited the property.

ITC (Inn & Travel Club Member)

Inn & Travel Club member property. If you are a guest member of the *Inn & Travel Club*, you will earn points for each net dollar of lodging or dining expenditure at the property. When booking your reservation, you need to indicate to the innkeeper that you are an *Inn & Travel Club* member.

DESCRIPTIVE SECTION NOTATIONS

COM This notation is applicable only for travel agents.

[I10IPTX1-1111] This group of letters is for the author's and inkeeper's information

INDEX SECTION NOTATIONS

A group of letters are included after the phone number in the Index Section. The group of letters are enclosed in brackets [ ] and have the following meaning.

Y/G/U/S = These letters are applicable only for travel agents

QA or QAR = Quality Assured Property /Quality Assurance Requested

ITC = Inn & Travel Club Member Property
Yes or No

We hope you enjoy using this guide book and the many pleasurable trips it brings for you. If you enjoy the book we hope you will share it and let other travelers know about it *and especially innkeepers*. Innkeepers are always anxious to know how you learned about them to decide which publications they should list information about their properties for travelers.

Travel agents have relied upon our publications for over ten years. This is the *only publication* to address your special needs - including a **commission guarantee program**. This and other special programs are available only to travel agents and when the guide book is purchased directly from Inn & Travel. Travel agents can call 800-431-8258 for more details and information.

New England

S___pring___ Peaceful fields with a haze of dew in early morning and a deer or two standing still; Tiny buds emerging on branches covering sleepy valleys with pale greens; Fresh mountain air and flowers everywhere; hiking through woods and wondering at the breathtaking views from the mountain tops.

S___ummer___ Cool mornings and warm afternoons; white, sandy beaches; babbling brooks; blue lakes; majestic mountains; art shows; antiques, auctions; summer country fairs; swimming, boating, fishing.

f___all___ Glorious colors everywhere as the green leaves turn to gold, red,yellow; pumpkins, hot cider, fall festivals; biking along winding roads and discovering the beauty and simplicity of a timeless world.

W___inter___ Blankets of snow covering sleeping villages, still lakes, silent brooks, shining mountains; alpine and cross-country skiing, snowmobiling, sleigh rides, ice skating; warm fireplaces at day end.

Marie A Kauk, Innkeeper
Hilltop Acres
Wentworth New Hampshire

Marblehead Massachusetts

Marblehead, an historic sea coast village on Boston's North Shore, has much to offer. Explore it's patriotic past as reflected in period architecture and historic sites. Enjoy the natural beauty of a rocky coastline studded with beaches and parks overlooking picturesque Marblehead harbor. Watch lobstermen pulling their traps, elegant yachts setting sail and small boats rounding race buoys. Walk charming old footpaths past lovely homes and gardens of traditional New England character. Browse the antique

©Inn & Travel Memphis, Tennessee

shops, art galleries and boutiques which offer treasures special to Marblehead. Relax over a bowl of New England clam chowder, feast on a boiled lobster or enjoy a gourmet dinner at local restaurants, offering both casual and elegant dining.

At *Abbot Hall*, the famous painting *The Spirit of '76* can be viewed. The *Jeremiah Lee Mansion* is an example of Georgian architecture with period furnishings. The *King Hooper Mansion*, an early 18th century mansion with slave quarters and a ballroom, now serves as an art gallery sponsored by the Marblehead Arts Association. Summer concerts are held at *Crocker Park*, overlooking the harbor and Marblehead Neck. *Fort Sewall* was built in the 1600's to ward-off pirates. Experience the unique character of Marblehead by staying in one of its many charming Bed and Breakfast homes.

Susan finds time to handle all the chores of operating her bed and breakfast while maintaining a schedule of activities ranging from dressmaking to competitive swimming - and everything in between. She admits to being *"a domestic person. I love my home and everything that goes along with making it a welcoming place to be, including baking, decorating and arranging flowers".* Rising early to greet guests and prepare breakfast isn't a problem - because she will have already been jogging or biking. Most days she can be found in a local pool training for Master's swim meets. She is a top-ten ranked national swimmer in over eight events and holds many New England records. Today, Susan is enthusiastic about her home, Marblehead and welcoming new guests to experience the adventure of visiting New England.

Susan Livingston, Innkeeper
Harborside House
Marblehead, Massachusetts

Boothbay Harbor Maine

The rock-bound coast of Maine and Boothbay Harbor is a popular destination for visitors yearning for fresh sea air, scenic lighthouses, lobsters and boating adventures. Popular since the turn-of-the-century, the Boothbay Region combines the economies of a working fishing village and a resort area.

In Spring, Summer and Fall, boat trips on big boats, little boats, sail boats, fishing boats - or your own rented boat, will transport you to offshore islands for hiking and picnicking or seal and puffin watching. Others will cruise along the rocky and spruce-treed coast to see lighthouses and off-shore for deep sea fishing. Golf, swimming, tennis, bird-watching, art galleries, antique shops, maritime museums add to the many activities in the Region. Within an hour's drive are white sandy beaches and shopping outlets including the famous LL Bean. In summer, yachts and windjammers visit the Harbor adding color and excitement for boat watchers. In winter, a quieter atmosphere prevails. The local country club is a great place to cross country ski, and West Harbor Pond finds ice skaters enjoying the crisp, clean air.

Boothbay Harbor is a working lobster fishing village. The lobstermen bring in the daily catch to local wharves where as you watch the sun set over the Harbor, you can relish the tender morsels dipped in butter. These activities can be seen from the shore near the Fisherman's Memorial or at many of the accommodations which are located right on the shore. You'll love Boothbay Harbor.

Diane Campbell, Innkeeper
Anchor Watch Bed & Breakfast
Boothbay Harbor Maine

Newport Rhode Island

To the visitor,
Newport offers the perspective of an island,
the excitement of a port,
world-class,
wealth,
and a blend of contemporary and past delights.

The town represents two eras in American history - downtown reflects the original 17th Century community and the mansions on Bellevue Avenue show the extravagance and spectacle of the Gilded Age.

Newport has more Colonial-era buildings than any city in the United States. Washington Square was the center of Colonial Newport. One end of the square is the Brick Market (1762), currently being restored as a museum. The other end of the square is the Old Colony House (1739). It was from the balcony of the Colony House that Rhode Island issued its own Declaration of Independence on May 4, 1776. Next to the Colony House on Broadway is the Wanton-Lyman-Hazard House, Newport's oldest house built in the 1690's. About a block up the hill from there is the Touro Synagogue built in 1759 and the oldest continuously operating synagogue in the U.S. Over on the Point, another historic area, is the Hunter House which served as headquarters for the French naval forces in 1780. Visit The Hunter House to see it's priceless collection of Townsend-Goddard furniture.

Strung along Bellevue Avenue are the famous Gilded Age Mansions. These are the magnificent summer *cottages* built by people like the Vanderbilts and the Astors. When visiting the Mansions, it is worth strolling along the Cliff Walk, a 3-1/2 mile footpath, which runs behind the Mansions and overlooks the ocean. Ocean Drive, a 10 mile drive around the south end of the island, has beautiful picturesque ocean. Stop for a picnic at Brenton Point Park.

If all this sightseeing has tired you out, you can take a relaxing boat ride on the Bay or visit one of several sandy beaches. Newport has something to offer everyone regardless of age, interests or time of year.

Sam & Rita Roger, Innkeepers
The Melville House
Newport, Rhode Island

Sandwich, Massachusetts

first town on Cape Cod

The town of Sandwich was founded in 1637, the first town on Cape Cod, and one of the oldest communities in America. It is picturesquely situated along historic Route 6A, the King's Highway, on the north shore of Cape Cod, at the eastern end of Cape Cod Canal.

A tour of the town might begin at the Village green and Town Hall Square, where you will find the Sandwich Glass Museum, First Church, with its *"Christopher Wren"* steeple, the Dexter Grist Mill, Thornton Burgess Museum, Hoxie House, oldest house on the Cape, Town Hall, itself of historical interest, and, a block away, the Doll Museum.

Heritage Plantation, nearby, maintains more than a thousand varieties of trees, shrubs and flowers on the grounds where Charles Dexter developed the internationally recognized Dexter rhododendrums. The plantation is also known for its three museums of Americana. The Antique Car Museum, in a Shaker round barn replica, houses forty antique and classic cars, including a stunning 1930 Dusenburg Tourester, once owned by Gary Cooper, and President William Howard Taft's White Steamer, the first official White House automobile. The Art and Military Museums display vintage treasures, including a restored and running 1912 carousel. The beach and Cape Cod Canal are within a mile of the
Village.

Elaine Dickson, Innkeeper
Capt. Ezra Nye House Bed & Breakfast
Sandwich, Massachusetts

National Edition   **Connecticut**

Eastover Farm B&B   Rt 132 Guilds Hollow Rd 06751   **Bethlehem CT**
Mr Mrs Erik Hawvermale   **Tel:** 203-266-5740

Gracious colonial c1773 on seventy acres of manicured lawns with farm animals, close to White Flower Farm, nature preserves, and plenty of New England hospitality from these lovely hosts. Continental breakfast included. **Seasonal:** No **Brochure:** Yes **Permitted:** Children **Payment**

Terms: Check MC/V [C11ACCT-921] **COM** Y **ITC Member:** No

Rates: Pvt Bath 7
Single $ 70.00
Double $ 80.00

Jared Cone House   25 Hebron Rd 06043   **Bolton CT**
Mrs Cinde Smith   **Tel:** 203-643-8538

Right off the Village Green is this colonial residence c1790's with spectacular views, fire-places, and plenty of hospitality for relaxing in the traditional New England style. Full breakfast included in rate. Close to plenty of fine shopping, antiquing, fine dining, and tennis, golf, and swimming. **Seasonal:** No **Reservations:** One night's deposit required at res time, refund if cancelled 10 days prior to arrival date. **Brochure:** Yes **Permitted:** Children, smoking **Payment Terms:** Check [C03ACCT-922] **COM** Y **ITC Member:** No

Rates: Pvt Bath 3
Single $ 55.00
Double $ 65.00

Four Roses Guest Inn   34 Summer Place 06011   **Bristol CT**
Wilma Flint   **Tel:** 203-572-0211

Prefect country setting for this New England farmhouse c1755 with original stone walls, fireplaces in every room, wood floors, with Early American furnishings. Your chance to really taste the frontier life! Wonderful homemade breakfast with original recipes handed down thru generations of Americans. Close to outdoor activities including boating, canoeing, fishing, golf on championship courses, and all winter sports within thirty minutes. Full breakfast included. **Seasonal:** No

CIRCA 1755 FARMHOUSE

Reservations: 50% deposit for length of stay required in 5 days, 10 day cancellation notice for refund. **Brochure:** Yes **Permitted:** Children, limited pets, and smoking **Payment Terms:** Check MC/V [X02BFCT-6585] **COM** U **ITC Member:** No

Rates: Pvt Bath 6
Single $ 65.00
Double $ 85.00

Riverwind Inn   209 Main St 06417   **Deep River CT**
Barbara Barlow   **Tel:** 203-526-2014
                                                                    Res Times 8am-8pm

Delightful setting for a restored 1850 Inn furnished with antique pieces, family heirlooms, and handicrafts in country theme. Fireplace in dining room, full New England breakfast includes Smithfield ham and other specialties of the hostess. **Seasonal:** No **Brochure:** Yes **Permitted:** Smoking, social drinking **Payment Terms:** Check MC/V [C11ACCT-929] **COM** Y **ITC Member:** No

Rates: Pvt Bath 4
Single $ 80.00
Double $ 90.00

Homestead Inn   420 Field Point Rd 06830   **Greenwich CT**
*Lessie Davison/Nancy Smith   **Tel:** 203-869-7500 **Fax:** 203-869-7500
                                                                    Res Times 8am-10pm

---

©*Inn & Travel Memphis, Tennessee*

Connecticut National Edition

Nestled on three acres of ancient maples and oaks is this unique c1799 homestead Colonial with Victorian cupola and wraparound porch additions features - just a stroll from Long Island Sound waters. Completely restored and featured in articles in *"Fortune'* 10/81, *"Colonial Homes"* 10/86, and *"Interior Design"* 4/80, are three charming buildings offering decor that includes antiques mostly with whimsical flair!! Nothing has been overlooked here, eg., beds have two pillows, one hard and one soft. Award-winning French dining on the premises by Chef Jacques Thiebeult offering extraordinary soups, diverse entrees, and an array of pure French Delight!! Close to Island Beach for short boat trips or antique shopping, guests are sure to find many points of interest. Inn is available for weddings and includes a honeymoon suite too!! **Seasonal:** No **Reservations:** Credit card to hold room, 24 hour cancellation for full refund **Permitted:** Limited children, smoking, and drinking **Conference:** Perfect setting for relaxing and exquisite business and social meetings **Languages:** German, French, Spanish **Payment Terms:** AE/DC/MC/V [A05ACCT-936] **COM** Y **ITC Member:** No

Award-wining chef

Rates:	Pvt Bath 23
Single	$ 90.00
Double	$ 105-165.00

Shore Inne 52 E Shore Rd 06340 Groton Long Point CT
Helen Ellison Tel: 203-536-1180
Res Times 8-8pm

Spectacular view of the coastal waters from this gracious Inn located on the water's edge. Relax all day long by visiting the local attractions, Mystic Seaport (3 miles), Marine Life Aquarium, Fort Griswold, or stroll along the beaches, fish, play tennis, golf. Or you can relax in the TV room, library, or sun room. Continental breakfast included. **Seasonal:** Open: Apr-Oct **Brochure:** Yes **Permitted:** Children, smoking, drinking **Payment Terms:** Check MC/V [C11ACCT-939] **COM** Y **ITC Member:** No

Rates:	Pvt Bath 3	Shared Bath 4
Single	$ 58.00	$ 52.00
Double	$ 62.00	$ 57.00

Old Mill Inn Hartford CT
Phyllis & Ralph Lumb Tel: 203-763-1473
Res Times 7am-10pm

Refer to same listing name under Somersville, CT for a complete description. **Seasonal:** No **Payment Terms:** Check [M01DPCT-6549] **COM** Y **ITC Member:** No

Rates:	Pvt Bath 3	Shared Bath 2
Single	$ 60.00	$ 50.00
Double	$ 60.00	$ 50.00

Tollgate Hill Inn Rt 202 & Tollgate Rd 06759 Litchfield CT
Frederick Zivic Tel: 860-567-4545 Fax: 860-567-8397
Res Times 8am-7pm

Listed on the *National Register of Historic Places* is this completely restored Inn, formerly the Captain Bull Tavern, c1745. Relive 1700's with pine paneled walls, dutch door fireplace, and a former historic schoolhouse next door that contains four of the guest rooms. Continental breakfast included. **Seasonal:** No **Reservations:** Deposit requested at reservation time with refund if cancelled & prior notice given **Brochure:** Yes **Permitted:** Children, pets, drinking **Payment Terms:** Check [C11ACCT-949] **COM** Y **ITC Member:** No

Historic Register

Rates:	Pvt Bath 10
Single	$ 85-95.00
Double	$ 85-95.00

1-6 ©*Inn & Travel Memphis, Tennessee*

National Edition   **Connecticut**

| **Tidewater Inn** | 949 Boston Post Rd 06443 | **Madison CT** |

Jean Foy & Rich Evans   **Tel:** 203-245-8457 **Fax:** 203-318-0265
                                                                                Res Times 8:30-8:30

The T*idewater Inn* is located in the village of Madison on the Connecticut shoreline. Decorated with a mixture of antiques and estate furniture, this former 1880's stagecoach stop offers a cozy and elegant atmosphere. Inside, the sitting room and two of the guest rooms have wood burning fireplaces. Outside, guests can relax in the English garden. All nine guest rooms provide private baths, TV, a/c and outgoing telephones. A full breakfast is served each morning. Guests can explore the area's colonial greens, historic homes, specialty

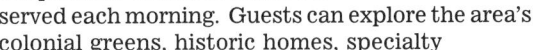

shops and shoreline restaurants. Browsing the antique shops is a popular activity. Guests have access to a state park beach and local town beaches on Long Island Sound, about one mile from the Inn. Additional attractions include the museums associated with Yale University, the colonial Whitfield Museum, the Essex Steam Train and Riverboat Ride, the Chamard Winery, and Gillette's Castle. Local theater includes Long Wharf and the Shubert in New Haven, the Goodspeed Opera House and Goodspeed at Chester for musicals, and the Yale Rep, all active at various times throughout the year. The Inn is located about fifteen minutes by car from New Haven, one hour from Hartford and two hours from Manhattan and two and a half hours from Boston. Midweek and business rates available. The Inn provides a smoke free environment for all guests and welcomes well behaved children over the age of seven. **Airport:** Bradley (Hartford)-1 hr **Discounts:** Midweek business rates **Reservations:** Full payment at time of reservation, two week cancel notice for refund, less than two week notice, refund only if rebooked. **Brochure:** Yes **Permitted:** Children 7+ **Payment Terms:** Check AE/MC/V [I05IPCT1-26851] **COM** U **ITC Member:** No

Rates: **Pvt Bath 9**
Single $ 70-160.00
Double $ 70-160.00

| **Tucker Hill Inn** | 96 Tucker Hill Rd 06762 | **Middlebury CT** |

Susan Cebelenski   **Tel:** 203-758-8334 **Fax:** 203-598-0652

Just off the village green is this classic center hall colonial serving guests for over forty years as a restaurant and guest house. Guest rooms are individually furnished in antiques including comfortable wing back chairs and balconies in some rooms. Full breakfast is served and includes a specialty of the hostess. Close to antiques, museums, and all outdoor sporting activities. **Seasonal:** No **Brochure:** Yes **Permitted:** Limited children, limited drinking **Conference:** Yes, up to 10 persons **Payment Terms:** Check [C11ACCT-952] **COM** Y **ITC Member:** No

Rates: **Pvt Bath 2**   **Shared Bath 2**
Single $ 75.00 $ 65.00

| **Harbour Inne & Cottage** | 15 Edgemont St 06355 | **Mystic CT** |

Charles Lecoures, Jr   **Tel:** 860-572-9253
                                                                                              Res Times 24 Hrs

The *Harbour Inne & Cottage* comprises "The Inne" or "Guest House" with five rental units, each of which has a full size bed, color cable TV, shower, lavatory, toilet and air conditioning. With room rental comes kitchen privileges and a social area with fireplace and antique piano. The three room cottage has two full size beds and a fireplace. The living room has a sofa which opens into a bed, cable color TV and air conditioning. Glider doors open onto a furnished deck with a six person hot tub

©*Inn & Travel Memphis, Tennessee*

jacuzzi spa. (Lavatory, shower and toilet; furnished kitchen and dining area). The Cottage and guest house overlook our picnic area with barbecue, picnic tables, gazebo with swing bench, table and chairs. We have over two hundred feet of Mystic River waterfront, boat dock and boats. We are two blocks from Historic Main Street in Downtown Mystic, minutes from the Mystic Seaport Museum and the Mystic Marine-life Aquarium and only eight country miles from "Foxwoods", the largest resort casino in the world. *Cottage rates: $150-250.00 **Discounts:** Off-season **Airport:** Groton/New London-20 mi **Seasonal:** Rates vary **Reservations:** Payment in full before arrival, 2 week cancel policy for refund less $25 service fee **Brochure:** Yes **Permitted:** Children, pets, drinking, smoking **Languages:** Greek **Payment Terms:** Check Tvlrs Ck [I10HP-CT1956] **COM Y ITC Member:** No

Rates: Pvt Bath 7
Single $ 65-105.00
Double $ 65-200.00

Red Brook Inn   PO Box 237 06372   Mystic CT
Ruth Keyes   Tel: 203-572-0349 Fax: 203-572-0349
                                                      Res Times 9am-9pm

If you're looking for a setting that provides a respite from the hectic pace of modern times, look no further than the *Red Brook Inn*. The Inn offers bed and breakfast lodging in two historic buildings: the Haley Tavern (c.1740) and the Cray Homestead (c.1770). Ruth Keyes, owner and innkeeper, as well as antiquarian and historian, has carefully restored these two eighteenth century Colonials to their original simplicity and elegance. The Inn has been personalized by Ruth's artistic stenciling ability, carefully selected period furnishings, hand-woven rugs and coordinating accessories. The Haley Tavern and Cary Homestead, both authentic center-chimney Colonials, feature lovely guest rooms, all of which are equipped with private baths and many with canopy beds and working fireplaces (firewood provided). Most quarters can accommodate a crib and a few have both a double and a single bed. Adjoining rooms can also be provided with advance notice. Each morning, full and hearty country breakfasts are served family-style in the Haley Tavern's Keeping Room. Pancakes, waffles or eggs, breakfast meats, fresh fruit, juice, cereal and coffee are all part of this delightful fare. On cold autumn and winter mornings, guests may enjoy their breakfast before an inviting fire in the great hearth. Ruth offers special weekend packages in the fall and winter, featuring traditional Colonial open-hearth cooking. Roast lamb and turkey are accompanied by homemade bread and pies served hot from the great hearth's brick oven. Over seven acres of wooded countryside surrounded by stone walls are yours to explore. Ruth is a grandmother herself and invites families of all ages to her Inn. The Tavern Room houses shelves of books, games and puzzles, as well as a color TV. A refrigerator to chill a bottle of wine or baby formula can also be found here. There are many attractions to keep a family on the go while in Mystic and the surrounding area, most notably, the Mystic Seaport Museum and the Mystic Marine Life Aquarium. Long Island Sound is a short distance from the Inn, as are antique shops, wineries and many day-trip excursions. **Airport:** TS Green-30 mi **Packages:** Colonial Dinners (Winter) **Seasonal:** No **Reservations:** 50% advance deposit, 7 day cancel policy for refund, check-in noon-8pm **Brochure:** Yes **Permitted:** Children, drinking **Conference:** Yes, groups to 25 persons **Payment Terms:** Check MC/V [K01HPCT1-980] **COM U ITC Member:** No

Rates: Pvt Bath 10
Single $ 85-169.00
Double $ 85-169.00

National Edition **Connecticut**

Maples Inn — 179 Oenoke Ridge 06840 — New Canaan CT
Joan Louleau
Tel: 203-966-2927
Res Times 8am-8pm

New England setting for this Country Inn with turn-of-the-century charm including country antique furnishings and family heirlooms and all modern amenities. Convenient location with Nature Center and town square within walking distances. Continental breakfast included. **Sea-sonal:** No **Brochure:** Yes **Permitted:** Children 10-up, smoking, drinking **Payment Terms:** Check AE/MC/V [C11ACCT-960] **COM** Y **ITC Member:** No

Rates:	Pvt Bath 22	Shared Bath 2
Single	$ 90.00-up	$ 80.00-up
Double	$ 100.00-up	$ 90.00-up

Greenwoods Gate — 105 Greenwoods Rd East 06058 — Norfolk CT
Ms Deanne P Raymond
Tel: 203-542-5439

Exciting 1797 colonial residence offering warmth and country elegance by a hostess who offers full hospitality to all guests. Guests rooms are furnished in period antiques, with deluxe suites including modern amenities. Homemade break-fasts awaken you while they are being prepared from family recipes. **Seasonal:** No **Brochure:** Yes **Permitted:** Limited children, limited smoking **Payment Terms:** Check AE/V [C11ACCT-970] **COM** Y **ITC Member:** No

Rates:	Pvt Bath 3
Single	$ 68-80.00
Double	$ 130-160.00

Manor House — Maple Ave 06058 — Norfolk CT
Diane & Hank Tremblay
Tel: 800-488-5690 203-542-5690

Fantastic baronial mansion c1898 rich in taste and design that still offers guests a glorious retreat on five acres, genuine Victorian antique furnishings fireplaces, many Tiffany and leaded glass windows, private elevator, balconies, and sleigh and carriage rides during the year. Full breakfast might include blueberry pancakes, homemade muffins or biscuits, orange-spiced waffles, or another specialty of the hosts. **Seasonal:** No **Brochure:** Yes **Permitted:** Children 12-up, limited smoking, limited drinking **Conference:** Yes, including evening dining. **Payment Terms:** Check MC/V [C11ACCT-971] **COM** Y **ITC Member:** No

Rates:	Pvt Bath 4	Shared Bath 2
Single	$ 75.00	$ 65.00
Double	$ 90-130.00	$ 75-95.00

Harbor House Inn — 165 Shore Rd 06850 — Old Greenwich CT
Dolly Stuttig/Dawn Browne
Tel: 203-637-0145 **Fax:** 203-698-0943
Res Times 7am-10pm

Harbor House Inn - "Your Home Away From Home". We are a lovely Bed & Breakfast located in an exclusive area by the water. A short walk to a charming New England town and train. Shops and fine restaurants are close by while the beach is just a ten minute walk. The lobby is filled with *"old world charm"*. A fully equipped kitchen and laundry are available for guests. A continental breakfast is included in your room rate. Antiques - this area is bountiful along with theaters, parks and lovely country roads for exciting New England sightseeing. New York City is just 45 mins away. Daily maid service is provided. **Airport:** Laguardia NYC-40 mins; West Chester County-125 mins **Discounts:** Seniors, AAA **Seasonal:** No **Reservations:** Credit card number or check for 50% of length of stay; 48 hr cancel policy for refund **Brochure:** Yes **Permitted:** Children, lim-

©Inn & Travel Memphis, Tennessee

1-9

Connecticut   National Edition

ited drinking **Conference:** Yes, for groups to 12 persons **Payment Terms:** AE/MC/V [I04IPCT1-976] **COM** YG **ITC Member:** No

Rates:	Pvt Bath 17	Shared Bath 6
Single	$ 79.00	$ 69.00
Double	$ 99.00	$ 79.00

Old Lyme Inn   85 Lyme St 06371   **Old Lyme CT**
Diana Atwood   **Tel:** 203-434-2600 **Fax:** 203-434-5352

Elegant restored empire mansion home to famous

elegant mansion . . .

impressionist painters and filled with paintings, period antiques, and perfect spot for seeing sights near Mystic, Gillettes Castle, Essex. Continental breakfast included. **Seasonal:** No **Brochure:** Yes **Permitted:** Children limited, smoking, and drinking **Payment Terms:** Check AE/MC/V/DC [C11A-CCT-978] **COM** Y **ITC Member:** No

Rates:	Pvt Bath 13
Single	$ 95.00
Double	$ 130.00

Captain Parkers Inn At Quinebaug   32 Walker Rd 06262   **Quinebaug CT**
David Parker/Bojeua Szmuniewska   **Tel:** 800-707-7303 203-935-5219
                                                                                   Res Times 24 Hrs

Captain Parker's Inn is located in a quiet, rural neighborhood in the most northeastern corner of Connecticut. Built by Captain Parker, it features beautiful varied hardwoods throughout. Although it is situated about an hour from the ocean, the decor portrays a nautical theme with a Victorian flair and an elegant atmosphere. The Inn lends itself to romantic getaways and small weddings. Each guest-room features a different hardwood flooring and trim and most have a bath ensuite. The more-than-ample common areas include a library with a wood stove, a large foyer with a baby grand piano, a relaxing entertainment room, formal dining room with a cozy fireplace and a hospitable kitchen. The private, manicured acre and a half of grounds can be enjoyed from a long screened-in front porch or from the rear deck with a built-in hot tub. The Captain takes breakfast seriously - starting with flavored coffee, juice, fresh bread and a choice of entrees that include eggs, omelettes, pancakes, Polish cuisine (the Polish speaking innkeeper means true European flavor can be included in the meals), hot cereal or a delicious healthy (low fat) meal. The New England countryside can be enjoyed with the complimentary bikes provided guests who can enjoy the miles of striking green farmland or the sights such as nearby Sturbridge Village, wine-tasting at Mellea Winery, close to Putnam Connecticut antiquing mecca and the beautiful fall foliage. Activities include hiking, fishing, golf, apple-picking, hayrides, sleigh rides and cross country skiing. Picnic lunches in a basket with beverages and a blanket are available at a reasonable rate. **Airport:** TF Green-30 mins **Packages:** Bicycling, Horseback Riding (trails and lessons available), Gourmet Cuisine Weekend **Seasonal:** No **Reservations:** 50% deposit to guarantee reservation, 14 day cancel notice for refund **Brochure:** Yes **Permitted:** Children 13-up, limited smoking **Conference:** Yes, groups to twenty **Languages:** Polish **Payment Terms:** Check MC/V [K08GPCT1-20080] **COM** Y **ITC Member:** No **Quality Assurance:** Requested

Rates:	Pvt Bath 4	Shared Bath 2
Single	$ 70.00	$ 55.00
Double	$ 75.00	$ 55.00

Old Mill Inn   63 Maple St 06072   **Somersville CT**
Ralph & Phyllis Lumb   **Tel:** 203-763-1473
                                                                          Res Times 7am-10pm

1-10   ©*Inn & Travel Memphis, Tennessee*

National Edition | **Connecticut - Maine**

Relax in a gracious old New England home located in a friendly north central Connecticut village setting, where comfort and hospitality are paramount. Twin beds or full double beds in well-appointed, air conditioned rooms. Upstairs sitting room has cable TV, phone and refrigerator. Downstairs living room has a stereo, fireplace and books everywhere. A beautiful dining room with hand-painted walls and a glass wall overlooks a vista of green lawn surrounded by gardens, flowering trees and shrubs. You're convenient to shopping and restaurants, Bradley Intl Airport, Trolley, Air and Indian Museums, golf and other attractions. Breakfast includes juice, fruit, pastries, cereals and hot beverages. **Seasonal:** No **Reservations:** One night's deposit to guarantee, 7 day cancel policy. Check-in 4pm, late check-in with prior arrangement. **Brochure:** Yes **Permitted:** Children over 5, drinking **Conference:** Can comfortably accommodate up to 20 persons. **Payment Terms:** Check [Z01DPCT-5905] **COM** Y **ITC Member:** No

Rates:	**Pvt Bath** 3	**Shared Bath** 2
Single	$ 60.00	$ 50.00
Double	$ 60.00	$ 50.00

Capt Stannard House　　138 S Main St 06498　　Westbrook CT
Tel: 203-399-4634
Res Times 8am-8pm

Lovely seacoast town Inn complete with New England traditional furnishings filled with antiques and family heirlooms. Dating c1889 and fully restored. You can relax directly upon the river bank or stroll to the beach nearby. Inn is close to some of the most interesting attractions in Connecticut. **Seasonal:** No **Brochure:** Yes **Per-mitted:** Children, smoking, and drinking **Payment Terms:** Check AE/MC/V [C11ACCT-1002] **COM** Y **ITC Member:** No

Rates:	**Pvt Bath** 7
Single	$ 70.00
Double	$ 85.00

Captain Parkers Inn At Quinebaug　　Woodstock CT
David Parker/Bojeua Szmuniewska
Tel: 800-707-7303 203-935-5219
Res Times 24 Hrs

Refer to the same listing name under Thompson, Connecticut for a complete description. **Seasonal:** No **Payment Terms:** Check MC/V [M08GPCT1-20106] **COM** Y **ITC Member:** No

Rates:	**Pvt Bath** 4	**Shared Bath** 2
Single	$ 70.00	$ 55.00
Double	$ 75.00	$ 55.00

Bayview Inn & Hotel　　111 Eden St Rt # 3 04609　　Bar Harbor ME
John Davis
Tel: 800-356-3585 207-288-3173
Res Times 8am-8pm

This gracious waterfront estate serves as an elegant and intimate Inn where former guests includes many world-leaders. Townhouses are available too. A con-tinental breakfast is included. There's swimming, tennis and complete dining facilities available. **Seasonal:** No **Brochure:** Yes **Per-mitted:** Children, smoking, drinking **Conference:** Yes including full facilities **Languages:** French/Spanish **Payment Terms:** Check AE/CD/DC/MC/V [X11ACME-3457] **COM** Y **ITC Member:** No

Rates:	**Pvt Bath** 32	**Shared Bath** 2
Single	$ 95-up	
Double	$ 105.00-up	

Holbrook House　　74 Mount Desert St 04609　　Bar Harbor ME
Jeani Ochtera
Tel: 800-695-1120 813-924-7847

Beautiful 1876 Victorian summer cottage within Bar Harbor and close to Acadia National Park.

©*Inn & Travel Memphis, Tennessee*

Furnished with period antiques and oriental rugs, guests can relax and enjoy the New England hospitality. Continental breakfast is served in a sunlit solarium. Tennis and swimming are available. **Discounts:** Seniors 10%. **Seasonal:** No **Reservations:** Deposit at res time to guarantee room. **Brochure:** Yes **Permitted:** Children 9-up, limited smoking, limited smoking **Payment Terms:** Check AE/MC/V [X11ACME-3464] **COM** Y **ITC Member:** No

Rates:	Pvt Bath 10	Shared Bath 2
Single		
Double	$ 90-up	$ 80-up

Maples 16 Roberts Ave 04609 Bar Harbor ME
Susan Sinclair
Tel: 207-288-3443
Res Times 9am-9pm

Beautiful Victorian residence just a short stroll to the ocean allows guests to unwind and relax in this great New England setting. If you're interested in the many sights, you can choose from Acadia National Park and the Nova Scotia Ferry for your pleasure. All the sporting activities are here; tennis, golf, swimming along with plenty of antiquing and interesting shops. **Seasonal:** Rates vary **Reservations:** Two night's deposit at res time with 10 day cancel policy. **Brochure:** Yes **Permitted:** Limited drinking **Payment Terms:** Check DISC/MC/V [X11-AXME-3467] **COM** U **ITC Member:** No

Rates: Pvt Bath 6
Single $ 60-140.00
Double $ 60-140.00

Mira Monte Inn & Suites 69 Mt Desert St 04609 Bar Harbor ME
Marian Burns
Tel: 800-553-5109 207-288-4263 **Fax:** 207-288-3115
Res Times 8am-9pm

Treat yourself to the simple elegance in this turn-of-the-century retreat that entertained those who could afford the luxury of summering in Bar Harbor. This 1864 structure is graced with wrap-around porches, balconies and bay windows and is nestled on grounds of beautiful sweeping lawns, paved terraces and lovely gardens. Guest rooms befit the lifestyle of the period with antique and period furnishings, wallpapers, private baths and lace curtains - without sacrificing the cleanliness, comfort and convenience of today. All rooms have a/c and phones. Guests can dream alongside one of the many fireplaces or spend a serene afternoon on the grounds, where the smell of salt air and flowers blend fragrances - long remembered! Morning brings a full breakfast buffet served on an elegant 1810 Federal Period server. Guests can choose a private patio, porch, balcony or a family-style table for breakfast. Just a five minute walk brings you to Bar Harbor's finest shops, restaurants and waterfront. The Acadia National Park offers 33,000 acres (just a five minute drive) for mountains, seashore, lakes, meadows, forests and a full schedule of Ranger-guided activities from June to early October. Enjoy climbing, hiking, boating, fishing, whale-watching, windsurfing, tennis, and golf. Two suites available in separate building on the property, each with parlor with fireplace, kitchenette unit, bedroom with lace canopy queen bed, two person whirlpool and a private deck overlooking the grounds. One two-bedroom housekeeping suite-weekly rental. **Packages:** Fly/Drive, Spring, Fall Honeymoon **Airport:** Bangor Intl-50 mi **Seasonal:** Clo 10/1-4/1 **Reservations:** First & last night deposit, 7 day cancel policy less $10 fee **Brochure:** Yes **Permitted:** Children, limited drinking, limited smoking **Conference:** Yes, separate building on the same ground for special functions. **Payment Terms:** Check AE/DISC/MC/V [I02HPME1-3468] **COM** YG **ITC Member:** No

Rates: Pvt Bath 14
Single $ 90-180.00
Double $ 90-180.00

National Edition *Maine*

Stratford House Inn	45 Mount Desert St 04609	**Bar Harbor ME**
Barb & Norm Moulton		**Tel:** 207-288-5189

Former home of *"Little Women"* publisher, this tudor-style residence is close to any woodland and water activity which might interest guests. Continental breakfast is included. Library and sitting room are for guests use. **Seasonal:** No **Reservations:** Deposit to guarantee room with 10 day cancel policy for refund less $10 service fee. **Brochure:** Yes **Permitted:** Children, limited pets, limited smoking **Payment Terms:** Check AE/MC/V [X11-ACME-3472] **COM Y ITC Mem-ber:** No

Rates:	**Pvt Bath 8**	**Shared Bath 2**
Single	$ 75.00-up	$ 65.00-up
Double	$ 85-110.00	$ 75-95.00

Granes Fairhaven Inn	N Bath Rd 04530	**Bath ME**
Jane Wyllie		**Tel:** 207-443-4391
		Res Times 8am-8pm

Lovely Country Inn for swimming, golfing and hiking if you like with all the country furnishings and plenty of home comfort and atmosphere with antique furnishings, handmade quilts and great New England hospitality. Continental breakfast is included with other meals available on the premises with prior notice. **Reservations:** 50% of stay required as deposit at res time. *Rates based on European Plan **Permitted:** Children, smoking **Payment Terms:** Check [X11ACME-3479] **COM Y ITC Member:** No

Rates:	**Pvt Bath 1**	**Shared Bath 2**
Single	$ 50.00	$ 40.00
Double	$ 50.00	$ 40.00

Belfast Bay Meadows Inn	90 Northport Ave 04915	**Belfast ME**
John & Patty Lebowitz	**Tel:** 800-335-2370 207-338-5715	**Fax:** 207-338-5715

Exemplary, very large, Shingled Down East "Cottage" offers wonderful international antique decor, fine paintings, colorful Persian rugs and comfortable furnishings. Breezy bright blue bay location by mottled forest. Cool summer mornings, spacious deck, big green umbrellas. Enjoy sweet, fresh local fruit, fancy muffins, creamy eggs with tender lobster and tasty sweet peppers. Stroll winding, grassy paths through 5-1/2 bay side acres, flowered meadows, gardens and forest to the cold blue waters of Penobscot Bay; wheeling gulls, white sailed schooners healing to the breeze, green shadowed island in bright morning mist. AAA and Mobil rated. Places to go and things to do. We can arrange for or direct you to: Rail and Sail (Belfast Moosehead Lake) R.R. and Voyager boat tour; Sailing Lessons (Sail boat rentals and charters, schooner rides); Horseback lessons and trail rides; tennis, golf, swimming, hiking, biking, cross country skiing, snowmobiling, Marine Museum, Fort Knox, antique stores, flea markets, Maskers Theater, fishing (Lake - summer, ice - winter), Deep Sea charters for striped bass, bluefish, mackerel, etc. Kayaking - rentals and guided excursions on the Penobscot Bay; Walking Tours-Architectural/Historical; Ferry boat rides to islands in Penobscot Bay; Day trips: Bar Harbor/Mount Desert Island, Camden/Rockland, Bangor, Augusta, Waterville, Freeport. **Discounts:** Mult-night stays, group rates **Seasonal:** Rates vary **Reservations:** One night deposit, one week cancel notice for refund **Brochure:** Yes **Permitted:** Children, pets, limited drinking **Conference:** New conference facilities for groups to 35 persons **Payment Terms:** Check AE/MC/V [I03HPM-E1-20154] **COM U ITC Member:** No

Rates:	**Pvt Bath 12**
Single	$ 60-125.00
Double	$ 60-125.00

©*Inn & Travel Memphis, Tennessee*

Maine   *National Edition*

Hiram Alden Inn	19 Church St 04915	**Belfast ME**
Jim & Jackie Lovejoy		**Tel:** 207-338-2151
		Res Times 24 Hrs

Enjoy New England in a stately 1840 Greek Revival home situated on an acre in Belfast's historical residential area and just minutes to the restored downtown commercial and waterfront district. The first in-town B&B in Belfast, it reflects the original owner's appreciation for quality craftsmanship and

blueberry nut pancakes

discerning eye for architectural style and beauty. Charming features include imported marble fireplace mantels, ornate tin ceilings, a "walk-in" butler's pantry, handcarved cherry wood staircase with a curved "pocket door". Your charming host's motto is *"accommodating you is not a hobby . . . but our full time occupation."* The formal dining room offers guests a full breakfast including house specialties of blueberry nut pancakes, ham on french toast, scrambled eggs, bacon/sausage, fresh fruit, juices and muffins with all the warm beverages prepared just to each guest's taste. Summer adds fresh-picked berries to the menu! The town setting offers a panoramic view of Penobscot Bay, home to over 200 sailboats, lobster and working tugs. Must-sees are the historic home tour, a variety of galleries, arts and craft shops and a summer theater group. July features two festivals: The Bay Festival (carnival, crafts and music for the whole family) and the Holy Mackerel Fishing Tournament. And you shouldn't miss a cruise on the 110 foot ship Mount Katahdin for sightseeing the islands. **Seasonal:** No **Reservations:** One night's deposit with 7 day cancel policy, arrival after 6pm with notice **Brochure:** Yes **Permitted:** Children, drinking, limited pets, limited smoking **Conference:** Yes for groups to 15 persons **Payment Terms:** Check [R02BCME-3480] **COM** Y **ITC Member:** No

Rates:	**Shared Bath 8**
Single	$ 40.00
Double	$ 55-60.00

Anchor Watch	3 Eames Rd 04538	**Boothbay Harbor ME**
Diane Campbell		**Tel:** 207-633-7565
		Res Times 10am-8pm

Lighthouse beacons, lobster boats, and islands with fir trees provide the setting for our cozy Bed & Breakfast on the prettiest shore of the Harbor. Country quilts and stencilling set the style inside. Breakfast features a baked cheese omelette or perhaps a baked orange french toast or blueberry blintz. Enjoy an intimate table for two or sit with other guests from all over the world at an oceanview window. The lawn slopes down to the water ending with a pier and float. Within a five minute walk are shops, boat trips, Monhegan ferry and many fine restaurants. Within an hour's drive are white sandy beaches, maritime museums and the famous LL Bean and Freeport shopping outlets. Your host, Captain Bob, operates the Maranbo II and Balmy Days II, excursion boats taking sightseeing and dinner cruises from Pier 8. Guests receive a "special fare" discount on the Harbor Tour. When Diane isn't at the B&B, she'll be found sailing in the Harbor or at the boat trip ticket booth at Pier 8. Bob and Diane live in the house next door to the Anchor Watch and in summer, Diane's dad stays at the B&B. Therefore, during off-season, the Anchor Watch kitchen is available for guests to use for snacks, or even cooking lobsters. *"This charming seaside Captain's house offers a warm welcome to travelers from afar."* **Packages:** Spring Boat Trip (one hour cruise) **Seasonal:** No **Reservations:** One night's deposit, one week cancel policy for refund or if less, only if room is rebooked **Brochure:** Yes **Permitted:** Drinking **Payment Terms:** Check MC/V [Z08GPME-6084] **COM** Y **ITC Member:** No

Rates:	**Pvt Bath 4**
Single	$ 75-95.00
Double	$ 80-100.00

Hilltop Guest House	44 McKnown Hill 04538	**Boothbay Harbor ME**
Mrs Cora Mahr		**Tel:** 207-633-2914
		Res Times 9am-7pm

1-14   ©*Inn & Travel Memphis, Tennessee*

National Edition *Maine*

Family oriented farmhouse lodging overlooking Boothbay Harbor and town with a relaxed setting. Large comfortable rooms and even a tree swing in the yard. **Seasonal:** No **Reservations:** Deposit required at res time. **Brochure:** Yes **Permitted:** Children, limited smoking, limited drinking **Payment Terms:** Check [X11ACME-3506] **COM** Y **ITC Member:** No

Rates:	Pvt Bath 1	Shared Bath 5
Single	$ 45.00	$ 38.00
Double		$ 38.00

L Ermitage   219 Main St 04416   **Bucksport ME**
Virginia & James Conklin   **Tel:** 207-469-3361
Res Times 9am-10pm

Patterned after traditional European Inns, this turn-of-the-century white colonial from the 1830s comforts guests with antique furnishings, oriental carpets and many collectibles your hosts enjoy sharing with guests. Full breakfast included. On Penobscot Bay near Fort Knox. **Seasonal:** No **Brochure:** Yes **Permitted:** Limited smoking, drinking **Languages:** French **Payment Terms:** Check MC/V/DC [X11ACME-3527] **COM** Y **ITC Member:** No

Rates:		Shared Bath 3
Single		$ 45.00
Double		$ 50.00

Belfast Bay Meadows Inn   **Camden ME**
John & Patty Lebowitz   **Tel:** 800-355-2370 207-338-5715

Refer to the same listing name under Belfast, Maine for a complete description. **Seasonal:** Rates vary **Payment Terms:** Check AE/MC/V [M03HPME1-22306] **COM** U **ITC Member:** No

Rates:	Pvt Bath 12
Single	$ 60-125.00
Double	$ 60-125.00

Goodspeeds Guest House   60 Mountain St 04843   **Camden ME**
Innkeeper   **Tel:** 207-236-8077
Res Times 7am-9pm

This 1879 Federal-style farmhouse has been restored and offers a great location for visiting the attractions in the quaint town of Camden. Interior detail includes stained-glass windows, wide pine planked floors, delightfully colored wallpapers with touches of antiques and heirloom furnishings. The guest rooms are furnished with a variety of wicker, canopy and cannon ball beds with several offering wonderful views of the nearby mountains. The hosts/owners collection of antique clocks and other collectibles create the warmth and feeling of old world charm. A continental breakfast is included and can be enjoyed outdoors in the wonderful Maine sunshine. Activities include excellent restaurants, shops, sailing, hiking, swimming, picnicking, cycling, antiquing, county fairs and Shakespearean performances. One of Camden's original grave yards next door makes for an interesting glimpse into Camden's history. Fall brings brilliant color and unforgettable memories of New England. A quiet location-just five blocks from the harbor. **Seasonal:** Open 6/1-10/15 **Reservations:** One night's deposit (if longer 50% of length of stay) plus 7% tax, required. 7 day cancel policy for full refund. **Brochure:** Yes **Permitted:** Drinking, children 12-up and limited smoking **Languages:** French **Payment Terms:** Check [Z11CPME-3536] **COM** Y **ITC Member:** No

Rates:	Pvt Bath 1	Shared Bath 7
Single		$ 49.00
Double	$ 75.00	$ 65.00

Hawthorn Inn   9 High St 04843   **Camden ME**
Ken & Abigail Stern   **Tel:** 207-236-8842 **Fax:** 207-236-6181
Res Times 9am-9pm

©*Inn & Travel Memphis, Tennessee*

Relive the Queen Victorian period in this gracious mansion with turrets dating from 1894, created by a prosperous coal merchant as his estate. The Inn has antiques through out and has recently been listed on the *National Register of Historic Places*. Inside, two large parlour rooms invite you to linger, perhaps over tea or lemonade, in conversation or while listening to music played on the beautiful grand piano. There are four bright and airy rooms off the second floor which overlook Camden Harbor or Mount Battie and two garden rooms (one with clawfoot tub) downstairs. Beautiful spiral staircase and dining room that removes the morning chill during breakfast complete the downstairs. A beautifully furnished carriage house with four rooms with full harbor views, fireplaces, whirlpool jacuzzis, cable TV and VCRs. A full breakfast is included with muffins hot from the oven, fresh fruit and artful egg dishes. On sunny days, you'll enjoy dining on the deck that offers a great harbor view. Nearby, and next to the grounds is the Bok Amphitheater for summer concerts and Shakespearean plays; with the town center just a five minute walk - to schooners, shops, restaurants and Mount Battie. The *Hawthorn Inn* is a very special place ... and all of our guests are very special people. **Airport:** Portland-85 mi; Bangor-57 mi **Seasonal:** No **Reservations:** Advanced 2 night payment as deposit, one week cancel policy for refund, check-in 3-6pm, prior notice required if later, check-out 10:30am **Brochure:** Yes **Permitted:** Children 12+, limited drinking, no smoking please **Conference:** Perfect setting for memorable weddings, social engagements and small seminars. **Payment Terms:** Check AE/MC/V [I05HPME-1-8645] **COM YG ITC Member:** No

Rates: Pvt Bath 10
Single $ 75-175.00
Double $ 75-175.00

Norumbega Inn   Rt 1 04843   Camden ME
Murry Keatings   **Tel:** 207-236-4646
                                                       Res Times 9am-7pm

This romantic Victorian *"castle by the sea"*, is fashioned of heroic proportions from local stone and overlooks Penobscot Bay and islands. Listed on the *National Register of Historic Places*, guests enjoy the delightful mythical city of Norumbega created by Joseph Sterns, a prosperous inventor who built his castle in 1866. Mr. Sterns furnished his mansion with the best of what he experienced in the manor houses of England and castles along the Rhine. Renovated by the Keatinges in 1987 as a luxury inn, it stands today as a tribute to the fine craftsmanship and antique period furnishings of the nineteenth century. From the ornate fireplaces in the downstairs parlors to the handsome library with wrap-around balcony and glass windows - the dramatically wood paneled public rooms, reminiscent of an English manor house, and the balconies and porches with their spectacular views - each guest feels at home in *"their own castle"*. Thirteen country-guest rooms include king-size beds, sitting areas, private bath with some rooms offering private balconies, fireplaces and picture-window views. An exciting penthouse suite sits above the treetops and is furnished in modern color and style with bold floral wallcoverings, subtle mint carpeting and a regal bath with ebony jacuzzi and shower. Morning brings a delicious royal fare of a variety of teas, coffee, juices, seasonal fruit, home-baked breads and muffins, egg dishes, meats and other culinary delights all served outdoors on the stone terrace or in the main dining room. Afternoon brings tea, beverages and hors d'oeuvres for guests to enjoy while planning their evening dining at one of Camden's excellent restaurants. A friendly helpful staff is ready to assist you ... and to make sure your bed is turned-down before retiring ... chill your favorite beverage ... arrange your dinner reservations. We want your visit to be a special and memorable experience - a castle to call home. **Airport:** Bangor-60 mi; Portland Jetport-80 mi. **Packages:** Weekend, Mid-Week, Holiday, Mystery **Seasonal:** No **Reservations:** Deposit required to confirm res, 10 day cancel policy less $20 service fee.

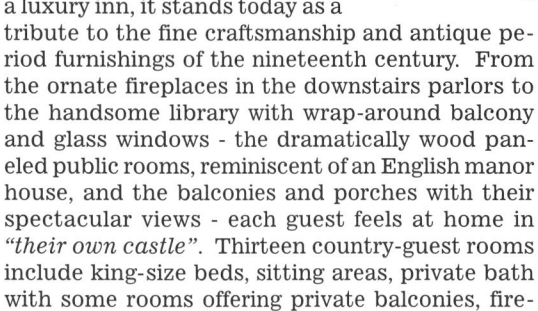

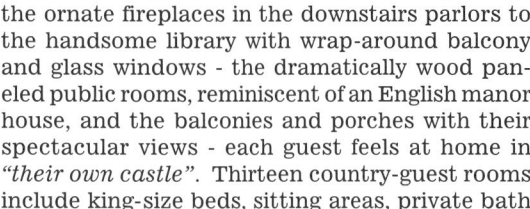

Brochure: Yes **Permitted:** Children 7-up, smoking, social drinking **Conference:** Excellent facilities for intimate business or social meetings. **Payment Terms:** Check AE/MC/V [I03E-PME-3543] **COM** Y **ITC Member:** No

Rates:	Pvt Bath 13
Single	$ 175.00-up
Double	$ 175.00-up

Wooden Goose Inn	Rt 1 03902	**Cape Neddick ME**
K Rippetow & A Sienicki		**Tel:** 207-363-5673
		Res Times 9am-8pm

A 19th Century farmhouse, former home of a sea captain, has been restored and furnished with crystal, oriental carpeting with plenty of nostalgia. Three course full breakfast begins each day and includes choices of eggs Benedict, omelette or Florentine with homemade breads. Close to Portsmouth and Ogunquit. Airport pickups with advance notice. **Seasonal:** No **Reservations:** One night's deposit required at res time. **Brochure:** Yes **Permitted:** Children, smoking, drinking **Payment Terms:** Check [X11ACME-3551] **COM** Y **ITC Member:** No

Rates:	Pvt Bath 6
Single	$ 75-85.00
Double	$ 85.00-up

Craignair Inn	533 Clark Island Rd 04859	**Clark Island ME**
Norman & Terry Smith		**Tel:** 207-594-7644 **Fax:** 207-596-7124
		Res Times 9am-9pm

This quaint Maine village offers guests a year-round opportunity to enjoy New England hospitality at the *Craignair Inn* nestled on four acres of shorefront coastline. Originally a boarding house for workers at nearby quarries, it was converted into an inn in 1940 offering cheery rooms overlooking the picturesque water setting and gardens. Guest rooms are simple and comfortable offering quilt covered beds, colorful wall coverings, hooked rugs on the floors and antique furnishings. A perfect locale for artists, writers and naturalists seeking a change of pace enjoying the sailboats, lobster fishermen, clammers, shore birds and the abundant wildlife on the islands, tidal pools, meadows and woodlands. Winter brings cross-country skiing, ice skating, downhill at the Camden Snow Bowl (just a short drive) and a crackling fire in the large library which provides refuge from the silent fog that slowly rolls onto land in the evening. A full breakfast is included with dinner available in the dining room on the premises which specializes in local seafood, meats, homemade sauces, breads, pastas and pastries. There's plenty to see with antiquing, galleries, golf, miles of hiking, riding, tennis, sailing, concerts, museums and numerous country fairs and a special granite quarry of deep saltwater for a warm swim in the afternoon before dinner. email address: craignair@-midcoast.com **Airport:** Portland Jetport-80 mi **Seasonal:** Closed Feb **Reservations:** One night's deposit by check in mail, 1 week cancel policy for refund. **Brochure:** Yes **Permitted:** Children, pets, drinking, smoking **Conference:** Yes for small conferences **Payment Terms:** Check AE/MC/V [K05IPME1-35-62] **COM** Y **ITC Member:** No

Rates:	Pvt Bath 8	Shared Bath 14
Single	$ 76.00	$ 42.00
Double	$ 86.00	$ 62.00

Brannon Bunker Inn	HCR 64 Box 045M 04543	**Damariscotta ME**
Jeanne & Joseph Hovance		**Tel:** 207-563-5941
		Res Times 9am-9pm

The *Brannon-Bunker Inn* is an intimate, relaxed country B&B, rurally situated in Maine's mid-coast region, just five miles off Rt 1 south of Damanscotta on Rt 129. The original Cape cottage portion (c1820) has been home to many generations of Mainers. The 1920's owners turned the barn into a dance hall, "La Hacienda". Over the intervening years, the barn and carriage house were converted into comfortable sleeping rooms with private and shared baths. Today, eight sleeping rooms are furnished in themes reflecting the charm of yesterday with the comforts of today, with a selection of queen, double and twin beds. The quiet beauty of stenciled walls, quaint wallpapers, homemade quilts, dried flowers and country crafts sets off the warmth and solid comfort of the carefully selected antique furnishings. One of the sitting areas reflects Joe's interest in World War I military collectibles. A complimentary "Continental-plus" breakfast features juices, cold cereals, fresh fruit in season, hot beverages and great homemade muffins - with time for conversation and mapping out the days' activities. You're just ten mins to the lighthouse, historic fort, sandy beaches, golf, Audubon Center, boating trips, canoe rentals, antique shop right at the Inn, fine dining and beautiful New England scenery. **Airport:** Portland Jetport-40mi **Seasonal:** Closed Christ-mas **Reservations:** 50% of stay as deposit at res time to confirm res with 7 day cancel policy for refund **Brochure:** Yes **Permitted:** Children, drinking **Payment Terms:** Check AE/MC/V [I03GPME1-3566] **COM** Y **ITC Member:** No

Rates:	Pvt Bath 5	Shared Bath 2
Single	$ 60.00	$ 50.00
Double	$ 65.00	$ 55.00

Artists Retreat 29 Washington St 04631 Eastport ME
Joyce Webster Tel: 207-853-4239

Step back in time to 1846 in this Victorian home, just two blocks from Eastport's waterfront, that is a Victorian buff's delight with touches of ornately carved and marble-topped furnishings. There are many special examples of Victorian Renaissance, like the bedsteads with high carved backs brought back following trips South after the Civil War! The guest rooms are on the second & third floors with a small library, sitting area with an Artist's Retreat on the fourth floor. Well-lit with skylights, guest artists are welcomed to use it! Enjoy this tranquil village setting that once vied with New York as the busiest port in the 19th century. While the tall ships are gone now, the harbor is a hub of activity, especially with fishing boats and their fresh "New England Catch" ready for dinner at one of the many local restaurants. Boat excursions are available for nature-trips and bird-watching (also whales & seals), fishing trips or just for exploring nearby islands and the wildlife in the surrounding undeveloped coastlines. A full New England breakfast starts your day. **Seasonal:** No **Reservations:** 25% deposit of entire stay at res time, 7 day cancel policy, less $10 service fee. **Brochure:** Yes **Permitted:** Children, drinking, limited smoking **Conference:** Large living room that's perfect for groups to 40 persons. **Payment Terms:** Check MC/V [R02B-CME-3574] **COM** Y **ITC Member:** No

Rates:		Shared Bath 5
Single		$ 50.00
Double		$ 60.00

High Meadows B&B Rt 101 03903 Eliot ME
Elaine Raymond Tel: 207-439-0590
  Res Times 9am-7pm

c1730's colonial country residence in a great locale for outdoor enthusiasts with walking trails, cross country skiing nearby. Plenty of fine shopping, dining and theaters close by. Just six miles to historic Portsmouth. Continental breakfast included. **Seasonal:** No **Brochure:** Yes **Permitted:** Smoking, social drinking **Payment Terms:** Check [X11-ACME-3579] **COM** Y **ITC Member:** No

Rates:	Pvt Bath 2	Shared Bath 2
Single	$ 60.00	$ 55.00
Double	$ 70.00	$ 65.00

National Edition *Maine*

Atlantic Seal B&B	**Freeport ME**
Capt Thomas & Gaila Ring	**Tel:** 207-865-6112
	Res Times 7:30-9pm

Refer to the same listing name under South Freeport, Maine for a complete description. **Seasonal:** Closed Christmas **Payment Terms:** Check [M09-CPME-11610] COM Y **ITC Member:** No

Rates: Pvt Bath 2   Shared Bath 2
Single $ 90.00 $ 55.00
Double $ 100-125.00 $ 65-85.00

Bagley House	1290 Royalsborough Rd 04222	**Freeport ME**
Susan Backhouse/Suzanne O'Connor	**Tel:** 800-765-1772 207-865-6566	**Fax:** 207-353-5878
		Res Times 8am-10pm

Six acres of lovely fields and woods surround this magnificent 1772 country home offering guests a peaceful stopping place to recall another era. Rooms are individually decorated with antiques, handmade quilts, wide pumpkin pine floors and fresh flowers. One room boasts its own working fireplace for cozy winter evenings. All have private baths (two have full baths, two are outside of the room), three queen size beds, one double bed and one double and a three-quarter bed. Full breakfast is served around the kitchen's huge free standing fireplace and beehive oven. All baked goods are homemade, specializing in sourdough baking. Individual dietary needs can be complied with. The

Bagley House is *"near enough but far enough"* from downtown Freeport, LL Bean and more than one hundred upscale shops and outlets. Bowdoin and Bates Colleges are a convenient thirty minute drive, Colby College is one hour away. Four state parks, several museums, island cruising, summer music theater, music festivals, country fairs, small-town bean suppers, auctions and antiquing keep guests busy. The *Bagley House* offers guests a convenient setting for enjoying New England hospitality. **Packages:** Call for Dinner Weekend details **Airport:** Portland Jetport-35 min **Discounts:** 5% AARP **Seasonal:** No **Reservations:** One night's deposit or credit card, 7 day cancel policy for full refund **Brochure:** Yes **Permitted:** Children, drinking **Conference:** Ideal for small retreat for groups to 7-10 persons **Payment Terms:** Check AE/DISC/MC/V [I07HPME1-7406] COM YG **ITC Member:** No

Rates: Pvt Bath 5
Single $ 70-85.00
Double $ 85-100.00

Bayberry Inn	8 Maple Ave 04032	**Freeport ME**
Frank Family		**Tel:** 207-865-6021

Welcome to the *Bayberry Inn*, located in the village district, just a three minute walk to LL Bean and all the fine shops and restaurants. We invite you to enjoy traditional New England charm and warmth. You will find beau-tiful oak, walnut, maple, ash and wide plank floors. Comfortable cheery bedrooms, all tastefully decorated with either king, queen, double or twin beds. All rooms have a private bath. Relax in our cozy sitting room with cable television, VCR, books, games or just good conversation. Several telephones in hall and guest rooms. Ample parking is located in front of the Inn. Enjoy a leisurely afternoon in our colorful garden with blooming shrubs and flowers. A continental breakfast is served between 8:00 - 9:00 am. Families are welcomed. Freeport has a beautiful coastline with spectacular views, harbour cruises, sailing, fishing, golf,

©Inn & Travel Memphis, Tennessee

Maine | *National Edition*

biking, hiking, whale watching, seal watching and sunset cruises. Restaurants with their outdoor tables line Main Street in summer. Freeport has more than one hundred outlets, factory stores, craft shops and boutiques, pottery, porcelain, leather, silver, antiques and world famous LL Bean, open 24 hours every day. The mellow atmosphere, the warmth, the charm and the whole experience will stay with you long after you leave. Spend a memorable week, weekend or midweek in our delightful and cozy Inn. We look forward to welcoming you to Freeport and the *Bayberry Inn*. Approved AAA, ABBA **Discounts:** Extended stays - 4 or more nights **Airport:** Portland Jetport-20 mi **Packages:** Yes, inquire at res time **Seasonal:** Rates vary **Reservations:** One night's lodging to confirm reservation, 5 day cancel policy for refund **Brochure:** Yes **Permitted:** Children, drinking **Payment Terms:** Check MC/V [I03HPME1-19569] COM YG ITC **Member:** No **Quality Assurance:** Requested

Rates: Pvt Bath 5
Single $49-95.00
Double $49-95.00

Captain Josiah Mitchell House	188 Main St 04032	Freeport ME
Alan & Loretta Bradley		Tel: 207-865-3289
		Res Times 9am-9pm

In-town Freeport, you're just a five minute walk to LL Bean Co along tree-shaded sidewalks that border beautiful old sea captains' homes. From the moment you arrive, you'll know you've discovered a very special place. This lovely former captain's residence is furnished with period antiques, four-poster beds, Victorian period satins and velvets, beautiful oil paintings and an exquisite collection of Oriental rugs covering the original floors. A gracious and grand dining room with a magnificent chandelier is the setting for breakfast. After shopping in the quaint shops, spend time relaxing on the large veranda furnished with antique wicker and a *"remember-when"* porch swing or rest in our screened gazebo! Plenty of shopping, hiking trails, golfing and dining spots (offering great lobster). The summer theater and Bowdoin College is nearby and you're just two hours from terrific skiing. Year-round sights include the wonderful Maine

munity of the Bounty fame

beaches, just 30 mins by car. Your gracious host will be most helpful to tell you the history of the famous Capt Mitchell, whose diary was used for writing *"Mutiny of the Bounty"*. For a treat, try the Mark Twain Room! **Airport:** Portland-20 mi **Discounts:** Lower winter rates **Seasonal:** Rates vary **Reservations:** Full payment in advance or credit card number to guarantee, arrive by 8 pm, two weeks advance in summer **Brochure:** Yes **Permitted:** Limited children, limited drinking **Payment Terms:** Check MC/V [I10HPME1-6119] COM YG **ITC Member:** No

Rates: Pvt Bath 7
Single $59.00-up
Double $69.00-up

Isaac Randall House	5 Independence Dr 04032	Freeport ME
Glyn & Jim Friedlander	Tel: 800-865-9295 207-865-9295	Fax: 207-865-9003
		Res Times 7am-10pm

The *Isaac Randall House* is a lovely Federal-style farmhouse built 171 years ago as a wedding present for Isaac, Jr and his bride, Betsy Cummings. Later, the home became a stop on the underground railway helping slaves escape into Canada. In years past, the property has been a dairy farm, a prohibition and depression-era dance hall and a tourist court. Today, restored as a Country Inn, its friendly ambience welcomes guests year-round. This historic farmhouse is located just off Rte 1, on six acres of land with a spring-fed pond. All of the guest rooms are charmingly appointed with antiques, oriental rugs and quilts. All have private bath, phone and a/c in season. Some include working fireplaces and TV. The Inn is within walking distance to the famous LL Bean and many other luxury factory outlet stores. Guests can relax outdoors and enjoy the beautiful New England weather, walk among the wildflowers along the path to the pond, broil a steak on our barbeque, make a snack in the guest service-kitchen or just sit back and enjoy games or conversation in the common room. Open year-round, near-by are beaches, golf, summer theatre, mountain parks and seashore preserves. Excellent dining is just a stroll away! **Packages:** Specials Available, inquire at res time **Discounts:** Yes, seniors and stays of 4 nights and longer **Airport:** Portland's Jetport-13 miles **Seasonal:** Rates vary **Reservations:** Deposit or credit card number to guarantee reservation *Caboose $125.00 **Permitted:** Limited children, pets in certain rooms, limited drinking **Conference:** Seminars can be accommodated for groups to twenty persons **Languages:** French, Spanish **Payment Terms:** Check DISC/MC/V [I09HPME1-3589] **COM** U **ITC Member:** No

Rates:	Pvt Bath 8	Caboose
Single	$ 60-105.00	
Double	$ 75-115.00	$ 125.00

Dark Harbor House Inn   PO Box 185   04848   Isleboro ME
Matt Skinner   **Tel:** 207-734-6669

An elegant example of a summer Georgian Revival Mansion off the Maine coast on it's own island setting for a quiet and peaceful setting. Continental breakfast is included. Complimentary bikes and wine. **Seasonal:** No **Brochure:** Yes **Permitted:** Limited smoking, limited drinking **Payment Terms:** Check [X11ACME-3601] **COM** Y **ITC Member:** No

Rates:	Pvt Bath 4	Shared Bath 3
Single	$ 70.00	$ 65.00
Double	$ 85.00	$ 75.00

Alewife House   1917 Alewive Rd Rt 35 04043   Kennebunk ME
Maryellen & Tom Foley   **Tel:** 207-985-2118
                                                                  Res Times 7am-11pm

Step back in time in this 1756 farmhouse nestled on six acres of rolling hills, gardens including a babbling brook - between area lakes and the ocean. Our B&B has enchanted guests for the past five seasons. Antique furnishings, pumpkin pine floors, stenciled walls and six fireplaces offer comfort and charm to guests from California to England, Russia and Sweden. Each guestroom accommodates two adults. Our accommodations have been selected by *"Yankee"* magazine and Bernice Chessler's B&B guide as a favored place to visit. A waterfall, small country church, old barns and stone fences are a few of the rural delights within walking distance. We are located about ten minutes by car from area beaches of Kennebunk and Kennebunkport. The *Alewife House* en-vironment is a treasure in all four seasons where guests are always made to feel special. A continental plus breakfast with fresh fruit and perked coffee is served on our sun porch each morning. Visit The Ashes of Roses Antiques Shop on our grounds. *Alewife House* is conveniently located 90 miles north of Boston, 45 mins south of LL Bean (Freeport ME) and 30 mins south of Portland. **Airport:** Portland-20 mi **Seasonal:** No **Reservations:** Deposit for entire stay required at res time, 14 day cancel policy for refund. If less than 14 day notice, 90% refund if re-rented. Check-in 5pm, check-out 11am. **Brochure:** Yes **Permitted:** Children 13-up, drinking, Smoke-free environment, no pets **Payment Terms:** Check MC/V [Z05FG-ME-3605] **COM** Y **ITC Member:** No

Rates:	Pvt Bath 2	Shared Bath 1
Single	$ 75.00	$ 75.00
Double	$ 75.00	$ 75.00

Lake Brook Guest House   57 Western Ave 04043   Kennebunk ME

Maine   National Edition

Carolyn McAdams   Tel: 207-967-4069

A great location, just one mile from Kennebunk Beach, just 1/2 mile from downtown Kennebunkport with many fine galleries, shops and restaurants. All rooms have private baths, ceiling fans and comforters for chilly Maine nights. **Seasonal:** No **Reservations:** Deposit to hold room **Brochure:** Yes **Permitted:** Children, limited smoking **Payment Terms:** Check [C11ACME-1390] **COM** Y **ITC Member:** No

Rates: Pvt Bath 4
Single $ 75.00
Double $ 85-95.00

1802 House B&B	PO Box 646-A 04046-1646	Kennebunkport ME
Ron & Carol Perry		Tel: 800-932-5632 207-967-5632
		Res Times 8am-10pm

1802 House - is informal, secluded, delightfully quiet and completely smoke-free. The Inn, bounded by the Cape Arundel Golf Club on two sides (non-members may play), is a ten minute walk from Dock Square. A morning choir of songbirds gets guests from the dewy fairways that roll past the breakfast room. The fresh ocean breeze and clean Maine sunshine bathes the Inns' decks and gardens. Each of the six recently remodeled, updated and cheerful guest rooms includes a private bathroom. Some rooms have fireplaces with queen size beds, others have four poster queen size beds and some rooms have two beds. The Inn and all guest rooms are furnished with antiques; each room offers the privacy and amenities that make the *1802 House A "Down-East" home away from home*. A full country breakfast awaits our guests each morning and consists of juices, coffee, tea and hot chocolate; a fresh fruit course; a main dish that might be Bavarian Apple Pancake with bacon or Baked Eggs Florentine gratine with ham; each served with freshly baked muffins and breads. Popular local activities include sightseeing along the coastline, including former President Bush's seaside home, swimming, boating, fishing, antiquing, shopping and delicious dining. Please inquire about our off-season dinner packages. **Airport:** Portland Jetport-25 mi **Packages:** Off-Season Dinner **Seasonal:** No **Reservations:** Full deposit for stays to 2 days, 50% for 3 days or longer stays, 14 day cancel policy for refund **Brochure:** Yes **Permitted:** Children 12-up, drinking **Conference:** Limited **Languages:** Some French, German **Payment Terms:** Check AE/MC/V [I03GPME-5934] **COM** Y **ITC Member:** No **Quality Assured:** Yes

Rates: Pvt Bath 6
Single $ 55-105.00
Double $ 65-125.00

Captain Fairfield House	PO Box 1308 04046	Kennebunkport ME
Bonnie & Dennis Tallagnon		Tel:800-322-1928 207-967-4454
		Res Times 9am-8pm

This gracious 1813 Federal Mansion is in Kennebunkports placid historic district. Conveniently located and only steps to the Village and Harbour, guests are a few minutes walk to Dock Square Marinas, shops, area restaurants and beaches. This Inn is ideal for those who wish to be near activities, yet seek a peaceful and quiet retreat. Graceful and elegant, the Inn's common rooms and bedrooms are individually and beautifully decorated with Period furnishings and wicker, which lend an atmosphere of tranquility and charm. Fireplaces are available in some rooms with complimentary firewood (except July and August) for cozy evenings. Guests may relax in our living-room, browse

1-22   ©*Inn & Travel Memphis, Tennessee*

in the library, or enjoy the tree-shaded grounds and gardens, following an active day on the Maine Coast. Guests awaken to birdsong from the gardens, the smell of fresh sea air and the aroma of gourmet coffee brewing in the kitchen. A full complimentary breakfast is always a treat - fresh fruits and juices, homemade breads, muffins and preserves; omelettes, crepes, pancakes, waffles and other specialties begin your day. The guest refrigerator is stocked with iced tea, chilled spring water and ice. Truly - home away from home! Exceptional and unique restaurants and shops abound. After a visit to this historic seaport one appreciates why former President Bush chose Kennebunkport as his summer retreat. **Airport:** Portland Intl-30 mins driving **Seasonal:** No **Reservations:** One nights deposit within 7 days of booking, 10 day cancel policy for refund less $10 service fee, two day min July & Aug weekends and holidays, arrival 2-8pm, later arrival by prior arrangement **Brochure:** Yes **Permitted:** Alcoholic beverages, children 7-up, limited smoking **Payment Terms:** Check AE/MC/V [I05FPME-3610] **COM Y ITC Member:** No

Rates: Pvt Bath 9
Single $ 70-145.00
Double $ 75-149.00

Captain Lord Mansion   PO Box 800 04046-0800   Kennebunkport ME
Bev Davis/Rich Litchfield   Tel: 207-967-3141 Fax: 207-967-3172
                                                                                 Res Times 8am-11pm

The Captain Lord Mansion is an intimate and stylish Inn situated at the head of a sloping village green, overlooking the Kennebunk River. Built during the War of 1812 as an elegant private residence, it is now listed on the *National Historic Register*. The large, luxurious guest rooms are furnished with rich fabrics, European paintings and fine period antiques, yet have modern comforts such as private baths, oversized beds, telephones, and gas working fireplaces. Six deluxe rooms overlook the green and Kennebunk River. These are the most sought after accommodations at the Inn. Gracious hosts and innkeepers, Bev Davis and husband Rick Litchfield, and their friendly, helpful staff are eager to make your visit enjoyable. Your greeting at the Inn will be warm and cheerful. The innkeepers and their staff also are pleased to help map out itineraries for shopping, walking, biking or driving. They also can point you to great restaurants, antique shops and out-of-the-way sights. Family-style full three-course breakfast are served in an atmospheric country kitchen. Breakfast begins with a choice of fresh fruit, creamy, French-vanilla yogurt, and a flavorful muesli cereal. The second course consists of made-from-scratch muffins, served piping hot from the oven to the table. The main course varies day to day and one of the following scrumptious dishes is served: Belgian waffles or buckwheat pancakes with fresh apples of blueberries, or Texas-size cinnamon French toast, or vegetable quiche. The Inn has been awarded the AAA 4-Diamond Award for fifteen consecutive years. *Andrew Harper's Hideaway Report* awarded the Inn it's *"Best B&B in the US"* citation in 1992. The Inn has been given the *"star"* choice by *Fromers* and *Fodors*. Warm hospitality, delicious breakfasts and incredible rooms are combined with meticulous attention to cleanliness and room details, making the Inn an engaging and memorable vacation spot. **Packages:** Yes, inquire at res time **Seasonal:** No **Reservations:** Deposit by credit card to guarantee res, 15 day cancel policy for refund less $15 service fee, min 2 night stay weekends year-round, $25 extra charge per person **Brochure:** Yes **Permitted:** Limited children, drinking **Conference:** Yes, groups to fourteen persons with board room style conference table, complete a/v and lunch with prior arrange-

Maine   *National Edition*

ments **Payment Terms:** Check AE/DISC/MC/V [J12GPME1-1380] **COM** YG **ITC Member:** No

Rates: Pvt Bath 16
Single $ 75-275.00
Double $ 75-275.00

| *Farm House B&B* | RR 1 Box 656   04046 | **Kennebunkport ME** |

Bart Panzenhagen   **Tel:** 207-967-4169

A gracious family Inn close to all points of interest, just ten mins from historic Dock Square. Continental breakfast is included. **Seasonal:** No **Reservations:** One night's deposit at res time **Brochure:** Yes **Permitted:** Limited smoking, limited drinking **Payment Terms:** Check [C11ACME-1384]

COM Y **ITC Member:** No

Rates: Pvt Bath 2
Single
Double $ 85.00

| *Inn At Harbor Head* | RR 2 Box 1180 Pier Rd   04046 | **Kennebunkport ME** |

Joan & Dave Sutter   **Tel:** 207-967-5564   **Fax:** 207-967-8776
                                                    Res Times 9:30-9:30

The nostalgia of a bygone era lingers in this picturesque fishing village inviting guests to relax and savor the feeling of *"letting go,"* so essential for a good vacation or important getaway. Your charming artist/innkeeper has beautifully decorated and furnished the Inn with original sculpture, family portraits, marine paintings, Oriental carpets, antique furniture and hand-painted murals on guestroom walls. The ocean and harbor are in view from the windows and a stroll down the yard will put you at the water's edge. The guest rooms are furnished with queen or king size beds, one with a raised whirlpool tub surrounded by hand-painted ceramic tiles. Fresh coffee begins the day at 7:30 with a gourmet's delight at 9:00, set with china and silver, to befit a typical offering of fresh squeezed orange juice, broiled grapefruit or bananas and a main course of stuffed french toast covered with fresh fruit or freshly made roast-beef hash with poached egg and salsa - guests come back just for breakfast! Full service is assured with nightly turn-down service, Godiva Chocolates and a champagne split for special occasions. Parking passes for Goose Rocks Beach (complimentary chairs and towels) area maps and a basketful of menus to sample the freshest fish and best lobster in the world! **Seasonal:** Closed Christmas **Reservations:** Strongly recommended, one night's deposit within 10 day, 10 day cancel policy for refund, two night min. 3-7pm check-in; 11am check-out **Brochure:** Yes **Permitted:** Drinking **Payment Terms:** Check MC/V [R02CPME-1387] **COM** Y **ITC Member:** No

Rates: Pvt Bath 4
Single $ 85-150.00
Double $ 85-150.00

| *Inn On South Street* | PO Box 478A   04046 | **Kennebunkport ME** |

Jacques & Eva Downs   **Tel:**800-963-5151 207-967-5151
                                                    Res Times 9am-9:30pm

Combine charm and romance in this 19th Century Greek Revival home fully restored and listed on the *National Register of Historic Places* in a picture-perfect setting. The interior decor reflects the area's connection with a maritime past and offers three uniquely furnished guest rooms with queen-sized beds, antique and period furnishings in each room. Also one luxurious three room suite-apartment with fireplace, whirlpool tub, queen-sized four-poster bed. Early risers find steaming coffee at 7:30 am. A full gourmet breakfast later includes Jack's home-baked breads, pancakes or other Downs family specialties. You'll enjoy breakfast in the country kitchen with a lovely ocean and river view or if you're in the honeymoon suite, you'll have a private breakfast overlooking the herb gardens. Each guest room is complete with fresh flowers, fluffy comforters, pillows and towels. Complimentary: Afternoon tea, wine or lemonade. Convenient, quiet location, within easy walking distance of shops, restaurants, beaches and the historic village areas. Closed Christmas and March. Featured in *"Country Inns Bed & Breakfast"*, Fall'87, Summer 1990 issue *"Discerning Traveller"* and *"Down East"*, 1994. Rated A+ by ABBA. **Discounts:** Yes, for week long stays **Airport:** Portland ME-30 mi; Boston Logan-80 mi **Seasonal:** See Below **Reservations:** 50% deposit or one night's rate (whichever is greater) or credit card to hold room, 14 day cancel policy for refund, two night min on weekends, holidays and in-season (6/21-10/28) **Brochure:** Yes **Permitted:** Older children **Languages:** German, Spanish, Russian **Payment Terms:** Check MC/V [I06HPME1-1388] **COM YG ITC Member:** No

Rates: Pvt Bath 4
Single
Double $ 85-185.00

Kennebunkport Inn	One Dock Square 04046	Kennebunkport ME
Rick & Martha Griffin	Tel: 800-248-2621 207-967-2621 Fax: 207-867-3705	Res Times 24 Hrs

Situated in the heart of Kennebunkport, just off the Kennebunk River, near the shop and historic district, the Inn was originally built as a sea captain's house in 1899. Today it maintains its' warmth and charm with late Victorian decor and antiques throughout. The guest rooms have private baths, color TV, a/c, phones and many include four-poster beds. The restaurant, one of the finest in the area, is well-known for its' regional cuisine, fresh native seafood, scrumptious Maine lobsters and features an extensive wine list. The charming dining ambiance is accented by fireplaces and candlelight. The dining room is open and serves a full breakfast and dinner from mid-May through late October. A continental breakfast is served during the off season. Outdoor dining on the patio for lunch and warm summer nights is also available. The turn-of-the-century Pub lounge, is a great spot to unwind in the evening. From mid-June through late October, nightly entertainment at the Piano Bar is provided. During the Spring, entertainment is provided on Friday and Saturday nights. There is a small outdoor pool with a large deck area for relaxation. Daytime activities include shopping at the numerous shops at your doorstep featuring antiques, arts and crafts and clothing. You can choose swimming in the pool or nearby beaches, golf, tennis, boating, horseback riding, bicycling, theaters or sightseeing along the rocky coast and country roads. **Discounts:** 10% AARP & AAA **Airport:** Logan-80 mi **Packages:** Two, Three and Four Night Stays include all breakfasts, one evening dinner, taxes, gratuity and lobster boat ride **Directions:** Rt 9E into Kennebunkport, over small bridge, through the square, past monument. Inn is the first building on the left, after the square. **Seasonal:** Yes, rates vary **Reservations:** One night's deposit, 14 day cancel policy less $10 service fee, 3-day min stay on Summer and holidays weekends; 2-day min stay on Spring & Fall weekends; Off season rates $79.50-179.00 **Brochure:** Yes **Permitted:** Children, drinking, limited smoking **Conference:** Yes, November to April, groups to 20 persons **Languages:** French **Payment Terms:** Check AE/MC/V [J11HPME1-3611] **COM YG ITC Member:** No

Rates: Pvt Bath 34
Single $ 79-139.00
Double $ 89-219.00

Kilburn House	6 Chestnut St 04046	Kennebunkport ME
Samuel & Shirey Minier		Tel: 207-967-4762
		Res Times 8am-10pm

©Inn & Travel Memphis, Tennessee

Centrally located just outside of Dock Square in town, the *Kilburn House* was the home of artists Margaret Kilburn-Fisher and William Fisher. Margaret was skilled in etching, stained glass and various arts and crafts while William is noted for his American scenes in oil and water colors. Today their works along with other works from their favorite artists are displayed through-out the house and the B&B is proudly run by William Fisher's immediate family. There are four guest rooms on the second floor and a delightful and airy suite encompassing the entire third floor with views in all directions. A warm, fresh full breakfast is served each morning and is included in the room rate. A short walk from the *Kilburn House* are many exquisite shops and restaurants while a short drive takes you to the fishing village of Cape Porpoise, Goose Rocks, Kennebunk Beaches and to Portland, Freeport (home of LL Bean) and Ogunquit. **Discounts:** Yes **Airport:** Portland ME-25 mi **Seasonal:** *5/15-10/12 **Reservations:** One night's deposit required, * closed 10/13-5/14 **Brochure:** Yes **Permitted:** Children, drinking **Payment Terms:** Check AE/MC/V [R11EPMA-1389] COM Y ITC **Mem-ber:** No

Rates:	Pvt Bath 2	Shared Bath 2
Single	$ 75.00	$ 45-60.00
Double	$ 75.00	$ 60.00

Maine Stay Inn & Cottages   34 Maine St 04046-1800   Kennebunkport ME
Carol & Lindsay Copeland   Tel: 800-950-2117 207-967-2117 **Fax:** 207-967-8757
                                                                Res Times 8am-10pm

Beautiful 1860 Victorian Inn with Italianate hip roof, accentuated by Queen Ann period flying staircase, wrap around porch, bay windows and masterful architectural detail. The *Maine Stay* offers a variety of air conditioned accommodations, from charming rooms and suites in the main house, to delightful one-bedroom cottages, some with fireplaces and separate kitchens. A sumptuous full breakfast plus afternoon tea and desserts are included. Cottage guests can have breakfast basket delivered to their door or enjoy breakfast with the rest of our guests in the dining room. Our living room, which is often filled with the aroma of our home baked goodies, is a comfortable place to sit and meet fellow travelers or enjoy a fire on a cold winter day. The Inn is perfectly situated in Kennebunkport's historic district. Our spacious grounds offer a peaceful resting spot amid the gigantic Maine pines. Our location, four blocks from the village, allows guests a leisurely walk to the shops, galleries, restaurants and the harbor. Golf, tennis and beautiful swimming beaches are all within one mile. Scenic Kennebunkport can be viewed via guided trolley car ride or by boat cruise. Other activities include boating, whale watching, visiting local museums, antiquing, and walking tours of the historic district. Bicycling, horseback riding, cross country skiing and ice skating are available in the area. **Airport:** Portland Jetport 25 mi, Boston Logan 75 mi. **Packages:** "Romance Renewed Package" includes two night's lodging, one dinner for two at local restaurant, gifts, breakfast, tea from Nov to May **Seasonal:** No **Reservations:** 50% deposit or one night's stay (which ever is larger) within 7 mailing days, 14 day cancel policy for refund less $15 service fee **Brochure:** Yes **Permitted:** Children **Conference:** Yes, for small groups (10-15 persons) in dining room, living room and fireplace suite **Payment Terms:** Check AE/DISC/MC/V [J11HPME1-1391] COM YG TC **Member:** No

Rates:	Pvt Bath 17
Single	$ 85-210.00
Double	$ 85-210.00

Olde Garrison House   Cape Porpoise 04014   Kennebunkport ME
Louise & Lyman Huff   Tel: 207-967-3522
                                                           Res Times 8am-8pm

1-26   ©*Inn & Travel Memphis, Tennessee*

National Edition   **Maine**

Relaxed New England atmosphere in this Cape Cod-style cottage overlooking a cove with plenty of salty air, gulls and lobster. The owners are lobster fishermen and you're at the right place if you're a lobster lover! Your hosts will lead you to the best ones around! **Seasonal:** 5/15-10/15 Open **Reservations:** Full payment in advance of date, 15 day cancel notice for full refund less $20 service fee **Brochure:** Yes **Permitted:** Children 12-up, drinking, smoking **Payment Terms:** Check [X11ACME-1394] **COM** Y **ITC Member:** No

Rates:	Pvt Bath 3	Shared Bath 2
Single	$ 62.00	$ 50.00
Double	$ 68.00	$ 58.00

White Barn Inn	PO Box 560C 04046	**Kennebunkport ME**
Laurie Cameron		Tel: 207-967-2321

A restored and renovated barn offers a casual yet elegant atmosphere. Dining is excellent; winner of 1983 Silver Spoon Award! Continental off-season. **Seasonal:** No **Reservations:** One night's deposit at res time *Rates based on European Plan **Brochure:** Yes **Permitted:** Children, smoking, drinking **Payment Terms:** Check AE/MC/V [C11ACME-1399] **COM** Y **ITC Member:** No

Rates:	Pvt Bath 24
Single	$ 90.00
Double	$ 110.00

Inn On Winters Hill	Winters Hill 04947	**Kingfield ME**
		Tel: 207-265-5421
		Res Times 7am-11pm

Originally designed by the Stanley Brothers, developers of the Stanley Steamer automobile, this charming Victorian mansion offers New England elegance and atmosphere with modern amenities. Listed on the *National Register of Historic Places*. Meals available on the premises with added cost. **Seasonal:** No **Reservations:** Deposit or credit card to hold room, 48 hour cancel policy **Brochure:** Yes **Permitted:** Children, smoking **Languages:** French **Payment Terms:** Check AE/MC/V [C11ACME-1403] **COM** Y **ITC Member:** No

Stanley Steamer fame mansion

Rates:	Pvt Bath 9	Shared Bath 2
Single	$ 90.00	$ 75.00
Double	$ 105.00	$ 85.00

Melfair Farm	365 Wilson Rd 03904	**Kittery ME**
Claire Cane		Tel: 207-439-0320

This 1871 New England traditional farmhouse in rolling pasture provides guests with warmth and hospitality. Close to shopping, beaches and historical Portsmouth. Continental plus gourmet breakfast. **Seasonal:** No **Reservations:** Deposit required at res time **Brochure:** Yes **Permitted:** Children 11-up, smoking, drinking **Languages:** French **Payment Terms:** Check [C11ACME-1404] **COM** Y **ITC Member:** No

Rates:	Shared Bath 4
Single	$ 70.00
Double	$ 75.00

Penury Hall	PO Box 68 04679	**Mount Desert Island ME**
Gretchen & Toby Strong		Tel: 207-244-7102

An 1830 frame home furnished in a traditional mixture of antiques, family heirlooms and original art. Friendly and hospitable, your hosts make for an enjoyable visit to this charming town. Full breakfast included. **Seasonal:** No **Reservations:** Deposit required at res time **Brochure:** Yes **Permitted:** Children over 16, smoking, drinking **Payment Terms:** Check [C11ACME-1423] **COM** Y **ITC Member:** No

©*Inn & Travel Memphis, Tennessee*

Rates:
Single $ 45.00
Double $ 50.00

Shared Bath 3

Songo B&B House   PO Box 554 04055   Naples ME
Judy & Ben Garron   Tel: 207-693-3960
                                                                Res Times 9am-8pm

Rustic country setting for this residence offering year-round activities for the entire family. Close to historic Songo Locks, swimming, tennis and golf are available with excellent skiing in winter. Full breakfast included. Just off Rt 302. **Seasonal:** No **Brochure:** Yes **Permitted:** Limited children **Payment Terms:** Check [C11ACME-1429] **COM** Y **ITC Member:** No

Rates:	Pvt Bath 2	Shared Bath 3
Single	$ 70.00	$ 65.00
Double	$ 80.00	$ 75.00

Captains House   19 River Rd 04553   Newcastle ME
Joe Sullivan/Susan Rizzo   Tel: 207-563-1482

Grand Greek Revival styling in this former sea captain's residence on the Damariscotta River, c1840. Large sunny guest rooms with excellent views overlooking the river setting. Full country breakfast included. Visit local sights and beaches nearby. **Seasonal:** No **Reservations:** 50% deposit required within 7 day of booking **Brochure:** Yes **Permitted:** Limited children **Payment Terms:** Check [C11ACME-1433] **COM** Y **ITC Member:** No

Rates: **Shared Bath 5**
Single $ 60.00
Double $ 70.00

Newcastle Inn   River Rd 04553   Newcastle ME
Ted & Chris Sprague   Tel: 800-832-8669 207-563-5685 Fax: 207-563-5685
                                                                 Res Times 10am-6pm

When you come to The *Newcastle Inn* you will find more than a welcome . . .. you will find a welcome home. We personally invite you to come and enjoy our fine small Inn . . . to share in our tradition of genuine hospitality. At the end of your day's travels, a warm greeting, an exceptional dinner, and a pampering atmosphere await you, here by the Damariscotta River. Come indulge your senses, where our nationally-acclaimed, four-star, five-course, fireside dinner is always an occasion to celebrate. Before dinner, gather in The Briar Patch, an intimate pub. In the morning, you'll awaken to our famous multi-course breakfast, guaranteed to stand you in good stead for the day's activities. We offer a cozy fireplaced living room, overlooking the river, a common room with beautifully stenciled floor and a wicker-filled sunporch which invites relaxation and conversation; and in the summer, a hammock from which to enjoy the perennial gardens and the river - - all at an unhurried pace. This quiet corner of Maine's famous Mid Coast is just enough off the well-trodden path that you'll have the pleasure of discovering your own special hideaways. Your memories will be filled with lighthouse-crowned ocean points, islands in the bay and authenticaside villages where things haven't changed much in a long time. We sincerely hope that your stay will soothe your body as well as your spirit. We look forward to having you as our guest. **Airport:** Portland Jetport-60mi **Packages:** New Year's Eve, Windjammer, Cooking **Reservations:** One night's deposit required. 7 day cancel policy less $20 service fee, if room is re-rented, deposit may be used for credit within 6 months of cancelled stay **Permitted:** Limited drinking **Conference:** Yes, seasonal from 11/1-5/30 **Payment Terms:** Check MC/V [I07HPME1-7443] **COM** YG **ITC Member:** No **Quality Assured:** Yes

Rates: **Pvt Bath 15**
Single $ 55-125.00
Double $ 60-135.00

Blue Shutters
Jean Dahler

6 Beachmere Place 03907

Ogunquit ME
Tel: 207-646-2163

This tranquil setting offers spectacular views, great New England hospitality and beautiful scenery year-round. Quaint beaches just a short stroll away. **Seasonal:** No **Brochure:** Yes **Permitted:** Smoking, drinking **Payment Terms:** Check [C11-ACME-1447] **COM** Y **ITC Member:** No

Rates: **Pvt Bath 5**
Single $ 70.00
Double $ 75.00

Hartwell House
Trisha & Jim Hartwell

116 Shore Rd 03907

Ogunquit ME
Tel: 207-646-7210 Fax: 207-646-6032

Elegant residence offers genuine antiques from England and Early Americana. Perfect setting to relax while visiting New England with over two acres of sculptured gardens. Continental breakfast is included. Swimming and tennis available. **Seasonal:** No **Brochure:** Yes **Permitted:** Limited smoking, limited drinking **Conference:** Yes for business or social events including gourmet dining **Payment Terms:** Check V [C11ACME-1453] **COM** Y **ITC Member:** No

Rates: **Pvt Bath 9**
Single $ 120.00
Double $ 140.00

Morning Dove B&B
Peter & Eeta Schon

30 Bourne Lane 03907-1940

Ogunquit ME
Tel: 207-646-3891
Res Times 9am-9pm

The *Morning Dove* is a tastefully restored 1860's farmhouse formerly owned by the Moses Littlefield family. It has light airy rooms furnished with antiques and European accents. The owner is an ASID interior designer and has designed each room to be totally unique. Antique collectibles such as brass beds, quilts, lace curtains and art by local artists are some of the furnishings. Breakfast is served cafe-style on the Victorian porch or in the elegant dining room. The Inn is conveniently located on a quiet side street and surrounded by spectacular and now famous gardens. Its a short stroll to the beaches, the Marginal Way, Perkins Cove, the Playhouse, shops, galleries and restaurants. The trolley stops on the corner. Candies and welcoming wine are complimentary. Hiking, tennis, outlet shopping and Mount Argamenticus for fall foliage are all nearby. Its an easy drive to Kennebunkport, Portsmouth's Strawberry Banke, Freeport, Kittery and Portland. The Portland Jetport is just 35 minutes and Boston's Logan Airport is and hour and fifteen minutes. **Seasonal:** No **Reservations:** 50% deposit within 7 days of booking to hold room, 10 day cancel policy for refund less $10 service fee; min stay during peak periods (mid-June to Labor Day) discounts for long stays. **Brochure:** Yes **Permitted:** Drinking, children 12-up **Languages:** Conversational French **Payment Terms:** Check AE/DISC/MC/V [Z08GPME-6831] **COM** U **ITC Member:** No

Rates: **Pvt Bath 4**   **Shared Bath 2**
Single $ 75-105.00 $ 55-80.00
Double $ 75-105.00 $ 55-80.00

Seafair Inn
Jeff Walker

24 Shore Rd 03907

Ogunquit ME
Tel: 207-646-2181

Beautiful restored Victorian residence and Inn complete with antique furnishings and period pieces. Close to all sights, shops, antiques and fine dining. Beach nearby. Continental breakfast in-

Maine   *National Edition*

cluded. Afternoon high tea and pastry. **Seasonal:** No **Brochure:** Yes **Permitted:** Children, smoking, limited drinking **Languages:** French **Payment Terms:** Check MC/V [C11ACME-1461] **COM** Y **ITC Member:** No

Rates:	Pvt Bath 16	Shared Bath 3
Single	$ 75.00	$ 60.00
Double	$ 95.00	$ 70.00

Yardarm Village Inn   142 Shore Rd 03907   **Ogunquit ME**
LC & PC Drury   Tel: 207-646-7006

Yardarm Village Inn - With old New England atmosphere is adjacent to Perkins Cove in Oqunquit and offers comfortable accommodations in this quiet part of Ogunquit, yet guests are just a short walk from the Marginal Way, Perkins Cove and the town beaches. All of the guest rooms include private baths, cable TV, refrigerators and air conditioning. A continental breakfast is included and the breakfast coffee and famous homemade blueberry muffins are a must! *Yardarm Village Inn's* Wine and Cheese Shop offers domestic and international wines of distinction. **Airport:** Portland-29 mi **Brochure:** Yes **Permitted:** Children, drinking, limited smoking **Payment Terms:** Check [R10EPME-1465] **COM** U **ITC Member:** No

Rates:	Pvt Bath 8
Single	$ 59.00-up
Double	$ 59.00-up

Inn At Parkerspring   135 Spring 04101   **Portland ME**
Judy & Bob Riley   Tel: 207-774-1059

c1845 townhouse in the center of town in a unique three-story design, one of Portland's finest. Fresh flowers, night-time chocolates and comfy towels are just a few pleasant touches this charming hostess provides her guests. Continental breakfast included. **Seasonal:** No **Brochure:** Yes **Permitted:** Children 5-up, smoking, drinking **Payment Terms:** Check MC/V [C11ACME-1474] **COM** Y **ITC Member:** No

Rates:	Pvt Bath 5	Shared Bath 2
Single	$ 85.00	$ 75.00
Double	$ 100.00	$ 85.00

York Harbor Inn   **Portland ME**
Garry Doninquez   Tel: 800-343-3869 207-363-5119 Fax: 207-363-3545
                                                                                       Res Times 8am-11pm

Refer to the same listing located under York Harbor, Maine for a complete description. **Seasonal:** Rates vary **Payment Terms:** Check AE/CD/DC/ER/MC/V [M08GCME-8252] **COM** Y **ITC Member:** No

Rates:	Pvt Bath 29	Shared Bath 6
Single	$ 79.00	$ 69.00
Double	$ 99.00	$ 89.00

Craignair Inn   **Rockland ME**
Norman & Terry Smith   Tel: 207-594-7644
                                                                                       Res Times 9am-9pm

Refer to the same name listed under Clark Island, Maine for a complete description. **Seasonal:** Clo Feb **Payment Terms:** Check AE/MC/V [M08BCE-8800] **COM** Y **ITC Member:** No

Rates:	Pvt Bath 8	Shared Bath 14
Single	$ 76.00	$ 42.00
Double	$ 86.00	$ 62.00

Lakeshore Inn   184 Lakeview Dr Rt 17 04841   **Rockland ME**
Paula Nicols/Joe McCluskey   Tel: 207-594-4209

We place our emphasis on personalized attention and our delicious full gourmet breakfasts *". . . so you can skip lunch."* Our four beautifully appointed and tastefully decorated guest rooms have queen size beds with private bath and air conditioning. Each of these lovely rooms has a view of the lake and two open out onto a deck. Unwind in front of one of the fireplaces after a day of winter fun. In warm weather, the colorful garden patio offers a pleasant atmosphere in which to visit with friends and fellow guests, or just lean back and relax or read within view of the Inn's orchard. In season, the views from the deck, sunroom or the outdoor patio include a beautiful array of wildbirds and wildlife, including numerous deer. The original structure of the *Lakeshore Inn* was built in 1767 by Rockland's first settlers, the Tolman family. It is reported to be one of the first buildings constructed in the town and it has undergone several cycles of additions and renovations. The latest cycle is the most recent renovation of this old New England farmhouse - into the *Lakeshore Inn* for the 1994 season. Join us at 184 Lakeview Drive in Rockland, Maine (Lakeview Drive is State Route 17) The Inn is about two miles north of the city, just one hundred yards south of the Rockport town line and six miles south of Camden. **Discounts:** Extended stays **Airport:** Portland & Bangor ME-1-1/2 hrs; Knox County (Owls Head)-20 min **Seasonal:** No **Reservations:** One nights deposit for stays to 2 nights, 3+ nights, 50% of stay; 14 day cancel policy for refund less $10 service fee, check payments must be received within 7 days of booking **Brochure:** Yes **Permitted:** Children 10+ **Conference:** Small bridal shower and social functions **Languages:** Greek **Payment Terms:** Check MC/V [I04IPME1-23219] **COM** U **ITC Member:** No

Rates: **Pvt Bath 4**
Single $ 85-90.00
Double $ 85-90.00

Sign Of The Unicorn   191 Beauchamp Ave 04856   **Rockport ME**
Winnie Easton   **Tel:** 207-236-8789

Great location for visiting Rockport. Overlook Rockport Harbor and enjoy sailing, fishing, golf, theater, tennis with fine dining at many excellent seafood restaurants. Full gourmet breakfast included. Sitting room and piano for guests use. **Seasonal:** No **Brochure:** Yes **Permitted:** Children, limited smoking, drinking **Payment Terms:** Check [C11ACME-1484] **COM** Y **ITC Member:** No

Rates:	**Pvt Bath 2**	**Shared Bath 2**
Single	$ 75.00	$ 70.00
Double	$ 80.00	$ 75.00

Crown 'n' Anchor Inn   121 North St 04072-0228   **Saco ME**
John Barclay/Marth Forester   **Tel:** 207-282-3829
                                                                                        Res Times 24 Hrs

Dating from 1827-28, this Greek Revival two-story home was built by George Thacher, Jr, descendent of the First Congressman from the district of Maine and is a fine example of rich detail and delicate lightness typical of the Federal/Adamesque-style and with a temple front. Listed on the *National Register of Historic Places* in the State of Maine, ornate Victorian furnishings, double parlors with twin mirrors and a bountiful country breakfast provide lasting memories for guests after departing. The Normandy Suite on the second floor is a favorite, offering Indian shutters, fireplaces and a private adjacent whirlpool bath. All rooms at the *Crown 'N' Anchor Inn* are furnished with period antiques, many collectibles and provide both a homelike atmosphere and luxurious pampered comfort while vacationing or takg time for a special weekend. Located on North Street,

Maine   *National Edition*

the *Crown 'N' Anchor Inn* is at the hub of local attractions. The York Institute Museum, Thornton Academy and the Dyer Library are all a leisurely walk from the center of the lovely tree-lined main street of Saco, a treasure-trove of 18th and 19th Century architecture. A short drive brings guests to the ocean beaches of Saco or Old Orchard Beach. Kennebunkport, Wells, Oqunquit and the shopping malls of Kittery and Freeport are but minutes away. **Packages:** Yes, inquire at res time **Seasonal:** No **Reservations:** One night deposit to guarantee, 10 day cancel policy; less than 10 day cancellation, 50% refund; no refund for non-arrival **Brochure:** Yes **Permitted:** Limited children, limited pets, limited drinking, no smoking **Conference:** Groups to fifty persons **Languages:** French **Payment Terms:** Check MC/V [I11IPME1-12828] **COM** U **ITC Member:** No

Rates:	Pvt Bath 6
Single	$ 50-85.00
Double	$ 50-85.00

Homeport   Rt 1 E Main St 04974   Searsport ME
Edith & George Johnson   Tel: 800-742-5814 207-548-2259

This sea captain's residence with widow's walk has been fully restored and is listed on the *National Historic Register*. Your charming hosts operate their Inn as a traditional English and Scottish "Bed & Breakfast" which has been open to the public for sixteen years. *Homeport* continues to offer guests a rare opportunity to enjoy the warm, homey, hospitable atmosphere while visiting New England. The guest rooms are complete with antique furnishings, family heirlooms, canopy beds, crystal chandeliers and lace curtains. Guests can enjoy the family room with its English Pub, The Mermaid and the dining room, both on the lower level. A porch or patio setting is offered for breakfast which includes exquisite views of the Bay. A full breakfast is included. Year-round activities include sailing, tennis, golf, cruises on the Bay, pleasant walks along the shore, forest trails and hills with visits to interesting antique and gift shops. October offers brilliant Fall foliage while Winter offers fine cross country skiing. A Victorian oceanside cottage is availle for weekly rental at $450.00. **Discounts:** 10% travel agents; 5% Seniors; 5% weekly stays **Airport:** Bangor Intl Airport-40 mins **Seasonal:** No **Reservations:** $25 non-refundable deposit for each night's stay in advance required **Brochure:** Yes **Permitted:** Limited children, limited smoking, limited drinking **Conference:** Yes, small groups **Payment Terms:** Check AE/ER/MC/V [I08GPME-1488] **COM** Y **ITC Member:** No

Rates:	Pvt Bath 6	Shared Bath 4
Single	$ 37.00	$ 30.00
Double	$ 60-75.00	$ 55.00

Atlantic Seal B&B   25 Main St 04078   South Freeport ME
Capt Thomas & Gaila Ring   Tel: 207-865-6112
                                                                                       Res Times 7:30am-9pm

Lovely harbor views await you in each cozy bedroom of our 1850's Cape Cod home, located on the ocean in historic South Freeport Village and furnished with antiques and nautical collections of our seafaring family. "The Glen" has an antique full-size sleigh bed and a shared bath. "The Heart's Desire" has a queen-sized four-poster pineapple bed and a windowseat, and may have a shared or private bath. "The Dash" has a full-size and queen-size bed and private bath, complete with a Jacuzzi whirlpool bath for two and a separate shower. All three guest rooms feature sea breezes, fresh flowers, thick towels, comfortable beds, homemade quilts and down comforters. Enjoy our friendly downeast hospitality, complimentary snacks & beverages by the fireplace in our old-fashioned parlor, hearty sailor's breakfast and exciting cruises of Casco Bay. Just a five minute drive to outlet stores. Resident dog and cat. Open year-round. **Seasonal:** Clo Xmas **Reservations:** One night's deposit, 14 day cancel notice for refund less $10 service charge. Late arrival by prior arrangement. **Brochure:** Yes **Permitted:** Limited children, smoking outside **Payment Terms:** Check [R09CPME-10012] **COM** Y **ITC Member:** No

National Edition *Maine*

Rates:	Pvt Bath 2	Shared Bath 2
Single	$ 90.00	$ 55.00
Double	$ 100-125.00	$ 65-85.00

Claremont   **Southwest Harbor ME**
Mr Mrs Allen McCue   **Tel:**207-244-5036

An 1844 summer inn on the Sound Shore offering traditional New England styling and atmosphere and the home for the Annual Croquet Tournament. Full breakfast included. Other meals available with added cost. **Seasonal:** No **Brochure:** Yes **Permitted:** Children, smoking and drinking **Payment Terms:** Check AE/MC/V [C11ACME-1499] **COM** Y **ITC Member:** No

Rates:	Pvt Bath 23	Shared Bath 3
Single	$ 110.00	$ 85.00
Double	$ 110.00-up	$ 95.00

Broad Bay Inn & Gallery   Main St 04572   **Waldoboro ME**
Jim & Libby Hopkins   **Tel:** 207-832-6668
                                                     Res Times 8am -8pm

Lovely colonial Inn offering candlelight dinners on the weekends. Sunny guest rooms are filled with Victorian furnishings with canopy beds in some rooms. Close to Maine's coastal sights and points of interest which include artist's workshops, Camden Shakespeare Theatre, summer stock and jazz concerts. Full breakfast included with other meals available at added cost. Complimentary bikes, tea or sherry outdoors in the early evening

Seasonal: No **Reservations:** One night's deposit at res time **Brochure:** Yes **Permitted:** Children 16-up, limited smoking **Payment Terms:** Check MC/V [X09BCME-1523] **COM** Y **ITC Member:** No

Rates:	Pvt Bath 1	Shared Bath 4
Single	$ 70.00	$ 45-65.00
Double	$ 75.00	$ 55-65.00

Le Vatout B&B   Rt 32 South 04572   **Waldoboro ME**
Don Slagel   **Tel:** 207-832-4552
                                            Res Times 8am-10pm

A rural setting midway between Brunswick and Belfast (perfect stopping place for exploring the scenic peninsulas of mid-coast Maine) is the locale for this restored pre-Civil War home on the village edge. Just a half mile off Rt 1, you'll enjoy the coast and the quiet Maine countryside. Enjoy meeting this interesting host who dabbles in most everything including his landscaped yard and gardens (included in the Annual Garden Tour Event). He also has a musical background and experience as an actor, singer, musician and teacher. Full breakfast included. **Seasonal:** No **Reservations:** Credit card to hold room, 24 hr cancel policy for refund, late arrival only if guaranteed with advanced payment **Brochure:** Yes **Permitted:** Children, limited drinking, limited smoking **Languages:** French, German, Spanish **Payment Terms:** Check MC/V [X02BCME-1520] **COM** Y **ITC Member:** No

Rates:	Pvt Bath 1	Shared Bath 3
Single	$ 75.00	$ 45.00
Double	$ 75.00	$ 55-65.00

Stacked Arms   Birch Point Rd 04578   **Wiscasset ME**
Dee, Sean, Pat Maguire   **Tel:** 207-882-5436
                                            Res Times 8am-9pm

A saltbox cabin that was moved to this beautiful hilltop location around the turn-of-the-century and has had three additions. All of the bedrooms are decorated in different styles and colors. Enjoy New England charm year-round & its gorgeous fall foliage and summer flower gardens in this setting just one mile from town. Full breakfast is served in a large sunny dining room which overlooks beautiful flower gardens, terraces and even a pond! You're close to everything here: plenty of shopping for pottery and antiques and museums. Just 20 mins from Boothbay Harbor and coastal New England, LL Bean, swimming and beaches at Reid State Park and great cross country skiing trails nearby with bike and walking trails during the summer months. Experience New England hospitality in this peaceful and serene setting shared with a military family who enjoy sharing their home with new friends. Picnic lunches and dinner available at added cost. **Seasonal:** No **Reservations:** One night's deposit with 48 hr cancel policy; arrival before 9 pm unless prior arrangements have been made **Brochure:** Yes **Permitted:** Limited children, limited smoking, limited drinking **Payment Terms:** Check MC/V [A03DPME-36-14] **COM** Y **ITC Member:** No

picnic lunches and dinner

Rates:	Shared Bath 5
Single	$ 45-50.00
Double	$ 65-80.00

Wild Rose Of York　　78 Long Sands Rd 03909　　York ME
Fran & Frank Sullivan　　Tel: 207-363-2532

This 1814 residence captures ocean breezes while nestled atop its hillside setting and offers guests cozy guest rooms with antique beds, patchwork quilts and fireplaces. Close to deep sea fishing, golf, hiking and plenty of shops and restaurants for an enjoyable visit in New England. Your host is a biology professor. Continental breakfast is included. Complimentary tea, sherry and cookies in afternoon. **Seasonal:** No **Brochure:** Yes **Permitted:** Children, smoking & drinking **Payment Terms:** Check [X11ACME-3617] **COM** Y **ITC Member:** No

Rates:	Pvt Bath 2	Shared Bath 2
Single	$ 48.00	$ 38.00
Double	$ 56.00	$ 46.00

York Harbor Inn　　Rt 1A 03911　　York Harbor ME
Gary Dominquez　　Tel: 800-343-3869 207-363-5119 **Fax:** 207-363-3545
　　Res Times 8am-11pm

For over one hundred years, the historic charm and hospitality of *The York Harbor Inn* have welcomed those seeking distinctive lodging and dining experiences. Nestled in the heart of York Harbor, amid classic oceanfront estates and the sights and sounds of the Atlantic - - the *York Harbor In* enjoys a truly auspicious natural setting. A short walk takes you to a peaceful, protected beach. A stroll long Marginal Way reveals hidden coastal scenes and fine properties. Golf, tennis, biking, deep-sea fishing and outlet shopping are all close by. Each of the guest rooms is furnished with fine antiques, some offering Ocean Views, fireplaces and jacuzzis. The oceanfront Dining Room offers top-rated cuisine and fine wines; and the downstairs tavern, The Wine Cellar, features pub-style comfort and entertainment. **Discounts:** Seniors **Airport:** Boston Logan Intl- 55 mi; Portland Jetport-50 mi **Packages:** Yes, inquire at res time **Seasonal:** No **Reservations:** 50% deposit required (100% for one night) at res time, 14 day cancel policy for refund, late check-in available, *off-season rates available; Fax: Extension 295 **Brochure:** Yes **Permitted:** Children, drinking, limited smoking **Conference:** Yes, five meeting rooms, 5000 square feet **Languages:** Spanish, French **Payment Terms:** Check AE/CB/DC/ER/V [I08HPME1-3625] **COM** Y **ITC Member:** No

Rates:	Pvt Bath 29	Shared Bath 6
Single	$ 79.00	$ 69.00
Double	$ 99.00	$ 89.00

Allen House Victorian Inn	599 Main 01002	**Amherst MA**
Allen & Ann Zieminski		**Tel:** 413-253-5000
		Res Times 24 Hrs

Featured in the *"New York Times"* Travel section (May 8, 1994), *"Fodors"* '94 and *"Bon Appetit"* (featured Christmas Inn, 1994) - The *Allen House Victorian Inn*, in the heart of Amherst on over three landscaped acres with its many peaked gables, ornately carved Austrian verge board, oriental Chippendale and multiple relief shingles, is one of the finest examples of Queen Anne - Stick-style architecture. The interior was restored with historic precision to every last detail to reflect the Aesthetic Movement, the Victorian subculture that emphasized art in the interior decor. The original handcarved cherry wood fireplace mantels are catalogued by the Metropolitan Museum of Art in New York City. This 1886, eighteen room architectural gem offers seven spacious museum-quality guest rooms with private bath and air conditioning. A full formal breakfast, afternoon and evening tea and refreshments are served at guest's convenience. Free pick-up service from the nearby Amtrack Train and bus stations. Free local bus transportation, walk to nearby Emily Dickinson Homestead, Amherst College, the Univ of Massachusetts, fine galleries, museums, theaters, concerts, shops and restaurants. Visit nearby Mount Holyoke, Smith and Hampshire Colleges, Northampton, Historic Deerfield and Old Sturbridge Village. *"1991 Historic Preservation Award Winner"*; AAA 3-Diamond, ABBA Rated Excellent; Mobil Quality Approved **Airport:** Hartford-Springfield-45 mins **Seasonal:** No **Reservations:** Call for information **Brochure:** Yes **Permitted:** Children 10-up, drinking, smoking on outside verandas **Payment Terms:** Check AE/DC/DISC/MC/V [I03HPMA1-16699] **COM** U **ITC Member:** No **Quality Assured:** Yes

Rates: Pvt Bath 7
Single $ 45-95.00
Double $ 55-115.00

Capt Samuel Eddy House Inn	609 Oxford St S 01501	**Auburn MA**
Diedre & Mike Meddaugh		**Tel:** 508-832-7282 508-832-3149
		Res Times After 4 pm

Let us make your expectations in lodging your most memorable Country Inn experience. Step back in time to the warmth and charm of the 18th century. Soft music enhances the evening for your candlelight dinner in the dining room or private parlors. Our chef will prepare a portion of dinner on the open hearth and breads in the bee hive oven. Breakfast is never ordinary, with favorites of stuffed French toast with berries and cream or ham and egg souffle. The bed chambers offer oak and canopy beds king, queen & twin sizes. Antique furnishings adorn the chambers, that include private baths and sitting areas. You'll find turned-down beds, chocolates, and a gift on your pillow, encouraging champagne dreams. Country walks, ice skating, yard games and a refreshing pool are just a few activities offered for your relaxation. Visit the country store with antiques, crafts, period clothing and herbs. The Inn is located less than 45 minutes from Boston, ten minutes from Worcester and fifteen minutes from Sturbridge, all which have a wide variety of interesting places to explore. Brimfield has an antique flea market (May, July, Sept) which is the largest in New England, with over 4000 dealers. Special events include *"Stew & Stories"*, murder weekends, small weddings and rehearsal dinners. Dinner, MAP, full breakfast and evening tea. **Discounts:** Yes, 10-15% extended stays **Airport:** Boston Logan-50 mins; Worcester-15 mins **Seasonal:** No **Reservations:** 50% deposit, late arrivals must call ahead. **Brochure:** Yes **Permitted:** Children welcomed, limited smoking limited drinking **Conference:** Yes, including dining **Payment Terms:** Check MC/V [Z06EPMA-6544] **COM** Y **ITC Member:** No

Rates: Pvt Bath 5
Single $ 52.00
Double $ 67-90.00

Massachusetts National Edition

Cobbs Cove — Rt 6A 02630 — Barnstable MA
Evelyn Chester/HJ Studley
Tel: 508-362-9356 Fax: 508-362-9356
Res Times 9am-9pm

Wonderful secluded Timbered Colonial Inn, just a delightful get-away for couples on Cape Cod's historic Northside District. Lovely waterviews everywhere and of Barnstable Village harbor. You can enjoy all the beach activities with just a short walk to the bathing beach, charter fishing facility, or whale watch from the Inn. Fine shopping at the nearby village stores and dining in unique Cape Cod restaurants and delicious seafood!! All accommodations are spacious with whirlpool tubs in all baths with imported bath oils and terry robes. Gratuitous refreshments daily. Large Count Rumford fireplace in Keeping Room for guests. Fabulous library area for guests' use. Hearty full Yankee breakfasts served in garden-patio area. Dinner for guests only, upon request. **Seasonal:** No **Reservations:** A $100.00 deposit per night seven days prior to arrival **Brochure:** Yes **Permitted:** Drinking, limited smoking **Conference:** Yes, small groups **Languages:** French **Payment Terms:** Check AE/MC/V [A08GPMA-1632] **COM** Y **ITC Member:** No **Quality Assurance:** Requested

Rates: Pvt Bath 6
Single
Double $ 149-189.00

Honeysuckle Hill — Barnstable MA
Barbara Rosenthal
Tel: 508-362-8418

Refer to the same listing name under West Barnstable, Massachusetts for a complete description. **Seasonal:** No **Payment Terms:** Check AE/DC/MC/V [M10EPMA-16414] **COM** U **ITC Member:** No

Rates: Pvt Bath 3
Single $ 90-105.00
Double $ 90-105.00

Belvedere B&B — 167 Main St 02664 — Bass River MA
Judy & Dick Fenuccio
Tel: 617-398-6674
Res Times 8am-7pm

Perfect Federal design colonial c1820 nestled on a country lane owned by a sea captain, Capt Isaiah Baker, that remains much the same as it did then. Furnished with period antiques, you'll step back in time when you stay here. Hearty New England breakfast included. **Seasonal:** No **Brochure:** Yes **Permitted:** Limited children, limited drinking

Payment Terms: Check [C11ACMA-1637] **COM** Y **ITC Member:** No

Rates:	Pvt Bath 2	Shared Bath 3
Single	$ 55.00	$ 45.00
Double	$ 65.00	$ 55.00

Captain Isaiahs House — 33 Pleasant St 02664 — Bass River MA
Alden & Marge Fallows
Tel: 617-394-1739

Restored sea captain's home in historic district with plenty of ambience for the late 1800's. Fire-

sea captain's house

places in all rooms to warm those hearty spirits. Continental breakfast include with homebaked breads and breakfast rolls to start each day. **Seasonal:** No **Brochure:** Yes **Permitted:** Children, smoking, drinking **Payment Terms:** Check [C11ACMA-1638] **COM** Y **ITC Member:** No

Rates:	Pvt Bath 6	Shared Bath 2
Single	$ 45.00	$ 40.00
Double	$ 55.00	$ 50.00

1810 House B&B — Boston MA
Susanne & Harold Tuttle
Tel: 617-659-1810

National Edition ***Massachusetts***

Refer to the same listing name under Norwell, Massachusetts for a complete description. **Seasonal:** No **Payment Terms:** Check [M08HPMA1-17769] **COM YG ITC Member:** No

Rates:	Pvt Bath 2	Shared Bath 1
Single	$ 65-80.00	$ 60-75.00
Double	$ 65-80.00	$ 60-75.00

Allen House Boston MA
Christine Gilmour Tel: 508-545-8221
 Res Times 8am-10:30am

Refer to the same listing name under Scituate, Massachusetts for a complete description. **Seasonal:** Clo March **Payment Terms:** Check AE/DISC/MC/V [M03HPMA-16688] **COM YG ITC Member:** No

Rates:	Pvt Bath 4	Shared Bath 2
Single	$ 89-149.00	$ 79-119.99
Double	$ 89-149.00	$ 79-119.00

Beacon Hill B&B 27 Brimmer St 02108 Boston MA
Susan Butterworth Tel: 617-523-7376

Beacon Hill B&B is an 1869 Victorian six-story townhouse overlooking the Charles River. It lies on *"the Flat"* within the historic district of Beacon Hill, a downtown residential neighborhood known for its architectural elegance, gaslit, tree-lined streets, brick sidewalks, wrought iron railings, window boxes and hidden gardens. The location is Boston's Best - a short walk to Boston Common and the Public Garden, *"Cheers"*, the State House and Freedom Trail connecting historic sites including Quincy Market, downtown, Filene's Basement, Theater District and the Back Bay and Convention Center. Charles Street, lined with antique and

short walk to Cheers

flower shops, restaurants and boutiques, is one block away; located there is a public garage and a subway stop connecting you within 15 mins to Harvard, the Museum of Fine Arts and the Isabella Stewart Gardner Museum, Symphony Hall, Kennedy Library, hospitals, universities and even Logan Airport. The three guest rooms are very spacious sitting rooms with private baths & fireplaces, eleven or twelve foot ceilings, original doors, moldings and hardware. They are attractively furnished with an eye to comfort. TV is available as well as an elevator for toting baggage. A full complimentary breakfast featuring homemade granola and baked goodies is served in the coral dining-sitting room with a river view, crystal chandelier, oriental rug and family antiques. Your hostess, who has lived here for 26 years, is a caterer and a former French teacher who spent her childhood in Paris. She looks forward to sharing her intimate knowledge of Boston with her guests. **Discounts:** 10% for stays 8 days and longer **Airport:** Boston Logan-15 mins **Seasonal:** No **Reservations:** One night's deposit in advance, 21 day cancel notice for refund less $10 service fee. 2 night min weekends/3 day min on holidays **Brochure:** Yes **Permitted:** Children, limited drinking **Languages:** French **Payment Terms:** Check [I07HPMA1-12003] **COM YG ITC Member:** No

Rates:	Pvt Bath 3
Single	$ 125-160.00
Double	$ 125-160.00

Cape Cod Sunny Pines Boston MA
Jack & Eileen Connell Tel: 800-356-9628 508-432-9628
 Res Times 9am-9pm

©*Inn & Travel Memphis, Tennessee*

Massachusetts National Edition

Refer to the same listing name under Harwich, Massachusett for a complete description. **Seasonal:** No **Payment Terms:** Check AE/MC/V [M05FCMA-11835] **COM** Y **ITC Member:** No

Rates: Pvt Bath 8
Single $ 75-95.00
Double $ 85-100.00

Harborside House Boston MA
Susan Livingston
Tel: 617-631-1032
Res Times 8am-8pm

Refer to the same listing name under Marblehead, Massachusetts for a complete description. **Seasonal:** No **Payment Terms:** Check [M04-HCMA1-14781] **COM** YG **ITC Member:** No

Rates:
Single
Double

Shared Bath 2
$ 60-65.00
$ 70-75.00

Land's End Inn Boston MA
David Schoolman
Tel: 508-487-0706
Res Times 9am-10pm

Refer to the same listing name under Provincetown, Massachusetts for a complete description. **Seasonal:** No **Payment Terms:** Check MC/V [M02HPMA-6553] **COM** YG **ITC Member:** No

Rates: Pvt Bath 16
Single $ 82-250.00
Double $ 82-250.00

Manor On Golden Pond Boston MA
David & Bambi Arnold
Tel: 800-545-2141 603-968-3348
Res Times 9am-9pm

Refer to the same listing name under Holderness, New Hampshire for a complete description. **Seasonal:** No **Payment Terms:** Check AE/MC/V [M10EPNH-16450] **COM** U **ITC Member:** No

Rates: Pvt Bath 27
Single $ 110-175.00
Double $ 155-220.00

Oasis Guest House 22 Edgerly Rd 02115 Boston MA
Joe Haley
Tel: 617-267-2262 Fax: 617-267-1920
Res Times 8am-midnight

The *Oasis Guest House* was designed and decorated with a clear understanding of the special needs of the traveler. Comfort, quality, cleanliness and an affordable price. Totally renovated, the *Oasis* is conveniently close to Prudential Center (Hynes Convention Center) in Boston's Back Bay. Our lobby, living room, outdoor decks and accommodations are handsomely appointed with comfortable furnishings blended with modern conveniences. Amenities include all new private and shared baths, central a/c, color TVs and a computer phone system. A complimentary breakfast is served each morning and includes coffee, juice and Danish while complimentary set-ups (BYOB) and hors d'oeuvres are offered each evening. A friendly staff is always available to assist you. Come experience the rewards of staying in an atmosphere that caters to your lifestyle and budget. Like many of the finer hotels in Boston, we are centrally located in the Back Bay - yet unlike the finer hotels, our rates are substantially lower. **Discounts:** Yes, inquire at res time **Airport:** Logan-10 mins **Seasonal:** No **Reservations:** One night deposit required to guarantee reservation, 24 hour check-in **Brochure:** Yes **Permitted:** Drinking, limited smoking **Payment Terms:** Check AE/MC/V [Z03HPMA1-7243] **COM** YG **ITC Member:** No

Rates:	Pvt Bath 11	Shared Bath 5
Single	$ 78.00	$ 50.00
Double	$ 78.00	$ 55.00

©Inn & Travel Memphis, Tennessee

National Edition **Massachusetts**

York Harbor Inn			Boston MA
Garry Dominquez		Tel: 800-343-3869 207-363-5119	**Fax:** 207-363-3545
			Res Times 8am-11pm

Refer to the same listing located under York Harbor, Maine for a complete description. **Seasonal:** Rates vary **Payment Terms:** Check AE/DC/MC/V [M08BCME-8253] **COM Y ITC Member:** No

Rates:	**Pvt Bath** 29	**Shared Bath** 6
Single	$ 79.00	$ 69.00
Double	$ 99.00	$ 89.00

Captain Freeman Inn	15 Breakwater Rd RR#4 02631	Brewster MA
Carol Covitz		Tel:508-896-7481

Built in 1860 without concern for expense in including details such as imported plaster moldings and two-tone inlaid wood floors, you can enjoy the restoration the present owner hosts are completing. Ideal for family stays in this Village Green locale; continental breakfast included outdoors around pool, weather permitting. **Seasonal:** No

Brochure: Yes **Permitted:** Children 12-up **Payment Terms:** Check [C11-ACMA-1650] **COM Y ITC Member:** No

Rates:	**Pvt Bath** 7	**Shared Bath** 3
Single	$ 60-70.00	$ 50.00-up
Double	$ 70-80.00	$ 60.00-up

Isaiah Clark House	1187 Main St 02631	Brewster MA
Chas & Ida Dicesare		Tel: 508-896-2223

Guests return to the *Isaiah Clark House* time and time again because of the charming Colonial ambiance, the five acres of landscaped grounds and the delicious Full American breakfasts served on the deck or in the 1780 Keeping Room. The seven guest rooms are decorated differently with antiques and canopy beds. Fluffy robes, evening chocolates, Afternoon Tea and complimentary use of bicycles are some of the amenities that have made this Inn so popular. Walk to beautiful Cape Cod Bay or bike the nearby Cape Cod Bike Trail. A sunset at Paine's Creek Beach is unforgettable. The Inn is a great location whether you choose to relax in a hammock or explore the many natural attractions of the Cape. All bedrooms are air conditioned for summer comfort and three have working fireplaces. Honeymooners are offered a special five night package! This historical Inn makes for a great Holiday anytime of the year. Recommended as *"Best of the Outer Cape"* by *Innsiders Guide to Cape Cod.* **Airport:** Hyannis/Barnstable-15 mins; Boston's Logan-90 mins **Discounts:** 10% Seniors (62 +) **Seasonal:** No **Reservations:** Deposit required, 10 day cancel policy for refund. **Brochure:** Yes **Permitted:** Children 13-up, **Conference:** Meeting room available. **Languages:** Italian, German, French **Payment Terms:** MC/V [R10EPMA-1652] **COM Y ITC Member:** No

Rates:	**Pvt Bath** 7
Single	$ 82-100.00
Double	$ 82-100.00

Ocean Gold B&B	RR #2 02631	Brewster MA
James & Margaret Geisler		Tel: 508-255-7045

Charming two story contemporary home in a lovely wooded suburban area with whirlpool, fireplace and country fresh eggs and hosts that will make your visit an event. Suite available with private entrance. Close to Atlantic and Bay for all water activities including lobstering. Full breakfast included. **Seasonal:** No **Brochure:** Yes **Permitted:** Limited drinking **Payment Terms:** Check [C11A-CMA-1653] **COM Y ITC Member:** No

Rates:	**Pvt Bath** 1	**Shared Bath** 2
Single	$ 75.00	$ 55.00
Double	$ 85.00	$ 65.00

Old Manse Inn	1861 Main St 02631	Brewster MA

©*Inn & Travel Memphis, Tennessee*

Massachusetts   *National Edition*

Sugar & Doug Manchester   **Tel:** 508-896-3149
                       Res Times 8am-10pm

Brewster on Cape Cod is called the *"sea captain's town"* for its historical role for world-travelling ship captains of the China-trade era. One such home is the *Old Manse Inn*, built in the early 1800s by Capt Winslow Lewis Knowles - has been renovated by the present owners to provide nine guest rooms and two gracious dining rooms. A warm cozy atmosphere has been created by the antique furnishings, hand-braided and Oriental rugs, patchwork quilts and old-fashioned print wallpapers. Each guest room is individually appointed and incudes a private bath, with fireplaces in some. Rooms with canopy Queen beds available. Six rooms have TV, all rooms are air conditioned. The common rooms are a favorite gathering area with their early spring and late fall fires, comfortable sofas and original prints and paintings. Dinner At *The Manse* features a gourmet menu and candle-light dining and has been recommended by *"Travel & Leisure"*, *"Boston Herald"* and the *"LA Times"* and is Mobil 3 Star rated. The Chef de Cuisine prepares elegant selections of mussel, fontina, plum tart; ginger marinated breast of chicken served on lemon pasta with apricot sauce and a bittersweet chocolate mousse meringues. A full complimentary breakfast is included with choice of two breakfast entrees. Sugar and Doug invite you to share their delightful manse, the fine food and friendly surroundings, the heritage of this famous "sea captain's town" and hope you will return often to renew fond memories of your stay with them. **Discounts:** Special midweek rate for three night min **Airport:** Hyannis-30 mins; Boston Logan-2 hrs **Seasonal:** Yes **Reservations:** 50% deposit, bal upon arrival, two week cancel policy for refund, commissionable only for min of 2 night stay, late arrivals (after 9 pm) only with prior arrangements, weekly rates available **Brochure:** Yes **Permitted:** Children 6-up, drinking, limited smoking **Payment Terms:** Check AE/DISC/MC/V [I08HPM-A1-1654] **COM** YG **ITC Member:** No

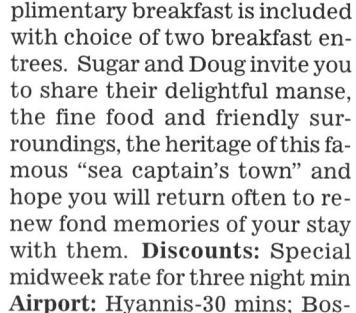

Rates: Pvt Bath   9
Single $ 70-100.00
Double $ 90-110.00

Beacon Inns   1087 & 1750 Beacon St   02146   **Brookline MA**
Hy Gloth   **Tel:** 617-566-0088
                                                        Res Times 9-9pm

These spacious turn-of-the-century townhouses have been converted into two of Brookline's most charming guest houses. The original woodwork is reminiscent of their 19th century construction with fireplaces in the lobby extending a friendly welcome to all guests. There are large, comfortable furnished guest rooms that offer bright sunny surroundings at a surprisingly affordable price. The Inns are on Beacon Street and just minutes from downtown Boston on the MBTA green lines from Beacon or Riverside Streets. The area offers a wide variety of restaurants, shops, museums, theaters, and other attractions. Boston's major hospitals are easily accessible by public or private transportation. Free parking available. No meals are available. **Seasonal:** No **Reservations:** Check for full payment 10 days in advance of arrival; arrival after 8:00 pm subject to $10.00 additional charge. **Permitted:** Children, limited smoking, limited drinking **Payment Terms:** Check MC/V [A07ACM-A-1656] **COM** Y **ITC Member:** No

Rates: Pvt Bath   8   Shared Bath   16
Single $ 65.00 $ 58.00
Double

Salty Dog Inn   Cotuit   02635   **Cape Cod MA**
Lynn & Jerry Goldstein   **Tel:** 508-428-5228
                                                        Res Times 9an-9pm

Experience *"The Cape"* in the town that *"Yankee"* magazine referred to as *"... one of the most beau-*

tiful (settings) in America." This charming and quaint Inn was owned by a sea captain and eventually converted into a gracious small Inn, offering guest rooms that are spacious and comfortable, including king-size beds and four-poster beds in some rooms. All of the Cape's attractions are nearby: antiquing, artists' colonies to explore, boutiques to visit or just relaxing beneath the 300-year-old oak on the grounds. Complimentary breakfast.

Seasonal: No **Reservations:** Full payment for one night, 10-day cancellation policy. **Brochure:** Yes **Payment Terms:** Check MC/V [X02BCMA-1680] **COM** Y **ITC Member:** No

Rates:	Pvt Bath 1	Shared Bath 4
Single	$ 60-75.00	$ 45-55.00
Double	$ 60-75.00	$ 50-60.00

Amerscot House — Concord MA
Doreen & Jerry Gibson
Tel:508-897-0666
Res Times 9am-6pm

Refer to the same listing name under Stow, Massachusetts for a complete description. **Sea-sonal:** No **Payment Terms:** AE/MC/V [M03CPMA-10689] **COM** Y **ITC Member:** No

Rates:	Pvt Bath 3
Single	$ 75-90.00
Double	$ 80-95.00

Anderson Wheeler Homestead   154 Fitchburg Turnpike 01742   Concord MA
David & Charlotte Anderson
Tel:508-369-3756

Original Whipple Tavern rebuilt after a fire in 1890. Served as a stagecoach stop and continues to offer guests antique furnishings mixed with four poster or canopy beds with working fireplaces in all rooms. Thoreau's cabin and Walden's Pond are just a short distance. Continental plus breakfast included. **Seasonal:** No **Brochure:** Yes **Permitted:** Children and social drinking **Payment Terms:** Check MC/V [X11ACMA-1674] **COM** Y **ITC Member:** No

Rates:	Shared Bath 5
Single	$ 65.00
Double	$ 65.00

Swift River Inn   151 South St 01026   Cummington MA
Brenda Burdick
Tel: 800-532-8022 413-634-5751 **Fax:** 413-634-5300

The *Swift River Inn* is a former turn-of-the-century gentleman's dairy farm that we restored for guest lodging, dining and recreation. Our twenty-two suites and guest rooms are uniquely decorated and are named after local artists, attractions and authors. Our restaurant specializes in fresh fish and regional cuisine. Breakfast, lunch and dinner are served, in addition to a bountiful Sunday Brunch. A continental breakfast of fresh home-made pastries is included in our room rates. The Lodge At Swift River Inn, added in November, 1992, serves as the recreation center. During the winter months, we offer cross country skiing on six hundred acres with 25km of impeccably groomed trails. In addition, we have snowmaking on 5km and night skiing on 2.5km. Two New England favorites, sleigh rides and ice skating are also available. Summer and fall recreation programs include: tennis, swimming, mountain biking, nature walks, fishing, volley ball, badminton, boccie ball, horseshoes and more! The setting of the *Swift River Inn* is ideal for corporate meetings, executive retreats, weddings and family reunions. The Meadowbrook Room is ideal for small meetings and receptions. The Hayloft Ballroom, with its open-beamed ceiling and the Pinnacle Room of the Lodge are perfect for parties and weddings, accommodating groups to 175 persons. The Trailside Tavern has a casual, relaxed atmosphere and serves food and drinks with entertainment on most weekends. **Discounts:** AAA, AARP, Off-season, midweek, corporate rates **Airport:** Hartford CT Brad-

Massachusetts   *National Edition*

ley-62 mi **Packages:** Cross Country Skiing, Family, Romance B&B, MAP inquire at res time **Seasonal:** Rates vary **Reservations:** Last night's deposit required; 14 day cancel policy for refund **Brochure:** Yes **Permitted:** Children, drinking **Conference:** Four rooms available for 8 to 165 persons **Payment Terms:** Check AE/DC/MC/V [I07GPMA-17202] **COM**

Y **ITC Member:** No

Rates:	Pvt Bath	22
Single	$ 69.00	
Double	$ 69.00	

Four Chimneys Inn   946 Main St Rt 6A 02638   Dennis MA
Russell & Kathy Tomasetti   Tel: 508-385-6317
     Res Times 7am-10pm

The *Four Chimneys Inn* is a charming Queen Anne Victorian located on Historic Rt 6A in Dennis, Massachusetts. It is located across from Scargo Lake which offers some of the best fresh water fishing on Cape Cod. The bay beaches, Dennis Village, the Cape Playhouse, the Cape Art Museum, restaurants and shops are all a short walk away. As you walk through the antique double front doors, the large entrance foyer with its unique staircase is very inviting. Eleven foot ceilings with medallions, spacious rooms with marble fireplaces and large windows add to the charm of the Inn. The living room has a working fireplace. The library has a TV with VCR and eight foot French doors leading to the screened porch. Enjoy breakfast in the dining room or on the porch. All bedrooms are located on the second and third floors. Six spacious bedrooms have private showers or tub baths. The two cozier rooms share a hall bath. The bedrooms have a queen bed or a queen and a twin bed. The smaller guest rooms have a double bed. All guest rooms offer garden, wooded or lake views. **Airport:** Boston Logan-90 mi; Cape Cod Airport-10 mi **Seasonal:** No **Reservations:** Full deposit for two days and three day weekends, 50% deposit for three days or longer **Brochure:** Yes **Permitted:** Children 7-up, limited drinking, limited smoking **Conference:** Common rooms can accommodate fifty persons **Payment Terms:** Check AE/DISC/MC/V [Z04GPMA-1688] **COM** Y **ITC Member:** No

Queen Anne Victorian

Rates:	Pvt Bath 6	Shared Bath 2
Single	$ 95.00	$ 55.00
Double	$ 95.00	$ 55.00

Isaiah Hall B&B Inn   152 Whig St 02638   Dennis MA
*Marie Brophy   Tel: 800-736-0160 508-385-9928
     Res Times 8:30am-10pm

Come share the delight of Cape Cod's past. Sleep on antique white iron and brass beds warmed by quilts. Wake to the sound of birds and the smell of coffee. Breakfast on hearty breads and muffins in a spacious antique-filled dining room evoking a bygone era. Take a leisurely walk past beautiful old homes to our beach or village. These simple country pleasures await you at the *Isaiah Hall Bed & Breakfast Inn*. Tucked away on a quiet historic street, this lovely 1857 farmhouse has had a tradition as an Inn since 1948 with cheerful guestrooms in both the Main House and Carriage House. Today, it continues as a romantic country refuge where you may chose to relax on a porch rocker, in front of a Victorian stove in the converted carriage house great room with white wicker furniture and knotty pine walls. The guestrooms are decorated with charming country antiques with most having private baths and queen beds. Three rooms have two beds, four rooms include balconies and one has a fireplace. Non-smoking rooms are available. A walk through the village will provide you with fine restaurants, antiques, crafts and one-of-a-kind shops, as well as the Cape Museum of Fine Arts, and in summer, the Cape Playhouse. Close by you

1-42   ©*Inn & Travel Memphis, Tennessee*

can enjoy bike trails, tennis and golf. Located in the heart of the Cape, Dennis offers a central homebase for day trips to other scenic, recreational and historic points of interest. **Discounts:** Yes, inquire at res time **Airport:** Hyannis /Barnstable-8 mi **Packages:** Spring, Sunday to Thursday Special Note: For aspiring innkeepers, your hostess also conducts seminars on operating and owning your own Bed & Breakfast **Seasonal:** Clo 10/16-4/7 **Reservations:** One night's deposit at res time or 50% if longer, 10 day cancel notice for refund, late arrival with advance notice **Brochure:** Yes **Permitted:** Children 7-up, drinking, limited smoking **Conference:** Yes, for small groups **Payment Terms:** Check AE/MC/V [I08HPMA1-1689] COM YG ITC **Member:** No **Quality Assurance:** Requested

Rates:	Pvt Bath 10	Shared Bath 1
Single	$ 64-96.00	$ 52-54.00
Double	$ 74-112.00	$ 57-59.00

Rose Petal B&B 152 Sea St 02639 **Dennisport MA**
Gayle & Dan Kelly   Tel: 508-398-8470
                                                     Res Times 8am-9pm

A traditional New England home complete with picket fence, Guests are invited to share this historic 1872 residence built for Almond Wixon, whose family was among Dennisport's original settlers. Wixon was lost at sea with all on board the Cross Rip Light Ship in 1918. Your hosts (formerly university administrators) completely restored and decorated in 1986 to accommodate guests in a delightful seaside resort neighborhood. Stroll past century-old houses and cottages to the warm water beaches of Nantucket Sound. Guest rooms offer queen size beds, antiques and lace, air conditioning, hand stitched quilts and spacious baths, There is a comfortable parlor to enjoy TV, piano or current magazines. A full homemade breakfast is prepared each morning where Dan, an expert baker and pastry chef, tempts your senses with his culinary expertise. Freshly ground coffee, specialties, cereals, juices and fresh fruit accompany a special entree and home-baked pastries. A short drive takes you to the ferries to Nantucket and Martha's Vineyard. Nearby are bike trails, golf courses, antique and craft shops and restaurants offering a variety of dining experiences. **Discounts:** Off-season (Sept 15-June 15th) **Airport:** Boston Logan **Packages:** Restaurants, Whale Watching and others **Seasonal:** Rates vary **Reservations:** Full deposit in advance for 1 to 3 nights, 50% for longer stays, bal upon arrival, 14 day cancel policy, including partials. *Off-season rates available **Permitted:** Children, drinking **Languages:** Some French **Payment Terms:** Check AE/MC/V [I03HPMA1-11078] COM YG ITC **Member:** No

Rates:	Pvt Bath 2	Shared Bath 1
Single	$ 89.00	$ 65.00
Double	$ 89.00	$ 65.00

Parsonage 202 Main St 02643 **East Orleans MA**
Innkeeper   Tel:508-255-8217

Lovely tree-lined street with period homes of sea captains and early residents, this Cape Cod home is reminiscent of the 1770's with low ceilings, huge walls, wavy glass windows, and antique furnishings and heirlooms. Breakfast includes cranberry muffins, a homemade delight, and fresh brewed coffee. **Seasonal:** No **Payment Terms:** Check MC/ [C1-1ACMA-1695] COM Y ITC **Member:** No

Rates:	Pvt Bath 2	Shared Bath 4
Single	$ 55.00	$ 50.00
Double	$ 60-70.00	$ 55.00

Ship's Knees Inn PO Box 756 02643 **East Orleans MA**
                               Tel:508-255-1312 Fax:508-240-1351
                               Res Times 8am-9pm

©*Inn & Travel Memphis, Tennessee*

Massachusetts *National Edition*

Built over 170 years ago, this restored sea captain's home invites guests to an old-style New England lodging surrounded with the charm of yesteryear but with the convenience of today. This intimate setting, just a short stroll to scenic Nauset Beach on Cape Cod, offers lantern-lit doorways to eighteen rooms, each individually appointed in special colonial colors and authentic antiques. There are beamed ceilings, quilts and old four-poster beds. Several rooms include beautiful ocean views and fireplaces. In-addition, overlooking the Orleans Cove is the Cove House with three rooms and a one-bedroom apartment and two housekeeping cottages providing the total escape. Seclusion and serenity await the less adventuresome vacationer at Nauset Bay, one of the finest in North America. Swimming pool and tennis on the premises with horseback riding, boating and lovely Cape Cod for shopping and fine restaurants. High Season rates are 5/2-10/30, lo-season rates are approx 25% less. Cottages and apartments are available weekly in-season and daily off-season **Discounts:** Yes, inquire at res time **Airport:** Hyannis Regional- 20 mi **Seasonal:** Rates vary **Reservations:** One night's deposit at res time (2 nights if more than 3 days), bal due upon arrival, 15 day cancel policy for refund. Cove House, cottages and efficiencies available. **Brochure:** Yes **Permitted:** Children in Cove House, cottages & efficiencies, drinking, smoking. **Payment Terms:** Check MC/V [J08HPMA1-2978] **COM YG ITC Member:** No **Quality Assured:** Yes

Rates:	Pvt Bath 12	Shared Bath 9
Single	$ 70-100.00	$ 70-100.00
Double	$ 70-100.00	$ 55-80.00

Overlook Inn   Country Rd Rt 6   02642   Eastham MA
Ian & Nan Aitchison   **Tel:** 800-356-1121   508-255-1886
    Res Times 9am-9pm

The *OverLook Inn* is a finely restored captain's mansion in Eastham, on the beautiful outer cape. Located across from the Cape Cod National Seashore, the Inn has 1-1/2 acres of beautiful treed grounds. The ten bedrooms are furnished with antiques, brass beds, down comforters, terry towel bath robes and all have private baths. On the main floor, there is a parlor where afternoon tea is served each day, a library, a Victorian billiard room and a large dining room overlooking the garden area. Nan enjoys making Scottish dishes for breakfast and her scones (made from her grandmother's recipe, which shouldn't be missed) are served at tea time. There are beautiful nature trails and bike trails nearby. **Seasonal:** No **Reservations:** Full deposit for less than three nights; 50% deposit if longer; 10 day cancellation policy, less 10% service fee for refund. **Permitted:** Limited drinking, smoking **Conference:** Yes, for small groups **Languages:** French/Spanish **Payment Terms:** Check AE/DISC/MC/V [I02HPMA1-1692] **COM YG ITC Member:** No

Rates:	Pvt Bath 10
Single	$ 75-125.00
Double	$ 75-125.00

Whalewalk Inn   220 Bridge Rd   02642   Eastham MA
Richard & Carolyn Smith   **Tel:** 508-255-0617   **Fax:** 508-240-0017
    Res Times 10am-8pm

©*Inn & Travel Memphis, Tennessee*

National Edition   ***Massachusetts***

The *Whalewalk* is located in the heart of the unspoiled "Outer Cape", considered by many to be one of the country's most beautiful places. Stretching for over forty miles, the shoreline lies within the 27,000 acre Cape Cod National Seashore. In this area you can find an abundance of outdoor activities. The dedicated bike trails are a haven for cyclists, joggers and walkers. A variety of beaches is found on the Atlantic Ocean, Cape Cod Bay, Pleasant Bay, and many local freshwater ponds. All of this provides a perfect setting for *The Whalewalk Inn*. Its own site consists of over three acres of lawns, gardens, specimen trees, meadowlands; located on a quiet back road only minutes by car or bike to beaches, bike trails or Orleans Village. Utilizing a unique blending of styles and periods, the guest rooms provide a range of individual accommodations. Seven guest rooms, all with private bath, are available and are furnished with either twin, double or queen beds. Four large suites, all with fully equipped kitchens, are located in the Barn and Guest House. A salt box studio cottage is also available, offering maximum privacy. A daily complimentary full breakfast is included with each guest room. **Airport:** Logan Intl, Boston, two hrs **Discounts:** Yes, for travel agents during the off-season **Reservations:** 50% deposit of entire stay, late arrival okay with prior notice **Brochure:** Yes **Permitted:** Children 12-up, drinking, limited smoking **Conference:** Yes, for small groups **Payment Terms:** Check [R10DPMA-1693] **COM Y ITC Member:** No

Rates:	Pvt Bath 12
Single	$ 75-150.00
Double	$ 75-150.00

Arbor   222 Upper Main St 02539   **Edgartown MA**
Peggy Hall   **Tel:** 508-627-8137
                                                                                                        Res Times 8am-8pm

Some say it was floated over on a barge from the adjoining island of Chappaquiddick at the turn of the century. Others say it was pulled by oxen on a sled of sorts across the icy narrows of Katama Bay. History abounds at the *Arbor*, but it cannot touch the warmth and hospitality which exists today. Innkeeper, Peggy Hall, is 100% responsible for this and has transformed this once gentle farmhouse into a very lovely friendly Inn. Victorian English Country in decor, Peggy has restored where possible, renovated to keep up with the times and added-on when necessary. Eight of the ten guest rooms have private baths and only two rooms share a bath. You will enjoy a delicious continental breakfast in the fireplaced dining room or charming muraled breakfast room painted by a local artist or outside in the English tea garden. A highlight of your visit could be the social hour in the living room with its balconied library. Just a short stroll to the enchanting village of Edgartown with its chalk white picket fences heralding the gateway to old whaling captain's homes, fine restaurants and the bustling activity of its scenic harbor. Or you may just want to nap in a hammock in the *Arbor's* rear garden, relax on a rocking chair on the front porch, or browse in the antique shop in the back. Peggy will gladly direct you to unspoiled beaches, walking trails, sailing, fishing and all of the delights of this storybook island of Martha's Vineyard. *One guest cottage available $700-$900/week. **Airport:** Matha's Vineyard Airport-7 mi **Seasonal:** Yes **Reservations:** Full deposit 3 days or less, 50% if longer; 3 day min stay (7/1-8/31) and two day min other times (5/1-6/14 & 9/16-10/31. Two week cancel policy for refund less 10% service fee **Brochure:** Yes **Permitted:** Children 12-up, drinking, limited smoking **Payment Terms:** Check MC/V [I05HPMA1-6832] **COM YG ITC Member:** No **Quality Assurance** Yes

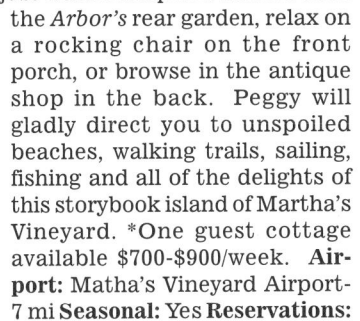

Rates:	Pvt Bath 8	Shared Bath 2
Single	$ 135-150.00	$ 95.00
Double	$ 135-150.00	$ 95.00

Capt Dexter House/Edgartown   35 Peases Pt Way 02539   **Edgartown MA**
Rick   **Tel:**508-627-7289
                                                                                                        Res Times 9am-9pm

Built in 1840 by a seafaring merchant, this historic country colonial Inn on the island of Martha's Vineyard offers a wonderful vacation any time of the year. The home is traditionally New England - from its white clapboard siding and black shutters to its original double-width floor boards. The home is located on a quiet residential street, yet it is only a short stroll to the Harbor, shops and restaurants of town. The rooms have been decorated to provide the feeling of a bygone era, but with today's conveniences. The landscaped garden is a haven for relaxing after a day at the beach, bicycling, horseback riding or taking one of the island's numerous nature walks. Guests start each day with a home-baked continental breakfast in the elegant dining room setting. Upon returning to the inn during the day, guests are offered complimentary aperitif and lemonade. The hospitality and personal service of the live-in innkeepers is nationally known. **Airport:** Martha's Vineyard-2 mi **Discounts:** Yes, inquire at res time **Packages:** Off-season, inquire at res time **Seasonal:** 3/1-12/31 **Reservations:** Full deposit for 3 nights or less, 50% for 4+ nights. *Hi-season May-October; off-season rates $65-130.00; 14 day cancel policy for refund, arrival before 10pm **Brochure:** Yes **Permitted:** Children, drinking, limited smoking **Conference:** Yes, if booking entire property, facility for groups to twelve **Payment Terms:** Check AE/DC/MC/V [Z04GPMA-11966] **COM** Y **ITC Member:** No

Rates:	Pvt Bath 11
Single	$ 65-190.00
Double	$ 65-190.00

Colonial Inn	38 N Water St 02539	Edgartown MA
Linda Malcouronne	**Tel:** 800-627-4701 508-627-4711	**Fax:** 508-627-5904
		Res Times 8am-12am

"No effort will be spared to promote the comfort and pleasure of all guests" was part of the Inn's first advertisement in 1911 and still holds true today. The *Colonial Inn* has undergone numerous changes throughout the years but still retains its original charm combined with modern day convenience and *"Affordable Luxury"*, with its latest upgrade completed in the spring of 1996. Located in the heart of Edgartown's Historic District, overlooking the harbor, all rooms include heat, air conditioning, telephone with modem, color cable TV, am/fm clock radio and full private bath. Many rooms also include harbor views and mini-fridges. A sumptuous complimentary continental breakfast is served daily in the solarium, which opens onto a garden courtyard. The Inn also offers six shops, Chesca's Restaurant and a unisex hairstylist. The Inn's three verandas (two offering fabulous harborview beckon you to return to the slower pace of yesteryear for which the Vineyard is famous. The Island provides something for everyone - water sports, golf, tennis, fishing, riding, bicycling, as well as fairs, festivals, performing arts, galleries, museums; in addition to a myriad of shops and restaurants. For more information on becoming a part of the tradition that is *The Colonial Inn*, call today. **Airport:** Martha's Vineyard-8 mi **Discounts:** Groups of six or more rooms **Packages:** Home For The Holidays (11/1-12/9), Colonial Christmas, Happy Haunting Weekend **Seasonal:** 4/1-12/31 **Reservations:** One night's deposit by credit card, 2 week cancel policy for refund, closed 1/1-3/31 **Brochure:** Yes **Permitted:** Children, drinking, limited smoking **Conference:** To twenty five on-site and to two hundred off-site **Languages:** French, Spanish, Portuguese **Payment Terms:** Check AE/MC/V [I10HPMA1-1700] **COM** YG **ITC Member:** No

Rates:	Pvt Bath 43
Single	$ 90-225.00
Double	$ 90-225.00

Point Way Inn	104 Main St 02539	Edgartown MA
Linda & Ben Smith		**Tel:** 508-627-8633 **Fax:** 508-627-8579

A charming 150 year-old sea captain's house whose hosts/owners add a magical touch to each guest's stay in a remodeled Inn and their year-round home. The Inn offers a variety of accommodations including a two-room suite, French doors and decks, fireplaces in most rooms, period wall coverings, New England antiques with four-poster canopy beds in some and a decanter of sherry on each night stand.

Make yourself at home in the gracious living room with a large fireplace, fridgefor ice or your libations and the library with an intriguing 500 piece custom-made wooden jigsaw puzzle. Breakfast is Linda's treat with one of her recipes for breakfast breads, New England popovers, fresh squeezed orange juice and plenty of fresh hot coffee, all served outdoors in the gazebo, a backyard walled garden, before a crackling fireplace or on the front porch swing for avid people watchers! In summer, afternoons bring lemonade and cookies in the gazebo; in winter, a traditional tea in the living room. Plenty to see but leave your car; these hosts offer a car for guests to use on a first come first serve basis so you don't really need one with great hosts who share their town with guests before venturing out. *High season rates (6/30-9/7) rates vary down to $70-125.00 (11/3-3/31), with 10% discount for singles. Holiday rates slightly higher **Discounts:** Seniors, AAA **Seasonal:** Rates vary **Reservations:** Full deposit less than 3 days stay, 50% if 4 days or longer, bal due upon arrival 14 day cancel policy for refund less 10% service fee. Rates do not include Mass Tax **Brochure:** Yes **Permitted:** Children, drinking, smoking, boarding can be arranged nearby for pets **Conference:** Limited facilities **Payment Terms:** Check AE/MC/V [I02HP-MA1-1709] **COM** YG **ITC Member:** No

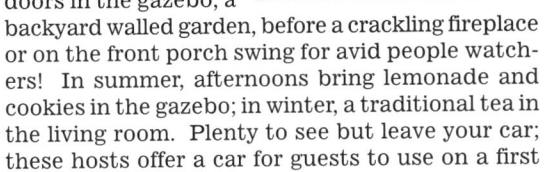

Rates:	Pvt Bath 15
Single	$ 120-205.00
Double	$ 125-250.00

Edgewater B&B 2 Oxford St 02719 Fairhaven MA
Kathy Reed Tel: 508-997-5512

Located in the historic Poverty Point section of Fairhaven, *Edgewater B&B* offers unique accommodations for tourists, visiting friends and relatives as well as business people, looking for a friendly, homelike atmosphere. This gracious waterfront home was originally built by Elnathan Eldredge in the 1760's as his home and store where he supplied the whaleships that were being constructed at the foot of Oxford Street. It is truly on the edge of the water on the very banks of the Acushnet River with the Fairhaven skyline on one side and at night, the glimmering lights of New Bedford on the other. You will find *Edgewater* the perfect year-round vacation spot. **Reservations:** Deposit required, 72 hr cancel policy for refund **Brochure:** Yes **Permitted:** Drinking, children 4-up **Payment Terms:** Check AE/MC/V [R07GPMA-1711] **COM** Y **ITC Member:** No **Quality Assurance:** Requested

Rates:	Pvt Bath 5
Single	$ 60.00
Double	$ 80.00

Capt Tom Lawrence House 75 Locust St 02540 Falmouth MA
Barbara Sabo-Feller **Tel:** 800-266-8139 508-540-1445 **Fax:** 508-457-1790
Res Times AM & PM

Beautiful 1861 whaling captain's residence is now an intimate Inn for those who appreciate warm hospitality and delicious breakfasts. Close to the beach, bikeway, island ferries, shops, restaurants and bus station. Explore entire Cape Cod, Vineyard and Plymouth by day trips. Elegant spacious corner guest rooms, all with private bath, firm beds (king, queen and twin sizes), some of which include canopies. Laura Ashley and Ralph Lauren linens. The living room includes a Steinway piano, antiques and working fireplace. Our full breakfast will be the highlight of your morning. It includes fresh fruit, homemade granola and a variety of creative entrees such as seafood crepes, eggs florentine or quiche Gisela. We grind our flour from organically grown grain which gives extra freshness to our homebaked breads, muffins, pancakes or Belgian waffles served with a scrumptious warm strawberry sauce and whipped cream. We invite you to stay in our congenial home that blends New England tradition with continental hospitality - a peaceful spot to relax in all sea-

Massachusetts

sons. Innkeeper is fluent in German. **Discounts:** Yes, inquire at res time **Packages:** Yes **Airport:** Boston Logan-75 mi **Seasonal:** Clo 1/1-1/31 **Reservations:** One night's deposit or 50% of stay, bal due upon arrival; 14 day cancel policy for refund, two night min 5/31 to 10/9, 5% T/A commission with two night min **Brochure:** Yes **Permitted:** Children 12-up, drinking **Languages:** German **Payment Terms:** Check MC/V [KI08HPMA-2979] COM Y ITC **Member:** No

Rates: Pvt Bath 6
Single $ 70-95.00
Double $ 80-115.00

Grafton Inn 261 Grand Ave S 02540 Falmouth MA
Liz & Rudy Cvitan
Tel: 800-642-4069 508-540-8688 **Fax:** 508-540-1861
Res Times 10am-9pm

Oceanfront - Historic Queen Anne style Victorian. Miles of beautiful beach and breathtaking views of Martha's Vineyard. Eleven air conditioned guest rooms are attractively furnished with period antiques and comfortable beds. Each has a private bath. Thoughtful amenities enhance your comfort and relaxation. A sumptuous full breakfast is served at private tables on our sun-drenched enclosed porch overlooking Nantucket Sound. Fresh flowers, handmade chocolates, afternoon wine and cheese. We are on the bike path and provide complimentary bicycles, as well as sand chairs and towels for the beach. Peruse the Inn's library of area menus, theaters and attractions. We are happy to make dinner arrangements and reservations. TV with cable and videos is on the porch and in the living room. A public phone is located in the common area. It is steps away to two fine restaurants and a five minute walk to the Island ferry. Shops, year round golf courses, deep sea fishing are a few minutes from the Inn, Falmouth Village is 1/2-3/4 mile. Planned daily itineraries to suit your interests. Discount tickets to attractions are available to guests. AAA & Mobil Rated **Airport:** Boston Logan-70 mi; TF Green to Falmouth-75 mi **Seasonal:** Clo 12/15-2/15 **Reservations:** 50% deposit, check-in 2-7pm, after 7 by prior arrangement **Brochure:** Yes **Permitted:** Drinking, children 16-up, smoking outdoors only **Conference:** Yes for groups to 20 persons **Languages:** Croation **Payment Terms:** Check AE/MC/V [K08HPMA1-1714] COM U ITC **Member:** No **Quality Assurance** Requested

Rates: Pvt Bath 11
Single $ 75-149.00
Double $ 75-149.00

Peacocks Inn On The Sound 313 Grand Ave 02541 Falmouth MA
Phyllis & Bud Peacock
Tel: 508-457-9666
Res Times Noon-9pm

Ocean Front million dollar view and miles of beaches at your doorstep! Located on a bluff overlooking the Vineyard Sound - guests choose one of the ten newly renovated guest rooms offering private baths and decorated in a country comfort theme. The spacious rooms, most with ocean views, include queen size beds, country decor with dust ruffles, comforters, baskets of flowers, homemade afghans, teddy bears with fireplaces and hardwood floors in some. A common room with a massive stone fireplace, color cable TV and seating areas is the perfect gathering place for breath-taking views of the ocean while sipping lemonade in summer or snuggled before the fireplace with hot cider and a novel from the library. Morning begins with coffee or tea outdoors, if you like, in the morning sea and salt air before returning to the cozy country dining room for a gourmet feast where you'll enjoy fresh seasonal fruit, special juice combinations, homemade blueberry and apple muffins, sticky buns, cream cheese coffee cake and a special entree such as Belgian waffles with fruit butter, banana stuffed French toast with blueberry compote or eggs Florentine. After a leisurely breakfast, there are endless opportunities to relax by lounging on the beach, swimming, fishing, sailing, exploring the Falmouth area by bike or by wandering through the many shops in Falmouth Village. Within 90 minutes are numerous day trips while Martha's Vineyard ferry is within walking distance and offers exciting trips to the towns and countryside of this lovely island. Mobil and ABBA Rated **Airport:** Boston Logan-1-1/2 hr drive **Package:** Honeymoon **Seasonal:** Rates vary **Reservations:** Full deposit to 3 nights, 50% 4 nights & longer with 2 night minimum; 14 day cancel policy for refund less 10% or $15 minimum fee **Brochure:** Yes **Permitted:** Drinking, limited children, smoking outdoors only **Payment Terms:** Check AE/DC/MC/V [I06FPMA-12509] **COM Y ITC Member:** No

Rates: Pvt Bath 10
Single $ 75-105.00
Double $ 95-125.00

Seekonk Pines Inn	142 Seekonk Cross Rd 01230	Great Barrington MA
Linda & Chris Best		**Tel:** 800-292-4192 413-528-4192
		Res Times 8am-9pm

Seekonk Pines is the life's work of Linda and Chris Best, artist, gardener, musician, electrician and sign craftsman. Since 1978 they have been pouring their many talents into creating a relaxing and unique haven for those visiting the Berkshires. The home consists of a restored 1830 farmhouse with a Dutch Colonial addition. Rooms are lovingly decorated with Linda's watercolors, quilts made by three generations of women in Linda's family and antiques collected from over the years and refinished in the Inn's picturesque barn. The grounds offer a full-size inground pool, beautiful gardens and picnic tables. Guests may either bring their own bikes or borrow one of the Inns, to enjoy the lovely backroads. The Inn's four acres are surrounded by 325 acres of a neighboring estate which welcomes hikers and cross country skiers. Breakfast is the social event of the day. A full country breakfast leaning towards a heart-healthy menu is served family-style at one large country table. Linda's heart-healthy blueberry souffle and Chris' multi-grain pancakes are featured. In season, guests may enjoy fresh-picked strawberries, blueberries, blackberries, raspberries and peaches - all grown on the property. Other times there is a guest pantry and small refrigerator stocked with beverages, hot water dispenser and a huge selection of teas and coffee. Located nearby are New England's prettiest villages, scores of antique shops, three state forests, two downhill ski slopes, Tanglewood Music Center, a wide selection of fine restaurants and all the myriad of cultural events made famous in the Berkshires. **Discounts:** Extended stays: 5 nights 5%; 7 nights 10% **Airport:** Hartford Bradley or Albany-50 mi **Seasonal:** No **Reservations:** One night deposit for stays to 4 nights - 50% deposit for longer stays; 14 day cancel policy (30 days July-Aug) for refund less $10 service fee, late arrivals okay with prior notice **Brochure:** Yes **Permitted:** Children, drinking **Languages:** German **Payment Terms:** Check MC/V [I03HPMA1-1729] **COM Y ITC Member:** No **Quality Assurance:** Requested

Rates: Pvt Bath 7
Single $ 50-up
Double $ 70-140.00

Miles River Country Inn	823 Bay Rd Box 149 01936	Hamilton MA
Gretel & Peter Clark		**Tel:** 508-468-7206 **Fax:** 508-468-3999

This 200 year old rambling colonial on thirty-plus acres adjoins many more of meadows, woodlands and wetlands. Sweeping lawns are graced with seven gardens and two ponds. The Miles River flows through the property. Set among Boston's fabled North Shore estates, the Inn is a haven for travelers and wildlife alike. One sees or hears Great Blue Heron, countless varieties of duck, great horned and screech owls right from the Inns' windows. There are shaded garden terraces where breakfast is served in warm weather. A glassed-in porch, framed by giant iron filigree panels from New Orleans, is a cheery spot for afternoon tea in the winter sun. Much of the decoration in this twenty-four room house is authentic colonial American with the addition of typical turn-of-the-century bathroom fixtures. The walls of the study are covered with 19th Century wooden bedsteads imported from Brittany. Many of the house's twelve working fireplaces are in the bedrooms. There is a flock of chickens that lay fresh eggs for your breakfast, gardens that produce fresh fruit for your cereal and an apiary (that the Innkeeper tends) oozing with golden honey for your toast. Hamilton and nearby communities offer opportunities for those who wish to hike, bike, birdwatch, bathe on pristine ocean beaches, canoeing, sailing or cross country ski. One can antique, golf, whale watch on special cruises and see world-class horse events such as carriage driving competitions, polo matches and pre-olympic Three Phase Eventing. A full complimentary breakfast included. **Discounts:** Extended stay **Airport:** Boston Logan-25 mi **Reservations:** One night deposit to guarantee reservation **Brochure:** Yes **Permitted:** Children, limited drinking **Conference:** Yes, for groups of 16-18 persons **Languages:** Spanish, French, some German **Payment Terms:** Check AE/DISC/MC/V [I04HPMA1-16718] **COM** U **ITC Member:** No

Rates:	Pvt Bath 3	Shared Bath 5
Single	$ 80-90.00	$ 65.00
Double	$ 80-90.00	$ 70-85.00

House Of Coffey	95 Broadway 02339	Hanover MA
Don & Faith Coffey		Tel: 617-826-3141

Lovely colonial residence located in the historic district of Hanover is filled with antique furnishings and includes twin and king size beds. Ten miles from the Atlantic Ocean you can visit the sights including Plymouth Rock, twenty-five miles from Cape Cod and Boston. Continental breakfast included. **Seasonal:** No **Brochure:** Yes **Permitted:** Children, limited pets, limited smoking **Payment Terms:** Check [C11ACMA-1733] **COM** Y **ITC Member:** No

Rates:		Shared Bath 5
Single		$ 40-60.00
Double		$ 50-85.00

Cape Cod Sunny Pines Inn	77 Main St 02671	Harwich MA
Jack & Eileen Connell		Tel: 800-356-9628 508-432-9628 **Fax:** 508-432-9628
		Res Times 9am-9pm

Irish hospitality is featured in this beautiful Victorian residence which offers guests a warm, friendly stopping place that's like visiting old friends. Reminiscent of a small Irish manor, furnishings include antiques, oriental rugs, lace doilies, a/c, refrigerators and color TV. The present Captain Jack has sailed the world for twenty years researching the ocean floor with a famous oceanographic institute located on the Cape. Your hostess, Eileen, is a registered nurse and now enjoys making sure all of her guests enjoy their stay. Centered on Cape Cod's south side, guests can walk to a warm beach, excellent area restaurants and the quaint village of Dennisport. A full complimentary Irish breakfast is served by candlelight on fine china and crystal! You'll dine on mixed grilled meats, eggs, juice, beverages, Irish soda bread made from an old family recipe served with Irish jams and jellies. Omelettes are a specialty along with hot Irish oatmeal with cranberry conserve in cool weather. Relax in the living room by the fireside or on the wrap around porch which overlooks the gardens, jacuzzi and pool. There's excellent golf, antiquing, arts and crafts, fishing, whale watching and trips to the islands. Fully licensed and inspected ABBA. Opened in 1991, Claddagh Tavern to further enhance your visit to *Sunny Pines,* serving light fair and beverages in the authentic Irish Pub! *Rooms are all suites. **Discounts:** Off-rack rate $100.00 **Packages:** Whale watch coupons and picnic lunches available **Airport:** Logan & Green-80mi **Seasonal:** No **Reservations:** Full payment in advance if less than one week; 50% if longer. **Brochure:** Yes **Permitted:** Drinking, children 12-up **Conference:** Groups of 20-30 persons. **Payment Terms:** Check AE/MC/V [I05FPMA-3712] **COM** Y **ITC Member:** No

Rates: **Pvt Bath 8**
Single $ 75-95.00
Double $ 85-100.00

Coach House   74 Sission Rd 02646   Harwich Port MA
Mrs Calvin Ayer   Tel: 508-432-9542

Perfect location for touring the New England Coast and excellent spot for whale watching. Attractive New England colonial home with king and queen beds in a quiet and natural setting. Bike trails, nature walks, and island hopping are all possible here. Continental breakfast included. **Seasonal:** 5/1-10/15 **Reservations:** Deposit at res time with refund if cancelled 10 days prior to arrival date.

Brochure: Yes **Permitted:** Limited smoking **Payment Terms:** Check MC/V [C11ACMA-1736] **COM** Y **ITC Member:** No

Rates: **Pvt Bath 4**
Single $ 75.00
Double $ 75.00

Harbor Walk Guest House   6 Freeman St 02646   Harwich Port MA
Marilyn & Preston Barry   Tel: 508-432-1675
    Res Times 7am-10pm

An enjoyable Victorian Summer Guest home c1880, built by Ensign Rogers in the beautiful and picturesque Wychmere Harbor area of Harwich Port. The harbor is just a few steps away offering a spectacular view and fine beaches of Nantucket Sound. *Harbor Walk* offers the discriminating traveler an opportunity to relax in quiet comfort in a quaint Cape Cod with eclectic furnishings of handmade quilts, antiques with twin and king size beds in the rooms. An attractive garden area and porch are perfect for sitting, lounging and reading. A continental breakfast is included and usually includes your host's specialty of home baked kuchen. Activities include a 22 mile bike path sure to introduce you to all of Harwich. There's excellent bird watching, two golf courses, three harbors for boating, fishing and sand beaches with tennis nearby. **Seasonal:** May - Oct **Reservations:** One night deposit at res time **Brochure:** Yes **Permitted:** Drinking, children 4-up, limited smoking **Languages:** French **Pay-ent Terms:** Check [Z10CPMA-1739] **COM** Y **ITC Mem-ber:** No

Rates: **Pvt Bath 4**   **Shared Bath 2**
Single $ 60.00 $ 40.00
Double $ 60.00 $ 45.00

Inn On Bank Street   88 Bank St 02646   Harwich Port MA
Arky & Janet Silverio   Tel: 508-432-3206
    Res Times 8am-10pm

A sprawling Cape Cod contemporary with library and guest rooms furnished in country style/modern touches. Close to sights, restaurants. Just a five minute walk to the ocean, theater and art galleries too. Full breakfast includes special cranberry crisp, French toast, and fresh homemade breads. **Seasonal:** No **Brochure:** Yes **Permitted:** Children 8-up, smoking, drinking **Languages:** Italian, Spanish **Payment Terms:** Check MC/V [C11ACMA-174-0] **COM** Y **ITC Member:** No

Rates: **Pvt Bath 5**   **Shared Bath 1**
Single $ 60-100.00 $ 55.00
Double $ 60-110.00

Massachusetts															National Edition

Capt Ezra Nye House
Elaine & Harry Dickson

Hyannis MA
Tel: 800-388-2278 508-888-6142
Res Times 9am-9pm

Refer to the same listing name under Sandwich, Cape Cod Massachusetts for a complete description. **Seasonal:** No **Payment Terms:** Check AE/DC/MC/V [M06BPMA-9376] **COM** Y **ITC Member:** No

Rates:	Pvt Bath 5	Shared Bath 2
Single	$ 70-90.00	$ 55-70.00
Double	$ 70-90.00	$ 55-70.00

Captain Sylvester Baxter House
156 Main St 02601
N Krojewski/R Arenstrup

Hyannis MA
Tel: 508-775-5611
Res Times 9am-6pm

Built in 1855 as the homestead of a deep water sailor, state senator and community leader, you'll be in the center of all the activities in this lovely setting. Historically the oldest settlement in Hyannis, the east end of Main Street retains the charm of another era. The setting is of a small village with granite curbs, flagstone walks and Colonial-styled lanterns in a comfortable and charming atmosphere. Enjoy the high ceilinged rooms in the main house or choose one of the cottages or efficiencies available. You're just a short stroll from the Cape Cod shores, the harbor area, ferries to the islands, and the town of Hyannis itself. All modern amenities are here including a/c, color TV,

...the center of activities

and an inground pool, picnic tables, barbecue, lawn chairs, and laundry facilities. A continental breakfast is included. **Seasonal:** *Rates vary **Reservations:** 25% of total rental required within 7 days of making reservation, 14 day cancel notice for full refund. *Season 5/26-10/09; Off-Season rates are 30% lower. **Brochure:** Yes **Permitted:** Children, smoking, drinking **Payment Terms:** Check MC/V [A10APMA-1746] **COM** Y **ITC Member:** No

Rates:	Pvt Bath 4
Single	$ 69-89.00
Double	$ 69-89.00

Sea Breeze By The Beach
397 Sea Street 02601
Martin & Patricia Battle

Hyannis MA
Tel: 508-771-7231

Perfect New England shingle Cape Codder, you'll enjoy the atmosphere in this quaint Inn close to all activities and ocean beaches in this famous resort area. Continental breakfast included. **Seasonal:** No **Brochure:** Yes **Permitted:** Children, smoking, drinking **Payment Terms:** Check [C11C-MA-1750] **COM** Y **ITC Member:** No

Rates:	Pvt Bath 3	Shared Bath 3
Single	$ 65.00	$ 55.00
Double	$ 70.00	$ 60.00

Simmons Homestead Inn
288 Scudder Ave 02647
Bill Putman

Hyannis Port MA
Tel: 800-637-1649 508-778-4999 Fax: 508-790-1342
Res Times 8am-10pm

The *Simmons Homestead* is an 1820 Sea Captain's estate that has been lovingly transformed into the nicest Bed & Breakfast Inn on Cape Cod. Ten wonderful bedrooms all with their own bathrooms. Rates include a full breakfast in the morning and complimentary wines in the evening. The only Inn in Hyannis Port, yet only two minutes from the beach, downtown Hyannis and the Harbor with ferries to the Islands. We are in the center of the Cape and convenient to everything. All rooms are uniquely furnished with antiques, canopy beds, fireplaces, huge common rooms. Grand porches surround the Inn and overlook the spacious grounds and pond. We can help plan your vacation, go whale watching, beaching, antiquing, day trips to Nantucket and Martha's Vineyard, biking

©Inn & Travel Memphis, Tennessee

or shopping. We'll steer you to the right restaurants, shops, beaches and craftspeople. The Inn is traditionally New England, full of charm, artworks and pleasant company. This is the nicest Inn on Cape Cod. Simply wonderful with knowledgeable host, Bill Putman, Innkeeper. **Seasonal:** No **Reservations:** Full deposit if less than 3 days, 3 or more days, 50% deposit; 14 day cancel policy less 10%. *Credit card for deposit only, payment required in cash or check. Special off-season rates available. **Brochure:** Yes **Permitted:** Drinking, limited smoking **Conference:** Yes in off-season (11/1-4/30) for entire house at special package rates-call for details. **Payment Terms:** Check AE/MC/V* [Z03HPMA1-8475] **COM YG ITC Member:** No

Rates:	Pvt Bath 10
Single	$ 80.00
Double	$ 130.00

Bayfront Inn — PO Box 4782 01240 — Lenox MA
Walter & Helen Wheeler   Tel: 413-637-4822 Fax: 413-642-1717

A fun time is guaranteed for everyone staying at this unique country inn. Listed in the *National Historic Register*, the Inn has been complete renovated and retored to its original glory. Furnished with period antiques and family heirlooms, its difficult for guests to realized they are living in the 1990's - except for all of the modern amenities that have been thoughtfully updated. Each of the ten guest rooms are individuall furnished and decorated in New England charm and themes. Choose from canopy beds to antique brass - all queen size offering the best night's rest you've ever had with the best mattresses available. When returning to your room each evening you'll find turndown service, a candy mint and a bottle of sherry on the night stand. A full breakfast is served in the dining room or can be served ensuite. Daytime activities include all of the outdoor sports on or near the Inn along with great shopping and dining. **Permitted:** Children, drinking, smoking outdoors only **Languages:** German, French **Payment Terms:** AE/MC/V **Reservations:** First and last night's deposit required at reservation time, 7 day cancel policy, refund less $10 service fee. [Z01FGMA-12221] **COM Y ITC Member:** No

Rates:	Pvt Bath 10
Single	$ 85.00
Double	$ 125.00

Birchwood Inn — 7 Hubbard St 01240 — Lenox MA
Joan, Dick & Dan Toner   Tel: 800-524-1646 413-637-2600
    Res Times 7am-9pm

Drive through the quaint village of Lenox and at the top of Main Street, across from the Old Church on the Hill, you'll find *The Birchwood Inn* -- a 230 year old home. Cozy fireplaces welcome guests in all of the public rooms and a parlor beckons you to read or browse while the den offers color TV for "must-see" events. Guest rooms are lavishly furnished and decorated including canopy beds and fireplaces, all with private baths. Two economical dormer rooms are available with shared baths. Guests can leisurely enjoy a complimentary breakfast offering a buffet laden with juice, coffee, tea, cereals, fruit and homemade muffins. For a real experience let our chef prepare his daily hot entrees where you can savor one of his specialties like Tarte d'Alsace, Eggs au Chasseur or Huevos Albuquerque! Summer evenings bring wine and cheese and wonderful breezes while relaxing outdoors on the large porch. Lenox hosts a variety of cultural events each summer including the Boston Symphony at Tanglewood, dance and Shakespeare theaters. The area also boasts museums, golf, tennis, fishing, swimming and factory outlet shopping. The unmatched beauty of autumn is a perfect time for hiking and biking. Winter offers cross country and downhill skiing. **Discounts:** 10% for weekly stays **Airport:** Albany 1 hr, Hartford-Springfield 1-1/2 hrs **Packages:** Winter "Getaway Weekends", Skiing, Hiking & Mountain Biking **Seasonal:** No **Reservations:** One night's deposit bal due with reservation, 10 day cancel policy for refund less 10% service fee, 3-day min during Tanglewood Festival; 2-day min Autumn and holiday weekends **Brochure:** Yes **Permitted:** Drinking, limited children

Conference: Yes; ideal for off-site business meetings, seminars and retreats. **Payment Terms:** Check AE/DISC/MC/V [I08HPMA1-1759] **COM** U **ITC Member:** No **Quality Assurance** Requested

Rates:	Pvt Bath 10	Shared Bath 2
Single	$ 80-199.00	$ 60-99.00
Double	$ 80-199.000	$ 60-99.00

Brook Farm Inn   15 Hawthorne St 01240   Lenox MA
Joe & Ann Miller   Tel:413-637-3013

Quaint 100-year-old Inn for those seeking solace with a pool, English Tea, shaded glen, fall foliage, fireplaces, and over five hundred volumes of poetry and over sixty poets on tapes to enjoy during your stay. Close to Tanglewood and museums. Full breakfast included. Library, swimming pool, sitting rooms **Seasonal:** No **Brochure:** Yes **Permitted:** Children 16-up **Payment Terms:** Check MC/V [C11A-CMA-1761] **COM** Y

Gables Inn   103 Walker St 01240   Lenox MA
Frank & Mary Newton   Tel: 800-382-9401 413-637-3416 **Fax:** 413-382-9401
                                                          Res Times 8am-8pm

This former home of author Edith Wharton has been fully restored to its original turn-of-the-century appearance. Edith's upstair's bedroom is one of the most attractive and includes a four-poster canopy bed in pink and white and a deep plum sofa next to the fireplace. Guests can visit the unusual eight-sided library where the author wrote some of her short stories. All of the guest rooms include private bath and each guest room has a unique theme. The "Jocky Club Suite" has a brass bed and an ample sitting area which includes a big-screen TV and two sofas. A private entrance from the backyard assures privacy. Another room, the "Show Business Room", is filled with autographed photos of movie stars along with a library of show-biz volumes which guests can enjoy reading during their stay. A complimentary continental breakfast includes goodies such as banana bread or sour-cream cake. Your hosts enjoy socializing with their guests and often become a willing partner for tennis in the back yard. An enclosed solar-heated swimming pool, jacuzzi are available for the guests year-round enjoyment. **Packages:** Yes, inquire at res time **Seasonal:** Rates vary **Reservations:** Deposit required at res time, 3 night min stay in season (July-August) **Brochure:** Yes **Permitted:** Children over 12, drinking, smoking **Languages:** Spanish **Payment Terms:** Check DISC/MC/V [Z02HPM-A1-14820] **COM** U **ITC Member:** No

Rates:	Pvt Bath 18
Single	$ 75-195.00
Double	$ 75-195.00

Garden Gables Inn   141 Main St 01240   Lenox MA
Mario & Lynn Mekinda   Tel:413-637-0193 **Fax:**413-637-4554
                                                          Res Times 8am-10pm

Garden Gables, a 220-year-old gabled Inn, was built originally as a private estate. Located in the historic district of Lenox, the Inn is well back from the main road on five wooded acres, dotted with gardens, maples and fruit trees. It's a perfect place for guests looking for a peaceful and relaxing atmosphere. The common rooms, with an abundance of books, magazines and board games, have several fireplaces and are beautifully furnished with antiques and 18th-century Dutch oil paintings. Guests are served a full breakfast in the beautiful dining room which overlooks the front and side gardens. Tanglewood is one mile away and summer brings guests outdoors to enjoy the large 72 ft swimming pool! Operated as an Inn since 1947, *Garden Gables* has eighteen cozy bedrooms - all

National Edition   ***Massachusetts***

with private baths. All bedrooms are uniquely decorated with choices between twin, double, queen and king-size beds, phones, fireplaces, porches, a/c and CATV in some rooms. **Discounts:** Weekly and monthly stays **Seasonal:** No **Reservations:** Full deposit at res time with cancel policy **Brochure:** Yes **Permitted:** Limited drinking, limited smoking **Languages:** German, French, Croatian **Payment Terms:** Check AE/DC/DISC/MC/V [I05HPMA-1-1767] **COM** U **ITC Member:** No

Rates: **Pvt Bath 18**
Single $ 65-175.00
Double $ 70-200.00

Walker House   74 Walker St 01240   Lenox MA
Richard & Peggy Houdek   **Tel:** 800-235-3098 413-637-1271

Become pampered in this country setting on three acres within walking distance of all points of interest. Great location for year round activities from fall foliage to summer hiking in the great outdoors. Bikes, piano, and sitting rooms are available. A continental breakfast is included with your room. **Seasonal:** No **Brochure:** Yes **Permitted:** Children 8-up, limited smoking, limited drinking **Payment Terms:** Check [C11ACMA-1772] **COM** Y **ITC Member:** No

Rates: **Pvt Bath 8**
Single $ 55-75.00
Double $ 65-130.00

Harborside House   23 Gregory St 01945   Marblehead MA
Susan Livingston   **Tel:** 617-631-1032
                                                                   Res Times 8am-8pm

This 1850 colonial overlooks the picturesque harbor in the historic district of Marblehead, yachting capital of America. Guests enjoy waterviews from the wood panelled and beamed living room, the period dining room, sunny breakfast porch and the third story deck. Antique furnishings and reproduction wallpapers enhance the charm of this comfortable quiet home. Generous breakfast includes juice, fresh fruit, homebaked breads and muffins, choice of cereals. Bedside Harbor Sweets candy at bedtime. Large twin bed guest room views the harbor. Romantic double bed guest room with antique mirrored dressing table looks out on flower gardens and deck. Quaint shops, gourmet restaurants and the historic sites of Old Town are just a pleasant stroll away. Marblehead also offers beaches, Audubon Bird Sanctuary, wind-surfing and sailing lessons. Whale-watching excursions and harbor cruises are available nearby. Half-hour travel time to Logan Airport; 45 mins to Boston. Hostess/owner is a thirty-year reident, Historical Society member, professional dressmaker and nationally-ranked competitive Master swimmer. *Harborside House* offers warmth and hospitality in gracious surroundings. Special events include: Marblehead Arts Festival (July 4th wknd), Race Week (mid-July) Halloween Celebration in Salem and Christmas Walk (early Dec). **Discounts:** Extended stays, travel agents **Seasonal:** No **Reservations:** Full deposit if 2 nights or less, if more, 50%. 10 day cancel policy less 15% service fee. 2pm check-in, 11am check-out **Brochure:** Yes **Permitted:** Children over 10, limited drinking **Languages:** French **Payment Terms:** Check [I04HPMA1-1782] **COM** YG **ITC Member:** No **Quality Assured:** Yes

Rates: **Shared Bath 2**
Single $ 60-65.00
Double $ 70-75.00

Massachusetts *National Edition*

Spray Cliff On The Ocean	25 Spray Ave 01945	**Marblehead MA**
Sally & Roger Plauche	**Tel:** 800-626-1530 617-631-6789 **Fax:** 617-639-4563	

This 1910 Victorian Tudor is set high above the Atlantic providing guests with mesmerizing views, quiet ocean front gardens, and a warm, friendly atmosphere. Each guest room is "light-filled" with a feeling of space, simplicity and elegance - with many nooks and corners to curl up in and read or listen to the ocean. When the Plauches purchased this B&B in 1994, they redecorated "everything but the view" with fresh flowers, fine fabrics, linens; comfortable wicker and sisal; with checks, plaids and lots of white. The gathering room usually has a fire burning in the fireplace and breakfast includes Nancy's homemade muffins, breads, quiches and stratas, along with fresh fruits and cereals. Bicycles are complimentary and beaches are just steps away in historic Marblehead. Sally and Roger, who have lived in various areas of the country have created a perfect setting for business travelers or that romantic getaway. **Discounts:** AAA, Corporate **Airport:** Boston Logan-13 mi **Seasonal:** No **Reservations:** One night's deposit within one week of reservation. Bal due on arrival for full period, 7 day cancel notice for refund less $15 service fee. **Brochure:** Yes **Permitted:** Drinking **Conference:** Excellent conference facilities for groups to 20 persons **Payment Terms:** Check AE/MC/V [I10HPMA1-1781] **COM** YG **ITC Member:** No

Rates: Pvt Bath 7
Single $ 149-199.00
Double $ 149-199.00

Arbor	**Marthas Vineyard MA**
Peggy Hall	**Tel:** 508-627-8137
	Res Times 8am-8pm

Refer to the same listing name under Edgartown, Massachusetts for a complete description. **Seasonal:** Yes **Payment Terms:** Check MC/V [M05HPMA1-9462] **COM** YG **ITC Member:** No

Rates: Pvt Bath 8   **Shared Bath** 2
Single $ 90-135.00 $ 90-95.00
Double $ 115-135.00 $ 90-95.00

Thorncroft Inn	278 Main St 02568	**Marthas Vineyard MA**
Karl & Lynn Buder		**Tel:** 800-332-1236 508-693-3333
		Res Times 9am-9pm

Thorncroft Inn is a nineteen room, antique appointed, romantic and intimate Bed & Breakfast Country Inn comprised of four restored homes in two locations all on the enchanting island of Martha's Vineyard, seven miles off the coast of Mass. Each building has a distinct non-commercial atmosphere enhanced by authentic restoration and architectural integrity. Each room decor is unique. Many rooms have four poster canopied beds, balconies and working wood-burning fireplace for off-season enjoyment and all rooms are fully a/c. There are suites that include color TV, phones, a jacuzzi for two or a private hot tub. Room prices include afternoon tea, evening turndown service and the morning paper! AAA Four Diamond Rating, it is the only lodging establishment on the Island to achieve this award. A full breakfast is served at both locations. The storybook island of Martha's Vineyard is a vacationer's delight. With miles of unspoiled beaches and lack of new building and development, it's a throwback to simpler times. There are many fine restaurants, out-of-the-way shops, galleries and boutiques. The Vineyard is considered as a final point of destination for vacationers and not an overnight trip because of it's remote and charming location. **Seasonal:** Rates vary **Reservations:** 100% for 1-2 nights, 50% for longer periods, due prior to arrival, two week cancel policy for refund. *Off season rates are $129-219.00. **Brochure:** Yes **Permitted:** Limited children, drinking, smoking **Payment Terms:** Check AE/MC/V [Z06EPMA-1785] **COM** Y **ITC Member:** No

National Edition *Massachusetts*

Rates: **Pvt Bath 19**
Single $ 129-299.00
Double $ 129-299.00

Centerboard Guest House 8 Chester St 02554 Nantucket MA
Ms Marcia Wasserman **Tel:** 508-228-9696
  Res Times 7am-9pm

The Centerboard is a charming Victorian home lovingly renovated and restored in 1986, located on the quiet perimeter of the Historic District just a few blocks from the cobblestoned shopping streets, white sand beaches, museums, galleries, and fine restaurants. You can choose from seven beautifully appointed guest rooms designed expressly for luxury and guest comfort. Individually decorated, each room provides a queen bed or two double beds, telephone, refrigerator, color TV, all within a gentle romantic ambiance. Choose the two room suite with white-on-white bedroom decor, huge four poster canopied bed, green marble bath complete with an oversized shower, jacuzzi bath and extraordinary accessories. A continental buffet breakfast is offered guests and includes breads and muffins, cereal, fresh fruits and a fine selection of morning beverages served in the softly lit dining room. Each Season is special here . . . with plenty to do year round! **Seasonal:** Rates vary **Reservations:** Rates based on double occupancy, $25.00 for added person, deposit of first and last night or 50% entire stay, (greater amount), 21 day cancel notice for refund or if re-rented. Off season $85-125.00 **Brochure:** Yes **Permitted:** Children 12-up **Conference:** Yes with full house rental for 11-20 persons **Payment Terms:** Check AE/MC/V [A03F-PMA-179-5] **COM** Y **ITC Member:** No

Rates: **Pvt Bath 7**
Single
Double $ 145-245.00

Century House 10 Cliff Rd 02554 Nantucket MA
Jean & Gerry Heron Connick **Tel:** 508-228-0530

Serving weary travelers since the mid-1880's and still offering antique period furnishings, Laura Ashley print wallcoverings and fabrics, you'll be close to the ocean and all activities in this resort setting. Continental breakfast included. **Brochure:** Yes **Permitted:** Children, limited drinking **Payment Terms:** Check [X11ACMA-2981] **COM** Y **ITC Member:** No

Rates:	**Pvt Bath 2**	**Shared Bath 3**
Single	$ 80.00	$ 70.00
Double	$ 90-135.00	$ 80.00

Lynda Watts B&B 10 Upper Vestal St 02554 Nantucket MA
Mrs Lynda Watts **Tel:** 508-228-3828

Contemporary home offering a great family stopover with king beds, TV, sunny patio, and a gracious hostess. Walking distance to all sights in town center. Plenty of the outdoor activities, swimming, tennis, golf, and sightseeing. Continental breakfast included. **Seasonal:** No **Permitted:** Children, limited smoking **Payment Terms:** Check [C11ACMA-1814] **COM** Y **ITC Member:** No

Rates:	**Pvt Bath 1**	**Shared Bath 1**
Single	$ 60.00	$ 60.00
Double	$ 68.00	

Phillips House 54 Fair St 02554 Nantucket MA
Mary Phillips **Tel:** 508-228-9217

Quaint 200 year old whaler's residence just minutes from the village green and within walking distance of all sights. Providing New England hospitality to every guests, activities include with golf, tennis, swimming nearby. Continental breakfast included. **Seasonal:** No **Brochure:** Yes **Permitted:** Limited

Massachusetts   *National Edition*

children, limited smoking **Payment Terms:** Check [X11ACMA-2982] **COM** Y **ITC Member:** No

Rates:	Pvt Bath 1	Shared Bath 2
Single	$ 60.00	$ 55.00
Double	$ 75.00	$ 65.00

Quaint Cape Victorian Inn   688 S Main St 02554   Nantucket MA
Bob Pickle   Tel: 508-322-0123
     Res Times 8am-5pm

Beautiful Victorian with breath-taking views of the Cape and ocean takes guests back in time and elegance to the Victorian era! Perfectly furnished with period antiques and family heirlooms - with all the important details, such as original gas lights, marble mantels, stained glass windows, spiral stairwell, carved oak woodwork and fine examples of oriental rugs covering the highly polished original oak floors. Guest rooms include king-size beds with either four-poster or canopy details and all modern amenities. Full New England breakfast is served in the formal dining room or "in-bed" if you like and includes fresh home-baked family recipes for muffins, breads and waffles. You're within easy strolling distance of all the Cape's sights, so you can park your car on the premises. **Seasonal:** No **Reservations:** 50% deposit for entire stay within 5 days of booking to hold reservation; check-in by 6pm; 5-day cancellation policy for refund. **Brochure:** Yes **Permitted:** Limited children, limited drinking **Conference:** Yes, for small groups **Languages:** French **Payment Terms:** Check AE/MC/V [G02BFMA-6576] **COM** Y **ITC Member:** No

Rates:	Pvt Bath 4	Shared Bath 2
Single	$ 65.00	$ 45.00
Double	$ 70.00	$ 60.00

Seven Sea Street   7 Sea St 02554   Nantucket Island MA
Matt & Mary Parker   Tel: 508-228-3577
     Res Times 8am-10pm

Featured in *The New York Times* Travel Section - *Seven Sea Street Inn* offers travelers a chance to make their time special - a trip that they will fondly remember for a long time after. Your hosts pride themselves on attentive service and elegant accommodations to make your stay on the island - unforgettable. Travelers to Nantucket Island will relive the *"- Early American Spirit"* while staying in this newly constructed red oak post and beam cozy Country Inn, reminiscent of a bygone period. Colonial furnishings combined with modern comforts and conveniences in each of our guest rooms and suites, provide a cozy respite on this romantic island, thirty miles at sea. Amenities include queen size canopy bed, cable TV, small refrigerator and private bath. Spectacular views of Nantucket Harbor abound from the rooftop "widow's walk". The cozy common rooms provide a perfect fireside visiting, reading and letter writing area - while the full-size heated Jacuzzi is enjoyable any time of the day. The Inn is centrally located, just a block from Nantucket Yacht Club and only a five minute walk to Main Street, Children's Beach and the Steamship Ferry Terminal. An elegant continental breakfast consisting of fresh fruit and juices, home-baked bread and muffins with coffee, tea and milk, is served in the common area or in your room, if you like. Our rates are neither the lowest nor the highest to be found on Nantucket Island, but they represent an excellent value for travelers and fond memories upon your return home. **Discounts:** Yes, off-season (Oct 13 to June 25) 15% for weekly stays and 10% for 3 or more weekdays, Sun to Thur **Airport:** 3 miles to island airport **Seasonal:** No **Reservations:** Full payment for two days or less, 50% deposit if longer, 14 day cancel policy less 10% service fee. **Brochure:** Yes **Permitted:** Drinking, limited children **Conference:** Yes, for special events, meetings, parties, wedding groups requiring eight rooms and function rooms. Hors d'oeuvres, full dinners, outdoor BBQ and authentic New England Clambakes. Full AV available. **Languages:** French **Payment Terms:** Check AE/MC/V [J02EPMA-7153] **COM** N **ITC Member:** No

National Edition   **Massachusetts**

Rates: **Pvt Bath 8**
Single $ 85-155.00
Double $ 95-165.00

Windsor House   38 Federal St 01950   **Newburyport MA**
John & Judith Harris   **Tel:** 508-462-3778   **Fax:** 508-465-3443
                                                                                           Res Times 8am-8pm

A former Continental Army Officer's home c1796, guests enjoy the Federal Period styling, gracious antique furnishings reminiscent of early colonial times. Each room is furnished with a different theme, one is an original ship's chandlery. Family dining at breakfast where guests are offered a hearty New England full meal to begin the day. **Seasonal:** No **Reservations:** Two night min on weekends **Brochure:** Yes **Permitted:** Children **Payment Terms:** Check MC/V [C09BCMA-1842] **COM** Y **ITC Member:** No

Rates:	**Pvt Bath 3**	**Shared Bath 3**
Single	$ 90.00	$ 83.00
Double	$ 95.00	$ 89.00

1810 House B&B   147 Old Oaken Bucket Rd 02061   **Norwell MA**
Susanne & Harold Tuttle   **Tel:** 617-659-1810
                                                                                           Res Times 8am-9pm

The *1810 House* is a comfortable bed and breakfast home lovingly restored and added to by the owners, Harold and Susanne Tuttle. The antique half-cape with it's original beamed ceilings, three working fireplaces, wide pine floors and hand-stenciled walls was recently featured on the Christmas Tour of Norwell homes. The house is furnished with antiques, beautiful oriental carpets and interesting accessories collected over a period of many years. Harold is a woodworker and refinisher who has done extensive restoration in the house, while Susanne is a seamstress who has created the custom window treatments. Three bright, cheery rooms, one with a canopy bed, one with twin beds and one with an antique spool bed share two full baths, The two rooms on the second floor are ideal for two couples traveling together or families. A full New England breakfast is served by the kitchen fireplace or on the screened porch. Norwell, a beautiful historic town, is located half-way between Plymouth and Boston on Massachusetts South Shore. It is an ideal spot for day trips to Cape Cod, Newport Rhode Island, Concord, Lexington, Salem and Rockport - all a short drive away. Public transportation to Boston via a subway or commuter boat is close by. A tour of the area in Harolds restored 1915 Model T depot hack adds to the feeling of a bygone era and is part of the fun of staying at the *1810 House B&B*. Featured in *"Country"* magazine, Aug/Sept 1993 **Airport:** Boston Logan-25 mi **Seasonal:** No **Reservations:** One night's deposit to guarantee reservation, 7 day cancel policy for refund **Permitted:** Children 6-up **Payment Terms:** Check [I07HPMA1-13172] **COM** YG **ITC Member:** No

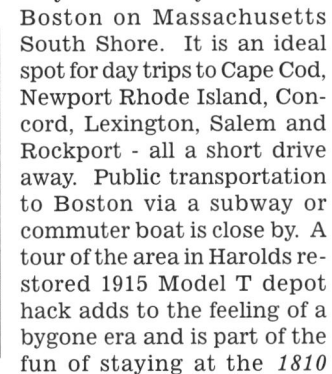

Rates:	**Pvt Bath 2**	**Shared Bath 1**
Single	$ 65-80.00	$ 60-75.00
Double	$ 65-80.00	$ 60-75.00

Oak House   Seaview & Pequot Aves 02557   **Oak Bluffs MA**
Betsi Convery-Luce   **Tel:** 508-693-4187

Enter the romance of a yesteryear seaside holiday at our Victorian Bed & Breakfast Inn, the richly restored 1872 beachfront summer home of Governor Claflin. Elegant oak paneled interior, authentic antiques, leaded glass windows, wide wrap around porches and balconies, offer sweeping

©*Inn & Travel Memphis, Tennessee*

Massachusetts *National Edition*

views of the ocean and nearby beach, complement our charming ten guest rooms. All uniquely furnished in various themes, each guest room has its own private bath. A continental breakfast is included along with Victorian high tea served each afternoon on the wicker-filled & stain glassed sun porch, just perfect for relaxing away the day. Guests can leisurely stroll to the nearby ferry, beaches, bike paths, Oak Bluff's shopping area and to exciting restaurants featuring fresh New England seafood entrees. *Closed late Fall and Winter. **Seasonal:** Yes* **Reservations:** 50% deposit required, balance due upon arrival (3 days or less full deposit) with 14 day cancel policy for refund less 10%. Rates subject to tax & gratuities. *25% discount 5/15-6/20 & 9/20-10/14. **Brochure:** Yes **Permitted:** Drinking, smoking, limited children **Conference:** Yes **Payment Terms:** Check MC/V [Z11C-PMA-1857] **COM** Y **ITC Member:** No

Rates: Pvt Bath 10
Single $ 85-175.00
Double $ 85-175.00

Onset Pointe Inn 9 Eagle Way 02558-1450 Onset MA
Debbie & Joe Lopes Tel: 800-35-ONSET 508-295-8442

The *Onset Pointe Inn* is situated on Point Independence in the village of Onset, Massachusetts, surrounded by miles of sandy beaches. Since Onset is just before the Bourne Bridge, you are able to avoid the bottle neck traffic jams that frequently occur at the high traffic times on weekends. Another plus is that Onset is a quiet seaside village off the beaten path, yet in the center of everything. Within minutes you can be at restaurants, a championship golf course, canal cruise, a water park, weekend entertainment, antique and specialty shops. Within an hour's drive you can be at almost any Cape Cod location or Plymouth, New Bedford, Fall River, Boston and Newport or Providence, Rhode Island. There are historic sites, outlet malls, bike trails, walking trails, whale watching, fishing, museums, entertainment and much more. Our facilities include a great diversity and all are directly on the beach. The *Onset Point Inn* itself is located at the end of a dead end street, The B&B "Mansion" with seven unique rooms, two with balconies, includes a hearty continental breakfast and is located at the furthest most end of the Point. Next to it is a two unit "Cottage" (the original carriage house), plus a "Guest House" which has five units. All fourteen of our rooms have waterviews, private baths and three have kitchens, with something in everyone's price range. In addition, we have two off the premise cottages. One is on an island and includes its own boat. It is completely furnished, three bedrooms and on the beach. The other was originally a houseboat, which has now been put onto it's own foundation. It has two bedrooms, and is completely furnished and just steps to the beach. If you're hoping to do a little bit of everything, including relaxing, we may be just the spot you've been looking for. **Discounts:** Seniors, midweek, corporate, off-season **Airport:** New Bedford-20 min; Providence-1 hr; Hyannis-30 min **Packages:** Yes, inquire at res time **Seasonal:** Yes, rates vary **Reservations:** 50% deposit, 14 day cancellation policy less $15 service fee, special terms for large groups, inquire at reservation time. Cottages available only by the week **Brochure:** Yes **Permitted:** Children welcomed in cottages and guest house, mansion reserved for adults only, limited drinking **Conference:** Facilities for small informal meetings & conferences to twenty; wedding and party groups to 50 or 150 with tents **Payment Terms:** Check AE/DISC/MC/V [I11HPMA1-17974] **COM** YG **ITC Member:** No

Rates: Pvt Bath 14
Single $ 75-150.00
Double $ 75-150.00

The Farm House 163 Beach Rd 02653 Orleans MA
Dot Standish Tel: 508-255-6654
Res Times 9am-10pm

Come and enjoy this nineteenth century farmhouse that has been carefully restored and furnished to provide a unique blend of country life in a seashore setting. An outside deck is used for a breakfast of freshly baked coffee cake with steaming coffee as well as for guests activities while enjoying a peeking view of the ocean. A short walk (1/2 mi) to beautiful Nauset Beach. Guests are close to sailing, golf, tennis, fine restaurants, shops, museums, beach strolling and surfing!! Guests can experience the best lobsters, quahaugs, chowders and an always fresh "catch of the day" in one of many fine nearby restaurants - which your hostess will kindly recommend - if needed. The guest rooms offer twin, double or king size beds finished with handmade quilts, afghans and bed ensembles. Some rooms provide ocean views. The Farmhouse is a licensed bed and breakfast awaiting guests who would like to enjoy Cape Cod to the fullest. *"Be Our Guests!"* **Discounts:** Yes, inquire at res time **Airport:** Boston Logan-2 hrs **Seasonal:** No **Reservations:** Deposit required and advance reservations advised **Brochure:** Yes **Permitted:** Children (6-up), drinking, limited smoking **Payment Terms:** Check MC/V [Z06GPMA-1859] **COM** Y **ITC Member:** No

Rates:	Pvt Bath 4	Shared Bath 4
Single	$ 60-95.00	$ 32-65.00
Double	$ 60-95.00	$ 32-65.00

Boggastowe Farm — Shattuck St 01463 — **Pepperell MA**
John & Shirley Ritichie — **Tel:** 508-433-9987
Res Times 8am-8pm

Hideaway in this charming c1790 country farm home and experience New England at it's best - just 60 minutes from Boston, on the Massachusetts and New Hampshire border. This 200 year old farmhouse sits atop a grassy knoll and is surrounded by giant maple trees and beautiful meadows. Guests enjoy watching the sheep and horses graze or feeding the ducks around the large farm pond. In March, guests may help make maple syrup. Two large bedrooms have adjoining baths and two bedrooms have private baths. Two bedrooms, a guest living room, dining room and kitchen have working fireplaces. Antique furnishings. Your hosts, a retired engineer and teacher, prepare a hearty full breakfast with farm-fresh eggs from the hen-house -- maple syrup made in their own sugarhouse. The scenery is beautiful year-round and the quaint country towns nearby have plenty of antiquing, shopping and national historic parks for outdoor activities and sports. Guests are conveniently located to Lowell and Concord (30 mins) and Nashua New Hampshire (20 mins). **Seasonal:** No **Reservations:** One night's deposit with 7 day cancel policy less 10% service fee. **Brochure:** Yes **Permitted:** Children, pets, limited drinking, limited smoking **Payment Terms:** Check [R09CPMA-11288] **COM** U **ITC Member:** No

Rates:	Pvt Bath 2	Shared Bath 2
Single	$ 55.00	$ 45.00
Double	$ 65.00	$ 55.00

Winterwood At Petersham — N Main St 01366 — **Petersham MA**
Robert Day — **Tel:** 617-724-8885

Greek Revival mansion in the center of town, it is listed on *National Register of Historic Places* and offers guests the warmth of antique furnishings and fireplaces in all rooms. Continental breakfast included. **Seasonal:** No **Brochure:** Yes **Permitted:** Children, limited smoking, limited drinking **Conference:** Yes, including dining and social hours **Payment Terms:** Check [X11ACMA-1863] **COM** Y **ITC Member:** No

Rates:	Pvt Bath 5
Single	$ 75.00
Double	$ 85.00

Allen House — **Plymouth MA**
Christine Gilmour — **Tel:** 508-545-8221
Res Times 8am-10:30am

Refer to the same listing name under Scituate, Massachusetts for a complete description. **Seasonal:** Clo March **Payment Terms:** Check AE/DISC/MC/V [M03HPMA1-16687] **COM** YG **ITC Member:** No

©*Inn & Travel Memphis, Tennessee*

Massachusetts   *National Edition*

Rates:	Pvt Bath 4	Shared Bath 2
Single	$ 89-149.00	$ 79-119.00
Double	$ 89-149.00	$ 79-119.99

Cranberry Cottage   10 Woodbine Dr 02360   **Plymouth MA**
Nanci & Capt Ray Reid   Tel: 508-747-1726   Fax: 508-747-1726

The *Cranberry Cottage* is nestled in a rural area of Plymouth Massachusetts. There are many activities and attractions nearby. These include Plimoth Plantation - a village re-enacting the way life was in 1620. The Plymouth Wax Museum and other museums have artifacts from when the settlers arrived on the Mayflower, including a replica of the Mayflower which was built in England and sailed from Plymouth, England to Plymouth, Massachusetts approximately forty years ago. Plymouth offers beautiful white sandy beaches with all sorts of boating, charters, kayaking and parachute rides over the harbor. The *Cranberry Cottage* is within a short walking distance to working cranberry bogs and Billington Sea. Just a couple of miles from downtown Plymouth, visitors can tour Cranberry World which depicts the history of farming cranberries. There are four guest rooms prices at $50-70.00 per night which includes a bountiful breakfast served in the fireplaced breakfast room or poolside. *Cranberry Cottage* has a large pool and spa. In the afternoon, high tea and light refreshments are available. Activities include horseshoes, volleyball, ping pong or badminton or a stroll along the cranberry bogs. A common room features cable TV and an electric organ and a working fireplace. The parlor is tastefully decorated in different periods, with Count Montgolfiere chairs, Louis XV chairs, a Victorian curio cabinet, Trumeau Mirrors set over Napoleon chests. Your hosts, Captain Ray and Nanci Reid are Ocean Spray cranberry growers. Captain Ray is a US licensed Captain and can arrange fishing charters on the Ray's Lure. **Airport:** Boston Logan Intl-60 mi; Warwick RI Great Airport-60 mi **Packages:** Autumn Season **Seasonal:** Yes, rates vary **Reservations:** $50 deposit required or credit card guarantee, 7 day cancel policy for refund **Brochure:** Yes **Permitted:** Children, drinking, limited smoking **Payment Terms:** Check AE/MC/V [I05HP-MA1-22048] **COM** YG **ITC Member:** No

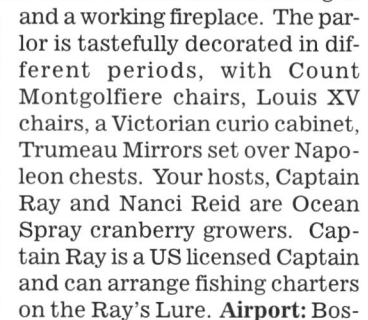

Rates:		Shared Bath 4
Single		$ 50-60.00
Double		$ 50-70.00

Morton Park Place   1 Morton Park Rd 02360   **Plymouth MA**
James & Janine Smith   Tel: 800-736-3276 508-747-1730
    Res Times 9am-5pm

Lovely New England Colonial situated at the entrance to Little Pond, you're just a short walk to fresh water ponds for swimming, boating, fishing while visiting "America's Hometown." Situated on a large lot that provides secluded areas for privacy, lawn games, and cookout if you like while here. This home has been completely restored and furnished with Victorian and 20th century antiques with guest rooms offering Red Maple Colonial and oak veneer Art Deco pieces. Location is everything here!! You're just a 15 minute walk from the center of Plymouth, the Mayflower, and Plymouth Rock. Plenty of antique shopping, fine restaurants and unique boutiques and unusual shops. Continental breakfast included. Baby-sitting and limo services are available at extra cost. **Seasonal:** Rates vary **Reservations:** 25% deposit, two weeks in advance of res date, 7 day cancellation for full refund. Add 9.7 tax, 4 pm check-in. **Brochure:** Yes **Permitted:** Limited children, limited drinking, limited smoking **Payment Terms:** Check MC/V [A11CPM-A-1867] **COM** Y **ITC Member:** No

Rates:	Pvt Bath 2	Shared Bath 2
Single	$ 55-65.00	
Double	$ 90-110.00	

Bradford Gardens Inn   178 Bradford St 02657   **Provincetown MA**

©*Inn & Travel Memphis, Tennessee*

National Edition
Massachusetts

Susan Culligan

Tel: 508-487-1616
Res Times 9am-9pm

Built in 1820, Provincetown's historic Bradford Gardens Inn brings true hospitality with all the comfort and convenience of a gracious country home. All the rooms are unique in character combining charm (working fireplaces in most rooms) with period and modern conveniences. The Morning Room with its fireplace and large bay window is a delightful setting for guests to mingle and enjoy the full complimentary country breakfast. Guests can enjoy the year-round scenery (Spring and Summer flowering cherry and fruit trees) and the fabulous Fall for enjoying the unhurried shopping and natures brightest colors. *Guests can choose one of the cottage rentals ($82-118) with maid service, firewood, parking and a full breakfast included. Add 8% Mass tax to rates. Activities include biking, exquisite walking trails, boating, fishing and neighboring towns of Truro and Wellfleet. **Seasonal:** Rates vary **Reservations:** One night's deposit (or 50% if longer) with reservation; 14 day cancel policy for refund; add $25 per day in high season (6/24-Mem Day and $10 per day 9/6-10/31, off-season mid-week rates available **Brochure:** Yes **Permitted:** Limited children, limited smoking, limited drinking **Payment Terms:** Check [X06BCMA-1874] COM Y ITC **Member:** No

Rates:	Pvt Bath 8
Single	$ 84-102.00
Double	$ 84-102.00

Lamplighter Guest House 26 Bradford St 02657 **Provincetown MA**
Mike Novik/Joe Czarnecki
Tel: 508-487-2529 **Fax:** 508-487-0079
Res Times 8:30am-11pm

Our charming Sea Captain's home, built in 1853, offers panoramic views of Provincetown, the Bay and all of Cape Cod. The Mayflower is anchored right in front of our Inn and the Pilgrims came ashore nearby. Activities abound such as whale watching, unique shopping, biking, sightseeing, swimming or strolling our numerous beaches. Our Inn provides two suites, rooms with private or semi-private baths, plus a separate cottage which is fully equipped to sleep four. The grounds surrounding the Inn are groomed daily and called the loveliest in Provincetown. Maid service, a continental breakfast and parking are provided. Reservations are required and free pick-up at the local airport, ferry or bus depot is provided with advance arrangements. **Discounts:** Off-season. **Airport:** Provincetown Airport-2 mi; Boston's Logan-2 hrs **Packages:** Off-season, inquire at res time **Seasonal:** Rates vary **Reservations:** 50% deposit required; *check acceptable for deposit. **Brochure:** Yes **Permitted:** Drinking, smoking **Conference:** Seasonal roof deck provides a unique setting. **Payment Terms:** Check* AE/MC/V [R10EPMA-1879] COM Y ITC **Member:** No

Rates:	Pvt Bath 8	Shared Bath 2
Single	$ 95.00	$ 55.00
Double	$ 95.00	$ 55.00

Land's End Inn 22 Commercial St 02657 **Provincetown MA**
Anthony Arakguan
Tel: 508-487-0706
Res Times 9am-10pm

Land's End Inn commands a splendid wind-swept breath-taking site with views of Provincetown and Cape Cod Bay. Built in the shingled-bungalow style

collection of oriental carvings

of the late Victorian Period by Charles Higgins, a Boston merchant, *Lands End* still houses part of his extensive collection of oriental wood carvings and stained glass. The Inn's large and airy living room is comfortably and informally furnished for relaxation, contemplation and quiet socializing before a large stone fireplace. The guest rooms are filled with antique furnishings and period decor providing a comfortable and lived-in feeling; where books abound - and the modern world doesn't intrude. Situated in the quiet residential West End of Provincetown, *Land's End* is close to the surrounding National Seashore beaches and numerous New England towns for fine restaurants and great *seafood!* Continental breakfast is included in rate. **Airport:** Boston Logan 130 mi; Provincetown Municipal-3mi **Seasonal:** No **Reservations:** 50% deposit at res time to hold room; min

©*Inn & Travel Memphis, Tennessee*

Massachusetts National Edition

2 day weekends, 3 day holidays and 7 day summer periods **Brochure:** Yes **Permitted:** Drinking, limited children **Conference:** Yes, for small groups **Payment Terms:** Check MC/V [Z02GHMA-1880] **COM** U **ITC Member:** No

Rates: **Pvt Bath** 16
Single $ 82-250.00
Double $ 82-250.00

Allen House Quincy MA
Christine Gilmour Tel: 508-545-8221
Res Times 8am-10:30am

Refer to the same listing name under Scituate, Massachusetts for a complete description. **Seasonal:** Clo March **Payment Terms:** Check AE/DISC/MC/V [M03HPMA1-16686] **COM** YG **ITC Member:** No

Rates:	**Pvt Bath** 4	**Shared Bath** 2
Single	$ 89-149.00	$ 79-119.00
Double	$ 89-149.00	$ 79-119.00

Gilberts B&B 30 Spring St 02769 Rehoboth MA
Jeanne & Martin Gilbert Tel: 800-828-6821 508-252-6416

c1840s farmhouse nestled on 70 acres of pastoral and wooded fields just outside of Providence, Rhode Island furnished with period antiques and family heirlooms. Pleasant hosts offer inground pool, pony rides for children and a full country breakfast with farm-fresh eggs you'll gather yourself. **Seasonal:** No **Reservations:** One night's deposit to guarantee room. **Brochure:** Yes **Permitted:** Children, limited smoking, limited pets **Payment Terms:** Check [X11ACMA-1891] **COM** Y **ITC Member:** No

Rates:	**Pvt Bath** 3	**Shared Bath** 4
Single	$ 50.00	$ 42.00
Double	$ 57.00	$ 50.00

Inn On Cove Hill 37 Mt Pleasant St 01966 Rockport MA
John & Marjorie Pratt Tel: 508-546-2701

Overlook the historic harbor area of Rockport from this delightful 200 year old Inn furnished in period decor with antique and canopy beds in some of the guest rooms. Continental breakfast is served on antique china indoors or, weather permitting, outdoors. Activities include golf, tennis and plenty of sight-seeing. **Seasonal:** Opn: 4/1-10/15 **Reservations:** Deposit to hold room, 10 day cancel policy **Brochure:** Yes **Permitted:** Children 15-up, limited smoking **Payment Terms:** Check [X11ACMA-189-9] **COM** Y **ITC Member:** No

Rates:	**Pvt Bath** 9	**Shared Bath** 2
Single	$ 60-74.00	$ 55.00
Double	$ 70-85.00	$ 65.00

Sally Webster 34 Mt Pleasant St 01966 Rockport MA
Tel: 508-546-9251

Colonial residence c1830s restored and furnished with antiques recall another era. Short stroll to water, beaches and village center. Continental breakfast included. **Seasonal:** No **Brochure:** Yes **Permitted:** Children 16-up, smoking, drinking **Languages:** French **Payment Terms:** Check [X11AC-MA-5891] **COM** Y **ITC Member:** No

Rates:	**Pvt Bath** 6
Single	
Double	$ 68.00

Seafarer Inn 86 Marmion Way 01966 Rockport MA

1-64 ©*Inn & Travel Memphis, Tennessee*

National Edition   *Massachusetts*

Tel: 508-546-6248
Res Times 9am-9pm

A distinctive Inn built in 1890s rests directly on Gap Cove at the end of a quiet residential coastal road in one of Rockport's most desirable areas. Guests can fully relax in this peaceful waterfront setting with its invigorating salt air, fragrant wild roses combined with bright sunshine while gulls cry overhead, lobstermen tend their traps and sailboats catch quick ocean breezes. All the guest rooms are bright and airy for watching perfect sunrises and sunsets over the ocean. Guest rooms are comfortably furnished with two lovely large rooms on the third floor which include kitchenettes and charming breakfast nooks. There's a small cottage-like efficiency apartment with a private entrance available too - all suitable for a weekly or seasonal use. A continental breakfast is included. Your hostess has gathered restaurant menus for guests to help make their choice before departing for town which is just a short stroll away. Favorite sights include the second largest artists colony in the USA with over 100 galleries and studios and favorite activities include nature trails, bird watching, jogging and rock sitting for refreshing ocean sprays. **Seasonal:** No **Reservations:** One night's deposit or credit card to guarantee res, 14 day cancel policy for refund. **Brochure:** Yes **Permitted:** No pets, children, smoking **Languages:** French **Payment Terms:** Check MC/V [R07BCMA-2630] **COM** Y **ITC Member:** No

Rates: **Pvt Bath 8**
Single $ 50-70.00
Double $ 60-80.00

Harborside House   Salem MA
Susan Livingston   **Tel:** 508-631-1032
                                                                         Res Times 8am-8pm

Refer to the same listing name under Marblehead, Massachusetts for a complete description. **Seasonal:** No **Payment Terms:** Check [M04HCMA1-14782] **COM** YG **ITC Member:** No

Rates: **Shared Bath 2**
Single $ 60-65.00
Double $ 70-75.00

Salem Inn   7 Summer St 01970   Salem MA
Richard & Diane Pabich   **Tel:**800-446-2995 508-741-0680 **Fax:**508-744-8924
                                                                         Res Times 8am-8pm

Located in the heart of one of America's oldest seaport cities, *The Salem Inn* offers accommodations rich in history and with a proud tradition of service and comfort. Built in 1834 by sea captain Nathaniel West, the lovely Captain West House blends the warmth and charm of yesterday with the comfort and convenience of today. All rooms are spacious, comfortable and individually decorated featuring antiques, period detail and homey touches. Guest suites, complete with kitchens, are ideal for families. All rooms have a queen or dual-king bed, air conditioning, direct dial telephones, color cable TV and private bath. Several rooms contain working fireplaces. Tucked away in the original kitchens of the West House is our restaurant, the Courtyard Cafe. The two intimate dining rooms open onto a gardened courtyard with outdoor dining during warm weather. Set in Salem's fashionable McIntire Historic District, the 1854 Curwen House of *The Salem Inn*, is a fine example of Italianate revival architecture. Details, such as quoined corner, hipped roof and large double portico supported by Corinthian columns, distinguish its facade. Acquired by *The Salem Inn* in 1994, this three-story building on the *National Register of Historic Places,* was lovingly restored, while maintaining the period appeal, original architectural detail and historical integrity. The lovely Curwen House, a smoke free environment, offers ten tastefully decorated guestrooms in a serene and

Massachusetts National Edition

gracious environment, each with queen bed and private bath. The three honeymoon suites feature canopy beds, double Jacuzzi bath and working fireplaces. Antiques, clawfoot tubs, coffee makers, cable TV's and direct dial phones provide a luxurious, comfortable escape for the modern day traveler. **Discounts:** AAA **Airport:** Boston Logan-17 mi **Packages:** Dinner, Family **Web Address:** http://www.star.net/salem/biz/saleminn; e-mail: Saleminn-@earthlink.net **Seasonal:** Rates vary **Reservations:** One night's deposit with 7 day cancel policy for refund less a $15 service fee **Brochure:** Yes **Permitted:** Children, drinking, limited smoking, limited pets **Conference:** With special arrangements **Payment Terms:** Check/AE/DC/DISC/JCB/MC/V [K05IPMA1-3637] **COM** U **ITC Member:** No

Rates:	Pvt Bath 29
Single	$ 119-175.00
Double	$ 119-175.00

Capt Ezra Nye House	152 Main St 02563	Sandwich MA
Elaine & Harry Dickson		Tel: 800-388-2278 508-888-6142 **Fax:** 508-888-2940
		Res Times 9am-9pm

Selected as one of the *Top Fifty Inns in America* by *"The Inn Times"* and winner, **Best Bed & Breakfast, Upper Cape,** *"Cape Cod Life"* magazine, 1993, 1994 also featured in *"Glamour"*, *"Innsider"*, and *"Cape Cod Life"* magazines, this 1829 Inn is a classic example of the stately Federal period homes built by sea captains of yore. The seven guest rooms are furnished with antiques. Three have canopy beds, another a queen four-poster, with a working fireplace. A suite with private entrance has a queen bed in one room and a small sitting room with a single sofa bed. Common rooms are the parlor with piano, a cozy den with fireplace, library and cable TV, and a large dining room where either an 8 or 9 am breakfast is served. Cape Cod Bay and the canal bike trail are one mile. **Discounts:** 10% for five or more days or three midweek day stay **Airport:** Boston Logan-60 miles **Seasonal:** No **Reservations:** Guaranteed with credit card, 48 hr cancel policy for refund, late arrival with advance notice **Brochure:** Yes **Permitted:** Children 6-up, drinking **Languages:** Spanish **Payment Terms:** Check AE/DC/MC/V [Z06GPMA-6543] **COM** Y **ITC Member:** No **Quality Assurance:** Requested

Rates:	Pvt Bath 5	Shared Bath 2
Single	$ 70-90.00	$ 55-70.00
Double	$ 70-90.00	$ 55-70.00

Six Water Street	6 Water St 02563	Sandwich MA
Linda & Mike Levitt		Tel: 508-888-6808

Romantic setting on Shawnee Pond, this elegant residence offers romantic candlelight breakfast, rowing on pond, and a decanter of sherry in each guest room. Continental breakfast included. Complimentary tennis, sitting room, rowboats. **Seasonal:** No **Brochure:** Yes **Permitted:** Children 16-up **Payment Terms:** Check [X11ACMA-3644] **COM** Y **ITC Member:** No

Rates:	Pvt Bath 2
Single	$ 60.00
Double	$ 100.00

Summer House	158 Main St 02563	Sandwich MA
David & Kay Merrell		**Tel:** 508-888-4991
		Res Times 9am-10pm

Twice featured in *"Country Living"* magazine, this residence is an exquisite example of c1835 Cape Cod Greek Revival architecture in a setting of equally stunning historically significant homes and public buildings. Centrally located in the heart of historic Sandwich, a quintessential New England village (settled in 1637) and within strolling distance of restaurants, museums, shops, pond and gristmill and boardwalk to the beach. Antique furnishings, hand-stitched quilts, spacious airy rooms, original woodwork, latch hardware, wavy handfashioned glass window panes and seven fireplaces evoke a gracious homelife. Full breakfast of freshly ground coffee, English or herbal teas, fruit juice, fresh seasonal fruit, entree of stuffed French toast, strata, Belgian waffles, quiche, garden fritatta, eggs benedict and two homebaked items (scones, muffins, yeast breads, fruit cobbler) are elegantly served in the sunny breakfast room (on cloudy days by candlelight). Special diets happily accommodated with advance notice. Complimentary English-style afternoon tea, brewed in antique silver pots, or iced, is served at an umbrella table in the garden or on the wicker furnished sunporch overlooking antique roses seldom seen today. Secluded hammocks beckon guests to daydream in the sun or shade. Small library, boa games, local newspapers, restaurant menus and color TV are available in the guest parlor. Tranquil Sandwich village makes an excellent "base" from which to explore all of the Cape Cod, the Islands and Plymouth - Boston and Providence are 60 miles away. **Discounts:** Travel agents **Airport:** Hyannis-15 mi; Boston or Providence RI-60 mi **Seasonal:** No **Reservations:** Credit card or check for deposit of 50% of stay to hold, 10 day cancel notice for refund. Refund with less than 10 day notice only if rebooked **Brochure:** Yes **Permitted:** Drinking, limited children, limited smoking **Payment Terms:** Check AE/DC/MC/V [I04EPMA-3645] **COM** Y **ITC Member:** No

Rates:	Pvt Bath 1	Shared Bath 4
Single	$ 55-65.00	$ 40-50.00
Double	$ 65-75.00	$ 50-60.00

Allen House   18 Allen Place 02066   **Scituate MA**
Ian & Christine Gilmour   **Tel:** 508-545-8221
Res Times 8am-10:30am

Don't pay in stress and dollars to stay, drive and park in Boston when you can stay 30 miles south in a quiet unspoilt fishing town, sleep peacefully and enjoy a fabulous gourmet breakfast before driving comfortably to a commuter boat and going to the city center in 35 minutes of civilized, stylish and comfortable sightseeing across Boston Harbor. Scituate is a beautiful small historic town on the South Shore where the Gilmours, gourmet caterer Christine and former journalist and corporate writer Ian, opened The *Allen House* primarily to provide engaging hospitality and a warm English welcome for visitors and friends of local families and businesses. Just six rooms, four with private baths, overlook the town center, harbor and ocean beyond. Working fireplaces in the parlor and dining room make winter visits almost as wonderful as eating a summer breakfast on their sun-filled porch. Restaurants, shops and most of the town's services are within a three minute walk. Reservations of three or more nights (excluding Fridays and Saturdays) enjoy discount rates. **Discounts:** Yes **Airport:** Boston Logan-30 miles **Seasonal:** Clo March **Reservations:** Deposit required (check preferred, minimum one week prior to arrival) or credit cards, rates are reduced for winter season **Brochure:** Yes **Permitted:** Children 14+, drinking - smoking is not permitted **Languages:** Little French, German, Spanish **Payment Terms:** Check AE/DISC/MC/V [I03HP-MA1-12510] **COM** YG **ITC Member:** No

Rates:	Pvt Bath 4	Shared Bath 2
Single	$ 89-149.00	$ 79-119.00
Double	$ 89-149.00	$ 79-119.00

Race Brook Lodge   864 Undermountain Rd 01257   **Sheffield MA**
Ernie Couse   **Tel:** 888-RBLODGE 413-229-2916 **Fax:** 413-229-6629

Rustic and elegant . . . Race Brook Lodge is a place you can rest your feet and feel reborn. This 18th Century Berkshire barn has been beautifully restored offering guest rooms furnished in warm country-style with textured fabrics, quilts, rugs, handhewn beams, original artwork and stenciling. The owner-architect, Dave Rothstein, retained the hand hewn beams, thick plan floors, hideaway corners - creating rooms and suites designed especially for 90's family reunions, small group retreats

Massachusetts *National Edition*

and quite getaways. The Barn Suite, Hayloft Suite and Harness Barn offer a range of two to four bedroom suites, perfect for extended families, friends or groups. A hearty breakfast buffet is featured daily and includes fruits, juices, granola, bagels, homemade muffins, great tea and our own special blend coffee, while Sundays frequently feature lively jazz sessions accompanied by Sunday papers and interesting refreshments. Located on scenic Undermountain Road between Salisbury Connecticut and South Egremont, Massachusetts, the old custom of changing stagecoach horses every seven miles explains our wonderfu location. Hikers can cross the foot bridge from the lodge and hike to Race Brook Falls on the Appalachian Trail; skiers are 15 mins from Catamount or Butternut and just 20 miles from Tanglewood - and close to many great town and country restaurants offering gourmet to family style meals. *Race Brook Lodge* with its whispering brook and old maples invite you to renew and refresh by finding your cozy corner, put your feet up and recharge - while in this rural wonderland. **Airport:** Albany-45 min **Packages:** Ski, Hunting, Antique Shopping **Meals**: Available for groups upon request. Extensive facilities for small or large workshops, seminars, executive retreats, featuring intimate setting for privacy. **Seasonal:** No **Reservations:** Credit card number to secure reservation, 7 day cancel policy for refund (14 days cancel notice for holiday period) email: rblodge@bcn.net **Brochure:** Yes **Permitted:** Children, limited pets, limited drinking, limited smoking **Conference:** Informal dress down accommodations for workshop retreats, task force/team building and creative brainstorming **Languages:** Spanish **Payment Terms:** Check AE/MC/V [K03IPMA1-18782] **COM** U **ITC Member:** No

Rates:	Pvt Bath 17	Shared Bath 2
Single	$ 79-119.00	$ 69-99.00
Double	$ 89-129.00	$ 79-119.00

Unique B&B — Undermountain Rd 01257 — Sheffield MA
May Stendardt — Tel: 413-229-3363

Custom designed log home snuggled in wooded pines at foothills of Mount Everett, you are able to relax and enjoy the beautiful scenery. Close to antiquing, skiing, hiking, trail walking, and fine dining. **Seasonal:** No **Brochure:** Yes **Payment Terms:** Check MC/V [X11ACMA-3654] **COM** Y **ITC Member:** No

Rates:	Pvt Bath 2	Shared Bath 1
Single	$ 85.00	$ 55.00
Double	$ 95.00	$ 65.00

Wyndemere House — 718 Palmer Ave 02540 — Sippewissett MA
Tel: 508-540-7069

Completely restored in 1980, this Paul Revere colonial built c1790's offers guests a true New England feeling with fine antique furnishings, and English pieces accenting the rooms. You might relax on the patio or in the library or TV room, with complimentary tea, coffee, sangria. Full breakfasts include host's specialty of Eggs Benedict if you like. Close to beaches and sights. **Reservations:** Reduced weekly rates. **Brochure:** Yes **Permitted:** Children 13-up, smoking, drinking; airport pick-up. **Payment Terms:** Check [X05ACMA-3657] **COM** Y **ITC Member:** No

Rates:	Pvt Bath 1	Shared Bath 2
Single	$ 65.00	$ 45.00
Double	$ 75.00	$ 65.00

Bull Frog B&B — South Ashfield MA
Lucille & Moses Thibault — Tel: 413-628-4493

Exciting 225 year farmhouse offering guests all the comfort of home with king size beds and plenty of

©*Inn & Travel Memphis, Tennessee*

National Edition   *Massachusetts*

New England hospitality. Furnished with a collection of country antiques and warmth, you'll enjoy visiting with the hosts who tend to all your interests. Full hearty New England break-ast is prepared by Lucille. Close to five colleges in Northhampton and Amherst with great outdoor activities nearby. **Seasonal:** Closed Jan/Tanks **Reservations:** Deposit for 50% of stay within ten days of reservation. **Permitted:** Limited children **Payment Terms:** Check [X11ACMA-3658] **COM Y ITC Member:** No

Rates:	Shared Bath 2
Single	$ 55.00
Double	$ 65.00

Ye Olde Nantucket House	2641 Main St 02659	South Chatham MA
Steve & Ellen Londo		Tel: 508-432-5641
		Res Times 9am-9pm

Midway between Cape Cod and Provincetown is an ideal location especially when guests can stay in this classic Greek Revival traditional Cape home moved to its present location in 1867 from Nantucket. Located in a designated Historic District, the atmosphere is friendly, informal and delightful. The stenciled walls, wide-pine plank floors, antique furnishings and attractive window and wall coverings combine into a unique Victorian flavor, fitting for a traditional stay on The Cape! Just a short walk to Nantucket Sound beach and the conveniently located areas for dining, shopping, golfing and fishing. An ideal location for visiting fine shops, restaurants, summer band concerts, picturesque lighthouses, concerts and plays, church suppers and great summer festivals, surfing and sailing, craft and nautical antique shops, as well as ordinary antiques. Plymouth and Boston are within easy driving range and daily ferry trips will bring guests to Martha's Vineyard and Nantucket. A complimentary continental breakfast includes seasonal fresh fruit and juice, home-baked goods and hot beverages. Off-season rates are $10 less, special winter rates are available. **Seasonal:** No **Reservations:** One night's full deposit or 50% if longer to confirm res; 2 day min on high season weekends and 3 day min on major holidays. 7 day cancel policy for full refund, early departures subject to no refund. **Brochure:** Yes **Permitted:** Children 8-up, drinking, limited smoking **Payment Terms:** Check MC/V [R06BCMA-3659] **COM Y ITC Member:** No

Rates:	Pvt Bath 5
Single	$ 70-82.00
Double	$ 70-82.00

Little Red House	631 Elm St 02748	South Dartmouth MA
Meryl Amoroso		Tel: 508-996-4554
		Res Times 9am-9pm

Charming New England red gambrel colonial home overlooking a horse and cow pasture is located in the lovely coastal village of Padanaram. This home is beautifully furnished with many country accents, antiques, a lovely living room with corner fireplace, luxuriously comfortable four-poster or brass and iron beds. A gazebo in the backyard offers a perfect setting for relaxing moments. A full homemade breakfast served in the candlelit dining room satiates the appetite. Each morning you'll awake to the aroma of freshly brewed coffee and a surprise treat of sausage and biscuits with a special sauce, french toast, mushroom and spinach quiche, egg and sausage strata, buttermilk pancakes or apple fritters accompanied by juices, fresh fruit dishes and Meryl's special raisin bran muffins, cranberry bread, scones and homemade preserves. Close to the harbor and superb restaurants, beaches, historic sites, and just a short distance to major tourist areas such as New Bedford, Newport, Plymouth, Boston and Cape Cod. The ferry to Martha's Vineyard is just ten minutes away. Centrally located for many a day's excursion, your friendly hospitable hosts will welcome you back with late afternoon tea and cookies or a refreshing cool drink. **Airport:** Providence RI Green Airport-45 mins **Seasonal:** No **Reservations:** One night's deposit or 50% of length of stay; 14 day cancel policy for refund less 10% service fee. 11 am checkout. **Brochure:** Yes **Permitted:** Limited drinking, children 16-up **Payment Terms:** Check [Z05GP-MA-10932] **COM Y ITC Member:** No

Rates:	Shared Bath 2
Single	$ 55.00
Double	$ 65.00

©*Inn & Travel Memphis, Tennessee*

Massachusetts   *National Edition*

Federal House Inn	Rt 102 01260	**South Lee MA**
Robin Slocum & Ken Almgren		**Tel: 617-350-6657**

Early 19th Century brick Federal building furnished with bright and cheerful touches including wallcoverings and family heirloom antiques such as Robin's great grandfather's sleigh bed. Full gourmet country breakfast includes specialties prepared by Ken, a professional chef who also prepares delightful entrees and appetizers included in their complete luncheon and dinner menu. Close to cross country skiing, Shakespeare and other sights. **Seasonal:** No **Brochure:** Yes **Permitted:** Limited smoking, limited drinking **Payment Terms:** Check [X11ACMA-3664] **COM** Y **ITC Member:** No

Rates: Pvt Bath 7
Single $ 55-up
Double $ 65-145.00

Captain Farris House	308 Old Main St 02664	**South Yarmouth MA**
Scott Toney		**Tel:** 800-350-9477 508-760-2818 **Fax:** 508-398-1262

Built in 1845 by a sea captain, this Greek Revival and French Second Empire home offers luxurious guest rooms with beautiful antique furnishings reflecting the international travels of a world-travelled sea captain of the mid-1800's. Guests will find a myriad of styles, countries of origins and period prior to the 1850's. The many uses and additions to the original houses have been brilliantly incorporated to create a unique and special place for guests. The two houses offer ten guest rooms, including one and two bedroom suites, with a variety of amenities which include jacuzzi bathtubs with fine soaps and bath salts for luxurious soaking, canopy beds, private terraces, while all rooms offer private and semi-private entrances, cable TV and phones. A complimentary gourmet breakfast is served in the dining room or the open-air courtyard in season. A wrap around veranda offers relaxation anytime of the day - while the beautiful nearby sights offer plenty of shopping, museums and dining. Great location for travel, guests are only forty-five minutes from both Plymouth and Provincetown; twenty minutes to Hyannis and Nantucket Sound. Within a few minutes are nearby ferries, Bass River offering classic Cape Cod scenery and great fishing and complimentary bikes bring the beaches with a ten minut ride - while golf, canoeing, bird-watching, beach hiking and antiquing are within an easy drive. The *Captain Farris House* is an exceptionally appointed bed and breakfast for escapes, vacations, tours, special occasions, weekends, honeymoons or whatever you desire. **Airport:** Boston Logan-80 mi **Seasonal:** No **Reservations:** One night non-refundable deposit, two night min weekends, three night min holidays **Brochure:** Yes **Permitted:** Children 12-up, drinking **Payment Terms:** Check AE/MC/V [I02HPMA1-18181] **COM** YG **ITC Member:** No **Quality Assured:** Yes

Rates: Pvt Bath 10
Single $ 75.00
Double $ 225.00

Old Mill Inn		**Springfield MA**
Phyllis & Ralph Lumb		**Tel:** 203-763-1473
		Res Times 7am-10pm

Refer to same listing name under Somersville, Connecticut for complete description. **Seasonal:** No **Payment Terms:** Check [M01DPCT-6550] **COM** Y **ITC Member:** No

Rates: Pvt Bath 3   **Shared Bath** 2
Single $ 60.00 $ 50.00
Double $ 60.00 $ 50.00

Amerscot House	61 W Acton Rd 01775	**Stow MA**

National Edition   *Massachusetts*

Doreen & Jerry Gibson   **Tel:** 508-897-0666
                                                                                            Res Times 9am-6pm

Amerscott House is a beautiful early American farmhouse built in 1734. Come home from a day of business or vacationing and enjoy the ambiance and warmth of the past. Linger over a glass of sherry or tea and scones by the fire. Antiques, handmade quilts and fresh flowers reflect Amerscot's personal touch. Each guest room has a fireplace, full private bath, phone and cable TV. The Lindsay suite has a sitting room and bath with jacuzzi. The Barn Room will accommodate up to sixty people for conferences or private parties. Visit historic sites, shop in the select stores of Concord and Boston, golf on any of the four top-flight courses, canoe, hike and enjoy fresh-picked apples from the nearby orchards. Stow is only five minutes from Rt 495 and Rt 2. Business services available include conference facilities, secretarial, copier and fax. A full breakfast is included with fresh fruit, homemade granola, bread, muffins and an entree. **Seasonal:** No **Reservations:** Reservations must be guaranteed with a deposit, 7 day cancel policy for refund, corporate & extended-stay special rates are available, check-in 4-9pm, check-out by 11 am **Brochure:** Yes **Permitted:** Children **Conference:** The Barn Room is a multi-function room perfect for business or social meetings, private parties for groups to 60 persons **Payment Terms:** AE/MC/V [R03CPMA-10637] **COM** Y **ITC Member:** No

Rates: **Pvt Bath** 3
Single $ 75-90.00
Double $ 80-95.00

Captain Parkers Inn At Quinebaug   Sturbridge MA
David Parker/Bojeua Szmuniewska   **Tel:** 800-707-7303 203-935-5219
                                                                                            Res Times 24 Hrs

Refer to the same listing name under Thompson, Connecticut for a complete description. **Payment Terms:** Check MC/V [M08GPCT1-20105] **COM** Y **ITC Member:** No

Rates: **Pvt Bath** 4   **Shared Bath** 2
Single $ 70.00 $ 55.00
Double $ 75.00 $ 55.00

Col E Crafts Publik House   Fiske Hill Rd 01566   Sturbridge MA
David Lane   **Tel:** 508-347-3313

Spectacular views from atop Fiske Hill are offered in this 1786 restored country farmhouse with deluxe accommodations which include swimming pool, piano and continental plus breakfast. **Seasonal:** No **Brochure:** Yes **Permitted:** Children, smoking, drinking **Languages:** French **Payment Terms:** Check AE/MC/V [X11ACMA-3675] **COM** Y **ITC Member:** No

Rates: **Pvt Bath** 8
Single $ 85.00
Double $ 95.00

Sturbridge Country Inn   530 Main St 01566   Sturbridge MA
Kevin MacConnell   **Tel:** 508-347-5503
                                                                                            Res Times 7am-11pm

Close to Old Sturbridge Village, on the old "Boston Post Road" (530 Main St), lies this mid-19th century Country Inn offering gracious surroundings. This grand structure is now known as the *Sturbridge Country Inn*. We welcome you to enjoy a respite in our luxurious accommodations where we have preserved the charm of the past while providing all of the fine comforts of today. All rooms are tastefully decorated with period colonial furnishings, a private fireplace, vaulted ceilings and whirlpool tubs. For the more discriminating guest, the Corner rooms offer a large whirlpool tub, sun porch and breakfast ensuite if desired. The Loft Suite with its king-size bed, skylights, sitting room, wet bar and breakfast ensuite provides elegance beyond your expectations. We encourage your special occasion, whether it is a wedding, anniversary, birthday, executive retreat or a weekend getaway.

Massachusetts   *National Edition*

Complimen-tary champagne greets each guest upon their arrival and your hosts can look after any details ranging from limousine and airport service, VCR rentals, Old Sturbridge Village tickets to fresh flowers. The perfect location for your affordable weekend getaway or special occasion. **Airport:** Bradley or Logan-60mi **Seasonal:** No **Reservations:** 50% deposit at res time with 14 day cancel policy for refund. **Brochure:** Yes **Permitted:** Children, drinking, smoking **Languages:** Spanish **Payment Terms:** Check AE/DC/DISC/MC/V [I04HPMA-18242] **COM YG ITC Member:** No

Rates: Pvt Bath 9
Single $ 89.00
Double $ 159.00

Longfellow's Wayside Inn	Wayside Inn Rd 01776	Sudbury MA
Robert Purrington		**Tel:** 508-443-1776 **Fax:** 508-443-2312

Longfellow's Wayside Inn, immortalized in 1863 by Longfellow in his *"Tales of a Wayside Inn"*, is located off US Rt 20 on Wayside Inn Rd. Next to the Inn, there's a working gristmill (open April-November) and the red stone school house of *"Mary and Her Little Lamb"* fame (open in seasonal weather). The Martha Mary Chapel is available for weddings and special events. The *Wayside Inn* offers facilities for small meetings and functions. Reservations for lodging or dining should be made well in advance. Our entire staff looks forward to welcoming you and showing you the hospitality that has made the *Wayside Inn* a special place for nearly three hundred years. **Airport:** Boston Logan-25 mi **Reservations:** Deposit required **Brochure:** Yes **Permitted:** Children, drinking, smoking **Conference:** Meeting and conference rooms available. **Payment Terms:** Check AE/DC/MC/V [R11EPMA-3679] **COM Y ITC Member:** No

Rates: Pvt Bath 10
Single $ 75.00
Double $ 85.00

Lothrop Merry House	Owen Park 02568	Vineyard Haven MA
Mary & John Clarke		**Tel:** 508-693-1646

18th century guest house nestled right on a hilltop setting with its own private beach and overlooking the harbor. All rooms offer guests lovely views, fireplaces, and quaint furnishings. Continental breakfast included with homemade breads. **Seasonal:** No **Permitted:** Children, limited smoking, drinking **Conference:** Yes **Payment Terms:** Check MC/V [X11ACMA-3691] **COM Y ITC Member:** No

Rates: Pvt Bath 2   Shared Bath 1
Single
Double $ 85-120.00 $ 70.00

The Hanover House	#10 Edgartown Rd 02568	Vineyard Haven MA
Kay & Ron Nelson		**Tel:** 508-693-1066
		Res Times 8am-10pm

Recommended by the *New York Times*, *The Hanover House* is a large old Inn that has been fully renovated offering guests modern convenience with the quaintness and personalized hospitality of the lovely old inns of yesteryear. All rooms include private baths, color cable TV, a queen size bed or two double beds, a/c and individual heat controls. Vineyard Haven is a quaint and unspoiled island/town which is reached by the Wood's Hole Ferry. The town is filled with craft shops, fine restaurants and theaters. *The Hanover House* is within walking distance of the ferry, island tours and shuttle buses to Oak Bluffs and Edgartown. Activities include sailing, windsurfing, swimming, fishing, biking, tennis, golf and horseback riding. Fully-equipped housekeeping units including kitchens are available for longer stays. A homemade continental breakfast is included. **Seasonal:**

©*Inn & Travel Memphis, Tennessee*

National Edition   *Massachusetts*

No **Reservations:** Full deposit 1-3 days, 50% - 4 days or longer received within 7 days of booking. 14 day written cancel notice for refund less 20% ($20 min). No refunds for early departure. **Brochure:** Yes **Permitted:** Children, limited drinking, non-smoking **Payment Terms:** Check AE/MC/V [Z04GPMA-3690] **COM** Y **ITC Member:** No

Rates: Pvt Bath 15
Single $ 95-158.00
Double $ 95-158.00

Honeysuckle Hill	591 Main St 02668	West Barnstable MA
Barbara Rosenthal		Tel: 508-362-8418

"Country Elegance at its Best" - Honeysuckle Hill was originally built in the early 1800s as a farm house near the great salt marshes of Cape Cod. Completely restored, the Inn is a comfortable, rambling place, decorated in a Cape Cod version of English Country: chintz, antiques, cushions, comfortable chairs, feather beds and down comforters, two shaggy dogs named Fred and Annie and a tin of homemade cookies at every bedside. The theme guest rooms are named Peter Rabbit (filled with antique furnishings and Peter Rabbit memorabilia); Rose Room featuring a working fireplace perfect for a romantic weekend; the very private Cape Cod Room tucked away on the second floor. In addition to fluffy ***feather beds and down comforters*** terry robes, each private bath includes a basket of English toiletries, fresh flowers in each guest room when in season, a carafe of ice water and a bedside tin of homemade cookies. Complimentary beach towels, beach chairs, umbrellas are always on the porch - along with a bulletin board of area events. Hearty Country breakfasts featuring memorable entrees such as sausage souffles or blueberry pancakes and traditional afternoon tea are served in the dining room. A wrap-around screen porch filled with wicker furniture provides summer relaxation while winter has everyone gathering in comfortable chairs around the fireplace in the Great Room with its game table and large screen TV. Located in Old Kings Highway historic district on Rt 6A, guests are still close to the dunes of Sandy Neck Beach, Hyannis, historic Sandwich Village while Boston and Provincetown are just an hour's drive. A perfect starting point for all of the Cape's excitement of whale watching, antiquing, beaches, golf, tennis and country auctions. **Airport:** Boston Logan-65 mi; Providence-75 mi **Discounts:** Off-season **Seasonal:** No **Reservations:** One night's deposit to confirm reservation **Brochure:** Yes **Permitted:** Limited children, limited pets, limited smoking **Conference:** Facility for small groups in a large great room setting **Languages:** Some French, Italian. **Payment Terms:** Check AE/DC/MC/V [I10EPMA-3699] **COM** Y **ITC Member:** No

Rates: Pvt Bath 3
Single $ 90-105.00
Double $ 90-105.00

Lions Head Inn	186 Belmont Rd 02671	West Harwich MA
The Dentons		Tel: 800-321-3155 508-432-7766
		Res Times 9am-9pm

The *Lion's Head Inn* is a delightfully romantic Inn with a sense of history . . . blended with the quiet elegance and updated amenities of a tastefully decorated country manor. Built in the 1800's as a Cape Half House, it was the home of Thomas L Snow, a sea captain of Orient-bound schooners. The architectural characteristics of the early 1800's are evident throughout the Inn. Adding to the original flavor are the furnishings, some of which are period antiques, and the tastefully decorated guest suites and common areas. A warm atmosphere awaits each guest at the *Lion's Head Inn*. Each morning a bountiful breakfast is served. Since the *Lion's Head Inn* is centrally located on the Cape, one's choice of pastime is close at hand. Whether in the warm waters of Nantucket Sound, a half-mile from the Inn, enjoying a dip in the Inn's swimming pool, riding nearby bicycle paths, fishing or sailing in the Cape Cod Bay or the Sound waters, whale watching, enjoying a round of golf,

©*Inn & Travel Memphis, Tennessee*

Massachusetts *National Edition*

shopping or antiquing, enjoying local theatre or dining at the area's superb restaurants, visitors will find their stay relaxing or full as they wish it to be. Rated Excellent by ABBA. **Airport:** Boston Logan-70 mi **Reservations:** 50% deposit at time of reservation. **Permitted:** Children over 4, drinking, limited smoking **Payment Terms:** Check AE/MC/V [R11EPMA-3711] **COM** Y **ITC Member:** No

Rates:	Pvt Bath 6
Single	$ 60-100.00
Double	$ 70-110.00

Card Lake Inn & Restaurant   29 Main St 01266   **West Stockbridge MA**
Ed & Lisa Robbins   **Tel:** 413-232-0272

The *Card Lake Restaurant and Country Inn*, in beautiful West Stockbridge, offers guests fine food and lodging in the Berkshires. Your innkeepers at *Card Lake* provide guests with charming, clean, comfortable guest rooms (most of which have brass beds and antique furnishings) and a delicious continental breakfast. The restaurant, open daily from 11am until 9pm, offers hearty country cuisine and tempting desserts along with a fine selection of liquors, wines, beer and plenty of good company and cheer. Just minutes away from attractions such as Tanglewood, Rockwell Museum, Jackob's Pillow, and major ski areas. **Airport:** Albany-1 hr **Seasonal:** Rates vary **Reservations:** First night deposit, min two night stay on weekends in season (May-Oct), one week cancel policy for refund **Brochure:** Yes **Permitted:** Children, drinking, limited smoking **Payment Terms:** Check DC/MC/V [I04GPMA1-7213] **COM** Y **ITC Member:** No

Rates:	Pvt Bath 4	Shared Bath 4
Single	$ 95-125.00	$ 70-80.00
Double	$ 95-125.00	$ 70-80.00

Worthington Inn/Four Corners   Old North Rd 01098   **Worthington MA**
Debi & Joe Shaw   **Tel:** 413-238-4441

Nestled on fifteen acres where the Hampshire hills meet the Berkshires, the *Worthington Inn* is central to this quaint New England town and accessible to Springfield, Williamstown and Pittsfield and the five college area of Amherst and Northampton. Dating from 1780 and fully restored, it is listed on the *Massachusetts Register of Historic Sites*. You'll enjoy the picture-postcard setting that offers guests billowy European down comforters and the delicious aroma of homemade gourmet breakfasts being served in the fireplaced dining room. There's plenty to do: x-country skiing, canoeing, swimming and hiking, as well as plenty of antiquing. **Seasonal:** No **Reservations:** One night's deposit at res time. **Brochure:** Yes **Permitted:** Limited children, limited smoking, drinking okay **Languages:** German **Payment Terms:** Check MC/V [X01BCMA-3733] **COM** Y **ITC Member:** No

Rates:	Pvt Bath 4
Single	$ 80.00
Double	$ 80.00

Liberty Hill Inn On Cape Cod   77 Main St 02675   **Yarmouth Port MA**
Jack & Beth Flanagan   **Tel:** 800-821-3977 508-362-3976
  Res Times 8am-10pm

Elegant, historic and romantic, this Bed & Breakfast Inn offers distinctive accommodations for the most discriminating traveler. Featured in many guidebooks such as *Fodor* and in magazines such as *Colonial Homes*. *"Best Bed & Breakfast"* - *"Insider's Guide to Cape Cod"*. AAA Approved, Mobil 3-Stars. The Greek Revival style, mini-mansion has high ceilings, modern private baths and spacious rooms filled with early American antiques. History is celebrated everywhere on Cape Cod but especially on the Old Kings Highway in the village of Yarmouth Port. Nearby are historic

National Edition   *Massachusetts - New Hampshire*

restorations, conservation areas, golf courses, fine beaches, whale watching, professional theatre, restaurants and gift shops. A full complimentary breakfast is included while lunches are available at added cost. You'll find cable TV in the Common Room, attraction brochures, maps of the area and menus from local restaurants. Guest telephone available, plenty of off-street parking. **Airport:** Boston Logan-77 mi; Barnstable County Airport-3 mi, free airport pick-up with prior arrangement **Packages:** Sunday-Thursday, 5 nights for the price of 4; Golf, Theatre **Seasonal:** No **Reservations:** One night's deposit if less than 4 days, 50% deposit if longer; 14 day cancel policy for refund **Brochure:** Yes **Permitted:** Children, drinking, limited smoking **Conference:** Yes, for groups to twelve with fax and copy machine nearby, guest phone **Payment Terms:** Check AE/MC/V [I06FPMA-3739] **COM** Y **ITC Member:** No

Rates: **Pvt Bath 5**
Single $ 50-70.00
Double $ 70-125.00

Wedgewood Inn	83 Main St 02675	Yarmouth Port MA
Milt & Gerrie Graham		Tel: 508-362-5157 Fax: 508-362-9178
		Res Times 24 Hrs

The *Wedgewood Inn* is a handsome Greek Revival built in 1812 on the historic north side of Cape Cod and is listed in the *National Registry of Historic Places*. This romantic Inn has two-plus beautifully landscaped acres of lawn and gardens, with a gazebo for the guest's enjoyment. There are six rooms, all with private baths. Most of the rooms have working fireplaces, wide board floors, and pencil post or canopy beds. Two full suites and a junior suite offer private porches and private sitting rooms. The decor is formal Country with antiques and oriental rugs. Fresh fruit is placed in each room, as is an Afternoon Tea tray. A sunny dining room with a large bay window provides a pleasant setting for a multi-course full breakfast. Homebaked goods, fresh fruit and a choice of entrees such as Belgian waffles with strawberries and whipped cream are featured. Nearby area activities include antique shops, fine restaurants, art galleries and of course, water sports and whale watching. Nature trails, bird watching and bicycle trails are also popular attractions. **Discounts:** *Off-season rates $90-135.00, travel industry, extended stays over 5 nights **Airport:** Boston Logan-70 mi; Hyannis-3 mi **Seasonal:** Rates vary **Reservations:** One night's deposit to 3 night stay, over 3 nights, 50% deposit **Brochure:** Yes **Permitted:** Children 10-up, drinking, limited smoking **Conference:** Yes for small groups **Payment Terms:** Check AE/DC/MC/V [I04HPMA1-3744] **COM** YG **ITC Member:** No

Rates: **Pvt Bath 6**
Single $ 105-150.00
Double $ 105-150.00

Stone Rest B&B	652 Fowler River Rd 03222	Alexandria NH
Richard Clarke		Tel: 603-744-6066

Quiet country setting with picturesque view of Mt. Cardigan with queen-size beds and a bunkroom. Fly fishing in the backyard, cross-country trails, nearby. Full breakfast included. Dinner avail-able, at added cost. **Seasonal:** No **Brochure:** Yes **Permitted:** Children 10-up. **Payment Terms:** Check [X-11ACNH-2259] **COM** Y **ITC Member:** No

Rates: **Shared Bath 4**
Single $ 50.00
Double $ 50.00

Glynn House Inn	43 Highland St 03217	Ashland NH
Betsy & Karol Paterman		Tel: 800-637-9599 603-968-3775 Fax: 603-968-9338
		Res Times 24 Hrs

©*Inn & Travel Memphis, Tennessee*

New Hampshire *National Edition*

Enjoy the gracious elegance of the 1890s in a beautifully restored Victorian Inn tucked away in the quaint New England village of Ashland, **The Heart of The White Mountains** - just minutes from year-round activities - and Squam Lake, of *"On Golden Pond"* fame. A picture-perfect example of the Victorian era, guests marvel at the Inn's cupola towers and gingerbread wrap-around porch. Upon arrival, guests are greeted by a magnificent foyer accented with carved oak woodwork and pocket doors. The Inn is beautifully furnished with Queen Anne furniture and ornate oriental wallpaper offering guests the warmth and hospitality of being "home" in the 1890s! Each bedroom has its own mood, distinguished by unique interior decor, period furnishings and amenities. A full gourmet breakfast is included and served in an elegant sunny dining room. Year-round activities include world-class downhill and cross country skiing, swimming, fishing, biking & hiking nature trails, gorgeous fall foliage, tennis golf and plenty of antiquing. Guests are centrally located between the Lakes and White Mountains and just two hours from Boston, four hours from Hartford or Montreal and six hours from NYC I-93 exit 24. Come discover and share the Victorian Love Affair your hosts have preserved! **Seasonal:** No **Reservations:** 50% deposit to confirm reservation, 14 day cancel policy for refund, 3pm check-in, 11am check-out **Brochure:** Yes **Permitted:** Children 12+, limited drinking **Languages:** Polish, Russian **Payment Terms:** Check DC/MC/V [K05HP-NH1-11476] **COM YG ITC Member:** No

Rates: Pvt Bath 8
Single $ 75.00
Double $ 85-145.00

Bradford Inn   11 West Main St 03221   **Bradford NH**
Connie & Tom Mazol   **Tel:** 800-669-5309 603-938-5309
  Res Times 9am-11pm

The *Bradford Inn* is a rural country hotel that was opened in May 1898. It offers guests a choice of twelve guest rooms (all with private bath) each tastefully decorated to reflect the charm and character of its turn-of-the-century beginning. Most of the guest rooms are on the second and third floor and vary in size from rooms with bath to parlor (mini) suites. The first floor is dedicated to the guests enjoyment and relaxation in either of the two large parlors which includes a fireplace and fine old antique and casual country furnishings. Wicker furniture beckons guests outdoors on sunny days. J Alberts restaurant serves a continental cuisine with an emphasis on cuisines of Eastern Europe. The full breakfast is never a disappointment. Fresh juices, breads and pastries, cereals, egg and meat dishes and delicious coffee are just some of the items guests might find on the morning menu. Enjoy New England's finest natural display year-round here with strolls along country lanes, antique shop browsing, driving the gentle rolling hills and mountains offers breath-taking vistas and the seasonal colors! There's swimming, sailing, golf, summer theater, lake cruises with great cross country or downhill skiing in winter. **Meals:** Dinner and other meals available **Discounts:** Yes, for multiple night stays **Packages:** Ski with maps available **Seasonal:** No **Reservations:** One night deposit to guarantee room, 14 day cancel policy less $10 service fee; less than 14 day notice, refund only if room is rented **Brochure:** Yes **Permitted:** Children, drinking, smoking, limited pets **Conference:** Yes for groups to 75 persons **Languages:** Arabic **Payment Terms:** Check AE/DC/DISC/MC/V [Z08HPNH1-2272] **COM YG ITC Member:** No

Rates: Pvt Bath 12
Single $ 59.00
Double $ 69-79.00

Mountain Fare Inn   Mad River Rd 03223   **Campton NH**
Susan & Nick Preston   **Tel:** 603-726-4283
  Res Times 8am-10pm

1-76   ©*Inn & Travel Memphis, Tennessee*

Your professional skier/hosts invite guests to share their year-round village farm house c1840's. Typical of the white clapboard New England style, with black shutters, multi-gabled roof line and a long open porch. Nestled on six acres at the edge of Campton Village, a charming town that grew up in the days of logging and steam engines. The decor is purely country, simple, cheerful, clean and full of handicrafts, with woodstoves and fireplaces to keep everyone toasty in winter! The guest rooms vary in size (with some accommodating 4-5 persons), and are well-furnished with attractive and homey touches of lovely fabrics, country antiques and crafts. Hearty New England breakfasts are included and start-off your day right with a treat of fresh fruit garnished with herbs and flowers in the summer; carbo-high for skiers in winter. During ski season, dinner is served on Saturday nights. Perfect locale for outdoor activities year-round. In the winter you have a lodge for active alpine or cross country. In the spring, fall and summer, the White Mountains offer a peaceful retreat for hiking, biking, fishing, golfing, canoeing, horseback riding and plenty of wildflowers and gardening on the Inn's grounds. Your hosts keep busy teaching the Freestyle Skiing program for Waterville Valley Ski Club and keep active year-round with all the other outdoor activities. We specialize in family reunions year-round for up to twenty persons and offer guided hiking week-ends May-October. We'll pack trail lunches and offer candlelight dining including garden-fresh vegetables Summer and Fall. **Seasonal:** No **Reservations:** $10 per night deposit, 10-day cancel policy for refund **Brochure:** Yes **Permitted:** Children, drinking **Conference:** Groups to 20 persons with dining. **Payment Terms:** Check [I07DPNH-2277] **COM** Y **ITC Member:** No

Rates:	Pvt Bath 5	Shared Bath 3
Single	$ 40.00	$ 30.00
Double	$ 56-64.00	$ 48-56.00

Farmhouse B&B	Page Hill Rd 03817	Chocorua NH
Kathie & John Dyrenforth		Tel: 603-323-8707

Pre-Civil War homestead in country setting of lakes and mountains with hiking, canoeing, fishing, and skiing nearby. Farm fresh breakfast includes pancakes and maple syrup fresh from the farm. **Seasonal:** No **Brochure:** Yes **Permitted:** Children, smoking, and drinking. **Payment Terms:** Check [X1-1ACNH-2284] **COM** Y **ITC Member:** No

Rates:	Shared Bath 4
Single	$ 50.00
Double	$ 60.00

Bradford Inn		Concord NH
Connie & Tom Mazol		Tel: 800-669-5309 603-938-5309
		Res Times 9am-11pm

Refer to the listing name located under Bradford, New Hampshire for the complete description. **Seasonal:** No **Payment Terms:** Check AE/DC/DISC-/MC/V [M08HPNH1-8254] **COM** YG **ITC Member:** No

Rates:	Pvt Bath 12
Single	$ 59.00
Double	$ 69-79.00

Kancamagus Swift River Inn	PO Box 1650 03018	Conway NH
The Beckenbach's		Tel: 800-255-4236 603-447-2332
		Res Times 24 Hrs

A newly constructed Inn located in the scenic White Mountain National Forest offers travelers quality lodging in a stress-free environment for enjoying the beauty of New Hampshire year-round.

New Hampshire *National Edition*

This Mount Washington Valley location offers fishing, bathing, nature trails, cross country skiing, exciting picnic areas, spectacular views, artist studios, antique shops and convenience while located along the Kancamagus Highway, claimed to be the most beautiful highway in all of New Hampshire. Nearby are five major ski areas, bargain factory outlet stores and many picturesque covered bridges. Accommodations offer new large rooms, each with a private bath and shower, two full size beds, TV, individual heat and a complimentary continental breakfast served in the Inn's dining room. **Seasonal:** No **Reservations:** One night's deposit to confirm room, 5 day cancel policy for refund. Less than 5 day's notice, refund only if room is rebooked. **Brochure:** Yes **Permitted:** Children, smoking, limited drinking **Languages:** Polish **Payment Terms:** Check [Z05FPNH-7372] **COM** Y **ITC Member:** No

Rates: **Pvt Bath 10**
Single $ 65.00
Double $ 65.00

Village House		Conway NH
Robin Crocker		Tel: 800-972-8343 603-383-6666

Refer to the same listing name under Jackson, New Hampshire for a complete description. **Seasonal:** No **Payment Terms:** Check DISC/MC/V [M08GP-NH-15321] **COM** Y **ITC Member:** No

Rates: **Pvt Bath 13**   **Shared Bath 2**
Single $ 50-125.00 $ 50-125.00
Double $ 50-125.00 $ 50-125.00

Chase House B&B	RR #2 Box 909 03745	Cornish NH
Bill & Barbara Lewis		Tel: 603-675-5391
		Res Times 8am-8pm

History buffs will love this darling Inn built 1766!! *Listed on National Register of Historic Places*, the Chase family tree includes the Governor of Ohio, Secretary of Treasury for Lincoln, the Chase from Chase Manhattan Bank, and a Chief Justice of the Supreme Court. Perfectly furnished for recalling our past, you'll enjoy making a trip just to stay here. **Seasonal:** No **Reservations:** Deposit required at time of reservation **Brochure:** Yes **Permitted:** Limited children **Payment Terms:** Check MC/V [X11ACNH-2290] **COM** Y **ITC Member:** No

Rates: **Pvt Bath 4**
Single $ 75.00
Double $ 95.00

Inn At Danbury	Rt 104 03230	Danbury NH
Joan & George Issa		Tel: 603-768-3318

Tranquil town setting for this turn-of-the-century farmhouse offering pleasant and comfortable surroundings and hospitality. Outdoor activities include skiing, fishing, swimming, canoeing, nature trails, biking, and hiking. Great home-cooked meals available including full breakfast, all served family style. **Seasonal:** No **Brochure:** Yes **Permitted:** Children, smoking, drinking **Payment Terms:** Check [X11ACNH-2292] **COM** Y **ITC Member:** No

Rates: **Shared Bath 8**
Single $ 37.00
Double $ 45.00

Highland Lake Inn	Maple St 03231	East Andover NH
The Petras Family		Tel: 603-735-6462 Fax: 603-735-5355

Built in 1767 and expanded in 1805, this classic building, set atop twelve acres, overlooks Highland Lake, Kearsarge, Tucher and Ragged Mountains. Exquisitely decorated, the Inn has been recently renovated to include private baths in each of its ten spacious guest rooms. Rooms are furnished with king, queen or two twin beds; several rooms have four-poster beds. Extra rollaways are available. A sumptuous and different breakfast is served each morning. Cross country ski or hike trails on our twen-ty-one acre nature conservancy, sit in front of our large hearth fireplace of enjoy one in your room, and in summer, frolic on the beach. Swim at our secluded beach. Cycle through the Sunapee and Lakes Region of New Hampshire. Bring your boat and your fishing gear, the Highland Lake boat ramp is closeby. The area boasts two first-class 18 hole golf courses and is central to several fine downhill ski areas and less than an hour from the major slopes of the White Mountains. Antique, craft fairs and outlet shopping are nearby. Located just twenty-three miles northwest of Concord, we are easy to reach from Rts 89, 91 and 93, yet we are tucked away in a rich, rural landscape surrounded by fields, barns and century-old farmhouses. Enjoy the perfect New England getaway. **Airport:** Manchester-50 mi **Seasonal:** No **Reservations:** One night's stay or 50% deposit within 7 days of booking require to guarantee reservation, 14 day cancel policy less $10 service fee, $20 per additional person in room **Brochure:** Yes **Permitted:** Children 8-up, drinking **Languages:** Greek **Payment Terms:** Check AE/DISC/MC/V [I07HPNH1-18981] **COM** U **ITC Member:** No

Rates:	Pvt Bath 10
Single	$ 85-100.00
Double	$ 85-100.00

Moose Mountain Lodge   Moose Mountain 03750   Etna NH
Peter & Kay Shumway   **Tel:** 603-643-3529

Splendid views of Green Mountains and Connecticut River Valley from this wood and stone lodge built from materials on the property in 1938. Fireplaces, log beds, and great meals make for a memorable visit. All outdoor activities are available year-round. Near Hanover and Dartmouth Colleges. American Plan and MAP option available for all meals. **Seasonal:** No **Brochure:** Yes **Permitted:** Children 5-up, limited smoking **Languages:** Spanish, Swedish, French. **Payment Terms:** Check MC/V [X11ACNH-2300] **COM** Y **ITC Member:** No

Rates:	Shared Bath 12
Single	$ 40.00
Double	

Bungay Jar B&B   Easton Valley Rd 03580   Franconia NH
Lee Strimbeck & Kate Kerivan   **Tel:** 603-823-7775 **Fax:** 603-444-0100
Res Times Anytime

Built in 1969 from a century-old barn of post and beam construction and nestled among eight acres of woodlands, bounded by the Franconia Range of the White Mountain National Forest. You'll be treated to spectacular views of the rivers, forests and mountains! Choose from one of the unique guest rooms with antiques, four-poster beds or the shared bathrooms, all of which share a sauna and balcony that overlooks the garden area that one of the hosts tends (a landscape architect by profession). Relax before a roaring fire with the aroma of mulled cider in the two-story living room reminiscent of a hayloft, or find an antique that interests you, because many are for sale. Your hosts are avid hikers and skiers, so you'll benefit from their expert knowledge of the local AMC trails, wildlife and woodlands. Full breakfast included, with dinner by prior arrangement. **Seasonal:** No **Reservations:** 50% deposit; 7-day cancellation policy; 2 night min weekends/holidays & foliage season. **Brochure:** Yes **Permitted:** Limited children, drinking okay **Payment Terms:** Check AE [X02B-CNH-2307] **COM** Y **ITC Member:** No

Rates:	Pvt Bath 2	Shared Bath 2
Single	$ 75-85.00	$ 55.00
Double	$ 75-85.00	$ 65.00

Franconia Inn   Easton Valley Rd 03580   Franconia NH

New Hampshire *National Edition*

Richard & Alec Morris **Tel:** 800-473-5299 603-823-5542 **Fax:** 603-823-8078
Res Times 9am-10pm

The *Franconia Inn* has been welcoming guests since 1886. Today, the *Franconia Inn* is operated by Alec and Richard Morris, third generation innkeepers. Nestled on 107 acres in the Easton Valley just below the White Mountain's famed Franconia Notch, home of the *"Old Man of the Mountain"*. White clapboards and green shutters; three stories, thirty rooms and three suites. Living room, Library, Dining Room, Rathskeller, Lounge and two spacious verandas with spectacular mountain views. Guests enjoy Elegant American Cuisine, Bach, Classic Wines and attentive, friendly service - all part of the *Franconia Inn's* unpretentious dining experience. Guests are encouraged to partake from the wealth of recreational activities on the property. Summer brings tennis, horseback riding, swimming, fishing, soaring (gliding), croquet, badminton, bicycles and lots of hiking. Winter offers cross country Ski Tour Center with 60km of groomed trails, horse-drawn sleigh rides, ice skate and snow shoe rentals, hot tub, hot buttered rums and of course roaring fireplaces in each common room. Honeymoon suites and extended stay packages are available. AAA 3-Diamond, Guide To Recommended Country Inns of New England, Inn Spots and Special Places, Family Inns of America. The Inn is located 2-1/2 hours north of Boston and 3-1/2 hours south of Montreal **Seasonal:** Rates vary **Reservations:** One night's deposit at res time, 14 day cancel policy for refund **Brochure:** Yes **Permitted:** Children, drinking, limited smoking **Conference:** Yes for groups to 65 persons including spectacular mountain views **Languages:** German **Payment Terms:** Check AE/MC/V [I02HPNH1-2309] **COM YG ITC Member:** No

Rates: Pvt Bath 34
Single $ 65-up
Double $ 75-up

Horse & House Inn   Off Rt 18 Cannon Mtn 03580   Franconia NH
The Larson Family   Tel: 603-823-5501

Natural setting for this year-round Inn set close to ski lifts and other activities including hand gliding, water sports on nearby lake, and a cable car for spectacular viewing. Robert Frost's home is just a short distance. Swimming, tennis, golf and other sports are available. Continental breakfast included with restaurant on premises for other meals. **Seasonal:** No **Reservations:** Deposit for one night required at res time. **Brochure:** Yes **Permitted:** Smoking, drinking **Payment Terms:** Check MC/V [X11ACNH-2311] **COM Y ITC Member:** No

Rates:	Pvt Bath 6	Shared Bath 5
Single	$ 60.00	$ 55.00
Double	$ 75.00	$ 65.00

Maria W Atwood Inn   RFD 2 Rt 3A   03235   Franklin NH
Andy LaBrie   Tel: 603-934-3666

Large brick Federal residence c1880 fully restored and furnished with antique pieces and family heirlooms, fireplaces, two formal gardens, sitting rooms, library. Close to skiing and antiquing, swimming. Full breakfast included. **Seasonal:** No **Brochure:** Yes **Permitted:** Children **Payment Terms:** Check AE/MC/V [X11ACNH-2315] **COM Y ITC Member:** No

Rates: Pvt Bath 8
Single $ 62.00
Double $ 69.00

Cartway House   Old Lake Shore Rd 03246   Gilford NH
Shortway Family   Tel: 603-528-1172

1-80   ©*Inn & Travel* Memphis, Tennessee

Great skiing Inn that's been renovated since its original 1771 beginning with a French Country kitchen just added. Some guest rooms have bunk beds for groups of skiers or larger family groups with the private beaches, and plenty of mountains for skiing in winter. Full breakfast includes specialties such as Eggs Benedict. **Seasonal:** No **Reservations:** Deposit of 50% length of stay required. **Brochure:** Yes **Permitted:** Children, smoking, drinking **Languages:** French, Italian **Payment Terms:** Check MC/V [X11ACNH-2319] **COM** Y **ITC Member:** No

Rates:	Pvt Bath 5	Shared Bath 5
Single	$ 60.00	$ 52.00
Double	$ 70.00	$ 58.00

Greenfield Inn   Forest Lane Rt 31 03047-0156   Greenfield NH
Barbara & Vic Mangini   Tel: 603-547-6327

Beautifully restored Victorian mansion situated on three acres of lawn in the lovely Valley of Monadnock Mountains (Crotched, Temple and Monadnock). Relax while viewing the mountain country from the spacious veranda with white wicker chairs and rockers. Peaceful retreat for the first and second honeymooners. Visited twice by Bob and Dolores Hope!! Beautiful Victorian setting offering a quiet togetherness, comfort, and good dining. Large rooms, some with king size beds and all with modern amenities. TV in some. Street level bedrooms and suites available. Very close to skiing, swimming, hiking, tennis, golf, biking, and antique shopping at bargain prices. Manchester, Keene, Peterborough and Nashua nearby, just 80 minutes to Boston, five hours plus to NYC. Delightful full breakfast included with excellent dining nearby. **Seasonal:** No **Reservations:** $25.00 per nite stay deposit at res time, 4pm check-in, after 9pm by arrangement **Brochure:** Yes **Permitted:** Children, limited smoking, limited drinking **Conference:** Groups to twelve indoor or open veranda and lawn with gourmet catering available **Languages:** Stock Market and antiques **Payment Terms:** Check MC/V [A11DPNH-2329] **COM** Y **ITC Member:** No

Rates:	Pvt Bath 4	Shared Bath 4
Single		
Double	$ 79-100.00	$ 59-69.00

Oceanside   356 Ocean Blvd 03842   Hampton Beach NH
Deborah & Duane Windemiller   Tel: 603-926-3542

Fabulous restored New England Inn right on the ocean beach. Room decor includes antiques and modern pieces with modern amenities. Continental breakfast included. **Seasonal:** No **Brochure:** Yes **Permitted:** Children limited **Payment Terms:** Check MC/V [X11ACNH-2334] **COM** Y **ITC Member:** No

Rates:	Pvt Bath 10
Single	$ 95.00
Double	$ 105.00

Silver Maple Lodge-Cottages   Hanover NH
Scott & Sharon Wright   Tel: 800-666-1946 802-333-4326
Res Times 7am-10pm

Refer to the same listing name under Farilee, Vermont for a complete description. **Seasonal:** No **Payment Terms:** Check AE/MC/V [M11CPNH-1183-7] **COM** Y **ITC Member:** No

Rates:	Pvt Bath 12	Shared Bath 2
Single	$ 48-58.00	$ 36-38.00
Double	$ 52-62.00	$ 42-44.00

Inn On Golden Pond   PO Box 680 Rt 3 03245   Holderness NH
Bill & Bonnie Webb   Tel: 603-968-7269
Res Times 8am-10pm

New Hampshire *National Edition*

A gracious home built in 1879 and nestled on fifty wooded acres offering guests a traditional New England setting where you can escape and enjoy warm hospitality and personal service of the resident hosts. Each room is individually decorated for your comfort and pleasure. Common rooms include a game room, sitting room with a roaring fire during the winter months, and a 60 ft screened porch to enjoy the outdoors during the summer. Close to Squam Lake (setting for *"On Golden Pond"*), you can enjoy all the outdoor sporting activities year-round. You're only 15 minutes from Tenney Mountain Ski area and 30 minutes from the best skiing in New Hampshire. Squam Mountain Range and the White Mountain National Forest are close by for any water or land sports year-round, including ice fishing and cross-country skiing. Hearty New England breakfast includes homemade breads, muffins, jams, and farm fresh eggs. **Airport:** Boston Logan-2hrs; Manchester NH-1hr **Seasonal:** No **Reservations:** One night's deposit or 50% if two nights or longer, refunded if cancelled 14 days prior to arrival **Brochure:** Yes **Permitted:** Drinking; Not permitted, smoking, children or pets **Payment Terms:** Check AE/MC/V [K03HPNH1-2346] **COM** YG **ITC Member:** No

Rates:	Pvt Bath 8
Single	$ 75.00
Double	$ 105.00

Manor On Golden Pond   Rt 3 Box T 03245   Holderness NH
David & Bambi Arnold   Tel: 800-545-2141 603-968-348 Fax: 603-968-2116
                                                                Res Times 9am-9pm

Nestled on the gentle slopes of Shepherd Hill, rising above the western shore of pristine Squam Lake (site of the movie *On Golden Pond*), the estate commands a panoramic 65-mile view of the lake and surrounding mountains. Built as a private home in 1903 by wealthy Englishman Isaac Van Horn, this stately old mansion embodies the elegant yet casual charm of a typical English country estate. *The Manor House* offers seventeen invitingly decorated guest rooms and common rooms with magnificently carved moldings, rich wood paneling and grand fireplaces - an ambience and heritage from the past which cannot be duplicated today. Spacious grounds (13 acres) provide a tranquil, dramatic setting for the mansion's outdoor pool and clay tennis court set among ancient pines. A separate lakefront cottage and boathouse complement the private sandy beach. Whatever season, you'll find the *Manor a country Inn of uncommon quality.* Summer activities include all water sports, golf, horseback riding, hiking, biking, browsing antique shops, while winter brings downhill and cross country skiing, ice skating, sleigh rides and a relaxed apres ski atmosphere. Since its completion, the estate has passed though many hands and the present owners, David and Bambi Arnold have dedicated themselves to restoring the traditional grace and beauty of the original home. They hope you will visit *The Manor* and invite you to establish your own tradition of returning each season. They look forward to providing a truly memorable experience. **Airport:** Manchester NH-1 hr; Boston Logan-2 hrs **Packages:** Holidays & some Special Events **Reservations:** One night's deposit, 50% deposit for longer stays. *Rates based on MAP **Permitted:** Limited children, drinking, limited smoking **Conference:** Available for groups to twenty. **Payment Terms:** Check AE/MC/V [I10EPNH-2347] **COM** Y **ITC Member:** No

Rates:	Pvt Bath 27
Single	$ 110-175.00
Double	$ 155-220.00

Wildflowers Guest House   N Main St 03845   Intervale NH
Eileen Davies & Dean Frank   Tel: 603-356-2224

1-82   ©*Inn & Travel Memphis, Tennessee*

National Edition **New Hampshire**

Turn-of-the-century residence with New England charm and warmth from the wood-burning stove that's still working in the cozy parlor. Enjoy the year-round beauty of New England with these gracious hosts that will guide you to all the sights and interests while here. Continental breakfast included. **Reservations:** One night's deposit required at res time with refund if cancelled. **Brochure:** Yes **Permitted:** Children, smoking **Payment Terms:** Check [X11ACNH-2350] **COM** Y **ITC Member:** No

Rates: Pvt Bath 2   Shared Bath 4
Single $ 65.00 $ 55.00
Double $ 75.00 $ 65.00

Inn At Jackson   Main St At Thorn Hill 03846   **Jackson NH**
Lori & KR Tradewell   **Tel:** 800-289-8600 603-383-4321
Res Times 8am-10pm

This Stafford White Mansion, c1906, has been renovated into a quaint Country Inn snuggled in the White Mountains and offers New England country atmosphere, decor, great hospitality and fine dining. The spacious guest rooms, all with private bath and public rooms, offer fireplaces and vistas at every turn. Offering year-round activities, guests can choose skiing at one of the four challenging downhill areas or cross country right at the doorstep. A horsedrawn sleigh ride brings unforgettable memories of the snow covered mountains. Spring blossoms bring out the nature lover in everyone and shopping Specials at the nearby outlet malls! Summer provides outdoor sporting and nature watching events. And the Fall shouldn't be missed! The splendid foliage is breath-taking in this area of New Hampshire and makes for a perfect outing. A full New England breakfast is served fireside in the dining room or in summer in the glassed-in porch with picturesque views. **Discounts:** Yes, inquire at res time. **Airport:** Portland-1-1/2 hrs **Packages:** Three, Four, Five Night Midweek Specials **Seasonal:** Rates vary **Reservations:** 50% deposit, 14 day cancel policy for refund **Brochure:** Yes **Permitted:** Children, drinking, limited smoking **Payment Terms:** Check AE/DC/DISC/MC/V [Z08GPNH-2355] **COM** Y **ITC Member:** No

Rates: Pvt Bath 12
Single $ 49-129.00
Double $ 59-129.00

Village House   PO Box 359 Rt 16A 03846   **Jackson NH**
Robin Crocker   **Tel:** 800-972-8343 603-383-6666 **Fax:** 603-383-6464

When you cross the red covered bridge and enter into Jackson Village, you are at *The Village House*. We have been serving guests here for over 100 years. Our Inn offers the amenities of a large resort but with the warmth and friendliness of a small Country Inn. Thirteen of our guest rooms have private baths and include queen and king size beds. Five new rooms include a combination of the following: family suites with kitchenettes, doubles with kitchenettes and doubles with jacuzzi tub. We offer a delightful living room area with a guest refrigerator, cable TV and warm fire in winter. Enjoy breakfast in our sunroom or out on the front porch. Winter breakfast is a traditional full country meal, while summer breakfast offers more flexibility with a continental-style array of fresh fruits, homemade cereals, breads and home baked pastries. In the summer you can enjoy our swimming pool, tennis court and jacuzzi. Nearby are many local Mount Washington Valley attractions, as well as hiking, biking, canoeing and scenic drives. In winter, cross country skiing begins right at your front door and nearby are four major mountains offering excellent downhill skiing. Don't miss out on the excitement of sleigh rides, ice skating, warming-up in the outdoor jacuzzi or peaceful evenings at the local pubs all right here in our Village. **Meals:** Full meals are available for groups and with prior arrangements. **Airport:** Portland-1-1/2 Hrs; Boston-2-1/2 Hrs **Packages:** Yes, inquire at res time **Discounts:** Groups **Seasonal:** No **Reservations:** 50% deposit of length of stay required by credit card or check prior to arrival, two week cancellation policy for refund, $10/night cancel charge for any cancellation **Brochure:** Yes **Permitted:** Drinking, limited smoking, limited pets, children **Conference:** Yes, for small groups **Payment Terms:** Check DISC/MC/V [I04HPNH1-2358] **COM**

©Inn & Travel Memphis, Tennessee

New Hampshire *National Edition*

YG **ITC Member:** No

Rates: **Pvt Bath 13** **Shared Bath 2**
Single $ 50-125.00 $ 50-125.00
Double $ 50-125.00 $ 50-125.00

Benjamin Prescott Inn   Rt 124 E   03452   **Jaffrey NH**
Barry & Jan Miller   **Tel:** 603-532-6637
   Res Times 8am-9pm

Fashioned in the Greek Revival style, this family home of Colonel Benjamin Prescott of Revolutionary War fame, stands shaded by maples. Enter by the front steps, graced with Old Glory stirring in the breeze and travel back into America's infancy. Inside, careful attention has been taken to see that the early American atmosphere has been preserved through use of color and design. All guest rooms in the Inn have private bath, complete with classic toiletries the discerning traveler has come to expect. Each room is decorated and furnished to bring out the individuality and charm. Antiques abound and lend credence to the ever-present feeling one has stepped back in time. Suites are available for those wanting to feel even more at home. After a hearty New England breakfast with home made fruit breads, enjoy the quiet countryside surrounding the Inn. For the adventurous, there is Mt Monadmock, the most climbed mountain in America, the most beautiful and challenging golf course in New Hampshire, and cross country skiing. For those seeking quiet reflection, a leisurely stroll up Witt Hill Road, a stonewall-lined lane that passes by the Inn, is a must during one's visit. It provides spectacular views of the mountains and the century-old operating dairy farm. For those seeking culture, enjoy the Amos Fortune Forum, Monadnock Music, Peterborough Players, Sharon Art Center, and Cathedral of the Pines. Antiques and local artisans abound. **Airport:** Boston Logan-2 hrs, Manchester-1 hr **Seasonal:** No **Reservations:** One night's deposit, 10-day cancellation policy for refund; 2 night min some weekends **Brochure:** Yes **Permitted:** Children 8-up, limited smoking, drinking **Conference:** Executive conferences for groups to eight persons **Payment Terms:** Check AE/MC/V [I02HPNH1-2360] **COM** YG **ITC Member:** No

Rates: **Pvt Bath 9**
Single $ 65-130.00
Double $ 65-130.00

Lilac Hill Acres   5 Ingalls Rd   03452   **Jaffrey NH**
Frank & Ellen McNeil   **Tel:** 603-532-7278

Farm life at its best in this five star location at the base of Mount Monadnock. Furnished with family heirlooms and antiques. Year-round activities. Full breakfast included. **Seasonal:** No **Brochure:** Yes **Permitted:** Children, smoking, social drinking **Payment Terms:** Check [X11ACNH-2364] **COM** Y **ITC**

Member: No

Rates: **Pvt Bath 1**   **Shared Bath 5**
Single $ 65.00 $ 50.00
Double $ 70.00

Mill Pond Inn   50 Prescott Rd   03452   **Jaffrey NH**
S Fitzgerald/E A Woodruff   **Tel:** 603-532-7687

Overlook this scenic mill pond from an 1825 homestead nestled on a five acre setting bordering Mount Monadnock and Annett State Park for year-round beauty. Gracious hosts make your stay en-

National Edition **New Hampshire**

joyable and they are prepared for helping you find "your thing" whether it's skiing, boating, nature trails or whatever. Fireplaces in several guest rooms with antique furnishings, plants, and family treasures in many rooms. Full breakfast included. **Seasonal:** No **Reservations:** 2 night min 9/1-10/30 & holidays, deposit for one night at res time

Brochure: Yes **Permitted:** Children, limited drinking **Payment Terms:** Check [X11ACNH-2365] COM Y ITC **Member:** No

Rates:	Shared Bath 5
Single	$ 55.00
Double	$ 65.00

Applebrook B&B Rt 115A 03583 **Jefferson NH**
Sandra Conley/Martin Kelly **Tel:** 800-545-6504 603-586-7713
  Res Times 7am-10pm

"Bring the children if you like . . . the more the merrier", for an unforgettable experience in this Victorian farmhouse where casual comfort (put-your-feet-up) reigns. In-addition to individual rooms, a great dormitory brings kids together and provides an economical choice for biking, hiking and ski groups. A spacious sunny living room with stained glass windows, beautiful sunset views of Mount Washington, plenty of books and magazines and an evening fire becomes the favorite gathering place for socializing. Located on acres of meadows and woods in the Northern White Mountains, this is truly a four-season vacation area. Winter provides three major downhill and cross country ski areas within 30 minutes (Bretton Woods, Wildcat, Cannon Mountain) - snowmobiles with direct access to the roads; moonlight toboggan rides and ice skating in the village center. Warm weather brings streams for trout fishing, swimming, canoeing or kayaking and mountain trails for hiking, biking and delicious mid-summer wild raspberries. Fall foliage in the White Mountains is spectacular - and shouldn't be missed! Still adding improvements, your hosts recently completed a cross country trail on their property, a campfire area and a hot tub for your pleasure. Nearby activities include golf, antiquing, theater and for children, Six Gun City and Santa's Village. A complimentary hearty New England breakfast served each morning usually includes French Toast, eggs or pancakes with home-fries, hot or cold cereal, fresh fruit, muffins, coffee, juice and assorted teas. Home cooked family style dinners are available at additional cost and with advance notice. We hope you will consider us when planning your next ski trip, reunion, bike trip or quiet weekend getaway in the mountains. **Discounts:** Group rates **Airport:** Boston Logan-165 mi **Packages:** Biking, hiking and skiing groups, including gourmet dinner **Seasonal:** No **Reservations:** 50% deposit appreciated **Brochure:** Yes **Permitted:** Children, well-mannered pets, drinking **Payment Terms:** Check MC/V [I09EPNH-15540] COM Y ITC **Member:** No

Rates:	Pvt Bath 3	Shared Bath 9
Single	$ 50.00	$ 20-40.00
Double	$ 60.00	$ 40-50.00

Issiac Merrill House PO Box 8 03847 **Kearsage NH**
Richard Levine **Tel:** 800-328 9041 603-356-9041
  Res Times 9am-9pm

A Classic Country Victorian Inn dating from 1775 (the guest book dates from 1875) offers relaxing New England Hospitality! This charming Inn is nestled in the heart of Mt Washington Valley near the quaint village of North Conway which offers spectacular year-round scenery and activities. Most of the guest rooms of this 215 year old period mansion have been lovingly restored and furnished with a variety of brass or canopy beds, antique rockers or skylights! Your hosts have created a warm, romantic and intimate atmosphere for their guests. They enjoy celebrations too, so if you have a special occasion, let them know and they'll have cake or champagne ready! There are breath-taking views of the sunsets over the Moat Mountains from within the Inn and if you like, splash in the babbling brook across the road! A hearty New England full breakfast begins each day and comp-

©Inn & Travel Memphis, Tennessee

limentary beverages, cheese and crackers are served each afternoon next to the large fireplace in the common room. Nearby activities include passes to Mount Cranmore Recreation Center for indoor swimming, racquetball or tennis, sauna and whirlpool. On your departure - don't be surprised if you find a package of cookies or fresh fruit packed by your hosts for you to enjoy on your trip home! *Special Package Rates, eg: stay 2 nights receive a 3rd night *free*; stay 3 nights and receive the next 2 nights *free*! **Seasonal:** Rates vary **Reservations:** Full payment in advance; 20 day cancel notice for credit refund for future use, less $20 service charge per room. **Brochure:** Yes **Permitted:** Children, drinking, limited smoking **Conference:** Yes, for groups to 30 persons. **Payment Terms:** Check AE/DISC/MC/V [R12CPNH-3749] **COM** Y **ITC Member:** No

Rates:	Pvt Bath 14	Shared Bath 4
Single	$ 74-118.00	$ 74-118.00
Double	$ 84-118.00	$ 84-118.00

Ammonoosuc Inn   Bishop Rd 03585   **Lisbon NH**
Ann & Wayne Monrad   **Tel:** 800-COBLERS 603-838-6118
Res Times 8am-4pm

Nestled in a quaint valley among the scenic White Mountains of New Hampshire is this charming Country Inn. A one hundred year old farmhouse, newly renovated, overlooks the Ammonoosuc River. Each guest room is individually decorated and includes a private bath. Stepping outside, guests find a challenging golf course designed by Ralph M Bartin because, located at the Inn, is the Lisbon Village Country Club complete with all facilities. Try the spectacular course, outdoor pool, tennis, fine fishing, game rooms and in winter, cross country skiing right at the door! Within minutes are The Old Man and The Mountain, The Tramway at Cannon Mountain, Mount Washington and Franconia Notch State Park for picturesque nature trails, climbing, hiking, swimming, horseback riding, canoeing and sailplane rides. In winter, skiers are just fifteen minutes to Cannon Mountain and thirty-five minutes to Loon and Bretton Woods. Part-time and full-time relaxing is encouraged on the spacious porch, filled with plenty of wooden rockers. A continental breakfast with coffee cake. Danish and plenty of fresh coffee is served while the Cobbler, an on premises restaurant, specializes in fine New England fare, including homemade breads and deserts to complement your mouth-watering dinner. Top all this off with warmth, hospitality and attentive service and you'll agree this is the perfect getaway. **Discounts:** Yes, inquire at res time **Airport:** Boston Logan-3 hrs **Packages:** Golf & Meal Plans, Ski & Meal **Seasonal:** No **Reservations:** 50% deposit or credit card to guarantee res and hold a room, 14 day cancel policy for refund, must call if arriving after 4pm, two night min on some weekends **Permitted:** Children, drinking, limited smoking **Payment Terms:** AE/DISC/MC/V [K07HP-NH1-2376] **COM** YG **ITC Member:** No

Rates:	Pvt Bath 9
Single	$ 40-69.00
Double	$ 59-79.00

Beal House Inn   247 W Main St 03561   **Littleton NH**
Barbara & Ted Snell   **Tel:** 603-444-2661
Res Times 7am-11pm

Live the White Mountains with us in our 1833 Federal Renaissance farmhouse! Relaxation and quiet elegance are balanced with a zest for adventure and the charm of this lovely little village. In our thirteen guest rooms, you will find antique furnishings, canopy beds, down comforters and special touches that will encourage you to feel right at home here. Tradition at the *Beal House,* an Inn since 1938, allows you to purchase many of the furnishings and native artwork that may catch your fancy as they decorate the Inn. Our parlor, game room and enclosed porch invite you to unwind, visit with other travelers and enjoy our treasures and collections. Breakfast gatherings by fire and candlelight feature Belgian waffles made fresh by your Belgian host, in addition to a bountiful buf-

National Edition *New Hampshire*

fet. Evening dining in our jazzy little dining room celebrates robust European fare, with very special classic French creations and a wine list of over three hundred wines. So close to so much in the White Mountains, revitalize yourself with fresh air while hiking, skiing, biking, fishing, playing golf, antiquing and visiting the many sites and attractions. Three hours by car from both Montreal, Quebec and Boston. **Discounts:** Yes, groups and extended stays **Airport:** Manchester NH-2 hr **Seasonal:** No **Reservations:** 50% deposit of stay at res time to guarantee, 15 day cancel policy for refund, less than 15 days, 50% refund **Brochure:** Yes **Permitted:** Children, drinking **Conference:** Business gatherings to 24 persons with meetings in dining room **Languages:** French **Payment Terms:** Check MC/V [Z04GPNH-2378] COM Y ITC Member: No

Rates:	Pvt Bath 9	Shared Bath 4
Single	$ 45-50.00	$ 40.00
Double	$ 55-80.00	$ 50-60.00

Lyme Inn Rt 10 03768 **Lyme NH**
Fred & Judy Siemons **Tel:** 603-795-2222

Quaint Country Inn in small New England town offering traditional style furnishings in guest rooms. Full breakfast included. Dinner available on premises. **Seasonal:** No **Brochure:** Yes **Permitted:** Children 8-up, smoking, drinking **Payment Terms:** Check AE/CD/DC/MC/V [X11ACNH-2382]

COM Y ITC Member: No

Rates:	Pvt Bath 10	Shared Bath 5
Single	$ 58.00	$ 48.00
Double	$ 65.00	$ 55.00

Blue Goose Inn 24 103 B Box 2117 03772 **Mount Sunapee NH**
Meryl & Ron Caldwell **Tel:** 603-763-5519

The ideal location of *The Blue Goose Inn* is only one of the many reasons to stay here during your next visit to the Lake Sunapee Area. Situated on a private 3.5 acres, this early 19th Century farmhouse provides the perfect setting for a fun and relaxing get away. The five guest rooms, three of which have private baths, are furnished in a quaint country-style and are cozy and comfortable. No matter what season, your stay at The *Blue Goose Inn* will be highlighted by a hearty old-time breakfast of pancakes, scrambled eggs, Canadian-style bacon, coffee, tea and juice with lighter fare such as granola, fresh fruit and yogurt available too. Guests can snuggle-up with a book before the fire or ski Mount Sunapee in winter to enjoying games on the spacious lawn or walk to the nearby beach, barbecue and picnics in summer. In addition, the area offers golf, tennis, antiquing, summer theatre, dinner cruises, auctions and gourmet dining. With so many reasons to stay, it's hard to decide which is the best - but travelers in the "know" enjoy the affordable rates too! **Airport:** Manchester Lebanon NH-30 mi **Packages:** Murder Mystery Weekends, Ski & Stay, call for details **Seasonal:** No **Reservations:** 50% deposit or credit card number to guarantee reservation. Handicap accessible **Brochure:** Yes **Permitted:** Children, drinking, limited smoking **Payment Terms:** Check MC/V [Z04HPNH1-12913] COM YG ITC Member: No

Rates:	Pvt Bath 3	Shared Bath 2
Single	$ 43.20	$ 40.00
Double	$ 55.00	$ 50.00

Inn At New Ipswich Porter Hill Rd 03071 **New Ipswich NH**
Steve & Ginny Bankuti **Tel:** 603-878-3711
Res Times 7am-10pm

This gracious 1790 farmhouse, with classic red barn, instantly welcomes you. Rolling grounds are bordered by stone walls, gardens, and fruit trees. Its six guest rooms are comfortably furnished with firm beds and cozy, country-style antiques. (Two guest rooms have working fireplaces) Play chess or scrabble by the parlor fire. Choose a book from the well-stocked shelves. In summer, enjoy the sun on the front porch rockers or evening breezes on the screened porch. If peaceful getaways are your pleasure, The *Inn at New Ipswich* is the perfect place to relax. The Inn is located a short distance from

©Inn & Travel Memphis, Tennessee

New Hampshire

myriad activities in the Monadnock Region, including golf, antiques, Summer Theater, concerts, arts and crafts, and auctions. Mount Monadnock (the most-climbed mountain in North America) offers fine hiking trails. Fall foliage here is unsurpassed and, in winter, cross country and downhill skiing is nearby. Guests awaken to aromas of fresh-baked muffins or breads and superb coffee. To quote guests, *"Breakfast alone is worth the trip"*. Also, tea, coffee and snacks are offered upon your arrival. **Airport:** Manchester NH 30 mi; Boston Logan Intl 65 mi **Discounts:** 15% weekday business rate, 15% preferred rate for travel agents **Reservations:** First night's deposit in full within 7 days to hold room; 10 day cancel policy for refund less $5 service charge. **Brochure:** Yes **Permitted:** Children over 8, limited drinking **Languages:** Hungarian **Payment Terms:** Check MC/V [Z05FPNH-12914] **COM** Y **ITC Member:** No

Rates: **Pvt Bath 6**
Single $ 45.00
Double $ 65.00

Inn At Coit Mountain — 423 N Main St 03773 — Newport NH
James Forman — Tel: 800-367-2364 603-863-3583

The Inn was the summer home of Cheronnet-Champollion family, well-known in France for deciphering the Rosetta Stone and in the United States for Austin Corbin and the Long Island Railroad, Coney Island and Corbin Park. This classic Georgian Inn is elegant yet comfortable with five guest rooms. The Library has fifteen foot ceilings, is panelled in oak and has a granite fireplace. Some bedrooms have fireplaces. A full hearty gourmet breakfast is included. Located in the Sunapee Region, year round activities are many. Lunch and dinner are available with prior notice and at added cost. **Discounts:** Mid-week ski; extended stays, stay one week, the 7th night is free **Airport:** Manchester NH-1 hr **Packages:** Ski packages begin at $55.00 pppd **Seasonal:** No **Reservations:** One night deposit applied to last day of stay; 10 day cancel policy for refund. **Brochure:** Yes **Permitted:** Children, drinking, limited smoking **Payment Terms:** Check AE/MC/V [R12EPNH-2396] **COM** Y **ITC Member:** No

Rates:	**Pvt Bath 2**	**Shared Bath 5**
Single	$ 100-120.00	$ 70-100.00
Double	$ 120-140.00	$ 85-115.00

Indian Shutters Inn — Rt 12 03603 — North Charleston NH
Farnsworth Elliot — Tel: 603-826-4445

Beautifully restored 1791 stagecoach stop with lovely antique furnishings in traditional New England style. Exceptional dining with beef and seafood entrees and all homemade from family recipes. Full breakfast included, with other meals available. **Seasonal:** No **Brochure:** Yes **Permitted:** Children smoking, drinking and limited pets. **Payment Terms:** Check MC/V [X11ACNH-2398] **COM** Y **ITC Member:** No

Rates:	**Pvt Bath 8**	**Shared Bath 4**
Single	$ 63.00	$ 54.00
Double	$ 74.00	$ 65.00

Cranmore Inn — Kearsarge St 03860 — North Conway NH
Chris & Virginia Kanzler — Tel: 800-526-5502 603-356-5502
Res Times 9am-9pm

There is a uniqueness about this authentic Inn, that surrounds you with a tradition of warm New England hospitality that has kept guests returning since the Inn opened in 1863. Centrally located in North Conway Village, in the heart of New Hampshire's spectacular White Mountains, guests can walk to village shops, restaurants, theatres, golf, playground and attractions. The Inn has retained much of its historic charm through period furnishings, dating from the 1800's through the 1940's. There are no televisions or telephones in the guest rooms, however these amenities are available to guests in our public sitting rooms. There is an outdoor pool where you can relax with iced tea or lemonade in summer, or relax by the fireplace with hot coffee or cocoa in winter, from our

National Edition | **New Hampshire**

afternoon tea service. You will find New England charm with Yankee hospitality. **Discounts:** Groups **Airport:** Portland Jetport-50 mi **Seasonal:** Clo Christmas **Reservations:** Deposit or credit card number at res time to guarantee. **Brochure:** Yes **Permitted:** Children, limited smoking, limited drinking (BYOB) **Conference:** Public sitting areas for small groups **Payment Terms:** Check MC/V [R05FPNH-2402] **COM** Y **ITC Member:** No

Rates:	Pvt Bath 14	Shared Bath 4
Single	$ 39-69.00	$ 39-52.00
Double	$ 49-79.00	$ 39-52.00

Stonehurst Manor PO Box 1937 Off Rt 16 03860 North Conway NH
Peter Rattay Tel: 800-525-9100 603-356-3271 **Res Times** 24 Hrs

Stonehurst Manor: **A Landmark in Lodging, Food and Spirits for over 46 years offering traditional hospitality in the Grand Manor!** The Staff of *Stonehurst Manor* invite you to enjoy the luxury of their elegant, turn-of-the-century mansion. Originally part of carpet baron Erastus Bigelow's summer estate, guests are surrounded with beautiful stain and leaded glass, hand-carved oak woodwork, a multitude of stone fireplaces - created by European craftsmen at the turn-of-the-century. Set on thirty-three secluded acres of pine forest, the Manor offers a truly unique and unforgettable White Mountain's vacation. From our exceptional mountain views to the peace and quiet of the fireplaced Library Lounge, you'll be surrounded by beauty and comfort. (Seven of the guest rooms also have working fireplaces). Chef Brian Coffey has created a wonderful approach to eating out here at the Manor. It's elegant yet casual, combining delicious tradition with inventive taste discoveries, and presented in a relaxing atmosphere of timeless ease enhanced by superb service and style. Watch us as we make our famous wood-fired gourmet pizza in our outdoor patio oven in summer and in our indoor brick oven in winter. Enjoy the pleasures of our large outdoor pool, hot tub, tennis court and walking trails leading from our door ... in winter, you'll cross country ski these trails for 65 scenic kilometers. At the Manor we also offer one to five day guided walking and hiking vacations, through beautiful countryside and the unspoiled wilderness of the White Mountains. Discover what it's like to live in royal-style without paying a king's ransom. We promise it's an experience you won't soon forget! The S*tonehurst Manor* has been recommended by *"Bon Appetit"* and *"Country Inn of New England."* **Discounts:** Yes, inquire at res time **Airport:** Portland ME-60 mi; Boston-125 mi **Packages:** Yes, $48.00 per night includes breakfast and dinner off regular menu, Walking and Hiking Tours **Seasonal:** No **Reservations:** One night's deposit, 14 day cancel policy for refund **Brochure:** Yes **Permitted:** Children, drinking, smoking **Conference:** Perfect setting for weddings and private parties to 200; conferences and meetings to 75 persons **Languages:** French, German **Payment Terms:** Check AE/MC/V [K03IPNH1-2409] **COM** U **ITC Member:** No

Rates:	Pvt Bath 24
Single	$ 75.00
Double	$ 75.00-up

Follansbee Inn Keyer Rd 03260 North Sutton NH
Sandy & Dick Reilein Tel: 603-927-4221

New England farmhouse c1840 on Kezar Lake, with old fashioned porch and charming bedrooms for true Yankee hospitality. Off I-89 at exit 10, close to Dartmouth, skiing, antiques and Mount Sunapee State Park. Full breakfast included. Other meals available by chef on the premises. **Seasonal:** No **Brochure:** Yes **Permitted:** Children 8-up **Payment Terms:** Check MC/V [X11AC-NH-

©*Inn & Travel Memphis, Tennessee*

New Hampshire *National Edition*

2411] **COM** Y **ITC Member:** No

Rates: **Pvt Bath** 11   **Shared Bath** 12
Single
Double $ 70.00 $ 60.00

Wilderness Inn B&B   Rt 3 & Courtney Rd 03262   **North Woodstock NH**
Michael/Rosanna Yarnell   **Tel:** 800-200-WILD 603-745-3890
    Res Times 7am-10pm

A year-round retreat snuggled within the White Mountain National Forest offers guests a true New England Experience while staying in *"turn-of-the-century elegance"*. The 80-year old *Wilderness Inn* has seven uniquely decorated guest rooms, family suites and a cottage with private baths and views of the Inn's gardens or nearby mountains. Lost River flows through the backyard and offers guests swimming or a pleasant afternoon picnic spot. In winter, ski downhill at Loon Mountain (3 miles) or Cannon Mountain (8 miles) or cross country ski nearby. Enjoy tea or hot mulled cider fireside upon your return. A complimentary full breakfast is served of freshly ground coffee, muffins, omelettes or cranberry-walnut pancakes with pure maple syrup. Just 2-1/2 hrs from Boston, 3-1/2 hrs from Portland & Providence, 6-1/2 hrs from NYC and 3 hrs from Montreal. **Packages:** Winter Skiing **Airport:** Logan-120mi **Seasonal:** Rates vary **Reservations:** One night's deposit at reservation time; 14 day cancel policy for refund **Brochure:** Yes **Permitted:** Children welcomed, drinking **Conference:** Yes for groups to 15 persons **Languages:** French, Italian, Bengali, Amharic **Payment Terms:** Check AE/MC/V [I02HPNH1-7341] **COM** YG **ITC Member:** No

Rates: **Pvt Bath** 6   **Shared Bath** 2
Single $ 50-80.00 $ 40-60.00
Double $ 50-90.00 $ 40-60.00

Meadow Farm B&B   Jenness Pond Rd 03261   **Northwood NH**
Doug & Hanet Briggs   **Tel:** 603-942-8619

Traditional New England farm house c1770, set on 50 acres of pasture and woods, built with beamed ceilings, fireplaces, and wide plank floors. Relax in this natural setting offering private beach on lake and cross country skiing in winter. Ideal location for travelers to Concord seacoast or mountain areas. **Seasonal:** No **Brochure:** Yes **Permitted:** Children, limited pets, smoking, drinking **Payment Terms:** Check [C11ACNH-2414] **COM** Y **ITC Member:** No

Rates: **Pvt Bath** 20   **Shared Bath** 8
Single $ 50.00 $ 45.00
Double $ 62.00 $ 57.00

Home Hill Country Inn   River Road 03781   **Plainfield NH**
Roger Nicolas   **Tel:** 603-675-6165
    Res Times 24 Hrs

Home Hill Country Inn and French Restaurant is a meticulously restored circa 1800 mansion on the banks of the Connecticut River. Nestled on twenty-five secluded acres, the Inn is a perfect getaway for those seeking an escape to the tranquility of a picture postcard perfect New England countryside. Each of the nine guest rooms are beautifully appointed with antiques and collectibles and includes a private bath. A two room suite, separate guest house and a pool house are also available. Ideally located for enjoying four season activities, *Home Hill* has a pool, clay tennis court and in winter,

©*Inn & Travel Memphis, Tennessee*

National Edition   *New Hampshire*

cross-country ski trails on the grounds with downhill skiing minutes away. Nearby there is canoeing, fishing, hiking and golf. Guests are invited to enjoy the complimentary continental breakfast in the Inn's country-style kitchen. Evening's offer the widely acclaimed French cuisine in one of three intimate dining rooms, where guests savor fine wines from the discriminating wine cellar or enjoy spirits from the fully licensed library bar. **Packages:** Yes, inquire at res time **Seasonal:** No **Reservations:** Prepayment to 2 nights, if longer, first and last night's deposit, 14 day cancel policy less $15 service fee; less than 14 days, refund only if rebooked **Brochure:** Yes **Permitted:** Limited children, drinking, limited smoking **Conference:** Perfect for intimate, secluded events featuring excellent dining **Languages:** French **Payment Terms:** Check MC/V [I10EPNH-2291] **COM** U **ITC Member:** No

Rates: **Pvt Bath 9**
Single $ 105-120.00
Double $ 105-120.00

Colonel Spencer Inn	RR 1 Box 206 03264	**Plymouth NH**
Carolyn & Alan Hill		**Tel:** 603-536-3438
		Res Times 8am-10pm

This historic 1764 colonial home was built by Colonel Joseph Spencer, an early settler to the Pemigewasset River Valley, who fought at Bunker Hill with General Washington and at the battle of Cambridge during the Revolution. Rurally located in the White Mountain Region, a short drive from Franconia Notch, major mountain and lake attractions, and three miles from Plymouth State College and the Holderness School, the *Colonel Spencer* is an ideal location for downhill and cross country skiing, skating, hiking, climbing, tennis, swimming, boating, cycling and leaf-peaking. Within view of the Pemigewasset River and the mountains, the Inn is a cozy retreat furnished with period antiques and country decorations. Guests may enjoy a full country breakfast served in a fireplaced dining room overlooking a country pond. Afternoon tea and evening coffee are also served. Tastefully restored architectural features include hewn post and beam construction, Indian shutters, wainscoting, paneling, gunstock corners, wide pine floors, Christian doors and secret passageways. Seven bedrooms, two with fireplaces and one suite with a kitchenette, welcome guests with New England warmth and charm. Whether you plan to spend a night or stay a week, you'll find the *Colonel Spencer* a relaxing and inviting refuge. **Discounts:** Three nights or longer **Airport:** Man-chester -60 mi; Boston Logan-110 mi **Packages:** Skiing **Seasonal:** No **Reservations:** $25 deposit required prior to arrival **Brochure:** Yes **Permitted:** Children, drinking **Payment Terms:** Check [I03HPNH1-13946] **COM** YG **ITC Member:** No

Rates: **Pvt Bath 7**
Single $ 30-40.00
Double $ 45-65.00

Governors House B&B	32 Miller Ave 03801	**Portsmouth NH**
Nancy & John Grossman		**Tel:** 603-431-6546 **Fax:** 603-427-0803
		Res Times 7am-10pm

Walk into John and Nancy Grossman's stately Georgian Colonial Revival home and enjoy the relaxed elegance shared by all. Its quiet location is a short walk from virtually everything there is to do in Portsmouth. The gracious dining room has a *"bottomless"* cookie jar and afternoon tea or lemonade. The cozy living room, with its fireplace, beckons with welcoming warmth and the library is a wonderful place to curl up and read, savor early morning coffee and meet other guests. Each bedroom, deco-

©*Inn & Travel Memphis, Tennessee*

New Hampshire   *National Edition*

rated with antiques, has a different motif, with queen-sized beds and unique private baths, one with a jacuzzi, proclaiming bold ceramic designs created by Nancy, a professional tile painter and artist. Nestled amidst pines and cedars is a tennis court, hammock and a quiet sitting area. After a delicious full New England breakfast, walk into historic Portsmouth to enjoy antiquing, Strawberry Banke Museum, historical tours, harbor cruising, a horse-drawn carriage ride, shopping, theatre and many fine restaurants. Close by is the breathtaking Wentworth By The Sea Golf Course and Kittery shopping outlets. **Discounts:** Groups **Airport:** Boston Logan-1-1/4 hrs; Portsmouth-10 min **Reserva-tions:** One night's deposit, 14 day cancel policy for refund **Brochure:** Yes **Permitted:** Children 14+, drinking **Payment Terms:** AE/MC/V [I08GPNH-18203] **COM** Y **ITC Member:** No

Rates: Pvt Bath 4
Single $ 65-130.00
Double $ 75-140.00

Hilltop Inn   Sugar Hill Rd 03585   **Sugar Hill NH**
Mike & Meri Hern   **Tel:** 603-823-5695
Res Times 9am-10pm

This charming Victorian Country Inn, built circa 1895, is furnished throughout with turn-of-the-century antiques making each of the six guest rooms unique and the common rooms comfortable and inviting. The Inn is close to all activities, including alpine and Nordic skiing, swimming, canoeing, fishing, biking, hiking, horseback riding, wind surfing, glider rides, Cannon Mountain, the Tramway, the Old Man of the Mountain and the flume. After a day exploring the White Mountains, you can relax in the Victorian parlor or enjoy the scenery from front porch rockers - where beautiful sunsets are guaranteed! Evening brings friendly conversation beside the cozy fireplace or fine candlelight dinner in the intimate dining room. All room rates include a large country breakfast each morning. Your hosts are professional caterers so there are always delicious surprises. **Airport:** Boston-3 Hrs; Burlington-1-1/2 Hrs **Packages:** Ski discount tickets **Seasonal:** Closed 4/1-5/15 **Reservations:** Deposit required, eight day cancel policy for refund, check-in 2-5:30 pm **Brochure:** Yes **Permitted:** Children 4-up, drinking, limited pets, limited smoking **Payment Terms:** Check AE/DISC/MC/V [R03EPNH-2439] **COM** U **ITC Member:** No

Rates: Pvt Bath 6
Single $ 50-75.00
Double $ 60-110.00

Village House At Sutton Mills   Box 151 Grist Mill Rd 03221   **Sutton Mills NH**
Peggy & Norm Forand   **Tel:** 603-927-4765
Res Times 9am-9pm

Our 1857 Country Victorian Guest House overlooking a quaint New England village affords our guests privacy, charm and the opportunity to be pampered. The guest rooms are tastefully decorated with antiques while everyone enjoys a selection from our antique quilt collection. Guests can enjoy yard games on our private four acres in summer, while winter offers cross country skiing, snowshoeing and snowmobiling right from the front door. Excellent downhill and cross country skiing establishments are just minutes away. A Skiers Delight Package offers three nights for the price of two, Sunday through Thursday, in season. Choose from among the many restaurants offering excellent dining while enjoying the great antiquing, shopping and strolling through yesteryear at the many old mill streams, water falls, mill ponds and miles of old stone walls. Outdoor activities include biking, boating, swimming and fishing. Room rates include a memorable full country breakfast with home

©Inn & Travel Memphis, Tennessee

National Edition **New Hampshire**

baked bread and muffins along with maple syrup made right in the backyard. Dinner is available at a nominal added cost and with prior arrangements. Treat yourself to a memorable and comfortable retreat! *Three guest rooms share two baths **Discounts:** Yes, inquire at res time **Packages:** Ski Season (Sunday-Thursday, stay three nights for the price of two) **Seasonal:** No **Reservations:** One night's deposit, two week cancel notice for refund less $10 service fee **Brochure:** Yes **Permitted:** Limited children, limited drinking **Payment Terms:** Check [I04IPNH1-2451] **COM** U **ITC Member:** No

Rates:	Shared Bath 3
Single	$ 45.00
Double	$ 60.00

Tamworth Inn	Main St 03886	Tamworth NH
Kathy Bender		Tel:800-933-3902 603-323-7721

Picture perfect New England setting for this quaint Inn between Mount Washington Valley and Lake Winnipesaukee, offering guests full time outdoor activities year-round. Hiking, nature trails, and swimming pool available, with excellent cross-country skiing in winter. Continental breakfast and other meals available at added cost. Bar on premises. **Seasonal:** No **Brochure:** Yes **Permitted:** Children 7-up, limited smoking, drinking **Payment Terms:** Check MC/V [X11ACNH -2452] **COM** Y **ITC Member:** No

Rates:	Pvt Bath 10	Shared Bath 11
Double	$ 60-90.00	$ 60-90.00

Hilltop Acres	East Side & Buffalo Rd 03282	Wentworth NH
Marie A Kauk		Tel:603-764-5896

Hilltop Acres is a peaceful country retreat located in picturesque Wentwoth, snuggled in the White Mountains. The home was built in 1806 and was one of the first settlements in town and offers easy access to the many tourist attractions in the Lakes and Mountains Regions. Located on 20 acres of field and pine forest, the surroundings are relaxing and inspirational. All of the guest rooms are comfortably furnished and offer beautiful views of the surrounding landscape. There is an extensive library, a large pine-panelled recreation room with fireplace, antique piano, games and cable TV. Outdoors, there's a spacious lawn area which is well-tended and surrounded by a beautiful pine forest and brook;. A continental plus breakfast begins each morning. Your hostess is pleased to help with directions to all of the year-round activities which include swimming, hiking, boating, mountain biking, fishing, snowmobiling, skiing, antiquing and fine dining. Your hostess can arrange special guided tours of the area and points of interest. *Cozy house-keeping cottages are available and offer a pine-panelled room with a kitchen unit, fireplace, full separate bathroom, bedroom and a screened-in porch. **Airport:** Manchester or Lebanon-1 hr-15 minutes **Packages:** Ski Packages **Seasonal:** No **Reservations:** Deposit required to hold reservation with a 7 day cancel policy for refund, less than 7 day notice is received, deposit will not be refunded unless room is resold for that evening **Brochure:** Yes **Permitted:** Children, drinking **Conference:** Yes **Languages:** German, French **Payment Terms:** Check MC/V [K04GPNH-12525] **COM** Y **ITC Member:** No

Rates:	Pvt Bath 5	Suite
Single	$ 65.00	$ 80.00
Double	$ 65.00	

Wentworth Inn & Art Gallery	Off Rt 25 03282	Wentworth NH
Barbara & Jim Moffat		Tel: 800-542-2331 603-764-9923
		Res Times 6:30pm-9:30pm

©*Inn & Travel Memphis, Tennessee*

1-93

New Hampshire - Rhode Island

In the foothills of the White Mountains and the beautiful Baker River Valley, where the pace is a little slower and life is more serene, is this stately old white Colonial Inn and art gallery. Surrounded by the scenic beauty of the mountains and the babbling streams nearby, you can taste the true New England flavors year-round. The Federal-design home offers guests comfort and time to converse with the hosts who are local artists, that display the works of other artists and craftsmen. Full country breakfast starts off your day with other gourmet choices for Inn guests only with a table d'haute menu to select. Other meals available. **Seasonal:** No **Reservations:** One night's deposit at booking for guarantee; 10-day cancellation notice, less 10% service fee. **Brochure:** Yes **Permitted:** Limited children **Conference:** Yes, groups to 40 persons. **Payment Terms:** Check AE/DC/MC/V [X02-BCNH-3758] **COM** Y **ITC Member:** No

Rates:	Pvt Bath 3	Shared Bath 4
Single	$ 75.00	$ 65.00
Double	$ 75.00	$ 65.00

Tall Pines Inn	752 Old Rt 3 03289	Winnesquam NH
Kent & Kate Kern	**Tel:** 800-722-6870 603-528-3632	**Fax:** 603-538-8550
		Res Times 10am-10pm

Tall Pines Inn is a homestay Bed & Breakfast Country Inn located in the heart of New Hampshire's "Lakes Region". The Inn is situated on the southern shore of Lake Winnisquam and features an outstanding view of the lake and mountains to the north. The Inn has three guest rooms and your innkeepers (Kent & Kate) have taken great care to create an atmosphere reflecting their hospitality and interest in having guests feel welcomed and at home. The guest rooms are bright, clean and comfortable with handmade quilts and "all you can eat" full country breakfasts. Guest rooms are designed for adult couples or single travelers. Special dinners are available with advance reservation and business travelers can join the innkeepers for dinner "du jour" at a nominal additional charge. The "Lakes Region" is a four-seasons destination area for recreational visitors with something for everyone. Additionally, the Inn is centrally located for business or recreational day trip travel ranging from Boston, MA to Concord, Manchester and Portsmouth, New Hampshire, Portland, Maine or White River Vermont. Reservations are recommended and a phone call with your credit card number will confirm your reservation. Prepayment of full rental guarantees your reservation. Toll-free reservation phone: 800-722-6870 **Discounts:** Weekly rates and mid-week business rates are available **Airport:** Manchester NH 50 mi; Portland ME 90 mi; Boston's Logan 90 mi **Seasonal:** No **Reservations:** Deposit to guarantee reservation; two week cancel policy for full refund. Two night min holidays & foliage season **Brochure:** Yes **Permitted:** Drinking, limited smoking **Payment Terms:** Check DISC/MC/V [Z02HPNH1-13953] **COM** YG **ITC Member:** No

Rates:	Pvt Bath 1	Shared Bath 2
Single	$ 60.00	$ 50.00
Double	$ 65.00	$ 55.00

Tuc' Me Inn	68 N Main St 03894	Wolfeboro NH
Terrille Foutz		**Tel:** 603-569-5702

Oldest summer resort town in USA offers a beautiful early 1800's colonial, tastefully decorated for comfort and warmth. Beautiful year-round area with water and snow sporting activities. Two blocks from town and scenic Lake Winnipesaukee. Exciting steam train ride through countryside. Full breakfast to start off your day. **Seasonal:** No **Brochure:** Yes **Permitted:** Children 12-up, smoking, drinking **Payment Terms:** Check MC/V [X11ACN-H-5873] **COM** Y **ITC Member:** No

Rates:	Pvt Bath 2	Shared Bath 4
Single	$ 65.00	
Double	$ 72.00	$ 59.00

Blue Dory Inn	Dodge Street 02807	Block Island RI
Ann Loedy		**Tel:** 800-992-7290 401-466-5891

Crescent Beach - where miles of white sand meet clear blue water - at the head of this famous beach, within a few feet of the sea is the charming *Blue Dory Inn*, a Victorian Inn dating from the turn-of-the-century. Newly renovated and furnished with antiques, fixtures and decorations, guests easily become enchanted by the Victorian charm within - evoking a time gone by. Spacious guest rooms provide town or ocean views, plush antique decor, private baths, wall-to-wall carpeting and all modern comforts. The eat-in kitchen welcomes guests each morning to a continental breakfast of fresh brewed coffee, breakfast rolls, fresh fruits, assorted juices, herbal teas and a bottomless pot of coffee. Located in the historical district, there are many fine shops, restaurants and sights within easy walking distance. Your hosts will arrange everything from Island Tours to bike rentals and can make numerous recommendations on sights to see and places to visit. Block Island has something for everyone. As a sportsman's paradise with unexcelled sailing and deep-sea fishing, or the beachcomber's delight with dunes and beaches to explore - its the perfect place to unwind during the day. Unwinding in the evening means trying one of the excellent restaurants where specialties include lobster, swordfish and quahogs. **Airport:** Providence-1 hr **Discounts:** Inquire at res time **Packages:** Inquire at res time **Seasonal:** Rates vary **Reservations:** 50% deposit within 7 days of booking **Brochure:** Yes **Permitted:** Children, pets, drinking, smoking **Conference:** Yes, for small groups **Payment Terms:** Check AE/MC/V [R12EPRI-4634] **COM** Y **ITC Member:** No

Rates:	Pvt Bath 15
Single	$ 65-170.00
Double	$ 65-170.00

Gables Inn & Gables II　　　　PO Box 516 Dodge St 02807　　　　**Block Island RI**
Barbara & Stan Nyzio　　　　　　　　　　　　　　　　　　　　　　**Tel:** 401-466-2213

A wonderful summer vacation - perfect for families, this spot has been a summer retreat for the past twenty-five years. Your hosts provide guests will all the essentials for enjoying the island. A variety of accommodations meet every need, ranging from single rooms to cottages - all guaranteed to provide a memorable experience. Each room or cottage is located on the ground floor and has its own outside entrance and porch. The beach and water are nearby and all of the activities of Block Island. **Discounts:** Yes, off-season and weekdays in season **Airport:** Block Island State Airport-1 mi **Seasonal:** *See Below **Reservations:** Full deposit to two nights, 3 nights or more require 50% deposit within 5 days of booking, bal due upon check-in, 15 day cancel policy less $20 service fee **Brochure:** Yes **Permitted:** Smoking, drinking, children **Payment Terms:** Check MC/V [R04GPRI-4636] **COM** U **ITC Member:** No

Rates:	Pvt Bath 10	Shared Bath 40
Single	$ 75-115.00	$ 40-60.00
Double	$ 75-115.00	$ 65-85.00

Seacrest Inn　　　　　　　207 High St 02807　　　　　　**Block Island RI**
　　　　　　　　　　　　　　　　　　　　　　　　　　　　　　Tel: 401-466-2882

Old Harbor section in the historic district offers picturesque views and strolling distance to all the sights. Victorian gazebo for relaxing outdoors in the ocean breezes. A continental breakfast is included. Complimentary bikes for guests use. **Seasonal:** May-Oct **Brochure:** Yes **Payment Terms:** Check [X11ACRI-4647] **COM** Y **ITC Member:** No

Rates:	Pvt Bath 18
Single	$ 68-80.00
Double	$ 68-80.00

Sheffield House　　　　　　High St 02807　　　　　　　　**Block Island RI**
The McQueenys　　　　　　　　　　　　　　**Tel:** 401-466-2494 **Fax:** 401-466-5067
　　　　　　　　　　　　　　　　　　　　　　　　　　　　Res Times 9am-2pm

The *Sheffield House* is an 1888 Queen Anne Victorian quietly set among perennial gardens within the Historic District of Block Island. It's seven guest rooms and country kitchen are furnished with antiques and family heirlooms along with a collection of local artists' works. Your hosts, Steve and Claire McQueeny, are knowledgeable and willing to help guests plan their relaxation or exploration. From the *Sheffield House* it is a five minute walk to the quaint village, ferry dock, many fine restaurants, interesting shops and galleries and the island's fine bathing beaches. Before setting out for your day, guests are invited to enjoy a generous complimentary continental breakfast in our country kitchen. The Irish sideboard provides an overflowing buffet-style breakfast of homebaked pastries, exquisite jams, fresh fruit, juices, herbal teas and freshly brewed coffee. Following a day of pursuing your favorite activities, guests can relax and enjoy pleasant conversation and a cool beverage on the wrap-around porch or in the private garden. While summer is the main season, don't forget the off-season. Not only are costs lower and the island less crowded, you'll soon learn why Native Americans called Block Island *"The Island of the Little God"*. **Discounts:** Senior citizens, week stays, members of Nature Conservancy **Airport:** Providence RI-30 mi **Packages:** Off-season (10/15-4/30) Four nights for the price of three; Other packages upon request **Seasonal:** No **Reservations:** Full deposit, 3 nights or longer 50% deposit to guarantee reservation, 14 day cancel notice for refund less $25 service fee **Brochure:** Yes **Permitted:** Drinking, limited smoking **Payment Terms:** Check AE/DC/MC/V [Z04GPRI-4648] **COM** Y **ITC Member:** No

Rates:	Pvt Bath 5	Shared Bath 2
Single	$ 50-140.00	$ 50-100.00
Double	$ 50-140.00	$ 50-100.00

Joseph Reynolds House   956 Hope St 02809   Bristol RI
Richard & Wendy Anderson   Tel: 401-254-0230

A *National Historic Landmark* that served as the headquarters of General Lafayette in 1778 and is the oldest three-story structure, c1693, in New England. Beautifully furnished with antiques, the hosts are very active in historical preservation and offer guests a complete history of the surrounding area. Continental breakfast is included. **Seasonal:** No **Brochure:** Yes **Permitted:** Children **Payment Terms:** Check [X11ACRI-4650] **COM** Y **ITC Member:** No

Rates:	Pvt Bath 4
Single	$ 55-90.00
Double	$ 55-90.00

Country Goose B&B   563 Greenend Ave 02840   Middletown RI
Paula Kelly   Tel: 401-846-6308
    Res Times 24 Hrs

The *Country Goose* is a charming country farmhouse built in 1898 which is the original farmhouse that was used to farm this land for three generations. It is nestled in a quiet country setting trimmed with its original gingerbread trim and old fashioned front porch, furnished in wicker and surrounded by flowers and trees. A distant view of the beach allows our guests to relax after a busy day in a comfortable setting and receive a quiet night's rest. The quaint country rooms are furnished with family heirlooms and antiques and with the large shared bathrooms, our guests feel *"right at home."* The *Country Goose* is located only minutes from the beaches, mansions, shopping, Tennis Hall of Fame, Norman Bird Sanctuary, yachting center and all other attractions on the island. Complimentary wine and cheese awaits your arrival, with a continental breakfast served each morning in surroundings of traditional country decor. **Airport:** Green-30 mins **Packages:** Weekdays, Two days or more, less 15% with coupons to mansions and other Newport attractions **Reservations:** Full payment for weekends, one night deposit weekdays and weekends if late booking, 5 day cancel policy for refund, less than five day cancel notice, refund only if rebooked, rates do not include tax **Permitted:** Children, social drinking **Payment Terms:** Check MC/V [I09FPRI-12553] **COM** U **ITC Member:** No

Rates:	Pvt Bath 6	Shared Bath 3
Single	$ 65-95.00	$ 65-95.00
Double	$ 65-95.00	$ 65-95.00

National Edition   *Rhode Island*

Lindseys Guest House	6 James St 02840	**Middletown RI**
Anne & David Lindsey		**Tel:** 401-846-9386

Enjoy a charming split level home in a residential setting with off-street parking and a large yard. Close to the famous sights in Newport and the famous Bellevue Avenue with its mansions, wharfs, boat tour operators, shops and well-known restaurants. The charming host/couple raised their seven children here and enjoy visiting with guests. Once guests walk through the front door, they are no longer strangers. A complimentary breakfast includes orange juice, cereals, muffins, jams (often homemade) coffee cake. **Reservations:** One night's deposit are res time, 14 day cancel policy for refund less 10% **Brochure:** Yes **Permitted:** Children, limited drinking and smoking **Payment Terms:** Check MC/V [X09BCRI-4661] **COM** Y **ITC Member:** No

Rates: Pvt Bath 1   Shared Bath 2
Single $ 65.00 $ 55.00
Double $ 75.00 $ 65.00

Ilverthorpe Cottage	41 Robinson St 02882	**Narragansett RI**
Chris & Rich Raggio		**Tel:** 401-789-2392

Restored Victorian residence c1886 just three blocks from the beach offering guests stenciled walls, fresh flowers, beautiful antique furnishings with lacy touches. Close to fine Newport restaurants and the finest mansions. A full breakfast is included. **Seasonal:** 5/15-10/15 Open **Brochure:** Yes **Permitted:** Children, drinking and limited smoking **Payment Terms:** Check [X11ACRI-4671] **COM** Y **ITC Member:** No

Rates: Pvt Bath 3   Shared Bath 3
Single $ 65.00 $ 50.00
Double $ 70.00 $ 60.00

Brinley Victorian Inn	23 Brinley St 02840	**Newport RI**
Peter Carlisle/Claire Boslem		**Tel:** 800-999-8523 401-849-7645
		Res Times 9am-9pm

Turn-of-the-century picture-perfect restoration for this Victorian residence where the host owners haven't overlooked anything, including beautiful Victorian period gardens. The inside has been perfectly decorated with antiques reminiscent of its former elegance including lace and satin window treatments. Amenities include evening mints, fresh flowers and champagne and wine for your special occasions (added cost). Continental plus breakfast is included. **Seasonal:** No **Reservations:** One night's deposit at res time, 10 day cancel policy for refund **Brochure:** Yes **Permitted:** Children 12-up, limited drinking **Payment Terms:** Check [X1-1ACRI-4690] **COM** Y **ITC Member:** No

Rates: Pvt Bath 5   Shared Bath 4
Single $ 85-95.00 $ 75-85.00
Double $ 95-105.00 $ 75-85.00

Cliff Walk Manor	82 Memorial Blvd 02840	**Newport RI**
Bryan Babcock		**Tel:** 401-847-1300
		Res Times 24 Hrs

Spectacular 1855 mansion setting on five acres of grounds atop the world-famous Cliff Walk where you'll have exciting views of the water and Newport's famous mansions. A full-service resort that tends to each guests's needs including full gourmet dining on the premises, hot tub, and entertainment. **Seasonal:** 3/1-11/30 **Res-ervations:** Deposit to hold room 48 hr cancel policy *Rates based on European Plan **Brochure:** Yes **Permitted:** Children, drinking, limited smoking **Languages:** Italian **Payment Terms:** Check AE/DC/MC/V [X1-1ACRI-4694] **COM** Y **ITC Member:** No

Rates: Pvt Bath 25
Single $ 85.00
Double $ 95.00

Rhode Island   *National Edition*

Cliffside Inn B&B	2 Seaview Blvd 02840	**Newport RI**
Stephan Nicholas	**Tel:** 800-845-1811 401-847-1811 **Fax:** 401-848-5850	
	Res Times 8am-9pm	

The *Cliffside Inn* was built in 1880 by the Governor of Maryland as a summer home. Later, it became the permanent residence of Beatrice Turner, an eccentric artist who painted over 1000 self-portraits during her lifetime. Today, *Cliffside* has been transformed into a beautiful Victorian Inn with fabulous period antiques and exquisite draperies. The parlor is a comfortable gathering place where the guest meet for afternoon appetizers and for the full gourmet breakfast in the morning. Some of the guest rooms feature such amenities as whirlpool tubs, fireplaces, skylights, clawfoot tubs, canopy beds and televisions. The *Cliffside Inn* is located on a quiet residential street near the beach and the famous Cliff Walk. Experience the grace, charm, beauty and elegance which is the *Cliffside Inn*. **Airport:** TF Green Airport-45 mi **Seasonal:** No **Reservations:** One night's deposit or 50% if staying longer than two nights to guarantee room; cancellation policy: deposits non-refundable but can be applied to future reservation within 12 months *Suites available **Brochure:** Yes **Permitted:** Children (13-up), limited drinking **Conference:** Yes, The Governor's Suite hosts executive meetings and is a fully equipped conference facility. **Languages:** German, French **Payment Terms:** Check AE/DC/MC/V [K05HPRI1-15545] **COM YG ITC Member:** No

Rates:	**Pvt Bath** 12	**Suites**
Single	$ 145-325.00	
Double	$ 145-325.00	

Gardenview	8 Binney St 02840	**Newport RI**
Mary & Andrew Fitzgerald		**Tel:** 401-849-5799
		Res Times 24 hrs

Gardenview is located on a quiet, residential street - a short distance from the mansions, beaches and the famous Ocean Drive. A large yard is filled with flowers, a fish pond, with a waterfall and many birds to view and enjoy. We offer two quiet rooms for guests. The Garden Room overlooks various gardens and includes a shared bath and king size bath. The Spiral Suite consists of a large private living room connected to the bedroom by a spiral staircase. A bathroom with jacuzzi and sitting room is also included. Amenities include a furnished patio for our guests to enjoy as well as fresh flowers and wonderfully scented soaps to choose from in the bathrooms. Daily newspapers are provided. The suite features a fireplace and both bedrooms have skylights, TV, stereos as well as antique furnishings and handmade quilts. The full complimentary breakfast includes homemade French toasts such as Belgium, almond, various homemade donuts and coffee cakes, fresh fruit, cold cereals and fresh squeezed orange juice. **Airport:** TF Green-45 mins **Packages:** Valentine Day, Christmas In Newport **Seasonal:** Yes, rates vary **Reservations:** 50% deposit required, 10 day cancellation policy for refund **Brochure:** Yes **Permitted:** Limited children, drinking **Payment Terms:** Check [I07HPRI1-22213] **COM YG ITC Member:** No

Rates:	**Pvt Bath** 1	**Shared Bath** 1
Single	$ 165.00	$ 95.00
Double	$ 165.00	$ 95.00

Hydrangea House Inn	16 Bellevue Ave 02840	**Newport RI**
Grant Edmondson/Dennis Blair	**Tel:** 800-945-4667 401-846-4435 **Fax:** 401-846-4435	
	Res Times 9am-10pm	

©Inn & Travel Memphis, Tennessee

National Edition **Rhode Island**

Located at the top of the Historic Hill, the *Hydrangea House Inn* is at the center of Newport's *"Walking District"*, with some 80% of its sights and attractions accessible by foot, right from our front door. This Victorian townhouse, built in 1876, has been carefully restored. It's six guest rooms, all with private baths, are elegantly decorated each with its own sumptuous personality. Plush carpeting, thick cozy towels, crystal water glasses, long-stemmed goblets for your wine set-up and complimentary refreshments are some of the amenities for you to enjoy. The quiet sophistication and uniqueness of the Inn's decor reflects the careers of its innkeepers, who are art and antique dealers. The non-smoking policy assures each guest a fresh, clean atmosphere. Your day will start with our gratifying hot buffet breakfast served in the contemporary fine art gallery. For your enjoyment, we will serve you our own blend of fresh-ground *Hydrangea House Coffee*, fresh-squeezed orange juice, home baked bread and granola - as well as our incredible raspberry pancakes, perhaps, or seasoned scrambled eggs. The gallery also serves as a unique setting for small conferences and business meetings. We know you'll love it here, because we do. The *"Boston Globe"* said of the Inn *"... in a city renowned for its lodging, the Hydrangea House Inn is not to be missed"!* AAA 3-Diamond Inspected and Approved, 1994 **Airport:** Providence RI-45 min **Seasonal:** No **Reservations:** One night deposit, 50% deposit for stays longer than 3 days, 14 day cancel policy for refund, check-in 2pm to not later than 8pm, check-out 11am, min stays 2 days weekends, 3 days on holidays & events **Brochure:** Yes **Permitted:** Children, drinking **Payment Terms:** Check MC/V [R10HPRI1-14030] **COM YG ITC Member:** No

Rates:	Pvt Bath	6
Single	$ 55-139.00	
Double	$ 55-139.99	

Melville House 39 Clarke St 02840 Newport RI
Vincent C DeRico/David J Horan **Tel:** 401-847-0640 **Fax:** 401-847-0956
Res Times 7:30am-10pm

Staying at the *Melville House* is a step back into the past. The *Melville House*, built c.1750, is listed on the *National Register of Historic Places*. We are located in the heart of the Historic Hill section of Newport, the streets of which, are still lit by gas. The French General Rochambeau quartered some of his troops here when they fought in the Revolutionary War under President George Washington. The Vernon House, where Washington, Rochambeau and Major General Marqis de Lafayette met, is across the street. Just down the block is the building that still houses America's oldest military unit in continuous service under its original charter in 1741, the Newport Artillery Company. Although the *Melville House* is situated on one of the quietest streets in Newport, it is only one block away from Thames Street and the harborfront where many of the city's finest restaurants, antique shops and galleries can be found. We are also within walking distance to Newport's many places of worship such as Touro Synagogue (the oldest in the U.S.), Trinity Church (built in 1726) and St Mary's Church (where President John F Kennedy married Jacqueline). The Tennis Hall of Fame, the famous and lavish mansions of the Vanderbilts, Astors and the Belmonts, The Naval War College and Newport's finest ocean beaches are just a very short drive. The seven rooms of the *Melville House* are furnished in traditional Colonial style. Off-street parking is available. Breakfast features homemade granola, muffins and various other baked items such as buttermilk biscuits, bagels, scones, stuffed French toast, Portuguese quiche, Yankee cornbread and Rhode Island Johnnycakes. An afternoon "tea" is served every day. Guests can enjoy refreshments or a glass of sherry and biscotti, as we discuss the days' activities and our favorite places for dinner. **Discounts:** Weekdays, off-season, long term stays **Airport:** Providence TF Green-25 mi **Seasonal:** No **Reservations:** One night's deposit, check in by 8pm, 14 day cancel policy **Brochure:** Yes **Permitted:** Children 13+, drinking **Conference:** Yes, call for information **Payment Terms:** Check AE/MC/V [I03H-PRI1-4707] **COM YG ITC Member:** No **Quality Assured:** Yes

Rates:	Pvt Bath	5	Shared Bath	2
Single	$ 60-125.00		$ 50-100.00	
Double	$ 60-125.00		$ 50-100.00	

©Inn & Travel Memphis, Tennessee

Rhode Island   *National Edition*

On The Point B&B	102 Third St 02840	**Newport RI**
Sheila & George Perry		**Tel:** 401-846-8377

On The Point Bed & Breakfast is conveniently located just one and one half blocks from Narragansett Bay and a very short walk to downtown Newport. This one hundred year old Victorian is in one of Newport's most historic districts. The "Point Area" was subdivided by the Quakers in the early 1700's and has more restored homes of the era than any other area. *On The Point Bed & Breakfast* has relaxing, beautifully furnished accommodations with either king size or twin beds in all rooms. Breakfast, which includes a fresh fruit salad and wonderful pastries, is served in antique wicker surroundings. There are nearby public tennis courts and Newport's best gourmet and seafood restaurants are a short walk. Your hosts are local history buffs and love to share their extensive collection of early Newport prints and turn-of-the-century photographs. Guests are also invited to enjoy the collection of Newport inspired books in the Victorian ambiance of this charming home. **Discounts:** 40% off-season (Nov-April), extended stays (min week) **Airport:** Providence-40 min **Packages:** Dinner Package, off-season **Seasonal:** Rates vary **Reservations:** First nights deposit or credit card number to guarantee reservation, bal due upon arrival **Brochure:** Yes **Permitted:** Children, drinking **Payment Terms:** Check MC/V [Z04HPRI1-16934] **COM** YG **ITC Member:** No

Rates:	**Pvt Bath** 2	**Shared Bath** 2
Single	$ 90-110.00	$ 70-90.00
Double	$ 95-125.00	$ 75-95.00

Rhode Island House	77 Rhode Island Ave 02840	**Newport RI**
John Rich/Michael Dupre		**Tel:** 401-848-7787 **Fax:** 401-849-3104
		Res Times 8am-8pm

Dating from 1881, the summer home for Thomas R Hunter and his family, guests can enjoy a traditional stay in this Grand Victorian residence while vacationing at this traditional resort area. Large and spacious, your hosts have recently decorated the entire home to make guests comfortable in this elegant residence with large bay windows that filter sunlight into the light and airy rooms with wide open porches for relaxing during the day and early evenings. This residence is just blocks from Easton Pond, near First Beach on Historic Hill. Historic Newport offers guests a chance to tour many of the fine mansions, the Tennis Hall of Fame, Newport Art Museum and experience traditional New England seafood cuisine at it's finest. A breakfast is included. **Seasonal:** Rates vary **Reservations:** One night's deposit or 50% of entire length of stay **Brochure:** Yes **Permitted:** Limited children, drinking **Conference:** Yes **Languages:** French, Spanish **Payment Terms:** Check AE/MC/V [R08GPRI-8412] **COM** Y **ITC Member:** No

Grand Victorian Residence

Rates:	**Pvt Bath** 5
Single	$ 105-225.00
Double	$ 105-225.00

Waterview	10 Cliff Terrace 02840	**Newport RI**
Emma & Frank Aponowich		**Tel:** 401-847-4425

Overlook Newport Beach from this spectacular vantage point at the beginning of Cliff Walk in a gorgeous Victorian home which has been completely restored and furnished in appropriate antiques. One of the most prestigious sections of Newport. A full breakfast is included. **Seasonal:** May-Sept **Brochure:** Yes **Permitted:** Limited children and drinking **Payment Terms:** Check [X11ACRI-4720] **COM** Y **ITC Member:** No

Rates:	**Pvt Bath** 3
Single	$ 63.00
Double	$ 63.00

State House Inn	43 Jewett St 02908	**Providence RI**
Frank & Monica Hopton		**Tel:** 401-785-6111 **Fax:** 401-351-4261
		Res Times 9am-10pm

©*Inn & Travel Memphis, Tennessee*

Enjoy your stay in the capitol city of Rhode Island in this conveniently located 100 year old Inn. The State House Neighborhood is currently being considered for a Historic Neighborhood Designation. Your hosts have completely restored and renovated this historic location into a charming Bed & Breakfast Inn offering king and queen beds, Colonial and Shaker reproduction furnishings with fireplaces and canopy beds in some of the guest rooms. This perfect location is convenient to all of the state offices and sights in downtown Providence. A hearty and healthy full breakfast is included in the rate. **Airport:** Providence (Green Airport) just 5 miles **Seasonal:** No **Reservations:** 50% deposit, check-in by 10pm **Brochure:** Yes **Permitted:** Children, drinking, limited smoking **Payment Terms:** Check AE/MC/V [I07-HPRI1-11948] **COM YG ITC Member:** No

Rates:	Pvt Bath 10
Single	$ 65-95.00
Double	$ 65-95.00

The Villa	190 Shore Rd 02891	Westerly RI
Jerry Maidrano		Tel: 800-722-9240 401-596-1054 **Fax:** 401-596-6268
		Res Times 9am-9pm

From the moment you arrive at *The Villa*, you will fall in love with their *"wonderful land of Armore"*. Escape to this perfect romantic hideaway of flower gardens, Italian porticos and verandas, where you can swim in a sparkling sapphire pool, surrounded by lush green plants and spectacular sunshine. Where soothing, hot waters calm and massage you while you relax in the outdoor spa. Open year-round, *The Villa* is the ideal setting for weddings, honeymoons and rekindling romance. Imagine yourself in a cozy, private suite in the middle of winter, gazing at the hypnotic flames of a sensuous, cracking fire. Summers here are warm and golden with cool ocean breezes and festive nights of music and Italian cuisine. Of *The Villa's* five attractive suites, some offer fireplaces and jacuzzi and all have cable TV, a/c and private baths. A pleasing complimentary buffet breakfast is served at the pool house, at poolside or in your private room. The romance of Italy awaits you. Experience the magic yourself. *The Villa* is located at the crossroads of historic Westerly and Watch Hill and is close to Mystic, Misquamicut Beach and foxwoods Resort and Casino. **Discounts:** AAA, weekly stays, corporate, travel agents **Packages:** Romantic Rendezvous (Two night's stay, champagne and dinner for two) **Seasonal:** No **Reservations:** Deposit required to guarantee reservation **Brochure:** Yes **Permitted:** Behaved children, limited pets, limited smoking, limited drinking **Languages:** Italian **Payment Terms:** Check AE/MC/V [I04IPRI1-14035] **COM YG ITC Member:** No

Rates:	Pvt Bath 7
Single	$ 70-200.00
Double	$ 75-205.00

Cookie Jar B&B	64 Kingstown Rd 02898	Wyoming RI
Dick & Madelein Sohl		Tel: 800-767-4262 401-539-2680
		Res Times 10am-9pm

The heart of our home, the living room, was built in 1732 and served as a blacksmith's shop for many years. Later, the forge was removed and a large granite fireplace was built by an American Indian stone-mason. The original wood ceiling, handhewn beams and granite walls remain today. Initially, the property was called The Perry Plantation and yes, they had two slaves who lived above the blacksmith shop. Over the generations, rooms were added to the smithy and some 65 years ago this building was used as a restaurant and called The Cookie Jar Tea Room; therefore, we thought it appropriate to call our Bed and Breakfast *The Cookie Jar*. There are only some three acres left of the original plantation. On the property we have two homes, a barn, swimming pool, fifty plus fruit trees, grape vines, berry bushes, a flower garden and an acre of grass. A perfect environment for rest and relaxation. Nearby are many beautiful white sand beaches, scenic drives, shoreline attractions and historical sights. Take day trips to see the Newport Mansions, Mystic Seaport or Cape Cod. Visit the fishing villages of Gaulee or Stonington, take a ferry to Block Island or go deep sea fishing. **Airport:** TF Green-25 min **Discounts:** 10% off for 4 nights or longer, 7th night free **Seasonal:** Rates vary **Reservations:** 50% deposit required within 5 days of booking to guarantee reservation **Brochure:** Yes **Permitted:** Children, drinking **Payment Terms:** Check [R09FPRI-18171] **COM** Y **ITC Member:** No

Rates:	Pvt Bath 1	Shared Bath 2
Single	$ 58.50	$ 54.00
Double	$ 65.00	$ 60.00

Inn At Highview　　　　　RR 1 Box 201A 05143　　　　　Andover VT
Greg Bohan　　　　　　　　　　　　　　　　　　　　　Tel: 802-875-2724

High on East Hill, with panoramic views of the surrounding mountains, sits *The Inn at Highview*, an immaculately restored 18th Century farmhouse filled with antique furnishings, but relaxingly unpretentious and comfortable. *Highview* is truly a step back in time to a Vermont you thought only existed in your dreams and in Hollywood movies, at the same time being convenient to all of the modern reasons for visiting Vermont . . . Okemo Mountain Ski Area, the Villages of Weston (home to the Weston Playhouse, Weston Priory and Vermont Country Store), and Chester are all within a fifteen minute drive. Winding through the Inn's seventy-two acres is a network of breath-taking hiking and cross country ski trails which connect with others for an uninterrupted network comprising 15 km. After you've had your exercise, put your feet up and relax by the fire, enjoy our sauna, or, in summer, have a dip in our rock garden swimming pool overlooking the valley below. Our country dining room has become well-known for its excellent Italian cuisine available only to Inn guests to guarantee attentive service. For small retreats and business meetings, we offer an excellent conference facility with full conference support services. A full complimentary breakfast is included. **Discounts:** Yes, inquire at res time **Airport:** Hartford CT-100 mi, 2 hrs **Packages:** Meeting, Summer Week and Holiday Weekends **Seasonal:** No **Reservations:** One night's deposit or credit card number; 10 day cancel policy for refund, less than 10 day notice, refund only if room is rebooked **Brochure:** Yes **Permitted:** Limited children, limited pets, drinking **Conference:** Full conference facility; complete audio/video, fax, copier and services (word processing, chart & graph making) **Languages:** English, Italian, Spanish **Payment Terms:** Check MC/V [Z06HPVT1-16520] **COM** YG **ITC Member:** No

Rates:	Pvt Bath 8
Single	$ 80-115.00
Double	$ 90-125.00

Arlington Inn　　　　　Historic Rt 7A 05250　　　　　Arlington VT
Mark & Deborah Gagnon　　　　　　　　Tel: 800-443-9442 802-375-6532
　　　　　　　　　　　　　　　　　　　　　Res Times 10am-10pm

This beautiful Greek Revival Mansion is the perfect place to step back in time and relive yesteryear. Once you enter the Inn with its gleaming wood floors and splendid Victorian antique furnishings, you begin to imagine yourself as part of a bygone era. Your hosts have taken care of every detail for a memorable stay - including beautifully furnishing and decorating each guest room in its own special way - including private baths for all rooms. The Inn boasts an award-winning (*Travel Holiday*) dining room where guests sample delectable gourmet delicacies during an evening of romantic candlelight dining. Your chef uses only fresh provisions to create his sumptuous fare. In Spring, Summer and Fall, the beautiful grounds surrounding the Inn offer tennis on the grounds as well as nearby hiking, biking, golf, swimming, canoeing and fishing. Winter brings the magic of snow with world-class cross-country and downhill skiing nearby. Although the Town of Arlington has remained the picture of "small town America" that lives in all of our thoughts, its close proximity to Manchester and Bennington provide a myriad of things to see and do, including exciting antique-hunting. A full complimentary breakfast starts your day. **Packages:** Inquire at res time **Airport:** Albany-1 hr **Discounts:** Inquire at res time **Seasonal:** No **Reservations:** One night's deposit, 14 day cancel policy for refund **Brochure:** Yes **Permitted:** Children, drinking **Conference:** Yes, inquire for details **Languages:** French **Payment Terms:** Check AE/DC/DISC/MC/V [I08-HPVT1-2797] **COM YG ITC Member:** No

Rates: Pvt Bath 13
Single $ 80-185.00
Double $ 80-185.00

Shenandoah Farm	Battenkill Rd 05250	Arlington VT
Woody Masterson		Tel: 802-375-6372
		Res Times 8am-5pm

Experience New England at its peak in this lovingly restored 1820 Colonial nestled in the rolling hillside country overlooking the valleys and Battenkill River. Wonderful "Americana" year-round whether its Spring flowers, Summer strolling, Autumn's brilliant foliage or skiing in Winter. Beautifully finished, this residence greets you with warmth and hospitality of the 1800s, complete with period antique furnishings that remind you of another era. You'll be close to skiing, golf and all other sporting activities. There's a sitting room and library to enjoy aswell, along with a piano. Full "farm-fresh" breakfasts are served daily and are included with your room. Complimentary wine and tea. **Seasonal:** No **Reservations:** Yes, including deposit **Brochure:** Yes **Permitted:** Children **Payment Terms:** Check [A08GPVT-2800] **COM Y ITC Member:** No

Rates: Pvt Bath 4   Shared Bath 1
Single $ 40.00 $ 40.00
Double $ 65.00 $ 55.00

Blue Haven Christian B&B	Rt 1 Box 328 05101	Bellows Falls VT
Helene Champagne		Tel: 802-463-9008

Innkeeper and artist, Helene, warmly welcomes guests to her creatively decorated and furnished Inn - a former country school. The lovingly restored series of clapboard buildings retain the hardy aura of the 1830 school house. Your charming hostess has personalized every corner with personalized touches to insure the guests comfort and enjoyment. The country feeling begins with original wide-plank flooring in the common rooms and a working, massive stone fireplace that boasts stones from travels here and abroad. Special touches of goose-down comforters, coverlets, bed canopies of wonderful fabrics, Helene's art and hand-painted furniture appear throughout the Inn as she tried to make each guest room a "little jewel." A festive breakfast is set with colorful antique dishes and includes special recipes for homemade granola, pancakes or French toast, Apple-Cranberry-Pecan muffins - and in season, wild blackberries and raspberries picked fresh from nearby - all served with plenty of conversation in a beautiful rambling, wood warm country kitchen. Daytime activities nearby include art shows, canoeing, cycling, fishing, flea markets, hiking, historic walking tours, Christmas shops, antiquing, swimming, theater, skiing, cross country and downhill, or simply getting comfortable. Sip mulled cider and put-up your feet and browse a broad art library, play a tune on the mellow upright piano, watching TV and games, whatever you please. **Discounts:** AARP, AAA, mid-week, off-season **Airport:** Hartford's Bradly 1.5 hrs; Boston 2 hrs; Keene NH 20 min **Packages:** Yes, please inquire at res time **Seasonal:** No **Reservations:** One night's deposit **Brochure:** Yes **Permitted:** Children, drinking **Conference:** Yes for 12-30 persons. **Languages:** French **Payment Terms:** Check AE/MC/V [I10DPVT-14498] **COM Y ITC Member:** No

Rates:	**Pvt Bath** 4	**Shared Bath** 2
Single	$58.00	$48.00
Double	$78.00	$68.00

Eastwood House   River Street 05032   **Bethel VT**
Christine & Ron Diamond   **Tel:** 802-234-9686

Beautiful Federal-style architecture in this 1816 residence built as a stagecoach stop-over and still serving travelers today! Five working fireplace (four in the bedrooms), original floors, hardware and hand-stenciled walls reminds guest of another era. You'll be surrounded by beautiful scenery including mountains just in the distance. A full Yankee breakfast gets everyone off to a fresh start each day. **Seasonal:** No **Reservations:** Deposit required to hold room **Brochure:** Yes **Permitted:** Children, limited smoking **Payment Terms:** Check AE/MC/V [X11ACVT-2809] **COM** Y **ITC Member:** No

Rates:	**Pvt Bath** 5	**Shared Bath** 2
Single	$40-65.00	$40-65.00
Double	$40-65.00	$40-65.00

Alpenrose Inn   Winhall Hollow Rd 05340   **Bondville VT**
Rosemarie Strine   **Tel:** 802-297-2750

Cozy atmosphere in this hideaway that's convenient and within minutes of the Volvo Tennis Tournament and ski slopes. Full breakfast included, MAP winters. Fireplace in dining room and lounge. Tennis and swimming are nearby. **Brochure:** Yes **Permitted:** Children and limited smoking **Languages:** German **Payment Terms:** Check MC/V [X11ACVT-2813] **COM** Y **ITC Member:** No

Rates:	**Pvt Bath** 9
Single	$45-65.00
Double	$45-65.00

Thatcher Brook Inn   **Burlington VT**
Pete & Kelly Varty   **Tel:** 800-292-5911 802-244-5911
    Res Times 10am-5pm

Refer to the same name listed under Waterbury, Vermont for a complete description. **Seasonal:** No **Payment Terms:** Check DISC/MC/V [M11BPVT-8574] **COM** Y **ITC Member:** No

Rates:	**Pvt Bath** 24
Single	$60-115.00
Double	$75-165.00

Hugging Bear Inn & Shoppe   Main St 05143   **Chester VT**
Georgette Thomas   **Tel:** 800-325-0519 802-875-2412
    Res Times 9am-10pm

Bed, Breakfast & Bears! This lovely Victorian Inn, built in 1850, is located on the green and is set in the heart of Chester's historic district. It is difficult to miss as there are bears on the lawn, bears on the porch, bears peering out of the windows and bears in every nook and cranny of the Inn. The six bedrooms have private baths and are simply furnished with various teddy bear motifs, including a teddy bear in every bed. There are three family rooms for guests with TV, toys, games and a fireplace. Sun streams in the bay window of the dining room where a hearty Vermont breakfast is served. Some of the favorite entrees are apple pancakes and French toast. The attached shop has four rooms with over four thousand different types of teddy bears and *bear-*

aphernalia. It is a collector's paradise, as well as fun for the playful at heart. Nearby guests can enjoy skiing, sledding, swimming, antiquing and delightful shopping. The *Hugging Bear* will be a part of the peasant memories of childhood for those fortunate enough to spend some magical nights in bear country, Vermont style. **Children of all ages are welcomed. Airport:** Boston Logan-3 hrs; Albany-2 hrs; Hartford-2 hrs **Seasonal:** Thanksgiving and Christmas **Reservations:** 50% non-refundable deposit required within 7 days of booking, two day min on holidays and high season weekends, closed Thanksgiving and Christmas **Brochure:** Yes **Permitted:** Children, drinking **Payment Terms:** Check AE/DC/MC/V [I03HPVT1-2832] **COM** U **ITC Member:** No

Rates:	Pvt Bath 6
Single	$ 55-65.00
Double	$ 75-95.00

Inn At Highview
Greg Bohan

Chester VT
Tel: 802-875-2724

Refer to the same listing name under Andover, Vermont for a complete description. **Seasonal:** No **Payment Terms:** Check MC/V [M06HPVT1-17784] **COM** YG **ITC Member:** No

Rates:	Pvt Bath 8
Single	$ 80-115.00
Double	$ 90-125.00

Inn Victoria
Catherine Hasbrouck

On The Green 05143

Chester VT
Tel: 800-732-4288 802-875-4288

"The most romantic Inn in Southern Vermont", *Vermont Green Mountain Guide*. Inn Victoria, the perfect getaway, where upon arrival you can relax with afternoon tea, sit on the front porch in antique wicker and watch the world go by, take a nap in a queen-size bed with embroidered pillows, or soak in the rose-scented bubbles in a sunken tub for two. A perfect start to the first day on your stay is a sumptuous breakfast served on antique china. From our "on the green" location in picturesque Chester, you can walk to shops and restaurants. In the surrounding area, go antiquing, golfing, boating, swimming, biking or hiking on the Appalachian or the Long Trail. Attend an auction, summer theatre or polo, or drive the short distance to three major ski areas. There are many interesting things to add to your enjoyment while at the *Inn Victoria*. On Saturday evening, your hosts KC & Tom open the *Inn Victoria*, by reservation only, to a very elegant dinner party where the menu might include Vermont Smokehouse specialties, Maple Apple Pie and always Champagne and Chocolate. We also host special weekends throughout the year - Overture to Christmas, Murder Mysteries, Cotry Fairs, Beer Brewing, a Quilt Festival, Victorian Tea Party and a Vintage Fashion Show. Each is a special opportunity to getaway, relax and have some interesting activities scheduled. *Inn Victoria's* own Teapot Shop is just next door and features teapots for collectors and drinkers from local artists, as well as from artisans around the world. **Discounts:** Yes, inquire at res time **Airport:** Albany NY-2 hrs; Bradley-1-1/2 hrs; Boston-3 hrs **Reservations:** Credit card number for one night's deposit to guarantee reservation, 7 day cancel policy for refund **Brochure:** Yes **Permitted:** Children, drinking, smoking **Conference:** Large room with fireplace, conversation table, comfortable seating with a kitchen - perfect for cooking class **Payment Terms:** Check MC/V [I04GPVT-1406-3] **COM** Y **ITC Member:** No

Rates:	Pvt Bath 7
Single	$ 65-150.00
Double	$ 65-150.00

Stone Hearth Inn
Don & Janet Strohmeyer

Rt 11 West 05143

Chester VT
Tel: 802-875-2525
Res Times 8am-10pm

Vermont — *National Edition*

Relax and leave stress, problems and the phone behind and visit this lovely, informal 1810 Country Inn known for its traditional Vermont Hospitality! All the rooms have been lovingly restored while retaining the original features including beams, fireplaces and wide-pine floors. An attached barn has been converted into a comfortable common room providing guests with a perfect New England atmosphere including a fieldstone fireplace for chilly evenings. Guest can relax or enjoy some of the many activities such as table tennis, pool or one of the many board games. Every room invites guests to relax and enjoy your home away from home. An inviting library awaits your choice for curling up with before the original "Stone Hearth". Outdoor activities abound year-round for everyone's taste. Bike tours, walking tours, cross country and alpine skiing, sledding, snowmobiling and for that perfect experience, an evening candle-light sleigh ride that's superb! A full country breakfast is included with other meals available in the English Pub or a candlelight dining room for dinner (advanced res required). Guests won't forget the "Nutcracker Suite" featuring German nutcrackers, cuckoo clocks and a collection of fine beer steins. **Seasonal:** No **Reservations:** One night's deposit in advance, 14 day cancel policy for refund. **Brochure:** Yes **Permitted:** Children, drinking, limited smoking **Conference:** Yes for groups to 20 persons. **Languages:** German, French, Dutch **Payment Terms:** Check DISC/MC/V [Z05FPVT-2834] **COM** Y **ITC Member:** No

Rates: Pvt Bath 10
Single $ 45-60.00
Double $ 60-100.00

Inn On The Common   Main St   05827   Craftsbury VT
Michael & Penny Schmitt   Tel: 800-521-2233 802-586-9619
                                                       Res Times 24 hrs

Enjoy New England in this quaint Inn that pampers guests with beautiful antique furnishings, elegant decor and gourmet dining located on the premises. Delightful and gracious accommodations for those looking for the best. Swimming, tennis, library, sauna, white water rafting and golf nearby. A full breakfast is included with other meals available. **Seasonal:** No **Reservations:** One night's deposit or credit card number, 48 hr cancel policy for refund. **Brochure:** Yes **Permitted:** Children 12-up, smoking, drinking **Payment Terms:** Check MC/V [X11ACVT-2839] **COM** Y **ITC Member:** No

Rates: Pvt Bath 18
Single $ 95.00
Double $ 100-135.00

Waybury Inn   Rt 125   05740   East Middlebury VT
Jim & Betty Riley   Tel: 802-388-4015
                                                       Res Times 7am-11pm

Traditional New England Inn c1810 that had it's beginning as a stagecoach stop located at the foot of the Green Mountains, that still carries on its tradition of fine service. Beautiful interior decor includes original wood beams with antique furnishings in all the rooms. Close to all the sights, guests will find tennis, golf, excellent fishing, mountain hiking, nature walks, antiquing, skiing, and exciting Fall foliage that's perfect for picnicking. A full breakfast includes scrumptious blueberry pancakes prepared from a wonderful family recipe. **Seasonal:** No **Reservations:** One night's deposit required **Brochure:** Yes **Permitted:** Limited children, smoking and drinking **Payment Terms:** Check AE/MC/V [X11ACVT-2856] **COM** Y **ITC Member:** No

Rates: Pvt Bath 14
Single $ 80.00-up
Double $ 90-135.00

Berkson Farms   RFD 1   05450   Enosberg Falls VT
Connie Rand   Tel: 802-933-2522

Relax in our 150 year-old farmhouse on a working dairy farm located on 600 acres of meadowland surrounded by a variety of animals, nature and warm hospitality. Guests can help out with the chores or just enjoy the friendly atmosphere, picnic, hike through the fields, bike in the warmer months, cross country ski and sled in the winter. We serve a hearty home-style full breakfast using our maple syrup and farm fresh dairy products. We are located just a few miles from the Canadian border. Swimming, golf and major ski areas are nearby, Children and pets are welcome. Reservations are suggested. We are open year round. Dis- counts: Weekly rates **Airport:** Burlington-1 hr **Seasonal:** No **Reservations:** Deposit required **Brochure:** Yes **Permitted:** Children, pets, drinking **Payment Terms:** Check [Z04GPVT-2857] **COM** Y **ITC Member:** No

Rates:	Pvt Bath 1	Shared Bath 3
Single	$ 45.00	$ 40.00
Double	$ 65.00	$ 55.00

Maplewood Inn   Rt 22A S   05743   Fair Haven VT
Cindy Baird   Tel: 800-253-7729 802-265-8039   Fax: 802-265-8210
    Res Times 9am-9pm

Rediscover romance in this exquisite 1843 Greek Revival-style Inn which is listed on the Vermont Register of Historic Places. Once part of a prosperous dairy, *Maplewood* was transformed into a warm and inviting Inn in 1986 after remaining in one family for over 100 years. Experience panoramic country views, spectacular sunsets and a romantic and intimate atmosphere amid many fine antiques. Conveniently located in Central Vermont's Lakes Region near many recreational attractions such as Lakes Bomoseen, St Catherine and Champlain, Killlington and Pico ski areas, historical sites, museums, shopping and great restaurants. Close to many New York State destinations, such as Lake George and Fort Ticonderoga. Our first class accommodations are expertly decorated in outstanding period decor. Doubles feature four-poster and brass beds, private baths, seating areas and most have working fireplaces. Suites feature a full living room, large bedroom, bath and fireplace. All accommodations have a/c, fans, radios, color TV and in-room phone available on request. Fine touches such as evening turn-down, mints, custom toiletries, bicycles and a canoe are our standard. Several lovely common rooms include Keeping Room with fireplace; Gathering Room with library; Parlor with Complimentary Cordial Bar and games and BYOB Tavern area. Our bountiful Breakfast Buffet will begin your morning. Featured in *"Country"*, *"New England Getaways"*, *"Americana"* and *Inn-sider"* magazines, many fine guidebooks and Mobil 3 Star, AAA 3 Diamond, ABBA 3 Crown **Discounts:** Groups, extended stays **Airport:** Burlington VT-70 mi; Albany NY-85 mi **Packages:** Off-season between Nov-April (except holidays), inquire at res time **Seasonal:** No **Reservations:** 50% deposit within 7 days of booking or credit card number, 14 day cancel policy for refund less $15 service fee. Less than 14 days refund only if rebooked **Brochure:** Yes **Permitted:** Limited children, limited smoking, drinking **Conference:** Yes, common rooms available for groups of 10-12 **Payment Terms:** Check/AE/ CB/DC/DISC/MC/V [I02HPVT1-13623] **COM** YG **ITC Member:** No **Quality Assurance:** Requested

Rates:	Pvt Bath 5
Single	$ 70-105.00
Double	$ 75-115.00

Inn At Buck Hollow Farm   RR 1 Box 680   05454   Fairfax VT
Dody Young/Bradley Schwartz   Tel: 802-849-2400
    Res Times 24 Hrs

We are an intimate New England Country Inn. Nestled on 400 spectacular acres just thirty miles from Burlington, the Inn is truly a four-season retreat. Whether you walk our wooded trails, cuddle a spring lamb, listen to a brook or sit by the heated pool and watch the birds, you will appreciate our special country atmosphere. Come fall, foliage is awe-inspiring, especially on country roads. After hiking, biking or walking, you may decide to sit before the fire, browse through the antique shop or simply enjoy the sounds of migrating geese. Winter offers cross-country skiing on our property with major ski areas close by. Watch the production of maple syrup in our sugar house and taste the re-

Vermont   *National Edition*

sults on your pancakes the next morning. A glass of wine, a crackling fire and a friendly cat welcome you at the end of the day. The Inn occupies a 1790's carriage house with the original beams left exposed. The guest rooms are decorated with antiques, queen-size canopy beds, quilts and color TVs. Guests can relax in the two-person jacuzzi. Children are welcome and love both the fenced-in play area and complimentary pony rides. A full complimentary breakfast is included. The *Inn At Buck Hollow Farm* -- A Special Place. **Discounts:** Yes, inquire at res time **Airport:** Burlington Intl-30 mins **Seasonal:** No **Reservations:** 1 night's or 50% of stay, which ever is greater; 14 day cancel policy. Less than 14 days, refund if rebooked or deposit held for future booking. **Brochure:** Yes **Permitted:** Children, drinking, limited smoking **Payment Terms:** Check MC/V [R05EPVT-15466] **COM Y ITC Member:** No

Rates:	Shared Bath 4
Single	$ 45.00
Double	$ 55.00

Hillside View Farm   South Rd 05455   **Fairfield VT**
Jacqueline Tretreault   **Tel: 802-827-4480**

Your chance to experience the excitement of "rolling hills" of a Vermont farm with beautiful year-round New England scenery. This charming home and hostess offers warmth and hospitality to all guests while visiting their working dairy farm. Just minutes from St Albans in a quiet village setting, you'll relish the peace and tranquility of this picturesque setting. Interesting and helpful hosts welcome you to New England and their farming life-style. And they'll make sure you see all the sights while here. A continental breakfast is included. Close to Stowe (an hour drive) and Montreal QU (two hour drive). **Seasonal:** No **Brochure:** Yes **Permitted:** Children **Languages:** French **Payment Terms:** Check [A05ACVT-2860] **COM Y ITC Member:** No

Rates:	Shared Bath 2
Single	$ 50.00
Double	$ 50.00

Silver Maple Lodge-Cottages   S Main St 05045   **Fairlee VT**
Scott & Sharon Wright   **Tel: 800-666-1946 802-333-4326**
                                                                                 Res Times 7am-10pm

Historic Bed & Breakfast Country Inn located in scenic four-season resort area in the Upper Connecticut River Valley between the Green Mountains and the White Mountains, built in the late 1700s. Choose one of the freshly renovated rooms in a quaint antique farmhouse or one of the knotty pine cottages with wide-plank floors made from lumber cut on the property. Guests can lounge on a wrap-around porch or picnic among the apple trees. All outdoor activities are here including lawn games of badminton, croquet, horseshoes and water sports at nearby Lake Morey and Lake Fairlee. (1 and 4 miles). Appalachian Trail, gliding and flying lessons and great cross country skiing are just a mile away and its just ten miles to a full downhill ski area. Vermont hospitality flourishes with these special hosts. A continental breakfast is included. AAA approved. **Packages:** Hot air balloon, Inn to Inn walking, bicycle or canoe, Summer Specials, Golf. **Discounts:** Senior Citizens, AAA, travel agents **Airport:** Burlington VT 80-mi **Seasonal:** No **Reservations:** One night's deposit 1-4 days, 50% deposit if longer, 14 day cancel policy for refund less $2 service fee. **Brochure:** Yes **Permitted:** Children, drinking, limited smoking **Conference:** Meetings to 15 persons. **Payment Terms:** Check AE/MC/V [A11DP-VT-2865] **COM Y ITC Member:** No

Rates:	Pvt Bath 12	Shared Bath 2
Single	$ 48-58.00	$ 38.00
Double	$ 52-62.00	$ 42-44.00

Blueberry Hill Inn   RD 3 05733   **Goshen VT**
Tony Clark   **Tel: 800-448-0707 802-247-6735**
                                                                                 Res Times 8am-10pm

Located in the tranquility of the Green Mountain National Forest, our twelve rooms are artistically fashioned with antiques, warm quilts and private baths. The greenhouse is just off the kitchen, with

National Edition — **Vermont**

brick walkway and every-blooming plants, bringing the outdoors inside. It is a favorite gathering place in winter with a cup of tea, a chocolate chip cookie and the warmth of the woodstove. With 75km of groomed and tracked trails, a full service ski shop and complimentary hot homemade soup offered each day, the Inn is a cross country skier's paradise. The activities are endless - with the famous New Years Eve night ski and bonfire on Hogback Mountain, to the American Ski Marathon. In summer, the ski trails are used for hiking, walking, running and mountain biking. In October, *Blueberry Hill* hosts the Knobby Rock, a cross country mountain bike race. And in July, the Annual Goshen Gallop, a 10km cross country run through some of the most scenic trails in Vermont. Dinner is served in our cozy dining room which boasts a large fieldstone fireplace and the imaginative upside-down garden of straw flowers and herbs hanging from the ceiling beams. There are four creative courses served in an unhurried pace, always using as many local producers as possible, including the *Blueberry Hill* gardens. Herbs, lettuces, vegetables and edible flowers all will grace the cuisine. Breakfast is an event also, served in courses beginning with juice, fruit, followed by homemade granola, a pastry and main course. As you exit the dining room, be sure to stop at the ever-full chocolate chip cookie jar, taking one to savor later on your walk or hike. Visit the blacksmith's shop next door for various *Blueberry Hill* items you can purchase - including the handcrafted coffee mugs, dried herbs and prints. In summer, step out the back door and pick blueberries to your heart's content or relax by the pond and take a swim. *"Come to Blueberry Hill Inn and share our special way of life."* **Discounts:** Groups, Corporate rates **Airport:** Burlington Intl-55 mi **Packages:** Cross Country Skiing **Reservations:** $45 per night per person deposit, refund only if rooms are re-rented *Rates based on MAP **Brochure:** Yes **Permitted:** Children, drinking (BYOB) **Conference:** Groups to forty persons **Languages:** French, Czech, German **Payment Terms:** Check MC/V [R08GPVT-2870] **COM Y ITC Member:** No

cross country skier's paradise

Rates:	Pvt Bath 12
Single	$ 84-105.00
Double	$ 168-210.00

Tyler Place	PO Box 45 05460	**Highgate Springs VT**
Tyler Family		Tel: 802-868-3301
		Res Times 8am-9pm

Built over 160 years ago, this restored sea captain's home invites guests to an old-style New England lodging surrounded by the charm of yesteryear while offering the convenience of today. This intimate setting, just a short stroll to scenic Nauset Beach on Cape Cod offers lantern-lit door-ways to nineteen rooms, each individually appointed in special colonial colors and authentic antiques. There are beamed ceilings, quilts, and old four poster beds. In addition, overlooking the Orleans Cove, is the Cove House with three rooms and a one-bedroom apartment and two housekeeping cottages offering the escape. Seclusion and serenity await the less adventure some vacationer at Nauset Beach, one of the finest in North America. Swimming pool on the premises is available to guests, with golf, horseback riding, tennis, lovely Cape Cod shopping and sightseeing nearby. **Seasonal:** Rates Vary **Reservations:** One night's deposit, balance upon arrival, min of two night's when Sat is included in-season, canc notice of 14 days for refund, *season 5/2-10/30, off season rates 25% lower **Brochure:** Yes **Permitted:** Children 12-up, drinking, smoking **Payment Terms:** Check [C12-CCVT-2878] **COM Y ITC Member:** No

Rates:	Pvt Bath 8	Shared Bath 3
Single	$ 78.00	$ 48.00
Double	$ 82-92.00	$ 52-70.00

Fitch Hill Inn	Fitch Hill Rd 05655	**Hyde Park VT**
Richard A Pugliese/Stanley Corklin		Tel: 800-639-2903 802-888-3834
		Res Times 8am-8pm

Historic elegance - at affordable rates! Charles Kuralt, on one of his much publicized tours, described Hyde Park as one of several villages in which he would be happy to live. Situated in the lovely Lamoille River Valley, on a hill overlooking the magnificent Green Mountains, *Fitch Hill Inn*

©Inn & Travel Memphis, Tennessee

Vermont *National Edition*

offers a special opportunity to enjoy the true Vermont experience. Set in four acres of woodland and central to Vermont's all-season vacation country, you can choose from any number of activities.

historic elegance . . .

You can ski, fish, hike, bike, canoe, play tennis or golf, visit a country auction or browse the many barn sales and antique shops. Four tastefully unique decorated guest rooms and one two bedroom suite with living room. A colonial dining room, a Federalist-style living room with fireplace and a comfortable library full of video tapes and books provided for your viewing and reading. A hearty complimentary breakfast is provided while four course candlelight gourmet dinners are prepared by your innkeeper, available at additional charge and with prior reservation. Whether for a night, weekend or an extended stay - you will find *Fitch Hill Inn* to be a very special place in a very special world. **Airport:** Burlington Intl-40 mi **Discounts:** Weekdays, extended stays, AAA **Packages:** Ski, Canoeing **Seasonal:** Yes, rates vary **Reservations:** One night's deposit, 14 day cancel policy for refund, late arrival only by prior arrangement **Brochure:** Yes **Permitted:** Children, drinking, no smoking **Conference:** For groups to ten persons **Languages:** Spanish, French **Payment Terms:** Check AE/MC/V [Z07HPVT1-2879] **COM U ITC Member:** No **Quality Assured:** Yes

Rates:	Pvt Bath 1	Shared Bath 4
Single	$ 75-95.00	$ 50-65.00
Double	$ 85-105.00	$ 59-75.00

Henry M Field House B&B Rt 2 Box 395 05465 Jericho VT
Mary Beth & Terrence Horan Tel: 802-899-3984
Res Times *See below

The picturesque New England village of Jericho is the setting for this beautiful Victorian Italianate circa 1875 offering guests all of the ambiance of the Victorian era. The interior features tall ceilings, ornamental plaster, etched glass, curved windows, large paneled doors and mouldings of mahogany and chestnut. Gleaming wood floors set-off the beautiful colors chosen for the rooms, each filled with period furnishings and lighting. From original sinks to sunlit entry foyer - you'll relax in wicker and palm-filled surroundings. The guest rooms offer queen size beds and period furnishings while the two parlors and library provide for relaxation or socializing with other guests. The dining room is large and family-style full breakfasts are served here or the outdoor porch in summer. Gardens and 3-1/2 acres of woods and meadow surround the home which is adjacent to Brown's River. Year-round activities at Mt Mansfield and nearby Lake Champlain include golf, cycling, swimming, hiking, skiing, boating with excellent antiquing and shopping available. Nearby schools include Univ of Vermont, Champlain College, Trinity College, Vermont College, St Michaels College and many others. Burlington is twelve miles. Your hosts enjoy meeting people and have flexible schedules to assure your comfortable stay. **Discounts:** Extended stays; $5 deduct if breakfast is not desired **Airport:** Burlington Intl **Packages:** When renting to groups for longer than two nights *Reservation Time: 7/1-8/30, 24 Hrs; 9/1-6/30, after 5pm *Closed: 12/23-1/3 **Seasonal:** *See below **Reservations:** 50% deposit of stay required, 14 day cancel policy less $5 service fee, minimum stay holidays & peak season, check-in after 10pm only with prior arrangement **Brochure:** Yes **Permitted:** Responsible children, drinking **Payment Terms:** Check MC/V [Z05HPVT1-10861] **COM U ITC Member:** No

Rates:	Pvt Bath 3
Single	$ 55-75.00
Double	$ 65-85.00

Inn At Long Trail Rt 4 Box 267 05715 Killington VT
The McGrath Family Tel: 800-325-2540 802-775-7181
Res Times 8am-11pm

Situated high in the Green Mountains of Vermont alongside the famous Appalachian and Long Trails which meet just a few hundred yards into the woods, from the Inn. Spectacular Fall foliage is every where at this elevation and in Winter, you're fortunate because you're right between Pico (1/4 mi) and Killington (1 mi) ski resort areas. This 1938 ski lodge setting was the first in Vermont! Everything is here for your leisure, including wood-panelled common rooms, candlelight dining areas,

©*Inn & Travel Memphis, Tennessee*

an Irish Pub, hot tub, wonderful year-round mountain views and fireplaces are in some of the guest rooms. New England specialties are offered at the restaurant on the premises and a full breakfast is included with your room. Owned and operated by the McGraths since 1977, this lovely Country Inn is perfect for travelers who love the natural setting at 2200 foot elevation. Immaculate rooms are sure to satisfy everyone. Nearby activities include antiquing and Vermont postcard scenery. Closed: 4/15-6/20 and 10/25-11/20. *Mid-week rates $46-98.00 and $294-384.00 MAP packages for winter weekends **Airport:** Burlington Intl-1-1/2 hrs; Albany-2-1/2 hrs **Seasonal:** See below **Reservations:** One night's deposit, 50% if more than one night, 14 day cancel policy, less $15 service fee **Brochure:** Yes **Permitted:** Children, drinking, limited smoking **Conference:** Yes for groups to 30 persons **Payment Terms:** AE/MC/V [A04GCVT-2889] **COM** Y **ITC Member:** No

Rates:	Pvt Bath 20
Single	$ 46-98.00
Double	$ 56-98.00

The Vermont Inn — Rt 4 05751 — **Killington VT**
Susan & Judd Levy — **Tel:** 800-541-7795 802-775-0708
Res Times 8am-10pm

The *Vermont Inn* is a small Country Inn located on six acres in the mountains of Killington. Originally a farmhouse built in 1840, the Inn provides country charm, a warm atmosphere and gourmet dining in a beautiful mountain setting. The parlor, lounge and dining room have fireplaces or wood-burning stoves. The dining room has spectacular views and a Three Diamond Award from AAA. The restaurant also won first place in Killington Korbel Champagne Dine-Around Contest in 1990 and 1991. The Inn's own herb garden provides fresh flavorings for many of the award-winning dishes. Specialties include fresh fish, veal and duckling. Everything is homemade including the herb rolls and desserts. An extensive wine list is available. Complimentary tea and warm cookies are offered every afternoon. This family operated Inn offers excellent year-round facilities including a sauna, hot tub, tennis court and swimming pool. Winter brings downhill skiing at Pico (2 mi) or Killington (8 mi). In summer and fall, guests enjoy lawn games, a PGA Championship Golf Course, summer theatre, ballet, farmer's market, Norman Rockwell Museum, great discount shopping and many other attractions. The Inn is centrally located in Vermont so guests can stay several days and easily tour the countryside with trips to nearby Woodstock, Manchester and Burlington. This is one of the few Inns in Vermont offering a handicap accessible room. **Discounts:** Yes, for 3 & 5 days stays **Airport:** Rutland-18 mi **Packages:** 3 & 5 days **Seasonal:** Clo 4/15-5/15 **Reservations:** 50% deposit at res time, 14 day cancel policy for refund less $25 service fee **Brochure:** Yes **Permitted:** Children 6-up, drinking, **Conference:** Yes for small group meetings including dining **Payment Terms:** Check AE/MC/V [I06EPVT-4842] **COM** Y **ITC Member:** No

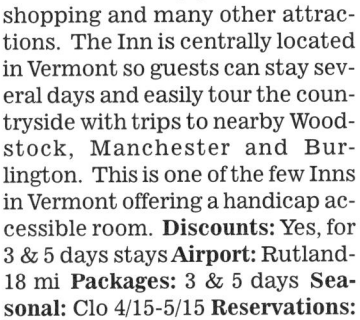

Rates:	Pvt Bath 15	Shared Bath 4
Single	$ 70-130.00	$ 60-90.00
Double	$ 80-150.00	$ 60-100.00

Echo Lake Inn — PO Box 154 05149 — **Ludlow VT**
Chip Connely/John & Yvonne Pardieu — **Tel:** 800-356-6844 802-228-8602 **Fax:** 802-228-3075
Res Times 7am-10pm

An Historic 1840's Country Inn with four stories and a gabled roof on a scenic route near Echo Lake and surrounded by spacious lawns, a tennis court and swimming pool. The twenty five guest rooms range from suites to family units have been individually decorated, some with antiques. Sit by the fire and read a book, enjoy a cocktail in the intimate lounge, or relax in one of the antique red rocking chairs on the front porch and watch the birds feeding in the evening. Stroll through the fall foliage, play a game of tennis, relax in the jacuzzi or take a steam bath before dinner. Take a picnic to Echo Lake Island in a complimentary canoe or hike, jog or bike through the woods. The full service dining room offers cocktails and a full wine list and features gourmet cuisine served by candlelight with porch dining dur-

Vermont   *National Edition*

ing the summer. Sample culinary delights such as fresh Lobster Ravioli, Rainbow Trout sauteed with artichoke hearts and sundried tomatoes, or our famous Roast Country Duckling. In the morning, enjoy a full breakfast with an omelette du jour, Vermont buttermilk pancakes or waffles with sauteed fresh fruit. **Airport:** Rutland-20 mi; Lebanon, NH-30 mi **Packages:** Fly Fishing, Skiing **Seasonal:** *See below **Reservations:** Deposit required *MAP, plus tax and service **Brochure:** Yes **Permitted:** Limited children, drinking, limited smoking **Conference:** Yes, groups to 12 **Payment Terms:** Check AE/DISC/MC/V [Z03HPVT1-4815] **COM YG ITC Member:** No

Rates:	Pvt Bath 11	Shared Bath 14
Single	$ 70-130.00	$ 59-101.00
Double	$ 118-260.00	$ 100-168.00

Inn At Highview   **Ludlow VT**
Greg Bohan   **Tel: 802-875-2724**

Refer to the same listing name under Andover, Vermont for a complete description. **Seasonal:** No **Payment Terms:** Check MC/V [M06HPVT1-17783] **COM YG ITC Member:** No

Rates:	Pvt Bath 8
Single	$ 80-115.00
Double	$ 90-125.00

Inn At Manchester   Rt 7A PO Box 41   05254   **Manchester VT**
Stan & Harriet Rosenberg   **Tel: 800-273-1793 802-362-1790 Fax: 802-362-3218**
                                                                         Res Times 8am-10pm

Welcome to this Historic Inn which was built in 1880 as a summer home and in succeeding years served as a private residence and as an Inn. This Victorian gem, listed on the *National Register of Historic Places*, was meticulously restored in 1978 by Stan and Harriet with over 450 rolls of wallpaper and countless gallons of paint. Their efforts returned the proud Inn to its former glory and elegance while adding the modern amenities guests expect when staying in a fine lodging. The Carriage House, built in 1867 was renovated in 1985 under the auspices of the Vermont Dept of Historic Preservation adding more guest rooms. Today, each guest room has a unique personality named for wildflowers growing in the meadow surrounding the Inn. Guests can choose the Blackeyed Susan, Blue Phlox, Sunflower, Primrose and others. A five-window view of the Green Mountains is seen from the Primrose Suite. Guests staying in the Carriage House and Inn will find original antique furnishings throughout - with a romantic star-gazing window set in the soaring ceilings of the Sweet William room. A full complimentary breakfast brings guests together each morning with a sample menu of fresh juice, homemade granola, old fashioned oatmeal, apple butter-milk pancakes with original Vermont Maple Syrup, sausage patty and plenty of hot beverages. Outdoor activities include swimming in the pool or the nearby abandoned Marble Quarry or Emerald Lake with sand beaches, boating and picnic areas. Bike enthusiasts will find complete packages and routes prepared by your hosts which include lunch stops and dinner. Winter brings excellent skiing at Bromley Mountain and Stratton areas. There's plenty of shopping at the factory outlets, entertainment, auctions, estate sales, craft shows and Robert Todd Lincoln's estate of Hildene for touring. **Airport:** Albany-70 mi **Discounts:** Corporate midweek 20% **Packages:** Ski & Stay, Stay & Play Summer Package, Golf, Tennis & Theatre, Mix & Match **Seasonal:** No **Reservations:** Two night's deposit except special occasions when full payment in advance is required; 14 day cancel policy less $5 service fee per room per night **Brochure:** Yes **Permitted:** Drinking, children over 8, smoking outdoors only **Conference:** Yes, perfect for Corporate Retreats and small conferences to groups of 25 persons **Payment Terms:** Check AE/DISC/MC/V [I04IPVT1-4859] **COM YG ITC Member:** No

©*Inn & Travel Memphis, Tennessee*

Rates: Pvt Bath 18
Single $ 95-110.00
Double $ 95-110.00

Manchester Highlands Inn	Highland Ave 05255	Manchester VT
Patricia & Robert Eichorn	**Tel:** 800-743-4565 802-362-4565 **Fax:** 802-362-4028	

Welcome to Manchester's best kept secret! Perched on a hill overlooking the town, away from the crowds, the *Manchester Highlands Inn* is unforgettable. Upon entering this lovely Victorian, you feel the special atmosphere with classical music in the background; Humphrey, the cat, curled up on the sofa and the aroma of something delicious baking in the oven. The Inn and Carriage House guest rooms have been recently refurbished with such amenities as feather beds, down comforters and lace curtains. The living room, sun-filled wicker room, game room and pub are comfortable spots for relaxing, snoozing or meeting fellow guests. In summer, you can laze by the pool, try croquet on the lawn or rock the evening away on the porch while enjoying the sunset over Mount Equinox. A full breakfast includes your host's selection of an entree such as Morning Glory Muffins, Banana Oat Bran Pancakes, Cheddar Souffles - all with plenty of Vermont syrup . . while afternoon brings delicious homemade snacks. Dinner available for parties of eight or more, with prior arrangements. As a year-round vacation destination, the famous Battenkill offers excellent fishing, canoeing, hiking and biking along beautiful back roads. Swimming, golf, tennis, craft fairs, antique car shows, polo, flea markets, country auctions and summer theatre and concerts make for a full day. Autumn brings brilliant sugar maple red and gold mantles - slowly turning winter's white with the first snow fall. Stratton and Bromley ski areas, just minutes away, offer miles of downhill and cross country skiing. Manchester's fine restaurants, shops and galleries await you - as does our warm and gracious hospitality. Sharing our home is what we like best - so please come and discover us - we won't be a secret for long! **Discounts:** Commercial, off-season, mid-week **Packages:** Mid-week, Ski, Christmas Prelude Weekends and others, inquire at res time **Seasonal:** No **Reservations:** One night or 50% of length of stay, deposit applied to last night of stay; 14 day cancel policy for refund less $10 service fee. Visit web site at: http//www.jover.net/~manhiinn. **Permitted:** Children, drinking **Conference:** Small groups 10-15 persons; perfect for family reunions, special celebrations and memorable business meetings. **Languages:** French, German **Payment Terms:** Check AE/MC/V [I04IPVT1-4860] **COM** YG **ITC Member:** No

Rates: Pvt Bath 15
Single $ 75-105.00
Double $ 95-135.00

Northfield Inn		Montpelier VT
Aglaia Stalb		**Tel:** 802-485-8558

Refer to the same listing name under Northfield, Vermont for a complete description. **Seasonal:** Rates vary **Payment Terms:** Check DISC/MC/V [M05HPVT1-17770] **COM** U **ITC Member:** No

Rates: Pvt Bath 8
Single $ 55-75.00
Double $ 75-85.00

Northfield Inn	27 Highland Ave 05663	Northfield VT
Aglaia Stalb		**Tel:** 802-485-8558

Restored to its original grand style, this lovely turn-of-the-century Victorian offers guests elegance and luxurious period furnishings and decor that includes all private baths, antiques and brass or carved wood beds with European feather bedding. Nestled in the heart of the Green Mountains, the *Northfield Inn* is just minutes from Montpelier, the state capital and Barre, the granite capital of the world. Framed by scenic mountains, the Inn is nestled on a hillside over-looking the village of Northfield and the historic campus of Norwich University, America's first private military college. Guests step back to an era of *"elegance, comfort and congeniality"* when *people had time for afternoon tea and pleasant conversation.* Our library, parlors, game room and formal dining room are filled with fine music and a cozy fire that will warm your heart and spirit on those chilly evenings. A complimentary hearty, old-fashioned multi-course breakfast begins your day. Panoramic views, scenic valleys, wildflower meadows, lovely gardens, bird songs, wind chimes and the outdoors can be enjoyed from the porch rockers. Northfield's historic district and charming village offers shopping and sightseeing, covered bridges, and a full offering of lawn games, mountain trails to explore, hiking, fishing, tennis, golf and an old swimming hole. There is sledding on our hillside, sleigh rides and cross country skiing. Winter brings world-class skiing at nearby Sugarbush, Mad River Glen or Stowe. **Discounts:** Groups & extended stays **Airport:** Burlington-37 mi **Packages:** Four Nights with breakfast in queen size bedroom $169.00 per person; Stay seven nights - the 7th night is free **Seasonal:** Rates vary **Reservations:** First and last night deposit required, late arrival only with prior arrangement, 14 day cancel policy for refund, two suites available **Brochure:** Yes **Permitted:** Children 15-up, BYOB social drinking, smoking outdoors & nearby kennel boarding can be arranged for pets **Conference:** Yes, groups to thirty persons **Languages:** Greek **Payment Terms:** Check DISC/MC/V [I05HPVT1-13626] **COM U ITC Member:** No

Rates: Pvt Bath 8
Single $ 55-75.00
Double $ 75-85.00

Brookside Farms   Hwy 22A 05760   Orwell VT
Joan & Murray Korda   Tel: 802-948-2727 Fax: 802-948-2015
                                                                        Res Times 24 hrs

This stately neo-classical Greek Revival mansion rests proudly with its shimmering white Ionic columns on a 300-acre working farm and celebrated its 200th Anniversary in 1989 - dating from 1789! Listed on the *National Register of Historic Places*, it has been meticulously restored and maintained as a fabulous showplace of yesterday's elegance while including today's conveniences. The main house and an adjacent guest house are furnished with classical antiques from its history. The guest house is part of the antique shop and everything is for sale - including the bed you sleep in! You can even try your hand at the first Bosendorfer piano brought into the USA before the war! Or browse through the extensive 10,000 volume library for a favorite novel. The full breakfast is a real treat offering farm-fresh eggs, maple syrup from the trees on the 300 acres and the tastiest bacon you've ever eaten - all prepared just to each guest's taste. Spend the day strolling the well manicured grounds with spectacular views and lush countryside. Boating and fishing are nearby, swimming, horseback riding, skiing, ice skating and your own cross-country trails right on the property. Sights include Morgan Horse Farm, Vermont Marble Exhibit, Frog Hollow Craft Center, Lake Champlain, Mount Independence and Fort Ticonderoga. Meals: Lunch and dinner available, all home prepared by your hostess **Discounts:** 10% to travel agents **Airport:** Burlington Intl **Pack-**

National Edition *Vermont*

ages: Yes, inquire at res time **Seasonal:** No **Reservations:** One night deposit at res time to hold room, two week cancellation policy *One suite available **Brochure:** Yes **Permitted:** Children, drinking, limited smoking **Conference:** Yes for groups to fifty persons **Languages:** French, Spanish, Italian, Hungarian, Russian, Greek, Hebrew, German **Payment Terms:** Check Travelers Check [I04HPVT1-7533] **COM** YG **ITC Member:** No

Rates:	Pvt Bath 2	Shared Bath 3
Single	$ 75-100.00	$ 50.00
Double	$ 125-150.00	$ 85.00

Gwendolyns B&B Rt 106 PO Box 225 05151 Perkinsville VT
Laurie, Win & Gwen Tel: 802-263-5248
Res Times 7am-12am

"We came to admire, We leave enchanted", Lynn Jordan, writer, Seattle Washington. Our 1872 Victorian, graced with veranda and grand curved stairway, opens it's doors, enter a romantic era, recapturing the charm and elegance of it's day. Fine linens and antiques enhance the ambience of this stately mansion. Each guest room has been given individual attention, adorned with canopy and timeless cherished treasures, patiently collected by Laurie over many years, with her dream of one day opening a B&B Inn, expressly in mind. Our Country water gardens lend certain charm. Take in the scent of our lovely flowers while relaxing by our fish pond, the perfect respite for the weary traveler, just what the doctor ordered! The aroma of home baking complements a distinctive breakfast always served on our finest antique china, silver and lovely linens. The attention and special service we offer is incomparable, evidence of the love and care we relish, welcoming travelers, our friends. Our warm-welcoming atmosphere *Welcomes you home*. Picnic lunches, BBQ, private dining room service available upon request and advance notice. Year-round activities include antiquing, art galleries, hiking, swimming, biking, downhill and cross country skiing and great New England dining within moments. By car: Albany or Hartford, 2-1/4 hrs, Boston, 2-1/2 hrs, Providence 3 hrs, New York 4-3/4 hrs, Philadelphia 6-1/2 hrs. Pickups by bus in Springfield VT, by train at Bellows Falls VT, by plane into Lebanon or Burlington VT and by private plane at Hartness Airport, just 2 miles from the Inn. **Discounts:** Check at res time for seasonal, promotional and midweek. **Packages:** Ski, Honeymoon, Equestrian **Reservations:** 50% deposit required within 7 days of booking. Train, bus and plane pick-ups available with advance notice. **Permitted:** Children, drinking, limited smoking, stable boarding available on premises **Conference:** Yes for groups to 16 persons for weddings, social and business functions. Phones, fax and copier available. **Languages:** Limited French **Payment Terms:** Check DC/MC/V [I02EPVT-14502] **COM** Y **ITC Member:** No

Rates:	Pvt Bath 4	Shared Bath 2
Single	$ 65.00	$ 60.00
Double	$ 92.00	$ 82.00

Inn At Weathersfield Rt 106 PO Box 165 05151 Perkinsville VT
Mary Louise & Ron Thorburn Tel: 800-477-4828 802-263-9217 Fax: 802-263-9219
Res Times 8am-11pm

Built in 1795, the Inn is a re-creation in architecture and spirit of the 1790's to the 1860's with exposed beams, period antiques and a functional cooking hearth with beehive bake oven. Here, Mary Louise master-minds complete meals using period recipes on winter holidays. High English tea, five-course Nouvelle Cuisine dinners, and four-course grand buffet breakfasts, included in your room rate, are served near one of the twelve working fireplaces. The Inn's own farm-raised pheasants and partridges are featured, along with fresh salmon, rack of lamb, filet mignon and a vegetarian stir fry, for example. Nestled at the base of Hawks Mountain on twenty-one acres, there are hiking trails, a pond for fishing and swimming, and horses for sleigh and carriage rides. Nearby recreational activities abound with hiking on Ascutney Mountain, Alpine and cross country skiing, two highly acclaimed golf courses, and tennis courts. Historic places to visit include the home and studio of

©*Inn & Travel Memphis, Tennessee* 1-115

America's most famous sculptor, Augustus St Gaudens; Robert Todd Lincoln's home and gardens; Billings Farm, a museum and farm depicting life in Vermont around 1890; Pres Coolidge's birthplace and summer White House; and Weston Priory's Benedictine Monks. The Inn's library of several thousand volumes keeps guests busy. The fitness center features aerobic equipment and a Finnish sauna. A fully licensed tavern, extensive wine cellar and two grand pianos providing nightly entertainment, round out the ultimate country inn experience. **Discounts:** Weekdays, multiple night stay, business. **Airport:** Boston Logan; Hartford Bradley Field, Lebanon NH

Packages: Five Day Stay beginning Sunday depart Friday, stay five nights, pay for four **Seasonal:** Yes **Reservations:** One night deposit on all reservations **Brochure:** Yes **Permitted:** Limited children, limited pets, drinking, limited smoking **Conference:** Two meeting rooms for groups to forty, including AV (projector, easel, boards, screens and etc **Languages:** German **Payment Terms:** Check AE/CB/DC/MC/V [I08GPVT-4978] **COM** Y **ITC Member:** No

Rates:	Pvt Bath 12
Single	$ 120-170.00 MAP
Double	$ 175-190.00 MAP

Parker House Inn/French Restaurant   16 Main St   05059   Quechee VT
Barbara & Walt Forrester   Tel: 802-295-6077

The *Parker House Inn*, a registered *National Historic Site*, was built in 1857 by Vermont Senator Joseph C Parker. The Ottaquechee River flows along the rear of the property. Each room is charming with furnishings that reflect the era. The guest rooms have private baths and either king or queen size beds. A sitting room with TV, VCR, books and games is available for guests use. The dining room and pub are lovely. A porch, shaded by an awning, is available for dining outside and featuring glorious sunsets! Breakfast is served in the sun-filled pub or porch, overlooking the Ottaquechee River. Your hosts combine their talents (Walt is a recent graduate of the Culinary Institute of America and Barbara is a pastry chef) - to prepare unforgettable dining. The cuisine can best be described as American Comfort. The menu is ever-changing and reflects seasonal ingredients and fresh local products. For starters, the grilled portabello mushrooms served on a spinach salad topped with warm Vermont goat cheese, is recommended. Entrees include Rack of Lamb, Moulard Duck Breast, Seared Sea Scallops, Vermont Rabbit and Lobster Ravioli topped with a lobster sauce. Dessert, especially the Creme Brubie, are to die for! Guests at the Inn enjoy club privileges at nearby Quechee Club. It has two 18 hole golf courses (one of which is rated #1 in Vermont), tennis, skiing, swimming and indoor and outdoor fitness centers. The area is a mecca for bikers, canoeing and fly fishing. The Inn is surrounded by quaint shops - including the famous glass artist Simon Pearce, next door! Located in the heart of the Green Mountains - spectacular views abound. **Packages:** Sports Widow, Golf, Tennis **Airport:** W Lebanon NH-10mi **Reservations:** One night deposit (50% if longer) to guarantee reservation, 10 day cancel policy for refund, early departures charged full rate for remaining days **Brochure:** Yes **Permitted:** Children, drinking **Payment Terms:** Check AE/MC/V [J12GPVT1-6485] **COM** U **ITC Member:** No

Rates:	Pvt Bath 7
Single	$ 100.00
Double	$ 125.00

National Edition   *Vermont*

Inn At Buck Hollow Farm		**Saint Albans VT**
Dody Young/Brad Schwartz		**Tel:** 802-849-2400
		Res Times 24 Hrs

Refer to the same listing name under Fairfax, Vermont for a complete description. **Seasonal:** No **Payment Terms:** Check MC/V [M05EPVT-15509] **COM** Y **ITC Member:** No

Rates:
Single
Double

Shared Bath 4
$ 45.00
$ 55.00

1860 House	School St 05672	**Stowe VT**
Innkeeper		**Tel:** 800-248-1860 802-253-5177
		Res Times 7am-11pm

Enjoy year-round activities in this Center Village residence, charmingly restored and listed on the *National Historic Register*. There are five beautifully furnished and a/c guest bedrooms, with private bath and a choice of king, queen and twin beds with firm mattresses and Vermont handmade quilts. All rooms are furnished with antiques or reproductions and silver accent pieces. A wonderful romantic retreat for couples. Guests enjoy friendly conversation in the sunny dining room or the spacious plant-filled living room or outside, on the patio surrounded by lovely flower gardens. There's a quiet reading nook in the living room, an antique writing or game table, an excellent upright piano, stereo with classical choices and a large comfy couch to relax before a crackling fire. Enjoy the nearby health club and pool at no additional cost, a six mile walking path and four tennis courts close-by for guests use. Just strolling distance to all the Stowe Village shops, restaurants and sights. A light breakfast includes fresh fruit, orange juice, fresh baked breads and pastries, whole grain cereals and hot beverages. Kitchen privileges, daily housekeeping services, along with plenty of parking, washer/dryer and a workroom for bikes on the premises are included. **Seasonal:** No **Reservations:** 50% of total due at booking time, balance due 30 days prior to arrival. 30 day cancel policy for refund less 10% service fee. **Brochure:** Yes **Permitted:** Children, drinking, limited pets, No Smoking. **Conference:** Yes when entire home is rented by one group **Languages:** German **Payment Terms:** Check MC/V [Z01DPVT-4936] **COM** Y **ITC Member:** No

Rates: Pvt Bath 5
Single $ 65-115.00
Double $ 85-115.00

Brass Lantern Inn	717 Maple St 05672	**Stowe VT**
Andy Aldrich		**Tel:** 800-729-2980 802-253-2229
		Res Times 7:30am-9:30pm

Enjoy a traditional Bed & Breakfast Inn surrounded by the Green Mountains. The Inn is an award-winning AAA 3-diamond and received the *1995 Gourmet Society of North America Award.* Included in this restoration of an early 1800's farmhouse and carriage barn are nine guest rooms, each room offers a private bath, planked floors, antiques and handmade quilts; fireplaces and whirlpool tubs are available in three guest rooms. The Inn is fully air-conditioned and rooms are individually heated. A full traditional Vermont breakfast awaits each guest, made with fresh Vermont products and produce. There are spectacular views of Mount Mansfield from the Inn. The Inn is located 1/2 mile from the village center of Stowe. Guests may engage in many activities, including skiing, biking, hiking, shopping, antiquing, golf, tennis, horseback riding and sightseeing. In the late afternoon, guests relax by the fireplace in the living room or watch the sunset over Mount Mansfield from the patio, while enjoying complimentary coffee, tea, hot chocolate and fresh-baked goods. In the evening, guests can sample one of the over forty restaurants in Stowe, the great nightlife and night skiing. Try one of our packages. Amenities include gym priv-

Vermont *National Edition*

ileges for stays of two or more days; a check-out day guest bathroom and shower. **Airport:** Burlington Intl-30 mi **Packages Discounts:** Ski, Alpine, Cross Country, Golf, Honeymoon, Sweetheart, Summer Fun, Dinner, Theater and others, inquire at res time **Seasonal:** Rates vary **Reservations:** Deposit required, refundable if cancelled 15 days prior to arrival, 30 days for Christmas season; arrival after 9pm only with prior arrangements **Brochure:** Yes **Permitted:** Children (adult environment normally), drinking **Conference:** Yes, for groups to twenty four **Payment Terms:** Check AE/MC/V [I04HPVT1-11172] **COM** YG **ITC Member:** No

Rates:	Pvt Bath 9
Single	$ 65-165.00
Double	$ 75-175.00

Edson Hill Manor   1303 Edson Hill Rd 05672   Stowe VT
Eric & Jane Landee   **Tel:** 800-621-0284 802-253-7371 **Fax:** 802-653-2694

A romantic Country Inn on a 300-acre private estate used for filming Alan Alda's *"The Four Seasons"*. Guest rooms include private bath, fireplaces and picture windows filled with mountain views. Take advantage of the swimming pool, the stocked stream, hiking trails and riding stable. There's tennis and golf nearby. Winter brings horseback riding, sleigh rides, cross country touring (rentals and lessons are available). Excellent cuisine - AAA and Mobile rated. Secluded location but close to all of Stowe's attractions. Meals: Meals available on the premises when on EP or MAP rate. **Seasonal:** No **Brochure:** Yes **Permitted:** Children, smoking and drinking **Conference:** Yes **Payment Terms:** Check AE/MC/V [A11CPVT-4940] **COM** Y **ITC Member:** No

Allen Alda's The Four Seasons

Rates:	Pvt Bath 25
Single	$ 90-120.00
Double	

Fitch Hill Inn   Stowe VT
Richard A Pugliese   **Tel:** 802-888-3834 802-888-3834

Refer to the same listing name under Hyde Park, Vermont for a complete description. **Seasonal:** Rates vary **Payment Terms:** Check AE/MC/V [M05-GPVT1-16413] **COM** U **ITC Member:** No

Rates:	Pvt Bath 1	Shared Bath 6
Single	$ 75-95.00	$ 50-63.00
Double	$ 85-105.00	$ 59-75.00

Logwood Inn   199 Edison Hill Rd 05672   Stowe VT
Melanie & Sam Kerr   **Tel:** 800-426-6697 802-253-7354

Lovely year-round resort in beautiful a New England country lodge secluded on five acres of lawn with mature trees and beautiful country gardens. Babbling mountain brook in your "own backyard" along with super year-round activities including World-Class alpine and cross country ski areas at Mount Mansfield (highest mountain in Vermont). Summer offers Championship 18-hole golf, riding, hiking, bike-touring, (with rentals available) canoeing and clay tennis courts. You can choose to relax in the heated pool or in front of the fieldstone fireplace in the handsome main lodge that still includes the original wide-plank floors, with open and comfortable sitting areas, separate TV lounge with cable, game room and a bar area (BYOB). Guest rooms are comfortably furnished and include handmade quilts for snuggling in winter! A full breakfast is included with dinner available, at added cost from 12/15-4/10. **Seasonal:** No **Reservations:** One night's deposit, 14 day cancel policy for refund. Late arrival notice appreciated. **Brochure:** Yes **Permitted:** Children, drinking, smoking **Payment Terms:** Check MC/V [A05FPVT-4950] **COM** Y **ITC Member:** No

Rates:	Pvt Bath 25	Shared Bath 4
Single	$ 70-90.00	$ 55-65.00
Double	$ 70-90.00	$ 55-65.00

National Edition *Vermont*

Thatcher Brook Inn — Stowe VT
Pete & Kelly Varty
Tel: 800-292-5911 802-336-5911
Res Times 10am-11pm

Refer to the same listing name under Waterbury, Vermont for a complete description. **Seasonal:** No **Payment Terms:** Check DISC/MC/V [M11CPVT-8424] **COM** Y **ITC Member:** No

Rates:	Pvt Bath 24
Single	$ 60-115.00
Double	$ 75-165.00

Strong House Inn — Rt 22A 05491 — Vergennes VT
*Mary & Hugh Barigiel
Tel: 802-877-3337
Res Times 7am-10m

Experience New England in this comfortable, elegant lodging, c1834 Federal-style home on the *National Register of Historic Places*. Built by Samuel Paddock Strong, the son of General Samuel Strong who directed the Vermont militia at the Battle of Plattsburgh during the war of 1812 and who made his mark in banking and railroads. Located in the Lake Champlain Valley on a slight ridge which commands fine views of the Green Mountains to the east and the Adirondack Range to the west, the Strong family passion for building grand houses is reflected in this elegant residence. Some of the interior details include the free-standing main staircase with curly maple railings, the formal fireplace over which a portrait of Samuel Strong as a young man hangs and the elegant mouldings and doors throughout. The residence has been tastefully decorated with antiques, family heirlooms and handcrafts to portray the feeling and spirit of Vermont. A full breakfast is included along with other meals available with prior notice. Centrally located to enjoy all of Vermont's year-round sights and pleasures, guests are just seven miles from the shores of Lake Champlain and 30 miles from Sugarbush/Mad River Valley Ski areas. The Vermont outdoors offers brisk mountain streams, canoeing, hiking Mount Philo, cycling the gently rolling hills and valleys, wandering down country lanes during Vermont's incomparable fall foliage and an unparalled variety of alpine and cross country ski trails. Cultural and heritage activities offer the renowned Vermont Mozart Festival, village band on the greens, Champlain Shakespeare Festival and Shelburne Museum with 35 historic buildings, the nation's oldest village museum. Vermont's fine restaurants, art galleries and country antique auctions round-out an unforgettable trip which brings travelers back again and again. **Seasonal:** No **Reservations:** $45 deposit per room night to confirm res with 14 day cancel policy for refund **Brochure:** Yes **Permitted:** Children, limited drinking **Payment Terms:** Check AE/MC/V [I06GPVT-4961] **COM** Y **ITC Member:** No

Rates:	Pvt Bath 5	Shared Bath 2
Single	$ 80.00-up	$ 65.00-up
Double	$ 80.00-up	$ 65.00-up

Newtons 1824 House Inn — Rt 100 Box 159 05673 — Waitsfield VT
Lawrence & Susan McKay
Tel: 800-426-3986 802-496-7555 **Fax:** 802-496-5124

Enjoy relaxed elegance. On the Mad River are fifty-two scenic acres in the heart of Vermont's best ski area. This white clapboard historical, two-story "telescope" farmhouse with 10 gables offers the warm charm of yesteryear. Antiques and period furniture fill each room along with Oriental rugs gracing the floors and museum-quality art adorning the walls, all creating an atmosphere of warmth and elegance. The Inn was featured in *"Los Angeles Times"*, *"Glamour"*, *"Skiing"* and *"Vermont Life"* '93 publications. Awake from behind the soft, puffy continental quilt in the morning to the smell of fresh muffins baking and see the picture-perfect views of winter's blanket of snow or the magical colors of autumn in this natural wonderland. Your hosts prepare gourmet breakfasts of souffle, blueberry pancakes with pure Vermont maple syrup and fresh squeezed orange juice served in the sunny dining room or on the porch overlooking a lovely setting. Outdoors, guests can try a dip

Vermont   *National Edition*

in the Inn's swimming hole, catch a trout or two or picnic along the river bank. Year-round activities include all the sports (Sugarbush, Stowe, Mad River Glen) and sights (Ben & Jerry's, Lake Champlain and the Trapp Family Lodge) within easy driving distance. AAA 3-Diamond, Mobile 2-Star **Packages:** Sun-Thur 5 weekday stay, less 20% **Airport:** Burlington VT 30 mi **Seasonal:** No **Reservations:** 50% deposit, 14 day cancel policy for refund, full daily rate charged on late arrivals or early departures **Brochure:** Yes **Permitted:** Limited children, limited drinking **Languages:** Spanish **Payment Terms:** Check AE/MC/V [I07G-PVT-8365] **COM Y ITC Mem-ber:** No

Rates: **Pvt Bath 6**
Single $ 65-115.00
Double $ 75-125.00

Northfield Inn   Waitsfield/Warren VT
Aglaia Stalb   Tel: 802-485-8558

Refer to the same listing name under Northfield, Vermont for a complete description. **Seasonal:** Rates vary **Payment Terms:** Check DISC/MC/V [M05HP-VT1-17771] **COM YG ITC Member:** No

Rates: **Pvt Bath 8**
Single $ 55-75.00
Double $ 75-85.00

White Rocks Inn   RD 1 Box 297   05773   Wallingford VT
June & Alfred Matthews   Tel: 802-446-2077

Escape to this century old elegant farmhouse whose renovation carefully preserved the wide board floors, wainscoting, ornate moldings and high ceilings. Rooms are lovingly decorated and furnished with antiques, oriental carpeting and canopied beds with the convenience of modern private baths. Panoramic view of the White Mountains across a valley setting brings guests to nature everywhere they turn. A country breakfast is served outdoors in summer overlooking the spotted cows that graze nearby and in winter guests relax in the antique furnished dining room. Guests can enjoy wintry horse drawn sleigh rides. **Seasonal:** Closed Nov **Reservations:** One night's (or 50% if longer than one night) with 14 day cancel policy, full deposit forfeited if cancelled less than 48 hrs. **Brochure:** Yes **Permitted:** Children 10-up, BYOB drinking **Languages:** French and Spanish (some) **Payment Terms:** Check MC/V [X06BCVT-4972] **COM Y ITC Member:** No

Rates: **Pvt Bath 5**
Single $ 70-95.00
Double $ 70-95.00

Grunberg Haus   RR 2 Box 1595 Rt 100S   05676   Waterbury VT
Mark Frohman/Christopher Sellers   Tel: 800-800-7760 802-244-7726
           Res Times 10am-10pm

Bavaria in Vermont! This picture-postcard Tyrolian-style B&B is tucked on a hillside in Vermont's Green Mountains and is the perfect location to reach Stowe (six miles), Smugglers' Notch, family-style Bolton Valley, Mad River Glen and Sugarbush just down the road. Wonderful views are offered year-round from the traditional wood balcony extending around the stucco and wood-trimmed chalet while inside the giant stone fireplace is a favorite gathering place for guests. Individually decorated guest rooms include antiques, quilts, cozy comforters and collectibles - with all rooms opening onto the balcony. A morning wake-up call from the Guinea hens (they also provide the fresh eggs) announces a full gourmet breakfast with frequent selections of spiced fruit bowl, apple cheddar muffins, lemon-ricotta pancakes or grape fruit ambrosia, pancake bread or ginger cakes! Guests come back just for breakfast. The evening fire warms up the Steinway Grand, Chris (a professional vocalist) and all guests so inclined to participate. Activities include spectacular autumn leaf-peaking, cross country skiing on the premises, golf, boating, bicycling, soaring, canoeing, hiking, antiquing, outlet shopping and visiting Ben & Jerry's ice cream factory.

Evening home-style dinners are available with prior arrangements and additional cost. **Discounts:** Seniors, extended stays, travel industry **Airport:** Burlington Intl-23 mi; Burlington Amtrak and bus-3 mi **Packages:** Ski Escape: Lifts, lodging, meals and fireside entertainment, Sweet Deal: Lodging, meals, wine, candy, Bed & Jerry's factory tour, Golf Getaway: Green fees, meals, lodging **Seasonal:** Rates vary **Reservations:** Deposit required, 14 day cancel policy less service fee, no-shows will be billed room rate plus tax **Brochure:** Yes **Permitted:** Limited children, limited smoking, drinking **Conference:** For groups to twenty-five **Payment Terms:** Check AE/DISC/MC/V[I11EPVT-2849] **COM** Y **ITC Member:** No

Rates:	Pvt Bath 5	Shared Bath 10
Single	$ 45-85.00	$ 35-55.00
Double	$ 75-135.00	$ 55-85.00

Inn At Blush Hill Blush Hill Rd 05676 **Waterbury VT**
Pam & Gary Gosselin Tel: 800-736-7522 802-244-7529
Res Times 9am-9pm

The *Inn at Blush Hill* was once a stagecoach stopover between Waterbury and Stowe, and now this c1790 Cape Cod is a haven for travellers seeking comfort and hospitality. Select a book from the library and curl-up in a comfortable chair in one of the Inn's many common rooms. The living room, with a roaring fire on chilly days, invites guests to relax on the overstuffed couches. The dining room, with antiques and wide-planked floors also has a fireplace and chairs for reading or chatting. There is a large front porch with rockers to watch the golfers on the adjacent nine hole public course or view the manicured perennial gardens. Nearby you can swim, fish or canoe on an 880 acre reservoir. The cozy guest rooms are filled with country antiques and coordinating fabrics and wallpapers.

There are fresh flowers in the summer and heated mattress pads in the winter. One room offers a working fireplace, another, spectacular mountain views. A full country breakfast is included. **Seasonal:** No **Reservations:** Advance payment or guarantee with credit card, 12 day cancel policy except 9/15-10/15 & holidays when 21 day cancel policy required for refund. **Brochure:** Yes **Permitted:** Children 7-up, drinking, limited smoking **Conference:** Yes for groups to ten persons **Payment Terms:** Check AE/MC/V[Z11CPVT-4976] **COM** Y **ITC Member:** No

Rates:	Pvt Bath 4	Shared Bath 2
Single	$ 60-100.00	$ 50-80.00
Double	$ 65-110.00	$ 55-85.00

Thatcher Brook Inn Rt 100 Rd #2 Box 62 05676-0490 **Waterbury VT**
Pete & Kelly Varty Tel: 800-292-5911 802-244-5911
Res Times 10am-11pm

An exquisitely restored Victorian gem that's listed on *Vermont's Register of Historic Buildings* offers guests a true romantic New England experience. No expense was spared in the construction of this beautiful example of Victorian architecture including unique touches of a beautiful hand carved fireplace and stairway that remain intact today. Numerous kinds of woods are used throughout and include oak, bird'seye maple, spruce, quarter-sawn maple, cherry and birch - all tastefully blended together. One of the most striking features of the Inn is the twin gazebo-type front porch which overlooked the railroad cars which use to pass the front yard on the way to Stowe. Things remain much the same today - enjoying another era and experiencing fine gourmet dining, Yankee hospitality and the pleasant year-round seasonal changes. A deluxe continental breakfast is included with each overnight stay. Rooms with fireplaces or whirlpools are available. Nearby there's skiing, biking, hik-

Vermont *National Edition*

ing, golf, tennis, riding, fishing, canoeing, gliding and fine antiquing. **Seasonal:** No **Reservations:** 50% of stay must be received within 7 days of booking, 10 day cancel policy less $10 service fee, **Brochure:** Yes **Permitted:** Children 6-up, smoking **Conference:** Yes for groups to 75 persons for weddings, social and business **Payment Terms:** Check DISC/MC/V [I11DPVT-7040] **COM** Y **ITC Member:** No

Rates:	Pvt Bath 24
Single	$ 60-115.00
Double	$ 75-165.00

Weathervane Lodge 57 Dorr Fitch Rd 05356 **West Dover VT**
Liz & Ernie Chabot **Tel: 802-464-5426**

A true *"year-round resort"* Weathervane Lodge is a paradise of outdoor activities as a getaway for couples and full family vacations. Only four miles from Mount Snow Haystock and Corinthia for Alpine skiing in winter, summer offers wonderful mountain biking uphill and over seventy miles of cross country trails throughout the valley - including trails beginning just outside the back door! This Tyrolean-style ski lodge is decorated with authentic antiques and a warm blend of colonial and modern charm. Guests are welcomed to make themselves at home in the lounge, dining and recreation room with a cozy fireplace, BYOB bar (complimentary set-ups are provided) and microwave for snacks. Summer brings lakeside swimming, boating, fishing, tennis, golf (three nearby courses) horseback riding, museums and the Marlboro Music Festival. The spectacular Fall Foliage shouldn't be missed. Tranquility is assured on the spacious landscaped grounds that include outdoor picnic tables and a gas grill for cooking. Your *hosts are "seasoned" pro's, hosting guests for the past thirty-two years from all over the world.* **Airport:** Hartford, 1-1/2 Hr; Albany, 1-1/2 Hr **Packages:** Off Season Midweek **Seasonal:** No **Reservations:** $50 deposit per room at res time, 7 day cancel policy for full refund **Brochure:** Yes **Permitted:** Children, drinking, limited smoking **Payment Terms:** Check [I04HPVT1-4985] **COM** U **ITC Member:** No

Rates:	Pvt Bath 4	Shared Bath 5
Single	$ 50-64.00	$ 25-32.00
Double	$ 50-64.00	$ 25-32.00

Stonecrest Farm B&B 119 Christian St 05088 **Wilder VT**
Gail Sanderson **Tel: 800-730-2425 802-295-2600 Fax: 802-295-1135**

Located 3.5 miles from Dartmouth College in

GUESTS INCLUDED
PRESIDENT
COOLIDGE AND
AMELIA EARHART

Hanover New Hampshire, this gracious historic 1810 country home with handsome barns was formerly a dairy farm. Here, Arthur Stone, a prominent local citizen, entertained guests such as President Coolidge and Amelia Earhart. *Stonecrest*, in a village on the Connecticut River, is convenient to many year-round recreation and cultural activities. We participate in a summer "inn-to-inn" two-day canoeing trip. Your well-traveled host, a former headmaster's wife and a practicing attorney, has welcomed many Dartmouth alumni and parents, and visitors as far away as China. Six graciously decorated guest rooms, all with private

©*Inn & Travel Memphis, Tennessee*

baths, are furnished comfortably with antiques, down comforters, quilts and lots of reading material. Choose a queen bed, a canopied double bed or twin beds all with private baths. Apres ski, bikes or hikes, snuggle-up with a book next to the fireplace, play the baby grand. Scout the antique shops. In warm weather, relax on our stone terrace, surrounded by flowers and fine old trees. Savor nearby views of New Hampshire mountains. Enjoy a full breakfast of vegetable frittata, filled french toast, berry pancakes, homemade scones, muffins, fresh fruit and such in our sunny dining room. **Discounts:** Week stays get last night free **Airport:** Lebanon-4 mi, connects to Boston, New York **Packages:** Inn-to-Inn Trips **Seasonal:** No **Reservations:** Credit card deposit to guarantee, 14 day cancel policy for refund less $10 service fee; check-in 3-7pm **Brochure:** Yes **Permitted:** Children 8+, drinking **Languages:** Limited German, French **Payment Terms:** Check AE/MC/V [I11HPVT1-16460] **COM** YG **ITC Member:** No

Rates:	Pvt Bath 6
Single	$ 90-105.00
Double	$ 105-120.00

Charleston House   21 Pleasant St 05091   Woodstock VT
Bill & Barb Hough
Tel: 802-457-3843
Res Times 8am-9pm

Fine craftsmanship and beautiful surroundings combine with warmth and hospitality reminiscent of a family homecoming. This 1835 Greek Revival townhouse is listed on the *National Historic Register* and is located in the picturesque Village of Woodstock - regarded as one of the most beautiful villages in the USA by National Geographic Magazine. Completely restored to provide modern comfort along with maintaining historic authenticity, the Inn offers period antique furnishings, fine reproductions and an eclectic selection of art and Oriental rugs. In Woodstock, you can leave your car parked and walk throughout the town, listening to the Revere Bells ring out on the hour, sit on a river bank watching the water slide by, relax on the town Green - the site of winter yule festivals and summer social events, as well as relaxed conversation between villagers. A hearty full breakfast at our common table or a continental breakfast in bed and hospitality usually extended only to "kith and kin" which become cherished memories as year pass. **Airport:** Lebanon NH-15 mi **Discounts:** Mid-week reservation **Brochure:** Yes **Permitted:** Drinking, limited children **Payment Terms:** Check AE/MC/V [R10EPVT-5010] **COM** Y **ITC Member:** No

Rates:	Pvt Bath 7
Single	$ 90.00
Double	$ 145.00

Woodstocker B&B   Rt 4 05091   Woodstock VT
Jerry & JaNoel Lowe
Tel: 802-457-3896   Fax: 802-457-4432
Res Times 24 hrs

Located in a historic colonial New England village, this inviting and charming Bed & Breakfast offers great New England warmth and hospitality. The nine guest rooms are comfortably furnished and spacious while reflecting New England decor. There are two suites which include a living room, kitchen and deck for the ideal setting for an intimate family vacation. Year-round activities are at your doorstep: skiing, fishing, biking, hiking, swimming and a sports center for racquetball and other indoor activities. At day's end, you can plan your evening events while refreshing in the whirlpool and enjoying your favorite beverage and snack. Common rooms include TV, a wide array of fascinating books and plenty of board games. **Meals:** A complimentary breakfast buffet includes fresh fruit, homemade cereals, quiche, breads and muffins. **Seasonal:** Rates vary **Reservations:** 50% deposit at res time with 14 day cancel policy. **Brochure:** Yes **Permitted:** Drinking, limited children **Conference:** For groups to 25 persons are well organized and welcomed **Languages:** Italian **Payment Terms:** Check MC/V [Z05FPVT-5012] **COM** Y **ITC Member:** No

Rates:	Pvt Bath 9
Single	$ 60-110.00
Double	$ 65-120.00

Connecticut *Bold Name - Description appears in other section*

CONNECTICUT

Ashford
Henrietta House B&B
860-429-0031

Ashford/Strafford
Buck Homestead

Bantam
Rockwood Farm B&B

Barkhamsted
Rose & Thistle Inn
203-379-4744

Bethlehem
Dutch Moccasin B&B
203-266-7364

Eastover Farm B&B
203-266-5740-[Y--]

Bolton
Jared Cone House
203-643-8538-[Y--]

Bristol
Chester Village B&B
860-526-9770

Chimney Crest Manor
860-582-4219

Four Roses Guest Inn
860-572-0211

Brooklyn
Barrett Hill Farm

Tannerbrook
860-774-4822

Chester
Inn At Chester
800-949-STAY

Clinton
Captain Dibbell House
860-669-1646

Colchester
Hayward House Inn
860-537-5772

Cornwall Bridge
Cornwall Inn & Restaurant
800-786-6884

Cos Cob
Harbor House Inn
203-661-5845

Coventry
Maple Hill Farm B&B
800-742-0635

Mill Brook Farm B&B
860-742-5761

Deep River
Riverwind Inn
860-526-2014-[Y--]

Durham
Daniel Merwin House B&B
860-349-8415

Durham B&B
860-349-3513

East Haddam
Bishops Gate
860-783-1677

Gelston House
860-873-1411

Stonecroft Inn
860-873-1754

Whispering Winds Inn
860-526-3055

East Hartford
Town Hall Inn
860-528-1776

East Killingly
Holland House

East Lyme
Red House

The Island

East Windsor
Stephen Potwine House
860-623-8722

Essex
Griswold Inn
860-767-1776

Farmington
Barney House
860-677-9735

Glastonbury
Butternut Farm
860-633-7197

Greenwich
Homestead Inn
203-869-7500-[Y--]

Stanton House Inn
203-869-2110

Groton Long Point
Shore Inne
860-536-1180-[Y--]

Hartford
Cobbie Hill Farm
203-379-0057

Mark Twain B&B
860-231-1475

Old Mill Inn
203-763-1473-[G--]

Ivoryton
Copper Beech Inn
860-767-0330

Ivoryton Inn
860-767-0422

Kent
1741 Saltbox Inn
860-927-4376

Chaucer House
860-927-4858

Constitution Oak Farm
860-354-6495

Country Goose B&B
860-927-3040

Flanders Arms
860-927-3040

Kent (Litchfield Hill)
Fif'n Drum Inn
860-927-3509

Lakeville
Wake Robin Inn
860-435-2515

Ledyard
Abbeys Lantern Inn
860-572-0483

Applewood Farms Inn
860-536-2022

Litchfield
Litchfield Inn
860-567-4503

On The Green
860-567-9151

Tollgate Hill Inn
860-567-4545-[Y--]

Madison
Dolly Madison Inn
203-245-7377

Madison B&B
203-245-0896

Madison Beach Hotel
203-245-1404

Stevens Inn At Cafe Lafayette

Tidewater Inn
203-245-8457

Manchester
Duck Harbor
860-783-3495

Middlebury
Tucker Hill Inn
203-758-8334-[Y--]

Middletown
Buckleys B&B
860-346-8479

Rowson House
860-346-8479

Moodus
Fowler House
860-873-8906

Mystic
Adams House
800-321-0433

Brigadoon B&B
860-536-3033

Comolli House
203-536-8723

Harbour Inne & Cottage
860-572-9253

Inn At Mystic
800-237-2415

Pequot Hotel B&B

Bold Name - Description appears in other section **Connecticut**

860-572-0390

Red Brook Inn
860-572-0349

Steamboat Inn
860-536-8300

Whalers Inne
203-536-1506

New Canaan
  Maples Inn
  203-966-2927-[Y--]

  Melba B&B Inn
  203-966-8413

  Roger Sherman Inn
  203-955-4541

New Hartford
  Highland Farm B&B
  860-379-6029

New Haven
  Inn At Chapel Hill West
  203-777-1201

New London
  Griffin House
  860-447-9797

  Lighthouse Inn
  860-443-8411

  Queen Anne & Antiques
  800-347-8818

New Milford
  Buck Rock Inn
  860-354-9831

  Heritage Inn
  860-354-8883

  Homestead Inn
  860-354-4080

New Preston
  Birches Inn
  860-868-0229

  Boulders Inn
  860-868-0541

  Hopkins Inn
  860-868-7295

  Inn On Lake Waramagu
  800-LAKE-INN

Newton
  Hawley Manor Inn
  860-426-4456

Noank
  Palmer Inn
  860-572-9000

Norfolk
  Blackberry River Inn
  860-542-5100

  Greenwoods Gate
  860-542-5439-[Y--]

  Manor House
  860-488-5690-[Y--]

  Mountain View Inn
  860-542-5595

  Weavers House
  860-542-5108

North Stonington
  Antiques & Accommodations
  860-535-1736

  Randalls Ordinary
  860-599-4540

Norwalk
  Silvermine Tavern
  203-847-4558

Norwich
  Norwich Inn & Spa
  800-892-5692

Old Greenwich
  Harbor House Inn
  203-637-0145-[G--]

Old Lyme
  Bee & Thistle Inn
  800-622-4946

  Hidden Meadow Inn
  860-434-8360

  Janes B&B
  860-434-7269

  Old Lyme Inn
  860-434-2600-[Y--]

Old Mystic
  Old Mystic Inn B&B
  860-572-9422

Old Saybrook
  Sandpiper Inn
  860-399-7973

Saybrook Point Inn
800-243-0212

Plainfield
  French Renaissance ConnecticutHouse
  860-564-3277

Plymouth
  Shelton House B&B
  860-283-4616

Pomfret
  Clark Cottage At Wintergreen
  860-928-5741

  Cobbscroft
  860-928-5560

Pomfret Center
  Karin In B&B
  860-928-5492

  Selah Farm
Portland
  Croft
  203-342-1856

Putnam
  Felshaw Tavern
  860-982-3467

  Kings Inn
  860-928-7961

  Thurber House
  860-928-6776

Quinebaug
  Captain Parkers Inn At Quinebaug
  800-707-7303-[G-QAR-]

Ridgefield
  Elms Inn
  203-438-2541

  Farview Manor
  203-438-4753

  Horse Shoe Farm

  Marley B&B
  203-438-9486

  Stonehenge
  203-438-6511

  West Lane Inn
  203-438-7323

Salisbury
  Ragamont Inn

860-435-2372

Undermountain Inn
860-435-0242

White Hart Inn
860-435-0030

Yesterdays Yankee
860-435-9539

Sharon
  1890 Colonial B&B
  860-364-0436

  Alexanders B&B
  800-727-7292

Sherman
  Barnes Hills
  860-354-4404

Simsburg
  Simsbury House
  800-TRY-1820

Simsbury
  Merrywood B&B
  860-651-1785

Somers
  Victorian Sentiment
  860-763-2762

Somersville
  Old Mill Inn
  860-763-1473-[Y--]

South Windsor
  Cumon Inn
  860-644-8486

South Woodstock
  Inn At Woodstock Hill
  860-928-0528

Southington
  Chaffees B&B

Staffordville
  Winterbrook Farm
  860-684-2124

Stamford
  Inn At Mill River

  Windswept Farm Inn
  203-332-4984

Stonington
  Farnan House
  860-535-0634

Stonington Village
  Lasburys B&B

©Inn & Travel Memphis, Tennessee

Connecticut - Maine

Bold Name - *Description appears in other section*

860-535-2681

Storrs
Altavegh Inn
860-429-4490

Farmhouse On The Hill
860-429-1400

Thompson
Cortiss Inn
860-935-5652

Lord Thompson Manor
860-923-3886

Samuel Watson House
860-399-7565

Taste Of Ireland
860-923-2883

Tolland
English Lane B&B
860-871-6618

Old Babcock Tavern
860-875-1239

Tidewater Inn
860-872-0800

Tolland Inn
860-872-0800

Torrington
Yankee Peddler Inn
860-489-9226

Uncasville
1851 Guest House
860-848-3849

Warren
Evies Turning Point Inn
860-868-7775

Turning Point Farm

Waterbury
House On The Hill
203-757-9901

Seventy Hillside B&B
203-596-7070

Watertown
Clarks

Graham House

860-274-2647

West Cornwell
Hilltop Haven B&B
860-672-6871

West Hartford
Yankee B&B
860-561-1006

West Mystic
Bakers River Lodge
860-536-7296

Leventhal B&B

West Woodstock
Ebenezer Stoddard House
860-974-2552

Westbrook
Capt Stannard House
860-399-4634-[Y--]

Talcott House
860-399-5020

Welcome Inn
860-399-2500

Westport
Antique House
203-454-2727

Cotswold Inn
203-226-3766

Inn At Longshore
203-226-3316

Wethersfield
Chester Bulkley House
860-563-4236-[Y--]

Windsor
Charles R Hart House
860-688-5555

Winsted
B&B By The Lake
860-738-0230

Provincial House
860-379-1631

Woodbury
Curtis House
203-263-2101

Merryvale B&B Inn
203-266-0800

Woodstock
Captain Parkers Inn At Quinebaug
800-707-7303-[G--]

English Neighborhood
860-928-6959

Inn At Woodstock Hill
860-928-0528

Abbott Village
Elderberry Inn
207-876-4901

MAINE

Addison
Pleasant Bay B&B
207-483-4490

Alfred
Blue Door Inn
207-490-2353

Hirams House
207-490-1126

Old Berry Inn
207-324-0603

Andover
Andover Arms B&B
207-392-4251

Aquia
Inn At Cold Stream Pond
207-732-3595

Augusta
Willows B&B
207-495-7753

Bailey Island
Captain York House B&B
207-833-6224

Driftwood Inn
207-833-5461

Johnson House
207-833-6053

Lady & The Loon
207-833-6871

Log Cabin Lodging
207-833-5546

Bangor
Country Inn
207-941-0200

Phenix Inn
207-947-3850-[Y--]

Bar Harbor
Atlantean Inn
207-288-3270

Bass Cottage, In The Field
207-288-3705

Bay Ledge Inn & Spa
207-288-4204

Bayview Inn & Hotel
800-356-3585-[Y--]

Black Friar Inn
207-288-5091

Breakwater 1904
800-238-6309

Briarfield Inn
207-288-5297

Canterbury Cottage
207-288-2112

Castlemaine Inn c1865
207-288-4563

Cleftstone Manor
800-962-9762

Cove Farm Inn
207-288-5355

Graycote Inn
800-GRA COTE

Hearthside Inn
207-288-4533

Heathwood Inn
207-288-5591

Holbrook House
800-695-1120-[Y--]

Kay Lodging
207-288-3531

Kedge
207-288-5180

Ledgelawn Inn
207-288-4596

Manor House Inn
800-437-0088

1-126

©Inn & Travel Memphis, Tennessee

Bold Name - Description appears in other section *Maine*

Maples
207-288-3443

Mira Monte Inn & Suites
800-553-5109-[Y--]

Morgan House Inn
207-288-4325

Nannau-Seaside B&B
207-288-5575

Pachelbel Inn
207-288-9655

Primrose Cottage Inn
207-288-4031

Ridgeway Inn
207-288-9682

Shady Maples
207-288-3793

Stratford House Inn
207-288-5189-[Y--]

Thornhedge Inn
207-288-5398

Tides
207-288-4968

Town Guest Huose
800-458-8644

Ullikana In The Field
207-288-9552-[Y--]

Wayside Inn
207-288-5703

White Columns Inn
207-288-4648

Bass Harbor
Barr Harbor Inn
207-244-5157

Bass Cove Farm B&B
207-244-3460

Little Island House
207-244-4021

Pointy Head Inn
207-244-7261

Bath
1024 Washington B&B
207-443-5202

Bath B&B
207-443-4477

Elizabeths B&B
207-443-1146

Glad II
207-443-1191

Granes Fairhaven Inn
207-443-4391-[Y--]

Inn At Bath
207-443-4294

Packard House B&B
207-443-6069

Sebastian & Friends

Belfast
Adaline Palmer House
207-338-5790

Belfast Bay Meadows Inn
800-335-2370

Daniel Faunce House
207-338-4205

Frost House
207-338-4159

Hiram Alden Inn
207-338-2151-[Y--]

Horatio Johnson House
207-338-5153

Jeweled Turret Inn
800-696-2304

Northport House
800-338-1422

Belgrade Lakes
Wings Hill
207-495-2400

Bethel
Abbott House
207-824-7600

Bakers B&B
207-824-2088

Bethel Inn & Court
207-654-0125

Chapman Inn
207-824-2657

Douglas Place
207-824-2229

Four Seasons Inn
207-824-2755

Hammons House
207-824-3170

Holidae House Country Inn
207-824-3400

L Auberge Country Inn
207-824-2774

Norseman Inn
207-824-2002

Pointed Fir B&B
207-824-2251

Sudbury Inn
207-824-2174

Sunday River Inn
207-824-2410

Telemark Inn
207-836-2703

Bieeldfordpool
Lodge
207-284-7148

Bingham
Mrs Frances Gibson
207-672-4034

Mrs Gs B&B
207-672-4034

Blue Hill
Arcady Down East
207-374-5576

Blue Hill Farm Country Inn
207-374-5126

Blue Hill Inn
207-374-2844

John Peters Inn
207-374-2116

Boothbay
Captain Sawyer Place
207-633-2290

Coburn House Inn
207-633-2120

Kenniston Hill Inn
207-633-2159

Linekin Bay Resort
207-633-3681

Sea Witch B&B
207-633-7804

Spruce Point Inn & Lodges
207-633-4152

Thistle Inn
207-633-3541

Boothbay Harbor
Admirals Quarters
207-633-2474

Anchor Watch
207-633-7565-[Y--]

Atlantic Ark Inn
207-633-5690

Boothbay Harbor Inn
207-633-6302

Green Shutters Inn
207-633-2646

Harbour Towne Inn
207-633-4300

Hilltop Guest House
207-633-2914-[Y--]

Hodgdon Island Inn
207-633-7474

Howard House
207-633-3933

Johnathans B&B
207-633-3588

Seafarer B&B
207-633-2116

Topside
207-633-5404

Welch House
207-633-3431

Westgare Guest House
207-633-3552

©*Inn & Travel Memphis, Tennessee*   1-127

Maine ***Bold Name** - Description appears in other section*

Brewer
Brewer Lodge
207-989-3550

Bridgton
Noble House
207-647-3733

Tarry-a-While Resort
207-647-2522

Bristol
Bristol Inn
207-563-1125

Old Cape Of Bristol Mills B&B
207-563-8848

Brownfield
Alecias B&B
207-935-3969

Brownville
Carousel B&B
207-965-7741

Brunswick
Aaron Dunning House
207-729-4486

Bowdinn
207-725-4656

Brunswick B&B
800-299-4914

Captain Daniel Stone Inn
207-725-9898

Dove B&B
207-729-6827

Harborsgate B&B
207-725-5894

Harriet Beecher Stowe House
207-725-5543

Samuel Newman House
207-729-6959

Buckfield
Buckfield Inn
207-336-2456

Bucksport
L Ermitage
207-469-3361-[Y--]

Old Parsonage Inn
207-469-6477

River Inn
207-469-3783

Camden
A Little Dream
207-236-8742

Abigails
207-236-2501

Aubergine
207-236-8053

Belfast Bay Meadows Inn
800-355-2370

Belmont
207-236-8053

Blackberry Inn
207-236-6060

Blue Harbor House
800-248-3196

Camden Harbour Inn
800-236-4266

Castleview By The Sea
800-272-8439

Chestnut House
207-236-6137

Edgecomb-Coles House
207-236-2336

Elms
207-236-6250

Goodspeeds Guest House
207-236-8077-[Y--]

Harbor View
207-236-9689

Hartstone Inn
207-236-4259

Hawthorn Inn
207-236-8842-[G--]

High Tide Inn
207-236-3724

Highland Manor
207-236-3724

Hosmer House B&B
207-236-4012

Inn At Sunrise Point
80043LOBSTER

Lord Camben Inn
207-236-4325

Maine Stay B&B
207-236-9636

Mansard Manor
207-236-3291

Norumbega Inn
207-236-4646-[G--]

Owl and The Turtle
207-236-4769

Whitehall Inn
207-236-3391

Windward House
207-236-9656

Cape Elizabeth
Crescent Beach Inn
207-799-4779

Cape Neddick
Cape Neddick House
207-363-2500

Pine Hill Inn Of Ogunqiut
207-361-1004

Sea Chimes B&B
207-646-5378

Wooden Goose Inn
207-363-5673-[Y--]

Cape Newagen
Newagen Seaside Inn
207-633-5242

Cape Rosier
Hiram Blake Camp

Caribou
Old Iron Inn
207-492-4766

Rivers Bend B&B
207-498-6405

Carrabassett Valley
Sugarloaf Inn
207-237-2701

Castine
Castine Inn
207-326-4365

Holiday House
207-326-4335

Manor Inn
207-326-4861

Pentagoet Inn
207-326-8616

Center Lovell
Center Lovell Inn
207-925-1575

Westways On Kezar Lake
207-928-2663

Chamberlain
Ocean Reefs On Log Cove
207-677-2386-[Y--]

Chebeague Island
Cheabeague Inn By The Sea
207-846-5155

Cherryfield
Black Shutter Inn

Ricker House
207-546-2780

Clark Island
Craignair Inn
800-320-9997-[Y--]

Copper Mills
Claryknoll Farm
207-549-5250

Corea
Black Duck
207-963-2689

Cornish
Cornish Inn
207-625-8501-[Y--]

Cranberry Isles
Red House B&B
207-244-5297

Crouseville
Rum Rapids Inn
207-455-8096

Cumberland Center
Sunrise Acres Farm
207-829-5594

Cutler
Little River Lodge

1-128 ©*Inn & Travel Memphis, Tennessee*

Bold Name - Description appears in other section Maine

207-259-4437

Damariscotta
Barnswallow B&B
207-563-8568

Brannon Bunker Inn
207-563-5941-[G--]

Downeasters Inn

Elizabeths B&B
207-563-1919

Oak Gables B&B
207-563-1476

Deer Isle
Eggemoggin Inn
207-348-2540

Kings Row Inn
207-348-7781

Pilgrims Inn
207-348-6615

Deer Isle Village
Laphroaig B&B
207-348-6088

Dennysville
Lincoln House Country Inn
207-726-3953

Dexter
Brewster Inn Of Dexter
207-924-3130

Dixfield
Von Simm's

Victorian Inn B&B
207-562-4911

Dixmont
Ben-Loch Inn
207-257-4768

Dover Foxcroft
Birches

Crawford Farm

Eagle Lake
Camps Of Acadia
207-444-5207

East Boothbay
Five Gables Inn
207-633-4551

Limekin Village

B&B
207-278-7624

Ocean Point Inn
207-633-4200

Sailmakers Inn
207-633-7390

East Broadbay
Treasure Island

East Machais
East River B&B
207-255-8467

East Waterford
Waterford Inne
207-583-4037

Eastport
Artists Retreat
207-853-4239-[Y--]

Milliken House
307-853-2955

Run At Eastport
207-853-4307

Todd House
207-853-2328

Weston House
207-853-2907

Eliot
Ewenicorn Farm B&B
207-439-1337

Farmstead
207-439-5033

High Meadows B&B
207-439-0590-[Y--]

Paul Moses Inn
207-439-1861

Ellsworth
Eagles Lodge
207-667-3311

Victorias B&B
207-667-5893

Farmington
Blackberry Farm B&B
207-778-2035

Country Seat Inn
207-778-3901

Five Islands
Coveside

Grey Havens Inn
207-371-2616

Fort Fairfield
Ma Meres B&B
207-473-7902

Fort Kent
Daigles B&B
207-834-5803

Foxcraft
Foxcroft B&B
207-564-7720

Freeport
181 Main Street
207-865-1226

Atlantic Seal B&B
207-865-6112-[Y--]

Bagley House
800-765-1772-[G--]

Bayberry Inn
207-865-6021-[G-1-]

Brewster House B&B
207-865-4121

Captain Josiah Mitchell House
207-865-3289-[G--]

Cottage Street Inn
207-865-0932

Country At Heart B&B
207-865-0512

Harraseeket Inn
800-342-6423

Holbrook Inn B&B
207-865-6693

Isaac Randall House
800-865-9295

Kendall Tavern
207-865-1338

Lucerne Inn
800-325-5123

Maple Hill B&B
207-856-3730

Monarch Landing B&B
207-865-4338

Nicholson Inn
207-865-6404

Old Red Farm
207-865-4550

Porters Landing B&B
207-865-4488

White Cedar Inn
207-865-9099

Friendship
Harbor Hill By The Sea B&B
207-832-6646-[Y--]

Outsiders Inn
207-832-5197

Fryeburg
Admiral Peary House
800-237-8080

Oxford House Inn
207-935-3442

Wood Doctors Country Inn
207-935-3334

Glen Cove
Old Granite Inn
207-594-9036

Gorham
Country Squire B&B
207-839-4855

Gouldsboro
Sunset House
207-963-7156

Grand Lake Stream
Leens Lodge
207-796-5575

Weatherby/Fishing Resort

Greenville
Chesuncook Lake House

Devlin House
207-695-2229

Evergreen Lodge B&B
207-695-3241

Greenville Manor

©Inn & Travel Memphis, Tennessee   1-129

Maine *Bold Name - Description appears in other section*

207-695-2206

Lodge At Moosehead
207-695-4400

Northern Pride Lodge
207-695-2890

Sawyer House B&B
207-695-2369

Guilford
Trebor Inn
207-876-0470

Guliford
Guliford B&B
207-876-3477

Hallowell
Maple Hill Farm B&B
207-622-2708

Hampden
Bleak House B&B
207-862-3860

Hancock
Crocker House
207-433-6806

Ledomaine
207-422-3395

Hancock Point
Crocker House Country Inn
207-422-6806

Harrington
Harrington House
207-483-4044

Harrison
Harrison House
207-583-6564

Snowbird Lodge
207-583-2544

Tolman House Inn
207-583-4445

Hartford
Green Acres Inn
207-597-2333

Haven
Haven
207-646-4194

Hope
Blanchard B&B

207-763-3785

Hulls Cove
Inn At Canoe Point
207-288-9511

Twin Gables Inn
207-288-3064

Isle Au Haute
Keepers House
207-367-2261

Isleboro
Dark Harbor House Inn
207-734-6669-[Y--]

Moss Inn
207-734-6410

Isleford
Island B&B
207-244-9283

Jefferson
Jefferson House
207-549-5768

Jonesboro
Chandler River Lodge
207-434-2651

Jonesport
Great Bar Farm
207-497-2170

Tootsies B&B

Kennebunk
Alewife House
207-985-2118-[Y--]

Arunder Meadows Inn
207-965-3770

Captain Littlefield Inn
207-985-3937

Kennebunk Inn 1799
207-983-3351

Lake Brook Guest House
207-967-4069-[Y--]

Merryfields Inn

Waldo Emersons Inn
207-985-4250

Kennebunkport
1802 House B&B
800-932-5632-[YQA]

Alewife House
207-985-2118-[Y--]

Breakwater
207-967-3118

Bufflehead Cove
207-967-3879

Captain Fairfield House
800-322-1928-[Y--]

Captain Jefferds Inn
207-967-2311

Captain Lord Mansion
207-967-3141-[G--]

Chetwynd House Inn
207-967-2235

Clarion Nonantum Inn
207-967-4050

Colony
207-967-3331

Cove House
207-967-3704

Dock Square Inn
207-967-5773

English Meadows Inn
207-967-5766

English Robin
207-967-3505

Falkeyard Farm
207-967-5965

Farm House B&B
207-967-4169-[Y--]

Green Heron Inn
207-967-3315

Harbor Inn
207-967-2074

Inn At Goose Rocks
207-967-5425

Inn At Harbor Head
207-967-5564-[Y--]

Inn On South Street
800-963-5151-[G--]

Kennebunkport Inn
800-248-2621-[G--]

Kilburn House
207-967-4762-[Y--]

Kylemere House 1818
207-967-2780

Maine Stay Inn & Cottages
800-950-2117-[G--]

North Street Guest House

Ocean View
207-967-2750

Old Fort Inn
800-828-3678

Old Parsonage Guest House
207-967-4352

Olde Garrison House
207-967-3522-[Y--]

Port Gardens
207-967-3358

Schooners Inn
207-967-5333

Seaside Inn
207-967-4461

Shawmut Inn

Sundial Inn
207-967-3850

Tides Inn By The Sea
207-967-3757

Village Cove Inn
207-967-3993

Welby Inn
207-967-4655

White Barn Inn
207-967-2321-[Y--]

Kents Hill
Aunt Marthas B&B
207-897-5686

Echo Lake Lodge

1-130

©Inn & Travel Memphis, Tennessee

Bold Name - Description appears in other section　　　　　　　　　　　　　　　　　　　　　　　　　　　　　　　　　　　　　　　*Maine*

207-685-9550

Kingfield
Herbert Inn
207-265-2000

Inn On Winters Hill
207-265-5421-[Y--]

One Stanley Avenue

River Port Inn
207-265-2552

Three Stanley Avenue
207-343-5541

Wunters Inn
207-265-5421

Kittery
Deep Water Landing B&B
207-439-0824

Enchanter Nights B&B
207-439-1489

Gundalow Inn
207-439-4040

Melfair Farm
207-439-0320-[Y--]

Kittery Point
Harbour Watch
207-439-3242

Whaleback Inn B&B
207-439-9570

Lewiston
Farnham House B&B
207-782-9495

Mom & Dads Guest House
207-783-3032

Limerick
Colonial House
207-793-8515

Lincolnville
Cedarholm Cottages
207-236-3886

Red House
207-236-4621

Sign Of The Owl

207-338-4669

Spouter Inn
207-789-5171

Victorian B&B
800-382-9817

Youngstown Inn
207-763-4290

Litchfield
Old Tavern Inn
207-268-4965

Longville
Longville
207-235-3785

Lubce
Bayviews
207-733-2181

Lubec
Breakers-By-The-Bay
207-733-2487

Due East-Bailey's Mistake
207-733-2413

Home Port Inn
207-733-2077

Hugel Haus B&B
207-733-4965

Overview
207-733-2005

Peacock House
207-733-2403

Machias
Clark Perry House
207-255-8458

Madison
Colony House
207-474-6599

Matinicus
Tuckanuck Lodge
207-366-3830

Medomak
Roaring Brook B&B
207-529-5467

Milbrige
Moonraker B&B
207-546-2191

Millbridge
Bayside Inn

207-546-7852

Millinocket
Big Moose Inn Cabins
207-723-8391

Sweet Lillian
207-723-4894

Milo
Down Home B&B
207-943-5167

Monhegan
Monhegan House
207-594-7983

Monhegan Island
Island Inn
207-596-0371

Shining Sails Inc
207-596-0041

Trailing Yes

Mount Desert
Clopver
207-244-5650

Collier House
207-288-3162

Long Pond Inn
207-244-5854

Mount Desert Island
Penury Hall
207-244-7102-[Y--]

Mount Vernon
Feather Bed Inn
207-293-2020

Naples
Augustus Bove House
207-693-6365-[Y--]

Charmwoods On Long Lake
207-693-6798

Haven
207-693-6602

Inn At Long Lake
800-437-0328

Lamb's Mill Inn
207-693-6253

Songo B&B House
207-693-3960-[Y--]

New Harbor
Bradley Inn
207-677-2105

Gosnold Arms
207-677-3727

New Portland
Gilamn Stream B&B
207-628-6257

Newcastle
Captains House
207-563-1482-[Y--]

Elfinhill
207-563-1886

Glidden House
207-563-1859

Markert House
207-563-1309

Mill Pond Inn
207-563-8014

Newcastle Inn
800-832-8669-[GQA]

Riversedge
207-563-5671

Newport
Lake Seabsticook B&B
207-368-5507

Norridgewock
Bear Spring Camp
207-397-2341

Norridgewock Colonial Inn
207-634-3470

North Anson
Carrabassett Inn
207-635-2900

North Edgecomb
Channelridge Farm
207-882-7539

North Haven
Pulpit Harbor Inn
207-867-2219

North Waterford
Olde Rowley Inn
207-583-4143

Northeast Harbor
Asticou Inn
207-276-3702

©*Inn & Travel Memphis, Tennessee*　　1-131

Maine **Bold Name -** *Description appears in other section*

Grey Rock Inn
207-276-9360

Harborside Inn
207-276-3272

Maison Suisse Inn
207-276-5223

Oakland
Pressey House - 1850
207-465-3500

Ogunquit
Admirals Inn
207-646-7093

Admirals Loft
207-646-5496

Bayberry
207-646-8158

Beachcrest
207-646-2156

Beauport Inn
207-646-8680

Blue Shutters
207-646-2163-[Y--]

Blue Water Inn
207-646-5559

Channing Hall
207-646-5222

Clipper Ship Guest House
207-646-9735

Dune On The Waterfront Gazebo
207-646-3733

Hartwell House
207-646-7210-[Y--]

High Tor
207-646-8232

Inn At Fieldstone

Inn At Two Village Square
207-646-5779

Juniper Hill Inn
207-646-4501

Leisure Inn
207-646-2737

Morning Dove B&B
207-646-3891

Ogunquit House
207-646-2967

Old Village Inn
207-646-7088

Puffin Inn
207-646-5496

Rockmere Lodge
207-646-2985

Seafair Inn
207-646-2181-[Y--]

Shore House
207-646-6619

Strauss Haus
207-646-7756

Terrace By The Sea
207-646-3232

Trellis House
207-646-7909

Yardarm Village Inn
207-646-7006

Yellow Monkey Inn
207-646-9056

Old Orchard Beach
Atlantic Birches
207-934-5295

Carriage House B&B
207-934-2141

Oquossoc
Horsefeather Inn
207-864-5465

Oquossacs Own B&B
207-864-5584

Orono
Highlawn B&B
207-866-2272

Orrs Island
Orrs Island B&B
207-833-2940

Otisfield
Claiberns B&B
207-539-2352

Otter Creek

Otter Creek Inn
207-288-5151

Peaks Island
Kellers B&B
207-766-2441

Moonshell Inn
207-766-2331

Pemaquid Falls
Little River Inn & Gallery
207-677-2845

Phippsburg
Captain Drummond House
207-389-1394

Riverview

Poland Spring
Poland Spring Inn
207-998-4671

Port Clyde
Copper Light
207-372-8510

Ocean House
207-372-6691

Portland
Andrews Lodging - B&B
207-797-9157

Inn At Parkerspring
207-774-1059-[Y--]

Inn At Saint Joun
207-773-6481

Inn On Carleton
800-639-1779

Ponegranate Inn
207-772-1006

West End Inn
207-772-1377

York Harbor Inn
800-343-3869-[G--]

Princeton
Mihku Lodge
207-796-2701

Prospect Harbor
Oceanside Meadows Inn
207-963-5557

Prouts Nech

Black Point Inn

Rangeley
Country Club Inn
207-864-3831

Farmhouse Inn
207-864-5805

Mallorys B&B
207-864-2121

Northwoods B&B
800-295-4968

Rangeley Inn
800-MOMENTS

Raymond
North Pines Health Resort
207-655-7624

Robbinston
Brewer House Inn
207-454-2385

Robinhood
Benjamin Riggs House
207-371-2256

Rockland
Craignair Inn
207-594-7644-[G--]

Lakeshore Inn
207-594-4209

Rockport
Bread & Roses B&B
207-236-6116

Rosemary Cottage
207-236-3513

Sign Of The Unicorn
207-236-8789-[Y--]

Twin Gables B&B
207-236-4717

Rockwood
Kineo House
207-534-8812

Round Pond
Briar Rose B&B
207-529-5478

Saco
Crown 'n' Anchor Inn
800-561-8865

Saint Francis

1-132   ©Inn & Travel Memphis, Tennessee

Bold Name - Description appears in other section *Maine*

Dallas B&B
207-398-3399

Sanford
Allens Inn
207-342-2160

Sargentville
Oakland House
207-359-8521

Scarborough
Higgins Beach
207-883-6684

Searsport
Brass Lantern Inn
207-548-0150

Captain Albert
Vinal Nickels
207-548-6691

Carriage House Inn
207-548-2289

Homeport
800-742-5814-[Y--]

McGilvery House
207-548-6289

Sea Captains Inn
207-548-0919

Thurston House B&B
207-548-2213-[Y--]

William & Mary Inn
207-548-2190

Sebagco Estates
Rock Gardens Inn
207-389-1339

Sebagco Lodge
207-389-1161

Sedgewick
Barlows Lanter Lane
207-359-8834

Sedgewick B&B

Short Sands Beach
Homestead Inn B&B
207-363-8952

Skowhegan
Brick Farm B&B
207-474-3949

Helens B&B
207-474-0066

South Berwick
Academy Street Inn
207-384-5633

Anic B&B

South Brooksville
Breezemere Farm Inn
207-326-4618

Bucks Harbor Inn
207-326-8660

South Casco
Migis Lodge
207-655-4524

Thomas Inn & Playhouse
207-655-7728

South Freeport
Atlantic Seal B&B
207-865-6112 [Y--]

South Gouldsboro
Bluff House
207-963-7805

South Harpswell
Harpswell House
207-833-5509

Senter B&B
207-833-2874

South Thomaston
Weskeag Inn
207-596-6676-[Y--]

South Waldoboro
Barn
207-832-5781

Southport
Albonegon Inn
207-633-2521

Southwest Harbor
Claremont
207-244-5036 [Y--]

Harbor Lights Home
207-244-3835

Harbour Cottage Inn
207-244-5738

Harbour Woods
207-244-5388

Inn At Southwest
207-244-3835

Island House
207-244-5180

Island Watch B&B
207-244-7229

Kingsleigh Inn
207-244-5302

Lambs Ear
207-244-9828

Lindenwood Inn
207-244-5335

Moorings
207-244-5523

Two Seasons
207-244-9627

Springfield
Old Farm Inn
207-738-2730

Stockton Springs
Hichborn Inn
207-567-4183

Stonington
Burnt Cove B&B
207-367-2392

Captains Quarters Inn
207-367-2420

Stratton
Tranquility B&B
207-246-4280

Widows Walk
207-246-6901

Strong
Copper Horse Inn
207-684-3300

Sullivan
Sullivan Harbor Farm
207-422-3591

Sullivan Harbor
Island View Inn
207-422-3031

Sunset
Goose Cove Lodge
207-348-2508-[Y--]

Surry

Surry Inn
207-667-5091

Tenants Harbor
Church Hill B&B
207-372-6256

East Wind Inn & Meeting House
207-372-6366

Mill Pond House
207-372-6209

The Forks
Crab Apple Acres Inn
207-663-2218

Thomaston
Bedside Manor Inn
207-354-8862

Cap'n Frost's B&B
207-354-8217

Gracies B&B
207-354-2326

Topsham
Middaugh B&B
207-725-2562

Walker Wilson House
207-729-0715

Twin Mountain
Partridge House Inn

Van Buren
Farrell-Michaud House
207-868-5209

Vinalhaven
Fox Island Inn
207-686-2122

Libby House B&B
207-863-4696

Morning Glory B&B
207-863-2051

Waldoboro
Blackford Inn
207-832-4714

Broad Bay Inn & Gallery
207-832-6668-[Y--]

Le Vatout B&B
207-832-4552-[Y--]

Letteney Farm

©Inn & Travel Memphis, Tennessee

Maine - Massachusetts   **Bold Name** - *Description appears in other section*

Vacations
207-832-5143

Medomak House
207-832-4971

Roaring Lion
207-832-4038

Snow Turtle Inn
207-832-4423

Tide Watch Inn
207-832-4987

Walpole
Bittersweet Inn
207-563-5552

Washington
Windward Farm
207-845-2830

Waterford
Kedarburn Inn
207-583-6182

Lake House
800-223-4182

Waterville
Lamplighter B&B
207-872-2432

Weld
Kawanhee Inn
207-778-4306

Lake Webb House B&B
207-585-2479

Weld Inn
207-585-2429

Wells
Bayview Inn B&B
207-646-9260

Beach Farm Inn
207-646-7970

Grey Gull Inn
207-646-7501

Holiday Guest House
207-646-5582

Purple Sandpiper Guest House
207-646-7990

Sand Dollar Inn
207-646-2346

West Bath
Bakke B&B
207-442-7185

New Meadows Inn
207-443-3921

West Bethel
Kings Inn
207-836-3375

West Boothbay Harbor
Lawnmeer Inn
800-633SMILE

West Forks
Dead River B&B
207-663-4480

West Gouldsboro
Sunset House
207-963-7156

West Paris
Bradford House
207-674-3696

West Summer
Morrill Farm B&B
207-388-2059

Winter Harbor
Main Stay Inn
207-963-5561

Winterport
Colonial Winterport Inn
207-223-5307

Wiscasset
Marston House American
207-882-6010

Sheepscot B&B
207-882-6024

Squire Tarbox Inn
207-882-7693

Stacked Arms
207-882-5436-[Y--]

Yarmouth
Homewood Inn
207-846-3351

York
Canterbury House
207-363-3505

Dockside Guest Quarters
207-363-2868

Franklin Guest House
207-363-6075

Hannahs Loft
207-363-7244-[Y--]

Hutchins B&B
207-363-3058

Scotland Bridge Inn
207-363-4432

Summer Place
207-363-5233

Wild Rose Of York
207-363-2532-[Y--]

York Beach
Beach Homestead B&B
207-363-8952

Candleshop Inn
207-363-4087

Golden Pineapple Inn
207-363-7837

Katahdin Inn
207-363-1824

Lighthouse Inn
207-363-6023

O'Regans Inn
207-363-5706-[Y--]

York Harbor
Bell Bouy
207-363-7264

Canterbury House
207-363-3505

Edwards Harborside Inn
207-363-3037

Inn At Harmon Park
207-363-2031

Moorelowe
207-363-2526

York Harbor Inn
800-343-3869-[G--]

MASSACHUSETTS

Adams
Butternut Inn

Agawam
Hartleys Guest House

Alford
Hidden Acres B&B
413-528-1028

Amherst
Allen House Victorian Inn
413-253-5000-[-QA-]

Amity House
413-549-6446

Ivy House B&B
413-549-7554

Andover
Andover Inn
508-475-5903

Ashfield
Apple Inn
413-628-4729

Gold Leaf Inn
413-628-3392

Attleboro
Col Blackinton Inn
508-222-6022

Emma C'S B&B
508-226-6365

Auburn
Capt Samuel Eddy House Inn
508-832-7282-[Y--]

Barnstable
Ashely Manor
508-362-8044-[Y--]

B&B On Beautiful Cape Cod
508-362-6556

Beechwood Inn
508-362-6618

Chas Hinkley House
508-362-9924

Cobbs Cove
508-362-9356-[G-1-]

Goss House B&B
508-362-8555

Honeysuckle Hill
508-362-8418

1-134   ©Inn & Travel Memphis, Tennessee

Bold Name - Description appears in other section   **Massachusetts**

Lamb & Lion
508-326-6823

Thomas Huckins House
508-362-6379

Barre
Olde Jenkins Guest House
508-355-6444

Bass River
Anchorage
617-398-8265

Belvedere B&B
617-398-6674-[Y--]

Captain Isaiahs House
617-394-1739-[Y--]

Old Cape House
617-398-1068

Becket
Canterbury Farm
413-623-8765

Long House

Bedford
Baird Tavern B&B
617-848-2096

Belchertown
Ingate Farm B&B
413-253-0440

McFadyens

Berlin
Stonehedge
508-838-2574

Billerica
Billerica B&B
508-667-7317

Boston
1810 House B&B
617-659-1810-[G--]

463 Beacon Street Guest House
617-536-1302

Allen House
508-545-8221-[G--]

Baileys Copley B&B
617-422-0646

Baileys II Boston House

617-262-4534

Beacon Hill B&B
617-523-7376-[G--]

Bostonian Hotel
800-343-0922

Buckminster Inn
617-236-7050

Cape Cod Sunny Pines Inn
800-356-9628-[G--]

Chandler Inn
800-842-3450

Emma James House
617-288-8867-[Y--]

Farrington Inn
800-767-5337

Harborside House
617-631-1032-[G--]

John Jeffries House
617-627-5536

Lafayette Hotel
617-451-2600

Land's End Inn
508-487-0706-[G--]

Lenox Hotel
800-225-7676

Manor On Golden Pond
800-545-2141

Newbury Guest House
617-437-7666

Oasis Guest House
617-267-2262-[G--]

Omni Parker House
617-227-8600

Terrace Townhouse
617-350-6520

Victorian B&B
617-247-1599

York Harbor Inn
800-343-3869-[G--]

Brewster
Beechcroft Inn
508-896-9534

Beechcroft Inn
508-896-9534

Bramble Inn
508-896-7644

Brewster Farmhouse Inn
508-896-3910

Candleberry Inn
508-896-3300

Cape Cod Ocean Gold B&B
508-255-7045

Captain Freeman Inn
508-896-7481-[Y--]

High Brewster Inn
508-896-3636

Isaiah Clark House
508-896-2223-[Y--]

Ocean Gold B&B
508-255-7045-[Y--]

Old Manse Inn
508-896-3149-[G--]

Old Sea Pines Inn
508-896-6114

Poore House
508-896-2094

Brookline
Beacon Inns
617-566-0088-[Y--]

Beacon Plaza
617-232-6550

Beech Tree Inn
800-544-9660

Brookline Manor House
617-232-0003

Buckland
1797 House
413-625-2697

Scott House
413-625-6624

Buzzards Bay
Cape Cod Canalside B&B
508-759-6564

Pond House
508-759-1994

Cambridge
Bettinas B&B

Cambridge B&B
617-491-6108

Cambridge Bed & Muffin
617-576-3166

Cambridge House
800-232-9989-[Y--]

Hamilton House B&B
617-491-0274

Irving House At Harvard
617-547-4600

Margarets B&B
617-876-3450

Mary Prentiss Inn
617-661-2929

Cape Cod
Salty Dog Inn
508-428-5228-[Y--]

Castleton
Blue Knoll Farm
703-937-5234

Cataumet
Wood Duck Inn
508-564-6404

Centerville
Adams Terrace Garden
508-775-4707

Carver House
508-775-9414

Copper Beech Inn
508-771-5488

Inn At Fernbrook
508-775-4334-[Y--]

Old Hundred House
508-775-6166

Terrace Gardens Inn
508-775-4707

Charlemont
Forest Way Farm
413-337-8321-[Y--]

©Inn & Travel Memphis, Tennessee   1-135

Massachusetts **Bold Name** - *Description appears in other section*

Inn At Charlemont
413-339-5796

Chatham
Bow Roof House
508-945-1346

Captains House Inn
800-315-0728

Chatham Bars Inn
508-945-0096

Chatham Guest House
508-945-3247

Chatham Town House Inn
800-527-4884

Cranberry Inn At Chatham
800-332-4667

Cyrus Kent House
800-338-5368

Inn Among Friends
508-945-0792

Inn At The Dolpin
508-945-0070

Moses Nickerson House
508-945-5859

Old Harbor Inn
800-942-4434

Queen Anne Inn
508-945-0394

Ships Inn At Chatham
508-945-5859

Wequassett Inn
Chatham Center
Bradford Inn
800-562-4667-[Y--]

Chelmsford
Westview Landing
508-256-0074

Cheshire
Beechwood Country B&B
413-743-1998

Chestnut Hill
Pleasant Pheasant
617-566-4178

Chilmark
Breakfast At Tiasquam
508-645-3685

Captain D Larson House
508-645-3484

Captain Flanders House
508-645-3123

Duck Inn
508-645-9018

Outermost Inn
508-645-3511

Cohasset
Actors Row B&B
617-383-9200

Colrain
Grandmothers House
416-624-3771

Concord
Amerscot House
508-897-0666-[G--]

Anderson Wheeler Homestead
508-369-3756-[Y--]

Col Roger Brown House
800-292-1369-[Y--]

Colonial Inn
508-369-9200

Hawthorne Inn
508-369-5610-[Y--]

Stow Away Inn
508-897-1999

Conway
Poundsworth B&B
413-369-4420

The Merriams
413-369-4052

Cummaquid
Ackworth Inn
508-362-3330

Anderson Acres
508-362-4394

Waratah House
508-362-1469

Cummington
Cumworth Farm
413-634-5529

Hidden Brook Inn
413-634-5653

Hill Gallery
413-238-5914

Inn At Cummington Farm Village
800-562-9666

Swift River Inn
800-532-8022-[G--]

Windfields Farm
413-684-3786

Cuttyhunk
Allen House Inn & Restaurant
508-996-9292

Dalton
Dalton House
413-684-3854

Danvers
Appleton Inn
508-777-8630

King's Grant Inn
800-782-7841

Salem Village B&B
617-774-7851

Dedham
Iris B&B
617-329-3514

Deerfield
Deerfield Inn
800-926-3865

Tea House Inn
413-772-2675

Deerfield-South
The Yellow Gabled House
413-665-4922

Dennis
Four Chimneys Inn
508-385-6317-[Y--]

Isaiah Hall B&B Inn
800-736-0160-[G-1-]

Soft Breezes Inn
508-385-5246

Weatherly House
508-385-7458

Dennisport
By The Sea Guests
508-398-8685

Rose Petal B&B
508-398-8470-[G--]

Duxbury
Campbells Country B&B
617-934-0862

Winsor House Inn
617-934-0991

East Falmouth
Petersons B&B
508-540-2962

East Orleans
Areys Pond Relais
508-240-0599

Nauset House Inn
508-255-2195

Parsonage
508-255-8217-[Y--]

Shepherds Inn
508-823-8777

Ship's Knees Inn
508-255-1312
[GQA-]

East Sandwich
Azariah Snow House
508-888-6677

Wingscorton Farm Inn
508-888-0534-[Y--]

Eastham
Great Pond House B&B
508-255-2967

Overlook Inn
800-356-1121-[G--]

Whalewalk Inn
508-255-0617-[Y--]

Edgartown
Arbor
508-627-8137
[G-QA-]

Ashley Inn
508-627-9655

1-136   ©Inn & Travel Memphis, Tennessee

Bold Name - *Description appears in other section*   *Massachusetts*

Capt Dexter House/ Edgartown
508-627-7289-[Y--]

Chadwick House
800-627-5656

Charlotte Inn
508-627-4751

Colonial Inn
800-627-4701-[G--]

Daggett House
508-627-4600

Edgartown Heritage Hotel
508-627-5161

Edgartown Inn
508-627-4794-[Y--]

Governor Bradford Inn
508-627-9150

Harborside Inn
508-627-4321

Jonathan Munroe Guest House
508-627-5536

Katama Guest House
508-627-5158

Kelly House
508-627-4394

Meeting House Inn
508-627-8626

Point Way Inn
508-627-8633-[G--]

Shiretown Inn
800-541-0090

Shiverick Inn
508-627-3797

Victorian Inn
508-627-4784

Vineyard Vines B&B
508-627-3172

Essex
George Fuller House
508-768-7766-[Y--]

Fairhaven

Edgewater B&B
508-997-5512-[G-1-]

Falmouth
Amherst
508-548-2781

Capt Tom Lawrence House
800-266-8139-[Y--]

Commonwealth House
508-548-2300

Coonamessett Inn
617-548-2300

Elm Arch Inn
508-548-0133

Gladstone Inn
508-548-9851

Grafton Inn
800-642-4069-[--1-]

Hastings By The Sea
508-548-1628

Hawthone Lodge
508-548-0389

Inn
508-540-7469

Inn At One Main Street
508-540-7469

Moorings Lodge
508-540-2370

Mostly Hall B&B Inn
508-548-3786

Palmer House Inn
800-4RB-ANDB

Peacocks Inn On The Sound
508-457-9666-[G--]

Scalloped Shell
508-548-8245

Swan Point Inn
508-540-5528

Village Green Inn
508-548-5621

Wildflower Inn B&B

800-294-LILY

Woods Hole Passage
508-548-9575

Worcester House
508-540-1592

Falmouth Heights
Beach House B&B At Falmouth Heights
800-351-3426

Gloucester
Blue Shutters Inn
508-281-2706

Gray Manor
508-283-5409

Harborview Inn
800-299-6696

Riverview B&B
508-281-1826

Schooner Inn
508-281-8097

Williams Guest House
508-283-4931

Goshen
Innamorata
413-268-0300

Whale Inn
413-268-7246

Great Barrington
Baldwin Hill B&B
413-528-4092

Bread & Roses
413-528-1099

Coffing-Bostwick House
413-528-4511

Ellings Guest House
413-528-4103

Greenmeadows
413-528-3897

Littlejohn Manor
413-528-2882

Millstones Guest House
413-229-8488

Red Bird Inn

413-229-2433

Seekonk Pines Inn
800-292-4192-[Y-1-]

Thornwood Inn
413-528-3828

Turning Point Inn
413-528-4777

Wainwright Inn
413-528-2062

Windflower Inn
800-992-1993

Greenfield
Brandt House B&B
413-773-8184

Hitchcock House
413-774-7452

Groton
Greenview
Hamilton

Miles River Country Inn
508-468-7206

Hancock
Kirkmeade B&B
413-738-5420

Mill House Inn
518-733-5606

Hanover
House Of Coffey
617-826-3141-[Y--]

Harvard
Two Deerfoot B&B
508-456-3669

Harwich
Bide A Wee

Cape Cod Sunny Pines Inn
800-356-9628-[G--]

The Winstead
508-432-4586

Harwich Center
Victorian Inn At Harwich
508-432-8335

Harwich Port
#10 B&B
508-432-9313

©Inn & Travel Memphis, Tennessee   1-137

Massachusetts *Bold Name -* *Description appears in other section*

Augustus Snow House
800-320-0528

Bayberry Shores
800-992-6550

Beach House Inn
508-432-4444

Captains Quarters
800-992-6550

Coach House
508-432-9542-[Y--]

Country Inn Acres
508-432-2769

Drangea House

Dunscroft Inn
800-432-4345

Grey Gull Guest House
508-432-0222

Harbor Breeze Inn
800-992-6550

Harbor Walk Guest House
508-432-1675-[Y--]

Inn On Bank Street
508-432-3206-[Y--]

Shoals Guest House
508-432-3837

Holyoke
Yankee Peddler Inn
413-532-9494-[Y--]

Housatonic
Christines Guest House
413-274-6149

Huntington
Paulson B&B
413-667-3208

Hyannis
Capt Ezra Nye House
800-388-2278-[G--]

Captain Sylvester Baxter House
508-775-5611-[Y--]

Cranberry Cove
508-775-7049

Fairbanks Inn
508-487-0386

Inn On Sea Street
508-775-8030

Mansfield House
508-771-9455

Salt Winds Guest House
508-775-2038

Sea Breeze By The Beach
508-771-7231-[Y--]

Hyannis Port
Simmons Homestead Inn
800-637-1649-[G--]

Kingston
Black Poodle

Lancaster
Carter-Washburn House
508-365-2188

Lanesboro
Amc-Bascom Lodge
413-743-1591

Tuckered Turkey
413-442-0260

Lanesborough
Towny Farm

Lee
Applegate
413-243-4451

Chambery Inn
413-243-2221

Donahoes
413-243-1496

Haus Andreas
413-243-3298

Inn At Laurel Lake
413-243-1436

Morgan House
413-243-0181

Parsonage On The Green
413-243-4364

Ramsey House
413-243-1598

Tollgate Inn
413-243-0715

White Horse Inn
413-443-0961

Lenox
Amadeus House
800-205-4770

Amity House
413-637-0005

Apple Tree Inn
413-637-1477

Bayfront Inn
413-637-4822

Birchwood Inn
800-524-1646
[-QAR-]

Blantyre
413-637-3556

Brook Farm Inn
413-637-3013-[Y--]

Candlelight Inn
413-637-1555

Chesapeake Inn Of Lenox
413-637-3429

Cliffwood Inn
413-637-3330

Cornell House
413-637-0562

Cranberry Goose
413-637-2812

Forty-Four St Annes Ave
413-637-3381

Gables Inn
800-382-9401

Garden Gables Inn
413-637-0193

Gateways Inn
413-637-2532

Kemble Inn
800-353-4113

Rockwood Inn
413-637-9750

Strawberry Hill
413-637-3381

Summer Hill Farm
413-442-2057

Underledge Inn
413-637-0236

Village Inn
413-637-0020

Walker House
800-235-3098-[Y--]

Wheatleigh
413-637-0610

Whippletree Inn
413-637-0610

Whistlers Inn
413-637-0975

Leverett
Hannah Dudley House
413-367-2323

Lexington
Ashleys B&B
617-862-6488

Halewood House
617-862-5404

Innval Hill

Littleton
Littleton Inn
508-486-4715

Lowell
Barnes House
508-453-9763

Sherman Berry House
508-459-4760-[Y--]

Lunenberg
Coach House Inn
508-582-9921

Lynn
Bayside Inn
617-581-5555

Diamond District B&B
800-666-3076

Manchester
Old Corner Inn
508-526-4996

Marblehead
10 Mugford Street

1-138   ©Inn & Travel Memphis, Tennessee

Bold Name - Description appears in other section   *Massachusetts*

B&B
617-631-5642

Harbor Light Inn
617-631-2186

Harborside House
617-631-1032-[G-2-]

Lindseys Garrett
617-631-2653

Pleasant Manor
B&B
617-631-5843

Sea Street B&B
617-631-1890

Spray Cliff On The Ocean
800-626-1530-[G--]

State Street B&B
617-639-0357

Stillpoint
617-631-2653

Marion
  Peregrine B&B

Marshfield Hills
  Woodlands Inn
  617-834-8971

Marstons Mills
  Prince House

Marthas Vineyard
  Arbor
  508-627-8137-[G-2-]

  Farmhouse
  508-693-5354

  Thorncroft Inn
  800-332-1236-[Y--]

Melrose
  Windslow House

Menemsha
  Beach Plum Inn
  508-645-9454

  Menemsha Inn
  508-645-2521

Merrimac
  Benjamin Choate House
  508-462-4786

Middlefield
  Strawberry Banke Farm
  413-623-6481

Monterey
  Mountain Trails B&B
  413-528-2928

Monument Beach
  Bay Breeze Guest House

Nantucket
  76 Main Street
  508-228-2533

  Anchor Inn
  508-228-0072

  Atlantic Mainstay
  508-288-5451

  Beachside
  508-228-2241

  Brant Point Inn
  508-228-5442

  Brass Lantern Inn
  508-228-4064

  Carlisle House
  508-228-0720

  Carriage House
  508-228-0326

  Centerboard Guest House
  508-228-9696-[Y--]

  Centre Street Inn
  800-298-0199

  Century House
  508-228-0530-[Y--]

  Cliffside Beach Club
  508-228-0618

  Corner House
  508-228-1530

  Country Island Inn
  508-228-0889

  Dolphin Guest House
  508-228-4028

  Eighteen Gardner Street
  508-228-1155

  Four Ash Street
  508-228-4899

  Four Chimneys Inn
  508-228-1912

  Great Harbor Inn
  508-228-6609

  Hallidays Nantucket House
  508-228-9450

  Harbor House
  508-228-1500

  Hawthorne House
  508-228-1468

  House Of Seven Gables
  508-228-4706

  Hungry Whale
  508-228-4206

  Hussey House-1795
  508-228-0747

  India House
  508-228-9043

  Ivy Lodge
  508-228-0305

  Jared Coffin House
  508-228-2405

  Le Languedoc Inn
  508-228-2552

  Lynda Watts B&B
  508-228-3828-[Y--]

  Martins Guest House
  508-228-0678

  Nantucket Landfall
  508-228-0500

  Nesbitt Inn
  508-228-0156

  Nesbitt Inn
  508-631-6655

  Parker Guest House
  508-228-4625

  Periwinkle Guest House
  508-228-9267

  Phillips House
  508-228-9217-[Y--]

  Quaint Cape

  Victorian Inn
  508-322-0123-[Y--]

  Quaker House Inn
  508-228-9156

  Roberts House
  508-228-9009

  Safe Harbor Guest House
  508-228-3222

  Sherburne Inn
  508-228-4425

  Ships Inn
  508-228-0400

  Spring Cottage
  508-325-4644

  Stumble Inne
  508-228-4482

  Ten Hussey
  508-228-9552

  Ten Lyon Street Inn
  508-228-5040

  Tuckernuck Inn
  800-228-4886

  Union Street Inn
  508-228-9222

  Wake Up On Pleasant Street
  508-228-0673

  West Moor Inn
  508-228-0877

  Wharf Cottages
  617-228-4620

  White Elephant Resort
  508-228-5000

  White House
  508-228-4677

  Woodbox
  508-228-0587

Nantucket Island
  Beachway Guest House
  508-228-1324

  Chestnut House
  508-228-0049

  Cliff Lodge

©Inn & Travel Memphis, Tennessee

Massachusetts   **Bold Name** - *Description appears in other section*

508-228-9480

Cobblestone Inn
508-228-1987

Fair Gardens
508-228-4258

Le Petite Maison
508-228-9242

Seven Sea Street
508-228-3577

Wauwinet
800-426-8718

Woodbox Inn
508-228-0587

Nantucket-Siasconset
  Summer House
  508-257-9976

Needham
  Brocks B&B
  617-444-6573

New Bedford
  Durant Sail Loft Inn
  508-999-2700

  Melville House B&B
  508-990-1566

New Marlborough
  Gedney Farm
  413-229-3131

  Old Inn On The Green
  800-752-1896

Newburyport
  Clark Currier Inn
  508-465-8363

  Essex Street Inn
  508-465-3145

  Garrison Inn
  508-327-6929

  House By The River
  508-463-9624

  Market House
  508-465-5816

  Morrill Place Inn
  508-462-2808

  Windsor House
  508-462-3778-[Y--]

Newtonville

  Sage & Thyme
  617-332-0695

North Adams
  Twin Sisters Inn
  413-663-6933

North Eastham
  Penny House
  508-255-6632-[Y--]

North Falmouth
  Captains Inn
  508-564-6424

  Fiddlers Cove Marina
  508-564-6326

  Wingate Crossing
  508-540-8723

North Scituate
  Wright Place

Northampton
  Autumn Inn
  413-584-7660

  Knoll
  413-584-8164-[Y--]

  Northampton B&B
  413-586-6190

Northfield
  Centennial House
  413-498-5921

  Northfield Country House
  413-498-2692

Norwell
  1810 House B&B
  617-659-1810-[G--]

Oak Bluffs
  Attleboro House
  508-693-4346

  Circuit House
  508-693-2966

  Dockside Inn
  508-693-2966

  Inn At Dockside
  800-245-5979

  Narraganset House
  508-693-3627

  Nashua House
  508-693-0043

  Oak Bluffs Inn
  508-693-7171

  Oak House
  508-693-4187-[Y--]

  Sea Spray Inn
  508-693-9388

  Ships Inn
  508-693-2760

  Summer Place Inn
  508-693-9908

  Tivoli Inn
  508-693-7928

Onset
  Onset Pointe Inn
  800-35-ONSET
  [G--]

Orleans
  Anchorage On The Cove
  508-255-1442

  Edgars B&B

  Morgans Way B&B
  508-255-0831

  The Farm House
  508-255-6654-[Y--]

Osterville
  East Bay Lodge
  508-428-6961

Otis
  Joyous Garde B&B
  413-269-6852

  Stonewood Inn
  413-269-4894

Pepperell
  Boggastowe Farm
  508-433-9987

Peru
  Chalet d'Alicia
  413-655-8292

  Stall Inn
  413-655-8008

Petersham
  Winterwood At Petersham
  617-724-8885-[Y--]

Pittsfield
  Greer B&B
  413-443-3669

  White Horse Inn
  413-442-2512

Plainfield
  Rolling Meadow Farm
  413-634-2166

Plymouth
  Allen House
  508-545-8221-[G--]

  Another Place Inn
  508-746-0126

  Campbell Guest & Muffin House
  508-747-3293

  Colonial House Inn
  508-746-2087

  Cranberry Cottage
  508-747-1726-[G--]

  Foxglove Cottage
  508-747-6576

  Halls B&B
  508-746-2835

  Hawthorne Hill B&B
  508-746-5244

  Litchfield House

  Morton Park Place
  800-736-3276-[Y--]

Pocasset
  Sterling Rose
  508-564-6691

Princeton
  Harrington Farm
  800-736-3276

  Hill House
  508-464-2061

Provincetown
  1807 House
  508-487-2173

  Admirals Landing Guest House
  508-487-9663

  Asheton House
  508-487-9966

  Bed N Breakfast
  508-487-9555

Bold Name - Description appears in other section   **Massachusetts**

Bradford Gardens
800-432-2334

Cape Codder Guest House
508-487-0131

Captain Lysander Inn
508-487-2253

Crosswinds Inn
508-487-3533

Elephant Walk
508-487-2543-[Y--]

Elliot House
508-487-4029

Gabriels
508-487-3232

Hargood House
508-487-9133

Lamplighter Guest House
508-487-2529-[Y--]

Land's End Inn
508-487-0706

Monument House
508-487-9664

Oceans Inn
508-487-7800

Red Inn
508-487-0050

Rose & Crowns Guest House
508-487-3322

Sandpiper Beach House
508-487-1928

Six Webster Place
508-487-2266

Somerset House
508-487-0383

Sunset Inn
508-487-9810

Three Peaks Inn
508-487-1717

Twelve Center Inn
508-487-0381

Victoria House

508-487-1319

Watership Inn
508-487-0094

Westwinds-On Gull Street
508-487-1841

White Wind Inn
508-487-1526

Windjammer House
508-487-0599

Quincy
Allen House
508-545-8221-[G--]

Rehoboth
Gilberts B&B
800-828-6821-[Y--]

Perryville Inn
508-252-9239

Richmond
A B&B In Berkshires
413-698-2817

Cogswell Guest House
413-698-2750

Inn At Richmond
413-698-2566

Rockport
1770 Inn
508-546-3227

Addison Choate Inn
508-546-7543-[Y--]

Beach Knoll Inn
508-546-6939

Cable House
508-546-3895

Eden Pines Inn
508-546-2505

Granite Houe
508-451-0395

Inn At Seven South Street
508-546-6708

Inn On Cove Hill
508-546-2701-[Y--]

Lantana House
508-546-3535

Linden Tree Inn
508-546-2494

Mooringstone For Nonsmokers
508-546-2479

Old Farm Inn
508-546-3237

Peg Leg Inn

Pleasant Street Inn
508-546-3915

Ralph Waldo Emerson Inn
508-546-6658

Rockport Lodge
508-546-2090

Rocky Shores Inn
508-546-2823

Sally Webster
508-546-9251-[Y--]

Seacrest Manor
508-546-2211

Seafarer Inn
508-546-6248-[Y--]

Seaward Inn
508-546-3471

Seven South Street Inn
508-546-6708

Rutland
General Rufus Putnam House
508-886-4256

Sagamore Beach
Bed & Breakfast
508-888-1559

Widows Walk B&B
508-888-3888

Salem
Amelia Payson Guest House
508-744-8304

Clipper Ship Inn
508-745-8022

Coach House Inn
800-688-8689

Harborside House

508-631-1032-[G--]

Nathaniel Bowditch Guest House

Salem Inn
800-446-2995

Stephen Daniels House
508-744-5709

Stepping Stone Inn
508-741-8900

Suzannah Flint House
508-744-5281

Sandisfield
New Boston Inn
413-258-4477

Sandwich
Bay Beach B&B
508-888-8813-[Y--]

Capt Ezra Nye House
800-388-2278-[Y-1-]

Daniel Webster Inn
800-444-3566

Dillingham House
508-833-0065

Hawthorn Hill
508-888-3333

Isaiah Jones Homestead
800-526-1625-[Y--]

Quince Tree
508-888-1371

Seth Pope House
508-888-5916

Six Water Street
508-888-6808-[Y--]

Stitchery In Sandwich Village
508-888-4647

Summer House
508-888-4991-[Y--]

The Inn at Sandwich Center
508-888-6958

Village Inn At Sandwich

©*Inn & Travel Memphis, Tennessee*   1-141

Massachusetts

Bold Name - Description appears in other section

800-922-9989

Wind Song B&B
508-888-3567

Scituate
Allen House
508-545-8221-[G--]

Raspberry Inn
508-545-6629

Seekonk
Historic Jacob Hill Farm
508-336-9165

Simeons Mansion House
508-336-6674

Sheffield
Berkshire Willows Inn
413-229-3137

Bow Wow Road Inn
413-229-3339

Centuryhurst Guest House
413-229-8131

Colonel Ashley Inn
413-229-2929

Ivanhoe Country House
413-229-2143

One Of A Kind B&B
413-229-2711

Orchard Shade B&B
413-229-8463

Race Brook Lodge
888-RBLODGE

Stagecoach Hill Inn
413-229-8585

Staveleigh House
413-229-2129

Unique B&B
413-229-3363-[Y--]

Shelburne Centre
Parson Hubbard House
413-625-9730

Shelburne Falls

Country Comfort
413-625-9877

Sippewissett
Wyndemere House
508-540-7069-[Y--]

Somerset
Poplars
508-675-7269

South Ashfield
Bull Frog B&B
413-628-4493-[Y--]

South Chatham
Ye Olde Nantucket House
508-432-5641-[Y--]

South Dartmouth
Little Red House
508-996-4554-[Y--]

Padanaram Guest House
508-993-9009

Salt Marsh Farm B&B
508-992-0980

South Deerfield
Orchard Terrace B&B
413-665-3829

Sunnyside Farm B&B
413-665-3113

Yellow Gabled House B&B
413-665-4922

South Dennis
Country Pineapple Inn
508-760-3211

South Egremont
1780 Egremont Inn
413-528-2111

Egremont Inn
413-528-2111

Weathervane Inn
413-528-9580

Windflower Inn
800-992-1993

South Hadley
Grandmarys B&&B
413-533-7381

South Harwich
House On The Hill
508-432-4321

South Lancaster
College Town Inn
508-368-7000

Deershorn Manor B&B
508-365-9022

South Lee
Federal House Inn
617-350-6657-[Y--]

Historic Merrell Tavern Inn
413-243-1794-[Y--]

South Orleans
Hillbourne House B&B
508-255-0780

South Sudbury
Wayside Inn
508-443-8846

South Yarmouth
Captain Farris House
800-350-9477-[GQA-

Four Winds B&B
508-394-4182

River Street Guest House
508-398-8946

Southampton
Dianthas Garden B&B
413-529-0093

Southfield
Langhaar House
413-229-2007

Springfield
Old Mill Inn
203-763-1473-[Y--]

Sterling
Sterling Inn
508-422-6592

Sterling Orchard
508-422-6595

Stockbridge
Arbor Rose B&B
413-298-4744

B&B Old Lamplighter
413-298-3053

Berkshire Thistle Inn
413-298-3188

Broad Meadows
413-298-4972

Cherry Hill Farm
413-298-5452

Inn At Stockbridge
413-298-3337

Olde Lamplighter
413-298-3053

Red Lion Inn
413-298-5545

Roeder House B&B
413-298-4015

Stirling Moffat Guest House

Taggart House
413-298-4303

Woodside B&B
413-298-4977

Stow
Amerscot House
508-897-0666-[Y--]

Stow Away Inn
508-897-1999

Sturbridge
Captain Parkers Inn At Quinebaug
800-707-7303-[G--]

Chamberlain House
508-347-3313

Col E Crafts Publik House
508-347-3313-[Y--]

Lakeshore B&B
508-347-9495

Sturbridge Country Inn
508-347-5503-[G--]

Sudbury
Checkerberry Corner
508-443-8660

1-142

©Inn & Travel Memphis, Tennessee

Bold Name - Description appears in other section **Massachusetts**

Coach House Inn
508-443-2223

Longfellow's Wayside Inn
508-443-1776-[Y--]

Sudbury B&B
508-443-2860

Swampscott
  Cap'n Jacks Waterfront Inn
  617-595-7910

  Marshall House
  617-595-6544

  Oak Shores
  617-599-2677

Taunton
  Inn At Cedar Street
  508-823-8966-[Y--]

Townsend
  Wood Farm
  508-597-5019

Truro
  B&B In Truro

  Parker House
  508-349-3358

  South Slope B&B
  508-487-3498

Tyringham
  Golden Goose
  413-243-3008

Uxbridge
  Capron House
  508-278-2214

Vineyard Haven
  Aldworth Manor
  508-693-3203

  Captain Dexter House
  508-693-6564

  Crocker House Inn
  508-693-1151

  Deux Noisettes Chez Vous
  508-693-0253

  Gazebo B&B
  508-693-6955

  Hanover Houes
  508-693-1066

  High Haven House
  508-693-9204

  Lothrop Merry House
  508-693-1646-[Y--]

  Nancys Auberge
  508-693-4434

  Ocean Side Inn
  508-693-1296

  Post House Inn
  508-693-5337

  The Hanover House
  508-693-1066-[Y--]

  Tisbury Inn
  508-693-2200

  Tuckerman House
  508-693-0417-[Y--]

  Twin Oaks Inn
  508-693-8633

Ware
  Antique 1880 B&B
  413-967-7847

  Wildwood Inn
  800-999-3416

Wareham
  Little Harbor Guest House
  508-295-6329

  Mulberry B&B
  508-295-0684

Warren
  Deer Meadow Farm
  413-436-7129

Wellfleet
  Cahoon Hollow B&B
  508-349-6372

  Holden Inn
  508-349-3450

  Inn At Duck Creeke
  508-349-9333

West Barnstable
  Gentleman Farmer B&B
  508-362-6955

  Honeysuckle Hill
  508-362-8418-[Y--]

West Boyleston
  Rose Cottage
  508-835-4034

West Brookfield
  Deer Meadow Farm

West Dennis
  Beach House
  508-398-8321

  Christian Hill

  Lighthouse Inn
  508-398-2244

West Falmouth
  Elms
  508-540-7232

  Inn At West Falmouth
  508-540-7696

  Old Silver Beach B&B
  508-540-5446

  Sjoholm Inn
  508-540-5706

West Gouldsboro
  Sunset House
  207-963-7156

West Harpswell
  Vigarage East Ltd

West Harwich
  Barnary Inn
  508-432-6789

  Lions Head Inn
  800-321-3155-[Y--]

  Sunny Pines B&B
  508-432-9628

  Tern Inn
  508-432-3714

  Willow House B&B
  508-432-2517

West Hawyley
  Stump Sprouts Lodge
  413-339-4265

West Newton
  Withington House
  617-332-8422

West Stockbridge
  Card Lake Inn & Restaurant
  413-232-0272-[G--]

  Shaker Mill Tavern Inn
  800-322-8565

  Williamsville Inn
  413-274-6118

West Stockbrige
  Marble Inn
  413-232-7092

West Tisbury
  Blue Goose
  508-693-3223

  Lamberts Cove
  508-693-2298

  Old Parsonage B&B
  508-696-7745

West Yarmouth
  Manor House
  508-771-3433

Westhampton
  Outlook Farm B&B
  413-527-0633

Westminster
  Westminster Village Inn
  508-874-5911

Weston
  Webb Bigelow Place

Westport
  Harbor Inn
  508-636-5915

Whatley
  Sunnyside Farm
  413-665-3113

Wilbraham
  B&B Bob & Barb
  413-228-7283

Williamsburg
  Helen S Gould
  413-268-7314

  Twin Maples B&B
  413-268-7925

Williamstown
  Field Farm Guest House
  413-458-3135

  Goldberrys B&B
  413-458-3935

©Inn & Travel Memphis, Tennessee

Massachusetts - New Hamphsire

Bold Name - *Description appears in other section*

House On Main Street
413-458-3031

Le Jardin
413-458-8032

Riverbend Farm
413-458-5504

Steep Acres Farm
413-458-3772

Williamstown B&B
413-458-9202

Winchester
Inn Of The Seven Seas

Woburn
Appleton Inn
617-932-3200

Woods Hole
Marlborough
508-548-6218

Worthington
Country Cricket Village Inn
413-238-5356

Franklin Burrs
413-238-5826

Inn Yesterday
413-238-5529

Worthington Inn / Four Corners
413-238-4441-[Y--]

Yarmouth
Dockside Guest Quarters

Yarmouth Port
Colonial House Inn
800-999-3416

Crook Jaw Inn
508-362-6111

Joshua Sears Manor
508-362-5000

Lanes End Cottage
508-362-5298

Liberty Hill Inn On Cape Cod
800-821-3977-[Y--]

Old Yarmouth Inn

508-362-8201

Olde Captains Inn
508-362-4496

One Centre Street Inn
508-362-8910

Village Inn
508-362-3182

Wedgewood Inn
508-362-5157-[Y--]

NEW HAMPSHIRE

Alexandria
Mount Cardigan B&B
603-744-5803

Stone Rest B&B
603-744-6066-[Y--]

Alstead
Darby Brook Farm
603-835-6624

Alton Bay
Oak Birch Inn

Andover
Andover Arms Guest House
603-735-5953

English House
603-735-5987

Antrim
Antrim Inn
603-588-8000

Breezy Point Inn
603-478-5201

Maplehurst
603-588-8000

Steele Homestead Inn
603-588-2407

Uplands Inn
603-588-6349

Ashland
Cheney House
603-968-7968

Country Options
603-968-7958

Cynthia Willey

House

Glynn House Inn
800-637-9599-[G--]

Haus Trillium
603-968-2180

Barnstead
Barnstead Parade Inn
603-435-6631

Bartlett
Country Inn At Bartlett
603-374-2353-[Y--]

Notchland Inn
603-374-6131

Bedford
Bedford Village Inn
603-472-2001

Bethlehem
Adair
603-444-2600

Gables of Park & Main
603-869-3111

Highlands Inn
603-869-3978

Mulberry Inn
603-869-3389

Mulburn Inn
603-869-2647

Wayside Inn
800-448-9557

Bradford
Bradford Inn
800-669-5309-[G--]

Candlelite Inn B&B
603-938-5571

Dogwood Country Inn

Massasecum Lodge

Mountain Lake Inn
800-662-6005

Rosewood Country Inn
603-936-5253

Bretton Woods
Bretton Arms

Country Inn
800-258-0330

Lodge At Bretton Woods

Bridgewater
Pasquaney Inn
603-744-2712

Bristol
Bristol Guest House

Pleasant View B&B
603-744-5547

Victorian
603-744-6157

Campton
Amber Lights Inn
603-726-4077

Campton Inn
603-726-4449

Mountain Fare Inn
603-726-4283-[Y--]

Osgood Inn
603-726-3543

Campton Village
Village Guest House
603-726-0444

Canaan
Inn On Canaan Street
603-523-7310

Towerhouse Inn
603-523-7244

Canterbury
Sleepy Hollow B&B
603-267-6055

Center Conway
Lavender Flower Inn
800-729-0106

Center Harbor
Dearborn Place
603-253-4900

Kona Mansion Inn
603-253-4900

Red Hill Inn
603-279-7001

Watch Hill B&B
603-253-4334

Center Ossipee

©Inn & Travel Memphis, Tennessee

Bold Name - *Description appears in other section*

New Hampshire

Effingham Inn
603-539-2141

Hitching Post Village Inn
603-539-4482

Center Sandwich
Corner House Inn
603-284-6219

Charlestown
Maplehedge B&B
603-798-4951

Chesterfield
Chesterfield Inn
800-365-5155

Chichester
Hitching Post B&B
603-798-4951

Chocorua
Farmhouse B&B
603-323-8707-[Y--]

Staffords In The Field
800-332-0355

Chocoura
Mount Chocoura View House
603-323-8350

Claremont
Goddard Mansion B&B
603-543-0603

Poplars
603-543-0858

Colebrook
Ma & Pa Cormiers Inn

Monadnock B&B
603-237-8216

Concord
Bradford Inn
800-669-5309-[G--]

Hitching Post B&B
603-798-4951

Wyman Farm
603-783-4467

Conway
Darby Field Inn
800-426-4147

Eastman Inn

800-562-1300

Foothills Farm B&B
207-935-3799

Kancamagus Swift River Inn
800-255-4236-[Y--]

Merrill Farm Resort
800-445-1017

Mountain Valley Manner B&B
603-447-3922

Village House
800-972-8343-[Y--]

Cornish
Chase House B&B
603-675-5391-[Y--]

Danbury
Inn At Danbury
603-768-3318-[Y--]

Dover
Silver Street Inn
603-743-3000

Durham
Hanna House B&B
603-659-5500

University Guest House
603-868-2728

East Andover
Highland Lake Inn
603-735-6462

Patchwork Inn
603-735-6426

East Sullivan
Delford Inn
603-847-9778

East Wakefield
Lake Ivanhor Inn
603-522-8824

Easton
Blanches B&B
603-823-7061

Eaton Center
Inn At Crystal Lake
800-343-7336

Palmer House Inn
603-447-2120

Rockhouse

Mountain Farm
603-447-2880

Elkins
Limner Haus
603-526-6451

Enfield
Kluges Sunset Hill Inn
603-632-4335

Epping
Haley House Farm
603-679-8713

Epsom
The Quiet Place B&B & Antiques
603-736-9696

Etna
Moose Mountain Lodge
603-643-3529-[Y--]

Exeter
Exeter Inn
603-772-5901

Inn By The Bandstand
603-772-6352

Fitzwilliam
Amos A Parker House
603-585-6540

Barntique

Fern Hill

Fitzwilliam Inn
603-585-9000

Hannah Davis House
603-585-3344

Francestown
Crotched Mountain Inn
603-588-6841

Francestown B&B
603-547-6333

Inn At Crotched Mountain
603-588-6840

Franconia
Blanches B&B
603-823-7061

Bungay Jar B&B
603-823-7775-[Y--]

Cannon Mountain Inn & Cottage
603-823-9574

Franconia Inn
800-473-5299-[G--]

Horse & House Inn
603-823-5501-[Y--]

Lovetts By Lafayette Brook
603-823-7761

Main Street B&B
603-823-8513

Pinestead Farm Lodge
603-823-5601

Sugar Hill Inn
603-823-5621

Franconia Village
Inn At Forest Hills
800-280-9550

Franklin
Maria W Atwood Inn
603-934-3666-[Y--]

Webster Lake Inn
603-934-4050

Freedom
Freedom House
603-539-4815

Freedom Hill
Knob Hill B&B
603-539-6576

Gilford
Cartway House
603-528-1172-[Y--]

Gunstock Inn
603-527-1086

Kings Grant Inn
603-293-4431

Gilmanton
Historic Tavern Inn
603-267-7349

Glen
Bernerhof Inn
800-548-8007

Covered Bridge

©*Inn & Travel Memphis, Tennessee*

1-145

New Hampshire *Bold Name - Description appears in other section*

House
603-383-9109

Gorham
Gorham House Inn
800-453-0023

Pinkham Notch
Camp
603-466-2727

Goshen
Cutters Loft
603-863-5306

Grafton
Grafton Inn

Greenfield
Greenfield Inn
603-547-6327-[Y--]

Greenland
Captain Folsom Inn
603-436-2662

Thomas Ayers
House
603-436-5992

Guild
Drum Inn
603-863-3881

Hampstead
Stillmeadow B&B
603-329-8381

Hampton
Blue Heron Inn
603-926-9666

Elmdale Guest
House
603-926-2507

Griffin House
603-926-2868

Inn At Elmwood
Corners
800-253-5691

Jaffrey Manor Inn
603-532-8069

Lamies Inn &
Tavern
603-926-0330

Victoria Inn At
Hampton
603-929-1437

Hampton Beach
Boars Head

603-926-3911

Century House
603-926-6874

Grayhurst
603-926-2584

Oceanside
603-926-3542-[Y--]

Roy Family B&B
800-235-2897

Hancock
John Hancock Inn
800-525-1789

Hanover
Hanover Inn
603-643-4300

Silver Maple Lodge-Cottages
800-666-1946-[Y--]

Stonecrest Farm
B&B
802-295-2600-[Y--]

Harrisville
Harrisville Squire
Inn
603-827-3925

Haverhill
Animal Track Inn
603-989-3351

Haverhill Inn
603-989-5961

Hebron
Six Chimneys
603-744-2029

Henniker
Colby Hill Inn
800-531-0330

Hanscom House
B&B

Henniker House
603-428-3198

Meeting House Inn
603-428-3228

Hill
Maple Tree Farm
603-744-6566

Snowbound B&B
603-744-9112

Hillsborough
Stonebridge Inn
603-464-3155

Stonewall Farm
Holderness

Inn On Golden Pond
603-968-7269-[G--]

Manor On Golden Pond
800-545-2141-[Y--]

Hopkinton
Windyledge B&B
603-746-4054

Intervale
Forest A Country
Inn
800-448-3534

Mountain Vale Inn
800-545-6033

New England Inn
603-356-5541

Riverside Country
Inn
603-356-9060

Wildflowers Guest House
603-356-2224-[Y--]

Invervale
Old Field House
603-356-5478-[Y--]

Jackson
Blake House
603-383-9057

Christmas Farm Inn
800-HI ELVES

Dana Place
800-537-9276-[Y--]

Eagle Mountain
House
603-383-9111

Ellis River House
B&B
800-233-8309

Inn At Jackson
800-289-8600-[Y--]

Inn At Thorn Hill
800-289-8990-[Y--]

Jackson House
B&B
800-338-1268

Nestlenook Inn
603-383-9443

Paisley & Parsley
603-383-0859

Village House
800-972-8343-[G--]

Whitneys Village Inn
800-252-5622

Wildcat Inn &
Tavern
603-383-4245

Jaffrey
Benjamin Prescott Inn
603-532-6637-[G--]

Galway House
603-532-8083

Gould Farm
603-532-6996

Lilac Hill Acres
603-532-7278-[Y--]

Mill Pond Inn
603-532-7687-[Y--]

Woodbound Inn
800-252-3033

Jaffrey Center
Monadnock Inn
603-532-7001

Jefferson
Applebrook B&B
800-545-6504-[Y--]

Davenport Inn
603-586-4320

Jefferson Inn
800-729-7908

Stag Hollow Inn /
Llama Keep
603-586-4598

Katonah
723 House
914-232-8864

Kearsage
Issiac Merrill House
800-328 9041-[Y--]

1-146 ©Inn & Travel Memphis, Tennessee

Bold Name - Description appears in other section   **New Hampshire**

Keene
   289 Court
   603-357-3195

   Carriage Barn Guesthouse
   603-357-3812

   Goose Pond Guest House
   603-352-2828

   Noah Cooke Inn
   603-357-3117

Laconia
   Ferry Point House
   603-524-0087

   Hickory Stick Farm
   603-524-3333

   Laran Farm

Lancaster
   A Touch Of Home

Lebanon
   B&B Of Bank Street
   603-448-2041

Lincoln
   Beacon
   603-745-8118

   Mill House Inn
   800-654-6183

Lisbon
   Ammonoosuc Inn
   800-COBLERS
   [G--]

Littleton
   1895 House
   603-444-5200

   Beal House Inn
   603-444-2661-[Y--]

   Ravens Inn
   800-209-5112

   Thayers Inn
   800-634-8179

Loudon
   Inn At Loudon Ridge
   603-267-8952

Lyme
   Dowd's Country Inn
   603-795-4712

   Lyme Inn
   603-795-2222-[Y--]

   Marjories House
   603-795-2141

Madison
   Madison Carriage House
   800-851-1088

Manchester
   Susse Chalet Inn
   800-5-CHALET

Marlborough
   Peep Willow Farm
   603-876-3807

   Thatcher Hill Inn
   603-876-3361

   Tolman Pond

Meredith
   Hathaway Inn
   603-279-5521

   Inn At Mill Falls

   Nutmeg Inn
   800-642-9229

Milford
   Ram In The Thicket
   603-654-6440

   Victoria Place

Mirror Lake
   Hardie House B&B
   603-569-5714

   Pick Point Lodge
   603-569-1338

Monroe
   Silver Birches B&B

Moultonboro
   Olde Orchard Inn
   800-598-5845-[Y--]

Mount Sunapee
   Blue Goose Inn
   603-763-5519-[G--]

Mount Vernon
   Zahns Alpine Guest House
   603-673-2334

Munsonville
   Old Mill House
   603-847-3224

Nashua
   Home Away From Home B&B
   800-345-2127

New Boston
   Colburn Homestead B&B
   603-487-5250

New Ipswich
   Inn At New Ipswich
   603-878-3711-[Y--]

New London
   Hide-way Lodge
   603-526-4861

   Maple Hill Farm
   603-526-2248

   New London Inn
   800-526-2791

Newbury
   Andrew Brook Lodge
   603-938-2920

Newmarket
   Helgas B&B
   603-659-6856

Newport
   Back Side Inn
   603-863-5161

   Inn At Coit Mountain
   800-367-2364-[Y--]

North Charleston
   Indian Shutters Inn
   603-826-4445-[Y--]

North Conway
   1785 Inn
   800-421-1785

   Buttonwood Inn
   800-258-2625-[Y--]

   Cabernet Inn
   603-356-4704

   Center Chimney 1787
   603-356-6788

   Cranmore Inn
   800-526-5502-[Y--]

   Cranmore Mountain Lodge
   800-356-3596

   Eastern Slope Inn

   Foothills Farm B&B
   207-935-3799

   Nereledge Inn
   603-356-2831-[Y--]

   New England Inn
   800-82-NEINN

   Old Red Inn & Cottages
   603-356-2642

   Scottish Lion Inn
   603-356-6381

   Stonehurst Manor
   800-525-9100

   The Forest
   800-448-3534

   Victorian Harvest Inn
   603-356-3548-[Y--]

   Wyatt House English Inn
   603-356-7977

North Sutton
   Follansbee Inn
   603-927-4221-[Y--]

North Woodstock
   Birch Hill Cottages

   Birches B&B
   603-745-6603

   Cascade Lodge
   603-745-2722

   Ledgeland
   603-745-3951

   Rivers Edge B&B
   603-745-2208

   Three Rivers House
   603-745-2711

   Wilderness Inn B&B
   800-200-WILD-[Y--]

   Woodstock Inn
   603-745-3951

Northwood
   Aviary
   603-942-7755

   Lake Shore Farm

New Hampshire   **Bold Name** - *Description appears in other section*

603-942-5921

Meadow Farm B&B
603-942-8619-[Y--]

Nostalgia B&B
603-942-7748

Resort At Lake
Shore Farm
603-942-5921

Orford
  White Goose Inn
  603-353-4812

Ossipee
  Acorn Lodge
  603-539-2151-[Y--]

Pelham
  Florence Lepore

Peterborough
  Apple Gate B&B
  603-924-6453

  Salzburg Inn

  Willows Inn

Pittsburg
  Glen

Pittsfield
  Appleview B&B
  603-435-7641

Plainfield
  Home Hill Country Inn
  603-675-6165

Plymouth
  Colonel Spencer Inn
  603-536-3438-[G--]

  Crab Apple Inn
  603-536-4476

  Northway House
  603-536-2838

Portsmouth
  Bow Street Inn
  603-431-7760

  Clef B&B
  603-772-8850

  Governors House B&B
  603-431-6546-[Y--]

  Inn At Christian
Shore
603-431-6770

Inn At Goodwin
Park

Inn At Strawberry
Banke
603-436-7242

Martin Hill Inn
603-436-2287

Sheafe Street Inn
603-436-9104

Sise Inn
603-433-1200

Treatre Inn
603-431-5846

Rindge
  Cathedral House
  603-899-6790

  Grassy Pond House
  603-899-5166

  Tokfarm Inn
  603-899-6646

Rochester
  Governors Inn B&B
  603-332-0107

Rye
  Cablehouse
  603-964-5000

  Rock Ledge Manor B&B
  603-431-1413

Seabrook Beach
  Bellingham At The Bay B&B

Shelburne
  Philbrook Farm Inn
  603-466-3831

Snowville
  Snowvillage Inn
  800-447-4345

Stafford
  Province Inn
  603-664-2457

Stark
  Stark Inn
  603-636-2644

Stratham
  Maple Lodge B&B
603-778-9833

Stratham Hill
Farm
603-772-3999

Sugar Hill
  Cannon View Inn
  603-823-8039

  Foxglove, A
  Country Inn
  603-823-8840

  Hilltop Inn
  603-823-5695

  Homestead
  603-823-5564

  Inn At Skunk
  Hollow
  800-551-3084

  Ledgeland
  603-823-5341

  Southworths B&B
  603-823-5344

  Sugar Hill
  603-823-5654

  Sunset Hill House
  603-823-5522

  The Sunset Hill
  House
  800-SUN-HILL

Sunapee
  Dexters Inn
  800-232-5571

  Haus Edelweiss
  B&B
  603-763-2100

  Inn At Sunapee
  603-763-4444

  Old Governors
  House
  603-763-9918

  Seven Hearths Inn
  800-237-2464

  Times Ten Inn
  603-763-5120

Suncook
  Suncook House
  603-485-8141

Sutton Mills
**Village House At
Sutton Mills**
603-927-4765

Tamworth
  Edgehill Inn

  Highland House
  603-323-7982

  Tamworth Inn
  800-933-3902-[Y--]

  Whispering Pines
  B&B
  603-323-7337

Tamworth Village
  Gilman Tavern
  603-323-8940

Temple
  Birchwood Inn
  603-878-3285

Tilton
  Black Swan Inn
  603-286-4524

  Country Place
  603-386-8551

  Tilton Manor
  603-286-3457

Troy
  Inn At East Hill
  Farm
  603-242-6495

Twin Mountain
  Carlsons Lodge

  Northern Zermatt
  Inn
  800-535-3214

  Partridge House Inn
  603-846-2277

Wakefield
  Jonathan Gilman
  Homestead
  603-522-3102

  Wakefield Inn
  603-522-8272

Walpole
  1801 House

  Great Brook House
  603-756-4721

  Josiah Bellows
  House

Bold Name - Description appears in other section   **New Hampshire- Rhode Island**

603-756-4250

Warner
Jacobs Ladder B&B
603-456-3494

Warren
Black Iris B&B
603-764-9366

Blue Spruce B&B
603-764-5756

Waterville Valley
Silver Squirrel Inn
603-236-8325

Snowy Owl Inn
603-236-8383

Valley Inn & Tavern

Wentworth
Hilltop Acres
603-764-5896-[G--]

Hobson House
603-764-9460

Wentworth Inn &
Art Gallery
800-542-2331-[Y--]

West Canaan
Chalet At Goose
Pond
603-632-4966

West Chesterfield
Chesterfield Inn
800-365-5515

West Franklin
Strolling Woods On
Webster Lake
800-540-5548

West Ossippee
Phoenix Inn
603-539-2874

West Ossippee
Country Inn
603-539-2874

Whitefield
1875 Mountain Inn
603-837-2220

General Lafayette
Inn
603-837-9300

Kimball Hill Inn
603-837-2284

Maxwell Haus
603-837-9717

Spalding Inn &
Club
603-837-2572

Wilson Mills
Bosebuck Mountain
Camps

Wilton
Greys Corner
603-654-6773

Wilton Center
Stepping Stones
603-654-9048

Winnesquam
Tall Pines Inn
800-722-6870-[G--]

Wolfeboro
Inn Of New Durham

Isaac Springfield
House
603-569-3529

Lakeview Inn
603-569-1335

Tuc' Me Inn
603-569-5702-[Y--]

Wolfeboro Inn
800-451-2389

Woodstock
The Birches B&B
603-745-6603

Woodsville
Green Pastures

RHODE ISLAND

Block Island
1661 Inn
401-466-2421

Adrian
401-466-2693

Art Construction
Studio
401-466-2924

Atlantic Inn
401-466-5883

Ballards Inn
401-466-2231

Barrington
401-466-5510

Bayberry Heath
401-466-2838

Bellevue
401-466-2389

Blue Dory Inn
800-992-7290-[Y--]

Capt Willis House
401-466-5883

Continental B&B
401-466-5136

Corner House
401-466-2624

Driftwind Guests
401-466-5548

Estas At Old
Harbor
401-466-2651

F Casey Inn
401-466-5502

**Gables Inn &
Gables II**
401-466-2213

Gothic Cottage
Ocean Villa
401-466-2918

Guest House
401-466-2676

Harbor View Guest
House
401-466-2807

Hardy Smith House
401-466-2466

Highview Country
Inn
401-466-5912

Hotel Manisses
401-466-2063

Inn At Old Harbor
401-466-2212

Island Home
401-466-5944

Island Manor
Resort
401-466-5567

Islander
401-466-2897

Lewis Farm Guest
House
401-466-2113

Lilac Cottage
401-466-5954

Mill Pond Cottages
401-466-2423

Mitchell Cottage
401-446-5053

National Hotel
800-252-2449

Neptune House
401-466-2988

New Shoreham
House Inn
800-272-2601

Old Town Inn
401-466-5958

Pond View B&B
401-466-2927

Rose Farm Inn
401-466-2021

Samuel Peckham
Inn
401-466-2439

Sasafrash
401-466-5486

Sea Breeze Inn
401-466-2275

Seacrest Inn
401-466-2882-[Y--]

Sheffield House
401-466-2494-[Y--]

Smugglers Cove
401-466-2828

Spring House
800-234-9263

Star Cottage
401-466-2842

Water Street Inn
800-825-6254

White House
401-466-2653

©*Inn & Travel Memphis, Tennessee*   1-149

Rhode Island

Bold Name - Description appears in other section

Willow Grove
401-466-2896

Bristol
Joseph Reynolds House
401-254-0230-[Y--]

Rockwell House Inn
401-254-0230

Williams Grant Inn
401-253-4222

Carolina
Brendas B&B
401-364-3608

Charlestown
General Stanton Inn
401-364-8888

Hathaways
401-364-6665

Inn At The Meadow
401-789-1473

Inn The Meadow
401-789-1473

Nordic Lodge
401-783-4515

One Willow By The Sea B&B
401-364-0802

Windswept Farm
401-364-6292

Exeter
Dovecrest
401-539-7795

Glocester
Freeman Farm B&B
401-568-6561

Hopkinton City
Gen Thurston House-1763
401-377-9049

Jamestown
Bay Voyage Inn
401-423-2100

Candlewick
401-423-2692

Jamestown B&B
410-423-1338

Lionel Champlin House
401-423-2782

Mary W Murphy
401-423-1338

Kingston
Admiral Dewey Inn
401-783-2090

Hedgerow B&B
401-783-2671

Lincoln
Whipple-Cullen Farmstead
401-333-1899

Little Compton
Ballyvoreen
401-655-4396

Roost
401-635-8407

Middletown
Atlantic House
401-847-7259

B&B N'More
401-846-3646

Bartrams B&B
401-846-2259

Bliss Mine Road House
401-846-2979

Briar Patch
401-841-5824

Country Goose B&B
401-846-6308

Finnegans Inn Shadow Lawn
401-847-0902

Hedgegate
401-846-3906

Lindseys Guest House
401-846-9386-[Y--]

Maude Kerrs B&B
401-847-5997

Pickhams Guest Home
401-846-2382

Pollys Place
401-847-2160

Sea Breeze
401-847-5628

Seaview Inn
401-846-5000

Stone Towers
401-846-3227

Stoneyard
401-847-0494

Wolcott House By The Sea
401-846-9376

Misquamicut
Andrea Hotel
401-348-8788

Misquamicut Beach
Ocean View
401-596-7170

Narragansett
1900 House
401-789-7971

23 Perkins
401-783-9158

Casa Marabele
401-782-6852

Chestnut House
401-789-5335

Duck Harbor
401-783-3495

Edward Earle House
401-789-4363

Endless Summer
401-789-0615

Four Gables
401-789-6948

Grinnell Inn

Historic Home
401-789-7746

House Of Snee
401-783-9494-[Y--]

Ilverthorpe Cottage
401-789-2392-[Y--]

Kenyon Farms
401-783-7123

Lindemere
401-783-2798

Louis Sherry Cottage
401-783-8626

Maison Bienvenue
401-783-1190

Mon Reue
401-783-2846

Murphys B&B
401-789-1824

Nansea By The Bay
401-783-4045

Old Clerk House B&B
401-783-8008

Phoenix House
401-783-1918

Phoenix Inn
401-783-1918

Pier House
401-783-4704

Pleasant Cottage
401-783-6895

Regina Cottage
401-783-1875

Richard/Joyce Saint Onge
401-789-7695

Rnyners Guest House
401-783-6001

Rockport Cottage
401-783-2647

Sea Gull Guest House
401-783-4636

Seafield Cottage
401-783-2432

Southwest Wind Acres
401-783-5860

Starr Cottage Inn
401-783-2411

Stephen Farmer
401-789-0763

Bold Name - Description appears in other section *Rhode Island*

Swan Cottage B&B
401-783-4391

Twenty Three Perkins
401-763-9158

Victorian Lady
401-789-6222

White Rose
401-789-0181

Newport
1812 House
401-847-1188

1855 Marshall Slocum House
401-847-3787

503 Spring
401-847-3132

Admiral Benbow Inn
800-343-2863

Admiral Farragut Inn
800-343-2863

Admiral Fitzroy
800-343-2863

Admiral Weaver Inn
401-849-0051

Ailinas
401-847-3903

Alexander Jack Jr House

Ancestral Woodbine Manor

Beachstone

Belle Reve Inn
401-846-4262

Bellevue House
401-847-1828

Bethshan B&B
401-846-1777

Bittersweet Guest House
401-849-7567

Bliss Cottage
401-846-6932

Blue Stone B&B
401-846-8250

Brinley Victorian Inn
800-999-8523-[Y--]

Burbank Rose
401-849-9457

Castle Keep
401-846-0362

Clarke Cooke House
401-849-2900

Clarkston
401-848-5300

Cliff View Guest House
401-846-0885

Cliff Walk Manor
401-847-1300-[Y--]

Cliffside Inn B&B
800-845-1811-[G--]

Clover Hill Guest House
401-847-7094

Commodore Perry Inn
800-343-2863

Covell Guest House
401-847-8872

Eastons Inn On The Beach
401-846-0310

Ellery Park House
401-847-6320

Elliott Boss House
401-849-9425

Elm Street Inn
401-849-7397

Elm Tree Cottage
800-882-3ELM

FG Hanson
401-846-6932

Flag Quarters
401-849-4543

Flower Garden Guests
401-846-3119

Francis Malbone House
401-846-0392

Garden Cottage

Gardenview
401-849-5799-[G--]

Halidon Hill Guest House
401-847-8318

Hammett House Inn
800-548-9417

Harborside Inn
401-846-6600

Harris B&B
401-847-5626

Hospitality House
401-849-9439

Hydrangea House Inn
800-945-4667-[G--]

Inn At Castle Hill
401-849-3800

Inn At Shadow Lawn
800-828-0000

Inn On Long Roof
800-225-3522

Inntowne
800-457-7803

Irish Dandelion
401-846-2050

Ivy Lodge
401-849-6865

Jailhouse Inn
401-847-4638

James B Finch House
800-235-1274-[--]

Jenkins Guest House
401-847-6801

John Banister House
401-846-0050

John Easton House
401-849-6246

La Forge Cottage
401-847-4400

Lowell Manor
401-849-8155

Ma Gallaghers
401-849-3975

Mariner House B&B
401-847-6938

Marions Guest House
401-847-6938

Marshall Slocum Guest House
401-841-5120

Martins B&B
401-847-5630

Melville House
401-847-0640-[GQA]

Merritt House Guests
401-847-4289

Mill Street Inn
401-849-9500

Moulton Weaver House
401-847-0133

Mount Vernon Inn
401-846-6314

Nelsons B&B
401-849-2982

Newfoundlander
401-846-2483

Oceancliff
401-849-9000

Old Dennis House
401-846-1324

On The Point B&B
401-846-8377-[G--]

One Bliss
401-846-5329

Osborn House
401-847-4199

Pilgrim House
800-525-8373

Poplar Street Guest

Rhode Island

Bold Name - Description appears in other section

House
800-537-1430

Queen Anne Inn
401-846-5676

Rhode Island House
401-848-7787-[Y--]

Rickys Place
401-846-2114

Rose Island Lighthouse
401-847-4242

Samuel Honey House
401-847-2669

Sanford-Covell Villa Maria
401-847-0206

Sarah Kendal House
401-846-7976

Spring Street Inn
401-847-4767

Stella Maris Inn
401-849-2862

Sunnyside Mansion
401-849-3114

Thames Street Inn
401-847-4459

Turn-Of-The-Century
401-846-6113

Victorian Ladies
401-849-9960

Villa Liberte
401-846-7444

Waterview
401-847-4425-[Y--]

Wayside
401-847-0302

William Fludder House
800-225-5087

Willows Of Newport
401-846-5486-[Y--]

Yankee Peddler Inn
401-846-1323

Yellow Cottage
401-847-6568

North Kingstown
Bittersweet Farm
401-885-0053

John Cozzens House B&B
401-295-1369

Meadowland B&B
401-294-4168

Morans
401-294-3497

William Holloway House
401-295-1528

Peacedale
Going My Way
401-789-3479

Portsmouth
2108 House
401-683-0849

Browns Bayview Guest House
401-683-0155

Holidays B&B
401-683-2416

Millstones
401-683-9225

Twin Spruce Tourist
401-683-0673

Providence
Cady House
401-273-5398

Church House Inn
401-351-5505

Helen Meier B&B
401-751-5914

Lansing House
401-421-7194

Last Resort By The Bay
401-433-1577

Old Court B&B
401-757-2002

State House Inn
401-785-6111-[G--]

Richmond

Country Acres B&B
401-364-9134

Saunderstown
Quarry House B&B
401-295-2805

Smithfield
Past Thymes
401-231-2173

South Kingstown
Almost Heaven
401-789-9272

Narrow River Cottage
401-783-9751

Tiverton
Bonniefield Cottage
401-624-6364

Squire Chate House
401-624-9873

Wakefield
BB Highland
401-783-2408

Gardner House
401-789-1250

Larchwood Inn
401-783-5454

Roads End
401-783-7547

Shanamar
401-789-8059

Whippoorwill Farm
401-789-8331

Warren
Nathaniel Porter Inn
401-245-6622

Warwick
Demasi Lodging
401-781-8433

Enchanter Cottage
401-732-0439

Open Gate Inn
401-884-4490

Pawtuxet B&B
401-941-4011

Watch Hill
Hartleys Guest House
401-348-8253

Inn At Watch Hill
401-596-0665

Narragansett Inn
401-596-0665

Ocean House
401-348-8161

Watch Hill Inn
800-356-9314

Weekapaug
Weekapaug Inn
401-322-0301

West Kingston
Stone Cottage
401-789-0039

West Warwick
Muriel Powers
401-828-6521

Westerly
Cornerstone Inn
401-322-3020

Grandview B&B Inn
401-596-6384

Harbour House
401-348-8998

J Livingstons Inn
401-322-0249

Longvue Guest House
401-322-0465

Seven Granite Street B&B
800-441-6384

Shelter Harbor Inn
401-322-8883-[Y--]

Shore Inn
401-348-8637

The Villa
800-722-9240-[G--]

Thirty Seven Elm
401-596-6849

Woody Hill Guest House
401-322-0452

Wickford
John Updike House
401-294-4905

Bold Name - Description appears in other section   **Rhode Island - Vermont**

Meadowland
401-294-4168

Sparrows Nest
401-295-1142

Wyoming
Cookie Jar B&B
800-767-4262-[Y--]

Way Stop
401-539-7233

VERMONT

Alburg
Auberge Alburg
802-796-3169

Thomas Mott
Homestead
800-348-0843-[Y--]

Ye Olde Greystone
B&B
802-796-3911

Andover
Hillside
802-875-3844

Inn At Highview
802-875-2724-[G--]

Arlington
Arlington Inn
800-443-9442-[G--]

Arlington Manor
House
802-375-6784

Evergreen
802-375-2272-[Y--]

Hill Farm Inn
800-882-2545

Inn At Sunderland
802-362-4213

Inn On Covered
Bridge Green
802-375-9489

Ira Allen House
802-362-2284

Keelan House B&B
802-375-9029

Shenandoah Farm
802-375-6372-[G--]

West Mountain Inn
802-375-6516

Willow Inn B&B
802-375-9773

Bakersfield
Village B&B
802-827-3206

Barnard
Silver Lake House
802-234-9957

Barnet
Old Homestead Inn
802-633-4100

Barre
Woodruff House
802-476-7745-[Y--]

Barton
Barton Inn
802-525-4721

Fox Hall B&B
802-525-6930

Lafonts Dairy Farm
B&B

Bellows Falls
**Blue Haven
Christian B&B**
802-463-9008-[Y--]

Horsefeathers B&B
802-463-9776

River Mist B&B
802-463-9023

Belmont
Leslie Place
802-259-2903

Parmenter House
802-259-2009

Bennington
Bakers At
Bennington
802-442-5619

Bennington House
802-447-7972

Molly Stark Inn
802-442-9631

Mount Anthony
Guest House
802-447-7296

Mt Anthony Guest
House
802-447-7396

Munro Hawkins
House
802-447-2286

Safford Manor
802-442-4934

South Shore Inn
802-447-3839

Benson
Green Mountain
B&B

Meadowbrook Farm

Bethel
Eastwood House
802-234-9686-[Y--]

Greenhurst Inn
802-234-9474

Poplar Manor
802-234-5426

Bondville
Alpenrose Inn
802-297-2750-[Y--]

Barn Lodge
802-297-1877

Bromley View Inn
802-297-1459

Bradford
Merry Meadow
Farm
802-222-4412

Village Inn of
Bradford
802-222-9303

Brandon
Brandon Inn
802-247-5766

Churchill House Inn
802-247-3078

Cox Mountain Inn

Gazebo Inn
802-247-3235

Hivue B&B
802-247-3042

Le Relais

Moffett House
802-247-3843

Old Mill Inn
802-247-8002

Rosebelles
Victorian Inn
802-247-0098-[Y--]

Stone Mill Farm
802-247-6137

Brattleboro
Forty Putney Road
802-254-6268

Bridgewater Corners
October Country
Inn
800-648-8412

Bristol
Crystal Palace
Victorian B&B
802-453-4131

Long Run Inn
802-453-3233

Maplewood Farm
B&B
802-453-2992

Brookfield
Green Trails
Country Inn
802-276-3412-[Y--]

Brownsville
Inn At Mt Ascutney
802-484-7725

Mill Brook B&B
802-484-7283-[Y--]

Southview B&B
802-484-7934

Burlington
Burlington B&B
802-862-3646

Howden Cottage
802-864-7198

Thatcher Brook Inn
800-292-5911-[Y--]

Truax Tourist Home
802-862-0809

Yellow House

Calais
White House At

©*Inn & Travel Memphis, Tennessee*   1-153

Vermont *Bold Name - Description appears in other section*

Kents Corner
802-229-9847

Cavendish
Cavendish Inn
802-226-7329

Charlotte
Charlottes Web B&B
802-425-3341

Green Meadows B&B
802-425-3059

Inn At Charlotte
802-425-2934

Chelsea
Shire Inn
800-441-6908

Chester
Chester House
802-875-2205-[Y--]

Greenleaf Inn
802-875-3171

Henry Farm Inn
800-723-8213

Hugging Bear Inn & Shoppe
800-325-0519

Inn At Highview
802-875-2724-[Y--]

Inn At Long Last
802-875-2444

Inn Victoria
800-732-4288-[Y--]

Madrigal Inn
802-463-2231

Night With A Native

Second Wind B&B
802-875-3438

Stone Hearth Inn
802-875-2525-[Y--]

Chittenden
Mountain Top Inn
800-445-2100

Tulip Tree Inn
800-707-0017

Colchester

On The Lamb B&B
802-586-2848

Coventry
Heermansmith Farm
802-754-8866

Craftsbury
Brass Knocker B&B
802-586-2814

Craftsbury B&B On Wylie Hill
802-586-2206

Craftsbury Inn
800-336-2848

Fitchingfield B&B
802-586-7763

Gary Meadow Dairy Farm
802-586-2536

Inn On The Common
800-521-2233-[Y--]

One Akre Farm

Cuttingsville
Maple Crest Farm
802-492-3367

Shrewsbury Inn

Danby
Quails Nest B&B
802-293-5099

Silas Griffin Inn
802-293-5567

Derby Line
Derby Village Inn
802-873-3604

Dorset
Barrows House
802-867-4455

Cornucopia Of Dorset
802-867-5751

Dorset Inn
802-867-5500

Dovetail Inn
802-867-5747

Little Lodge At Dorset
802-867-4040

Marble Inn
802-867-4155

Village Auberge
802-867-5715

Dover
Doveberry Inn
802-464-5652

Duxbury
Boomsburg B&B
802-244-7726

East Barnett
Inwood Manor
802-633-4047

East Burke
Blue Max Farm
802-626-5542

Burke Green Guest House
802-467-3472

Darion Inn

Garrison Inn
802-626-8329

House In The Woods

Nutmegger

Old Cutter Inn
802-626-5152

Village Inn Of East Burke
802-626-3161

East Calais
Lake House B&B

East Dorset
Kiln Guest House
802-362-4889

East Dover
Cooper Hill Lodge
802-348-6333

East Fairfield
Whispering Pines
802-827-3827

East Hardwick
Brick House
802-472-5512

East Middlebury
By The Way B&B
802-388-6291

Lords B&B

October Pumpkin Inn
802-388-9525

Robert Frost Mountain B&B

Waybury Inn
802-388-4015-[Y--]

East Montpelier
Cherry Tree Inn
802-233-0549

East Poultney
Eagle Tavern On The Green
802-287-9498

East Saint Johnsbury
Echo Ledge Farm Inn
802-748-4750

Enosberg Falls
Berkson Farms
802-933-2522-[Y--]

Rick Lansings B&B

Essex Junction
Country Comfort B&B
802-878-2589

Inn At Essex
802-878-1100

Tandys B&B
802-878-4729

Varnums
802-899-4577

Fair Haven
Fairhaven Inn
802-265-3833

Haven Est 1948
802-265-3373

Maplewood Inn
800-253-7729-[GQAR-]

Vermont Marble Inn
800-535-2814

Victorian Marble Inn

Fairfax
Buck Hollow Farm
802-849-2400

1-154 ©Inn & Travel Memphis, Tennessee

Bold Name - Description appears in other section **Vermont**

Foggy Hollow Farm

Inn At Buck Hollow Farm
802-849-2400-[Y--]

Fairfield
Hillside View Farm
802-827-4480-[Y--]

Fairlee
Aloha Manor
802-333-4478

Rutledge Inn
802-333-9722

Silver Maple Lodge-Cottages
800-666-1946-[Y--]

Ferrisburg
1810 Farmhouse Inn
802-877-2576

Forest Dale
Blake House B&B
802-247-3152

Franklin
Fair Meadows Farm
802-285-2132

Gassetts
Old Town Farm Inn
802-875-2346

Gaysville
Cobble House Inn
802-234-5458

Laolke Lodge
802-234-9205

Goshen
Blueberry Hill Inn
800-448-0707-[Y--]

Grafton
Bandywine Inn
802-843-2250

Eaglebrook Of Grafton
802-843-2564

Hayes House
802-843-2461

Old Tavern At Grafton
800-843-1801

Woodchuck Hill Farm

802-843-2398

Greensboro
Greensboro House
802-533-7155

Highland Lodge
802-533-2647

Guildhall
Guildhall Inn
802-676-3720

Hancock
Kincraft Inn
802-767-3734-[Y--]

Hardwick
Kahagon At Nichols Pond
802-472-6446

Somerset House B&B
802-472-5484

Hartford
House Of Seven Gables
800-325-2540

Harwick
Carolyns B&B
802-472-6338

Hero
Thomas Mott B&B
802-372-5777

Highgate Springs
Tyler Place
802-868-3301-[Y--]

Huntington
Camels Hump Nordic Center
802-434-2704

Hyde Park
Fitch Hill Inn
800-639-2903-[-QA-]

Irasburg
Brick House
802-754-2108

Irasburg Green B&B
802-754-6012

Jacksonville
Candlelight B&B
802-368-7826

Jamaica
Sunnybrook Loge

802-874-4891

Three Mountains Inn
802-874-4140

Jay
Jay Village Inn & Restaurant
802-988-2643

Woodshed Lodge
802-988-4444

Jeffersonville
Jefferson House
802-644-2030

Mannsview Inn
800-937-MANN

Smugglers Notch Inn
802-644-2412

Sterling Ridge Inn
802-644-8265

Windridge Inn
802-644-8281

Jericho
Eaton House B&B
802-899-2354

Henry M Field House B&B
802-899-3984

Homeplace
802-899-4694

Millikens
802-899-3993

Saxon Inn
802-899-3015

Killington
Chalet Killington
800-451-4105

Cortina Inn
800-451-6108

Grey Bonnett Inn
800-342-2086

Inn At Long Trail
800-325-2540-[Y--]

Inn Of Six Mountains

Mountain Meadow Lodge

802-775-1010

Mountain Morgans

Sherburne Valley Inn
802-422-9888

The Vermont Inn
800-541-7795-[Y--]

Landgrove
Nordic Inn
802-824-6444

Village Inn At Landgrove
802-824-6673

Londonderry
Blue Gentian Lodge
802-824-5908

Country Hare
802-824-3131

Highland House
802-824-3019

Inn On Magic Mountain

Village Inn
800-669-8466

Lower Waterford
Flower Cottage B&B
802-748-8441

Rabbit Hill Inn
800-76-BUNNY

Ludlow
Andrie Rose Inn
800-223-4846

Black River Inn
802-228-5585

Combes Family Inn
802-228-8799

Echo Lake Inn
800-356-6844-[G--]

Fletcher Manor
802-228-3548

Inn At Highview
802-875-2724-[G--]

Jewell Brook Farm
802-228-8926

Okemo Inn

©Inn & Travel Memphis, Tennessee

Vermont *Bold Name - Description appears in other section*

802-228-8834

Old Farmhouse Inn
802-228-8700

Lyndon
Branch Brook Inn
802-626-8316

Lyndonville
Wildflower Inn
800-627-8310-[Y--]

Manchester
1811 House
800-432-1811

Birch Hill Inn
800-372-2761

Book N Hearth Inn
802-362-3604

Equinox
800-362-4747

Inn At Manchester
800-273-1793-[G--]

Inn At Willow Pond
802-362-4733

Manchester Highlands Inn
800-743-4565-[G--]

River Meadow Farm
802-362-3700

Seth Warner Inn
802-362-3830

Skyline Inn
802-362-1113

Village Country Inn
800-379-0300

Wilburton Inn
800-648-4944

Manchester Center
Brook N Hearth B&B
802-362-3604

Inn At Ormsby Hill
802-362-1163

Manchester Village
Charles Orvis Inn
802-362-4700

Reluctant Panther
802-362-2568

Marlboro
Longwood Inn
802-257-1545

Tamarack House
802-257-1093

Whetstone Inn
802-254-2500

Mendon
Red Clover Inn
800-752-0571

Middleburg
Peaceful Acres
802-388-2076

Middlebury
Middlebury Inn
800-842-4666

Point Of View

Swifthouse Inn
802-388-9925

Montgomery
Fallbrook House
802-326-4616

Phineas Swan B&B
802-326-4306

Montgomery Center
Eagle Lodge
802-326-4518

Inn On Trout River
800-338-7049

Seven Bridges Inn
802-326-4166

Zacks On The Rocks

Montgomery Village
Black Lantern Inn
802-326-4507

Montpelier
Betsys B&B
802-229-0466

Inn At Montpelier
802-223-2727

Montpelier B&B
802-229-0878

Northfield Inn
802-485-8558

Moretown
Camels Hump View Farm
802-496-3614

Honeysuckle Inn
802-496-6200

Morgan
Seymour Lake Lodge
802-895-2752

Morrisville
Lepines Inn Brook
802-888-5862

Mount Holly
Austria Haus
802-259-2441

Hortonville Inn
802-259-2587

Hounds Folly
802-259-2718

New Haven
Horn Farnsworth House
802-388-2300

New Haven B&B
802-453-5495

Newbury
A Century Past
802-866-3358

Century Past
802-866-3358

Newfane
Four Columns Inn
802-365-7713

Inn At South Newfane
802-348-7191

Old Newfane Inn
802-365-4427

West River Lodge
802-365-7745

North Ferrisburg
Dunn-Inn
802-425-2902

North Hero
Charles Northland Lodge
802-372-8822

North Hero House
802-372-8237

North Thetford
Stone House Inn
802-333-9124

North Troy
North Troy Inn
802-988-2527

Rose Apple Acres Farm
802-988-4300

Northfield
Longway Inn
802-485-3559

Northfield Inn
802-485-8558

Northfield Falls
Four Bridges Inn
802-485-8995

Norwich
Inn At Norwich
802-649-1143

Old Bennington
Four Chimneys Inn
802-447-3500

Orleans
Valley House Inn
800-545-9711

Orwell
Brookside Farms
802-948-2727-[G--]

Perkinsville
Gwendolyns B&B
802-263-5248-[Y--]

Inn At Weathersfield
800-477-4828-[Y--]

Peregrines Restaurant
802-263-5784

Peru
Johnny Seesaws
802-824-5533

Wiley Inn
802-824-6000

Pittsfield
Pittsfield Inn
802-746-8943

Swiss Farm Lodge
802-226-7744

Pittsford
Fox Bros Farm

Bold Name - Description appears in other section Vermont

802-483-2870

Plainfield
Yankees Northview B&B
802-454-7191

Plymouth
Hawk Inn & Mountain Resort
800-685-4295

Plymouth Towne Inn
802-672-3059

Salt Ash Inn
802-672-3748

Snowy Owl Lodge
802-672-5018

Post Mills
Lake House
802-333-4025

Poultney
Lake St Catherine Inn
802-287-9347

Stonebridge Inn
802-287-9849

Tower Hall B&B
802-287-4004

Pownal
Gail & Irv Tabzmen B&B

Inn At Oak Hill
802-823-7849

Proctor
Yankee Willow
802-459-2959

Proctorsville
Allens Proctorsville Inn
802-226-7970

Castle Inn
802-226-7222

Depot Corner Inn
802-226-7970-[Y--]

Golden Stage Inn
800-253-8226

Okemo Lantern Lodge
802-226-7770

The Castle
802-226-7222

Whitney Brook B&B
802-226-7460

Putney
Hickory Ridge House
802-387-5709

Mapleton Farm B&B
802-257-5252

Misty Meadow B&B
802-722-9517

Putney Inn
802-387-6617

Quechee
Annies Sugar Pine Farm
802-295-1266

Country Garden Inn
802-295-3023

Parker House Inn/ French Restaurant
802-295-6077

Quechee Inn At Marshland Farm
800-235-3133

Quechee Lakes

Quechee Village
Abel Barron House
802-295-1337

Randolph
Placidia Farm B&B
802-728-9883

Three Stallion Inn
802-728-5575

Rawsonville
Bear Creek Inn

Reading
Greystone B&B
802-484-7200

Hapgood Cottage

Peeping Cow Inn
802-484-5036

Readsboro
Old Coach Inn
802-423-5394

Richford
Troy Street B&B
802-848-3557

Richmond
Black Bear Inn
800-395-6335

Bolton Valley Resort
800-451-3220

Ripton
Chipman Inn
802-388-2390

Rochester
Harveys Mountain View Inn
802-767-4273

Kingsburys Forest Home B&B

Liberty Hill Farm
802-767-3926

New Homestead
802-767-4751

Tupper Farm Lodge
802-767-4243

Roxbury
Inn At Johnnycake Flats
802-485-8961

Johnny Cake Flats Inn
802-485-8961

Royalton
Fox Stand Inn
802-763-8437

Rutland
Hillcrest Guest House
802-775-1670

Inn At Rutland
802-773-0575

Red Clover Inn
802-775-2290

Saint Albans
Bayview B&B
802-524-5609

Bellevue
802-527-1115

Inn At Buck Hollow Farm

802-849-2400-[Y--]

Island View

Saint Johnsbury
Broadview Farm B&B
802-748-9902

Echo Ledge Farm Inn
802-748-4750

Heart 'n Hand
802-748-4487

Looking Glass Inn
802-748-3052

Saxtons
Saxtons River Inn
802-869-2110

Shaftsbury
Country Cousin B&B
802-375-6985

Shelburne
Hullcrest B&B

Inn At Shelburne Farms
802-985-8498

Shelburne House
802-985-8498

Shorham
Shoreham Inn
800-255-5081

Shrewsbury
Buckmaster Inn B&B
802-492-3485

Simonsville
Roerlld Inn
802-875-3658

South Burlington
Lindenwood A Country Inn
802-862-2144

South Hero
Paradise Bay B&B
802-372-5393

South Londonderry
Londonderry Inn
802-824-5226

South Newfane
Inn At South

©Inn & Travel Memphis, Tennessee 1-157

Vermont   **Bold Name** - *Description appears in other section*

Newfane
802-348-7191

South Strafford
Watercourse Way
800-562-5110-[Y--]

South Wallingford
Green Mountain
Tea Room
802-446-2611

South Woodstock
Kedron Valley Inn
802-457-1473

Springfield
Hartness House Inn
800-732-4789

Starksboro
Millhouse B&B
802-453-2008

Stockbridge
Scarborough Inn
802-746-8141

Stockbridge Inn
802-746-8165

Wild Berry Inn
802-746-8141

Stowe
1860 House
800-248-1860-[Y--]

Andersen Lodge
Austrian Inn
802-253-7660

Baas' Gasthaus
802-253-8376-[Y--]

Bittersweet Inn
802-253-7787

Brass Lantern Inn
800-729-2980-[G--]

Butternut Inn At
Stowe
800-3 BUTTER

Cottage In Magical
Forest
802-253-9577

Edson Hill Manor
800-621-0284-[Y--]

Fiddlers Green Inn
802-253-8124

Fitch Hill Inn

802-888-3834

Fountain B&B
802-253-9285

Foxfire Inn
802-253-4887

Gables Inn
800-GABLES 1

Golden Kitz Lodge
800-KITS LOV

Green Mountain Inn
800-445-6629

Grey Fox Inn
802-253-8921

Guest House Cristel
Horman
802-253-4846

Hadleigh House
B&B
802-253-7703

Hob Nob Inn
802-253-8549

Inn At Turner Mill
802-253-2062

Innsburck Inn
802-253-8582

John M Henzel
802-253-7574

Logwood Inn
800-426-6697-[Y--]

Nichols Lodge
802-253-7683

Plum Door
802-253-9995

Put At Stowe
802-253-8669

Raspberry Patch
B&B
802-253-4145

Scandinavia Inn &
Chalet
800-544-4229

Siebeness
800-426-9001-[Y--]

Ski Inn
802-253-4050

Spa At Stowe/Green
Mountain Inn

Spruce Pond Inn
802-253-4828

Stowe Away Lodge
802-253-7547

Stowe Bound Lodge
800-72-STOWE

Stowehof Inn
802-253-9722

Ten Acres Lodge
800-327-7357

Thatcher Brook Inn
800-292-5911-[Y--]

Timberholm Inn
802-253-7603

Topnotch At Stowe
802-253-9649

Ye Old England
Inne
800-477-3771-[Y--]

Yodler
802-253-4836

Stratton Mountain
Birkenhaus
802-297-2000

New Life Spa
Program

Sugarbush
Sugartree A
Country Inn
802-583-3211

White Horse Inn
802-496-2476

Taftsville
Applebutter Inn
802-457-4158

Maitland Swan
House
802-457-5181

Thetford Hill
Fahrenbrae
802-785-4304

Tinmouth
Five M Farm

Townshend
Boardman House

802-365-4086

Townshend Inn
802-365-4087

Troy
Friedlich Haus
802-744-6113

Underhill
Sinclair Inn
802-899-2234

Underhill Center
Haus Kelley B&B
802-899-3905

Vergennes
Emersons Guest
House
802-877-3293

Strong House Inn
802-877-3337-[Y--]

Waitsfield
Battleground

Honeysuckle Inn
802-496-6200

Hyde Away Inn
800-777-HYDE

Inn At Round Barn
Farm
802-496-2276

Knoll Farm Country
Inn
802-496-3939

Lareau Farm
Country Inn
800-833-0766-[Y--]

Mad River Barn
802-496-3310-[Y--]

Millbrook Inn
802-496-2405

Mountain View Inn
802-496-2426

**Newtons 1824 House
Inn**
800-426-3986-[Y--]

Round Barn Farm
802-496-2276

Snuggery Inn
802-496-2322

Tucker Hill Lodge

1-158   ©*Inn & Travel Memphis, Tennessee*

Bold Name - *Description appears in other section*   **Vermont**

802-496-3983-[Y--]

Valley Inn
802-496-3450

Waitsfield Inn
802-496-3979

Weathertop Lodge
802-496-4909

Waitsfield/Warren
Northfield Inn
802-485-8558-[Y--]

Wallingford
Victorian Inn
802-446-2099

White Rocks Inn
802-446-2077-[Y--]

Warren
Beaver Pond Farm Inn
802-583-2861

Christmas Tree Inn
802-583-2211

Rynes B&B
802-496-6042

Sgt Peppers Lodge

South Hollow Farm
802-496-5627

Sugarbush Inn
800-451-4320

Waterbury
Black Locust Inn
802-244-7490-[Y--]

Grunberg Haus
800-800-7760-[Y--]

Inn At Blush Hill
800-736-7522-[Y--]

Old Stagecoach Inn
802-244-5056

Thatcher Brook Inn
800-292-5911-[Y--]

Waterbury Center
May Farm Lodge
802-244-7306

Weathersfield
Theodore Lillemoe

West Arlington
Four Winds Country Inn
802-375-6734

West Brattleboro
Captain Henry Chase House
802-254-4114

West Charleston
Hunts Hideaway
802-895-4432

West Dover
Austin Hill Inn
800-332RELAX

Deerhill Inn
802-464-3100

Doveberry Inn
802-464-5652

Gray Ghost Inn
802-464-2474

Inn At Sawmill Farm
802-464-8131

Shield Inn
802-464-3984

Snow Den Inn
800-852-9240

Snow Lake Lodge
802-464-3333

Waldwinkel Inn
802-464-5281

Weathervane Lodge
802-464-5426

West Dover Inn
802-464-5207

West Glover
Rodgers Dairy Farm

West Halifax
Shearer Hill Farm
802-464-3253

West Hartford
Half Penny B&B
802-295-6082

West Rutland
Silver Fox Inn
802-438-5555

West Townshend
General Fletcher Homestead
802-874-4853

Windham Hill Inn
800-944-4080

Weston
1830 Inn On The Green
802-824-6789

Colonial House
802-824-6286

Darling Family Inn
802-824-3223

Inn At Highview
802-875-2724-[G--]

Inn At Weston
802-824-5804

Wilder Homestead Inn
802-824-8172

White River Junction
Serenity Hill Farm

Wilder
Stonecrest Farm B&B
800-730-2425-[G--]

Williamstown
Autumn Crest Inn
802-433-6627

Rose Wood Inn
802-433-5822

Williamsville
Country Inn At WIlliamsville
802-348-7148

Williston
Partridge Hill
802-878-4741

Wilmington
Brook Bound/ Hermitage
802-464-3511

Inn At Quail Run
800-34ESCAPE [Y--]

Misty Mountain Lodge
802-464-3961

Nordic Hills Lodge
802-464-5130

Nutmeg Inn
802-464-3351

Trails End Lodge
800-859-2585

Vermont House
802-464-9360

White House Of Wilmington
802-464-2135

Windsor
Juniper Hill Inn
800-359-2541

Wolcott
Golden Maple Inn
802-888-6614

Woodstock
1830 Shire Town Inn
802-457-1830

Canterbury House
802-457-3077

Carriage House of Woodstock
802-457-4322

Charleston House
802-457-3843-[Y--]

Deerbrook Inn
802-672-3713

Jackson House
802-457-2065

Lincoln Covered Bridge Inn
802-457-3312

Three Church Street B&B
802-457-1925

Village Inn Of Woodstock
802-457-1255

Winslow House
802-457-1820

Woodstock House B&B
802-457-1758

Woodstock Inn & Resort
800-448-7900

Woodstocker B&B
802-457-3896-[Y--]

- E N D -

©*Inn & Travel Memphis, Tennessee*

Mid-America

Discover What You're Missing In Illinois!

*Illinois, America's prairie land.
And one of the most diverse states in the United States.*

From Chicago to Carlyle, Galesburg to Golconda, and Peoria to Pickneyville, Illinois boasts history, antiques, rich fertile farmland, high-tech shopping areas, cuisine from around the world and many outdoor recreation areas.

Chicago is a mecca of international travel - A blend of small town Americana and the cosmopolitan. Northern Illinois - the stops to make are many. Freeport, where the second Lincoln-Douglas debates were held; Mt. Carroll that was once dubbed, **"The New England of the Midwest"**, laying amidst gently rolling hills; or the ever-popular Galena where over sixty antique shops and forty Bed & Breakfast establishments wait for your visit. Traveling south along the Mississippi River you can traverse the Great River Road which runs through Illinois' countryside from East Dubuque on the Wisconsin border to Cairo at the southern tip of Illinois, where the Ohio River joins the Mississippi River. You will find some Illinois' most memorable scenery. Century-old Victorian homes stand watch over the scenic drive. Cities such as Nauvoo with its wealth of history.

Central Illinois is where the history of Abraham Lincoln comes to life. At the age of twenty, Abe Lincoln arrived in 1830 to this part of the great state of Illinois. Visit cities like Petersburg, Decatur, Clinton, CharlesLena, Lincoln, and Springfield, where history once again comes to life while you are there. Or visit the Amish country of Arcola and Arthur. Traveling northwest of Springfield you will find wonderful stops in Galesburg, the birthplace of Carl Sandburg; or Bishop Hill, listed as a National Historic Landmark. Southern Illinois, you know you are there when the smooth gently rolling prairie land disappears and the woods, valleys, dales and hills begin to appear. Southern Illinois is a special place of peace and tranquility, of down-home hospitality and a gentle prairie spirit. While you drive through southern Illinois you will find the history of cities like Vandalia, the site of Illinois' second state capitol; Salem, home of William Jennings Bryan; Kinmundy, where a collection of log cabins from through-out

©Inn & Travel Memphis, Tennessee

southern Illinois invite you to step into an 1800's cobbler's shop, apothecary, or blacksmith.

Recreation can be found in southern Illinois - sailing, boating, fishing, swimming, hiking and rock climbing are just a few of the many outdoor activities to be found in this southern wonderland. Carlyle Lake is Illinois' largest inland lake, with 26,000 acres of water and 11,000 acres of public land - and the site of the 1994 Olympic Sailing Festival. Shawnee National Forest will transport you back in time to the days of the glaciers. Fantastic rock formations, grand wooded hills and peaceful still valleys make up Shawnee National Forest, as does swamp land that looks as if it were transported from Louisiana just for your visit. Hiking trails and rock climbing expeditions are favorite activities in the Ozark Mountain foothills of southern Illinois. A trip from the northern tip to the southern edge of Illinois will infuse your life with a little peace, a little wonder, a little history and a big dose of prairie land hospitality.

Vickie Cook, Innkeeper ***Country Haus Bed and Breakfast,*** Carlyle Illinois

Vickie, her husband Ron, eleven year old Jessica and Sammie, a pound puppy soon to be two years old operate *Country Haus Bed and Breakfast* following their sixteen year career in retail management. **"Carlyle needed a bed and breakfast and we loved the area. So here we are."** Ron and Vickie are both active in the Carlyle Chamber of Commerce, the Illinois Bed & Breakfast Association, the Professional Association of Innkeepers International and local literacy efforts. Vickie is co-chairperson of the Christmastown, USA events held each December in Carlyle which includes open house of the *Country Haus* as well as other tour homes.

Westhampton Beach, New York

I love the area of Long Island, New York because of the numerous activities offered residents and travelers alike. The Atlantic Ocean beach is one of the most beautiful beaches in the world. Soft white sand, warm to the touch on a sunny day, with the blue of the ocean is one of the best reasons to come to Long Island. A drive on the famous Dune Road, next to the ocean where there is often a surprisingly designed modern home which overlooks the Atlantic Ocean and the inland waterways. Shop in the small picturesque villages and enjoy lunch. Nature walk at the Quoque Wildlife Refuge - enjoy the wild animals, feed the ducks and geese. Bring a picnic lunch and a loaf of bread for the ducks. You can spend several hours following the trails through scenic woodside. A trip to Montauk Point will take several hours. Touring the many old English-style communities along Rt 80E approximately 47 miles to the point. This is one of the biggest tourist attractions in the northeast. Once you reach Montauk, take a walk on the rock beach, see the famous lighthouse, shop in the nearby stores and enjoy a meal at Gosman's Dock. An interesting area is Sag Harbor where you can visit the whaling museum and see some of the oldest surviving whaling artifacts, ship models and records.

You can continue to Main Street and then to ferry road to the end where a short ferry ride will take you to Shelter Island. Enjoy the scenic boat trip over to the island then continue on Rt 114 across the island to the Greenport ferry. Greenport is the home of a former ship building village. You may want to walk along Main Street, visit the docks and ships along the waterfront. As you go back, heading west to Riverhead, you will pass vineyards and farms. Be sure to stop in at anyone of the vineyards for a demonstration on how wine is produced. Antique shops are a special part of your visit to Long Island, New York, as they tell their own story of our past history.

Each day is an adventure here on Long Island. Come and see us soon!

Elsie Collins, Innkeeper
1880 Seafield House
Westhampton Beach, New York

Ocean Grove New Jersey

Ocean Grove has been designated an historic community. It is a Victorian, turn-of-the-century resort community on the Atlantic Ocean with Old World Charm

There are more authentic Victorian homes preserved here than almost any other square mile. Because of the many restrictions, Ocean Grove did not attract a resort crowd until quite recently. Because of this, builders did not come in and the original Victorian homes are still here - as well as the slow pace and friendliness of the past.

Ocean Grove is one of the two largest Methodist Retreat Centers in the U.S, established in 1869. At that time, ten families gathered for rest and religious activities over the summer months. Ocean Grove has approximately one mile of oceanfront. Until 1977, vehicular traffic of any kind was not permitted on Sunday .... creating a strange sight each Saturday evening, as cars were lined-up as they prepared to leave Ocean Grove and to be parked in neighboring communities for twenty four hours. Swimming wasn't permitted, nor could individuals work on their homes or gardens on the Sabbath.

Sunday life revolved around the *Great Auditorium*, named thus, because it is the largest wooded structure (7,000 seats) in the U.S. with a roof span of 40,400 square feet. Past presidents, including Woodrow Wilson and Grover Cleveland, stayed in Ocean Grove and spoke in the Auditorium. The Auditorium as well as Ocean Grove are national and New Jersey historical landmarks. A tent colony, consisting of 114 tents, each of which is attached in back to a wooden shed, surrounds the Auditorium and were built to commemorate the workers who lived in tents during the summer months while building the Auditorium. Today, some tents are decorated like Victorian summer cottage, with oak and wicker furniture as fine as that seen in the gingerbread houses of Ocean Grove itself. Come visit us .... and enjoy the unique flavor of Ocean Grove yourself!- Doris Chernik, Innkeeper

The Cordova
Ocean Grove New Jersey

A Trip to the Adirondacks ......

..... North we headed to beat the heat!

We, being the adventurous type, left our cares behind and locked our door, bound for somewhere; anywhere away from the city. .... 100 miles north of Albany, New York, the serious/exciting search began. Lake Placid ... Olympics, Adirondack Mountains ....

"Hey honey, wake up, I found it". Off the interstate exit and onto an unexpectedly scenic mountain thorough-fare, our auto magnetically edging ever closer to our destined haven away from our hectic lives. *"Tom, look at those beautiful white birch trees along the edge of that lake! ... Let's stop." "Those are white trees Marge, but let's keep moving on to Lake Placid, my stomach is growling".*

Winding our way along the main street shopping area left us wondering at the unexpected charm which we found ourselves surrounded by. Lunch overlooking one of natures most pristine mountain lakes created yet another type of hunger - a yearning for an establishment to spend the night. *"Say - Tom, let's stay in a country inn ... remember that weekend two years ago ... how romantic?" "Marge, that's just what I was thinking ...."*

.... next day.

After a second helping of homemade pancakes, we headed out for a look around the area. Golf, tennis, boating, hiking, horseback riding, walking, shopping, eating, olympic village, amusement attractions - and just relaxing. We had many items from our Adirondack menu to choose from. We chose the lake, lunch and shopping. In between, we re-booked our room and took advantage of the hot tub spa. Candle lit romantic dining capped-off our mountain escape, making us wish it was Friday afternoon once again.

Your Adirondack Travellers

Ted Blazer, Innkeeper
Highland House Inn, Lake Placid NY

The Endless Mountains of Pennsylvania

Northeast Pennsylvania

*offers 4500 square miles of green mountains
and lush valleys,
laced with silvery rushing streams and lakes of cool, pure water,
dotted with picturesque farms, parks, game lands
and bisected from northwest to southeast by the wide, slow moving and beautiful Sesquehanna River.*

*The first inhabitants of the area, the Delaware Indians, were the first to call the area **"the endless mountains"**, and interchanged that identity with **"the land of paradise"** because of the abundance of game and fish. Those identities are as valid today as when the name* Endless Mountains *appeared on maps more than two centuries ago.*

The traveler who values the serenity of the mountains, uninterrupted by the trappings of gross commercialism, will find these attributes in the *Endless Mountains*. As a bonus (characterized by Mike Shoup of the *Philadelphia Inquirer*), the traveler will see several people and places with enduring character. This is a land where the bed & breakfast hosts (26 as of this writing), are resident on their property and most likely life-long residents of the mountains. They are representative of the area, where folks say hello to strangers on the street and the doors are not locked by deadbolts at night. They live in places where, at breakfast, you are likely to find yourself looking at a herd of buffalo, a family of deer or a gaggle of geese - not to mention cows, chickens and horses.

As you travel the roads, you will invariably meet a farmer with a tractor or pick-up truck tending to chores or a logging truck full of native hemlock, oak, maple or cherry logs for America's appetite of fine wood products. The diners, restaurants and shops are places to eat or buy what you need, not tourist attractions. Although many are surprised at the quality of art and antiques available in this backwater country.

The towns you visit, like Tunk-hannock, Towanda, Dushore, Montrose, Nicholson, Laceyville and Beaumont, all reflect the influence of the native American, French and other European settlers. The flavor and values of small-town America are alive and well - all with their white, columned court houses, clock & bell towers - surrounded by the town commons adorned with band shells and the antique cannon.

The mountains are a treasure for outdoor persons and families, regardless of the preferred activity: golf, swimming, canoeing, cross country or downhill skiing and ice skating. Not only can you enjoy the recreation inherent to the seemingly pervasive game lands and state parks (hiking, camping, fishing, hunting, bird/animal watching) but there are man-made wonders as well. You can visit the area, still somewhat remote, where aristocratic refugees from the

French Revolution built a sanctuary in hopes Marie Antoinette and her family could join them. In fact, it is named the French Azilum and is located on the bank of the Susquehanna River. There is also the "oldest house" in Laceyville, which is architecturally intact after more than two centuries. It served river travelers and later, the railroad and is now a historical landmark. The house is a stark reminder of the lack of comfort available to residents and travelers when the American republic was formed. There is the Farm Museum at Troy. The museum and collections of tools and memorabilia from the past, all still in working order, or illustrated as to its use, were all donated by residents of the mountains. Operation and maintenance are paid by donations from guests to the museum with labor still donated by local residents.

The bridge enthusiast will find the area dotted with covered bridges, most notable being Luther's Mills. However, for sheer grandeur, the Nicholson Bridge is the largest poured concrete bridge in the world.

It is still in use since it was built in 1915. Another bridge is a true wonder, Starruca Viaduct. Built in 1848 completely of stone - each piece was laid in place by hand - and still in full use today. Of course, the fall colors are unmatched. When viewed from the top of one of the mountains, the foliage truly spreads out in an endless carpet of rolling, flaming colors.

The Endless Mountains are easy to reach; from the north, Rts 15, 220. 11, 81 - and from the south, Rts 15, 220, 11, 81, 9. Rts 6 and 11 follow the Susquehanna River though the region, southeast/northwest. Rt 17 runs just north of the area through New York state and Rt 80 runs just south of the area through Pennsylvania. Rt 84 ends at the *Endless Mountains* after its journey through Connecticut and New York. Rt 118 ends at the *Endless Mountains* after its journey from Williamsport, the home of Little League Baseball. The area is 3 hours from New York; 2-1/2 hours from Philadelphia; 4 hours from Washington DC. The Wilkes-Barre Intl Airport is on the eastern edge of the mountains.
Cliff Rowland, Innkeeper

Ponda-Rowland Bed & Breakfast
Dallas, Pennsylvania

National Edition   **Delaware**

Addy Sea	99 Ocean View Parkway 19930	Bethany Beach DE
Mr Leroy Gravette III		Tel: 302-539-3707 703-354-8500

Right on the ocean is this c1905 restored Victorian family operated Inn offering gorgeous ocean views from all rooms, antique furnishings throughout, and plenty of warmth and hospitality. Continental breakfast included. **Seasonal:** No **Brochure:** Tes **Permitted:** Children 8-up, and limited smoking **Payment Terms:** Check [C11ACDE-1009] **COM** Y **ITC Member:** No

Rates:	Pvt Bath 2	Shared Bath 12
Single	$ 70.00	$ 60.00
Double	$ 80.00	$ 70.00

Darley Manor Inn B&B	3701 Philadelphia Pike 19703	Claymont DE
Ray & Judith Hester		Tel: 800-824-4703 302-792-2127 Fax: 302-798-6143
		Res Times 10am-10pm

Southern-style hospitality and service abound in this Historic Register, 1790's colonial home. It was the home of Felix Darley, mid-1800 America's most famous illustrator. He illustrated for Poe, Cooper, Irving, Hawthorne, Longfellow, Charles Dickens and others; Dickens visited Darley here for two weeks in 1867. The elegant two bedrooms and four suites (2 with fireplace), are furnished with antiques and reproductions. All rooms have queen-size beds (full or wall-canopied), a/c, CATV, VCR, private baths and phones. The Inn's common areas include two parlors, meeting room, porch and azalea garden with gazebo and swing. There is well-lighted off-street parking. AAA 3-Diamond rating. There are refreshments upon arrival, evening sherry and a 24 hour *"hospitality table."* The full complimentary breakfast has time and entree selections. Guests most often compliment the Inn's food, comfort, attention to details, and convenience; the Inn is truly *"close to everything ... yet it is a century away."* Special attention is given to the business travelers' needs, in both the Inn's design and service. Located in suburban north Wilmington (10 min), nearby I-495, I-95, Rt 202, provides quick and easy access to all Brandywine Valley attractions, Winterthur, Longwood Gardens, Brandywine River (Wyeth Museum), good restaurants, historic Philadelphia and the airport. Pennsylvania Amish Country, Atlantic City and Baltimore are just 90 minutes away. New York City-2-1/2 hrs, Innkeepers, Ray and Judith, are always available for recommendations, maps and directions and to discuss the house's history and renovations. **Airport:** Philadelphia-15 mins **Packages:** Some weekends, inquire at res time **Discounts:** Corporate, extended stays of 7 days and longer **Reservations:** One night's deposit, 3 day cancellation policy for refund less $10 service fee **Brochure:** Yes **Permitted:** Children 10+, drinking, limited smoking **Conference:** Yes, small meeting room **Payment Terms:** Check AE/DC/DISC/MC/V [I01HPD-E1-21455] **COM** YG **ITC Member:** No

Charles Dickens visited here in 1867

Rates:	Pvt Bath 6
Single	$ 69-99.00
Double	$ 69-99.00

David Finney Inn	216 Delaware St 19720	New Castle DE
Judy & Kurt Piser		Tel: 800-334-6640 302-322-6367
		Res Times 24 Hours

Historic village setting for this famous c1685 Inn offering history complete restoration including antique furnishings in guest rooms. Continental breakfast or full breakfast on weekends. Gourmet restaurant on premises offering lunch and dinner, and entertainment. **Seasonal:** No **Brochure:** Yes **Permitted:** Children, smoking, drinking **Languages:** Spanish **Payment Terms:** Check AE/MC/V/DC [C11ACDE-1017] **COM** Y **ITC Member:** No

Rates:	Pvt Bath 17
Single	$ 70-130.00

©*Inn & Travel Memphis, Tennessee*

Delaware *National Edition*

William Penn Guest House
Mr Mrs Richard Burwell

206 Delaware St 19720

New Castle DE
Tel: 302-328-7736

1682 residence where William Penn stayed and you can share that same room today! Restored and listed on the *National Register of Historic Places*, you enjoy the antique furnishings that let you step back in time. Just two blocks from the water and on the Village Green. Continental breakfast included. **Seasonal:** No **Reservations:** One night's deposit refunded if cancelled with minimum 10 day notice less handling fee. **Brochure:** Yes **Permitted:** Children 7-up, limited drinking **Payment Terms:** Check [C11A-CDE-1018] **COM** Y **ITC Member:** No

Rates:	Pvt Bath 4
Single	$ 45.00
Double	$ 50.00

Inn At The Canal
Mary & Al Ioppolo

Newark DE
Tel: 410-885-5995

Refer to the same listing name under Chesapeake City, Maryland for a complete description. **Seasonal:** No **Payment Terms:** Check AE/DC/MC/V [M02FPM-D-16744] **COM** U **ITC Member:** No

Rates:	Pvt Bath 6
Single	$ 70-100.00
Double	$ 75-105.00

Cantwell House
Carole F Coleman

PO Box 2 19730

Odessa DE
Tel: 302-378-4179
Res Times 9am-9pm

Completely restored c1840 residence by interior designer and hostess in keeping with historical significant surroundings of Winterthur Museum. Guests can choose second floor rooms decorated in country antiques or a suite with private bath on the third floor with whirlpool tub, terry robes, TV, queen size bed, hidden ref, a/c and spectacular views of the surrounding town. Don't miss breakfast here! Your hostess prepares homemade specialties of muffins, croissants, french toast stuffed with bananas, nut breads, cinnamon buns along with fresh fruit and all the coffee you can hold. A fireplace warms guests during breakfast in winter while summer brings guests onto a screened porch overlooking flower gardens. Guests can visit the local Historical Houses, Bombay Hook (National Wildlife Refuge), St Andrews Boarding School, auctions (your hostess is an auctioneer and gladly offers hints on shopping). **Seasonal:** No **Reservations:** One night's deposit at res time to hold room, 14 day cancel policy. **Brochure:** Yes **Permitted:** Limited drinking, children limited **Payment Terms:** Check [X06BCDE-1019] **COM** Y **ITC Member:** No

Rates:	Pvt Bath 1	Shared Bath 2
Single	$ 75.00	$ 65.00
Double	$ 85.00	$ 75.00

Lord Baltimore Lodge
James & Doris Douns

16 Baltimore Ave 19971

Rehoboth Beach DE
Tel: 302-227-2855
Res Times 8am-5pm

Perfect seashore location for summer relaxing that's close to the beaches and boardwalk. Relive another era in this turn-of-the-century residence now offering guests a quaint and economical locale to all seaside activities. Golf, tennis, and all water sports and activities are here. Continental breakfast included. **Seasonal:** Rates vary **Reservations:** Deposit required at res time for first night's stay. **Brochure:** Yes **Permitted:** Children, smoking, drinking **Payment Terms:** Check MC/V [C11ACDE-1023] **COM** Y **ITC Member:** No

Rates:	Pvt Bath 5	Shared Bath 3
Single	$ 67.00	$ 55.00
Double	$ 77.00	$ 65.00

Tembo Guest House — 100 Laural St 19971 — Rehoboth Beach DE
Don & Gerry Cooper
Tel: 302-227-3360

Two story beach cottage nestled among shade trees just a block from the beach. Breakfast (full) served outdoors, weather permitting, with homemade raisin-bran muffins and oatmeal-date scones, and freshly brewed coffee/tea. **Seasonal:** No **Permitted:** Children, smoking, drinking, limited pets. Airport pick-ups at nominal charge. **Payment Terms:** Check [C11ACDE-1027] **COM** Y **ITC Member:** No

Rates:		Shared Bath 4
Single		$ 55.00
Double		$ 55.00

Darley Manor Inn B&B — Wilmington DE
Ray & Judith Hester
Tel: 800-824-4703 302-792-2127 Fax: 302-798-6143

Refer to the same listing name under Claymont, Delaware for a complete description. **Seasonal:** No **Payment Terms:** Check AE/DC/DISC/MC/V [M03H-PDE1-22309] **COM** YG **ITC Member:** No

Rates:	Pvt Bath 6
Single	$ 69-99.00
Double	$ 69-99.00

Adams Inn — 1744 Lanier Pl NW 20009 — Washington DC
Gene & Nancy Thompson
Tel: 800-578-6807 202-745-3600 Fax: 202-332-5867
Res Times 8am-9pm

The *Adams Inn* is a mid-city townhouse version of the American favorite - the Country Inn - in the British tradition of emphasis on hospitable and comfortable surroundings in a personal atmosphere. Located in a multi-cultural neighborhood with turn-of-the-century homes and stately trees, many diplomats, radio/TV personalities, professors, attorneys and government workers reside nearby. Guest rooms are furnished homestyle, some with private bath while others have a wash basin in the room and a shared bath. A sitting parlor is available for guests to relax and socialize or enjoy the paper, a book from the library, a puzzle or game. Your hosts enjoy helping sightseers make plans on what to see and where to dine. Located just two miles north of the White House, guests can take the Woodley-Zoo Metro on the Red Line or one of the many bus lines. Guests are within walking distance of three major convention hotels (Shoreham, Washington-Hilton, Washington-Sheraton) and within two blocks are fine boutiques, antique and international shoppes and the cuisine of many cultures. A continental breakfast is included and served in the spacious dining room. **Airport:** Washington National, Dulles, Baltimore-Washington **Seasonal:** No **Reservations:** One night deposit at res time, 72 hour cancel policy for refund, late arrival with prior arrangements **Brochure:** Yes **Permitted:** Children **Payment Terms:** AE/DC/DISC/MC/V [K04HPDC1-5042] **COM** YG **ITC Member:** No

Rates:	Pvt Bath 12	Shared Bath 13
Single	$ 60.00	$ 45.00
Double	$ 70.00	$ 55.00

Kalamore Guest House-Kalorama Park — 1854 Mintwood PL NW 20009 — Washington DC
*Tami Wood, John, Carlotta
Tel: 202-667-6369 Fax: 202-319-1262
Res Times 9am-9pm

Built at the turn-of-the-century, this group of charming Victorian Inns provides a cozy home-away-from-home. They are located on a quiet tree-lined street in a lovely downtown residential neighborhood, just a short stroll for a host of restaurants and neighborhood businesses. The guest rooms have been decorated to the provide the feeling of a bygone era but with today's conveniences. Most bedrooms have original fireplace mantels and period antiques. The garden is a sunny spot to enjoy the Inn's complimentary continental breakfast at the start of each day, or a complimentary aperitif and tea at day's end. The working fireplace in the parlor sets the same warm and friendly tone that is continued by the hospitality and personal service of the live-in innkeepers. Guests may walk to the White House. All of the Smithsonian museums and monuments are just 10 minutes away. **Airport:** Washington Natl-7mi; Dulles-25 mi **Discounts:** Senior citizens **Packages:** Yes, for groups **Seasonal:** No

Reservations: Deposit required, two weeks written cancel notice required for full refund**Brochure:** Yes **Permitted:** Children, drinking, limited smoking**Conference:** Yes, from 10-15 persons; groups may rent an entire house (6-15 bedrooms) **Payment Terms:** AE/DC/MC/V [Z11GP-DC1-5046] **COM** Y **ITC Member:** No

Rates:	**Pvt Bath 12**	**Shared Bath 19**
Single	$ 55-85.00	$ 40-65.00
Double	$ 60-95.00	$ 45-75.00

Morrison House — Washington DC
Robert & Rosemary Morrison
Tel: 800-367-0800 703-838-8000
Res Times 24 Hrs

Refer to the same listing name under Alexandria, Virginia for a complete description. **Seasonal:** No **Payment Terms:** Check AE/DC/MC/V [M11-BCVA-6350] **COM** Y **ITC Member:** No

Rates:	**Pvt Bath 45**
Single	$ 135-200.00
Double	$ 135-200.00

Prince George Inn B&B — Washington DC
Bill & Norma Grovermann
Tel: 410-263-6418

Refer to the same listing name under Annapolis, Maryland for a complete description. **Seasonal:** No **Payment Terms:** Check MC [M02BCMD-6379] **COM** Y **ITC Member:** No

Rates:	**Shared Bath 4**
Single	$ 50.00
Double	$ 60.00

Swiss Inn — 1204 Massachusetts Ave NW 20005 — Washington DC
Ralph Nussbaumer
Tel: 800-955-7947 202-842-0151
Res Times 24 Hrs

Experience the old European charm of this beautifully reconstructed Town House. Conveniently located near museums, restaurants and the White House. All suites include individual climate control, private baths and fully equipped kitchenettes. No meals included. Conveniently located on prestigious Massachusetts Avenue. **Seasonal:** No **Reservations:** One night's deposit at res time. **Brochure:** Yes **Permitted:** Children, drinking, limited smoking **Languages:** French, Arabic **Payment Terms:** Check AE/MC/V [X09BCDC-5050] **COM** Y **ITC Member:** No

Rates:	**Pvt Bath 6**
Single	$ 58.00
Double	$ 68.00

Country Haus — 1191 Franklin 62231 — Carlyle IL
Ron & Vickie Cook
Tel: 800-279-4486 618-594-8313
Res Times 8am-10pm

Country Haus B&B is located one mile from Carlyle Lake, Illinois' largest man-made lake. With over 24,000 acres of water, outdoor activities abound such as water sports, swimming, fishing, boating, sailing and skiing. Carlyle Lake was named the premier sailing lake of the Midwest. Visitors can also choose between two golf courses, tennis courts, and a swimming pool - all open to the public. *Country Haus* is located just one block from the picturesque downtown shopping area and the Historical Society

National Edition   *Illinois*

Museum. Built at the turn of-the-century in the Eastlake-style, the original stained glass windows, pocket doors and hardwood floors are found throughout. For relaxation, a library complete with TV and stereo is on the first floor. A hot tub awaits you on the back deck. The five guest rooms are individually decorated with cozy country themes, complete with toiletries, hair dryers and robes. Each guest room has its own private bath. A full breakfast is served in the first floor dining room. A gift shoppe features craft items from local crafts people as well as souvenirs and suntan lotion. Carlyle is located 50 miles east of St. Louis. **Discounts:** Yes, business travelers and singles **Airport:** St Louis Lambert-60 mi **Reservations:** First night's deposit or cc number to guarantee res, 48 hr cancel policy for refund. **Permitted:** Children, limited drinking **Payment Terms:** Check AE/DC/DISC/MC/V [I04GPIL-12965] **COM** Y **ITC Member:** No

Rates:	Pvt Bath 5
Single	$ 53.00
Double	$ 58.00

Wright Farmhouse   Rt 3 62321   Carthage IL
John & Connie Wright   **Tel:** 217-357-2421

Turn-of-the-century farmhouse being restored by the hosts to represent original period furnishings and decor. Relaxed and warm hospitality are offered by these pleasant hosts and include the opportunity to live a short period on a working farm in Illinois. Nearby sights include craft festivals, antique shops, swimming, golf, and historic Mormon sights. Continental breakfast of homemade family recipes including biscuits and blueberry pancakes. **Seasonal:** No **Brochure:** Yes **Permitted:** Children **Payment Terms:** Check [C11ACIL-1240] **COM** Y **ITC Member:** No

Rates:	Pvt Bath 3
Single	$ 40.00
Double	$ 50.00

TC Smith Historic B&B Inn   Chicago IL
Marks Family   **Tel:** 800-423-0233 414-248-1097

Refer to the same listing name under Lake Geneva, Wisconsin for a complete description. **Seasonal:** No **Payment Terms:** Check AE/DC/DISC/MC/V [M04G-PWI-17196] **COM** YG **ITC Member:** No

Rates:	Pvt Bath 8
Single	$ 85-225.00
Double	$ 95-250.00

The Margarita European Inn   Chicago IL
Judith Baker   **Tel:** 847-869-2273 **Fax:** 847-869-2353

Refer to the same listing name in Evanston, Illinois for a complete description. **Payment Terms:** Check AE/MC/V [M05IPIL1-26842] **COM** YG **ITC Member:** No

Rates:	Pvt Bath 16	Shared Bath 34
Single	$ 70-105.00	$ 55.00
Double	$ 80-115.00	$ 65.00

Longwell Hall   Chicago IL
Neil McFadden/Eileen Pembroke   **Tel:** 708-386-5043
    Res Times 9am-5pm

Refer to the same listing name under Oak Park, Illinois for a complete description. **Payment Terms:** Check [M01EPIL-15182] **COM** U **ITC Member:** No

Rates:	Pvt Bath 1	Shared Bath 2	Suite 1
Single	$ 75.00	$ 60.00	$ 125.00
Double	$ 85.00	$ 65.00	$ 150.00

©*Inn & Travel Memphis, Tennessee*

Illinois National Edition

Wheaton Inn
Julie Green

Chicago IL
Tel: 312-690-2600

Refer to the same listing name under Wheaton, Illinois for complete description. **Seasonal:** No **Payment Terms:** Check AE/DC/D/MC/V [M02BCIL-6560] **COM** Y **ITC Member:** No

Rates: **Pvt Bath 16**
Single $ 99-160.00
Double $ 99-160.00

Fannies House
Mary & Don Noonan

300 N Front St 60930

Danforth IL
Tel: 815-269-2145
Res Times To 8:30am/after 5:30*

Escape to *Fannie's House*, just two hours south of Chicago's loop. Relax and savor the simple *"Prairie Home Companion" charm* of this small one hundred year old home in a peaceful little country town setting. The house has a kitchen stove and refrigerator for your use, should you want to prepare some special treats. A continental breakfast is included and is served in the dining room. Choose either the secluded upstairs bedroom and private bath or the cozy downstairs bedroom. They both have comfortable queen sized beds. Good restaurants are within five to ten minutes driving time. A listing of interesting things to see and do in the nearby area is available. Fields of grain, farm animals, wooded areas, ponds and streams are all around and make for fine bicycling or easy hiking. **Discounts:** Yes, inquire at res time **Airport:** Chicago O'Hare-2 hrs; Champaign IL Willard-1-1/4 hrs **Seasonal:** No **Reservations:** Advance deposit required to guarantee reservation, *call anytime on weekends **Brochure:** Yes **Permitted:** Limited children and drinking **Payment Terms:** Check [R01EPIL-14885] **COM** Y **ITC Member:** No

Rates: **Pvt Bath 2**
Single $ 50.00
Double $ 60.0

Hobsons Bluffdale
Bill & Lindy Hobson

Rt 1 Eldred-Hillview Rd 62027

Eldred IL
Tel: 217-983-2854

c1828 farmhouse constructed from native limestone by J. Russell, well-known poet whose writings appeared in McGuffys Readers and whose guests often included Charles Dickens. Now a working farm with all the required animals, you'll relive childhood adventures while staying here. Continental breakfast included. **Seasonal:** No **Reservations:** Deposit required at res time, refund if cancelled. **Brochure:** Yes **Permitted:** Limited children, limited smoking **Payment Terms:** Check [X11ACIL-2955] **COM** Y **ITC Member:** No

Rates: **Pvt Bath 8**
Single $ 45.00
Double $ 55.00

The Margarita European Inn
Judith Baker

1566 Oak Ave 60201

Evanston IL
Tel: 847-869-2273 **Fax:** 847-869-2353

Warm as a European Country Inn ... as quaint as an English bed and breakfast ... the *Margarita's* historical vibrance has been carefully restored by the present owners. From noble arched French doors to vintage period moldings, the Margarita's architectural significance is complemented throughout with tasteful antiques offering guests friendly, relaxing accommodations in a cozy setting. *The Margarita* has forty sleeping rooms with either private or European-style shared bath arrangements. A pleasant continental breakfast is served each morning in the parlor with other meals available in Va Pensiero, the *Margarita* in-house regional Italian ristorante. *The Margarita's* location offers guests the best of both worlds - the moderate pace of a suburban setting along with the vitality of a university town immediately next door to a major city. Points of interest and activities include beautiful Lake Michigan, golf, indoor and outdoor tennis, fishing piers, 86 parks and recreation centers, art galleries, eight theatre companies, outstanding schools (Northwestern, Kendall, National-Lewis,

National Edition   *Illinois*

Garrett Evangelical, Seabury Western Seminary) and downtown Evanston shops, galleries and restaurants. Public transportation to nearby Chicago and all of its sights and activities is just two blocks from the Inn. **Airport:** O'Hare Intl-15 mi (30 mins) **Seasonal:** No **Reservations:** One night's deposit or credit card guarantee required, 24 hr cancel policy for refund *Suite available **Brochure:** Yes **Permitted:** Children, drinking, smoking **Conference:** Yes, seating to 15 persons **Payment Terms:** Check AE/MC/V [Z05-IPIL1-7588] **COM** YG **ITC Member:** No

Rates:	Pvt Bath 16	Shared Bath 34
Single	$ 70-105.00	$ 55.00
Double	$ 80-115.00	$ 65.00

Aldrich Guest House   900 Third St 61036   Galena IL
Sandra & Herb Larson   Tel: 815-777-3323

Wonderful Greek Revival furnished with family heirlooms and period antique pieces and complete with all the period touches including working fireplaces. US Grant often entertained here and his troops marched in the front yard on numerous occasions. Full breakfast served in formal dining room or on the screened porch. **Seasonal:** No **Reservations:** Deposit required to hold room. **Brochure:** Yes

Ulyssus S Grant often entertained here

Permitted: Children 10-up, limited smoking, limited drinking **Payment Terms:** Check MC/V [C11ACIL-1250] **COM** Y **ITC Member:** No

Rates:	Pvt Bath 3	Shared Bath 2
Single	$ 55.00	$ 45.00
Double	$ 65.00	$ 55.00

Log Cabin Guest House   11661 W Chetlain Lane 61036   Galena IL
Mary Alice Bernard   Tel: 815-777-2845

Authentic 1832 servant's house with a woodstove in the kitchen, fireplace, and period furnishings, but with all the other modern amenities including showers, TV, and air conditioning. Continental breakfast included. **Seasonal:** No **Brochure:** Yes **Permitted:** Children, limited smoking, social drinking **Payment Terms:** Check [C11ACIL-1249] **COM** Y **ITC Member:** No

Rates:	Pvt Bath 2
Single	$ 55.00
Double	$ 60.00

Stillmans Country Inn   513 Bouthillier 61036   Galena IL
Janette Mueller   Tel: 815-777-0557

Gorgeous Victorian mansion built by wealthy businessman where Ulysses S. Grant often dined and visited as a guest of the hosts. Today the guest rooms contain period antique furnishings including porcelain bowls and working fireplaces. The house tower was often used as a lookout for runaway slaves in the underground railway. Continental breakfast included. **Seasonal:** No **Reservations:** Credit card for guarantee to hold room with 48-hour cancellation notice. **Brochure:** Yes **Permitted:** Smoking, drinking, children 12-up **Conference:** Yes, up to 20 persons including dining for luncheons or dinners. **Payment Terms:** Check AE/DISC/MC/V [C11ACIL-1266] **COM** Y **ITC Member:** No

Rates:	Pvt Bath 5
Single	$ 60.00
Double	$ 70.00

The Poor Farm Bed & Breakfast   Poor Farm Road 62863-9803   Mount Carmel IL
Liz & John Stelzer   Tel: 800-646-FARM 618-262-HOME **Fax:** 618-262-8199
    Res Times 24 Hrs

A gracious glimpse of yesteryear awaits those fortunate enough to visit the *Poor Farm Bed & Breakfast*. From 1857, the first year of James Buchanan's only term, until 1949, the first year of Harry

©*Inn & Travel Memphis, Tennessee*

Illinois   *National Edition*

Truman's second term, the Wabash County Poor Farm served as the home for the homeless. Today, *The Poor Farm Bed & Breakfast* is home for the modern traveler who enjoys authentic country charm and genuine old-time hospitality. Enjoy luxury in one of the four room suites or gracious double rooms, all with private bath. Children are welcome! Located within walking distance of the historic Wabash River, two city parks, fishing, swimming, tennis, a driving range and perhaps the finest 18 hole municipal golf course in Illinois, this stately old 35 room brick structure will enchant you as you discover the simple joys of simpler times. Roam the 90 foot hallway and browse through the many artifacts, curl up with one of the hundreds of books, or enjoy an old-fashioned sing-along around the antique player piano. Within 45 mins you can experience nearby historic old New Harmony, Indiana or try your luck at riverboat gaming in Evansville, Indiana. Awaken to the aroma of freshly-brewed coffee and prepare yourself for a hearty Country Breakfast. Whether vacationing, on a business trip or a romantic weekend getaway, the ambiance, location and your hosts' sincere concern for your comfort will help you understand why *The Poor Farm Bed & Breakfast* is known as *"The Inn place to stay."* **Airport:** Evansville IN-35mi **Packages:** Golf **Seasonal:** No **Reservations:** Deposit required, when calling, ask for cancel policy **Brochure:** Yes **Permitted:** Children, limited drinking, limited smoking, limited pets, wheel chair and handicapped accessible **Conference:** Two meeting rooms, including dining for groups to 36, meetings, receptions on 2-1/2 acres outdoors **Payment Terms:** Check AE/DISC/MC/V [I02HPIL1-18772] **COM** YG **ITC Member:** No

Rates:	Pvt Bath 5
Single	$ 45-85.00
Double	$ 45-85.00

Longwell Hall   301 N Scoville Ave 60302   Oak Park IL
Neil McFadden/Eileen Pembroke   **Tel:** 708-386-5043
                                                                                   Res Times 9am-5pm

Formerly Toad *Hall, Longwell Hall* is a great location for architecture and literature buffs, business travelers, university student parents and "extra" out-of-town guests. Built in 1909 by a prominent villager, its lustrous history includes visits by Ernest Hemingway who courted Kathryn, one of family's daughters. Carefully maintained and restored, this gracious brick colonial home is furnished with antiques, Oriental rugs and Laura Ashley wallpapers. Guest rooms have comfortable reading chairs, luxurious linens, and a/c. Guests are welcomed to relax in the wicker on the porches, practice on the putting green or curl up near a fireplace with a borrowed book. A continental breakfast, with your choice of time, is served in the oak-paneled dining room. Centrally located in the Frank Lloyd Wright District, *Longwell Hall* is within walking distance of twenty-five Wright masterpieces, dozens of architecturally significant buildings, the Ernest Hemingway Museum, lovely shops, fine restaurants and public transportation to downtown Chicago. A romantic fireplaced-suite with a private porch is perfect for honeymoons and weekend getaways. Your host is a Chicago native and glad to help travelers find area attractions and dining hot spots! **Airport:** O'Hare Intl and Midway-20 mins. **Reservations:** One night's deposit, 14 day cancel policy for refund. **Brochure:** Yes **Permitted:** Children, Drinking **Payment Terms:** Check [I11IPIL1-6680] **COM** G **ITC Member:** No **Quality Assurance:** Requested

Rates:	Pvt Bath 1	Shared Bath 2	Suite 1
Single	$ 75.00	$ 60.00	$ 125.00
Double	$ 85.00	$ 65.00	$ 150.00

Inn On The Square   3 W Montgomery 61943   Oakland IL
Gary & Linda Miller   **Tel:** 217-346-2289

National Edition   *Illinois*

We specialize in fine food and friendly atmosphere - best of all, its the return of Bed and Breakfast and Tourism. Blending the old with the new, we offer you warm hospitality and simple country pleasures, as well as historical sites, recreational activities, shopping excursions and plain old *"sittin' and rockin'."* Our Bed & Breakfast features three upstairs bedrooms, comfortably furnished for country living, each with its own "down the hall" private bath. Relax in the Library with a good book, jigsaw puzzle, or the evening local news. Wander our "forest" out back of the Inn or sit under the trees on the town square. Antiques, gifts, flowers, crafts and ladies apparel shop will pique your curiosity, while our Tea Room offers simple but elegant luncheons and dinners for you and your friends. Open 11am to 2pm, Mon through Sun and 5pm to 8pm, Friday and Saturday. Private dinner parties are our specialty. Within easy walking or driving distance, you can visit landmarks which appear on the *National Historical Register*. There's golf, swimming and Walnut Point - a beautiful conservation park. Located 20 mins from Eastern Illinois Univ at Charleston. **Reservations:** Credit card number required to guarantee reservation **Brochure:** Yes **Permitted:** Children, drinking, limited smoking **Conference:** Yes, groups of 10 to 50 persons **Payment Terms:** Check MC/V [R11EPIL-1279] **COM** Y **ITC Member:** No

Rates: Pvt Bath 3
Single $ 45.00
Double $ 50.00

Little House On The Prairie   RR 2 Patterson Rd 61951   Sullivan IL
Guy S Little Jr/Kirk McNamer   **Tel:** 217-728-4727
Res Times 10am-6pm

The *Little Home* dates from 1894 and the fourth generation now calls it his home after forty years of being involved in the world of show business. This Queen Anne farmhouse remains the same today - furnished with beautiful original antiques and art work along with theatrical memorabilia Guy has collected throughout his career. Broadway and Hollywood stars of the '60s and '70s enjoyed dinner parties here including Alan Alda, June Allyson, Bob Cummings, Ann Miller and dozens of others. All of the rooms are elegantly appointed and three of the guest rooms open onto a large sunroom which features a jacuzzi and entertainment center with TV, VCR and a stereo while outdoors a 40 x 20 ft pool and accompanying cabana are available for guest use. The grounds are beautifully maintained with flowering trees, tulips and flowering gardens spring through fall - with acres of woods beyond the grounds for pleasant walks, picnic lunches, biking and even a pond. Afternoon tea or complimentary wine is served daily. Guests are invited to enjoy the extensive theatre library or listen to Broadway's greatest hits. A full breakfast is offered 8-11 and guests have their choice of eating in the formal dining room, sunroom, the patio in summer or enjoy breakfast in bed! Central Illinois has much to offer guests including Lake Shelbyville with three marinas and large beaches just a few miles away. An outstanding golf course is just around the corner where your host will make arrangements for you or at other local courses. The only Amish colony in Illinois is just 15 mi with many interesting attractions. The Little Theatre-On The Square will celebrate its 37th year in 1994 - and your host/former producer-director will make sure you know about the upcoming performances before your arrival. **Seasonal:** Clo 1/2-3/31 **Reservations:** 50% deposit required with a 5 day cancel policy for refund less $20 service fee, check-in 4pm, check-out 11am **Brochure:** Yes **Permitted:** Drinking, limited children, limited smoking **Conference:** Small conferences indoors and outdoors in summer around the 40 x 20 ft pool grounds. **Payment Terms:** Check [I09DPIL-12162] **COM** Y **ITC Member:** No

Rates: Pvt Bath 4
Single $ 50.00
Double $ 60.00

Wheaton Inn   301 W Roosevelt Rd 60187   Wheaton IL
Linda Matzen   **Tel:** 312-690-2600   **Res Times** 24 hrs

©*Inn & Travel Memphis, Tennessee*

Illinois - Indiana   *National Edition*

Located in historic Wheaton, just 25 miles west of Chicago, the *Wheaton Inn* has welcomed guests with its gracious Williamsburg ambiance since opening in 1987. Each of the Inn's sixteen spacious, elegantly appointed bedrooms has a private bath, phone, remote control TV, VCR hook-up and towel warmer. Eleven rooms include working fireplaces and a number have jacuzzi tubs. A continental plus breakfast is served each morning in the cheery breakfast room which is located adjacent to an outdoor patio. Guests are served snacks and hors d'oeuvres with flavored coffees and teas available around the clock. An ideal setting for retreats and seminars for groups to four persons. A wood-paneled library with fireplace and large screen TV hosts intimate groups up to twelve. An exceptional catering staff works with each group to plan menus which meet all meal requirements. An abundance of cultural and recreational activities of the Chicago Metro area are available including golf, cross-country skiing or even cycling on the extensive Prairie Path - all located close to the Inn. Forest preserves, polo fields, arboretum, theatres, museums and shopping areas are within fifteen minutes driving. Meals available upon request and advance notice. **Seasonal:** No **Reservations:** Credit card or deposit at res time, 7-day cancellation policy for refund **Brochure:** Yes **Permitted:** Children, smoking, limited drinking **Conference:** For groups to 45 persons. **Payment Terms:** Check AE/DC/D/MC/V [R02BCIL-1289] **COM** Y **ITC Member:** No

Rates:	Pvt Bath 16
Single	$ 99-160.00
Double	$ 99-160.00

Dunes Shore Inn   33 Lakeshore County Rd 46301-0807   **Beverly Shores IN**
Fred & Rosemary Braun   **Tel:** 219-879-9029
                                                                           Res Times 8am-8pm

Dunes Shore Inn ... where nature, friendship and a heartfelt welcome are found. A casual Bed & Breakfast in secluded Beverly Shores, one block to Lake Michigan. Surrounded by Indiana Dunes State and National Parks, one hour from Chicago, three hours from Indianapolis. A four-season oasis - miles of wooded trails and beaches await you. The Inn has ten comfortable guest rooms on the upper two floors with a guest lounge on each floor. In summer, guests enjoy the patio, screen house and the picnic area with grill. For those who want more privacy, we offer our summer apartment adjacent to the Inn, available from May - October. We welcome family reunions, small groups and cater to the midweek retreat or low-key business meeting. Restaurants, antique shops, Lighthouse Place, outlet mall, Michigan City Marina, the zoo, golf, summer stock theatre, tennis, inland lakes are all within ten miles. Come and experience the new life of spring, the long sandy beaches of summer, the fall color burst and the wonders of winter! Spectacular sunrises and sunsets upon an ever-changing lake are guaranteed year round! Open since 1985. A continental breakfast is included. **Discounts:** Yes, AARP (5%) and Weekly (15%) **Airport:** Chicago O'Hare-70 miles **Seasonal:** No **Reservations:** Full deposit, 50% for extended stays; 14 day cancel policy less 25% service fee. **Brochure:** Yes **Permitted:** Children, drinking **Conference:** Yes, small groups. **Languages:** German **Payment Terms:** Check MC/V [R02EPIN-1291] **COM** Y **ITC Member:** No

Rates:	Pvt Bath 1	Shared Bath 10
Single	$ 72.00	$ 42.00
Double	$ 83.00	$ 46.00

Gray Goose Inn   350 Indian Boundry Rd 46304   **Chesterton IN**
Tim Wilk/Chuck Ramsey   **Tel:** 800-521-5127 219-926-5781 **Fax:** 219-926-4845
                                                                           Res Times 10am-9pm

Located in the heart of the Dunes Country. Leave the hurried pace of everyday life behind. Enter a world of tranquility. A world where the spirit and gracious traditions of our colonial heritage are yours to savor and enjoy. Century-old oaks embrace an English country house overlooking picturesque Lake Palomara. Upon entering the front hall you immediately sense the qualities that set the *Gray Goose* apart from the ordinary. Traditional English decor, fresh flowers and sincere friendly hospitality. Choose from a four-poster 18th Century rice bed, a four-poster washed pine in the Shaker tradition, or a four-poster French Country style. Three suites have fireplaces, one with fireplace and jacuzzi. All rooms feature private phones, TV's, some with VCR. Our library has a selection of books, magazines and videos. Breakfast is always a special time at the *Gray Goose*, it's always gourmet! Take peaceful walks around the lake, feed the geese, take a paddle boat ride. Near Indiana Dunes State and national Lakeshore. There are fine antique shops, cross country and downhill skiing nearby along with fine dining within walking distance. Whatever your pleasure, we wish to share a truly beautiful corner of "Dunes Country" with you. **Packages:** Weddings **Discounts:** Midweek, two day min **Airport:** Chicago O'Hare-90 mins; South Bend-50 min **Seasonal:** No **Reservations:** One night's deposit required within 7 days of booking reservation to guarantee, 10 day cancel policy for refund **Brochure:** Yes **Permitted:** Children 12-up, limited smoking, drinking **Conference:** Small parties, weddings, group meetings **Payment Terms:** Check AE/DISC/MC/V [I02HPIN1-1293] **COM YG ITC Member:** No **Quality Assurance** Requested

Rates: Pvt Bath 8
Single $ 80-135.00
Double $ 80-135.00

Columbus Inn	445 Fifth St 47201	Columbus IN
*Paul Staublin		Tel: 812-378-4289

The Columbus Inn offers luxury accommodations and the finest of hospitality in the former town City Hall of 1895. The Inn's thirty-four rooms and suites feature grand architectural details and are furnished with elegant Victorian antiques and fine reproductions. Each guest room has its own thermostat and private bath. Guests enjoy daily tea and a full Heartland breakfast featuring fresh fruits, home-baked pastries and hot casseroles. A library containing historic books keeps many guests busy. This Inn is located in the heart of a nationally-renowned collection of contemporary architecture, and is convenient to golf, antique shopping, buggy ride, the theatre, scenic railroads and plenty of midwest warmth and hospitality. AAA Four Diamond Lodge Rated. **Seasonal:** No **Reservations:** Deposit or credit card # to guarantee room at res time; 48 hr cancel notice required for refund. **Brochure:** Yes **Permitted:** Children, **Payment Terms:** Check AE/DC/MC/V [Z05EPIN-1296] **COM U ITC Member:** No

Rates: Pvt Bath 34
Single $ 83-132.00
Double $ 93-160.0

Candlewyck Inn	331 W Washington Blvd 46802	Fort Wayne IN
Jan & Bob Goehringer		Tel: 219-424-2643

Beautiful 1914 California Craftsman style bungalow lovingly restored and listed on the National Register offering beveled and stained glass throughout, oak beamed ceilings in several rooms, and furnished by the host/interior designer by profession, with plenty of antiques, brass furnishings, wallcoverings and accessories. You're walking distance to Grand Wayne Convention Center and Embassy Theatre Botanical Conservatory, and the Allen County Library for tracking genealogies. Gracious hosts extend their hospitality to everyone and where a night's stay is always welcome..a homecoming! Breakfast is continental plus and full on weekends. **Seasonal:** No **Reservations:** 50% deposit at res time with full refund on 48hr notification, res held until 6:00 pm without guarantee. Arrival 4-6:00pm, 10% senior discount. **Brochure:** Yes **Permitted:** Limited smoking **Conference:** Yes, up to eight persons. **Payment Terms:** Check AE/MC/V [A01DPIN-1301] **COM YG ITC Member:** No

Rates: Shared Bath 5
Single $ 45.00
Double $ 55-60.00

Checkerberry Inn	62644 County Rd 37 46526	Goshen IN
The Graffs		Tel: 219-642-4445
		Res Times 8:30-5:30pm

Rated as one of the *Ten Best Nationally* by "Inn-review", at the *Checkerberry Inn* you will find a

Indiana   *National Edition*

unique atmosphere unlike anywhere else in the midwest. The fourteen individually decorated rooms and suites will please even the most discerning guests. Each room has a breath-taking view of the unspoiled rolling countryside. The restaurant serves only the freshest foods using herbs and other ingredients from the local countryside including an extensive wine list. Situated off of a sparsely traveled road in a serene and secluded Amish farmland, guests can experience the uncluttered culture of the Amish, where horse and buggy are the way of life. A continental breakfast of fresh juice, coffee and tea, fresh baked muffins, nut and fruit breads - served with strawberry butter, cereal and fresh fruit are included. The Inn has its own outdoor pool, professional croquet court and tennis court. Fine walking, cycling, jogging paths are available. Excellent golfing and shopping are within 10-20 mins. In a nutshell - The Checkerberry Inn is a destination offering the tranquility of pastoral countryside rest and relaxation. **Packages:** Yes, on special dinner events **Seasonal:** No **Reservations:** Credit card or deposit to guarantee, 24 hr cancel policy for refund **Brochure:** Yes **Permitted:** Children, drinking **Conference:** Yes for groups to 30 persons. **Payment Terms:** Check AE/MC/V [Z11DPIN-6529] **COM** Y **ITC Member:** No

Rates: **Pvt Bath 14**
Single $ 72-90.00
Double $ 96-120.00

Nuthatch B&B   7161 Edgewater Pl 46240   Indianapolis IN
Joan & Bernie Morris   Tel: 317-257-2660   Fax: 317-257-2677
    Res Times 24 Hrs

The *Nuthatch is a Bed & Breakfast* home in a resort-like setting minutes north of downtown Indianapolis. A 1920's French country cottage with arched windows and leaded glass doors, the Nuthatch overlooks the White River as it winds it way south past the quaint village of Broad Ripple, home of some of the best restaurants in the city. Fragrant flower and herb gardens surround the house and grounds. This quiet riverside setting provides an ideal four-season getaway. Breakfasts are very special here! Your host, Joan, is a cooking teacher and culinary herbalist who honed her cooking skills in classes as far away at Bangkok, Thailand and Bali, Indonesia. Yes, she will cook a Thai breakfast for you on request, but her American breakfasts can be just as unusual. This is especially true when she is trying something new from the extensive herb gardens she grows just outside the front door. Tours of these gardens can be a fun part of your stay. There are only two guest rooms so your hosts, Joan and husband Bernie, can make your every visit a special occasion. The Adirondack suite is reminiscent of Joan's former summer home on Lake George; barn-siding on the walls, old Indian rugs, white iron bed and natural wicker furniture complete its cottage atmosphere. The Wren's Nest, on the other hand, reflects Joan's Florida heritage with soft tropical colors, parquet floor from an old hotel ballroom, gas light fixtures and clawfoot tub mix happily with modern wicker for coziness and comfort. A quiet workspace can be arranged for you, complete with fax, should you be in our area on business. But if you are able, just grab your camera or fishing gear, leave all the work and stress behind, prop your feet up on the deck and watch the river meander by! **Airport:** Indianapolis-20 mi **Discounts:** Corporate rates available **Packages:** Winter Midweek: Book two rooms for two nights - Free Cooking Class **Seasonal:** Rates vary **Reservations:** One night deposit, 7 day cancel policy for refund, rates vary for special events: e-mail bbmorri@indyvax.iupui.edu **Brochure:** Yes **Permitted:** Limited children, limited pets, limited drinking, limited smoking **Languages:** Yiddish **Payment Terms:** Check AE/DISC/MC/V [I06HPIN1-11055] **COM** YG **ITC Member:** No

Rates: **Pvt Bath 2**
Single $70-85.00
Double $ 80-95.00

Old Hoosier House   Rt 2 Box 229-1 46148   Knightstown IN
Jean Lewis   Tel: 800-755-3515   317-345-2969

Quiet relaxation in an ideal central location for true Indiana country living and sightseeing, the *Old Hoosier House* offers guests a hearty country breakfast and gracious common rooms (library, sitting room, dining room) and sunny patio. With four tastefully decorated guest rooms to choose, guests can select from rooms with fireplaces, king or queen-size beds and one room with a splendid view of the countryside. Fine golf at Royal Hylands is available at a reduced rate and is just across the pond from this residence. Hiking, biking, bird-watching and plenty of antiquing for the true enthusiast. **Seasonal:** No **Reservations:** One night's tariff as deposit with 25% cancel fee **Brochure:** Yes **Permitted:** Children, limited smoking, limited drinking **Payment Terms:** Check [E06BCIN-1306] **COM** Y **ITC Member:** No

Rates:	Pvt Bath 3	Shared Bath 1
Single	$ 58.00	$ 48.00
Double	$ 68.00	$ 58.00

Beiger Mansion Inn 317 Lincoln Way E 46544 Mishawaka IN
Ron Montandon/Phil Robinson **Tel:** 800-437-0131 219-256-0365 **Fax:** 219-259-2622
Res Times 8am-8pm

Gracious accommodations for travelers looking for a blend of history and cultural personality in a romantic and nostalgic mansion from the turn-of-the-century, listed in the *National Register of Historic Places*. Built for his wife in 1903-06, after she fell in love with similar homes in Newport Rhode Island, the four-story neo-classical stone and columned exterior offers a palatial ambience. Inside reflects the grandeur of gala affairs of the 1900s with ornate Victorian beauty of original imported wall coverings, impressive floor designs and inlays, working fireplaces, a spectacular staircase, verandas overlooking the grounds and antique furnishing throughout, including many family originals. In keeping with Susie Beiger's love of fresh flowers, each guest room is named for a flower which has maintained popularity since the 1900s. Guests are served a full or continental breakfast in the Trameisus Room on the Mall Level. The Inn is just a short walking distance of downtown with delightful restaurants and only a few driving-minutes from Notre Dame, St Mary's College, Indiana University of South Bend, Bethel College and downtown South Bend. **Seasonal:** No **Reservations:** One night's deposit at res time, 10 day cancel policy otherwise 50% refund for 2 days notice. Two night min stay for all Notre Dame home football games. **Brochure:** Yes **Permitted:** Children, drinking, smoking is not allowed **Conference:** Perfect setting for special occasions including complete A/V facilities and dining. Home to many lecture, performing theatre groups and service clubs that regularly reside here. **Payment Terms:** Check AE/MC/V [R09BCIN-1319] **COM** Y **ITC Member:** No

Rates:	Pvt Bath 5	Shared Bath 5
Single	$ 65-125.00	$ 55.00
Double	$ 70-125.00	$ 60.00

Greenmeadow Ranch R 2 State Rd 5 Box 592 46565 Shipshewana IN
Paul & Ruth Miller **Tel:** 219-768-4221

A lovely brick colonial home set on twenty acres of ranch land that includes chickens, ducks, donkeys, and miniature horses. Set in the middle of Amish country, your hosts will direct you to the local sights that include the largest flea markets in the country every Tuesday and Wednesday during the summer. Continental breakfast is included. **Seasonal:** No **Brochure:** Yes **Permitted:** Children **Languages:** PA Dutch **Payment Terms:** Check [C11ACIN-1333] **COM** Y **ITC Member:** No

Rates:	Shared Bath 7
Single	$ 35.00
Double	$ 50.00

Morton Street B&B 140 Morton St 46565 Shipshewana IN
Joel, Kim, Esther Mishler **Tel:** 800-447-6475 219-768-4391
Res Times 8:30am-5pm

In the heart of Amish Country, *Morton Street Bed & Breakfast* is within walking distance of all shops and the famous Shipshewana Auction and Flea Market. Three old homes offer you a choice of periods; Country, Antique or Victorian hospitality. A full complimentary breakfast is provided at the Buggy Wheel

Restaurant where you may choose from a medley of Amish/Mennonite home prepared dishes. Between sight-seeing, guests at the Wolfe Home can unwind in the Garden Gazebo, on the spacious front porch of the Davis Home or in the courtyard behind the Morton Home. Peace and quiet is preserved by not having TVs in the homes - so you can enjoy the simplicity of your surroundings and fully appreciate the uniqueness of *Morton Street Bed & Breakfast*. **Airport:** South Bend-1 hr **Discounts:** Travel agents **Packages:** Winter Weekend Special: Friday and Saturday nights, double occupancy $89.00 (Nov-April) **Seasonal:** No **Reservations:** 50% deposit required within 2 weeks of booking or credit card at res time **Brochure:** Yes **Permitted:** Children **Payment Terms:** Check DC/MC/V [I10EPIN-1334] **COM** Y **ITC Member:** No

Rates:	Pvt Bath 9
Single	$ 34-60.00
Double	$ 59-85.00

Mont Rest B&B   300 Spring St 52031   Bellevue IA
Christine & Bob Gelms   Tel: 319-872-4220

This Queen Anne mansion nestled on a nine acre hillside setting, overlooks the Mississippi River. Built in 1890's and restored and furnished with period antiques and family heirlooms - all for sale! Beautiful grounds include all forms of wildlife including eagles. Spectacular views from all the rooms and the wraparound porch. Museums, parks, antique shops, skiing, golfing, and local caves give guests plenty to do. Full breakfast included with room. Lunch and dinner available upon advance notice. **Seasonal:** No **Reservations:** Deposit required to hold room, check-in 2:00 pm with arrival before 8:00 pm unless prior arrangements have been. **Brochure:** Yes **Permitted:** Limited smoking **Payment Terms:** Check MC/V [X11ACIA-2958] **COM** Y **ITC Member:** No

Rates:	Pvt Bath 2	Shared Bath 5
Single	$ 75.00	$ 50.00
Double	$ 85.00	$ 60.00

Robins Nest Inn B&B   327 9th Ave 51501   Council Bluffs IA
Wendy Story   Tel: 712-323-1649

Grand Victorian residence within strolling distance to Dodge House and Haymarket Square with turn-of-the-century frontier furnishings and a hearty full breakfast of homemade breads and pastries. Dinner by prior arrangement. **Seasonal:** No **Brochure:** Yes **Permitted:** Children. **Payment Terms:** Check MC/V [C11ACIA-1351] **COM** Y **ITC Member:** No

Rates:	Shared Bath 3
Single	$ 45.00
Double	$ 55.00

River Oaks Inn   1234 E River Dr 52803   Davenport IA
Bill & Suzanne Pohl   Tel: 800-352-6016 319-326-2629

Overlook the Mississippi from this combination of Italianate and Victorian architecture listed on the *National Register of Historic Places* and fully restored and complete with antique furnishings and family heirlooms. Full breakfast served in the country kitchen. Plenty of local activities. **Seasonal:** No **Brochure:** Yes **Permitted:** Limited children, social drinking **Payment Terms:** Check MC/V [C11ACIA-1352] **COM** Y **ITC Member:** No

Rates:	Pvt Bath 4
Single	$ 45-45.00
Double	$ 55-70.00

Iowa

| *Redstone Inn* | 504 Bluff 52001 | **Dubuque IA** |

Tel: 319-582-1894
Res Times 24 hrs

This special treat in Iowa awaits everyone and needs to be included at least once in a lifetime! A classic Victorian mansion built c1894 takes guests back in time year-round. Beautifully furnished with antique period furnishings, it boasts it has the *"most luxurious bridal suite in the Midwest"* including a turret sitting room, and a charming bathroom featuring a double whirlpool bath! Christmas time is a real Victorian event that shouldn't be missed! Guest rooms are all spectacularly furnished, but try the one with a special brass and onyx queen size bed you won't see anywhere else! Breakfast is included with guest suites, but everyone receives coffee in their room in the morning. A real treat awaits guests in the dining room that serves as an on-the-premises European-style Cafe, where guests can select from a variety of homemade treats. Breakfast and tea menu. **Seasonal:** No **Reservations:** Deposit at res time; 48-hr cancellation policy **Brochure:** Yes **Permitted:** Children **Conference:** Yes **Languages:** Spanish **Payment Terms:** Check AE/DC/MC/V [I11BCIA-1357] **COM** Y **ITC Member:** No

Rates: Pvt Bath 15
Double $ 46-160.00

| *Rainbow H Ranch & Campground* | RR 1 Box 89 51531 | **Elk Horn IA** |
| Mark & Cherie Hensley | | **Tel:** 712-764-8272 |

A weary traveler can expect to receive more than just a place to rest here! They'll have a wonderful opportunity to become acquainted with the peaceful charm of the Iowa countryside in this grand brick home. Adults will enjoy a game of horseshoes or a crackling fire in the large rec room in winter. Children will enjoy exploring the outdoors and watching the varied livestock, including some of the best examples of Texas Longhorns. There is a/c, a private entrance, color TV and a large rec room. A hearty country breakfast is included with country fresh eggs, homemade jams and jellies, fresh baked breads, or you can enjoy a lighter continental breakfast with a Danish pastry. **Seasonal:** No **Reservations:** $10.00 deposit at res time **Brochure:** Yes **Permitted:** Smoking, limited children, limited drinking **Languages:** Spanish **Payment Terms:** Check [X02-BCIA-1360] **COM** Y **ITC Member:** No

Rates: Pvt Bath 2
Single $ 36.00
Double $ 42.00

| *Kingsley Inn* | 707 Ave H 52627 | **Fort Madison IA** |
| Myrna Reinhard | | **Tel:** 800-441-2327 319-372-7074 **Fax:** 319-372-7096 |

Res Times 8am-11pm

Experience complete relaxation in 1860's Victorian luxury. The "President James Madison" or "Blackhawk" rooms are just two of the fourteen individually decorated and appointed rooms named for persons of local historical significance. Spacious rooms with modern comforts overlook the sweeping Mississippi River or balconies over a quaint courtyard. Meticulous "million dollar" restoration and authentic furnishings recall the opulent period when steamboats tied-up just across the street. Walk to the replica of the 1808 Fort, Train Depot Museum, Steam Engine, Marina, parks, unique shops, galleries, antique malls and Riverboat Casinos. Ten minute drive to Nauvoo, Illinois, the "Williamsburg of the Midwest", with forty restored 1840's shops and homes. Awake to the aroma of Kingsley Blend coffee and greet the day with a specialty breakfast in the elegant Morning Room. Enjoy an array of homemade coffee cakes, muffins, fruit breads, our own granola, fruits and beverages. Enjoy a lunch or dinner at Alphas on the Riverfront, our restaurant. All guest rooms have private baths (some with whirlpools) CATV, a/c, phones, king, queen and extra-long double beds, sprinklers, alarms and elevator. Fax

Iowa   *National Edition*

is available. AAA 3-Star Rates **Discounts:** Corporate, AAA, AARP **Airport:** Burlington Municipal-30 mins **Packages:** Yes, inquire at res time **Seasonal:** No **Reservations:** Credit card number to guarantee reservation **Brochure:** Yes **Permitted:** Drinking, children 12-up **Payment Terms:** Check AE/DISC/MC/V [K03HPIA1-15616] **COM** YG **ITC Member:** No

Rates:	Pvt Bath 14
Single	$ 70-115.00
Double	$ 70-115.0

Wilson Home   RR 1 Box 132   50849   **Greenfield IA**
Wendy & Henry Wilson   **Tel: 515-743-2031**
                                                                Res Times 5:00-10:00 pm

A relaxful country atmosphere awaits all travelers in this perfect get-away. Dating from 1918 - today this retreat includes a forty foot indoor pool for refreshing swimming year-round. Each spacious bedroom is air conditioned and includes TV, phone, private bath and each room has sliding glass doors onto a large upper deck. The indoor pool is on the lower deck. Whether you're on a business trip, vacation, hunting trip, honeymoon or just passing through - the living is great in southwest Iowa. Complimentary beverages are offered guests in the fully stocked kitchenette and a complimentary breakfast is included each morning which can be served poolside. Nearby sights include an antique airplane museum, a Heritage Museum, Henry Wallace and John Wayne's birthplaces plus plenty of excellent fishing, quail and pheasant hunting and excellent golf. **Airport:** Des Moines-50mins **Seasonal:** Opn 1/15-10-15 **Reservations:** $25.00 deposit within 7 days to hold reservation, 48 hr cancel policy for refund. Payment by cash, check, travelers check; credit cards not accepted; check-in 4-6pm (other by prior arrangements) **Permitted:** Children, drinking (BYOB), limited smoking **Payment Terms:** Check [Z05GPIA-12500] **COM** Y **ITC Member:** No

Rates:	Pvt Bath 2
Single	$ 75.00
Double	$ 75.00

Decker House Inn   128 N Main   52060   **Maquoketa IA**
Troy Theede   **Tel: 319-652-6654**
                                                 Res Times 8am-8pm

1874 Hotel listed on *National Register of Historic* places and completely restored to permit you to step back in time and enjoy the turn-of-the-century feeling. Authentic antique furnishings including clawfoot tubs and period pieces everywhere. Close to the center of town and fine restaurants and shops. Outdoor activities year-round include fishing, canoeing, and snow skiing. Continental breakfast included. Dinner available at add cost. **Seasonal:** No **Brochure:** Yes **Permitted:** Children, pets, limited smoking, limited drinking **Payment Terms:** Check AE/MC/V [C11ACIA-1369] **COM** Y **ITC Member:** No

Rates:	Pvt Bath 15
Single	$ 60-70.00
Double	$ 65-75.00

Loy B&B   RR 1   52301   **Marengo IA**
Loy & Robert Walker   **Tel: 319-642-7787**

Enjoy this modern farm home, built in 1976, in the heartland of Iowa while visiting a "real working farm"! You'll hear the corn growing in season on this large farming operation, but the main residence is surrounded by expansive lawns offering great views of the "countryside". Guests begin each day

©*Inn & Travel Memphis, Tennessee*

with a hearty breakfast prepared right at home and served in the kitchen or screened porch, weather permitting. Enjoy the pool table, table tennis, shuffleboard and the many table games the hosts enjoy sharing with all guests. Loy will pack your lunch, if you want, for a day's outing. And you can participate in all the farming chores if you or the children want! Other meals available with advanced notice. **Seasonal:** No **Reservations:** $20 deposit at res time, refund with one-week cancellation and limited drinking. **Brochure:** Yes **Permitted:** Children **Payment Terms:** Check [X02BCIA-1370] **COM** Y **ITC Member:** No

Rates:		Shared Bath 3
Single		$ 40.00
Double		$ 55.00

Old World Inn 331 S Main St 52168 Spillville IA
Juanita J Loven Tel: 319-562-3739 319-562-3186
Res Times 8am-5pm

Don't miss this great ethnic B&B located in a *National Historic Registered* building c1871 used as the General Store and since renovated in 1987 as a historic Inn. The ground floor is the home of a Czech restaurant that tempts guests with traditional specialties such as roast pork, sauerkraut and dumplings, home rye breads, kolaches, poppyseed cake and also the "best beer" Pilsner Urquel, imported from Czechoslovakia. The guest rooms are located on the second floor and include modern amenities including a/c and individual heating control with each individually decorated room. One suite has a sink, refrigerator, table and room for sleeping cots. You're walking distance of the world-famous Billy Clock/Anton Dvorak Exhibit and lovely St Wenceslaus Church. Spillville is a Czech village located near Decorah in scenic northeast Iowa. Many historic, scenic and recreational attractions are here, including Vesterheim Norwegian Museum, the smallest church, Laura Ingals Wilder Museum, Spook Cave, Effigy Mounds National Park, and the mighty Mississippi River. **Seasonal:** No **Reservations:** One night's deposit at res time; 3-day cancellation policy for refund; latter requires service fee. **Brochure:** Yes **Permitted:** Children, limited drinking, limited pets **Languages:** Czech **Payment Terms:** Check MC/V [X02BCIA-1375] **COM** Y **ITC Member:** No

Rates:	Pvt Bath 4
Single	$ 45.00
Double	$ 55.00

Cimarron Hotel 203 N Main St 67853 Caimarron KS
Kathleen Holt Tel: 316-855-2244

c1887 brick hotel recently restored complete with antique furnishings and wallcoverings and great hospitality from this family operation, including their cat. Complete dining is available with wonderful tasting pan fried chicken. Full breakfast with homemade biscuits is served daily. **Seasonal:** No **Brochure:** Yes **Permitted:** Children, limited pets, limited smoking, limited drinking **Payment Terms:** Check [X11ACKS-3032] **COM** Y **ITC Member:** No

Rates:	Pvt Bath 5	Shared Bath 5
Single	$ 45.00	$ 40.00
Double	$ 50.00	$ 45.00

Crystles B&B 508 W 7th St 66901 Concordia KS
Joan Rhys Tel: 913-243-2192
Res Times 4pm-6pm

This charming turn-of-the-century home includes traditional mid-western hospitality in an historic Kansas town that's like visiting Grandmas! Dating from the 1880's, it has remained in the McClean family since 1920 and today the fourth generation has opened its doors to friends and travelers alike. The home is furnished with antiques and family heirlooms reminiscent of a bygone era including the guest rooms located on the second floor. The common rooms are warm and charming, inviting guests to relax and visit with the other guests or to curl up with a cup of tea and a good book, or to enjoy the 1916 Steinway. A delicious breakfast is included and can be enjoyed in your room, the spacious dining

Kansas   *National Edition*

room or the sunny front porch, weather permitting. You will find plenty of help available to plan your day while enjoying your second cup of coffee. In addition to the many interesting places to visit, the area offers recreational activities including hunting, fishing, golf, tennis, swimming and a health club in town. Special occasion arrangements can be made for flowers, candy or other surprises. A small gift show displays the work of local artists. **Discounts:** Business travelers or booking entire house **Airport:** Kansas City MO-4 hrs **Packages:** Yes, inquire at res time **Reservations:** 50% deposit within 5 days of making reservation, 7 day cancel policy for refund less $10 service fee **Brochure:** Yes **Permitted:** Children, drinking **Payment Terms:** Check DC/MC/V [R05FPKS-7968] COM U **ITC Member:** No

Rates:	Pvt Bath 1	Shared Bath 2
Single	$ 45.00	$ 35-40.00
Double	$ 45.00	$ 35-40.00

Cottage House Hotel	24 N Neosho 66846	Council Grove KS
Connie Essington		Tel: 800-888-8162 316-767-6828

Charming Victorian hotel c1876 that has been beautifully restored and is complete with antique furnishings from the period and a perfect starting point for a Western trip, at the beginning of the Santa Fe Trail! Famous Hays Restaurant is nearby offering fine dining to please all guests. Continental breakfast is included. Handicap access. **Seasonal:** No **Reservations:** Deposit required to hold room, 48 hr cancel policy for full refund. **Brochure:** Yes **Permitted:** Children, pets, smoking, drinking **Conference:** Yes, for groups to 35 persons including gourmet dining. **Payment Terms:** Check MC/V [X11ACKS-3033] COM Y **ITC Member:** No

Rates:	Pvt Bath 35
Single	$ 48.00
Double	$ 58.00

Halcyon House B&B	1000 Ohio St 66044	Lawreance KS
Esther Wolfe & Gail Towle		Tel: 913-841-0314
		Res Times 7-9:30

A real treat in Kansas by these charming hostesses who see to every guests' wishes! Their 100 year-old architectural masterpiece has been fully restored with each guest room having unique decor and ambience. The common rooms are bright and spacious and the magnificent kitchen with vaulted ceiling to floor with a glassed-Southern exposure brings everyone together in the morning for a great homemade experience. The full breakfast begins with fresh homemade muffins and preserves, coffee and tea, juices, and your choice of omelettes, eggs or cereal. You're close (3 blocks) to University of Kansas and all the downtown shops and restaurants. **Seasonal:** No **Reservations:** 50% deposit, cancel policy of 14-day notice, less 10% fee. **Brochure:** Yes **Payment Terms:** Check AE/MC/V [X02BCKS-3038] COM Y **ITC Member:** No

Rates:	Pvt Bath 2	Shared Bath 6
Single	$ 80.00	$ 50.00
Double	$ 80.00	$ 50-65.00

Inn At The Park	3751 E Douglas 67218	Wichita KS
Michelle Hickman		Tel: 800-258-1951 316-652-0500 Fax: 316-652-0610
		Res Times 7am-11pm

The *Inn at the Park* is a full service hotel which features twelve suites, each uniquely decorated by a different designer. The Inn is a historic mansion which was built in 1910 by the Beachy family, founders of Steffen's Dairy. In 1988 it underwent a complete renovation and was named one of the *Ten Best New Inns* in the country by *Inn Review*. Some of the amenities offered include; fireplaces, a hot tub and a jacuzzi bath and of course, a continental breakfast offering homemade baked goods and fresh fruits. The *Inn at the Park* is centrally located in Wichita. It is just minutes from the downtown business district and most of Wichita's other major businesses. The Inn is within walking distance of quaint neighborhood shops and College Hill Park. There are many fine dining establishments nearby. We feel the *Inn at the Park* is a luxurious retreat for weekend getaways or an enjoyable change of pace for

National Edition   *Knasas - Kentucky*

tired travelers seeking an Inn of distinction. **Discounts:** Corporate **Airport:** 10 mi to Wichita Mid-Continent **Seasonal:** No **Reservations:** One night's deposit to guarantee, 24 hr cancel policy for refund **Brochure:** Yes **Permitted:** Children, drinking, smoking in some rooms **Conference:** Yes, for groups to 20 persons. **Payment**

Rates:	Pvt Bath 12
Single	$ 75.00
Double	$ 85.00

Terms: Check AE/MC/V [K03-HPKS1-9025] **COM** Y **ITC Member:** No

---

The Castle Inn Riverside	1155 N River Blvd 67203	Wichita KS
Terry & Paula Lowry		Tel: 316-263-9300 Fax: 316-263-4998

The Castle, of Richardsonian Romanesque architectural style, was constructed in 1886-1888 by cattle baron, Col. Burton Campbell and is listed on the local, state and *National Register of Historic Places. The Castle* and its one and a half acre lawn sit on the bank of the Little Arkansas River and provide an ideal setting for the "perfect wedding", or for a romantic stroll while enjoying aperitifs and light refreshments. There are fourteen uniquely appointed guest rooms in the *Castle* and carriage house, each with a private bath, color TV and VCR. Twelve of the fourteen rooms have a fireplace and six rooms have jacuzzi tubs for two. Special touches include fresh flowers, luxury soaps and toiletries and European linens. Common areas in the *Castle* include the parlor (a perfect setting for afternoon tea), the library, solarium, coffee bar, dining room and the billiards room. Stained glass windows, European fireplaces, parquet hardwood floors and intricately carved fret and woodwork grace the entire *Castle*. A gourmet breakfast, including fresh fruits and juices, yogurt, homemade granola and muffins, freshly ground and brewed coffee, and an entree specialty is served daily. Gift shop and seminar rooms with business necessities are all on the premises. Golf and tennis are nearby. **Packages:** Honeymoon, Anniversary, Birthday, Reunion, Design Your Own **Seasonal:** No **Reservations:** One night's deposit to guarantee reservation, 72 hr cancel policy for refund **Brochure:** Yes **Permitted:** Limited children, limited drinking, limited smoking **Conference:** Business suite, seminar rooms, fax, modems, copier, a/v, conference phoning **Payment Terms:** Check AE/DISC/MC/V [I04HPKS1-22063] **COM** YG **ITC Member:** No

Rates:	Pvt Bath 14
Single	$ 125-225.00
Double	$ 125-225.00

Lamplighter Inn	103 W 3rd St 41002	Augusta KY
Alan, Chas, Doris Tongret		Tel: 606-756-2603
		Res Times 8am-7pm

The *Lamplighter Inn* is situated in Augusta, on one of the Ohio River's loveliest spots. Featured is the Saint Charles Restaurant, serving breakfast, lunch and dinner seven days a week under one of the area's top chefs. The cozy lobby is dominated by a stone fireplace, dating from 1800, and has an ornate

©*Inn & Travel Memphis, Tennessee*   2-25

Kentucky *National Edition*

pressed-tin ceiling. The nine guest rooms, richly furnished with antiques, are individually styled and include the Shaker Room, Starboard Berth and the Victorian Room. The Inn is fully protected with fire sprinklers. There is a forty-two seat banquet room and dining room that makes the Inn ideal for retreats, conferences, receptions and any social or business meetings and dining up to forty persons with smaller rooms also available. Continental breakfast included, with others available on the premises. **Seasonal:** No **Reservations:** One night's deposit, 7-day cancellation policy for refund, less $10.00 service fee **Brochure:** Yes **Permitted:** Children, drinking, limited pets, limited smoking **Conference:** Yes, for meetings and dining up to 40 persons with smaller rooms also available. **Payment Terms:** Check MC/V [R02-BCKY-3047] **COM** Y **ITC Member:** No

Rates:	Pvt Bath 9
Single	$ 55.00
Double	$ 60.00

Talbot Tavern — Court Square 40004 — **Bardstown KY**
The Kelley Family — Tel: 502-348-3494

Fine food and lodging since 1779 - the *Old Talbot Tavern* is the oldest western stagecoach stop in America dating from Patrick Henry, who granted the tavern its operating permit! President George Washington directed exiled King Louise Phillippe to see the Western Frontier and the murals painted by them still remain on the upstairs wall - except for the bullet holes made by Jesse James, as legend tells it - when he used them for target practice. Other famous guests include the Lincoln family, Daniel Boone, John Fitch the inventor of the steamboat, General George Rogers Clarke, Stephen Foster, John J Audubon, General George Patton and authors Washington Irving and Theodore O'Hare, author of Bivouac of the Dead. As mid-America's oldest restaurant - we're in our Third Century of service offering fine recognized recipes at reasonable prices. Fifty years ago, renowned food critic Duncan Hines recommended the *Talbot Tavern* - and more recently, the *Chicago Tribune* described our menu as indescribably delicious. Seven overnight accommodations are still in use today - all with Colonial furnishings including antiques, brass beds, fireplaces, footed bath tubs. A continental breakfast is included. **Airport:** Louisville Standiford Field-40 mi **Reservations:** 50% deposit or credit card number to guarantee, 48 hour cancel policy for refund **Permitted:** Children, smoking, drinking **Conference:** Memorable meetings, seminars and social occasions. **Payment Terms:** AE/MC/V [I07F-PKY-3050] **COM** U **ITC Member:** No

Rates:	Pvt Bath 11	Shared Bath 2
Single	$ 50.00-up	$ 89.00
Double	$ 50.00-up	$ 89.00

Alpine Lodge — 5310 Morgantown Rd 42101-8201 — **Bowling Green KY**
Dr & Mrs David Livingston — Tel: 502-843-4846
Res Times 9am-9pm

Alpine Lodge is a Swiss Chalet located on nine acres of beautiful flower gardens and nature trails with deer stands. The home has over six thousand square feet that includes five bedrooms, large den with big screen TV, living room with a grand piano, large country kitchen, screened-in porch, deck, gazebo, and an above the ground pool. The furniture is all antique. We are twenty five minutes to Mammoth Cave, one hour to Nashville, sixteen to Shakertown, twenty five to Horse Cave theatre and eighteen to Dueling Ground Horse Track. We are the home of the Corvette! Call us up! **Airport:** Nashville TN-70 **Seasonal:** No **Reservations:** $20 deposit to hold reservation. **Brochure:** Yes **Permitted:** Children, pets, drinking, smoking in special areas **Payment Terms:** Check [Z04GPKY-11553] **COM** Y **ITC Member:** No

Rates:	Pvt Bath 3	Shared Bath 2
Single	$ 45.00	$ 35.00
Double	$ 65.00	$ 55.00

National Edition **Kentucky**

Doe Run Inn	Rt 2 Box 287 40108	**Brandenburg KY**
Kimberly & Keith Hager		Tel: 502-422-2982

Charming Country Inn on a thousand acres for roaming at your leisure along with a stream next to the inn for cooling splashes in the hot sun or for perfect picnics. Furnished with period antiques, you can unwind and relax in this country atmosphere. Full breakfast included and other meals available in the dining room on the premises. **Seasonal:** No **Reservations:** Credit card for room guarantee with 48-hour cancellation. **Brochure:** Yes **Permitted:** Children, smoking **Conference:** Yes, for groups to 25 person including dining. **Payment Terms:** Check AE/MC/V [X11ACKY-3053] **COM** Y **ITC Member:** No

Rates:	Pvt Bath 8	Shared Bath 7
Single	$ 58.00	$ 50.00
Double	$ 60.00	$ 60.00

Broadwell Acres B&B	Rt 6 Box 58 41031	**Cynthiana KY**
George & Nancy Hehr		Tel: 606-234-4255
		Res Times 8am-7pm

Your own cabin that's listed on the *National Register of Historic Places* with room for four-five persons, 1-1/2 baths and your own kitchenette in the middle of horse country. Filled with antique furnishings, you can enjoy the natural setting and your lovely hosts who will share the history of the cabin and all the antiques. Stocked kitchen lets you prepare your own throughout your stay. **Seasonal:** 4/1-10/30 Open **Reservations:** Deposit for each night's stay at res time **Brochure:** Yes **Permitted:** Children**Payment Terms:** Check [X11ACKY-3055] **COM** Y **ITC Member:** No

Rates:	Pvt Bath 1
Single	$ 90.00
Double	$ 90.00

B&B At Sills Inn	**Frankfort KY**
Tony Sills	Tel: 800-526-9801 606-873-4478 **Fax:** 606-873-7099
	Res Times 10am-10pm

Refer to the same listing name under Versailles, Kentucky for a complete description. **Seasonal:** No **Payment Terms:** Check AE/DISC/DC/MC/V [M03G-PKY-15983] **COM** YG **ITC Member:** No

Rates:	Pvt Bath 12
Single	$ 79-119.00
Double	$ 79-119.00

Blackridge Hall B&B	4055 Paris Pike 40324	**Georgetown KY**
Jim D Black		Tel: 800-768-9308 505-863-2069
		Res Times 10am-10pm

This Southern Georgian-style mansion, situated on five acres in the heart of horse country, exemplifies the high-style and elegant living of a true Kentucky horse farm. Filled with 18th and 19th century antique and reproduction furnishings, *Blackridge Hall's* five guest rooms, two of which are luxury master suites with whirlpool tubs, look out upon the rolling Bluegrass landscape. Travelers feel the southern hospitality as they enjoy the cheerful sun room, formal dining room and the family gathering room. A full gourmet breakfast is served on fine china and crystal in the dining room, breakfast room or perhaps our picturesque veranda. Complimentary soft drinks and snacks are always available in the cozy guest kitchen. *Blackridge Hall* is easily accessible by interstate (4 minutes from I-75 and 10 minutes from I-64) and conveniently located only minutes from downtown Lexington, Kentucky Horse Park, Keeneland and Red Mile Race Tracks, Univ of Kentucky, Toyota Motor Corporation tours and historic Georgetown antique shops. **Discounts:** Corporate rates Sun-Thursday **Airport:** Lexington-20 min **Seasonal:** No **Reservations:** Credit card or payment in full required to guarantee reservation, 7 day cancel policy for refund. **Brochure:** Yes **Permitted:** Drinking, limited children, smoking outdoors only, no pets **Payment Terms:** Check AE/DC/MC/V [R07FPKY-16986] **COM** Y **ITC Member:** No

©*Inn & Travel Memphis, Tennessee*

Kentucky   *National Edition*

Rates:	**Pvt Bath** 3	**Shared Bath** 2
Single	$ 109-159.00	$ 89.00
Double	$ 109-159.00	$ 89.00

Log Cabin B&B   350 N Broadway 40324   **Georgetown KY**
Clay & Janis McKnight   **Tel:** 502-863-3514

c1800 log cabin cottage at the edge of the former frontier complete with huge fieldstone fireplace, shake shingle roof, and restored logs. Fully restored and furnished with period antiques, the kitchen area offers new appliances. Close to Kneeland and Kentucky Horse Parks and other historical sites. Master bedroom and bath on ground floor with loft bedroom for two more. Continental breakfast. **Seasonal:** No **Brochure:** Yes **Permitted:** Children, pets, smoking, drinking **Payment Terms:** Check [X11ACKY-3057] **COM** Y **ITC Member:** No

Rates:	**Pvt Bath** 1	**Shared Bath** 1
Single	$ 50-70.00	
Double		

---

547   547 N Broadway 40501-0147   **Lexington KY**
Ruth & Joseph Fitzpatrick   **Tel:** 606-255-4152
     Res Times 24 Hrs

A Bed and Breakfast, *547* is a small private apartment in a restored Victorian home near Translvania University, just five blocks from Victorian Square in downtown Lexington. Guest accommodations are spacious, air conditioned bedroom with brass double bed and featuring a sunny bay-windowed eating area and self-contained small kitchen, well-stocked with breakfast foods to prepare at your leisure, while a large modern bath includes a large walk-in tile shower. Your hosts are a professor of painting and drawing at he University of Kentucky and a government program manager. Guests are welcomed to browse through their extensive collection of books and art work. On-street parking and easy access to Broadway bus. **Discounts:** Extended stays; stay six nights, 7th night free **Airport:** Lexington Bluegrass-1-1/2 mi **Seasonal:** No **Reservations:** One night's deposit, 7 day cancel policy for refund **Brochure:** Yes **Permitted:** Limited children, limited drinking, limited smoking **Languages:** French, Hebrew, English, some Spanish and Italian **Payment Terms:** Check [R11FPKY-18063] **COM** Y **ITC Member:** No

Rates:	**Pvt Bath** 3	**Shared Bath** 1
Single	$ 70.00	$ 45.00
Double	$ 70-85.00	$ 45.00

B&B At Sills Inn   **Lexington KY**
Tony Sills   **Tel:** 800-526-9801 606-873-4478 **Fax:** 606-873-7099
     Res Times 10am-10pm

Refer to the same listing name under Versailles, Kentucky for a complete description. **Seasonal:** No **Payment Terms:** AE/DISC/DC/MC/V [M04IPY1-15982] **COM** YG **ITC Member:** No

Rates:	**Pvt Bath** 12
Single	$ 79-119.00
Double	$ 79-119.00

Maple Hill Manor   **Lexington KY**
Bob & Kay Carroll   **Tel:** 606-336-3075

Refer to the same name listed under Springfield, Kentucky for a complete description. **Seasonal:** No **Payment Terms:** Check MC/V [M07BCKY-8756] **COM** Y **ITC Member:** No

Rates:	**Pvt Bath** 7
Single	$ 45.00
Double	$ 55.00

Maple Hill Manor		**Louisville KY**
Bob & Kay Carroll		**Tel:** 606-336-3075

Refer to the same name listed under Springfield, Kentucky for a complete description. **Seasonal:** No **Payment Terms:** Check MC/V [M07BCKY-8756] **COM** Y **ITC Member:** No

Rates: Pvt Bath 7
Single $ 45.00
Double $ 55.00

Mello Inn	2856 Nolin Dam Rd	**Mammoth Cave KY**
Rhonda & Scott Mello		**Tel:** 502-286-4126

The *Mello Inn* is a newly constructed and delightful folk Victorian Bed & Breakfast at Nolin Lake, Kentucky, just minutes from Mammoth Cave National Park. The five guest rooms are finely appointed with antique and reproduction antique cherry furnishings and include private bath in all rooms. One of the guest rooms, the Master Suite, includes a mirrored jacuzzi, tray ceiling and canopy bed. The common and dining room, sunroom, gingerbread front porch and spacious back deck are available for your leisure and pleasure. A full country breakfast is served in the dining room and is included with your stay. Nearby activities include fishing, canoeing, jet ski, boating, swimming, horseback riding, hiking and cave tours. Located on twelve acres, guests are within twenty five minutes of restaurants and shopping. **Airport:** Leitchfield KY-20 min; Warren County Regional-30 mins **Packages:** Canoeing, Fishing, Horseback Riding, Mammoth Cave Tours **Reservations:** Credit card number for 50% deposit of length of stay **Brochure:** Yes **Permitted:** Children, limited drinking, limited smoking **Payment Terms:** Check AE/DC/MC/V [R07GPKY-19747] **COM** U **ITC Member:** No

Rates: Pvt Bath 5
Single $ 65-75.00
Double $ 65-75.00

Victorian Mansion	851 Winchester Rd Hwy #60 40353	**Mount Sterling KY**
		Tel: 606-498-5383

Beautiful Victorian mansion nestled on five elegant acres of grounds with rolling hills and beautiful scenery surrounding the residence that's filled with antique furnishings for your enjoyment. Stroll the fields or golf nearby if you like. Patio and picnic area let guests unwind at their own pace. Full breakfast included with rate. **Seasonal:** No **Reservations:** 50% deposit required, refunded if cancelled with 5 day notice. **Brochure:** Yes **Permitted:** Limited children, drinking **Payment Terms:** Check MC/V [X11ACKY-3062] **COM** Y **ITC Member:** No

Rates:	Pvt Bath 2	Shared Bath 2
Single	$ 55.00	$ 50.00
Double	$ 65.00	$ 60.00

Barnes Mill B&B Guest House	1268 Barnes Mill Rd 40475	**Richmond KY**
Christine Sowers		**Tel:** 606-623-5509
		Res Times 7am-10pm

Located only one-half mile from I-75 (exit 87), *Barnes Mill Bed & Breakfast* is surrounded by a picturesque farm of black fences, grazing cattle and rolling hills. Built in 1916, the Victorian home has been completely and beautifully renovated and exquisitely decorated with period antiques. Just minutes from Lexington to our north, you could cheer your favorite horse to victory at Keenland Race Track, tour the homes of Henry Clay or Mary Todd Lincoln, visit the campus of University of Kentucky, shop the numerous shopping complexes and malls in the city or meander through a luscious horse farms. To our south, discover Berea. Just a short fifteen minute drive could send you through numerous antique malls and craft shops. Watch dulcimers being built or dine at the famous Boone Tavern. Not far from Berea will take you to foot-stomping, hand-clapping delightful Renfro Valley where there is a barn dance every Saturday night. Back in Richmond, visit old Fort Boonesboro, world-famous Bybee Pottery. Specialties of the house are homemade bread, in-season fruit and cheese grits. Ex-

Kentucky - Maryland

perience the original Victorian elegance seasoned with Old Southern Charm. **Discounts:** Yes, inquire at res time **Airport:** Lexington-20 mi **Seasonal:** No **Reservations:** 10% deposit reservation fee required **Brochure:** Yes **Payment Terms:** Check [R10EPKY-16070] **COM** Y **ITC Member:** No

Rates:	Pvt Bath 1	Shared Bath 2
Single	$ 60.00	$ 50.00
Double		

Maple Hill Manor Perryville Rd Rt 150 40069 **Springfield KY**
Bob & Kay Carroll **Tel:** 606-336-3075
Res Times 24 hrs

This hilltop manor, a *Kentucky Landmark Home* (c.1851) on the *National Historical Register*, is located on fourteen tranquil acres in the scenic Bluegrass Region. It's ten foot doors, thirteen foot ceilings, cherry spiral staircase, ten foot windows, decorative stenciling in the foyer, three crystalline and brass chandeliers and nine fireplaces make it one of the best preserved brick Revival homes with Italianate detail in Kentucky. Guest rooms are large, airy and warmly decorated with antique furnishings and include a Honeymoon room with a beautiful canopy bed, jacuzzi and a private entrance. Awake to the aroma of freshly brewed coffee and oven fresh muffins as your hosts prepare your full breakfast which is served on their fine china in a formal Dining Room. In the evening, relax with your hosts and enjoy a complimentary beverage and a homemade dessert. Within one hour of both Louisville and Lexington, guests can visit Lincoln Homestead Park, Perryville Battlefield, Shaker Village and My Old Kentucky Home. There's also entertainment, playhouses, golf, tennis, fishing, and great antiquing. **Seasonal:** No **Reservations:** One night deposit, late arrival with prior notice. **Brochure:** Yes **Permitted:** Children **Conference:** Yes, call for information. **Payment Terms:** Check MC/V [R07BCKY-8514] **COM** Y **ITC Member:** No

Rates:	Pvt Bath 7
Single	$ 45.00
Double	$ 55.00

B&B At Sills Inn 270 Montgomery Ave 40383 **Versailles KY**
Tony Sills/Vicky Cozadd **Tel:** 800-526-9801 606-873-4478 **Fax:** 606-873-7099
Res Times 10am-10pm

Guests are treated to true Southern Hospitality as soon as they step into this restored 1911, three-storied Victorian Inn in downtown Versailles, the center of bluegrass horse country, just seven minutes from the Bluegrass Airport, Keenland Race Track and ten minutes from Lexington area. Each of the twelve guest rooms are highly decorated with their own private bath, with eight suites offering a double jacuzzi. A full gourmet breakfast is served on the sun porch or breakfast room on china, crystal and linen. The guests are also treated to fresh baked chocolate chip cookies, refrigerator stocked with soft drinks, hot drinks, popcorn and anything they are in need of as a snack. The pampering continues as the dinner reservations are called for the guest, with a map highlighting their way to their choice from the restaurant menu book. Guests fall asleep reading previous comments from the guest diaries... those wonderful blue berry muffins and eggs benedict waiting for them, only a few hours away. **Airport:** Blue Grass-7 mins **Seasonal:** No **Reservations:** Deposit on credit card at res time, 7 day cancel policy for refund; Special Events require full payment in advance with 30 day cancel notice **Brochure:** Yes **Permitted:** Limited children, drinking, limited smoking **Conference:** Yes, groups to 40 **Payment Terms:** AE/DISC/DC/MC/V [I03IPKY1-11557] **COM** YG **ITC Member:** No

Rates:	Pvt Bath 12
Single	$ 79-119.00
Double	$ 79-119.00

Casa Bahia 262 King George St 21401 **Annapolis MD**

2-30 ©*Inn & Travel Memphis, Tennessee*

National Edition | ***Maryland***

Mel Clark/Gene Lohman **Tel:** 410-268-3106 410-268-8941

Casa Bahia is an 1880's three story home located in the historic Annapolis district with three rooms available all the time and the entire home can be rented for Naval Commissioning Week, Annual Boat Show, weddings or other special occasions. Contemporary decor is representative of your hosts' Southwestern heritage with original art by Gene, who is a multi-media artist, some of which is available for purchase. A greenhouse/breakfast room is flooded with morning sun and overlooks a fish pond in the side yard fed from a small stream with waterfall. Close to major sights such as the Naval Academy (1 block), Maryland State Capitol (2 blocks), Annapolis City Dock (5 blocks) across the street from St John's College. A self-service continental buffet breakfast is included with each room. **Seasonal:** No **Reservations:** Entire house may be rented, 3 day min plus refundable security deposit. **Brochure:** Yes **Permitted:** Children **Languages:** Spanish **Payment Terms:** Check [R06BCMD-6320] **COM** Y **ITC Member:** No

Rates:	Pvt Bath 1	Shared Bath 3
Single	$ 85.00	$ 70.00
Double	$ 85.00	$ 70.00

College House-Historic District　　　One College Ave 21401-1603　　　Annapolis MD
Don & Jo Anne Wolfrey **Tel:** 410-263-6124
Res Times 10am-4pm

College House Suites is located in the Historic District nestled between the US Naval Academy and St John's College (AAA 3-Diamond Rated). The elegant brick townhome features eclectic decor with a flair including antiques, contemporary pieces and a collection or orientals which cover the mirror-finished antique softwood floors. The Annapolitan Suite with a private ivy-covered courtyard includes a fireplace in the sitting room, antique brass bed and floral chintz covered furnishings. A collection of French impressionist prints, white wicker and floor coverings of layered sisal and oriental rugs enhance the decor and ambiance of this lovely suite. Other features include a full wet bar, VCR, private telephone line and answering machine. The Colonial Suite includes silk and antique orientals, an antique Victorian dresser and a mask collection from three continents. The bedroom has a cherry four-poster bed, antique curly maple chest, ivory medallion Kirman oriental and window seats. It is decorated with unusual collections from throughout the world that adorn the floors, walls, shelves and seating. The bath has a rose Italian marble floor and pedestal sink with brass and porcelain fixtures. *College House Suites* is a short walk to the city dock, Pace House and Gardens, fine restaurants, fascinating shops and boutiques, art and antique galleries, museums, historic buildings, churches and theatre. **Discounts:** Extended stays 7 days or longer **Airport:** Baltimore Wash Intl-20 mi **Seasonal:** No **Reservations:** Full deposit for min 2 nights, 50% deposit if longer - 21 day cancel policy less 10% service fee for refund, less than 21 days, refund only if rebooked. *$25 deduction for "breakfast-out" option **Brochure:** Yes **Permitted:** Drinking, no smoking **Payment Terms:** MC/V [K03HPMD1-6115] **COM** YG **ITC Member:** No

Rates:	Pvt Bath 2
Single	$ 160.00
Double	$ 160.00

Green Street Inn　　　172 Green St 21401　　　Annapolis MD
Stephanie Ann Bowe **Tel:** 410-263-9171

A fine example of Victorian design is this masterpiece, located in the historic district of this quaint town, just one block from the City Dock area. Furnished with period decor and family heirlooms, guests will enjoy staying at this charming Inn and the nearby sightseeing. Continental breakfast is included. **Seasonal:** No **Reservations:** One night's deposit required to guarantee reservation **Brochure:** Yes **Permitted:** Limited children **Payment Terms:** Check [C11ACMD-1544] **COM** Y **ITC Member:** No

©*Inn & Travel Memphis, Tennessee*

Maryland National Edition

Rates: **Pvt Bath 2**
Single $ 65.00
Double $ 75.00

Prince George Inn B&B 232 Price George St 21401 **Annapolis MD**
Janet Coughlin **Tel:** 410-263-6418

Add variety to your travel itinerary by visiting Annapolis and enjoy your stay in this Victorian townhouse c1884, the first licensed Bed & Breakfast in the City. Refresh yourself on a *"wind-down weekend"* or weekday for tourists and business travelers. Enjoy a crackling fireplace in the parlour in winter or sip a cool refreshment in the courtyard during the summer. This historic residence offers guest rooms filled with antique beds, armories, chests, collectibles and family heirlooms. Awake each morning to the aroma of fresh-brewed coffee awaiting you in the breakfast room. A continental buffet-style breakfast (included with your room) will get you off to a fresh start of sightseeing in the famous town. Bring good walking shoes because you're within strolling distance of all the sights. You can visit the US Naval Academy, board a ship at City Dock for a cruise of Annapolis Harbor, see an 18th century Statehouse, visit museums and find plenty of fine shopping in picturesque areas with boutiques, galleries and gift shops. Or to get-away, you can try a full-day of sailing to the Eastern Shore. Don't miss the great seafood specialties native to this region! Your gracious hosts are more than happy to help with your travel plans while here. **Seasonal:** No **Reservations:** One night's deposit within 10 days of booking; 24 hr cancel policy, check-in 3-6pm (advise if other), check-out noon **Brochure:** Yes **Permitted:** Children 12-up, limited drinking, limited smoking **Conference:** Yes for groups to eight persons **Payment Terms:** Check MC [R02BCMD-1546] **COM** Y **ITC Member:** No

Rates: **Shared Bath 4**
Single $ 50.00
Double $ 60.00

William Page Inn 8 Martin St 21401 **Annapolis MD**
Greg Page/Rob Zuchelli **Tel:** 800-364-4160 410-626-1506

Built in 1908, the turn-of-the-century, wood-frame structure has been handsomely renovated offering a feeling of quiet hushed elegance and Victorian splendor. It's wrap-around porch, finished Adirondak chairs and striped canvas awnings present a distinctive appearance especially in a Historic District where a fair number of the buildings are brick. The Inn is carefully furnished in genuine antiques and period reproductions and features a first floor entry foyer and open stairway flanked by crystal chandeliers and art work. The Inn has five distinctively appointed guest rooms from the third-floor spacious, light-filled room with dormer windows, window seat, sky light, sitting area, cable TV, whirlpool tub to a first floor room with private bath and porch access - convenient for persons who might find stairs difficult. All accommodations include queen size bed, sitting areas, daily housekeeping, central a/c and heating, off-street parking and a full complimentary buffet breakfast each morning. The Inn is located in the Historic District of Annapolis, just fifty yards from the visitors Gate #1 to the Naval Academy and within two blocks of the downtown waterfront. Mobil, AAA and ABBA rated and approved. **Discounts:** Business, mid-week and winter **Airport:** Balt Wash Intl-45 min **Packages:** Winter Dinner **Reservations:** Deposit required to guarantee reservation **Brochure:** Yes **Permitted:** Limited children, drinking **Conference:** Yes, 2-12 persons with office service and audio visual equipment **Payment Terms:** Check MC/V [I07FPMD-8527] **COM** Y **ITC Member:** No

Rates: **Pvt Bath 3** **Shared Bath 2**
Single $ 80-140.00 $ 65-75.00
Double $ 80-140.00 $ 65-75.00

Admiral Fell Inn 888 S Broadway 21231 **Baltimore MD**
Dominik Eckenstein **Tel:** 800-292-INNS 410-522-7377 **Fax:** 410-522-0707
Res Times 24 Hrs

In the Fell's Point Section of the city is the *Admiral Fell Inn*. This Historic Inn is composed of four build-

2-32 ©*Inn & Travel Memphis, Tennessee*

ings, dating from 1850-1910, a blend of Victorian and Federal architectures. Originally a boarding house for sailors, later a YMCA and then a vinegar bottling plant, this delightful facility was completely renovated and refurbished in 1985. The public areas include an antique filled lobby as well as a library and an English-style pub for light fare and a restaurant specializing in New American Cuisine. **Discounts:** Yes, inquire at res time **Airport:** Baltimore Intl-20 mins **Packages:** Yes, inquire at res time **Seasonal:** No **Reservations:** One night's deposit, 24-hr cancel policy for refund **Brochure:** Yes **Permitted:** Children, smoking, drinking **Conference:** Groups to 50 persons including dining **Languages:** German, French, Spanish **Payment Terms:** Check AE/DISC/MC/V [Z05EPMD-1551] **COM Y ITC Member:** No

Rates: Pvt Bath 36
Single $ 89-125.00
Double $ 125-155.00

Betsys B&B　　　　　　　　1428 Park Ave 21217　　　　　　　　**Baltimore MD**
Betsy Grater　　　　　　　　　　　　　　　　　　　　**Tel:** 410-383-1274 **Fax:** 410-728-8957

A petite estate in a historic residential downtown neighborhood, just seven minutes driving time to the Inner Harbor, Fells Point or walking distance to museums, theater, the opera house, restaurants and antique row. This four-story brick row house with white marble steps and brass rail was built by 1870. The rooms are spacious and include twelve foot ceilings, ceiling medallions, moldings and a center hall stair which opens to a sky light. A freshly prepared breakfast is served in the dining room decorated with antique quilts, brass rubbings and artifacts. A hot tub is available. **Airport:** BWI-10 mi **Seasonal:** No **Reservations:** Credit card to guarantee one night's deposit **Brochure:** Yes **Permitted:** Children **Conference:** Yes, for groups to six persons **Payment Terms:** Check [K05HPMD1-1552] **COM U ITC Member:** No

Rates: Pvt Bath 3
Single $ 65.00
Double $ 85.00

Casa Bahia　　　　　　　　　　　　　　　　　　　　　　　　**Baltimore MD**
Mel Clark/Gene Lohman　　　　　　　　　　　　　　　　　　**Tel:** 410-268-3106

Refer to the same listing name under Annapolis, Maryland for a complete description. **Payment Terms:** Check [M06BCMD-8530] **COM Y ITC Member:** No

Rates: Pvt Bath 1　　Shared Bath 3
Single $ 85.00　　　　　$ 70.00
Double $ 85.00　　　　　$ 70.00

Mr Mole B&B　　　　　　　1601 Bolton St 21217　　　　　　　　**Baltimore MD**
Collin Clarke/Paul Bragaw　　　　　　　　　　　　　　**Tel:** 410-728-1179 **Fax:** 410-728-3379
　　　　　　　　　　　　　　　　　　　　　　　　　　　　　　Res Times 8am-8pm

Mr Mole Bed & Breakfast is a renovated Baltimore row house (built about 1870) which provides gracious accommodations for discriminating visitors. The house is located in the historic Bolton Hill District, close to the Inner Harbor, Orioles Park, Antique Row, Johns Hopkins University, Meyerhoff Symphony Hall and other attractions. *Mr Mole B&B* is a licensed B&B and an inspected and approved member of The Maryland B&B Association. *Mr Mole B&B* has appeared in *Travel Holiday* magazine and was selected by *"The Discerning Traveler"* as a **"Romantic Hideaway"** and by *Inn Marketing* as one of the **Ten Outstanding New Inns**. Collin has decorated the house in a comfortable English-style, complete with 18th and 19th Century antiques. On the first floor, the living room, breakfast room and parlor with their fourteen foot ceilings, bay windows and marble fireplaces are at the guests' disposal.

Maryland   National Edition

The five suites are all spacious and include private bath. Each is individually decorated according to its theme. The London Suite and The Print Room include a private sitting room and two bedrooms. Garage parking with an automatic garage door opener is included, as is a large, Dutch-style continental breakfast served on the main floor. **Airport:** BWI-15mi **Seasonal:** Clo: 1/15-31 **Reservations:** One night deposit to guarantee, 7 day cancel policy except holidays and special events require 14 days, if less, refund only if rebooked **Brochure:** Yes **Permitted:** Limited children, limited drinking **Languages:** French, German, Dutch **Payment Terms:** Check AE/DISC/MC/V [R04GPMD-15516] **COM** Y **ITC Member:** No

Rates:	Pvt Bath 5
Single	$ 75-100.00
Double	$ 90-130.00

Upstream At Waters Gift	3604 Dustin Rd 20866	Burtonsville MD
Marceline Murphy		Tel: 410-421-9562

One of the most beautiful settings in Maryland - this Bed & Breakfast with its fifty-three acres, is one of Maryland's most respected show horse breeding farms. Dating from 1753, Samuel Water's home, a chestnut log-and-beam home and is home to your hosts. *Upstream, the Bed & Breakfast Inn* on the grounds, is a contemporary design home providing spectacular views, antique yellow pine planks, massive beams and cathedral ceilings. The two guest rooms have private baths and offer informal elegance with modern conveniences. The owners, Larrine and Russ Abolt, traveled Europe and the US extensively staying only in B&Bs - just to find out what travelers enjoyed - and included the best ideas in Upstream! Guests are spoiled with beds that can be automatically adjusted to the guest's desired firmness, oversized bath sheets, a great basket of necessities in case you forgot something, a hospitality bar filled with sparking juices, tea, homemade sweets and fruits, turn-down service, picnic hampers on request and a full breakfast offering fresh-squeezed orange juice, several types of homemade muffins and perhaps the innkeeper's speciality - a Dutch Baby (a large pancake-like puff filled with fresh fruit and topped with confectioner sugar)! While horseback riding is not permitted - guests are welcomed in the barns and to roam the rolling pastures. Year-round activities include sitting by the fire, spring-time foals, summer relaxation or visits to nearby Baltimore and DC and autumn's colors enjoyed by hiking or picnicking. Join in the harmony of nature and hospitality at *Upstream At Waters Gift* during the week - or for a romantic weekend. **Discounts:** Seniors **Airport:** BWI-30 mins; Dulles Intl-45 mins **Packages:** Weekly stays, pay for 4 nights - next three nights are free **Seasonal:** No **Reservations:** One night's deposit, 2 week cancel policy for refund, check-in after 3pm, check-out 11am **Brochure:** Yes **Permitted:** Limited children (less than 6 mos and over 6 years) **Conference:** Yes, for groups to 15 with catering available **Payment Terms:** Check MC/V [R09EPMD-15302] **COM** Y **ITC Member:** No

Rates:	Pvt Bath 2
Single	$ 80-100.00
Double	$ 80-100.00

Inn At The Canal	104 Bohemia Ave 21915-0187	Chesapeake City MD
Mary & Al Ioppolo		Tel: 410-885-5995 Fax: 410-885-3585

Sprung from the banks of the Chesapeake and Delaware Canal, Chesapeake City is not a reconstruction of replicas but rather is alive with the pride of restoration. The *Inn At The Canal* is locally known as the Brady-Rees House. Henry Brady promised his wife a new grand home should she present him with a son - and this lovely home was built as a result of that fulfilled promise. Reminiscent of the 19th Century, guests find architectural and decorative details that bespeak of the elegant taste with which the house was designed. Your hosts have filled their Inn with antique quilts and furnishings and display a large collection of old baking and cooking implements on the fireplace wall of their kitchen. All six bedrooms are unique and feature private baths and individually controlled a/c and heating. Outdoor porches offer canal views along with three of the guest rooms. *Inn At The Canal* offers much more than a comfortable night's lodging and a mouthwatering full breakfast - it offers a walk through history and a balm to the spirit. A canal town sprinkled with delightful shops and fine restaurants (four within walking distance, two of which provide entertainment), you'll enjoy the Canal Museum, relaxing by the water, or biking the gentle rolling countryside past well-known horse farms, home to Northern Dancer and Kelso. **Discounts:** Corporate Sun-Thur **Airport:** Phila Intl-50 mi; Balt-Wash BWI-70 mi **Packages:** Winter Getaway (Dec-March) **Seasonal:** No **Reservations:** One night's deposit by credit card or check within 5 days of booking, 10 day cancel policy for refund, less $15 service fee **Brochure:** Yes **Permitted:** Children 10-up, drinking, smoking outdoors only **Conference:** Room seats to twelve persons comfortably at conference table **Payment Terms:** Check AE/DC/MC/V [R02FPMD-8869] **COM** U **ITC Member:** No

Rates:	Pvt Bath 6
Single	$ 70-100.00
Double	$ 75-105.00

Great Oak Manor	Rt 2 Box 766 21620	Chestertown MD
		Tel: 800-778-5796 410-778-5769

Maryland's eastern shore holds this grand mansion offering spectacular views of the Chesapeake Bay with great sand beaches, croquet, hunting, golf and tennis for relaxing. Continental plus breakfast is served in-bed if you like. **Seasonal:** No **Reservations:** Credit card to hold room, 48-hr cancel policy for refund. **Brochure:** Yes **Permitted:** Children, smoking, drinking **Payment Terms:** Check AE/MC/V [C11ACMD-1568] **COM** Y **ITC Member:** No

Rates:	Pvt Bath 9
Single	$ 95.00-up
Double	$ 105-155.00

Dukesdale Farm	PO Box 220 21625	Cordova MD
Deon & Howard Harper		Tel: 410-820-2349

This clapboard colonial has been restored to its original charm and glamour with high ceilings, wood floors and working fireplaces. These gracious hosts are anxious to make every guest feel at home. Close to Tuchahoe River for canoe rides, Wye Plantation and Tuchahoe State Park offer scenic nature trails. A full breakfast is included. **Seasonal:** No **Brochure:** Yes **Permitted:** Limited children **Payment Terms:** Check [C11ACMD-1576] **COM** Y **ITC Member:** No

Rates:	Pvt Bath 2	Shared Bath 2
Single	$ 58.00	$ 50.00
Double	$ 61.00	$ 60.00

Inn At The Canal		Elkton MD
Mary & Al Ioppolo		Tel: 410-885-5995

Refer to the same listing name under Chesapeake City, Maryland for a complete description. **Seasonal:** No **Payment Terms:** Check AE/DC/MC/V [M02FP-MD-16743] **COM** U **ITC Member:** No

Rates:	Pvt Bath 6
Single	$ 70-100.00
Double	$ 75-105.00

Mayland Farm	5000 Sheppard Lane 21403	Ellicott City MD
Louis & Dorothy Mobley		Tel: 410-531-5593

Country living is offered in this large manor home furnished with contemporary and family heirlooms providing a comfortable visit with these charming hosts. Both are retired and have traveled extensively. An inviting outdoor pool invites everyone during the summer months. A full breakfast is included. **Seasonal:** No **Brochure:** Yes **Permitted:** Children, social drinking **Payment Terms:** Check [C11ACMD-1580] **COM** Y **ITC Member:** No

Rates:	Pvt Bath 1	Shared Bath 2
Single		$ 25.00
Double	$ 45.00	$ 65.00

Maryland   *National Edition*

Middle Plantation Inn	9549 Liberty Rd 21701-3246	**Frederick MD**
Shirley & Dwight Mullican		**Tel:** 301-898-7128
		Res Times 4pm-7pm

Nestled on twenty-six acres just several miles east of Frederick in Mount Pleasant, known for its beautiful horse farms, is this charming stone and log home offering guests a peaceful setting and weekend retreat. Guests step into a delightful setting which includes Addion's Run, a nearby brook, beautiful in any season. You'll wake each morning to the sound of birds (and an occasional rooster) and see nature in all its glory. Your hosts have visited some of the finest B&Bs in the Mid-Atlantic region and take great pleasure in sharing their antique furnishings they've collected during their many travels. Each guest room offers a delightful 19th century ambiance combined with modern conveniences of private baths, queen size beds, a/c and television. In room phones available upon request. Guests enjoy the privilege of a private entry to their rooms. A massive stone fireplace, stain glass windows and skylights highlight the Keeping Room, a public room within the Inn where guests unwind or socialize. A deluxe continental breakfast of seasonal fruits, fresh-baked breads or muffins, cheese, yogurt, cereal and granola is served each morning. Whether you are enroute to another destination or simply need a getaway weekend, Shirley and Dwight will make certain your stay is pleasant. **Discounts:** Multiple night stays, corporate, midweek, room without breakfast less $15.00 **Airport:** BWI-40mi, Dulles-40mi, National-40mi **Packages:** Special Corporate package **Seasonal:** No **Reservations:** One night's deposit with 7 day cancel policy less $10 service fee; less than 7 day, transferable; less than 48 hr non-refundable; check-in other than 4-7pm by prior arrangement only **Brochure:** Yes **Permitted:** Drinking, children 15+, smoking outdoors [I11I-PMD1-10969] **Payment Terms:** Check MC/V **ITC Member:** No

Rates:	**Pvt Bath 4**
Single	$95-110.00
Double	$95-110.00

Lewrene Farm B&B	9738 Downsville Pike 21740	**Hagerstown MD**
Irene Lehman		**Tel:** 301-582-1735
		Res Times 24 hrs

Located in Washington County farming country; Rt 632, 4 miles south of Hagerstown, *Lewrene Farm B&B* is a 125 acre crop farm. We, Irene and Lewis Lehman think people are important. We will be glad to serve tea, coffee, etc and help you plan your stay in our area. We want you to feel at home in our uniquely furnished thirteen room Colonial-style house. Enjoy our spacious living room; fireplace, piano and plenty of space for relaxing. From here an open stairway leads up to "Rose Retreat", our deluxe bedroom with a cherry canopy queen size bed, refrigerator with sodas and private bath with whirlpool tub. Next is "Lilac Haven" with private bath, two full size mahogany and cherry beds, one with a canopy. Then to our three bedrooms with shared bath. Guest rooms include heat, a/c and bedside snacks each evening. You'll awake to cooking aromas from our complimentary full breakfast served family-style. Then it's your choice: visit Antietam Battlefield, Harper's Ferry. Gettysburg, outlet stores, antique shops, Valley Mall or you can select a handmade quilt and collectibles from your hostess. Washington and Baltimore are just 90 mins away. **Discounts:** Available on stays over two nights **Airport:** BWI-70 mi; Hagerstown airport-12mi **Seasonal:** No **Reservations:** $25 deposit within 5 days of booking reservation. **Brochure:** Yes **Permitted:** Children **Conference:** Yes, up to 14 persons in large 26 x 30 room. **Languages:** Spanish **Payment Terms:** Travelers Check [R07DPMD-1590] **COM** Y **ITC Member:** No

Rates:	**Pvt Bath 2**	**Shared Bath 3**
Single	$ 60-70.00	$ 40-45.00
Double	$ 65-78.00	$ 50-55.00

Sunday's B&B	39 Broadway 21740	**Hagerstown MD**

National Edition **Maryland**

Bob Ferrino

Tel: 800-221-4828 301-797-4331
Res Times 24 Hrs

This elegant 1890 Queen Anne Victorian home is situated in the historic north end on a street lined with grand old homespun Hagerstown, less than ninety mins from Washington DC and Baltimore. Relax in your room or in any of the many public rooms and porches. You may also want to explore the many attractions in the area, such as the National Historic Parks of Antietam, Harper's Ferry and C&O Canal. Many other historic sites and antique shops, fishing areas, golf courses, museums, shopping outlets, theater and Whitetails Ski Resort are all nearby. You'll experience special hospitality and find many personal touches - reminiscent of a gracious past. Many personalized services for special occasions and numerous packages are available. Sausage quiche, apple French toast and orange whole wheat pancakes are a just samples of the dishes you'll awaken to. Experience afternoon tea served with homemade breads, tea cookies and other delicious treats. A selection of local wines and cheese are served in the parlor each evening while a cordial and truffle greet you each evening at bedside. **Discounts:** Yes, inquire at res time **Airport:** Baltimore and DC National-70 mi **Packages:** Corporate (Long or Short Term) **Seasonal:** No **Reservations:** One night's deposit required to guarantee reservation, two week cancel notice for full refund; less than two week, credit applied to future stay; less than one week, no refund **Brochure:** Yes **Permitted:** Limited children, limited drinking, limited pets, smoking outdoors only **Payment Terms:** Check [R09FPMD-15307] **COM Y ITC Member:** No

Rates:	Pvt Bath 1	Shared Bath 2
Single	$ 65-75.00	$ 65.00
Double	$ 75-95.00	$ 65-75.00

National Pike Inn	9-11 Main St 21774	New Market MD
Terry & Tom Rimel		Tel: 301-865-5055

Antique capital of Maryland, this home offers the convenience of Washington DC and Baltimore, both just an hour away. Relax in this country setting with golf, tennis and plenty of antiquing everywhere. Continental plus breakfast is included. **Seasonal:** No **Reservations:** One night's deposit at res time with 5 day cancel policy for refund. **Brochure:** Yes **Permitted:** Limited children, limited smoking **Payment Terms:** Check [C11ACMD-1597] **COM Y ITC Member:** No

Rates:	Pvt Bath 2	Shared Bath 2
Single	$ 65.00	$ 50.00
Double	$ 70.00	$ 60.00

Elmwood c1770 B&B	Locust Point 21853	Princess Anne MD
Mr Mrs Stephen Monick		Tel: 410-651-1066

Perfect brick Federal designed residence c1770 which has been restored and furnished with period decor and pieces. Former home of Confederate Gen Arnold Elzey and nestled on the waterfront, guests enjoy the wildlife and beaches while here. Perfect spot for crabbing, boating, fishing and nature trails. Continental breakfast is included. **Seasonal:** No **Reservations:** 50% deposit for length of stay within 5 days of booking **Brochure:** Yes **Permitted:** Limited children and drinking **Languages:** French **Payment Terms:** Check [C11ACMD-1602] **COM Y ITC Member:** No

Rates:	Pvt Bath 3	Shared Bath 2
Single	$ 85.00	$ 70.00
Double	$ 95-100.00	$ 80.00

Wells House	102 Aberdeen Rd	Rockville MD
Nadean Pedersen		Tel: 301-251-1033
		Res Times 5pm-10pm

This Victorian farmhouse dating from 1887 was built on twenty two acres of farmland outside of the county seat of Rockville but today is within the city of Rockville - set on a third acre lot filled with spectacular azaleas and dogwoods - with splendid boxwoods lining the walkways to the house and patio.

Maryland — National Edition

An ideal location for business travelers and tourists alike who appreciate living in a quiet, private setting but need to be close to the office or transportation. Both the local Ride-On bus and Metrobus stops are just two minutes away. A full array of shops, restaurants and major high tech and bio tech companies are within the general area including many federal agencies. Nearby points of interest include Gettysburg, Annapolis, Eastern Shore and Richmond. A continental breakfast is included. **Discounts:** Yes, extended stays **Airport:** Dulles-25 min; Washington Natl-20 mi; Baltimore-40 mi **Seasonal:** No **Reservations:** One week advance reservation with 24 hour confirmation; 2 night min stay **Brochure:** Yes **Permitted:** Drinking **Languages:** Basic Danish **Payment Terms:** [R07FPMD-14972] **COM** Y **ITC Member:** No

Rates: Pvt Bath 2
Single $ 50.00
Double $ 60.00

Castle Rd 36 PO Box 578 21545 Savage MD
Bill & Andrea Myer **Tel:** 301-759-5946

A *National Historic Landmark*, this 115 year old stone manse is set on twenty acres of sumptuous estate grounds with rare horticultural specimen trees and plantings all surrounded by twenty foot high wall. Inside guests find fabulous and rare antique furnishings, family heirlooms including four-poster or canopy beds in the guest rooms. A continental plus breakfast is included. Croquet and putting are permitted on grassed areas. **Seasonal:** No **Brochure:** Yes **Permitted:** Children 12-up **Payment Terms:** Check MC/V [C11ACMD-1595] **COM** Y **ITC Member:** No

Rates: Pvt Bath 4 Shared Bath 2
Single $ 75-100.00 $ 60-85.00
Double $ 85-125.00 $ 70-95.00

Inn At Antietam 220 E Main 21782 Sharpsburg MD
Betty Fairbourn **Tel:** 410-342-6601

Relive the history in this famous setting from the wrap-around porch on this restored Victorian nestled in the Blue Ridge Mountains, next to the National Cemetery and surrounded by Antietam Battlefield. Fully restored and furnished with period antiques and family heirlooms, guests step back in time while visiting this B&B jewel. Close to C&O Canal and Harper's Ferry. Continental breakfast is included. Complimentary bikes, picnic lunches available at nominal added cost. **Seasonal:** No **Reservations:** One night's deposit to guarantee room **Brochure:** Yes **Payment Terms:** Check AE [C11ACMD-1609] **COM** Y **ITC Member:** No

Rates: Pvt Bath 4 Shared Bath 2
Single $ 45.00 $ 40.00
Double $ 65-75.00 $ 55.00

River House Inn 201 E Market St 21863 Snow Hill MD
Larry & Susanne Knudsen **Tel:** 410-632-2722

Enjoy an elegant but casual getaway at this *Maryland Trust Home* on the wild and scenic Pocomoke River. Located in a 300 year-old village that has serenity and charm, yet is close to golf, beaches, biking and hiking, you can be as relaxed or active as you choose. Canoes can be rented nearby, there are 100 marked miles of bike trails in the county and some of the East Coast's most beautiful beaches are only 1/2 hour away. Lovely, spacious rooms with queen size beds, fireplaces, ceiling fans and antique furnishings have all the amenities to make your stay comfortable. Screened porches on first and second floors overlook water gardens, With nine guest rooms, two of which are suites, to choose from, we can suit any fancy. A hearty country breakfast is included, featuring fresh fruits in season and special egg dishes. Box lunches and dinner are available with prior arrangement. Free tie-up at our waterfront for guests. **Airport:** Salisbury-16 mi **Dis-**

©*Inn & Travel Memphis, Tennessee*

counts: AAA, AARP **Packages:** Holidays (Thanksgiving, New Years, Christmas) include festive dinner; Biking, Golf, Heritage, Canoeing, River Tour **Seasonal:** No **Reservations:** One night deposit, 7 day cancel policy unless rerented; check-in 3-7pm, check-out noon. **Brochure:** Yes **Permitted:** Children, drinking, smoking allowed only on porches and outdoors **Conference:** Facilities for small meetings, seminars and conference **Payment Terms:** Check MC/V [I04HPMD-12604] **COM** Y **G ITC Member:** No

Rates: Pvt Bath 9
Single $ 75.00
Double $ 130.00

Tilghman Island Inn   Coopertown Rd 21671   Tilghman Island MD
Tel: 800-866-2141   410-886-2141
Res Times 9am-7pm

Not a typical Bed & Breakfast but an intimate resort that's contemporary and luxurious offering all the modern amenities while situated in a quaint 19th Century fishing village - home of the country's last working sailing boat fleet. Situated right on the water at Knapps Narrows and the Chesapeake Bay, there are docking facilities, formal and casual dining rooms, private tennis court, swimming pool, croquet court, fishing, biking and great dining experiences awaiting everyone. The Dining Room overlooks the water setting and offers the best of seasonal local produce, prime meats, fresh seafood prepared in creative and traditional ways. Continental breakfast is included. Guests can drive or arrive by boat at this private and luxurious Inn, where service, food and drink will exceed your highest expectations. **Reservations:** One night's deposit or credit card for guarantee, 48 hr cancel policy except holidays requiring 10 day notice **Permitted:** Children, smoking, drinking, limited pets **Conference:** Yes for small groups to 20-25 persons. **Payment Terms:** Check AE/MC/V [R09BCMD-7751] **COM** Y **ITC Member:** No

Rates: Pvt Bath 20
Single $ 85-95.00
Double $ 95-105.00

Clements Inn   1712 Center Ave M-25 48609   Bay City MI
Brian & Karen Hepp   Tel: 517-894-4600   Fax: 517-895-8535

The *Clements Inn* was built in 1886 by William and Jessie Clements. This Queen Anne style Victorian home features six fireplaces, magnificent woodwork, an oak staircase, amber-colored glass windows, working gas lamps, organ pipes, two clawfoot tubs and a third floor ballroom. Each bedroom is named after an author, in honor of William Clement's love of books, and includes CATV, phone and a private bath. The Emily Bronte Room is decorated in white wicker, lace and ivy and features a working in-room gas fireplace. The five hundred square foot Elizabeth Barrett Browning Suite boasts a king size bed, love seat, gas fireplace and an in room whirlpool tub. The ballroom and adjoining rooms have been converted into the twelve hundred square foot Alfred Lord Tennyson Suite and includes the bedroom and bath, a fully furnished kitchen, and a living room/dining room area complete with a queen futon. The other guest rooms feature in room recliners and desks. Awaiting your arrival will be a colorful gift bag of treats on your pillow, cookies on the bureau and small tokens on the nightstand in honor of that birthday, anniversary or honeymoon. Romance starts with candles and herbal bath grains in the evening and continues with a candlelight breakfast in the morning. Days will find you enjoying antique and craft shops, a wide assortment of riverfront activities or walks along historic Center Avenue with its collection of late 1800's Victorian homes. **Discounts:** 20% for booking entire house **Airport:** Tri-City Intl-20 min **Reservations:** One night's deposit, 7 day cancel policy for refund, less than 7 days notice, refund only if rebooked **Permitted:** Children, drinking **Conference:** Meeting space for groups to 30 with lodging for groups to 15+ **Payment Terms:** AE/DISC/MC/V [I08GPMI-10717] **COM** Y **ITC Member:** No

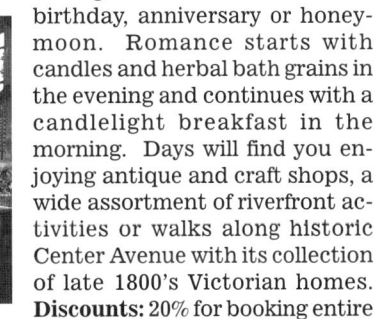

Rates: Pvt Bath 6
Single $ 70-125.00
Double $ 70-125.0

Michigan National Edition

Stonehedge Inn	924 Center Ave (M-25) 48708	Bay City MI
Ruth Koerber		**Tel:** 517-894-4342
		Res Times 8am-9:30pm

Proudly standing today, *Stonehedge Inn*, built in 1889, remains a fine example of English Tudor architecture but updated to include modern comforts and amenities. Soft mauve and cream interior colors portray the essence of the turn-of-the-century ambiance along with original electric and gas lighting fixtures, hand carved woodwork, fireplaces and clawfoot tubs. Guest rooms are furnished with antiques, collectibles and family heirlooms with a choice of brass, oak and antique beds. A continental-plus breakfast includes fresh fruit, cereals, homemade muffins and breads and a bottomless cup of coffee. The quaint town of Bay City offers numerous museums, antique shops, restaurants and boating, fishing and excellent strolling. **Discounts:** Corporate, group rates **Airport:** Freeland MBS-20 mi **Seasonal:** No **Reservations:** 50% deposit or credit card number to guarantee reservation, 48 hr cancel policy. Arrival before 11pm except bridal couples. **Brochure:** Yes **Permitted:** Children, limited smoking **Conference:** Yes, meetings, bridal showers, birthdays, small weddings and parties. **Payment Terms:** Check AE-/DC/MC/V [R07FPMI-6535] **COM** Y **ITC Member:** No

Rates:		**Shared Bath** 7
Single		$ 60.00
Double		$ 85.00

Silver Creek Lodge B&B	4361 US 23S 48721	Black River MI
Kim, Jim, Bill Moses		**Tel:** 517-471-2198 517-724-6430
		Res Times 10am-6pm

Situated on eighty tranquil wooded acres adjoining 5200 acres of beautiful Federal Forests is this unique homey lodge. Nestled in the Black River foothills, it features spacious carpeted rooms gracefully accented with antiques, paintings and crafts. Here you may buy the very bed you sleep in - you see this B&B is also an antique shop! You'll enjoy a panoramic view of this peaceful and natural setting while enjoying the **Deluxe full breakfast!** These hosts prepare their specialties of pecan waffles, perfect homemade popovers, breads and jams for each guests delight! Spring, summer and fall, guests can stroll the hiking trails, enjoy wildlife in their natural setting and picnic next to a spring fed brook. There's horseback riding through the hardwoods and in winter you can enjoy the ski trails that begin right outside of the front door! Watch deer and turkey while sipping coffee by the massive stone fireplace in the great room. Nature truly abounds at this tranquil woodland setting. *Silver Creek* was one of fourteen Michigan B&Bs (selected from over 250 in Michigan) for Laura Zahn's third book "*Wake-up And Smell The Coffee*". At *Silver Creek* these charming hosts make your stay memorable and offer special packages for anniversary, birthday or a romantic getaway weekend! Located just ten miles from Neqweghon Park, 10 mi of Virgin Lake Huron shoreline for swimming and hiking. **Seasonal:** No **Reservations:** Deposit required, credit card to guarantee room if late arrival after 7pm. **Brochure:** Yes **Permitted:** Drinking, limited smoking (certain rooms) **Payment Terms:** Check MC/V [R03BCMI-6835] **COM** Y **ITC Member:** No

Rates:	**Pvt Bath** 2	**Shared Bath** 4
Single	$ 55.00	$ 50.00
Double	$ 65.00	$ 60.00

Dewey Lake Manor B&B	11811 Laird Rd 49230	Brooklyn MI
Phillips Family		**Tel:** 517-467-7122
		Res Times 24 Hrs

This century-old home sits atop a knoll overlooking picturesque Dewey Lake surrounded by eighteen acres of rolling land. Guests step back in time and relax in an aura of yesteryear - a time of lamplight and lace, love songs and flowers, picnics and sunsets. Four guest rooms feature comfortable country Victorian decor. A glass enclosed porch, with a view of the lake, provides a pleasant place to enjoy a summer breakfast or to just relax. Other common rooms include a parlor with a piano and a sitting room with a bay window overlooking the lake. There are eighteen acres to wander on and a picnic area by the lake shore. In the Irish Hills of Southern Michigan, Dewey Lake Manor is located 40 minutes from Ann Arbor, MI; 45 minutes from Toledo, Ohio; and 30 minutes from Jackson, Michigan. The

©*Inn & Travel Memphis, Tennessee*

National Edition **_Michigan_**

central location of Irish Hills offers antiquing, fifty-two spring fed lakes, golfing, fishing, hunting, cross-country skiing and much more. Car enthusiasts are just 3 miles away from the Michigan International Speedway. Come visit us - where your hosts have prepared an atmosphere with a country flavor. Whether you enjoy the sweet sound of the summer nights or the quiet stillness of the frozen lake - your stay will be a pleasant one to remember. A generous continental plus breakfast is included in your room rate. **Discounts:** Off-season, "Whole House" booking, weekly stays **Packages:** Golf, Dinner, Honeymoon **Seasonal:** No **Reservations:** 50% deposit at res time with a 5 day cancel policy for refund **Brochure:** Yes **Permitted:** Children, limited drinking **Conference:** Yes for groups to 25 persons **Payment Terms:** Check AE/MC/V [I03HPMI1-12002] **COM** YG **ITC Member:** No

Rates:	Pvt Bath 4
Single	$ 50-70.00
Double	$ 55-70.00

American Inn B&B	312 E Cass St 49601	Cadillac MI
Mike & Cathy Feister		**Tel:** 616-779-9000
		Res Times 8am-10pm

A turn-of-the-century home offers travelers a chance to step back in time and experience Cadillac's limber era. Original oak carvings, hardwood floors, pocket doors, stained glass and antiques throughout. Our tastefully appointed guest rooms have private baths, cable/HBO, a/c and queen or king size beds. Guests may relax and unwind in the hot tub and sauna available on an enclosed porch. Our luxurious suite offers a private spa with spiral stairway to a walk-out deck, cathedral ceiling, skylights - the perfect romantic getaway. The Inn is centrally located, just a short walk to shops, restaurants and Lake Cadillac. Golf, boating, skiing are available nearby. A hearty continental breakfast is included. **Discounts:** Corporate and Seasonal - 11/1-5/20 **Airport:** Traverse City-50 mi; Grand Rapids Airport-90 mi **Seasonal:** No **Reservations:** One night's deposit to guarantee reservation, 7 day cancel policy for refund **Brochure:** Yes **Permitted:** Children, drinking, limited smoking **Payment Terms:** Check MC/V [R07FPMI-11299] **COM** Y **ITC Member:** No

Rates:	Pvt Bath 5
Single	$ 55-75.00
Double	$ 65-150.00

Chicago Pike Inn	215 E Chicago 49036	Coldwater MI
Rebecca Schultz		**Tel:** 517-279-8744
		Res Times 7am-11pm

Enjoy a night or weekend in this turn-of-the-century Colonial mansion located in quiet historical residential neighborhood. This national award-win-

| *recommended by* |
| *Chicago Sun Times* |

ning Inn has been recommended by the *"Chicago Sun Times","Oakland Press"*, among others, and it was ***a featured and a cover Inn*** for *"Innsider."* Restored to Victorian elegance, guests find a sweeping cherry staircase, stained glass windows, parquet floors, gas and electric chandeliers and beautiful Victorian antique furnishings throughout. Choose a guest room to match your mood or pleasure - you'll find queen size beds, four pillows (two hard and two soft), lace curtains at all windows, paddle fans, TV and clock radios, comfortable chairs and sitting areas and private baths - including the recently added jacuzzi rooms in the adjacent Carriage House. Special arrangements are always available for romantic picnics, a room full of your favorite bouquets and scents or a *"do not disturb"* sign. Mornings bring fresh ground brewed coffee and morning paper for early risers - while a full country breakfast is served in the formal dining room and features fresh fruit, freshly brewed flavorful ground coffee, spiced teas and a homemade "specialty of the day" entree. Afternoon seasonal refreshments are served either by the warmth of the fireplace or in the cool comfort of our many porches. Year-round outdoor activities abound since Coldwater is surrounded by rich

Michigan National Edition

farmland and picturesque lakes. **Airport:** Kalamazoo-55 mi; Ft Wayne-65 mi; Detroit-130 mi **Packages:** Summer Theater, July and Aug **Seasonal:** No **Reservations:** One night's deposit, 7 day cancel policy; gift certificates available **Brochure:** Yes **Permitted:** Limited children, limited drinking, limited smoking **Conference:** The perfect setting for unforgettable occasions such as weddings, rehearsal dinners and lodging for out of town guests; excellent site for private small business meetings and accommodations **Payment Terms:** Check AE/MC/V [Z02-HPMI1-9606] **COM** U **ITC Member:** No

Rates:	Pvt Bath 8
Single	$ 80-165.00
Double	$ 80-165.00

Our Old House B&B	285 MIll St 49042	Constantine MI
Liz Cruce/Micki Britt		Tel: 616-435-5365

"Our Old House" is a quiet elegant historical home in the tree lined village of Constantine on the St Joseph River, nine miles north of the Indiana-Ohio turnpike on US 131. This lovely 150 year old home has been redecorated and renovated with comfort in mind, by Liz and Micki, who are sisters. The most popular guest room is the Renaissance Room with an antique queen bed, bay window and an adjoining jacuzzi bath on the first level. The guest rooms offer wicker furnishings (Evergreen Room) while the shared-bath guest rooms (Oriental Poppy Room, Iris Room and Blue Rose Room) are furnished with comfort in mind. A full nutritious complimentary breakfast of homemade breads, muffins, fruits in season and a variety of entrees freshly prepared for each guest is available each morning. Complimentary refreshments are provided throughout the day and while relaxing with a good novel or watching TV in the comfy living room beside a fire. Within easy driving distance are many antique centers in Schoolcraft Michigan, a renowned flea market and the Centreville antique show while Shipshewana, Indiana offers shopping at the Amish and Mennonite villages. Your hostesses welcome travelers to take a break and enjoy the old-fashioned swing and wicker furniture on their wrap around front porch. **Airport:** Kalamazoo and South Bend-35 mi **Seasonal:** No **Reservations:** Deposits are requested; arrival time flexible but hostesses desire prior arrangements **Brochure:** Yes **Conference:** Capabilities for small meetings **Payment Terms:** Check [R10EPMI-15422] **COM** U **ITC Member:** No

Rates:	Pvt Bath 2	Shared Bath 2
Single	$ 65-95.00	$ 45-55.00
Double	$ 65-95.00	$ 45-55.00

Country Lane B&B		Dearborn MI
Julius & Veronica Laroy		Tel: 313-753-4586
		Res Times 8am-9pm

Refer to the same listing name under Romulus, Michigan for a complete description. **Seasonal:** No **Payment Terms:** Check MC/V [M07FPMI-17778] **COM** YG **ITC Member:** No

Rates:	Shared Bath 2
Single	$ 35.00
Double	$ 45.00

Hidden Pond B&B	5975 128th Ave 49408	Fennville MI
Priscilla & Larry Fuerst		Tel: 616-561-2491
		Res Times 8am-10pm

Hidden Pond Bed & Breakfast is set on twenty-eight acres of woods, perfect for bird-watching, hiking, cross-country skiing, or just relaxing in a rowboat on the pond. This sprawling thirteen room house was designed to provide visitors with privacy and rest. Guests have exclusive use of seven entry-level rooms, including bedrooms and baths, a living room with fireplace, the dining room, library room, and breakfast porch. Priscilla and Larry, who work for rival airlines, understand the importance of a soothing, calm and slow-paced overnight. They enjoy pleasing guests and creating an atmosphere of quiet elegance. There are no schedules; breakfast is served when you wake up. Unwind and take in the sun on the outdoor deck and patio. Behind the house is a ravine with a pond, where you might see a deer or two. Or take a brief excursion; this lovely retreat is near the beaches on Lake Michigan, the boutiques of Saugatuck and the winery and cider mill in Fennville. Turndown service, complimentary soft drinks, tea, hot chocolate or an evening sherry is there for you. A full hot breakfast is served in the sun-washed garden room includes fresh fruits, breads, muffins and a hot entree, served at your leisure. After breakfast, relax on the patio amongst the terrace garden full of seasonal blooms with over 300 spring bulbs, or enjoy the view from the 60 ft deck overlooking the fishing pond. In the winter, relax by the fireplace after a cross country ski adventure on our grounds. **Discounts:** Extended stays-3 days and longer **Airport:** Grand Rapids and Kalamazoo MI-1 hr **Seasonal:** Yes, rates vary **Reservations:** 50% deposit within 7 days, 10 day cancel policy less 15% service fee, 3pm check-in **Brochure:** Yes **Permitted:** Limited children, drinking, limited smoking **Conference:** Yes, for groups of 8-12 persons **Payment Terms:** Check [I02HP-MI1-16006] COM YG **ITC Member:** No

Rates:	Pvt Bath 2
Single	$ 64-110.00
Double	$ 64-110.00

B&B At The Pines 327 Ardussi St 48734 **Frankenmuth MI**
Richard & Donna Hodge **Tel:** 517-652-9019
Res Times 9am-7pm

Guests are welcomed to this charming home offering a friendly casual atmosphere surrounded by pines and strolling distance to restaurants and the main tourist attractions. Guest rooms include beautiful heirloom quilts and ceiling fans. A home made continental breakfast includes baked breads, seasonal fruit and beverages. **Seasonal:** No **Reservations:** Deposit of $10.00 at res time; check-in after 2pm **Brochure:** Yes **Permitted:** Children, limited pets **Payment Terms:** Check [X06BCMI-1936] COM Y **ITC Member:** No

Rates:	Pvt Bath 1	Shared Bath 1
Single		
Double	$ 45.00	$ 45.00

Dutch Colonial Inn 560 Central Ave 49423 **Holland MI**
Bob & Pat Elenbaas **Tel:** 616-396-3664

Relax and enjoy a gracious 1928 Dutch Colonial, an award-winning B&B, located in a quiet residential neighborhood. Your hosts have elegantly decorated their home with family heirloom antiques and furnishings from the 1930s. Guests enjoy the relaxing atmosphere of the lovely common rooms or the cheery sun-porch, which includes a TV and VCR. Air conditioning assures year-round comfort. Each of the five guest rooms is unique in decor and includes a private bath (some with whirlpool tubs for two). Double, queen and king-size beds are available, complete with lovely linens. Try the "Hideway Suite" during your visit or your "Special Getaway"! Special festive touches are everywhere during the Christmas Holiday Season - offering travelers a *"home away from home"*, while traveling. A delicious full breakfast is included and served in the formal dining room. Guests will enjoy the nearby Windmill Island, Wooden Shoe Factory, Delftware Factory, Tulip Festival, Hope College, Michigan's finest beaches, bike paths and cross-country ski trails. **Seasonal:** No **Reservations:** Business people are welcomed and special corporate rates are available. **Brochure:** Yes **Permitted:** Limited children **Payment Terms:** Check MC/V [R06FPMI-11202] COM U **ITC Member:** No

Rates:	Pvt Bath 5
Single	$ 60-85.00
Double	$ 60-85.00

Reka's B&B 300 N 152nd Ave 49424 **Holland MI**
Rein & Kay Wolfert **Tel:** 616-399-0409

Michigan   *National Edition*

"True Dutch Atmosphere" abounds in this contemporary Bed and Breakfast which shouldn't be missed in Holland. Newly decorated, the guest rooms offer king and queen size beds, air conditioning and walkouts to the patio for enjoying the beautiful view. Your interesting hosts look forward to your visiting them - and experience true hospitality like so many other guests. Marcia and Rob G. comment, *"Had a wonderful and relaxing time. We felt that we were staying with friends rather than staying at a hotel. The room was comfortable and warm as were the two of you". "Having a great stay! Will tell everyone about you"*, John and Paula G. Carol and Ann (mother and daughter) commented *"Thank you both so very much for your warm hospitality. We enjoyed our stay with you and the Tulip Festival." "We had a wonderful time. The hospitality was super and the food was great!"* says Joe and Lauren H. For a true Holland Michigan experience, don't miss Reka's and great hosts Rein and Kay and a breakfast that will bring you back again and again. Proximity to Chicago and Detroit - 200 miles. **Airport:** Park Township Airport, private-1 mi; Grand Rapids Kent County Airport-35 mi **Seasonal:** No **Reservations:** 50% deposit or credit card number to guarantee reservation **Brochure:** Yes **Permitted:** Children **Conference:** For small groups **Languages:** English, Dutch, German, some Spanish and French **Payment Terms:** Check MC/V [I07FPMI-16793] **COM** Y **ITC Member:** No

Rates:	Pvt Bath	3
Single	$ 80.00	
Double	$ 80.00	

The Parsonage 1908   6 E 24th St 49423   **Holland MI**
Bonnie Verwys   **Tel: 616-396-1316**
     Res Times 9-12am/5-9pm

Experience a true European-style Bed and Breakfast Inn. This beautiful older residence built c1908 as a church parsonage is situated in a quiet street "A-1" neighborhood. Guests consistently rate this Inn as superior for hospitality, cleanliness and overall impression. Inside, guests find the glowing warmth of rich oak woodwork, antique furnishings, leaded glass windows, two cozy sitting rooms, an antique fireplace and country kitchen, with a lovely summer porch for relaxing, that's perfect for business travelers looking to relax after a day's activity. A full breakfast is served in the formal dining room or outdoors on the garden patio and your charming hostess will prepare it to meet the needs of health-conscious guests! Holland is located on the shores of Lake Michigan and beautiful Lake Macatawa. Excellent location offers guests swimming, charter boating, golf, tennis canoeing, hiking, art and craft shows, antiques, cross-country skiing and exceptional dining and shopping. Just five minutes from Hope College or Hedcore business district and only ten miles south of Saugatuck. Arriving by plane? Just ten minutes by taxi will bring you from the Holland airport. Call ahead and your hostess will arrange dinner at one of the many delightful restaurants. **Seasonal:** 5/1-10/31 Open **Reservations:** Deposit at res time; late arrival by prior arrangement; 48 hr cancel policy **Brochure:** Yes **Permitted:** Limited drinking **Conference:** Yes, for small groups or luncheons. **Payment Terms:** Check [RO1BCMI-1951] **COM** Y **ITC Member:** No

Rates:	Pvt Bath 1	Shared Bath 3
Single	$ 60-80.00	$ 55-60.00
Double	$ 80-90.00	$ 65-70.00

Stagecoach Stop   4810 Leonard Rd W 49430   **Lamont MI**
Marcia Ashby   **Tel: 616-677-3940**

Midway between Grand Rapids and Grand Haven, this current Inn built in 1859 served as the stagecoach stop-over and much of the original house remains today. Decorated with period antiques offering warmth and traditional comfort for weary travelers today too. Full breakfast included. **Seasonal:** No **Brochure:** Yes . **Payment Terms:** Check MC/V [X11ACMI-1964] **COM** Y **ITC Member:** No

Rates:	Pvt Bath 1	Shared Bath 2
Single	$ 55.00	$ 55.00
Double	$ 65.00	$ 60.00

©*Inn & Travel Memphis, Tennessee*

National Edition   *Michigan*

Cloghaun	PO Box 203 49757	Mackinac Island MI
James Bond		Tel: 906-847-3885
		Res Times 8am-9:30pm

The Irish greeting Caid Mille Failte, meaning a hundred thousand welcomes has been given a new meaning at the *Cloghaun* for over a century. A large Victorian home with spacious grounds, situated on Market Street, it is one block from the harbor and close to many fine restaurants and shops. The Shepler Boat Line is one block away. The name Cloghaun is Gaelic and means **"Land of Little Stones"**. It is pronounced Clah Hahn. Cloghaun was a little town in County Galway, Ireland which Thomas and Bridgett Donnelly left in 1848, the year of the great famine. They came to Mackinac Island, where a relative, Charles O'Mally was already a prosperous trader and hotel owner (The Island House). They purchased a large tract of land in 1852 and in 1884 the *Cloghaun* was built to house their large Irish family. We have eleven guest rooms which can accommodate twenty-four guests. All of our rooms connect and can be rented as suites. Eight rooms have private baths while the other rooms share baths. All rooms have hand basins. Most of our guests return year after year. In fact, one guest has stayed with us for forty consecutive years! The quiet peace of Mackinac life with no cars or motor vehicles allows visitors to recharge themselves for city living and provides a restful interlude for their busy lives. All the facilities of the Grand Hotel, golf, swimming and dancing are open to all guests of the island. The *Cloghaun* is but a short walk from the Grand. A continental plus breakfast is included. Come to *Cloghaun* to enjoy the ambiance and elegance of anther generation. **Airport:** Pelston Airport-20 mi **Seasonal:** Open 5/15 to 10/31 **Reservations:** One night's deposit to guarantee reservation and a 15 day cancel notice is required for refund less $15 service fee **Brochure:** Yes **Permitted:** Children, smoking on outdoor porch **Conference:** Yes, for small groups to 24 persons with separate meetings rooms available **Payment Terms:** Check [I04IPMI1-14290] **COM U ITC Member:** No

Rates:	Pvt Bath 9	Shared Bath 2
Single	$ 100-110.00	$ 70.00
Double	$ 100-110.00	$ 70.00

McCarthys Bear Creek Inn	15230 C Dr North 49068	Marshall MI
Mike & Beth McCarthy		Tel: 616-781-8383

A 1940's estate built by a wealthy inventor and situated on 15 acres just outside of town, you'll enjoy this relaxed atmosphere and rural setting for hiking in summer and spring and sleigh rides in the winter. Furnished with a mixture of antiques, artists' crafts, and family treasures, these lovely hosts make sure every guest is pleased. Full breakfast is served outdoors on the porch in a family style service. **Seasonal:** Closed Christmas **Reservations:** Deposit for one night's stay. **Brochure:** Yes **Permitted:** Children, limited smoking **Payment Terms:** Check [X11ACMI-1982] **COM Y ITC Member:** No

Rates:	Pvt Bath 7
Single	$ 70.00
Double	$ 80.00

1873 Mendon Country Inn	440 W Main St 49072	Mendon MI
Richard & Dolly Buerkle		Tel: 616-496-8132 Fax: 616-496-8403

Featured in Jan 1986 *"Country Living"* magazine, this inn c1873 features high ceilings, eight foot windows, winding walnut staircase, and beautiful antique furnishings in guest rooms. Set on four acres, you can canoe off their dock at no added cost. **Seasonal:** No **Brochure:** Yes **Permitted:** Limited smoking, drinking. **Payment Terms:** Check AE/MC/V [X11ACMI-1986] **COM Y ITC Member:** No

Rates:	Pvt Bath 6	Shared Bath 5
Single	$ 50.00	$ 40.00
Double	$ 70-80.00	$ 50-60.00

©*Inn & Travel Memphis, Tennessee*

Michigan   *National Edition*

Yesterdays Inn 518 N 4th St 49120		Niles MI
Elizabeth Baker		Tel: 616-683-6079

Turn-of-the-century Italianate residence with eclectic decor providing comfort and hospitality to all guests. Close to Notre Dame, plenty of shops, and antique stops. Full breakfast included daily. **Seasonal:** No **Brochure:** Yes **Permitted:** Children **Payment Terms:** Check MC/V [X11ACMI-1994] **COM** Y

ITC Member: No

Rates:		**Shared Bath** 4
Single		$ 47.00
Double		$ 52.00

Bear & The Bay	421 Charlevoix Ave 49770	Petoskey MI
		Tel: 616-347-6077

Quaint clapboard Victorian with all the gingerbread c1900 nestled above Bear River. Antique furnishings decorate all the rooms with guest rooms complete with terry cloth robes, down comforters, fresh flowers, and canopied beds. Full breakfast included. Complimentary PM wine, sherry, tea. **Brochure:** Yes **Permitted:** Limited smoking **Payment Terms:** Check V [X11ACMI-2010] **COM** Y **ITC Member:** No

Rates:	**Pvt Bath** 2	**Shared Bath** 2
Single	$ 60.00	$ 55.00
Double	$ 50.00	$ 65.00

Victorian Inn	1229 Seventh St 48060	Port Huron MI
Shelia Marinez		Tel: 810-984-1437 Fax: 810-982-5830

Lovely 1890's Queen Anne three story completely restored including antique furnishings. Victorian dining in restaurant on premises, with quaint Pub in lower level. **Seasonal:** No **Brochure:** Yes **Permitted:** Children, smoking, drinking **Payment Terms:** Check AE/MC/V [X11ACMI-2017] **COM** Y **ITC Member:** No

Rates:	**Pvt Bath** 2	**Shared Bath** 2
Single		
Double	$ 50-60.00	$ 50-60.00

Country Lane B&B	32285 Sibley Rd 48174	Romulus MI
Julius & Veronica Laroy		Tel: 313-753-4586
		Res Times 8am-9pm

A warm welcome awaits guests at our charming cape cod home on a twenty acre farm. Large comfortable air conditioned guest rooms include TV, radio and desks. A hearty all-you-can-eat full breakfast is served family-style when you arise. Typical entrees are waffles with strawberry preserves, apple fritters or blueberry pancakes, plus homemade bread, muffins, coffee, tea and juice. The farm is a working pumpkin farm with wooded trails for year-round strolling and an apple grove with a nice area for a relaxing picnic or barbecue. Guests can enjoy the nearby all-sports park system and several golf courses. Airport pick-up is available at Ann Arbor, Dearborn and Detroit Metropolitan airports with prior arrangement. Special package discount for nearby historical Henry Ford Museum/Greenfield Village. Your well-traveled host and hostess enjoy visiting with guests and joy-riding in their 1923 Model T convertible or tractor and wagon. There are stalls and outdoor facilities for pets. **Pacakge:** Henry Ford Museum, Greenfield Village Tour **Seasonal:** No **Reservations:** One night deposit required to guarantee reservation **Brochure:** Yes **Permitted:** Children, outdoor kennel for pets, drinking, smoking **Payment Terms:** Check MC/V [R07FPMI-14303] **COM** Y **ITC Member:** No

Rates:		**Shared Bath** 2
Single		$ 35.00
Double		$ 45.00

South Cliff Inn B&B	1900 Lake Shore Dr 49085	Saint Joseph MI

©*Inn & Travel Memphis, Tennessee*

National Edition   *Michigan*

Bill Swisher   **Tel:** 616-983-4881

Welcome to St Joseph's first Bed & Breakfast, *South Cliff Inn*, a 75 year-old large brick English Cottage-style home located on a bluff overlooking peaceful Lake Michigan. A year-round Inn where you experience a soothing relaxation within its luxurious accommodations. Each guest room has been individually decorated with imported fabrics and all furnishings were designed and tailored specifically for the room. Choose from a variety of guest rooms, one of which includes a whirlpool tub overlooking Lake Michigan. Guests are welcomed to share the living room with other guests or your hosts or curled-up before the glowing embers of a wintry fire with a good novel. Located on an acre of land surrounded with fieldstone fences in a charming residential area. Take a leisurely stroll to either a quiet private beach or a nearby public beach. A continental breakfast is served in the Sun Room each morning - where you'll watch the many boats traveling the Lake and the commercial fishing boats gathering their nets. Whatever your plans include ... don't forget the most important point ... to simply relax and enjoy yourself. **Discounts:** Corporate with prior approval **Airport:** South Bend-40 mi; Chicago O'Hare-100 mi; **Seasonal:** No **Reservations:** One night deposit by credit card number **Brochure:** Yes **Permitted:** Children, drinking, limited smoking **Payment Terms:** AE/DISC/MC/V [Z04GPMI-11086] **COM** Y **ITC Member:** No

Rates:	**Pvt Bath 7**
Single	$ 70-110.00
Double	$ 70-110.00

Homestead B&B	9279 Macon Rd 48176	**Saline MI**
Shirley Grossman		**Tel:** 313-429-9625

1850 farmhouse with country charm and Victorian elegance on fifty acres of pasture land full of wildflowers and fauna. Close to Ann Arbor and Ypsilanti, 45 mins to Detroit and Toledo. Full country breakfast included. Complimentary beverages, cheese and crackers **Seasonal:** No **Brochure:** Yes **Permitted:** Smoking, limited drinking **Payment Terms:** Check [X11ACMI-2025] **COM** Y **ITC Member:** No

Rates:	**Shared Bath 6**
Single	$ 40-45.00
Double	$ 50-55.0

Bayside Inn	618 Water St 49453	**Saugatuck MI**
Kathy & Frank Wilson		**Tel:** 800-548-0077 616-857-4321 **Fax:** 616-857-1870
		Res Times 8am-7pm

Once a charming boathouse now an elegant and contemporary waterfront Bed & Breakfast at the water's edge - guests are treated to a perfect location and all of the comforts of home. Seven of the guest rooms have a magnificent waterfront view that provide year round enjoyment whether watching the wildlife, mute swans or passing boats - while snuggled in your own private little world next to a cozy fireplace. Each guest room has a private bath, deck, cable TV, phone and a spacious central living area. Located just footsteps from downtown restaurants and shops, guests are still close to marinas, beaches and nature trails. Once an important shipping and fishing port, complete with its own shipyards, today Saugatuck is a "modern port" complete with charter fishing, marinas and shops of every size and description and with a variety of fine and casual dining choices. Four golf courses, special art exhibits, winery tours, exploring the nearby countryside and the numerous forests and fruit farms tucked away in the rolling hills and Lake Michigan's sand dunes, beaches and water sports offer a wide range of activities for even a long stay.

©*Inn & Travel Memphis, Tennessee*

Michigan   *National Edition*

A complimentary continental breakfast is included. **Packages:** *"Wine Lover's Weekend"*, Two night's lodging for two, complimentary bottle of champagne upon arrival, personalized tasting tour at Fenn Valley Vineyards, dinner at Toulouse French restaurant and special wine purchase discounts, $250 per couple. (Available Nov through May) Special midweek rates are available - call for details. **Discounts:** Midweek Nov-April **Seasonal:** No **Reservations:** One night or 50% of length of stay deposit, 7 day cancel notice (30 days for holiday, festival weekends and weekly stays), $10 service fee, 2 night min on weekends in July and August **Brochure:** Yes **Permitted:** Children, drinking, smoking **Conference:** Perfect setting for group gatherings or mini-conventions to enjoy Saugatucks year-round activities **Payment Terms:** Check AE/DISC/MC/V [I02HPMI1-16032] **COM YG ITC Member:** No

Rates:	Pvt Bath 10
Single	$ 55-185.00
Double	$ 55-185.00

Hidden Pond B&B   Saugatuck MI
Priscilla & Larry Fuerst   Tel: 616-561-2491
       Res Times 8am-10pm

Refer to the same listing name under Fennville, Michigan for a complete description. **Seasonal:** Yes, rates vary **Payment Terms:** Check [M02HPMI1-22640] **COM YG ITC Member:** No

Rates:	Pvt Bath 2
Single	$ 64-110.00
Double	$ 64-110.00

Maplewood   428 Butler St 49453   Saugatuck MI
Catherine Simon/Sam Burnell   Tel: 616-857-1771 Fax: 616-857-1773
      Res Times 9am-5pm

Step into the 1860's during Michigan's busy lumberman's era when the *Maplewood* served as the luxury resort hotel and continues today. Located on the quiet village green, this excellent example of Greek Revival with its three story front and four massive pillars, the interior remains much as it did then with crystal chandeliers, period furnishings, and tailored carpeting. All guest rooms are filled with period antique furnishings made in Grand Rapids, and offer fireplaces, canopied beds, and double jacuzzi in various rooms. Outdoor lap pool and wood deck for poolside sunbathing, glass enclosed sun porch furnished with rattan and potted ferns or the Parkside Porch offers a lazy summer afternoon viewing onto the public square. Full breakfast included and is served in the gourmet dining room. Other meals available at added cost. **Airport:** Kent County Intl-Grand Rapids MI **Seasonal:** Rates vary **Reservations:** Deposit required, cancellation 7 days prior to arrival for refund. Late arrivals only with prior arrangements. **Brochure:** Yes **Permitted:** Children, drinking **Conference:** Yes, available for small groups off season **Payment Terms:** Check AE/MC/V [A02HPMI1-2990] **COM YG ITC Member:** No

Rates:	Pvt Bath 15
Single	$ 65.00
Double	$ 155.00

Red Dog B&B   132 Mason St 49453   Saugatuck MI
Gary Kott   Tel: 616-857-8851
      Res Times 9am-10pm

The *Red Dog Bed & Breakfast* carries on the Saugatuck tradition of hospitality offering six comfortable air conditioned rooms to choose from, four with private bath. There's a large living room with fireplace that's perfect for warming-up following a winter afternoon of cross country skiing. A lovely second floor porch runs the length of the house, providing an ideal place for relaxing on summer evenings. In the morning, guests gather in the beautiful dining room to enjoy the complimentary continental breakfast. Located in the heart of Saugatuck, less than one block from the shops and restaurants on Butler Street, and just steps away from the boardwalk along Lake Kalamazoo, guests have many enjoyable walking tours available to them. Saugatuck is a resort town that's the perfect escape anytime during the year. Rolling sand dunes, winding waterways, beaches, boating, unique shops and restaurants have attracted summer enthusiasts for over a century. After the crowds have gone home and the days grow shorter, you'll discover the quiet side of Saugatuck - sipping cider from a local orchard while marveling at the stunning fall foliage. Whatever the season, your stay at the *Red Dog B&B* will be memorable. **Discounts:** Nov-April, stay one night, 50% off the second night **Seasonal:** No **Reservations:** One night's deposit, 7 day cancel policy for refund **Brochure:** Yes **Permitted:** Children, drinking **Payment Terms:** Check DC/MC/V [Z04GPMI-13907] **COM** Y **ITC Member:** No

Rates:	Pvt Bath 4	Shared Bath 2
Single	$ 70-85.00	$ 55.00
Double	$ 70-85.00	$ 55.00

Sherwood Forest B&B	938 Center St 49453	Saugatuck MI
Keith & Susan Charak		Tel: 800-838-1246 616-857-1246
		Res Times 9am-10pm

Nestled by woods, the *Sherwood Forest B&B* is a beautiful Victorian home built in 1900. The five guest rooms are furnished with antiques and comfortable decorative touches to add to the relaxing surroundings. Each room includes a private bath and queen-sized bed, while the Black and White Room boasts a spacious jacuzzi and the Apricot Room has a beautiful fireplace with an oak mantle. A continental breakfast of homemade breads and muffins, cereals, juices, fresh fruit and aromatic coffee and teas is served each morning. Guests can enjoy breakfast in the sun filled dining room or on the gracious wraparound porch. Behind the house is a heated swimming pool with a painted mural of dolphins riding the ocean waves, while the eastern shore of Lake Michigan and the public beaches are 1/2 block away. The wide white sand beach is a perfect place for strolling, swimming or watching spectacular sunsets. A separate cottage is also available that sleeps seven. Sherwood Forest Bed & Breakfast also offers *"The Famous Chefs of Saugatuck Gourmet Dinner Package"* November through April. *Sherwood Forest* is AAA and ABBA Inspected and Approved. If a day in town in on the agenda, Saugatuck is just minutes away, with art galleries, antique and gift shops and an array of restaurants. **Airport:** Kent County Airport-40 mi **Packages:** Famous Chefs of Saugatuck Gourmet Dinner **Seasonal:** No **Reservations:** 50% deposit, 10 day cancel policy for refund less service fee **Brochure:** Yes **Permitted:** Drinking, limited smoking **Conference:** Groups to ten persons **Payment Terms:** Check DISC/MC/V [I08GPMI-14859] **COM** Y **ITC Member:** No

Rates:	Pvt Bath 5
Single	$ 70-130.00
Double	$ 70-130.00

Twin Gables Country Inn	900 Lake St 49453	Saugatuck MI
Michael & Denise Simcik		Tel: 800-231-2185 616-231-4346
		Res Times 10am-10pm

Overlooking Kalamazoo Lake, the family owned and operated State Historic *Twin Gables Country Inn* dates from 1865, is the only original mill in the area still standing from the busy lumbering era. Recently restored after being closed for almost two decades, the Inn features fourteen guest rooms with private baths in different country theme decor and named accordingly. Rooms have pretty wallpapers or stenciling with colour co-ordinated comforters and curtains and include antique and country furnishings. The Inn has over 3500 square feet of embossed tin ceilings, wainscoting and a cathedral window design. Summers brings beautiful sunsets on the front veranda overlooking the Lake while wintertime offers crackling fires for cross country skiers to enjoy - after a relaxing dip in the large indoor jacuzzi hot tub. A continental breakfast is included along with complimentary evening coffee and tea. Your hosts will gladly help with restaurant reservations, plays or charters and assist with information on activities. Three separate one and two bedroom cottages available too. **Airport:** Grand Rapids MI-40 mi. **Packages:** Murder Mysteries, Progressive Dinners **Seasonal:** No **Reservations:** 50% deposit for length

Michigan *National Edition*

of stay at least 3 wks prior to arrival, one week cancel policy for refund less service fee **Brochure:** Yes **Permitted:** Limited children **Conference:** Meetings and small weddings **Languages:** French, Italian, Maltese **Payment Terms:** Check AE/DISC/MC/V

[Z07GPMI-2032] **COM** Y **ITC Member:** No

Rates:	Pvt Bath 14
Single	$ 68-98.00
Double	$ 68-98.00

Wickwood Inn   510 Butler St 49453   Saugatuck MI
Julee Rosso-Miller/Bill Miller   Tel: 616-857-1456
                                                    Res Times 7am-10pm

"One of America's 10 best Inns", *"Glamour Magazine"* while the *"Chicago Tribune"* *"... a perfect place to escape the urban grind ... romantic rooms ... beautifully maintained"*. This truly elegant and stately Inn near beautiful Lake Michigan offers privacy, comfort and all of the amenities of your dream home. Filled with a few of our favorite things; French and English antiques, oriental rugs, overstuffed chairs, vases of fresh flowers, candlelight, an English library of books, fine music and original oils and drawings - choose your favorite of four living rooms in which to relax. Each guest room provides a unique decor - themed for a season, a country, or local historical interest - each with cozy down comforters and plump pillows, sure to please. While each season is featured at the Inn, Christmas extends from November 15th - January 15th, with a tradition of a special Christmas tree in every room. Each day begins on your own personal schedule with your favorite newspaper at your door and coffee in your room. Then you'll meet in the Garden Room for a memorable breakfast prepared from recipes in the *"Best-selling cookbook author"* and innkeeper, Julee Rosso-Miller, author of the *"The Silver Palate, "The Silver Palate Good Times Cookbook", "The New Basic Cookbook"* and *"Great Good Foods."* Julee and husband Bill are working towards all of their dreams and can't wait to welcome you. **Discounts:** Corporate, travel agents, weekdays (Jan-April) **Airport:** Grand Rapids Kent County Airport-45 mi **Seasonal:** Clo Christmas vary **Reservations:** First night's deposit, 10 day cancel policy less $10 service fee, check-in 3-10pm **Brochure:** Yes **Permitted:** Children 12+, drinking **Conference:** Yes, Garden Room for informal meetings to twelve **Payment Terms:** Check MC/V [I08HPMI1-2033] **COM** U **ITC Member:** No

Rates:	Pvt Bath 11
Single	$ 90.00
Double	$ 100.00

Seymour House   Blue Star Hwy 49090   South Haven MI
Tom & Gwen Paton   Tel: 616-227-3918 Fax: 616-227-3918
                                                    Res Times 8am-11pm

The *Seymour House* is a beautiful brick Italianate-style Victorian mansion built in 1862 by William Seymour who spared no expense in the construction of this stately home. The original wood floor remains in the dining room as well as intricate carved wood trim on doors and windows. The home has been recently redecorated in a style that complements the setting. Choose from five guest rooms with private baths, central a/c, some with TV/VCRs, fireplaces and jacuzzi. A two bedroom guest log cabin is also available for a more rustic experience. Enjoy nature and ultimate relaxation on our eleven acres of beautiful Michigan countryside, 1/2 mile from Lake Michigan. The grounds are complete with maintained nature trails and a stocked acre pond. Deer, wild turkeys, rabbits, woodchucks and a resident turtle call this beautiful property home. Relax on white wicker in the garden patio beneath giant oaks and weeping willows. Located one mile off I-96 and along scenic Blue Star Highway. Minutes to popular resort towns of Saugatuck and

South Haven (12 minutes to each). Explore the area's sandy beaches, boutiques, antique shops, galleries, restaurants, wineries, farm markets, orchards, biking/hiking, cross country trails and boating. A beautifully presented gourmet breakfast is served each morning the sunny dining room. Hand thrown pottery and photography are featured in the gift shop by the Innkeeper/artist. Whether you choose the Inn or the guest log cabin, Summer or Winter, we're sure your stay will be memorable. **Airport:** Grand Rapids, Kent County, O'Hare Chicago-2.5 hrs **Discounts:** Seniors, midweek, extended **Seasonal:** Reduced rates 11/1-5/1 **Reservations:** Credit card to guarantee, 7 day cancel policy for refund **Brochure:** Yes **Permitted:** Limited children, limited drinking **Payment Terms:** Check MC/V [I02-IPMI1-14306] **COM** YG **ITC Member:** No

Rates:	Pvt Bath 5
Single	$ 59-120.00
Double	$ 69-130.00

Victorian Villa Guesthouse   601 N Broadway St 49094   Union City MI
Ron Gibson   **Tel:** 800-34-VILLA 517-741-7283
    Res Times 8am-8pm

1876 Italianate mansion setting on sumptuous grounds that has been restored to former elegance offers guests a romantic setting for their visit here. Close to West Michigan, Kalamazoo and Albion College, relax in this peaceful setting and ask for the Tower Suite if it's available. Full breakfast included. **Seasonal:** Closed Jan-Feb **Brochure:** Yes **Permitted:** Limited children, limited drinking **Payment Terms:** Check MC/V [X11ACMI-2054] **COM** Y **ITC Member:** No

Rates:	Pvt Bath 4	Shared Bath 4
Single	$ 65.00	$ 55.00
Double	$ 75.00	$ 65.00

Fitgers Inn   600 E Superior St 55802   Duluth MN
Robert Hollis   **Tel:** 800-726-2982 218-722-8826

Complete resort on the shores of Lake Superior in the Fitger Brewing Complex with sensational views of the lake, specialty shops and restaurants reminiscent of the turn-of-the-century. **Seasonal:** Rates vary **Brochure:** Yes **Permitted:** Children, smoking, drinking **Payment Terms:** Check AE/MC/CB/V [X11-ACMN-2068] **COM** Y **ITC Member:** No

Rates:	Pvt Bath 48
Single	
Double	$ 70-80.00

Thorwood Inns   315 Pine 55033   Hastings MN
Dick & Pam Thorsen   **Tel:** 800-992-4667 612-437-3297

1880 French Empire mansion listed on *National Register of Historic Places* that overlooks the Mississippi River and bluffs offering antique furnishings, feather comforters, suite-sized rooms, with hearty full breakfast included. **Seasonal:** No **Permitted:** Children Complimentary wine, sherry, snacks, and airport pick-up, laundry service. **Payment Terms:** Check AE/MC/V [X11ACMN-2078] **COM** Y **ITC Member:** No

Rates:	Pvt Bath 3	Shared Bath 2
Single	$ 60.00	$ 55.00
Double	$ 70.00	$ 65.00

Evelos B&B   2301 Bryant Ave S 55045   Minneapolis MN
David & Sheryl Evelo   **Tel:** 612-374-9656

c1879 Victorian in Lowry Hill East area with period furnishings and plenty of hospitality. Full breakfast included. **Seasonal:** No **Brochure:** Yes **Permitted:** Children, limited drinking **Payment Terms:** Check [R11APMN-2087] **COM** Y **ITC Member:** No

Rates:	Shared Bath 4
Double	$ 35-40.00

©Inn & Travel Memphis, Tennessee

Minnesota   *National Edition*

Pratt Taber Inn	706 W 4th St 55066	**Red Wing MN**
Dick & Jane Walker		**Tel: 612-388-5945**

Quaint Country Inn complete with antique furnishings, fireplaces, and atmosphere in a turn-of-the-century setting. Skiing villages just twenty minutes, golfing close by. Continental plus breakfast. Complimentary beverages and bikes for touring. **Seasonal:** No **Brochure:** Yes **Permitted:** Children 6-up, limited smoking, pets, drinking **Payment Terms:** Check AE/MC/V [X11ACMN-2097] **COM Y ITC Member:** No

Rates:	**Pvt Bath 4**	**Shared Bath 2**
Single	$ 65.00	$ 60.00
Double	$ 75.00	$ 69.00

Driscolls For Guests	5522 Bald Eagle Blvd 55110	**Saint Paul MN**
Mina Driscoll		**Tel: 612-439-7486**

Historic Inn located in the town center dating to 1870's and still retaining much of its original splendor while providing guests with traditional service. Period furnishings, fireplaces and elegant dining are included. Full breakfast is included. **Seasonal:** No **Reservations:** Deposit at res time with refund if cancelled 10 days prior to arrival. **Brochure:** Yes **Permitted:** Limited children, smoking, drinking **Payment Terms:** Check [X11ACMN-2105] **COM Y ITC Member:** No

Rates:	**Pvt Bath 1**	**Shared Bath 2**
Single	$ 60.00	$ 55.00
Double	$ 70.00	$ 60.00

Lowell House B&B Inn	531 Wood St 55105	**Saint Paul MN**
Barbara Lowell		**Tel: 612-345-2111**

On the Mississippi River is this turn-of-the-century residence near Rochester and Twin Cities with large, cheerful guest rooms. Continental breakfast included. **Seasonal:** May-October **Brochure:** Yes **Permitted:** Limited children **Languages:** Spanish **Payment Terms:** Check [X11ACMN-2093] **COM Y ITC Member:** No

Rates:	**Pvt Bath 1**	**Shared Bath 3**
Single	$ 60.00	$ 55.00
Double	$ 75.00	$ 65.00

Park Row B&B	525 W Park Row 56082	**Saint Peter MN**
Ann Burckhardt		**Tel: 507-931-2495**

Innkeeper Ann Burckhardt is a newspaper food columnist who enjoys cooking so much that she bought a big yellow Victorian and started an inn just so she'd have folks to cook for! Her B&B is the first one in St Peter, which was once slated to become the capital of Minnesota. A charming town with many lovely old homes, it is the county seat and site of Gustavus Adolphus College. Park Row's rooms boast queen size beds, individual down comforters and terry cloth robes. The rooms are color-coordinated in cranberry red, wedgewood blue and creamy white. The English room, downstairs, has a day-bed to accommodate a third person. ($10 extra). The help-yourself cookie jar, always full of homemade chocolate chip cookies, is in the parlor. Breakfasts feature a blended juice (served in wine glasses), an egg casserole, hot bread and fruit dessert. Guests, writing in the guest room diaries, comment favorably on the warm hospitality, the pretty decor and the excellent food. Good restaurants in all price ranges are nearby. Friendly conversation, good reading (books, magazines and cookbooks) and old-fashioned relaxation are encouraged here. **Airport:** Minneapolis World Chamberlain Intl-60 mi **Seasonal:** No **Reservations:** $30 advance deposit to hold reservation. **Brochure:** Yes **Permitted:** Children, drinking **Payment Terms:** Check/DC [R12DP-MN-13744] **COM Y ITC Member:** No

Rates:		**Shared Bath 3**
Single		$ 40.00
Double		$ 65.00

©*Inn & Travel Memphis, Tennessee*

Palmer House Hotel	500 Sinclair Lewis Ave 56378	**Sauk Centre MN**
Al Tingley		**Tel:** 612-352-3431

Full service resort guest house and locale for Sinclair Lewis' "Main Street" setting in his novel. Full service dining on the premises. **Seasonal:** No **Brochure:** Yes **Permitted:** Children, smoking, drinking, pets **Languages:** German **Payment Terms:** Check [X11-ACMN-2102] **COM** Y **ITC Member:** No

Rates:	**Pvt Bath 4**	**Shared Bath 30**
Single		$ 34.00
Double		$ 45.00

James A Mulvey Residence Inn	622 W Churchill St 55082	**Stillwater MN**
Truett & Jill Lawson		**Tel:** 612-430-8008
		Res Times 8am-10pm

The *James Mulvey B&B* is located on 1-1/2 acres in the charming Victorian river town of Stillwater. The home was built in 1878 by James Mulvey, one of the town's prosperous lumbermen, when he returned home from the Civil War. The Lawsons, your innkeepers, are avid antique and art collectors and have filled their home with exquisite treasures. A crackling fire always burns in the grand parlour in the fall and winter months, in the magnificent Grueby Art tile fireplace. The fireplace is one of only two known in Minnesota, made by the Grueby Tile Company of Boston. Fabulously expensive in its day with a frieze of landscape tiles called "The Pines", it is truly a jewel. Breakfast is served in the summer months on the Victorian sunporch and in the formal arts and crafts dining room in cooler weather. A four-course gourmet breakfast is always finished-off with chocolate covered strawberries. Guests are welcomed by the smell of warm chocolate chip cookies and can choose from five stunning guest rooms, all furnished with private baths and featuring whirlpools, fireplaces and his and her clawfoot tubs. **Airport:** Minneapolis Intl-30 mi **Discounts:** Midweek discount $20.00 **Reservations:** Full payment to guarantee reservation, 7 day cancel policy for gift certificate, less than 7 days, gift certificate only if room is re-rented, handicap accessible rooms **Brochure:** Yes **Permitted:** Limited drinking **Payment Terms:** Check MC/V [I08GPMN-16327] **COM** U **ITC Member:** No

Rates:	**Pvt Bath 5**
Single	$ 85-129.00
Double	$ 95-139.00

Lowell Inn	102 N Second St 55082	**Stillwater MN**
The Palmer Family		**Tel:** 612-439-1100 **Fax:** 612-439-4686
		Res Times 8am-10pm

"An Inn for all seasons and occasions ... "The Lowell Inn is, indeed, one of those places - more than a red brick retreat with majestic collonnades, she is more than what history-filled Stillwater offers it daily visitors - and more than what the St Croix River Valley offers with the most glorious autumn-hued days. The *Lowell Inn* has become a national hallmark of family innkeeping representing all that is best of our American ways by welcoming and caring for others - a tradition the Palmer Family still continues today. A tribute to her loving founders, Arthur and Nelle Palmer - she is truly a place for romance. When those special times beckon us to go beyond wishful thinking for unforgettable weddings, anniversaries, birthdays and inexplicable spur-of-the-moment excursions of which dreams are made - the *Lowell Inn* will fulfill your wishes. Each of the lovely guest rooms and suites comfort the overnight sojourner - each a reflection of the intimate tastes of Nelle - French Provincial all softly blended to create a bit of fantasy for you. At the *Lowell Inn*, dining becomes a

Minnesota - Missouri   *National Edition*

culinary affair. In the George Washington Room - time stands still! For the insatiable romantic, The Garden Room, with its bubbling springs forming an indoor trout pool, provides a most natural setting while the Matterhorn Room invokes good spirits and inspires carefree camaraderie. *Holiday Award for 29 years, Ivy Award (Restaurant Hall of Fame).* **Discounts:** Corporate weekday **Airport:** Minneapolis-St Paul-45 min **Packages:** American Plan, High Season $219-289, double occupancy **Seasonal:** Rates vary **Reservations:** Full payment within 5 days of booking; refund only if room is rebooked, weekday and off-season rates lower, MAP available **Brochure:** Yes **Permitted:** Smoking, drinking **Payment Terms:** MC/V [K05FPMN-2106] **COM** Y **ITC Member:** No

Rates: **Pvt Bath 21**
Single $ 119-189.00
Double $ 119-189.00

Down Over Holdings   602 Main St 65320   **Arrow Rock MO**
John & Joyce Vinson   **Tel:** 816-837-3268

Historic town setting for this country residence, full of charm and hospitality for all guests, especially the young at heart and age. Tom Sawyer country includes free movie made on location in town. Continental breakfast included. Complimentary childrens' toys and bike built-for-two. **Seasonal:** 4/15-12/15 **Permitted:** Children, smoking, limited drinking

Payment Terms: Check [X11ACMO-2164] **COM** Y **ITC Member:** No

Rates: **Pvt Bath 2**
Single $ 55.00
Double $ 65.00

Brass Swan   202 River Bend Rd 65616   **Branson MO**
Dick & Gigi House   **Tel:** 800-280-6873 417-334-6873
                                                                            Res Times 8am-10pm

This elegant contemporary home offers every comfort and convenience you expect of a fine bed and breakfast. Your stay with us will be a delightful one (prepare to be pampered) and a long-remembered experience. We are in a beautiful setting.... wooded tranquility that complements the beauty of Lake Taneycomo - yes there is a view! So near yet so far! Away from the hustle and bustle for relaxation, guests are just minutes to all of the exciting music shows, shopping and fine restaurants on Branson's famous Seventy Six Country Boulevard! The spacious guest rooms offer sitting areas, remote control TV, radio and private bath. You'll relax in the privacy of the mirrored hot tub with its romantic mood lighting - or in the outdoor hot tub against the background of majestic shade trees. On cool evenings, nestle up to either fireplace while sipping hot apple cider. Make use of the wet bar, refrigerator and microwave with complimentary beverages and popcorn. An extravagant "family-style full breakfast" includes fresh fruit, juices and assorted homemade breads. We are open all year, and especially for the Ozark Mountain Christmas ... the most colorful Christmas celebration in Mid-America. But come any season and join us ... your hosts who care. We really do! **Airport:** Springfield-40 mi **Seasonal:** No **Reservations:** Deposit required, 14 day cancel policy for refund less 10%, less than 14 day notice, refund less 20% only if rebooked **Brochure:** Yes **Permitted:** Children 12-up, drinking, smoking outdoors only **Payment Terms:** Check DC/MC/V [I11FPMO-17915] **COM** Y **ITC Member:** No

Rates: **Pvt Bath 4**
Single $ 65-75.00
Double $ 70-80.00

Fifth Street Mansion   213 S Fifth St 63401   **Hannibal MO**
Mike & Donalene Andreotti   **Tel:** 800-874-5661 314-221-0445 **Fax:** 314-221-3335
                                                                                            Res Times 7am-10pm

National Edition   **Missouri**

Italianate style brick mansion listed on *National Register of Historic Places* with gracious interior period furnishings and paneled library. Walking distance to historic district in Mark Twain's hometown. **Seasonal:** 4/1-12/1 **Brochure:** Yes **Permitted:** Children, smoking, drinking **Payment Terms:** Check [X-11AXMO-2175] **COM** Y **ITC Member:** No

Rates:	Pvt Bath 2	Shared Bath 5
Single	$ 55.00	$ 45.00
Double	$ 65.00	$ 55.00

Basswood Country Inn   Kansas City MO
Don & Betty Soper   **Tel:** 816-431-5556
                               Res Times 6:30am-10pm

Refer to the same listing name under Platte City, Missouri for complete description. **Seasonal:** No **Payment Terms:** Check DISC/MC/V [M08BPMO-6567] **COM** YG **ITC Member:** No

Rates:	Pvt Bath 8
Single	$ 58-125.00
Double	$ 63-125.00

Doanleigh Wallagh Inn   217 E 37th St 64111   Kansas City MO
Terry Maturo/Cynthia Brogdon   **Tel:** 816-753-2667 **Fax:** 816-531-5185
                                     Res Times 24 Hrs

Enjoy the elegance of Kansas City's first bed and breakfast! This 1907 mansion is located in the heart of the city, between the famed Country Club Plaza and Hallmark Crown Center. Lovely European and American antiques enhance the Georgian architecture of the Inn. Each spacious guest room is beautifully furnished and offer such amenities as private bath, telephone and cable television. Some rooms also feature Jacuzzi tubs, fireplaces and balconies! A delicious full, gourmet breakfast awaits you each morning. Our Butler's pantry is always stocked with sodas, juices and snack foods. Evenings greet you with wine and tempting hors d'oeuvres! Whether traveling for leisure or business, *Doanleigh Wallagh Inn* will provide casual elegance while attending to all of your needs away from home. Pamper yourself during your stay as you curl up in our luxurious robes. Enjoy breakfast in bed! Enjoy a video from our library, or relax by the fireplace. The Inn offers free local phone and faxes as well as computer modem access in all rooms. Wake up calls with early morning coffee and newspaper service are also available. Your hosts at *Doanleigh Wallagh Inn* are known for their careful attention to detail and service. Come - enjoy the elegance and luxury of this 1907 Mansion. **Airport:** KCI-20-30 mins **Discounts:** AARP, AAA, Corporate **Packages:** Romance, includes roses, champagne and chocolates **Reservations:** One nights deposit or credit card number to guarantee, 7 day cancel notice **Brochure:** Yes **Permitted:** Limited children, drinking **Conference:** Business meetings to twenty persons, receptions to 125 **Payment Terms:** Check AE/DISC/MC/V [I05IPMO1-2183] **COM** YG **ITC Member:** No

Rates:	Pvt Bath 5
Single	$ 81-121.00
Double	$ 90-135.00

Southmoreland On The Plaza   116 E 46th St 64112   Kansas City MO
Susan Moehl/Penni Johnson   **Tel:** 816-531-7979 **Fax:** 816-531-2407
                                   Res Times 7am-10pm

This comfortable, 1913 New England Colonial is located in the heart of Kansas City's cultural, shopping, entertainment and emerging financial district. Just 1-1/2 blocks from the renowned Country Club

©*Inn & Travel Memphis, Tennessee*

Missouri *National Edition*

Plaza and Nelson-Atkins Museum of Art, Southmoreland is particularly suited to both the business and leisure traveler. Twelve unique guestrooms with either a private deck, fireplace, or double jacuzzi bath and telephone service. Amenities include: Complimentary wine and cheese reception at check-in; sherry, fresh flowers and fruit in the rooms, down comforters; fax and modem connections, copier; a/c, antique furnishings, common areas with fireplaces, TV, VCR and classic film library; expanded meeting, parking, sports and fine dining facilities are nearby at a historic, private club. *Only Mobil 4-Star Inn in twenty state region*, Awarded Gem of the Midwest Award by Association of Midwest Travel Writers; "Four Crown" Winner - ABBA. **Airport:** Kansas City-45 mins **Seasonal:** Rates vary **Reservations:** 50% deposit at res time guaranteed with credit card, 5 day cancel notice for refund less $20 service charge, late arrival by prior arrangement T/A commissions only for leisure guests **Brochure:** Yes **Permitted:** Drinking, limited children (13-up), non-smoking Inn **Conference:** Yes, special accommodations for day-long and overnight corporate retreats. **Payment Terms:** Check AE/MC/V [Z08H-PMO1-9612] **COM Y ITC Member:** No

Rates: Pvt Bath 12
Single $ 90-135.00
Double $ 100-145.00

Basswood Country Inn   15880 Interurban Rd 64079   Platte City MO
Don & Betty Soper   Tel: 816-431-5556 Fax: 816-431-5556
Res Times 6:30am-10pm

A former millionaire's estate, *Basswood* is the single most beautiful, secluded, wooded, private lakefront accommodation in the entire Kansas City area. Only ten minutes to the door of KCI Airport. Located three miles north of Hwy 92, halfway between I-29 and #169. The bed and breakfast is in a private home. It consists of the original 1935, two bedroom cottage that sits lakeside, with a woodburning fireplace and has been totally restored. Four Country French King Suites that include a sitting room, king bed, dining area, mini-kitchen and own deck. The Celebrity (triplex) house consists of 1550 square feet, The Truman Suite (with two jacuzzis) and the Rudy Vallee and the Bing Crosby Suites. Meeting rooms. Spring-fed and stocked fishing lakes, bring your own pole, small fee, no license required. Plenty of nature trails and an outdoor pool are on the property. AAA 3 Diamond Rated **Seasonal:** No **Reservations:** Deposit at res time, 72-hr cancellation policy for refund **Brochure:** Yes **Permitted:** Children, drinking, smoking **Payment Terms:** Check DISC/MC/V [Z08GPMO-2192] **COM Y ITC Member:** No

Rates: Pvt Bath 8
Single $ 58-125.00
Double $ 63-125.00

Camerons Crag B&B   PO Box 526 65726   Point Lookout MO
Kay & Glenn Cameron   Tel: 800-933-8529 417-335-8134 Fax: 417-335-8134

Cameron's Craig - A special Bed & Breakfast in a contemporary home perched high on a bluff overlooking Lake Taneycomo! Located just three miles from Branson, Missouri! Hosts Kay and Glen Cameron have three separate guest areas featuring spectacular scenery, hearty breakfasts, delightful accommodations with easy access to all area attractions. Each suite has a private entrance, private bath (tub and shower), king bed, TV/VCR/Video Library and bedroom and sitting area combo and its own Hot Tub. You can see the lake and valley from each guest suite and from each Hot Tub. Around The World has a private hot tub on a private outdoor deck. The Highland Rose Suite has an indoor hot tub in its own room with a wall of windows on all sides. Bird's-Eye View Suite is a private spacious suite in our unique, detached guest house with spectacular "Bird's-Eye View" from suite and private deck with a new Hot Tub! The fully equipped suite has sitting area, dining area, full-sized kitchen, private bath with shower and deluxe whirlpool tub for two! Each suite accommodates two persons. **Discounts:** Jan-March after third night and groups **Packages:** Special occasions-inquire at reservation time **Seasonal:** No **Reservations:** 50% deposit of total for length of stay required to guarantee reservation, 7 day cancel policy for refund less

2-56   ©*Inn & Travel Memphis, Tennessee*

National Edition   **Missouri**

10% service fee **Brochure:** Yes **Permitted:** Children 6+ **Payment Terms:** Check AE/DISC/MC/V [I08HP-MO1-21641] **COM YG ITC Member:** No

Rates: Pvt Bath 3
Single $ 70-90.00
Double $ 75-95.00

Clydes Pleasant Acres	PO Box 304 65559	**Saint James MO**
Clyde Brennan		Tel: 800-916-2345 573-646-3276
		Res Times 24 Hrs

Enjoy country ambiance and a touch of southern hospitality in this modern farmhouse overlooking 200 acres of nature's splendor. You'll have a magnificent view of thousands of trees that fill the countryside - majestic oaks, hickories, maples and many other species. Wander about the farm at you leisure. Travel over a pasture where the beef cattle are lazily grazing. Nearby you can observe the Bourbeuse River as it encounters a rock cliff and abruptly changes course from east to north. Explore the great outdoors on foot or by recreational vehicles. This gracious home has four bedrooms with private bath or showers and is beautifully decorated for the holidays of Christmas and Thanksgiving, Halloween and Easter. The farmhouse is air conditioned in summer and has fireplaces for use in winter (guest's option). Amenities include an outdoor hot tub year-round and a swimming pool (seasonal). In the great room, guests can enjoy their favorite music or check in on the lower level for sports' games. Early risers may catch a glimpse of the white tail deer grazing in the fields or wild turkeys scrambling for their breakfast. Adding to the delight of the picturesque surroundings are the sight and sounds of some native inhabitants - redbirds, bluebirds and wrens. Fresh, crisp morning air, soft river breezes, blue skies, wide open spaces, starlit nights, spectacular views from sunrise to sunset await guests! The farm is twelve miles from St James, a quaint retirement community serving as an entrance to the Ozark Mountains. Mark Twain National Park is only 15 miles away. Ten miles west of St James is the city of Rolla, with it University of Missouri campus and just down the road from the farm is Redbird, a tiny village proud of its large population of red Cardinals. A full country breakfast is included, other meals are available with prior arrangements and added cost. **Discounts:** 20% second night **Airport:** St Louis Lambert-100 mi; Rolla (Vichy)-25 mi **Packages:** Total house $350.00/night **Seasonal:** No **Reservations:** Inquire at reservation time **Brochure:** Yes **Permitted:** Children, drinking **Conference:** Yes, small groups **Payment Terms:** DISC/MC/V [I11HP-MO1-22622] **COM YG ITC Member:** No

Rates: Pvt Bath 4
Single $ 110.00
Double $ 125.00

Lafayette House	2156 Lafayette Ave 63104	**Saint Louis MO**
Bill, Nancy, Annalise		Tel: 800-641-8965 314-772-4429 **Fax:** 314-664-2156
		Res Times 8am-10pm

An 1876 historically significant brick Queen Anne residence *"In the Center of Things To Do in St Louis!"* Convenient to central St Louis and overlooking Lafayette Park. Tastefully furnished with antiques but including modern amenities: air conditioning, TV, VCR, extensive library and numerous owner/host collectibles to enjoy during your stay. Children welcomed with crib, high chair and play pen already here! Airport, bus, train pick-ups arranged for nominal extra charge. Owners' cats make it necessary to check if you want to bring pets. Complimentary soft drinks, wine, cheese and crackers included. Learn all about St Louis from these native hosts. Hearty full breakfast **Seasonal:** No **Reservations:** 20% deposit at res time, 7-day cancellation notice, refund less $10.00 charge. Check-in 4-10pm, other by prior arrangement *Suite is $65.00. **Brochure:** Yes **Permitted:** Children, drinking **Payment Terms:** Check [A11CPMO-2198] **COM Y ITC Member:** No

Rates: Pvt Bath 2   Shared Bath 3
Single $ 55.00 $ 50.00*
Double $ 65.00 $ 55.00

©*Inn & Travel Memphis, Tennessee*

Missouri   *National Edition*

Preston Place   1835 Lafayette Ave 63104   **Saint Louis MO**
Jenny Preston   **Tel:** 314-664-3429   **Fax:** 314-664-6929

This city oasis offers urban convenience with historical ambience. Victorian parlours are decorated in rich Moroccan colors while the bedrooms soothe with comfortable pastels. Each uncluttered guest room has a double bed and private bath with large shower. One includes a clawfoot tub and a selection of bubble baths. In-room TV is available upon request. Breakfasts can be traditional or heart-healthy, according to guest preference, and are served in a walnut and fir wainscotted dining area. Located in a National Historic District, this 1886 townhouse has been restored over the past twenty years by the owner. Old house buffs will love the restoration stories and the "before" pictures. Half a block away is Lafayette Park, predating the Civil War and completely surrounded by the original wrought iron fence. Its shaded paths and lagoons invite strollers and joggers. Preston Place is a 5-10 minute drive from any downtown or Clayton business, the Convention Center, or the sports' stadiums, with very easy access to four interstate highways. Business women find it especially amenable since phone and fax are available as well as ironing board and iron, steamer, hair dryer, curling iron and even a extra pair of stockings for emergencies. Off-street parking adds to the secure feeling of being at home while away from home. A full breakfast is included. **Airport:** Lambert St Louis Intl-20 mins **Seasonal:** No **Reservations:** One night's rate required, 5 day cancel policy for refund **Brochure:** Yes **Permitted:** Limited drinking, outdoor smoking only, no facilities for pets or children **Languages:** French **Payment Terms:** Check AE/DC/MC/V [I10-HPMO1-22331] COM YG **ITC Member:** No

A bed and breakfast establishment

Rates:	Pvt Bath 2
Single	$ 60.00
Double	$ 70.00

Winter House   3522 Arsenal 63118   **Saint Louis MO**
Sarah & Kendall Winter   **Tel:** 314-664-4399

Built in 1897, just prior to the St Louis World's Fair, this ten room Victorian home offers guests a taste of the past. All of the touches are here including pressed tin ceilings, a first floor dining room including a turret where a continental plus breakfast is served each morning. The Carrie Kimbrell room has a beautiful pineapple poster double bed including a crocheted bedspread and it has a large private bath adjoining. The Alma Culp Suite, on the second floor, offers a queen size bed and a 1904 sofa to accommodate two more. The room features the original coal burning fireplace (now decorative only), a wood print wall border, balcony and a private bath. A complimentary breakfast plus includes fresh squeezed orange juice, hot breads and muffins, fresh fruits, gourmet coffee and tea, jams, marmalades and grits too! Complimentary tea and beverages upon arrival and live piano with breakfast. The *Winter House* offers tea with live piano music with advance notice - featuring Mozart selections. There's plenty to see within walking distance, including Tower Grove Park with lighted tennis courts and fitness trails. The Missouri Botanical Garden. Anheuser-Busch Brewery, Busch Stadium, Gateway Arch and Museum, Union Station, Fox Theatre, Muny Opera, St Louis Symphony, Forest Park, the zoo, art museum are in the area. **Airport:** Lambert-18 mi **Discounts:** 10% after 2nd night **Reservations:** 50% deposit to guarantee reservation, 7 day cancel policy for refund **Brochure:** Yes **Permitted:** Children, limited drinking **Payment Terms:** Check AE/DC/MC/V [Z04GPMO-11100] COM Y ITC **Member:** No **Quality Assurance:** Requested

Rates:	Pvt Bath 3
Single	$ 60.00
Double	$ 65-80.00

Inn St Gemme Beauvais   78 N Main St 63670   **Sainte Genevieve MO**
Frankie & NB Donze   **Tel:** 314-883-5744

National Edition　　　　　　　　　　　　　　　　　　　　　　　　　　*Missouri - Nebraska - New Jersey*

Quaint Victorian Inn in historic French settlement just an hour outside of St. Louis. Full country breakfast included. Luncheon available upon request. **Seasonal:** No **Brochure:** Yes **Permitted:** Children, smoking, drinking **Payment Terms:** Check MC

[X11ACMO-2193] **COM** Y **ITC Member:** No

Rates:　**Pvt Bath 8**
Single　$ 58.00
Double　$ 66.00

Fort Robinson Inn　　　　　　Box 392 69339　　　　　　Crawford NE
　　　　　　　　　　　　　　　　　　　　　　　　　　　Tel: 308-665-2660

Former cavalry headquarters setting offers guests the chance to step back in history while relaxing in a pleasant setting. Gracious hosts see to all your needs. Cafeteria dining. Swimming, tennis, sightseeing, and camp bikes. **Seasonal:** Mem Day-Lab Day **Brochure:** Yes **Permitted:** Children, smoking, limited pets, drinking **Payment Terms:** Check MC/V [X11ACNE-2230] **COM** Y **ITC Member:** No

Rates:　**Pvt Bath 23**
Single　$ 55.00
Double　$ 64.00

Avon Manor Inn　　　　　　109 Sylvania Ave 07717　　　　　　Avon By The Sea NJ
Jim & Kathleen Curley　　　　　　　　　　　　　　　　　　　Tel: 908-774-0110
　　　　　　　　　　　　　　　　　　　　　　　　　　Res Times 9am-9pm

The *Avon Manor Inn*, circa 1907 was built in the Colonial Revival-style as a private summer residence. In 1948, it was converted to a full service Inn. As you pass through the Columned Portico, you'll begin to experience the serenity and the romance of a bygone era. Escape from your daily pressures to relax, unwind and enjoy a visit. A friendly and informal atmosphere will embrace you. Our parlor has a fireplace for cozy winter nights, a small library, antiques and some personal mementos. Enjoy a quiet time or socialize with other guests - the choice is yours. If the romantic style of years past appeals to you, then the *Avon Manor Inn* will be your special seaside getaway. Each of the eight bed chambers have been designed and furnished for your comfort and relaxation with antiques, period pieces, wicker and air conditioning. The aroma of the *Avon Manor's* special coffee blend gently awakens you from a seaside rest while a complimentary hearty breakfast (continental weekdays/full weekends) served in the sunny dining room is being prepared. The *"best kept secret of the Jersey Shore."* An all-season retreat offering summer fun with water activities, thoroughbred racing fun Great Adventure Park, antiques, wineries, Revolutionary Allaire Village - the Battle Site of Monmouth or Washington's Crossing. Whether arriving for a vacation or a corporate functions - you'll leave refreshed and renewed. We look forward to welcoming you to the *Avon Manor Inn* very soon. **Discounts:** Corporate, AARP, Travel agents **Airport:** Newark-45 min **Packages:** Midweek Specials, inquire at res time **Seasonal:** No **Reservations:** 50% deposit, full payment upon check-in, 14 day cancel policy for refund less $15 service fee. **Brochure:** Yes **Permitted:** Limited children, limited drinking **Conference:** Groups to twelve persons **Payment Terms:** Check AE/MC/V [I07FP-NJ-16437] **COM** Y **ITC Member:** No

Rates:　**Pvt Bath 6**　　**Shared Bath 2**
Single　$ 95.00　　　$ 70.00
Double　$ 112.00　　$ 80.00

Grenville Hotel & Restaurant　　　345 Main Ave 08742　　　　　Bay Head NJ
Joseph P Milza　　　　　　　　　　　　　　　　　　　　　　Tel: 908-892-3100
　　　　　　　　　　　　　　　　　　　　　　　　　　Res Times 24 Hrs

Escape to this striking Victorian Inn, built in the 1880's in the quaint town of Bay Head on the Jersey Shore, approx 65 miles south of New York City. Completely restored and renovated to a superb

©*Inn & Travel Memphis, Tennessee*

hotel which boasts of rich comfortable furnishings and excellent cuisine. The thirty-one rooms and two suites, accessible by elevator, offer choices which include balconies, gabled ceilings, authentic French antiques with all including TV, phone and private baths. A large entryway off the main lobby opens into a charming and elegant Victorian restaurant for gourmet dining. The seasonal menu offers creative American cuisine. Luncheon and dinner are available, with a continental breakfast included with your room. Just a block from the ocean and the sandy beaches, activities include all the water sports, bay fishing and boating. Shopping and antiquing make the Grenville Hotel and Restaurant a perfect spot for a memorable vacation or getway. Experience real luxury - often dreamt of but seldom found while reliving the exciting Victorian Era. **Packages:** Yes, Winter and Holidays, inquire at res time **Seasonal:** No **Reservations:** Deposit required; rates are seasonal **Brochure:** Yes **Permitted:** Children, drinking, smoking **Conference:** Yes for social, business, weddings to 100 persons **Payment Terms:** Check AE/DC/MC/V [Z04HPNJ1-7626] **COM** Y **ITC Member:** No

Rates:	Pvt Bath 33
Single	$ 57-209.00
Double	$ 57-209.00

Chalfonte Hotel 301 Howard St 08204 Cape May NJ
Ann LeDuc & Judy Bartella Tel: 609-884-8409 Fax: 609-884-4588
Res Times 8am-8pm

Built in 1876, and wrapped in verandas and gingerbread trimmings, the *Chalfonte* is a landmark among the six hundred buildings in Victorian Cape May. A rare retreat which many guests consider a second home, the *Chalfonte* offers simply appointed accommodations with ceiling fans, marble-topped dressers and original Victoriana. Children are most welcome guests of the hotel. The *Chalfonte* offers a separate supervised children's dining room for children ages six and under, and special childrens programs each July. Educational programs, exhibits, workshops and concerts are offered throughout the summer. Renowned for the southern fare prepared by the Dickerson Family, the *Chalfonte* Kitchen is headed by sisters Dorothy Burton and Lucille Thompson. Daughters of the late Helen Dickerson, Dot and Lucille are long-time *Chalfonte* Chefs who continue their mother's traditions of down-home southern cooking. Guests are invited to sample Southern Specialties including spoonbread, corn pudding, biscuits, homemade rolls, fried chicken and crab cakes. The *Chalfonte* enjoys a rich Southern tradition. Although built by a Northern hero of the war between the states, the *Chalfonte* was operated by the Satterfield Family of Virginia until 1972. At that time, a long time family friend, Anne LeDuc, and her fellow school teacher, Judy Bartella, began managing the property. Committed to preserving the architectural beauty, traditions and quirky charm of the *Chalfonte*, the pair describe their work as a "labor of love". Located in the heart of the historic district, the *Chalfonte* offers easy access to beaches, shoppes, tennis courts, horseback riding, golf, state parks and bird sanctuaries. **Discounts:** Yes, inquire at res time **Airport:** Atlantic City Intl-45 mi **Packages:** Variety of workshops, including Swedish Massage, Water Color, Country Cooking, Vintage Dance, Tea and Tour and Luncheons **Seasonal:** Opn 5/1-10/30 **Reservations:** One night's deposit; 2 night min weekends; 2 week cancellation policy for refund, less $15 fee, *MAP rates include breakfast and dinner **Brochure:** Yes **Permitted:** Children, drinking **Conference:** Yes, to 80 persons; wedding receptions/-dinners **Languages:** German **Payment Terms:** Check MC/V [I04HPNJ1-3891] **COM** YG **ITC Member:** No

Rates:	Pvt Bath 11	Shared Bath 66
Single	$ 129-140.00	$ 61-90.00
Double	$ 154-165.00	$ 81-152.00

Colvmns By The Sea 1513 Beach Dr 08204 Cape May NJ
Bernadette Brennan Kaschner Tel: 800-691-6030 609-884-2228 Fax: 609-884-4789
Res Times 8am-10pm

Fall asleep to the sounds of the surf and awake to a breathtaking view of the Atlantic. A turn-of-the-century oceanfront mansion accented by fluted columns, antique furnishings and Chinese ivory carvings - all of this balanced with modern comfort and informality. There are twelve foot ceilings and hand carved woodwork throughout. The *Colvmns* is away from the bustle of the town offering guests a place to relax, savor the pleasures of a long gone lifestyle and best of all, to sit on a rocker and watch crystals of ocean water dance as waves crash against a sea wall. A gourmet sit-down breakfast is included with afternoon refreshments and special treats. Complimentary bikes, beach towels, beach badges, a relaxful hot tub and off-street parking are provided. **Packages:** Off-Season Discounts and Christmas Gift. Certificates **Discounts:** AAA, AARP **Airport:** Atlantic City-40mi **Seasonal:** No **Reservations:** Deposit required to guarantee reservation, check-in 2pm-10pm, check out 11am **Brochure:** Yes **Permitted:** Drinking, children 10-up, limited smoking **Conference:** Seven meeting rooms and suites are perfect for business meetings, executive getaways and management seminars and other groups meetings. **Languages:** German **Payment Terms:** Check MC/V [I02HPNJ1-3892] **COM** YG **ITC Member:** No

Rates:	Pvt Bath 11
Single	$ 120-145.00
Double	$ 135-210.00

Leith Hall Historic Seashore Inn   22 Ocean St   08204   Cape May NJ
Susan & Elan Zingman-Leith

Tel: 609-884-1934
Res Times 9am-9pm

Visit our elegantly restored 1890's home in the heart of the Victorian Historic District. We offer ocean views, antiques, private baths, complimentary beach towels and chairs, full gourmet breakfasts and afternoon English teas. Only one half block from the beach and two blocks from the Mall. Described by *Inn Spots* as *"... working miracles with wallpaper and paint."* Described in *"Fromers Atlantic City"* and *"Cape May"* guide as *"... distinctive restoration ... stunning ... handsomely appointed."* *Leith Hall* sparkles with multi-patterned walls and shimmering gilded surfaces. Our opulent bedrooms are furnished with Victorian antiques including walnut or brass beds, hand carved mahogany tables, laces and linens, fringes and tassels. Our stained glass French doors open onto the shady verandahs. Amidst all this Victorial luxury, we haven't forgotten modern amenities. All of our rooms and suites feature private baths and several include refrigerators for cooling your beverages for the beach. Of course, one of our greatest amenities is the view of the ocean from every bedroom and from the verandah. Your hearty Victorian breakfast is served from antique silver, crystal and Royal Worcester china. The aroma of fresh brewing coffee and home-baked breads wakes you up while quiches, crepes, and egg entrees fortify you for the day. We offer beach chairs, towels and tags, if you're heading for the surf. We offer directions and advice if you're looking for antiques. Perhaps best of all, we offer a beautifully restored parlor and library and a very large wraparound porch if you're planning on doing absolutely nothing. There's a Victorian cabinet grand piano if you're feeling musical, hundreds of books if you're feeling literary, and extremely comfy chairs and ottomans if you're feeling like a nap. **Airport:** Atlantic City-45min, Philadelphia-1.5hrs **Discounts:** 10% weeks stay **Seasonal:** No **Reservations:** 50% deposit, two week cancel policy, 50% of deposit refunded in one week of reservation date **Brochure:** Yes **Permitted:** Limited children, drinking **Languages:** French, Yiddish **Payment Terms:** Check MC/V [J03HPNJ1-12608] **COM** U **ITC Member:** No

Rates: Pvt Bath 7   Suite 1   Single $ 75-135.00
                                          Double $ 85-145.00 $ 150.00

Mason Cottage	625 Columbia Ave 08204	Cape May NJ
Dave & Joan Mason		**Tel:** 800-716-2766 609-884-3358

This quaint National Historic Landmark City includes this charming 1871 former summer residence of a wealthy Philadelphia entrepreneur and remains the same today, with lofty ceilings, full-length windows and a sweeping veranda so characteristic of Victorian homes of the period. Much of the furnishings belonged to the original family and have been carefully restored. Your hosts purchased the home in the 1940's and have been welcoming guests to the "shore", since then. All guest rooms have a/c and private baths. You're just one block from the ocean and you'll be cooled by the summer breezes. Guests receive a full-breakfast buffet which may be enjoyed in the dining room or outdoors on the veranda. Guests are invited to use the hosts' beach passes and can park their bikes in a bike rack provided. Menus of many Cape May's favorite restaurants are available and your hosts will be glad to make reservations where appropriate. Experience the tree-shaded streets line with Victorian homes and shops of Cape May and the peace and solitude of another era. **Discounts:** Yes, 10% four nights or more; AARP 5% and mid-week **Airport:** Atlantic City Pomona-45 mi; Phila Intl-100 mi. Gift Certificates available **Seasonal:** 3/1-1/1 **Reservations:** 50% non-refundable deposit required, cancellations can be only rebooked; two night min weekends and three night min summer and holiday weekends *Suites available **Permitted:** Children 12-up, drinking, limited smoking (outdoors) **Payment Terms:** Check AE/MC/V [I08HPNJ1-6583] **COM YG ITC Member:** No

Rates:	**Pvt Bath 5**	**Shared Bath 4**
Single	$ 95-165.00	$ 145-265.00
Double	$ 95-165.00	$ 145-265.00

Jerica Hill B&B Inn	96 Broad St 08822	Flemington NJ
Judith Studer		**Tel:** 908-728-8234

Flemington's first bed and breakfast Inn offers a gracious character and a comfortable sense of well-being, joining its historic past to a friendly future. Off the beaten path, this turn-of-the-century Queen Anne-style Victorian home greet guests with warm country hospitality and a large measure of creature comforts. A graceful center hall staircase leads to bright, airy and spacious guestrooms. Canopy, brass and four poster beds, bay window, recesses, comfortable reading chairs, old-fashioned ceiling fans, flowers an greenery insure a restful and cheerful stay. Soft music, open fire, oriental rugs and deep wing chairs invite guests to unwind with a book from the well-stocked library or with the New York Times. Our lovely screened porch with white wicker and green plants beckons guests to enjoy a warm summer breeze, an evening aglow with fireflies or your morning breakfast. Mornings are heralded with a hint of freshly brewed coffee followed by a bountiful seasonal breakfast set out on the dining rooms' mahogany sideboard or served to you on the porch. We hope that sharing our enthusiasm for this area will make your stay at *Jerica Hill* very special. We're always happy to answer your questions or make suggestions about restaurants, shopping and the many wonderful activities in nearby New Hope, Lambertville, Peddler's Village and all of Hunterdon and Bucks counties. To make your stay more memorable, we offer two favorite pastimes - Hot Air Ballooning and Country Wine Tours. AAA 3-Diamond Rated. **Discounts:** Corporate, midweek periods, AARP (midweek only), AAA **Packages:** Hot Air Ballooning, Winery Tours **Reservations:** 50% deposit required, 10 day cancel policy for refund, 2 night min weekends and holidays **Permitted:** Children 12-up, drinking **Conference:** Small meetings and social events **Payment Terms:** Check AE/MC/V [R08GPNJ-3917] **COM Y ITC Member:** No

Rates: Pvt Bath 5
Single $ 70-105.00
Double $ 70-105.00

Hunterdon House	12 Bridge St 08825	Frenchtown NJ
Gene Refalvy		**Tel:** 800-382-0375 908-996-3632 **Fax:** 908-996-0942
		Res Times 10am-9pm

A distinctive Italianate-style true Victorian dating from 1864, the *Hunterdon House* will be an unforgettable experience. From the downstairs parlor where sherry is offered each evening, to the gracious dining room where a complimentary old-fashioned full breakfast is served, to the shaded sitting porch where time stands still, the Hunterdon House embraces its guests with the warmth of a bygone era. The lavish facade bespeak the luxury of time and craftsmanship now gone forever. Inside, rooms heavy with objects that delight the eye envelop us in comfort and testify to a gentler life. Period pieces, family memorabilia and antiques are everywhere - and guests are encouraged to explore the premises and wind their way up to the belvedere and tarry in private thought or conversation. Each guest room is uniquely furnished allowing guests to choose among a wrought iron bed, fireplaces, Italianate carved four poster canopy, Eastlake carved beds and sitting areas. Located in Frenchtown, half a block from the Delaware River, guests are in the *perfect "country getaway"*. Deep in the heart of antiquing territory - treasure-hunting is a pleasure. There's a wealth of local artists, craftsmen and specialty shops all along Bridge Street. Sports enthusiasts can enjoy fishing, boating, tubing, biking and hiking. Fine restaurants are plentiful - and an old-fashioned ride through the country shouldn't be missed. **Discounts:** Yes, inquire at res time **Airport:** Newark-1 hr; Philadelphia-1-1/2 hr **Packages:** Retreats, Business Conferences **Seasonal:** No **Reservations:** Check or one night's deposit required, 10 day cancel policy for refund, check-in 3-9pm unless other arrangements have been made **Brochure:** Yes **Permitted:** Limited drinking **Conference:** Large suite suitable for intimate meetings (6-7) and dining area (14-16) with group catering for lunch, evening dinner and breaks **Payment Terms:** Check AE/MC/V [Z05HPNJ1-3918] **COM** U **ITC Member:** No

Rates:	Pvt Bath 7
Single	$ 85-145.00
Double	$ 85-145.00

Serendipity B&B	712 Ninth St 08226-3554	Ocean City NJ
Clara & Bill Plowfield		**Tel:** 800-842-8544 609-399-1554

Serendipity is a beautifully renovated and immaculately maintained 1912 seashore Inn serving the finest of healthy and delicious natural foods. Nestled in the heart of Ocean City, one-half block from the beach and fun-filled boardwalk, Serendipity places you within easy walking distance of beaches, shopping, restaurants, theaters and the Music Pier. Each morning of your stay, *Serendipity's* complimentary breakfast of scrumptious, home-baked muffins, natural fruit juice, hot herbal teas and freshly brewed coffee awaits you in our cheerful dining room, where you can enjoy your breakfast and the morning paper in private or with other guests. A variety of selections are available from the daily breakfast menu, including multi-grain waffles, low-cholesterol omelettes, fresh fruit or carrot juice and lots more! Clara and Bill are first-rate natural cooks, and off-season will lovingly prepare your selections from the vegetarian dinner menu. *Serendipity's* six guest rooms are all air conditioned, comfortably furnished and tastefully decorated in wicker and seashore pastels. Relax on *Serendipity's* shade porch in the summertime or by the fireplace in the comfortable living room in the winter. Catch an incredible Ocean City sunrise, spend the day on the eight miles of clean, sandy beaches, enjoy a leisurely bike ride on a 2-1/2 miles boardwalk, or browse the unique shops along Asbury Avenue. You can plan a day trip an-tiquing or visiting nearby historical sites, and Atlantic Citys' shows and casinos are minutes away. Plan a very special Ocean City getaway or vacation - *Serendipity* style! **Discounts:** Off-season (Oct-May) **Meals:** Dinner available off-season **Airport:** Atlantic City-30 min **Packages:** Off-season, inquire at res time **Seasonal:** No **Reservations:** 50% deposit within 5 days, deposit refund only if room is rebooked less $10 service fee **Brochure:** Yes **Permitted:** Children 10+, drinking **Payment Terms:** Check DISC/MC/V [I03HPNJ1-21504] **COM** YG **ITC Member:** No

©Inn & Travel Memphis, Tennessee

New Jersey — National Edition

Rates:	Pvt Bath 2	Shared Bath 4
Single	$ 65-80.00	$ 48-65.00
Double	$ 65-80.00	$ 48-65.00

Cordova 26 Webb Ave 07756 Ocean Grove NJ
*Doris & Vlad Chernik
Tel: 908-774-3084 908-751-9577
Res Times 7am-10pm

The *Cordova* is a century-old four-story guest house located in a Victorian community of Old World Charm - just one block from the beach. The beautiful beach and boardwalk in this lovely community are designated as a Historic Landmark. Quiet and family-oriented, the *Cordova* was selected by *"New Jersey Magazine"* as *"... one of the seven best places to stay on the Jersey Shore"* and featured in *O'New Jersey* by Heidi Gilman. Many presidents (Wilson, Cleveland, Roosevelt) visited Ocean Grove and addressed audiences in the "Great Auditorium", the largest wooden structure in the USA, which seats 7000 persons. You're a family member here - - where you can enjoy reading, listening to music or watching TV in the living room - or make your special feast in the kitchen or the outdoor BBQ and with picnic tables in a private garden area or join us for Mystery Weekend in June or Halloween weekend. You're just 1-1/2 hours or less from Manhattan to the north, Philadelphia and Atlantic City to the south. Deluxe continental breakfast is included with your room and occasional BBQ, wine and cheese parties Saturdays and afternoon Sunday Tea. Two cottage apartments are available $525-650 per week. **Packages:** Seven day stays at the regular five day rate; 3 night special for weekdays! **Airport:** Newark-45 mins **Discounts:** Groups, Seniors **Seasonal:** Memorial thru September **Reservations:** 50% deposit at res time and advanced notice for late arrivals, winter season phone: 212-751-9577 **Brochure:** Yes **Permitted:** Children, drinking, limited smoking **Conference:** Small groups to twenty five **Payment Terms:** Check [I04HPNJ1-6051] **COM** YG **ITC Member:** No

Rates:	Pvt Bath 5	Shared Bath 11
Single	$ 70-85.00	$ 45-55.00
Double	$ 70-105.00	$ 50-65.00

Kenilworth 1505 Ocean Ave 07762 Spring Lake NJ
L Mason Mills & Ric Karr
Tel: 908-449-5327

Lovely oceanfront setting brings unobstructed spectacular views to all guests. Rock on the large front porch in this c1883 Victorian, reminiscent of a bygone period. Located in a conservative resort community, the ocean lets you escape and enjoy the serenity and peaceful ambience while close to all conveniences. There's nothing nicer than enjoying a "second home" at the shore! Full kitchen privileges allow you to make your meals when you please or even barbecue on the side lawn. Invite your friends to meet you on the beach or just relax on the porch overlooking the ocean. Abundant breakfast buffet is included and a complimentary afternoon beverage. Relax! Enjoy a restful visit shielded from those demanding phone calls. Sun and surf at the uncrowded beach. Walk or run the 2 mile boardwalk. **Seasonal:** No **Reservations:** 50% deposit for weekday stays, full payment in advance for weekends. **Brochure:** Yes **Permitted:** Children, smoking, drinking **Conference:** Yes, with or without dining. **Payment Terms:** Check MC/V [A09ACNJ-3944] **COM** Y **ITC Member:** No

Rates:	Pvt Bath 14	Shared Bath 9
Single	$ 80-100.00	$ 50-60.00
Double	$ 80-100.00	$ 55-65.00

Normandy Inn 21 Tuttle Ave 07762 Spring Lake NJ
Michael & Susan Ingnio
Tel: 800-449-1888 908-449-7172 **Fax:** 908-449-1070
Res Times 8:30am-10:30pm

The *Normandy Inn* was built as a summer rental home for the Audenreid family of Philadelphia and has recently been placed on the *National Register of Historic Places* by the US Department of the Interior. This Italianate villa with Queen Anne modifications currently has two suites which boast fireplace and fifteen guest rooms. Its present owner, Michael and Susan Ingino have undertaken an extensive and authentic restoration of both the interior and exterior. The prized furnishings of all guest rooms and common areas are original American Victorian antiques and are accented with reproduction Victorian wallpapers. Located just five houses from the beach, the *Normandy Inn* offers the experience of a true Victorian seaside resort. The full country breakfast fortifies the guest for the coming days' activities such as swimming, golf, tennis or exploring the picturesque town of Spring Lake on one of the Inn's bicycles. The *Normandy Inn* is also the perfect location for your next business seminar or corporate meeting. Full catering is available or dine in one of the areas many restaurants. Please contact Anne Marie for more information. **Discounts:** Yes, corporate, extended stays **Airport:** Newark Intl- 51 miles **Packages:** Inquire at reservation time **Seasonal:** No **Reservations:** Deposit upon reservation (50% of stay), 10 day cancel policy, late arrival (after 10:30pm) only with prior arrangement **Brochure:** Yes **Permitted:** Children, limited smoking, limited drinking **Conference:** Yes, two adequate meeting rooms for small seminar/meeting to thirty persons **Payment Terms:** Check AE/DC/DISC/MC/V [I05HPNJ1-3943] **COM** YG **ITC Member:** No

Rates: Pvt Bath 17
Single $ 74-252.00
Double $ 90-263.00

Sea Crest By The Sea	19 Tuttle Ave 07762	Spring Lake NJ
John & Carol Kirby		Tel: 908-449-9031
		Res Times 9am-9pm

A lovingly restored 1885 Victorian specializes in pampering guests seeking relaxation, romance or a special fantasy, while convenient to both New York City and Philadelphia. This luxurious Bed & Breakfast by the sea offers guests friendly, yet unobtrusive, warmth and hospitality. Guests are greeted with the soft strains of classical music, fresh flowers in their room, a collection of English and French antique furnishings and treasured family heirloom pieces. Each guest room offers a different fantasy - choose from The Victorian Rose, The Pussy Willow, The Washington or The Casablanca and be lulled asleep by the gentle surf while you snuggle in billowy starched linens of Egyptian cotton and Belgian lace. (Seven rooms also offer fireplaces). For diversion, the ocean and beach are just a half-block away and there's a stable of bikes for riding. A library with books and games and the porch are convenient places for developing new friendships during your stay. A full breakfast begins a 9am with freshly baked scones and muffins, fruit and Sea Crest granola, all served on family china, silver and crystal. Enjoy this year-round retreat - where Fall and Winter evenings are warmed by the fireplace with hot mulled cider and interesting conversation - or by memories of ocean walks shared only with the remaining gulls. **Seasonal:** Rates vary **Reservations:** 50% deposit of full amount is required at res time, with refund only if room is re-rented, full payment upon arrival, check-in 2pm check-out 11am **Brochure:** Yes **Permitted:** Drinking, limited smoking **Payment Terms:** Check AE/MC/V [I02HPNJ1-3946] **COM** U **ITC Member:** No

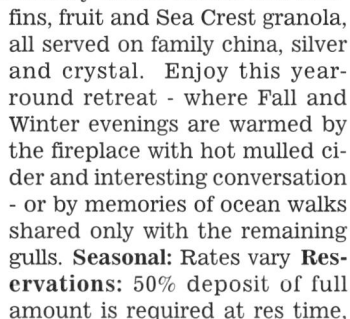

Rates: Pvt Bath 12
Single $ 110-239.00
Double $ 110-239.00

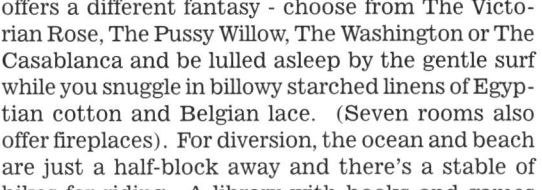

Whistling Swan Inn	110 Main St 07874	Stanhope NJ
Paula Williams & Joe Mulay		Tel: 201-347-6369

New Jersey - New York National Edition

Res Times 9am-6pm

Step back in time to a more genteel atmosphere that gives guests a feeling of being invited to a private home for a visit with friends, yet with privacy. A lovely Victorian structure, with a grand wrap-around porch, turrets, stone and white pillars, furnished with rockers for leisure. Each guest room is a special theme with some that include clawfoot tubs complete with terry robes and bubbles, if you like! Choose the Art Deco, Oriental Antique, White Iron or Brass room or from the others named for New Jersey locations. You're close to Waterloo Village, antiquing, skiing, boating, Lake Musconetcong, golf, horseback riding, state parks and forests, Morris Canal and many other sights. **Seasonal:** No **Reservations:** One night's deposit at res time, 48-hr cancellation policy for refund **Brochure:** Yes **Permitted:** Limited children, drinking, smoking **Conference:** Yes, for groups to twelve. **Payment Terms:** Check AE/MC/V [X02B-CNJ-3951] **COM** Y **ITC Member:** No

Rates: Pvt Bath 10
Single $ 65-80.00
Double $ 65-80.00

Colligans Stockton Inn 1 Main St 08559 Stockton NJ
Andy McDermott Tel: 800-368-7272 609-397-1250

Built c1710 as a residence and completely restored into an exciting Inn with the 1800's atmosphere. Furnished in authentic period decor that includes wall murals of 1800 scenes. Your hosts and five original fireplaces warm all guests. Outside are beautiful gardens and waterfalls for summer dining. Rich in history, Stockton was one of George Washington's launching points when crossing the Delaware River to Valley Forge! Gourmet meal selections and extensive wine list available. **Seasonal:** No **Brochure:** Yes **Permitted:** Children **Payment Terms:** Check AE/MC/V [X11ACNJ-3952] **COM** Y **ITC Member:** No

Rates: Pvt Bath 11
Single $ 70.00-up
Double $ 80-130.00

Mansion Hill Inn 115 Philip St at Park 12202 Albany NY
Maryellen & Steve Stofelano, Jr Tel: 518-465-2035 518-434-2334

This unique group of buildings once served as the residence of several of Albany's early extended families have been completely restored to its former glory as a three-story wood/brick Victorian design. The buildings have been completely rehabilitated by Maryellen and Steve and were awarded the 1986 Preservation Merit Award by Historic Albany Foundation and 1993 Award by New York State Museum. Located in the Mansion Neighborhood, a residential neighborhood just around the corner from the New York State Governor's Mansion, it's Albany's only downtown Inn. The *Mansion Hill Inn* is a focal point of the neighborhood and a perfect location for visitors, tourists and business travelers wanting to be "in town". The Inn features a variety of guest rooms from full suites with full kitchens, den and living rooms to comfortable rooms with queen sized beds, private baths, easy chair and desk. The five largest suites provide a view of Heidelberg Mountains, the Hudson River and the Berkshire Mountains. All rooms include cable color TV, HBO, phone and off-street parking. A full complimentary breakfast is included in the room rate. An exciting variety of lunch and appetizing evening entrees are offered in the restaurant where a wood-burning fireplace chases away the fall and winter chill. Conveniently located, the State Capitol, government offices, downtown Albany, shopping districts and historic sites are within a few walking minutes. **Packages:** Theatre and Symphony **Airport:** Albany County-20 mins **Discounts:** Yes, inquire at res time **Seasonal:** No **Reservations:** One night deposit with 7 day cancel policy Pick-ups at train station with prior arrangement. **Discounts:** Yes, inquire at res time. **Brochure:** Yes **Permitted:** Children, smoking, drinking **Conference:** Yes, seating for groups to 35 persons. **Languages:** French, Spanish, Italian **Payment Terms:** Check AE/DC/MC/V [Z05IPNY1-2458] **COM** Y **ITC Member:** No

Rates: Pvt Bath 13
Single $ 95.00
Double $ 185.00

©Inn & Travel Memphis, Tennessee

National Edition *New York*

Apple Inn	PO Box 18 RD#3 12009	Altamont NY
Laurie & Gerd Beckermann		Tel: 518-267-6557

An exciting 1765 colonial listed on the *National Historic Register*. Formerly a tavern and Inn offering guests spacious rooms and antique furnishings that are reminiscent of another period of time. Fireplace, wide-planked floors and a solarium, overlooking a stream and where a full breakfast is served make guests feel at home. You might visit the brass and iron bed store that's on the premises too.

There's a horse barn and tennis courts available. **Seasonal:** No **Brochure:** Yes **Permitted:** Children **Payment Terms:** Check MC/V [X11ACNY-2460] **COM** Y **ITC Member:** No

Rates:		Shared Bath	4
Single		$ 50.00	
Double		$ 60.00	

Mulligan Farm B&B	5403 Barber Rd 14414	Avon NY
Lesa & Jeff Mulligan		Tel: 315-226-6412

c1852 Greek Revival farmhome offering complete accommodations on a working dairy farm setting. Listed on the National Historic register, you'll find pleasing guest rooms, swimming pool, clay tennis courts and a library for your enjoyment. A full hearty farm-fresh breakfast is included to begin your day. **Seasonal:** No **Brochure:** Yes **Permitted:** Children, limited pets **Languages:** Spanish **Payment Terms:** Check [X11ACNY-2467] **COM** Y **ITC Member:** No

Rates:	Pvt Bath 2	Shared Bath	2
Single	$ 60.00	$ 55.00	
Double	$ 65.00	$ 60.00	

Chestnut Inn		Binghamton NY
Matt Akulonis		Tel: 800-467-7676 607-467-2500

Refer to the same listing name under Deposit, New York for a complete description. **Seasonal:** No **Permitted:** Children, drinking, limited smoking **Payment Terms:** Check AE/DC/DISC/MC/V [M06FPNY-18183] **COM** Y **ITC Member:** No

Rates:	Pvt Bath 7	Shared Bath	24
Single	$ 100.00	$ 85.00	
Double	$ 100.00	$ 85.00	

B&B On The Park	113 Prospect Park W 11215	Brooklyn NY
Liana Paolella		Tel: 718-499-6115

Located in Brooklyn's historic district of Park Slope is this lovely 1892 limestone landmark Victorian four-story Inn, just across from beautiful Prospect Park. Fully renovated and decorated in period antiques, oriental rugs, stained glass windows, original paintings, guests enjoy the ambience of old-world charm and gracious living from the turn-of-the-century. All rooms have the original mantles and woodwork with modern amenities of a/c, TV and phones. Guests are just twenty minutes from Manhattan, 1/2 mile from the Brooklyn Museum and Botanic Gardens and only two blocks from boutique shopping and a wide variety of restaurants. Each guest room offers a unique experience. There are two suites and four double rooms, one which has access to the roof-top garden for enjoying unlimited views of the Big Apple. Guests keep coming back to this charming Big Apple Inn to enjoy the gracious hospitality and luxurious, yet comfortable atmosphere. **Seasonal:** No **Reservations:** One night deposit at res time (50% if 4 nights or more), balance due upon arrival. 10 day cancel policy less a $25 service fee. **Brochure:** Yes **Permitted:** Children, drinking - smoking in common areas **Languages:** French **Payment Terms:** Check MC/V [R11DPNY-10059] **COM** U **ITC Member:** No

Rates:	Pvt Bath 4	Shared Bath	2
Single	$ 137-150.00	$ 100.00	
Double	$ 137-150.00	$ 110.00	

©*Inn & Travel Memphis, Tennessee*

New York — National Edition

Sutherland House — 3179 Bristol St 14424 — **Canandaigua NY**
Cor & Diane Van Der Woude — **Tel:** 800-396-0375 716-396-0375 **Fax:** 716-346-9281
Res Times 8am-10pm

Sutherland House is an 1885 renovated Victorian featuring comfort and charm. Our beautiful Victorian Parlor is brimming with whimsy. Lace curtains, curved glass, antique lights and collectibles are a feast for the eye as your attention flits from one item to the next. Don't forget to peek at the scrap book which chronicles the house's journey from haunted to Bed & Breakfast. All five air conditioned guest rooms feature private bath, remote controlled TV and clock radio. Two have private line telephones, ideal for corporate travelers. Two suites feature two person whirlpools and VCR; two guest rooms have fireplaces. Each morning a breakfast party is thrown in your honor. An assortment of homemade muffins, fresh fruit, breads and omelettes, french toast, tempting pancakes and seasonal favorites are offered. Centered on our own five acres of quiet and solitude, *Sutherland House* is surrounded by rolling farmland and mature trees. Just 30 minutes to Rochester NY, one hour to Syracuse NY and one hour to Buffalo NY. Located at the top of Canandaigua Lake, in the heart of the Finger Lakes areas, there is so much to do . . . come to ski, shop, visit restaurants, concert, attractions, winery festivals, foliage or do nothing at all! Welcome! Featured in *"Inn Spots & Special Places"*, AAA Rated 3-Diamond, ABBA-3 Crowns **Airport:** Rochester Intl-30 mins **Packages:** Ski, Mystery, Victorian Holiday **Discounts:** Midweek corporate. **Seasonal:** No **Reservations:** Credit card number to guarantee reservation, 2 week cancellation notice for refund **Brochure:** Yes **Permitted:** Limited children, drinking **Conference:** Small conferences and meetings **Languages:** Dutch **Payment Terms:** Check AE/DISC/MC/V [K10IPNY1-21107] **COM** G **ITC Member:** No

Rates:	Pvt Bath 5
Single	$ 85.00
Double	$ 90-165.00

Brae Loch Inn — 5 Albany St 13035 — **Cazenovia NY**
Jim & Val Barr — **Tel:** 315-655-3431 **Fax:** 315-655-4844
Res Times 9am-10pm

As close to a Scottish Inn you can get this far west of Edinburg. The *Brae Loch Inn* opened in 1946, adjacent to Cazenovia Lake, offers guests warmth and elegance but above all, a grand Scottish time! Guests enjoy delightful overnight accommodations, fine dining, banquets, seminars and meetings. Guests are greeted by Jim Barr and served dinner by attendants dressed in kilts and Glengarrie hats. There are twelve guest rooms on the second floor of this charming Inn, all with the old-time charm of antique furnishings, the classic luxury of Stickley furniture and the modern comfort of king-size beds, with canopied beds and fluffy lace comforters in selected rooms. The dining room is furnished with Victorian antiques, mellow tartan plaids, original stained glass, gleaming glassware, silver and pewter. Set in the quaint village of Cazenovia for shopping with golf and beach facilities. The Wee Gift and Antique House at the *Brae Loch* is a bit of the British Isles right on main street. Specialties include imported wools, tartan plaids and kilts, crystal and many other items. A continental breakfast is included each morning. **Discounts:** AAA, AARP **Airport:** Syracuse Intl-35 mins **Packages:** Deluxe king canopy bedroom, dinner for two $125.00 **Seasonal:** No **Reservations:** Full payment in advance of stay, 10 day cancel notice for refund **Brochure:** Yes **Permitted:** Children, drinking, limited smoking **Conference:** Yes, excellent atmosphere for social and business occasions up to 200 persons **Payment Terms:** Check AE/MC/V [I05HPNY1-2492] **COM** YG **ITC Member:** No

Rates:	Pvt Bath 12	Shared Bath 2
Single	$ 65.00	$ 65.00
Double	$ 75-125.00	$ 75.00

©*Inn & Travel Memphis, Tennessee*

National Edition   **New York**

Gasho Inn	Rt 32 Box M 10917	**Central Valley NY**
Marge Salamin		**Tel:** 914-928-2277

Step into an authentic Japanese inn located in Gasho Village which encompasses over twenty five lush acres of meditation areas, fish ponds, tea houses and traditional rock and Japanese gardens. A restaurant is on the premises serving American and many traditional Japanese courses. **Seasonal:** No **Reservations:** *Rates based upon European Plan **Brochure:** Yes **Permitted:** Children, smoking and drinking **Languages:** Japanese **Payment Terms:** Check AE/CB/DC/MC/V [X11ACNY-2494] **COM** Y **ITC Member:** No

Rates:	**Pvt Bath** 25
Single	$ 60.00
Double	$ 75.00

Thousand Islands Inn	PO Box 69 13624-0069	**Clayton NY**
Allen & Susan Benas		**Tel:** 315-686-3030

The only full-time Inn still operating on the island . . . and since 1897!! The location (you guessed it) from where Thousand Island Salad Dressing was developed--and the original recipe is still in use today. **Seasonal:** Opn: 5/30-10/31 **Reservations:** One night's deposit required at res time. *Rates based on European Plan **Brochure:** Yes **Permitted:** Children, smoking and drinking **Payment Terms:** Check CB/DC/MC/V [X11ACNY-2501] **COM** Y **ITC Member:** No

Rates:	**Pvt Bath** 8
Single	$ 42-52.00
Double	$ 47-60.00

Angelholm	14 Elm St 13326	**Cooperstown NY**
Fred & Jan Reynolds		**Tel:** 607-547-2483 **Fax:** 607-547-2309
		Res Times 8am-8pm

A beautiful 1815 colonial typical of this area that's in town and close to the sights, antique shops and restaurants, including the Baseball Hall of Fame. Perfectly furnished in period antiques including family treasures, you'll understand the host's enthusiasm in showing you around. A full breakfast is included. **Seasonal:** No **Reservations:** One night's deposit with 10 day cancel policy for refund. **Brochure:** Yes **Permitted:** Children, limited smoking **Payment Terms:** Check [X11ACNY-2511] **COM** Y **ITC Member:** No

Rates:	**Pvt Bath** 3	**Shared Bath** 2
Single	$ 75.00	$ 65.00
Double	$ 85.00	$ 75.00

Davenport Inn		**Cooperstown NY**
		Tel: 800-273-1746 607-278-5068
		Res Times 24 Hrs

Refer to the same listing name under Davenport, New York for a complete description. *800 only for New York state. **Seasonal:** No **Payment Terms:** Check DC/MC/V [M10DPNY-14643] **COM** YG **ITC Member:** No

Rates:	**Pvt Bath** 5	**Shared Bath** 2
Single	$ 38-48.00	$ 19-26.00
Double	$ 46-58.00	$ 38.00

JP Still House	63 Chestnut 13326	**Cooperstown NY**
Ms. Zucotti		**Tel:** 607-547-2633

An elegant restoration of an 1864 Italianate Victorian residence offers marble fireplaces, authentic handpainted wallcoverings and beautiful fine antique furnishings. Close to all the sights and just

---

©*Inn & Travel Memphis, Tennessee*

two blocks from the Baseball Hall of Fame. A full breakfast is prepared each morning for guests and is included with each room rate. **Seasonal:** No **Brochure:** Yes PPayment Terms: Check MC/V [X11AC-NY-3015] **COM** Y **ITC Member:** No

Rates:	**Pvt Bath** 2	**Shared Bath** 3
Single	$ 80.00	$ 69.00
Double	$ 80.00	$ 69.00

Alexander Hamilton House	49 Van Wyck St 10520	Croton-on-Hudson NY
Barbara Notarius		Tel: 914-271-6737 **Fax:** 914-271-3927
		Res Times 9am-9pm

The *Alexander Hamilton House*, circa 1889, is a sprawling Victorian home situated on a cliff overlooking the Hudson. Grounds include a mini-orchard, in-ground pool. The home has many period antiques and collections and offers: a queen bedded suite with fireplaced sitting room, two large rooms with queen beds (one with an additional day bed), and a bridal chamber with king bed, Jacuzzi, entertainment center, pink marble fireplace and lots of skylights. The master suite, with queen bed, fireplace, picture windows, stained glass, full entertainment center, Jacuzzi, skylight and a winter river views was just finished last year. A one bedroom apartment with double bed, living room with kitchen on one wall, private bath, and separate entrance is available for longer stays. Nearby attractions include West Point, the Sleepy Hollow Restorations, Lyndhurst, Boscobel, the Rockefeller Mansion, hiking, biking and sailing, and New York City, less than an hour away by train or car. A full breakfast is included. All rooms include: a/c, private bath, color CATV, phone. Off-street parking for guests. **Airport:** White Plains-15mi; LaGuardia-25mi Bridal Suite Photo: Courtesy Barbara Notarius and *Country Inns Bed & Breakfast*. **Seasonal:** No **Reservations:** Credit card guarantee, 7 day cancel policy, weekly and monthly rates available **Brochure:** Yes **Permitted:** Children, drinking **Conference:** Meeting room for groups to twenty persons **Languages:** French **Payment Terms:** Check AE/DISC/MC/V [I02HCNY1-12811] **COM** YG **ITC Member:** No **Quality Assured:** Yes

Rates:	**Pvt Bath** 7
Single	$ 75-100.00
Double	$ 95-250.00

Chestnut Inn	498 Oquaga Lake Rd 13754	Deposit NY
*James Gross, GM		Tel: 800-467-7676 607-467-2500 **Fax:** 607-467-5911
		Res Times 8am-10pm

Imagine a perfectly restored Country Inn set on a pristine mountain lake in the midst of the rolling hills of Central New York.... Experience the *Chestnut Inn* at Oquaga Lake. We've been attracting visitors for over 100 years. Whether you seek a relaxing and undisturbed retreat surrounded by some of New York's most magnificent scenery, or a dynamic lakefront resort with limitless activities to choose from, you'll find it at the *Chestnut Inn*. Our lobby welcomes you with its original chestnut woodwork, massive stone fireplace and warm atmosphere. Relax and enjoy ... we're at your service 24 hours a day. Our thirty-one gracious and relaxing guest rooms, each beautifully appointed, are cozy and restful just like a Country Inn should be. Whether you prefer the soft sounds of Oquaga Lake lapping against the shore or the soothing, peaceful sounds of nothingness, we offer you a choice of lakeside or woodland views. As is customary in a first-class resort, the pleasures of the table are never far. Relax in our main dining room, enjoy your meal while savoring the view from our lakeside sun room or experience the intoxicating cuisine from our distinctive water front terrace. Our executive chef and his competent staff prepare weekday meals and Sunday lunch - including our tantalizing dessert that has become a popular main attraction not to be missed. The lounge and patio are popular for dining and peaceful conversation. Activities include golf, tennis, boating, hiking, swimming, bicycling and sightseeing at nearby towns. **Discounts:** Groups, corporate **Airport:** Binghamton NY-25 mi **Packages:** Weekend, Midweek Golf, Foliage Tours and special promotions **Reservations:** Deposit or credit card number required to guarantee reservation, two night min weekends during social season and holidays **Brochure:** Yes **Permitted:** Children, drinking, limited smoking **Payment Terms:** Check AE/DC/DISC/MC/V [I06GPNY-18182] **COM YG ITC Member:** No

Rates:	Pvt Bath 7	Shared Bath 24
Single	$ 100.00	$ 85.00
Double	$ 100.00	$ 85.00

1819 Red Brick Inn	SRt 230 14837	Dundee NY
Peggy Albee & Ray Spencer		Tel: 697-243-8844
		Res Times 7am-5pm

In the heart of the Wine Country in upstate New York is this 1819 brick farmhouse built from bricks made right on the grounds that has been fully restored. Guest rooms are named for various wines and each decor is unique with many original paintings and antique furnishings, including canopy beds in some of the guest rooms. Great homemade pancakes from locally milled flour and homemade New York maple syrup shouldn't be missed with your complimentary breakfast. **Seasonal:** No **Reservations:** One night's deposit to hold with a 5 day cancel policy for refund **Brochure:** Yes **Permitted:** Children, limited smoking, limited drinking **Payment Terms:** Check [X11ACNY-2526] **COM Y ITC Member:** No

Rates:	Pvt Bath 2	Shared Bath 2
Single	$ 55.00	$ 45.00
Double	$ 65.00	$ 55.00

Highland Springs	Allen Rd 14055	East Concord NY
		Tel: 716-592-4323

Enjoy a peaceful and serene setting on 75 acres in Upstate NY. Forty miles south of Buffalo and Niagara Falls, there's rolling hillsides with pastureland and wood areas for a relaxful way of life. A continental plus breakfast is included. There's a sitting room for socializing or reading, piano and a swimming pond for old country dipping. **Seasonal:** No **Brochure:** Yes **Permitted:** Children **Payment Terms:** Check [X11ACNY-2531] **COM Y ITC Member:** No

Rates:	Pvt Bath 2	Shared Bath 1
Single	$ 62.00	$ 55.00
Double	$ 72.00	$ 65.00

Rufus Tanner House		Elmira NY
Bill Knapp/John Gibson		Tel: 607-732-0213
		Res Times 24 Hrs

Refer to the same listing name under Pine City, New York for a complete description. **Seasonal:** No **Payment Terms:** Check MC/V [M03FPNY-14592] **COM YG ITC Member:** No

Rates:	Pvt Bath 4
Single	$ 50.00
Double	$ 55-95.00

Battle Island Inn	RD 1 Box 176 13069	Fulton NY
Richard & Joyce Rice		Tel: 315-593-3699

The ordinary doesn't exist at *Battle Island Inn*. From our century-old rooms to our gourmet breakfasts, this inn is extraordinary in every way. Every antique-filled guest room has its own private bath,

TV, down-filled pillows and deep wool bed liners to assure you of the most restful sleep possible. Conduct business right from your room with a phone and desk area. You'll wake to a tantalizing breakfast, featuring different entrees daily. Sample the hosts' famous "made at the Inn" breads and jams! Relaxation comes easy at Battle Island Inn, where you can choose a view of the woods and gardens, or the golf course and river, from the porch and patio areas. Inside, three parlors allow plenty of meeting space, private reading or conversational areas with other guests. Conveniently located for business and pleasure trips. businesses, fishing and golfing - just across the road! After a hectic day of business or traveling, unwind at *Battle Island Inn*...your haven of home comfort and relaxation. **Seasonal:** No **Reservations:** 50% deposit or credit card deposit; 24-hr cancellation policy for refund. **Brochure:** Yes **Permitted:** Children, drinking **Conference:** Yes **Payment Terms:** Check MC/V [R02BCNY-6608] **COM** Y **ITC Member:** No

Rates: **Pvt Bath 6**
Single $ 55-65.00
Double $ 65-85.00

Geneva On The Lake   1001 Lochland Rd Rt 14S 14456   Geneva NY
Norberth Schickel Jr.   **Tel:** 800-3-GENEVA 315-789-7190
Res Times 24 hrs

Gorgeous Italian Renaissance mansion in a picture-perfect setting on ten acres of landscaped grounds that you shouldn't miss! A real treat that's perfect for that special romantic occasion or for spoiling yourself. Beautifully furnished guest rooms and personal attention by staff means you won't need to do anything except enjoy the amenities such as beautiful pool area, sailing on the lake, or just relaxing with excellent dining on the premises. Continental breakfast included with other meals available. **Seasonal:** No **Reservations:** Deposit required at res time, 48-hour notice for refund. **Permitted:** Children, smoking, drinking. Handicap access. **Payment Terms:** Check AE/DC/MC/V [X11ACNY-2553] **COM** Y **ITC Member:** No

Rates: **Pvt Bath 25**
Single $ 85.00
Double $ 95-130.00

Tepee   Rt 438 14070   Gowanda NY
Max & Phyllis Lay   **Tel:** 716-532-2168

Your hosts are Seneca Indians and their B&B reflects their Indian heritage and tradition and is located on the Cattaraugus Indian Reservation. All outdoor sporting activities are here, along with hot air ballooning. **Seasonal:** No **Brochure:** Yes **Permitted:** Children, limited smoking, limited drinking

Payment Terms: Check [X11ACNY-2556] **COM** Y **ITC Member:** No

Rates: **Pvt Bath 2**   **Shared Bath 2**
Single $ 45.00 $ 40.00
Double $ 52.00 $ 47.00

House On The Water   PO Box 106 11946   Hampton Bays NY
Mrs Ute   **Tel:** 516-728-3560
Res Times 9am-9pm

This quiet waterfront residence in the Hamptons (Shinnecock Bay) provides an excellent vacation or weekend getaway spot for locals and a great stop for travelers. Guests enjoy the large grounds and garden, outdoor terrace, beautiful views, complimentary bicycles, windsurfer and pedal boat, beach lounges and umbrellas, TV, barbecue and full kitchen facilities. Choose The Pink Room with joined twin beds, waterview, private entrance or The Mexican Room with twin beds, waterview and next to side-entrance. Extra beds are available at additional cost. Your hostess prepares a delicious morning feast including choices of English muffins, fresh fruit (in season), Danish, waffles, pancakes, granola,

French toast, your preference of egg entrees and cottage cheese fritters. **Discounts:** Off-season, weekly and monthly stays **Airport:** NY Kennedy-60 mi; McArthur-35 mi **Seasonal:** Open: 5/1-11/1 **Reservations:** One night's deposit, bal upon arrival; 2 night min, 3 night min July and Aug weekends, 4th July and Labor Day 4 night min **Brochure:** Yes **Permitted:** Drinking, limited smoking, adults only **Languages:** German, Spanish, French **Payment Terms:** Check Tvlr Cks [I03HPNY1-2568] **COM YG ITC Member:** No

Rates:	Pvt Bath 2	Shared Bath 1
Single	$ 70-90.00	$ 40.00
Double	$ 75-95.00	$ 50.00

Country Life B&B	237 Cathedral Ave 11550	Hempstead NY
Richard & Wendy Duvall		Tel: 516-292-9219
		Res Times 11am-9:30pm

This charming seventy year old Dutch Colonial is ideally situated in the center of Long Island on the Garden City border and has been twice honored by being chosen to be on the house tours because of the delightful decor and the genuine welcome guests receive while staying here. Each guest room offers special charm - one has an antique marble top dresser and twin four posters covered with hand crocheted spreads .... another has a king size bed and Queen Anne furnishings ... while some travelers prefer the adjoining den and parlor which can sleep four. All have color TV and air conditioning. Baby furniture is available for young guests. A complete, home-cooked breakfast is served in a sunny, plant-filled room starting with coffee brewed from freshly ground beans or a choice of teas. Complimentary village tours in a 1929 antique Ford introduces guests to the town sights. Featured in *"Newsday"*, *"New York Times"*, ABC TV *"Weekend Report"* and CBS *"This Morning Show"*, 1993; members of B&B Assoc of New York, National B&B Assoc and others. **Airport:** Kennedy-20 min; LaGuardia-40 min **Seasonal:** No **Reservations:** One night deposit required to guarantee reservation, 10 day cancel policy for refund, *check only for deposit **Brochure:** Yes **Permitted:** Children, drinking, no smoking **Languages:** Spanish, German **Payment Terms:** Check* [R07FPNY-2570] **COM Y ITC Member:** No

Rates:	Pvt Bath 3	Shared Bath 2
Single	$ 75-95.00	$ 70.00
Double	$ 75-95.00	$ 70.00

Inn At Green River	Green River Rd 12529	Hillsdale NY
Deborah Bowen		Tel: 518-325-7248

Your hostess owner relocated from Manhattan in 1988 to restore this 1830 Federalist farmhouse set in a quiet meadow overlooking Shepard Hill and an ancient cemetery. Exterior renovations and the landscaping continues, but the inside work is complete. The three guest rooms have been superbly furnished with antiques, oriental rugs, paintings, old family photos and each offers an unusual touch, such as a six-foot long soaking tub; a queen-size four poster bed in one room and antique cannonball and pineapple finial double beds in the other guest rooms. Regardless of the season, Green River is a good jumping-off point for visiting Tanglewood, Berkshire Festival, summer stock in New Lebanon, Chatham and Spencertown and the Norman Rockwell Museum and Shakespeare and Company at The Mount. Hiking to Bashbish Falls, Bartholomew's Cobble or Mount Greylock is beautiful Spring through Fall, while Winter brings cross country skiing right out the back door! A continental breakfast is included. Two cats are in residence. **Seasonal:** No **Reservations:** One night's deposit or 50% on longer stays to confirm reservation, 14 day cancel policy for refund less service fee **Brochure:** Yes **Permitted:** Drinking, limited children, a no smoking inn **Payment Terms:** Check [X04CCNY-10697] **COM Y ITC Member:** No

Rates:	Pvt Bath 1	Shared Bath 2
Single	$ 100.00	$ 75.00
Double	$ 100.00	$ 80.00

Breezy Acres Farm B&B	RD 1 Box 191 13788	Hobart NY
Joyce & David Barber		Tel: 607-538-9338
		Res Times 9am-9pm

The perfect place for a getaway - *Breezy Acres Bed & Breakfast* sits on 300 acres of rolling hills in Delaware County, known for its scenic beauty. You will be greeted by friendly hosts and made to feel immediately "at home". Then you will be shown through our immaculate rambling farmhouse with its many places for relaxing - a porch with a wicker swing, living room with fireplace, TV room with its incredibly comfortable leather sofa and sunny deck surrounded by perennial gardens. Each of our three individually decorated guest rooms has its own full bath. Wake up to the smells of coffee brewing and muffins baking. A full, homemade breakfast is lovingly prepared each morning by your hosts. Take a walk through our woods or take a soak in the spa - or set-off exploring. There are a surprising number of cultural events for so rural an area plus antique auctions, museums, fairs and festivals. Hunting, fishing, golf, skiing and tennis are all available nearby. Our guests feel so comfortable that they return again and again - we become a home away from home as a retreat from their stressful lives. ***Do experience country warmth and hospitality at its best - visit the Barbers at Breezy Acres***. AAA Rated 3-Diamond **Airport:** Albany-60 mi **Discounts:** Weekly stays **Seasonal:** No **Reservations:** One night deposit or credit card number to guarantee reservation, refund if cancelled two weeks prior or if less, only if rebooked **Brochure:** Yes **Permitted:** Limited children, limited drinking **Payment Terms:** Check MC/V [Z07GPNY-12808] **COM U ITC Member:** No

Rates: **Pvt Bath**   3
Single $ 40-55.00
Double $ 50-65.00

Peregrine House Victorian   140 College Ave   14850   Ithaca NY
Nancy Falconer   **Tel:** 607-272-0919
Res Times 9-12 am

Nestled in the heart of the city, surrounded by an iron fence, big, old shade trees, and pretty English gardens, this elegantly comfortable eight bedroom brick home provides travelers a unique experience. Dating from 1874, there's a beautiful wide front porch to enjoy and architectural highlights such as an original slate mansard roof. The guest bedrooms are Victorian too, with plump down comforters and pillows, firm new beds, lace curtains and Laura Ashely prints and air conditioning for your summer comfort. The bathrooms are brand new and you'll never have to walk down the hall to find them. Each room has a private full bath or private half bath with a shower room just outside your door. Guests are treated to a healthy or lavish breakfast around a huge oak table. Visitors from all over the world and various fields in the arts and sciences gather here for fascinating conversations. Wintertime brings hot tea or cider in the Victorian parlor before the fire while summer offers ice lemonade or tea while relaxing on the front porch wicker furniture. You'll be convenient to the new Cornell Performing Arts Center and the main entrance to Cornell's campus. Ithaca offers sparkling water falls, dramatic gorges and wildflower hikes. Cayuga Lake offers swimming, boating and several wineries. Off-street parking and TV available. AAA 3 Diamond rating **Discounts:** Extended stays **Airport:** Ithaca-4 mi; Syracuse-55 mi **Packages:** Winter and Holiday **Seasonal:** Rates vary **Reservations:** Credit card number required to guarantee reservation **Brochure:** Yes **Permitted:** Children over 7 **Conference:** Meeting room available for groups to fifteen **Payment Terms:** Check DISC/MC/V [Z02HPNY1-5960] **COM U ITC Member:** No

Rates: **Pvt Bath**   4   **Shared Bath**   4
Single $ 79-99.00 $ 69-89.00
Double $ 85-109.00 $ 69-89.00

Rose Inn   Rt 34 N Box 6576   14851-6576   Ithaca NY
Sherry & Charles Rosemann   **Tel:** 607-533-7905   **Fax:** 607-533-7908
Res Times 7am-11pm Mon-Sat

Elegant Italianate mansion built in the 1840's and surrounded by twenty landscaped acres with apple orchard and fishing pond, exquisitely furnished in period antiques and selected by "New Woman" magazine, January '88, as one of the "Ten most Romantic Inns of America"!! Selected by "Uncle Bens Rice" as one of the "Ten Best Inns in America" - two year in a row! New York State's only Mobil and AAA 4 Diamond Country Inn. Suites available: four bridal and *Deluxe Suites with Jacuzzi for two. An elegant prix fixe dinner is served in the candlelit dining room Tuesday thru Saturday at 7 pm. You'll be close to Cornell University and Ithaca College, Finger Lakes' wineries and Corning Glass Museum. Full breakfast included with other meals at added cost. *$125-175.00 weekends Easter thru Thanksgiving. Two night stay if your stay includes Saturday night. Holiday and Special University Weekends: Subject to a three night minimum stay. **Airport:** Ithaca-8 mi **Seasonal:** No **Reservations:** Full payment for stays to 3 days rec'd within 7 days of res, refund if cancelled prior to 14 days of arrival less $25.00 handling fee, local and state sales tax, add 11% plus 15% service charge **Brochure:** Yes **Permitted:** Children over 10, limited drinking, smoking is not permitted **Conference:** 1000 sq ft conference facility in 1840's restored carriage house with seating for 80 persons **Languages:** Fluent German, Spanish **Payment Terms:** MC/V [R04IP-Y1-2581] COM YG **ITC Member:** No

Rates:	Pvt Bath 14
Single	
Double	$ 100-150.00

High Meadows B&B	3740 Eager Rd 13078	Jamesville NY
Nancy Mentz		Tel: 315-492-3517 **Res Times** 8am-8pm

You are invited to enjoy country hospitality at *High Meadows B&B*, high in the tranquil hills just 10 miles south of Syracuse, New York. High Meadows offers two guest bedrooms with shared bathroom, a/c, fireplace, a plant-filled solarium and a wrap-around deck with a magnificent forty mile view. The Rose Room is tastefully and comfortably decorated and sleeps two in a queen size bed. The Green Room offers double bed comfort in a cozy home-like setting. Corporate and weekly rates are offered along with seniors' discounts. A continental breakfast is included in your room rate. We look forward to your stay with us and we are confident you will enjoy the area. Explore the Adirondack Mountains, Thousand Island resort area and wander the scenic back roads and lush vineyards of the Finger Lakes. Major annual events include New York State Fair, Hot-Air Balloon Festival, IRA Regatta, Winterfest and the Apple Festival. Central New York is a recreational paradise offering picturesque lakes, rivers, streams perfect for fishing boating and excellent hiking and nature trails for exploring. Winter offers great downhill and cross country skiing. **Airport:** Syracuse-15 mi **Discounts:** Yes, inquire at res time **Seasonal:** No **Reservations:** One night's deposit, 5 day cancel policy for full refund. Special events for Syracuse Univ increase daily rates by $10 per night **Brochure:** Yes **Permitted:** Children **Payment Terms:** Check [Z05FPNY-12532] COM Y **ITC Member:** No

Rates:	Shared Bath 2
Single	$ 35-40.00
Double	$ 40-50.00

Highland House Inn	3 Highland Place 12946	Lake Placid NY
Ted & Cathy Blazer		Tel: 800-342-8101 518-523-2377 **Fax:** 518-523-1863
		Res Times 7-9pm

The *Highland House Inn* is located in a lovely residential section, just above Main Street in the village of Lake Placid. The decor throughout the Inn, we describe as "Adirondack" - intrinsic to this area. Wallpapers are of rich green, rose and ivory backgrounds and use of birch tree furnishings abound. The main floor of the Inn consists of several little rooms off the main living space, where games are in progress and reading and conversation are invited. The dining area is a separate room just off the living room and runs the length of the house. Bordered by glass on three sides it is bright and sunny and full of plants for year round dining enjoyment. Breakfasts are served to order, including blueberry pancakes, french toast, eggs, sausages, cereals and etc. A huge deck spans the length of the Inn, wrapping around two clumps of birch trees and supports a wonderful seven person hot tub spa. The seven bedrooms are located on the second and third floors. They are each uniquely decorated and have either a private bathroom within the room or a private bath located directly across the hall from the room. A remote control color TV is available in each room, along with other necessary amenities, including hair dryers, for a comfortable stay. Adjacent to the Inn is the Highland Cottage. Decorated in the same style as the Inn, the Cottage is fully equipped with a kitchen, bedroom with queen size bed and a deck off the back. It has a fireplace for use in winter and air conditioning available in summer. The Cottage also has two televisions, a VCR and stereo tape player. All amenities offered at the Inn are included with a stay in the Cottage. **Airport:** Albany-2-1/2 hrs **Packages:** Ski, Golf **Seasonal:** No **Reservations:** 50% deposit by check 14 days prior arrival date or MC/V, 3 week cancellation policy for refund late arrival okay with prior notice **Brochure:** Yes **Permitted:** Children, drinking **Conference:** Small conferences for groups to 15 **Payment Terms:** Check MC/V [I10HPNY1-2591] **COM YG ITC Member:** No

Rates: Pvt Bath 8
Single $ 60.00
Double $ 105.00

Interlaken Inn	15 Interlaken Ave 12946	**Lake Placid NY**
Roy & Carol Johnson		**Tel:** 800-428-4369 518-523-3180

A quaint country inn c1906 situated in breathtaking Adirondack Mountains between picturesque Mirror Lake and historic Lake Placid. This lovely Victorian and former private summer residence has been restored, offering guests an intimate atmosphere in uniquely decorated and furnished guest rooms and common rooms, including a tin-ceilinged dining room and lace trim! Quiet and peaceful setting as a four-season resort unsurpassed in variety of outdoor activities including championship golf, fly fisherman's paradise, nature lover's palette of foliage colors in the Fall, and Olympic skiing! Enjoy the spectacular views from terraces available in some of the guest rooms. Fine dining available on the premises by your hosts and a full gourmet menu. **Seasonal:** Closed: 4/1-4/15 **Reservations:** One night's deposit to hold reservations, 2 week cancel policy for refund. *Rates based on MAP **Brochure:** Yes **Permitted:** Children 5-up, drinking, limited smoking **Conference:** Yes, depending upon group's size and function **Payment Terms:** Check AE/MC/V [A06EPNY-10890] **COM YG ITC Member:** No

Rates: Pvt Bath 12
Single $ 80.00
Double $ 100-160.00

South Meadow Farm Lodge	HCR 1 Box 44 Cascade Rd 12946-9703	**Lake Placid NY**
Tony & Nancy Corwin		**Tel:** 800-523-9369 518-523-9369
		Res Times 7am-9pm

South Meadow Farm Lodge is a cozy year-round farm and lodge located in the middle of the beautiful High Peaks Region of the Adirondack Park. The farm lies off Rt 73, halfway (7 miles) between Lake Placid and Keene and a half-mile east of Mount Van Hoevenberg Recreation Area. Accommodations are varied and include guest rooms for ten people in double rooms around a comfortable living room. The large fireplace in the living room offers plenty of warmth and socializing in the evening among guests and your hosts. A piano brings-out the musical talents of guests so inclined. A log cabin is available for the soft camper which is "winterized" with a wood stove, candlelight and sleeping loft with comfy mattresses. Freshwater and privy are nearby. Lodge guests begin each day with a complimentary delicious family-style full breakfast served with a country flair. Your hosts pride themselves in raising some of their own food (without preservatives) and they do their own homestyle baking, with far more honey that sugar. For the active and not so active person, there are plenty of year-round activities nearby from which to choose. Fifty km of Olympic cross county ski trails that cross the farm (free passes for the guests), a refreshing outdoor sauna among the birches, helping with the farm chores (horses, chickens and sheep), and soon learn the secrets of making maple syrup in their sugar bush, bread baking, haying, gardening tips, fishing, canoeing, swimming holes, golf, tennis, hiking, backpacking and in winter, there's plenty of ice skating, dog sled riding, sleigh rides, ice climbing and downhill skiing. Nearby is the sports complex used for the Olympic Bobsled and Luge Run as well as the Olympic Cross Country Ski Trails. **Discounts:** Yes, inquire at res time. **Airport:** Albany NY-120 mi, Saranac Lake-20 mi for commuter flights **Seasonal:** No **Reservations:** 50% deposit on length of stay, bal due at check-out. Cancel policy: 21 day notice for refund, no refund for early departure **Brochure:** Yes **Permitted:** Children, drinking (BYOB) **Payment Terms:** Check MC/V [I04IPNY1-2596] **COM YG ITC Member:** No

Rates:	Shared Bath 5
Single	$ 45-65.00
Double	$ 70-95.00

Spruce Lodge B&B   31 Sentinel Rd 12946   Lake Placid NY
Ms Carol Hoffman

Tel: 800-258-9850 518-523-9350
Res Times 1pm-later

Enjoy a homelike atmosphere in this cozy year-round lodge nestled in the Village of Lake Placid that's close to all outdoor activities for relaxing or experiencing. Whether it's hiking, golf, tennis, swimming, alpine skiing, x-country skiing, skating, hockey, fishing, sightseeing, boating or indoor shopping and antiquing, you'll be within ten miles of any activity here. You'll be close to Mt Van Hoevenberg Ski Jumps and just ten minutes to Whiteface ski area. Continental breakfast with hot and cold cereals, breads, and a variety of beverages is included.

Airport: Albany-2-1/2 hrs **Seasonal:** No **Reservations:** One night's deposit at least two weeks prior to res date. One week cancel policy for refund. *Cottage available that sleeps up to eight $99.00 per night, two night minimum stay **Brochure:** Yes **Permitted:** Children **Payment Terms:** Check MC/V [Z08-HPNY1-2594] **COM** U **ITC Member:** No

Rates:	Pvt Bath 2	Shared Bath 5
Single		
Double	$ 60-65.00	$ 45-50.00

Village Inn B&B   111 S Erie St Rt 394 14757   Mayville NY
Dean R Hanby

Tel: 716-753-3583
Res Times After 5pm

You are invited to spend a restful night in a turn-of-the-century home located near the shores of Lake Chautauqua and Erie in the village of Mayville. Comfort is assured in both single and double rooms in this quaint home furnished with many antiques and trimmed in woodwork crafted by European artisans. Just a five minute walk from the Inn, Chautauqua Lake offers all the water sports including wind surfing and sailing. Nearby is golfing, biking trails, boat excursions, tennis, hand gliding, wineries and vineyards and in winter, snowmobiling, ice fishing, hunting and sleigh rides with downhill skiing at Pean N Peak in the Cockaigne Ski Centers.

Before an active day begins, guests are treated to a continental breakfast of homemade waffles, nut kuchen and seasonal fruit with plenty of freshly-brewed coffee. A true year-round adventure in a 19th Century Victorian Home. **Seasonal:** No **Reservations:** $20 deposit **Brochure:** Yes **Permitted:** Children, drinking, smoking **Payment Terms:** Check [R07BCNY-6732] **COM** Y **ITC Member:** No

Rates:	Shared Bath 3
Single	$ 30.00
Double	$ 45.00

Landmark Retreat   6006 Rt 21 14512   Naples NY
Ann Albrecht

Tel: 716-396-2383
Res Times After 2pm

Beautiful country setting with spectacular view of Canandaigua Lake - located in the heart of the Finger Lakes. Close to wineries, theater, golf course, ski resort, auto and horse races, fishing, boating and hiking. Our 1830 residence offers contemporary comfort with a congenial Bavarian dining room atmosphere featuring a full breakfast and fruits, served family-style. Guests relax in three separate living rooms, one with a marble fireplace, the library, patio or porches along with enjoying the outdoors and grounds. **Discounts:** 10% for groups, senior citizens and extended stays **Airport:** Rochester-45 mi;

Syracuse-60 mi **Seasonal:** No **Reservations:** 50% deposit required to guarantee reservation **Brochure:** Yes **Permitted:** Limited children, limited pets, drinking, restricted smoking **Conference:** For small groups of 12-18 persons **Languages:** English, German **Payment Terms:** Check [R07FPNY-12758] **COM** Y **ITC Member:** No

Rates:	Pvt Bath 1	Shared Bath 6
Single	$ 40.00	$ 40.00
Double	$ 60.00	$ 60.00

New York   *National Edition*

B&B On The Park   New York NY
Liana Paolella   Tel: 718-499-6115

Refer to the same listing name under Brooklyn, New York for a complete description. **Seasonal:** No **Payment Terms:** Check MC/V [M11DPNY-10112] **COM U ITC Member:** No	**Rates:** Pvt Bath 4 Single $ 137-150.00 Double $ 137-150.00	**Shared Bath** 2 $ 100.00 $ 110.00

Broadway B&B Inn   264 W 46th St   10036   New York NY
Louis Rose   Tel: 800-826-6300   212-997-9200 **Fax:** 212-768-2807

Located in midtown, in the heart of Times Square, *Broadway Bed & Breakfast* is a modern European-style Inn comprising three floors above a quaint Irish Pub on the first level. Dating from 1918, the Inn was completely renovated in 1995. Tastefully furnished and decorated in a variety of textures with original restored brick walls and beautiful mahogany wood trim. The atmosphere is light and airy. The guest rooms are finished in subtle shades of ivory, green and gray and include private bath, a/c, cable TV, phones and daily maid service. A continental breakfast including juice, croissant or baguette and hot beverages is provided. Your hosts invite travelers to enjoy the homey atmosphere they have created in the center of The Big Apple. **Reservations:** Credit card number to guarantee, 24 hour cancel notice policy for deposit refund **Brochure:** Yes **Permitted:** Children, drinking, smoking **Languages:** French, Spanish, German **Payment Terms:** AE/DC/DISC/MC/V [I06IPNY1-26945] **COM YG ITC Member:** No

Rates: Pvt Bath 29
Single $ 75.00
Double $ 85.00

The Cameo Manor   Niagara Falls NY
Greg & Carolyn Fisher   Tel: 716-745-3034
     Res Times 9am-9pm

Refer to the same listing name under Youngstown, New York for a complete description. **Seasonal:** No **Payment Terms:** Travelers Check DISC/MC/V [M10HPNY1-20107] **COM YG ITC Member:** No	**Rates:** Pvt Bath 2 Single $ 80-125.00 Double $ 85-130.00	**Shared Bath** 2 $ 60.00 $ 75.00

Pollyanna   302 Main St   13421   Oneida NY
Doloria & Ken Chapin   Tel: 315-363-0524
    Res Times 8am-11pm

Enjoy a true Italian Villa of the Victorian period in historic Oneida with wonderful hosts who make sure each guest enjoys their stay and doesn't *"go to bed hungry!"* Filled with warmth, hospitality and memories, guests can enjoy outstanding features as brass door knobs with dogs' heads projecting, glass globes blown "into a frame", gas chandeliers, balloon (canvas) ceilings, marble fireplaces, and each guest room has its own unique decor of antiques and family heirlooms. Copper bed warmers and down quilts keep guests cozy in winter while summer refreshments include sipping lemonade and pleasant conversation on the veranda in the cool evening. Crafts and collections abound since your hostess, Mrs Chapin, is an artist, craftsman and teacher in spinning, bobbin lace and felting and Mr Chapin is a business consultant and woodworker. Fruit and flowers are in each guest's room while special books, games, music, puzzles fill an elegant parlor. Christmas begins Dec 1 with a 12' tree and a live tree is added to the parlor a week before the 25th. Outdoors guests can enjoy a beautiful Japanese Garden filled with a pool, fountain, zen lake and bonsai, window of heaven and hundreds of varieties of iris, lilies, roses, and sweet alyssum. A full breakfast is included with cookies and evening snacks. Just off I-90 Thruway and close to Syracuse, Rome and Utica, Colgate and Hamilton Colleges. Plenty of shopping, water, mountains, lakes, museums. **Seasonal:** No **Reservations:** Deposit with credit card (AE/MC/V), 15 day cancel policy for refund, partial refund if less. Call by 7pm if arriving late. Two day mins on college, homecoming and graduation weekends. **Brochure:** Yes **Permitted:** Children, limited pets **Conference:** Parlor and dining room for small groups. **Payment Terms:** Check [R08BCNY-3776] **COM** Y **ITC Member:** No

Rates:		Shared Bath 6
Single		$ 40.00
Double		$ 40-68.50

Davenport Inn   Oneonta NY
Tel: 800-273-1746 607-278-5068
Res Times 24 hrs

Refer to the same listing name under Davenport, New York for a complete description. *800 only for New York state. **Seasonal:** No **Payment Terms:** Check DC/MC/V [M10DPNY-14642] **COM** Y **ITC Member:** No

Rates:	Pvt Bath 5	Shared Bath 2
Single	$ 38-48.00	$ 19-26.00
Double	$ 46-58.00	$ 38.00

Rufus Tanner House   60 Sagetown Rd 14871   Pine City NY
Bill Knapp/John Gibson
Tel: 607-732-0213
Res Times 24 Hrs

Century old maples surround this 1864 Victorianized Greek Revival Farmhouse that provides a commanding position on a small knoll in up-state New York. Tastefully and comfortably updated residence still retains its wonderful Victorian charm. All of the guest rooms are tastefully decorated with period furnishings and are located upstairs. The downstairs Master Bedroom will be memorable with marble-topped high-Victorian furniture, white pine floors and period wallcoverings. The European-style bath has a two-person shower, whirlpool tub and a black marble floor. The common rooms offer unique furnishings including an ornate cookstove in the kitchen, a Victorian fireplace and wainscoting in the dining room, a baby grand piano in the living room and a plant filled sunroom with wicker furnishings and a weight machine for guests so inclined. A full complimentary breakfast is prepared daily and other meals are available at an extra charge and with prior notice. Elmira-Corning attractions are nearby with the National Soaring Museum, Mark Twain sites, Arnot Art Museum, Corning Glass Museum, Rockwell Museum, The Christmas House, two Four-Star restaurants and the myriad Finger Lake attractions including wineries and antique shops. **Discounts:** AAA, long stays receive 10% **Airport:** Elmira Corning-14 mi **Packages:** Getaway Weekend, Honeymoon **Seasonal:** No **Reservations:** One night's deposit required except race and graduation weekends require full advance payment. 48 hr cancel policy except race and graduation weekends which require 30 day notice for refund. **Brochure:** Yes **Permitted:** Children, drinking **Conference:** Yes, for groups of 10-12 persons. **Languages:** Some French **Payment Terms:** Check MC/V [Z03FPNY-12765] **COM** Y **ITC Member:** No

Rates:	Pvt Bath 4
Single	$ 50.00
Double	$ 55-95.00

Pine Hill Arms   Main St 12465   Pine Hill NY
Robert & Valeri Konefal
Tel: 918-254-9811

Nestled at the foot of Belleayre Mountain in the heart of the Catskill Mountains is this legendary resort established c1882 and one of the few remaining resorts reminiscent of the 1920's and 30's era but recently upgraded to include modern amenities without losing the flavor of yesteryear. Spacious grounds surround the Inn and include a grand swimming pool, private trout brook to test your skill and luck, horseback riding, tennis, hiking, antiquing, and tubing the Esopus River nearby. Lovely greenhouse dining room, bar, huge fireplaced lobby, gameroom, sauna and hot tub spa are included. Meals are not included but are available in the on-premises restaurant. **Seasonal:** Rates vary **Reservations:** Deposit required to guarantee at res time. *Rates increase during ski season. **Brochure:** Yes **Permitted:** Children, smoking, drinking **Conference:** Yes, groups to 50 persons **Payment Terms:** Check MC/V [A06AC-NY-3784] **COM Y ITC Member:** No

Rates: **Pvt Bath 20**
Single $ 45.00
Double $ 50.00

Inn On Bacon Hill	PO Box 1462 12866	**Saratoga Springs NY**
Andrea Collins-Breslin		**Tel:** 518-695-3693
		Res Times 8am-9pm

Close to historic Saratoga Springs, you'll find this lovely mid-Victorian home constructed during the Civil War, c1862, by a prominent New York State Legislator, Alexander Baucus. Recently restored to its original beauty and charm, guests will enjoy the many interesting architectural features including a guest parlor with its marble fireplace, high ceilings, antique chandeliers and original plaster and wood mouldings. A baby grand piano adorns the Victorian Parlor Suite. A hearty breakfast, including homemade muffins and jams, is served each morning at 8:45 in our country dining room, with wake-up coffee awaiting our early risers. A screened-in gazebo, surrounded by peaceful rural settings and the distant hills of Vermont is a perfect setting to enjoy your morning coffee or afternoon beverages. The Inn is located just 12 minutes east of Saratoga's racetracks and the city's many attractions and fine restaurants - close enough to the excitement of Saratoga Springs, yet far enough away for a restful night's sleep. Albany, Lake George or Vermont are all within a 45-minute drive. When not out on the town or visiting the sights, you can relax by browsing in the library of books, magazines, games or by enjoying the comfortable wicker on the porch or wandering through Mom's informal flower garden. **Discounts:** 10% off-season (Nov-March) **Airport:** Albany NY-40 mins **Packages:** 3-Day Weekend For Prospective Innkeepers (Spring and Fall) **Seasonal:** Rates vary **Reservations:** 1-2 nights/full deposit; 3-4 nights/2 night's deposit; more than 4 nights/50% deposit. Rates higher during race season (late July and August) **Brochure:** Yes **Permitted:** Drinking, smoking outdoor porch **Payment Terms:** Check MC/V [I04-GPNY-16681] **COM U ITC Member:** No

Rates:	**Pvt Bath 2**	**Shared Bath 2**
Single	$ 75-85.00	$ 65.00
Double	$ 75-85.00	$ 65.00

Lombardi Farm B&B	41 Locust Grove Rd 12866	**Saratoga Springs NY**
V&K Lombardi		**Tel:** 518-587-2074

The *Lombari Farm B&B* is a restored Victorian Farm two miles from the center of historic Saratoga Springs, New York. The large newly decorated rooms are all a/c with private baths. A gourmet breakfast is served daily in the Florida Room. There is an indoor hot tub/jacuzzi for guests to enjoy. The country setting is peaceful and quiet, yet it is within two miles of: National Museum of Dance, Saratoga Thoroughbred Racetrack, Saratoga Harness Track, Saratoga Polo Club, Skimore College, Yaddo, Artists Retreat and Gardens, Famous Saratoga Mineral Baths. There are parks, pools, lakes, golfing, restaurants, buses and trains within a short distance of the B&B. The *Lombardi Farm* is proud of its Nubian dairy goats and guests are welcomed to bottle feed a baby goat in the spring-time. The *Lombardi Farm B&B* is a member of the Greater Saratoga

National Edition *New York*

Chamber of Commerce, B&B RSO Worldwide, B&B Society Intl, American Country Collection of B&B, B&B Assoc of Saratoga, Lake George and Gore Mountain Region as well as the AAA. **Airport:** Albany-15 mi **Packages:** Yes, inquire at res time. **Seasonal:** No **Reservations:** One evening's deposit ($100) to guarantee reservation. **Brochure:** Yes **Permitted:** Drinking, smoking **Payment Terms:** [I05FPNY-7644] **COM YG ITC Member:** No

Rates:	Pvt Bath 4
Single	$ 100.00
Double	$ 100.00

Lakecrest Guest House	7589 N Ontario St 14555	Sodus Point NY
Bob & Carole Snyder		Tel: 315-483-6090

This Queen Anne Victorian guest house and Caretakers cottage provides a year round getaway with beautiful views of the historical lighthouse and Lake Ontario beaches from all of the rooms. Located a short distance from Syracuse and Rochester, guests can escape to a peaceful and tranquil setting where lazy Sunday afternoons are spent on the unique front porch while summer "Concerts in the Park" take place just across the street. Or, guests can relax beneath the giant shade trees while boats glide across beautiful Lake Ontario. All of the guest rooms include private baths and ceiling fans add to the Victorian charm. A continental breakfast is included and served in the parlor. The Caretakers Cottage is suitable for families and fishermen and includes a full kitchen, washer and dryer, two bedrooms, two full baths, cable TV and is available for weekly stays. **Airport:** Rochester Intl-40 mi **Reservations:** Deposit required with 14 day cancel policy. **Brochure:** Yes **Permitted:** Children, drinking **Payment Terms:** Check MC/V [R11DPNY-12770] **COM U ITC Member:** No

Rates:	Pvt Bath 4
Single	$ 55-75.00
Double	$ 55-75.00

Benedict House	1402 James St 13203	Syracuse NY
Terry & Bernie Gero		Tel: 315-476-6541
		Res Times 7am-10pm

Although we are located only 5-8 mins from downtown Syracuse, Syracuse University, and LeMoyne College, you will find the charm and pace of Benedict House relaxing and caring. We want to pamper you with an elegant atmosphere and delicious food all made by your hosts. Benedict House has three spacious, beautifully appointed bedrooms (one queen size, one full size and a twin-bedded room) with sitting and reading areas. A small conference room is available. Early coffee and juice is always ready at 7:30 - just help yourself. A full breakfast is served in the dining room at 8:30 (Time requests will be honored for your convenience). The breakfast menu changes daily. **Seasonal:** No **Reservations:** One night's deposit required with 72 hr cancel policy less $10 processing fee, min two night stay on special weekends **Brochure:** Yes **Permitted:** Limited children **Conference:** Yes for groups to 10 persons at no extra charge **Payment Terms:** Check [R09DSNY-12773] **COM Y ITC Member:** No

Rates:	Pvt Bath 2	Shared Bath 1
Single	$ 50.00	$ 45.00
Double	$ 55.00	$ 50.00

Merrill Magee House	2 Hudson St 12885	Warrensburg NY
Ken & Florence Carrington		Tel: 518-623-2449
		Res Times 8am-10pm

In a small (quaint) Adirondack Mountain village, tucked behind a tall white fence and shaded by century old maple trees this little Inn abounds with 19th century charm and 20th century comforts. From the inviting wicker chairs on the porch to the glowing fireplaces in the Victorian dining rooms, a warm welcome awaits you. The guest rooms are a romantic mix of antiques, lace and linen with decidedly 20th century comforts. Each room is uniquely decorated and accented by a warm crackling fireplace. All the rooms have private baths. There is a plant filled sunroom with a jacuzzi. For your quiet time, we have lots of books and games you can enjoy or just curl up by your fire and relax in peace and tranquility. Cocktails are served in the garden or on the porch set the tone for a special evening before your

©Inn & Travel Memphis, Tennessee

2-81

delightful candlelight dinner. Our romantic dining room, wonderful food and friendly, attentive service makes dinner at the *Merrill Magee House* memorable. Situated in the historic and scenic Adirondack Park, six million acres of outdoor recreation surround you and each season brings it special pleasures: Lake George is five miles away - whitewater rafting - antiquing - concerts - Saratoga - Performing Arts - Thoroughbred racing - outlet shopping - downhill and cross country skiing are just a few of the many activities close by. Listed on the *National Historic Register of Historic Places*, the *Merrill Magee House* is everything you thought a Country Inn would be. **Airport:** Albany-60mi **Discounts:** Corporate rate $65.00 **Packages:** Romantic Getaway, Two Day Break Handicap accessible room **Seasonal:** Rates vary **Reservations:** One night's deposit at res time, 7 day cancel policy for refund *Suite **Brochure:** Yes **Permitted:** Limited children, limited smoking, drinking **Conference:** Meeting room for groups of 10 to 50 guests **Payment Terms:** AE/DISC/MC/V [I11IPNY1-3854] **COM YG ITC Member:** No

Rates:	Pvt Bath 10	Shared Bath 1
Single	$ 85-95.00	$ 185.00*
Double	$ 102-125.00	

1880 House	2 Seafield Lane 11978	**Westhampton Beach NY**
Elsie Collins		**Tel:** 800-346-3290 516-288-1559 **Fax:** 516-288-0721

Only 90 minutes from Manhattan is this hidden 100-year-old country retreat that's perfect for a romantic hideaway, weekend of privacy or just a change of pace from the city. Your charming hostess caters to just two couples at a time and spoils everyone with her personal concern and interest in each guest. The lovely suites are individually decorated and include special touches: Victorian blue and delicate floral wallpapers, raised brass beds, sitting rooms, and private baths. A rustic panelled yellow suite has a loveseat couch, antique oak desk, swivel cane chair and a clawfoot tub. Both suites include handsome coverlets and quilts. You'll awake in the morning to the aroma of freshly-baking breads and rolls, along with a full breakfast of your choosing. Located in the exclusive Seafield Lane area, you can choose either swimming or tennis on the premises or a short stroll to the fine beaches. You're also close to numerous fine restaurants, shops, athletic facilities and your hostess will help direct you to any other activities or points of interest. **Seasonal:** No **Reservations:** One night's deposit within 5 days of booking; cancellation refunded as credit for future stay only. **Permitted:** Limited children, limited drinking **Conference:** Yes, small groups both indoors and outdoors **Payment Terms:** Check AE/MC/V [I04HPNY1-3865] **COM YG ITC Member:** No

Rates:	Pvt Bath 2
Single	$ 100.00
Double	$ 100.00

The Cameo Manor	3881 Lower River Rd 14174	**Youngstown NY**
Carolyn & Greg Fisher		**Tel:** 716-745-3034
		Res Times 9am-9pm

Our 1860's English Manor house on New York's Seaway Trail is located in an area of great historical significance. Just seven miles north of Niagara Falls, *Cameo Manor* is the perfect spot for that quiet getaway you've been meaning to treat yourself to. Situated on three secluded park-like acres, the *Manor* offers a Great Room with fireplaces at either end, a solarium, fireplaced library and an outdoor terrace for your enjoyment. Our beautifully appointed guestrooms include suites with adjoining private sunrooms and CATV. The dramatic decor and relaxing ambiance beckon guests to linger by the fire, enjoy the view of the river or simply stroll the grounds while awaiting the sumptuous breakfast served in the formal dining room. If Victoriana is more to your liking, we invite you to enjoy our second guest house, *The Cameo Inn*, located at 4710 Lower River Rd, Lewiston, NY (2-1/2 miles south on the same road at the *Cameo Manor*). Lovingly furnished with period antiques and family heirlooms, the *Cameo Inn* will charm you its quiet elegance and the view of the lower Niagara is worth the trip alone! Open full time in summer and as needed in the off-season, this location has four lovely guestrooms with private and shared baths, as well as a suite overlooking the river. Both the *Cameo Manor* and the *Cameo Inn* are ideally located for sightseeing, antiquing, fishing, boating, golf, biking or just relaxing by the river. Come and enjoy! **Discounts:** Yes, inquire at res time **Airport:** Buffalo Intl-40 mins **Packages:** Yes, inquire at res time **Reservations:** One night's deposit to guarantee reservation, 72 hr cancel policy for refund less $15 service fee **Brochure:** Yes **Permitted:** Drinking, smoking outside **Conference:** Groups to fifteen **Payment Terms:** Travelers Check DISC/MC/V [K10HPNY1-18838] **COM** YG **ITC Member:** No

Rates:	Pvt Bath 2	Shared Bath 2
Single	$ 80-125.00	$ 60.00
Double	$ 85-130.00	$ 75.00

Prospect Hill B&B Inn   408 Boal St 45210   Cincinnati OH
Gary & Tony   Tel: 513-421-4408
Res Times 8am-11pm

Nestled into a wooded hillside in downtown Cincinnati, this Italianate Victorian townhouse was built by Jacob DeBoor in 1867 on Prospect Hill, now a *National Historic District*. The Bed & Breakfast has been restored, keeping original woodwork, doors, hardware and light fixtures. Each room is furnished with period antiques from various decades. Our 1870's and 1940's rooms include woodburning fireplaces, skelton keys and spectacular views of downtown. The Penthouse Suite has a jacuzzi with a great view. Try the 1902's Room with queen bed and a large Victorian bath with clawfoot tub and shower. We are the oldest B&B operating within the city and are only a fifteen minute walk to Fountain Square on the Ohio River. The University of Cincinnati, Playhouse In The Park, music hall, Eden Park and most hospitals and museums are less than two miles away. There is plenty of off-street parking. *Prospect Hill B&B Inn* is surrounded by wooded park land so guests can relax beneath a shade tree or in our hot tub while taking in a view of the Queen City. A complimentary continental breakfast is included. **Discounts:** 10% for 7 day stay or longer **Airport:** Cincinnati Intl-12 mi **Reservations:** Credit card number or deposit to guarantee, 7 day cancel policy for refund, late arrival only with pior arrangements **Brochure:** Yes **Permitted:** Children 10-up, drinking outdoors only **Payment Terms:** Check AE/DISC/MC/V [K06IPOH-26948] **COM** Y **ITC Member:** No

Rates:	Pvt Bath 4
Single	$ 89-109.00
Double	$ 89-109.00

Tudor House   PO Box 18590 44118   Cleveland OH
Jane McCarroll   Tel: 216-321-3213
Res Times 9am-5pm

c1920's Tudor style residence listed on *Register of Historic Places* and beautifully furnished, offering convenience and comfort during your stay. Hosts are professional couple who have traveled widely and enjoy sharing their home with guests. Full breakfast included. **Seasonal:** No **Brochure:** Yes **Permitted:** Smoking, limited drinking **Payment Terms:** Check [X11ACOH-4202] **COM** Y **ITC Member:** No

Rates:	Pvt Bath 2
Single	$ 55-65.00
Double	

©*Inn & Travel Memphis, Tennessee*

Ohio *National Edition*

White Oak Inn	29683 Walhonding Rd 43014	**Danville OH**
Ian & Yvonne Martin		**Tel:** 614-599-6107
		Res Times 7am-10pm

Set in the rolling hills of the Walhonding Valley, the *White Oak Inn* is a turn-of-the-century farmhouse, crafted entirely from local timbers. It has a fifty foot long front porch with swings and rocking chairs, a screened gazebo and fourteen acres of woodlands for guests to explore. Each room is lovingly furnished with antiques, restored and upgraded to provide maximum comfort for today's guests. We pamper our guests with touches like extra large fluffy towels, feather pillows and homebaked cookies. Three of our guest rooms have fireplaces. The antique square grand piano is the focus for our cozy common room, where guests gather for complimentary refreshments in front of the fireplace. A hearty country breakfast is included with lodging; dinner available at added cost except for weekend packages below. Taste buds are tantalized by gourmet four-course candlelit dinners, prepared from the freshest local ingredients and including homebaked breads and desserts. Among our guests' favorite dishes are Peppered Apricot loin of pork and Rocky Road Cake with hot fudge sauce. We are always happy to cater to special dietary requests. A registered archaeological dig is located right on the Inn grounds. Nearby attractions include Ohio's Amish countryside, fishing, cycling trails and golf. **Airport:** Columbus- 50 mi. **Discounts:** Commercial rates **Packages:** Romantic, Naturalist, Wine, Trim-A-Tree, Cooking, Archaeological, Murder Mysteries **Meals:** Gourmet dinners by reservations Special Note: Your hostess Yvonne Martin and their Inn is featured in *"Country Inn Cooking"*, aired on public television stations beginning in 1996. **Seasonal:** No **Reservations:** Deposit secured with credit card number, two night min Sept-Oct and 4/15-5/30 **Brochure:** Yes **Permitted:** Limited children, drinking, no smoking **Conference:** Groups to twenty persons **Languages:** French **Payment Terms:** Check DISC/MC/V [I02HPOH1-4206] **COM YG ITC Member:** No

Rates: Pvt Bath 10
Single $ 65-125.00
Double $ 70-130.00

Buxton Inn	313 E Broadway 43023	**Granville OH**
Orville & Audrey Orr		**Tel:** 614-587-0001
		Res Times 8am-7pm

Built in 1812 as a tavern and stagecoach stop, you can still recall another era when you stay at this National Registered Historic Place. Fully restored and furnished with antiques, you can relax in this country atmosphere and be close to quaint shopping in the village shops, antique fairs, and plenty of fine country dining. Continental breakfast included. **Seasonal:** No **Brochure:** Yes **Permitted:** Children, limited smoking, limited drinking **Payment Terms:** Check AE/MC/V [X11ACOH-4211] **COM Y ITC Member:** No

Rates: Pvt Bath 15
Single $ 50.00
Double $ 60.00

Mainstay B&B	1320 E Main St 44641	**Louisville OH**
Joe & Mary Shurilla		**Tel:** 216-875-1021

A beautifully restored century-old Queen Anne Victorian offering spacious rooms, original tin ceilings, richly carved oak woodwork and antiques galore. Louisville was the home town of Charles Julliard, the founder of New York City's music school bearing his name. Mary and Joe, both educators, greet guests with a complimentary fruit and cheese basket upon arrival, a sparkling beverage, a le petit

©*Inn & Travel Memphis, Tennessee*

dejeuner or full breakfast served between 7 and 9:30 am, with coffee available at 6 am for early risers. Local sights include Julliard's home, listed on the National Register of Historic Places, offers tours by prior arrangement; the Pro Football Hall Of Fame in nearby Canton. **Discounts:** Yes, extended stays of 3 days or longer **Airport:** Akron-Canton Regional-16 mi. Private entrance with personal key. **Seasonal:** No **Reservations:** Deposit required, 4-9pm check-in, late arrival only with prior arrangements, check-out 11am **Brochure:** Yes **Permitted:** Children, drinking **Payment Terms:** Check [R02FPOH-16294] **COM** Y **ITC Member:** No

Rates:	Pvt Bath 1	Shared Bath 2
Single	$ 40.00	$ 35.00
Double	$ 50.00	$ 45.00

Inn At The Green 508 S Main St 44514 **Poland OH**
Steve & Ginny Meloy **Tel:** 216-757-4688
Res Times 12pm-9pm

A classic 1876 Victorian "Baltimore" townhouse surrounded with a sweeping view of Main Street and Western Reserve Colonials, Federal and Greek Revival dating from the 19th century. The residence has been completely restored and includes twelve foot ceilings, beautiful crown moldings, five Italian marble fireplaces and the original popular floors. All the guest rooms are uniquely furnished and are light and airy with poster beds and antiques, and Sealy Posture-pedic mattresses for guests' comfort. Mornings begin with a complimentary breakfast of fruit juice, croissant and muffins, french jams and coffee, served outdoors on a wicker-furnished porch, if weather permits. Complimentary pm aperitif gets the guests ready for selecting from one of the many restaurants nearby. You can enjoy plenty of year-round activities: jogging, cross country skiing, antiquing, golf, tennis, fly fishing, canoeing and sailing. You may also visit museums, such as the Butler Institute, that houses the nation's finest American Art Collection. **Seasonal:** No **Reservations:** One night's deposit at res time, within 7-days; 7-day cancellation policy. **Brochure:** Yes **Permitted:** Drinking, smoking, limited children **Conference:** Yes **Payment Terms:** Check MC/V [X01BCOH-4234] **COM** Y **ITC Member:** No

Rates:	Pvt Bath 2	Shared Bath 2
Single	$ 55.00	$ 45.00
Double	$ 60.00	$ 50.00

Azorean B&B 242 W Walnut St 43072 **Saint Paris OH**
Bob & Alda Bondaruk **Tel:** 513-663-5448
Res Times 10am-8pm

An excellent place for adults who enjoy the company of each other to that of other travelers or just escaping for the weekend. A place where you are made to feel special because you are! Where gourmet Portuguese dining is available with prior arrangement. This quiet, cozy, romantic, fully-restored and renovated 1875 house offers four completely private guest rooms, each with private bath, furnished largely with antiques and items of European origin. Where you can enjoy polite conversation in Portuguese, Spanish, or English as suits your fancy. The spacious guest rooms are located on both the first and second floors for added convenience. The large front porch provides for restful enjoyment of ones book, partner or solitude. Located on the Simon Kenton Historic Corridor; the quaint village shops offer peaceful shopping while the country-side beckons with canoeing, horseback riding, sail boating or nature walks at Kiser Lake State Park. **Discounts:** Yes, extended stays **Airport:** Dayton Intl-40 mi **Seasonal:** No **Reservations:** Prefer two weeks in advance if dining, full deposit guarantee, refunded if situation warrants, preferred rates for travel agents; discounts for extended stays **Brochure:** Yes **Permitted:** Limited smoking, drinking with meals **Conference:** Limited space for up to ten **Languages:** Portuguese, Spanish **Payment Terms:** Check MC/V [R02FPOH-16270] **COM** Y **ITC Member:** No

Rates:	Pvt Bath 4	
Single	$ 49.00	
Double	$ 52.00	

Wagners 1844 Inn 230 E Washington St 44870 **Sandusky OH**
Barb & Walt Wagner **Tel:** 419-626-1726 **Fax:** 419-626-3465
Res Times 24 Hrs

This beautiful and elegant Italianate-style home dating from 1844 welcomes guests to the quaint town of Sandusky where time stands still. Listed on the *National Register of Historic Places*, this vintage Bed and Breakfast features turn-of-the-century grace and pleasant solitude with its antique furnishings including a billiard room, Victorian Parlour, antique piano, living room with woodburning fireplace, screened-in porch and enclosed courtyard. The three spacious guest rooms include air conditioning, private baths along with modern amenities. Morning brings a complimentary continental breakfast of homemade baked goods, fresh fruit and plenty of warm beverages. You can dine in formal elegance of the dining room or relax in the casual atmosphere of the screened in porch. The Inn is just one block from Sandusky's historic downtown and two blocks from Sandusky Bay where you can catch a ferry to Cedar Point or Lake Erie islands. Downtown Sandusky offers numerous restaurants, boutiques and antique shops - and even a wave pool when temperatures rise. Within a short drive there are abundant recreational, cultural and historical attractions including golf, swimming, sailing, fishing, hiking, nature trails and birding at two nearby nature reserves - plus numerous wineries offering both tours and sampling. As a small Inn, your hosts, a practicing attorney and a registered nurse, extend personalized attention to all of their guests. **Discounts:** Yes, corporate weekdays **Airport:** Cleveland-60 min; Toledo-60 min **Seasonal:** No **Reservations:** Full payment in advance in summer; partial payment winter, one week cancel policy for refund **Brochure:** Yes **Permitted:** Limited pets (resident cat and dog), drinking **Payment Terms:** Check DC/MC/V [Z04HPOH1-13527] **COM** YG **ITC Member:** No

Rates:	Pvt Bath 3
Single	$ 50-90.00
Double	$ 65-100.00

Sugar Camp Cottage 319 Collett Rd 45068 **Waynesville OH**
Mr Mrs Mckay Collett **Tel:** 513-382-6075
Res Times 8am-8pm

City getaway - enjoy this farmhouse in the country for a weekend or a week! *Sugar Camp Cottage* sleeps up to eight persons and includes two baths, kitchen, living room, dining room, screened porch and washer/dryer. Set in a corner of 80 acres of woods, there's pasture and a stream - a mile from the nearest road. Guests can feed the cows, collect eggs, shear the sheep, feed the chickens or walk through the woods and sample the wonderful wildflowers. Indoor activities include board games, video tapes and books. Nearby, you'll find Kings Island, Wilmington College, Caesars Creek State Park, swimming, canoeing and numerous restaurants and antique shops in Lebanon and Waynesville. The kitchen is fully equipped with a microwave, electric stove and frige. A full complimentary breakfast including eggs fresh from the farm and such dishes as sausage casserole with fried apples, cheesy egg bake, banana blueberry muffins and fresh fruit bowl. **Airport:** Greater Cincinnati-50 mi **Seasonal:** No **Reservations:** $50 deposit, 48 hr cancel policy for refund; *two shared guest rooms are included **Brochure:** Yes **Permitted:** Children, limited drinking **Conference:** Yes, for groups to twenty persons **Payment Terms:** Check MC/V [R02FPOH-16307] **COM Y ITC Member:** No

Rates:	Pvt Bath 1	Shared Bath 2
Single	$ 70.00	
Double	$ 70.00	

Cider Mill B&B Second St 44697 **Zoar OH**
Ralph & Judy Kraus **Tel:** 216-874-3133

Surround yourself with the memories of Ohio's early settlers in this charming village and Inn dating from 1863, originally a mill and cabinet shop for hardy, religious pioneers. Renovated in 1972, guest rooms are highlighted by the original exposed ceiling beams and furnished with tastefully selected antique pieces. Common areas include a unique three-story spiral staircase and a stone hearth in the family room for relaxing at day's end. Complimentary continental breakfast is served from the appealing country kitchen. Close-by, you'll find antiques and gift shops, two public golf courses, scenic bike paths, well-stocked fishing spots and the Amish area with the National Football Hall of Fame close at hand. Other meals available with advanced notice. **Seasonal:** No **Reservations:** One night's deposit at res time, non-refundable. **Brochure:** Yes **Payment Terms:** Check AE/MC/V [X02BCOH-4256] **COM Y ITC Member:** No

Rates:
Single
Double

Shared Bath 2
$ 50.00
$ 55.00

Spring House
Ray Constance Hearne

Muddy Creek Forks 17302

Airville PA
Tel: 717-927-6906
Res Times 8am-9pm

Ten years of restoration by this charming and witty hostess/owner introduces guests to a countryside setting and historic inn. The farm girl, turned art student (Antioch College) and now innkeeper, was introduced to bed and breakfast inns while on a walking trip through England. She has brought all of her ideas together to create an inn every traveler needs to visit. Constructed by a legislator in 1798 of local warm-colored fieldstone, the *Spring House* retains its history with country antique furnishings, handwoven rugs, paintings, cheerful antique quilts and featherbeds that offer a cloud of comfort in winter. Dining is exceptional at breakfast (plum cobbler or sweet corn timbale) also homemade jams/jellies, kugelhopfs, pies and breads, sparkling cider, all prepared from farm-fresh ingredients and home-prepared on a woodburning stove. Theme weekends offer lessons in bread baking, vegetarian Indian cooking, use of herbs, wreath-making, tours and wine tasting, stenciling, Christmas tree gathering and decorating and special Welsh musical happenings. Ray invites everyone to enjoy her transplanted yellow primroses, Ullyses, the resident dog and tour guide, the purring cats, the sounds of spring peepers, the smell of farm-fresh breakfast cooking on the wood stove, the bright Milky Way and the wild and cultivated fruit she has gathered. Country comforts are not a thing of the past at *Spring House*! Sightseeing in nearby York, Gettysburg and Lancaster includes the Amish landscape, wineries, antique shops with horseback riding, golf and hiking. Restored scenic railroad right at the front door! (Ma & Pa). **Airport:** Baltimore/Wash Intl-60 mi **Seasonal:** No **Reservations:** Full payment at time of reservation, 7 day cancel policy refund less 10% service fee; otherwise, refund if room is filled **Brochure:** Yes **Permitted:** Children, drinking **Conference:** Yes, a dining room a huge ships table **Languages:** Spanish **Payment Terms:** Check [Z06GPPA-4398] **COM** Y **ITC Member:** No

Rates:	Pvt Bath 3	Shared Bath 2
Single	$ 75.00	$ 50.00
Double	$ 85.00	$ 60.00

Bedford House
Lyn & Linda Lyon

203 W Pitt St 15522

Bedford PA
Tel: 814-623-7171
Res Times 10am-10pm

This 200 year old brick residence and the present owners (only the sixth family privileged to own this lovely home) invite travelers to come home to the Bedford House. The ambience remains much the same as in 1803 - where guests can relax in the Early American living room in a wingback chair by the fireplace or converse with the hosts and other guests or read in a quiet corner. The guest room decor varies with the size and includes a double or queen size bed all with private shower-baths, and some with fireplaces and TV. Furnishings include some antiques, reproductions and family heirlooms to rekindle the historical spirit. In the morning, guests are treated to a full breakfast of seasonal fruits, homemade muffins and bread and the *"Chef's Choice"* entree in the large country kitchen. Located in the National Historic District of Bedford Borough, guests are just a five minute walk from Fort Bedford Museum and Park, local shops, restaurants, churches and the post office. Nearby attractions include Old Bedford Village, Fort Bedford, Shawnee State Park, Coral Caverns and Blue Knob Ski Resort. Activities include golf, hiking, swimming, fishing, hunting, craft and antique shopping, winter sports and fall foliage **Airport:** Pittsburgh-97 mi west **Seasonal:** No **Reservations:** One night's deposit required, 3 day cancel policy for refund less $10 service fee **Brochure:** Yes **Permitted:** Drinking, children 12-up, limited smoking **Payment Terms:** Check AE/DISC/MC/V [R12EPPA-14472] **COM** Y **ITC Member:** No

Rates:	Pvt Bath 8
Single	$ 35-65.00
Double	$ 45-75.00

Pennsylvania
National Edition

Vietersburg Inn B&B	1001 E Main St 15530	**Berlin PA**
Kathy & Larry Ogline		**Tel: 814-267-3696**
		Res Times 6-10:30pm

Meet a charming couple who welcome all guests as members of their family in their c1860's home that includes twelve foot ceilings, spacious rooms, gorgeous woodwork, winding staircases and two guestrooms, all furnished with antiques, family heirlooms, and handcrafted accessories. One room is furnished with a lovely iron and brass bed and the other offers two double beds with a beautifully carved oak fireplace mantel with antique details. A hearty country breakfast is prepared just for each guest's taste and includes fresh fruit, juice, eggs, potatoes, toast with homemade jams and jellies, beverages, and homebaked pastries. **Seasonal:** No **Reservations:** $10.00 deposit for each night's stay. **Brochure:** Yes **Permitted:** Children, drinking, smoking **Payment Terms:** Check [X02B-CPA-4409] **COM Y ITC Member:** No

Rates:	Pvt Bath 1	Shared Bath 1
Single	$ 50.00	$ 45.00
Double	$ 50.00	$ 45.00

Mulberry Farm	616 Flohrs Church Rd 17307	**Biglerville PA**
Mimi Agard		**Tel: 717-334-5827**

This 1817 brick colonial home was used during The Battle of Gettysburg as a rest stop . . . and continues to be a rest stop - Beautifully restored, the Inn offers a serene atmosphere in a busy community. Six miles west of Gettysburg, Pennsylvania, our guests spend the day visiting the battlefields and come "home" to comfort. Five bedrooms filled with antiques and some furnishings made by your host, Jim Agard. Jim's an artist and has restored ten houses and teaches at Gettysburg College while Mimi has been in public relations since college. They owned The Brafferton Inn in Gettysburg for nine years and purchased *Mulberry Farm* and a home in the Caribbean (available for weekly rentals). *Mulberry Farm* is a classic Williamsburg restoration, has four acres to roam with beautiful perennial gardens; country lanes to walk - making for a memorable visit to this area of Pennsylvania. A full breakfast is served on white Wedgewood accented by a mixed collection of variegated blue cups, saucers and bowls while candles glow, soft music plays - all set on a drop-leaf cherry table. Full breakfast specialties might include crepes with rosy apple sauce topping and French toast with mulberries. On warm mornings, guests may prefer to dine on the terrace or, for a special occasion, request breakfast in bed. Local sights always include the historic Gettysburg, a local winery and summer theater. **Airport:** BWI/Baltimore; Dulles/DC; Harrisburg **Seasonal:** No **Reservations:** 50% deposit to guarantee, 7 day cancel policy for refund less $15 service fee, check-in 3-6pm, check-out 11am **Brochure:** Yes **Permitted:** Children, drinking, smoking outside only **Payment Terms:** Check [I10HPPA1-19416] **COM YG ITC Member:** No

Rates:	Pvt Bath 5
Single	$ 100-125.00
Double	$ 100-125.00

Greystone Manor	2658 Old Philadelphia Pike 17505	**Bird In Hand PA**
Ann Treier		**Tel: 717-393-4233**
		Res Times 8am-8pm

In the Heart of the Pennsylvania Dutch Country is this spectacular French (Second Empire) Victorian mansion with segmented arches, high Victorian windows, imposing bay windows and stately columns typical of the post-Civil War Period. Built in c1883, the interior touches remain much the same today. Cut crystal doors, intricate woodwork carvings, antique bath fixtures, molded plaster ceilings, antique lighting fixtures, beveled glass doors and lovely antique furnishings and family heirlooms are throughout the Inn. All of the rooms are a/c and color TV is available. A carriage house is available for guests

2-88 ©*Inn & Travel Memphis, Tennessee*

seeking privacy. A continental breakfast is served in the beautiful dining room and a quilt and craft store is located in the basement for easy shopping. Just five miles from Lancaster, you're close to all of the sights, including: Amish Farms, farmers' markets, Strasburg Railroad, Dutch Wonderland, Hershey (45 mins) and many Amish quilt and craft shops. Multiple room suites are available for families. **Seasonal:** No **Reservations:** One night's deposit at res time, 72 hr cancel policy. Less than 72 hr notice, refund only if the room is rebooked. Call if arriving after 8pm. **Brochure:** Yes **Permitted:** Drinking, limited smoking, limited children **Conference:** Yes for groups to 14 persons. **Payment Terms:** Check MC/V [Z11DPPA-4412] **COM** Y **ITC Member:** No

Rates: Pvt Bath 13
Single $ 55-65.00
Double $ 75-90.00

Village Inn Of Bird In Hand	2695 Old Philadelphia Pike 17505	**Bird In Hand PA**
Richmond & Janice Young	Tel: 800-914-2473 717-293-8369	**Fax:** 717-768-1117
		Res Times 7am-9pm

Enjoy the hospitality of our 18th Century Country Inn located in the heart of the rolling farmlands of Lancaster County Pennsylvania. Dating back to 1734, the Inn was originally a stop for stage coaches on their way to the "frontier" of Lancaster from Philadelphia. Inns were built every few miles along the way as convenient rest stops for travelers. It is listed on the *National Register of Historic Places*. Today, your innkeepers continue to reside in the Inn and provide guests with the finest hospitality. Fresh flowers greet you in our Inn's eleven uniquely decorated guest rooms. Each room has it's own private bath and deluxe down-filled bedding. Four of our rooms are suites, three with king-size beds and two with whirlpool baths. Each morning we served a continental-plus breakfast in the common area, the Sun Porch. All guests can enjoy free use of indoor and outdoor pools and tennis courts located within walking distance of the Inn. We also offer a complimentary two hour tour of the surrounding Amish Farmlands. Although the town of Bird-in-Hand is small (pop 300), there are many things for guests to do. Adjacent to the Inn is a farmer's market, a country store and a number of quilt and craft shops. And within minutes of our Inn are numerous antique shops, museums and outlet shopping. The Inn is great for get-aways and special occasions like honeymoons and anniversaries. **Airport:** Harrisburg Intl-45 min **Packages:** Yes, includes meals and attractions **Reservations:** Deposit required to guarantee reservation, 48 hr cancel policy for refund E-mail: Smucker @ Bird-in-Hand.com **Brochure:** Yes **Permitted:** Children, limited smoking, limited drinking **Payment Terms:** Check AE/DISC/MC/V [I04H-PPA1-11939] **COM** YG **ITC Member:** No

Rates: Pvt Bath 11
Single $ 59-144.00
Double $ 59-144.00

Indian Mountain Inn	Tripp Lake Rd 18812	**Brackney PA**
Dan & Nancy Strnatka		Tel: 717-663-2645 **Fax:** 717-663-3123
		Res Times 9am-8pm

Indian Mountain Inn is located at the top of the *"Endless Mountains"* in Susquehanna County of Northeastern Pennsylvania. It is twelve miles north of the county seat of Montrose, twelve miles south of Binghamton, New York and just twelve miles from I-81. Sequestered in over 3500 acres of undeveloped countryside, its dining room overlooks the far hillside where deer, wild turkey and other wild animals are frequently viewed. The outdoors lovers will plenty of space for hiking, mountain biking, cross country skiing and just relaxing. Fishing enthusiasts will find closeby Quaker Lake a haven of trout, Salt Springs State park is only six miles away with hiking trails, water falls, and the only stand of virgin hemlock in the entire state of Pennsylvania. It, along with the Thompson Wet Lands in nearby

Pennsylvania *National Edition*

Thompson, Pennsylvania, make *Indian Mountain Inn* an ideal Eco-tourist destination. The Inn has an excellent reputation for fine dining at its best. The menu includes such items as Charbroiled lamb tenderloin with fresh mint demigalce, Salmon Dijonaise and Shrimp and Scallop Provencale. Owners Nancy and Dan Strnatka are part of the Binghamton exchange program with sister-city La Teste de Buch in the Bordeaux Region of France. In 1994 they were the guests of the French city for two weeks where they learned the fined points of French wines, food and oysters! Nancy is an accomplished potter and items from her studio are available for sale in the gift shop and demonstrations are available upon request. 1995 will see the beginning of art workshops for pottery, painting and writing. 1996 will be a great time to come out and watch the production of maple syrup. September and October offer the most vibrant fall colors of anywhere in the USA. Come and check them Out! The Inn is located between Elk Mountain and Greek Peak for excellent downhill skiing and Quaker Lake is often ideal for the ice-boating enthusiast. Last but not least, there are antique shops galore. **Airport:** Greater Broome County- 20 mi **Packages:** Midweek, 2 nights with dinner and breakfast $210.00; weekends $249.00 *Pets must be crate trained and small. **Seasonal:** No **Reservations:** One night deposit or credit card number required to guarantee reservations, 14 day cancellation policy, full refund less $10 service fee *Suite $125.00 **Brochure:** Yes **Permitted:** Drinking, pets* **Conference:** Yes, small groups to 25 persons **Payment Terms:** Check MC/V [V05HPPA1-6465] **COM YG ITC Member:** No

Rates:	Pvt Bath 6	Shared Bath 4
Single	$ 85-95.00	$ 75.00
Double	$ 95.00	$ 85.00

Pine Knob Inn   Rt 447 PO Box 275 18325   Canadensis PA
*John Garman   Tel: 800-327-8358 717-595-2532

An historic Civil War Period Inn of distinction - nestled in a picturesque setting in the heart of the beautiful Pocono Mountains creates a perfect year-round resort. The Inn offers guests simple hospitality and comfort with antique furnished guest rooms. The friendly and informal atmosphere highlights the inn's charm and uniqueness has guests returning year after year. Continental cuisine such as rack of lamb, roast ducking, daily fresh seafood and veal are featured in the nigthly five-course gourmet dinner prepared by the inn's chef, served in the candlelit dining room accompanied by a selection of music unique to Pine Knob. A hearty full breakfast begins each day, featuring homemade breads, blueberry pancakes, fresh fruits and much more. The inn's grounds offer a pool, tennis court, horseshoes and other lawn games while there are plenty of shade trees, a trout stream and trails for hikers, birders and nature walks. Nearby are excellent golf courses, boating, horseback riding, the Pocono Playhouse Theatre, Promiseland State Park with winter sports at Alpine Mountain Ski Area, Jack Frost, Camelback and Shawnee ski areas. Anytime of the year - your hosts are ready to make you feel at home with their pleasant surroundings, delicious dining and gracious service. **Airport:** ABE-Bethlhem-1 hr **Seasonal:** No **Reservations:** $100 deposit required to confirm reservation *Rates based on MAP **Brochure:** Yes **Permitted:** Children 8-up, drinking, smoking **Conference:** Groups to thirty easily accommodated for weddings, receptions, private parties, conferences**Payment Terms:** Check MC/V [Z04GPPA-4424] **COM Y ITC Member:** No

Rates:	Pvt Bath 18	Shared Bath 4
Single	$ 80.00	$ 60.00
Double	$ 160.00	$ 120.00

Clarion River Lodge   Clarion PA
Ellen O'Day   Tel: 800-648-6743 814-744-8171
   Res Times 24 hrs

©*Inn & Travel Memphis, Tennessee*

National Edition   *Pennsylvania*

Refer to same listing name under Cooksburg, Pennsylvania for a complete description. **Seasonal:** No **Payment Terms:** Check AE/MC/V [M05FPPA-6564] **COM** Y **ITC Member:** No

Rates: Pvt Bath 20
Single $ 64-109.00
Double $ 74-129.00

Tara - A Country Inn	3665 Valley View Rd 16113	**Clark PA**
*Donna & Jim Winner		**Tel:** 800-782-2803 412-962-3535
		Res Times 8am-8pm

Tara is a **World-Class Country Inn** based on the greatest movie of our time "Gone With The Wind". Each of our twenty-seven guest rooms are lovingly named and decorated in honor of characters in the movie or themes inspired by the Civil War Era. There are three distinct restaurants at Tara. Ashley's is our Gourmet Dining Room, boasting an elegant seven course meal, table-side flambes and the most extensive wine list in Western Pennsylvania. Stonewall's Tavern was inspired by the 1850's roadside pubs. We serve an a la carte menu in a perfect atmosphere for a quiet afternoon or evening of conversation. The Old South Restaurant is our family-style dining area. The waitresses serve up bountiful helpings of Southern cooking, just like Mammy would - all you can eat. A visit to Tara, whether for a weekend getaway, a dining experience or corporate business, will indulge you in the lifestyles of a by-gone era. You will encounter Southern Hospitality in its truest form and be treated like belles and gents of the Antebellum South. *Tara* is a virtual museum of rare antiques, works of art and collectibles of the Golden Days of the South. **Seasonal:** No **Reservations:** Deposit within 5 days of booking, 7 day cancel policy for refund, *call for special package and corporate rates **Brochure:** Yes **Permitted:** Drinking, limited smoking **Conference:** Specialized convention and meeting service, extensive spa facilities available, fax, copier and AV equipment on property, phones in all rooms **Payment Terms:** Check DC/MC/V [I03FPPA-4429] **COM** YG **ITC Member:** No

Rates: Pvt Bath 27
Single $ 75-198.00
Double $ 75-198.00

Victorian Loft	216 S Front St 16830	**Clearfield PA**
Tim & Peggy Durant		**Tel:** 800-464-1268 814-765-4805
		Res Times 9am-11pm

Step back in time to an era when life had more grace .... as it might have been at the turn-of-the-century. Elegant 1894 Victorian home on the river in historic district featuring double-decker Gingerbread porches, hand-carved cherry staircase, original stained glass windows and lots of Victorian charm throughout. In addition to warm hospitality, amenities include: memorable full breakfast in the full formal dining room; air conditioned rooms with skylights featuring antique linens, books and rocking chairs; private kitchen and dining area; guest entertainment center with family movies provided; grand piano, billiards and spacious bath with whirlpool tub. Guests interested in textiles may visit our sewing studio which was recently featured in *"Threads"* magazine. Discover how wool, silk and linen are spun into yarn for weaving of knitting of garments and household items. Spinning and weaving demonstrations by request. Also: Off premises, completely equipped post and beam three bedroom cabin on eight forested acres adjacent to State Parks available for one party only. Five hours from Philadelphia, NYC, DC, Baltimore and Toronto. Easily accessible from Pittsburgh, Harrisburg, Erie and just two hours from the Ohio border. **Airport:** Pittsburgh Intl-85 mi **Seasonal:** No **Reservations:** Credit card number or one night's prepaid lodging, late arrival by prior arrangement only *800 number from 8am-5pm only **Brochure:** Yes **Permitted:** Children, limited pets **Languages:** Conversational Spanish **Payment Terms:** Check MC/V [R11FPPA-16231] **COM** Y **ITC Member:** No

Rates: Pvt Bath 2   Shared 2
Single $ 45-55.00 $ 35-45.00
Double $ 55-65.00 $ 45-55.00

©Inn & Travel Memphis, Tennessee

Clarion River Lodge	HC 1 Box 22D 16217	Cooksburg PA
Ellen O'Day		**Tel:** 800-648-6743 814-744-8171
		Res Times 24 hrs

Small, romantic Inn nestled in a clearing above the Clarion River. Originally built as an executive private estate. The main building features open, spacious architecture with native stone and timbers - anchors twenty well-appointed most comfortable lodging units as well as a full service restaurant. The Lodge is adjacent to Cook Forest State Park, which has the largest remaining virgin pine and hemlock stand in the East and where outdoor recreational activities abound: canoeing, horseback riding, hiking, snowmobiling, swimming, water slides, rafting, fishing, bicycling, hunting, golfing, cross country skiing, theatre programs, historic sites and museums. The twenty rooms have all the amenities necessary for a most comfortable stay at Cook Forest including TV, phone, refrigerator, a/c, and private bath. The Lodge has a full restaurant and beverage service featuring a refined menu of meat, seafood and pasta entrees. Innkeeper Ellen O'Day and her friendly staff can help you plan your day. Mid-week, the Lodge is ideal for seclusion in a spectacular natural setting. Other meals available on the premises; continental breakfast included. AAA 3-Diamond Award inn. **Seasonal:** No **Reservations:** $50 deposit within one week of booking res **Brochure:** Yes **Permitted:** Children 12-up, smoking, drinking **Conference:** Yes, for groups to 100 persons and a special River Room for groups to 40 persons **Payment Terms:** Check AE/MC/V [Z05G-PPA-6563] **COM** Y **ITC Member:** No

Rates: Pvt Bath 20
Single $ 74-129.00
Double $ 74-129.00

Ponda-Rowland B&B	RR 1 Box 349 18612-9604	Dallas PA
Jeanette & Cliff Rowland		**Tel:** 800-854-3286 717-639-3245 **Fax:** 717-639-5531
		Res Times 11am-11pm

Rowland Farm is located in the Endless Mountains region of Northeast Pennsylvania. It provides year-round spectacular scenery as the setting for a family farm vacation, a restful stay for business travelers, or a romantic retreat. A thirty acre wildlife sanctuary has been established, complete with trails and wild creatures. These include majestic blue herons, swans, snow geese, deer and fawn, fox, and the occasional bear or coyote. In addition, there are plenty of domestic farm animals: horses, goats, sheep, turkey, chicken, dogs, cat, pot-bellied pig and ferret. The Inn features museum-quality American Colonial country furnishings and antiques abound with special touches in each guest room. The Amish Room has a king size bed or two twin cannonball beds, an 18th Century armoire and a fantastic view of the wildlife sanctuary. The Autumn Room has a king size bed and a similar view. The Spring Room overlooks the farm fields and has a double bed and dresser in bird'seye maple. Two new rooms (the Mallard and the Swan Room) each have king size beds, fireplaces, armoires and great views of the wildlife sanctuary. Each of these rooms is connected to a separate room with beds for additional adults and/or children. Guests are treated to a full country breakfast by candlelight, which includes homemade pancakes, French toast, eggs, cereals, a beautiful fruit platter, juices and beverages. Special and vegetarian diets are available with prior notice. Complimentary afternoon and evening beverages and snacks in any of the six large common rooms, two with satellite TV and one with the great stone fireplace (the Great Room). Activities include hiking, fishing, canoeing, hay rides, pony rides, children play areas, indoor games, tobogganing, ice skating, down hill and cross country skiing. **Airport:** Wilkes-Barre, Scranton Intl just 20 miles **Reservations:** Deposit or credit card , 14 day cancel policy **Permitted:** Children, drinking, limited pets **Conference:** Yes, to 12 persons and lodging **Payment Terms:** Check AE/DISC/MC/V [I02HPPA1-12551] **COM** YG **ITC Member:** No **Quality Assured:** Yes

Rates: Pvt Bath 5
Single $ 65-95.00
Double $ 65-95.00

National Edition **Pennsylvania**

Crestmont Inn	Crestmont Drive 17731	Eagles Mere PA
John & Jane Wiley		Tel: 800-522-8767 717-525-5519
		Res Times 8am-10pm

Since the turn-of-the-century, visitors from Philadelphia, Washington DC, Baltimore, Harrisburg and New York City have made Eagles Mere home. Poised on the highest point in Sullivan County is Crestmont Inn where a comfortable atmosphere, gracious hospitality and a warm welcome await you. As Norman Simpson, renowned as the *"father of country inns"* said, **"Eagles Mere is one of the last unspoiled resorts in the East".** On the Crestmont Inn grounds, guests have full privileges of our 60 x 30 pool, six expertly maintained Har-Tru tennis courts and three shuffle board courts. Within a three minute drive is Eagles Mere Country Club with a splendid eighteen hole course full of beautiful hardwood forests, views and meticulously maintained greens. Guests can enjoy the ten acres of lawns, gardens and nature trails of the Inn and the adjacent 18,000 acre Wyoming State Forest. Guest accommodations range from cozy bedrooms to spacious suites, all tastefully appointed with baths offering old-fashioned tiger paw tubs and showers reminiscent of the early part of the century. Candlelight and flowers from the gardens grace the Inn's beautifully appointed tables. Just three blocks from the Inn is the charming Victorian village of Eagles Mere, complete with gaslight lamps lining the streets. The 19th Century shops feature antiques, handmade woolens from Ireland, herb and perennial plants, homemade jams and jellies, handmade quilts and collectibles from our country and abroad. Members of PAII and IIA **Discounts:** Mid-week corporate rates **Airport:** Williamsport/Lycoming-33 mi **Packages:** Golf, Murder Mystery Weekend **Seasonal:** No **Reservations:** One night's deposit for short stays, 50% for long stays, 15 day cancel policy for refund except Dec-April, deposit is non-refundable *Rates based on MAP **Brochure:** Yes **Permitted:** Children, drinking, limited pets **Conference:** Yes, groups to sixty **Payment Terms:** Check MC/V [K11FPPA-16969] **COM** U **ITC Member:** No

Rates:	Pvt Bath 18
Single	$ 115.00
Double	$ 145.00

Bechtel Mansion Inn	400 W King St 17316	East Berlin PA
Ruth Spangler		Tel: 800-873-2392 717-259-7760
		Res Times 9am-6pm

A magnificent Queen Anne Victorian Mansion c1897, listed on the *National Historic Register*. Popular with honeymooners, anniversary couples and guests interested in the local historical, architectural and Pennsylvania Dutch atmosphere of Lancaster, York and Gettysburg. All rooms are handsomely furnished with period antiques, numerous porcelains, oriental rugs, handmade Mennonite Quilts, and with modern amenities such as a/c. Located on the Western frontier of the 18th century Pennsylvania Dutch Country, East Berlin is noted for examples of Pennsylvania German and Victorian architecture and the charming, scenic and historical role when both Union and Confederate troops passed by prior to the Battle of Gettysburg! **Airport:** Philadelphia-100 mi; Baltimore BWI-70 mi; Wash DC National-105 mi**Reservations:** Full deposit or guarantee with credit card at res time; 72-hr (prior to 1:00 pm check-in time) cancel policy for refund. 10% discounts for AARP/Senior Citizens. **Brochure:** Yes **Permitted:** Children, drinking, limited smoking **Conference:** Yes, for groups up to 12 rooms of cyclists or bird watchers in group reservations. Gift Certificates are available for those special persons and occasions in life. **Payment Terms:** Check AE/DISC-/MC/V [I11DPPA-4443] **COM** Y **ITC Member:** No

Rates:	Pvt Bath 7	Shared Bath 2
Single	$ 65-95.00	$ 55.00
Double	$ 75-130.00	$ 70-85.00

©*Inn & Travel Memphis, Tennessee*

Pennsylvania   *National Edition*

Spencer House B&B	519 W 6th St 16507	**Erie PA**
Pat & Keith Hagenbuch		**Tel:** 800-890-7263 814-454-5984 **Fax:** 814-456-5091

When it was built in 1876, the old house at 519 West Sixth Street was one of the showiest homes in the city. Judah Colt Spencer, founder and president of Erie's First National Bank, constructed the home as a wedding gift for his son William. Over the course of the next 117 years, the home was occupied but never with residents so willing to share its beauty and hospitality as now. Erie's first B&B - the *Spencer House B&B* remains an architectural showplace. Keith is a full time physics professor at Penn State-Behrend, the B&B becomes Pat's full time vocation - one which is her dream-come-true. *"I like serving people, taking care of people and having people in my home."* The complete restoration Pat undertook preserved the historic integrity of the home. While the original woodwork and historic features captivate guests - each guest bed room is individually decorated with themes ranging from the Niagara to the Keyna Room. Guests are invited to join the Hagenbuch family in the elegant living room, with its fireplace and baby grand piano, or to enjoy a good book in the comfortable library. And before you leave, stop by the quaint gift shop, featuring locally made items and *Spencer House* memorabilia. Home cooked breakfast is frequently the best reason for staying at the *Spencer House*. Guests are treated to an individually prepared breakfast consisting of fresh juice, coffees and homemade baked goodies served daily. The *Spencer House* is the perfect location for small weddings, business luncheons, workshops and seminars - providing participants with a truly unforgettable experience. The harried business traveler to Erie will find the home comforts and relaxed surrounds an enjoyable change of pace. Located close to Presque Isle and the Erie Bayfront, it is the ideal home base for visiting hikers, boaters, cross country or downhill skiers and sightseers. For guests who prefer their entertainment closer to home, the wide inviting front porch is the perfect place to watch the world pass on a sunny Erie afternoon. **Discounts:** Corporate 10%, Extended stays **Airport:** Erie Intl-5mi **Seasonal:** No **Reservations:** $50 deposit per room within 7 days of booking, 7 day cancel policy for refund less $10 service fee **Brochure:** Yes **Permitted:** Well behaved children, drinking (BYOB), limited smoking **Conference:** Small groups for memorable and special occasions **Payment Terms:** Check AE/DISC/MC/V [U02HPPA1-16227] **COM YG ITC Member:** No

Rates: **Pvt Bath 6**
Single $ 70-125.00
Double $ 75-130.00

Duling-Kurtz House	146 S Whitford Rd 19341	**Exton PA**
Tish Morescalchi		**Tel:** 610-524-1830 **Fax:** 610-524-6258
		Res Times 9am-9pm

A cozy parlor welcomes guests to this Inn offering fifteen individually decorated guest rooms, each with its own warmth and charm. Each guestroom, named after historical figures, has been comfortably furnished with beautiful period reproductions and a selection of rooms offering fireplaces (decorative only), old-fashioned clawfoot tubs, jacuzzis, four-poster and canopy beds and suites that include your own private outdoor courtyard. All baths are private. A fine Continental breakfast of fruits, juices, home-baked pastries, rich coffees and fragrant teas are offered each morning. Guests can experience old-style candlelight dining in the intimate rooms of our lovely stone home. You may enjoy a view of our formal gardens from one of the glass-enclosed porches or from one of four dining rooms featuring working fireplaces. Anywhere in the Inn, you'll dine elegantly on the

©Inn & Travel Memphis, Tennessee

National Edition   *Pennsylvania*

best foods and spirits. We welcome you to be our guest. Our staff will assure you a wonderful visit. *Duling-Kurtz House and Country Inn* is conveniently located to the many historic sights, museums, galleries and theaters throughout Chester County and the surrounding countryside and is just a short drive from Center City Philadelphia. Our private banquet and meeting facilities provide a special comfort and intimacy. Whether it be a romantic garden wedding or a successful business meeting, our coordinator's special attention to details guarantees a memorable occasion. **Airport:** Phila Intl-50 mi **Packages:** Dining Packages **Seasonal:** No **Reservations:** Seventy-two hour cancel policy (prior to 3pm 72 hrs before reservation date) **Brochure:** Yes **Permitted:** Children 3+, drinking, smoking **Payment Terms:** AE/DC/DISC/MC/V [I08GPPA-4457] **COM YG ITC Member:** No

Rates:	Pvt Bath 15
Single	$ 55-120.00
Double	$ 55-120.00

Bechtel Mansion Inn   Gettysburg PA
Ruth Spangler   **Tel:** 800-873-2392 717-259-7760
                                                               Res Times 9am-6pm

Refer to the same listing name under East Berlin, Pennsylvania for a complete description. **Seasonal:** No **Payment Terms:** Check AE/DISC/MC/V [M11D-PPA-6558] **COM YG ITC Member:** No

Rates:	Pvt Bath 7	Shared Bath 2
Single	$ 65-95.00	$ 55.00
Double	$ 75-130.00	$ 70-85.00

Beechmont Inn   Gettysburg PA
William & Susan Day   **Tel:** 800-553-7009 717-632-3013
                                                               Res Times 9am-9pm

Refer to the listing name under Hanover, Pennsylvania for a complete description. **Seasonal:** No **Payment Terms:** Check AE/DISC/MC/V [M05HC-A1-13086] **COM YG ITC Member:** No

Rates:	Pvt Bath 7
Single	$ 80-135.00
Double	$ 80-135.00

Brafferton Inn   44 York St 17325   Gettysburg PA
Jane & Sam Back   **Tel:** 717-337-3423
                                                               Res Times 9am-9pm

A sculpture of Colonel Brafferton directs guests safely to the front door of the *Brafteron Inn*, where they are warmly greeted by new hosts, Jane and Sam Back. Having purchased the Inn in February 1993, the Back's have renovated it to include ten guest rooms, each with a private bath, while retaining all of the convincingly historic charm of this eclectic bed and breakfast. In fact, in one of the upstairs guest rooms (aptly called the "Bullet Room"), curious guests will discover a Union bullet lodged in the mantel of the fireplace, from the July 1863 Battle of Gettysburg. All of the rooms are handsomely furnished and decorated with a large collection of 18th and 19th century antiques. The four walls surrounding the breakfast room are covered with a primitive mural depicting historic Gettysburg landmarks and scenes painted by local artist Virginia Jacobs McLoughlin, who also designed the 18th century stencils that adorn the guest rooms. Guests will enjoy relaxing in the atrium with a skylight roof and exposed brick walls or behind the house on the patio, amidst the herb and flower garden. **Airport:** DC National-90 mi **Discounts:** Yes, inquire at res time **Seasonal:** No **Reservations:** 50% deposit of length of stay at res time or credit card number for guarantee, 7 day cancel policy for refund **Brochure:** Yes **Permitted:** Children 9-up, drinking, limited smoking **Conference:** Yes for groups of 10-12 persons **Languages:** French **Payment Terms:** Check MC/V [I03HPPA1-4464] **COM YG ITC Member:** No

©*Inn & Travel Memphis, Tennessee*

Pennsylvania National Edition

Rates: Pvt Bath 10
Single $ 80.00-up
Double $ 90.00-up

Mulberry Farm B&B — Gettysburg PA
Mimi & Jim Algard — Tel: 717-334-5827

Refer to the same listing name under Biglerville, Pennsylvania for a complete description. **Seasonal:** No **Payment Terms:** Check [M10GPPA1-21424] **COM YG ITC Member:** No

Rates: Pvt Bath 5
Single $ 100-125.00
Double $ 100-125.00

Tannery B&B — 49 Baltimore St 17325 — Gettysburg PA
Ryan Raffensperger — Tel: 717-334-2454
Res Times 8am-10pm

Built in the mid 1800s - guests recall the Battle of Gettysburg when, on the 3rd day of the Battle, John Rupp (the original owner) hid in the cellar while Union men occupied the porch and Confederate soldiers occupied the rear of the original Rupp house. Located just four blocks south of the center of town - the Battlefield complete surrounds *The Tannery*! Today, Jule, Charlotte and their family welcome guests to share their family home and the history of Gettysburg. You'll feel right at home with these charming hosts who have decorated their home for your comfort with traditional furnishings. Guests relax on a spacious front porch with a tall lemonade or iced tea and enjoy wine and cheese before dinner, in the parlor. You'll awake each morning to a delicious continental plus breakfast. Well-know landmarks are within walking distance and include Evergreen Cemetery where Lincoln gave his famous Gettysburg Address, Jenny Wade's home and the town center is just four blocks away. Tour buses for the Battleground and Pres Eisenhower's home are within one block. Lutheran Theological Seminary, Gettysburg College along with golf, Caledonia State Park for hiking, swimming or an afternoon picnic in the mountains, beautiful farmlands and fruit orchards. **Distances:** Harrisburg 35 mi, Washington DC 70 mi and Baltimore 60 mi. **Reservations:** $20 per night deposit at res time, 14 day cancel policy for refund.**Brochure:** Yes **Permitted:** Drinking, children 8-up, smoking outdoors only **Payment Terms:** Check MC/V [I05DPPA-8863] **COM Y ITC Member:** No

Rates: Pvt Bath 5
Single $ 55.00
Double $ 65-85.00

Huntland Farm B&B — RD 9 Box 21 15601 — Greensburg PA
Robert & Elizabeth Weidlein — Tel: 412-834-8483
Res Times 9am-6pm

Nestled in the foothills of the Allegheny Mountains, one hundred acre *Huntland Farm* is three miles northeast of Greensburg, Pennsylvania. The house, built in 1848 and listed in Historic Places of Western Pennsylvania, is furnished with antiques. A large living room as well as porches and gardens are available for guest's use. Four large corner bedrooms make it comfortable for up to eight people. Each bathroom accommodates two bedrooms. *Huntland Farm* is ideal for out-of-town guests coming for weddings or reunions and visitors to Seaton Hall College, St Vincent College or the Univ of Pittsburgh at Greensburg. It is a convenient halfway stop for travelers going to or from the midwest to the east coast. The property is in the western section of the Laurel Highlands Recreational Area and contains many scenic and historical sites, such as: Fort Ligonier, Bushy Run, Seven Springs, Ohiopyle water raft-

National Edition   *Pennsylvania*

ing and Fallingwater, Frank Lloyd Wright's masterpiece. Skiing, jogging and walking trails are close by. Hot air ballooning, Westmoreland Museum of Art and excellent restaurants and antique shops are nearby. **Discounts:** Yes, weekly stays **Airport:** Pittsburgh-50 mi **Seasonal:** No **Reservations:** One night's deposit **Brochure:** Yes **Permitted:** Children 12-up, social drinking, limited smoking **Languages:** French **Payment Terms:** Check AE [Z04GPPA-8858] COM Y **ITC Member:** No

Rates:	Shared Bath 4
Single	$ 55.00
Double	$ 70.00

Inn At Elizabethville   Halifax PA
Beth & Jim Facinelli   **Tel:** 717-362-3476 717-362-3477 **Fax:** 717-362-4571
                                                                                                       Res Times 8am-8pm

Refer to the same listing name under Elizabethville, Pennsylvania for a complete description. **Seasonal:** No **Payment Terms:** Check MC/V [M11CPPA-11818] COM YG **ITC Member:** No

Rates:	Pvt Bath 5
Single	$ 55.00
Double	$ 60.00

Beechmont Inn   315 Broadway (Rt 194) 17331   Hanover PA
William & Susan Day   **Tel:** 800-553-7009 717-632-3013
                                                                                                       Res Times 9am-9pm

All sixteen rooms of this gracious Federal Period home, built in 1834, were completely redecorated with soft period colors, artwork, and furnishings. Restored to its former elegance, *Beechmont* offers guests a bridge across time. There are four large bedrooms and three suites; one with a working fireplace, one with a private balcony, and one with a private kitchenette. Common rooms include a formal parlor, a library and the dining room. All rooms are air-conditioned for comfort. Much attention is given to small details such as 18th century books in the library, extra pillows on the queen-sized beds, a collection of Civil War and local memorabilia and complimentary tea and sweets served in the afternoon. Outdoors, guests relax and enjoy breakfast under a vine-covered trellis, the wicker-filled porch and a flagstone patio sheltered by a 125 year-old magnolia tree. Herb and flower gardens and even an old-fashioned glider swing are on the landscaped grounds. The full breakfast is still the special event it was in the 18th century. The full multi-course breakfast often includes hot entrees of apricot puff pancakes, herb cheese tarts, or shirred eggs in bread baskets. *Beechmont* will enjoy pampering you. Conveniently located to Gettysburg Battlefield, Hershey Park and Lancaster County's PA Dutch countryside. Enjoy antiquing in nearby New Oxford and affordable outlet shopping in both Hanover and York. Numerous golf courses and wineries are in the area. Lake Marburg, only three miles away, offers swimming, boating and fishing. **Airport:** 40 mi to Baltimore-Washington and Harrisburg. **Packages:** Anniversary, Honeymoon, Weekend and Golf **Seasonal:** No **Reservations:** Deposit required by check, 48 hr cancel policy. **Brochure:** Yes **Permitted:** Drinking, limited children **Conference:** A large dining area or a small library are available, depending upon the group size; copier on the premises **Payment Terms:** Check AE/DISC/MC/V [I05HPPA1-4477] COM YG **ITC Member:** No

Rates:	Pvt Bath 7
Single	$ 80-135.00
Double	$ 80-135.00

Hen-Apple B&B   Harrisburg PA
Flo & Harold Eckert   **Tel:** 717-838-8282
                                                                                 Res Times 9am-9pm

©*Inn & Travel Memphis, Tennessee*

Pennsylvania National Edition

Refer to the same listing name under Palmyra, Pennsylvania for a complete description. **Seasonal:** No **Payment Terms:** MC/V [M02HPPA1-16885] **COM** YG **ITC Member:** No

Rates:	**Pvt Bath 6**
Single	$ 65.00
Double	$ 75.00

Academy Street B&B	528 Academy St 18428	Hawley PA
*Judith Lazan		Tel: 717-226-3430

A premium Bed and Breakfast Inn offering gourmet breakfast and afternoon tea and cakes in a completely restored 1863 Victorian residence that's nestled in the beautiful lake region of the Poconos! All of the guest rooms are furnished with lovely canopied brass or antique beds and include air conditioning and CATV. Victorian flair-with beautiful paneling and molding throughout. You don't want to miss the house specialties for a buffet breakfast which includes blueberry french toast and rum raisin pudding! Convenient to I-84 and all the Pocono attractions, Lake Wallenpaupack and recreational activities. Member of PMVB and listed in most B&B brochures. **Seasonal:** Yes **Reservations:** Deposit required at res time for 3-day weekends. Winter phone 609-395-8590 **Brochure:** Yes **Permitted:** Limited drinking, limited smoking **Payment Terms:** Check MC/V [Z04IPPA1-4480] **COM** YG **ITC Member:** No

Rates:	**Pvt Bath 4**	**Shared Bath 3**
Single	$ 75.00	$ 45.00
Double	$ 75-80.00	$ 65.00

Settlers Inn	4 Main Ave 18428	Hawley PA
Jeanne/Grant Genzlinger		Tel: 800-833-8527 717-226-2993

Standing as a monument to the grand hotels of the 1920's, the Tudor-style *Settlers Inn* remains much the same today. The Inn's eighteen guest rooms are tastefully furnished with "early attic" antiques offering comfort with private baths. There's an upstairs sitting room and an airy front porch for guests to socialize, sip a cool drink and enjoy a cool afternoon breeze. A spacious lobby with specialty shops and a massive stone fireplace evokes an *"English hotel" atmosphere - stately but not stuffy!* An on premises restaurant offers amiable service and excellent homemade recipes that include seasonal specialties and renown homemade breads. Live piano music entertains guests in the dining room at each meal. Gothic oak chairs and tables covered with lace cloths and handmade crafts and art works by local artists decorate the dining room area. This Lake Region offers a multitude of year-round activities which include skiing, ice skating, water skiing, boating, swimming, hiking, and Fall Foliage! At the end of a busy day, the fireplace in the tavern is the perfect gathering location. **Reservations:** Deposit or credit card guarantee, 24 hr cancel policy **Brochure:** Yes **Permitted:** Children, drinking **Languages:** German/French **Payment Terms:** Check AE/MC/V [R06BCPA-4481] **COM** Y **ITC Member:** No

Rates:	**Pvt Bath 18**
Single	$ 50.00
Double	$ 75-85.00

Hen-Apple B&B		Hershey PA
Flo & Harold Eckert		Tel: 717-838-8282
		Res Times 9am-9pm

Refer to the same listing name under Palmyra, Pennsylvania for a complete description. **Seasonal:** No **Payment Terms:** MC/V [M02HCPA1-16979] **COM** YG **ITC Member:** No

Rates:	**Pvt Bath 6**
Single	$ 65.00
Double	$ 75.00

Ash Mill Farm	Rt 202 18928	Holicong PA
Pat & Jim Auslander		Tel: 215-794-5373
		Res Times 9am-8pm

2-98 ©*Inn & Travel Memphis, Tennessee*

National Edition **Pennsylvania**

An invitation to tranquility and a gracious country welcome awaits you at our c1790 stone manor home set amidst eleven bucolic sheep filled acres of meadows, nurseries, deer, bunnies, berries and wild flowers. Featured in *"Gourmet"* and *"Family Circle"* magazines. Full gourmet breakfast and afternoon tea to the strains of Brahms, Mozart or Vivaldi in front of the walk-in fireplace in winter; or on the flower-strewn patio summers. Five accommodations including two-room suites are tastefully decorated with treasures collected in Ireland, England and America. Minutes away from the famous Peddler's Village and New Hope. In an area renown for its antique shops, arts and crafts boutiques, and galleries, their is something for everyone's taste. **Discounts:** Extended stays **Airport:** Phila Intl-23 mi; Newark Intl-65 mi **Reservations:** MC or V, one night deposit to confirm room/s **Permitted:** Children over 15 **Payment Terms:** Check MC/V [Z04GPPA-4485] **COM** Y **ITC Member:** No

Rates:	Pvt Bath 5
Single	$ 90-145.00
Double	$ 90-145.00

Inn At Jim Thorpe   24 Broadway 18229   **Jim Thorpe PA**
David Drury   **Tel:** 717-325-2599 **Fax:** 717-325-9145
Res Times 6am-10pm

Discover the elegance of *The Inn at Jim Thorpe*. Our hotel, painstakingly and lovingly restored, recalls that highflying era of gaslights and horse-drawn carriages, black diamonds and Victorian opulence. Built in the 1840's, it has provided comfort to some of the 19th Century's most influential and colorful people. Each of the rooms at the Inn is elegantly appointed with furnishings reminiscent of the Victorian Age. Our private baths are complete with pedestal sinks and genuine marble floors. Of course, the comforts of home are here as well: a/c, cable TV and phone are found in each room. . With our stunning Victorian architecture and picturesque setting, Jim Thorpe has been called the *"Switzerland of America"*. For the adventurous, Jim Thorpe has some of the best mountain biking and whitewater rafting in the Northeast plus Skirmish (paintball) is nearby. **Discounts:** Yes, inquire at res time **Airport:** ABE-25 mi **Packages:** Ski, Whitewater Rafting, Mountain Biking, Golf, Ski and Special Entertainment **Seasonal:** No **Reservations:** One night's deposit (25% if stay is over 4 days) at res time, 14 day cancel policy **Brochure:** Yes **Permitted:** Children, drinking, limited smoking **Conference:** Yes, for groups to 75 persons **Payment Terms:** AE/DC/DISC/MC/V [R04EPPA-14019] **COM** Y **ITC Member:** No

Rates:	Pvt Bath 21
Single	$ 65-125.00
Double	$ 65-125.00

Meadow Spring Farm   201 E Street Rd 19348   **Kennett Square PA**
Anne Hicks/Deborah Hicks Axelrod   **Tel:** 610-444-3903
Res Times 3pm-later

Picture-perfect rustic stone farmhouse c1836 is nestled on a 150-acre working farm complete with all the animals and all in the heart of Brandywine Country with a delightful hostess who is an accomplished cook, decorator and craftswoman. Anne enjoys entertaining and she extends great hospitality to all guests for a day trip or longer. Her home is delightfully furnished with antiques that include a queen size sleigh bed and a Chippendale canopied queen-size bed fitted with handmade Amish quilts. The other guest rooms are complete with Laura Ashley prints, linens and quilts, with wedding gown wall-hangings. Nothing is overlooked by Anne and you'll enjoy the details such as fresh flowers year-round in all the guest rooms. Activities include antiquing, tennis, golf, skiing, canoeing and tubing and museums aplenty. Featured in *"Country Time Magazine"*, *"New York Times"* and *"Pennsylvania Magazine."* **Seasonal:** No **Reservations:** $20 deposit at res time, check-in after 3pm **Brochure:** Yes **Permitted:** Children, drinking, limited smoking **Payment Terms:** Check [I06FPPA-4496] **COM** U **ITC Member:** No

Rates:	Pvt Bath 4	Shared Bath 2
Single	$ 65.00	$ 55.00
Double	$ 75.00	$ 65.00

Pennsylvania   National Edition

Australian Walkabout Inn   837 Village Rd 17537   Lampeter PA
Richard & Margaret Mason   **Tel:** 717-464-0707 **Fax:** 717-464-2678
Res Times 9am-9pm

An authentic Australian-style B&B in the heart of the Amish Countryside - just as the Australian word Walkabout means: to go about and discover new places, you too can easily embark on your own walkabout from our conveniently located Inn. Beautifully furnished and decorated throughout with antique furniture, canopy and queen size beds for your comfort along with private bath and cable TV with jacuzzi and fireplaces available in some rooms. A two-bedroom suite is also available. Each morning guests find a romantic candlelight full breakfast served in the *Walkabout* dining room. Maggie's home recipes feature homemade Australian and British pastries, muffins, jellies and jams after which you can relax on the wrap-a-round porch and sip a cup of imported Australian tea while watching the passing Amish buggies or while enjoying the English Country garden and patio. Eight person outdoor jacuzzi for relaxation. Nearby activities offer historic sites, country auctions, shopping outlets, many fine restaurants and a nine hole executive golf course. Your hosts have provided tour information and money-saving coupons for their guests. Dinner available with prior arrangements and additional cost. AAA Three Diamond Property. **Airport:** Lancaster-10 mi **Packages:** Halloween, Thanksgiving, Amish dinner, Tour; Two-Night Special includes dinner with Plain People, 3 hour Tour, full breakfast each morning. Honeymoon/Anniversary Specials. **Discounts:** AAA **Packages:** Dec-April: Double Special Two Nights-Two Breakfasts-Buggy Ride-Dinner One Night $259.00 **Seasonal:** No **Reservations:** One night's deposit, 7 day cancel notice less $35 service fee, less than 7 day notice, refund only if rebooked **Brochure:** Yes **Permitted:** Children 9-up, drinking, limited smoking (outdoor porch) **Conference:** Yes, for groups to ten **Languages:** Some Spanish **Payment Terms:** Check AE/MC/V [I07HPPA1-4503] **COM YG ITC Member:** No

Rates:	Pvt Bath 5
Single	$ 69-129.00
Double	$ 89-149.00

Australian Walkabout Inn   Lancaster PA
Richard & Margaret Mason   **Tel:** 717-464-0707 **Fax:** 717-464-2678
Res Times 9am-9pm

Refer to the same listing name under Lampeter, Pennsylvania for a complete description. **Seasonal:** No **Payment Terms:** Check AE/MC/V [M07HCPA1-16449] **COM YG ITC Member:** No

Rates:	Pvt Bath 5
Single	$ 69-129.00
Double	$ 89-149.00

Buona Notte B&B   2020 Marietta Ave 17603   Lancaster PA
Joe & Anna Kuhns Predoti   **Tel:** 717-295-2597

Plenty of warmth and hospitality with these charming hosts who offer their home to all guests during their trip through the Amish country. Plenty of sightseeing while visiting the Pennsylvania Dutch. A great continental breakfast is included which features homemade breads, jams, jellies and granola. **Seasonal:** No **Brochure:** Yes **Permitted:** Children 2-up **Languages:** Italian, French **Payment Terms:** Check [X11AXPA-4505] **COM Y ITC Member:** No

Rates:	Pvt Bath 1	Shared Bath 3
Single		$ 50.00
Double	$ 70.00	$ 60.00

2-100   ©*Inn & Travel Memphis, Tennessee*

National Edition   *Pennsylvania*

Hillside Farm B&B   Lancaster PA
Gary & Deb Lintner   Tel: 717-653-6697
Res Times 24 Hrs

Refer to the same listing name under Mount Joy, Pennsylvania for a complete description. **Seasonal:** No **Payment Terms:** Check Tvlrs Check [M04GPPA-18783] **COM** Y **ITC Member:** No

Rates:	Pvt Bath 3	Shared Bath 2
Single	$ 62.50	$ 50.00
Double	$ 62.50	$ 50.00

Witmers Tavern Historic 1725 Inn   2014 Old Philadelphia Pike 17602   Lancaster PA
Brant E Hartung   Tel: 717-299-5305
Res Times 8am-8pm

Pre-Revolutionary travelers stopped here in 1725 and the Inn remains much the same today and is listed on the *National Historic Register*. One of the remaining original inns on the first turnpike to Philadelphia. Fireplaces everywhere (including all the guest rooms) antique furnishings, beautiful original hardware (locks and hinges) and traditional six over nine windows. A continental breakfast is include with the room rate. **Seasonal:** No **Reservations:** Deposit required at res time, 10 day cancel policy for refund **Brochure:** Yes **Permitted:** Children 12-up, limited smoking, limited drinking **Payment Terms:** Check [X11ACPA-4510] **COM** Y **ITC Member:** No

Rates:	Pvt Bath 3	Shared Bath 2
Single	$ 75.00	$ 65.00
Double	$ 85.00	$ 75.00

The Whistlestop B&B   195 Broad St 15056   Leetsdale PA
Steve & Joyce Smith   Tel: 412-251-0852
Res Times 8am-10pm

The *Whistlestop Bed & Breakfast* is a quaint brick Victorian built in 1888 by the Harmonist Society, a Christian communal group similar to the Shakers. It features two guest suites, both with CATV, a/c, private bath and phones. In keeping with a train theme, the "Upper Berth" is a third floor suite with a small kitchen and a dining area. The "Lower Berth" has a sofa bed and private entrance on the first floor. Children are welcome and stay free in their parent's room. The home is smoke-free and resident pets prefer that you leave your pets at home. Your hostess is well known for her country cooking, specializing in homemade breads, muffins, pastries and jams which you'll enjoy for breakfast which is served in the family dining room or outdoors beneath magnificent walnut and oaks. Leetsdale is located on the Ohio River, twelve miles west of Pittsburgh and close to the classic American village of Sewickley where fine examples of historic architecture are well maintained. While in the area, guests can visit Old Economy Village, a state historic site and the last home of the Harmonists. Directions: Follow I-79 to Pittsburgh, exit 19 to Sewickley, turn right onto the Ohio River Blvd (Rt 65) North, drive seven miles. Turn right on Spencer Street and right on Broad Street, Leetsdale. **Airport:** Pittsburgh Intl-20 min **Reservations:** $25 deposit required 10 days in advance **Brochure:** Yes **Permitted:** Children, limited drinking **Payment Terms:** Check Tvlr Ck [R08GPPA-18992] **COM** U **ITC Member:** No

Rates:	Pvt Bath 2
Single	$ 50.00
Double	$ 60.00

Alden House   62 E Main St 17543   Lititz PA
Harold & Joy Coleman   Tel: 800-584-0753 717-627-3363
Res Times 1pm-9pm

Old-fashioned, old-town hospitality with modern conveniences blend together in this stately brick residence (c1850) in historic Lititz, a street and town reminiscent of everyone's dream hometown of yesteryear. A town where lovingly restored homes still line quiet streets, bedecked with window boxes of

Pennsylvania   *National Edition*

brightly colored flowers. Where friendly neighbors still tip their hat warmly as you relax on the porch almost frozen in the good life in this slower - less hectic pace! A part of Main Street, the *Alden House* has been painstakingly restored to her original Civil War-era charm and elegance. Her guests enjoy a continental plus breakfast buffet served in the breakfast nook or outdoors on one of her three porches. Guests will especially enjoy the gardens and sightseeing in this peaceful and quaint hometown. **Reservations:** 50% deposit within 7 days of res; 7 day cancel policy for full refund; 72 hr cancel refund less 10%, less than 72 hr, no refund. 2 nite min on holiday weekends (1 nite surcharge $10); off-season rates from 11/1-3/31 offers $10 discount from rates for two nights, holidays excluded. *Suite of quad 90-95.00. **Seasonal:** No **Brochure:** Yes **Permitted:** Children 7-up, smoking and drinking. **Payment Terms:** Check MC/V [R06BCPA-4520] **COM Y ITC Member:** No

Rates:	Pvt Bath 5	Shared Bath 2
Single	$ 75-85.00	$ 75.00
Double	$ 75-85.00	$ 75.00

General Sutter Inn   14 E Main St 17543   **Lititz PA**
Tel: 717-626-2115
Res Times 9am-9pm

The oldest continuously operating Inn in Pennsylvania, 1764 where guests step back in time with the Gaslight Pub on the premises offering fine dining. The Inn is furnished with authentic Victorian antiques and family treasures creating a warm and hospitable feeling for guests. A continental breakfast is included. **Seasonal:** No **Reservations:** One night's deposit at res time with a 5 day cancel policy for a refund. **Brochure:** Yes **Permitted:** Limited children, smoking and drinking **Payment Terms:** Check MC/V [X11ACPA-4521] **COM Y ITC Member:** No

Rates:	Pvt Bath 4	Shared Bath 2
Single	$ 65.00	$ 55.00
Double	$ 70.00	$ 65.00

Black Bass Hotel   River Rd Rt 32 18933   **Lumberville PA**
Herbert E Ward   **Tel: 215-297-5770**
Res Times 8am-7pm

Dating from the 1740's when weary river travelers were pursued by hostile Indian bands and early fur traders travelled the paths, this inn still offers guests comfort, warmth, hospitality, fine gourmet dining and plenty of ambience. All of the rooms remind guests of the exciting history of this beautiful Buck's County area with period antiques. This is *perhaps the Only Inn where George Washington didn't sleep* because the owners were loyal to the Crown of England and wouldn't let George in! You'll have a breath-taking view of the Delaware River and enjoy the specialties of the inn. This is one piece of history travelers shouldn't miss! A continental breakfast is included. **Seasonal:** No **Reservations:** One night's deposit with 2 week cancel policy for refund. Late arrival (after 10pm) with prior arrangement. **Brochure:** Yes **Permitted:** Pets, drinking, limited smoking **Conference:** Yes with excellent dining for business and social groups looking for that special experience. **Payment Terms:** Check AE/DC/MC/V [R01BCPA-4525] **COM Y ITC Member:** No

Rates:	Pvt Bath 3	Shared Bath 7
Single	$ 125-175.00	$ 55-80.00
Double	$ 125-175.00	$ 55-80.00

Eaglesmere   RR 3 Box 2350 19355   **Malvern PA**
Dr. Mary Gillespie   **Tel: 610-296-9696**
Res Times 24 Hrs

Hidden away on a deeply wooded cul-de-sac in historic Chester County is this unique twenty-one sided contemporary home overlooking the Great Valley and Valley Forge Mountain. The unusual architecture, designed by Paul L 'Esperance, includes three cathedral ceilings, exposed beams, four decks and window walls for year-round scenery. Guests can choose the Garden Suite with soft greens, mauves and lush foliage and Andrew Wyeth's prints. A toe heater in the adjacent full bath warms frosty feet!

2-102   ©*Inn & Travel Memphis, Tennessee*

The Jungle Suite includes dramatic greys and blacks, myriad woodland plants, unusual animal and primitive masks and picture windows. There is an unusual faux marble nine-sided clock-radio cube and a supplemental heater for toasty showers. Guests can relax in the Great Room with music, an interesting library, pocket billiards on the Olhausen table, exercise on the NordicTrack or Schwinn Exercycle and a sauna too soothe-away any aches! A full breakfast is included along with creature comforts your practicing psychologist hostess has included, such as: bath gels, pre-heated beds, guest robes, original and limited edition art. The perfect place for business travel or romantic weekend getaways. Philadelphia, Valley Forge, Wilmington DE and Lancaster are all within 10-45 mins. **Seasonal:** No **Reservations:** $25 per night deposit to hold reservation, 7 day cancel policy for refund **Brochure:** Yes **Permitted:** Limited children, pets and drinking. No Smoking. **Payment Terms:** Travelers Check [R08BCPA-6885] **COM** Y **ITC Member:** No

Rates: **Pvt Bath** 2
Single $ 75.00
Double $ 75.00

Herr Farmhouse Inn   2256 Huber Dr 17545   Manheim PA
Barry & Ruth Herr   **Tel:** 800-584-0753 717-653-9852
Res Times 12pm-9pm

Relax. A world away doesn't have to be far! Nestled on eleven and one-half acres of rolling farmland in Lancaster county - the *Farmhouse Inn* presents a peaceful, quiet and tasteful setting for weary travelers. From each window in this stone home, guests experience a special world - one of pastoral horizons broken only by an occasional barn or silo - one that is well known for its intrinsic tranquility in life. Dating back to 1738, the Farmhouse Inn has been restored with the greatest care and attention to detail. The ambiance is due, no doubt in part, to such distinctive features as the fanlights adorning the entrance, the six working fireplaces and the original wide plank pine floors. Whether guests desire a cozy winter's night spent by the fireplace or a bright summer's morning spent sipping tea in the sun room, the *Herr Farmhouse* is the perfect location. A continental breakfast is included. **Seasonal:** No **Reservations:** One night's deposit required at res time. **Brochure:** Yes **Permitted:** Children, limited smoking, limited drinking **Payment Terms:** Check MC/V [R06BCPA-4527] **COM** Y **ITC Member:** No

Rates: **Pvt Bath** 2   **Shared Bath** 2
Single $ 85-95.00 $ 75.00
Double $ 85-95.00 $ 75.00

Magoffin Guest House   129 S Pitt St 16137   Mercer PA
Jacquie McCelland   **Tel:** 412-662-4611

A lovely Victorian home snuggled on a tree-lined street opposite the town court house and next to the museum. Antique furnishings are featured throughout the residence which are available for purchase. A continental breakfast is included. Close to I-79, I-80 in western PA. **Seasonal:** No **Brochure:** Yes **Permitted:** Children **Payment Terms:** Check [X11ACPA-4531] **COM** Y **ITC Member:** No

Rates: **Shared Bath** 4
Single $ 44.00
Double $ 53.00

Carriage House At Stonegate   RD 1 Box 11A 17754   Montoursville PA
Harold & Dena Mesaris   **Tel:** 717-433-4340 **Fax:** 717-433-4536
Res Times Evenings

Dating to the late 1700's and including Pres Herbert Hoover as a descendent, this converted carriage house welcomes guests to the oldest farm in the Loyalsock Creek Valley. Guests have full use of the 1400 square foot two-level facility just thirty yards from the main house nestled on thirty acres for hiking and creek wading. There are two bedrooms upstairs with a queen and double bed with a full modern bath. Downstairs is a complete living/dining area, complete kitchen and a half-bath. Guests can relax in the living area and look out onto the many flower gardens and the rolling meadows.

Pennsylvania   *National Edition*

Cribs and extra beds are available for larger families as the unit is rented to just one private party at a time. Guests will enjoy the beautiful outdoor activities year-round. The area is the gateway to extensive Game Lands of North Central Pa offering great canoeing, fishing, hunting, hiking, golfing, biking, skiing, tennis, antique hunting and interesting factory outlets. There are numerous restaurants from exquisite to local fare. Williamsport, just 6 miles west is the Little League Baseball Headquarters including its museum and a major league farm-team that calls it home. Lycoming, Bucknell, Penn State and Bloomsburg colleges are close-by. A seasonally appropriate continental breakfast is included. **Seasonal:** No **Reservations:** One nite's deposit, 7 day cancel policy less 10% fee. **Brochure:** Yes **Permitted:** Children, pets, smoking, drinking, (smoking in bed is not permitted **Languages:** Spanish **Payment Terms:** Check [Z11CPPA-4540] **COM** Y **ITC Member:** No

Rates:	Pvt Bath 2
Single	$ 50.00
Double	$ 70.00

Montrose House	26 S Main St 18801	Montrose PA
Rick & Candy Rose		**Tel:** 717-278-1124
		Res Times 7am-10pm

Built around the turn-of-the-century, the Montrose House has a colorful and interesting history with a tradition of friendly hospitality. Set in the heart of the Endless Mountains in northeastern Pennsylvania, this area has become a favorite year-round place for sport enthusiasts and vacationers. Winter brings downhill and cross country skiing and year-round antique shopping, auctions, hiking, picnics, hunting, fishing, golf and tennis. The Inn offers an Early American setting for cozy comfort and candlelight dining. A full country breakfast is served daily and weekenders are treated to a Sunday Country Brunch Buffet - - all prepared and supervised by Rick, a graduate of the Culinary Institute of America. There are twelve guest rooms (eight with private baths) and most rooms have a/c and color TV. The friendly and attentive staff insures each guest's comfort and with banquet facilities to 200 persons, this is an ideal location for conferences, banquets, weddings, class reunions, rehearsal dinners and anniversaries. Nearby activities include nature walks at Woodburne; waterfalls, hiking, fishing, swimming at Salt Springs; skiing at Elk Mountain; the Harford Fair and Annual Blueberry Festival each August. **Seasonal:** No **Reservations:** One night's deposit required, 48 cancel notice for refund **Brochure:** Yes **Permitted:** Children, pets, smoking, drinking **Conference:** Excellent banquet and meeting facilities for social and business functions with seating capacity of 200 **Payment Terms:** Check AE/DC/MC/V [R09CPPA-11281] **COM** Y **ITC Member:** No

Rates:	Pvt Bath 8	Shared Bath 4
Single	$ 42-60.00	$ 35-40.00
Double	$ 42-60.00	$ 35-40.00

Hillside Farm B&B	607 Eby Chiques Rd 17552	Mount Joy PA
Gary & Deb Lintner		**Tel:** 717-653-6697
		Res Times 24 Hrs

Dating from 1863, the two and a half-story farmhouse has an interesting history as an operating dairy farm, fruit orchard - while today its offers travelers a quiet country get-away where rabbits, squirrels, woodchucks meander in the yard. Situated off the main road, the two acre grounds provide seclusion and an opportunity to relax to the evening sounds of bullfrogs calling from the old dam at the nearby Chiques Creek - whose water, along with song birds, provide your morning wake-up call. All of the guest rooms are comfortably furnished on the second and third floors, featuring cozy bedrooms with twin, king, double and queen size beds and each features a tranquil view of the surrounding dairy farms. Located in the Pennsylvania Dutch area, all of the Amish attractions are nearby. There's hiking, biking, shopping malls, antiquing, wining, dining, swimming and golf - enough to keep everyone busy for days. A full complimentary breakfast is served in the sunny dining room each morning at 8:30. **Reservations:** One night's deposit within 7 days of booking to guarantee, bal due upon arrival. 14 day cancel policy for refund, check-in 4pm (5:30 weekdays), check-out 11am **Permitted:** Children 10-up **Payment Terms:** Check Tvlrs Check [R04GPPA-13558] **COM** Y **ITC Member:** No

Rates:	Pvt Bath 3	Shared Bath 2
Single	$ 62.50	$ 50.00
Double	$ 62.50	$ 50.00

National Edition *Pennsylvania*

Bodine House	307 S Main St 17756	Muncy PA
David & Marie Louise Smith		**Tel:** 717-546-8949

In the historic district of Muncy, this colonial residence c1805 has been beautifully restored with working fireplaces and a candlelight living room that is reminiscent of another era. A side courtyard in the Williamsburg style provides an interesting area for relaxing and conversing with your hosts. A full breakfast is included. **Seasonal:** No **Brochure:** Yes

Permitted: Children 6-up, limited social drinking
Payment Terms: Check AE/MC/V [X11ACPA-4547]
COM Y **ITC Member:** No

Rates:	**Pvt Bath** 3	**Shared Bath** 1
Single	$ 45.00	$ 35.00
Double	$ 55.00	$ 45.00

Ash Mill Farm		New Hope PA
Pat & Jim Auslander		**Tel:** 215-794-5373
		Res Times 9am-8pm

Refer to the same listing name under Holicong, Pennsylvania for a complete description. **Seasonal:** No **Payment Terms:** Check MC/V [M04EPPA-15062] **COM** YG **ITC Member:** No

Rates:	**Pvt Bath** 5
Single	$ 95-145.00
Double	$ 95-145.00

Joseph Ambler Inn	1005 Horsham Rd 19454	North Wales PA
Steve & Terry Katz		**Tel:** 215-362-7500

Beautiful estate c1734 with antique furnishings that were carefully selected to insure an authentic period atmosphere. Stenciled walls and private entrances for guest's rooms. Nestled on twelve rolling acres. A full country breakfast is included. **Seasonal:** No **Reservations:** One night's deposit required. **Brochure:** Yes **Permitted:** Children 11-up, limited drinking **Payment Terms:** Check MC/V [I11AXPA-4539] **COM** Y **ITC Member:** No

Rates:	**Pvt Bath** 15
Single	$ 85-130.00
Double	$ 92-130.00

Hickory Bridge Farm	96 Hickory Bridge Rd 17353	Orrtanna PA
Robert & Mary Martin		**Tel:** 717-642-5261
		Res Times 9am-9pm

Hickory Bridge Farm provides year-round Bed'n Breakfast and Country Dining. Located in the foothills of the Appalachian mountains in south central Pennsylvania, nine miles west of Gettysburg, guests relax and enjoy the year round peaceful atmosphere. Country cottage guest rooms are located in the woods overlooking a well-stocked mountain trout stream, while there are several guest rooms in the antique furnished farmhouse. Meals are offered in a unique and charming century-old barn decorated with farm antiques. On weekends, dinner is served the old fashioned way - homestyle with many of the fresh fruits and vegetables grown on the grounds or neighboring farms. Year-round activities include spring apple blossoms, antique flea markets, trout fishing; summer days begin with breakfast outdoors to enjoy the singing birds and later, there's golf, swimming, sightseeing at Gettys-burg or visiting the

Pennsylvania *National Edition*

Totem Pole Playhouse. Fall foliage flames the mountains with blazing colors and signals guests to begin evening fires in the Franklin stoves located in each cottage. A wintery blanket of snow transforms the farm into a picturesque wonderland and nearby ski resorts provide great skiing. **Airport:** Harrisburg-65 mi **Seasonal:** Yes **Reservations:** $35 per night deposit within 10 days of booking, 7 day cancel policy for refund, check-in 3-10pm, check-out 11am, two night min stay weekends **Permitted:** Children, drinking **Conference:** Yes, to 125 persons **Payment Terms:** Check MC/V [I04HP-PA1-4563] **COM U ITC Member:** No

Rates:	Pvt Bath 7
Single	$ 50.00
Double	$ 79-88.00

Hen-Apple B&B   409 S Lingle Ave 17078-9321   Palmyra PA
Flo & Harold Eckert   **Tel:** 717-838-8282
Res Times 9am-9pm

The *Hen-Apple* is a beautifully restored Georgian-style farmhouse offering a peaceful stay in a country setting. The house is filled to the brim with decorating delights (Stencilling, baskets, candles, wicker, antiques, quilts, braided rugs and etc). Outside you'll find lots of flowers, an herb garden, an old orchard complete with a tree swing and lawn chairs. There are a lot of things to do here, from riding our river boat, Hershey attractions, antiquing to fishing and many places of interest within driving distance - Lancaster, Harrisburg, York, Gettysburg, Carlisle, Mount Gretna with summer *"off-broadway"* shows, craft shows, good dining and a lake. Guests breathe a sigh of relief when they walk through our front door and always leave smiling, hoping to return. The Inn offers several common rooms and a huge screened porch for guest's enjoyment. A stay here is like visiting family! We serve a wonderful full course breakfast on very lovely dishes with special touches and soft music playing. The holiday season is a real treat here! We love Christmas and to decorate takes a full week. It's a real Country Christmas House. This is a true Bed and Breakfast where guests are treated real fine whether they're here for one night or a week. The rooms are all tastefully decorated with private baths, a/c and am/fm clock radios and have very comfortable bedding. There are no public phones in the B&B and only one TV in the Parlor - so this really is a place to relax and get away - with nothing more to worry about other than being on time for breakfast! **Airport:** Philadelphia Intl-2-1/2 hrs; Harrisburg Intl-15 mi **Reservations:** 50% of total amount due by check or credit card, *checks accepted only for deposit **Payment Terms:** MC/V [I02IPA1-16239] **COM YG ITC Member:** No

Rates:	Pvt Bath 6
Single	$ 65.00
Double	$ 75.00

Maple Lane Farm   505 Paradise Lane 17562   Paradise PA
Marion & Edwin Rohrer   **Tel:** 717-687-7479

In the center of the Amish settlement is this working dairy farm and guest house furnished with antiques which includes streams, woodlands and farm fresh products. A continental breakfast includes homemade breads and freshly brewed coffee. **Brochure:** Yes **Permitted:** Children **Payment Terms:** Check [X11ACPA-4564] **COM Y ITC Member:** No

Rates:	Pvt Bath 2	Shared Bath 2
Single	$ 45.00	$ 35.00
Double	$ 45.00	$ 45.00

©*Inn & Travel Memphis, Tennessee*

National Edition *Pennsylvania*

Academy Street B&B — Philadelphia PA
Judith Lazan
Tel: 717-226-3430 609-395-8590

Refer to the same listing name under Hawley, Pennsylvania for a complete description. **Seasonal:** Yes **Payment Terms:** Check MC/V [M09BPPA-6551] **COM YG ITC Member:** No

Rates:	Pvt Bath 4	Shared Bath 3
Single	$ 75.00	$ 45.00
Double	$ 75-80.00	$ 65.00

Eaglesmere — Philadelphia PA
Dr. Mary Gillespie
Tel: 610-296-9696
Res Times 24 Hrs

Refer to the same listing name under Malvern, Pennsylvania for a complete description. **Seasonal:** No **Payment Terms:** Travelers Check [M08BCPA-8716] **COM Y ITC Member:** No

Rates:	Pvt Bath 2
Single	$ 75.00
Double	$ 75.00

Hen-Apple B&B — Philadelphia PA
Flo & Harold Eckert
Tel: 717-838-8282
Res Times 9am-9pm

Refer to the same listing name under Palmyra, Pennsylvania for a complete description. **Seasonal:** No **Payment Terms:** MC/V [M02HPPA1-16886] **COM YG ITC Member:** No

Rates:	Pvt Bath 6
Single	$ 65.00
Double	$ 75.00

Independence Park Inn   235 Chestnut St 19106   Philadelphia PA
Thierry Bompard
Tel: 800-624-2988 215-922-4443
Res Times 24 Hrs

Philadelphia's Great Little Hotel located in the heart of America's most historic square mile near Independence Hall, Liberty Bell, Penn's Landing and Society Hill. The Inn perfectly mixes the charm and warmth of a small Inn with the modern state-of-the-art amenities of a large hotel. Discover our thirty six distinctively decorated rooms. Each designed with every comfort in mind from our king or queen Rice poster beds, Chippendale writing tables, remote controlled color TV, high ceilings and specially selected non-smoking rooms. The *Independence Park Inn* is listed on the National Register of Historic Places, an authentic Victorian landmark. Guests begin their day in our glass enclosed courtyard with a scrumptious complimentary European breakfast and finish the day lounging in our parlor lobby on leather settees, sipping tea and nibbling on cucumber sandwiches by the fireplace. The *Independence Park Inn* is a full-service Inn offering modern meeting room facilities to meet every need. We believe Small Meetings Succeed in Small Hotels because we offer the flexibility and privacy such meetings demand! Make your next meeting an unforgettable experience in this charming landmark facility. **Seasonal:** No **Reservations:** Credit card guarantee to hold room. 24 hr cancel policy for refund. **Brochure:** Yes **Permitted:** Children, drinking, limited smoking **Conference:** Yes. Three meeting rooms, two board rooms and one conference room for groups of 10-25 person **Payment Terms:** AE/DC/MC/V [K05CCPA-6746] **COM Y ITC Member:** No

Rates:	Pvt Bath 36
Single	$ 100.00
Double	$ 120.00

©*Inn & Travel Memphis, Tennessee*

Pennsylvania *National Edition*

Priority-A City Inn	614 Pressley St 15212	Pittsburgh PA
Mary Ann/Suzanne Graf		Tel: 412-231-3338

A restored Victorian Priory in a National Historic Registered District offering great city views, courtyards, antique furnishings and plenty of hospitality and warmth. A continental breakfast is included. Library, fireplaces, parking, shuttle and sitting rooms are included. **Seasonal:** No **Brochure:** Yes **Permitted:** Children, smoking and drinking **Payment Terms:** Check AE/DC/MC/V [X11ACPA-4572] **COM** Y **ITC Member:** No

Rates: Pvt Bath 25
Single $ 55-up
Double $ 65-95.00

The Whistlestop B&B		Pittsburgh PA
Steve & Joyce Smith		Tel: 412-251-0852
		Res Times 8am-10pm

Refer to the same listing name under Leetsdale, Pennsylvania for a complete description. **Brochure:** Yes **Payment Terms:** Travelers Check Pers Ck [M08-GPPA-20110] **COM** U **ITC Member:** No

Rates: Pvt Bath 2
Single $ 50.00
Double $ 60.00

Hunter House	118 S Fifth St 19602	Reading PA
Ray & Norma Staron		Tel: 610-374-6608

Located in downtown's historic Callowhill, this elegant 1846 Greek Revival restoration offers the warmth and friendliness of a private home coupled with the furnishings and privacy required to maintain a comfortable and relaxed atmosphere. The individually and tastefully decorated rooms and suites - with TV and a/c - blend yesterday's ambiance with todays' comforts. We are just minutes from Reading's famous outlet centers, antique markets, historic sites, fine restaurants, fashionable shops, galleries and museums . . . and just up the road is Amish Country. *Hunter House* is a unique and sheltered urban experience. A full breakfast is included in the room rates. **Discounts:** Mon-Thur and 20% disc Jan to May **Airport:** Reading-3 mi; Philadelphia Intl-60 mi; Allentown ABE-35 mi; Harrisburg Intl-40 mi **Seasonal:** Rates vary **Reservations:** Credit card or 25% deposit to hold res. 3 day cancel notice for single rooms, 14 day notice for multiple rooms. **Brochure:** Yes **Permitted:** Limited children, drinking, smoking **Languages:** Italian **Payment Terms:** Check MC/V [Z11DPPA-10872] **COM** Y **ITC Member:** No

Rates: Pvt Bath 2   Shared Bath 2
Single $ 60.00 $ 50.00
Double $ 70.00 $ 60.00

Brownstone Corner B&B	590 Galen Hall Rd 17569	Reinholds PA
Jane, Vicki, Barb		Tel: 215-484-4460
		Res Times 8am-9pm

Our 200 year old brownstone home offers four bedrooms with private and shared baths. Enjoy this country setting located on over seven acres of quiet Amish countryside. All of the rooms are tastefully furnished and decorated with lovely antiques and personal treasures. Join us for complimentary full breakfast in our large country kitchen with a walk-in fireplace. A private sitting room is waiting for you and your family. Brownstone Corner B&B is located just minutes from more than 2500 antique markets, farmers' markets, Pennsylvania Dutch Country-style restaurants famous for their generous smorgasbords, exciting sightseeing and lovely golf courses and country clubs. Reading, the *"Outlet Capital of the World"* is just 10 mi to the east. Lancaster, 20 mi to the west, offers many historical sights, with Gettysburg, Hershey, Harrisburg and Philadelphia just a short drive away. **Seasonal:** No **Brochure:** Yes **Permitted:** Drinking, children 12-up, smoking on outdoor porch **Payment Terms:** Check

MC/V [R10DPPA-13101] **COM** Y **ITC Member:** No

Rates: Pvt Bath 1   Shared Bath 2
Single $ 65.00 $ 50-55.00
Double $ 65.00 $ 50-55.00

Tara - A Country Inn   Sharon PA
Donna & Jim Winner   **Tel:** 800-782-2803 412-962-3535
                                                                        Res Times 8am-8pm

Refer to the same listing name under Clark, Pennsylvania for a complete description. **Seasonal:** No **Payment Terms:** Check DC/MC/V [M03DPPA-12138] **COM** Y **ITC Member:** No

Rates: Pvt Bath 27
Single $ 75-198.00
Double $ 75-198.00

Applebutter Inn   152 Applewood Lane 16057   Slippery Rock PA
Gary & Sandy McKnight   **Tel:** 412-794-1844
                                                                        Res Times 9am-10pm

Nestled in the rolling green meadows of rural Western PA, *Applebutter Inn* offers a window to the past. Built in 1844, the original six room farmhouse has been restored and expanded but still retains the fine millwork, flooring and brick fireplaces while furnished with antiques and authentic canopy beds setting a mood of gracious tranquility. All guest rooms have private baths and offer the luxury of today's comfort with the elegance of yesterday's charm. Your gracious hosts provide close attention to personal service yet allow guests to enjoy their privacy and relaxation. The meadow pond nearby, where geese frequently light, offers a beautiful and serene locale. Nearby sights include Slippery Rock Univ and Grove City College, Moraine State Park, McConnell's Mills State Park, the Amish Country and Wendell August Forge. Activities include: golf on nearby private club, biking, tennis, cross-country skiing. A full gourmet breakfast is provided each morning. *Special rates for Two Night Packages, 10% senior discounts, gift certificates. Handicap accessible. *Weekday rates quoted, weekends slightly higher. **Seasonal:** Clo: Thanksgiving and Christman **Reservations:** Night's deposit within 7 days, 14 day cancel policy for refund less $10 service charge. If less, may rebook anytime within 6 mos. **Brochure:** Yes **Permitted:** Children, drinking; no smoking **Payment Terms:** Check MC/V [R06-BCPA-7584] **COM** Y **ITC Member:** No

Rates: Pvt Bath 11
Single $ 65-86.00
Double $ 89-119.00

Carnegie House   100 Cricklewood Dr 16803   State College PA
Peter & Helga Schmid   **Tel:** 800-229-5033 814-234-2424 **Fax:** 814-231-1229
                                                                        Res Times 8am-10pm

Every day is special at *Carnegie House*. This old world country estate, nestled in the woods overlooking the 17th green of Toftrees Golf Course, offers the comfort and charm of a European Country Home. It's twenty guest rooms and two suites, each with private bath, are individually decorated and tastefully furnished with *Carnegie House's* own collection of beautiful antiques. The luxuriously comfortable accommodations and spectacular views will encourage you to linger. The hospitality and charm of *Carnegie House* are evident in our library where the glowing embers in the fireplace and elegantly comfortable furnishings invite you to pause to savor the delights of gracious conversation and pleasant libation with friends old and new. Our goal is to create the perfect retreat from the everyday experience. *Carnegie House* offers a complete food fare.

Pennsylvania   *National Edition*

From daily continental breakfasts to leisurely luncheons and elegantly unhurried dinners served Thursdays through Saturday in a gracefully luxurious dining room. Sunday morning's full Scottish breakfast is a particular treat. Guests may choose to relax on the veranda and enjoy the restful view down the tree-lined rolling fairway, or you can enjoy golf, hiking, cross country skiing, jogging or strolling the two mile fitness trail. Should shopping or business take you away from this serenity, the *Carnegie House* courtesy van can provide your transportation. Special occasions make your visit even more memorable - as the perfect setting for holidays, reunions, intimate getaways or corporate retreats. **Airport:** University Park-5 mi **Packages:** Yes, inquire at res time **Seasonal:** No **Reservations:** One night deposit, 14 day cancel policy for refund, late arrival only by prior arrangement **Brochure:** Yes **Permitted:** Limited children, drinking, limited smoking **Conference:** Board room for group to fourteen persons **Languages:** German, French **Payment Terms:** Check AE/MC/V [I03HPPA1-19313] **COM** YG **ITC Member:** No

Rates:	Pvt Bath 22	Suite
Single	$ 150.00	$ 225.00
Double	$ 150.00	

Strasburg Village Inn   Centre Square 17579   Strasburg PA
John Gerhardt   Tel: 800-541-1055 717-687-0900

c1788 homestead with elegant furnishings is located on the village green of this National Historic Listed District. Adjacent to the original Country Store and Creamery, guests are in the center of all the activities of this historic area. A continental breakfast is included. A porch, patio and jacuzzi are available in two suites. **Seasonal:** No **Brochure:** Yes **Permitted:** Children, smoking, drinking **Payment Terms:** Check MC/V [X11AC-PA-4601] **COM** Y **ITC Member:** No

Rates:	Pvt Bath 11
Single	$ 69-100.00
Double	$ 69-100.00

Pace One Restaurant Inn   Thornton Rd 19373   Thornton PA
Ted Pace   Tel: 610-459-3702 **Fax:** 610-558-0825
    Res Times 9am-5pm M-F

Start with a 250 year-old fieldstone barn - set it in Brandywine Valley's rich history and natural beauty - add an innovative innkeeper and chef and you'll understand *Pace One Restaurant and Country Inn's* success. Predating the Civil War, the building's thick walls retain boarded-up vents that may have been used as musket slots during the nearby Battle of Brandywine, original wide planked floors and stucco walls with museum lighted drawings and watercolors complete this country setting. *Bed & Breakfast Pace One* style means a room with charm, modern conveniences and a continental breakfast of fresh fruit, orange juice, breakfast cake and coffee to start your day. The nearby Brandywine Museum in Chadds Ford houses the world-famous collection of paintings and illustrations - particularly works by the Wyeth family - many inspired by the beauty of the area itself. Minutes away you'll find Longwood Gardens, renowned for breathtaking horticultural exhibits. Favorable reviews from the Philadelphia Enquirer and selected the **Readers Choice Restaurant Award** by the *Wilmington News Journal* - Ted's *"country imaginative"* cooking is the heart of all they do and shouldn't be missed. The entrees are fresh, the soups homemade, and the desserts astounding - including the now-famous Pace One New England pudding; hot cobbler made with apples, pineapple and walnuts and topped with rich vanilla ice cream that slowly melts into a wonderful gooey mess. Whether dining or resting overnight, guests will find the Inn a gracious, comfortable place to stay. **Airport:** Phila Intl-25 mins **Discounts:** Corporate rates,

2-110   ©*Inn & Travel Memphis, Tennessee*

extended stays **Seasonal:** No **Reservations:** Credit card deposit to guarantee reservation, 2 day cancel policy for full refund **Brochure:** Yes **Permitted:** Children, smoking and drinks only purchased through the restaurant bar **Conference:** Yes, six rooms plus full facilities for banquets to parties, weddings, reunions, graduation and bar mitzvah - all designed to suite your needs **Payment Terms:** Check AE/DC/MC/V [I02HPPA1-6469] **COM** U **ITC Member:** No

Rates:	Pvt Bath 6
Single	$ 65.00
Double	$ 85.00

Victorian Inn B&B   205 S Home Ave 19562   **Topton PA**
Ron & Linda Knecht   **Tel:** 610-682-6846
   Res Times 24 Hrs

Mid-way between Reading and Allentown is this 1912 Grand Victorian home where the hosts pamper you just like Grandma! Beautiful beveled glass windows and an antique-tiled entry welcomes guests to a "Home away from Home". Each of the four guest rooms has a unique decor, from Oriental to Revolutionary themes. A spacious suite 12 x 28 is available with a fireplace, private bath and cable TV. Guests can unwind by soaking in a clawfoot tub, enjoying the antique piano or relaxing outdoors in the rose garden your hosts pride themselves on. An outdoor spa and a wonderful porch capture cooling breezes during the summer. Your hosts haven't overlooked anything. Hospitality and VIP treatment is assured each guest. After a relaxing night, you'll awaken to the smell of freshly brewed coffee and you'll enjoy the homemade breads and pastries that will delight every palate; and a complimentary copy of the local newspaper. Guests can enjoy the nearby activities, including basketball and tennis courts, golf and miniature golf, hiking, horseback riding, skiing, swimming and walking, just to name a few. Within a short driving distance are the famous Reading Discount Markets, fabulous antiquing and yearly events you should see, like the Kutztown Fair. **Seasonal:** No **Reservations:** $25 advance deposit, with a 10 day cancel policy for refund. **Brochure:** Yes **Permitted:** Limited children, limited drinking, limited smoking **Conference:** Yes for groups to 5-7 persons. **Payment Terms:** Check MC/V [R11C-PPA-10954] **COM** Y **ITC Member:** No

Rates:	Pvt Bath 1	Shared Bath 3
Single	$ 70.00	$ 40.00
Double	$ 80.00	$ 50.00

Carriage House At Stonegate   **Williamsport PA**
Harold & Dena Mesaris   **Tel:** 717-433-4340
   Res Times Evenings

Refer to the same listing name under Montoursville, Pennsylvania for a complete descrip-tion. **Seasonal:** No **Payment Terms:** Check [M11CPPA-8405] **COM** YG **ITC Member:** No

Rates:	Pvt Bath 2
Single	$ 50.00
Double	$ 70.00

Hollileif B&B   677 Durham Rd Rt 413 18940   **Wrightstown PA**
Richard & Ellen Butkus   **Tel:** 215-598-3100
   Res Times 9am-10pm

An 18th century plaster and fieldstone farmhouse on 5-1/2 acres of rolling Bucks County countryside where romantic ambience, four course gourmet breakfasts, fresh flowers, fireplaces, evening turndown service, central a/c and private baths combine with gracious personal service and attention to detail. Each guest room is beautifully appointed with antiques and country furnishings. During warm weather, guests may enjoy a game of croquet, volleyball, badminton or horseshoes on our spacious grounds. In winter, the Inn boasts a gentle hill, perfect for sledding. For serious joggers or walkers, several lovely state parks are within a ten minute drive. Enjoy complimentary afternoon refreshments by the fireside or on the arbor-covered patio. Relax in a hammock hung lazily in the meadow overlooking a peaceful stream. At day's end, view a vibrant sunset and occasional wildlife. Bucks County offers a wealth of historical attractions, exquisite scenery, recreational pleasures and cultural activities.

Pennsylvania - West Virginia — *National Edition*

Fine dining and shopping abound. *Hollileif* is situated six miles west of New Hope and five miles south of Peddler's Village. **Discounts:** Corporate, extended stay available upon request **Airport:** Philadelphia Intl 40 mi; Newark 58 mi **Seasonal:** No **Reservations:** One night's deposit at res time; 7 day cancel policy less $15 fee. 2:30-10pm check-in, late arrival only with prior arrangements. Travel agent commission only on weekday stays. **Brochure:** Yes **Permitted:** Drinking, limited children **Conference:** For groups to 15 persons. **Languages:** Some Spanish **Payment Terms:** Check MC/V [R07DPPA-6627] **COM** Y **ITC Member:** No

Rates:	Pvt Bath 5
Single	$ 75-120.00
Double	$ 75-120.00

Bechtel Mansion Inn — York PA
Ruth Spangler
Tel: 717-259-7760
Res Times 9am-6pm

Refer to the same listing name under East Berlin, Pennsylvania for a complete description. **Seasonal:** No **Payment Terms:** Check AE/DISC/MC/V [M11B-CPA-6559] **COM** YG **ITC Member:** No

Rates:	Pvt Bath 7	Shared Bath 2
Single	$ 65-95.00	$ 55.00
Double	$ 75-130.00	$ 70-85.00

Beechmont Inn — York PA
William & Susam Day
Tel: 800-553-7009 717-632-3013
Res Times 9am-9pm

Refer to the same listing name located under Hanover, Pennsylvania for a complete description. **Seasonal:** No **Payment Terms:** Check AE/DISC/MC/V [M05HPPA1-10816] **COM** YG **ITC Member:** No

Rates:	Pvt Bath 7
Single	$ 80-135.00
Double	$ 80-135.00

Briarwold B&B — 5400 Lincoln Hwy 17406 — York PA
Marion Bischoff
Tel: 717-252-4619
Res Times 9am-9pm

Stay in a lovely 1836 colonial home situated on three acres of wooded and cared for lawn between Hallam and Wrightsville, Pennsylvania. This quaint farmhouse offers travelers large common rooms, a large living room and fireplace and all the history of the area along with modern amenities of air conditioned rooms for those hot summer nights. Your hosts are interested in helping you with directions and information to all of the sights in York County, Lancaster's Pennsylvania Dutch and Amish settlements in adjacent Lancaster County. Nearby sights include Gettysburg, Baltimore, Washington DC and Ski Roundtop in Central Pennsylvania. **Reservations:** 50% deposit required to guarantee reservation, 24 Hr cancellation policy for refund **Brochure:** Yes **Permitted:** Children, limited drinking **Payment Terms:** Check V [R07FPPA-13563] **COM** U **ITC Member:** No

Rates:	Shared Bath 3
Single	$ 60.00
Double	$ 60.00

Hendersons Heritage Herbs B&B — RR 1 Box 44H 26710 — Burlington WV
Mickie & Steve Henderson
Tel: 304-289-5100
Res Times 8:30am-9pm

Our Bed & Breakfast features a charming, eclectic mix of antiques and "country" with two guest rooms, a guest library with fireplace, a great room with huge stone fireplace, comfortable dining areas indoors or out, and the ubiquitous satellite TV. Enjoy our casual relaxed atmosphere, mountain views, country hospitality and outstanding food. A full breakfast is included. We also offer, at nominal costs and with prior arrangement, lunches and dinners you will be extremely pleased with. Dig around a bit in our herb nursery; take a herb plant home with you. Try the challenging walking trail; cross country ski or play croquette and horseshoes. Relax in the outdoor spa and wait for deer to amble by. Foliage is magnificent in three seasons, especially during the Fall - and nothing can match the beauty of winter and snow-covered mountains. There are Saturday auctions where great bargains can still be found. Golf is just ten minutes away - with nearby state parks. Almost equidistant from Washington, Baltimore and Pittsburgh - we're located just eleven miles west of Romey Wedy Virginia. We invite you to escape the big city and spend a relaxed, pampered and refreshing time at our Bed & Breakfast - all at a very affordable rate. **Airport:** Washington DC Dulles-100 mi; Baltimore 2-1/2 hrs; Pittsburgh-3 hrs **Packages:** MAP **Seasonal:** Clo Xmas **Reservations:** One night deposit required within one week of booking; 7 day cancel policy for refund less service fee of 10% of deposit **Brochure:** Yes **Permitted:** Limited smoking **Languages:** English, Farsi **Payment Terms:** Check [R07FPWV-17788] **COM** Y **ITC Member:** No

Rates:	Shared Bath 2
Single	$ 70-90.00
Double	$ 75-95.00

Gilbert House Of Middleway   PO Box 1104 25414   **Charles Town WV**
Bernie Heiler
Tel: 304-725-0637
Res Times 9am-9pm

The *Gilbert House* is near Harper's Ferry, Antietam Battlefield, Charles Town Races, the George Washington Family homes and lush Shenandoah Valley countryside. This magnificent Georgian Greystone townhouse c.1760 is pivotal to the Middleway National Historic District and is listed in the Historic American Building Survey. The home is filled with antiques, master paintings, rich tapestries, oriental rugs and fireplaces. Each large room is decorated so you may never want to leave. The Bridal Suite includes a clawfoot tub. A full breakfast is included with refreshments available from your host at any time. Guests often relax on the porch while enjoying the beautiful garden. An old log house is at the rear of the property. A gazebo and a stream with a millwheel are one block away. This 18th century village was founded as a hemp mill site by members of first European settlement party into Shenandoah Valley (1729). The Village is on Indian trails and the original settlers trail into the valley. Harpers Ferry and Jefferson County have several major arts and crafts fairs every year. The Historic House Tour is in April. Skyline Drive is one hour away; DC is less than two hours away. Area offers excellent scenic and historic sightseeing, canoeing, white-water rafting, golf, antiquing, theater, music and etc. Your host is a Harvard-grad-gone-country who pampers guests with hospitality and attention. Ask about pre-Civil War graffiti in the house and the village ghost story. **Airport:** Dulles Intl-48 mi **Seasonal:** No **Reservations:** Advance payment or credit card for deposit, two week cancel policy for refund **Permitted:** Limited drinking, limited smoking, limited children **Languages:** Spanish, German **Payment Terms:** Check AE/MC/V [I04HPWV1-8540] **COM** YG **ITC Member:** No

Rates:	Pvt Bath 3
Single	$ 70-130.00
Double	$ 80-140.00

Hutton House B&B   Rt 219/250 26273   **Huttonsville WV**
Loretta Murray/Dean Ahren
Tel: 800-234-6701 304-335-6701
Res Times 7am-11pm

The *Hutton House*, a Queen Anne Victorian listed on the *National Register of Historic Places*, was completed in 1901. Sitting majestically above Huttonsville, it commands a broad view of the mountains and the valley. The home features original oak woodwork, a three-story turret, arched pocket doors, wrap around porch and a winding staircase. The *Hutton House* is meticulously restored and antiques abound. Each guest room has its own individual style and it is not unusual for guests to photograph their personal favorite before departing. The *Hutton House*, only seventeen miles south of Elkins, is conveniently located in a four seasons area rich with activity. Travelers visit state and national parks, ride the railroad and tour the national radio observatory. They pursue outdoor events like skiing at Snowshoe, golf, canoeing, hunting and fishing. Guests can attend festivals, take classes at the Augusta heritage Workshops and explore Civil War sites. Come and enjoy the easy atmosphere. Guests set their own schedule and are invited to linger over a gourmet breakfast. They are encouraged to relax on the grounds or common rooms while being served refreshments at their leisure - not at predetermined times. **Airport:** Pittsburgh-3 hrs **Packages:** Various packages are available, suited to each guests' interests **Reservations:** One night's deposit at res time **Brochure:** Yes **Permitted:** Children, limited smoking, limited drinking **Payment Terms:** Check MC/V [R11DPWV-14790] **COM** Y **ITC Member:** No

Rates:	Pvt Bath 3	Shared Bath 4
Single	$ 52-57.00	$ 42-47.00
Double	$ 60-65.00	$ 50-55.00

Hampshire House 1884 165 N Grafton Street 26757 Romney WV
Jane & Scott Simmons Tel: 304-822-7171

You're invited to treat yourself to the personal attention and amenities offered by this lovely Inn with all the graciousness and charm of the 1880's in a quiet sleepy town of 2800 population. A 19th century home furnished with period antiques, family heirlooms, period lighting and modern amenities with central a/c and heating. Each of the four guest rooms are individually decorated, some with their own fireplace and all with complimentary sherry before retiring. The common rooms include a music room with an antique pump organ, reading materials, games, TV and VCR. Private TV in bedchamber upon request. A private patio with an intimate garden lets guests enjoy this peaceful setting. Your hosts love to pamper guests and offer therapeutic massages. A full gourmet breakfast is standard fare. Activities include hiking, golf, cross country skiing, fishing, hunting, canoeing, nature trails in 1600 acres of public wildlife areas. You can visit interesting antique shops in the area. Romney is the oldest town in West Virginia and changed sides fifty-six times during the Civil War. Home of West Virginia School for Deaf and Blind. Complimentary snacks, lunch and dinner available with prior notice. **Seasonal:** No **Brochure:** Yes **Permitted:** Wine license, smoking outdoors only **Conference:** Yes for business and social events /meetings including gourmet dining **Payment Terms:** Check AE/MC/V [R07BCWV-8243] **COM** Y **ITC Member:** No

Rates:	Pvt Bath 5
Single	$ 50-55.00
Double	$ 60-65.00

Washington House Inn W 62 N 573 Washington Ave 53012 Cedarburg WI
*Wendy Porterfield Tel: 800-554-4717 414-375-3550
Res Times 24 Hours

In the heart of Cedarburg Historic District is this fully-restored Country Victorian Inn c1886 and listed on the *National Register of Historic Places*, ready to greet guests today in comfort and the elegance of a bygone era. You'll be greeted with Victorian furnishings throughout the inn, marble-trimmed fireplaces (in some guest rooms, too) and a helpful, friendly staff to make your visit memorable. Each guest room is tastefully appointed in period antiques, with king and queen-sized beds fitted with down comforters and with all modern amenities such as whirlpool baths, cable TV hidden in antique armories and finished-off with fresh-cut flowers in each room. Afternoon complimentary wine and cheese is provided in the warmth of the "gathering room" and includes homemade recipes for muffins, cakes, juices and all beverages are included. You'll enjoy visiting Historic Cedarburg's antique shops, Cedar Creek Settlement, local winery and fine restaurants and still you'll be just 20 miles north of Milwaukee. Two guest rooms are handicap-accessible. **Discounts:** 10% AARP, AAA **Airport:** 40 mins **Packages:** Victorian Interlude **Seasonal:** No **Reservations:** One night's deposit or credit card number for guarantee, 24-hour cancellation policy for refund **Brochure:** Yes **Permitted:** Children, drinking, smoking **Conference:** Yes; two meeting rooms are available **Payment Terms:** Check AE/DISC/DC/MC/V [A06GPWI-3309] **COM** Y **ITC Member:** No

Rates:	Pvt Bath 34
Single	$ 59-159.00
Double	$ 59-159.00

Wisconsin

Lodge At Canoe Bay	W16065 Hogback Rd 54728	Chetek WI
Dan & Lisa Dobrowolski	**Tel:** 800-568-1995 715-924-4594 **Fax:** 715-924-2078	
	Res Times 8am-10pm	

Wisconsin's ultimate getaway ... your hosts want to share the seclusion of this special hideaway with guests who want the very best .... including important details such as the very best beds, premiere over-sized whirlpools (not just glorified bathtubs) and even the finest of towels. The Inn is built in the grand traditions of northern lodges with a 30-foot tall fieldstone fireplace and natural cedar ceilings. The furniture if oversized and meant to be used - not just admired. A small library includes the best national magazines and daily newspapers for every interest. Your hosts have even included access to a fax machine, copier for guests who just can't leave business at the office - along with a satellite TV and VCR for entertainment. Sitting on the shore of a fifty acre crystal-clear spring-fed private lake and just eight miles from the town of Chetek, the Inn is surrounded by a 280 acre forest of oak, aspen and maple full of blackberries, wildflowers and deer. The grounds are completely private - for use by guests only. All recreational facilities are just outside your door including cross country skiing, skating, ice fishing and sledding; summer offers swimming, boating, canoeing, fishing and biking. Fall brings exquisite foliage: a series of nature walks cut through the forest and along the lake will leave you breathless. The Inn itself is built in the grand tradition of northern lodges with a huge thirty-foot tall field stone fireplace and natural cedar ceilings. Nearby activities include golf, downhill skiing and casino gambling. A continental breakfast is included. Two hours from the Twin Cities; three hours from Madison; four and one half hours from Milwaukee. **Discounts:** Yes, inquire at res time **Airport:** Eau Claire WI Municipal-35 mi; Minn/St Paul Intl-98 mi **Seasonal:** No **Reservations:** One night's deposit within 7 days of booking to guarantee; 7 day cancel policy for refund **Brochure:** Yes **Permitted:** Children 13-up, limited drinking **Conference:** Excellent facility for groups to 16; satellite equipped, fax, copier and computer available **Payment Terms:** Check DC/MC/V [I03FP-WI-16753] **COM Y ITC Member:** No

Rates:	Pvt Bath 4	Shared Bath 3
Single	$ 89-129.00	$ 59-79.00
Double	$ 89-129.99	$ 59-79.00

The Manor House	6536 3rd Ave 53143	Kenosha WI
Kathy & Rikki Thompson		**Tel:** 414-658-0014
		Res Times 8-5pm M-Sat

Stately brick Georgian Mansion overlooking Lake Michigan c1920's, built for JT Wilson, of Nash Motor Co (forerunner AMC). Fully restored to its original splendor with authentic antiques and listed on *National Register of Historic Places*, you can choose from the Purple Room with its four-poster queen bed or the Rose Room with a 1780 Sheraton queen-size canopied bed, overlooking the rose garden-just perfect for wedding and anniversary guests! Continental breakfast is served in the formal dining room amidst crystal chandeliers and oak paneling. The outdoors is stunning with landscaped acres, water fountain, and picturesque gazebo for strolling while enjoying the beauty of nature's fragrances. In the Heart of Kenosha's Lakeshore Historical District, you're close to charter fishing, marinas, miles of public beaches and parks, and with complimentary bikes, you can ride anywhere or get into shape with jogging nearby, tennis, downhill and cross country skiing and indoor ice rink. **Discounts:** Corporate **Airport:** Chicago O'Hara 40 min; Milwaukee Michell 40 min. **Seasonal:** No **Reservations:** Full payment for Fri or Sat, in advance: 50% deposit weekdays, 21 day cancel notice for refund less $15 service fee **Brochure:** Yes **Permitted:** Limited children, restricted areas for smoking **Conference:** Yes, dining by special arrangements, including receptions, weddings, parties for groups to 85 indoors and to 225 outdoors. **Payment Terms:** Check AE/MC/V [A11DPWI-3329] **COM Y ITC Member:** No

Rates:	Pvt Bath 4
Single	$ 90-130.00
Double	$ 90-130.00

Wisconsin   *National Edition*

Eleven Gables Inn On The Lake	493 Wrigley Dr 53147	**Lake Geneva WI**
A Fasel Milliette		Tel: 414-248-8393 **Fax:** 414-248-6096
		Res Times 8am-8pm

Nestled in evergreens amid giant oaks, this lakeside 1847 Carpenter's Gothic Compound, built as a private residence, coachhouse, ice house and greenhouse between 1847-1852 was converted into a Bed'n Breakfast in 1966. A perfect location in the Edgewater Historical District, this small jewel provides a peaceful lakeside residential atmosphere. A short two block shoreline stroll reaches restaurants, boutiques and entertainment. The varied traditional accommodations offer Romantic "Bedrooms, Bridal Chamber", and quaint 2-3 bedroom "Country Cottages." (One is handicap accessible). All have tile baths, gas log fireplaces, plump down comforters, TV, cocktail refrigerators or wet bars, a/c or ceiling fans. Many rooms include private entrances, lattice courtyards, balconies or lakeviews. A complimentary breakfast is served in the Tea Room during the warmer months and before the fireplace in the Drawing Room in winter. The Inn's private pier provides exclusive swimming, sunning, fishing and boating. Fringed by multi-million dollar estates, this "Newport of the Midwest" lake area abounds all seasons with twenty-two golf courses, tennis courts, equestrian activities, hunt clubs, stock theatre, sailing and boating. There are magnificent autumn-color tours, biking, hiking and winter sports during the pristine white snows of winter. **Discounts:** Midweek stays **Airport:** Milwaukee Mitchell-1 Hr; Chicago O'Hare-2 Hrs **Packages:** 9/8-6/30, Sun through Thursday special rates **Reservations:** Full deposit one night, 50% deposit longer periods required to guarantee reservation; 14 day cancel notice less 10% total reservation amount; Closed Christmas Eve and Thanksgiving Eve **Brochure:** Yes **Permitted:** Limited children, drinking, limited smoking **Conference:** Yes, groups to eighteen persons for inhouse business meetings with dinners and luncheons available **Payment Terms:** AE/DC/MC/V [I04HPWI1-6786] **COM** YG **ITC Member:** No

Rates: Pvt Bath 12
Single $ 69-149.00
Double $ 69-255.00

TC Smith Historic Inn B&B	865 Main St 53147	**Lake Geneva WI**
Marks Family		Tel: 800-423-0233 414-248-1097 **Fax:** 414-248-1672
		Res Times 7am-11pm

Experience classic elegance and recapture the majestic 19th Century ambience at this 1845 downtown lakeview historic mansion. The Inn is listed on the *National Register of Historic Places* for outstanding architectural, historical and artistic significance. You will experience 19th Century light fixtures, that once were gas lights, illuminating the parquet foyer floor, the magnificent hand-tooled black walnut balustrades and staircase, and handpainted walls with miniature oil paintings and original trompe d'oeil by famed Chicago artist John Bullock. As you enter the Grand Parlor with the glowing rose marble fireplace you truly sense the warmth, majesty and splendor of the Historic Inn. Feel the significance and depth of history created in the midst of hand painted mouldings, intricate woodwork, fine cabinetry and immense pocket doors. Live with crackling fireplaces, fine oriental carpets, museum-quality period antiques, objects d'art and paintings by renowned European artists. Traditional to the Grand Victorian era, the bright and spacious rooms are furnished with fine period antiques, Persian carpets and European paintings. All rooms have private baths, several of which include whirlpools. Sit leisurely sipping tea in the Grand Parlor under an authentic Strauss crystal chandelier, before a marble fireplace hearth or enjoy breakfast on the veranda surrounded by colorful flowers and plantings with wild birds singing in the courtyard. For special occasions, the Renoir Garden Suite, a magnificent honeymoon suite has a columned Grecian-style marble and walnut 6' x 10' lighted whirlpool spa. Outdoors, guests relax in the gazebo and courtyard garden shaded by a variety of trees while listening to the gentle sounds of the waterfall fountain in the midst of neo-classic statues. An outdoor courtyard deck has a spacious and luxurious patio spa for twelve guests which overlooks the water garden. Delight in the colorful array of fish in the granite and Bedford limestone pool. True relaxation awaits you on the teakwood couches set on the private rooftop deck. The Inn is within a block of the acclaimed Riveria Beach, shops, restaurants, theatres, museums and nightly entertainment. Within a block are public parks, walking paths, tennis courts, playgrounds, boat rentals, jet skies, dinner cruise tours and public boat launch. Nearby are championship golf courses and horse stables. At the Inn, enjoy the antique doll and porcelain collection, gift shoppe and bicycle rentals. **Discounts:** Off-season (11/1-5/15), Weekdays, extended stays 3 days or more, groups **Seasonal:** No **Reservations:** 50% of stay at upon reservation, bal due 30 days prior to arrival. Less than 45 days prior to arrival, full amount due; 30 day cancel policy less $20 fee, less than 30 days refund only if rebooked **Brochure:** Yes **Permitted:** Children, pets, limited smoking, drinking **Payment Terms:** Check AE/DISC/DC/MC/V [J04HPWI1-13707] **COM YG ITC Member:** No

Rates:	Pvt Bath 8
Single	$ 85-350.00
Double	$ 95-350.00

Arbor House, An Environmental Inn   3402 Monroe St 53711   Madison WI
John & Cathie Imes   Tel: 608-238-2981 Fax: 608-238-1175
Res Times 24 Hrs

One of Madison's oldest homes is also one of the city's most charming and unique Inns. Located across the street from the UW Arboretum (1280 acres of restored woodland and prairie), this 1800's landmark was originally a tavern and stagecoach stop. The Inn's original wood floors, natural stone fireplaces and sunny breakfast room are just some of the features admired by visitors. *Arbor House* is evolving into a model for urban ecology in the areas of architecture, landscaping, interior design, energy and water use and inn operations. An environmental annex will be added to the property. As a showcase for sustainable living, this award-winning structure offers three premium guest rooms which promise guests a truly unique and inspiring experience. All guest rooms have private baths, some with whirlpools and fireplaces. All rooms include Aveda and The Body Shop products and all guests are treated to complimentary Gehl's Iced Cappuccino and canoeing on Lake Wingra. Just minutes from the Capitol, just over a mile from the stadium and on the bus line, the Inn is convenient for both leisure and people doing business in Madison. *Arbor House* is the place to stay if you like to bike, hike, nature walk, bird-watch or cross-country ski. The Inn is within walking distance to popular restaurants and we offer a complete business center, breakfast at your convenience, meeting space and a value-added corporate rate. Its a fine choice for corporate travelers. *Arbor House* is perfect for use as a business retreat or for reunions with friends and family. And our gift certificate packages make wonderful gifts. **Discounts:** Corporate rate, Extended stays, Groups **Packages:** Inquire at reservation time **Seasonal:** No **Reservations:** One night deposit, 7 day cancel policy for refund (gift certificate), less than 7 days, deposit is forfeited **Brochure:** Yes **Permitted:** Children, drinking **Conference:** Yes, groups of 15-18 persons **Payment Terms:** Check AE/MC/V [I06HPWI1-3338] **COM** U **ITC Member:** No

Rates:	Pvt Bath 8
Single	$ 69-100.00
Double	$ 84-180.00

Hill House B&B	2117 Sheridan Drive 53704	Madison WI
Sutart Family		Tel: 608-244-2224
		Res Times 8am-8pm

A contemporary homestay in the traditional English style where the hosts spoil guests in the comfort of their own home, nestled atop a setting that offers beautiful views of the valley, water and woodlands below. On the edge of Madison's most beautiful park area, year-round outdoor activities are available while here, with downtown just ten minutes away by car. The grounds offer a picturesque garden setting, including a gazebo where special events are held. Guest rooms are uniquely furnished with antiques and offer great views! Breakfast is *all full country* with fresh-squeezed orange juice, fruit, egg strata and Annie's famous homemade baked goods, along with all the hot beverages you want - and the morning paper. **Seasonal:** No **Reservations:** Non-refundable one night deposit; check-in 4-6 pm - other by prior arrangement; check-out 12 pm. **Brochure:** Yes **Permitted:** Children, drinking, limited smoking **Payment Terms:** Check MC/V [X02BCWI-3336] **COM** Y **ITC Member:** No

Rates:	Pvt Bath 2	Shared Bath 1
Single	$ 75.00	$ 65.00
Double	$ 80.00	$ 70.00

Mansion Hill Inn	424 N Pinckney St 53703	Madison WI
Janna Wojtal		Tel: 800-798-9070 608-255-3999 **Fax:** 608-255-2217
		Res Times 7am-11pm

An outstanding example of Romanesque Revival architecture crafted in 1858 in this elegant Inn filled with Victorian atmosphere and furnishings. This show case setting is complete with marble and hardwood carvings throughout, period antique furnishings, and pure delight created by the warm hospitality you'll relish while here. Situated high on the isthmus between two lakes with a panoramic view from the belvedere, you are located in downtown Madison, just a few blocks from the state capital, cultural events, business offices, the university campus. All guest rooms have modern amenities, including sumptuous baths with whirlpool tubs, cable and stereo, 24-hour valet service, frequent traveler program, and a complimentary shoe shine to start each day. Silver service continental breakfast is served in your room daily. Afternoon refreshments are served daily. Madison's only 4-Diamond Accommodation **Airport:** Dane County Reg Airport 10 mins **Seasonal:** No **Reservations:** One night's deposit or credit card for guarantee, 48-hour cancellation policy **Brochure:** Yes **Permitted:** Drinking, children over 12 **Payment Terms:** Check AE/MC/V [A02HPWI1-3337] **COM** YG **ITC Member:** No

Rates:	Pvt Bath 11
Single	$ 80-250.00
Double	$ 100-270.00

Morning Glory	346 E Wilson St 53207	Milwaukee WI
Marie M Mahan		Tel: 414-483-1512
		Res Times 8am-8pm

Your first view of *Marie's Bed & Breakfast* is certain to charm and delight you. Located in the homey and diverse atmosphere of Milwaukee's historic Bayview district. This single family dwelling was built in 1896 by William Grange, a prominent real estate developer of the time. Completely restored by your hostess and owner who brings an interesting sense of history to the house through her use of antique furnishings, collectibles, family heirlooms and vivid splashes of original artwork. Exceptionally convenient, Maries is perfectly located just seven minutes from the airport and six minutes from downtown Milwaukee for both leisure and business travelers. All universities are within 15-20 minutes. Guests will enjoy the full gourmet breakfast served in the Fan Room, or during the warm months, in the outdoor garden setting. **Seasonal:** No **Reservations:** Deposit at res time with 2 week cancel policy; less than 2 week notice, deposit refunded less $10 handling fee **Brochure:** Yes **Permitted:** Children, drinking, smoking outdoors only **Conference:** Yes, with prior arrangement up to 8 persons. **Payment Terms:** Check [R10BCWI-8652] **COM** Y **ITC Member:** No

Rates:	Shared Bath 4
Single	$ 45-55.00
Double	$ 45-55.00

TC Smith Historic Inn B&B — Milwaukee WI
Marks Family — Tel: 800-423-0233 414-248-1097
Res Times 7am-11pm

Refer to the same listing name under Lake Geneva, Wisconsin for a complete description. **Seasonal:** No **Permitted:** Children, pets, smoking, drinking **Payment Terms:** Check AE/DISC/DC/MC/V [M04GPWI-16982] **COM** YG **ITC Member:** No

Rates:	Pvt Bath 8
Single	$ 85-350.00
Double	$ 95-250.00

Dreams Of Yesteryear B&B — 1100 Brawley St 54481 — Stevens Point WI
Bonnie & Bill Maher — Tel: 715-341-4525 Fax: 715-344-3047
Res Times 9am-10pm

This elegant 1901 Victorian Queen Anne is listed on the *National Historic Register* and was given an **Historic Preservation Certificate of Commendation in 1996.** The tasteful renovation of this 4000 square foot home was featured in "Victorian Home" magazine. Today "Dreams" offers Victorian ambiance on three floors and is within walking distance of historic Stevens Point, Wisconsin River parks, Point Brewery, university and the twenty-seven mile Green Circle hiking/biking trails. Visitors to the third floor Ballroom Suite enjoy the architectural beauty of this spacious suite with cathedral ceilings, queen size bed, whirlpool tub, sculptured tile and romantic burgundy and lavender decor. The Heritage Suite offers third floor quiet with sitting room, queen size wicker bed, leaded glass windows, bathroom with a large brass and glass shower that follows the contour of the roof and luscious peach and green decor. The Isabella Room with a bay, is decorated in navy and mauve and has a cherry and mahogany queen size bed, hardwood floors and antique bathroom with a footed tub and high-tank pull chain toilet. The Florence Myrna, decorated in forest green and gardenia wallcoverings, has a double bed, private bath with neo-angular shower and forest green and white ceramic tile. Gareld's Balcony Room is decorated in French blue wallcoverings and has two twin beds (or one king). The Maid's Quarters is simply peach with an antique double bed and antique furnishings. Gareld's Room and the Maid's Quarters share a first floor bath with a large tub and separate walk-in shower. **Discounts:** Wisconsin State employees **Airport:** Central Wisconsin-20 mi **Packages:** Biking **Seasonal:** No **Reservations:** One night deposit, 7 day cancel policy for refund **Permitted:** Children 13+, drinking, limited smoking **Conference:** Parlors available for groups to 25 persons **Payment Terms:** Check AE/DISC/MC/V [I04IPWI1-19177] **COM** YG **ITC Member:** No

Rates:	Pvt Bath 4	Shared Bath 2
Single	$ 65-129.00	$ 55-60.00
Double	$ 65-129.00	$ 55-60.00

Victorian Swan On Water — 1716 Water St 54481 — Stevens Point WI
Joan Ouellette — Tel: 715-345-0595

Wisconsin

The *Victorian Swan on Water* is an inviting bed and breakfast tourist home situated at the gateway to Wisconsin's vacationland. This restored 1889 home showcases original crown mouldings, wood floors with black walnut inlays, hidden wood shutters, beautiful woodwork throughout with antique furnishings. Don't miss trying the guest room with the hidden Roman Bath containing a whirlpool tub and fireplace. With comfort as the main ingredient, guests can leisurely stroll the riverwalks along the Wisconsin River, relax in the rose garden during a lazy summer afternoon or cozy near the fireplace in autumn and winter. Downtown is just a few blocks with the local university, brewery and other attractions just minutes away. Business travelers will enjoy the peace and comfortable surroundings in this quiet, calm atmosphere. The Swan can provide meeting rooms for creative business sessions. Lunches can be catered. A full delicious breakfast is included with your room. Local activities include six golf courses, miles of cross-country skiing trails within minutes. When away from home for business or pleasure, you will always find a warm welcome at the *Victorian Swan* on Water. **Airport:** Steven's Point (private planes only) Airport-2 mi **Seasonal:** No **Reservations:** One night deposit or credit card number **Brochure:** Yes **Permitted:** Limited children, limited drinking **Conference:** Small conference room available for groups to twenty **Payment Terms:** Check AE/DC/MC/V [Z08GPWI-3366] **COM Y ITC Member:** No

Rates: Pvt Bath 4
Single $ 45-110.00
Double $ 50-120.00

Bold Name - Description appears in other section   *Delaware - District of Columbia - Illinois*

DELAWARE

Bethany Beach
Addy Sea
302-539-3707-[Y--]

Homestead Guests
302-529-7248

Sand Box & Sea Vista Villas
302-539-3354

Camden
Jonthan Wallace House
302-697-2921

Centreville
Buckleys Tavern
302-656-9776

Claymont
Darley Manor Inn B&B
800-824-4703-[G--]

Dagsboro
Beckys Country Inn
302-732-3953

Dewey Beach
Barrys Gull B&B
302-227-7000

Dover
Biddle B&B
302-736-1570

Inn At Meeting House Square
302-678-1242

Harrington
Eli Country Inn

Laurel
Spring Garden
302-875-7015

Lewes
Inn At Canan Square
302-645-8499

Kings Inn
302-645-6438

New Devon Inn
302-645-6466

Savannah Inn
302-645-5592

Seaport Inn
302-644-1000

Milford
Banking House Inn

Causey Mansion
302-422-0979

The Towers
800-366-3814

Milton
Drawing Room
302-684-0339

Montchanin
Inn At Montchanin Village
800-COWBIRD

New Castle
David Finney Inn
800-334-6640-[Y--]

Janvier-Black House B&B
302-328-1339

Jefferson House B&B
302-323-0999

River House
302-328-2323

Ross House
302-322-7787

Terry House B&B
302-322-2505

William Penn Guest House
302-328-7736-[Y--]

Newark
Inn At The Canal
410-885-5995

Odessa
Cantwell House
302-378-4179-[Y--]

Rehoboth Beach
Abby
302-227-7023

Beach House
302-227-7074

Beach House Bedroom
302-227-0937

Corner Cupboard Inn
302-227-8553

Gladstone Inn
302-653-8294

Lord & Hamilton Seaside Inn
302-227-6960

Lord Baltimore Lodge
302-227-2855-[Y--]

O Conners B&B
302-227-2419

Pleasant Inn lodge
302-227-7311

Rehoboth Guest House
302-227-4117

Sand In My Shorts Inn
302-226-2006

Silver Lake Guesthouse
302-226-2115

Tembo Guest House
302-227-3360-[Y--]

Shelbyville
Victorian Rose Guest House
302-436-2558

Smyrna
Main Stay
302-653-4293

Wilmington
Boulevard B&B
302-656-9700

Creek View B&B
302-994-5924

Darley Manor Inn B&B
800-824-4703-[G--]

DISTRICT of COLUMBIA

Adams Inn
800-578-6807-[G--]

Canterbury

202-393-3000

Capitol Hill Guest House
202-547-1050

Castlestone Inn
202-483-4706

Connecticut Woodley
202-667-0218

Embassy Inn
800-423-9111

Hereford House
202-543-0102

Kalamora Guest House-Woodley Park
202-328-0860

Kalamore Guest House-Kalorama Park
202-667-6369-[G--]

Little White House B&B
202-583-4074

Megs Intl Guest House
202-232-5837

Morrison House
800-367-0800-[Y--]

Morrison-Clark Inn
800-322-7898

Normandy Inn
800-424-3729

Prince George Inn B&B
410-263-6418-[Y--]

Swiss Inn
800-955-7947-[Y--]

Tabard Inn
202-785-1277

Windsor Inn
800-423-9111

ILLINOIS

Alton
Haagen House B&B
618-462-2419

Jackson House

©*Inn & Travel Memphis, Tennessee*

2-121

Illinois *Bold Name - Description appears in other section*

800-462-1426

Anna
Goddard Place
618-833-6256

Arcola
Curleys Corner
217-268-3352

Flower Patch
217-268-4876

Arthur
Favorite Brother Inn
217-543-2938

Athens
Bailey House
217-636-7695

Atwood
Harshbarger Homestead
217-578-2265

Bartlett
Cead Mile Failte
708-289-3009

Batavia
Villa Batavia
708-406-8182

Beardstown
Enchanted Crest
618-736-2647

Nostalgia Corner
217-323-5382

Belle River
Enchanted Crest
618-736-2647

Belvidere
Victorian 1897 House
815-544-6600

Bishop Hill
Holdens Guest House
309-927-3500

Browning
Friddle Creek Lodge B&B
217-323-4232

Cairo
Windham
618-734-3247

Carbondale
Sassafras Ridge B&B
618-529-5261

Carlyle
Country Haus
800-279-4486-[Y--]

Victorian Inn B&B
800-594-8505

Carthage
Wright Farmhouse
217-357-2421-[Y--]

Casey
Cumberland Trail B&B
217-932-5522

Champaign
Alices Place
217-359-3332

Barb'S B&B
217-356-0376

Glads B&B
217-586-4345

Grandma Joan's Homestay
217-356-5828

Normas Hideaway
217-359-5876

Shurts House B&B
217-367-8793

Charleston
Charleston B&B
217-345-6463

Lincoln Land B&B
217-345-2711

Chester
Betsys Sugar Wood
618-826-2555

Sugar Wood
618-826-2555

Chicago
Hotel Tremont House
800-621-8133

House Of Two Urns
312-235-1408

Hyde Park House
312-363-4595-[Y--]

Lakeshore Drive B&B
312-404-5500

Lincoln Park B&B
312-327-6564

Magnolia Place
312-334-6860

TC Smith Historic Inn B&B
800-423-0233-[G--]

The Margarita European Inn
847-869-2273-[G--]

Longwell Hall
708-386-5043

Villa Toscana Guest House
312-404-2643

Wheaton Inn
312-690-2600-[Y--]

Cisco
Country House
317-364-0461

Collinsville
Happy Wanderer Inn
618-344-0477

Maggies B&B
618-344-8283

Maries B&B
618-344-8238

Dallas City
1850s Guest House
217-852-3652

Danforth
Fannies House
815-269-2145-[Y--]

Decatur
Weedons B&B
217-422-4930

Dixon
Medusa Manor
815-288-7111

Riverview Guest House
815-288-5974

Rose Colonial Inn
815-652-4422

Du Quoin
Francies B&B Inn
618-542-6686

Dundee
Ironhedge Inn B&B
847-426-7777

Dwight
Voyager B&B
815-584-2239

East Dubuque
Captain Merry Guest House
815-747-3644

Eldred
Bluffdale Vacation Farm
217-983-2854

Hobsons Bluffdale
217-983-2854-[Y--]

Elizabeth
Brookside B&B
815-845-2251

Elizabeth Guest House
800-318-9993

Far Ninety Guest House
815-858-3604

Flint Hill Farms Country Inn
815-858-3471

Forget-Me-Not B&B
815-858-3744

Locker Knoll B&B
815-598-3150

Ridgeview B&B
815-598-3150

Elizabethtown
River Rose Inn
618-287-8811

Williams Village Inn
618-287-7088

Elsah
Corner Nest B&B
618-374-1892

Green Tree Inn
618-374-2821

Maple Leaf Cottage Inn
619-374-1684-[Y--]

Eureka

2-122 ©Inn & Travel Memphis, Tennessee

Bold Name - *Description appears in other section* *Illinois*

Dickinson House
309-467-3116

Evanston
The Margarita European Inn
847-869-2273-[G--]

Fairfield
Glass Door Inn
618-847-4512

Franklin Grove
Whitney B&B
815-456-2526

Freeburg
Westerfield House
618-539-5643

Galena
Aldrich Guest House
815-777-3323-[Y--]

Amber Creek Farm
815-598-3301

Avery Guest House
815-777-3883

Bedford House
815-777-2043

Belle Aire Mansion
815-777-0893

Brierwreath Manor
815-777-0608

Byrne B&B
815-777-9080

Captain Gear Guest House
800-794-5656

Captain Harris Guest Cottage

Chestnut Mountain Resort
815-435-2914

Cloran Mansion Inn
815-777-0583

Colonial Guest House
815-777-0336

Country Gardens
815-777-3062

Country Valley Guest Home
815-777-2322

Country Valley Homestead
815-777-1915

Craig Cottage
815-777-1461

Desoto House
800-343-6562

Dezoya House B&B
815-777-1203

Eagle Ridge Inn

Early American Settlement
800-366-LOGS

Farmers Home Hotel
800-373-3456

Farsters Executive Inn
800-545-8551

Felt Manor
815-777-9093

Fireside Country Inn
800-342-2632

Five In The Woods
815-786-7196

Four Oaks
815-777-9567

Gallery Guest Suite
815-777-1222

Goldmoore
800-397-6667

Grandview Guest House
800-373-0732

Hellman House
815-777-3638

Homestead
815-777-3638

Inn At Irish Hollow
815-777-6000

John Henry Guest House
815-777-3595

LeFevre Inn & Resort
800-619-9500

Log Cabin Guest House
815-777-2845-[Y--]

Logan House
815-777-0033

Main Street Inn
815-777-3454

Mars Avenue Guest House
815-777-2808

Mothers Country Inn
815-777-3153-[Y--]

Park Avenue Guest House
800-359-0743

Pats Country Guest Home
815-777-1030

Pine Hollow Inn
800-789-2975

Queen Ann Guest House
815-777-3849

Rainbow & Roses
815-857-3707

Renaissance Riverboat Suites
815-777-0123

Robert Scribe Harris House
815-777-1611

Ryan Mansion Inn
815-777-2043

Spring Street Guest House
815-777-0354

Steamboat House
815-777-3128

Stillmans Country Inn
815-777-0557-[Y--]

Tripps Country Inn
815-777-3149

Victorian Mansion Guest House
800-373-6906

Vineyard Guest House
815-858-3649

Wild Turkey
815-858-3649

Will House
815-209-1618

Galesburg
Seacord House
309-342-4107

Geneva
Herrington
708-208-7433

Oscar Swan Country Inn
708-232-0173

Gibson City
Stolt Home
815-784-4502

Golconda
Mansion Of Golconda
618-683-4400

Silk Stocking B&B
618-683-2231

Goodfield
Brick House Inn
815-965-2545

Grafton
Shafer Wharf Inn
618-374-2821

Wildflower Inn
618-465-3719

Grant Park
Bennett Curtis House
815-465-6025

Grayville
Founders Mansion
618-375-3291

Greenville
Prairie House

Country Inn
618-664-3003

Gurnee
Sweet Basil Hill Farm
800-228-HERB

Hanna City

©*Inn & Travel Memphis, Tennessee*

2-123

Illinois   **Bold Name** - *Description appears in other section*

Double D Country Inn
309-565-4022

Harrisburg
Harts White Lace Inn
618-252-7599

House of Nahum
618-252-1414

Havana
McNutt Guest House
309-543-3295

Highland
Phyllis B&B
618-654-4619

Hindsboro
Breakfast In The Country
217-346-2739

Hopedale
Rose Manor Inn
309-449-5522

Huntley
Croaking Frog
847-669-1555

Jerseyville
Homeridge
618-498-3442

Junction
Thomas House
800-866-6716

Kewanee
Bishops Inn
309-832-5201

Knoxville
Walnut Tree House
309-289-6933

Lake Forest
Dear Path Inn
847-234-2280

Lake Zurich
China Cup Inn
708-550-1107

Lanark
Standish House
800-468-2307

Victorian Lace
815-493-2546

Lena

Sugar Maple Inn
815-369-2786

Lincoln
Prairie Fields Inn
217-732-7696

Lyons
Aherns B&B
708-442-1170

Macomb
Brockway House
309-837-2375

Pineapple Inn Inc
309-837-1914

Maeystown
Corner George Inn
800-458-6020

Marengo
Harmony Hills Farm
815-923-4369-[Y--]

Marseilles
Annie Tiques Hotel
815-795-5848

Connie Tique Hotel
815-795-5848

McLeansboro
Rebeccas Guest House
618-643-3249

Mendota
Elizabeths B&B
815-539-5555

Lord Stockings
815-539-7905

Metamora
Stevenson House
309-367-2831

Metropolis
Isle of View B&B
618-524-5383

Moline
River Drive Guest House
309-762-8503

We Share B&B
309-762-7059

Momenca
Supernaut B&B
815-472-3156

Wilkstrom Manor

815-472-3156

Monmouth
Carr Mansion Guest House
309-734-3654

Monticello
Lindas Country Loft B&B
217-762-7316

Morrison
Hillendale B&B
815-772-3454-[Y--]

Mossville
Old Church House Inn
309-579-2300

Mount Carmel
Legacy Homestead
618-298-2476

Living Legacy Homestead B&B
618-298-2476

The Poor Farm Bed & Breakfast
800-646-FARM-[Y--]

Mount Carroll
Captains Quarters
815-244-2692

Country Palmer House
815-244-2343

Prairie Path Guest House
815-244-3462

Ravens Grin Inn
815-244-4746

Tuk-A-Way Center
815-244-2577

Mount Morris
Kable House
815-734-7297

Mount Pulaski
Dorseys B&B
217-792-3347

Moweaqua
Dowd House
217-768-3821

Mundelein
Round Robin Guesthouse

847-566-7664

Naperville
Die Blaue Gans
312-355-0835

Harrison House B&B
708-420-1117

Oak Cove Resort
616-674-8228

Nashville
Mill Creek Inn
618-327-8424

Story Inn
812-988-2273

Nauvoo
Ancient Pines
217-453-2767

Hotel Nauvoo
217-435-2211

Mississippi Memories
217-453-2771

Parley Lane B&B
217-453-2277

Oak Park
Cheney House
708-524-2067

Elan Affilates B&B
708-848-4732

Longwell Hall
708-386-5043
[GQAR-]

Under The Ginko Tree
708-310-9010

Oakland
Inn On The Square
217-346-2289-[Y--]

Johnsons Country Home
217-346-3276

Oblong
Welcome Inn
618-592-3301

Olney
Richs Inn
618-392-3821

Oregon
Lyndel Mansion

Bold Name - *Description appears in other section*   *Illinois*

815-732-7313

Pinehill B&B
815-732-2061

Paris
  Tiara Manor B&B
  800-531-1865

Paxton
  Westlawn Manor
  217-379-2594

Pekin
  Herget House
  309-353-4025

Peoria
  Bit Of Country
  B&B
  217-632-3771

  Ruths B&B
  217-632-5971

Petersburg
  A Bit Of Country
  B&B
  217-632-3771

  Caermodys Clare
  Inn
  217-632-2350

  Carmodys Clare Inn
  217-632-2350

  Oaks B&B
  217-632-4480

  Robert Frackelton
  House
  217-632-4496

Pickneyville
  Oxbow B&B
  618-357-9839

Pleasant Hill
  Pleasant Haven
  B&B
  217-734-9357

Plymouth
  Plymouth Rock
  Resort
  309-458-6444

Port Byron
  Frederick La Verne
  Waldbusser
  309-523-3236

  Old Brick House
  309-523-3226

Prairie Du Rocher
  La Maison du
  Roucher
  618-284-3463

Princeton
  Yesterdays
  Memories
  815-872-7753

Quincy
  Kaufman House
  217-223-2502

  Petzoldts
  217-222-4665

Rantoul
  Better 'n Grandmas
  217-893-0469

Red Bud
  Das Busche Haus
  618-282-2181

  Magnolia Place
  618-282-4141

Robinson
  Bertram Arms B&B
  618-546-1122

  Heath Inn
  618-544-3410

Rock Island
  Potter House
  800-747-0339-[Y--]

  Top O' The Morning
  309-786-3513

  Victorian Inn
  800-728-7068

Rockford
  Bayberry Inn
  815-964-7243

  Victorias B&B
  815-963-3232-[Y--]

Rossville
  Farmhouse
  217-748-6505

Rushville
  Bottenberg B&B
  217-322-6100

Saint Charles
  Charleston Guest
  House
  708-377-1277

  Stagecoach Inn

312-584-1263

Saint Joseph
  Alice Vernon
  217-469-2402

Salem
  Badollet House
  618-548-0982

Savanna
  Carroll County B&B
  815-273-5000

  Granny O'Neils
  River Inn
  815-273-4726

Scales Mound
  Franklin House
  B&B
  815-845-2304

Sesser
  Hill House
  618-625-6064

Springfield
  Corinnes B&B
  217-527-1400

  Henry Mischler
  House
  217-523-0205

  Inn At 835
  217-523-4466

  Mischler House
  217-523-5616

Stockton
  Hammond House
  815-947-2032

  Herrings Maple
  Lane Farm
  815-947-3773

  Maple Lane
  815-947-3773

  Memory Lane Lodge
  815-947-2726

Streator
  Dicus House
  800-BNB-1890

Sullivan
  **Little House On The
  Prairie**
  217-728-4727-[Y--]

  Miss Connies B&B
  217-728-8582

Sycamore
  Country Charm
  B&B
  815-895-5386

  Stratford Inn
  815-895-6789

Thomasboro
  Burkes Country Inn
  B&B
  217-643-7257

Tolono
  Aunt Zelmas
  Country House
  217-485-5101

  Rockwell Victorian
  B&B
  309-286-5201

Trenton
  Jefferson House
  618-224-9733

Urbana
  Shurts House B&B
  800-339-4156

Villa Grove
  Fair Oaks Inn
  217-832-9313

Warren
  Amos & Company
  B&B
  815-745-2881

  Nonis B&B
  815-745-2045

  Stagecoach Corners
  Guest House
  815-745-2090

Waterloo
  Senator Rickert
  Residence
  618-939-8242

Wenona
  Hart Of Wenona
  815-853-4778

West Salem
  Thelams B&B
  618-456-8401

Wheaton
  Wheaton Inn
  312-690-2600-[Y--]

Williamsville
  B&B At Edies

Illinois - Indiana **Bold Name** - *Description appears in other section*

217-566-2538

Wilmette
La Bri
800-732-7328

Winnetka
Chateau des Fleurs
312-256-7272

Woodstock
Bundling Board Inn
815-338-7054

Concorde Country Inn
815-338-1100

Springshire Inn
815-337-8839

Yorkville
Silver Key B&B
708-553-5612

INDIANA

Alexandria
Interurban Inn
317-724-2001

Sycamore Hill Inn
317-724-2001

Angola
Potawatomi Inn
219-833-1077

Attica
Apple Inn B&B
317-762-6574

Auburn
Hill Top Country Inn
219-281-2529

Batesville
Beechwood Inn
812-934-3426

Sherman House
812-934-2407

Berne
Schug House Inn
812-589-2448

Bethlehem
Inn At Bethlehem
812-293-3975

Beverly Shores
Dunes Shore Inn
219-879-9029-[Y--]

Stoney Point B&B
219-879-9120

Bloomington
Baure House- A B&B
812-336-4383

Grant Street B&B Inn
812-334-2353

Hoosier Hospitality B&B
812-339-1491

Quilt Haven
812-876-5802

Scholars Inn
800-765-3466

Bluffton
Wisteria Manor
219-824-4619

Bristol
Milburn House
219-848-4026

Tylers Place B&B
219-848-7145

Brookville
Duck Creek B&B
317-647-6497

Centerville
Lantz House Inn
800-495-2689

Chesterton
Gray Goose Inn
800-521-5127
[GQAR-]

Wingfields Inn B&B
219-348-0766

Clinton
Pentreath House
317-832-2762

Columbus
Columbus Inn
812-378-4289

Lafayette Street B&B
812-372-7245-[Y--]

Connersville
Maple Leaf Inn
317-825-7099

Corydon

Kinter Inn
812-738-2020

Warren Cabin B&B
812-738-2166

Crawfordsville
Davis House
317-364-0461

Sugar Creek Queen Ann B&B
317-362-4095

Yount's Mill Inn
317-362-5864

Culver
Culver House B&B
219-842-4009

Dana
Castle Inn B&B
317-665-3282

Danville
Magnolia Manor
317-745-2347

Decatur
Cragwood Inn
219-728-2000

Evansville
Brigadoon B&B Inn
812-422-9365-[Y--]

Rivers Inn B&B

Fishers
Frederick Talbot Inn
317-776-1765

Fort Wayne
Candlewyck Inn
219-424-2643-[Y--]

Carol Lombard House
219-426-9896

Maysville Manor
219-493-8814

Roebuck Inn
219-485-9619

Union Chapel B&B
219-627-5663

Fowler
Pheasant Country Inn
317-884-0908

Franklin

Oak Haven B&B
317-535-9491

Goshen
Amish Country B&B
219-533-1631

B&B On The Farm
219-862-4600

Checkerberry Inn
219-642-4445-[Y--]

Country B&B
219-862-2748

Country Lane B&B
219-533-1631

Flower Patch B&B
219-534-4207

Garbers Guest House
219-831-3740

Indian Creek B&B
219-875-6606

Lakeside Haven
219-642-3678

Martins Heritage Guest House
219-533-8915

Ol' Barn
219-642-3222

Ramers
219-831-4801

Royers BnB
219-533-1821

Spring View B&B
219-642-3997

Timberidge B&B
219-533-7133

Tylers Place B&B
219-848-7145

Waterford B&B
219-533-6044

Whippoorwill
219-875-5746

White Birch B&B
219-533-3763

Woody Acres
219-875-8294

Bold Name - *Description appears in other section* **Indiana**

Grabill
Amandas Country Inn
219-627-2704

Grandview
Grandview Guest House
812-649-2817

River Belle B&B
800-877-5165

Granger
1900 House
219-277-7783

Grayville
Founders Mansion Inn
618-375-3291

Greencastle
Brick Inn
317-653-3267

Seminary Place
317-653-3177

Walden Inn
317-653-2761

Hagerstown
Teetor House
800-824-4319

Hartford City
Decoys B&B
317-348-2164

Whispers B&B
317-348-2349

Howe
Lasata B&B
219-562-3655

Huntington
Purviance House B&B
219-356-4218

Indianapolis
Barn House
317-823-4898

Friendliness With A Flair
317-356-3149

Hoffman House
317-635-5659

Holland House
317-685-9326

Le Chateau Delaware Inn
317-636-9156

Manor House
317-634-1711

Nuthatch B&B
317-257-2660-[G--]

Old Northside B&B
317-635-9123

Osborne House
317-924-1777

Pairadux Inn
317-259-8005

Tranquil Cherub
317-923-9036

Jasper
Artists Studio B&B
812-695-4500

Kendallville
Olde McCray Mansion Inn
219-347-3647

Knightstown
Main Street Victorian B&B
317-345-2299

Old Hoosier House
800-755-3515-[Y--]

Olde Country Club
317-345-5381

Kokomo
Bavarian Inn
317-453-4715

Koontz Lake
Koontz House
219-586-7090

La Grange
1886 INN
219-463-4227

Atwater Century Farm B&B
219-463-2743

M&N B&B
219-463-2961

Weavers Country Oaks
219-768-7191

Lafayette

McIlwains

LaPorte
Arbor Hill Inn
219-362-9200

Leavenworth
Ye Old Scotts Inn
812-739-4747-[Y--]

Ligonier
Minuette B&B
219-894-4494

Solomon Meir Manor B&B
219-894-3668

Loogootee
Stone Ridge Inn
812-295-3382

Madison
Autumnwood
812-265-5262

Broadway House
812-265-2207

Cliff House
812-265-5272-[Y--]

Clifty Inn
812-265-4135

Elderberry Inn
812-265-6856

Heritage House
812-265-2393

Main Street B&B
800-362-6246

Millwood House
812-265-6780

Old Mansion House
812-265-6874

Schussler House B&B
800-392-1931

Marion
Golden Oak B&B
317-651-9550

Marshall
Turkey Run Inn
317-597-2512

Metamora
Publik House
317-647-6269

Thorpe House
317-647-5425

White Rose Inn
317-647-3292

Michigan City
Creekwood Inn
219-874-8357

Hutchinson Mansion Inn
219-879-1700

Plantation Inn
219-874-2487-[Y--]

Middlebury
Bee Hive B&B
219-825-5023

Bittersweet Hill B&B
219-825-5953

Bontreger Guest House
219-825-2647

Coneygar B&B
219-825-5707

Country Victorian B&B
219-825-2568

Das Dutchman Essenhaus
219-825-9471

Empty Nest B&B
219-825-1042

Essenhaus Country Inn
219-825-9471

Four Woods B&B
219-593-2021

Hergest Ridge
219-825-2929

Kings B&B
219-825-7304

Lookout B&B
219-825-9809

Marys Place
219-825-2429

Mill Street B&B
219-625-5359

Patchwork Quite Country Inn

©Inn & Travel Memphis, Tennessee

2-127

Indiana   **Bold Name** - *Description appears in other section*

219-825-2417

Tayler House
219-825-7296

Varns Guest House
219-825-9666

Yoder's Zimmer Mit Frustuck
219-825-2378

Zimmer Haus B&B
219-825-7288

Middletown
  Maple Hill
  317-354-2580

Mishawaka
  Beiger Mansion Inn
  800-437-0131-[Y--]

  Kamms Island Inn
  219-256-1501

Mitchell
  Spring Mill Inn

Monon
  Bestemors House
  219-253-8351

Monticello
  1887 Black Dog Inn
  219-583-8297

  Countree Aire Resort
  219-583-3097

  Zimmer Frei Haus
  219-583-4061

Morgantown
  Rock House
  812-597-5100

Moscow
  Story Inn
  812-988-2273

Muncie
  Elizabethan Inn
  317-289-9449

  Old Franklin House
  317-286-0277

  Sourgeon Inn
  317-747-5089

Nappanee
  Homespun Country Inn
  219-773-2034

  Indiana Amish Country B&B
  219-773-4188

  Market Street Guest House
  219-773-2261

  Olde Buffalo Inn B&B
  219-773-2223

  Victorian Guest House
  219-773-4383

Nashville
  5th Generation Farm
  800-437-8152

  Abe Martin Lodge
  812-988-4418

  Allison House Inn
  812-988-0814

  Always Inn
  812-988-2233

  Chestnut Hill Log Home
  812-988-4995

  Cornerstone Inn
  812-988-0300

  Days Star Inn
  812-988-0403

  McGinleys Cabins
  812-988-7337

  Mindheism Inn
  812-988-2590

  Old Loom B&B
  812-988-8367

  Plain & Fancy
  812-988-4537

  Seasons
  812-988-6516

  Story Inn
  812-988-2273

  Sunset House
  812-988-6118

  Victoria House
  812-988-6344

  Wraylyn Knoll

  812-988-0733

New Albany
  Honeymoon Mansion
  812-945-0312

New Harmony
  Harmonie B&B
  812-682-3730

  New Harmony Inn
  812-682-4491

  Old Rooming House
  812-682-4724

Newburg
  Phelps Mansion Inn
  812-853-7766

North Manchester
  Fruitt Basket Inn B&B
  219-982-2443

North Salem
  Retreat House
  317-676-6669

Paoli
  Braxton House Inn
  812-723-4677

Peru
  Rosewood Mansion Inn
  317-472-7151

Plymouth
  Driftwood
  219-546-2274

Portland
  Sandy Hollow Inn B&B
  219-726-9444

Richland
  Country Homestead
  812-359-4870

Rising Sun
  Jelly House Country Inn
  812-438-2319

Roachdale
  Victorian House
  317-522-1225

Rockport
  Rockport Inn
  812-649-2664

Rockville

  Suits Us B&B
  317-569-5660

Rossville
  Wildwood B&B
  317-296-2134

Salem
  Lanning House
  812-883-3484

Shipshewana
  Four Woods B&B
  219-593-2021

  Greenmeadow Ranch
  219-768-4221-[Y--]

  Morton Street B&B
  800-447-6475-[Y--]

  Old Carriage Inn
  800-435-0888

  Old Davis Hotel
  219-768-7300

  Shipshewana Log Cabin
  219-768-7770

South Bend
  Book Inn
  219-288-1990

  Home B&B
  219-291-0535

  Jamison Inn
  219-277-9682

  Oliver Inn B&B
  219-232-4545

  Queen Anne Inn
  800-582-2379

  The Book Inn
  219-288-1990

Spencer
  Canyon Inn
  812-829-4881

Syracuse
  Anchor Inn B&B
  219-457-4714

  Victoria Bay B&B
  219-457-5374

Terre Haute
  Cruft House B&B
  812-234-3484

Bold Name - *Description appears in other section*   **Indiana - Iowa**

Tippecanoe
Bessingers Hillfare Wildlife B&B
219-223-3288

Valparaiso
Inn At Aberdeen
219-465-3753

Vevay
Captains' Quarters B&B
812-427-2900

Ogle Haus Inn
812-427-2020

Swiss Hills B&B
812-427-3882

Wakarusa
Farm Wood B&B
219-862-2981

Wengers B&B
219-862-2981

Wappanee
Amish Acres
219-267-2906

Warsaw
Candlelight Inn
800-352-0640

White Hill Manor
219-269-6933

Washington
Haven B&B
812-254-7770

West Lafayette
Kent House
317-743-3731

Westfield
Camel Lot
317-873-4370

Country Roads Guesthouse
317-846-2376

Winamac
Tortuga Inn
219-946-6969

Winona Lake
Gunn Guest House
219-267-2023

Zionsville
Brick Street Inn
317-873-5895

IOWA

Adair
Lalley House B&B
515-742-5541

Adel
Walden Acres
515-987-1567

Allerton
Inn Of The Six-Toe Cat
515-873-4900

Alta
Addies Place
712-284-2509

Ames
Green Belt B&B
515-232-1960

Anamosa
Shaw House
319-462-4485

Atlantic
Chestnut Charm
712-243-5652

SF Martin House
712-243-5589

Audubon
John James Audubon B&B
712-563-3674

Battle Creek
Inn At Battle Creek
712-365-4949

Bedford
Old Settlers Inn
712-523-2451

Bellevue
Mont Rest B&B
319-872-4220-[Y--]

Our House
319-872-5612

Spring Side B&B
319-872-5452

Bettendorf
Abbey Hotel
319-355-1291

Boone
Barkley House B&B
800-753-8586

Hancock House
515-432-4089

Brayton
Hallock House
712-549-2449

Brooklyn
Hotel Brooklyn
515-522-9229

Buckingham
ABC Country Inn
319-478-2321

Burlington
Lakeview B&B
319-752-8735

Mississippi Manor B&B
319-753-2218

Calmar
Calamar Guesthouse
319-562-3851

Calrinda
Colonial White House B&B
712-542-5006

Carlisle
Tuttle House B&B
515-287-5162

Cedar Falls
Carriage House
319-277-6724

Taylor Manor
319-266-0035

Townsend Place B&B
319-266-9455

Cedar Rapids
Gwendolyns B&B
319-363-9731

Snoozies B&B
319-364-2134

Centerville
One Of A Kind
515-437-4540

Paint'n Primitives
515-856-8811

Clarinda
Country Gables B&B
712-542-5006

Westcott House
712-542-5323

Clayton
Claytonian

Clear Lake
Larch Pine Inn
515-357-7854

Noe House B&B
515-357-8368

Norsk Hus-By The Shore
515-357-8368

North Shore House
515-357-4443

Clermont
Mill Street B&B
319-423-5531

Miller House B&B Inn
319-423-7275

Colo
Martha's Vineyard B&B
515-377-2586

Corning
Pheasants Galore Inn
515-322-3749

Council Bluffs
Lions Den B&B Suite
712-322-7162

Robins Nest Inn B&B
712-323-1649-[Y--]

Terra Jane Country Inn
712-322-4200

The Terra Jane
712-322-4200

Dallas Center
Hartman House B&B
515-992-3900

Davenport
Beiderbecke Inn B&B
319-324-2454

Bishops House
319-324-2454

©Inn & Travel Memphis, Tennessee

2-129

Iowa **Bold Name** - *Description appears in other section*

Fultons Landing
319-322-4069

River Oaks Inn
800-352-6016-[Y--]

De Witt
Wagoneer Guest House
319-659-5555

Decorah
Broadway House B&B
319-382-2329

Montgomery Mansion
319-382-5088

Vanaheim Inn
319-382-4191

Victoria Cottage B&B
319-382-4897

Delmar
Lears Retreat
319-674-4157

Denison
Connors Corner B&B
712-263-8826

Queen Belle B&B
712-263-6777

Des Moines
Brownswood Country B&B
515-285-4135

Carter House
515-288-7850

Jardin Suite
515-289-2280

Dubuque
Alta Monte
319-582-6851

B&B On Juniper Hill
319-582-4405

Hancock House
319-557-8989

Juniper Hill Farm
800-572-1449

L'Auberge Mandolin
319-556-0069

Lore House-Valleyview
319-583-7327

Mandolin Inn
800-524-7996

Martin Anthony
319-583-5336

Oak Crest Cottage
319-582-4207

Redstone Inn
319-582-1894-[Y--]

Richards House B&B
319-557-1492

Ryan House
319-556-5000

Dunlap
Get-Away
712-643-5584

Durango
Another World Paradise Valley Inn
970-552-1034

East Dubuque
Capt Chas Merry Guest House
815-747-3644

Elgin
Country Swiss Guest House
319-426-5712

Elk Horn
Rainbow H Ranch & Campground
712-764-8272-[Y--]

Traveling Companion
712-764-8932

Elkader
Little House Vacation
319-783-7774

Elkhorn
Joys Morning Glory B&B
712-764-5631

Emmetsburg
Queen Marie B&B
712-852-4700

Essex
Essex House
800-309-3311

Estherville
Hoffman Guest House
712-362-5994

Fairfield
Bountiful B&B Inn
515-472-7737

Happy Hearth B&B
515-472-9386

Pollys B&B
515-472-2517

Fort Atkinson
Cloverleaf Farm
319-534-7061

Fort Madison
Kingsley Inn
800-441-2327-[G--]

Mississippi Rose & Thistle Inn
319-372-7044

Morton House
319-372-9517

Galva
Pioneer Farm B&B
712-282-4670

Garden Grove
McClung House
515-443-2277

Garner
Mrs Bs B&B
515-923-2390

Greenfield
Wilson Home
515-743-2031-[Y--]

Grinnell
Carriage House
515-236-7520

Clayton Farms B&B
515-236-3011

Guttenburg
Old Brewery B&B
319-252-2094

Hampton
Spring Valley Farm B&B
515-456-4437

Harper
Harper B&B
515-635-2619

Hartley
Time Out B&B
712-728-2213

Hawkeye
Hawkeye House Inn
319-427-3787

Homestead
De Heimat Country Inn
319-622-3937

Rawsons B&B
319-622-6035

Independence
Riverside B&B
319-334-4100

Iowa City
Bella Vista Place
319-338-4129

Golden Haug
319-338-6452

Haverkamps Linn St Homestay
319-337-4363-[Y--]

Sugar Woods B&B
319-338-3164

Jefferson
Johnson House B&B
515-386-4759

Keokuk
Grand Anne B&B
319-524-6310

Keosauqua
Hotel Manning
319-293-3232

Mason House Inn
319-592-3133

Keota
Elmhurst
515-636-3001

Knoxville
Le Grande Victorian B&B
515-842-4653

Lake View
Lakeside B&B
712-657-2835

2-130

©Inn & Travel Memphis, Tennessee

Bold Name - *Description appears in other section* *Iowa*

Midway Farm B&B
712-657-2389

Lansing
Fitzgeralds Inn
319-538-4872

Kuhlmans Decker House Inn
319-538-4263

Lansing House
319-538-4263

LaPorte
Brandts Orchard B&B
319-342-2912

Brandys Orchard Inn
319-342-2912

Le Claire
Country Inn B&B
319-289-4793

Latimers B&B
319-289-5747

McCaffrey House
319-289-3011

Mississippi Sunrise B&B
319-332-9203

Mohrhaur Monarch B&B
319-289-3011

River Rest B&B
319-289-5865

Leighton
Heritage House
515-626-3092

Long Grove
DeScheppers Night On The Farm
319-285-4377

Luana
Bs B&B
319-864-3681

Malcom
Pleasant Country B&B
515-528-4925

Manchester
Homestead House

Maquoketa
Decker House Inn
319-652-6654-[Y--]

Squires Manor B&B
319-652-6961

Marengo
Loy B&B
319-642-7787-[Y--]

Marion
L-Mar Farm International
319-377-2055

Massena
Amdors Evergreen Inn
712-779-3521

Mayward
Boedeckers Bungalow West
319-637-2711

McGregor
Little Switzerland Inn
319-873-3670

McGregor Rivertown Inn
319-873-2385

Rivers Edge B&B
319-873-3501

Middle Amana
Dusk To Dawn B&B
319-622-3029

Rettig House
319-622-3386

Missouri Valley
Apple Orchard B&B
712-642-2418

Hilltop B&B
712-642-3695

Mitcheville
Whitaker Farms
515-967-3184

Montezuma
English Valley B&B
515-623-3663

Montpelier
Varners Caboose
319-381-3652

Moorehead

Loess Hills B&B
712-886-5495

Nevada
Queen Anne B&B
515-684-8893

New London
Old Brick B&B
319-367-5403

Newton
Lacorsette Masion Inn
515-792-6833

Nichols
Townsend Nichols House B&B
319-723-4503

Oakland
Spalti House
712-482-3758

Oskaloosa
Mansion On The Hill
515-673-9294

Ottumwa
Guest House B&B
515-684-8893

Panora
Hudson House
515-755-2797

Pella
Strawtown Inn
515-628-2681

Postville
Old Shepherd House
319-864-3452

Postville B&B
319-864-7146

Princeton
Woodlands
800-257-3177

Red Oak
Heritage Hill B&B
800-721-6035

Rockwell City
Pine Grove B&B
712-297-7494

Ruthven
Brotts Country Inn
712-837-5225

Rutland
Heart & Home

515-332-3167

Sac City
Brick Bungalow B&B
712-662-7302

Drewry Homestead
712-662-4416

Saint Ansgar
Blue Belle Inn
515-736-2225

Schaller
Pioneer Farm B&B
712-275-4611

Seymour
Seymour B&B
515-898-7682

Shenandoah
Garrisons House
712-246-1820

Gibson House B&B
712-246-1820

Slater
Bestmamoer Haus
515-685-3794

South Amana
Babis B&B
319-662-4381

Spencer
Hanna Marie Country Inn
712-262-1286-[Y--]

Spillville
Old World Inn
319-562-3739-[Y--]

Taylor Made B&B
319-562-3958

Spirit Lake
Francis Hospitality Manor
712-336-4345

Moorelands Country Inn
515-847-4707

Stratford
Hooks Point Farmstead B&B
800-383-7062

Valkommen House
515-838-2440

©*Inn & Travel Memphis, Tennessee*

Iowa - Kansas **Bold Name** - *Description appears in other section*

Swedesburg
Carlson House
319-254-2451

Swisher
Terra Verde Farm
319-846-2478

Tama
Hoskins House
800-461-3797

Thurman
Plum Creek Inn
800-829-0646

Tipton
Victorian House Of Tipton
319-886-2633

Titonka
Mile-Away Farm
515-928-2447

Open Space
515-928-2502

Ricklefs B&B
515-928-2864

Ricks House
515-928-2185

Turin
Country Homestead B&B
712-353-6772

Walnut
Antique City Inn B&B
712-784-3722

Walnut Creek Station B&B
800-395-8056

Washington
Quiet Sleeping Rooms
319-653-3736

Roses & Lace B&B
319-653-2462

Waterloo
Daisy Wilton Inn
319-232-0801

Wellington B&B
319-234-2993

Waukon
Allamakee B&B
319-568-3103

Waverly
Villa Fairfield B&B
319-352-0739

Webster City
Centennial Farm
515-832-3050

West Branch
Inn At Nearby Wapsinonoc
319-643-7484

West Des Moines
Ellendale B&B
515-225-2219

Ellendale Scandinavian B&B
515-225-2219

Whitting
Lighthouse Marina Inn
712-458-2066

Williamsburg
Lucilles Bett Und Breakfast
319-668-1185

Woodbine
Four Pines B&B
712-647-2295

KANSAS

Abilene
Balfours House
913-263-4262

Dora Theay Ah's B&B
913-263-0226

Old Glory Guest House
913-263-0226

Spruce House
913-263-3900

Victorian Reflections B&B
913-263-7774

Alma
Stuewe Place
913-765-3636

Ashland
Rolling Hills B&B
316-635-2859

Slaton House
316-635-2290

Wallingford Inn
316-635-2129

Atchison
Williams House
913-367-1757

Atwood
Country Corner
913-626-9516

Flower Patch B&B
913-626-3780

Goodnite At Irenes
913-626-3521

Baldwin City
Grove House
913-594-2947

Barnes
Glorias Coffee & Quilts
913-763-4569

Basehor
Bedknobs & Biscuits
913-724-1540

Bern
Lear Acres B&B
913-336-3903

Burlington
Victorian Memories
316-364-5752

Cambridge
Grouse Creek Ranch B&B
316-467-2276

Caney
Caney B&B
316-879-5478

Cassoday
Sunbarger Guest House
316-735-4499

Chapman
Windmill Farm B&B
913-263-8755

Cimarron
Cimarron Hotel
316-855-2244-[Y--]

Clyde
Clyde Hotel
913-446-2231

Columbus
Meriwether House B&B
316-429-2812

Concordia
Crystles B&B
913-243-2192

Cottonwood Falls
Carols Country Inn
316-273-6683

Council Grove
Cottage House Hotel
800-888-8162-[Y--]

Flint Hills B&B
316-767-6655

Dodge City
Boot Hill B&B
316-225-7600

Dorrance
Country Inn
913-666-4468

Dover
Sage Inn
913-256-6336

Elkhart
Cimarron
405-696-4672

Emporia
Plumb House B&B
316-342-6881

White Rose Inn
316-343-6336

Enterprise
Ehrsam Place B&B
800-470-7774

Eureka
123 Mulberry Street B&B
800-283-7515

Fort Scott
Bennington House
316-223-1837

Chenault Mansion
316-223-6800

Country Quarters
316-223-2889

Courtland B&B Inn
316-223-0098

2-132 ©Inn & Travel Memphis, Tennessee

Bold Name - *Description appears in other section* *Kansas*

Huntington House
316-223-3644

Lyons House
800-78-GUEST

Fowler
Creek Side Farm B&B
316-646-5586

Garnett
Kirk House
913-448-5813

Glasco
Rustic Remembrances
913-546-2552

Goodland
Heart Haven Inn
913-899-5171

Great Bend
Peaceful Acres B&B
316-793-7527

Walnut Brook B&B
800-300-5901

Halstead
Heritage Inn & Restaurant
316-835-2118

Murray Way B&B
316-835-2027

Hiawatha
Pleasant Corner
913-742-7877

Hill City
Pheasant Run B&B
913-674-2955

Pomeroy Inn
800-675-2099

Hillsboro
Nostalgic B&B Place
316-947-3519

Holton
Dodds House
800-341-8000

Hotel Josephine
913-364-3151

Holyrood
Holyrood House
913-252-3678

Hutchinson
Bowman House B&B
316-663-5824

Rose Garden
316-663-5317

Independence
Rosewood B&B
316-331-2221

Lakin
Country Pleasures B&B
316-355-6982

Lawrence
Halcyon House B&B
913-841-0314-[Y--]

Leavenworth
Salt Creek Valley Inn
913-651-2277

Lenora
Barbeau House
913-567-4886

Liberal
Bluebird Inn
316-624-0720

Lincoln
Woody House B&B
913-524-4744

Lindsborg
Smoky Valley B&B
800-532-4407

Swedish Country Inn
913-227-2985

Lucas
Lucas Country Inn
913-525-6358

Madison
Flinthills B&B
316-437-2735

Manhattan
Cliff Kimble B&B
913-539-3816

Kimble Cliff
913-539-3816-[Y--]

Marion
Country Dreams
316-382-2250

Melvern

Schoolhouse Inn
913-549-3473

Meriden
Village Inn
913-876-2835

Minneola
Homestead Inn
316-885-4537

Moran
Hedgeapple Acres B&B
316-237-4646

Newton
Hawk House B&B
800-500-2045

Nickerson
Hedricks B&B Inn
316-662-1881

Olathe
Martin Van Buren Parker B&B
913-780-4587

Pickering House
913-829-7800

Osage City
Rosemary Inn
913-528-4498

Osborne
Loft B&B
913-346-5984

Oskaloose
Stone Crest B&B
913-863-2166

Overbrook
Pinemoore Inn
913-463-2304

Parsons
Painted Lady
316-421-3958

Pittsburg
Victorian Gardens B&B
800-709-1961

Pleasanton
Cedar Crest
913-352-6706

Pratt
Pratt Guest House
316-672-1200

Riley

Trixs Riley Roomer
913-485-2654

Rose Hill
Queen Anne Lace B&B
316-733-4075

Salina
Hunters Leigh B&B
800-889-6750

Seneca
Country Charm B&B
913-336-2480

Stafford
Henderson House B&B
800-473-8003

Sylvan Grove
Spillman Creek Lodge
913-277-3424

Syracuse
Braddock Ames B&B
316-384-5218

Tonganoxie
Almedas B&B Inn
913-845-2295-[Y--]

Topeka
Brickyard Barn Inn
913-235-0057

Elderberry B&B
913-235-6309

Four Woods B&B
219-593-2056

Heritage House
913-233-3800

Holliday Park B&B
913-234-8384

Sunflower B&B
913-357-7509

Ulysses
Fort Cedar View
316-356-2570

Forts Cedar View
316-356-2570

Valley Center
Broadway B&B
316-755-1000

Valley Falls

©Inn & Travel Memphis, Tennessee

Kansas - Kentucky   **Bold Name** - *Description appears in other section*

Barn B&B Inn
800-869-7717-[Y--]

Victoria
Das Younger Haus
913-735-2760

Wakeeney
Thistle Hill B&B
913-743-2644

Wakefield
Nuttall B&B
913-461-5732

Rock House BNB
913-461-5732

Wakefields Country B&B
913-461-5533

Washington
More Ballard Inn
913-325-3292

Wathena
Carousel B&B
913-989-3537

Wichita
Holiday House-Res B&B
316-721-1968

Inn At The Park
800-258-1951-[Y--]

Inn of Willowbend
800-553-5775

Max Paul, An Inn
316-689-8101

Strafford House Inn
316-942-0900

The Castle Inn Riverside
316-263-6219-[G--]

Vermillion Rose
316-267-7636

Winfield
Iron Gate Inn
316-221-7202

KENTUCKY

Allensville
Pepper Place
502-265-9859

Auburn

Auburn Guest House
502-542-6019

David Williams House
502-542-6019

Augusta
Augusta Ayre B&B
606-756-3228

Augusta Landing B&B
606-756-2510

Doniphan Home
606-756-2409

Lamplighter Inn
606-756-2603-[Y--]

Swan Song Guest Cottage
606-735-3551

Bardstown
1790 House
502-348-7072

Amber Leann B&B
800-828-3330

Bruntwood 1802
502-348-8218-[Y--]

Coffee Tree Cabin
502-348-1151

Jailers Inn
502-348-5551

Kenmore Farms
502-348-8023

Mansion
502-348-2586

McLean House
502-348-3494

Shadow Lawn
502-348-2267

Talbot Tavern
502-348-3494

Victorian Lights
502-348-8087

Beaver Dam
Old Hartford Inn
502-274-5500

Bellevue
Welle Haus B&B

606-431-6829

Berea
Boone Tavern Hotel
800-366-9358

Holly Tree B&B
606-986-2804

Mansion House
606-986-9851

Morning Glory
606-252-5042

Bloomfield
Vintage Rose
502-252-5042

Bowling Green
Alpine Lodge
502-843-4846-[Y--]

Bowling Green B&B
502-781-3861

Walnut Lawn B&B
502-781-7255

Brandenburg
Doe Run Inn
502-422-2982-[Y--]

East Hill Inn
502-422-3047

Bronston
Annies Of Lake Cumberland
606-561-9966

Burkesville
Cabin Fever
502-737-8748

Cadiz
Round Oak
502-924-5850

Campbellsburg
Ridgeview House
502-532-6404

Campbellsville
Yellow Cottage
502-789-2669

Carrollton
Baker House Inn
502-732-4210

Carrollton Inn
502-732-6905

Pt Baker House
800-74-BAKER

Cave City
Maple Grove Inn
502-678-7123

Covington
Amos Shinkle Townhouse
606-431-2118-[Y--]

Carmeal House
606-431-6130

Claire House
606-491-0168

Quinn B&B
606-491-0168

Sanford House
606-291-9133

Cynthiana
Broadwell Acres B&B
606-234-4255-[Y--]

Seldon Renaker Inn
606-234-3752

Danville
Empty Nest
606-236-3339

Pasicks
606-236-0074

Randolph House
606-236-9594

The Cottage
606-236-9642

Twin Hollies B&B
606-236-8954

Deatsville
Deatsville Inn
502-348-6382

Dowson Springs
Ridley House
502-797-2165

Elizabethtown
Bethlehem Academy Inn
502-862-9003

Olde Bethlehem Academy Inn
800-662-5670

Pams Cabin Fever
502-737-4980

2-134   ©*Inn & Travel Memphis, Tennessee*

Bold Name - *Description appears in other section* **Kentucky**

Eminence
Eminence Inn B&B

Frankfort
B&B At Sills Inn
800-526-9801-[G--]

Olde Kentuckie
B&B Inn
502-227-7389

Taylor Compton
House
502-227-4368

Franklin
College Street Inn
502-586-9352

Georgetown
**Blackridge Hall
B&B**
800-768-9308-[Y--]

Jordan Horse Farm
502-863-1944

Log Cabin B&B
502-863-3514-[Y--]

Pineapple Inn
502-863-5453

Ghent
Ghent House B&B
502-347-5807

Historic Ghent
House
606-291-0168

Glasgow
"307"
502-651-5672

B&B Country
Cottage
502-646-2940

Country Cottage
502-646-2677

Four Seasons
Country Inn
502-678-1000

Hall Place c1852
502-651-3176

Glendale
Petticoat Junction
502-369-8604

Grays Knob
Three Deer Inn
606-573-6666

Harrodsburg
Beaumont Inn
800-352-3992

Canaah Farm B&B
606-734-3984

Jailhouse
606-734-7012

Ms Jesta Belles
606-734-7834

Shaker Village
Pleasant Hill
606-734-5411

Hazard
Pleasure Cove
606-439-2345

Hazel
Outback B&B
502-436-5858

Hickman
Laclede B&B
502-236-2902

Hindman
Quilt Maker Inn
606-785-5622

Hodgenville
Lakeside
502-358-3711

Hopkinsville
Oakland Manor
502-885-6400

Independence
A Touch Of Country
B&B
606-356-7865

Cullys Country
Retreat
606-356-7848

Kuttawa
Davis House
502-388-4468-[Y--]

Lancaster
Perkins Place Farm
800-762-4145

Lebanon
Myrtledene
502-692-2223

Lewisport
Hayden House
502-295-3939

Lexington
547
606-255-4152-[Y--]

B&B At Sills Inn
800-526-9801-[G--]

B&B In Lexington
606-255-4152

Cherry Knoll Farm
B&B
606-253-9800

Homewood
606-255-4152

Maple Hill Manor
606-336-3075-[Y--]

Rokeby Hall
606-252-2368

Sycamore Ridge
606-231-7714

Liberty
Liberty Greystone
Manor
606-787-5444

Louisville
Angelmelli Inn
800-245-9262

Inn At The Park
800-700-7275

Maple Hill Manor
606-336-3075-[Y--]

Old Louisville Inn
502-635-1574

Old Stone Inn
502-722-8882

Rose Blossom
502-636-0295

St James Court
502-636-1742

Victorian Secret
B&B
502-581-1914

Mammoth Cave
Mello Inn
502-286-4126

Manchester
Blairs Country Log
Home
606-598-2854

Marion
Lafayette Heights
Clubhouse
502-965-3889

Maysville
Blue Licks
Battlefield State
Park
606-289-5507

Middlesborough
Ridge Runner
606-248-4299

Midway
Holly Hill Inn
606-846-4732

Morehead
Appalachian House
606-784-5421

Morgantown
Helm House B&B
800-441-4786

Mount Sterling
Colonial Inn

Trimble House
606-498-6561

Victorian Mansion
606-498-5383-[Y--]

Munfordville
Farm Retreat
502-524-3697

Murray
Diuguid House B&B
502-753-5470

New Haven
Sherwood Inn
502-549-3386

Newport
Gateway
606-581-6447

Nicholasville
Cedar Haven Farm
606-858-3849

Sandusky House
606-223-4730

Oak Grove
Tuckaway Farm
B&B
502-439-6255

Old Kuttawa

©*Inn & Travel Memphis, Tennessee*

Kentucky - Maryland | **Bold Name** - *Description appears in other section*

Silver Cliff Inn
502-388-5858

Olive Hill
Oak Hills
606-286-6294

Owensboro
Razberry Butterfly
502-771-5590

Weatherberry
502-684-US60

Owensburg
Friendly Farm &
Tennis House
502-771-5590

Paducah
Ehrhardts B&B
502-554-0644-[Y--]

Farley Place
502-442-2844

Paducah Harbor
Plaza B&B
502-442-2698

Perryville
Elmwood Inn
606-332-2400

Princeton
Maples
502-365-2758

Richmond
**Barnes Mill B&B
Guest House**
606-623-5509-[Y--]

Jordan Hill Farm
606-623-8114

Rockfield
Victorian Oaks
502-781-8465

Russell Springs
White Pillars
502-866-7231

Russellville
Log House
502-726-8483

Stone Mountain
Estate
502-726-2559

Washington House
502-726-7608

Sandy Hook

Charlenes Inn
606-738-6674

Shelbyville
Muir House
502-633-7037

Wallace House
502-633-1132

Simpsonville
KHC Farm
502-722-3793

Somerset
Marcum Porter
House
606-376-2242

Osbornes Of Cabin
Hollow
606-382-5495

Shadwick House
606-678-4675

South Union
Shaker Tavern
502-542-6801

Springfield
Glenmar Plantation
B&B
800-828-3330

Maple Hill Manor
606-336-3075-[Y--]

McChord Carriage
House Inn
606-336-3290

Waltons West Wind

Taylorsville
B&B At Taylorsville
502-477-2473

Bowlings Villa B&B
502-477-2636

Versailles
B&B At Sills Inn
800-526-9801-[G--]

Rose Hill Inn
800-526-9801

Shepherd Place
606-873-7843

Victorian Rose
800-526-9801

West Point
Ditto House Inn

502-922-4939

Wilmore
Scott Station Inn
606-858-0121

Winchester
Windswept Farm
606-745-1245

MARYLAND

Accident
Alberts House
301-746-8655

Adelphi
Monkes
301-434-5558

Allen
Allendale Cottage
B&B
410-860-2800

Annapolis
American Heritage
B&B
410-280-1620

Annapolis B&B
410-269-0669

Ark & Dove
410-268-6277

Barn On Howards
Cove
410-266-6840

Casa Bahia
410-268-3106-[Y--]

Charles Inn
410-268-1451

Chesapeake By
Lighthouse B&B
410-757-0248

Chez Amis B&B
410-263-6631

**College House-
Historic District**
410-263-6124-[G--]

Flaghouse Inn
410-280-2721

Gatehouse B&B
410-280-0024

Gibson's Lodging
410-268-5555-[Y--]

Green Street Inn
410-263-9171-[Y--]

Heart Of Annapolis
B&B
410-268-2309

Hunter House
410-626-1268

Johan Williams
House
410-269-6020

Little Guest House
410-268-2128

Maggie Molly
410-263-5410

Magnolia House
410-268-3477

Maryland Inn
800-638-8902-[Y--]

Maryrob B&B
410-268-5438

Murphys B&B
410-974-9030

One-Four-Four B&B
410-268-8053

**Prince George Inn
B&B**
410-263-6418-[Y--]

Samuel Hutton
House
410-266-3796

Scotland Inn
410-268-5665

Severn B&B
410-757-9487

Shaws Fancy
410-268-9750

Southgate B&B
410-263-3126

William Page Inn
800-364-4160-[G--]

Baltimore
Admiral Fell Inn
800-292-INNS-[Y--]

Agora Inn
301-234-0515

Ann Street B&B

Bold Name - *Description appears in other section* *Maryland*

410-342-5883

Betsys B&B
410-383-1274

Bolton Hill B&B
410-669-5356

Casa Bahia
410-268-3106
[G--]

Celies Waterfront
B&B
800-432-0184

Chez Claire
410-837-0996

Eagles Mere B&B
410-322-1618

Hendersons
Wharf
800-522-2088

Mr Mole B&B
410-728-1179-[Y--]

Mulberry House
410-576-0111

Paulus Gasthaus
410-467-1688

Rachels Dowry
410-385-2656

Shirley Guest
House
800-868-5064

Society Hill
Hopkins
410-235-8600

Twin Gates
800-635-0370

Union Square
House B&B
410-233-9064

Bel Air
  Tudor Hall
  410-838-0466

Berlin
  Atlantic Hotel
  410-641-3589

  Holland House
  410-641-1956

  Merry Sherwood
  Plantation

  410-641-2112

Bethesda
  Sea Voice Inn
  301-220-4121

  Windsow Home
  301-229-4654

Betterton
  Lantern Inn
  410-348-5809

  Ye Lantern Inn
  410-348-5809

Bridgetown
  Chesapeake Gun
  Club
  800-787-INNS

Buckeystown
  Catoctin Inn
  301-874-5555

  Inn At Buckeystown
  800-272-1190

Burtonsville
  Upstream At Waters
  Gift
  410-421-9562-[Y--]

Cambridge
  Commodores
  Cottages
  410-228-6938

  Glasgow Inn
  800-225-0575

  Lodgecliffe
  410-228-1760

  Oakley House
  410-228-6623

  Sarke Plantation
  410-228-7020-[Y--]

Cascade
  Bluebird On The
  Mountain
  800-362-9526

  Inwood Guest
  House
  301-241-3467

Cecilton
  Anchorage B&B
  410-275-1972

Centerville
  Academy B&B
  410-758-2791

  Kendall House On
  Corsica
  410-758-0159

  Locust Hill B&B
  410-758-2777

  Rose Tree B&B
  410-658-3991

  Wharf Lodge B&B
  Inn
  410-758-1111

Chesapeake City
  Blue Max Inn
  800-885-2781

  Bohemia House
  410-885-3024

  Inn At The Canal
  410-885-5995

  McNulty House
  410-885-2200

Chestertown
  Brampton B&B
  410-778-1860

  Claddaugh Farm
  B&B
  410-778-4894

  Cole House
  410-928-5287

  Country Inn At
  Rolphs Wharf
  410-778-6347

  Drop The Anchor
  Inn
  410-778-1004

  Flyway Lodge
  410-778-5557

  Great Oak Manor
  800-778-5796-[Y--]

  Hills Inn
  800-778-INNS

  Homestead Tavern
  410-778-5518

  Imperial Hotel
  410-778-5000

  Inn At Mitchell
  House
  301-778-6500-[Y--]

  Lauretum Inn
  410-778-3236

  Radcliffe Cross
  410-778-5540

  White Swan Tavern
  Inn
  410-778-2300

  Widows Walk Inn
  410-778-6455

Chevy Chase
  Chevy Chase B&B
  301-656-5867

  Smiths
  301-656-5690

Church Creek
  Loblolly Landings &
  Lodge
  410-397-3033

Clear Springs
  Wilson House B&B
  301-582-4320

Clinton
  Tall Oaks B&B
  301-868-1922

Cordova
  Dukesdale Farm
  410-820-2349-[Y--]

Crisfield
  My Fair Lady B&B
  410-968-3514

  The Islander
  410-968-3314

Cumberland
  Colonial Manor

  Inn At Walnut
  Bottom
  800-286-9718

  Mount Aerie
  301-724-5397

  Red Lamp Post
  301-777-3262

Deale
  Makai Pierside
  410-867-0998

East New Market
  Friendship Hall
  410-943-4843

Easton

©*Inn & Travel Memphis, Tennessee*

Maryland   *Bold Name - Description appears in other section*

Ashby 1663
410-822-4235

Bishops House
410-820-7290

Gross Coat
Plantation
800-580-0802

John S McDaniel
House
800-822-3704

Thanksgiving Farm

Edgewater
Almost Home B&B
410-956-6038

Edgewater Beach
Cliftara At Cedar
Point
410-269-2854

Edgewood
Victorian Lady B&B
410-676-4661

Elkton
Inn At The Canal
410-885-5995

Sinking Springs
Herb Farm
410-398-5566

Ellicott City
Hayland Farm B&B
410-531-5593

Mayland Farm
410-531-5593-[Y--]

Wayside Inn
410-461-4636-[Y--]

White Duck
410-992-8994

Emmitsburg
Silver Fancy Inn
301-447-6627

Stonehurst Manor
301-447-2880

Ewell
Ewell Tide Inn B&B
410-425-2141

Guys Guest House
410-425-2751

Pitchfort Inn

Fairplay
Candlelight Inn
301-582-4852

Fallston
Broomhall B&B
800-552-3965

Frederick
121 Record Street

Middle Plantation
301-898-7128-[G--]

Spring Bank
301-684-0440

Turning Point Inn
301-874-2421

Tyler-Spite House
301-831-4455

Freeland
Freeland Farm
410-357-5364

Heartland Farm
301-695-9315

Gaithersburg
Gaithersburg
Hospitality B&B
301-977-7377

Georgetown
Kitty Knight House
410-648-5777

Glaena
Rosehill Farm
410-648-5538

Grantsville
Casselman Valley
Farm
301-895-5055

Greensboro
Riverside Inn

Hagerstown
Beaver Creek House
B&B
301-797-4764

Lewrene Farm B&B
301-582-1735-[Y--]

Sunday's B&B
800-221-4828-[Y--]

Wingrove Manor
301-733-6328

Harwood

Oakwood
301-261-5338-[Y--]

Havre De Grace
Spencer Silver
Mansion
410-939-1097

Susquehanna
Trading Co Guest
House
410-939-4252

Vandiver House
410-939-5200

Huntington
Ches Bayvu
410-535-0123

Hurlock
Hunters Cove
410-651-9644

Keedysville
Antietam Overlook
Farm
800-878-4241

Keymar
Bowling Brook
Country Inn
410-848-0353

Kingsville
Briarmeade
410-592-6818

Leonard
Matoaka Cottages

Lutherville
Twin Gates
800-635-0370

McHenry
Country Inn
301-387-6694

Savage River Inn
B&B
301-245-4440

Middletown
Stone manor
301-473-5454

New Market
National Pike Inn
301-865-5055-[Y--]

Strawberry Inn
301-865-3318

North Beach
Angels In The Attic

B&B
410-257-1069

North East
Chesapeake Lodge
410-287-5433

Mill House B&B
301-287-3532

North Bay B&B
410-287-5948

Oakland
Alpine Vilalge
301-387-5534

Cornish Manor
301-334-3551

Deer Park Inn
301-334-2308

Harley Farm
301-387-9050

Mountain Village Inn
301-334-8518

Oak & Apple
301-334-9265

Red Run Inn
301-387-6606

Ocean City
Annabells
410-289-8894

Conners Inn
410-289-7721

His Honors Place
410-289-2630

Taylor House B&B
410-289-1177

Olney
Thoroughbred B&B
301-774-7649-[Y--]

Tranquil Forest
301-774-6052

Oxford
1876 House
410-226-5496

Oxford Inn
410-226-5220

Robert Morris Inn
410-226-5111

Pasadena

2-138   ©*Inn & Travel Memphis, Tennessee*

Bold Name - *Description appears in other section*   *Maryland*

Waterview B&B
410-437-3526

Phoenix
Barn House
410-527-0873

Prince Frederick
Hutchins Heritage B&B
410-535-1759

Princess Anne
Elmwood c1770 B&B
410-651-1066-[Y--]

Hayman House B&B
410-651-1107

Hyland House
410-651-1056

Washington Hotel & Inn
410-651-2525

Queenstown
House Of Burgess
410-827-6834

Rising Sun
Chandlee House
410-658-6958

Rock Hall
Bay Breeze Inn
410-639-2061

Black Duck Inn
410-639-2478

Huntingfield Manor Inn
410-639-7779

Inn At Asprey
410-639-2194

Littleneck Lodge
410-639-7577

Napley Green Country Inn
410-639-2267

Swan Point Inn
410-639-2500

Rockville
Wells House
301-251-1033-[Y--]

Royal Oak
Pasadena Inn & Conference Center
410-745-5053

Saint Michaels
208 Talbot
410-745-3838

Barretts B&B Inn
410-745-3322

Fox Run Farm
410-745-2381

Getaway
410-745-2094

Hambleton Inn
301-245-3350

Inn At Perry Cabin
800-722-2949

Kemp House Inn
410-745-2243

Palmer House
410-745-3319

Parsonage Inn 1883
800-234-5519

Tarr House
410-745-2175

Two Swan Inn
410-745-2929

Victorian Inn
410-745-3368

Victoriana
410-745-3368

Wades Point Inn
410-745-2500

Salisbury
White Oak Inn
410-742-4887-[Y--]

Savage
Castle
301-759-5946-[Y--]

Scotland
Old Kirk House
301-872-4093

St Michaels Manor
301-872-4025

Sharpsburg
Ground Squirrel Holler
301-432-8288

Inn At Antietam
410-342-6601-[Y--]

Jacob Rohrbach Inn
301-432-5079

Silver Spring
Johnsons
301-384-2824

Northwood Inn
301-593-7027

Windswept
301-604-7788

Smithsburg
Blue Bear B&B
301-824-2292

Snow Hill
Chanceford Hall B&B
410-632-2231

River House Inn
410-632-2722-[G--]

Snow Hill Inn
410-632-2102-[Y--]

Solomons
Black Creek Inn
410-326-2022

Locust Inn
410-326-9817

Solomons Island
Davis House
410-326-4811

Stevenson
Gramercy B&B
410-486-2405

Mensana Inn
410-653-2403

Stevensville
Kent Manor Inn
410-643-5757

Still Pond
Still Pond
410-348-2234

Sykesville
Long Way Hill
410-795-8129

Tall Timbers
Potomac View Farm
301-994-0418

Taneytown

Antrim 1844
410-756-6812

Glenburn
410-751-1187

Thurmont
Cozy Country Inn
301-271-4301

Tilghman
Chesapeake Wood Duck Inn
410-886-2070

Harrisons Country Inn
410-886-2123

Lazy Jack Inn
410-886-2215

Tilghman Island
Black Walnut Point
410-886-2452

Sinclair House B&B
410-886-2147

Tilghman Island Inn
800-866-2141-[Y--]

Wood Duck B&B
800-956-2070

Uniontown
Newel Post
410-775-2655

Vienna
Governors Ordinary
301-376-3530

Tavern House
410-376-3347

Westminster
Avondale
410-848-4475

Judge Thomas House
410-876-6686

Westminster Inn
410-876-2893-[Y--]

Winchester Country Inn
410-876-7373-[Y--]

Williamsport
Wolfs End B&B
301-223-6888

Wittman

©Inn & Travel Memphis, Tennessee   2-139

Maryland - Michigan   **Bold Name** - *Description appears in other section*

Christmas Farm
301-822-4470

Woodsboro
Rosebud Inn
301-845-2221

MICHIGAN

Adrian
Briar Oaks Inn
517-263-1659

Ahmeek
Sand Hills Lighthouse
906-337-1744

Albion
Ds B&B
207-629-2976

Alden
Torch Lake B&B
616-331-6424

Touch Timbers B&B
616-331-4050

Algonac
Lindas Lighthouse Inn
810-794-2992

Allegan
Castle In The Country
616-673-8054

Delano Inn
616-673-2609

Winchester Inn
800-582-5694

Allen
Olde Brick House Inn
517-869-2349

Alma
Candlelight Cottage B&B
517-463-3961

Saraville
517-463-4078

Ann Arbor
B&B On Campus
313-994-9100

Cambridge B&B
313-663-1932

Gladstone House
313-769-0404

Hexagon House B&B
313-668-1616

Reynolds House
313-995-0301

Urban Retreat
313-971-8110

Woods Inn
313-665-8394

Atlanta
Briley Inn B&B
517-785-4784

Au Train
Pinewood lodge
906-892-8300

AuGres
Point Augres Hotel
517-876-7217

Bad Axe
Cross House
517-269-9466

Battle Creek
Greencrest Manor
616-962-8633

Maple Street B&B
616-963-2603

Old Lamplighters
616-963-2603

Bay City
Benders Haus
517-652-8897

Clements Inn
517-894-4600-[G--]

Stonehedge Inn
517-894-4342-[Y--]

Bay Port
Bay View Country Inn
517-656-9952

Bay View
Gingerbread House
616-347-3538

Terrace Inn
616-347-2410

Bellaire
Bellaire B&B

800-545-0780

Grass River B&B Inn
616-533-6041

Lake B&B
616-533-6167

On The Lake B&B
616-533-6167

Benzonia
Crystal B&B

Willowfen B&B
616-882-7169

Beulah
Brookside Inn
616-882-7271

Windermere Inn
616-882-9000

Big Bay
Big Bay Point Lighthouse
906-345-9957

Big Rapids
Taggart House
616-796-1713

Birch Run
Church Street Manor
517-624-4920

Black River
Silver Creek Lodge B&B
517-471-2198-[Y--]

Blaney Park
Celibeth House
906-283-3409

Blissfield
Hathaway House
517-486-2141

Hiram D Ellis Inn
517-486-3155

Boyne City
Duley's State Street Inn
616-582-7855

Boyne Falls
Arman House B&B
616-549-2764

Brighton
Log House B&B

810-229-2673

Brooklyn
Chicago Street Inn
800-252-5674

Dewey Lake Manor B&B
517-467-7122-[G--]

Buchanan
Four Flags Farm B&B
616-471-5711

Cadillac
American Inn B&B
616-779-9000-[Y--]

Essenmachers B&B
616-775-3828

Hermans's European Cafe
616-775-9563

Calumet
Bostrom-Johnson House
906-337-4651

Calumet House
906-337-1936

Thimbleberry Inn
906-337-1332

Caro
Garden Gate B&B
517-673-2696

Caseville
Carkner House
517-856-3456

Country Charm Farm
517-856-3110

Cedar
Jarrold Farm
616-228-6955

Victoria Creek B&B
616-228-7246

Central Lake
Coulter Creek B&B
616-544-3931

Darmon Street B&B
616-544-3931

Twala's B&B
616-599-2864

Centreville

2-140   ©*Inn & Travel Memphis, Tennessee*

Bold Name - *Description appears in other section*   *Michigan*

Centreville Inn
616-467-4071

Charlevoix
Aaron's Windy Hill Lodge
616-547-2804

Bay B&B On Lake Michigan
616-599-2570

Belvedere House
800-280-4667

Bridge Street Inn
616-547-6066

Charlevoix Country Inn
616-547-5134

La Bergerie
616-547-2251

MacDougall House
616-547-5788

Patchwork Parlour B&B
616-547-5788-[Y--]

Wildflower
616-547-2667

Chassell
Hamar House B&B
906-523-4670

Chatham
Pacific House
906-439-5599

Cheboygan
Algomah Wheelhouse Inn
616-627-3643

Burt Lake B&B
616-238-9680

Chesaning
Bonnymill Inn
517-845-7780

Johnston Farm B&B
517-845-2180

Clinton
Clinton Inn
517-456-4151

Clio
Chandlier Guest House
810-687-6061

Coldwater
Batavia Inn
517-278-5146

Chicago Pike Inn
517-279-8744

Columbiaville
Redwing
810-793-4301

Commerce Two
Victorian Rose
810-360-8221

Conklin
Miller School Inn B&B
616-677-1026

Constantine
Our Old House B&B
616-435-5365

Crystal Falls
Crystal Inn B&B
906-875-6369

Curtis
Aunt Beas Long Pointe B&B
906-586-9849

Chamberlins Olde Forest Inn
906-586-6000

Davison
Oakbrook Inn
810-658-1546

Dearborn
Country Lane B&B
313-753-4586-[Y--]

Dearborn Inn
313-271-2700

York House
313-561-2432

Detroit
Blanche House Inn
313-822-7090

Country Lane B&B
313-753-4586-[Y--]

Dobson House
313-965-1887

Dewitt
Griffin House
517-669-9486

Diamondville
Bannicks B&B
317-646-0224

Douglas
Douglas Dunn Resort
616-857-5685

Goshorn House B&B
616-857-1326

Rosemont Inn
616-857-2637

Valentine Lodge
616-857-4598

Dundee
Dundee Guest House
313-529-5706

Eagle River
Eagles Nest B&B
906-337-4441

East Jordan
Easterly Inn B&B
616-536-3434

East Lansing
Coleman Corners B&B
517-339-9360

East Tawa
East Tawas Junction B&B
517-362-8006

Eastport
Sunrise B&B
616-599-2706

Torch Lake Sunrise B&B
616-599-2706

Eaton Rapids
Dustys English Inn
517-663-2500

Elberta
Summer Inn

Elk Rapids
Carin House B&B
616-264-8994

Widows Walk
616-264-5767

Ellsworth
Ellsworth House

B&B
616-588-7001

House On The Hill
616-588-6304

Empire
Empire House
616-326-5524

Southbar Manor
616-326-5304

Erie
Lotus Inn
313-848-5785

Evart
B&B At Lynch's Dream
616-734-5989

Farmingthon Hills
Botsford Inn
810-474-4800

Fennville
Crane House
616-561-6931

Grandmas Houes
616-543-4706

Heritage Manor Inn
616-543-4384

Hidden Pond B&B
616-561-2491-[G--]

J Paules, Fenn Inn
616-561-2836

Kingsley House
616-561-6425

Porches
616-543-4162

Fenton
Pine Ridge
810-629-8911

Flint
Avon House
810-232-6861

Courtyard
810-238-5510

Frankenmuth
B&B At The Pines
517-652-9019-[Y--]

Bavarian Town B&B
517-652-8057

©*Inn & Travel Memphis, Tennessee*   2-141

Michigan *Bold Name - Description appears in other section*

Bender Haus
517-652-8897

Das Kueffner Haus
517-652-6839

Franklin Haus
517-652-3939

Kueffner Haus B&B
517-652-6839

Frankfort
Haugens Haven B&B
616-352-7850

Hotel Frankfort
616-882-7271

Morningside B&B
616-352-4008

Pierside Lodging
616-352-4778

Summer Inn
616-352-7279

Trillium
616-352-4976

Fremont
Gerber House B&B
616-924-2829

Fruitport
Village Park B&B
616-865-6289

Galesburg
Byrd House
616-665-7052

Pine Arbor
800-541-7463

Garden
Summer House
906-644-2457

Gaylord
Heritage House B&B
517-732-1199

Nroden Hem Resort
517-732-6794

Glen Arbor
Glen Arbor B&B
616-334-6789

Sylvan Inn
616-334-4333

Walkers White Gull B&B
616-334-4486

White Gull Inn
616-334-4486

Gobles
Kal-Haven B&B
616-628-4932

Grand Blanc
Country Inn Of Grand Blanc
810-694-6749

Grand Haven
Boyden House B&B
616-846-3538

Harbor House Inn
800-841-0610

Highland Park Hotel B&B
616-846-1473

Shifting Sands B&B
616-842-3594

Washington Street Inn
616-842-1075

Grand Marais
Lakeview Inn
906-494-2612

Grand Rapids
Fountain Hill
616-458-6621

Hampton Inn
616-956-9304

Heald-Lear House
800-551-5126

Morning Glory Inn
616-894-8237

Ubran Retreat B&B
616-363-1125

Grass Lake
Coppys Inn
517-522-4850

Grawn
Ancient Mariner
616-263-5111

Grayling
Borcher's Au Sable B&B

Greenville
Gibson House
616-754-6691

Winter Inn
616-754-7108

Grosse Isle
Bishops Cottage
313-671-9191

Harbor Beach
Wellock Inn
517-479-3645

Harbor Springs
Four Acres B&B
616-526-6076

Harbour Inn
616-526-2107

Kimberly Country Estate
616-526-7646

Harrisville
Red Geranium Inn
517-724-6153

Springport Inn
517-724-6308

Widows Watch B&B
517-724-5465

Hart
Courtland House
616-873-4746

Wells 602 House B&B

Hartland
Farmstead B&B Ltd
810-887-6086

Hillsdale
Shadowlawn Manor B&B
517-437-2367

Holland
Dutch Colonial Inn
616-396-3664

Historic Old Holland Inn
616-396-6601

McIntyre B&B
616-392-9886

Old Holland Inn
616-396-6601

Reka's B&B
616-399-0409-[Y--]

The Parsonage 1908
616-396-1316-[Y--]

Holly
Historic Holly B&B
810-634-9375

Side Porch B&B
810-634-0740

Homer
Grist Guest House
517-568-4063

Grist Mill Inn
517-568-4063

Houghton
Charleston House B&B
906-482-7790

Hudson
Baker Hill B&B
517-448-8536

Suttons Weed Farm B&B
800-826-FARM

Interlochen
Betsie Valley B&B
616-275-7624

Interlochen Aire
616-276-6941

Lake & Pines Lodge
616-275-6671

Ionia
Union Hill Inn
616-527-0955

Iron River
Pine Willow B&B
906-265-4287

Ithaca
Chaffins Balmoral Farm
517-875-3410

Jackson
Country Hearth Inn
517-783-6404

Summer Place
517-787-0468

Jonesville
Munro House B&B
517-849-9292-[Y--]

2-142 ©Inn & Travel Memphis, Tennessee

Bold Name - *Description appears in other section* *Michigan*

Kalamazoo
Bartlett-Upjohn House
616-342-0230

Bluebird Inn
616-345-6173

Hall House B&B
800-421-4414

Kalamazoo House
616-343-5426

Stuart Avenue B&B
616-342-0230

Kearsage
Belknaps Garnet House
906-337-5607

Kearsarge
Garnet House B&B
906-337-5607

Lake City
B&B In The Pines
616-839-4876

Lake Leelanau
Centennial Inn
616-271-6460

Snowbird Inn B&B
616-256-9773

Lakeland
Sunset Cove
810-231-3802

Lakeside
Pebble House
616-469-1416

White Rabbit Inn
616-469-4620

Lamont
Riverview B&B
616-677-3921

Stagecoach Stop
616-677-3940-[Y--]

Lansing
Maplewood
517-372-7775

Lapeer
Hart House
810-667-9106

Laurium
Keweenaw House B&B
906-337-4822

Laurium Manor B&B
906-337-2549

Leland
Highlands
616-256-7632

Manitou Manor
616-256-7712

Riverside Inn
616-256-9971

Lewiston
Lakeview Hills Country Inn
517-786-2000

Lexington
Britannia English House
810-359-5772

Centennial B&B
810-359-8762

Governors Inn B&B
810-359-5770

Powell House B&B
810-359-5533

Vickie Vans B&B
810-359-5533

West Wind B&B
810-359-5772

Lowell
McGee Homestead B&B
616-897-8142

Ludington
B&B At Ludington
616-843-9768

Doll House Inn
616-843-2286

Grandma Mary's B&B
616-845-6577

Hamlin Lake Cottage
616-845-7127

Inland Sea Getaway
616-845-7569

Inn At Ludington
616-845-7055

Lamplighter B&B
616-843-9792

Ludington 1878 B&B
800-827-7869

Snybers Shoreline Inn
616-845-1261

Mackinac Island
Bay View At Mackinac
906-847-3295

Bogan Lake Inn
906-847-3439

Chateau Lorraine
906-847-8888

Cloghaun
906-847-3885

Haan 1830 Inn
906-847-6244

Iroquois Hotel On The Beach
906-847-3321

Lilac House
906-847-3708

Metivier Inn
906-847-6234-[Y--]

Small Point B&B
906-847-3758

Stone Cliff Resort

Mancelona
Cedar Bend Farm
616-687-5709

Manistee
Doubille EE House B&B
616-723-8654

Gubalts B&B
616-723-2006

Inn-Wick-a-Te-Wah
616-889-4396

Ivy Inn B&B
616-723-8881

Manistee Country House
616-723-2367

Manistique
Marina Guest House
906-341-5147

Maple City
Country Cottage B&B
616-228-5328

Leelanau Country Inn
616-228-5060

Marine City
Heather House
313-765-3175

Marlette
Country View B&B
517-635-2468

Marquette
Blueberry Ridge B&B
906-249-9246

Michigamme Lake Lodge
906-225-1393

Marshall
McCarthys Bear Creek Inn
616-781-8383-[Y--]

National House Inn
616-781-7374

McMillan
Helmer House Inn
906-586-3204

Mecosta
Blue Lake Lodge B&B
616-972-8391

Mendon
1873 Mendon Country Inn
616-496-8132-[Y--]

Mendon Country Inn
616-496-8132

Menominee
Gehrkes Gasthaus
906-863-6345

Metamora
Arizona East
810-678-3107

Michigamme
Cottage On The Bay

Michigan   ***Bold Name*** *- Description appears in other section*

906-323-6191

Michigan City
Duneland Beach Inn
219-874-7729

Midland
Bramble House B&B
517-832-5082

Castle B&B
800-892-9824

Henrietta B&B
517-631-0795

Jays B&B
517-496-2498

Milford
Hibbard Tavern
810-685-1435

Montague
Schillers Country Inn
616-894-2101

Mount Pleasant
Country Chalet
517-772-9259

Granary
517-772-3298

Roycroft Inn
517-772-3298

Munising
Homestead B&B
906-387-2542

Muskegon
Blue Country B&B
616-744-2555

Emery House
616-722-6978

Village B&B
616-726-4523

New Buffalo
Bauhaus On Barton
616-469-6419

Sans Souci B&B
616-756-3141

Sea Gull Inn
616-469-0485

Tall Oaks Inn B&B
616-469-0097

Newberry
MacLeod House
906-293-3841

Niles
Woods & Hearth B&B
616-683-0876

Yesterdays Inn
616-683-6079-[Y--]

Northport
Apple Beach Inn
616-386-5022

Birch Brook
616-386-5188

Hutchinsons Garden
616-386-5534

Mapletree Inn
616-386-5260

Northshore Inn
616-386-7111

Old Mill Pond
616-386-7341

Plum Lake Inn
616-386-5774

Vintage House
616-386-7228

Wood How Lodge
616-386-7194

Northville
Atchison House
810-349-3340

Carriage Stop

Nunica
Stonegate Inn
616-837-9267

Omena
Frieda's B&B
616-386-7274

Omena Shores B&B
616-386-7311

Omer
Rifle River B&B
517-653-2911

Onekama
Lake Breeze House
616-889-4969

Oscoda

Huron House
517-739-9255

Ossineke
Fernwood B&B
517-471-5176

Owosso
Merkel Manor
517-725-5600

Mulberry House
517-723-4890-[Y--]

Parkers Victorian Splendor
517-725-5168

R&R Farm Ranch
517-723-2553

Sylverlynd
517-723-1267

Victorian Splendor
517-725-5168

Parma
Hilltop Farm
517-531-5820

Paw Paw
Carrington's Country House
616-657-5321

Pentwater
Candlewyck House B&B
800-348-5827

Nickerson Inn
616-869-8241

Pentwater Abbey
616-869-6731

Pentwater Inn
616-869-5909

Pequaming
The Bungalow
906-524-7595

Petoskey
Apple Tree Inn
616-347-2900

Bear & The Bay
616-347-6077-[Y--]

Bear River Valley B&B
616-348-2046

Cozy Spot

616-347-3869

Gulls Way
616-347-9891

Staffords Bay View Inn
800-456-1917

Pinckney
Bunn-Pher Hill
313-878-9263

Plainwell
1882 John Crisp House
616-685-1293

Plymouth
Mayflower B&B Hotel
800-456-1620

Pontiac
Emlys B&B
810-333-7499

Port Austin
Garfield Inn
517-738-5254

Lake Street Manor
517-738-7720

Questover Inn
517-738-5253

Port Hope
Stafford House Inn
517-428-4554

Port Huron
Victorian Inn
810-984-1437-[Y--]

Port Sanilac
Raymond House Inn
810-622-8800

Prescott
Duncans B&B
517-873-4237

Prudenville
Spring Brook Inn
800-424-0218

Rapid City
Buck Stops Here B&B
906-446-3360

Redford
Country Keepsakes

Reed City

2-144   ©*Inn & Travel Memphis, Tennessee*

Osceola Inn
616-832-5537

Rochester Hills
Paint Creek B&B
810-651-6785

Rockford
Grandmas House
616-866-4111

Village Rose B&B
616-866-7041

Romeo
Country Heritage B&B
810-752-2879

Romulus
Country Lane B&B
313-753-4586-[Y--]

Roscommon
Tall Trees
517-821-5992

Saginaw
Brockway House
517-792-0746

Heart House
517-753-3145

Montague Inn
517-752-3939

Saint Clair
Hopkins Inn
810-329-3490

Murphy Inn
810-329-7118

River House B&B
810-329-4253

St Clair Inn
313-963-5735

Saint Ingnace
Colonial House Inn & Motel
906-643-6900

Saint James
McCann House
616-448-2387

Saint Johns
Classic B&B
517-224-6879

Saint Joseph
Chestnut House
616-983-7413

South Cliff Inn B&B
616-983-4881-[Y--]

Saline
Homestead B&B
313-429-9625-[Y--]

Saugatuck
Bayside Inn
800-548-0077-[G--]

Beechwood Manor
616-857-1587

Fairchild House
616-857-5985

Four Seasons Inn
616-857-1955

Hidden Pond B&B
616-561-2491-[G--]

Kemah Guest House
616-857-2919

Kirby House
616-857-2904

Maplewood
616-857-1771-[G--]

Marywood Manor
616-857-4771

Moores Creek Inn
616-857-2411

Newman Inn
800-877-4149

Newnahm Sun Catcher Inn
616-857-4249

Park House
800-321-4535

Red Dog B&B
616-857-8851-[Y--]

Rosemont Inn
616-857-2637

Sherwood Forest B&B
800-838-1246-[Y--]

Twin Gables Country Inn
800-231-2185-[Y--]

Twin Oaks Inn
616-857-1600

Twin Oaks Inn
616-857-1600

Wickwood Inn
616-857-1456

Sault Ste Marie
Water Street Inn
906-632-1900

Scottville
Amber Acres B&B
616-757-9343

Sebewaing
Rummels Tree Haven
517-883-2450

Shelby
Elmhurst B&B
616-861-4846

Little Village B&B
616-861-5332

Shelbyville
Mill Pond Inn
616-792-9552

South Haven
Arundel House
616-637-4790

Country Place B&B
616-637-5523

Elmhurst Farm Inn
616-637-4633

Last Resort B&B Inn
616-637-8943

North Beach Inn & Restaurant
616-637-6989

Old Harbor Inn
616-637-8480

Pigozzis North Beach Inn
616-637-6738

Ross B&B House
616-637-2256

Seymour House
616-227-3918-[G--]

Victoria Resort
800-593-7376

Yelton Manor
616-637-5220

Spring Lake
Alberties Waterfront
616-846-4016

Royal Pontaluna
800-865-3545

Seascape B&B
616-842-8409

Stanton
Clifford Lake Hotel
517-831-5151

Stephenson
Cstalos' Csarda
906-753-2170

Top Of The Hill
906-753-4757

Sturgis
Christmere House
800-874-1882

Suttons Bay
Cottage B&B
616-271-6348

Country House
616-271-4478

Lee Point Inn
616-271-6770

Open Windows B&B
616-271-4300

Swartz Creek
Pink Palace Farm
810-655-4076

Tawas City
Sarahs Countryside B&B
517-362-7123

Tecumseh
Boulevard Inn
517-423-5169

Stacy Mansion
517-423-6979

Toivola
Lost Bowl Farm
906-288-3604

Traverse City
Bass Lake Inn
616-943-4790

Bowers Harbor B&B
616-223-7869

Michigan - Minnesota *Bold Name - Description appears in other section*

Cherry Center Farm
616-223-4195

Cherry Knoll Farm
800-847-9806

Cherryland Lodge
616-922-7330

Cider House B&B
616-947-2833

Grainary
616-946-8325

Hillside B&B
616-228-6106-[Y--]

L'Ds Ru B&B
616-046-8999

Linden Lea On Long Lake
616-943-9182

Mission Point B&B
616-223-7526

Neahtwanta Inn
616-223-7315

Peninsula Manor
616-929-1321

Queen Annes Castle
616-946-1459

Stonewall Inn
800-432-2466

Tall Ship Malabar
616-941-2000

Victoriana
616-929-1009

Warwickshire Inn
616-946-7176

Weathervane Home
616-946-4090

Wooden Spoon B&B
616-947-0357

Trenton
 Bear Haven
 313-675-4844

Union City
 Victorian Villa Guesthouse
 800-34-VILLA-[Y--]

Union Pier
 Country Comfort

 Cottages
 708-952-0492

 Garden Grove B&B
 616-469-6346

 Garden Grove B&B
 616-469-6346

 Gordon Beach Inn
 616-469-3344

 Inn At Union Pier
 616-469-4700

 Pine Garth Inn
 616-469-1642

 Union Pier Summer House
 616-469-5520

Wakefield
 Medford House
 906-224-5151

Walled Lake
 Villa Hammer
 810-624-1070-[Y--]

Walloon Lake
 Masters House
 616-535-2944

 Walloon Lake Inn
 616-535-2999

Webberville
 Basic Brewer B&B
 517-468-3970

West Branch
 Curtis B&B
 517-345-1411

 Green Inn
 517-345-0334

 Rose Brick Inn
 517-345-3702

White Cloud
 Crows Nest
 616-689-0088

 Shack Country Inn
 616-924-6683

White Pigeon
 River Haven
 616-483-9104

Whitehall
 Music Box Inn
 616-894-6683

 Timekeepers Inn Clock Shop
 616-894-5169

Williamston
 Capital B&B

Ypsilanti
 Cricket House
 313-484-1387

 Parrish House Inn
 313-480-4800

MINNESOTA

Afton
 Afton House Inn
 612-436-6964

 Dees Country B&B
 612-426-6964

 Mulberry Pond On River Road
 612-436-8086

Albert Lea
 Fountain View Inn
 507-377-9425

 Victorian Rose Inn
 507-373-7602

Alexandria
 Carrington House
 612-846-7400-[Y--]

 Robards House
 612-763-4073

Annadale
 Thayer Hotel
 800-944-6595

Anoka
 Bendermere On Mississippi
 800-453-9962

Backus
 Pine Mountain B&B Inn
 218-947-3050

Battle Lake
 Page House
 218-864-8974

Baudette
 Rainy River Lodge
 218-634-2730

Blooming Prairie

 Pine Springs Inn
 507-583-4411

Brainerd
 Pleasant Acres
 218-963-2482

 Woods Of Interlachen
 218-963-7880

Breezy Point
 Breezy Point Resort
 218-562-7811

Brooklyn Center
 Inn On The Farm
 800-428-8382

Caledonia
 Inn On The Green
 507-724-2818

Cannon Falls
 Candlewick Country Inn
 507-263-0879

 Country Quilt Inn
 612-258-4406

 Quill & Quilt
 800-488-3849

Carver
 Carousel Rose Inn
 612-448-5847

Chaska
 Bluff Creek Inn
 612-445-2735

Chatfield
 Lunds Guest House
 507-867-4003

Cold Spring
 Pillow, Pillar & Pine House
 612-685-3828

Copas
 Crabtrees Kitchen

Crookston
 Elm Street Inn
 800-568-4476

Crosby
 Hallett House
 218-546-5433

Dassel
 Gabrielsons B&B
 612-275-3609

2-146 ©*Inn & Travel Memphis, Tennessee*

Bold Name - *Description appears in other section*　　　　　　　　　　　　　　　　　　　　　　　　　　　　　　*Minnesota*

Deerwood
　Walden Woods B&B
　800-8 WALDEN

Dent
　Heart 'O Lakes Farm
　218-758-2121

Detroit Lakes
　Grandmas Attic
　218-847-1229

Dodge Center
　Eden B&B
　507-527-2311

Duluth
　Barnum House
　800-879-5437

　Ellery House
　800-355-3794

　Fitgers Inn
　800-726-2982-[Y--]

　Manor On The Creek Inn
　218-728-3189

　Mansion
　218-724-0794

　Mathews S Burrows 1890 Inn
　218-724-4991

　Olcott House
　612-825-2743

　Stanford Inn
　218-724-3044

Dundas
　Martin Oaks B&B
　507-645-4644

Elmare
　Kuchenbecker Farm

Ely
　Burntside Lodge
　218-365-3894

　Our Moms B&B
　218-365-6510

　Three Deer Haven B&B
　218-365-6464

Excelsior
　Christopher Inn
　612-474-6816

　Murry Street Gardens Inn
　612-474-8089

Fairbault
　Hutchinson House
　507-332-7519

Falcon Heights
　Rose B&B
　800-966-2728

Faribault
　Cherub Hill
　800-332-7254

　Hutchinson House
　507-332-7519

Finlayson
　Giese B&B
　612-233-6429

Frazee
　Acorn Lake B&B
　218-334-3238

Glenviewe
　Glenview B&B
　507-629-4808

Glenwood
　Country Inn
　800-356-8654

　Peters Sunset Beach Hotel
　612-634-4501

Good Thunder
　Cedar Knoll Farm
　507-452-3813

Graceville
　Lakeside B&B
　612-748-7657

Grand Marais
　Cascade Lodge
　218-387-1112

　Clearwater Lodge
　800-527-0554

　East Bay Hotel
　218-387-2800

　Gunflint Lodge
　800-328-3325

　Naniboujhou Lodge
　218-387-2688

　Pincushion Mountain B&B
　800-542-1226

　Superior Overlook B&B
　218-387-1571

　Youngs Island
　800-322-8327

Grand Marias
　Dream Catcher B&B
　800-682-3119

Grand Rapids
　Judge Thwing House
　218-326-5618

Harmony
　Selvig B&B Inn
　507-886-2200

Hastings
　Heartwood
　612-437-1133

　River Rose
　612-437-3297

　Rosewood Inn
　800-657-4630

　Thorwood Inns
　800-992-4667-[Y--]

Hendricks
　Triple L Farm
　507-275-3740

　Wahlstrom House
　507-275-3769

Herman
　Lawndale Farm
　612-677-2687

Hibbing
　Adams House B&B
　218-263-9742

Hinckley
　B&B Lodge
　612-384-6052

　Dakota Lodge
　612-384-6052

Houston
　Addies Attic
　507-896-3010

　Bunkhouse Inn
　507-896-2080

Hovland
　Trovalls Inn

　218-475-2344

Hutchinson
　Harrington House
　612-587-2400

Jackson
　Old Railroad Inn
　507-847-5348

Kasson
　Jacobs Inn
　507-634-4920

Kensington
　Runestone B&B Inn
　612-965-2358

Lake City
　Evergreen Knoll Acres
　612-345-2257

　Pepin House
　612-345-4454

　Victorian B&B
　612-345-2167

Lake Shore
　Sherwood Forest Lodge
　218-963-2516

Lanesboro
　Birch Knoll Ranch B&B
　507-467-2418

　Cady Hayes House
　507-467-2621

　Carrolton Country Inn
　507-467-2257

　Galligan House
　507-467-2299

　Historic Lanesboro Inn
　507-467-2154

　Mrs B's Historic Landsboro Inn
　800-657-4710

　Scanlan House B&B
　800-944-2158

Le Sueur
　Cosgrove
　612-665-2763

　Country Oaks Inn
　612-665-2763

©*Inn & Travel Memphis, Tennessee*

Minnesota *Bold Name - Description appears in other section*

Lindstrom
Boat House B&B
612-257-9122

Little Falls
Pine Edge Inn
612-632-6881

Little Marais
Stone Hearth Inn
218-226-3020

Lutsen
Caribou Lake B&B
218-663-7489

Cascade Lodge
218-387-1112

Lindgrens B&B
218-663-7450

Mabel
Mabel House B&B
507-493-5768

Mankato
Butler House
507-387-5055

Mantorville
Grand Old Mansion
507-635-3231

Marine on St Croix
Asa Parker House
612-612-5248

McGregor
Savanna Portage Inn
800-428-6108

Minneapolis
1900 Dupont
612-374-1973

Brasie House
612-377-5946

Coe Mansion
612-871-4249

Elmwood B&B
612-822-4558

Evelos B&B
612-374-9656-[Y--]

Heatherwood B&B
612-874-7167

Inn On The Farm
800-428-8382

Le Blanc House
612-379-2570

Nans B&B
800-214-5118

Nicollet Island Inn
612-331-1800

Morris
American House
612-589-4054

Nevis
Park Street Inn
612-599-4763

New Prague
Schumachers New Prague Hotel
612-758-2133

New York Mills
Whistle Stop Inn
218-385-2223

Nisswa
Victorian Villa Inn
218-963-3953

North Branch
Red Pine B&B
612-583-3326

Northfield
Archer House
800-247-2235

Moses House B&B
507-663-1563

Oakdale
Oakdale Tanners Lake
612-739-0193

Olivia
Sheep Sheddle Inn

Onamia
Cour du Lac
320-532-4627

Osace
Lady Slipper Inn
800-531-2787

Owatonna
Northrop House
507-451-4040

Park Rapids
Dickson Viking Huss B&B
800-426-2019

Dorset Schoolhouse
218-732-1377

Grandmas B&B
218-732-0987

Heartland B&B
218-732-5305

Red Bridge Inn
218-732-0481

Pelican Rapids
Prairie View Estate
218-863-4321

Pequot Lakes
Stonehouse B&B
218-568-4255

Pine City
Black Cow Inn
612-629-7421

Pipestone
Calmut
800-535-7610

Preston
Intown Lodge
507-765-4412

Jail House
507-765-2181

Sunnyside Cottage
507-765-3357

Princeton
Oakhurst Inn
800-443-2258

Rum River Country B&B
612-389-2679

Ray
Bunts B&B
218-875-3904-[Y--]

Red Wing
Candlelight Inn
612-388-8034

Gold Lantern Inn
612-388-3315

Hungary Point Inn
612-388-7857

Pratt Taber Inn
612-388-5945-[Y--]

Sprague House
612-388-3115

Redwood Falls
Stanhope B&B
507-644-2882

Rochester
Canterbury Inn B&B
507-289-5553

Round Lake
Prairie House On Round Lake
507-945-8934

Rush City
Grant House
612-358-4717

Rushford
Meadows Inn
507-864-2378

River Trail Inn
800-584-6764

Saint Charles
Victorian Lace Inn
507-932-3054

Saint Joseph
Lambs B&B
612-363-7924

Saint Paul
Como Villa
612-647-0471

Driscolls For Guests
612-439-7486-[Y--]

Garden Gate B&B
612-227-8430

Lowell House B&B Inn
612-345-2111-[Y--]

Miller B&B
612-227-1292

Priors On Desoto
612-774-2695

Saint Peter
Engesser House
612-374-9656

Park Row B&B
507-931-2495-[Y--]

Sauk Centre
Palmer House Hotel
612-352-3431-[Y--]

Shafer
Country B&B
612-257-4773

2-148

©*Inn & Travel Memphis, Tennessee*

Bold Name - *Description appears in other section*

Minnesota- Missouri

Shakopee
Apple Hill B&B
612-445-4487

Nicholas House B&B
612-496-2537

Valley Manor
612-496-2936

Sherburn
Four Columns Inn
507-764-8861

Side Lake
McNairs B&B
218-254-5878

Silver Bay
Guest House B&B
218-226-4201

Inn At Palisade
218-226-3505

Sleepy Eye
Woodland Inn
507-794-5981

Spicer
Green Lake Inn
320-796-6523

Spicer Castle
800-821-6675

Spring Grove
Touch Of The Past
507-498-5146

Spring Lake
Anchor Inn
218-798-2718

Spring Valley
Chases
507-346-2850

Stacy
Kings Oakdale Park
612-462-5598

Stephen
Grandmas House
218-478-2743

Stillwater
Ann Bean House
612-430-0355

Battle Hollow
612-439-0449

Elephant Walk B&B

612-430-0359

Heirloom Inn B&B
612-430-2289

James A Mulvey Residence Inn
612-430-8008

Laurel Street Inn
612-351-0031

Lowell Inn
612-439-1100-[G--]

Outing Lodge At Pine Point
612-439-9747

Overlook Inn
612-439-3409

Rivertown Inn
800-562-3632-[Y--]

William Sauntry Mansion
800-828-2653

Taylors Falls
Hudspeth House B&B
612-465-5811

Old Jail Company B&B
612-465-3112

Tyler
Babettes Inn
800-466-7076

Utica
Ellsworth B&B
800-342-2318

Vergas
Log House On Spirit Lake
218-342-2318

Wabash
Bridgewater B&B Inn
612-565-4208

Wabasha
Anderson House
800-535-5467

Walker
Chase On The Lake Lodge
218-547-1531

Peacecliff B&B

218-547-2832

Tianna Farms B&B
218-547-1306

Welch
Hungary Point Inn
612-437-3660

Wells
Siebert Inn
507-553-3788

Westbrook
Parkview B&B
507-274-6221

Winona
Carriage House B&B
507-452-8256

The Hotel
507-452-5460

MISSOURI

Arcadia Valley
White House
314-546-7978

Arrow Rock
Airy Hill Inn
816-837-3458

Borgmans B&B
816-837-3350

By Hammer And Hand
816-837-3441

Cedar Grove B&B
816-837-3441

Down Over Holdings
816-837-3268-[Y--]

Miss Nelles B&B
816-837-3280

Augusta
Augusta Haus
314-228-4467

Lindenhof Country Inn
314-228-4617

Aurora
Hollister House
417-678-6819

Beaufort

Wild Wind Farms B&B
314-484-3110

Bethany
Downtown B&B
816-425-3676

Bethel
Bethel Colony B&B
816-284-6493

Blackwater
Kusgen Farm B&B
816-846-3061

Bolivar
Apple Orchard B&B
417-326-5490

Bonne Terre
1909 Depot
314-731-5003

Lamplighter Inn B&B
314-358-4222

Mansion Hill Country Inn
314-731-5003

Boonville
Doll House B&B
816-882-5482

Lady Goldenrod
816-882-5764

Morgan Street Repose
800-248-5061

River City Inn
816-882-5465

Rose Cottage
816-882-2280

Bourbon
Meramc Farm B&B
314-732-4765

Branson
Aunt Sadies Garden Glade
800-944-4250

Bradford Inn & General Store
417-338-5555

Branson Hotel
417-335-6104

Branson House

©Inn & Travel Memphis, Tennessee

2-149

Missouri

Bold Name - Description appears in other section

B&B
417-334-0959

Brass Swan
800-280-6873-[Y--]

Country Gardens
800-727-0723

Emory Creek
800-484-9469

Fall Creek Inn
417-334-3939

Gaines Landing B&B
800-825-3145

Inn At Fall Creek Country B&B
800-280-3422

Josies-Peaceful Getaway
800-289-4125

Lodge At We Lamb Farm
417-334-1486

Ozark Mountain Country Inn
800-695-1546

Rhapsody Inn
417-335-2442

Schrolls Lakefront B&B
800-285-8830

Stratford House Inn
417-334-3700

Thurman House
800-238-6630

Bridgeton
Boone Terre Mansion
314-731-5003

Brighton
Eden B&B
417-467-2820

Bristol
Bristol House
314-427-1981

Bunceton
Ravenswood Inn
816-427-5627

California

Memory Lane B&B
314-796-4233

Camdenton
Blatherskite Pointe B&B
314-374-2678

Lakeside Guest House
314-346-3767

Ramblewood B&B
314-346-3410

Cape Girardeau
Bellevue B&B
800-768-6822

Olive Branch
314-335-0449

Carthage
B&B On The Square
417-358-1501

Brewwer Maple Lane Farms
417-358-6312

Grand Avenue Inn
417-358-7265

Leggett House
417-358-0683

Cedarcreek
Some Day Ranch
800-325-3305

Clarksville
Ressell-Carroll House
314-242-3854

Clayton
Seven Gables Inn
314-863-8400

Columbia
Teddy Bear B&B
314-772-4429

Concordia
Fannie Lee B&B
816-463-7395

De Soto
Arlington Inn
314-586-8390

Defiance
Country Porch B&B
314-987-2546

Dixon

Rock Eddy Bluff B&B
314-759-6081

Eminence
Cedar Stone Lodge
314-226-5656

Hawkins House
314-226-3793

Maple Tree B&B
314-226-3644

Rivers Edge B&B
314-226-3233

Ethel
Recess Inn
800-628-5003

Excelsior Springs
Crescent Lake Manor
816-637-2958

Fayette
Doll House B&B
816-248-2887

Fredericktown
Cordelias B&B
314-783-2568

Fulton
Loganberry Inn
314-642-9229

Gainesville
Zanoni Mill Inn
417-679-4050

Grandview
Fountains
816-763-6260

Gravois Mills
Linderlong
314-372-2481

Hamiltom
Grants Touch Of Country
816-583-2333

Hannibal
Cliffside Mansion
573-248-1461

Fifth Street Mansion
800-874-5661-[Y--]

Garth Woodside Mansion
573-221-2789-[Y--]

Queen Annes Grace
573-248-0756

Riverfront Inn
573-221-6662

Harpers Ferry
Filmore Street B&B
314-535-2768

Hartsburg
Globe Hotel B&B
314-657-4529

Hartville
Frisco House
417-741-7304

Hermann
1868 White House
314-468-3200

Aunt Lotties B&B
573-943-6953

Bid-A-Wee B&B
314-486-3961

Birks Goethe St Gasthaus
800-748-7883

Capt Wohlt Inn
314-486-3357

Captain Wohlt Inn
573-486-3357

Das Brownhaus
573-486-3372

Das Delaney Haus
573-486-2242

Das Rhein Haus
573-486-3976

Die Gillig Heimat (Homestead)
314-943-6942

Esthers Ausblick
573-486-2170

John Bohlken Inn
573-486-3903

Klos B&B
573-486-5532

Kolbe Guest Haus
573-486-3453

Larks Nest B&B
573-943-6305

2-150

©Inn & Travel Memphis, Tennessee

Bold Name - Description appears in other section **Missouri**

Maurers Hideaway
573-486-2964

Meyers 4th Street B&B
573-486-2917

Meyers Hilltop Farm
314-486-5778

Mumbrauger Gasthaus
573-486-5246

Pelze Nichol Haus B&B
573-486-3886

Reiff House
573-486-2994

Schmidts Guesthouse
314-486-2146

White House Hotel B&B
573-486-3200

White Roses B&B
573-486-3875

William Klinger Inn
314-486-5930

Historic Weston
Benner House B&B
816-386-2616

Hollister
Red Bud Cove B&B
800-677-5525

Sherrys Log Cabin B&B
417-335-3769

Wee Lamb Inn
417-334-1485

Independence
Arthurs Horse & Carriage
816-461-6814

English Pines Inn
816-833-4366

House Of Hoyt
816-461-7226

Serendipity B&B
816-833-4719

Woodstock Inn
800-276-5202

Ironton
Green Roof Inn
573-546-7670

Jackson
Trishas B&B
800-651-0804

White House
573-243-4329

Jamesport
Richardson House
816-684-6664

Jefferson City
Peacock Inn
314-659-4444

Joplin
Victorian Inn
417-781-1898

Visages
417-624-1397

Kahoka
Fox Valley Meadows B&B
816-727-3533

Kansas City
Basswood Country Inn
816-431-5556-[Y--]

Behms Carriage House
816-753-4434

Carriage Hill B&B
816-454-1629

Doanleigh Wallagh Inn
816-753-2667-[Y--]

Dome Ridge
816-532-4074-[Y--]

Faust Townhouse
816-741-7480

Hotel Savoy
816-842-3575

Milford House
816-753-1269

Pridewell
816-931-1642

Southmoreland On The Plaza
816-531-7979-[Y--]

Willow Creek Manor
816-943-1212

Kimberling City
Anderson House
417-739-4298

Cinnamon Hill
800-925-1556

Kimmswick
Kimmswick Korner Inn
314-467-1027

Wenom-Drake House B&B
314-464-1983

Kirkwood
Eastlake Inn B&B
314-965-0066

Fissys Place
314-821-4494

Koshkonong
Richardson House
417-867-5656

Lafayette Square
Napoleons Retreat
314-771-2075

Lampe
Grandpas Farm
800-280-5106

Lathrop
Parkview Farm
816-664-2744

Lesterville
Wilderness Lodge
573-637-1195

Lexington
Graystone
816-259-3476

Linwood Lawn B&B Inn
816-259-4290

Liberty
Liberty Inn
816-792-1081

Liberty Inn
816-792-1081

Lindgrens Landing
816-781-8742

Sugar Tree Inn
816-781-9553

Wynbrick Inn B&B
816-781-4900

Lockwood
Prairie Chicken B&B
417-232-4925

Louisiana
Louisiana Guest House
573-754-6366

Serandos House
573-754-4067

Macomb
Bartlett Farm
417-746-4161

Macon
St Agnes Hall B&B
816-385-2774

Mansfield
Antique Rose
417-924-8446

Friendship House B&B
417-924-8511

Marble Hill
Ricketts House
573-238-2355

Marionville
White Squirrel Hollow B&B
417-462-7626

Marquand
Castor Haven B&B
314-783-4179

Marshfield
Dickey House
417-468-3000

Marthasville
Concord Hill
314-932-4228

Countryside B&B
314-433-5156

Grammas House
314-433-2675

Matthews
Falutline Farms B&B
573-472-4880

©*Inn & Travel Memphis, Tennessee*

2-151

Missouri

Bold Name - Description appears in other section

Mexico
Hylas House B&B Inn
314-581-2011

Rosalie B&B Inn
314-581-2735

Moberly
Miller Burke House
816-263-2292-[Y--]

Mount Vernon
Farmhouse B&B
417-466-7577

Lane Tree Farm
417-466-7589

Mountain Grove
Cedar Hill Farm
417-926-6535

Mountain View
Jacks Fork
417-934-1000

Nevada
Cherry Street Inn
417-667-3030

New Franklin
Rivercene
800-531-0862

New Haven
125 Front Street Inn
573-237-2783

Augustin River Bluff Farm
573-239-3452

Welcome Haus
573-237-2771

Nixa
Country View
417-725-1927

North Kansas City
Barbaras Hotel
816-221-6544

Owensville
Sylvias B&B
314-437-4677

Ozark
B&B At Merrywoods
800-381-BEAR

Country Lane Cabin B&B
800-866-5903

Dears Rest B&B
800-588-2262

Parkville
Down-To-Earth-Lifestyles
816-891-1018

Parkville B&B
816-587-0463

Perry
Perrys Guest House
573-565-3191

Platte City
Basswood Country Inn
816-431-5556-[Y--]

Pleasant Hill
Pleasant Stay Inn
816-987-5900

Point Lookout
Birds Eye View B&B
800-933-8529

Camerons Crag B&B
800-933-8529-[G--]

Poplar Bluff
Stuga
314-785-4085

Potosi
Bust Inn
314-438-4457

Roanoake
Roanoake Guest House
816-273-2447

Rocheport
School House B&B
314-698-2022

Yates House B&B
314-698-2129

Rogersville
Anchor Hill Lodge
417-753-2930

Rosebud
Rosebud Inn
314-764-4144

Saint Charles
Boones Lick Trail Inn
800-336-2427-[Y--]

Lococo House II Of Saint Charles
314-946-0619

Quilt B&B
314-946-1612

St Charles House
314-946-6221

Sugartree Haus
314-946-6221

Saint James
Clydes Pleasant Acres
800-916-2345-[G--]

Ferrigno Winery
314-256-7742

Saint Joseph
Harding House
816-232-7020

Strawberry Patch
816-233-9788

Saint Louis
Doelling Haus
314-894-6796

Falcon Inn
314-771-1993

Geandaugh House
314-771-5447

Lafayette House
800-641-8965-[Y--]

Lehmann House B&B
314-231-6724

Lister House B&B
314-361-5506

Old Convent Guesthouse
314-772-3531-[Y--]

Overland Trail B&B
314-427-3918

Park Avenue B&B
314-241-6814

Parkside Cottage
314-772-1304

Preston Place
314-664-3429-[G--]

River Country Inn
314-965-4328

Soulard Inn
314-773-3002

Soulard Manor
314-664-9738

Winter House
314-664-4399-[YQAR-]

Sainte Genevieve
Belle River B&B
573-883-3830

Bellerive B&B
573-883-3830

Captains Retreat
573-883-7108

Creole House B&B
573-883-7171

Hotel St Genevieve

Inn St Gemme Beauvais
573-883-5744-[Y--]

John Neal Gasthaus
573-883-5881

Main Street Inn
573-883-9199

Memory House

Southern Hotel
800-275-1412

Steiger Haus
573-883-5881

Salem
Brewer Inn
573-729-8168

Polk Place B&B
573-729-4456

Spring Creek Inn
573-729-5209

Sedalia
Sedalia House
816-826-6615

Shell Know
Shore Hollow B&B
417-858-2415

Smithville
Basswood Country Inn

2-152

©Inn & Travel Memphis, Tennessee

Bold Name - *Description appears in other section* **Missouri - Nebraska**

816-431-5556-[Y--]

Springfield
Cottage B&B
800-593-6346

Elfindale Mansion
800-443-0237

Mansion At Elfindale
417-831-5400

Walnut Street Inn
800-593-6346

Wildwood Manor
417-889-8652

Yorkshire B&B
417-887-1369

Steelville
Hanson House
573-775-2330

Hideaway House
573-775-5898

Wicker House
573-775-2166

Stockton
Our Happy House B&B
417-276-3345

Sullivan
Sleepy Seal B&B
573-468-7585

Whip Haven Farm
573-627-3717

Wildflower
573-468-7975

Trenton
Hyde Mansion
816-359-5631

Van Buren
Inn At Park Place

Skyline Lodge
573-323-4144

Versailles
Hilty Inn
573-378-2020

Walnut Shade
Branson House
417-334-0959

Light In The

Window B&B
417-334-7341

Old House
417-561-8283

Warrensburg
Camel Crossing B&B
816-429-2973

Cedarcroft Farm
800-368-4944

Washington
125 Front Street Inn
314-237-3534

Gustin River Bluff Farm
314-239-3452

Pogue B&B
314-239-0668

Schwegmann House B&B Inn
800-949-ABNB

Washington House
314-239-2417

Weirick-Hoelscher Estate B&B
800-791-4469

Zachariah Foss Guest House
314-239-6499-[Y--]

Waynesville
Home Place B&B
573-774-6637

West Plains
Blue Spruce Inn
417-256-3209

Pinebrook Lodge
417-257-7769

Twin Bridges
417-256-7507

Weston
Apple Creek B&B
816-386-5724

Hatchery
816-386-5700

Zanoni
Zanoni Mill Inn
417-679-4050

NEBRASKA

Ainsworth
Curio Cupboard B&B
402-387-0454

Alliance
Hendersons
308-487-3932

Bartley
Nelms
308-692-3278

Beatrice
Carriage House
402-228-0356

Beemer
Behrens Inn
402-528-3212

Bellgrade
Bel Horst Inn
308-357-1094

Big Springs
Phelps Hotel
308-889-3246

Blair
Nostalgia Inn
402-426-3280

Brewester
Uncle Bucks Lodge
308-547-2210

Brewster
Eliza Cottage
888-999-2432

Sandhills Country Cabin
308-547-2460

Broken Bow
Pine Cone Lodge
308-872-6407

Brownville
Thompson House
402-825-6551

Callaway
Chesleys Lodge
308-836-2658

Travelers Inn[--ITC]
308-836-2200

Cambridge
Cambridge Inn
308-697-3220

Cedar Rapids
Cedar Valley B&B
308-358-0488

River Road Inn
308-358-0827

Chadron
Olde Main Street Inn
308-432-3380

Chappell
Cottonwood Inn
308-874-3250

Clarkson
Annies B&B
402-892-3660

Columbus
Valley View
402-563-2454

Crawford
Butte Ranch
308-665-2364

Butte Ranch B&B
308-665-2364

Fort Robinson Inn
308-665-2660-[Y--]

Crete
Johnston-Muff House
402-826-4155

Parsons House
402-826-2643

Parsons House
402-826-2634

Crofton
Argo Hotel
800-607-2746

Crookston
B&B Guest Ranch
402-425-3353

Dannebrog
Heart Of Dannebrog
308-226-2303

Nestle Inn
308-226-8252

Dixon
Georges
402-584-2625

Elgin
Plantation House B&B

©Inn & Travel Memphis, Tennessee

2-153

Nebraska *Bold Name - Description appears in other section*

402-843-2287

Eustis
Hotel Eustis
308-486-5345

Fairbury
Park House
402-729-5516

Presonett House
402-729-2902

Falls City
Matthes Manor
402-245-5449

Fremont
B&B Of Fremont
402-727-9534

Funk
Uncle Sams B&B
308-996-5568

Gering
Monument Heights B&B
308-635-0109

Gordon
Meadow View Ranch
308-282-0679

Spring Lake Ranch
308-282-0835

Gothenburg
Swede Hospitality B&B

Grand Island
Kirschke House B&B
308-381-6851

La Bleu Bonnett
308-873-5590

Grant
Prairie Jeans B&B
308-352-2355

Gretna
Bundys B&B
402-332-3616

Hastings
Grandmas Victorian B&B
402-462-2013

Hemingford
Hansen Homestead
308-487-3805

Hickman
Farabees Country Inn
402-792-2911

Holdrege
Crows Nest
308-995-5440

Hooper
Empty Nest B&B
402-664-2715

White House
402-654-2185

Howells
Prairie Garden
402-986-1251

Kearney
George W Frank Jr House
308-237-7545

Walden West
308-237-7296

Laurel
Kraemer Estates
402-256-3585

Leigh
B&B On The Farm
402-487-2482

Lexington
Memories
308-324-3290

Lincol
Atwood House B&B
402-438-4567

Lincoln
Capitol Guesthouse
402-476-6669

Gran
402-476-7873

Rogers House
402-476-6961-[Y--]

Sweet Dream
402-438-1416

Yellow House On The Corner
402-466-8626

Long Pine
Pine Valley Resort
402-273-4351

Loup City

Enchanted Retreat
308-745-0850

Madrid
Clown 'N Country
308-326-4378

McCook
Park House Guest House
308-345-6057

Merna
Country Nest
308-643-2486

Merriman
Twisted Pine Ranch
308-684-3482

Minden
Home Comfort
308-832-0531

Prairie View
308-832-0123

Murdock
Farm House
402-867-2062

Nebraska City
Whispering Pines
402-873-5850

Neligh
Mary Mahoneys Thissen House
402-553-8366

North Bend
Platte Valley Guernsey B&B
402-652-3492

North Platte
Knolls Country Inn
800-337-4526

Watson Manor Inn
308-532-1124

Oakland
Benson B&B
402-685-6051

Omaha
Clairmont B&B
402-341-8990

Offutt House
402-553-0951

Ord
Shepherds Inn
308-726-3306

Osmond
Willow Way
402-748-3593

Oxford
North York Farm B&B
308-337-2380

Pawnee City
My Blue Heaven
402-852-3131

Paxton
Gingerbread Inn
308-239-4265

Petersburg
Wirges B&B
402-386-5524

Pierce
Willow Rose B&B Wichman
402-329-4114

Plainview
Rose Garden Inn
402-582-4708

Ravenna
Aunt Bettys B&B
800-632-9114

Red Cloud
Meadowlark Manor
402-746-3550

Saint Libory
Quiet Country Farm House
308-687-6085

Sidney
Snuggle Inn
308-254-0500

Spalding
Esch House
308-497-2628

Springview
Big Canyon Inn
800-437-6023

Steinauer
Convent House
402-869-2276

Stromsburg
Strombers Vardhus
402-764-8167

Stuart
Sisters House

2-154 ©Inn & Travel Memphis, Tennessee

Bold Name - *Description appears in other section* *Nebraska - New Jersey*

402-924-3678

Sutton
Maltby House
402-773-4556

Tekamah
Deer Run B&B
402-374-2423

Trenton
Blue Colonial B&B
308-276-2533

Flying A Ranch
800-434-5574

Valentine
Boardman Springs Ranch
402-376-1498

Elysian B&B
402-376-3210

Hill Haben Ldoge
402-376-1942

Stone House Inn
402-376-1942

Town House B&B
402-376-2193

Verdigre
Commercial Hotel
402-668-2386

Waterloo
JC Robinson House B&B
800-779-2705

Wayne
Grandma Butches
402-375-2759

Swansons B&B
402-584-2277

Weeping Water
Lauritzens Danish American Inn
402-267-3295

West Point
Von Schweiger Haus
402-372-5945

Wilber
Hotel Wilber
402-821-2020

NEW JERSEY

Absecon

White Manor Inn
609-748-3996

Alloway
Josiah Reeve House
609-935-5640

Andover
Crossed Keys
201-786-6661

Hudson Guide Farm
201-398-2679

Asbury Park
Hermitage Guest House
908-776-6665

Atlantic City
Another Time B&B
609-345-4700-[Y--]

Avalon
Golden Inn
609-368-5155

Avon By The Sea
Atlantic View Inn
908-774-8505

Avon Manor Inn
908-774-0110-[Y--]

Cashelmara Inn
800-821-2976

Dunrovin
908-776-9360

Ocean Mist Inn
908-775-9625

Sands Of Avon
908-776-8386

Summer House
908-775-3992

Victoria Hotel
908-988-9798

Bay Head
Bay Head Gables
908-892-9844

Bay Head Harbor Inn
908-899-0767

Bay Head Sands
908-899-7016

Bentley Inn
908-892-9589

Conovers Bay Head Inn
908-892-4664

Gray Goose Inn
908-899-0767

Grenville Hotel & Restaurant
908-892-3100-[G--]

Rooming House

The Bentley Inn
908-892-9589

Beach Haven
Amber Street Inn
609-492-1611

Barque
609-492-5216

Bayberry Barque
609-492-5216

Green Gables
609-492-3553

Heather House
609-492-2474

Island Guest House
609-444-9427

Magnolia House
609-492-2226

Magnolia House
609-492-0398

Pierrot-By-The-Sea
609-492-4424

St Rita Hotel
609-492-9192-[Y--]

Victoria Guest House
609-492-4154

Belmar
Carols Guest House
908-681-4422

Down The Shore B&B
908-681-9023

Gallaghers Guest House
908-681-2655

Inn At The Shore
908-681-3762

Neier Seasonal Guest House
908-681-7003

Seaflower B&B Inn
908-681-6006

Sheppards Guest House
908-681-1140

Treetops Guest House
908-681-4137

Bernardsville
Bernards Inn
908-766-0002

Old Mill Inn
908-221-1100

Bradley Beach
Bradley Inn
908-774-7000

Cape May
7th Sister Guesthouse
609-884-2280-[Y--]

Abbey
609-884-4506

Abigail Adams B&B
609-884-1371

Albert G Stevens Inn
609-884-4717

Alexanders Inn
609-884-2555

Angel Of The Sea
800-848-3369

Barnard Good House
609-884-5381

Bedford Inn
609-884-4158

Bell Shields House
609-884-8512

Belmont Guest House
609-884-7505

Brass Bed
609-884-8075

Buttonwood Manor
609-884-8075

Captain Mey's Inn

New Jersey

Bold Name - Description appears in other section

609-884-7793

Carroll Villa B&B Hotel
609-884-5970

Chalfonte Hotel
609-884-8409-[G--]

Cliveden Inn
609-884-4516

Columbia House
609-884-6211

Colvmns By The Sea
800-691-6030-[G--]

Dormer House
609-397-7446

Duke Of Windsor Inn
800-826-8973

Fairthorne B&B
800-438-8742

Garnard Good House
609-884-5381

Gingerbread House
609-884-0211-[Y--]

Hanson House
609-884-8791

Heirloom B&B
609-884-1666

Henry Sayer Inn
609-884-5667

Holly House
609-884-7365

Humphrey Hughes House
609-884-4428

Inn at 22 Jackson
800-452-8177

Inn at Jackson Street
800-452-8177

Jerimiah Hand Guest House
609-884-1135

John F Craig House
609-884-0100

John Wesley Inn

609-884-1012

King's Cottage a Seaside B&B
609-884-0415

Leith Hall Historic Seashore Inn
609-884-1934

Mainstay Inn
609-884-8690

Manor House Hughes Street
609-884-4710

Manse Inn
609-884-0116

Mason Cottage
800-716-2766-[G--]

Merry Widow
609-884-2789

Mission Inn
609-884-8380

Mooring Guest House
609-884-5425

Open Hearth Guest House
609-884-4933

Periwinkle Inn
609-884-9200

Perry Street Inn
609-884-4590

Poor Richards Inn
609-884-3536-[Y--]

Primrose
609-884-8288

Prince Edward Victorian Suites
609-884-2131

Puffin
609-884-2664

Queen Victoria
609-884-8702

Sea Holly Inn
609-884-6294

Springside
609-884-2654

Stetson B&B Inn

609-884-1724

Summer Cottage Inn
609-884-4948

Summer Station
800-248-8801

The Kings Cottage
609-884-0415

Thorn & Rose
800-884-8142

Twin Gables
609-884-7332

Victorian Lace Inn
609-884-1772

White Dove Cottage
800-321-DOVE

White House Inn
609-884-5329

Wilbraham Mansion
609-884-2046

Windward House
609-884-3368

Wooden Rabbit
609-884-7293

Woodleigh House
609-884-7123

Cardiff
Inn Of The Dove
609-645-1100

Chatham
Parrot Mill Inn
201-635-7722

Chester
Publick House Inn
908-879-6878

Clinton
Amber House
908-735-7881

Creamridge
Country Meadows
609-758-9437

Craig House
609-522-8140

Earth Friendly
609-259-9744

Denbille

Lakeside B&B

Edgewater Park
Whitebriar B&B
609-871-3859

Flemington
Cabbage Rose Inn
908-788-0247

Jerica Hill B&B Inn
908-728-8234-[Y--]

Franklin
Sullivans Gas Light Inn
201-827-8227

Frenchtown
Hunterdon House
800-382-0375

National Hotel
201-996-4871

Glenwood
Apple Valley Inn
201-764-3745

Haddonfield
Queen Anne Inn
609-428-2195-[Y--]

Hampton
Place At The Quarry
908-537-6944

Haworth
Needlework House

Highlands
Sea Bird Inn
908-872-0123

Hope
Inn At Millrace Pond
908-459-4884-[Y--]

Island Heights
Studio Of John F Peto
908-270-6058

Jobstown
Daffodil
609-723-5364

Lambertville
Bridgestreet House
609-397-2503

Chimney Hill Farm B&B
609-397-1516

Coryell House

2-156 ©Inn & Travel Memphis, Tennessee

Bold Name - *Description appears in other section*   *New Jersey*

609-397-2750

Inn At Lambertville Station
800-524-1091

Inn Of The Hawke
609-397-9555

York Street House
609-397-3007

Long Valley
Neighbor House
908-876-3519

Longport
Winchester Hotel
609-822-0623

Lyndhurst
Jeremiah J Yercance House
201-438-9457

Manahawkin
Goose 'N Berry Inn
609-597-6350

Mays Landing
Inn At Sugar Hill
609-625-2226

Milford
Chestnut Hill
908-995-9761

Millville
Country Inn
800-456-4000

Montclair
Marlboro Inn
201-783-5300

Moorestown
Victorian Lady
609-235-4988

Newton
Tall Pines Farm

North Wildwood
Candlelight Inn
800-992-2632-[Y--]

Ocean City
Adelmans
609-399-2786

Barnagate B&B
609-391-9366

Beach Club Hotel
609-399-8555

Beach End Inn
609-391-1016

Bradburys

Delancey Manor
609-398-9831

Ebbie Guest House
609-399-4744

Enterprise
609-398-1698

Hotel Scarborough
800-258-1558

Laurel Hall
609-399-0800

Mary Ellen's Victorian Rooms
609-399-0764

Mayfair Guest House
609-825-3084

New Brighton Inn
609-399-2829

Northwood Inn
609-399-6071

Sandaway Inn B&B
609-399-2779

Sandy Nook Guest House
609-391-1314

Scarborough Inn
609-399-1558

Seahorse Inn
609-398-4889

Serendipity B&B
800-842-8544-[G--]

Terrace B&B
609-399-4246

Ocean Grove
Albatross Hotel
908-775-2085

Amherst
908-988-5297

Ashling Cottage
908-449-3553

Atlantic House Hotel
908-449-8500

Bellvue Stratford Inn
908-775-2424

Carol Inn
908-776-6174

Carriage House
908-449-1332

Cordova
908-774-3084-[G--]

Grand Victorian
908-449-5327

Hamilton House Inn
908-449-8282

Heather Lodge
908-988-6609

House by the Sea
908-775-2847

Keswick Inn
908-775-7506

Laingdon Hotel
908-774-7974

Lillagaard
908-774-4049

Manchester Hotel
908-775-0100

Moulton House
908-449-5177

Ocean Park Inn
908-988-5283

Ocean Plaza Hotel
908-774-6552

Ocean Pride
908-774-0491

Ocean Vista Hotel
908-776-2500

Pine Tree Inn
908-775-3264

Quaker Inn
908-755-7525

The Innkeeper
908-775-3232

White Lilac Inn
908-449-0211

Ocean View

Major Gandys
609-624-1080-[Y--]

Pennington
Baily B&B
609-737-9439

Pittstown
Seven Springs Farm
908-735-7675

Point Pleasant Beach
Gull Point Inn
908-899-2876

Steepleview
908-988-8999

Sun Ray B&B
908-899-0108

Princeton
Nassau Inn
800-843-6664

Peacock Inn
609-924-1707-[Y--]

Red Maple Farm
908-329-3821

Readington
Holly Thorn House
908-534-1616

Red Bank
Molly Pitcher Inn
908-747-2500

Shaloum Guest House
908-530-7759

Salem
Abbotts At Tide-Mill Farm
609-935-2798

Browns Historic Home
609-335-8595

Ma Bowmans B&B
609-935-4913

Sea Girt
Beacon House
908-449-5835

Ridgewood House
908-449-8710

Sea Grit
Holly Harbor Guest House
908-449-9731

©*Inn & Travel Memphis, Tennessee*   2-157

New Jersey - New York **Bold Name** - *Description appears in other section*

Sea Isle City
Bayview Harbor

Colonnade Inn
609-263-0460

Continental Guest House
609-263-6945

Somers Point
Sutors Island Inn
609-927-3440

South Belmar
Hollycroft Inn
908-681-2254

Spring Lake
Amherst
908-988-5297

Ashling Cottage
800-237-1877

Atlantic House Hotel
908-449-8500

Bath Avenue House
908-775-5833

Carriage House
908-449-1332

Chateau
908-974-2000

Grand Victorian
908-449-5327

Heather Lodge
908-988-6609

Hollycroft B&B
908-681-2254

Johnson House
908-449-1860

Kenilworth
908-449-5327-[Y--]

La Maison
908-449-0969

Moulton House
908-449-5177

Normandy Inn
800-449-1888-[G--]

Sandpiper Inn
908-449-6060

Sarann Gueste House
908-449-9870

Sea Crest By The Sea
908-449-9031

Stone Post Inn
908-449-1212

Victoria House
908-974-1882

Villa Park House
908-449-3642

Walden On The Pond
908-449-7764

Warren Hotel
908-449-8800

Spring Lake Beach
Colonial Ocean House
908-449-9090

Stanhope
Whistling Swan Inn
201-347-6369-[Y--]

Stewartsville
Stewart Inn
908-479-6060

Stockton
Colligans Stockton Inn
800-368-7272-[Y--]

Wolverton Inn
609-861-5847

Stone Harbor
Fairview Guest House
609-696-5000

Toms River
Plain & Fancy
908-363-9275

Town Centre
Isaac Hillard House B&B
609-894-0736

Wenonah
Sand Castle Guest House
609-884-5451

Wildwood Crest
Pope Cottage B&B

609-523-9272

Woodbine
Henry Ludlam Inn
609-861-5847

NEW YORK

Acra
New Mohegan House
518-622-3393

Adams Basin
Canalside Inn
716-352-6784

Addison
Addison Rose B&B
607-359-4650

Albany
Mansion Hill Inn
518-465-2035-[Y--]

Pine Haven B&B
518-482-1574

Riells B&B
518-869-5239

State Street Mansion
518-462-6780

Albion
Friendship Manor B&B
716-589-7973

Alexandria Bay
Bachs Alexandria Bay Inn
315-482-9697

Mug 'n Muffin
800-884-8843

SS Suellen
315-482-2137

Alfred
Hitchcock House
607-587-9102

Saxon Inn
607-871-2600

Alpine
Fontainebleu Inn
607-594-2008

Altamont
Apple Inn
518-267-6557-[Y--]

Altmar
Stone House Inn
315-298-6028

Amagansett
21 House
800-888-8888

Amagansett House
516-267-3808

Bluff Cottage
516-267-6172

Mill Garth Mews Inn
516-267-3757

Sea Breeze Inn
516-257-3892

Amenia
Marshfield
914-868-7833

Troutbeck
914-373-9681

Angelica
Angelica Inn
716-466-3295

Ashland
Ashland Farmhouse
518-734-3558

Ashville
Green Acres
716-782-4254

Astoria
Breezy Point Inn
603-478-5201

Athens
Stewart House
518-945-1357

Auburn
Fays Point Beach House
315-253-9525

Irish Rose Inn
315-255-0196

Springside Inn
315-257-7247-[Y--]

Aurora
Aurora Inn
315-364-8842

Averill Park
Ananas Haus B&B
518-766-5035

Bold Name - *Description appears in other section*   New York

Gregory House
800-497-2977

Avoca
 Patchwork Peace
 B&B
 607-566-2443

Avon
 Avon Inn
 315-226-8181

 Charleton B&B
 716-226-2838

 Mulligan Farm B&B
 315-226-6412-[Y--]

Bainbridge
 Berry Hill Farm
 315-733-0040

Baldwinsville
 Pandoras Getaway
 315-635-9571

Barneveld
 Sugarbush
 315-896-6860

Barryville
 All Breeze Farm
 914-557-6485

 Rebers
 914-557-8111

Bearsville
 Bearsville B&B

Beaver Dams
 Vrede Landgoed
 607-535-4108

Belfast
 Belfast B&B
 716-365-2692

Bellport
 Great South Bay
 Inn
 516-286-8588

 Shell Cottage
 516-286-9421

Bengall
 Beaverbrook House
 914-868-7677

Berkshire
 Kinship B&B & Doll
 Shop
 800-493-2337

Berlin
 Sedgewick Inn
 800-845-4886

Big Indian
 Alpine Inn
 914-254-5026

 Applachian
 Mountain Club

 Catskill Mountain
 Lane B&B
 914-254-5498

 Slide Mountain
 Forest House
 914-254-5365

Binghamton
 B&B Adagio
 607-724-5803

 Chestnut Inn
 800-467-7676-[G--]

Blue Mountain Lake
 Hedges On Blue
 Mountain Lake
 518-352-7325

 Hemlock Hall
 518-352-7706

 Potter On Blue
 Mountain Lake
 518-352-7331

 Potters Resort
 518-352-7331

Boiceville
 Cold Brook Inn
 914-657-6619

Bolton Landing
 Hayes B&B Guest
 House
 518-644-5941-[Y--]

 Hilltop Cottage
 518-644-2492

Booneville
 Greenmeadow Inn
 315-733-0040

Bouckville
 Ye Olde Landmark
 Tavern
 315-893-1810

Bovina Center
 Churchside
 607-832-4231

 Country House
 607-832-4371

 Swallows Nest
 607-832-4547

Branchport
 Four Seasons B&B
 607-868-4686

 Gone With THe
 Wind/Keuka Lake
 607-868-4603

Brant Lake
 Tumble Brook Farm
 518-494-3020

Brockport
 Portico B&B
 716-637-0220

 The Victorian
 716-637-7519

 Victorian B&B
 800-836-1929

 Vintage Manor B&B
 716-637-5156

 White Farm B&B
 716-637-0459

Brookfield
 Bivona Hill B&B
 315-899-8921

 Gates Hill
 Homestead
 315-899-5837

Brooklyn
 AJ Bluestone Inn
 718-499-1401

 B&B On The Park
 718-499-6115

 Brooklyn B&B
 800-248-3026

 Providence House
 718-284-6688

Buffalo
 B&B Of Niagara
 Frontier
 716-836-0794

 Beau Fleuve B&B
 716-882-6116

 Bettys B&B
 716-881-0700

 Bryant House 1895
 716-885-1540

 EBs B&B
 716-882-1428

Burdett
 Country Gardens
 607-546-2272

 Red House Country
 Inn
 607-546-8566

Burlington Flats
 Chalet Waldheim
 607-965-8803

Burt
 Inn On The Hill
 716-688-7900

 Plum Durr B&B

Caledonia
 Annindale B&B
 716-538-4593

Callicoon
 Tonjes Farm
 914-482-5357

Cambridge
 Battenkill B&B
 518-677-8868

 Cambridge Inn
 518-677-5741

 Maple Ridge Inn
 518-677-3674

Camden
 Erie Bridge Inn
 315-245-1555

 Village Inn

Camillus
 Green Gate Inn
 315-672-9276

Campbell Hall
 Point Of View
 800-294-6259

 Tara Farm B&B
 914-294-6482

Canaan
 Inn At Shaker Mill
 Farm
 518-794-9345

 Mountain Home
 B&B

©*Inn & Travel Memphis, Tennessee*   2-159

New York *Bold Name - Description appears in other section*

518-392-5136

Woodbine Inn
518-781-4748

Canandaigua
Acorn
716-398-9910

Canfield Manor
716-493-1793

Clawsons B&B
800-724-6379

Cricket Club Tea Room/B&B

Habersham Country Inn
716-394-1510

JP Morgan House B&B
800-233-3252

Nottingham Lodge
716-374-5355

Oliver Phelps Country Inn
716-396-1650

Sutherland House
800-396-0375-[G--]

Thendara Inn & Restaurant
716-394-4868

Wilder Tavern
716-394-8132

Canaseraga
Country House
607-545-6439

Canastota
Goldie Days B&B
315-697-3802

Candor
Edge Of Thyme
800-722-7365

Canton
Green Acres B&B
315-386-4955

Cape Vincent
Buccaneer
315-654-2975

Dodge Bay Farmhouse
315-654-2084

Featherbed Shoals
315-654-2983

Point Street Manor
315-654-2982

Sunny Morn B&B
315-654-2477

Tymes Remembered B&B
315-654-4354

Caroga Lake
Nick Satoner B&B
518-835-8000

Castile
Eastwood House
716-493-2335

Glen Iris Inn
716-493-2622

Cazenovia
Brae Loch Inn
315-655-3431-[G--]

Brewster Inn
315-655-9232

Country Bumpkin
315-655-8084

Leland House
315-655-8171

Lincklaen House
315-655-3461

Central Valley
Gasho Inn
914-928-2277-[Y--]

Chaffee
Butternut Inn
716-496-8987

Chappaqua
Crabtrees Kittle House
914-666-8044

Chateaugay Lake
Banner House Inn
518-425-3566

Chatham
Old Chatham Sheepherding Co Inn
518-794-9774

Rosehill B&B
518-392-3060

Wolfes Inn
518-392-5218

Chautauqua
Longfellow Inn
716-357-2285

Summer House
716-357-2101

Chestertown
Balsam House Inn
800-441-6856

Chester Inn
518-494-4148

Friends Lake Inn
518-494-4751

Chichester
Maplewood
914-688-5433

Cincinnatus
Alices Dowry B&B
607-863-3934

Clarence
Asa Ranson House
716-759-2315

Coventry Tea Room
716-759-8101

Claverack
Martindale B&B
518-851-5405

Clayton
Greystone Inn
315-686-2408

Thousand Islands Inn
315-686-3030-[Y--]

Cleveland
Cobblestone B&B
315-678-8638

Melody Inn
315-675-8616

Clinton
Clinton House
315-853-5555

Hedges
315-859-5909

Westward Mansion
315-853-3016

Clinton Corners

Bed & Breakfast
914-266-3922

Clintondale
Greens Victorian B&B

Orchard House
914-883-6136

Cobleskill
Gables B&B Inn
518-234-4467

Cochecton
Blue Spruce B&B
914-932-8236

Cold Spring
Hudson House
914-365-9355-[Y--]

Olde Post Inn
914-265-2510

One Market
914-265-3912

Pig Hill
914-265-9247

River View

Village Victorian
914-265-9159

Colden
Back Of The Beyond
716-652-0427

Conesus
B&B AtSBlue Stone
716-346-6929

Bluestone B&B
716-346-6929

Conesus Lake B&B
716-346-6526

Cooperstown
Adalaide B&B
607-547-1215

Angelholm
607-547-2483-[Y--]

Bassett House Inn
607-547-7001

Brown-Williams House B&B
607-547-5569

Cooper Motor Inn
607-547-2567

2-160

©*Inn & Travel Memphis, Tennessee*

Bold Name - Description appears in other section **New York**

Creekside B&B
607-547-8203

Davenport Inn
800-273-1746-[G--]

Green Apple Inn
607-547-1080

Hickory Grove Inn
607-547-8100

Hill & Hollow Farm
607-547-2129

Inn At Brook Willow Farm
607-547-9700

Inn At Cooperstown
607-547-5756-[Y--]

JP Still House
607-547-2633-[Y--]

Main Street B&B
800-867-9755

Middlefield Guest House
607-286-7056

Phoenix Inn At River Road
607-547-8250

Thistlebrook B&B
607-547-6093

Tunnicliff Inn
607-547-9611

Wynterholm B&B
607-547-2308

Corfu
Hens Nest
716-599-6417

Corinth
Agape Farm B&B
518-654-7777

Inn At Edge Of The Forest
800-654-3343

Corning
1865 White Birch B&B
607-962-6355

Delevan House
607-962-2347

Laurel Hill B&B
607-936-3215

Rosewood Inn
607-962-3253

Victoria House
607-962-3413

Cornwall on Hudson
Cromwell Manor
914-534-7136

Cortland
Countryview B&B
607-844-8286

Manor House B&B
607-756-2908

Croton-on-Hudson
Alexander Hamilton House
914-271-6737-[GQA-]

Crown Point
Crown Point B&B
518-597-3651

Cuba
33 South
716-968-1387

Rocking Duck Inn
716-968-3335

Cuddleback
Deerpark Farms Resort
914-754-8357

Dandee
Red Brick Inn
607-243-8844

Davenport
Davenport Inn
800-273-1746-[Y--]

DeBruce
De Bruce Country Inn
914-439-3900-[Y--]

Delhi
Creekside Acres
607-746-3309

Deposit
Alexanders Inn
607-467-6023

Chestnut Inn
800-467-7676-[G--]

White Pillars Inn

607-647-4191

Dolgeville
Adriana B&B
315-429-3249

Dover Plains
Mill Farm
914-832-9198

Old Drovers Inn
914-832-9311

Downsville
Adams Farmhouse
607-363-2757

Juniper Hill B&B
607-363-7646

Victoria Rose B&B
607-363-7838

Dryden
Candlelight Inn
800-579-4629

Margaret Thatchers Spruce B&B
607-844-8052

Sarah Dream B&B
607-844-4321

Serendipity B&B
607-844-9589

Dundee
1819 Red Brick Inn
697-243-8844-[Y--]

Country Manor B&B
607-243-8626

Glenora Guests B&B
607-243-7686

Lakeside Terrace
607-292-6606

Tree Farm B&B
607-243-7414

Willow Cove
607-243-8482

Durhamville
Towering Maples B&B
315-363-9007

Eagle Bay
Big Moose Inn
315-357-2042

East Aurora
Roycroft Inn
716-652-9030

East Bloomfield
Enchanted Rose Inn
716-657-6003

Holloway House
716-657-7120

East Concord
Highland Springs
716-592-4323-[Y--]

East Durham
Evans Palm Inn

Kennedys B&B
518-622-2360

East Hampton
1770 House
516-324-1770

Bassett House
516-324-6127

Centennial House
516-324-9414

Hedges House
516-324-7100

Hunting Inn
516-324-0410

Maidstone Arms
516-324-5006-[Y--]

Mill House Inn
516-324-9766

Phillip-Taylor House

The Pink House
516-324-3400

East Hanpton
East Hampton House
516-324-4300

East Marion
Seahouse

East Meredith
Old Stageline Stop
607-746-6856

East Quogue
Caffrey House
516-728-1327

East Windham

New York

Bold Name - *Description appears in other section*

Point Lookout Inn
518-734-3381

Eaton
Eaton B&B
315-684-7228

Eden
Eden Inn
716-992-4814

Edmeston
Owls Nest Inn
607-965-8720

Pathfinder Village
Country Inn
800-965-8378

Elbridge
Fox Ridge Farm
B&B
315-673-4881

Elizabethtown
Stoneleigh B&B
518-873-2669

Stony Water B&B
518-873-9125

Elk Park
Redcoat Return
518-589-9858

Elka Park
Redcoats Return
518-589-9858

Windswept
518-589-6275

Ellenburg Depot
McGregor House
B&B
518-594-7673

Ellicottville
Ellicottville Inn
716-699-2373

Ilex Inn
716-699-2002

Elmira
Breinlingers B&B
607-733-0089

Lindenwald Haus
B&B
607-733-8752

Rufus Tanner House
607-732-0213-[G--]

Strathmont
607-733-1046

Essex
Stonehouse B&B
518-963-7713

Fair Haven
Black Creek Farm
315-947-5282

Browns Village Inn
315-947-5817

Frost Haven Resort
315-947-5331

Isaac Turner Inn
315-947-2553

Pleasant Beach Inn
315-947-5592

Fairport
Woods Edge
716-223-8877

Woods Edge B&B
716-223-8877

Fault Point
Mill At Bloomvale
Farms
914-266-4234

Fayetteville
Beard Morgan
House B&B
800-775-4234

Ravenswood B&B
315-637-2836

Findley Lake
Nelsons Tin Cup Inn
716-769-7764

Fleischmanns
Highland Fling Inn

River Run
914-254-4884

Fly Creek
Litco Farms B&B
607-547-2501

Lost Trolley Farm
607-547-5729

Forestbaugh
Inn At Lake Joseph
914-791-9506-[Y--]

Fosterdale
Fosterdale Heights
House
914-482-3369

Frankfort
Frankfort Hill B&B
315-733-0040

Fredonia
White Swan Inn
716-672-2103

Freeville
LoPinto Farms
Lodge
800-551-5806

Friendship
Merry Maid Inn
716-973-7740

Fulton
Aunt Ts B&B
315-592-2425

Battle Island Inn
315-593-3699-[Y--]

Doneys B&B
315-593-7419

Galway
Salt Hill Farm
518-882-9466

Garrison
Bird & Bottle Inn
914-424-3000

Golden Eagle Inn
914-424-3067

Gasport
Country Cottage
B&B
716-772-2251

Geneseo
American House
716-243-5483

Oak Valley Inn
716-243-5570

Geneva
Cobblestones
315-789-1896-[Y--]

Geneva On The Lake
800-3-GENEVA-[Y]

Inn At Belhurst
Castle
315-781-0201

Virginia Dean B&B
315-789-6152

Gilboa
Windy Ridge B&B
607-588-6039

Glenfield
Keystone Manor
315-376-8326

Glens Falls
Crislips B&B
518-793-6869

East Lake George
House
518-656-9452

Gorham
Gorham House
716-526-4402

Goshen
Anthony Dobbins
Stagecoach Inn
914-294-5526

Gowanda
Tepee
716-532-2168-[Y--]

Graham
Victoriana
716-526-4531

Greenfield
Wayside Inn
518-893-7249

Greenfield Park
Greenfield Pole Hunt
Club
914-647-3240

Greenhurst
Sheldon Hall B&B
716-664-4691

Spindletop B&B
716-484-2070

Greenport
Bartlett House Inn
516-477-0371

Townsend Manor Inn
516-477-2000

White Lions
516-477-8819

Greenville
Greenville Arms
518-966-5219

Homestead
518-966-4474

2-162   ©*Inn & Travel Memphis, Tennessee*

Bold Name - *Description appears in other section* **New York**

Groton
Austin Manor B&B
607-898-5786

Benn Conger Inn
607-898-5817

Gale House B&B
607-898-4904

Tinkering "A"
607-898-3864

Guilford
Tea & Sympathy B&B
607-895-6874

Hadley
Saratoga Rose
800-942-5025

Hague
Trout House
518-543-6088

Haines Falls
Huckleberry Hill Inn
518-589-5799

Halcottsville
Carriage House of Halcottsville
607-326-7992

Susans Pleasant Pheasant Farm
800-693-3781

Hamburg
Misserts B&B
716-649-5830

Hamden
Bella Vista Ridge B&B
607-746-2553

Hamilton
Colgate Inn
315-824-2134

Hamlin
Sandy B&B
716-964-7528

Sandy Creek Manor House
800-594-0400

Hammondsport
Another Tyme B&B
607-589-2747

Blushing Rose B&B
800-982-8818

Bowmans B&B
607-569-2516

Bully Hill Vineyard B&B
607-868-3337

Cedar Beach B&B
607-868-3228

JS Hubbs B&B
607-569-2440

Lake Keyua Manor
607-868-3276

Pleasant Valley Inn
607-569-2282

Switzerland Inn
607-292-6927

Wheeler B&B
607-776-6756

Hampton Bays
House On The Water
516-728-3560-[G--]

Poulsens Place
516-728-5285

Twin Forks B&B
516-728-5285

Hancock
Cranberry Inn
607-637-2788

Silver Lake Lodge
607-467-5390

Hannibal
Stone Manor Inn
315-564-5850

Hartsdale
Krogh's Nest
914-946-3479

Hempstead
Country Life B&B
516-292-9219-[Y--]

Henderson
Dobson House
315-938-5901

Sandy's Camo Fa'Lodge
315-846-5775

Henderson Harbor
Gill House Inn
315-938-5013

Herkimer
Bellinger Woods B&B
315-566-2770

Heuvelton
Veras Oswegatchie B&B
315-393-0780

High Falls
Brodhead House
914-687-7700

Capt Schoonmakers B&B
914-687-7946

House On The Hill
914-687-9627

Highland
Fox Hill B&B
914-691-8151

Hillsdale
Creekside At Hillsdale
518-325-6334

Inn At Green River
518-325-7248-[Y--]

L Hostellerie Bressane

Linden Valley
518-325-7100

Swiss Hutte Inn
518-325-3333

Hobart
Breezy Acres Farm B&B
607-538-9338

HR Sugarbush
607-538-9829

Holcomb
Billys B&B
716-229-2408

Homer
David Harum House
607-749-3548

Quagmire Manor B&B
607-749-2844

Stoddard House
607-749-4354

Honeoye
Greenwoods
716-229-2111

Hoosick Falls
Gypsy Lady Inn
518-686-4880

Hopewell Junction
Bykenhulle House
914-226-3039

Le Chambord Inn
914-221-1941

Hornell
Williams Inn
518-324-7400

Horseheads
Birch Hill B&B
607-739-2504

Muse
607-739-1070

Howes Cave
Cavern View B&B & Antiques
518-296-8052

Hudson
Inn At Blue Stores
518-537-4227

Hunter
Featherstones B&B
518-246-6898

Fitch House
518-263-5032

Sedgewick House
518-263-3871

Hyde Park
Fala B&B
914-229-5937

Ilion
Chesham Place
315-894-3552

Indian Lake
Zullo 1870 House
518-648-5377

Inlet
Cinnamon Bear B&B
315-357-6013

Ithaca
Buttermilk Falls
607-272-6767

©*Inn & Travel Memphis, Tennessee*

New York   **Bold Name** - *Description appears in other section*

Elmshade Guest House
607-273-1707

Federal House
607-533-7362

Glendale Farm B&B
607-272-8756

Hanshaw House B&B
800-273-1437

Hillside Inn
607-272-9507

Hound & Hare
607-257-2821

Latourelle A Country Inn
607-237-3777

Lily Hill
607-273-7128

Log Country Inn
607-589-4771

Peregrine House Victorian
607-272-0919

Pierce House
607-273-0824

Ritas Country B&B
800-231-6674

Rose Inn
607-533-7905-[G--]

Sweet Dreams
607-272-7727

Thomas Farm
607-539-7477

Varna Inn
607-277-7735

Welcome Inn
607-257-0250

Jacksonville
  Pleasant Grove
  800-398-3963

Jamaica
  Paradise Farm Resort

Jamesville
  High Meadows B&B
  315-492-3517-[Y--]

Jay
  Book & Blanket B&B
  518-946-8323

Jefferson
  Wind In The Willows
  607-652-2533

Johnson
  Elaines Guest House
  914-355-8811

Keene
  Bark Eater Inn
  518-576-2221-[Y--]

Keene Valley
  Champagnes High Peaks Inn
  518-576-2003

  High Peaks Inn
  518-576-2003

  Trails End
  518-576-9860

Keeseville
  Apple Muffin B&B
  518-834-7160-[Y--]

Kenmore
  Village B&B
  716-875-5860

Kerhonkson
  Maybrook Lodge
  914-626-9823

Kinderhook
  Kinderhook B&B
  518-758-1850

Kingston
  Rondout B&B
  914-331-2369

Lacona
  Boylestown Bunkhouse
  315-387-5835

Lake Clear
  Lodge On Lake Clear
  518-891-1489

Lake George
  Corner Birches B&B Guests
  518-668-2837

  McEnaneys Lincoln Log
  518-668-5326

  Timothys B&B
  518-668-5238

Lake Luzerne
  Lamplight Inn
  800-BNB INNV

Lake Placid
  Adirondak Lodge
  518-523-3441

  Blackberry Inn
  518-523-3419

  Empty Nest

  Highland House Inn
  800-342-8101-[G--]

  Interlaken Inn
  800-428-4369-[Y--]

  Lake Placid Manor
  518-523-2573

  Mountain Hearth Inn
  518-523-1114

  Mt Van Hoevenberg B&B
  518-523-9572

  Solitude On The Lake
  518-523-3190

  South Meadow Farm Lodge
  800-523-9369-[G--]

  Spruce Lodge B&B
  800-258-9850

  Stagecoach Inn
  518-523-9474

Lake Pleasant
  Hummingbird Hill
  518-548-6386

Lansing
  Bay Horse B&B
  607-533-4612

  Cuddle Duck Cottage
  607-257-2821

  Cuddy Duck B&B
  607-364-7085

  Decker Pond Inn
  607-273-7133

  Federal House B&B
  800-533-7362

Laurel
  Gandaldf House
  516-298-4769

Lawyersville
  Stone House B&B
  518-234-2603

Leeds
  Leeds Country Inn
  518-943-2099

Leonardsville
  Horned Dorset Inn
  315-855-7898

LeRoy
  Edson House
  716-768-8579

Lew Beach
  Beaverkill Valley Inn
  914-868-7677

Lewiston
  Cameo Inn
  716-745-3034

  Country Club Inn
  716-285-4869

  Kelly House
  716-754-8877

  Ridgeside Country Acres
  716-754-9114

  The Little Blue House
  716-754-9425

Lisbon
  Tilden Stage At Iroquois Farm
  315-393-4346

Lisle
  Dorchester Farm
  607-692-4511

Little Falls
  Buttermilk Bear
  315-823-3378

  Gansevoort House
  315-823-1833

Little Valley
  Old Homestead In Napoli

©*Inn & Travel Memphis, Tennessee*

Bold Name - *Description appears in other section* New York

Livingston Manor
Lanzas Country Inn
914-439-5070

RM Farm
914-439-5511

Livonia
Briar Root Farm B&B
716-346-2762

Lockport
Chestnut Ridge Inn
716-439-9124

Hambleton House
716-439-9507

Maplehurst B&B
716-434-3502

National Centennial House
716-434-8193

Lodi
Maxsons B&B
607-582-6248

Long Eddy
Rolling Marble Guest House
914-887-6016

Long Lake
Inn On The Hill
518-624-4684

Lowman
Notch House B&B
607-529-3428

Lowville
Hinchings Pond B&B
315-376-8296

Zehrcroft B&B
315-376-7853

Lynbrook
Ricks Heartside
516-593-6721

Lyons
Roselawne B&B
716-946-4218

Macedon
Iris Farm
315-986-4536

Madison
Abigails Straw Hat
315-893-7707

Magraw
Hathaway House
607-836-6006

Mahopac
Mallard Mansion
914-628-3595

Maine
Killarney B&B
607-862-4528

Malone
Kolburn Manor
518-483-4891

Maple Springs
Lake Side B&B
716-386-2500

Marathon
Dukes Coop B&B
607-849-6775

Three Bear Inn
607-849-3258

Marcellus
Debevic Homestead B&B
315-673-9447

Marcy
Towne & Country Lodge
315-724-9207

Margaretville
Margaretville Mountain Inn
800-766-8642

Marlboro
Shady Brook Farm
914-236-3690

Massapequa
Harbor House

Mattituck
Mattituck B&B
516-298-8785-[Y--]

Mayville
Inn On Hobnobbin Farm
716-753-3800

Plumbush B&B At Chautauqua
712-789-5309

Stuart Manor B&B
716-789-9902

Village Inn B&B
716-753-3583-[Y--]

Medina
Crafts Place
716-735-7343

Meridale
Old Stage Line Stop B&B
607-346-6856

Middleport
Canal Country Inn
716-725-7572

Milford
1860 Spencer House
607-286-9402

Cats Pajamas B&B
607-286-9431

Maple Shade B&B

Millbrook
A Cat In Your Lap
914-677-3051

Calico Quail Inn
914-677-6016

Cottonwood Inn
914-677-3919

Evensong B&B
914-677-5720

Millerton
Simmons Way Village Inn
518-789-6235

Mohawk
Country Hills B&B
315-866-1386-[Y--]

Montauk
Beach Plum Inn
516-668-4100

Green Hedges
516-668-5013-[Y--]

Hewitts Ruschmeyers Inn

Shepherds Neck Inn
516-668-2105

Wavecrest Resort

Montgomery
Wards Bridge Inn
914-457-3488

Montour Falls
Catharine Creek B&B

Mount Morris
Allens Hill B&B Inn
716-658-4591

Mount Tremper
Mount Temper Inn
914-688-5329

Mount Vision
B&B Twin Falls
607-293-8009

Mumford
Genesee Country Inn
716-538-2500

Naples
Landmark Retreat
716-396-2383-[Y--]

Vagabond Inn
716-538-2500

Nelliston
Historian B&B
518-993-2233

New Harford
The Globe
315-733-0040

New Hartford
Roughhouse
315-724-4441

New Haven
Brickie House Inn
315-963-8592

New Lebanon
Churchill House
518-766-5852

New Lebanon Inn
518-794-9550

Palmer House
518-794-9385

New Paltz
Audreys B&B
914-255-1103

Jingle Bell Farm
914-255-6588

Mohonk Mountain House
914-225-1000

Nanas B&B

©Inn & Travel Memphis, Tennessee

2-165

New York   *Bold Name - Description appears in other section*

914-255-5678

Nieuw Country Loft
914-255-6533

Ujjalas B&B
914-255-6360

New Rochelle
Rose Hill Guest House
914-632-6464

New Windsor
Empty Nest
914-496-9263

Old Stone House
914-496-9694

New York
Abode Inn
212-472-2000

B&B On The Park
718-499-6115

Bed of Roses B&B
212-421-7604

Box Tree
212-758-8320

Broadway B&B Inn
800-826-6300-[G--]

Chelsea Inn
800-777-8215

City Lights B&B
212-737-7049

Incentra Village House
212-206-0007

Inn At Irving Place
212-533-4600

Malibu Studio Hotel
212-992-3455

Penington Friends House
212-673-1730

The James House
212-213-1484

Newark
Twin-Steeples Farm B&B
315-597-2452

Newburgh
Early Settler B&B

800-824-9934

Kelsays House Of Nations
914-562-1477

Morgan House
914-561-0326

Stockbridge Ramsdell House/ Croton
914-561-3462

Newfane
Creekside B&B
716-778-9843

Newfield
Decker Pond Inn
607-273-7133

Historic Cook House
607-564-9926

Newport
What Cheer Hall
315-845-8312

Niagara Falls
Bonnies B&B
716-297-5426

Manchester House B&B
716-282-5717

Old Niagara House
716-285-9408

Park Place B&B
716-282-4626

Rainbow Guest House
800-724-3536

Red Coach Inn
716-282-1459

The Cameo Manor
716-745-3034-[G--]

Thomsan Place
716-285-3935

Nichols
Fawns Grove B&B
607-699-3222

River Tree B&B
607-699-7484

Nicholville
Chateau Lesperance
315-328-4669

North Creek
Copperfield Inn
518-251-5200

Goose Pond Inn
518-251-3434

North Granville
Chateau Fleur de Leys
518-642-1511

North Hudson
Pine Tree Inn
518-532-9255

North River
Garnet Hill Lodge
518-251-2821

Highwinds Inn
518-251-3760

Pascales B&B
518-251-4296

Toags Lodge B&B
518-251-2496

Northville
Inn At The Bridge
518-863-2240

Trailhead Lodge
518-863-2198

Norwich
Cedar Court
607-336-3333

Nunda
Butternut B&B
716-468-5074

Ocean Beach
Four Seasons B&B
516-583-8295

Place In The Sun Inn
516-583-5716

Off Shelter Island
Rams Head Inn
516-749-0811

Ogdensburg
Maple Hill Country Inn
315-393-3961

Salty Dog B&B
315-393-1298

Way Back Inn

315-393-3844

Olcott
Bayside Guest House
716-778-7767

Old Chatham
Depot Lane B&B
518-794-8336

Locust Tree House
518-794-8671

Old Forge
Pine Shadows Lodge
315-369-3551

Olean
Castle Inn
518-422-7853

Olde Library Inn
716-373-9804

Oneida
Pollyanna
315-363-0524-[Y--]

Oneida Castle
Governors House B&B
800-437-8177

Oneonta
Agnes Hall Home
607-432-0655

Cathedral Farms Country Inn
800-FARMS-90

Christohpers
607-432-2444

Davenport Inn
800-273-1746-[G--]

Long Winter Farm B&B
607-263-2463

Ontario
Tummonds House
315-524-5381

Windy Shores B&B
315-524-2658

Orchard Park
Mansard Inn
716-828-1115

Oswego
Chestnut Grove Inn
315-342-2547

Bold Name - *Description appears in other section* **New York**

Kings Inn
315-342-6200

Ovid
Silver Strand
800-283-LAKE

Tillinghast Manor
607-869-3584

Owego
Pumpelly House
607-687-0510

Oxford
Whitegate
607-843-6965

Oyster Bay Cove
Woodland Residence
516-922-1905

Painted Post
Dannfield
607-962-2740-[Y--]

Stiles Guest House
607-962-1894

Palenville
Arlington House B&B
518-678-9081

Palenville House
518-678-5649

Pearls Place B&B
518-678-5549

Palmyra
Canaltown B&B
315-597-5553

Parksville
Arrow Head Ranch
914-292-6267

Patchogue
Halcyon Manor
516-289-9223

Peconic
1867 House

Penfield
Strawberry Castle
716-385-3266

Penn Yan
Fintons Landing
315-536-3146

Fox Inn B&B
800-901-7997

Fox Run Vineyards B&B
315-536-2507

Heirlooms
315-536-7682

On The Beach

Wagener Estate B&B
315-536-4591

Wilkins Keuka Cove

Phelps
Tower B&B
315-548-8888

Phoenix
Main Street House
315-695-5601

Pierrepont Manor
Pierrepont Manor
315-465-5000

Pine Bush
Milton Bull House
914-361-4770

Netherfield
914-733-1324

Pine City
Rufus Tanner House
607-732-0213-[Y--]

Pine Hill
Birch Creek Inn
914-254-5222

Colonial Inn
914-254-5577

Pine Hill Arms
914-254-9811-[Y--]

Pine Plains
Hammertown Inn
518-398-7539

Pines
518-398-7677

Piseco
Irondequoit Club Inn
518-548-5500

Pittsford
Oliver Louds Inn
716-248-5200

Plattsburg

Sunny Side Up B&B
518-563-5677

Port Jefferson
Captain Hawkins House
516-473-8211

Compass Rose B&B
516-474-1111

Danfords Inn
516-928-5200

Port Jervis
Educators Inn East
914-856-5543

Portageville
Genesee Falls Hotel
716-493-2484

Poughkeepsie
Inn At The Falls
914-462-5770

Preble
Martin House B&B
607-749-7137

Pulaski
Salmon River Anglers Lodge
315-298-3044

Sequoia Inn
315-298-4407

Shillelaugs & Shamrocks B&B
315-298-7040

Way Inn
315-298-6073

Pulteney
Vineyard House B&B
607-868-3714

Purling
Shepherds Croft
518-622-9504

Putman Valley
Living Springs Retreat
914-526-2800-[Y--]

Queensbury
Sandfords Ridge B&B
518-793-4923

Randolph
Highland View Farm

B&B
716-358-2882

Raquette Lake
Sagamore Lodge
315-354-5311

Red Hook
Red Hook Inn
914-758-8445

Remsen
Stor Felen
315-831-5443

Remsenburg
Pear Tree Farm
516-325-1443

Rensselaer
Tibbitts House Inn
518-472-1348

Rexford
Rexford Crossings B&B
518-399-1777

Rhinebeck
Aunt Sallys B&B
914-876-8340

Beekman Arms
914-876-7077

Delamater House
914-876-7077

Hellers
914-876-3468

Lakehouse
914-266-8093

Mansakenning Carriage House
914-876-3500

Mary Sweeney B&B
914-876-6640

Montgomery Inn Guest House
914-876-3311

Seapacot Farms
914-876-4592

Stanford Whites Carriage House
914-876-7257

Veranda House B&B
914-876-4133

Village Victorian Inn

New York *Bold Name - Description appears in other section*

914-876-8345

Whistle Wood Farm
914-876-6838

Rhinecliff
Rhinecliff B&B
914-876-3716

Richfield
Summerwoods B&B
315-858-2024

Richfield Springs
Canadarago Lake House
315-858-1761

Country Spread B&B
315-858-1870

Jonathan House
315-858-2870

Wolfe Hall
315-858-1510

Riverhead
Libby House

Rochester
428 Mount Vernon B&B
800-836-3159

Dartmouth House B&B
800-724-6298-[Y--]

Highland B&B
716-442-4813

Rose Mansion & Gardens
716-546-5426

Swan Walk
716-865-7552

Wynderly
716-224-0758

Rock Stream
Reading House
607-535-9785

Vintage View
607-535-7909

Rocky City Falls
Mansion Inn
518-885-1607

Rome
Little Schoolhouse

B&B
315-336-4474

Maplecrest B&B
315-337-0070

Roscoe
Baxter House B&B
607-498-5911

Open Door B&B
607-498-5772

Rosendale
Astoria Hotel
914-658-8201

Round Lake
Olde Stone House Inn
518-899-5048

Round Top
Pickwick Lodge
518-622-3364

Winter Clove Inn
518-622-3267

Roxbury
Scudder Hill House
607-326-4215

Rush
B&B At Bonnie
716-533-1990

Rushford
Klartag Farms B&B
716-437-2946

Rushville
Lakeview Farm B&B
716-554-6973

Sabael
Burkes Cottages
518-583-1890

Sackets Harbor
Old Stone Row Country Inn
315-646-1234

Sag Harbor
Sag Harbor Inn
516-725-2949

Saint Johnsville
Fiveacre Farm B&B
518-568-7162

Saint Regis Falls
Adirondack House
315-328-4459

Salem
Angelas
518-854-3802

Griffin House
518-854-7688

Sandy Creek
All Season Lodge
315-387-5850-[Y--]

Pink House Inn
315-387-3276

Tug Hill Lodge
315-387-5326

Saranac Lake
Fogartys B&B
518-891-3755

Lands End
800-859-9224

Point
800-255-3530

Porches
518-891-2973

Sunny Pond B&B
518-891-1531

Saratoga
Adelphi Hotel
518-587-4688

Saratoga B&B
518-584-0920

Saratoga Springs
Chestnut Tree Inn
518-587-8681

Highclere Inn
518-696-2861

Inn At Saratoga
518-583-1890

Inn On Bacon Hill
518-695-3693

Lombardi Farm B&B
518-587-2074-[Y--]

Six Sisters B&B
518-583-1173

Union Gables B&B
518-584-1558

Washington Inn
518-584-9807

Westchester House
518-587-7613-[Y--]

Saugerties
High Woods Inn
914-246-8655

House On The Quarry
914-246-8584

Sacks Lodge
914-246-8711

Sauquoit
Hayfield House B&B
315-737-8289

Schenectady
Widow Kendall House
518-370-5972

Schoharie
Maples B&B
518-295-7352

Marsh House
518-295-7981

Wedgewood Inn
518-295-7663

Schroon Lake
Schroon Lake Inn
518-532-7042

Schroon Lodge
Woods Lodge
518-532-7529

Schuylerville
Fish Creek Inn
518-581-0297

Scio
Scio House B&B
716-593-1737

Senca Falls
Gurion House B&B
315-568-8129

Seneca Falls
Chamberlain Mansion Hotel
315-568-9990

Goulds
315-568-5801

Locustwood Country Inn
315-549-7132

Severance

2-168   ©Inn & Travel Memphis, Tennessee

Bold Name - Description appears in other section **New York**

Sawmill B&B
518-532-7734-[Y--]

Shandaken
Auberge des Quatre Saisons
914-688-2223-[Y--]

Cooper Hood Inn
914-688-9962

Two Brooks B&B
914-688-7101

Sharon Springs
Clausen Farms B&B
518-284-2527

Shelter Island
Azalea House
516-749-4252

Bayberry B&B
516-749-3375

Chequit Inn
516-749-0018

House On Chase Creek
516-749-4379

Pridwin

Shelter Island Resort
516-749-2001

Shelter Island Heights
Belle Crest House
516-749-2041

Sherburne
Lok n Logs B&B
607-674-5111

Sherman
Weises Inn-Between
716-761-6255

Shinhopple
Peaceful Valley B&B
607-363-2211

Silver Creek
Grape Country Manor
716-934-3532

Sinclairville
Gray Gables B&B
716-962-8584

Skaneateles
Cozy Cottage B&B
315-689-2082

Gray House
315-685-0131

Sherwood Inn
315-685-3405

Slate Hill
Ridgebury Inn & Hunt Club
914-355-4868

Riding Habit Inn
914-355-4868

Slaterville Springs
Kestrel Hill B&B
607-539-7768

Sodus
Maxwell Creek Inn
315-483-2222

Silver Waters Guest House
315-483-8098

Sodus Point
Carriage House Inn
800-292-2990

Lakecrest Guest House
315-483-6090

South Dayton
Greystone Mansion

Town & Country B&B
716-988-3340

South Durham
Glen Durham
518-622-9878

South Nyack
Eleanors
914-353-3040

South Otselic
Northwest Corners B&B
315-653-7775

Southampton
Bayberry Inn Southampton
516-283-4220

Mainstay B&B
516-283-4375

Old Post House Inn
516-283-1717

Village Latch Inn
516-283-2160

Southold
Goose Creek Guesthouse
516-765-3356

Speculator
Inn At Speculator
518-548-3811

Zeisers Oak Mountain Lodge
518-584-7021

Spencer
Slice Of Home
607-589-6073

Spencertown
Spencertown Guests
518-392-2358

Spring Glen
Gold Mountain Chalet
914-395-5200

Springville
Franklin House B&B
716-592-5388

Staatsburg
Scenery Hill
914-889-4812

Stamford
Breezy Acres Farm B&B
607-538-9338-[Y--]

Dayton Farm Guest House
607-652-3631

Lanigan Farmhouse
607-652-7455

Majestic View B&B
607-652-7768

McLinden Lodge
607-652-4751

Stanfordville
Country Manor Lodge
914-876-1151

Lakehouse On Golden Pond
914-266-8093

Staten Island
Sixteen Firs

718-727-9188-[Y--]

Stephentown
Andersons Country House
518-733-6600

Berkshire Mountain House
518-733-6923

Keepsake Inn
518-733-6277

Millhof Inn
518-733-5606

Sterling
Whispering Pines Inn
315-947-6666

Stillwater
Lees Beer Run
518-584-7722

Stone Ridge
Bakers B&B
914-687-9795

Deerfield
914-687-9807

Hasbrouch House Inn
914-687-0055

Stony Brook
Three Village Inn
516-751-0555

Summit
Sawyer Hollow Ranch
518-287-1728

Syracuse
B&B And Music
315-474-4889

B&B Wellington
800-724-5006

Benedict House
315-476-6541-[Y--]

Giddings House B&B
800-377-3452

Ivy Chimney
315-446-4199

Russell Farrenkopf House
315-472-8001

©Inn & Travel Memphis, Tennessee

2-169

New York *Bold Name - Description appears in other section*

Tannersville
Deer Mountain Inn
518-589-6268

Eggery Inn
518-589-5363

Kennedy House
518-589-6082

Washington Irvings Lodge
518-589-5560

Tarrytown
Tarrytown House
914-591-8200

Thendara
Moose River House
315-369-3104

Van Aunens Inne
315-369-3033

Theresa
Reeds Rest
315-628-5312

Three Mile Bay
Le Muguet
315-649-5896

Ticonderoga
Bonnie View Acres B&B
518-585-6098

Tompkins Cove
Cove House B&B
914-429-9695

Troy
Pinewoods House
518-271-6881

Trumansburg
Archway
800-387-6175

Conifer Hill B&B
607-387-5849

Crester House
607-387-9666

Gothic Eves B&B
607-387-6033

Pillars
607-387-9342

Sage Cottage
607-387-6449-[Y--]

Taugahnnock Farms Inn
607-387-7711

Westwind B&B
607-387-3377

White Gazebo Inn
607-387-4952

Truxton
Milkland Farms B&B
607-842-6472

Tuckahoe
Beehive B&B

Tupper Lake
Green Gables B&B
518-359-7815

Turin
Pioneer Lodge
315-348-8649

Towpath Inn
315-348-8122

Ulster Park
Rennies B&B
800-447-8262

Union Springs
Ludwigs B&B
315-889-5940

Malabar House
315-889-7217

Utica
Adam Bowman Manor
315-738-0276

Herys & Hospitality
315-797-0079

Iris Stonehouse
800-446-1456-[Y--]

Valley Falls
Maggie Townes B&B
518-663-8369

Vernon
Jenkins House At Woodlawn
315-829-2459

Lavender Inn
315-829-2440

Trestle Acres
315-829-4807

Verona
Stones Throw Inn
315-363-6053

Victor
Golden Rule B&B
716-924-0610

Safari House B&B
716-924-0250

Sugar Tree
716-924-5546

Walden
Heritage Farm
914-778-3420

Wallkill
Audreys Farmhouse B&B
914-895-3440

Walton
Aching Acres
607-865-8569

Carriage Houes B&B
607-865-4041

Sunrise Inn B&B
607-865-7254

Wappinger Falls
Castle Hill B&B
914-298-8000

Wappingers B&B

Warrensburg
Bent Finial Manor
518-677-5741

Country Road Ldoge
518-623-2207

Donegal Manor B&B
518-623-3549

House On The Hill
518-623-9390

Merrill Magee House
518-623-2449-[G--]

White House Lodge
518-623-3640

Warwick
Peach Grove Inn
914-986-7411

Tranquility Guest Home
914-986-4364

Willow Brook Farm
914-853-7728

Washingtonville
Back In Time B&B
914-496-5867

Water Mill
Seven Ponds Inn
516-726-7618

Waterloo
Evergreens
315-539-8329

Front Porch Antiques/B&B

Hist James R Webster Mansion
315-539-3032-[Y--]

James Russell Webster Inn
315-539-3032

Watertown
Starbuck House
315-788-7324

Waterville
B&B Of Waterville
315-841-8295

Watkins Glen
Chalet Leon
607-582-6204

Clarke House B&B
607-535-7965

Farm Sanctuary
607-583-2225

Glen Manor B&B
607-535-9737

Red House Country Inn
607-546-8566-[Y--]

Rose Window B&B
607-535-4687

Vintage View B&B
607-535-7909

Webster
B&B At Country
716-265-4720

Country Schoolhouse

2-170　　　　　　　　　　　　　　　　　　　　　　©Inn & Travel Memphis, Tennessee

Bold Name - *Description appears in other section*

New York - North Dakota

716-265-4720

Denonville Inn
518-671-1550

Wells
  Abners Country Inn
  518-924-2206

  Adirondack
  Mountain Chalet
  518-924-2112

West Shokan
  Glen Atty Farm
  914-657-8110

  Haus Elissa B&B
  914-657-6277

West Winfield
  Five Gables B&B
  315-822-5764

  Old Stone House
  315-822-6748

Westfalls
  Pipe Creek Farm
  B&B
  716-652-4868

Westfield
  Brewer House
  716-326-2320

  Simpsons
  716-326-2532

  Westfield House
  716-326-6262

  William Seward Inn
  800-338-4151

Westhampton Beach
  1880 House
  800-346-3290-[G--]

Westport
  All Tucked Inn
  518-962-4400

  Inn On The Library
  Lawn
  518-962-8666

Wevertown
  Mountainaire
  Adventures
  800-950-2194

White Lake
  Bradstan Country
  Inn
  914-583-4114

Whitehall
  Apple Orchard Inn
  518-499-0180

Whitney Point
  Our Heritage Inn
  607-692-3049

Willet
  Woven Waters
  607-656-8672

Williamsville
  Heritage House Inn
  716-633-4900

Willsboro
  Champlain Vistas
  518-963-8029

Wilmington
  Whiteface Chalet
  518-946-2207

  Willkommen Hof
  518-946-7669

Windham
  Albergo Allegria
  518-734-4499

  Christmans
  Windham House
  518-734-4230

  Country Suite B&B
  518-734-4079-[Y--]

  Danske Haus
  518-734-6335

Wolcott
  Bonnie Castle Farm
  B&B
  315-587-2273

  Lake Bluff Inn
  315-587-2421

Woodbourne
  Chez Renux
  914-434-1780

Woodgate
  Red House B&B
  315-392-5479

Woodstock
  Parnassus Square
  Inn
  914-679-5078

  Twin Gables Of
  Woodstock
  914-679-9479

Wyoming
  Wyoming Inn B&B
  716-495-6470

Youngstown
  Mill Glenn Inn
  716-754-4085

  Ontario House
  716-745-9774

  The Cameo Manor
  716-745-3034-[G--]

Yulan
  Bear Paw Inn
  914-557-6002-[Y--]

NORTH DAKOTA

Bismark
  White Lace B&B
  701-258-4142

Bottineau
  Log Manor Inn
  701-263-4596

Bowman
  Logging Camp
  Ranch
  701-279-5702

Carrington
  Blue Swan Inn
  701-652-3978

  Kirkland B&B
  800-451-7150

Devils Lake
  Dakota Friend B&B
  701-662-6327

Fargo
  Bohligs B&B
  701-235-7867

Fessenden
  Belseker Mansion
  701-547-3313

Grand Forks
  511 Reever B&B
  701-772-9663

  Lord Byrons B&B
  701-775-0194

  Merrifield House
  B&B
  701-775-4250

Jamestown

  Country Charm
  B&B
  701-251-1372

Kemare
  Farm Comfort
  701-848-2433

Leonard
  Lady Bird B&B
  701-645-2509

Lidgerwood
  Kalers B&B
  701-538-4848

Luverne
  Grandmas House
  Farm
  701-845-4994

  Volden Farm B&B
  701-769-2275

McClusky
  Midstate B&B
  701-363-2520

Minnewaukan
  Minnewaukan B&B
  701-473-5731

Minot
  Broadway B&B
  701-838-6075

  Dakota Rose
  701-838-3548

  Muffin House
  701-839-0750

New Salem
  Prairie View B&B
  701-843-7236

Northwood
  Twin Pine Farm
  B&B
  701-587-6075

Oakes
  House Of 29 B&B
  701-742-2227

Reeder
  Rocking Chair B&B
  701-853-2204

Regent
  Pleasant View B&B
  701-563-4542

Scranton
  Hist Jacobson
  Mansion

©*Inn & Travel Memphis, Tennessee*

North Dakota - Ohio

Bold Name - Description appears in other section

701-275-8291

Stanley
Triple T Ranch
701-628-2418

Tower City
Tower City Inn
701-749-2660

Velva
Hagenhaus B&B
701-338-2714

Wahapeton
Adams Fairview Farm B&B
701-274-8262

OHIO

Akron
Helens Hospitality House
216-724-7151

O Neil House
216-867-2650

Portage House
216-535-1952-[Y--]

Albany
Albany House
800-600-4941

Andover
Vickerys B&B
216-293-6875

Archbold
Murbach House
419-445-5195

Ashland
Twin Oaks B&B
419-281-5333

Winfield B&B
419-281-5587

Ashtabula
Cahill B&B

Atwater
Buckeye Lady B&B
216-947-3932

Aurora
Bed & Breakfast & Tennis
216-562-7031

Walden

Avon Lake
Williams House
216-933-5089

Barnesville
Georgian Pillars B&B
614-425-3741

Bellefontaine
Whitemore House
513-592-4290

Belleville
Frederick Fitting House
419-886-2863-[Y--]

Rockledge Manor
419-892-3329

Bellevue
Britannia B&B
419-483-4597

Berlin
Amish Country Inn
216-893-3000

Donnas Country Inn
216-893-3068

Blue Rock
McNutt Farm II
614-674-4555

Bryan
Elegant Inn
419-636-2873

The Elegant Inn
419-636-2873

Bucyrus
Hideaway B&B
419-562-3013

Hideaway B&B
800-570-8233

Burton
Weishfield Inn

Cadiz
Family Tree Inn
614-942-3641

Cambridge
Leyshon B&B
614-432-7822

Salt Fork Park Lodge

Camden
Pleasant Valley B&B

513-787-3800

Celina
Winkeljohn House
419-586-2155

Centerville
Yesterday B&B
513-433-0785

Chagrin Falls
Inn Of Chagrin Falls
216-247-1200

Inn Of Chagrin Falls
216-247-1200

Chardon
Bass Lake Inn
216-285-3100

Charm
Charm Countryview Inn
216-893-3003

Watchmans Cottage
216-893-2717

Chillicothe
Blair House
614-774-3140

Chillicothe B&B
614-772-6848

Greenhouse B&B
614-775-5313

Old McDill Anderson Place
614-774-1770

Vanmeter B&B
614-774-3510

Victorian Manor
614-775-6424

Cincinnati
Neil House
513-961-4805

Parker House
513-579-8236

Prospect Hill B&B
513-421-4408

Prospect Hill B&B Inn
513-421-4408-[Y--]

Victoria Inn Of Hyde Park
513-321-3567

Circleville
Castle Inn
614-477-3986

Castle Kreistadt B&B
614-477-3986

Fireside Inn
614-474-6640

Penguin Crossing B&B
800-736-4846

Cleveland
Baricelli Inn
216-791-6500

Baricelli Inn
216-791-6500

Bass Lake Inn
216-338-5550

Dubonnet Garden
216-231-8900

Dubonnet Garden
216-431-1717

Glidden House
216-231-8900

Truebrooke Inn

Tudor House
216-321-3213-[Y--]

Columbus
50 Lincoln-A Very Small Hotel
614-291-5056

Belmont B&B
614-421-1235

Columbus B&B
614-443-3680

Goss House
614-299-9803

Harrison House
614-421-2202

House Of Seven Gables B&B
614-761-9595

Lansing Street B&B
614-444-8488

Penguin Crossing B&B

2-172

©Inn & Travel Memphis, Tennessee

Bold Name - *Description appears in other section* *Ohio*

614-261-7854

Victorian B&B
614-299-1656

Conesville
　Log House B&B
　614-829-2757

Conneaut
　Campbell Braemar B&B
　216-599-7362

Coshocton
　1890 B&B
　614-622-1890

　Apple Butter Inn
　614-622-1329

　Roscoe Village Inn
　800-237-7397

Cuyahoga Falls
　Studio 12 B&B
　216-928-5843

Danville
　White Oak Inn
　614-599-6107-[G--]

Dayton
　Chadlewick B&B
　513-233-9297

　Prices Steamboat House
　513-223-2444

　Steamboat House
　513-223-2444

DeGraff
　Rollicking Hills
　513-585-5161

Delaware
　Olentangy River Valley B&B
　614-885-5859

　Van Deman B&B
　614-363-2963

Dellory
　Dripping Rock Farm
　216-735-2987

Dellroy
　Candle Glow B&B
　216-735-2407

　Whispering Pines B&B
　216-735-2824

Dover
　Mowerys Welcome Home Inn
　216-343-4690

　Old World Inn
　216-343-1333

Dresden
　Corner House B&B
　614-754-2212

　Hemlock House B&B
　614-754-4422

　Village Victorian B&B
　614-754-2231

East Fultonham
　Hill View Acres B&B
　614-849-2728

East Liverpool
　Grannys Shanty B&B
　216-385-7722

Eaton
　Decoy B&B
　513-456-6145

Fort Recovery
　Main Street Inn
　419-375-4955

Fredericktown
　Heartland Country Resort

Freson
　Valley View Inn
　216-897-3232

Gahanna
　Lily Stone Inn
　614-476-1976

Galion
　Quarry Ridge B&B
　419-468-4623

　Rose Of Sherron B&B
　419-468-3973

Gambier
　Blossom Tyme
　614-427-3300

　Gambier House
　614-427-2668

Geneva-on-the-Lake

　Otto Court B&B
　216-466-8668

Glouster
　Countyline Farm B&B
　614-767-4185

Grand Rapids
　Mill House
　419-832-6455

Granville
　Buxton Inn
　614-587-0001-[Y--]

　Cream Station Antiques
　614-587-4814

　Granville Inn
　614-587-4677

　Porch House B&B
　614-587-1995

Greenfield
　Mertz Place
　513-981-2219

Hamersville
　Days Gone By B&B
　513-379-2025

Hillsboro
　Candlewick B&B
　513-393-2743

　Chanticleer B&B
　513-365-1308

Hiram
　Lily Ponds
　216-569-3272

Huron
　Beach House
　419-433-5839

　Captain Montagues B&B
　419-433-4746

Jackson
　Bowman House
　614-286-1916

　Maples B&B
　614-286-6067

Johnstown
　Pudding House B&B/For Writers
　614-967-6060

Kellys Island

　Beatty House
　419-746-2379

　Cricket Lodging
　419-746-2263

　Inn On Kellys Island
　419-746-2258-[Y--]

　South Shore B&B
　419-746-2409

　Sweet Valley Inn
　419-746-2750

Kent
　Editon House
　216-673-5544

Kings Mills
　Kings Manor
　513-459-9959

Kinsman
　Hidden Hollow
　216-876-8686

Lakeville
　Quiet Country
　216-378-2291

Lakewood
　Captains House
　216-521-1038

Lancaster
　Barbaras B&B
　614-687-1689

　Butterfly Inn
　614-654-7654

Laurelville
　Hocking House B&B
　614-332-1655

Lebanon
　1790 Log Home
　502-465-4221

　Golden Lamb
　513-932-5065

　White Tor
　513-932-5892

Lewisville
　Grandma Bettys
　614-567-3465

Lexington
　White Fence Inn
　419-884-2356

Logan
　Inn At Cedar Falls

©Inn & Travel Memphis, Tennessee

2-173

Ohio *Bold Name - Description appears in other section*

614-385-7489

Log Cabin
614-385-8363

Loudonville
Blackfork Inn
216-994-3252-[Y--]

Louisville
Mainstay B&B
216-875-1021-[Y--]

Lucasville
Olde Lamplighter
614-259-3002

Mansfield
B&B At Willow Pond
419-522-4644

Happy Hill
419-884-3916

Witmers Country Acres
419-884-2846

Marblehead
Idlewyld B&B
419-798-4198

Ivy House
419-798-4944

Lakeview Inn
419-798-5845

Old Stone House B&B
419-798-5922-[Y--]

Poor Richards Inn
419-798-5405

Rothenbuhlers Guest House
419-798-5404

Victorian Inn
419-734-5611

Marietta
Buckley House B&B
614-373-3080

First Steelement Inn
614-373-9377

Folgers Bantam Farm B&B
614-374-6919

House Of Seven Porches

614-373-1767

Larchmont
614-376-9000

Marion
Olde Towne Manor B&B
614-382-2402

Victoriana B&B
614-382-2430

Martins Ferry
Mulberry Inn
614-633-6058

McConnelsville
Outback Inn
614-962-2158

Medina
Oakwood B&B
216-723-1162

Mentor
Tolle House
216-657-2900

Mesopotamia
Truebrooke Inn
800-832-8690

Miamisburg
English Manor B&B
513-866-2288

Middlefield
Pine Grove Inn
216-632-0489

Walker Johnson House
216-632-5662

Milan
Coach House
419-499-2435

Gastier Farm
419-499-2985

Millersburg
Adams Street B&B
216-674-0766

Bingham House B&B
216-674-2337

Das Gasthaus B&B
216-893-3089

Inn At Honey Run
216-674-0011

Touch Of Time B&B
216-674-4311

Morrow
Country Manor B&B
513-899-2440

White Oak Farm B&B
513-899-4045

Mount Gilead
Holiday House
419-947-8804

Mount Sterling
Deer Creek Park Lodge

Mount Vernon
Accent House
614-392-6466

Mt Vernon House Inn
614-397-1914

Oak Hill B&B
614-393-2912

Russell Cooper House
614-397-8638-[Y--]

Stauffer House
614-397-9594

New Matamoras
Archers Fork Manor
614-865-3670

New Richmond
Hollyhock
513-553-6585

Newark
Pitzer-Cooper House
614-323-2680

Newtown
Winds Way B&B
513-561-1933-[Y--]

North Ridgeville
St George House
216-327-9354

Norwalk
Boos Family Inn
419-668-6257

Old Washington
Zane Trace B&B
614-489-5970

Orrville

Grandmas House
216-682-5112

Oxford
Alexander House, Country Inn

Duck Pond
513-523-8914

Painesville
Riders 1812 Inn
216-942-2742

Peebles
Bayberry Inn
513-587-2221

Peninsula
Centennial House
216-657-2506

Pettisville
Tudor Country Inn
419-445-2351

Piqua
Pickwinn Guesthouse
513-773-6137

Plain City
Yoders Spring Lake B&B
614-873-4489

Poland
Inn At The Green
216-757-4688-[Y--]

Pomeroy
Holly Hill Inn
800-445-8525

Port Clinton
Inn Of Chagrin Falls
419-734-2166

Old Island House Inn
419-734-2166

Powell
Buckeye B&B
614-548-4555

Put In Bay
Arlington House
419-285-2844

Bay House B&B
419-285-2822-[Y--]

Le Vent Passant
419-285-5511

Vineyard

2-174 ©*Inn & Travel Memphis, Tennessee*

Bold Name - *Description appears in other section*   *Ohio*

419-285-6181

Richfield
   Farnham Manor
   B&B
   216-237-7253

Ripley
   Baird House B&B
   513-392-4918

   Signal House
   513-392-1640

Rittman
   Crawford B&B
   216-925-1977

Rockbridge
   Glenlaurel
   800-908-REST

Sagamore Hills
   Inn At Brandywine
   Falls
   216-467-1812

Saint Clairsville
   My Fathers House
   B&B
   614-695-5440

Saint Paris
   Azorean B&B
   513-663-5448-[Y--]

Sandusky
   1890 Queen Anne
   B&B
   419-626-0391

   Big Oak
   419-627-0329

   Bogarts Corner
   B&B
   419-627-2707

   Pipe Creek B&B
   419-626-2067-[Y--]

   Red Gables B&B
   419-625-1189

   Wagners 1844 Inn
   419-626-1726-[G--]

Seaside
   10th Avenue B&B
   503-738-0643

Seville
   Colonial Manor

Sharon Center
   Hart & Mather

   Guest House
   800-352-2584

Sidney
   Great Stone Castle
   513-498-4728

Smithville
   Smithville B&B
   216-669-3333

Somerset
   Somertea B&B
   614-743-2909

South Amherst
   Birch Way Villa
   216-986-2090-[Y--]

South Charleston
   Houstonia B&B
   513-462-8855

Spring Valley
   3 B'S B&B
   513-862-4241

Stout
   One Hundred Mile
   House
   614-858-2984

Sugarcreek
   B&B Barn
   216-852-BEDS

Tahlequah
   B&B Tahlequah
   918-456-1309

Thornville
   Wal Mec Farm
   614-246-5450

Tiffin
   Zelkova Inn
   419-447-4043

Tipp City
   Willowtree Inn
   513-667-2957

Toledo
   Mansion View Inn
   419-244-5676

Troy
   Allen Villa B&B
   513-335-1181

   WH Allen Villa
   513-335-1181

Urbana
   At Home In Urbana
   800-800-0970

   Barnett Hill B&B
   513-653-7010

Vermilion
   Gilchrist Guest
   House
   216-967-1237

Walnut Creek
   Carlisle Village Inn
   216-893-3636

   Indiantree Farm
   216-893-2497

   Troyers Country
   View
   216-893-3284

Warren
   Shirlees Chambers
   216-372-1118

   Twin Maples B&B
   216-399-7768

Warsaw
   Mary Harris B&B
   614-824-4141

Waverly
   Governors Lodge
   614-947-2266

Waynesville
   **Sugar Camp
   Cottag**e
   513-382-6075-[Y--]

West Milton
   Locust Lane Farm
   B&B
   513-698-4743

West Union
   Murhyin Ridge Inn
   513-544-2263

Westerville
   Cormelias Corner
   B&B
   614-882-2678

Westserville
   Priscillas B&B
   614-882-3910

Williamsburg
   Lewis McKever
   Farmhouse B&B
   513-724-7044

Wilmington
   Cedar Hill B&B
   513-383-2525

   Grantstead Farm
   513-382-3548

   Historic South
   Street Manor
   513-382-7978

Wilmot
   Cranberry Cottage
   216-359-5171

Woodsfield
   Black Walnut Inn
   614-472-0002

Wooster
   Haueisens House
   216-345-8105

   Historic Overholt
   House
   330-263-6300

   Howey House
   330-264-8231-[Y--]

   Leila Belle Inn
   216-262-8866

   Wooster Inn

Worthington
   Am House
   614-885-5580

   Bufords
   614-885-5579

   Worthington Inn
   614-885-2600

Yellow Springs
   Morgan House B&B
   513-767-7509

Youngstown
   Boardman Manor
   216-758-2315

Zoar
   Cider Mill B&B
   216-874-3133-[Y--]

   Cowger House
   216-874-3542

   Garden Gate B&B
   216-874-2693

   Weaving House
   216-874-3318

Zoar Village
   Cobbler Shop Inn
   216-874-2600

©*Inn & Travel Memphis, Tennessee*

Ohio - Pennsylvania   **Bold Name** - *Description appears in other section*

Heartland Country Inn
216-768-9300

PENNSYLVANIA

Aaronsburg
Brick House B&B
814-349-8795

Adamstown
Adamstown Inn
800-594-4808

Airville
Spring House
717-927-6906-[Y--]

Akron
Boxwood Inn
717-859-3466

Allentown
Brennans B&B
610-395-0869

Coachouse
800-762-8680

Toby Valley Lodge
610-646-4893

Annville
Horseshoe Farm

Swatara Creek Inn
717-865-3259

Ardmore
Shamrock House B&B
610-642-2655

Atglen
Umble Rest
610-593-2274

Audubon
Blue Bonnet Farm
610-666-0361

Austin
Wavers Vag Hollow

Avella
Weatherbury Farm B&B
412-587-3763

Avondale
B&B Walnut Hill
215-444-3703

Springs Valley Inn
215-268-2597

Windswept B&B
610-869-2512

Bangor
Hurryback B&B
610-498-3121

Barto
Bally Spring Farm
610-845-7781

Beach Lake
Beach Lake Hotel
717-729-8239-[Y--]

East Shore House B&B
717-729-8523

Evergreen Lodge
717-729-8404

Bear Creek
Bischwind B&B
717-472-3820

Bedford
Bedford House
814-623-7171-[Y--]

Hist Chalybeate Springs
814-623-7792

Jean Bonnet Tavern
814-623-2250

Bellefonte
Aunt Junes B&B
814-355-1135

Emilys On Linn
814-355-4020

Yocums Victorian B&B
814-355-5100

Bendersville
Hist Paul Sorss Plantation
717-677-6688

Benton
Red Poppy B&B
717-925-5823

White House On North Mountain
717-925-2858

Berlin

Vietersburg Inn B&B
814-267-3696-[Y--]

Bernville
Sundays Mill Farm
610-488-7821

Bethlehem
Bethlehem Inn
610-867-4985

John Wiginton
610-868-4043

Wydnor Hall
610-867-6851

Biglerville
Mulberry Farm
717-334-5827-[G--]

Bird In Hand
Country Farm House
717-656-4625

Greystone Manor
717-393-4233-[Y--]

Village Inn Of Bird In Hand
800-914-2473-[G--]

Bloomsburg
Hotel Magee
717-784-3200

Inn At Turkey Hill
717-387-1500

Irondale Inn B&B
717-784-1977

Magees Main Street Inn
717-784-3200

Blossburg
John Deming House
717-638-3011

Mountain Laurel Inn
800-467-2698

Boalsburg
Colony House
814-466-2191

House On Top Of The Hill
814-466-2070

Springfield House
814-466-6290

Summer House B&B
814-466-3304

Boiling Springs
Allenberry Resort Inn
717-258-3211

Garmanhaus
717-258-3980

Highland House
717-258-3744

Boyertown
Chateau
610-367-5112

Little House
215-689-4814

Twin Turrets Inn
610-367-4513

Brackney
Indian Mountain Inn
717-663-2645-[G--]

Linger Longer
717-663-2844-[Y--]

Bradford
Fisher Homestead
814-368-3428

Brogue
Miller House
717-927-9646

Brookville
Bluebird Hollow
814-856-2858

Buck Hill Falls
Buck Hill Inn
800-233-8113

Buckingham
Inn Of Innisfree
215-297-8329

Mill Creek Farm B&B
800-562-1776

Buffalo Mills
Buffalo Lodge
814-623-2207

Cambridge Springs
Bethany Guest House
800-777-2046

Rider Hill Inn

2-176   ©Inn & Travel Memphis, Tennessee

Bold Name - *Description appears in other section*   **Pennsylvania**

814-398-4249

Canadensis
Brookview Manor B&B
717-595-2451

Dreamy Acres
717-595-7115-[Y--]

Laurel Grove Inn
717-595-7262

Merry Inn
800-858-4182

Nearbrook
717-595-3152

Overlook Inn
800-441-0177

Pine Knob Inn
800-327-8358-[Y--]

Pump House Inn
717-595-7501

Canton
Cantonian
717-673-4637

Rockgirt B&B
717-673-3930

Carbondale
Fern Hall
717-222-3676

Carlisle
Jacobs Resting Place
717-243-1766

Kellerhaus B&B
717-249-7481

Line Linousin Farm B&B
717-243-1281

Pheasant Field B&B

Cashtown
Historic Cashtown Inn (1797)
717-334-6566

Cedar Run
Cedar Run Inn
717-353-6241

Centre Hall
Laurels By The Mountain
814-238-1484

Nittany Meadow Farm
814-466-7550

Chadds Ford
Brandywine River Hotel
610-388-1200

Chadds Ford Inn
215-388-1473

Hedgerow B&B
215-388-6080

Chalfont
Butler Mill House
215-822-3582

Curley Mill Manor B&B
215-997-9015

Old Arcadia Inn
215-822-1818

Seven Oaks Farm B&B
215-822-2164

Simon Butler Mill House
215-822-3582

Chambersburg
Falling Spring Inn
717-267-3654

Shultz Victorian Mansion
717-263-3371

Christiana
Georgetown B&B
717-786-4570

Winding Glen Farm
610-593-5535

Churchtown
Churchtown Inn
800-637-4446

Foreman House B&B
215-445-6713

Inn At Twin Linden
215-445-7619

Clarendon
Timberline Lodge

Clarion
Clarion House B&B

814-226-4996

Clarion River Lodge
800-648-6743-[Y--]

Clark
Tara - A Country Inn
800-782-2803-[G--]

Clarks Summit
Linen Closet

Clearfield
Christopher Kratzner House
814-238-1484

Clearfield Country B&B
814-765-1712

Victorian Loft
800-464-1268-[Y--]

Clearville
Conifer Ridge Farm
814-784-3342

Coburn
Feathered Hook B&B
814-349-8757

Cochranton
Smith Mills Coach Stop
814-425-2377

Columbia
Columbian
800-422-5869

Confluence
Bali Hai Ranch
814-395-3353

Hannahouse Inn
814-395-5151

Riverrest B&B
814-395-3771

Rivers Edge B&B
814-395-5059

Cooksburg
Clarion River Lodge
800-648-6743-[Y--]

Gateway Lodge & Cabins
800-843-6862

Coudersport
Big Moores Run Lodge
814-647-5300

Cowansville
Garrotts B&B
412-545-2432

Cranberry
Cranberry B&B
412-776-1198

Cranesville
Carriage Hill Farm
814-774-2971

Cresco
Crescent Lodge
800-392-9400

Golden Goose Country Inn
717-595-3788

La Anna Guest House
717-676-4225

Dallas
Ponda-Rowland B&B
800-854-3286
[GQAR]

Danville
Pine Barn Inn
717-275-2071

Delaware Water Gap
Mountain House
717-424-2254-[Y--]

Shepard House
717-424-9779

Denver
Cocalico Creek B&B
717-336-0271

Dillsburg
Peter Wolford House
717-432-0757

Dilltown
Dillweed B&B
814-446-6465

Douglassville
Yellow House Hotel
610-689-9410

Dover
Danmar House
717-292-5128

Downingtown
Bradford Hills B&B

©Inn & Travel Memphis, Tennessee

Pennsylvania **Bold Name** - *Description appears in other section*

610-269-8207

Doylestown
Doylestown Inn
215-345-6610

Highland Farms
215-340-1354

Inn At Blueberry Hill
215-345-6200

Inn At Fordhook Farm
215-345-1766

Peace Valley B&B
215-230-7711

Pine Tree Farm
215-348-0632

Dunshore
Heritage Guest House
717-928-7354

Dushore
Cherry Mills Lodge
717-928-8978

Eagles Mere
Crestmont Inn
800-522-8767

Eagles Mere Inn
800-426-3273

Flora Villa Inne
717-525-3503

Shady Lane Lodge
717-523-3394

East Berlin
Bechtel Mansion Inn
800-873-2392-[Y--]

Lion & Lamb
717-259-9866

East McKeesport
Gate House B&B
412-824-9399

East Petersburg
George Zahn House
717-569-6026

East Stroudsburg
Inn At Meadowbrook
717-629-0296

Red Rock Inn

717-421-4976

East Towanda
Williamston Inn

Easton
Lafayette Inn
610-253-4500

Ebensburg
Noon-Collins Inn
814-472-4311

Edinboro
Raspberry House B&B
814-734-8997

Elizabethtown
Apples Abound Inn
717-367-3018

West Ridge Guest House
717-367-7783

Elizabethville
Inn At Elizabethville
717-362-3476-[Y--]

Elkland
Marigold Manor B&B
814-258-7144

Elm
Elm Country Inn
717-664-3623

Elverson
Rocky Side Farm
610-286-5362

Elysburg
Crab Apple Cove
717-672-2078

Emigsville
Emig Mansion
717-764-2226

Emlenton
Apple Alley B&B
412-867-9636

Barnard House B&B
412-867-2261

Whipple Tree Inn
412-867-9543

Emmanus
Leibert Gap Manor
610-967-1242

Macrobiotic B&B

610-967-4613

Epharata
Covered Bridge Inn
717-733-1592

Gerhart House B&B
717-733-0263-[Y--]

Ephrata
Clearview Farm B&B
717-733-6333

Doneckers of Ephrata
717-733-2231

Farmers Valley
717-354-0714

Guesthouse At Doneckers
717-789-9500

Hackmans Country Inn
717-733-3498

Historic Smithton
717-733-6094

Kimmell House
717-773-6358

Over Mountain Home
717-733-9611

Smithton
717-733-3333

Trout Run Inn
717-733-6135

Equinunk
Hills Twin Spruce Lodge
717-224-6044

Erie
Royal Acre Retreat

Spencer House B&B
800-890-7263-[G--]

Erwinna
Evermay On The Delaware
610-294-9100

Golden Pheasant Inn
610-294-9595

Isaac Stover House

610-294-8044

Everett
Newry Manor B&B
814-623-1250

Exton
Duling-Kurtz House
610-524-1830-[Y--]

Fairfield
Historic Fairfield Inn
717-642-5410

Fairfiled
Old Barn B&B
717-642-5711

Falls
Taylor Sisters B&B
717-388-6335

Farmington
Mount Summit Inn
412-438-8594

Fayetteville
Herb Cottage
717-352-7733

Fogelsville
Glasbern
610-285-4723-[Y--]

Fort Loudon
Richmond Hill Resort
717-369-2673

Fort Washington
Quaker Manor House

Franklin
Lamberton House
814-432-7908

Quo Vadis House Franklin B&B
814-432-4208

Freeport
Hobby Horse Farm
412-295-3123

Gap
Ben Mar Tourist Farm
717-768-3309

Fassitt Mansion
800-653-4139

Gardenville
Maplewood Farm
215-766-0477

2-178 ©*Inn & Travel Memphis, Tennessee*

Bold Name - Description appears in other section   *Pennsylvania*

Gardners
  Goose Chase B&B
  717-528-8877

Germantown
  Germantown B&B
  215-848-1375

Gettysburg
  Altland House
  717-259-9535

  Appleford Inn
  717-337-1711

  Baladerry Inn
  800-220-0025

  Bechtel Mansion Inn
  800-873-2392-[G--]

  Beechmont Inn
  800-553-7009-[G--]

  Brafferton Inn
  717-337-3423-[G--]

  Brierfield B&B
  800-247-2216

  Dobbin House Tavern
  717-334-2100

  Doubleday Inn
  717-334-9119

  Ends Of Gettysburg
  717-334-0050

  Farnsworth House
  717-334-8838

  Goose Chase
  717-528-8877

  Herr Tavern & Publik House
  717-334-4332

  Hist Farnsworth House
  717-334-8838

  Keystone Inn
  717-337-3888

  Mulberry Farm B&B
  717-334-5827-[G--]

  Old Appleford Inn
  717-337-1711-[Y--]

  Swinns Lodging
  717-334-5255

  Tannery B&B
  717-334-2454-[G--]

  Tiber House B&B
  717-334-0493

  Twin Elms
  717-334-4520

Gibsonia
  Sun & Cricket B&B
  412-443-8558

Gillett
  Carls Oldroyd Gillett House
  717-596-4428

Girard
  Victorian Inn
  814-774-2221

Glen Mills
  Crier In The Country
  610-358-2411

  Sweetwater Farms
  610-459-4711

Glen Moore
  Conestoga Horse B&B
  610-458-8535

Glen Rock
  Dogwood At Spotwood Farm
  717-235-6610

  Glen Rock Mill In
  717-235-5918

Gordonville
  Ebys Pequea Tourist Farm
  717-768-3615

  Osceola Mill House
  717-768-3758

Gouldsboro
  Country Surrey Inn
  717-842-2081

Greencastle
  Phaeton Farm B&B
  717-597-8656

  Welsh Run Inn
  717-328-9506

Greensburg
  Huntland Farm B&B
  412-834-8483-[Y--]

  Mountain View Inn
  412-834-5300

Greentown
  Halls Inn
  717-676-3429

  Hemlock Grove B&B
  717-676-4511

Greenville
  Phillips 1890 House
  412-588-4169

Grove City
  Snow Goose Inn
  412-458-4644

Gwynedd
  William Penn Inn
  215-699-9272

Halifax
  Bisking Family Farm B&B
  717-362-4136

  Inn At Elizabethville
  717-362-3476-[G--]

Hallstead
  Corner Inn

  Log Cabin B&B
  717-879-4167

Hanover
  Beck Mill Farm

  Beechmont Inn
  800-553-7009-[G--]

  Chestnut Hill Inn B&B
  717-632-8514

  Country View Acres
  717-637-8992

Harmony
  Neff House B&B
  412-452-7512

Harrisburg
  Abide With Me B&B
  717-236-5873

  Hen-Apple B&B
  717-838-8282-[G--]

Harrisville
  Gillray B&B

  412-735-2274

Hartleton
  Col Thomas Hartley Inn
  717-922-4477

Hartsville
  Bittersweeet Farm B&B
  215-672-2022

Harveys Lake
  Duck Inn
  717-639-2605

Hawley
  Academy Street B&B
  717-226-3430-[G--]

  Morning Glorys
  717-226-0644

  Old Mill Stream Inn
  717-265-1337

  Settlers Inn
  800-833-8527-[Y--]

Hershey
  Gibsons B&B
  717-534-1035

  Hen-Apple B&B
  717-838-8282-[G--]

  Horetskys Tourist Home
  717-533-5783

  Pinehurst Inn
  800-743-9140

Hesston
  Aunt Susies Country Vacations
  814-658-3638

Hickory
  Shady Elms Farm B&B
  412-356-7755

Hillsgrove
  Tannery B&B
  717-924-3505

Holicong
  Ash Mill Farm
  215-794-5373-[Y--]

  Barley Sheaf Farm
  215-794-5104

Hollidaysburg

©*Inn & Travel Memphis, Tennessee*   2-179

Pennsylvania **Bold Name** - *Description appears in other section*

Brun Run Estate

Hoenstines B&B
814-695-0632

Jackson Inn
814-695-1232

Holtwood
Country Cottage B&B
717-284-2559

Honesdale
Hotel Wayne
717-253-3290

Olivers B&B
717-253-4533

Howard
Curtinview
814-238-1484

Huntingdon
Yoders
814-643-3221

Intercourse
Carriage Corner B&B
800-209-3059

Jamestown
Villamayer
412-932-5194

Willowood Inn
412-932-3866

Jersey Shore
Sommerville Farms B&B
717-398-2368

Ye Olde Library B&B

Jim Thorpe
Harry Packer Mansion
717-325-8566

Hotel Switzerland
717-325-4563

Inn At Jim Thorpe
717-325-2599-[Y--]

The Dimmick House
717-325-2533

Tiffanys Grand Victoria
717-325-8260

Victoria Anns B&B
717-325-8107

Johnstown
Meadowbrook School B&B
814-539-1756

Kane
Kane Manor Country Inn
800-837-6815

Kempton
Hawk Mountain Inn
610-756-4424

Kennett Square
B&B At Lighted Holly
610-444-9246

Buttonwood Farms
610-444-0278

Longwood Inn
610 444-3515

Meadow Spring Farm
610-444-3903

Red Willos Farm
610-444-0518

Scarlett House B&B
610-444-9592

Kintersville
Bucksville House
610-847-8948

Lightfarm B&B
610-847-3276

Kinzer
Groff Tourist Farm House
717-442-8223

Sycamore Haven Farm House
717-442-4901

Kirkwood
White Rock Farm B&B
717-529-6744

Knox
Mitchells Pond
814-797-1690

Kutztown
Around The World B&B

610-683-8885

Ladenberg
Daybreak Farm B&B
610-255-0282

Tiptree Lodge
610-274-0240

Lahaska
Golden Plough Inn
215-794-4004

Peddlers Village Lodging

Lampeter
Australian Walkabout Inn
717-464-0707-[G--]

B&B - The Manor
717-464-9564

Lancaster
90 Greenfield
717-299-5964

Australian Walkabout Inn
717-464-0707

Buona Notte B&B
717-295-2597-[Y--]

Candlelite Inn
717-299-6005

Creekside Inn
717-687-0333

Gardens Of Eden
717-393-5179

Groff Farm Abend Ruhe
717-687-0221

Hollinger House
717-464-3050

Kings Cottage
800-747-8717-[Y--]

Lime Valley Cottage
717-687-6118

Lincoln Haus Inn B&B
717-392-9412

Maison Rouge B&B
717-399-3033

Meadowview Guest House
717-299-4017

New Life Homestead B&B
717-396-8928

Nisslys Olde Home Inn
717-392-2311

O'Flahertys Dingeldein House
800-779-7765

Patchwork Inn
717-293-9078

Witmers Tavern Historic 1725 Inn
717-299-5305-[Y--]

Landenberg
Cornerstone B&B
610-274-2143

Cornerstone B&B
610-274-2143

Daybreak Farm B&B
610-255-0282

Langhorne
Gertrude Garber

Lansford
Liberty Hill B&B
717-645-2346

Laughlintown
Ligonier Country Inn
412-238-3651

Lebanon
Zinns Mill Homestead
717-272-1513

Leesport
Loom Room
610-926-3217-[Y--]

Leetsdale
The Whistlestop B&B
412-251-0852

Leola
Millport Manor
717-627-0644

Turtle Hill Road B&B
717-656-6163

Lewisburg

2-180   ©Inn & Travel Memphis, Tennessee

Bold Name - *Description appears in other section*   *Pennsylvania*

Brookpark Farm B&B
717-523-0220

Inn At Fiddlers Tract
800-523-8200-[Y--]

Lewisburg Hotel
717-523-1216

Pineapple Inn
717-524-6200-[Y--]

Liberty
Hill Top Haven
717-324-2608

Ligonier
Grant House B&B
412-238-5135

Townhouse
412-238-5451

Lima
Hamanassett B&B
610-459-3000

Linfield
Shearer Elegance
610-495-7429

Lititz
Alden House
800-584-0753-[Y--]

Banner House B&B
717-626-REST

Carter Run Inn
717-626-8807

Dots B&B
717-627-0483

General Sutter Inn
717-626-2115-[Y--]

Sleepy Mill Farm
717-626-6629

Spahrs Century Farm B&B
717-354-4374

Swiss Woods B&B
800-594-8018

Little Britian
Little Britian Manor
717-529-2862

Lock Haven
Hoffmans Victorian B&B

800-237-8688

Partnership House B&B
717-748-1990

Rogers B&B
717-748-8688

Victorian Inn
800-237-8688

Loganton
Webb Farm B&B
717-725-3591

Loganville
Greystone B&B
717-428-3376

Lumberville
1740 House
215-297-5661

Black Bass Hotel
215-297-5770-[Y--]

Kirk House
215-297-5141

Macungie
Sycamore Inn
610-966-5177

Mahanoy City
Kaier Mansion
717-773-3040

Malvern
Blackberry Hill
610-647-0554

Eaglesmere
610-296-9696-[Y--]

Genearl Warren Inne
610-296-3637

Manheim
Country Pines Farm & Cottage
717-665-5478

Herr Farmhouse Inn
800-584-0753-[Y--]

Jonde Lane Farm
717-665-4231

Landis Guest Farm
717-898-7028

Manheim Manor
717-664-4168

Penn Valley Farm &

Inn
717-898-7386

Rose Manor
717-664-4932

Stauffers Country Home
717-665-7327

Stone Haus Farm
717-653-5819

Wengers B&B
717-665-3862

Mansfield
Crossroads B&B
717-662-7008

Marietta
Olde Fogie Farm
717-426-3992

Railroad House B&B Inn
717-426-4141

River Inn
717-426-2290

Vogt Farm B&B
717-653-4810

Mars
Strawberry Point B&B
412-935-4628

Maytown
Three Center Square Inn
717-426-3036

McClure
Mount Dale Farm
717-658-3536

McElhatten
Restless Oak B&B
717-769-6035

McKeesport
Easlers B&B
412-673-1133

Guest Home
412-751-7143

Meadville
Fountainside B&B
814-337-7447

Mechanicsville
Stoneymead
215-794-8081

Mendenhall
Fairville Inn
610-388-5900

Mendenhall Inn

Mendnehall
Le Clos Normand
610-347-2123

Mercer
Magoffin Guest House
412-662-4611-[Y--]

Stranahan House
412-662-4516

Mercersburg
Fox Run Inn
717-328-3570

Maplebrow B&B
717-328-3172

Mercersburg Inn
717-328-5231

Steiger House
717-328-5757

Mertztown
Blair Creek Inn
610-682-6700

Longswamp B&B
610-682-6197

Middlebury Center
Woods Rustic Inn
717-376-2332

Milford
Black Walnut Inn
800-866-9870

Cliff Park Inn
800-225-6535

Harford Inn
717-296-7757

Pine Hill Farm B&B
717-296-7395

Tom Quick Inn
717-296-6514

Vines
717-296-6775

Milheim
Milheim Hotel
814-349-5994

©*Inn & Travel Memphis, Tennessee*   2-181

Pennsylvania **Bold Name** - *Description appears in other section*

Millersburg
Victorian Manor Inn
717-692-3511

Millerstown
Sunbury Street B&B
717-589-7932

Millersville
Greenlawn B&B
717-872-7453

Walnut Hill B&B
717-872-2283

Millrift
Bonny Bank
717-491-2250

Mohnton
Windy Hill B&B
610-775-2755

Montoursville
Carriage House At Stonegate
717-433-4340-[Y--]

Montrose
Montrose House
717-278-1124-[Y--]

Montville
Mountville Antiques B&B
717-285-5956

Mount Bethel
Elvern Country Lodge
610-588-7922

Mount Gretna
Mount Gretna Inn
717-964-3234

Mount Joy
Betty & Abrham Groff
717-653-2048

Brenneman Farm B&B
717-653-4213

Cameron Estate Inn
717-653-1773

Cedar Hill Farm B&B
717-653-4655

Chrisken Inn
717-653-2717

Country Stay B&B
717-367-5167

Donegal Mills Inn
717-653-2168

Green Acres Guest Farm
717-653-4028

Hillside Farm B&B
717-653-6697-[Y--]

Nolt Farm Guest House
717-653-4192

Old Square Inn
717-653-4525

Rocky Acre Farm
717-653-4449

Mount Pocono
Country Road B&B

Farmhouse BNB
717-839-0796-[Y--]

Hampton Court Inn
717-839-2119

Muncy
Bodine House
717-546-8949-[Y--]

McCarty House Inn
717-546-5005

Walton House B&B
717-546-8114

Myerstown
Tulpehocken Manor Inn
717-392-2311

Navron
Jeric Inn
610-445-6840

Nazareth
Classic Victorian B&B
610-759-8276

Inn At Heyers Mill
610-759-6226

New Albany
Waltmans B&B
717-363-2295

New Berlin
Inn At Olde New Berlin
717-966-0321

New Bloomfield
Tressler House B&B
717-582-2914

New Cumberland
Farm Fortune
717-774-2683

New Holland
Smucker Farm Guest House
717-354-4374

New Hope
Aaron Burr Home
215-862-2343

Ash Mill Farm
215-794-5373-[G--]

Backstreet Inn
800-841-1874

Bucks County B&B
215-862-3390

Centre Bridge Inn
215-862-9139

Fox & Hound
215-862-5082

Hollileif B&B
215-598-3100-[G--]

Holly Hedge B&B
215-862-3136

Hotel du Village
215-862-9911

Ingham Woods B&B
215-862-2227

Inn At Phillips Mill
215-862-9919

Lexington House
215-794-0811

Logan Inn
215-862-2300-[Y--]

Mansion Inn
215-862-1231

Pam Minfords Hacienda
800-272-2078

Rambouillet
215-862-3136

Riverside B&B

215-862-0216

Umpleby House Inn
215-862-3936

Wedgewood Inn Collection
215-862-2570-[Y--]

Whitehall Inn
800-37 WHITE-[Y--]

New Oxford
Adams Apple
717-624-3488

New Tripoli
Around The World B&B
610-298-3365

New Wilmington
Behms B&B
412-946-8641

Gabriels B&B
412-946-3136

Tavern
412-946-2020

Newfoundland
White Cloud Sylvan Retreat
717-676-3162

Newtown
Brick Hotel
215-860-8313

Hollielf
215-598-3100

Temperance House
800-446-0474

Ye Olde Temperance House
215-860-0474

Newtown Square
Fifers Folly
610-353-3366

North East
South Shore Inn
814-725-1888

Village Inn
814-725-5522

North Wales
Joseph Ambler Inn
215-362-7500-[Y--]

Oakmont

2-182 ©Inn & Travel Memphis, Tennessee

Bold Name - *Description appears in other section* *Pennsylvania*

The Inn At Oakmont
412-828-6079

Orbisonia
Salvinos Guest House
814-447-5616

Orrtanna
Hickory Bridge Farm
717-642-5261

Orwigsburg
Patchwork Farm B&B

Ottsville
Auldridge Mead
610-847-5842

Farnkenfield Farm B&B
215-847-2771

Frankenfield Farm
610-847-2771

Oxford
Hersheys Log House
610-932-9257

John Hayes House
610-932-5347

Log House B&B
610-932-9257

Stonewall B&B
610-032-2924

Palmyra
Hen-Apple B&B
717-838-8282-[G--]

Shepherds Acres
717-838-5899

Paradise
Bart 896 B&B
717-786-7479

Creekside Inn B&B
717-687-0333

Maple Lane Farm
717-687-7479-[Y--]

Neffdale Farm
717-687-7837

Rayba Acres Farm
717-687-6729

Verdant View Farm

717-687-7353

Patton
Nationality House
814-674-2225

Peach Bottom
Pleasant Grove Farm
717-548-3100

Pennsylvania Furnace
Graysville Tollhouse
814-238-1484

Penryn
Newport Inn Of Penryn B&B
717-665-7413

Philadelphia
Abigail Adams B&B
215-546-7336

Academy Street B&B
717-226-3430-[G--]

Antique Row B&B
215-592-7802

Bag & Baggage B&B
215-546-3807

Chestnut Hill Hotel
215-242-5905

Eaglesmere
610-296-9696-[Y--]

Earl Grey B&B
215-732-8356

Hen-Apple B&B
717-838-8282-[G--]

Hotel La Reserve
215-735-0582

Independence Park Inn
800-624-2988-[Y--]

La Reserve
215-735-0582

Penns View Inn
800-331-7634

Shippen Way Inn
215-627-7266

Society Hill Hotel
215-925-1919-[Y--]

Steele Away B&B
215-242-0722

Thomas Bond House
800-845-BOND-[Y--]

Village Guest House B&B
215-755-9770

Phoenixville
Amsterdam B&B
610-983-9620

Pine Bank
Coles Log Cabin B&B
412-627-9151

Pine Grove
Forge
717-345-8349

Pine Grove Mills
General Potter Farm
814-238-1484

Split Pint Farm House B&B
814-238-2028

Pittsburgh
Columbus Inn
412-471-5420

Grandview Inn
412-431-3344

La Fleur B&B
412-921-8588

Oakwood
412-835-9565

Prioty-A City Inn
412-231-3338-[Y--]

Shadyside B&B
412-683-6501

The Whistlestop B&B
412-251-0852

Plumsteadville
Plumsteadville Inn
215-766-7500

Widow Browns Inn
215-766-7500

Pocopson
Lenape Springs B&B

610-793-2266

Point Pleasant
Carriage House
215-297-5367

Carriage House At Walnut Hill Farm
215-297-5367

Tattersall Inn
215-297-8233

Port Clinton
Union House
610-562-4076

Port Matilda
Martha Furnace House
814-692-4393

Potters Mills
General Potter Farm
814-238-1484

Pottstown
Coventry Forge Inn
610-469-6222

Fairway Farm B&B
610-326-1315

Quakertown
Sign Of The Sorrel Horse
215-536-4651

Quarryville
Bright Pine Hollow Farm
717-299-4501

Leroy & Marian Sensnig B&B
717-786-3128

Runnymede Farm Guest House
717-786-3625

Reading
El Shaddai
610-929-1341-[Y--]

Hunter House
610-374-6608-[Y--]

Inn At Centre Park
800-447-1094

Red Lion
Red Lion B&B
717-244-4739

Regent Square

©Inn & Travel Memphis, Tennessee

Pennsylvania   **Bold Name** - *Description appears in other section*

Bianconis B&B
412-731-2252

Reinholds
Brownstone Corner B&B
215-484-4460-[Y--]

Rexmont
Dishongs B&B
717-273-5065

Richlandtown
Richlandtown Hotel
215-536-6239

Ridgway
Faircroft B&B
814-776-2539

Post House
814-772-2441

Riegelsville
Riegelsville Hotel
610-749-2469

Villa Richard
610-749-2094

Roaring Spring
Spring Garden Farm B&B
814-224-2569

Rockwood
Carousel Inn
814-926-2666

Merchants Hotel
814-926-3473

Trenthoues Inn
814-352-8492

Ronks
Benners Country Home
717-299-2615

Calamus Creek Inn
717-687-8590

Candlelite Inn B&B
717-299-6005

Cherry-Crest Hist Dairy Farm
717-687-6844

Floys Guest House
717-687-6670

Kreiders Tourist Farm
717-687-7001

Wee Three Haus
717-687-8146

Saint Marys
Old Charm B&B
814-834-8429

Town House Inn
814-781-1556

Saint Thomas
Heavenly Scent
717-369-5882

Rices White House Inn
717-369-4224

Saxonburg
Main Stay
412-352-9363

Saxton
Weavers Ridge Resort B&B
814-635-3730

Sayre
Guthrie Inn
717-888-7711

Paetzell Haus B&B
717-888-4748-[Y--]

Park Place B&B
717-888-5779

Scenery Hill
Century Inn
412-945-6600

Schaefferstown
Franklin House
717-949-3398

Schellsburg
Bedfords Covered Bridge Inn
814-733-4093

Country Spun Farm B&B
717-428-1162

Scottdale
Pine Woods Acres
412-887-5404

Zephyr Glen B&B
412-887-6577

Sellersville
Almont Inn
215-794-5373

Sellingsgrove
Blue Lion Inn
717-374-2929-[Y--]

Sewickley
Greissingers Farm
412-741-2597

Sharon
Tara - A Country Inn
800-782-2803-[Y--]

Shartlesville
Haags Hotel
610-488-6692

Shavertown
Wee House B&B
717-696-4602

Shawnee On The Delaware
Eagle Rock Lodge
717-421-2139

Shippensburg
Field & Pine B&B
717-776-7179

McLean Houes
717-530-1390

Thornbury Farm
717-776-5617

Wilmar Manor
717-532-3784

Shunk
Shunk Kaiser Frazer B&B
717-924-3070

Sigel
Discoveries B&B
814-752-2632

Slippery Rock
Applebutter Inn
412-794-1844-[Y--]

Smethport
Blackberry Inn
814-887-7777

Smoketown
Homestead Lodging
717-393-6927

Old Road Guest Home
717-393-8182

Smoketown Village Home
717-393-5975

Solebury
Holly Hedge Estate
215-862-3136

Somerset
Bayberry Inn
814-445-8471

Glades Pike Inn
814-443-4978

Heart Of Somerset B&B
814-445-6782

Inn At Georgian Place
814-443-1043

Somerset Country Inn
814-443-1005

South Sterling
French Manor Serling Inn
800-523-8200

Spring Mills
General Potter Farm
814-238-1484

Spruce Creek
Cedar Hill Farm/ Spruce Creek
814-238-1484

Starlight
Inn At Starlight Lake
800-248-2519

Starrucca
Matta Streamside Manor
717-727-2330

Neithercott Inn
717-727-2211

State College
Carnegie House
800-229-5033-[G--]

Vincent Douglas House
814-237-4490

Strasburg
Decoy B&B
717-687-8585

Limestone Inn
717-687-8392

PJs Guest Home

2-184   ©*Inn & Travel Memphis, Tennessee*

Bold Name - *Description appears in other section*   *Pennsylvania*

717-687-8800

Siloan
717-687-6231

Strasburg Village Inn
800-541-1055-[Y--]

Stroudsburg
Academy Hill House
717-476-6575

Stroudsmoor Country Inn
717-421-6431

The Peetham
717-629-0483

Sumneytown
Kaufman House
215-234-4181

Susquehanna
April Valley B&B
717-756-2688

Swiftwater
Antlers Lodge
717-839-7243

Britannia Country Inn
717-839-7243

Terre Hill
Apple Blossom Inn
215-445-9466

Thompson
Burchman House
717-727-3200

Jefferson Inn
717-727-2625

Thorndale
Pheasant Hollow Farm
610-384-4694

Thornton
Pace One Restaurant Inn
610-459-3702

Three Springs
Aguhwich House
814-447-3027

Tidioute
Tidioute Friendly Eagle B&B
814-484-7130

Tinicum Township
Auldridge Mead
215-847-5842

Titusville
McMullen House
814-827-1592

Topton
Victorian Inn B&B
610-682-6846-[Y--]

Towanda
Victorian Guest House
717-265-6972

Transfer
Williman Jersey Farm
412-962-2556

Troy
Silver Oakleaf B&B
717-297-4315

Tunkhannock
Andersen Acres

Annmaries Gazebo
717-836-5730

Sharpes House
717-836-4900

Tyler Hill
Tyler Hill B&B
717-224-6418

Tyrone
Arch Springs Farm
814-238-1484

Eden Croft
814-238-1484

White House B&B
814-684-5155

Union Dale
B&B Carousel
717-679-2600

Hollymount B&B
717-222-4686

Wiffy Bog Farm
717-222-9865

Upper Black Eddy
Bridgeton House
610-982-5856

Driftin Del

Indian Rock Inn

610-982-5300

Tara
610-982-5457

Volant
Candleford Inn
412-533-4497

Walnutport
Anchor Inn
610-767-0575

Walusing
Wyalusing Hotel
717-746-1204

Warfordsburg
Buck Valley Ranch
717-294-3759

Warminster
Apple Bucket Country Inn
215-674-1799

Warren
Jefferson House & Pub
814-724-2268

Willows
814-726-2667

Warrington
The Warrington
800-333-1827

Washington
Bird Garden B&B
412-745-8381

Washington Crossing
Inn To The Woods B&B
800-982-7619

Woodhill Farms Inn
215-493-1974

Waterford
Altheim B&B
814-796-6446

Waterville
English Center B&B
717-634-3104

Point House
717-753-8707

Wayne
Wayne Hotel
800-962-5850

Waynesburg

Green Gables
412-627-4391

Wellsboro
Auntie Ms B&B
717-724-5771

B&B Stop Light
717-724-4202

Four Winds B&B
717-724-6141

Foxfire B&B
717-724-5175

Kaltenbachs B&B
717-724-4954

Penn Wells Hotel
717-724-2111

West Alexander
Saints Rest B&B
412-484-7950

West Chester
1810 House of Marshalltown
610-430-6013

Bankhouse B&B
610-344-7388

Barn
610-436-4544

Crooked Windsor
610-692-4896

Dilworthtown Inn
215-399-1390

Faunbrook B&B
215-436-5788

Franklin House
610-696-1665

Highland Farm B&B
610-610-7026

Highland Manor
215-686-6251

Marshalton Inn
215-692-4367

Monument House
610-793-2986

Quarry House
610-793-1725

Sadonjaree Farm
610-793-1838

©Inn & Travel Memphis, Tennessee   2-185

Pennsylvania - South Dakota   **Bold Name** - *Description appears in other section*

Victorian Guest House
610-692-5067

Whitewing Farm B&B
610-388-2664

Wexford
Coreys
412-935-5292

White Haven
Redwood House
717-443-7186

White Horse
Fassit Mansion B&B
717-442-3139

Williamsport
Carriage House At Stonegate
717-433-4340-[G--]

Reighard House
717-326-3593-[Y--]

Snyder Victorian House
717-326-0411

Thomas Lightfoot Inn
717-326-6396

Willow Street
Apple Bin Inn
800-584-0753

Cooks Guest House
717-464-3273

Country View Tourist Home
717-464-4083

Green Gables B&B
717-464-5546

Woodbury
Waterside Inn A B&B
814-766-3776

Woodbury Inn
814-766-3647

Woodward
Woodward Inn
814-349-8118

Wrightstown
Aberdare B&B
215-598-3896

Hollileif B&B
215-598-3100-[Y--]

Wrightsville
1854 House
717-252-4643

Roundtop B&B
717-252-3169

Wycombe
Wycombe Inn
215-598-7000

York
Bechtel Mansion Inn
717-259-760

Beechmont Inn
800-553-7009-[G--]

Briarwold B&B
717-252-4619

Inn At Mundis Mills
717-755-2002-[Y--]

Smyser-Bair House
717-854-3411

Sunstar B&B
717-755-7511

Twin Brook Inn
717-757-5384

Zelienople
Benvenue Manor
412-452-1710

SOUTH DAKOTA

Artesian
Rundell House
605-238-5855

Brookings
Beal House
605-692-6889

Canova
Skoglund Farm
605-247-3445-[Y--]

Canton
Kennedy Rose Inn
605-987-2834

Tree Top Retreat
605-987-4251-[Y--]

Chamberlain
Riverview Ridge
605-734-6084

Custer
Bavarian Inn
605-673-2802

Custer Mansion B&B
605-673-3333

Hartman Haven B&B
605-673-2714

Higgen Fortune B&B
605-666-4744

Rock Crest Lodge
605-673-4323

Sylvan Lake Resort
605-574-2561

De Smet
Prairie House B&B
605-854-9131

Deadwood
Adams House
605-578-3877

Freeman
Farmers Inn
605-925-7580

Hermosa
Bunkhouse B&B
605-342-5462

JD Guest Ranch B&B
800-261-3329

Hill City
Deerview B&B
605-574-4204

Heart Of The Hills
605-574-2704

Palmer Gulch Lodge
605-574-2525

The Homestead
605-574-4226

Hot Springs
Cascade Ranch B&B
605-745-3397

Villa Theresa Guest House
605-745-4633

Huron

Fair City B&B
605-352-1470

Interior
Prariise Edge B&B
605-433-5441

Keystone
Elk Haven Resort
605-666-4856

Triple R Dude Ranch
605-666-4605

Lemmon
The 49'er
701-376-3280

Martin
Cross Roads Inn
605-685-1070

Milesville
Fitch Farms
605-544-3227

FLying Horse
605-642-1633

Murdo
Landmark Country Inn
605-669-2846

Okaton
Roghari Herefords B&B
605-669-2529

Phillip
Thorsons Homestead
605-859-2120

Pierre
Cow Creek Lodge
605-264-5450

Spring Creek Resort
605-224-8336

Rapid City
Abigails Garden
605-343-6530

Audries Cranbury Corner B&B
605-342-7788-[Y--]

B&B Domivara
605-574-4207

Black Forest Inn
605-574-2000

Carriage House Inn

©*Inn & Travel Memphis, Tennessee*

Bold Name - *Description appears in other section*   **South Dakota - West Virginia**

605-343-6415

H Bar D Ranch
605-341-7580

Seneca
  Rainbow Lodge
  605-436-6795

Sioux Falls
  Pine Crest Inn
  605-336-3530

Spearfish
  Christensens
  Country Home
  605-642-2859

  Kelly Inn
  605-642-7795

Vermillion
  Goebel House B&B
  605-624-6691

Webster
  Lakeside Farm
  605-486-4430

Yankton
  Mulberry Inn
  605-665-7116-[Y--]

WEST VIRGINIA

Aurora
  Cabin Lodge
  304-735-3563

  Mountain Village
  Inn

Bartow
  Tranquility B&B
  304-456-3430

Beaver
  House Of Grandview
  304-763-4381

Beckwith
  Woodcrest B&B
  304-574-3870

Berkeley Springs
  Aarons Acre
  304-258-4079

  Aron's Acre
  304-258-4079

  Country Inn
  800-822-6630

  Folkstone B&B

304-258-3743

Glens B&B
304-258-GLEN

Highlawn Inn
304-258-5700

Manor
304-258-1552

Marias Garden &
Inn
304-258-2021

On The Banks 1875
Guesthouse
304-258-2134

Bramwell
  Bluestone Inn
  304-248-7402

  Perry House
  304-248-8145

  The Park House
  304-248-7252

  Three Oaks & A
  Quilt
  304-248-8316

Buchannon
  Henderson House
  B&B
  304-472-1611

  Post Mansion B&B
  304-472-8959

Buckhannon
  Deer Park B&B
  800-296-8430

Burlington
  **Hendersons
  Heritage Herbs
  B&B**
  304-289-5100-[Y--]

  Shellys Homestead
  304-289-3941

Caldwell
  Greenbrier River Inn
  304-647-5652

Cass
  Cass Inn
  304-456-3464

Charles Town
  Carriage Inn
  304-728-8003

Cottonwood Inn
304-725-3371

**Gilbert House Of
Middleway**
304-725-0637-[G--]

Hillbrook Inn
304-725-4223

Charleston
  Brass Pineapple
  B&B
  304-344-0748

Cheat Mountain
  Last Frontier
  304-456-4281

Crawley
  Oak Knoll B&B
  304-392-6903

Davis
  Bright Morning
  304-259-5119

  Twisted Thistle
  B&B
  304-259-5389

Elkins
  Cheat River Lodge
  304-636-2301

  Lincoln Crest B&B
  304-636-8460

  Marians Guest
  House
  304-636-9883

  Post House
  304-636-1792

  Retreat At Buffalo
  Run
  304-636-2960

  Tunnel Mountain
  B&B
  304-636-1684

  Wayside Inn B&B
  304-636-1618

Fairmont
  Acacia House
  304-367-1000

  Tichnells Tourist
  House
  304-366-3811

Fayetteville
  Foxglove B&B

304-574-1751

Morris Harvey
House B&B
304-574-1179

White Horse B&B
304-574-1400

Franklin
  Candlelight Inn B&B
  304-358-3025

Gauley Bridge
  Three Rivers Inn
  304-632-2121

Gerrardstown
  Prospect Hill B&B
  304-229-3346-[Y--]

Glen Ferris
  Glen Ferris Inn
  304-632-1111

Grandview
  House of Grandview
  B&B
  304-763-4381

Greenville
  Creekside
  304-832-6420

Harpers Ferry
  Between Two Rivers
  304-535-2768

  Filmore Street B&B
  304-337-8633

  Harpers Ferry Guest
  House
  304-535-6955

  Hilltop House
  800-338-8319

  Lee Stonewall Inn
  304-535-2532

  Ranson-Armory
  House B&B
  304-535-2142

  The View
  304-535-2688

Harrisville
  North Bend Pines
  B&B
  304-643-2102

Helvetia
  Beekeeper Inn
  304-924-6435

©*Inn & Travel Memphis, Tennessee*   2-187

West Virginia - Wisconsin *Bold Name - Description appears in other section*

Hillsboro
 Cranberry Mountain Lodge
 800-CALL-WVA

 Current
 304-653-4722

 Yew Mountain Lodge B&B
 800-Call-WVA

Hinton
 Jones House B&B
 304-466-2108

Huntersville
 Carriage House Inn
 304-799-6706

Huntington
 Heritage Station
 304-523-6373

Huttonsville
 Cardinal Inn
 304-335-6149

 Hutton House B&B
 800-234-6701-[Y--]

Jane Lew
 West Fork Inn
 304-745-4893

Lewisburg
 General Lewis
 304-645-2600

 Hide Away B&B
 304-645-7718

 Lynn's Inn B&B
 304-645-2003

 Minnie Manor
 304-647-4096

Logan
 Manor Haus
 304-752-5824

Lost Creek
 Crawfords Country Corner
 304-745-3017

Lost River
 Guesthouse
 304-897-5707

Marlinton
 Jerico B&B
 304-799-6241

 Old Marlinton Hotel
 304-799-6377

Martinsburg
 Aspen Hall
 304-263-4385

 Boydville Inn At Martinsburg
 304-263-1448

 Dunn Country Inn
 304-263-8646

Mathias
 Valley View Farm
 304-897-5229

Moorefield
 Hickory Hill Farm
 304-538-2415

 McMechen House Inn
 304-538-2417

Morgantown
 Chestnut Ridge School B&B
 304-598-2262

 Maxwell B&B
 304-594-3041

New Creek
 Maplewood Manor
 800-225-5982

Orlando
 Friend Sheep Farm B&B
 304-462-7075

 Kilmarnock Farms
 304-452-8319

Pence Springs
 Riverside Inn
 304-445-7469

Petersburg
 Smoke Hole Lodge

Pipestem
 Walnut Grove Inn
 304-446-6119

Princeton
 Sans Souci
 304-425-4804

Prosperity
 Prosperity Farmhouse
 304-255-4245

Romney
 Hampshire House 1884
 304-822-7171-[Y--]

Saint Albans
 Chilton House
 304-722-2918

Salty Fork
 Elk River Touring Center
 304-572-3771

Shepherdstown
 Bavarian Inn & Lodge
 304-876-2551

 Bellvue B&B
 304-876-2887

 Fuss n' Feathers
 304-876-6469

 Little Inn/Yellow Brick Bank
 304-876-2208

 Mecklenberg Inn
 304-876-2126

 Shang-Ra-La B&B
 304-876-2391

 Stonebrake Cottage Guest House
 304-876-6607

 Thomas Shepherd Inn
 304-876-3715

Sinks Grove
 Morgan Orchard
 304-772-3638

Sisterville
 Cobblestone On The Ohio
 304-652-1206

 Wells Inn
 304-652-3111-[Y--]

Snowshoe
 Whistlepunk Village & Inn
 800-624-2757-[G--]

Summersville
 Historic Brock House B&B
 304-872-4887

Summerville

 Old Wilderness Inn
 304-872-3481

Summit Point
 Countryside
 304-725-2614

Valley Chapel
 Ingberg Acres
 304-269-2834

Wellburg
 Drovers Inn
 304-737-0188

Wheeling
 B&B At 651 Main Street

 Stratford Springs Inn
 304-233-5100

 Yesterdays Ltd B&B
 304-233-2003

White Sulphur Springs
 James Wylie House B&B
 304-536-9444

Winona
 Garvey House
 800-767-3235

WISCONSIN

Albany
 Albany Guest House
 608-862-3636

 Oak Hill Manor
 608-862-1400

 Sugar River Inn
 608-862-1248

Algoma
 Amberwood Inn
 414-487-3471

Allenton
 Addison House B&B
 414-629-9993

Alma
 Gallery House
 608-685-4975

 Lane House Inn
 608-685-4923

Amherst
 Journeys End B&B

Bold Name - *Description appears in other section*   Wisconsin

715-824-3970

Appleton
Franklin Street Inn
414-739-3702

Queen Anne
414-739-7966

Avoca
Prairie Rose B&B
608-532-6878

Baileys Harbor
Potters Door Inn
414-839-2003

Baraboo
Baraboos Gollmar
Guest House
608-356-9432

Barristers House
608-356-3344

Frantiques
Showplace
608-356-5273

House Of Seven
Gables
608-356-8387

Pinehaven B&B
608-356-3489

Victorian Rose
608-356-7828

Barnes
Sunset Resort B&B
715-795-2449

Barnfield
The Garden
608-924-2408

Bayfield
Apple Tree Inn
715-779-5572

Baywood Place B&B
715-779-3690

Chez Joliet
715-779-5480

Cooper Hill House
715-779-5060

Gruenkes First
Street Inn
715-779-5480

Old Rittenhouse Inn
715-779-5111

Pinehurst Inn
715-779-3676

Thimbleberry Inn
715-779-5757

Belleville
Abendruh B&B
Swiss Style
608-424-3808

Cameo Rose B&B
608-424-6340

Birnamwood
Old Birnamwood
Inn

Black Creek
Old Coach Inn B&B
414-984-3840

Brantwood
Palmquists "The
Farm"
715-564-2558

Broadhead
Buckskin Lodge
B&B
608-897-2914

Browntown
Four Seasons
608-966-1680

Burlington
Foxmoor B&B
414-862-6161

Hillcrest B&B Inn
414-763-4706

Cable
Connors B&B

Cambridge
Knight Heron B&B
608-423-4141

Cambridge-Rockdale
Night Heron Bed,
Books & Breakfast
608-423-4141

Campbellsport
Mielke-Mauk House
414-533-8602

Newcastle Pines
414-533-5252

Cascade
Timberlake Inn
414-528-8481

Cashton
Cannondalen B&B
800-947-6261

Convent House
608-823-7906

Cassville
Geiger House
608-725-5419

River View B&B
608-725-5893

Cedarburg
Stagecoach Inn
414-375-0208-[Y--]

**Washington House
Inn**
800-554-4717-[G--]

Chetek
Annadale Inn
715-837-1974

Lodge At Canoe Bay
800-568-1995-[G--]

Ruthies B&B
715-924-2407

Trails End B&B
715-924-2641

Chippewa Falls
Wilson House
715-723-0055

Cochrane
Rosewood B&B
608-248-2940

Colfax
Son Ne Vale Farm
B&B
715-962-4342

Columbus
By The Okeag
414-623-3007

Maple Leaf Inn B&B
608-248-2940

Cornucopia
Village Inn
715-742-3941

Crandon
Courthouse Square
B&B
715-478-2549

Cross Plains

Enchanted Valley
B&B
608-798-4554

Past & Present Inn
800-316-3884

Cumberland
Rectory B&B
715-822-3151

De Pere
Birch Creek Inn
414-336-7575

DeForest
Circle B&B
608-846-3481

Delavan
Allyn House
414-728-9090

Jeremiah Mable
House
414-728-1876

Lakeside Manor Inn
414-728-2043

DePere
Astor House
414-432-3585

Door County
Harbor House Inn
414-854-5196

Downsville
Creamery
715-664-8354

Durand
Ryan House B&B
715-672-8563

Eagle
Eagle Centre House
414-363-4700

Eagle River
Brennan Manor
715-479-7353

Cranberry Inn
Resort
715-479-2215

Inn At Pinewood
715-479-4114

East Troy
Greystone Farm
414-495-8485

Mitten Farm

©*Inn & Travel Memphis, Tennessee*   2-189

Wisconsin   **Bold Name** - *Description appears in other section*

414-642-5530

Pine Ridge
414-594-3629

Eau Claire
Evergreen Acres
715-832-0034

Fanny Hill Inn
715-836-8184

Otter Creek Inn
715-832-2945

Edgerton
Olde Parsonage B&B
608-884-6490

Elkhart Lake
Eastlake Victorian B&B
414-876-2272

Siebkens
414-876-2600

Elkhorn
Ye Olde Manor House
414-742-2450

Ellison Bay
Country Woods B&B
414-854-5706

Griffin Inn
414-854-4306

Elron
East View B&B
608-463-7564

Waarviks Century Farm
608-462-8595

Elroy
Stillestad
800-462-4980

Elton
Deharts House
715-882-4781

Endeavor
Neenah Creek Inn
608-587-2229

Ephraim
Eagle Harbor Inn
414-854-2121

Ephraim Inn
414-854-4515

French Country Inn
414-854-4001

Hillside Hotel
800-423-7023

Evansville
Holmes Victorian Inn
608-882-6866

Fennmore
Gazebo B&B
608-822-3928

Ferryville
Mississippi Humble Bush
608-734-3022

Fish Creek
Birchwood
414-868-3214

Thorp House Inn
414-868-2444

Whistling Swan Inn
414-868-3442

White Gull Inn
414-868-3517

Florence
Lakeside B&B
715-528-3259

Fontana
Lazy Cloud B&B
414-275-3322

Fontana-On-Geneva Lake
Emerald view House
414-275-2266

Fort Atkinson
Lamp Post Inn
414-563-6561

Frederic
Gandy Dancer B&B
715-327-8750

Fremont
Candlelight Manor
414-446-2464

Galesville
Clark House B&B
608-582-4190

Gays Mills
Miss Mollys B&B
608-735-4433

Genoa City
House On The Hill
414-279-6466

Gills Rock
Harbor House Inn
414-854-5196

Glen Haven
Parsons Inn B&B
608-794-2491

Grand View
Hummingbird B&B

Green Bay
Astor House
414-432-3585

R&R Homestead
414-336-8244

Stonewood Haus
414-499-3786

Green Lake
Heidel House

McConnell Inn
414-294-6430

Oakwood Lodge
414-294-6580

Strawberry Hiill
414-294-3450

Hammond
Summit Farm B&B
715-796-2617

Hartford
Jordan House
414-673-5643

Hartland
Monches Mill House
414-966-7546

Hayward
Edgewater Inn B&B
715-462-9412

Lumbermans Mansion
715-634-3012

Mustard Seed
715-634-2908

Ross Teal Lake Lodge
715-462-3631

Spider Lake Lodge

800-OLD-WISC

Hazel Green
Dewinters Of Hazel Green
608-854-2768

Wisconsin House Stagecoach Inn
608-854-2233

Hazelhurst
Hazelhurst Inn
714-356-6571

Hillsboro
Masclones Hidden Valley
608-489-3443

Hollandle
Old Granary Inn
608-967-2140

Honey Creek
Honey Creek Acres
800-484-8081

Houlton
Shady Ridge B&B
715-549-6258

Hudson
1884 Phipps Inn
715-386-0800

Bluebird Cottage
715-749-4243

Boyden House
715-386-7435

Phipps Inn
715-386-0800

Stageline Inn
715-386-5203

Iola
Iris Inn
715-445-4848

Taylor House
715-445-2204

Irma
Swan Song B&B
715-453-1173

Iron River
Iron River Trout Haus
715-372-4219

Jamesville
Antique Rose

2-190   ©*Inn & Travel Memphis, Tennessee*

Bold Name - *Description appears in other section*   Wisconsin

Janesville
Jackson Street Inn
608-754-7250-[Y--]

Saltbox Inn
608-754-6929

Juneau
Country Retreat On Primrose Ln
414-386-2912

Kansasville
Linen & Lace B&B
414-534-4966

Kendall
Cabin At Trails End
608-427-3877

Kenosha
Black Swan Inn
414-656-0207

The Manor House
414-658-0014-[Y--]

Kewaskum
Country Ridge Inn B&B
414-626-4853

Kewaunee
Chelsea Rose B&B
414-388-2012

Duvall House
414-388-0501

Gables
414-388-0220

La Farge
Trillium
608-625-4492

La Pointe
Woods Manor
715-747-3102

Lac de Flambeau
Ty-Bach
715-588-7851

LaCrosse
Martindale House
608-782-4224

Lake Denton
Swallows Nest B&B
608-254-6900

Lake Geneva
Eleven Gables Inn On The Lake
414-248-8393-[G--]

Elizabethian Inn
414-248-9131-[Y--]

French Country Inn
414-245-5220

Geneva Inn
800-441-5881

Lazy Cloud Lodge
414-275-3322

Pederson Victorian B&B
414-248-9110

Roses, A B&B
414-248-4344

TC Smith Historic Inn B&B
800-423-0233-[G--]

Two Akers Of England

Lake Mills
Fargo Mansion Inn
414-648-3654

Lewis
Seven Pines Lodge
715-653-2323

Livingston
Oak Hill Farm
608-943-6006

Lodi
Prairie Garden B&B
608-592-5187

Victorian Treasure B&B
800-859-5199

Lomira
White Shutters
414-269-4056

Luxemberg
Bit Of The Bay
414-866-9901

Madison
Annies B&B
608-244-2224

Arbor House, An Environmental Inn
608-238-2981

Canterbury Inn
800-838-3850

Collins House
608-255-4230

Hill House B&B
608-244-2224-[Y--]

Lake House In Monona
800-397-8261

Livingston Victorian Inn
608-257-1200

Mansion Hill Inn
800-798-9070-[G--]

Stoney Oaks
608-278-1646

University Heights B&B
608-233-3340

Maiden Rock
Eagle Cove B&B
715-596-4302

Harrisburg Inn
715-448-4500

Manawa
Ferg Haus Inn B&B
414-596-2946

Mantiowoc
Arbor Manor B&B
414-684-6095

Jarvis House B&B
414-682-2103

Manwa
Gages Gardens & Gables B&B
414-682-3643

Marinette
Lauerman Guest House
715-732-7800

M&M Victorian Inn
715-732-9513

Mayville
Audubon Inn
414-387-5858

Menomonee Falls
Dorshels B&B Guest House
414-255-7866

Hitching Post B&B
414-255-1496

Menomonie
Cedar Trail Guesthouse
715-664-8828

Menomonie Falls
Katy May House B&B
715-235-1792

Mequon
American Country Farm
414-242-0194

Captain Ams

Sonnenhof Inn
414-375-4294

Merrill
Brick House
715-536-3230

Candlewick Inn
800-382-4376

Middleton
Middleton Beach Inn
608-831-6446

Milton
Chase On The Hill
608-831-6446

Milwaukee
Morning Glory
414-483-1512-[Y--]

Pfister Hotel
414-273-8222

Riley House
414-764-3130

TC Smith Historic Inn B&B
800-423-0233-[G--]

Mineral Point
Chesterfield Inn
608-987-3682

Cothren House
608-987-2612

Duke House
608-987-2821

House On The Brau-Meister
608-987-2913

Knudson Guest

©*Inn & Travel Memphis, Tennessee*

Wisconsin *Bold Name - Description appears in other section*

House
608-987-2733

Walker House
608-987-3794

Wilson House Inn
608-987-3600

Wm A Jones House
608-987-2337

Minocqua
Whitehaven B&B
715-356-9097

Monroe
Victorian Garden
608-328-1720

Montello
Westmont Farms B 'N B
414-293-4456

Montreal
The Inn
715-561-5180

Mount Horeb
HB Dahle House
608-437-8894

New Glarus
Jeanne-Maries B&B
608-527-5059

Linden Inn
608-527-2675

Spring Valley Creek
608-527-2314

Zentner Haus
608-527-2121

New Holstein
Krupp Farm Homestead
414-782-5421

New Lisbon
Evansen House
608-562-5202-[Y--]

New Richmond
Kettle Falls Hotel
800-322-0886

Newton
Rambling Hills Tree Farm
414-726-4388

Oconomowoc
Inn At Pine Terrace

414-567-7463

Ogema
Timms Hill B&B
715-767-5288

Onalaska
Lumber Baron Inn
608-781-8938

Ontario
Inn At Wildcat Mountain
608-337-4352

Osceola
Lessards On The Lake
715-294-2447

Pleasant Lake Inn
800-294-2545

St Croix River Inn
800-645-8820

Oshkosh
Marybrooke Inn
414-426-4761

Tiffany Inn
414-426-1000

Oxford
Halfway House
608-586-5489

Pardeeville
Gator Gully B&B
608-429-2754

Pepin
Summer Place
715-442-2132

Phelps
Hazen Inn
715-545-3600

Limberlost Inn
715-545-2685

Phillips
East Highland B&B
715-339-3492

Plain
Bettinger House
608-546-2951

Kraemer House
608-546-3161

Plainfield
Johnson Inn B&B
715-335-4383

Platteville
Cunningham House
608-348-5532

Walnut Ridge
608-348-9359

Plymouth
52 Stafford
414-893-0552

BI Nutt Inn
414-892-8566

Hillwind Farm B&B
414-892-2199

Spring Farm Cottage
414-892-2101

Yankee Hill B&B
414-892-2222

Port Washington
Captains Table B&B
414-284-3818

Grand Inn
414-284-6719

Inn At Old Twelve Hundred
414-268-1200

Port Washington Inn
414-284-5583

Portage
Breeze Waye B&B
608-742-5281

Country Aire
608-742-5716

Inn At Gradys Farm
608-742-3627

Poynette
Jamiseon House
608-635-4100

Prairie du Chien
Neumann House
608-326-8104

Prairie du Sag
Graff House B&B
606-643-6978

Prescott
Oak Street Inn
800-697-7521

Princeton

Ellisons Gray Lion Inn
414-295-4101

Racine
Lochnaiar Inn
414-633-3300

Mansards On The Lake
414-632-1135

Reedsburg
Parkview B&B
608-524-4333

Rhinelander
Cranberry Hill Inn
715-369-3504-[Y--]

Richland Center
Lambs Inn B&B
608-585-4301

Littledale
608-647-7118

Mansion
608-647-2808

River Falls
Knollwood House B&B
715-425-1040

Trillium Woods B&B
715-425-2555

Saint Croix Falls
Amberwood B&B
715-483-9355

Saint Germain
Saint Germain B&B
715-479-8007

Stonehouse B&B
715-542-3733

Shawano
Prince Edward
715-526-2805

Sheboygan
Scheele House
414-458-0998

Sheboygan Falls
Rochester Inn
414-467-3123

Siren
Forgotten Tymes B&B
715-349-5837

©*Inn & Travel Memphis, Tennessee*

Bold Name - Description appears in other section *Wisconsin*

Sister Bay
White Apron
414-854-5107

Soldier Grove
Pages Old Oak Inn
608-624-5217

Sparta
Blyton Park B&B
608-269-8159

Briar Patch B&B
608-269-1026

Franklin Victorian
800-845-8767

Just n Trails B&B
800-488-4521

Spooner
Aunt Marthas Guest House
715-635-6857

Green Valley Inn
715-635-7300

Spread Eagle
Lodge At Rivers Edge
715-696-3406

Spring Green
Deer Acres
608-588-7299

Hardyns House
608-588-7007

Hill Street B&B
608-588-7751

Silver Star
608-935-7297

Springbrook
Stout Trout
715-466-2790

Star Lake
Whip-Poor-Will Inn
800-788-5215

Stevens Point
Birdhouse
715-341-0084

Dreams Of Yesteryear B&B
715-341-4525-[G--]

Marcyannas B&B
715-341-9922

Victorian Swan On Water
715-345-0595-[Y--]

Stockholm
Hyggelig Hus
715-442-2086

Pine Creek Lodge
715-448-3203

Stone Lake
New Mountain B&B
715-865-2486

Stoughton
Stokstads B&B
608-884-4941

Strum
Lake House
715-695-3519

Sturgeon Bay
Barbican
414-743-4854

Bay Shore Inn
414-743-4551

Chanticleer Guest House
414-746-0334

Gandts Haus Und Hof
414-743-1238

Gray Goose B&B
414-743-9100

Hearthside B&B Inn
414-746-2136

Van Clay Guest House
414-743-6611

White Lace Inn
414-743-1105-[Y--]

Whitefish Bay Farm B&B
414-743-1560

Three Lake
Three Lakes Haven
715-546-2012

Tomahawk
Prides English Manor
715-453-7670

Two Rivers
Abbas Inn B&B

414-793-1727
Red Forest B&B
414-793-1794

Viola
Inn At Elk Run
608-625-2062

Viroqua
Eckhardt House B&B
608-637-3306

Serendipity Farm
608-637-7708

Viroqua Heritage Inn
608-637-3306

Washington Island
Island House B&B
414-847-2779

Washington Hotel & Resort
414-847-2346

Waterford
River View Inn
414-534-5049

Watertown
Brandt Quirk Manor
414-261-7917

Waupaca
Crystal River B&B
715-258-5333

Thomas Pipe Inn
715-824-3161

Whippoorwill Acres
715-256-0373

White Horse B&B
715-258-6162

Waupun
Rose Ivy Inn
414-324-2127

Wausau
Rosenberry Inn
715-842-5733

Stewart Inn
715-842-5733

Wautoma
Kristine Anns Inn
414-787-4901

West Bend

Mayer-Pick Haus
414-335-1524

West Salem
Wolfway Farm
608-486-2686

Westby
Westby House
608-634-4112

Westfield
Marthas Ethnic B&B
608-296-3361

White Lake
Wolf River Lodge
715-882-2182

Whitewater
Greene House B&B
800-468-1959

Hamilton House B&B

Victoria On Main
414-473-8400

Wilton
Pahls B&B
608-435-6434

Rices Whispering Pines B&B
608-435-6531

Wisconsin Dells
Dells Carver Inn
608-254-4766

Historic Bennett House
608-254-2500

House On River Road
608-253-5573

Sherman House
608-253-2721

Thunder Valley B&B
608-254-4145

Wisconsin Rapids
Nash House
715-424-2001

- E N D -

©*Inn & Travel Memphis, Tennessee*

2-193

South

St. Francisville Louisiana

In wonderful West Feliciana Parish, the heart of Louisiana's English Plantation Country

From the resonance of its name (Feliciana is Spanish for Happyland) to the romance of its antebellum plantation culture and unspoiled scenery, West Feliciana Parish at the heart of English Louisiana has enthralled visitors from its earliest days, combining history with hospitality and a happy climate, and today is the state's second most popular tourist destination year-round, ideally situated as it is on the Mississippi River between New Orleans and Natchez, Mississippi.

Settled first by the peaceful Houmas, who were driven out by the fierce Tunica Indian tribe, West Feliciana attracted both Spanish and French explorers beginning in the 16th century, and the area is rich in Indian artifacts bespeaking a thriving trade with European adventurers traversing the Mississippi and visiting its shores.

Its first formal settlement centered around a small fort, Ste. Reyne aux Tonicas, established by the French around 1729 and abandoned soon after. When France lost the rest of Louisiana to Spain, her vast territory east of the Mississippi, including West Feliciana, went to England in 1763 and became known as West Florida.

In the 1770's settlement began in earnest around a monastery and cemetery established by Spanish Capuchin monks, and for the rest of the century the area was dominated by Spain and England, both encouraging settlement with large land grants. In 1779 the governor of Spanish Louisiana, Bernardo de Galvez, ousted the British from that portion of West Florida he called Feliciana.

The challenge of taming the virgin Feliciana woodlands and tilling its rich river bottomlands attracted a fiercely independent and courageous lot, determined to carve from the wilderness settlements noted not just for agricultural subsistence but also for fine architecture, refined culture, educational achievement and a gracious standard of honorable living. The extent to which they succeeded may be remarked from the fact that the large planters who harvested immense acreages of cotton, sugar cane and indigo along the Great River Road from New Orleans to Natchez in the mid-1800's comprised more that two-thirds of America's known millionaires of that period.

These strong-willed pioneers, primarily English-speaking Anglo-Saxons, twice revolted after the Louisiana Purchase excluded their beloved Feliciana area and left it under Spanish dominion. The Kemper Brothers Rebellion of 1804 was more colorful than successful, but the Republic of West Florida stemmed from a more respectable rebellion, which pulled off a successful coup in 1810, establishing for 74 days an independent republic with its capital in St. Francisville. This led to the desired annexation of the Felicianas into the United States by President Madison. Becoming part of the state of Louisiana in 1812, West Feliciana would fly its own independent banner only once more, upon secession from the Union at the outset of the Civil War.

Along the banks of the Mississippi River developed rowdy Bayou Sara, at one point the largest port between New Orleans and Memphis, attracting heavy flatboat traffic as well as cargo barges and steamboats plying the waters of that era's most significant and well-travelled highway. Shipping point for the cotton and produce from the rich surrounding plantation country, arrival point for fine furnishings and other finished goods the wealthy planters imported to beautify their homes and lives, Bayou Sara was an important river port until the steamboat was replaced by the railroad; shelled during the Civil War, nearly wiped out by several disastrous fires levelling large blocks of commercial and residential structures, the Mississippi's floodwaters eventually obliterated every trace of this once-extensive town.

The parish seat of St. Francisville, fortunately, established itself beginning in 1807 on the bluffs towering above Bayou Sara, safe from rampaging spring floods and stretching along an undulating, narrow finger ridge as the town called "two miles long and two yards wide" with not much exaggeration. Oldest town charted in Florida Parishes, it was long the social, cultural and religious center for the cotton-rich plantation country surrounding it, and after Bayou Sara's demise became the commercial hub as well.

The high concentration of quaint 19th-century structures in town has resulted in large sections of town being protected as Historic Districts, listed on the National Register of Historic Places; maps available at the visitor center delineate a pleasant walking or driving tour through these areas. While fewer large working plantations exist in the surrounding countryside in the face of more modern land-use patterns, grazing cattle and growing crops still color the rolling landscape.

Happiest trend of all is the increasing importance of the tourist trade, with visitors being welcomed into a number of historic plantation homes, gardens and other significant structures on a year-round basis, while still other attractions open for special pre-arranged tours. The third weekend in March features the Audubon Pilgrimage through homes not normally accessible to the public, and throughout the Christmas season the little town of St. Francisville is transformed into a veritable winter wonderland with millions of tiny white lights.

There are several plantation homes open to the public on a regular basis, offering visitors a fascinating glimpse into history. Earliest of these are the raised rambling cottage-style plantations, called The Cottage, Butler Greenwood and The Myrtles, begun in the 1790's, still shaded by ancient live oaks and filled with fine antiques. Oakley House at Audubon State Park shows the tiny room occupied by artist-naturalist John James Audubon when he painted more that a third of his Birds of America studies here in 1821, so enthralled was he by the lush flora and fauna of the area. Later Greek Revival houses like Rosedown and rebuilt Greenwood exemplify the extravagance and elegance of the wealthy Cotton Kingdom, and yet another site, Afton Villa, illustrates the adaptive use of ruins (the flamboyant house here burned) as setting for one of the south's most glorious gardens.

Visitors to St. Francisville will find a wonderful array of shops lining the major thoroughfare through town, many housed in restored 19th-century structures, three historic churches and several fine restaurants.

Overnight accommodations provide a pleasing variety from historic to brand new, from restored plantations in the country to elegant townhouses within walking distance of all of St. Francisville's attractions, from modern lodges at golf resorts to cozy cottages scattered among moss-draped oaks. Bed & Breakfasts include Barrow House and Printer's Cottage; The Bluffs; Butler Greenwood Plantation; The Cottage Plantation; Green Springs; Hemingbough; Lake Rosemound Inn; The Myrtles; Propinquity; Shadetree; St. Francisville Inn. There is also a modern motel, St. Francis Hotel on the Lake, and a campground.

Tourist information is available from the West Feliciana Historical Society at its in-town museum headquarters on Ferdinand Street or by writing PO Box 338, St. Francisville, LA 70775, tel: 504-635-6330.

Anne Butler, Innkeeper,
Butler Greenwood Bed & Breakfast
St. Francisville, Louisiana

Anne Butler is a working journalist and author of ten published books, the two latest on crime and criminal justice called *Angola* and *Dying To Tell*. She began her writing career in Washington with AAA and is the author of two travel books on Louisiana and Mississippi. A native of Louisiana where she lives with her husband and children and operates a Bed & Breakfast on the 1790's plantation first established by her great-great-great-great grandparents, she has a BA in English from Sweet Briar College in Virginia and an MA in English from Humboldt State University in California. It's a good bet her next book will involve a Bed & Breakfast!

Akansas, the Natural State,

is small but has great natural beauty, and wonderful state parks that enhance the enjoyment of it's beauty.

©*Inn & Travel Memphis, Tennessee*

The Ozark Gateway Region (the northern mid-section of the state) is rich in forests, rolling Ozark foothills, streams, rivers and lakes but is not well known to the tourist. In addition to the scenery and outdoor activities, this area offers quaint towns to explore, interesting museums, historic sights and one of the nations most unique state parks, the Ozark Folk Center, where the old way of life is preserved and passed on. The Ozark Folk Center and the town of Mountain View are a treat for people wanting a peek at the *"Old Arkansas"*. You can observe craftspeople using the old methods to produce their wares. Calico colored rock cliffs along the White River provide a backdrop to the wonderful little town of Calico Rock.

Hardy, a colorful old railroad town along the Spring River, is a mecca of antique shops and local arts and crafts. The Arkansas Traveller Dinner Theater and the Ozark Jubilee Country Music Theater provide the best in both musical comedy and country music. Music fills the air when local musicians gather to play and everyone is invited to join in. Bring your musical instruments when travelling to Mountain Home or Hardy and join the fun. Rivers provide excellent canoeing and several golf courses accommodate the avid golfer. If you would like more information on the Ozark Gateway Region, an area of undiscovered wonders and pristine beauty, contact Gateway Tourist Council at 800-264-0316.

Peggy Johnson, Innkeeper
The Olde Stonehouse
Hardy, Arkansas

The Southeastern United States

The southeast reveals itself as a region rather than a group of states. Beginning in North Carolina with its treacherous out islands, its gentle Piedmont and ppalachian western area, the traveler can find contrast within one day's drive. At the North Carolina-Tennessee border the Great Smokey Mountain National Park, America's most popular, gives way to rolling midlands. In Nashville Tennessee, the traveler finds the country music capital of the world.

Traveling southwest into Mississippi, the lovely antebellum period homes of Natchez and the magnolia, both the state tree and the state flower, reveals a look at the Deep South. The stately cypress trees decorated with Spanish moss lead a traveler into Louisiana, the cradle of jazz and then to the beauties of Jackson Square and the French Quarter of New Orleans.

The humid, subtropical Gulf Coast of Louisiana and Mississippi lead into Alabama, the heart of Dixie. Huntsville, called Rocket City USA, offers thrills for adults and children. The Battleship Alabama anchored in Mobile Bay and saltwater fishing in the Gulf of Mexico provide a great diversity. Almost one-half of all Georgians live in the Atlanta area. Stone Mountain, the Augusta National Golf Tournament and the lovely restorations of Savannah give delight to the traveler.

Our southernmost state, Florida with its balmy climate and fabulous beaches as well as our nation's oldest city, St. Augustine, provide retirees and tourists alike with endless variety.

South Carolina with lovely Charleston full of old mansions and gardens and the seaside resorts of Myrtle Beach and Hilton Head bring the traveler full-circle around the Southeast. This beautiful region is brimming with delights and Bed and Breakfasts ready to serve you. Sample our hospitality!

Mary McElhinney, Innkeeper
McElhinney House
Charlotte, North Carolina

Treasures of the Tarheel State

Among the millions of travelers who visit North Carolina to partake of its diverse vacation charms, more and more are discovering the wealth of Bed & Breakfasts, guest houses and small country inns that dot the map, from the unspoiled Outerbanks to the western mountains.

From east to west, or as Tarheels put it, *"from Murphy to Manteo"*, visitors enjoy heart-warming welcomes in lodgings that are historic plantations, restored log tobacco barns, turn-of-the-century restored inns and Greek Revival town houses. Their innkeepers, typically proud of the riches of the *"Old North State"*, can direct guests to beach sites that once harbored Bluebeard the Pirate, to Revolutionary and Civil War sites, to tobacco auctions and museums, to Indian artifacts and to the farm where the Regulators fought the Royal Governor to win fair taxation and representation in the Colonial Assembly. In the center of the state, known as the Piedmont, vacationers have so many choices of attractions that they often extend their stay. Within minutes of the famous Research Triangle Park (a marvel of industrial planning that revitalized and re-shaped the Piedmont), are Duke University, the University of North Carolina at Chapel Hill and North Carolina State University, as well as a dozen other locally respected colleges. They all offer exciting arts calendars, museums, planetaria, gardens and handsome campuses for afternoon strolling.

For those who prize physical beauty above man-made attractions, the menu is rich indeed. Wide, empty beaches; acres of farm and woodland; small towns recalling the past; lakes and wildlife preserves; and blue-hazed mountains that lead the eye and the imagination westward - all these treasures and more are the secret that draws visitors from all over the world. But maybe the most appealing feature of all is the warm friendliness of Tarheels, which visitors quickly recognize and always appreciate.

Y'all come, hear?

Barbara B Ryan, Innkeeper,
husband Jerry and daughter Cathy.
Arrowhead Inn
Durham, NC
Photo: *Herald-Sun Photo,* Dan Charlson

©*Inn & Travel Memphis, Tennessee*

3-5

Alabama - Arkansas   *National Edition*

Rutherford Johnson House   Main St 36444   **Franklin AL**
Tel: 335-282-4423
Res Times 8am-5pm

Traditional Southern Victorian farmhouse still furnished with the original furniture nestled in a picturesque setting. There are nature trails, all the farm animals including horses for an exciting farm/country stay. Appetizing full country breakfast with farm-fresh ingredients. Meals: Dinners available upon request. **Seasonal:** No **Brochure:** Yes

Permitted: Limited children, limited smoking **Payment Terms:** Check [E11ACAL-3] **COM** Y **ITC Member:** No

Rates:	Pvt Bath 4	Shared Bath 1
Single	$ 65.00	$ 55.00
Double	$ 75.00	

Churchview   327 Church St 36701   **Selma AL**
Mrs. Henry   **Tel:** 334-875-2144

A beautifully restored three-story Victorian residence built in 1893 by Ernest Lamar. Inside you'll find all the Victorian trimmings with burled pine woodwork, parquet floors, original brass trim, fixtures and lovely stained glass windows. Listed on the *National Register of Historic Places*. **Seasonal:** No **Reservations:** One night's deposit at res time to hold reservation. **Brochure:** Yes **Permitted:** Limited children **Conference:** Yes, for groups to fifteen persons including luncheons and dinners. **Payment Terms:** Check MC/V [X11AXAL-13] **COM** Y **ITC Member:** No

Rates:	Pvt Bath 4	Shared Bath 2
Single	$ 65.00	$ 55.00
Double	$ 70.00	$ 60.00

Great Southern Hotel   127 W Cedar 72021   **Brinkley AR**
Stanley & Dorcas Prince   **Tel:** 501-734-4955
Res Times 8-7pm

Relive the grand style at the turn-of-the-century crossroads of southern train travel where guests like Jimmy Carter and Colonel Saunders (Kentucky Chicken fame) traveled at the beginning of their careers - where seven railroads brought 500 passengers daily! Midway between Memphis and Little Rock, *The Great Southern Hotel* has been resurrected to its former glory offering guests atmosphere of a bygone era and fine gourmet dining. The completed guest rooms have the original "ball & claw" bath tubs, the old-fashioned elevated-tank water closets and are furnished with antique period pieces with carefully chosen period wallcoverings and delicate lace curtains. The focal point of the Inn is the beautifully restored lobby area and the fine restaurant with tin ceilings reaching fifteen feet in the air, shellacked woodwork, marble wainscotting and where your host and hostess lovingly prepare each meal including Regional Southern Dishes of Trout Elvira, Delta Pork Tenderloin and Mississippi Fly Way Duck. A full complimentary breakfast is brought to your room or served in the dining room whenever you're ready. Make this a definite stop because it has already been written-up in *"Southern Living" "Arkansas Times"* and received the *"Best Overall Dining Award"* by the *Arkansas Times*, Jan 1989. **Seasonal:** No **Reservations:** $20 deposit or credit card with 24 hr cancel policy for refund **Brochure:** Yes **Permitted:** Limited children **Conference:** Yes, banquets up to 200 **Payment Terms:** Check AE/MC/V [R08BPAR-108] **COM** Y **ITC Member:** No

Rates:	Pvt Bath 4
Single	$ 40.00
Double	$ 45.00

Olde Towne B&B   567 Locust Ave 72032   **Conway AR**
Paul & Rosalie Revis   **Tel:** 501-329-6989
Res Times Morning

Olde Towne Bed and Breakfast is a 1922 Colonial Revival house built by the newspaper publisher, Frank E Robins for his family home. It is a two and a half story brick structure and is situated two

---

3-6   ©*Inn & Travel Memphis, Tennessee*

blocks from the old downtown area of Conway, Arkansas. The home is listed on the *National Register of Historic Places*. Conway is an old railroad town incorporated in 1875 and has maintained many of its old structures, commercial as well as residential. There are three colleges and several industries in the town of 33,000 population. Conway is a thirty minute drive to the capital city of Little Rock and forty minutes from the Little Rock Airport. *Olde Towne Bed and Breakfast* is conveniently located close to the junction of I-40 and Hwy 65. Conway is a short half-day drive from Branson, Missouri and from Eureka Springs, Arkansas. **Airport:** Little Rock Airport-40 mi **Seasonal:** No **Reservations:** One night's deposit required **Brochure:** Yes **Permitted:** Children, limited smoking (outdoors only) **Payment Terms:** Check MC/V [I06GPAR1-19417] COM YG **ITC Member:** No

Rates: Pvt Bath 4
Single $ 60-85.00
Double $ 60-85.00

Treischmann House B&B	707 Cedar 71635	Crossett AR
Pat & Herman Owens		Tel: 501-364-7592
		Res Times 24 Hrs

The *Trieschmann House* was built in 1903, the same year that Crossett incorporated, for Adam Trieschmann, an official of the Crossett Company. Crossett was a company-owned town. In 1946, the company sold the houses to its employees. The Trieschmann House at this time, was located on Pine Street and it was moved to its present location. The house sits on one and one-third acres surrounded by big old pecan trees. Picket fences accent the backyard which features a wicker swing, stone patio, hammock and fountain for relaxing. The house features original hardwood floors, ceiling, fans, ten and twelve foot ceilings, radiators for heating and a relaxing atmosphere. The front bedroom has a private bath and a sofa. The Rose Bedroom was originally a "sleeping porch" and has lots of windows. It is a very cheery room overlooking the backyard. It is real cozy in the winter with a fireplace with electric heater and a chair and ottoman nearby for reading. There is also a desk if you have any writing to do. A full complimentary breakfast is served every morning around a clawfoot oak table in the kitchen. The house is very quiet and a wonderful place to relax and get away from it all. Nearby activities include the Felsentahl Wildlife Refuge with fishing, hunting, tours and bird watching. **Seasonal:** No **Reservations:** Deposit required, 24 Hr cancel policy **Permitted:** Children **Conference:** Wedding receptions, luncheons and parties for groups of eight or more **Payment Terms:** Check MC/V [I05GPAR-15699] COM YG **ITC Member:** No

Rates: Pvt Bath 1   Shared Bath 2
Single $ 50.00 $ 50.00

---

5 Ojo Inn	5 Ojo St 72632	Eureka Springs AR
Paula Kirby Adkins		Tel: 800-656-6734 501-253-6734

Built circa 1890, the two restored Victorian homes and two newer cottages, all in a row, offer charming Bed & Breakfast accommodations in Eureka Springs Historic District. Located on Ojo Street on the Historic Loop (old 62B), it's just a 6-8 minute walk to the shops and galleries in the Historic Downtown area. A trolley stops in front of the Inn, if you'd rather not walk. Accommodations include ten guest rooms and suites, some with whirlpools and fireplaces - all with private bath, coffee maker, refrigerator, separate heat and a/c, cable color TV and period antique furnishings and memorabilia. A full elegant gourmet breakfast is served at 9am in the Sweet House dining room with

Arkansas — *National Edition*

other guests. Private dining is available upon prior request if desired. Other meals available by prior arrangements. A conversation area with books, games and phone are available in the Ojo House common area. Make new friends or greet old friends in the convivial outdoor garden setting. Use the hot tub, or just visit with other guests, or relax in the privacy of your spacious room. **Packages:** Honeymoon **Discounts:** Corporate rates and winter period **Seasonal:** Rates vary **Reservations:** Full payment required by credit card guarantee or check, 7 day cancel notice for refund, less $15 service fee. No refunds for early departures. Check in 4-6pm, check-out 11am **Brochure:** Yes **Permitted:** Drinking, smoking on outside veranda **Payment Terms:** Check with ID AE/DC/MC/V [I08IPA-R1-17507] **COM** YG **ITC Member:** No **Quality Assured:** Yes

Rates:	Pvt Bath 10
Single	$ 75-129.00
Double	$ 85-129.00

Cliff Cottage, A B&B Inn	42 Armstrong St 72632	Eureka Springs AR
Sandra CH Smith		**Tel:** 800-799-7409 501-253-7409
		Res Times 8am-11pm

Nestled against a timeless Ozark bluff surrounded by ageless trees, Cliff Cottage, an historic *"Painted Lady"* (built in 1892 and lovingly restored in 1991) offers elegant Victorian suites in the heart of this Victorian village's historic downtown. Take a blissful journey to a place of pampered solitude - all you need to fulfill a dream! Your innkeeper (a writer), just back from seven years of mostly singlehandedly sailing from San Francisco to Costa Rica, proffers you complimentary champagne, fruit baskets, fresh flowers and a lavish Continental breakfast. "The Place Next Door" provides exquisitely decadent breakfasts and complimentary afternoon sherry and evening brandy is served around the roaring fire in the Great Room. All suites and guestrooms are furnished with antiques and eclectic collectibles including double jacuzzi in three rooms. Victorian picnic lunches, intimate candlelit dinners available by special advance arrangement. Trout fishing guides, tennis and world-class golf available. **Discounts:** 10% Midweek (Mon-Thur) three night min **Airport:** Fayetteville-1 hr; Springfield MO-1-1/2 hr **Seasonal:** No **Reservations:** One night's deposit for three nights or less; 50% deposit if longer, 14 day cancel policy less $20 booking fee **Brochure:** Yes **Permitted:** Smoking in garden, drinking, no children, no pets **Languages:** French, Spanish, German, Love **Payment Terms:** Check MC/V [R09FPAR-18170] **COM** Y **ITC Member:** No

Rates:	Pvt Bath 4
Single	$ 85-125.00
Double	$ 85-125.00

Crescent Cottage Inn	211 Spring St 72632	Eureka Springs AR
Phyllis & Dr Ralph Becker		**Tel:** 501-253-6022
		Res Times 9am-9pm

"Elegance with history"... This premier-class Victorian *"Painted Lady"* home, dating from 1881, is a landmark property on the historic loop and photographic Spring Street, just a short walk from historic downtown Eureka Springs. Listed on the *National Register of Historic Places*, *Crescent Cottage Inn* was built for the first governor of Arkansas, Powell Clayton, following the Civil War. The home includes beautiful Victorian touches and offers breath-taking views of the valley and the East Mountains and has been featured in numerous magazines, books and is nationally rated. The common and guest rooms are beautifully furnished with Victorian period furnishings and guest rooms include modern amenities such as double jacuzzi spas in two of the guest rooms, queen beds, CATV, phones and air conditioning. The two inviting verandas overlook gardens, the valley, mountains and forests and are the perfect spot for swinging during the warm summer afternoons or while enjoying the beautiful foliage each fall. A full breakfast is included in your stay. Ralph, a professor emeritus and Phyllis, have traveled extensively, which is reflected in their home and wish you to enjoy their lovely home and to depart refreshed and ready to plan your return. Weddings and receptions under

the only remaining arch by Buell and/or on a large veranda overlooking valleys and mountain ranges with nothing but forest. AAA 3-Diamond and Mobil Quality Rated **Discounts:** 10% for extended stays 3+ days, off-season (Jan-March) **Airport:** Fayetteville-45 min Res Only: 800-223-3246 **Reservations:** 10 day cancel policy for refund less $20 processing fee; less than 10 days, refund only if rebooked for entire period, less service fee. Two night min weekends, three night min for special events **Brochure:** Yes **Permitted:** Limited children, limited drinking, smoking outdoors only **Languages:** Spanish, German **Payment Terms:** Check DISC/MC/V [K05HPAR1-116] COM YG ITC **Member:** No

Rates: **Pvt Bath 4**
Single $ 75-115.00
Double $ 75-115.00

Gardeners Cottage   c/o 11 Singleton 72632   **Eureka Springs AR**
Barbara Gavron   **Tel:** 800-833-3394 501-253-9111
    Res Times 24 Hrs

Located in Eureka Springs' historic district is this lovely *Gardener's Cottage* offering private accomm-odations. Ideal for honeymooners or a weekend getaway, this cozy private retreat features charming country antique decor with a fully furnished kitchen, beamed cathedral ceilings, skylights, TV, microwave and Jacuzzi tub. A stony path leads up to the spacious porch where the unusual railwork cut in the shape of flowers frames a porch swing and hammock for leisurely lounging. Tucked away on a wooded lot near a rippling stream, the *Gardener's Cottage* is only one block off the trolley line or a convenient walk to shops and sights. Reservations made for Dinner Train, Passion Play, Bath House and Music Shows. **Seasonal:** No **Reservations:** One night's deposit by check, two day min stay unless 1 day available; 3 day min on holidays & festivals, 14 day cancel policy **Brochure:** Yes **Permitted:** Well-behaved children, porch smoking only, drinking, no pets please **Payment Terms:** Check AE/DC/MC/V [K08HPAR1-12024] COM YG ITC **Member:** No

Rates: **Pvt Bath 1**
Single $ 95-125.00
Double $ 95-125.00

Jordan Drive Hideaway B&B   RR 4 102 Jordan Drive 72632   **Eureka Springs AR**
Lavonne St Clair   **Tel:** 800-245-5931 501-253-8918
    Res Times 8am-8pm

"Eureka Springs hideaway has peaceful site, enticing menu", explains Ellen Gayle Fly, in her article about the *Jordan Drive Hideaway* that she wrote for the *Tulsa Tribune*. Nestled off the "-beaten path" in a wooded setting of oaks and pine, *Jordan Drive Hideaway* is this snug brick Bed and Breakfast - just a stone's throw from the sights and excitement of Eureka Springs. At Jordan Drive Hideaway you'll experience comfort, serenity and a bountiful delicious breakfast that has guests coming back again. There are two, two-room suites which include jacuzzi baths, comfy pellet stoves for fires during the cooler months, cable TV, a small refrigerator and there's room for four persons. Guests are treated by Levonne to a breakfast served on your deck with its forest view, ensuite or upstairs with your hostess - for entertaining conversation and laughter. The full complimentary breakfast begins with a basket full of muffins, from poppy-seed and chocolate-chip banana to maple bran. Wonderfully-prepared egg dishes might include ham and mushroom quiches, baked eggs with broccoli and cheese or eggs baked with mushrooms and three cheeses - all with apple juice

Arkansas
National Edition

served in stemmed crystal - and a delicious Peaches Brulee finale. Just one block from the city trolley - a full day of activities await travelers to Eureka Springs. Your hostess will be glad to make advance reservations for area attractions. **Discounts:** 10% December-April **Airport:** Fayetteville-55 mi **Seasonal:** No **Reservations:** 50% deposit by credit card, 10 day cancel policy for refund; no refund with less than 10 day notice or early departures **Brochure:** Yes **Permitted:** Children **Payment Terms:** Check AE/MC/V [R11FPAR-17520] **COM** Y **ITC Member:** No

Rates: Pvt Bath 2
Single $ 85.00
Double $ 85.00

Pond Mountain Lodge	Rt 1 Box 50 72632	Eureka Springs AR
Judy Jones/Deb Clay		Tel: 800-583-8043 501-253-5877
		Res Times 9am-9pm

"Enjoy the best of two worlds." The charm, hospitality and personal service of a bed and breakfast inn plus the scenic expanse of an Ozark Mountain retreat. Set on 209 acres of gently rolling hills, meadows and hiking paths, *Pond Mountain Lodge & Resort* was a privately owned estate which has been renovated into elegant accommodations in a rustic setting with thirty mile vistas from the front veranda - while just two miles from the congestion. Each guest room and suite has a distinctive "personality", ranging from Monet's Eastern Shores to the rich warmth of Westwood's 1860's four poster cherry bed and dresser to the contemporary and elegant Mirage. Suites have an in-room private jacuzzi while all rooms include private bath, refrigerators, TV/VCRs, microwave, gourmet ground coffees with coffee makers and comfy room robes. Noted for gourmet breakfasts prepared by the former chef of Mimi's, a highly ranked restaurant - you can call upon her for catering your dining requests, whether for couples or groups - including special occasions such as weddings and anniversaries for groups to fifty. Activities nearby include all of the sights of Eureka Springs - and the relaxing country atmosphere of cane pole fishing the stocked artesian spring fed ponds or splashing in the 44 foot pool. From complimentary champagne (or non-alcoholic sparkling juice) upon arrival to your departure, you'll enjoy this *"unique lodging experience where unsurpassed elegance and serenity are a specialty"*. Conferences: Excellent facilities for family reunions, small wedding parties and receptions; educational workshops for groups to fourteen; business retreats - with catering of all meals, including the most discriminating palates **Airport:** Fayetteville or Springfield-35 mi **Discounts:** Midweek, winter, AARP, AAA **Packages:** Romance At The Pond, Groups, Extended Stays **Seasonal:** No **Reservations:** 50% deposit, 14 day cancel policy less $20 service fee, less than 14 days, only if rooms are rebooked **Brochure:** Yes **Permitted:** Children, drinking, limited smoking **Payment Terms:** Check AE/MC/V [R11FPAR-17526] **COM** Y **ITC Member:** No

Rates: Pvt Bath 5
Single $ 75-125.00
Double $ 75-125.00

Singleton House B&B	11 Singleton 72632	Eureka Springs AR
Barbara Gavron		Tel: 800-833-3394 501-253-9111
		Res Times 24 Hrs

Singleton House is an old-fashioned place with a touch of magic. Sheltering a hidden enchanted garden on a hillside in Eureka Springs' historic district, the 1890's Victorian home is whimsically decorated with an eclectic collection of cherished antiques and unexpected treasures. Light and airy guest rooms are uniquely furnished with romantic touches and homey comforts. Enjoy a full breakfast served on the balcony overlooking the fantasy wildflower garden, winding stone paths and a lily-filled goldfish pond. Browse through the small nature library and identify the feathered inhabitants of 50-some birdhouses scattered about the grounds. A short stroll down a scenic wooded footpath leads to shops and cafes. For would-be B&B'ers - your hostess offers an *"Apprenticeship Pro-*

gram" with hands-on training for everyone wanting to try on the innkeepers' hat before taking the plunge! For further information contact Barbara. Reservations made for Dinner Train and Passion Play, Bath House and Music Shows. **Seasonal:** No **Reservations:** One night's deposit to guarantee to hold room, arrival by arrangement, 14 day cancel policy **Brochure:** Yes **Permitted:** Well-behaved children, porch smoking only, drinking, no pets please **Payment Terms:** Check AE/DC/MC/V [I08HPAR1-142] COM YG **ITC Member:** No

Rates:	Pvt Bath 5
Single	$ 65.00
Double	$ 65-95.00

White Dove Manor	#8 Washington St 72632	Eureka Springs AR
Don Mackie		Tel: 800-261-6151 501-253-6151

This beautifully restored Victorian Inn Bed & Breakfast is in the heart of Eureka Springs. The ambience of the *White Dove Manor* and Eureka Springs make you feel the reverence and romance of the gentler Victorian Era. Guest rooms are beautifully furnished in antiques and Victorian Era decor. Amenities include golf privileges at Holiday Island, off-street parking, jacuzzi guest rooms, complimentary fruit, flowers and candy and entertainment and dining reservations. The Inn is conveniently located a beautiful walk to the quaint downtown area. For those who wish to conserve all of their energy for visiting the wonderful shops or sightseeing, a trolley ride if available. Come and experience what it must have been like in the Ozarks a century ago. We look forward to your coming to enjoy the town, its atmosphere and a true touch of Southern Hospitality! We love it here and you will too. **Packages:** Inquire at reservation time **Reservations:** One night's deposit, ten day cancellation policy for refund, no refunds for early departure, handicap accessible **Brochure:** Yes **Permitted:** Children, limited pets **Conference:** Conference facility for small groups **Payment Terms:** AE/DISC/MC/V [I08IPAR1-23470] COM YG **ITC Member:** No

Rates:	Pvt Bath 6	Shared Bath 1
Single	$ 75-85.00	$ 55.00
Double	$ 75-85.00	$ 55.00

Willow Ridge Luxury Lodging	85 Kingshighway 72632	Eureka Springs AR
Roy & Patty Manley		Tel: 800-467-1737 501-253-7737

Does a Victorian aura arouse your enthusiasm? Do you yearn for a glimpse of the Twenties? Are you searching for relaxing country charm? If you fit into one of these niches, we have just the room for you. All rooms of *Willow Ridge* have luxurious private bathrooms with elegant towels. Every room is equipped with color cable TV, remote control VCR, AM/FM clock radio, refrigerator, Mr Coffee and a microwave oven. In every room, a chandelier above a mirrored corner, lights a Jacuzzi for two. Coffee, tea, hot chocolate and fruit juice are provided in each room. Comfort is guaranteed by individually controlled heat and a/c, plush carpeting, smooth-textured bed linens or satin sheets, downy comforters, satiny and lacy, all bespeak ease and luxury. Each room offers a special adventure like the Morning Iris, with a private balcony, French doors to a Jacuzzi and a restful color scheme of sea-green, white and mauve. The Irish Rose offers a 1920's antique bedroom suite, soft lights from the chandelier above mirrored walls which enclose a Jacuzzi for two. A private balcony provides a romantic southern sunset. Located on fourteen wooded acres, the architecture of *Willow Ridge* takes advantage of the natural terrain so rooms on each story have a ground-level entry and parking space and each upper-story room has a private balcony. Lodgers are invited to use (for a small use fee), tennis courts, swimming pools, golf greens and other facilities of Holiday Island resort as our guests. **Seasonal:** No **Reservations:** Min 2 nights

Arkansas

National Edition

lodging, one night's deposit required to confirm res, 7 day cancel policy for refund; 20% T/A comm Nov-Mar (except holidays) **Brochure:** Yes **Payment Terms:** Check DC/MC/V [I12DPAR-14931] **COM YG ITC Member:** No

Rates: **Pvt Bath 7**
Single $ 125.00
Double $ 145.00

Turman House B&B	Hwy 167S 72532	Evening Shade AR
Jim Turman		**Tel:** 800-257-3405 **Fax:** 501-266-3405
		Res Times 9am-5pm M-F

Elegant and new luxurious two bedroom guest Inn set on nineteen rolling, wooded acres with cool breezes and tranquil surroundings. The *Turman House* is located just two miles south of Evening Shade and is set almost in the middle of the nineteen acres surrounded by pine and fruit trees, making this a very unique bed and breakfast indeed. The home has a wrap around porch and a large deck at the rear for the guests to enjoy. All guest rooms are air conditioned and have fans and queen size beds. Mornings begin with the aroma of freshly brewed coffee followed with a full country breakfast. You will be served in either the dining room or in the breakfast room - the choice is yours. Also, as an extra treat, a delightful evening dessert is served. **Discounts:** Seniors **Airport:** Little Rock-100 mi **Reservations:** 50% deposit per night stay within 10 days **Brochure:** Yes **Payment Terms:** Check MC/V [Z03HPAR1-19740] **COM YG ITC Member:** No

Rates: **Pvt Bath 2**   **Shared Bath 2**
Single $ 55-65.00 $ 55-65.00
Double $ 55-65.00 $ 55-65.00

Hideaway Inn	Rt 1 Box 199 72543	Hardy AR
Julia Baldridge		**Tel:** 501-966-4770
		Res Times 8am-8pm

Situated near Hardy, there's 376 acres of privacy with a variety of wildlife and birds, a private fishing hole and plenty of walking trails and picnic sites. Contemporary home features three guest rooms, individually decorated, one with private bath and two queen size beds, two with shared bath and queen size beds. There's central heat and a/c, complimentary full gourmet breakfast served in the dining room with optional lunch and dinner available at added costs and with prior arrangements. *"Come listen to the quiet, breathe the clean fresh air and experience the peace of country living".* While relaxing at the Inn, guests may enjoy browsing the small gift shop, library, TV/VCR and games. Get away from the stress of everyday city life. Area attractions include: Arkansas Traveller Dinner Theater, Ozark Jubilee Theater, Indian Culture Center, Mammoth Spring Park, Grand Gulf State Park, canoeing on Spring River, fishing, golf, boating, horseback riding, antiques and shopping the nearby area. Complimentary full breakfast is included. Lunch and dinners available at added cost and advance notice. **Packages:** Special Occasions, Groups, inquire at res time **Airport:** Memphis-3 hrs; Little Rock-3 Hrs **Seasonal:** No **Reservations:** 50% deposit, 7 day cancel notice for refund **Brochure:** Yes **Permitted:** Drinking (BYOB), children, pets, limited smoking **Payment Terms:** Check AE/DISC/MC/V [I02HPAR1-18843] **COM U ITC Member:** No

Rates: **Pvt Bath 1**   **Shared Bath 2**
Single $ 65.00 $ 50.00
Double $ 75.00 $ 55.00

Olde Stonehouse B&B Inn	511 Main St 72542	Hardy AR
Peggy & David Johnson		**Tel:** 800-514-2983 501-856-2983 **Fax:** 501-856-4036
		Res Times 8am-8pm

Main Street USA - in an old railroad town - guests walk to Spring River (just across the street) or through this quaint town with its unique shops. This Arkansas native stone home was built in the late twenties by a local banker and is original except for updated central air and heat. Your hosts have beautifully furnished the rooms with antiques. American oak pieces furnish the dining room including a claw foot dining table which is set the old fashioned way, with lace table cloths, china and silver - for morning breakfast. The six guest rooms are individually decorated and furnished with antiques and all have queen size beds, ceiling fans and private baths. "Aunt Bette's" room offers ornate Victorian furnishings and "Grandpa Sam's" room is furnished with 19th century oak - including a tall oak bed. "Aunt Tilly's" room contains walnut Victorian furniture, lots of crochet items and the original pedestal sink. "Aunt Jenny's" room is a pink & lace delight with its original claw foot tub and white iron bed and "Uncle Buster's" is the largest, decorated with depression era furnishings. The *"secret suites,"* located nearby, have sitting rooms with "mood setting fireplaces", large old fashioned baths and elaborate bedrooms. Perfect for honeymooners and other special occasions. Rates include a full breakfast plus evening snacks. A pot of coffee and a crock of iced tea are always available. Nearby attractions include Mammoth Spring and Grand Gulf State Park, Cherokee Village, Arkansas Traveller Theater and activities of canoeing and rafting on Spring River, fishing, boating, golf, horseback riding, antiques and craft shopping in Old Hardy Town. **Discounts:** Yes, non-peak periods **Airport:** Memphis, Little Rock, Springfield MO-2 to 3 hrs **Packages:** Yes, inquire at res time **Seasonal:** No **Reservations:** 50% deposit to guarantee reservation, 7 day cancel policy *Suite available **Brochure:** Yes **Permitted:** Drinking (BYOB), limited smoking, no pets or children, please **Conference:** Facilities for small meetings & conference **Payment Terms:** Check AE/DISC/MC/V [I08HPAR1-14900] COM YG **ITC Member:** Yes

Rates:	**Pvt Bath 7**	**Shared Bath 2**
Single	$ 55-65.00	$ 89.00
Double	$ 59-69.00	

Stitt House B&B Inn 824 Park Ave 71901 Hot Springs AR
Linda & Horst Fischer Tel: 501-623-2704 Fax: 501-623-2704

This Victorian jewel sits atop a hill surrounded by two acres of lush greenery in the heart of Hot Springs National Park. Built by entrepreneur Samuel Stitt in 1875, it remained in the family until Linda and Horst Fischer bought it in 1983. After restoring the 6000 square foot mansion to it's old grandeur, they operated a nationally recognized restaurant for eight years. Beginning February 1995, guests can enjoy the charm of this elegant mansion as a beautifully appointed four guest room Bed and Breakfast Inn. Relax in the library, parlor or any of the public areas amid rare antiques and step back in time. Whether you want to work off the sumptuous breakfast, served in your room the formal dining room or on the veranda, or linger with a book - you can do so in or around the heated swimming pool (open April-Sept). All rooms have private bath, lush his and her's terry cloth robes, TV, all day complimentary refreshments, as well as other amenities one would expect at a luxury hotel. The guest rooms are named after each of the host's children. Kai's Korner is a two-room suite with a wrought iron king size canopy bed draped with Battenburg lace. Michael's Manor contains a palatial mahogany poster bed and is decorated in rich warm colors. Loc's Loft" has slanted ceilings, mahogany king size bed and a bath room with a Jacuzzi tub, glass enclosed shower, skylights and polished brass fixtures. "Hong's Hideaway" is a charming room tucked away behind the library and is complete with a French hand-carved king bed with walnut burling and a pullout sofa in a window alcove, affording a view of the beautiful grounds. Restaurants, galleries and shopping are but a mile away. It will be our pleasure to pamper you! **Airport:** Hot Springs Memorial-3 mi; Little Rock-55 mi **Discounts:** 5% cash, corporate when rooms are available **Packages:** Honeymoon, Fun In The Sun **Reservations:** Credit card guarantee, 48 hr cancel policy for refund **Brochure:** Yes **Permitted:** Children 13+, drinking **Conference:** Yes **Languages:** German **Payment Terms:** AE/MC/V [I03-HPAR1-21521] COM YG **ITC Member:** No **Quality Assured:** Yes

Rates: Pvt Bath 4
Single $ 95-110.00
Double $ 95-110.00

1735 House	584 S Fletcher Ave 32034	Amelia Island FL
Tim & Marsha Stowers	Tel: 800-872-8531 904-261-4148	**Fax:** 904-261-9200
		Res Times 7am-11pm

Step into another era with the salt breeze, beaches and surf in this delightful oceanside nautical setting that even includes a lighthouse near the main house. This weathered white framed inn is a perfect place for unwinding by the sound of the waves. Decorated with nautical decor including marine charts, century-old sea chests, natural wicker, and old prints of sailing vessels filling the Georgia heart-pine panelled walls. There are five suites which sleep up to four persons, with private baths and a down-home style kitchen where guests can prepare their "fresh catch" or brew their own coffee. Swimming, fishing, boating, beachcombing, boat rentals and charters nearby or try your hand at treasure hunting! There is plenty of tennis, golf, sightseeing, shopping, horseback riding and touring. Complimentary beach towels, "shell collection bags" and drying lines available. Airport pick-up can be arranged in advance from Fernandina Beach airport. **Discounts:** AARP **Seasonal:** No **Reservations:** 50% deposit within 7 days of res; full payment for just one day; refunded if cancelled with advanced notice, check-in 4pm **Brochure:** Yes **Permitted:** Limited children, drinking, smoking **Payment Terms:** Check AE/DISC/DC/MC/V [I04IPFL1-6120] COM YG **ITC Member:** No

Rates: Pvt Bath 6
Single $ 100-120.00
Double $ 100-120.00

Elizabeth Pointe Lodge	98 S Fletcher 32034	Amelia Island FL
David & Susan Caples	Tel: 800-772-3359 904-277-4851	**Fax:** 904-277-6500
		Res Times 7am-11pm

David & Susan Caples, who originally founded the *1735 House* on Amelia Island, Florida have now put their talent to a new lodging experience. Opened January 1992, the Lodge is constructed in a 1890's "Nantucket shingle" style with a strong maritime theme. Porches surround the main floor with an abundance of rockers, sunshine and lemonade. Newspapers are delivered to your room to start each day. A complimentary breakfast is served homestyle in an oceanfront sun room. All twenty five guest rooms are different and it makes room hunting down the winding halls an interesting pastime. Books, personal effects and maritime photos are everywhere as has been the case with previous Caples creations. Fresh flowers, oversized tubs and homemade snacks are all part of the fun. Sitting prominently on the Atlantic Ocean, the Lodge is only steps from the barrier island sand

dunes. Long stretches of often deserted beaches

await the guest. Sailing, fishing charters, tennis, golf, and horseback riding are nearby. Touring bikes, beach equipment and airport pickup are always available for guests. Special tours, outings, and charters can be arranged to suit your adventure. The historic seaport of Fernandina is only a short bike ride away for dining & shopping. Susan and daughters Katie and Beth Ann have daily activities planned that you can participate in . . . for kids, or "big kids". **Airport:** Jacksonville FL 25 mi **Discounts:** Seniors -10%, travel agents-25% **Seasonal:** No **Reservations:** 50% deposit within 7 days of reservation; depending on length of stay, cancel notice is 2-14 day notice for refund. **Brochure:** Yes **Permitted:** Children, drinking, arrangements for pets can be made nearby **Conference:** Yes, excellent facilities as Executive Retreat with food and beverage catered to your needs; complete a/v, fax, copy and secretarial services available **Payment Terms:** Check AE/DISC/MC/V [I05HPFL1-14372] **COM** YG **ITC Member:** No

Rates: Pvt Bath 25
Single $ 90.00-up
Double $ 100.00-up

Duncan House B&B	1703 Gulf Dr 34217	**Bradenton Beach FL**
Becky & Joe		**Tel:** 813-778-6858
		Res Times 9am-9pm

Come spend some time with Becky, Joe and friends on beautiful Anna Marie Island. A relaxed area close to central Florida full of great restaurants to be savored. Walk our white sandy beaches, hunt for sharks teeth or enjoy the turquoise water and spectacular sunsets. A full breakfast awaits you in the morning with home made breads, muffins, fresh fruit, juice, coffee and a variety of entrees. Victorian decor with romantic furnishings and period antiques combine with modern comforts and conveniences in each of our guest rooms and suites, making your stay unforgettable. **Airport:** Sarasota/Bradenton-30 min; Tampa-1-1/2 hr **Reservations:** One night deposit (full deposit for holidays) with major credit card, 14 day cancel policy for refund **Permitted:** Limited children, limited pets, limited smoking, drinking **Conference:** Yes, to six couples **Payment Terms:** Check AE/MC/V [K07FPFL-11981] **COM** Y **ITC Member:** No

Rates: Pvt Bath 4
Single $ 55-95.00
Double $ 55-95.00

Cedar Key B&B	810 Third St 32625	**Cedar Key FL**
Lois & Bob Davenport	**Tel:** 800-453-5051 904-543-9000	**Fax:** 904-543-8070
		Res Times 9am-8pm

Located three miles out into the Gulf, Cedar Key is a small island community nestled among the many tiny Keys on the Nature Coast of Florida. The town is one of the oldest seaports in the state and today offers a rich history, tranquil life-style and an almost forgotten old Florida atmosphere. The house, built in 1880, is number twenty-three on the Cedar Key Historical District Walking Tour. It was built by the Eagle Cedar Mill entirely of native yellow pine as an employee and guest house. Later it was operated as a boarding house by the sister of David Levy Yulee. Prominent in the history of Florida, David Levy Yulee was one of Florida's first US Senators and for whom this county was named. Purchased by BC Wadley in 1919, the house remained in the same family until 1991. Lovingly and painstakingly restored, the home once again is offering gracious accommodations as a Bed & Breakfast. It is located within walking distance of all the unique shops as well as the "dock" and fishing pier. A full breakfast included. **Airport:** Gainesville Regional-60 mi **Seasonal:** No **Reservations:** One night deposit to confirm reser-

Florida *National Edition*

vation, 5 day cancel policy for refund, check-in 3-8pm, check-out 11am **Brochure:** Yes **Permitted:** Children 13-up, drinking, limited smoking **Payment Terms:** Check AE/MC/V [K04HPFL1-16881] **COM YG ITC Member:** No

Rates: Pvt Bath 5
Single $ 65-85.00
Double $ 65-85.00

Historic Island Hotel	PO Box 460 32625	Cedar Key FL
Tom & Alison Sanders		**Tel:** 352-543-5111
		Res Times 7am-11:30pm

A pre-Civil War building with Jamaican style architecture, the Island Hotel is one of the oldest hotels in Florida. Rustic and authentic, retaining much of the original structure, it is listed on the *National Register of Historic Places*. The hotel has a colourful history, beginning life as a general store and serving as a troop billet for both armies in the Civil War. The Hotel retains it's romantic ambiance, and staying with us is like stepping back in time, with muraled walls, paddle fans, French doors and a wide wrap-around porch which catches the gulf breezes. The rooms all have a/c and most have private baths, but there are few other concessions to the 20th Century. The hotel restaurant serves a gourmet seafood menu with local fish, fresh from the bay. The menu is distinctively Cedar Key, including soft shell crabs, stone crab claws, grouper and pompano in season. Jahn McCumbers, the chef, combines a French training with local knowledge and her own unique style to make dining a delightful experience. The bar is also worth a visit. Decorated with murals of Cedar Key painted in 1946, the Neptune lounge is cozy and informal. The bar is built of local cedar and serves a full range of wines, beers and cocktails. Set in the historical district of sleepy Cedar Key, the *Island Hotel* is relaxing, romantic and restful - the perfect place to get away from it all. **Airport:** Gainesville-70 mi; Tampa, Tallahassee, Orlando-3 Hrs **Packages:** Yes, Two night stay with B&B and dinner for two, $250.00 **Seasonal:** No **Reservations:** Credit card deposit **Brochure:** Yes **Permitted:** Limited children, drinking, smoking **Conference:** Groups to 200 nearby **Languages:** French, Japanese **Payment Terms:** Check AE/MC/V [I04HPFL1-1044] **COM YG ITC Member:** No

Rates: Pvt Bath 6   Shared Bath 4
Single $ 85-95.00 $ 75-85.00
Double $ 85-95.00 $ 75-85.00

Higgins House B&B		Daytona Beach FL
Walter & Roberta Padgett		**Tel:** 407-324-9238

Refer to the same listing name under Sanford, Florida for a complete description **Seasonal:** No **Payment Terms:** Check AE/DC/MC/V [M09FPFL-18174] **COM YG ITC Member:** No

Rates: Pvt Bath 1   Shared Bath 2
Single $ 70.00 $ 60.00
Double $ 85.00 $ 75.00

Live Oak Inn	444-448 S Beach St 32114	Daytona Beach FL
Del & Jessie Glock	**Tel:** 800-253-4667 904-252-4667	**Fax:** 904-255-1871
		Res Times 8am-10pm

Daytona's oldest residences (1871 & 1881) have been completely restored and welcome guests with historic gardens and verandas, fountains and a gazebo offering a romantic, relaxful and refined retreat - yet next to all of the sights and activities of the "World's Most Famous Beach." Located on the site on which Mathias Day began Daytona as a refuge from the ravages of the Civil War, these homes are listed on the *National Register of Historic Places*. The decor features significant periods of Florida's history and include period antiques, canopy beds and armories in many rooms.

All rooms have private baths with nine rooms offering either a whirlpool or antique soaking tub. Fourteen rooms have porches overlooking Daytona's new marina or the Inn's garden. Fine gourmet dining, high-tea, cafe, and banquet services indoors or in the outdoor garden are available. Amenities include an outdoor hot tub, bikes, bathrobes, flowers and fruit baskets, a continental breakfast and a complimentary beverage upon arrival. There's off-street parking, concierge and breakfast in-bed! Within walking distance are all of Daytona's sights, including museums, riverfront parks, beach areas, recreational activities and great shopping; 3/4 mi to beaches and 1-1/2 mi to Speedway and airport. Anyone seeking a retreat or reunion setting or parents seeking a holiday retreat will find this an ideal location. **Seasonal:** Rates vary **Reservations:** 25% deposit 2 wks prior to arrival, 7 day cancel policy less $10 service fee, late arrival by prior arrangement only **Brochure:** Yes **Permitted:** Children 12-up, limited smoking **Conference:** Ideal for groups to 30 persons **Payment Terms:** Check AE/MC/V [R08CPFL-11256] **COM** Y **ITC Member:** No

Rates: Pvt Bath 16
Single $ 55-160.00
Double $ 55-160.00

Sunbright Manor	606 Live Oak 32433	**DeFuniak Springs FL**
John & Byrdie Mitchell		**Tel:** 904-892-0656

Enjoy a lovely Queen Anne home from 1886 formerly owned by Florida Governor Sidney J Catts. This complete restored gem included a beautiful tower and porches with over 1600 spindles and thirty-three columns - that everyone passing stops to appreciate the beauty of this home. Listed on the National Register of Historic Places, all of the rooms are interestingly furnished with antiques from the Victorian Period, some of which are for sale! A continental breakfast is served in the formal dining room and includes fresh Florida juices, fresh-baked pastries, hot beverages, hot and cold cereals all served on original Jewel T China. An annual Chautauqua Festival is held in DeFuniak Springs which began in 1884. Evenings offer complimentary spiced tea on the front porch with your hosts, the Mitchells, who provide historical anecdotes about their lovely home and town. **Seasonal:** No **Brochure:** Yes **Payment Terms:** Check [C05C-CFL-10923] **COM** Y **ITC Member:** No

Rates: Pvt Bath 3   **Shared Bath** 1
Single $ 60-85.00 $ 60-85.00
Double $ 60-85.00 $ 60-85.00

Bailey House	28 S 7th St 32034	**Fernandina Beach FL**
Tom & Diane Hay		**Tel:** 904-261-5390

Center of historic district is this darling 1895 Queen Anne listed on *National Register of Historic Places* with all the amenities you'd expect including wonderful carved woodwork, brass beds, marble topped-tables, footed bath tubs, and beautiful antique furniture pieces to complete the Victorian period. You're close to the beach, horseback riding, shops, restaurants. **Brochure:** Yes **Permitted:** Children over 10, limited smoking, and drinking. **Payment Terms:** Check AE [C11ACFL-1055] **COM** Y **ITC Member:** No

Rates: Pvt Bath 4
Single $ 65.00-up
Double $ 75.00-up

1735 House		**Fernandnia Beach FL**
Gary & Emily Grable		**Tel:** 800-872-8531 904-261-4148
		Res Times 7am-11pm

Refer to the same listing name under Amelia Island, Florida for a complete description. **Seasonal:** No **Payment Terms:** Check AE/DISC/DC/MC/V [M05-BPFL-9459] **COM** YG **ITC Member:** No

Rates: Pvt Bath 6
Single $ 100-120.00
Double $ 100-120.00

Florida *National Edition*

Grandma Newtons B&B	40 NW 5th Ave 33034	Florida City FL
Mildred Newton		Tel: 305-247-4413
		Res Times 9am-4pm

Grandma Newton makes sure every guest enjoys Southern Florida by spoiling them with plenty of country-style hospitality and comfort. Her Historically Designated 1914 two-story pine home is surrounded by soaring palms and shrubs with a large grassy yard that's perfect for capturing the warm Florida breeze. All of the rooms have been renovated and comfortably furnished in a mixture of furnishings and styles and there is room for even the largest of families in a separate guest house! All rooms are a/c but guests can choose to open the windows or operate the ceiling fans if they like. Mornings bring the aroma of fresh coffee and home baked biscuits while a full breakfast is prepared just the way you like it! (If it's baking day - you'll get to try her specialty - green tomato pie!)

Grandma will help in all your sightseeing interests whether it's Miami's Goldcoast, Biscayne National Park, the Florida Keys or the Everglades National Park - you're just minutes away from them all! Don't miss this quaint home and it's charming hostess who guarantees 100% satisfaction for every guest! **Seasonal:** No **Reservations:** Deposit required, advise if late arrival. Discounts for longer stays. **Brochure:** Yes **Permitted:** Children, smoking, drinking **Payment Terms:** Check [R01C-PFL-1057] **COM** Y **ITC Member:** No

Rates:	Pvt Bath 6	Shared Bath 8
Single	$ 50.00	$ 45.00
Double	$ 65.00	$ 55.00

Magnolia Plantation B&B	309 SE Seventh St 32601	Gainesville FL
Joe & Cindy Montalto		Tel: 904-375-6653
		Res Times 8am-10pm

The *Magnolia Plantation B&B* is a completely restored French Second Empire Victorian dating from 1885, located in a National Register Historic District. Nestled among beautiful magnolias - the grounds were lovingly designed by Joe's father (a professional landscape architect) and are tended by Cindy's mother. You're in the comfort of waterfalls, a sixty-foot meandering pond and a gazebo - all perfect for a soothing cool drink late in the afternoon. The Inn offers six uniquely decorated guest rooms (still retaining their original 1885 configuration), satisfying the needs of the no-nonsense corporate traveler or the incurable romantic. Antiques and family heirlooms fill many of the rooms including antique fixtures and clawfoot tubs in the baths. All of the woodwork is original to the house as well as the ten fireplace mantels and tile work. Upon arrival you'll enjoy complimentary wine served in your room along with freshly baked goodies and snacks. A complimentary full (meatless) breakfast is served indoors or out with lunch available upon request and with added cost. Located six miles east of I-75 and 1.5 miles from the University of Florida, guests are within walking distance of downtown, the Hippodrome State Theatre, Matheson Historical Center and a fine selection of restaurants. *Magnolia Plantation* has been a true *"labor of love"- we love sharing with guests.* **Discounts:** Yes, inquire at res time **Airport:** Gainesville Regional-3 mi **Seasonal:** No **Reservations:** Credit card number or deposit for one night's stay to guarantee reservation, 7 day cancel policy for refund **Brochure:** Yes **Permitted:** Limited children, limited pets, limited smoking, drinking **Payment Terms:** Check AE/MC/V [Z05HPFL1-14876] **COM** YG **ITC Member:** No

Rates:	Pvt Bath 6
Single	$ 70-125.00
Double	$ 70-125.00

Harrington House	5626 Gulf Dr 34217	Holmes Beach FL
Jo & Frank Davis		Tel: 813-778-5444 813-778-6335

©Inn & Travel Memphis, Tennessee

This gracious 1925 beachfront home is snuggled on the unspoiled island of Anna Maria - beachfront locations - offering guests the best of Florida! Your hosts, Jo & Frank have completely restored their home and have lovingly furnished and decorated each room to please every taste. Each guest room offers a "special theme and decor" such as the Birdsong Room which offers a soft romantic setting or the Veranda Room that is furnished in casual wicker. Each room has a private bath, fan and most have French Doors leading to a balcony overlooking the Gulf of Mexico for a romantic evening sunset. Guests can just step outside the door and enjoy a stroll along the tranquil beach or take a refreshing dip in the pool. Evening brings guests around the fireplace where they enjoy hot chocolate and plenty of conversation with your charming hosts and other guests. Betty makes every guest feel at home each morning by preparing your full breakfast - just the way you like it! Nearby attractions include Ringling Mansion andMuseum, Bishops Planetarium and Shelby Gardens. Within a 2-hour drive, you'll reach the exciting world of Florida at Disney World Complex, Epcot Center, Busch Gardens and MGM Theme Park. Your hosts have plenty of tips to share about the area events, attractions and dining spots. **Seasonal:** Rates vary **Reservations:** One night's deposit, two week cancel policy. *High season rates (Dec-Apr). Low-season rates (May-Nov) $79-139.00, two night stay weekends & holidays **Brochure:** Yes **Permitted:** Children 12-up, drinking, smoking outside **Conference:** Yes for groups to 12 persons **Payment Terms:** Check MC/V [K05GPFL-6635] **COM** Y **ITC Member:** No

Rates:	Pvt Bath 8
Single	$ 79-139.00
Double	$ 129-159.00

1735 House   Jacksonville FL
Gary & Emily Grable   Tel: 800-872-8531 904-261-4148
Res Times 7am-11pm

Refer to the same listing name under Amelia Island, Florida for a complete description. **Seasonal:** No **Payment Terms:** Check AE/DISC/DC/MC/V [M05PFL-9460] **COM** YG **ITC Member:** No

Rates:	Pvt Bath 6
Single	$ 100-120.00
Double	$ 100-120.00

House On Cherry Street   1844 Cherry St 32205   Jacksonville FL
Carol Anderson   Tel: 904-384-1999
Res Times 8am-8pm

Older, restored Colonial home on beautiful St Johns River in Historic Riverside-Avondale area; just ten minutes from downtown, twenty minutes from the airport. Guests will enjoy period antique furnishings, canopy beds, oriental carpets, decoys, baskets, coverlets and other collectibles. Amenities include complimentary wine or soft beverage, snacks, a/c and ceiling fans and flowers in each guest room, which includes a sitting area. A full breakfast is served with entrees that include baked french toast, eggs benedict, and crepes. Fresh orange juice, fresh ground New Orleans coffee and various breads are included, also. You'll enjoy tennis, golf, hiking trails, fishing and fine restaurants nearby. Complimentary bikes are available for leisurely touring town. **Seasonal:** No **Reservations:** One night's deposit with 3-day cancellation policy for refund; two night min for special events **Brochure:** Yes **Permitted:** Drinking, smoking, limited pets, limited children**Payment Terms:** Check [R01BCFL-1066] **COM** Y **ITC Member:** No

Rates:	Pvt Bath 2	Shared Bath 2
Single	$ 80.00	$ 70.00
Double	$ 85.00	$ 75.00

Florida   *National Edition*

Jules' Undersea Lodge	51 Shoreland Dr 33037	**Key Largo FL**
Ian Koblick/Neil Monney		Tel: 305-451-2353 Fax: 305-451-4789
		Res Times 8am-5pm

The *world's first and* **only underwater** *hotel* invites you to experience an incredible adventure you will never forget .... a voyage to *Jules' Undersea Lodge*. . . five fathoms beneath the surface of the Emerald Lagoon at Key Largo Undersea Park. *Jules' Undersea Lodge* is designed to provide luxury air conditioned accommodations for up to six persons. Deluxe amenities include 40" diameter windows, a fully stocked galley, hot showers, telephone, stereo sound system and VCR. *Jules Undersea Lodge* is the perfect place to celebrate a birthday, anniversary or honeymoon. The Lodge also offers a unique elegance for underwater weddings. Cakes and flowers are available with prior arrangements. *"A very special place for very special people."* Once the private realm of marine scientists, the fascinating world of Innerspace is now opened to all divers. Dive with an unlimited air supply, using hookah diving gear to investigate Marine Lab, an operating research habitat. Listen to underwater music as you explore sunken wrecks and visit your aquatic neighbors. Live within the sea of the "experience of a lifetime." Become an Aquanaut by spending an entire day and night in underwater luxury. From 1pm to 11am, enjoy unlimited diving (certified divers only), a gourmet dinner and breakfast, snacks and beverages. Dinner is prepared and served by a "mer-chef." Each guest earns their personal Aquanaut certificate. Located in Key Largo Undersea Park, the site of Scott Carpenter Man In The Sea Program, operated by Marine Resources Foundation offering a one man sub, an undersea laboratory, commercial diving and submerging in a diving bell. **Airport:** Miami-55mi **Discounts:** Inquire at res time Note: Guests must scuba dive to enter the quarters. Three hour lesson available for guests not certified. **Seasonal:** No **Reservations:** 50% deposit at res time, full payment upon arrival. Full refund for cancellations 30 days and longer, less than 30 days notice, 50% refund, 7 days or less forfeit deposit *Rates based on American Plan **Brochure:** Yes **Permitted:** Children 12-up **Conference:** Yes, to 8 persons for *very private* meetings. **Payment Terms:** Check DISC/MC/V [I01BCFL-6101] **COM** YG **ITC Member:** No

Rates:	Pvt Bath 2	Shared Bath 2
Single	$ 195-295.00	
Double	$ 390-590.00	

Banyan Resort Of Key West	323 Whitehead St 33040	**Key West FL**
Martin J Bettencourt		Tel: 800-865-3993 305-296-7786 Fax: 305-294-1107
		Res Times 9am-9pm

The *Banyan Resort* is nestled in the heart of Historic Old Town Key West and includes eight elegantly refurbished Victorian homes, five of which are listed on the *National Historic Register*. The estate includes 38 contemporary suites each with French doors that open onto a private patio or veranda. The atmosphere is tranquil amid the lush tropical gardens which boast two massive Banyan trees and over 200 varieties of tropical flora, spring-fed and two heated swimming pools, a jacuzzi, waterfall and lily pond. Choose from a studio, one bedroom suite, or two bedroom suites with one or two baths. The *Banyan Resort* is within walking distance to restaurants, night-life, shops, boat tours, sightseeing and the beach. Located on Whitehead

©*Inn & Travel Memphis, Tennessee*

National Edition   ***Florida***

Street which runs from Mel Fisher's Treasure Saviors on the north to the southern most point of the USA and midway between the Audubon House and Hemingway's home. **Discounts:** Travel agents, airline employees **Airport:** Key West Intl-4 miles **Reservations:** One nights deposit with 14 day cancel policy for refund, *high season rates for 12/15-4/30, low season 115-165.00, *check for deposit only

Permitted: Limited children, limited drinking **Conference:** With prior arrangements **Languages:** Spanish **Payment Terms:** Check* AE/DC/MC/V [I05HPFL1-7122] **COM** YG **ITC Member:** No

Rates: Pvt Bath 38
Single $ 185-265.00
Double $ 185-265.00

Curry Mansion	511 Caroline St 33040	Key West FL
Edith & Al Amsterdam		Tel: 800-253-3466 305-294-5349 **Fax:** 305-294-4093

An oasis of quiet, beauty and sunshine, *The Curry Mansion*, *National Register residence*, guests step back in time when Florida's first millionaire built this magnificent residence. Your hosts/owners just completed a fifteen guest room wing that's attached to the Mansion with every room opening onto the fantastic outdoor pool/patio area, and like the Mansion, the rooms are furnished with period antiques, wicker, handmade patchwork quilts with modern amenities; a/c, phones, wet bar, cable TV and ceiling fans. Honeymooners will enjoy the special suite available just for them! Just a hundred feet from Duval Street and the excitement of the Keys. Complimentaries include Membership in the prestigious Pier House Beach Club with the most picturesque powder white beach in the Keys! Fresh orange juice, fruit, homemade muffins, cereal and plenty of freshly brewed coffee are served every morning. Your delightful hosts love entertaining their guests and offer a daily complimentary "Happy Hour" of snacks, chips, dip, wine, beer, rum, juices and soft drinks and a full bar. **Airport:** Key West-3mi **Reservations:** Deposit required to confirm reservation. **Permitted:** Children, drinking, smoking; barrier free handicap access **Languages:** Spanish, Italian, French, German **Payment Terms:** Check AE/DC/-MC/V [I11DPFL-8410] **COM** Y **ITC Member:** No

Rates: Pvt Bath 21
Single $ 140-200.00
Double $ 140-200.00

Eden House	1015 Fleming 33040	Key West FL
Michael Eden		Tel: 800-533-KEYS 305-296-6868 **Fax:** 305-294-1221
		Res Times 8am-11pm

A great place to slip away to - since 1930! Accommodations ranging from inexpensive, clean and simply decorated guest rooms to extravagant suites where Goldie Hawn's film, *Criss Cross* - your choice depends upon your needs and interest. Located deep in the Historic District of Key West - guests are close to the ceremonial sunsets at Mallory Square, the shops of Duval, a short bike ride to the famous beaches while removed from the crowds of Duval Street. Traditional Key West is served here - tropical plants, pool, Caribbean jacuzzi, decks, a gazebo and an exciting restaurant on the premises with a menu specialties of eggs Benedict or crepes with breast of chicken. Don't miss beginning your day in the traditional Key West manner by slowly sipping a cafe con leche (strong cappuccino with sugar from the nearby Five Brothers Cuban grocery store) while sitting in original green metal rockers on the front porch - enjoying the cool early morning breeze. If you need help with your plans, just ask Steve or Robin - they'll be

©*Inn & Travel Memphis, Tennessee*   3-21

sure to get you started in the right direction. Meals are available but not included in your room rate. **Discounts:** AAA, AARP, airline personnel, Prodigy Members, Seniors **Airport:** Key West Intl-15 min **Seasonal:** Rates vary **Reservations:** 50% deposit required within 7 days of booking, 14/20 day cancel policy for refund. Room rates quoted for high season; mid-season & off-season rates are lower. **Brochure:** Yes **Permitted:** Children, drinking, smoking, limited pets **Conference:** Facilities available for small groups (ten persons), call for details **Languages:** French, Spanish **Payment Terms:** Check* MC/V [K03HPFL1-1073] **COM** U **ITC Member:** No

Rates:	Pvt Bath 22	Shared Bath 20
Single	$ 125-250.00	$ 80-95.00
Double	$ 125-250.00	$ 80-95.00

Heron House   512 Simonton St 33040   **Key West FL**
Fred Geibelt   **Tel:** 800-294-1644 305-294-9227 **Fax:** 305-294-5692
Res Times 9am-9pm

Just one block off Duval Street, smack in the center of Key West, the *Heron House* offers travelers twenty guest rooms that are more like suites. There are large comfortable beds, inlaid wood and mirrored walls, high ceilings, ceiling fans, cool tiled floors, marble bathrooms, stained glass over slatted French doors, color TV and even a wet bar and refrigerator - an "instant escape" to the Keys. Combining three homes, your host provides every convenience including an outdoor pool area and spacious decks surrounded by a planned "tropical rainforest" garden fantasy including wild orchids, bougainvillea, jasmine and palms. A complimentary continental breakfast "spread" perfect for starting your day in Key West, is set out under a cool, slat-roofed porch. There are delicious sticky buns, warm bagels, bowls of fruit, bran and blueberry muffins, fresh juice and coffee. Centrally located, guests are within walking distance of the main drag filled with funky clothing shops, outdoor bars, eateries and "what's happening" in Key West - including a get-together at sunset where a full assortment of street performers, tourists and locals gather each evening to celebrate the day's end and the start of evening celebrations. **Airport:**- 2mi **Seasonal:** No **Reservations:** Two night's deposit at res time, 14 day cancel policy for refund. *Check accepted only in advance of arrival **Brochure:** Yes **Permitted:** Drinking, smoking **Payment Terms:** AE/DC/MC/V [U05HPFL1-1076] **COM** YG **ITC Member:** No

Rates:	Pvt Bath 21
Single	$ 95-225.00
Double	$ 95-225.00

Island City House   411 William St 33040   **Key West FL**
Stan & Jan Corneal   **Tel:** 800-634-8230 305-294-5702 **Fax:** 305-294-1289
Res Times 8am-8pm

Three unique guest houses share a private tropical garden with winding brick walkways throughout, a breakfast terrace with coral rock fountain, shaded porches, widows' walk, and crystal clear pool and Jacuzzi. The *Island City House* is a grand three-story Victorian mansion circa 1889 complete with hardwood floors, Bahama fans, lace curtains, period furnishings, and full amenities in all suites. The Arch House is the original carriage house to the mansion with gingerbread trimmed arched carriageway allowing the tropical breezes to reach inside. Balconies, Bahama fans, and casual island decor are what characterize these light and airy suites. The all-cypress Cigar House dates from 1980, but was built in the style of a cigar factory that once stood on that site. These spacious suites are furnished in an elegant tropical style with hardwood floors, Bahama fans, porches with hammocks overlooking the pool and Jacuzzi deck, and full amenities. All twenty four one and two bedrooms are full suites with kitchens, dining area, living area, bedroom and private bath. Additional amenities include private phone, color TV and air conditioning. A complimentary continental breakfast of fresh-baked breads, muffins, fruit, coffee and tea is served outside beneath the palms. **Airport:** Key West Intl-2 mi **Packages:** Honeymoon **Discounts:** Extended stays, AAA, Group **Seasonal:** Rates vary by season **Reservations:** One night's deposit at res time; 7-day cancellation policy for refund. *Off-season rates quoted **Brochure:** Yes **Permitted:** Children, smoking, drinking **Conference:** Yes, for small social or business meetings. **Payment Terms:** Check DC/DISC/MC/V [K03HPFL1-1077] **COM YG ITC Member:** No

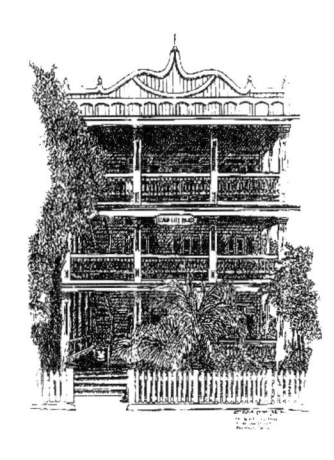

Rates:	Pvt Bath 24
Single	$ 95-145.00
Double	$ 95-145.00

Pilot House	511 Eaton 33040	Key West FL
		Tel: 800-648-3780 305-294-3800
		Res Times 8am-8pm

Handsome 1880's residence tastefully adapted to enhance Victorian character touches include rugs, fabrics, original art and antiques imported from England but with 20th Century of amenities private shower/bathroom, a/c, refrigerators, and your own porch, patio, or veranda. Listed on *National Register of Historic Places*, this Inn is internationally and nationally renowned and received the *"Architectural Restoration Award"* in 1983. **Reservations:** 1/3rd deposit with reservation, full refund with 14 day notice of cancellation or if re-booked (likely). **Brochure:** Yes **Permitted:** Drinking, smoking **Payment Terms:** Check AE/MC/V [X09ACFL-1072] **COM Y ITC Member:** No

Rates:	Pvt Bath 12
Single	$ 95-115.00
Double	$ 110-130.00

Popular House	415 Williams 33040	Key West FL
Jody Carlson	Tel: 800-438-6155 305-296-7274	Fax: 305-293-0306
		Res Times 9am-9pm

The *Popular House* is a 100-year old three-story Victorian home located in the center of Key West's historic district, within walking distance to beaches, shops, restaurants, bars and boats. Listed on the *National Register of Historical Places*, this lovely home was built by Bahamian shipbuilders and is located on a quiet, tree-shaded street in the heart of Key West's Old Town. Each guest room is uniquely decorated featuring high ceilings, hardwood floors, Caribbean-style furnishings and the exposed Dade County Pine walls complement the extensive collection of local art. Pastel porches, sundecks, lush gardens, jacuzzi and spa allows guests the pleasure of relaxing in tropical ease and splendor. A continental breakfast includes Cuban coffee, homebaked breads, cakes, seasonal fruits and fresh-squeezed orange juice, served at your leisure. **Discounts:** Yes, inquire at res time **Airport:** Key West Intl-15 min **Seasonal:** No **Reservations:** One night's deposit required, 14 day cancel policy for refund **Brochure:** Yes **Permitted:** Drinking, smoking, limited children **Conference:** Yes for groups to 17 persons **Languages:** German, French **Payment Terms:** Check AE/DC/DISC/MC/V [K05HPFL1-1083] **COM YG ITC Member:** No

Rates:	Pvt Bath 4	Shared Bath 5
Single		$ 49-79.00
Double	$ 79-250.00	$ 59-99.00

©Inn & Travel Memphis, Tennessee

Florida *National Edition*

Watson House	525 Simonton St 33040	Key West FL
Joe Beres/Ed Czaplicki	Tel: 800-621-9405 305-294-6712 **Fax:** 305-294-7501	
		Res Times 9-9

Built 1860 by William & Susan Watson, *The Watson House* was later sold and remolded as a Southern Colonial Mansion. The house was owned by several prominent Key West families until 1984, when it was purchased by the current owners, who fully restored and expanded it to the original Bahamian style. The *Watson House* is a distinctively furnished guest house in the Historic Preservation District of Old Key West. The House received the *"1987 Award For Excellence"* by the *Historical Florida Keys Preservation Board*. Entering through the rear gate, one will discover a heated swimming pool, heated jacuzzi, patio, decks and gardens. Accommodations include two separate suites on the second floor of the main house; a queen size bed in a one bedroom suite and a four room apartment. Separate from the main house is a Cabana, which is a four-room private apartment. All units have their own distinctive style and include a private bath and modern amenities: color cable TV, phones and a/c. Both apartments have full kitchens. Privacy prevails here - at this *"Adults Only" location.* Continental breakfast is included with full kitchen for guests to prepare any meals. AAA approved/High rating; ABBA A+ Rated **Airport:** Key West, 1.5 miles **Seasonal:** Rates vary **Reservations:** Two night deposit required within 7 days of booking for min of 2 night's lodging; 14-day cancel policy **Brochure:** Yes **Permitted:** Adults only, no pets, limited drinking, limited smoking **Payment Terms:** AE/MC/V [K05HPFL1-1086] COM YG **ITC Member:** No

Rates: Pvt Bath 3
Single $ 105-140.00
Double $ 105-380.00

Chalet Suzanne Country Inn	3800 Chalet Suzanne Dr 33853	Lake Wales FL
Bonnie Grenier	Tel: 800-433-6011 813-676-6011 **Fax:** 813-676-1814	

Discover Europe in the heart of Florida! This historic Country Inn is nestled on seventy acres of fragrant orange groves overlooking beautiful Lake Suzanne. Beginning with Bertha Hinshaw's Yankee Ingenuity and Southern Hospitality, a world traveler and gourmet cook, the Inn opened in the 1930's following The Stock Market Crash. The unlikely combination of today's architecture rambles in all directions and on at least fourteen different levels. Guests enjoy all the amenities of these unique lodgings where guest rooms are furnished with appointments from around the world. *Selected as one of Florida's top "Romantic Inns",* amenities include swimming pool, lake, artist's workshop, soup cannery, antique and gift shops, and a 2450' private airstrip. Guests are treated to award winning excellence in the dining room which has received the Mobil 4-star Award, *Travel/Holiday* **Fine Dining Award** and voted *Golden Spoon's* **Florida Top Ten Restaurants** for 24 consecutive years. Listed by Duncan Hines in the very first *"Guide To Good Eating"* in the USA and more recently, glowing reviews have appeared in *"Better Homes & Tampa Gardens", "Gourmet Life", "Time" and "Southern Living"*. **Uncle Ben's Top 10 National Award Winner.** A memorable experience. AAA-3 Diamond **Jetport:** Orlando-50mi **Packages:** Mini-Vacation, Honeymoon, Murder Mystery. **Discounts:** Groups, Summer Photo Credit: David Woods, Winter Haven FL **Seasonal:** No **Reservations:** One night's deposit required, 72 hour cancel policy for refund **Brochure:** Yes **Permitted:** Children, pets, smoking, drinking **Conference:** Yes, full capabilities for groups to forty persons **Languages:** German, French **Payment Terms:** Check AE/DC/DISC/MC/V [I08HPFL1-2949] COM YG **ITC Member:** No

Rates: Pvt Bath 30
Single $ 125-195.00
Double $ 125-195.00

©*Inn & Travel Memphis, Tennessee*

Miami River Inn	118 SW S River Dr 33130	Miami FL
Sallye Jude	Tel: 800-468-3589 305-325-0045 **Fax:** 305-325-9227	
		Res Times 10am-10pm

Miami River Inn, Miami's only B&B, is located in the ethnically diverse Miami River Neighborhood of East Little Havana. The Inn, originally built in 1908, was restored to its original splendor in the late 1980's by local preservationist and community activist Sallye Jude. Considered Miami's best kept secret, the Inn is now listed on the *National Register of Historic Places*. The *"compound"* consists of five wooden cottages surrounding a pool and Jacuzzi in a lush tropical environment flourishing with flowers, soaring palms and other native greenery. Guests can enjoy a lazy day by the pool, soaking up the suns' rays while being entertained by our extended family of cats and kittens. Or take a seat on a comfortable wicker couch on the front porch as the sun falls, with a complimentary glass of red wine, and watch the cargo ships squeeze through the Miami River aided by tugoats - - it's almost magical. Rooms are individually decorated with antiques and period pieces. Lace curtains, hardwood floors and painted ceilings outline the rooms with brass, wood and wicker furniture filling in the rest. Guests can take a first-floor room with a porch that opens to the garden area or choose a room on the second or third floors with a view to the east, overlooking the river and downtown. Room amenities include color TV, touch-tone phones, central air and heat and ceiling fans. Beaches, colleges, hospitals, air/sea-port, concert and sporting venues - all within 15 minutes. Gym, dry cleaning and business services are available also. Continental breakfast included. **Discounts:** AAA, AARP, Government **Airport:** Miami Intl-6 mi **Seasonal:** Yes, rates vary **Reservations:** Credit card or first night's deposit to guarantee res, 24 hr cancel policy for full refund *Five apartments available $250-350/week email: 100@ix.net-com.com **Brochure:** Yes **Permitted:** Children, drinking, smoking only on the porches or patios **Conference:** Two meeting rooms for groups of 5-60 persons **Payment Terms:** Check/AE/CB/DC/DISC-/MC/V [I09IPFL1-10948] COM YG **ITC Member:** Yes

Rates: Pvt Bath 38*
Single $ 69-99.00
Double $ 69-125.00

Herlong House	402 NE Cholokka Blvd 32667	Micanopy FL
HC (Sonny) Howard Jr	Tel: 800-HERLONG 904-466-3322 **Fax:** 904-466-3322	
		Res Times 8am-9pm

Surround yourself with the romance of A Great Southern Mansion snuggled in the heart of Florida during your visit to the Sunshine State! Just 12 miles south of Gainesville, Micanopy is a peaceful turn-of-the-century Southern town setting complete with Spanish moss draped oak and pecan trees with a sleepy two lane highway winding to one of perhaps Florida's most elegant Bed & Breakfast. Beginning in 1845 as a humble two-story home, the structure grew in size and grandeur with the Herlong family's fortune in citrus and timber. In 1910 the Classic Revival Mansion took shape by adding four two-story Roman Corinthian columns and a two-story veranda across the front. Today guests can enjoy the fine touches of 12' ceilings, mahogany inlaid oak and maple floors, ten fireplaces (still working today) and beautiful leaded glass windows. The guest rooms offer a unique decor and depending upon the room, touches like king canopy, cast iron or copper and brass beds, wicker, original clawfoot tub bathrooms, large front verandas & suites are available. Guest may relax before fireplaces in their antique furnished rooms or sip wine while socializing in the pleasant restfulness of the parlor. Each morning offers a delicious full breakfast including homemade pastries, croissants, fresh fruit and a fine selection of tea and coffees. There's plenty to see and your host is most

©*Inn & Travel Memphis, Tennessee*

Florida *National Edition*

interested in helping you find the points of interest such as the 16 Micanopy antique shops, Paynes Prairie State Preserve, Silver Springs, Univ Florida, Florida fresh water springs, Marjorie Kinnan Rawlings Home and the Thomas Center Gallery. **Airport:** Gainesville, 15 miles **Seasonal:** No **Reservations:** Credit card of check deposit to guarantee at res time, 7 day cancel policy for refund **Brochure:** Yes **Permitted:** Children, drinking, smoking outdoors only **Conference:** The entire Herlong Mansion may be reserved for weddings, special family events and conferences. **Payment Terms:** Check MC/V [I04HPFL1-12492] **COM** YG **ITC Member:** No

Rates: Pvt Bath 12
Single $ 50.00
Double $ 145.00

Inn By The Sea	287 11th Ave South 33940	Naples FL
Peggy Cormier		Tel: 813-649-4124
		Res Times 9am-9pm

Just 700 feet from the beach and fully a/c this beach house is nestled in a *"tropical setting"* surrounded by Coconut Palms, White Bird of Paradise and Bougainvillea. Dating from 1937 and listed on the *National Register of Historic Places,* this unique Inn was selected by the South Florida Chapter of American Society of Interior Designers as the site for its prestigious Designer's Showcase in 1989. Located in a quiet residential neighborhood of quaint "Old Florida cottages", all of the appointments are typical of the years past; yellow heart pine floors and ceilings, a tin roof, ceiling fans, brass and iron beds reminiscent of Naple's colorful past as an old fishing village. Plenty of relaxing, sightseeing, beachcombing, biking, snorkeling, windsurfing, sailing, fishing, tennis, golf, Everglades Natl Park, Greyhound Racetrack and the Thos Edison House. Begin your day with a "Tropical Continental" breakfast of homemade muffins and breads, vine-ripe fruit, freshly-squeezed orange juice, natural cereals and imported teas and coffees shared with other guests on the sun porch or beach-side. Complimentary bikes, fishing poles and beach chairs. **Seasonal:** Rates higher 12/21-4/30 **Reservations:** One night's deposit at res time with 7 day cancel policy for refund. Check in 3-7pm, late arrivals upon request. Check out 11 am. Airport pick-up with prior arrangement. **Brochure:** Yes **Permitted:** Children 17-up **Payment Terms:** Check MC/V [R05BCFL-8240] **COM** Y **ITC Member:** No

Rates:	**Pvt Bath** 4	**Shared Bath** 2
Single	$ 70-105.00	$ 55-75.00
Double	$ 70-105.00	$ 55-75.00

Higgins House B&B		Orlando FL
Walter & Roberta Padgett		Tel: 407-324-9238

Refer to the same listing name under Sanford, Florida for a complete description **Seasonal:** No **Payment Terms:** Check AE/DC/MC/V [M09FPFL-18175] **COM** Y **ITC Member:** No

Rates:	**Pvt Bath** 1	**Shared Bath** 2
Single	$ 70.00	$ 60.00
Double	$ 85.00	$ 75.00

Dancing Palms	34 Surfside Dr 32074	Ormond Beach FL
John & Barbara Pinney		Tel: 904-441-8800

Modern ranch home within a pleasant stroll of the ocean beach or the intracoastal waterway, private screened porch, and a full Florida breakfast served outdoors in pool enclosure. **Seasonal:** No **Payment Terms:** [C11ACFL-1104] **COM** Y **ITC Member:** No

Rates:	**Pvt Bath** 2	**Shared Bath** 1
Single	$ 50.00	$ 45.00
Double	$ 60.00	$ 55.00

Palm Beach Historic Inn	365 S County Rd 33480	Palm Beach FL
Melissa Laitman		Tel: 407-832-4009 Fax: 407-832-6255
		Res Times 9am-8pm

The *Palm Beach Historic Inn* is a charming, historic landmark building restored, with bright, individually and tastefully-furnished rooms and suites, all designed with your comfort in mind - - all with private baths, a/c, phones and cable TV. We are perfectly located right in the heart of Palm Beach - - 1 block from the beach, 2 blocks to world-famous Worth Avenue, right on the ocean block A1A, convenient to sports, cultural and boating activities, museums, the performing arts of every kind, spectacular shopping, exquisite dining, the exciting nightlife and unlimited recreational activities - just 10 mins from the airport. Enjoy fishing, sailing, yachting, deep-sea angling, powerboating, romantic sightseeing cruises, golfing, tennis, snorkeling, scuba diving, jai alai, greyhound racing, croquet, polo, theatre, concerts, ballet, opera, comedy clubs, supper clubs and more. Our convenient central location is walking distance from gourmet restaurants, art galleries, the beach and Worth Avenue. Whether you come for a relaxing getaway, a family vacation or a romantic weekend, the charming, beautifully-restored *Palm Beach Historic Inn* is the perfect place for you to feel comfortably at home, as you enjoy the picturesque beauty and tranquility of this tropical island paradise. **Discounts:** Yes, inquire at res time **Airport:** West Palm Beach-10 mins **Packages:** Yes, inquire at res time **Seasonal:** No **Reservations:** Deposit required to guarantee reservation **Brochure:** Yes **Permitted:** Limited children, limited smoking, drinking **Languages:** French **Payment Terms:** AE/DC/DISC/MC/V [I04HPFL1-15574] **COM** YG **ITC Member:** No

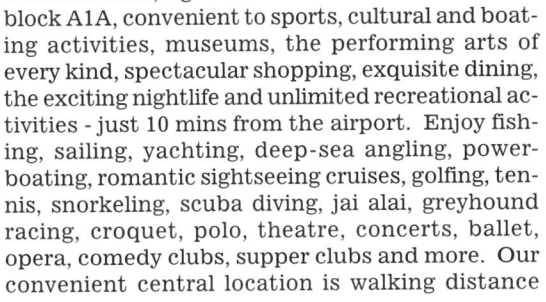

Rates:	Pvt Bath 9	Shared Bath 4
Single	$ 60-210.00	
Double	$ 60-210.00	

West Palm Beach B&B — **Palm Beach FL**
Dennis Keimel — Tel: 800-736-4064 407-848-4064 Fax: 407-842-1688
Res Times 8am-10pm

Refer to the same listing name under West Palm Beach, Florida for a complete description. **Seasonal:** No **Payment Terms:** Check AE/DC/MC/V [M06G-PFL1-20113] **COM** Y **ITC Member:** No

Rates:	Pvt Bath 4
Single	$ 75-115.00
Double	$ 75-115.00

Five Oaks Inn — 1102 Riverside Dr 34221 — **Palmetto FL**
Pam Colorito — Tel: 800-658-4167 813-726-1236

A classical Florida home c1910 complete with its Spanish tile roof and magnificent wrap-around porch filled with tropical furnishings and white wicker. Sitting on the Manatee River, towering Royal Palms and moss covered oaks create an elegant setting for a peaceful and relaxing stay. Furnished in period decor from the turn-of-the-century, fine craftsmanship is evident throughout with arches doorways, lead glass china closets and a graceful oak staircase leading to the guest rooms on the second floor. Perfect locale for romance, super for sports, convenient to colleges, efficient for business and always relaxing. Your interesting hosts make all guests a member of *"their family!"* Hearty full Florida breakfast included. **Seasonal:** No **Reservations:** Full deposit up to 2 nights within 7 days; 50% for longer period. 14 day cancel policy for refund less $3 service fee. Full amount due upon arrival. **Brochure:** Yes **Permitted:** Drinking, limited smoking **Payment Terms:** Check MC/V [X06BCFL-7861] **COM** Y **ITC Member:** No

Rates:	Pvt Bath 4
Single	$ 55-120.00
Double	$ 55-120.00

Homestead Inn — 7830 Pine Forest Rd 32526 — **Pensacola FL**
Mary Beth Paul — Tel: 904-944-4816 Fax: 904-944-0163

Homestead Inn offers that unique combination of comfort, atmosphere and southern hospitality in a manner that makes an over-night stay an event rather than just a stopover. Guest rooms feature wood floors, poster beds, fireplaces and garden tubs. Featuring Lancaster Pennsylvania Amish-Mennonite recipes in the Victorian restaurant on the premises, you'll enjoy skillet breakfasts, famous B-roasted chicken and real mashed potatoes with gravy. There's an outdoor pool and a Victorian Gift Shop with a variety of unusual gift items. **Discounts:** Yes, inquire at res time **Airport:** Pensacola-10 mi **Packages:** Yes, inquire at res time **Seasonal:** No **Brochure:** Yes **Permitted:** Children 12-up **Payment Terms:** Check AE/MC/V [R02EPFL-1105] **COM** Y **ITC Member:** No

Rates:	Pvt Bath 6
Single	$ 59-69.00
Double	$ 79-89.00

Alexander Homestead B&B — 14 Sevilla St 32084 — Saint Augustine FL
Bonnie J Alexander
Tel: 904-826-4147
Res Times 7am-9pm

Picture a rich parlor bursting with romantic detail; hear the crackling fire, glasses clinking, people talking. Enter the formal dining room and feel the warmth from the visual impact. Awaken each morning to the soul-stirring aroma of breakfast as it has been lovingly created. Each Victorian bedchamber has a faintly old fashioned air, hinting of lavender sachets tucked away in every drawer. You may choose between Alexander, with its romantic French Walnut antique furnishings, wood-burning fireplace, screened-in private porch and best of all, a modern jacuzzi bathtub with shower. Victoriana has an impressive bedstead with a built-up crested headboard, marble topped dresser, wood-burning fireplace, screened-ion private porch and magnificent bath facilities with grand oval tub plus separate shower. Queen Anne has perhaps the most Victorian feeling of all bedchambers with its four poster bed, hand crocheted bedspread, old fashioned Victorian soaking tub and French doors leading out onto its private porch. Sweet William embraces the coziness and warmth of wicker, lace, stained glass, braided rug and wrought iron bed. You'll enjoy the separate sitting room and its own private [porch. Fully air conditioned, queen size beds, cable TV and full complimentary gourmet breakfasts. AAA Approved **Airport:** Jacksonville & Daytona-60 mi **Seasonal:** No **Reservations:** One night deposit to guarantee, 7 day cancel policy **Brochure:** Yes **Permitted:** Limited children, drinking, smoking outdoor porches **Payment Terms:** MC/V [R03GPFL-17427] **COM** Y **ITC Member:** No

Rates:	Pvt Bath 4
Single	$ 75-135.00
Double	$ 75-135.00

Carriage Way B&B — 70 Cuna St 32084 — Saint Augustine FL
Diane & Bill Johnson
Tel: 904-829-2467
Res Times 8:30am-8:30pm

In the center of the historic district is this restored Victorian period gem c1883, with a casual and leisurely atmosphere in keeping with the feeling of Old St Augustine. You're in the center the historic district, close to Castillo de San Marcos, St George Street, all of the unique and charming shops, boutiques, historic sites, fine restaurants and nearby carriage rides. Each guest room is named after prior owners and includes overlooking the Victorian porch. All rooms have a private bath with claw foot tub or shower and antique or reproduction furnishings including brass, canopy or four poster beds. A full breakfast is served each morning and includes an entree, homemade white bread, jellies, homemade fruit bread or muffins, fresh fruit, orange juice, coffee and tea. Snacks (cookies or cake), newspapers, beverages and coffee and tea are available throughout the day. Complimentary bikes are available for guests. **Discounts:** Seniors, extended stays, weekdays and certain travel clubs **Airport:** Jacksonville-50 mi; Daytona-55 mi **Packages:** Honeymoon Breakfast in Bed, Gourmet Picnic Lunches, Sunset Beach Basket Dinner, Sweetheart Package **Seasonal:** No **Reservations:** Deposit required, 7 day cancel policy for refund (14 day for holidays); early departures & late arrivals charged as full stay **Permitted:** Drinking, limited children, limited smoking **Payment Terms:** Check AE/DISC/MC/V [Z10HPFL1-1108] **COM** YG **ITC Member:** No **Quality Assurance** Requested

Rates:	Pvt Bath 9
Single	$ 59-115.00
Double	$ 59-115.00

National Edition *Florida*

Castle Garden B&B	15 Shenandoah St 32084	**Saint Augustine FL**
Bruce Kloeckner/Kimmy VanKooten		**Tel:** 904-829-3829
		Res Times 8am-10pm

"Stay at a Castle and be treated like Royalty." Relax and enjoy the peace and quiet of *"Royal Treatment"* at our newly restored 100 year-old Castle of Moorish Revival design, where the only sound you'll hear is the occasional roar of a cannon shot from the ole fort, 200 yards to the South, or the creak of solid wood floors. Guests awaken to the aroma of freshly baked goodies as we prepare a full, mouth-watering country breakfast just like *"mom used to make."* The unusual coquina stone exterior remains virtually untouched while the interior of this former Castle Warden Carriage House boasts two beautiful bridal rooms complete with sunken bedrooms, soothing in-room jacuzzi and all of life's little pleasures. All rooms furnished with antiques. Other amenities include complimentary wine or champagne, chocolates on your pillow for sweet dreams, bikes for your touring pleasure and private fenced-in parking. **Discounts:** AAA, Seniors **Airport:** Jacksonville Intl-30 mi **Packages:** Anniversary, Honeymoon, Birthday Surprises. Picnic lunches, horse and buggy rides and unique and specialty gift baskets for all occasions for that "someone special". Baskets custom made to order, waiting on your bed!! **Seasonal:** No **Reservations:** One night deposit or 50% deposit for extended stays, 7 day cancel policy for refund, notify if arriving late **Brochure:** Yes **Permitted:** Limited children, limited drinking **Payment Terms:** Check AE/DISC/MC/V [I04H-PFL1-14839] **COM** YG **ITC Member:** No

Rates: Pvt Bath 6
Single $ 85-135.00
Double $ 85-135.00

Old City House Inn & Restaurant	115 Cordova St 32084	**Saint Augustine FL**
John & Darcy Compton		**Tel:** 904-826-0113 **Fax:** 904-829-3798
		Res Times 8am-9pm

We are located in the heart of town, nestled among some of the most beautiful, historic architecture in Northeast Florida ... former Flagler hotels. Our building, which was originally a stable in 1873, has been called by the City of St Augustine, a classic example of Colonial Revival architecture. In 1990, we restored it to the beautiful ivory stucco and red-tiled roofed building you enjoy today. The guest rooms are large and attractive, all with private baths and entrances. We are unique in that we have a Five-Star, award-winning restaurant on the premises. You are, therefore, able to dine in an atmosphere of charm and elegance just downstairs in the restaurant. A full complimentary breakfast is included with other meals available. The *Old City House* offers its guests the opportunity to experience New Florida cuisine in an Old Florida atmosphere. Although only in operation a little over five years, the restaurant has gained a solid reputation as an establishment featuring high quality food product, creative recipes and artistic presentation. **Discounts:** Midweek 10%, AAA **Airport:** Jacksonville-50 mi; Daytona-50 mi; St Augustine for private planes **Seasonal:** No **Reservations:** One night deposit or credit card number to guarantee reservation **Brochure:** Yes **Permitted:** Children, drinking, smoking outdoors only **Payment Terms:** Check AE/DC/DISC/MC/V [Z04HPFL1-12598] **COM** U **ITC Member:** No

Rates: Pvt Bath 5
Single $ 65-110.00
Double $ 65-110.00

Old Powder House	38 Cordova St 32084	**Saint Augustine FL**
		Tel: 800-447-4149 904-824-4149
		Res Times 8am-10pm

©*Inn & Travel Memphis, Tennessee*

3-29

Relive the past and enjoy the present in the Historic District of St Augustine where horse & buggy tours still pass beneath your window. This historic 1899 structure still retains much of its original character with high ceilings, verandas and elaborate woodwork extending to all the guest rooms which have their unique decor and theme. Each guest room offers a private entrance and bath, ceiling fans, antique furnishings and individual a/c and heating units. Our full gourmet breakfast consists of fresh fruit, homemade granola, muffins, juice, beverage and one of our delicious entrees. Afternoon tea and evening wine and appetizers are also a special treat. **Discounts:** Yes, inquire at res time **Airport:** JAX Intl-35 mi **Seasonal:** No **Reservations:** One night's deposit or credit card number for guarantee, 7 day cancel policy for refund, 14 day cancel policy for holiday weekends **Brochure:** Yes **Permitted:** Children 8-up, smoking limited to veranda **Payment Terms:** Check DISC/ MC/V [Z08GPFL-8425] COM Y ITC **Member:** No

Rates: Pvt Bath 9
Single $ 59-109.00
Double $ 59-109.00

St Francis Inn	279 St George St 32084	Saint Augustine FL
Joe Finnegan		Tel: 800-824-6062 904-824-6068
		Res Times 24 Hrs

Located in the heart of the Historic District in the nation's oldest city, the *St Francis Inn* is within easy walking distance of St Augustine Antigua, The Bay Front, great restaurants, historic sites and the unique shops of St Augustine. Built in 1791, the Inn is a Spanish Colonial structure with a private courtyard, balconies furnished with rocking chairs and the modern amenity of a swimming pool. The *St Francis* has a large selection of accommodations ranging from single rooms to two and three room suites to a separate two bedroom cottage - all with color/cable TV and many with fireplaces. The warmth and peacefulness of the Inn itself, the location of the Inn and the quality of the guests it attracts - makes the *St Francis Inn* the place to stay while visiting St Augustine. **Airport:** Jacksonville-45 mi **Seasonal:** No **Reservations:** One night's deposit, 7 day cancel policy for refund. **Brochure:** Yes **Permitted:** Limited children, drinking **Payment Terms:** Check MC/V [I03HP-FL1-1113] COM YG ITC **Member:** No

Rates: Pvt Bath 14
Single $ 55-125.00
Double $ 55-125.00

Westcott House	146 Avenida Menendez 32084	Saint Augustine FL
Sharon & David Dennison		Tel: 904-824-4301
		Res Times 8am-9pm

One of Saint Augustine's most elegant Guest Houses overlooking Matanzas Bay allows guests to step back to the turn-of-the-century and enjoy this romantic setting. Home of Dr John Westcott, this example of fine vernacular architecture from the 1880s is located in the Historical District perfect for leisurely strolling to the many historical sights, fine restaurants and quaint shops. Completely renovated and exquisitely furnished, each guest room includes American and European antiques, oriental rugs, brass, china and crystal and modern amenities such as Queen or King size beds, private baths, phones, TV and a/c. For water lovers, *The Westcott House* is located right on the Intracoastal Waterway, a half block from the city's Yacht Pier and within a short distance of Saint Augustine's fine beaches. A continental breakfast is included. **Discounts:** Yes, for weekday periods, except holidays, $95-115.00 **Airport:** Jacksonville Intl-35 mi **Seasonal:** No **Reservations:** Credit card at res time to guarantee one night's stay with 7 day cancel policy for refund **Brochure:** Yes **Permitted:** Children, drinking, limited smoking (outdoor porches) **Payment Terms:** Check MC/V [R05FPFL-1115] COM Y ITC **Member:** No

Rates: Pvt Bath 8
Single $ 95-135.00
Double $ 95-135.00

National Edition *Florida*

Bayboro House/Old Tampa Bay	1719 Beach Dr SE 33701	**Saint Petersburg FL**

Gordon & Antonia Powers
Tel: 813-823-4955 **Fax:** 813-823-4955
Res Times 24 hours

A beautiful three-story Queen Anne fully-furnished with antiques, oriental rugs and other furnishings your charming hosts have collected over the years because they like them. Step back to a more tranquil time, away from the bustle of town where a grand wrap around veranda invites guests to relax on one of the rockers or an old fashioned porch swing. Your hosts offer good old-fashioned Southern Hospitality. Walk out the front door to perfect sun bathing, beach combing, swimming and relaxation with refreshing tropical breezes. A continental plus breakfast includes fresh fruit, coffee or tea, delicious pastries and muffins served at your pleasure in the dining room or outdoors on the veranda. Each guest room includes color TV, a/c, beach chairs and beach towels with a refrigerator and laundry facilities available for guests use. Excellent sightseeing nearby offers Salvador Dali Museum, the Sunken Gardens, Busch Gardens, Ringling Museum (-Sarasota) Sea World and Disney World just 1-1/2 hrs away. *1 Bedroom apartment also available. **Airport:** Tampa Intl 25 mins **Seasonal:** No **Reservations:** Full deposit within 5 days of booking (50% on stays of 4 days or more) to confirm reservation. Bal due on arrival. 15 day cancel policy for refund; less than 15 days, refund only if rebooked* **Permitted:** Limited drinking, limited smoking **Payment Terms:** Check MC/V [I04HPFL1-1116] **COM** YG **ITC Member:** No

Rates:	Pvt Bath 4
Single	$ 95-115.00
Double	$ 95-115.00

Hunter Arms Inn	1029 New York Ave 34769	**Saint Cloud FL**

Marylou Buston/Hildy Drummond
Tel: 407-891-9655

Hunter Arms Inn is of Mediterranean Revival architectural style, popular in the 1902's when the building was constructed. Although the Inn contains forty-four rooms, only thirteen have been restored for your comfort. There is a pay phone in the lobby. Application for placement on the *National Register of Historic Places* has been accepted and placement is anticipated in the near future. There is an electric elevator in the entrance hall for convenient access to the guest rooms. All guest rooms include private bath and TV. The Spanish-style staircase descends to the lobby with its large coquina rock fireplace, commanding the attention of all who enter. The ceiling of the lobby and entrance hall is beamed with rare pecky cypress as is the cupola in the lobby which is of interest to all who view it. The second story floor is hard wood and the lobby and the entrance hall is of imported Spanish tile. Eight commercial stores are located at street level, including the Hunter Arms cafe, where guests of the Inn take breakfast each day, except Monday, when the Cafe is closed. The Inn is approximately 20 minutes from the Orlando International Airport and 35 minutes to many Central Florida attractions. Excellent golf courses are nearby and golfers will receive a discount card to one of the nicest. **Airport:** Orlando Intl-20 mins **Discounts**: 15% for stays of a week and longer **Seasonal**: No **Reservations**: One night deposit to guarantee, 72 hr cancel policy for refund **Permitted:** Limited children, limited drinking, limited smoking **Languages**: Limited Spanish [I12IPFL1-27182] **COM** G **ITC Member** No **Payment Terms:** Check, MC/V

Rates:	Pvt Bath 10	Suites 3
Single	$ 45.00	$ 95.00
Double	$ 55-70.00	$ 150.00

©*Inn & Travel Memphis, Tennessee*

Florida   National Edition

Higgins House B&B   420 S Oak St 32771   Sanford FL
Walter & Roberta Padgett   **Tel:** 407-324-9238

We invite you to enjoy the romantic ambience this magnificent turn-of-the-century Queen Anne residence offers. It was built in 1894 for James Cochran Higgins, superintendent of the railroad in Sanford. Sit in the large Victorian parlor and relive a time past. Breakfast in the elegant dining room. Enjoy the cozy pub room or meander outside and view beautiful Centennial Park from our porch swings. The upstairs veranda is a secluded spot just to sit, read or relax over a cup of coffee. It provides an excellent view of Holy Cross Episcopal, Sanford's earliest church. You'll also want to browse in our gift and antique shop upstairs. You may choose to sit on our large deck overlooking the Victoria box garden full of flowers and vegetables. Of course, a soak in our therapeutic spa is a splendid way to start or finish your day. *The Higgins House* offers three guest rooms and Cochran's Cottage. All guest rooms and the Cottage have queen size beds. A bountiful continental breakfast featuring fresh seasonal fruit, juice, hot steaming coffee, cereal, fresh baked muffins, breads and homemade jams and jellies is served in the elegant dining room each morning. Nearby activities include strolling along lovely Lake Monroe and enjoying the St John's River, sailing, pleasure boating, fishing and Big Tree Park. Daily and evening river cruises on the Rivership Grand Romance, canoeing excursions and nature and airboat tours of Central Florida's unspoiled scenery also available. **Airport:** Orlando-50 min; Daytona Beach-35 min **Seasonal:** No **Reservations:** One nights deposit to guarantee reservation, 5 day cancel notice for refund less $10 service fee per room. **Brochure:** Yes **Permitted:** Drinking, smoking outdoors, children in the cottage **Payment Terms:** Check AE/DC/MC/V [I09FPFL-16216] **COM** Y **ITC Member:** No

Rates:	Pvt Bath 1	Shared Bath 2
Single	$ 70.00	$ 60.00
Double	$ 85.00	$ 75.00

Song Of The Sea   883 E Gulf Dr 33957   Sanibel Island FL
Patricia Slater   **Tel:** 800-231-1045 813-472-2220 **Fax:** 813-472-8569
Res Times 8am-11pm

At *Sanibel's Song of the Sea*, the warmth and hospitality of Europe are blended with the dramatic beauty of sun-drenched Sanibel Island directly on the sparkling Gulf of Mexico. Our philosophy is simple. We focus on personal service, luxurious amenities and your comfort. The island does the rest. Our small inn and friendly, personal staff are part of our charm. In true European style, fresh flowers, wine and purified water awaits you in your studio or suite which are done in French Country; cozy and luxurious and include full kitchens and microwaves. Guests can choose to relax in the pool or outdoor whirlpool under swaying palms; choose a book of bestsellers from the extensive library; explore miles of the island with complimentary bikes; enjoy Sanibel's incredible wildlife which include dolphins, manatees, roseate spoonbills, otters, owls and loggerhead turtles; wash sea treasures from the Gulf in our private shell house; tennis & golf at nearby Dunes Golf & Tennis Club for a minimal fee. Each day begins with a scrumptious continental breakfast al fresco on the terrace along with complimentary newspapers. We understand privacy too ... so you'll only know we're there if you want us! **Airport:** Ft Myers SW Regional-45 mins. **Packages:** Nature, Island Romance, Fitness, Golf, Relax-Refresh-Renew. Complete phone, fax and message services are provided. **Seasonal:** Rates vary **Reservations:** Two night deposit required, 14 day cancel policy for refund **Brochure:** Yes **Permitted:** Children, drinking, smoking **Payment Terms:** Check AE/DC/MC/V [R06EPFL-15318] **COM** Y **ITC Member:** No

Rates:	Pvt Bath 30
Single	$ 114-263.00
Double	$ 114-263.00

©*Inn & Travel Memphis, Tennessee*

National Edition *Florida*

Harborfront Inn	310 Atlanta Ave 34994	Stuart FL
JoAyne Elbert		**Tel:** 407-288-7289 **Fax:** 407-221-0474
		Res Times 10am-8pm

Escape to the leisurely pace of days goneby at the *HarborFront Inn* for spacious accommodations, delightful dining and grounds overlooking the St Lucie River where your hosts, John, JoAyne and Amy Elbert are dedicated to making your stay at their home a truly relaxing and memorable experience with personal service and attention to your needs. Once accessible only by water, this *"Old Florida"* home is now in the heart of Stuart's historic district surrounded by the town's grandest homes. Great thought and care were exercised to maintain and preserve the original turn-of-the-century architecture while adding modern conveniences and amenities. Choose from among a variety of guest rooms, cottages, riverfront apartments and even a "bunk and board" aboard the Silver Lady, a 33' center cockpit O'Day sail boat. Guests at HarborFront Inn are cordially invited to share the view of the water from our large front porch or on cooler days, before the fireplace in the great room. Complimentary snacks and refreshments are served throughout the day along with a deluxe home cooked breakfast and refreshments at the water's edge while enjoying the evening sunset. Optional activities include Boat Charters, Sunset Sails, Candlelight Dinners, Massage Therapy, Fishing Charters, Tickets for Local Events. **Discounts:** Off-season, extended stays **Airport:** West Palm Beach-30 mi **Packages:** Great Getaway One & Two Nights; Holiday Weekends for Valentine Day, Memorial Day, Thanksgiving **Seasonal:** No **Reservations:** One night deposit with 10 day cancel policy for refund; 30% deposit for weekly or longer stays, 30 day cancel notice for refund less $10 service fee **Brochure:** Yes **Permitted:** Children 12-up, drinking, smoking outdoors **Conference:** Yes, common areas accommodate twenty persons **Payment Terms:** Check [R07FPFL-13850] **COM** Y **ITC Member:** No

Rates:	Pvt Bath 6
Single	$ 55-85.00
Double	$ 65-115.00

Duncan House B&B		Tampa FL
Becky & Joe		**Tel:** 813-778-6858 813-778-6335
		Res Times 9am-9pm

Refer to the same listing name under Bradenton Beach, Florida for a complete description. **Seasonal:** No **Payment Terms:** Check AE/MC/V [M07FPFL-17768] **COM** Y **ITC Member:** No

Rates:	Pvt Bath 4
Single	$ 79-139.00
Double	$ 79-159.00

Gram's Place B&B	3109 N Ola Ave 33603	Tampa FL
Mark Holland		**Tel:** 813-221-0596 **Fax:** 813-221-0596
		Res Times 24 Hrs

"A taste of Amsterdam and Key West." An artist's Retreat and Music Lover's Paradise for all. Named in honor of singer/songwriter Gram Parsons (1946-1973) who discovered Emmylou Harris and influenced the Rolling Stones, The Byrds, The Eagles and thousands of others worldwide. A Bed & Breakfast for those interested in music and the arts, with music played upon request in a relaxing, laid-back eclectic atmosphere. It is common to see and hear musicians, singers, actors, painters, classical, jazz, blues, rock, country, folk and gospel, to hear at home seconds upon arriving. Oversized jacuzzi, Tropical Courtyard/Bar, waterfall, sundeck - and inside you'll find skylights throughout the house and a fireplace. Located two miles northwest of Historic Ybor City and downtown Tampa. Open 24 hours **Airport:** Tampa Intl-8 mi **Discounts:** Yes, inquire at res time **Reservations:** One night's deposit **Brochure:** Yes **Permitted:** Children, well-groomed pets, drinking, smoking **Payment Terms:** Check AE/MC/V [R08GPFL-19587] **COM** Y **ITC Member:** No

Rates:	**Pvt Bath** 3	**Shared Bath** 9
Single	$ 75.00	$ 45.00
Double	$ 80.00	$ 50.00

©*Inn & Travel Memphis, Tennessee*

Florida - Georgia　　　　　　　　　　　　　　　　　　　　　　　　　　　　　　　　*National Edition*

West Palm Beach B&B	419 32nd St 33407-4809	**West Palm Beach FL**
Dennis Keimel	**Tel:** 800-736-4064 407-848-4064 **Fax:** 407-842-1688	
		Res Times 8am-9pm

".. a relaxing and fun place to kick-off your sandals!" West Palm Beach B&B is a cozy but deceptively large property reminiscent of a "Key West" guest house with poolside cottages. The main clapboard house is painted pastel pink with aqua stripped awnings, white picket fences and in 1993 received a ***Historic Restoration Award*** *by the City of West Palm Beach Historic Preservation Board.* Retaining much of its original character, it is decorated with an influence of tropical Florida and Caribbean Islands. The bright colors abound, along with the whimsical decorations and white wicker furniture make for a fun comfortable "island" atmosphere. West Palm Beach Bed & Breakfast is known for its unique coziness, sparkling clean accommodations, warm hospitality and the innkeepers attention to details. Four guest accommodations are available, all with private bath, queen size bed, color CATV, air conditioning and paddle fans, each with a unique style and personality. The Aqua Room and Amethyst Room are in the main house. Bonnie's Cottage is a secluded small out building off the lush tropical pool area with a mini-cathedral ceiling, refrigerator, French doors, and a cozy front porch. The Carriage House, a perennial favorite, with a living area, sleeping area and kitchenette, lofted ceiling, Mexican tile, with French doors directly to the pool. Guests enjoy a tropical breakfast buffet featuring fresh seasonal fruit, juices, hot steaming coffee, fresh muffins, breads, jams, jellies, and a variety of healthy cereals. *West Palm Beach Bed and Breakfast* is ideally located in the Old Northwood Historic District, just one block from the waterway, minutes from the tropical Atlantic beaches, the fabulous Palm Beach with world famous "Worth Avenue", and the revitalized downtown waterfront. The warm hospitality, ideal location and Caribbean flavor have made this B&B a favorite with Americans, Europeans and Canadians alike. West Palm Beach B&B offers weekday discounts to and welcomes corporate guests. **Airport:** Palm Beach Intl-5 mi; Tri-Rail-3 mi (Complimentary pick-up at airport & Tri-Rail with prior arrangements) **Discounts:** Weekdays, off-season **Seasonal:** Yes, rates vary **Reservations:** One night deposit to guarantee reservation, bal due upon arrival, 2 week cancel policy for refund **Brochure:** Yes **Permitted:** Drinking, limited smoking **Payment Terms:** Check AE/DC/MC/V [I03HPFL1-15443] COM YG **ITC Member:** No

Rates:	Pvt Bath 4
Single	$ 75-115.00
Double	$ 75-115.00

Beverly Hills Inn	65 Sheridan Dr NE 30305	**Atlanta GA**
Mit Amin		**Tel:** 800-331-8520 404-233-8520
		Res Times 24 hours

Atlanta's first little Inn, The *Beverly Hills Inn* is a charming retreat that provides an alternative to large hotels. Now travelers can enjoy the charm of Southern Hospitality with traditional European-style accommodations while visiting Atlanta. Often referred to by guests as "a three-star left-bank hotel in the middle of Buckhead" guests are conveniently located in a fine old residential neighborhood of Buckhead, just 15 minutes north of the central business district and close to the major attractions of Atlanta. Just three mins to the Atlanta Historical Society and the Governor's Mansion, five minutes to Lenox Square and Phipps Plaza, the South's premier shopping area offering Nieman-Marcus, Lord & Taylor, Saks Fifth Avenue, Macys, Richs and over 250 other fine shops. Downtown Atlanta, the State Capitol and the Atlanta-Fulton County Stadium are just fifteen minutes away. This city retreat provides eighteen uniquely decorated guest rooms include period furnishings, private baths, phones, and color TV. Suites are

©*Inn & Travel Memphis, Tennessee*

available too. Guests are treated to complimentary breakfast in the garden room each morning and can enjoy playing the piano. The friendly staff is available for suggestions on where to visit and where to dine at the many fine near-by restaurants. Definitely for those travelers seeking-out the unusual instead of the tired, tried and familiar. **Airport:** Atlanta's Hartsfield 15 mi **Seasonal:** No **Reservations:** First night's deposit or credit card guarantee; 72 hr cancellation policy for refund **Brochure:** Yes **Permitted:** Children, smoking, drinking **Languages:** French, Italian, Arabic **Payment Terms:** Check AE/DC/DISC/MC/V [I04G-PGA-1130] **COM YG ITC Member:** No

Rates: Pvt Bath 18
Single $ 59-74.00
Double $ 74-120.00

Inman Park-Woodruff Cottage B&B	100 Waverly Way 30307	Atlanta GA
Eleanor Quinn Mathews		**Tel:** 404-688-9498
		Res Times 7am-12pm

The honeymoon cottage of Robert Woodruff, Atlanta's famous anonymous donor and Coca Cola soft-drink magnet. A totally restored Victorian located in Historic Inman Park, Atlanta's first "street car suburb". One block from the subway station, guests are within walking distance to dining and shopping in the Little Five Points area - Atlanta's Soho district. Boarding for pets is just one block away. Listed on the *National Register of Historic Places, Woodruff Cottage* has 12 foot ceilings, fireplaces, heart of pine floors and woodwork, antiques, fine china, screened porch and a private garden. Secured on-site parking is provided. Your complimentary breakfast is continental in style: health-oriented baked goods, fruits, juices and beverages. About one mile to the Martin Luther King Jr grave site and the Carter Presidential Library. Two miles by bus or subway to downtown Atlanta; State Capital, Omni Coliseum, Georgia Dome Stadium, World Congress Center, Underground Atlanta and World Headquarters of Coca Cola. **Airport:** Atlanta Hartsfield-15 mi **Discounts:** Extended stay **Seasonal:** No **Brochure:** Yes **Permitted:** Children, drinking **Payment Terms:** MC/V [Z04HPGA1-15796] **COM YG ITC Member:** No

Rates: Pvt Bath 3
Single $ 70-90.00
Double $ 70-90.00

King Keith House B&B	889 Edgewood Ave NE 30307	Atlanta GA
Jan & Windell Keith		**Tel:** 404-688-7330
		Res Times 7am-10pm

Located in a National Register of Historic Place's neighborhood, the spectacular Queen Anne-style *King-Keith House* is one of the most photographed houses in Atlanta. It was built in 1890 by the local hardware magnate. Within walking distance of the funky Little Five Points commercial district, the B&B is close to Atlanta's most popular intown shopping, restaurant and theatre areas. Two miles from downtown and two blocks to MARTA (subway) station, transportation to the airport and downtown sporting, cultural and convention events is easily accessible. Your hosts are always available for pick-up at the MARTA station and for rides to the nearby events and excursions. The *King-Keith House* boasts twelve foot ceilings and carved fireplaces. The elegant public spaces include a baby grand piano for guests to enjoy. Spacious guest rooms are furnished with authentic period antiques and elegant accessories. The architect-owner and his wife have renovated/restored four homes - with this hopefully being their last! Your hosts enjoy antiquing, decorating, gardening, cooking and entertaining. Whether your visit to Atlanta is for a Braves game, an evening at the symphony or convention, your stay will be enriched by your visit to the *King-Keith House* - **where Southern Hospitality is alive and well.** **Discounts:** Government rates **Airport:** Harts-field-15 min **Reservations:** One night's deposit, 7 day cancel policy for refund **Brochure:** Yes **Permitted:** Children, drinking, smoking outdoors only **Payment Terms:** Check AE/MC/V [K08GPGA-20013] **COM** Y **ITC Member:** No **Quality Assurance:** Requested

Rates:	Pvt Bath 2	Shared Bath 1
Single	$ 75-95.00	$ 50.00
Double	$ 75-95.00	$ 55.00

Oakwood House B&B 951 Edgewood Ave NE 30307   Atlanta GA
Judy & Robert Hotchkiss   Tel: 404-521-9320 **Fax:** 404-688-6024
   Res Times 9am-9pm

This two-story 1911 frame home with Craftsman overtones has been a boarding house, travel agency and film-maker's studio. One former owner had an alcohol still in the basement! The house is in Atlanta's oldest planned suburb, Inman Park. Today, Inman Park has restored Victorian and turn-of-the-century homes, including the first Coca-Cola mansion and the mayor's home. This tree-lined enclave is just two miles east of downtown Atlanta. The owners have lived next door for over sixteen years and love renovation work. Their goal for the *Oakwood House B&B* was to make a home-away-from-home for guests. *Oakwood House* is a small historic Inn but there's little that resembles a hotel (except the little soaps!). Furnishing is traditional but not fussy. There are bookcases everywhere! Choose from a king, queen, double or two twin beds. Each room is uniquely furnished. In 1996, a new romance room with whirlpool tub was opened. A substantial continental breakfast is served on china with silver. *Oakwood House* is centrally located. Walk 1.5 blocks to the subway (MARTA) to reach downtown sites and conventions. It's a one mile drive to the Martin Luther King tomb and Jimmy Carter's Presidential Library. Downtown find the Underground, Coke Museum, CNN Studio tours and the zoo. Little Five Points, unique ethnic restaurants, theaters and shops are within a short walking distance. Virginia-Highland, Decatur and Buckhead are minutes away. So many reasons to visit... **Airport:** Hartsfield Intl-10 mi, via subway **Packages:** Fall & Winter: Theater Package - Two tickets to Seven Stages play, (when performing), with two night stay **Seasonal:** No **Reservations:** One night's deposit, 3 day cancel policy for refund, 7 day cancel policy for whole house rental, late arrival only with prior arrangement **Brochure:** Yes **Permitted:** Children (n/c for one in parent's room) drinking, pets boarded nearby, smoking outdoors **Conference:** Up to 20 persons with house rental; to 300 next door at The Trolley Barn, c.1887 **Payment Terms:** Check AE/MC/V [I05HPGA1-15797] **COM** YG **ITC Member:** No **Quality Assured:** Yes

Rates:	Pvt Bath 5
Single	$ 60-100.00
Double	$ 85-150.00

Sixty Polk Street, A B&B   Atlanta GA
Mary & Chet Ladd   Tel: 800-497-2075 404-419-0101
   Res Times 8am-8pm

Refer to the same listing name under Marietta, Georgia for a complete description. **Seasonal:** No **Payment Terms:** Check [M10EPGA-16319] **COM** U **ITC Member:** No

Rates:	Pvt Bath 4
Single	$ 75-85.00
Double	$ 75-85.00

Woodruff B&B Inn 223 Ponce de Leon Ave 30308   Atlanta GA
Douglas & Joan Jones   Tel: 800-473-9449 404-875-9449 **Fax:** 404-875-2882
   Res Times 8am-midnight

National Edition — ***Georgia***

Southern hospitality awaits you in historic Midtown Atlanta. Atlanta's *Woodruff Inn*, built at the turn-of-the-century, is a beautifully restored, three-story Victorian home. It was originally constructed by Norman Godfrey, Atlanta's premier architect at the turn-of-the-century. Upon completition, the house was featured in the 1908 Atlanta Journal and Constitution. In the following years, this charming dwelling, with its heart-carved stairways and open front porches, was the toast of Ponce de Leon Avenue. During the 1950's Bessie Lucille Woodruff purchased 223 Ponce de Leon Avenue and used the building for her business and home. Bessie Woodruff passed away in 1986 and left thirty years of wonderful memories and stories behind. We, the Jones', have restored the Bessie Woodruff home and look forward to sharing its history and treasures with you. A full breakfast is included. **Discounts:** AAA and AARP **Airport:** Atlanta Hartsfield-25 mins **Packages:** Special Occasion Suite, Private Hot Tub, Champagne, Flowers, Breakfast In Bed **Seasonal:** No **Reservations:** Credit card or deposit to guarantee reservation, 72 hr cancel policy for refund. Email RSVP@mindspring.com **Brochure:** Yes **Permitted:** Children, limited drinking **Conference:** Yes, for small groups, meetings, weddings, parties **Languages:** Spanish, French [K12IPGA1-17804] **COM** G **ITC Member** No **Payment Terms:** AE/DC/DISC/MC/V

Rates:	Pvt Bath 10	Shared Bath 4
Single	$ 89.00	$ 79.00
Double	$ 99-129.00	$ 89.00

Layside   611 River St 31723   Blakely GA
Ted & Jeanneane Lay   **Tel:** 404-723-8932
Res Times 8am-7pm

A lovely traditional 1900 Southern Colonial with all the trimmings including a ninety foot wrap around porch where guests rock all day long while relaxing with an ice tea or mint julep! These lovely hosts make each guest feel right at home with their Southern Hospitality and atmosphere. You'll be whistling Dixie here! Continental breakfast included. **Seasonal:** No **Reservations:** Deposit at res time, 2pm check-in, 7 day cancel policy **Brochure:** Yes **Permitted:** Limited children **Payment Terms:** Check [C09BCGA-1135] **COM** Y **ITC Member:** No

Rates:	Pvt Bath 4
Single	$ 65.00
Double	$ 70.00

Hummingbirds Perch B&B   Rt 1 Box 1870 31733   Chula GA
Frances Wilson   **Tel:** 912-382-5431
Res Times 3pm-10am

Whether you enjoy birdwatching, fishing or beautiful sunsets while strolling around the lake, Hummingbird's Perch will refresh the spirit and soothe the mind. This is modern country-living at its best with a touch of elegance. A full complimentary breakfast is included in your rate. Conveniently located (one mile off I-75) guests can enjoy visiting local sights such as Historic Tifton, Fulwood Park, Love Affair, Agirama, Rural Development Center, ABAC, Coastal Plains Experimental Station and the Sunbelt Expo. **Airport:** Atlanta-2-1/2 hrs; Tallahasse-1-1/2 hrs **Seasonal:** No **Reservations:** 50% deposit, late arrivals only with prior arrangements, additional guest per room $10.00 **Brochure:** Yes **Permitted:** Children 12-up, smoking outside only **Payment Terms:** Check AE/MC/V [R01FPGA-16124] **COM** Y **ITC Member:** No

Rates:	Pvt Bath 1	Shared Bath 2
Single	$ 40.00	$ 40.00
Double	$ 60.00	$ 60.00

Towering Oaks B&B Lodge   115 Windy Acres Rd 30528   Cleveland GA
Tel: 706-865-6760

©*Inn & Travel Memphis, Tennessee*

Center of Georgia mountain country on sixty acres is this lovely setting offering a tranquil and serene opportunity to relax and enjoy the outdoors. National Forest nearby, fishing, canoeing, golfing, tennis, or just relaxing while walking the many nature trails and enjoying the Southern climate. Full breakfast included. **Seasonal:** Jan 14-Thanksgiving **Brochure:** Yes **Permitted:** Children, smoking, drinking, limited pets **Payment Terms:** Check MC/V [C11ACGA-1139] **COM** Y **ITC Member:** No

Rates:	Pvt Bath 4	Shared Bath 1
Single	$ 55.00	$ 35.00
Double	$ 65.00	$ 45.00

Royal Guard Inn   203 S Park St 30533   Dahlonega GA
John & Farris Vanderhoff   Tel: 706-864-1713
      Res Times 10am-9pm

A Bed & Breakfast in the Scandinavian Style ... what better place than in the heart of the North Georgia Mountains with its valleys not unlike those of Southern Norway. Like those valleys, Dahlonega is reminiscent of bygone days centuries removed from much of the world today. Within one-half block of downtown, the Royal Guard Inn is a historic home restored and added to and sheltered by nearby huge magnolia trees. A stately pine guards the entrance. The look of yesteryear's British and European craftsmanship blend with todays technology promises a delightful and luxurious stay. Inside, the elegant decor, large rooms with private baths and cable color TV are enhanced by views of the surrounding area. Upon arriving you can relax in your room or on the porch while enjoying a complimentary wine and cheese tray. Your complimentary full breakfast is home-prepared in our own kitchen and includes coffee, juice, fruit, a daily fresh-baked egg and sausage casserole with delicious homemade muffins - all served on crisp table linen. The Inn is near the Welcome Center in easy walking distance of all of the sights, shops and restaurants. **Discounts:** Yes, inquire at res time **Airport:** Atlanta-80 mi **Packages:** Two rates available whether including breakfast **Seasonal:** No **Reservations:** One night deposit or credit card number to guarantee reservation, 72 Hr cancel policy for refund, taxes not included **Brochure:** Yes **Permitted:** Limited children, limited drinking **Payment Terms:** MC/V [R05FPGA-11400] **COM** Y **ITC Member:** No

Rates:	Pvt Bath 5
Single	$ 65-75.00
Double	$ 65-75.00

Oakwood House B&B   Decatur GA
Judy & Robert Hotchkiss   Tel: 404-521-9320 Fax: 404-688-6034
      Res Times 9am-9pm

Refer to the same listing name under Atlanta, Georgia for a complete description. **Seasonal:** No **Payment Terms:** Check AE/MC/V [M05HCGA1-16742] **COM** YG **ITC Member:** No

Rates:	Pvt Bath 5
Single	$ 60-100.00
Double	$ 65-150.00

Captain's Quarters B&B   13 Barnhardt Circle 30742   Fort Oglethorpe GA
Pam Humphry/Ann Gilbert   Tel: 706-858-0624
      Res Times 9am-10pm

Our home was built in 1902, as home for Captain's stationed at Fort Oglethorpe. The military post operated from 1902 to 1946. It was known as the most elite Army post of the period. We are adjacent to Chickamauga-Chattanooga National Military Park. All of the Chattanooga Tennessee attractions, like the new Tennessee Aquarium, Warehouse Row and Lookout Mountain are just fifteen minutes away. There are many antique shops in the area. Our guest rooms all have private baths, color TV, ceiling fans, alarm clocks and five have original mantels. Our decor leans toward Victorian and all have pretty wallpapers, pretty bed linen, lace curtains and special touches featuring hearts and needlework. One suite has a full kitchen and private entrance. One suite includes a sitting room. A full complimentary breakfast is included. **Discounts:** Seniors-10%; weekday business travelers-20%. **Airport:** Chattanooga Lovell Field-12 mi **Seasonal:** No **Reservations:** $25 deposit or credit card number, 7 day cancel policy for refund **Brochure:** Yes **Permitted:** Limited children, limited drinking **Payment Terms:** Check AE/MC/V [R07F-PGA-10792] **COM** Y **ITC Member:** No

Rates:	Pvt Bath 7
Single	$ 50-85.00
Double	$ 50-85.00

Sixty Polk Street, A B&B
60 Polk St 30064 — Marietta GA
Mary & Chet Ladd
Tel: 800-497-2075 404-419-0101

Relax, be at home, and enjoy elegant pampering where Sherman began his march on Atlanta. Visit the Kennesaw Mountain battle site just down the road, Get drenched on the water slides at White Water Park, just 2 miles away. Shop for antiques on the Square. Scare yourself silly on the five (so far!) roller coasters at Six Flags Amusement Park. Not a secluded location, *Sixty Polk Street* is in the heart of historic Marietta and within walking distance of the Square (also a Sherman bonfire) for shopping or business. It's two miles to I-75 and a fast 20 minutes to downtown Atlanta during non-rush hour for business or sporting events. Colleges? You bet - Kennesaw College, Southern Tech, Georgia Tech, Georgia State - all 10-20 minutes away. *Sixty Polk Street* is a French Regency Victorian, c1872. The four rooms are furnished with antiques and fine reproductions. The beds are so comfortable one guest went to the square and bought "her" bed the next day. One bath has a clawfoot tub, the other three have more modern showers. A king suite has the original 120 year old horizontal panelling and a working fireplace - a true log cabin feeling. Mary loves to cook so bring your appetite to the full-plus complimentary breakfast served in the red dining room or on the porch, weather permitting. Complimentary tea available. **Airport:** Hartsfield Intl-30 mins **Discounts:** Extended stays, booking all rooms and airline employees **Seasonal:** No **Reservations:** $25 deposit (cash/check), 24 hr cancellation policy for full refund; check-in not later than 10 pm **Brochure:** Yes **Permitted:** Drinking **Payment Terms:** Check [I10E-PGA-16137] **COM** Y **ITC Member:** No

Rates:	Pvt Bath 4
Single	$ 75-85.00
Double	$ 75-85.00

Stanley House
236 Church St 30060 — Marietta GA
Brigita Rowe
Tel: 404-426-1881

Since 1895, the *Stanley House* in Marietta has offered a delightful experience in Victorian elegance and charm for vacationers and local guest alike. This beautiful four-story Queen Anne home was originally built for President Woodrow Wilson's aunt, Felie Woodrow of Columbia South Carolina. Hospitality and comfort were the call of the day then, as friends and family weary from travel flocked to these unique quarters for holiday and weekend getaways. The tradition continues today - year round. One of Georgia's most elegant Victorian Inns, the 5000 square foot *Stanley House* was thoroughly renovated in 1985 and proudly retains its quaint, individual character and dignity. Six individual units grace the premises, each with private bath, spacious bedroom and decorated throughout with period antiques and wallpapers. Historic Marietta Square, just two blocks from the *Stanley House*, retains its reputation as one of the regions most charming shopping districts. Atlanta is just thirty minutes with all of its sights and attractions. Hiking and Civil War buffs enjoy exploring Kennesaw Mountains. White Water Park, just five minutes away, offers a cooling adventures during the Summer. A continental breakfast is included in the room rate. **Seasonal:** No **Reservations:** One night's deposit or credit card to confirm reservation, 24 Hr cancel notice for refund, except weekends (Fri & Sat nights), a 7 day cancel notice required **Brochure:** Yes **Permitted:** Limited children, limited smoking, limited drinking **Conference:** A memorable location for special oc-

Georgia   *National Edition*

casions - wedding receptions, bridal luncheons, business meeting. Accommodation for 150 at stand-up reception; 50 for plated luncheons /dinners; 20 for meetings. **Languages:** Latvian **Payment Terms:** Check MC/V [Z11DPGA-10793] **COM Y**

ITC Member: No

Rates: **Pvt Bath 6**
Single $ 65-75.00
Double $ 75-85.00

Goodbread House   209 Osborne Rd 31558   **Saint Marys GA**
George & Betty Krauss   **Tel:** 912-882-7490
                                                                                       Res Times 7am-10pm

The *Goodbread House* circa 1870 is in the heart of the National Historic District of St Marys Georgia. The town, a quiet fishing village founded in 1787, is thirty miles south of Brunswick Georgia and thirty miles north of Jacksonville Florida. The *Goodbread House* is ideally situated within walking distance of the ferry to Cumberland Island National Seashore. Kings Bay Sub Base, Okefenokee Swamp Park, the Golden Isles and Amelia Island are all a short drive away. Osprey Cove, the area's newest recreation attraction offers a par 72 hole golf course to the public - a Mark McCumber course. The *Goodbread House* is a carefully restored Victorian home. The high ceilings, seven fireplaces, wide pine floors and original wood trim and antique furnishings throughout add to it's ambience. Each antique-filled bedroom has its own fireplace and private bath. And of course . . . ceiling fans and air conditioning. Enjoy complimentary wine and cheese at cocktail time and in the morning, a continental breakfast and newspaper. **Discounts:** Military, AARP. **Airport:** Jacksonville or Brunswick-30 mi **Seasonal:** No **Reservations:** Phone reservations in advance are requested **Brochure:** Yes **Permitted:** Limited drinking **Payment Terms:** Check [R09EPGA-10753] **COM Y ITC Member:** No

Rates: **Pvt Bath 3**   **Shared Bath 1**
Single $ 65.00 $ 55.00

Little St Simons Island   PO Box 21078 31522   **Saint Simons Island GA**
Debbie & Kevin McIntyre   **Tel:** 912-638-7472 **Fax:** 912-634-1811
                                                                                               Res Times 8am-5pm

Your Own Private Island Awaits You . . . Virtually untouched for centuries, Little St Simon Island is a privately owned, 10,000 acre barrier island along the Georgia Coast. A rich and varied natural world, its pristine beaches, maritime forest, shimmering marshes and tidal creeks await your exploration. The owners of Little St Simon Island have welcomed family and friends since the early 1900's. Today, the tradition continues. We welcome special friends to experience a rare combination of complete privacy in an unspoiled wilderness - with the thoughtful service and Southern Hospitality of our professional staff. Accessible only by boat and allowing just 24 overnight guests, The Lodge at Little St Simon Island provides comfort in a natural setting. The classic Hunting Lodge, built in 1917, is the very heart of the Island life. Reminiscent of a Hemingway novel, its living room is the gathering sport for each evening's social hour. The Hunting Lodge's two guest bedrooms are filled with rustic furniture and family memorabilia. Nearby, the Michael Cottage with it sitting room and fireplace, two bedrooms and screened porch, is a favorite with honeymooners and families. The Cedar House and River Lodge each offer a common sitting room and spacious bedrooms with private baths. Relax in front of the tabby fireplace. Enjoy what is described at the Island's best sunset view from the porch. **Airport:** Jacksonville, FL-70 mi, Savannah GA-65mi, transportation can be arranged

©*Inn & Travel Memphis, Tennessee*

National Edition   *Georgia*

Meals: All meals included, snack, hor d'oeuvres, drinks and honor bar. Email 102063.467 @ CompuServe.com **Seasonal:** Yes, rates vary **Reservations:** Deposit required **Brochure:** Yes **Permitted:** Children (varies by season), drinking, limited smoking **Conference:** Yes, entire Island rental suitable for up to 24 persons: $3,150 to $4,550. Special midweek packages summer. **Payment Terms:** Check MC/V [K05HCGA-1166] **COM YG ITC Member:** No

Rates:	Pvt Bath 11
Single	$ 215-415.00
Double	$ 290-515.00

Ballastone Inn & Townhouse   14 E Oglethorpe 31401   Savannah GA
Richard Carlson/Tim Hargus   **Tel:** 800-822-4553 912-236-1484   **Fax:** 912-236-4626
    Res Times 7am-11pm

Enjoy gracious Southern Hospitality in sumptuous Victorian ambience at this unique c1838 restored Inn, where guests are pampered with everything from a glass of sherry upon arrival to complimentary shoe shines nightly, fresh flowers in each guest room, terry bath robes, and evening turndown service with chocolate and an evening cordial! Beautifully furnished with authentic antiques, four-poster beds, period wallcoverings, linens and curtains - all of the details that bring guests into another period of time. The charming courtyard is perfect for an afternoon lemonade or mint julep, while relaxing among the fragrant magnolias, gardenias, jasmine and wisteria. All modern amenities are tastefully included: TV, VCRs, phones, fireplaces in some rooms, whirlpools in some baths, sprinkler system, elevators, and concierge service. Choose from the main house upper floors, or garden level rooms in the former servant quarters for a most rustic setting. A continental plus breakfast is included and is offered in the courtyard or in *Bed!* Fresh fruits, juice, southern-style pastries and rich dark coffees with the morning paper are included. **Seasonal:** No **Reservations:** Credit card to guarantee room, 96 hr cancel policy *Suites available **Permitted:** Children 12-up, drinking, smoking **Payment Terms:** Check AE/MC/V [K04HPGA1-1171] **COM YG ITC Member:** No

Rates:	Pvt Bath 22	
Single	$ 85.00	$ 185-200.00
Double	$ 95.00	$ 185-200.00

Eliza Thompson House   5 West Jones 31401   Savannah GA
Carol & Steve Day   **Tel:** 800-348-9378 912-348-9378   **Fax:** 912-238-1920
    Res Times 24 Hrs

Cotton was "King" and Savannah was enjoying the prosperity of 1847 when Mrs. Eliza Thompson built her fabulous home nestled in this tranquil residential neighborhood. The lovely homes of Savannah were spared during General Sherman's *"March to the Sea"* and the charm and intrigue of the "Old South" is alive today at the Eliza Thompson House. This regally restored residence is one of the oldest inns in Savannah and where guest rooms offer rich heart pine floors and period furnishings but modern conveniences such as direct dial phones and color TV all with private baths. Guests are greeted each morning with a complimentary newspaper and the delicious aroma of rich brewed coffee and freshly baked butter croissants - along with an assortment of delicious pastries and homemade muffins along with fresh seasonal fruit and berries, cereals, juice and tea. Ideally located for walking through-out the Historic District guests can visit the quaint shops, antique stores, magnificent museum houses, Civil War memorials, beautiful old churches and the wonderful Southern and courtyard formal gardens of Savannah. A beautiful landscaped courtyard with a splashing fountain invites guests to relax after their daily excursions and enjoy afternoon tea or the daily wine and cheese reception at 5-7 pm. The owners and staff are available 24 hours and assist guests with dining suggestions and reservations as well as sightseeing information. Discover the timeless heritage of Savannah - The *Eliza Thompson House* has been featured in numerous articles in *"Southern Living", "Architectural Digest", "Bon Appetit", "House Beautiful", "New York Times"* and *"Travel & Leisure."* **Discounts:** AAA **Airport:** Savannah Intl-10 mi **Seasonal:** No **Reservations:** Credit card deposit with 72 hr cancel policy, late arrivals welcomed **Brochure:** Yes **Permitted:** Limited children **Conference:** Yes, for groups to 35 persons **Payment Terms:** Check AE/MC/V [I04IPGA1-1177] **COM** YG **ITC Member:** No

Rates: Pvt Bath 23
Single $ 89-149.00
Double $ 89-149.00

Liberty Inn 1834　　　128 W Liberty St 31401　　　Savannah GA
Janie & Frank Harris　　　　　　　　Tel: 800-637-1007 912-233-3331
　　　　　　　　　　　　　　　　　　　　Res Times 9am-6pm

....1834 Townhouse on Tour Route in the Nation's largest Landmark District. Savannah, one of the country's first planned cities, preserves the charm and pace of times gone by. In the heart of all this is the *Liberty Inn - 1834*. Restored in 1979 to the charm of yesteryear with the luxuries of today. Five suites: the two-room suites accommodate one couple or a family up to six and the three-room Suites accommodate two couples. Each bedroom adjoins a private bath. Each suite has a Family/Sitting Room plus kitchenette with Breakfast Fixin's...Orange Juice, Croissants, Whipped Butter, Strawberry Preserves and Coffee. Private Phone, TV & VCR with free movies. Private off-street parking and entrance via Garden-Courtyard with 8-ft spa and sundeck. **Reservations:** One night's cash deposit within 10 days of booking, a 10-day cancellation policy for refund. **Permitted:** Children, drinking, smoking **Conference:** Yes, in the two & three room Suites that accommodate up to eight persons. **Payment Terms:** Check AE/MC/V [Z05FPGA-6592] **COM** Y **ITC Member:** No

Rates: Pvt Bath 5
Single $ 95.00

Lions Head Inn　　　120 E Gaston St 31401　　　Savannah GA
Christy Dell'Orco　　　　Tel: 800-355-LION 912-232-4580 **Fax:** 912-232-7422
　　　　　　　　　　　　　　　　　　　　Res Times 24 Hrs

Featured in *"Country Inns Magazine"* (May 1993), this elegant 19th Century mansion is tastefully adorned with pristine Empire Period furniture and accessories. A collection of European and American art, Italian marble and French bronze sculptures and 19th Century lighting beautifying each room. The Inn boasts five luxurious guest rooms all with private baths, king or queen four poster beds, working fireplaces, cable television with HBO, private phones, free local calls and smoke-free rooms. Each morning a deluxe continental breakfast is served between 8:30 and 10 am family-style in the formal dining room which is lavishly accessorized with a Waterford crystal chandelier, a buffet and wine cellarette hand-crafted by Antoine Quervelle. Guests enjoy wine and cheese reception in the front parlor or on the sweeping veranda overlooking a lush marble courtyard. The *Lion's Head Inn* is located on Gaston Street, the prime residential street in the Historic District. Stroll across the street to picturesque Forsyth Park and enjoy all the attractions and amenities - all within walking distance. Enjoy gracious living at its best in a city and Inn - allowing one to experience true 19th Century grandeur. **Discounts:** Senior citizens, corporate weekday rate $70.00 any room **Airport:** Savannah Intl-7 mi **Seasonal:** No **Reservations:** One night's deposit or credit card number to guarantee reservation, 7 day cancel policy for refund; Check-in 2pm, late arrivals only with prior arrangements **Brochure:** Yes **Permitted:** Children, drinking, limited smoking

Conference: Large dining room and parlor great for special occasions and meetings **Payment Terms:** Check AE/MC/V [K05HPGA1-17284] COM YG ITC **Member:** No

Rates:	Pvt Bath 5
Single	$ 75-115.00
Double	$ 90-130.00

Veranda   252 Seavy Street 30276-0177   Senoia GA
Jan & Bobby Boal   Tel: 706-599-3905   Fax: 706-599-0806

Lovingly restored Victorian c1907 (formerly Hollberg Hotel) with traditional Southern touches of classical doric columns framing the spacious veranda. Some famous guests include William Jennings Bryan and Margaret Mitchell, who interviewed Civil War vets when she researched material for *"Gone With The Wind."* Just a short distance South of Atlanta, you step into another era in a town and Inn, both listed on the *National Register of Historic Place*. Guest rooms are furnished with period antiques and family heirlooms. Hosts offer wonderful Southern hospitality to all guests for dining or accommodations. Bobby dons her chef attire and prepares gourmet or pure Southern Country feasts from scratch and from home recipes. Be prepared for homemade breakfasts of sourdough french toast with muscadine syrup or enticing biscuits, cinnamon rolls or bran muffins. Featured in many magazines, *"Georgia Trend"*, 3/88 and *"Southern Homes"* 1/87 on fine accommodations and gourmet dining. Full breakfast included, other meals available. **Seasonal:** No **Reservations:** Deposit to hold reservation within 5 days of making reservation. **Brochure:** Yes **Permitted:** Children, smoking limited **Conference:** Yes, social or business to 20 persons. **Payment Terms:** Check MC/V [A06ACGA-1197] COM Y ITC **Member:** No

Rates:	Pvt Bath 9
Single	$ 65-85.00
Double	$ 75-95.00

Statesboro Inn   106 S Main St 30458   Statesboro GA
John J Tulip   Tel: 912-489-8628

c1904 restored Country Inn is listed on *National Register of Historic Places,* where you can relive the another era with period antique furnishings, and a local pine interior woodwork. Modern amenities include whirlpool baths, color TV remote, and ceiling fans for your comfort. Full breakfast daily. **Seasonal:** No **Brochure:** Yes **Permitted:** Children limited. **Payment Terms:** Check AE/MC/V [C11A-CGA-1198] COM Y ITC **Member:** No

Rates:	Pvt Bath 9
Single	$ 55-90.00
Double	$ 65-100.00

Deer Creek B&B   1304 Old Monticello Rd 31792   Thomasville GA
Bill & Gladys Muggridge   Tel: 912-226-7294
    Res Times 24 Hrs

Deer Creek B&B is located 1.2 miles from the Chamber of Commerce where plantation tours begin. A lovely custom-built home on two acres next to the second oldest golf course in the South. Guests enjoy a rare combination: woods in town which offer tranquility and beauty up in the trees on deck or a great view of the all-glassed southside by the fireplace. Furnishings are from host's own antique store. Complete privacy is assured - guest rooms are on the opposite end's from host's quarters and have private entrance. Enjoy rare books in the library, music or TV. Thomasville is one of the top resorts and living areas in the USA. Dating back to the 1800s, "Harper" magazine chose Thomasville as the third most desired area in the USA. Golfers will enjoy trying the adjacent course which has hosted celebrities such as Pres Eisenhower, Jackie Kennedy and many others. As a resort are there are many beautiful mansions and plantations open for tours. Full Southern breakfast includes home-cooked Mayhaw Jelly prepared from fresh-picked local berries. **Seasonal:** No **Reservations:** Call anytime, 7 days a week. **Brochure:** No **Permitted:** Children, smoking, drinking **Payment Terms:** Check [R10CPGA-11398] **COM Y ITC Member:** No

Rates:	Pvt Bath 2
Single	$ 48.00
Double	$ 48.00

White Castle Inn — Baton Rouge LA
Don & Linda Neahusan
Tel: 504-545-9932
Res Times 9am-8pm

Refer to the same listing name under White Castle, Louisiana for a complete description. **Seasonal:** No **Payment Terms:** AE/MC/V [M05HPLA1-16981] **COM YG ITC Member:** No

Rates:	Pvt Bath 4
Single	$ 55-60.00
Double	$ 65-75.00

Maison d'Andre Billeaud — 203 E Main 70518 — Broussard LA
Craig & Donna Kimball
Tel: 800-960-REST 318-837-3455
Res Times 8am-9pm

This beautifully restored Victorian home is just minutes from the best Cajun cuisine and entertainment in Acadiana. Located in the historic town of Broussard, guests are just five miles from the Lafayette airport, ten minutes from downtown Lafayette and twenty minutes from New Iberia. Broussard has more large Victorian homes, in a town of its size, than anywhere else in Louisiana and the city has mapped out walking tours of the town. This elegant bed and breakfast, with large spacious rooms, was built in 1903 and is listed on the *National Register of Historic Places*. The home is furnished throughout with period antiques. Suite One is very spacious and decorated in rich red and gold tones. The walls are covered in raw silk and it is furnished with an antique half tester bed. Suite Two is also a very spacious room decorated in dark burgundy and rich dark green tones. This room is furnished with an antique half tester bed. Suite Three (The Honeymoon Suite), is a unique four-sided stained glass room with an upstairs loft that leads out to a private balcony, which overlooks the courtyard. An antique bed also graces the loft and a complimentary bottle of champagne is included in the rate. This room offers a sitting area and a six foot claw foot tub, perfect for a relaxing soaking. It is the only suite with a private courtyard entrance. The room is furnished with a small refrigerator, coffee maker and refreshments. Complimentary hors d'oeuvres and wine are served to guests every evening in the New Orleans-style courtyard, shaded by a 150 year old like oak tree. A fabulous gourmet breakfast is prepared by the chef-owner, Chef Kimball. There is an antique and gift shop on the premises. Roll-aways available with added fee, handicap accessible. **Airport:** Lafayette-5 mi **Tours:** Tuesday through Saturday **Seasonal:** No **Reservations:** One night's deposit or credit card number to guarantee reservation *Suites available **Brochure:** Yes **Permitted:** Children are welcome, pet permitted if in portable kennel provided by guest **Conference:** Yes, beautiful setting for wedding receptions, rehearsal suppers, bridal luncheons - with catering and dining available **Payment Terms:** Check AE/DISC/MC/V [I08HPLA1-18117] **COM YG ITC Member:** No

Rates:	Pvt Bath 3
Single	
Double	$ 85-125.00

National Edition   **Louisiana**

La Maison de Campagne	825 Kidder Rd 70520	Carencro LA
Joeann & Fred McLemore		Tel: 800-368-3806 318-896-6529
		Res Times 8-8pm

Just a short distance from Lafayette and sitting atop the highest point in Lafayette Parish is this turn-of-the-century Victorian home, nestled among century-old live oaks and mature pecan trees creating a perfect country setting. Expanded in 1913-1915 and moved to its present nine acre setting atop the Couteau Ridge in 1974, guests can enjoy the beautiful views from the sweeping wrap around porch or the upstairs balcony. As you leave the "Wilderness Trail" and drive down the circular drive to the "Country House", you'll step back in time to the way things use to be! Built by Charles Landry II, a sugar cane farmer and expanded to meet his family's needs, your hosts have maintained the furnishings and decor reminiscent of this early period, The cozy guest rooms are furnished with antiques and offer private baths. Peaceful walks on the "place" near the coulee are especially relaxing before retiring in the evening. Complimentary afternoon refreshments are prepared by your Award-Winning Chef/Innkeeper hostess and include seafood and local delicacies to whet your appetite for the outstanding Cajun restaurants which are just minutes away! Mornings bring wake-up coffee and a sumptuous Cajun breakfast feast featuring homemade breads, rolls, pastries made from our own home-milled flour, homemade jellies and preserves. Following breakfast, your gracious hosts lend a hand at offering directions and information about the nearby attractions which includes Vermilionville, a living history museum depicting life in Acadiana 100-200 years ago, Acadian Village-a popular tourist attraction, Washington LA - a historic French community, Liberty Theater - the Cajun radio show at Eunice LA, swamp tours on Atchafalaya Basin, Jefferson Island Botanical Gardens and to famous Avery Island - home of Tobasco Hot Sauce! For dining - Enola Prudhomme's (Paul's sister) Cajun Cafe, Prejeans (great food and Cajun music for dancing) and Angelle (fine dining/dinner theater) - will whet your appetite to come back again! **Discounts:** Yes, inquire at res time **Airport:** Lafayette Regional-15-20 mins **Seasonal:** No **Reservations:** One night deposit to guarantee, 72 hr cancel notice for refund. **Permitted:** Children 12-up **Conference:** Teas, coffees for groups or clubs up to 20 persons by prior reservation. **Languages:** French with prior notice **Payment Terms:** Check MC/V [I11DPLA-14131] **COM** Y **ITC Member:** No

Rates: Pvt Bath 3
Single $ 70.00
Double $ 70.00-up

Tezcuco Plantation B&B	3138 Hwy 44 70725	Darrow LA
Debra & Chuck Purifoy		Tel: 504-562-3929
		Res Times 7am-11pm

Beautiful plantation setting with individual guest cottages surrounded with atmosphere and lush mature cypress & oaks that bring you into this wonderful bayou country. Cabins have been made from the cypress from the immediate area. All activities are here if you like including horseback riding, swimming, tennis and plenty of sights to visit. **Seasonal:** No **Reservations:** Credit card to hold room, 48 hour cancel policy for refund. **Brochure:** Yes **Permitted:** Children, smoking, drinking. Full breakfast is an added charge of $$4.50 with other local meals available in the restaurant on the premises **Payment Terms:** Check AE/MC/V [X11ACLA-3387] **COM** Y **ITC Member:** No

Rates: Pvt Bath 14
Single $ 70.00
Double $ 80-90.00

Asphodel Village	Rt 2 Box 89 70748	Jackson LA
Robert Couhig		Tel: 504-654-6868

Plantation Country Inn with cottages, a converted train station offering complete accommodations

---

©*Inn & Travel Memphis, Tennessee*   3-45

and dining while visiting. Main house dates c1820's in Greek Revival Cottage style and is restored and furnished with period antiques. Plenty of sights and hospitality included during your stay. Full hearty breakfast included. Five hundred acre estate grounds include swimming, creeks, and plenty of walking trails. **Seasonal:** Closed Christmas **Brochure:** Yes **Permitted:** Children, drinking, smoking **Payment Terms:** Check AE/MC/V [X11ACLA-3390] **COM** Y **ITC Member:** No

Rates:	Pvt Bath 11	Suites
Single		
Double	$ 50-80.00*	$ 90-120.00

Milbank Mansion	102 Bank St 70748	Jackson LA
Mr Mrs LeRoy Harvey		Tel: 504-634-5901

Originally a bank built in 1830, this beautiful structure had been completely renovated into a gorgeous antebellum mansion and one of the finest examples of this architecture in the state. Complete with period antique furnishings and family heirlooms, you can relive the true "Southern Feeling" here! Full breakfast included in the room rate. **Seasonal:** No **Reservations:** One night's deposit required at res time to hold. **Brochure:** Yes **Permitted:** Children 10-up, limited smoking **Payment Terms:** Check MC/V [X11ACLA-3391] **COM** Y **ITC Member:** No

Rates:	Pvt Bath 6	Shared Bath 3
Single	$ 85.00	$ 65.00
Double	$ 85.00	$ 65.00

Victoria Inn	Hwy 45 Box 0545 70067	Lafitte LA
Roy & Dale Ross		Tel: 504-689-4757 Fax: 504-689-3399
		Res Times 8am-9pm

"Come on Down to the Bayou and experience Cajun living!" Travel the route of the Baratarians. Explore the Bayous haunted by Jean Lafitte and relax in the elegant surroundings fit for the debonair pirate himself. Located in the small fishing village of Jean Lafitte, named for the famous pirate, this five bedroom Bed & Breakfast overlooks the water. You reach it by turning off Highway 45 and driving down a winding tree-shaded lane. The West Indies-style cottage is on six acres of landscaped grounds and overlooks one of the many bays and lakes in south Louisiana. As a little lagniappe (Cajun for "something extra") we serve afternoon drinks on the gallery or on our private pier. A full complimentary Cajun-style breakfast is graciously served every morning either on the gallery or in the Garden Room. Swamp Tours, chartered fishing, the Jean Lafitte National Park and a Cajun Fais Do Do every Saturday night and Sunday afternoon as well as wonderful seafood restaurants. **Airport:** New Orleans Intl-30 mins **Discounts:** Yes, inquire at res time **Seasonal:** No **Reservations:** 50% deposit, 30 day cancel notice for refund, less than 30 days, refund only if rebooked **Brochure:** Yes **Permitted:** Children, drinking, limited pets, limited smoking **Conference:** Yes, for special meetings, family reunions - featuring seafood boils! **Languages:** Spanish, English **Payment Terms:** Check MC/V [R09FPLA-18192] **COM** Y **ITC Member:** No

Rates:	Pvt Bath 2	Shared Bath 4
Single		$ 50.00
Double	$ 100-125.00	$ 65-75.00

Maison Marceline	442 E Main St 70560	New Iberia LA
Dan Broussard		Tel: 318-364-5922
		Res Times 24 Hrs

This Eastlake Victorian Town House is an elegant gingerbread design with all the trimmings including a gazebo surrounded by lush plants reminiscent of a tropical forest in this southern climate. The owner/host, an interior designer, has accented all the architectural highlights and has furnished all the rooms to perfection with antique period pieces. Located in the Historic District, one-half block from the Shadows On The Teche . . . downtown New Iberia. The one guest bedroom features an antique queen-size bed, a jacuzzi bath with a roll-away for a third person if desired. The full house is available for the guest's use including a private parlor and library. Guests receive the Royal

Treatment with a full breakfast that's served in the gazebo on fine china and silver. Nearby activities include Live Oak Garden, Avery Island and the Tabasco Plant, airboat tours of the swamps and great Cajun dining. Off-street parking is included. **Seasonal:** No **Reservations:** $20 deposit, non-refundable. **Brochure:** Yes **Permitted:** Pets, limited children **Conference:** Yes for a perfect occasion to 20 persons **Payment Terms:** Check [Z11DPLA-8433] **COM** Y **ITC Member:** No

Rates:	Pvt Bath 1
Single	$ 80.00
Double	$ 80.00

Hotel St Pierre	911 Burgundy St 70116	New Orleans LA
Ian Hardcastle	**Tel:** 800-225-4040 504-524-4401 **Fax:** 504-524-6800	
		Res Times 24 Hrs

This two hundred year-old Inn (former slave quarters) has been restored, offering 18th century guest room cottages in the heart of Veux Cairre (The French Quarter) - steps from Bourbon Street, Jackson Square and other sights. A maze of romantic courtyards form a restful oasis with lush tropical plants and two swimming pools, surrounded by guest cottages (some with balconies) offering native New Orleans ambience and hospitality. Arranged in clusters of Creole Cottages with exposed wood beams and original brick construction, each guest cottage is a spacious abode of refined taste reflecting that laid-back feeling indigenous to the Quarter. Guest rooms are appointed with antique reproductions with modern amenities (including color TV hidden away in an antique armoires) to provide for a pleasant lifestyle - including infamous ceiling fans to lull you to sleep.

A continental breakfast, complimentary champagne and off-street parking is included. A complimentary Happy Hour is provided in the courtyard daily, followed by a sophisticated dinner (additional cost) at The Empire, with its English Club atmosphere, situated on the site of the original New Orleans Jazz Museum. **Discounts:** Five or more rooms. **Airport:** New Orleans Moisant-25 mi **Packages:** Honeymoon, Christmas, New Orleans Cook School, Family Getaways. **Seasonal:** No **Reservations:** Deposit required **Brochure:** Yes **Permitted:** Children, pets, drinking, smoking **Languages:** French, Spanish **Payment Terms:** Check AE/DC/MC/V [R12EPLA-15728] **COM** Y **ITC Member:** No

Rates:	Pvt Bath 24
Single	$ 99.00
Double	$ 109.00

Lafitte Guest House	1003 Bourbon St 70116	New Orleans LA
John Maher	**Tel:** 800-331-7971 504-581-2678	
		Res Times 24 Hours

Originally constructed in 1849 as a grand private home - guests can enjoy the gracious hospitality and Victorian ambiance - in the center of the French Quarter - right on Bourbon Street. Meticulously restored to include every modern convenience without detracting from the graciousness - elegance abounds throughout. Each guest room is individually furnished with antiques and reproductions from around the world ranging from antique crown canopy beds, 19th Century furnishings, eclectic decor - to a balconied-room overhanging Bourbon Street. Whether you choose to have a complimentary breakfast of coffee and local delicate pastries on a wrought iron balcony while watching artists walking their canvases to famed Jackson Square or a more intimate setting in our beautiful courtyard setting - you'll experience the true feeling of the city. Get to know us at *Lafitte Guest House*. We're as New Orleans as street cars, jazz musicians and voodoo queens - and in the center of the Quarter's antique shops, museums and world-famous restaurants. Whether it's a quiet stroll

©*Inn & Travel Memphis, Tennessee*

Louisiana   *National Edition*

through rows of colorful Creole and Spanish cottages or the liveliness of the 24-hour night club scene on Bourbon Street ... you are only footsteps away at the Lafitte Guest House. **Discounts:** AAA **Airport:** New Orleans Intl-20 mins **Seasonal:** No **Reservations:** One night's deposit or credit card number to guarantee reservation; rates subject to change for special events **Brochure:** Yes **Permitted:** Children, drinking **Languages:** French **Payment Terms:** Check AE/DC/-MC/V [K07FPLA-3419] COM YG ITC **Member:** No

Rates: Pvt Bath   14
Single $ 85-165.00
Double $ 85-165.00

Mardi Gras House	40 Toulouse St 70121	New Orleans LA
Warren Charpee		Tel: 504-234-0192
		Res Times 8am-7pm

c1850s townhouse with French Creole flavor and decor complete with antiques, brass and four-poster beds, original art work and great food prepared on the premises by a former chef from a famous New Orleans dining establishment. Gourmet is the word here for both accommodations and dining experiences. Home recipes in traditional Creole style. Located within the French Quarter, so you only need to step out your door to be in the middle of everything. Full breakfast including choices of such favorites as Eggs Benedict, omelettes and homebaked cinnamon rolls and great beignets. **Seasonal:** No **Reservations:** 1 night's deposit at time of res, with full payment for guaranteed late **Brochure:** Yes **Permitted:** Smoking, drinking **Payment Terms:** Check [G02BFLA-6572] COM Y ITC **Member:** No

Rates: Pvt Bath   1   Shared Bath   12
Single $ 65.00 $ 45.00
Double $ 75.00 $ 52.50

PJ Holbrooks Olde Victorian Inn	914 N Rampart 70116	New Orleans LA
PJ Holbrook		Tel: 800-725-2446 504-522-2446

Whether you are visiting New Orleans again or for the first time - be ready for an exciting trip when you're met at the airport and delivered right to the door - all complimentary of course! This perfect "home away from home" in the historic French Quarter of New Orleans offers charm and elegance in the Victorian manner. Your engraved key ring brings you to one of the seven period guest rooms that are beautifully furnished and decorated - namely Chantilly, Wedgewood, Chelsea, Regency, Chateau, Somerset or Greenbriar - most rooms have fireplaces and three include balconies. Enjoy wine and cheese in the "Gathering Room" or in the beautiful courtyard where you can browse the menus your hostess has thoughtfully set out to help with your dinner plans. If you're uncertain where to go, PJ is around & ready with helpful recommendations and reservations at New Orleans famous - and best! While you're visiting the French Market or shopping Bourbon Street, PJ will make your reservations - from a lazy cruise up the "Mighty Mississippi" to a Louisiana bayou swamp adventure. Each morning brings the wonderful aroma of French coffees and a full complimentary breakfast of hot homemade breads, biscuits or coffee cakes, fresh fruit and juices, eggs, home fries, bacon, ham or perhaps crepes and your second or third cup of coffee. When your visit has ended - you'll be whisked back to the airport knowing you have a friend in New Orleans - and already planning your next visit. **Airport:** New Orleans Intl 20 mins. **Discounts:** Senior citizens, singles **Seasonal:** No **Reservations:** One night's deposit to secure stay, 10 day cancel policy for full refund. **Brochure:** Yes **Permitted:** Children, drinking **Payment Terms:** Check AE/MC/V [K09-DPLA-14395] COM YG ITC **Member:** No

Rates: Pvt Bath   7
Single $ 100.00
Double $ 100-150.00

National Edition   *Louisiana*

Prytania Inn I	1415 Prytania St 70130	**New Orleans LA**
Sally & Peter Schreiber		Tel: 504-566-1515 Fax: 504-566-1518
		Res Times 24 Hrs

"Old New Orleans Guest Homes" - built as private homes dating from the 1850's - the Inns have been restored to their pre-Civil War Glory during the past ten years. Just one block from St Charles and five minutes from the Quarter, the Inns are within an easy walking distance of the Garden District. *Prytania Inn One* received the Historic District Landmark Commission Award in 1984 for its restoration which includes the original hand-carved cornices, medallions and plasters - along with twin black fireplace mantels. Prytania Two is an historic mansion designed by Henry Howard, a noted architect for many Louisiana plantations, including Nottoway. Prytania Three is the former Harris-Maginnis Mansion with 38 rooms and is listed on the *National Historic Register*. All-in-all - three unique properties for travelers seeking the French Quarter and the excitement of New Orleans. A full-service property, daily laundry services are available, TV, tour and restaurant information. Full gourmet breakfast is available for additional $5.00 rate. **Discounts:** Weekly, monthly extended stays **Airport:** New Orleans Intl- 20 min **Seasonal:** No **Reservations:** Mail deposit or credit card number to guarantee reservation; latest arrival 11:30pm; 36 hr cancel policy required for refund. Rates vary for special events. **Brochure:** Yes **Permitted:** Children, pets, drinking, smoking **Languages:** German, French, Spanish, Japanese **Payment Terms:** Check AE/DC/MC/V [K07FPLA-3430] **COM** YG **ITC Member:** No

An Old New Orleans Guest House

Rates:	Pvt Bath 30	Shared Bath 10
Single	$ 35-39.00	$ 29.00
Double	$ 39-69.00	$ 30-40.00

Terrell House	1441 Magazine St 70130	**New Orleans LA**
Harry Lucas		Tel: 800-878-9859 504-524-9859
		Res Times 9am-9pm

Step into the New Orleans atmosphere in this Classical Revival-style residence on Magazine Street-"The Street of Dreams", filled with antique shops, art galleries, jazz clubs and fine restaurants. Dating from 1858 and a former residence of a cotton broker, it was restored in 1984 and furnished with elegance and authentic museum antiques by Prudent Mallard, a famous New Orleans craftsman whose workshop on Royal was patronized by the city's elite in 1840-50s. An original carriage house with four guest rooms, all furnished in a unique decor, open onto and overlook the lovely garden courtyard. The Servant's Quarters, located over the kitchen, include the original brick walls, hardwood floors with oriental carpeting. The rooms in the main mansion have fourteen foot ceilings, teastered beds, marble mantles, gold-leaf mirrors, gaslight-era chandeliers, paintings, antique furnishings, beautiful draperies and wall coverings of the period and Carnival memorabilia creating an "Old New Orleans ambience". Located in the Lower Garden District, this it the oldest "pure residential" neighborhood outside of the Quarter, rich in history and architectural treasures. A continental breakfast is included. **Seasonal:** No **Reservations:** Deposit at res time and advise arrival time. **Brochure:** Yes **Permitted:** Smoking, social drinking **Conference:** Yes for groups to 10 persons for social and business meetings. **Payment Terms:** Check AE/MC/V [I04DPLA-3434] **COM** Y **ITC Member:** No

Rates:	Pvt Bath 9
Single	$ 100.00
Double	$ 100.00

©*Inn & Travel Memphis, Tennessee*

Louisiana   *National Edition*

Victoria Inn   **New Orleans LA**
Roy & Dale Ross   **Tel:** 504-689-4757
                                                                                                              Res Times 8am-9pm

Refer to the same listing name under Lafitte, Louisiana for a complete description. **Seasonal:** No **Payment Terms:** Check MC/V [M09FPLA1-18209] **COM** Y **ITC Member:** No

Rates:	**Pvt Bath 2**	**Shared Bath 4**
Single		$ 50.00
Double	$ 100-125.00	$ 65-75.00

Bella Rose Mansion   255 N Eighth St 70454   **Ponchatoula LA**
Rose James   **Tel:** 504-386-3857
                                                                                                              Res Times 8am-8pm

"When only the best will do!" Thirty five minutes from New Orleans International Airport and only forty-five minutes from Baton Rouge, the *Bella Rose Mansion* offers 12,000 square feet of excitement and wonder. Formerly the home of a wealthy family that employed over 4,000 people in the strawberry business, the Mansion is listed on the *National Historic Register of the State of Louisiana*. The mansion has beautiful hand-carved mahogany paneling, a marble-walled solarium with a fountain of Bacchus, parquet and hardwood floors, Waterford Crystal chandeliers and a hand-carved spiral staircase crowned with a stained glass dome - one of the finest mansions in the South. Pick your suite to match your mood! The Primrose Bridal Suite is the ultimate, offering a heart-shaped Jacuzzi for two and plush terry cloth robes for lounging. The Veranda Suite features a black Jacuzzi for two and a Victoria's Secret decor. The Forget-Me-Not room provides a Laura Ashley theme while a masculine theme is feature in the Mallard Room. Godiva chocolates, a snack basket, fresh flowers and mylar balloons are complemented to each room. On weekends the Mansion is filled with guests, most of which are from the New Orleans and Baton Rouge elite. Rose, a natural entertainer and formerly in the restaurant business, offers a Silver Service Breakfast of Eggs Benedict, Banana Foster Crepes and Mimosas followed by a craps lesson on an original antique table. A complimentary bar is open 24 hours. Guests may enjoy playing shuffle board on the indoor court, reading in the library, relaxing by the pool or trying their hand at one of the finest collections of antique gaming equipment in the United States. The Monte Carlo High Rollers Collection of gaming memorabilia includes slot machines dating back to the early 1900's, a hand-crafted antique roulette wheel once owned by Jim Garrison, antique craps table and Blackjack table-each piece having Louisiana origins. For bargain hunters-antique buffs will enjoy Ponchatoula, known as the Antique Capital of the World, with a famous Saturday night Auction. *"If you are down in the dumps .... don't waste your money on a shrink .... spend a weekend at the Bella Rose Mansion."* **Discounts:** Inquire at res time **Packages:** Yes, inquire at res time **Seasonal:** No **Reservations:** One night's deposit or credit card number to guarantee reservation **Brochure:** Yes **Permitted:** Drinking, smoking in designated areas, children are not appropriate **Conference:** Yes, perfect for any special occasion or business meeting **Payment Terms:** MC/V [I08HPLA1-12430] **COM** YG **ITC Member:** No **Quality Assured:** Yes

Rates:	**Pvt Bath 4**
Single	$ 145-225.00
Double	$ 145-225.00

Butler Greenwood B&B   3345 US Hwy 61 70775   **Saint Francisville LA**
Anne Butler   **Tel:** 504-635-6312

3-50   ©*Inn & Travel Memphis, Tennessee*

National Edition   ***Louisiana***

Louisiana's English Plantation Country near St Francisville, offers the *National Register-listed Butler Greenwood* home, a working plantation of several thousand acres since 1796. The extensive oak-shaded grounds surround the antebellum home and two delightful B&B accommodations, each with private bath and partial or full kitchen. The Old Kitchen B&B is one of Audubon Country's most historical structures, an original detached kitchen built in 1796 under Spanish rule. An adaptive restoration has preserved the historic ambience with exposed brick, original aged beams, skylights overhung by moss-draped oak limbs. To the rear is the wood-frame shingle-roofed Cook's Cottage B&B - once home to the plantation cook who would rise early each morning and take a few steps to begin baking morning biscuits and the famous slow-dripping pungent Louisiana coffee. Overlooking a pond abloom with iris are the Gazebo B&B, built around three 9-foot tall stained glass windows from an old church and the Pond House B&B, gingerbread cottage with a big front porch and hammock perfect for watching the ducks and geese. At the edge of a steep wooded ravine is the Treehouse B&B with a wonderful four-tiered deck, fireplace and king size cypress four-poster bed. A continental breakfast, tour of the main home, and use of the swimming pool are included. Anne, your author-historian-innkeeper, provides guests with a wealth of delightful insights and history of the area. Featured recently in *"Southern Living"*, this area was the locale for eighty of John James Audubon's renderings that appeared in his famous *"Birds Of America,"* in 1821. **Airport:** Baton Rouge-25 mi **Packages:** Guided Birdwalks, Plantation Tours, Book Review Tours by resident author/historian. *Note: The innkeeper and St Francisville goodwill ambassador, has contributed a travel article about Saint Francisville.* **Seasonal:** No **Reservations:** Credit card deposit to guarantee reservation, 24 hr cancel policy for refund **Brochure:** Yes **Permitted:** Children, limited smoking, drinking, limited pets **Conference:** Pool pavilion with kitchen & bathrooms, can accommodate to 75 persons, attached gazebo **Languages:** Some French **Payment Terms:** Check AE/MC/V [I02HPLA1-15730] **COM** YG **ITC Member:** No

Rates:	Pvt Bath 5
Single	$ 80-90.00
Double	$ 80-90.00

Wolf Schlesinger House	118 N Commerce 70775	Saint Francisville LA
Patrick & Laurie Walsh		**Tel:** 800-488-6502 504-635-6502
		Res Times 7am-9pm

Located in Louisiana Plantation Country, the Saint Francisville Inn is on the edge of the Historic District. All rooms include canopy or poster beds, antique furnishings and all open onto a New Orleans-style courtyard in the rear of this 1880 building. In the main parlor there's a spectacular ceiling medallion decorated with Mardi Gras masks. Many antebellum plantations homes to tour are in the area along with a real opportunity to become part of the Louisiana culture with plenty of crawfish, gumbo and fine Cajun recipes. Complimentary continental breakfast included with your room. Listed in Mobile Travel Guide. Meeting room & conference facilities and the on-premises restaurant can accommodate bus groups with prior arrangements. Plenty of shopping and golf are nearby. Swimming pool on the premises. **Discounts:** Available **Airport:** 24 mi to Ryan Airport **Seasonal:** No **Reservations:** One night's deposit to confirm reservation; call if arriving after 10 pm **Brochure:** Yes **Permitted:** Children, smoking, drinking **Conference:** Meeting space; up to 25 persons **Payment Terms:** AE/DC/MC/V [R07DPLA-3442] **COM** U **ITC Member:** No

Rates:	Pvt Bath 9
Single	$ 49.00
Double	$ 59.00

Louisiana
National Edition

Fairfield Place	2221 Fairfield Ave 71104	**Shreveport LA**
Jane Lipscomb		**Tel: 318-222-0048**

Visitors to Shreveport have discovered *Fairfield Place Bed & Breakfast Inn*. Built before the turn-of-the-century, it is beautifully restored to bring you all the charm of a bygone era in a setting that offers lovely lodging accommodations. It is conveniently located near downtown, I-20, the medical centers and Louisiana Downs is only minutes away. We are within walking distance of fine restaurants and shops. Enjoy spacious rooms, individually decorated with European and American antiques. Relax in the oversized tubs and enjoy the casually elegant atmosphere. After a refreshing night's sleep, awaken to the aroma of rich Cajun coffee and fresh-baked, flaky croissants. Breakfast in the comfort and privacy of your room. Sip that last sip of coffee on the balcony or in the courtyard. Our staff is committed to providing personal, efficient service. Whether you come to us on an overnight business stay or you're looking for the perfect setting for that special occasion, we make every effort to insure a memorable visit. Try our wonderful alternative to traditional hotel lodging. We welcome the opportunity to serve you. When you call for reservations, you'll hear *"Welcome to Fairfield Place,"* and you'll think you're hearing *"Welcome Home."* We invite you to share the news of our accommodations with your friends and business associates. **Seasonal:** No **Reservations:** Deposit required to guarantee room, 7 day cancel policy for refund **Brochure:** Yes **Permitted:** Limited children and drinking. Smoking not permitted inside the building. **Payment Terms:** Check AE/MC/V [R05FPLA-3444] **COM** U **ITC Member:** No

Rates: Pvt Bath 6
Single $ 89.00
Double $ 135.00

Slattery House	2401 Fairfield Ave 71104	**Shreveport LA**
Bill & Adrienne Scruggs		**Tel: 318-222-6577 Fax: 318-222-7539**
		Res Times By Appt

Slattery House is a landmark of Shreveport located in the Highland Historic District. The history of the white turn-of-the-century house reaches back almost one hundred years. It was built in 1903 by attorney JB Slattery and is listed on the *National Register of Historic Places*. The white Victorian home features wrap around porch, library, parlor, formal dining room and four guest rooms, each with a private bath. It is situated on over an acre of land, including a private swimming pool, gardens and deck. Each spacious guest room is furnished with period antiques, queen size beds, CATV, private phones, imported toiletries. A fax and copier are available for our corporate guests. For the perfect honeymoon, a bridal suite is available, complete with a Jacuzzi and a honeymoon package. Guests can start their day with coffee, juice and the morning paper just outside their room, then head down stairs for a full country breakfast of homemade breads, eggs, bacon, sausage, grits and regional homemade jams grits and jellies. For restful moments, guests can retire to the upper gallery or front veranda, both filled with wicker furnishings and hanging ferns. Slattery House is only moments away from Riverboat Casinos, LA Downs, fine restaurants, antique malls, museums and theaters. **Airport:** Shreveport Regional-10 mins **Packages:** Honeymoon **Seasonal:** No **Reservations:** Credit card or cash deposit required, 48 hr cancel policy weekdays, 7 day notice for weekends **Brochure:** Yes **Permitted:** Limited children, drinking **Conference:** Yes **Payment Terms:** Check AE/DC/DISC/MC/V [I03IPLA1-22365] **COM** YG **ITC Member:** No

Rates: Pvt Bath 4
Single $ 85-150.00
Double $ 85-150.00

Twenty Four Thirty Nine	2439 Fairfield Ave 71104	**Shreveport LA**
Jimmy & Vicki Harris		**Tel: 318-424-2424**

National Edition   ***Louisiana***

Victorian Elegance combined with Southern Charm welcomes guests to a more gentle era on this beautiful avenue of splendid mansions and fine homes built at the turn-of-the-century. From the beautifully carved oak staircase, crystal chandeliers, Victorian swag drapes of lace and moire - guests enjoy the wonderful Victorian Era furnishings from Lalique, Sabino and Degenheart. Each guest room is uniquely furnished and yours may have a queen size four-poster bed, a wet bar, a view of one of the private gardens, an antique brass bed with a feather mattress or perhaps an 1860 petticoat vanity. Modern amenities include whirlpool baths, phones, fax, copier and cable TV (tucked away in the armoire). Morning brings the spicy aroma of gourmet breads being prepared for a proper English breakfast of fresh fruit, cheeses, home-made muffins, cereals, juice and coffee; followed by eggs, ham, sausage, fresh sauteed mushrooms and English muffins served with home-made jellies and butter. A luscious cup of hot tea from the kettle is the proper English way to end a delightful breakfast. Set your day to meet your interests: curl-up among down pillows and blankets with your favorite novel; handy phones and tables create a quiet work area; relax outdoors on one of the balconied rooms overlooking the lavish landscaped gardens which contain a Victorian swing, gazebo and water fountain or visit Line Avenue shopping corridor of unique shops and restaurants, just a few minutes away. Guests are conveniently located to downtown Shreveport, Bossier City Municipal Complex, Shreveport Airport, Barksdale Air Force Base, medical facilities, museums, art galleries, Louisiana Downs and Riverboat gambling. **Discounts:** Corporate rates **Package:** Honeymoon **Airport:** Shreveport Airport-10 mi **Seasonal:** No **Reservations:** Credit card number required if not paid in advance to guarantee, 7 day cancel policy for weekends, 48 hrs for weekdays **Brochure:** Yes **Permitted:** Children, pets, smoking, drinking are not permitted **Payment Terms:** Check AE/DC/DISC/-MC/V [Z04GPLA-14910] **COM Y ITC Member:** No

Rates: Pvt Bath   4
Single $ 95-150.00
Double $ 95-150.00

Nottoway Plantation Inn   Mississippi River Rd   70788   White Castle   LA
Cindy Hidalgo   Tel: 504-545-2730   Fax: 504-545-8632
                                                                                       Res Times 9am-5pm

Southern hospitality and genteel comfort lives in the Crowning Jewel of America's antebellum mansions - and listed on the *National Register of Historic Places*. Saved from destruction during the Civil War, Nottoway Plantation modestly contains 53,000 square feet of perfection which has been restored down to its intricate lacy plaster frieze work, hand-painted Dresden porcelain doorknobs, hand-carved marble mantles, twenty-two massive cypress columns and the Grand White Ballroom in which six of the prosperous owners' children were married. Ten years of construction (1849-1859) were required to complete this incomparable home and introduced such innovations to the South as indoor plumbing, gas lighting and coal fireplaces. All rooms remain furnished with period decor including the original furnishings still in the Master Bedroom. Choose a room or suite in the Mansion and Wings or the secluded Overseer's Cottage nestled beside the duck pond on the grounds. Room rates include a complimentary bottle of sherry on your night stand prior to your arrival. Morning wake-up call includes a Southern breakfast snack (sweet potato muffins), orange juice and coffee before enjoying your full plantation breakfast. A complimentary tour of the home is included. Honeymoon suite offers a private pool whether just married or not! Randolph Hall offers 19th century dining featuring Creole and Cajun specialties on the premises. Special group rates are available for lunch and dinner by advanced reservation. **Airport:** Baton Rouge-25 mi; New Orleans-70 mi **Reservations:** One night deposit at res time, 72 hr cancel policy for full refund. $25 service fee less than 72 hrs, no refund if cancelled within 24 hrs. **Permitted:** Children, drinking, smoking outdoors on the veranda only **Conference:** Yes: Special occasions that will never be forgotten, including special Candlelight Weddings and receptions **Payment Terms:** Check AE/DISC/MC/V [I08GPLA-3450] **COM YG ITC Member:** No **Quality Assured:** Yes

Rates: Pvt Bath   13
Single $ 95.00-250.00
Double $ 125.00-250.00

©Inn & Travel Memphis, Tennessee

Louisiana - Mississippi *National Edition*

White Castle Inn	55035 Cambre St 70788	White Castle LA
Don & Linda Neahusan		Tel: 504-545-9932
		Res Times 9am-8pm

Dating from 1897 as the Bank of White Castle when cypress lumber mills were booming, your hosts restored this picturesque building into a quaint Bed & Breakfast. Completely remodeled and refurbished - the first level consists of The Vault Gift Shop (formerly the bank's actual vault room), a quaint lobby area and the Blue Willow Dining Room where guests leisurely enjoy their complimentary continental breakfast among antique furnishings and the paintings of EJ Hutchinson and JC Olano. The second floor guest rooms are tastefully decorated with antiques, quilts and artwork, Each has a private bath, individually controlled a/c and a common sitting room and screened porch that provides a place to unwind and relax after a day of sightseeing. The Inn is located just off Hwy 1 in White Castle and within easy driving distance of all the River Road plantation homes of Nottoway, Houmas House, Tezcuco, Destrehan, San Francisco, Oak Alley and Ormand. **Discounts:** AARP **Airport:** Baton Rouge-25 mi; New Orleans Intl-60 mi **Seasonal:** No **Reservations:** Credit card number to guarantee full payment at time of reservation, 7 day cancel policy for refund **Brochure:** Yes **Permitted:** Drinking, limited children with prior notice, limited smoking, pets not permitted **Payment Terms:** AE/MC/V [Z05HPLA1-14135] **COM** YG **ITC Member:** No

Rates: Pvt Bath 4
Single $ 55-60.00
Double $ 65-75.00

Red Creek Colonial Inn		Biloxi MS
Dr & Mrs Karl Mertz		Tel: 800-729-9670 601-452-3080
		Res Times 8am-10pm

Refer to the same listing name under Long Beach, Mississippi for a complete description. **Seasonal:** No **Payment Terms:** Check [M06HPMS1-15384] **COM** YG **ITC Member:** No

Rates: Pvt Bath 3   Shared Bath 2
Single $ 39-69.00 $ 25.00
Double $ 49-79.00 $ 35.00

General's Quarters B&B & Restaurant	924 Filmore St 38834	Corinth MS
JL & Rosemary Aldridge		Tel: 601-286-3325
		Res Times 6-10pm M-Sat

Fabulous recently restored turn-of-the-century Edwardian Style residence in quaint Southern town full of *"Southern Comfort!"* All rooms are fully furnished in period antiques with modern conveniences and private baths. Located in historic area near Battery Fort Robinett and a pleasant country ride to famous Civil War battle area of Shiloh and its National Military sights. Close to Pickwick recreational area. Beautiful area for walking and jogging. There are plenty of shopkeepers offering antiques and flea markets nearby for important shopping while in Corinth. Just a short trip to Memphis or Jackson TN while enroute to perhaps Nashville or while traveling the Natchez Trace Parkway. Full Southern breakfast included with other meals available in the restaurant on the premises. **Discounts:** Yes, corporate rates upon approval of proprietor **Airport:** Memphis Intl-80 mi, Huntsville AL-90 mi **Seasonal:** No **Reservations:** Deposit required to confirm reservation, 24 hr cancel notice for refund. Corporate discounts upon approval of proprietor. **Brochure:** Yes **Permitted:** Children, smoking, limited drinking **Conference:** Yes, flexible for dining, business, or rehearsal dinners. **Payment Terms:** AE/MC/V [I04EPMS-2119] **COM** Y **ITC Member:** No

Rates: Pvt Bath 5
Single $ 75.00
Double $ 75.00

©*Inn & Travel Memphis, Tennessee*

National Edition ***Mississippi***

Doler B&B	Grenada MS
Ray & Vera Marcum	**Tel:** 601-637-2695
	Res Times 10am-10pm

Refer to the same listing name under Slate Springs, Mississippi for a complete description. **Seasonal:** No **Payment Terms:** Check MC/V [M01DPMS-12032] **COM** Y **ITC Member:** No

Rates: **Pvt Bath** 5
Single $ 75.00
Double $ 125.00

Redbud Inn	121 N Wells 39090-0266	Kosciusko MS
Rose Mary Burge/Maggie Garrett		**Tel:** 601-289-5086

An especially beautiful Queen Anne Victorian, listed on the *National Historic Register* as the Jackson-Nile House, it has enjoyed the distinction as one of the town's best examples of Victorian design since its inception in 1844. With its new identity as the *Redbud Inn*, it remains an eye-catcher for passers-by and receives enthusiastic praise from guests and visitors alike. The distinctive Victorian multi-color scheme will first catch your eye along with the beautiful gallery and balconies complete with balustrades, spindles and carved brackets. An octagonal corner tower rises three stories with a roofline that complements steep-pitched attic dormers, trimmed with fish scale shingles while wooden appliques in the popular sunrise motif provide final detail touches. The interior is just as impressive with a traditional wide center hall, heart-pine wainscoting, doors and woodwork, ornate mantles accented with tiles, windows which still retain the original interior blinds and a richly embellished square staircase - a unique example. As a bed & breakfast inn, its role as a travelers' haven is simply an extension of a purpose the house has served since the mid-1890s. Following the death of her husband in a politically-motivated duel, Lillie took in boarders to support herself and her four children. The tradition continued when the next owner, Miss Pattie Lee Sallis, opened the rooms of the big house to teachers and others in need of a place to stay. Today, your innkeepers continue the long tradition of having guests stay with them in this magnificent residence. There's an antique shop and a dining room which provides weekday lunches and Saturday night dinners. Nearby activities include antiquing, horseback riding, fishing/boating, golf, parks with walking tracks and sights such as Oprah Winfrey's birthplace! **Discount:** Yes, for two nights or more **Airport:** Jackson Intl-70 mi. Mile marker 160, Natchez Trace Parkway **Seasonal:** No **Reservations:** Deposit required **Brochure:** Yes **Permitted:** Children, limited drinking, limited smoking **Languages:** French **Payment Terms:** Check MC/V [I09EPMS-15481] **COM** Y **ITC Member:** No

Rates: **Pvt Bath** 2 **Shared Bath** 1
Single $ 60.00 $ 50.00
Double $ 75.00 $ 60.00

Red Creek Colonial Inn	7416 Red Creek Rd 39560	Long Beach MS
Dr & Mrs Karl Mertz		**Tel:** 800-729-9670 601-452-3080 **Fax:** 601-452-3080
		Res Times 8am-10pm

About an hour east of New Orleans and twenty minutes west of Biloxi is *Red Creek Colonial Inn*. This lovely three-story "raised French cottage" was built in 1899 and converted to an inn in 1989. Built by a retired Italian sea captain to entice his young bride away from New Orleans, Karl & Toni Mertz have owned the property since 1971. There is a 64 ft front porch with two porch swings and another swing is suspended from a registered live oak that spans 125 ft. Wooden radios, a Victorian organ and an Edison record player add to the Inn's charm. The antiques are usable and the atmosphere is relaxed. Toni's favorite part of the Inn is the front porch, *"... where I enjoy the shade of the beautiful magnolias and just swing to my heart's content, enjoying a tall drink and a thick novel."* Karl says his favorite way of enjoying his stay is "**... listening to the rain on the metal roof, reading in**

©*Inn & Travel Memphis, Tennessee*

Mississippi — *National Edition*

"Needing to get away from it all is something we understand completely." Karl, a regional manager with USDA's front of the fireplace, or just walking the beautiful grounds, especially in spring." Toni, the mother of two "grown sons", says Agricultural Research Service, adds, *"This place is our therapy for city-life and we want to offer our guests the same experience."* A continental-plus breakfast is included. **Discounts:** Yes, free 7th night. **Airport:** Biloxi-Gulfport-7 mi. **Packages:** Golf and Casino **Seasonal:** No **Reservations:** One night's deposit in advance, if possible **Brochure:** Yes **Permitted:** Limited children, drinking, smoking outside **Payment Terms:** Check [I06HPMS1-9034] **COM** YG **ITC Member:** No

Rates:	Pvt Bath 3	Shared Bath 2
Single	$ 39-69.00	$ 25.00
Double	$ 49-79.00	$ 35.00

Dunleith	84 Homochitto 39120	Natchez MS
Nancy Gibbs		Tel: 800-443-2445 601-446-8500 **Fax:** 601-446-6094
		Res Times 9am-5pm

Surrounded by forty acres of green pastures and weeded bayous, *Dunleith*, a stately white colonnaded Greek Revival temple stands on a terraced rise near the heart of Natchez. *Dunleith* is sometimes called the most photographed house in America and was cited by the *Southern Heritage Society* for the beauty and grace of its architecture and it has appeared in *Southern Accents* book, H*istoric Homes of the South*. Listed on the *National Register of Historic Places* and a *National Historic Landmark, Dunleith* has been the backdrop for such films as *Huckleberry Finn* and *Showboat*. Restoration work under the inspiration and guidance of William F Heins III, ushers in *Dunleith's* finest hour. There are eight guest rooms in the courtyard wing and three rooms in the main house. Each room is individually decorated and has a private bath, individual heat and a/c, color TV, fireplace and phone. A plentiful Southern breakfast is served in the restored poultry house. Guests receive complimentary refreshments and a tour of the home, Guests may relax in the wicker chairs on the gallery or roam the grounds which are lighted at night to give the feeling of moonlight. **Airport:** Baton Rouge-1-1/2 hr; Jackson, MS-2 hr **Seasonal:** Closed Sunday **Reservations:** One night's deposit to guarantee reservation, check-in 1pm-6pm, check-ins not accepted after 6pm, check-out 11am **Brochure:** Yes **Permitted:** Drinking, limited smoking **Conference:** Perfect for unforgettable private and intimate meetings, seminars, conferences **Payment Terms:** AE/DISC/MC/V [K08GPMS-2128] **COM** U **ITC Member:** No

Rates:	Pvt Bath 11
Single	$ 85-130.00
Double	$ 85-130.00

Mount Repose Plantation	1733 Martin Luther King 39120	Natchez MS
Shields Brown		Tel: 601-442-0097
		Res Times 8:30-5:30pm

Mount Repose is a fitting name for this 1824 antebellum plantation home tranquilly sitting in the midst of 250 acres of rolling hills, green pastures, tree-lined ponds, magnificent live oaks, and lovely magnolias. It is located on an old Spanish highway five miles north of Natchez, the oldest town on the Mississippi River. On a still night, guests may hear tug boat whistles on the river four miles distant. Guests may take a walking tour or carriage ride through historic downtown Natchez, experience the fine dining in the local pubs and restaurants, ride bikes on the Natchez Trace, ex-

©*Inn & Travel Memphis, Tennessee*

National Edition *Mississippi*

plore historic Indian Mounds or tour more than 30 antebellum homes on the famous Natchez Spring Pilgrimage. Upon arriving, guests are treated to complimentary beverages and a tour of this lovely residence. Three large bedrooms are located in the main house, furnished with fine period antiques, portraits and family heirlooms. A complimentary full Southern (or Continental - your choice breakfast is served in the formal dining room. This is the perfect weekend or special "Get-Away Place"! Great Southern dinners and picnic baskets are available upon request and added cost. **Seasonal:** No **Reservations:** One night's deposit; late arrival with prior notice **Brochure:** Yes **Permitted:** Children, limited drinking **Payment Terms:** Check AD/DC/MC/V [R02BCMS-2138] **COM** Y **ITC Member:** No

Rates:	Pvt Bath 3	Shared Bath 1
Single	$ 60-70.00	$ 40.00
Double	$ 65-75.00	

Oakland Plantation	1124 Lower Woodville Rd 39120	Natchez MS
Mr Mrs Andrew Peabody		Tel: 800-824-0355 601-445-5101
		Res Times 8am-7pm

"Most beautiful plantation home in Natchez," Sam Wilson, noted New Orleans architect, comments about this lovingly restored 1785 home of Abner Green, situated on a 360 acre game preserve full of nature's best in this Southern historic area. Beautifully furnished with period antiques and family heirlooms, you can relax inside or stroll the rolling hills and pastures and nature's trails. Bring your fishing pole here too for the pond!! Or else practice your tennis with lessons available by a USPTA instructor. Plantation tour included of this residence where Andrew Jackson courted Rachel Robards!! Just 8 miles south of Natchez. Full Southern breakfast to delight you each morning is included. **Seasonal:** No **Reservations:** First day's deposit, non-refundable **Brochure:** Yes **Permitted:** Children, drinking **Payment Terms:** Check MC/V [I10HPMS1-2139] **COM** YG **ITC Member:** No **Quality Assured:** Yes

Rates:	Pvt Bath 2	Shared Bath 1
Single	$ 65.00	$ 55.00
Double	$ 75.00	$ 65.00

Presbyterian Manse	307 S Rankin 39120	Natchez MS
		Tel: 601-446-9735
		Res Times 8am-5pm

This antebellum home c1830's has served as the home of the Presbyterian ministers since 1835 with the present pastor and his family in residence since 1980. The first guest room available is "The Study", built 1859 as a study for the pastor and is pleasantly furnished in period decor with two double beds and a single, with modern amenities included, and antique furnishings, with a private entrance. The second bedroom is beautiful, with Victorian period decor with double beds, and sitting room in the main house. Lovely Southern gardens are enjoyed while your continental breakfast is served outdoors, weather permitting. **Seasonal:** No **Reservations:** Yes, one night's deposit in advance, late arrival by prior arrangement **Permitted:** Well-behaved children, pets **Payment Terms:** Check MC/V [A05ACMS-2140] **COM** Y **ITC Member:** No

Rates:	Pvt Bath 2
Single	
Double	$ 95.00

Weymouth Hall	1 Cemetery Rd 39120	Natchez MS

©*Inn & Travel Memphis, Tennessee*

Mississippi *National Edition*

Mrs Gene Weber
Tel: 601-445-2304
Res Times 8am-7pm

Neo-Classic 1855 home is listed on *National Register of Historic Places* and is nestled on several acres of lawn on the most prominent point, offering spectacular vies of the Mississippi River. This residence has been restored and is furnished with authentic period pieces by John Belter, Chas Baudoine and P. Mallard. Beautiful porcelain collection by all the masters: Meissen, Dresden, Teplitz, Royal Bonn and Old Paris shared by the host with all guests. Guest rooms are in the main house and all include antique decor and full baths. Exciting plantation breakfast is included and served in the magnificent main dining room each morning. Complimentary tour of home and evening beverage. **Seasonal:** No **Reservations:** Advance reservations, 50% deposit, refunded if cancelled seven days prior to arrival. No late arrivals. **Brochure:** Yes **Permitted:** Social drinking **Payment Terms:** Check MC/V [A05ACMS-2147] **COM** Y **ITC Member:** No

Rates: Pvt Bath 5
Single $ 70.00
Double $ 80.00

Oak Square Plantation   1207 Church St 39150   **Port Gibson MS**
William Lum, Mgr
Tel: 800-729-0240 601-437-4350
Res Times 8am-10pm

Step back to an era of gracious living and antebellum splendor in this luxurious mansion built in 1850 and listed in the *National Register of Historic Places* and in *Mississippi's First National Historic District*. Restored to its original elegance by the owners, Mr & Mrs Lum, *Oak Square*, a Mansion of the Old South, bids visitors a quiet retreat to the past. Comprised of five buildings, main house, two guest houses, carriage house and quarters. Greek Revival style, six fluted Corinthian columns welcome guests inside where displayed are family heirlooms and exquisite antiques, including twenty-four canopy beds, a rare Chickering piano and spectacular chandeliers. Ornate mill work adorns the doors and ceilings and a divided white staircase leads to an unusual second floor minstrel gallery where musicians waltzed guests throughout the evening. Surrounding this elegant residence are beautiful grounds filled with magnificent oaks, courtyard, fountains and a gazebo for enjoying the evening breeze. Each spring, Oak Square hosts the 1800's Spring Festival on these beautiful grounds. Over 200 costumed participants performing music, dancing and merry-making of the 1800's. Relive a day in the past with fencing duels, Maypole dances, lawn games, 1800's fashion show and more. *"A Top Twenty Event"*, last weekend in March. A full southern breakfast begins your day of visiting the historic and quaint sights in this charming Southern town that General US Grant called "The town too beautiful to burn". Visit nearby Grand Gulf Military State Park, historic buildings, Civil War battlefields and museums. AAA 4-Diamond Rated **Airport:** Jackson MS-70 mi **Packages:** Yes, inquire at res time **Seasonal:** No **Reservations:** One night's deposit or credit card to guarantee reservation **Brochure:** Yes **Permitted:** Children, limited drinking, limited smoking (drinking and smoking not permitted in guest rooms) **Payment Terms:** Check AE/DISC/MC/V [I05HPMS1-2152] **COM** U **ITC Member:** No **Quality Assured:** Yes

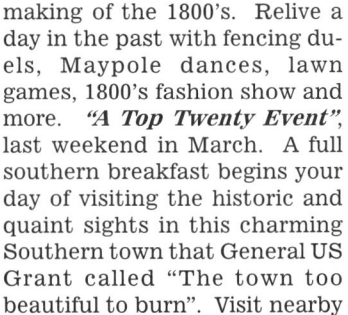

Rates: Pvt Bath 12
Single $ 85.00
Double $ 85-125.00

Cottage Inn   Rt 1 Box 40 38664   **Robinsonville MS**
*Ruth Lindley
Tel: 800-363-2900 601-363-5997
Res Times 24 Hrs

This charming, new, twenty room Country Inn, including suites, offers a unique approach to lodging. Conveniently located at Casino Center, *Cottage Inn* features ten charming cottages, each with

©*Inn & Travel Memphis, Tennessee*

two spacious and elegantly furnished guest rooms. Each bedroom and living room has private entrances, TV, phone, wet bar, refrigerator, coffee maker, microwave and other amenities. The Presidential Suite is the choice for special occasions, honeymoons and high-rollers offering fireplace, jacuzzi for two, living area, kitchen and etc. The gazebo, at the center point of the landscaping, has a fireplace, wet bar and grill and is available to all guests. Some rooms have fireplaces, laundry facilities. A complimentary continental breakfast is served each morning. **Airport:** Memphis Intl-40mi **Packages:** Yes, inquire at res time **Reservations:** Valid credit card or cash deposit required, 24 hr cancel policy **Brochure:** Yes **Permitted:** Children, pets, drinking, limited smoking **Payment Terms:** AE/DISC/MC/V [I02HP-MS1-20743] **COM** YG **ITC Member:** No

Rates: Pvt Bath 20
Single $ 59-up
Double $ 59-up

Doler B&B	PO Box 4605 38955	Slate Springs MS
*Ray & Vera Marcum		**Tel:** 601-637-2695
		Res Times 10am-10pm

Doler Bed & Breakfast Farm home was built in the 1890s on a 150 acres just three miles West of Slate Springs, Mississippi and 25 miles east of Grenada, Mississippi. The home is 45 miles from Mississippi State University at Starkeville and 125 miles south of Memphis Tennessee. The home is furnished with heirloom furniture and an antique doll collection. There are half-tester beds adorned with lace coverlets downstairs, and the curved staircase leads to a breath-taking view of the grounds of flowering shrubs and lilies. Seventy-five acres of trails let guests escape for a creekside picnic, to jog, bird watch and bike as well as walk the many nature trails. A beautiful conference room, porch swings and rocking chairs on the wrap around porch are just a few of the amenities available to the guests. Water sports, fishing and antique shopping can be arranged at an extra cost. Room rates are MAP and include a full country breakfast and evening dinner. Southern recipes are highlighted and include homemade biscuits, cornbread, cinnamon rolls and cobblers for dessert. Discounts for honeymooners with three days or longer stay and group or wedding activities. **Seasonal:** No **Reservations:** One night's deposit, 7 days cancel notice for refund; 4-9pm arrival unless arrangements for late arrival are made **Brochure:** Yes **Permitted:** Limited children, limited pets, no alcoholic beverages, smoking outside **Conference:** Yes; conference room available for business & social events including wedding receptions up to 40 persons **Payment Terms:** Check MC/V [R01DPMS-12029] **COM** Y **ITC Member:** No

Rates: Pvt Bath 5
Single $ 75.00
Double $ 125.00

Mocking Bird Inn B&B	305 N Gloster 38801	Tupelo MS
Sandy & Jim Gilmer		**Tel:** 601-844-5271 **Fax:** 601-840-4158
		Res Times 24 Hrs

Treat yourself to a *"Holiday in Paris, Africa, Venice or maybe even Athens,"* while visiting Tupelo, Mississippi either on business or leisure. Each of the seven intriguing guest rooms represents the decor from a different area of the world. Venice - An 1800's tapestry with Venetian gondolas and the Doge's Palace transport you to the City of Canals. This guest room has a fireplace. Mackinac Island - Surround yourself with the style of a white-washed cottage and relax on the porch swing in your guest room! It has a private ramp entrance and full handicap facilities as well. Paris - The Parisian Room draws inspiration from the artist, Toulouse LaTrec. A pewter wedding canopy bed and Victorian-style wicker chaise provide sweet dreams. Athens - Experience the atmosphere of old Greece in this guest room lavished in the architectural style from 1000 BC. In contrast, you'll enjoy the L-shaped double jacuzzi tub. Africa - Straight out of Isak Dinesen's "Out of Africa", experience a taste of the jungle with sensuous mosquito netting, zebra and leopard-like furs and rugs, as well as an interesting collection of African wood carvings. Sanibel Island - Awaken with the morning light peeking through the windows of this island room with verdigris iron bed and separate sitting area. Bavaria - Take a glimpse of the Alps while you awaken in your feather, sleigh bed. Knotty pine touches, antique wooden skis and lace curtains transport you to a little Bavarian village. Each guest room has a private bath, cable TV and phone, a delicious hardy full breakfast and evening refreshments are included. Fax machine available. Two upscale restaurants in quaint old residences are across the street, as well as the school where Elvis attended the 6th and 7th grades. The Inn is centrally located in Tupelo on Business 45 (Glouster), one block north of Hwy 6 (Main Street) and just off the Natchez Trace Parkway, halfway between Natchez and Nashville Tennessee. Three Civil War battlefields are within an hour's drive of the Mockingbird Inn. **Packages:** Honeymoon, Special Occasions **Seasonal:** No **Reservations:** One night's deposit within ten days of booking or one week prior to arrival whichever comes first, 3 day cancel policy for refund **Brochure:** Yes **Permitted:** Children 13-up, pets, drinking, smoking outdoors only **Conference:** Small meetings and get-togethers **Languages:** Some Spanish **Payment Terms:** Check AE/DISC/MC/V [K04GPMS-18855] COM YG ITC **Member:** No

Rates: Pvt Bath 7
Single $ 65-95.00
Double $ 65-95.00

Cedar Grove Mansion	2200 Oak St 39181-0833	Vicksburg MS
Ted Mackey		Tel: 800-862-1300 601-636-1000
		Res Times 7am-10pm

"Gone With The Wind" elegance lives on, in this grand 1840 antebellum mansion, nestled on four acres of gardens, gazebos, fountains; roof garden with a magnificent view of the Mississippi River. Relive the gracious 1800's in this twenty six room mansion, where a cannon ball fired by the Union gunboats remains lodged in the parlour wall! The former owners had guests, such as Jefferson Davis, who waltzed across the ballroom numerous times, and Ulysses Grant, who spent the night here after his Union troops captured the town. Today the furnishings remain the same, with many exquisite original antiques, original gaslight chandeliers, gold-leaf mirrors and fourteen Italian marble mantles. Guest rooms and suites, furnished in original and period antiques, some with canopy beds. A full Southern breakfast and tour are included. Gourmet candlelight dining and piano bar open after 6pm. Croquet and lawn tennis available. **Airport:** Jackson, MS-1 Hr **Seasonal:** No **Reservations:** Credit card number required to guarantee reservation at res time **Brochure:** Yes **Permitted:** Children 6-up, drinking, limited smoking **Conference:** Grand dining and common rooms are available for meetings and dining, perfect for groups 20-25 persons **Payment Terms:** Check AE/DISC/MC/V [Z08GPMS-2993] COM Y ITC **Member:** No

Rates: Pvt Bath 29
Single $ 75-150.00
Double $ 85-160.00

Corners	601 Klein St 39180	Vicksburg MS
Bettye & Cliff Whitney		Tel: 800-444-7421 601-636-7421

Stepback to 1783 in this beautiful Southern residence with its high ceilings, period antique furnishings, 65 foot verandas overlooking the Mississippi and fragrant gardens filled with blossoms throughout the summer. These gracious hosts introduce all of their guests to the traditional Southern Style of Living by encouraging guests to relax throughout their home, by selecting an interesting novel from their library, or by watching the Mississippi from the highback rockers standing guard on the broad gallery outdoors. Morning brings a full plantation breakfast served in the formal dining room followed by an enjoyable tour & historical narrative of the mansion & the original parterre gardens. **Seasonal:** No **Reservations:** One night's deposit within 5 days, 48 hour cancel policy for refund.

Brochure: Yes **Permitted:** Children, drinking, limited smoking **Conference:** An unforgettable setting for special business or social functions including wedding receptions and luncheons. **Payment Terms:** Check AE/MC/V [X06BCMS-2155] **COM** Y

ITC Member: No

Rates:	Pvt Bath 7
Single	$ 75-85.00
Double	$ 75-95.00

Alexander House	210 Green St 39192	West MS
Ruth Ray & Woody Dinstel		**Tel:** 601-967-2417
		Res Times Prior to 6pm

The *Alexander House* opened as a bed and breakfast in 1994 and dates from at least 1880. Named for Captain Joseph T Alexander, a Civil War veteran, he lived in the home after the was, as did many of his family. The guest rooms are named for his sons and daughters. The Captain Alexander room is downstairs and features some furniture original to the home. The downstairs also includes two kitchens - the original and a modern kitchen located in what used to be the smoke house - where inscribed on the door are notations about hams that were cured in 1936! Most of the furnishings have been collected by Ruth and Woody over the years - with everything fitting "like it belonged here" says Ruth. A full Southern breakfast is included and candlelight dinners are available at a nominal fee. Activities and sights include old homes, Holmes County State Park with plenty of fishing, Civil War sites of skirmishes, cemeteries, hospitals, Casey Jones wreck site and museum, Little Red Schoolhouse, birthplace of the Order of the Eastern Star, Natchez Trace and plenty of friendly people. **Seasonal:** No **Reservations:** Deposit required to guarantee reservation **Brochure:** Yes **Permitted:** Limited children, drinking **Conference:** Yes, groups to thirty **Payment Terms:** Check [I08GP-MS-20055] **COM** YG **ITC Member:** No **Quality Assurance:** Requested

Rates:	Pvt Bath 3	Shared Bath 2
Single	$ 65.00	$ 65.00
Double	$ 65.00	$ 65.00

Square Ten Inn	242 Depot St 39669	Woodville MS
Elizabeth M Treppendahl		**Tel:** 601-888-3993

c1830's townhouse offering New Orleans style courtyard, antique furnishings, and listed on the National Register of Historic Places. You're close to Rosemont, boyhood home of Jefferson Davis. Continental breakfast included. **Seasonal:** No **Brochure:** Yes **Permitted:** Children 6-up, smoking, drinking **Payment Terms:** Check [X11ACMS-2160] **COM** Y **ITC Member:** No

Rates:	Pvt Bath 3
Single	
Double	$ 50.00

Cover House	34 Wilson 28901	Andrews NC
Gayle Lay		**Tel:** 704-321-5302 **Fax:** 704-321-2145

Built at the turn-of-the-century, this beautiful Bed and Breakfast Inn beckons you to come and sit a spell while enjoying one of western North Carolina's most beautiful valleys. Located in Andrews, North Carolina, the *Cover House* is nestled among majestic mountains, sparkling lakes and white-water rivers offering a "down home" adventure where you can sit back, relax and enjoy the quiet of mountain living. Surrounded by unlimited recreational activities and adventures, the *Cover House* boasts convenient access to white water rafting, canoeing and kayaking. Or if you'd rather - spend the day at one our area lakes boating, fishing or water skiing. Whether you are a hiker, biker or golfer, or seek to learn more about our mountain arts and crafts, it's all conveniently lo-

North Carolina

cated near the *Cover House.* Unique is the heritage of the "mountain-folk" of Andrews. With a population of around 1,500, Andrews offers the advantages of a closely-knit community, as well as, the proximity of larger metropolitan areas. Major cities including Atlanta, Chattanooga, Knoxville, Asheville and Greenville are located within 150 miles. The Andrews Airport is licensed and insured by the FAA and offers charter flights throughout the country. Hanger and tie-down spaces are available at the facility, which features a 5,000 foot lighted air strip. The Great Smoky Mountain Railway has scheduled tours coming and going on a regular basis from the Andrews Train Station. Western North Carolina boasts the deepest gorge east of the Grand Canyon, numerous lakes, streams, waterfalls, the Blue Ridge Parkway, and the Great Smokey Mountains and as a guest of the *Cover House,* you can explore any of these area activities. Or if you're *"Fix'in to sit a spell,"* relax in our rocking chairs on the front porch or in your room. Restored to it's Victorian beauty with antique furnishings, charming rooms with private baths, fireplaces, mountain views and breathtaking sunsets, the *Cover House* **invites you to come and "sit a spell" and enjoy the quiet of mountain living.** Airport: Atlanta-2 hrs; Andrews-Murphy-5 mins **Packages:** Inquire at res time **Seasonal:** No **Reservations:** Credit card to guarantee reservation, 24 hour cancellation policy, late arrival okay with prior arrangements **Brochure:** Yes **Permitted:** Limited children, drinking, limited smoking **Conference:** Andrews Cultural Arts Center **Payment Terms:** MC/V [I11HPNC1-22317] **COM YG ITC Member:** No

Rates:	Pvt Bath 3	Shared Bath 2
Single	$ 75.00	$ 70.00
Double	$ 80.00	$ 75.00

Huntington Hall B&B Andrews NC
Bob & Kate DeLong Tel: 800-824-6189 704-837-9567
Res Times 24 Hrs

Refer to the same listing name under Murphy, North Carolina for a complete description. **Seasonal:** No **Payment Terms:** Check AE/DC/DISC/MC/V [M06H-PNC1-14550] **COM YG ITC Member:** No

Rates:	Pvt Bath 5
Single	$ 49-65.00
Double	$ 65-85.00

Blake House Inn 115 Royal Pines Dr 28704 Arden NC
Jack & Jan Bass Tel: 704-684-1847

Dating from 1847, this former summer estate and Confederate field hospital offers guests seclusion and ambience with fireside dining. Nestled in the mountains with 150 year-old sycamores and giant boxwoods, guests feel the warmth and hospitality offered by Jan Bass, a home economist/hostess who looks after every detail including the preparation of the meals. Guests can choose from regional specialties such as fresh local trout or country French entrees which change daily. Built of 22-inch thick stone walls, all of the rooms offer mahogany and heart pine woodwork, antique furnishings and family heirlooms. The large wrap around porch is a perfect place for relaxing with a fresh homemade dessert or in winter guests can choose the warmth of one of the many fireplaces. Fireplaces are available in some of the guest rooms too. A full breakfast is included in the room rate. Activities include nature tails, antique shopping and being just seven miles south of Asheville, Biltmore Estate, Carl Sandburg and all the other sights are just minutes away. **Seasonal:** Clo: 1/1-3/31 **Reservations:** Deposit at res time to hold room, late arrival notice in advance and rooms held until 7 pm. **Brochure:** Yes **Permitted:** Children during the week only, limited smoking, limited drinking **Conference:** Yes for small groups **Payment Terms:** Check MC/V [R08BCNC-2893] **COM Y ITC Member:** No

Rates:	Pvt Bath 2	Shared Bath 3
Single	$ 65.00	$ 55.00
Double	$ 65.00	$ 55.00

National Edition *North Carolina*

Albemarle Inn	86 Edgemont Rd 28801-1544	Asheville NC
Kathy & Dick Hemes		Tel: 704-255-0027

Albermarle Inn has graciously hosted guests for over fifty years, including the Hungarian composer Bela Bartol, who composed his Third Piano Concerto here in 1943, inspired by the mountain birdsong outside his window. Located in a beautiful historic residential area, Albemarle Inn is a handsome Greek Revival mansion with high airy ceilings, polished oak paneling, and an exquisite carved oak stairway with a unique circular landing and balcony. This distinguished Inn is on the *National Register of Historic Places*. Eleven spacious and comfortable guest rooms present romantic themes creating very special niches for its guests. Rooms provide modern amenities, including private baths with tub/showers, TV, phones and air conditioning. Sunrise Suite, Juliet's Chamber, Pink Parfait and the Royal Hideaway are very large and bright. Rooms feature king or queen size beds in a variety of styles including four posters, canopy, wicker, wood, iron and brass. A delicious full breakfast is served in the dining room or on the bright and airy sunporch where typical fare includes fresh fruit, chilled juice, delicate cream cheese stuffed French toast with sweet orange sauce and smoked sausage. For the sports-minded, the Inn has a refreshing swimming pool and is very near facilities for golf, horseback riding, tennis, bicycling and water sports. Others may enjoy fine dining, antique shopping and art galleries. Graciously hosted by Kathy and Dick Hemes, the *Albemarle Inn* is the epitome of stately elegance and relaxed charm where hospitality and service are the essence of the Inn. **Airport:** Asheville Regional-20min **Seasonal:** No **Reservations:** Deposit, 7 day cancel policy, special arrangements required for check-in after 9pm **Brochure:** Yes **Permitted:** Children 14-up, limited drinking **Payment Terms:** Check DISC/MC/V [K03HPNC1-4016] **COM** YG **ITC Member:** No

Rates: Pvt Bath 11
Single $ 85-140.00
Double $ 85-140.00

Black Walnut B&B	288 Montford 28801	Asheville NC
Janette Sypezak		Tel: 704-254-3878

The *Black Walnut Inn* is a unique turn-of-the-century shingle-style home built by architect Richard Sharp Smith. This special ten room home was restored into a four-guest room inn in 1992. Each room is decorated with a blending of antiques and traditional furniture. Three of the guest rooms have working fireplaces. Guests can choose from rooms that feature a whirlpool tub, an oversized clawfoot tub or a steam/shower bath room. Additional amenities include welcoming refreshments, TV in each guest room plus games, video and video tape library or enjoying a tune on our baby grand piano. Our full breakfast features homemade breads, jams and is served family style, allowing guests an opportunity to visit each morning. We look forward to your stay. **Discounts:** Yes, inquire at res time **Packages:** Yes, inquire at res time **Seasonal:** No **Reservations:** Deposit required to hold room, check-in 3-9 pm or upon prior arrangements. **Brochure:** Yes **Permitted:** Children, limited drinking **Languages:** Limited Polish, German, French **Payment Terms:** Check DC/MC/V [R12EPNC-1-6074] **COM** Y **ITC Member:** No

Rates: Pvt Bath 4
Single $ 60-90.00
Double $ 65-95.00

Claddagh Inn		Asheville NC
Vickie & Dennis Pacilio	Tel: 800-225-4700 704-697-7778	Fax: 704-697-8664
		Res Times 24 Hrs

©*Inn & Travel Memphis, Tennessee*

3-63

North Carolina

National Edition

Refer to the same listing name under Hendersonville, North Carolina for a complete description. **Seasonal:** No **Payment Terms:** Check AE/DISC/MC/V [M11CPNC-11839] **COM** Y **ITC Member:** No

Rates:	Pvt Bath 14
Single	$ 53-79.00
Double	$ 59-89.00

Richmond Hill Inn	87 Richmond Hill Rd 28806	Asheville NC
*Susan Michel		**Tel:** 800-545-9238 704-252-7313 **Fax:** 704-252-8726
		Res Times 9am-8pm

The grand Victorian mansion known as Richmond Hill was built in 1889 by Richmond Pearson, a former congressman and ambassador renowned for his political service to our nation. This century-old home stands proudly as Asheville's premier remaining example of Queen Ann-style architecture. Today *Richmond Hill Inn* welcomes guests in the grand style of a by-gone era, offering thirty-six comfortable rooms, each with a private bath and many with fireplaces. Other touches include fresh flowers and wonderful down pillows. The Inn's elegance gourmet restaurant, Gabrielle's, serves contemporary American cuisine with an emphasis on fresh ingredients available locally. Both the Inn and Gabrielle's have earned AAA's Four Diamond Award. Guests can enjoy exceptional dining in the mansion's formal Dining Room or on the glass-enclosed Sun Porch. A delightful full breakfast is included in each room rate. A lush, peaceful setting awaits guests in the new garden complex along with an additional fifteen guest rooms, a second restaurant, a brook and a large waterfall. *Richmond Hill* is just minutes away from the Biltmore House, downtown Asheville and the Blue Ridge Parkway. **Seasonal:** No **Reservations:** 50% deposit with a 72-hour cancellation policy **Brochure:** Yes **Permitted:** Children, drinking, smoking outdoors **Conference:** Handsome conference facilities (3000 sq ft) for executive retreats, seminars, banquets, weddings and receptions. Gabrielle's offers gourmet dining on the premises. Complete A/V facilities **Payment Terms:** Check AE/MC/V [I02HPNC1-11122] **COM** YG **ITC Member:** No

Rates:	Pvt Bath 36	Suites
Single	$ 130-350.00	
Double	$ 130-350.00	

Waverly Inn		Asheville NC
John & Diane Sheiry/Darla Olmstead		**Tel:** 800-537-8195 704-693-9193 **Fax:** 704-692-1010
		Res Times 9am-11pm

Refer to same listing located under Hendersonville, North Carolina for complete description. **Seasonal:** Rates vary **Payment Terms:** Check AE/DISC/MC/V [M10ICNC1-6547] **COM** YG **ITC Member:** No

Rates:	Pvt Bath 14	Suites
Single	$ 80.00	$ 145-185.00
Double	$ 79-139.00	$ 165-195.00

Archers Inn	Beech Mt Parkway 28504	Banner Elk NC
Bill Coleman		**Tel:** 704-898-9004
		Res Times 7am-11pm

Charming country inn just two miles from the best ski areas in NC offering guests spectacular views of surrounding mountains and scenery. Year-round resort activities include white-water rafting, tennis, fishing, golfing, horseback riding and swimming and exciting shopping nearby at quaint country shops. Full breakfast included. **Seasonal:** Rates vary **Reservations:** Deposit required to hold room,

©*Inn & Travel Memphis, Tennessee*

refunded if cancelled. **Permitted:** Children, limited smoking, limited smoking **Payment Terms:** Check [X11ACNC-4026] **COM** Y **ITC Member:** No

Rates:	**Pvt Bath 14**
Single	$ 50-95.00
Double	$ 50-95.00

Banner Elk Inn B&B	Rt 3 Box 1134 28604	Banner Elk NC
Beverly Lait		**Tel:** 800-547-8438 704-898-6223
		Res Times 24 Hrs

This lovely historic home built in 1912 and recently renovated with a stunning decor is centrally located in the mountain village of Banner Elk, in northwest North Carolina. A perfect location that's just six miles from the Blue Ridge Parkway & Grandfather Mountain, near Valle Crucis, Linville and halfway between the ski slopes of Sugar and Beech Mountain resorts, the ski capital of the South! This charming Inn is filled with antiques collected from around the world, tapestries and art works creating a personable and cozy atmosphere of old world European charm with modern amenities and Southern hospitality. Four pretty guest bedrooms are furnished with antiques, friendly fabrics and wallcoverings - two with private baths and two guest rooms share baths. The great room is a perfect spot for relaxing and enjoying the stone fireplace while socializing with your charming hostess and other guests, enjoying cable TV or reading a book available from the library. A small shop of fine quality handmade sweaters is within the Inn. A full breakfast of homemade breads, fresh fruit, a variety of specialty dishes is included with your room rate. There are several fine restaurants nearby. Local events include the Scottish Highland Games (July), golfing, craft fairs, Wooly Worm Festival (October), white-water rafting, hiking, antiquing and great winter skiing. **Seasonal:** No **Reservations:** One night's deposit to hold res, 7 day cancel notice for refund. 10% discount for one week stays, *check preferred **Brochure:** Yes **Permitted:** Limited drinking **Conference:** Yes for groups 8-10 persons **Languages:** Spanish & German **Payment Terms:** Check* MC/V [R04DPNC-12286] **COM** U **ITC Member:** No

Rates:	**Pvt Bath 2**	**Shared Bath 2**
Single	$ 60.00	$ 55.00
Double	$ 65-85.00	$ 55-75.00

Old Mill Inn	US Hwy 64 & 74 28710	Bat Cave NC
Walt Davis		**Tel:** 704-625-4256

Listen to the stream bubbling past this 1920's style chalet on the banks of Rocky Broad River while cooling-off your toes in the water. Pure country and pure relaxation. Continental breakfast included. River swimming allowed. **Seasonal:** 4/1-12/15 **Brochure:** Yes **Permitted:** Children, smoking, drinking, and limited pets **Payment Terms:** Check MC/V [X11ACNC-4028] **COM** Y **ITC Member:** No

Rates:	**Pvt Bath 5**	**Shared Bath 2**
Single	$ 45.00	$ 45.00
Double		

Cedars Inn	305 Front St 28516	Beaufort NC
Hugh Gray		**Tel:** 800-732-7036 919-728-7036

Located on the Outer Banks, this charming colonial seaport town boasts over 120 homes built in the 1700 and 1800's. The Cedars Inn, built in 1768 and 1851 was the home of William Borden, a shipwright and ancestor of the Borden milk company family. Beaufort is home to the North Carolina Maritime Museum, the Beaufort Restoration grounds and close by, Old Fort Macon and the North Carolina Aquarium. The *Cedars* is well known for it's hospitality, excellent accommodations and superb breakfasts. Rooms and suites range from $75 to $135.00 per night, in season. All accommodations boast private baths, complimentary sherry and sweets. **Discounts:** AARP and AAA. **Airport:** New Bern-45 min **Packages:** Midweek Vacation (Sun-Thur) **Seasonal:** No **Reservations:** Full deposit in advance. **Brochure:** Yes **Permitted:** Limited children, drinking, limited smoking, no pets **Conference:** Conference groups limited to twelve at the Inn but can accommodate up

North Carolina *National Edition*

to 100 in Beaufort **Payment Terms:** Check MC/V [R10EPNC-4034] **COM** Y **ITC Member:** No

Rates: **Pvt Bath 11**
Single $ 70-150.00
Double $ 70-150.00

B&B Over Yonder 433 N Fork Rd 28711 Black Mountain NC
Wilhelmena Headley **Tel:** 704-669-6762

Peaceful serenity is the theme in this 1920 American Craftsman mountain home of native stone and dutch siding and large windows everywhere. Secluded on eighteen acres of privacy, guests enjoy the spectacular views of the Black Mountain Range, craggy gardens filled with wildflowers, splendid outdoor breakfasts in warm weather and a gazebo with its own spring for relaxing with a good novel. Inside, this mountain home is handsomely furnished with English antiques, new beds, junk shop wonders and family antiques and heirlooms. The bedrooms have Laura Ashley fabrics or English lace, bright polished floors and large windows to bring in the wildflowers and informal rock gardens surrounding the home. The large living room has a big fireplace, plenty of books and great "sink-in" chairs. Guests will enjoy the fresh flowers and the touches added by your hostess who looks forward to sharing her homeplace with each guest and who is a retired RN and grandmother of eleven. Nearby are plenty of walking and hiking trails, white water rafting, swimming, tennis and golf course just a quarter-mile away. Asheville's Biltmore house is just 13 miles away. A full breakfast is included with fresh fruit (in season), juices, fresh baked bread, meat, egg casserole or waffles, pancakes and fresh mountain trout (mountain brown) upon request. **Airport:** Asheville-20 miles **Discounts:** $5 per night after 3rd night **Seasonal:** No **Reservations:** One night's deposit prior to arrival, 14 day cancel policy for refund. Arrival 4-6pm, notify if earlier or later. **Brochure:** Yes **Permitted:** Drinking, limited children, limited smoking **Payment Terms:** Check [Z04FPNC-6593] **COM** Y **ITC Member:** No

Rates: **Pvt Bath 5**
Single $ 40-55.00
Double $ 45-60.00

Engel House 303 Montreat Rd 28711 Black Mountain NC
Cheryl & Fred Engel **Tel:** 704-669-5960

Large Edwardian inn with wrap-around porch complete with antique furnishings and reproductions, ceiling fans, and comfortable rooms for relaxing. Local sights include Biltmore Estate, spectacular mountain ranges for hiking and trail walking, plenty of antique shops and fine restaurants. Continental breakfast includes freshly ground coffee, homemade breads, and sticky buns. **Seasonal:** No **Brochure:** Yes **Permitted:** Children 12-up, smoking, drinking **Payment Terms:** Check [X11A-CNC-4040] **COM** Y **ITC Member:** No

Rates: **Pvt Bath 12**   **Shared Bath 4**
Single $ 45.00 $ 40.00
Double $ 50.00 $ 48.00

Lions Dene PO Box 1327 28607 Boone NC
 Tel: 704-963-5785

Cozily secluded on a mountain ridge with spectacular views of Grandfather Mountain and Beech Mountain, guests can relax in this informal inn while enjoying the Great Outdoors year-round. Five miles from downtown Boone, this Lodge has three decks for perfect viewing with spacious and private guest rooms on two levels with a "Great Room" for everyone to relax by a fire and watch TV or socialize. Families with children are welcomed with babysitting available by local college students. Year-round activities include skiing, Tweetsie Railroad, Mystery Hill Museum are only minutes away. A full breakfast is included with light suppers available for an additional charge. **Seasonal:** No **Reservations:** One night's deposit at res time. **Brochure:** Yes **Permitted:** Children, smoking, drinking **Conference:** Great mountain retreat for business or social meetings for 15-20 persons. **Payment Terms:** Check MC/V [X06BCNC-8413] **COM** Y **ITC Member:** No

Rates: **Pvt Bath 5**
Single $ 65.00
Double $ 70.00

Inn Brevard	410 E Main St 28712	Brevard NC
Bertrand & Eileen Bourget		Tel: 704-884-2105
		Res Times 8am-10pm

National Register of Historic Places includes this turn-of-the-century Inn filled with nostalgia including original brass hardware, carved fireplaces, antique furnishings, and history. Full breakfast of country eggs and meats. Close to Pisgah National Forest and Blue Ridge Pkwy. **Seasonal:** Rates vary **Brochure:** Yes **Permitted:** Limited children, smoking, and drinking. **Conference:** Yes, groups to 125 persons with dinner and lunch by reservation. **Payment Terms:** Check [X11ACNC-4047] **COM** Y **ITC Member:** No

Rates: **Pvt Bath 12**   **Shared Bath 2**
Single $ 44-52.00 $ 44-52.00
Double $ 56-60.00 $ 56-60.00

Red House Inn	412 W Probart St 28712	Brevard NC
Mary Ong		Tel: 704-884-9349

The *Red House* on Probart Street was built in 1851 to be a trading post long before Brevard or Transylvania County were established. As the area developed, the Red House changed from the trading post to the railroad station, as trains came to Brevard; then transformed into the county's first court house, Brevard's first post office, a private school (the predecessor to Brevard College) and following years of neglect and attempts to destroy it during the Civil War - it has been lovingly transformed into a charming Bed & Breakfast. Each room has been decorated with a distinctive flavor of it's own and furnished with turn-of-the-century period antiques. Guests can choose from single or double bedrooms, one with a separate sitting room and private or shared bath. Convenient to many area sites of interest, it is within walking distance of downtown shops and restaurants. Nearby are numerous shopping outlets, the Blue Ridge Parkway, Asheville's Biltmore House, Flat Rock's Carl Sandburg Home, Pisgah National Forest and Brevard's one hundred-twenty waterfalls. Evening offers the famous Flat Rock Playhouse and the wonderful music of Brevard's very own nationally acclaimed Music Center. A full complimentary breakfast is served guests each morning. Come by and join us for a relaxing visit on our porch in the clear, clean air of our lovely mountains. **Discounts:** Extended stays - 7th night free **Airport:** Asheville-25 mi **Seasonal:** No **Reservations:** One night's deposit, 7 day cancel policy for full refund **Brochure:** Yes **Permitted:** Limited children, drinking **Payment Terms:** MC/V [R11EPNC-4048] **COM** Y **ITC Member:** No

Rates: **Pvt Bath 3**   **Shared Bath 4**
Single $ 55.00 $ 43.00
Double $ 65.00 $ 49.00

Estes Mountain Retreat	Rt 1 Box 1316A 28714	Burnsville NC
Bruce & Maryallen Estes		Tel: 704-682-7264
		Res Times 24 Hrs

Estes Mountain Retreat is a modern log home resting on the side of a mountain just west of Burnsville, North Carolina. Guests are surrounded by lush green trees and an infinite variety of wildflowers which bloom from April 'til October. In good weather, we eat breakfast on the front porch where we view the mountains and watch the gold finches and humming birds at the feeders. WE are in a fifty mile radius of Mt Mitchell, the highest peak east of the Mississippi, Asheville's Biltmore Estate, Carl Sandburg's home in East Flat Rock, Linville Falls, Grandfather Mountain, Chimney Rock and Asheville's Folk Art Center. Burnsville itself boasts two summer theaters and we're within twenty-five miles of the Southern Appalachian Repertory Theater in Mars Hill. Burnsville is also the location of the largest craft fair in Western North Carolina which is held annually during the first weekend in August. My husband has built a romantic trail in our woods where one can commune with nature and feel at peace with the world. The more intrepid guests can take the old logging trail to the top of the property where one can find mountain laurel, flame azaleas and wild blueberries in late spring or early summer. A full complimentary breakfast is included. Come, relax on our mountain! **Discounts:** Seniors, weekly stays **Airport:** Asheville-37 mi **Reservations:** One night's deposit **Brochure:** Yes **Permitted:** Children, 3+, limited drinking, smoking outdoors only **Languages:** Some Spanish, French **Payment Terms:** Check MC/V [R07GPNC-17042] **COM** U **ITC Member:** No

Rates:	Pvt Bath 1	Shared Bath 1
Single	$ 50.00	$ 45.00
Double	$ 60.00	$ 55.00

Fearrington House Country Inn
Richard M Delany

Chapel Hill NC
Tel: 919-542-2121 Fax: 919-542-2121
Res Times 24 Hrs

Refer to the same listing name under Pittsboro, North Carolina for a complete description. **Seasonal:** No **Payment Terms:** Check MC/V [M01D-PNC-9377] **COM** Y **ITC Member:** No

Rates:	Pvt Bath 14
Single	$ 125-295.00
Double	$ 125-295.00

Hampton Manor
3327 Carmel Rd 28211
Charlotte NC
Tel: 704-542-6299

Surround yourself with this luxurious accommodation while in Charlotte and the amenities that include fine antique furnishings, king size beds, hot tub, swimming pool, piano, and Rolls Royce limo service from the airport. Full breakfast included. **Seasonal:** No **Brochure:** Yes **Permitted:** Children, smoking, pets, drinking **Payment Terms:** Check AE/MC/V [X11ACNC-4063] **COM** Y **ITC Member:** No

Rates:	Pvt Bath 4
Single	
Double	$ 150-300.00

Homeplace
Frank & Peggy Dearien
5901 Sardis Rd 28270
Charlotte NC
Tel: 704-365-1936

The moment you drive up to this Country Victorian bed and breakfast, leave your cares behind and prepare to experience the warm friendly atmosphere of The Homeplace. Situated on two and one-half wooded acres in southeast Charlotte, this peaceful setting is an oasis on one of the South's fastest growing cities. Built in 1902 by RG Miller, a Presbyterian minister, this completely restored home includes a beautiful wrap-around porch and tin roof - awaiting an evening's downpour to lull you to sleep. Guests sleep in spacious bedrooms with ten foot ceilings, heart-of-pine floors and delightful blends of Country/Victorian decor. Special touches such as quilts, fine linens, handmade accessories, family antiques and original primitive paints by Peggy's father, John Gentry (1898-1989), evoke simpler times. Hot or cold refreshments greet guests upon arrival and into the evening and each day begin with a scrumptious gourmet breakfast. The *Homeplace* seems a world unto its own - while still being convenient to restaurants, shopping areas and fifteen minutes from uptown. Relaxation is assured with porch rockers, a secluded "cottage-style" garden with gazebo, brick walkways, a 1930's log barn and secluded gardens on the property. Whether you are a traveler, business executive or connoisseur of finer older homes, The Homeplace will make your stay in Charlotte a relaxing and unique experience you won't soon forget. **Airport:** Douglas-15 mi **Discounts:** 10% travel agents **Packages:** Honeymoon Special **Seasonal:** No **Reservations:** One night's deposit, 48 hr cancel policy for refund, holidays and special events require 2 night min stay and 7 day cancel notice **Brochure:** Yes **Permitted:** Limited children *Two bedroom unit, one bath **Conference:** Yes, small groups **Payment Terms:** Check AE/MC/V [R05-GPNC-4064] **COM** Y **ITC Member:** No

Rates: Pvt Bath 2
Single $ 78-88.00
Double $ 78-88.00

Inn On Providence — 6700 Providence Rd 28226 — Charlotte NC
Dan & Darlene McNeil
Tel: 704-366-6700

Beautiful three-story colonial nestled in a perfect Southern Exposure setting including verandas and an inground pool which serves as the backdrop for crisp early morning coffee and full breakfast. Guest rooms are furnished with antiques and family treasures these lovely hosts enjoy showing guests. **Seasonal:** No **Reservations:** Deposit at res time, refund if cancelled. **Brochure:** Yes **Permitted:** Limited children, limited smoking **Payment Terms:** Check MC/V [X11ACNC-4065] **COM** Y **ITC Member:** No

Rates:	**Pvt Bath** 2	**Shared Bath** 2
Single	$ 65.00	$ 50.00
Double	$ 75.00	$ 60.00

McElhinney House — 10533 Fairway Ridge Rd 28277 — Charlotte NC
Mary & Jim McElhinney
Tel: 704-846-0783
Res Times 7am-9pm

McElhinney House, located in convenient, southeast Charlotte, welcomes American and international guests, business travelers and families. Your hosts speak German, French and Italian. A spacious lounge area containing books, travel brochures and cable TV is available to our guests. A gas barbeque and laundry facilities are included at no cost. A delicious continental breakfast is served in the lounge or on our deck. We are located minutes from Piper Glen and Rain Tree golf courses and Providence Country Club. Close to the fine restaurants, museums, cultural and sports facilities of Charlotte. Just 25 minutes from Charlotte Douglas International Airport. Near I-77 and the Billy Graham Parkway. Personal checks and most major credit cards are accepted. A warm welcome and thoughtful attention await you at modest rates. **Airport:** Charlotte Douglas Intl-25 mins **Seasonal:** No **Reservations:** 25% deposit **Brochure:** Yes **Permitted:** Children, alcohol, limited smoking **Languages:** Host is fluent in Italian, German, French **Payment Terms:** Check MC/V [Z04F-PNC-15506] **COM** U **ITC Member:** No

Rates: Pvt Bath 2
Single $ 55.00
Double $ 65.00

Shield House — 216 Sampson St 28328 — Clinton NC
Anita Green/Juanita McLamb
Tel: 800-462-9817 910-592-2634
Res Times 24 Hrs

The Shield House is reminiscent of "Gone With The Wind" and is listed in the *National Register of Historic Places*. This spectacular classic revival home has many dramatic features, including: four dominating Corinthian fluted columns surrounding the entrance, twelve ionic columns wrapped around the corner porches - lined with rockers; an entrance highlighted with leaded glass; a large foyer with enclosed columns outlining a grand central flight staircase - whose red carpeted stairs twist up to a landing and then back to the front of the house. A guest lounge at the top of the stairs is naturally lighted through glass doors which open onto a balcony. Guests can relax and enjoy the evening sunset reflecting from the courthouse clock tower or the beautiful skyline view of the town. A full breakfast is served in a 22 foot dining room which includes a gorgeous crystal chandelier suspended from a coffer ceiling with sunlight sparkling through a beveled lead glass window. Six spacious guest rooms offer cable TV, phones and a comfortable seating area. An upstairs lounge and large parlor on the first floor are available for use by guests. There are many flowering shrubs and trees on the 1-1/2 acres surrounding this gracious Southern home - offering the elegance of bygone days. Downtown Clinton exudes down-home Southern hospitality with its quaint courthouse square and friendly people. Nearby are the towns of Raleigh, Wilmington, Fayetteville and Ft Bragg. Tennis

North Carolina *National Edition*

courts and golf privileges are available to guests. **Seasonal:** No **Reservations:** Two night's deposit (first & last night), 14 day cancel notice for refund. *Corporate discounts during the week. **Brochure:** Yes **Permitted:** Drinking, limited children, limited smoking **Conference:** The perfect setting for an unforgettable party, reception or business meeting. **Payment Terms:** Check DC/MC/V [R11CPNC-6385] **COM** Y **ITC Member:** No

Rates:	Pvt Bath 6
Single	$ 45-60.00
Double	$ 45-60.00

Windsong A Mountain Inn 120 Ferguson Ridge 28721 Clyde NC
Donna & Gale Livengood Tel: 704-627-6111 Fax: 704-627-8080
Res Times 8am-8pm

Windsong, our contemporary rustic log Inn (completed in 1989) at 3,000 foot on a rural mountainside near Maggie Valley NC overlooks miles of spectacular Smokey Mountain views. We are small and intimate but our rooms are large, bright and airy, with high beamed-ceilings and floors of Mexican tile. Each room has a unique accent in decor (Santa Fe, Alaska, Country and Safari) and each has a private deck or patio, VCR, fireplace, an oversize soaking tub and a separate shower. There is a Guest Lounge with wet bar and small refrigerator, a billiard table, books, games and a large VCR cassette library. Our full breakfast includes a hot entree with home baked croissants, hot breads and muffins, juices, fruits and fresh coffee. We have a wonderful quiet serenity, although our swimming pool, edged with huge boulders, the tennis court and the hiking trails offer activity for those who want it. Also available is a new deluxe two bedroom guest house. Nearby for our guest's enjoyment are the Great Smokey Mountain National Park, Blue Ridge Parkway, Biltmore House, Cherokee Indian Reservation, Maggie Valley and Gatlinburg, whitewater rafting and horseback riding on mountain trails. You'll love our llamas. **Discounts:** 10% for singles and six or more day stay **Airport:** Asheville NC-25 mi **Packages:** Llama Trekking Adventures **Seasonal:** No **Reservations:** Credit card or advanced deposit to hold room; 72 hr cancel policy for refund. *Guest House available **Brochure:** Yes **Permitted:** Children 8-up, social drinking, smoking only outside **Conference:** Yes, perfect secluded setting for small groups **Payment Terms:** Check DC/MC/V [Z10G-PNC-9990] **COM** Y **ITC Member:** No

Rates:	Pvt Bath 4	Suites
Single	$ 103.00	
Double	$ 115.00	$140-160.00

Jarrett House PO Box 219 28725 Dillsboro NC
Jim & Jean Hartbarger Tel: 800-972-5623 704-586-0265

Complete lodge famous for accommodations and dining since 1884 offers Great Southern dining, beautiful grounds, and plenty of rocking chairs on the wraparound porch for relaxing. Lunch and dinner are available. **Seasonal:** Easter-10/31 **Brochure:** Yes **Permitted:** Children 12-up **Payment Terms:** Check [X11ACNC-4071] **COM** Y **ITC Member:** No

Rates:	Pvt Bath 18
Single	$ 58.00
Double	$ 68.00

Arrowhead Inn 106 Mason Rd 27712 Durham NC
Jerry, Cathy, Barb Ryan Tel: 800-528-2207 919-477-8430 Fax: 919-477-8430
Res Times 10am-8pm

Set on four acres with 150 year-old magnolias is a c1775 award winning southern colonial featured in articles in *"House & Garden", "Food & Wine", "USA Today"* and recognized by Durham Historical Preservation Society for Adaptive Re-use. The main house of a former 2000 acre plantation - the "Great Path" was at its front door where Catawba and Waxhaw Indians travelled between Virginia and the mountains. Today, guests can choose one of the five guest rooms in the manor house, two in the carriage house or the two-room log cabin. The guest rooms are tastefully furnished and decorated in period interpretations from the Colonial to Victorian period and with modern sparkling baths. A rustic Land Grant Cabin is also available and is a perfect for a honeymoon couple or family. Guests are treated each morning to a full Carolina breakfast of juice, fruit, meat, eggs and plenty of homemade breads and muffins. Nearby sights include Duke Univ, UNC-Chapel Hill, Research Triangle Park, Hillsborough Historic District, Treyburn, North Carolina Museum of Life & Science and Bennett Place (where the generals signed the final surrender of the War Between the States). Complimentary afternoon tea is served and your hosts have a full guidebook of restaurant menus to help plan your evening dining. After dinner, the Keeping Room provides hours of enjoyment with good conversation, TV, videos or jigsaw puzzles. Our eleventh year of innkeeping! **Discounts:** After third night **Airport:** Raleigh-Durham 18 mi **Seasonal:** No **Reservations:** One night's deposit with 48 hr cancel policy for refund, check-in 3pm or by prior arrangement **Brochure:** Yes **Permitted:** Children, drinking, limited smoking **Conference:** Yes, groups of 8-12 persons for small meetings and social events in fireplaced rooms indoor or outdoors on a shaded patio **Languages:** French **Payment Terms:** Check AE/DC/DISC/MC/V [Z05HPNC1-4074] COM YG ITC **Member:** No

Rates: Pvt Bath 8
Single $ 90.00
Double $ 100-170.00

Lords Proprietor's Inn   300 N Broad Street 27932   Edenton NC
Arch & Jane Edwards   Tel: 919-482-3641 Fax: 919-482-2432
     Res Times 8am-8pm

The *Lord's Proprietors' Inn* is acclaimed by many to be the finest accommodations in North Carolina. The Inn offers twenty elegant and spacious guest rooms with private baths in three restored homes on an acre and one-half in the historic district of beautiful Edenton. These lovely homes are tastefully decorated and furnished, including large parlors for gathering for afternoon tea around the fireplace. The dining room is a separate and distinctly lovely building on a large brick patio in the center of the complex. A full breakfast served daily, rates include dinner Tuesday - Saturday (MAP).

Packages: Preservation weekends in December and January **Seasonal:** No **Reservations:** 50% deposit within 5 days, late arrivals will find instruction note. Commissionable except for Federal Holidays *Rates based on MAP **Brochure:** Yes **Permitted:** Children, drinking, limited smoking **Conference:** Yes **Payment Terms:** Check [Z08HPNC1-6090] COM YG ITC **Member:** No

Rates: Pvt Bath 20
Single $ 120-180.00
Double $ 165-215.00

Ellerbe Springs Inn & Restaurant   2537 N US Hwy 220 28338   Ellerbe NC
Neal & Beth Cadieu   Tel: 800-248-6467 910-652-5600 Fax: 910-652-5600
     Res Times 7am-9pm

Longleaf pines, hardwoods and wild flowering dogwoods stand gracefully on fifty rolling acres which surround the turn-of-the-century *Ellerbe Springs Inn and Restaurant*. Victorian style antiques accent the lobby, restaurant and fifteen lovely guest rooms and sparkling private baths. One of the nicest amenities is the large comfortable front porch and the second story side porches. Forget the stress and hustle of the city as you relax in one of our white wicker rocking chairs with your favorite book. Ask your Innkeeper about the annual events, such as Monthly Murder Mystery Weekend, Valentine Day Dinner, Ellerbe Springs Marathon, Santa Claus for the Kids and a New Year's Eve Celebration. Breakfast, lunch and dinner are served daily in the dining room overlooking the lush countryside. The spacious 125 seat dining room serves Southern Specialties such as fried chicken, grilled

North Carolina

salmon patties and infamous chicken and dumplings. A newly renovated Springhouse is perfect for reunions, meetings, parties and dances. Situated in North Carolina's Piedmont, Ellerbe Springs is within an easy drive from Charlotte, Greensboro, Raleigh and Myrtle Beach. A friendly community, Ellerbe is well-known for its antique shops, fresh farm produce and the Rankin Museum of American Heritage. Discover our unique blend of warmth and elegance. Family owned and listed on the *National Register of Historic Places*. Relax and relive the timeless tradition of Ellerbe Springs. **Airport:** Southern Pines Regional-35 mi **Discounts:** 15% corporate **Packages:** Yes, inquire at res time **Seasonal:** No **Reservations:** Credit card or deposit to guarantee, 24 hr cancel policy for refund; suites available **Brochure:** Yes **Permitted:** Children, drinking **Conference:** Yes, perfect place for family reunions, seminars, workshops, weddings, social affairs with dining for groups to 125 persons. **Payment Terms:** Check AE/DISC/MC/V [I05IPNC1-23820] **COM** Y **ITC Member:** No

Rates:	Pvt Bath 15
Single	$ 48-88.00
Double	$ 54-94.00

Woodfield Inn   PO Box 98   28371   **Flat Rock NC**
Wayne & Mary Lou Smith   Tel: 800-533-6016   704-693-6016

Just perfect for relaxing and wonderful dining, winner of Diner's Club of "America Silver Spoon Award." Wonderful nature trails, tennis, golfing, and white water rafting nearby. Continental breakfast included. Other meals available. **Seasonal:** No **Brochure:** Yes **Permitted:** Children, smoking, drinking, pets **Payment Terms:** Check AE/MC/V [X11ACNC-4079] **COM** Y **ITC Member:** No

Rates:	Pvt Bath 10	Shared Bath 8
Single		
Double	$ 75.00	$ 65.00

Franklin Terrace   Hwy 28 N   28734   **Franklin NC**
Ed & Helen Henson   Tel: 800-633-2431   704-524-7907

The *Franklin Terrace*, built as a school in 1887, is listed on the *National Register of Historic Places*. *The Terrace* is a lovely two-story Bed & Breakfast that offers nostalgic charm and comfortable accommodations. It's wide porches and large guest rooms are filled with period antiques reminiscent of another period when Southern Hospitality was at its finest. All guest rooms are furnished in period antiques and include private bath, color TV all and air conditioning. Your mornings begin with a complimentary continental plus breakfast which includes cold cereals, sausage, homemade muffins, sausage biscuits, banana bread, pumpkin bread, cake, croissants, fruit juices, plenty of delicious homemade jams & jellies and your choice of hot beverage. The Terrace offers a casual shopping experience where you can browse through the antiques, crafts and gifts for sale on the main floor of the Inn. Guests are within walking distance of Franklin's famous gem shops, clothing boutiques and fine restaurants. Located just 2-1/2 hrs north of Atlanta, guests can visit Cherokee Indian Reservation, The Smoky Mountain Railroad, Ruby Mines, Highlands Instant Theatre, Unto These Hills, Ghost Town, Bridal Veil Falls, The Tartan Museum or enjoy a short drive to nearby Highlands, Cherokee and Asheville. **Airport:** Atlanta Hartsfield 127 mi, Asheville 72 mi **Seasonal:** Opn 4/1-11/15 **Reservations:** Deposit to guarantee res, 72 Hr cancel policy for refund. Check-in 2pm, check-out 10:30am **Brochure:** Yes **Permitted:** Children, drinking, smoking **Payment Terms:** Check MC/V [Z06FPNC-4081] **COM** Y **ITC Member:** No

Rates:	Pvt Bath 9
Single	$ 52.00
Double	$ 56.00

Greenwood B&B   205 N Park Dr   27401   **Greensboro NC**
Vanda Terrell   Tel: 800-535-9363   910-274-6350   **Fax:** 910-274-9943
    Res Times Mornings

This fully restored home c1905 is located in Greensboro's Fisher Park Historical District and offers guests central location, just three minutes to downtown area and twenty minutes from the airport.

©Inn & Travel Memphis, Tennessee

Completely renovated in 1986, all modern amenities are here along with the host/owner's collection of original art and wood carvings from around the world, creating an elegant setting for guests to relax in during their stay. Common room includes cable TV. Guests have their own kitchen, phones in each room, and central air for summer and a relaxing fireplace for winter. Charming hosts on the premises offer complimentary beverages and cheese upon arrival and maps and touring information for local areas. Continental plus breakfast includes juices, fresh fruit, cereals, homemade waffles or muffins, coffee and tea. During summer periods, you can splash around in the pool too! **Seasonal:** No **Reservations:** One night's deposit or credit card guarantee, 24-hour notice for cancellation, check-in 4-6pm, other times by prior arrangement. **Brochure:** Yes **Permitted:** Limited children, drinking & smoking **Payment Terms:** Check AE/MC/V [A09ACNC-4090] **COM** Y **ITC Member:** No

Rates:	**Pvt Bath 4**	**Shared Bath 1**
Single	$ 50.00	$ 40.00
Double	$ 60-70.00	$ 45.00

Claddagh Inn   755 N Main St 28792   Hendersonville NC
Vickie & Dennis Pacilio   Tel: 800-225-4700 704-697-7778   **Fax:** 704-697-8664
Res Times 24 Hrs

The *Claddagh Inn* is a recently renovated meticulously clean B&B located two blocks from the Main Shopping Center of beautiful downtown Hendersonville. The friendly, home-like atmosphere of the Inn is complimented by a safe and secure feeling guests experience while here. The Claddagh Inn is listed on the *National Register of Historic Places* and is AAA Approved. Each guest room has a private bath, in-room phone, TV, overhead fan, a/c (in season) and a delicious all-you-can-eat full breakfast that awaits guests each morning. Guests can challenge one of the seven conveniently located golf courses, compete on the nearby tennis courts, swim in an olympic-size pool or experience the scenic Blue Ridge Mountains by exploring one of the many nature trails. Such tourist delights as the Biltmore House, Carl Sandburg's home, Chimney Rock, Grandfather Mountain, Blue Ridge Mountains and Parkway and Pisgah National Forests are pleasant day-outings from the Claddagh Inn. For culturally-minded guests, the Flat Rock Playhouse and Brevard Music Center perform June through Sept and the Hendersonville Symphony Orchestra satisfies music lovers year-round. Fax available. **Seasonal:** No **Reservations:** One night's deposit at res time. **Brochure:** Yes **Permitted:** Children, drinking, limited smoking **Conference:** Yes **Payment Terms:** Check AE/DISC/MC/V [Z11D-PNC-4091] **COM** Y **ITC Member:** No

Rates:	**Pvt Bath 14**
Single	$ 53-79.00
Double	$ 59-89.00

Echo Mountain Inn   2849 Laurel Parkway 28739   Hendersonville NC
Frank & Karen Kovacik   **Tel:** 704-693-9626
Res Times 8:30-830

Character and ambiance are the key words describing this 1886 stone and frame Inn on top of Echo Mountain - a full service Country Inn featuring gourmet dining, pool, shuffle board and liquor service. Our guest rooms are furnished with antiques and reproductions, many of which include fireplaces or spectacular mountain views. Family suites are available in a separate building and kitchen suites are available for larger groups or extended stays. Sweetheart Packages featured for those special occasions. Our staff is dedicated to providing personal service in a warm and relaxed environment. All outdoor activities are nearby, featuring golf, snow skiing and excellent whitewater rafting. AAA Approved. **Discounts:** AAA, AARP, Seniors, some travel clubs **Packages:** Sweetheart For Special Occasions, includes gourmet picnic basket, roses, champagne, wine, sparkling juice, fruit basket and special occasion cakes - perfect for anniversaries and honeymoons. **Seasonal:** No **Reservations:** Deposit required to guarantee reservation, cancel policy - 7 days, 14 days for holiday periods and season peaks **Brochure:** Yes **Permitted:** Children, drinking **Conference:** Meeting rooms for groups to one hundred, off-season only **Payment Terms:** Check DC/MC/V [R03GPNC-4092] **COM** Y **ITC Member:** No

Rates:	**Pvt Bath 37**
Single	$ 45-175.00
Double	$ 45-175.00

North Carolina *National Edition*

Ivy Terrace	**Hendersonville NC**
Diane & Herbert McGuire	**Tel:** 800-749-9542 704-749-9542
	Res Times 8am-9pm

Refer to the same listing name under Saulda, North Carolina for a complete description. **Seasonal:** Clo 1/1-3/31 **Payment Terms:** Check MC/V [M05GPNC-19319] **COM YG ITC Member:** No

Rates: Pvt Bath 8
Single $ 85-125.00
Double $ 85-125.00

Waverly Inn	783 N Main St 28792	**Hendersonville NC**
John & Diane Sheiry/Darla Olmstead	**Tel:** 800-537-8195 704-693-9193 **Fax:** 704-692-1010	
		Res Times 9am-9pm

Listed in the *National Register of Historic Places*, this Inn combines Victorian stateliness with the charm of the Colonial Revival period. Open all year, The *Waverly Inn* has something for everyone. Some of our rooms include clawfoot tubs, king and queen four poster canopy beds, turn-of-the-century spindle beds and much more. The front veranda, with its rocking chairs, invites guests to sit and chat. Relax and sample the cheese, nuts and fruit juices during the social hour each evening between 5 and 6 pm. Enjoy John's "all-you-can-eat" breakfast served in the beautifully decorated dining room. Special weekends with special rates include "Murder Mystery", "Wine Lovers" and "Winter Getaway". Charlestonians have come to this area to escape the heat of the South Carolina coast since the 1840's. Travelers still enjoy the cool summer evenings, and romantic winter getaways and everyone loves Darla's daily batch of freshly baked chocolate chip cookies! Folks also come for the North Carolina Apple Festival in September, "Home for the Holidays" in December, Color Season in October and the blooming laurel and wild flowers in April. Hiking, boating, fishing, golf and spectacular mountain scenery are at the top of the list. Convenient to The Biltmore Estate. Carl Sandburg's Home, Blue Ridge Parkway, Flat Rock Playhouse and plenty of antique shops and stores in town and over forty restaurants in the area some within walking distance. **Airport:** Asheville-8 mi; Greenville SC-45 mi **Packages:** Wine Lovers Weekend, Mystery Adventure Weekend, Winter Getaway **Seasonal:** Rates vary **Reservations:** Credit card guarantee or check prior to arrival with refund if cancelled 48 hrs prior to res date, email: waverlyinn@aol.com **Brochure:** Yes **Permitted:** Children, drinking, limited smoking **Payment Terms:** Check AE/DISC/MC/V [K10IP-NC1-4096] **COM YG ITC Member:** No **Quality Assurance:** Requested

Rates: Pvt Bath 14
Single $ 80.00 $ 145-185.00
Double $ 79-139.00 $ 165-195.00

Colonial Pines Inn	Hickory St At 4-1/2 28741	**Highlands NC**
Chris & Donna Alley		**Tel:** 704-526-2060

Country charm in this beautiful colonial with white columns stretching the length of an oversized veranda and set on two acres of lawns and plantings. Antique furnishings and spectacular views make your visit a pleasant experience. Full breakfast included. Compli-mentary pm coffee or tea. **Seasonal:** No **Brochure:** Yes **Permitted:** Limited children, smoking. **Payment Terms:** Check MC/V [X11-ACNC-4099] **COM Y ITC Member:** No

Rates: Pvt Bath 7
Single $ 68.00-up
Double $ 75-80.00

3-74   ©*Inn & Travel Memphis, Tennessee*

Ye Olde Stone House B&B	Rt 2 Box 7 28741	Highlands NC
Jim & Rene Ramsdell		Tel: 704-526-5911
		Res Times 8am-10pm

Ye Olde Stone House is situated at 4100 ft elevation in the mountains of western North Carolina. In the area, there are twenty seven waterfalls and the 250 million year old Whiteside Mountains. Located one mile from the center of town, guests are treated to a quiet, country-like atmosphere - perfect for enjoying the natural beauty of the Highlands The guest rooms are attractively decorated with bright and cheerful colors and include private baths. A cozy, glass-enclosed gazebo, porch and deck offer lots of comfortable chairs and rockers to enjoy the country air. Valley View Chalet, on the same grounds, is a three-story A-frame with two bedrooms (a king size and a loft for children), complete with all the country sounds of a nearby creek, frogs, crickets - to lull you to sleep. Within a day's drive (round-trip) are the towns of Asheville, Cherokee and the Great Smoky Mountains National Park. Convenient to town, guests will find the Nature Center, Highlands Playhouse, library, tennis courts, auction gallery and quaint shops offering antiques and mountain crafts - plus outstanding restaurants. Amenities include: TV, gas barbecue, croquet and horseshoes, adjacent fishing lake (per pound charge) and heart-warming fires to chose the chills on cool mountain evenings. A full country breakfast is included for guests in the main house only. **Discounts:** Yes, off-season, inquire at res time **Airport:** Asheville-60 mi; Atlanta-120 mi *Separate chalet rates **Seasonal:** No **Reservations:** One night's deposit to guarantee, 48 hour cancel policy for refund, 2 & 3 night minimum weekends and holidays **Brochure:** Yes **Permitted:** Children 11-up, drinking, smoking outdoors **Conference:** Special occasions, weddings, reunions **Payment Terms:** Check MC/V [R03G-PNC-17076] **COM U ITC Member:** No

Rates:	Pvt Bath 4	Shared Bath 2
Single	$ 65.00	$ 95.00
Double	$ 65-85.00	$ 95.00

Hillsborough House Inn	209 E Tryon St 27278	Hillsborough NC
Katherine Webb	Tel: 800-616-1660 919-644-1600	Fax: 919-644-1600
		Res Times 9am-6pm

A sweeping 80 foot wrap-around front porch greets guests to a completely renovated historic Inn, dating from the late 1700's. Its balanced expansion over the years and the beautiful columned porch is reminiscent of a late 19th century Italianate villa style architecture. Your hostess/artist/designer/decorator collected ideas, matcrials and furnishings from family homes to create an eclectic setting for family and guests alike. Today, skylights, original art works of the innkeeper and others, paper-maiche, heavy bevelled glass transoms from Mr Webbs' grandparents home in Raleigh, four-poster queen-size beds and dozens of yards of fabric create individual styles in each room. Each of the five guest rooms is named for a historical family member. The Miss Eliza's room or Joe's room offers a private porch overlooking the pool and summer kitchen, while Kate's room has its own private entrance. Elizabeth's room, done in crisp blue and white, features large old-glass double windows with a beautiful view of the surrounding woods. Annies room has a hand-painted bath floor and a pond just outside. All guest rooms include sitting areas, ceiling fans, original art, either queen or king beds, private bath and a/c. Guests feel at home whether reading a good book in front of the fireplace, watching a film, preparing a snack or gathering with other guests and friends in the library or den. This seven acre setting offers swimming and walking among the woods and gardens. A sumptuous continental plus breakfast is served each morning in the dining room, where Katherine decorated the walls with hand-painted murals. **Airport:** Raleigh-Durham 30 min **Seasonal:** Clo Xmas **Reservations:** MC or Visa card number for deposit to guarantee room, 7 day cancel policy *Suites available **Brochure:** Yes **Permitted:** Children 12-up, drinking, smoking outside only. Boarding nearby for pets.

North Carolina *National Edition*

Conference: Yes for groups to 12 persons. **Payment Terms:** Check MC/V [I05HPNC1-14452] **COM** YG **ITC Member:** No

Rates:	Pvt Bath 5	Shared Bath 1
Single	$ 95-105.00	$ 150.00
Double	$ 95-105.00	

Cherokee Inn   500 N Virginia Dare   27948   **Kill Devil Hills NC**
Kaye & Bob Combs   **Tel:** 800-554-2764 919-441-6127 **Fax:** 919-441-1072
Res Times 9am-10pm

Enjoy this charming large beach house just 600 ft from the ocean and surrounded by beaches, sand and public access beaches everywhere on this resort strip on a barrier island! The interior is furnished with soft cypress, a/c, complimentary bikes available, CATV and all six guest rooms, comfortably furnished with ceiling fans, occupy the second floor. Just the spot for a quiet, relaxing holiday. There's a great wrap-around porch and a sitting room for relaxing with a good book or friendly conversation with the other guests. Close-by you'll find the Wright Bros Memorial within easy walking distance, Jockey Ridge Sand Dunes, Cape Hatteras National Seashore, Roanoke Island and Lost Colony, Oregon Inlet fishing area for deep sea fishing charters, shipwrecks and bird watching and Ocracoke Island. All sporting activities are available: golf, tennis, fishing, diving, hang gliding and all water sports! Continental breakfast is included. **Seasonal:** Yes **Reservations:** Two night min (July, Aug) Three night min holidays; one night non-refundable deposit; senior $5 discount, except holidays **Brochure:** Yes **Permitted:** Limited children, drinking **Payment Terms:** Check AE/MC/V [Z02H-PNC1-4104] **COM** YG **ITC Member:** No

Rates:	Pvt Bath 6
Single	$ 60-90.00
Double	$ 65-95.00

Tranquil House Inn   Queen Elizabeth St   27954   **Manteo NC**
Don & Lauri Just   **Tel:** 800-458-7069 919-473-1404 **Fax:** 919-473-1526
Res Times 24 Hrs

Welcome to Breezy Porches, Southern Friendliness and Chantilly Comforts. Located right on the waterfront in downtown Manteo, you're surrounded by beautiful boardwalks, sailboats and the music of Shallowbag Bay lapping the shore. You're welcomed by innkeepers have been expecting you, and pampered by a staff whose very friendliness says plainly that you're a valued guest. Rooms are as individual as you .... where you can choose from rooms with canopies, four-poster beds, queens, kings and our suites with cozy sitting areas and sleep sofas and all are beautifully decorated with designer wallpapers, Oriental or Berber carpets and hand-tiled baths. Your mornings get off to a good start with a complimentary continental breakfast served in ensuite, on the porch or the Library. You are within walking distance of historic sites, great restaurants and some of the best shopping spots in the area. Most of our guests comment about the quiet - a tangible, wonderful part of what the *Tranquil House* is all about. Close enough to the excitement and activity of the beaches, yet you have a haven to return to where you can rejuvenate and relax without the hubbub and snuggle-up with a great novel. Selected as one of the *"Top Ten Inns In The USA"* by *Innsider* Publication. An evening wine and cheese reception and complimentary bikes for guest's use are provided. **Discounts:** Corporate, tours, groups **Airport:** Norfolk-1-1/2 hr **Packages:** Yes, groups and tours **Seasonal:** No **Reservations:** One night's deposit to hold reservation, 14 day cancel policy for refund **Brochure:** Yes **Permitted:** Children, drinking, limited smoking **Conference:** Yes, groups to twenty five **Payment Terms:** Check* AE/DC/MC/V [I08GPNC-6531] **COM** Y **ITC Member:** No

Rates:	Pvt Bath 28
Single	$ 69-149.00
Double	$ 69-149.00

North Carolina

Boxwood Lodge	132 Becktown Rd 27028	Mocksville NC
Martha Hofffner		Tel: 704-284-2031

Boxwood Lodge, a colonial revival twenty-five room Country Mansion by Delano, is situated on fifty-one acres of beautifully wooded land at the corners of Highway 601 and 132 Bucktown Road. The Lodge is convenient to I-85 or I-40 where travelers can relax and enjoy a nearby game of golf, leisure walks, fishing, a game of pool, afternoon tea, reading by the fireside in the library or just browsing, enjoying Edmund Osthaus original paintings. Fine location for special and memorable occasions such as weddings and receptions. **Airport:** Charlotte, Greensboro High Point **Packages:** Three Night Stays, inquire at res time **Seasonal:** No **Reservations:** Deposit to guarantee reservation, 24 hr cancel policy for refund, except during Market **Permitted:** Limited drinking, limited smoking **Payment Terms:** Check MC/V [I01HPNC1-21451] **COM** U **ITC Member:** No

Rates:	Pvt Bath 5	Shared Bath 3
Single	$ 75.00	
Double	$ 75-95.00	$ 65.00

Huntington Hall B&B	500 Valley River Ave 28906	Murphy NC
Bob & Kate DeLong		Tel: 800-824-6189 704-837-9567 **Fax:** 704-837-2527
		Res Times 24 Hrs

A great location near the Great Smoky Mountains, Murphy NC is a picture-postcard small town setting where travelers will find the understated elegance of Huntington Hall. Bob and Kate, your hosts, have looked after every detail and enjoy making every guest feel at home and at ease. Their five guest rooms have been individually decorated to suit the feeling of the room and are named after homes of the English countryside. Each spacious guest room offers a private bath, individual heating and a/c, cable TV. Some have tall windows and the original hardwood floors - all offer the individual charm of comfortable and inviting furnishings! Guests are invited to join their hosts and other guests in the living room each evening for complimentary beverages, relaxed conversation, and/or TV viewing. A wonderful breakfast is served in the dining room or on the sun porch daily. A short walk brings guests to the town shopping area, Cherokee Museum, business offices, and tennis courts. The Great Smoky Mountain Railway offers excursions which include Murphy. Outdoor activities abound with rafting, canoeing, fishing, golfing at Cherokee Hills Golf Course, the Joyce Kilmer Wilderness, Great Smoky Mountain National Park and plenty of spectacular mountain scenery year-round. **Packages:** Murder Mystery Weekends, Whitewater rafting, Theatre & Holidays **Discounts:** AAA, Senior, Corporate **Airport:** 120 mi to Atlanta's Hartsfield Intl **Seasonal:** No **Reservations:** One night's deposit required with 48 hr cancel policy for refund, full payment required upon arrival, check-in 3 pm, check-out 10:30am, *Diners Card accepted **Brochure:** Yes **Permitted:** Children, drinking, limited smoking on porch outdoors, pet boarding at local vet can be arranged **Conference:** Private glassed-in porch available for groups 10-15 after 10am **Payment Terms:** Check AE/DC/DISC/MC/V [Z03HPNC1-12536] **COM** YG **ITC Member:** No

Rates:	Pvt Bath 5
Single	$ 49-65.00
Double	$ 65-85.00

First Colony Inn	6720 S Virginia Dare Trail 27959	Nags Head NC
The Lawrences		Tel: 800-368-9390 919-441-2343 **Fax:** 919-441-9234
		Res Times 9am-10pm

The Outer Banks only historic B&B Inn affords comfortably elegant accommodations at the beach. Each guest room is individually appointed with English antiques and traditional furnishings with king, queen or twin beds, remote-controlled heat pumps, wet bars or kitchenettes, private tiled baths (jacuzzi available in some rooms), with heated towel bars and English toiletries. This handsome Single-style building, listed on the *National Register of Historic Places*, is wrapped by unique continuous double verandas. Begin your day at the *First Colony* with a complimentary extended continental breakfast in the sunny breakfast room, then stroll to the ocean for beachcombing, fishing or swimming. Sightsee or hike the Nag's Head Woods. Wind surf, hangglide, take an aero tour or go on a dolphin watching expedition. Or maybe you'd rather rock on the porch with a good book from our library or laze by the secluded pool. Spend your afternoon at the North Carolina Aquarium or in the Elizabethan Gardens and then return for tea. After dinner enjoy wine and cheese on the veranda while the sun sets over Roanoke Sound. East of US 158 at MP 16, we are near Fort Raleigh ("The Lost Colony"), and the Wright Brothers Memorial. Jockey's Ridge (tallest sand dune on the East Coast), Cape Hatteras National Seashore, wildlife refuges famous as the wintering ground for Canadian waterfowl and home to a varied population of other birds, "Elizabeth II" (a replica 16th Century ship) lighthouses, wild horses and a more are nearby. Honeymoons, weddings and small conference are specialties - we'll take care of all the arrangements while you relax and enjoy the event. Featured in *"Southern Living"*, July 1992; *Carolina Style*, Spring 1994, AAA-4 Diamond **Airport:** Norfolk VA-80 mi; complimentary pick-ups from local Dare County Regional Airport-10 mi and First Flight-9 mi **Discounts:** Stay 4 nights - 5th night free, Sun-Thurs only **Packages:** Honeymoon, Valentine, New Years **Seasonal:** Rates vary **Reservations:** Two night deposit to guarantee, 7 day cancel policy for refund, weekends & holidays require min stay, check-in 3-11pm, later with prior arrangements, check-out 11am *800 number for reservations only **Brochure:** Yes **Permitted:** Children, drinking **Conference:** Groups to twenty-five **Payment Terms:** Check DC/MC/V [I02HPNC1-6737] **COM** YG **ITC Member:** No

Rates:	Pvt Bath 26
Single	$ 75-225.00
Double	$ 75-225.00

Tranquil House Inn — Nags Head NC
Don & Lauri Just — Tel: 800-458-7069 919-473-1404
Res Times 24 Hrs

Refer to the same listing name under Manteo, North Carolina for a complete description. **Seasonal:** No **Payment Terms:** Check AE/DC/MC/V [M08BPNC-9452] **COM** Y **ITC Member:** No

Rates:	Pvt Bath 28
Single	$ 69-149.00
Double	$ 69-149.00

Ye Olde Cherokee Inn — Nags Head NC
Phyllis & Bob Combs — Tel: 919-441-6127

Refer to the same listing name under Kill Devil Hills, North Carolina for a complete description. **Seasonal:** Yes **Payment Terms:** Check MC/V [M11DPNC-6562] **COM** Y **ITC Member:** No

Rates:	Pvt Bath 4	Shared Bath 2
Single	$ 65.00	$ 95.00
Double	$ 65-85.00	$ 95.00

Kings Arms Inn — 212 Pollock St 28560 — New Bern NC
Richard & Patrica Gulley — Tel: 800-872-9306 919-636-4409

In the historic district is this spacious c1850 home offering excellent Southern Dining and hospitality. Some rooms date back to the early 1800's and the tavern is said to have hosted members of the First Continental Congress. Three blocks from Tryon Palace. Continental breakfast included. **Seasonal:** No **Brochure:** Yes **Permitted:** Children, smoking, drinking **Payment Terms:** Check AE/MC/V [X11A-CNC-4124] **COM** Y **ITC Member:** No

Rates: Pvt Bath 8
Single $ 65.00
Double $ 75.00

Tar Heel Inn   205 Chruch St 28571   Oriental NC
Robert Hyde   Tel: 919-249-1078
Res Times 9am-9pm

This quiet fishing village, located on the Pamlico Sound near the outer banks, Kitty Hawk, and Cape Hatteras, is the perfect spot for enjoying the coast and is the sailing capital of North Carolina. This quaint c1899 Inn, restored to capture the feeling of an English-style Country Inn, contains heavy beams and comfortable common rooms with games, books, TV & VCR. There are brick terraces, gardens, lawn games, and even bicycles you can borrow. The guest rooms are furnished in different themes using Laura Ashley prints for wallcoverings and fabrics. There are king or queen-size four poster or canopy beds and private baths with each guest room. There is year-round sailing and cruising, golf, tennis, fishing, and hunting. Warmth and hospitality are assured with your hosts. Dave's background is in engineering and he enjoys canoeing, being a handyman, and an innkeeper. Patti is a former art teacher. She enjoys collecting recipes, walking, and working in some art form. Full breakfast included. **Seasonal:** Rates vary **Reservations:** One day's deposit at res time or 50% of total. Late arrival room guarantee only with fully paid deposit. **Brochure:** Yes **Permitted:** Children 12-up, pets by prior arrangement. Smoking only outdoors. **Payment Terms:** Check [A05-ACNC-4135] **COM** Y **ITC Member:** No

Rates: Pvt Bath 6
Single $ 65.00
Double $ 75.00

Tranquil House Inn   Outer Banks NC
Don & Lauri Just   Tel: 800-458-7069 919-473-1404
Res Times 24 Hrs

Refer to the same listing name under Manteo, North Carolina for a complete description. **Seasonal:** No **Payment Terms:** Check AE/DC/MC/V [M11BPNC-9453] **COM** Y **ITC Member:** No

Rates: Pvt Bath 28
Single $ 69-149.00
Double $ 69-149.00

Pines Country Inn   719 Hart Rd 28768   Pisgah Forest NC
Mary & Tom McEntire   Tel: 704-877-3131
Res Times 10-10pm

A trip thru the woods to grandmother's home!! Family operated Inn surrounded by mountains and overlooking Little River Valley offers guests a main house and four cabins. All with porches, fireplaces, beautiful woods, and plenty of mountains. Close to Blue Ridge Parkway, and Biltmore House. Full breakfast included. **Seasonal:** 5/1-10/31 **Brochure:** Yes **Permitted:** Children, smoking, social drinking **Payment Terms:** Check [X11ACNC-4139] **COM** Y **ITC Member:** No

Rates: Pvt Bath 17
Single $ 68.00
Double

Fearrington House Country Inn   Fearrington Village Center 27312   Pittsboro NC
RB & Jenny Fitch   Tel: 919-542-2121 Fax: 919-542-4202
Res Times 24 Hrs

Nestled in the quiet rolling hills south of Chapel Hill, you can relax in this village setting of renovated buildings c1780's, offering gourmet dining and European Country Inn style accommodations.

North Carolina *National Edition*

The original homeplace offers the finest cuisine, which has been featured in "Gourmet", "House Beautiful", and "Food & Wine" and received excellent reviews by Craig Claibourn in the "New York Times!" Each of the guest rooms are individually designed to capture distinctive moods with a blend of antiques, original art and tasteful appointments to assure your comfort. You'll also find the Market & Cafe country store, a deli and cafe, next to McIntyre's Fine Books and the Pringle Pottery, A Stone's Throw and Dovecote - all for country shopping! This tranquil setting is completed by mature plantings of hollyhocks, and bluebirds and unique Belted Galloway Cows from the Highlands of Scotland (reportedly the oldest breed of beef cattle). A true gourmet European country venture! Continental breakfast included, with all other meals available on premises. **Seasonal:** No **Reservations:** Full deposit within 7 days of booking; 7-day cancellation policy for refund. Kennels nearby for pets. **Brochure:** Yes **Permitted:** Drinking **Conference:** Yes, groups up to 50 person. **Languages:** French, Spanish, German **Payment Terms:** Check MC/V [Z01DPNC-4140] **COM** Y **ITC Member:** No

Rates:	Pvt Bath 14
Single	$ 125-295.00
Double	$ 125-295.00

Acadian House B&B — Raleigh NC
Johanna & Leonard Huber
Tel: 919-975-3967
Res Times 8am-8pm

Refer to the same listing name under Washington, North Carolina for a complete description. **Seasonal:** No **Payment Terms:** Check AE/DISC/MC/V [M04FPNC-16804] **COM** U **ITC Member:** No

Rates:	Pvt Bath 3	Shared Bath 1
Single	$ 45.00	$ 85.00
Double	$ 55.00	

Oakwood Inn 411 N Bloodworth St 27604 Raleigh NC
Terry Jones, Mgr
Tel: 919-832-9712

An 1871 charming Victorian residence on the *National Register of Historic Places* furnished with period antiques that take you back to another era. Located within historic home district with numerous other examples of Victorian period homes. Full breakfast included. **Seasonal:** No **Brochure:** Yes **Permitted:** Children 12-up **Payment Terms:** Check AE/MC/V [X11ACNC-4142] **COM** Y **ITC Member:** No

Rates:	Pvt Bath 6
Single	$ 70-80.00
Double	$ 80-90.00

Old Plough B&B 40 Main St W 27605 Raleigh NC
Marie & Ed Brida
Tel: 919-221-1212
Res Times 8am-5pm

Turn-of-the-century Gothic Revival colonial with huge white columns surrounding the wide veranda leading into fully restored and antique furnished guest quarters including dining at the gourmet restaurant on the premises. Continental breakfast included. **Seasonal:** Rates vary **Brochure:** Yes **Permitted:** Children, pets, limited smoking, limited drinking **Conference:** Yes, business facilities for groups to 12 persons. **Payment Terms:** Check MC/V [G02BFNC-6573] **COM** Y **ITC Member:** No

Rates:	Pvt Bath 2	Shared Bath 3
Single	$ 48.00	$ 39.00
Double	$ 52.00	$ 43.00

The Shield House — Raleigh NC
Anita Green/Juanita McLamb
Tel: 800-462-9817 910-592-2634
Res Times 24 Hrs

©*Inn & Travel Memphis, Tennessee*

Refer to the same listing name under Clinton, North Carolina for a complete description. **Seasonal:** No **Payment Terms:** Check DC/MC/V [M11-CPNC-11929] **COM** Y **ITC Member:** No

Rates: Pvt Bath 6
Single $ 45-60.00
Double $ 45-60.00

Rowan Oak House	208 S Fulton St 28144	Salisbury NC
Bob & Les Coombs		**Tel:** 800-786-0437 704-633-2086
		Res Times 9am-9pm

Experience this magnificently detailed eclectic Queen Anne in a beautiful historic setting that is picture-perfect! It will be love at first sight when you view the columned wrap-around porch with rocking chairs, flowers and ferns: the octagonal cupola high above the trees; granite foundations and steps leading to an exquisitely carved oak door surrounded with stained glass. Each of the three guest rooms is furnished with antiques, historic wall coverings, sitting areas, duvet with down comforters, fresh fruit and flowers. One includes a double jacuzzi. All are a/c, heated and have phone jacks, and TV in the lounge. You'll be treated in the morning to a gourmet continental feast of homemade breads, seasonal fresh fruits, juices and beverages. You may choose to eat on china with silver and crystal, in the grand dining room which is decorated with 1901 wallpaper, and oil portrait of Queen Louise of Prussia, leaded glass windows and wainscotting. Or your hosts will provide coffee, breakfast and the morning paper in bed! **Seasonal:** No **Brochure:** Yes **Payment Terms:** Check MC/V [R01BCNC-6392] **COM** Y **ITC Member:** No

Rates: Pvt Bath 3
Single $ 60-80.00
Double $ 65-75.00

Ivy Terrace	Hwy 176 Main Street 28773	Saluda NC
Diane & Herbert McGuire		**Tel:** 800-749-9542 704-749-9542 **Fax:** 704-749-2017
		Res Times 8am-9pm

Surrounded by stone terraces and hidden under towering cedars, spruces and firs, *Ivy Terrace* is a perfect escape from everyday challenges. Originally constructed in 1890, it has been completely renovated to provide modern conveniences yet its charm has been retained. After settling into your room decorated with comfortable and homey furnishings, plan your evenings' activities over afternoon refreshments, listening to the chirping of robins from our porches or patios. Enjoy a play at Flat Rock Playhouse and a fine dinner close-by. Unwind in front of a crackling fire in our parlor on chilly evenings before retiring. Awake to the aroma of fresh local cider, hazelnut oatmeal pancakes with sauteed apples and fresh link sausage, and coffee brewing. Leisurely enjoy your meal in the spacious dining room or outdoors on stone terraces. Your days' excursions may include sightseeing at Carl Sandburg, Thomas Wolfe or the Biltmore House. Nature lovers can hike Pearsons' Falls or tour the Blue Ridge Parkway. Shop at outlets, antique and craft stores. Walk "Old Timey" Saluda with its turn-of-the-century homes and where the merchants and townspeople will greet you with a friendly word. A full complimentary breakfast is included, other meals available for conferences. **Airport:** Asheville NC-30 mi **Seasonal:** Clo 1/1-3/31 **Reservations:** One night deposit, 24 hour cancel policy **Brochure:** Yes **Permitted:** Children, drinking **Conference:** Full conference facility in separate building for groups of 4-40 **Payment Terms:** Check MC/V [R05GPNC-19247] **COM** Y **ITC Member:** No

Rates: Pvt Bath 8
Single $ 85-125.00
Double $ 85-125.00

B&B At Laurel Ridge	Rt 1 Box 116 27344	Siler City NC
David Simmons/Lisa Reynolds		**Tel:** 800-742-6049 919-742-6049
		Res Times 24 Hrs

Laurel Ridge is a beautiful, serene bed and breakfast centrally located between the Triade area (Greensboro, High Point, Winston-Salem) and the Research Triangle Park (Raleigh, Durham and

Chapel Hill) of North Carolina. Located on a twenty-six acre site that borders the Rocky River with a large and beautiful stand of native Mountain Laurel, hiking trails to the river and an English Country Garden. The post and beam country home features the Rose Suite, a large elegant master suite with a jacuzzi and balcony overlooking the river. Smaller but equally elegant rooms are named the Jewel Room and the Pine Room. *Laurel Ridge* is owned and operated by Lisa Reynolds, a physical therapist and David Simmons, a professional chef with extensive experience in all phases of the culinary arts. In 1993, David was a member of a culinary team that won the Gold & Silver Medals at the International Food Olympics in Frankfurt, Germany. Informal cooking classes are conducted which culminate in a luscious feast that evening. Every effort is made to use the highest quality products that are organic and locally produced, with an abundance of gourmet vegetarian items. Your hosts are dedicated to providing the best atmosphere and food in central North Carolina. The full complimentary breakfast offers fresh squeezed orange juice, specialty roasted coffees, bread baked daily, Laurel Ridge poppyseed pancakes and creative omelettes, quiches and frittata. The Triangle area is home to the Univ of NC at Chapel Hill, Duke Univ and NC State Univ and offers Burlington Outlet stores for great shopping, horseback riding, golf and parks and museums. **Airport:** Greensboro or Raleigh, Durham-1 Hr **Seasonal:** No **Reservations:** One night deposit required, 3 day cancel notice for refund less a $5.00 service fee, less notice, refund only if rebooked **Brochure:** Yes **Permitted:** Children, drinking, limited pets, smoking outdoors only **Conference:** Groups of 6-12 persons **Payment Terms:** Check MC/V [R0GPNC-18854] COM U ITC **Member:** No **Quality Assurance** Requested

Rates:	Pvt Bath 1	Shared Bath 2
Single	$ 85.00	$ 30-45.00
Double	$ 95.00	$ 40-55.00

Richmond Inn   101 Pine Ave 28777   Spruce Pine NC
Bill Ansley/Lenore Boucher   Tel: 704-765-6993

Snuggled in the Blue Mountains are luxurious accommodations in the main lodge and cabins. Spectacular scenery with outdoor activities that include panning for gemstones (garnets and amethysts) in the gemstone capital of the USA. Full breakfast included. **Seasonal:** No **Brochure:** Yes **Permitted:** Children, smoking, drinking **Languages:** German, French **Payment Terms:** Check MC/V [X11ACNC-4155] COM Y ITC **Member:** No

Rates:	Pvt Bath 7
Single	$ 55.00
Double	$ 70.00

Cedar Hill Farm   778 Elmwood Rd 28677   Statesville NC
Brenda & Jim Vernon   Tel: 800-484-8457 704-873-4332
   Res Times 8am-10pm

Welcome to *Cedar Hill Farm*, a quiet country setting close to three interstate highways. You will find a three-story Federal farmhouse, circa 1840, log barn and outbuildings on thirty-two acres of rolling green pasture dotted with our sheep. Your accommodations will be a private cottage with porch or a bedroom in the main house. The cottage is air conditioned, has a private bath and antique furnishings in the sleeping and sitting areas - tucked away under your tin roof - ready for those cozy rainy nights. If you're traveling with children, there's a twin and a trundle bed available as well. If you choose to stay in the farmhouse, your room is the only bedroom on the first floor, giving you added privacy. Amenities include a/c, cable TV, telephone and private bath. We serve a full complimentary breakfast of locally cured ham, sausage, farm-fresh eggs, fruit, potatoes and delicious homemade buttermilk biscuits with homemade preserves. After breakfast, relaxing is in order with the nearby hammock, porch rocker or you can try the pool, badminton, horseshoes or a hike through the woods - while evening serenades include tree frogs, bull frogs and crickets - not to mention daily chime of four resident geese and rooster. **Reservations:** One night's deposit or credit card number*after dialing the 800 number, dial 1254 after the tone **Permitted:** Children, drinking, limited pets, limited smoking **Payment Terms:** Check MC/V [R05FPNC-16844] COM Y ITC **Member:** No

Rates:	Pvt Bath 1	Shared Bath 9
Single	$ 55.00	$ 70.00
Double	$ 55.00	$ 70.00

National Edition   **North Carolina**

Acadian House B&B	129 Van Norden St 27889	**Washington NC**
Johanna & Leonard Huber		**Tel:** 919-975-3967
		Res Times 8am-8pm

Newly renovated, *Acadian House* invites you to enjoy a relaxed pace in this 1902 home furnished with antiques and local crafts. Guests can visit nearby historic sites, the beautiful Pamlico River, one block away and other attractions by walking or using the complimentary bikes - or relax on the porch swing while enjoying the lovely garden. Acadian House is in "Little" Washington's Historic District and is on the Historic Albermarle Tour Route. The comfortable parlor is for guests to enjoy and is the gathering place for complimentary "T Time" daily at 5:30pm. A Victorian staircase leads to the guest rooms and the library where books and games are available. The business traveler will find writing tables and phones readily available with nearby fax and copy machine facilities. Hosts Johanna and Leonard Huber, both transplanted New Orleanians, serve beignets, cafe-au-lait, pan perdu and other southern Louisiana specialties along with traditional breakfast food. *Fourth guest room available as suite for 3-4 persons combined with a private guest room at $85.00. **Airport:** Greenville-20 mi; Raleigh-50 mi **Seasonal:** No **Reservations:** Confirm res with 50% deposit, 48 hr cancel policy; 4pm check-in, 11am check-out, arrangements for early or late arrival. *MC/V accepted only for deposit, cash or check for balance *Suites available **Brochure:** Yes **Permitted:** Children 12-up, social drinking, smoking outdoors only, no pets **Payment Terms:** Check AE/DISC/MC/V [Z04HPNC1-16720] **COM YG ITC Member:** No

Rates:	Pvt Bath 3	Shared Bath 1
Single	$ 45.00	$ 85.00
Double	$ 55.00	

Grandview Lodge	809 Valley View Circle Rd 28786	**Waynesville NC**
Stan & Linda Arnold		**Tel:** 800-255-7826 704-456-5212 **Fax:** 704-456-5212
		Res Times 7am-10pm

Snuggled in the mountains, guests feel like they're visiting Grandma's home at this 100 year-old house offering a quiet, scenic, peaceful and restful setting that's ideal for vacations, reunions, meetings and special occasions. *Grandview Lodge* is set on 2-1/2 acres of rolling land with its own apple orchard, grape arbors and rhubarb patch with access to year-round golfing, tennis, outlet shopping with plenty of rockers and cool mountain breezes to share on the grand front porch. The guest rooms are tastefully decorated and include mahogany poster beds, color TV in each room with choices of rooms on the porch, in the Lodge, and two one-bedroom apartments. Your hostess (graduate home economist and publisher of several cookbooks) promises to please your palate with her favorite recipes while catering to any special dietary need. Guests meet around the dinner table twice a day, with family-style dining that includes locally grown fresh fruits and vegetables, homebaked biscuits, muffins & breads and home-prepared jams, jellies and relishes. Don't miss the whole-grain pancakes for breakfast!! **Airport:** Asheville-40 mi **Packages:** Golf Special (- Waynesville CC and Laurel Ridge CC) **Seasonal:** No **Reservations:** One night's deposit within 5 days (6 days or more $150) 14 day cancel policy for refund less 15% service charge, 10am check-out, 1pm check in, subject to NC & Haywood Cty tax. *Rates based on MAP **Brochure:** Yes **Permitted:** Children, drinking (BYOB), limited smoking **Conference:** Yes with dining available for business & social events, eg: wedding receptions & rehearsals **Languages:** Polish, Russian, German **Payment Terms:** Check [I02HPNC1-4168] **COM YG ITC Member:** No

Rates:	Pvt Bath 11
Single	$ 70-75.00
Double	$ 95-105.00

Swag Country Inn	Rt 2 PO Box 280A 28786	**Waynesville NC**

©*Inn & Travel Memphis, Tennessee*

North Carolina *National Edition*

Deener Mathews

Tel: 704-926-0430 Fax: 704-926-2036
Res Times 8am-10pm

The Swag, named *"Country House Hotel of The Year"* by Andrew Harper in his December, 1993 issue of *"The Hideaway Report,"* is located on top of a 5000 foot private mountain and commands fifty mile views. The Inn is made of hand-hewn logs from original Appalachian structures. From the massive stone fireplace in the living room to the original North Carolina art work, the atmosphere of *The Swag* is a beautiful blend of mountain authenticity and rustic elegance. Our guest rooms and private cabins are all individually decorated with handmade quilts, woven rugs and unique pieces of art - enhancing the home-like environment. Hair dryers, coffee makers and grinders, plush bathrobes and your own refrigerator are all delightfully convenient. Many rooms feature private balconies, woodstoves, fireplaces, jacuzzi tubs and steam showers. Dining is sensational at *The Swag*. Authentic regional cuisine is presented in an imaginative and innovative style. Our room rates include three meals a day for the two of you. Complimentary hors d'oeuvres before dinner are also included. *The Swag* has a private entrance to the 500,000 acre Great Smokey Mountains National Park with trails that will delight everyone. Gentle wilderness trails reveal views and vistas that enchant each guest. Afternoons can be enjoyed on the indoor racquet ball court, paying badminton or croquet, floating on the secluded spring-fed pond or relaxing in a hammock our sauna. Each day presents different opportunities to discover beauty, seclusion and a quieter pace. **Airport:** Asheville-1 hr *__Seasonal:__ Closed 11/1-5/15 **Seasonal:** *See Below **Reservations:** One night deposit, 14 day cancel policy less 15% service fee *Rates based on American Plan **Permitted:** Children limited, drinking (BYOB, no liquor license) **Conference:** Yes for groups to thirty **Payment Terms:** Check MC/V [I03GPNC-4175] **COM** Y **ITC Member:** No

Rates: Pvt Bath 14
Single $ 125.00
Double $ 125.00

Kingsley House Victorian B&B   312 S Third St 28401   Wilmington NC
Jeanne & Elizabeth DiFerdinando

Tel: 800-763-6603 910-763-6603
Res Times 10am-10pm

Discover historic downtown Wilmington at its finest when you visit the *Kingsley House*, a Victorian Italianate Bed and Breakfast. Built in 1837, this home is lovingly tended by innkeepers Jeanne and her mother Elizabeth. Elegant original antique furniture adorn each room. Full gourmet country breakfast is served mornings in the formal dining room accented by fine china and crystal. Complimentary refreshments are served in the afternoon and evening. Relax in the parlor over a game of chess and the puzzle of the day or lounge on one of our many porches with a good book or daily paper. Breath-taking antique Empire bed suites add Victorian ambiance enhanced by spacious sitting areas, private baths, fireplace, CATV/HBO, a/c, ceiling fans and phones to each of our guest rooms. The *Kingsley House* hosts weddings, bridal showers, small office parties and business meetings, corporate travelers and holiday packages. Recently the *Kingsley House* has become host to the Mystery Weekend. Guests assume "the identity" and spend the weekend solving a "who dunnit"! Wilmington activities include antique shops, the USS North Carolina, Chandlers Wharf, Cotton Exchange, horsedrawn carriage tours, Henrietta II Riverboat excursions, Cape Fear Museums, Thalian Hall Center for Performing Arts, Wrightsville, Carolina and Kure beaches as well as fine restaurants. Events include Azalea Festival, Chili Cook-off, music and jazz festivals, Riverfest, holiday firework celebrations, Halloween festivals, holiday flotilla, Christmas festival, Santa parade and Candlelight Tour of Historic Homes. "Step back in time to an Era of Elegance and Hospitality". **Discounts:** 10% seniors **Packages:** Mystery Weekend, Holiday, Corporate **Airport:** New Hanover-10 mins **Packages:** 4,5 & 7 Nights, Mystery Weekend, Holiday **Reservations:** One night deposit with credit card, 7 day cancel policy for refund **Brochure:** Yes **Permitted:** Children 13-up, limited drinking, limited smoking **Conference:** Groups to eight persons **Languages:** Italian **Payment Terms:** Travelers Check MC/V [K06HPNC1-20088] **COM YG ITC Member:** No

Rates: **Pvt Bath 3**   **Shared Bath 1**
Single $ 75.00
Double $ 85-105.00 $ 115-155.00

Taylor House Inn   14 N 7th 28401   Wilmington NC
Glenda Moreadith   Tel: 800-382-9982 910-763-7581

Innkeeper Glenda Moreadith has created the perfect place for exploring the Cape Fear Coast. The *Taylor House Inn*, a comfortable, romantic, turn-of-the-century home built in 1908 by a local merchant John Allen Taylor as his private residence, is located in Wilmington Historic District. Here you will find excellent food, cozy rooms, friendship and genuine hospitality. Imagine a day at the North Carolina Coast after a full English breakfast, taking a short walk into downtown Wilmington to explore antique shops, galleries, the Old Cotton Exchange, Chandler's Wharf and much more, or take a fifteen minute drive to one of North Carolina's finest beaches. As your day comes to a close, imagine returning to the *Taylor House Inn*, with its inviting warmth of golden oak fireplaces, staircase, inlaid parquet and heart of pine floors. The comfortable public rooms invite you to read or relax. Of course, there is an old fashion porch complete with swings and rockers for summer enjoyment. Luxury awaits you in the Jacobean Room with it's king size bed, or in the inviting Queen's Suite, which has a queen size pine poster bed and an adjoining room with a European-style queen size bed. The Garden Room is quite cozy with its brass bed and fireplace. All rooms have private baths and lighted sitting areas, Fine linens and top quality mattresses provide excellent sleeping comfort. Glenda is fulfilling her dream as an innkeeper after raising her family and working as a Certified Registered Nurse Anesthetist. Her artistic style of decorating and attention to detail make this the perfect place to stay. Guests are treated each morning to breakfast served on bone china, sparkling crystal, linen napkins and candles - her way of saying "thank you for visiting Taylor House Inn" - and please come again. Shooting locale for the film *"Against Her Will."* **Discounts:** Corporate, Extended Stays - 3-up nights **Airport:** New Hanover Intl-8mi **Seasonal:** No **Reservations:** One night deposit, 7 day cancel policy **Brochure:** Yes **Permitted:** Limited children, limited drinking, no smoking **Payment Terms:** Check AE/MC/V [I01HPNC1-21447] **COM U ITC Member:** No **Quality Assurance** Requested

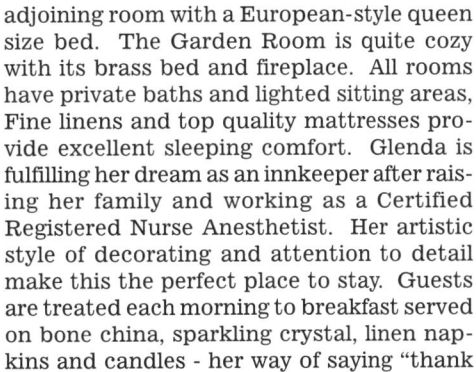

Rates: **Pvt Bath 4**
Single $ 65.00
Double $ 85.00

Worth House   412 S Third St 28401   Wilmington NC
Francie & John Miller   Tel: 800-340-8559 910-762-8562 **Fax:** 910-763-2173

The *Worth House*, a gracious and comfortable Victorian bed and breakfast Inn, is located in the heart of Wilmington's Historic District. Originally settled in 1732, the Historic District is one of the largest in the US with many 18th and 19th Century homes. The *Worth House* was built in 1893 and is a three-story Queen Anne style home with bay windows, turrets, porches and gardens. The first floor includes a parlor, library and formal dining room furnished with antiques and period art. For the enjoyment of guests, the parlor has a Victorian era pump organ and the library has a large screen TV.

Another large sitting room with a game table and TV is located on the third floor. Each of the seven guest rooms has its own personality. All have private baths and telephones, and most have fireplaces and sitting areas. A full breakfast is served in the morning and refrigerators on each floor are stocked with complimentary soft drinks and snacks. For the convenience of the business traveler, fax service is available as well as the use of the laundry. The Inn is a five minute walk from restaurants, antique shops and entertainment available in downtown Wilmington and the Cape Fear River waterfront area, including walking tours, horse and carriage rides. Weightsville Beach and other ocean beaches are just a fifteen minute drive. The Cape Fear area boasts a number of international class golf courses, museums and the Wilmington campus of the University of North Carolina. **Discounts:** Seniors, Corporate rates Sun-Thur **Airport:** Wil-mington-10 mins **Seasonal:** No **Reservations:** Deposit required, 72 hr cancel policy for refund **Brochure:** Yes **Permitted:** Children 9+, drinking **Payment Terms:** Check MC/V [K05HP-NC1-4181] **COM** YG **ITC Member:** No

Rates: Pvt Bath 7
Single $ 65-105.00
Double $ 70-110.00

Miss Betty's B&B Inn   600 W Nash St 27893-3045   Wilson NC
Betty & Fred Spitz   Tel: 800-258-2058 919-243-4447
Res Times 7am-10pm

Selected as *"one of the best places to stay in the South."* Located on a gracious lot in the downtown historic section, *Miss Betty's,* comprised of four beautifully restored homes, the National Registered Davis-Whitehead Harris House (circa 1858) the Riley House (circa 1900), Queen Ann (circa 1891) and the Rosebud (circa 1942) is a recapture of the elegance and style of an era gone by. Quiet Victorian elegance and charm abound in an atmosphere of all modern day conveniences. Guests can browse for antiques in any of the numerous antique shops that have given Wilson the title of *"Antique Capital of North Carolina."* A quiet eastern North Carolina town also known for its famous barbecue. Wilson, with its four beautiful golf courses and numerous tennis courts, "is ideally located midway between Maine and Florida, along the main North-South Route I-95." A full breakfast is included. Handicap accessible. **Airport:** Raleigh / Durham-60 mi **Packages:** Golf, Tennis, Anniversary, Birthday, Holiday Gift Certificates **Seasonal:** No **Reservations:** *800 number only for reservations, full deposit via check or guaranteed by credit card **Brochure:** Yes **Payment Terms:** Check/AE/CB/DC/DISC/MC/V [I08GPNC-4182] **COM** U **ITC Member:** No

Rates: Pvt Bath 10
Single $ 50-65.00
Double $ 60-75.00

Arcadian Inn B&B   328 E First St 73034   Edmond OK
Martha & Gary Hall   Tel: 800-299-6347 405-348-6347
Res Times 9am-6pm

Basking in the Oklahoma breeze, across from the University of Central Oklahoma, The Arcadian Inn is a step back in time to old-fashioned service and hospitality. From the grand wrap-around front porch and it's swing, guests may enjoy the lovely view overlooking the City of Edmond, known as the *"Crown Jewel of Central Oklahoma."* Martha Hall has decorated each of the five antique filled rooms to reflect Victorian romance and luxury. With modern comforts and antique settings, the Arcadian Inn provides private, peaceful accommodations for business or relaxation. Amenities include jacuzzi, clawfooted tubs, fireplaces, queen and king size beds, in room phones and free local calls. Breakfast is a true occasion, with homemade entrees and breads, fresh fruit, juice and coffee. Private candlelight dinners may be arranged with prior notice and added cost. Enjoy the stars in the Garden spa or a puzzle in the parlor. Four blocks from downtown Edmond, antique tours are available. Golf, tennis and swimming are nearby - and just minutes from Oklahoma City and Guthrie attractions. Edmond's summer attractions include Theatre Ala Carte, Shakespeare in the Park, a spectacular Fourth of July Celebration Parade and fireworks occur right in front of the Inn. Martha and Gary Hall welcome you to their Inn. **Airport:** Will Rogers-15 mi **Seasonal:** No **Reservations:** One night deposit required, 5 day cancel policy for refund **Brochure:** Yes **Payment Terms:** Check AE/DISC/MC/V [R05GPOK-16665] **COM** Y **ITC Member:** No

Rates: Pvt Bath 5
Single $ 60-110.00
Double $ 65-120.00

Arcadian Inn B&B   Oklahoma City OK
Marth & Gary Hall   Tel: 800-299-6347 405-348-6347
                                                                                    Res Times 9am-6pm

Refer to the same listing name under Edmond, Oklahoma for a complete description. **Seasonal:** No **Payment Terms:** Check AE/DISC/MC/V [M05GPOK-19320] **COM** YG **ITC Member:** No

Rates: Pvt Bath 5
Single $ 60-110.00
Double $ 65-120.00

Rose Stone Inn   120 S 3rd St 74601   Ponca City OK
David Zimmerman   Tel: 800-763-9922 405-763-9922 Fax: 405-762-0240
                                                                                    Res Times 24 Hrs

This European-style Inn is famous for its tranquil luxury. From the handmade furniture to the airport limousine pick-up, one is made to feel like an Oklahoma Oil Baron. Located in a renovated historic bank, each room has a theme of people, places and things to discover in the Rose Stone State. Styles vary from baronial to Victorian to Art Deco. Ponca City was at the vortex of the Chisholm Trail, the Cherokee Outlet Land Run and the Oil Boom. Downtown is a romantic haven for window shoppers, diners, antique hunters of a jumping-off point for walkers to visit attractions: Ponchan Theatre - live performances most weekends; Pioneer Woman Statue and museum - celebrates the women who won the West; Marland Mansion - fabulous home of oilman and Oklahoma's tenth governor; Cann Botanical Gardens; Indian Museum - tribes of the Cherokee Strip; Conoco Refinery - the last refinery open to the public in the USA; Tallgrass Prairie Preserve. Summers: Balloon Festival and Fly-in, Iris Festival, Kaw Lake Festival, Three Pow-wows, PRCA Rodeo, Grand National Motocross Championship. Business travelers are within walking distance to banks and Conoco, a full-service health club. Derricks restaurants and other fine dining nearby. Evening snacks available. **Discounts:** Yes, inquire at reservation time **Airport:** Ponca City-3 mi; Wichita Intl-85 mi **Packages:** Sweetheart Spree, Petroleum From Ground to Glamour; Petticoats and Lace **Seasonal:** No **Reservations:** Credit card to guarantee, cancellation policy - cancel prior to 6 pm date of arrival **Brochure:** Yes **Permitted:** Children, drinking, limited drinking **Conference:** Yes, four conference rooms seating 8-90 persons **Payment Terms:** Check/AE/BAR CB/DC/DISC/MC/V [I03IOK1-22940] **COM** YG **ITC Member:** No

Rates: Pvt Bath 25
Single $ 66.00
Double $ 71.00

Beaufort Inn   809 Port Republic St 29901-1257   Beaufort SC
*Debbie & Russell Fielden   Tel: 803-521-9000 Fax: 803-521-9500
                                                                                    Res Times 7am-11pm

Nestled in the downtown Historic Landmark District, the *Beaufort Inn* is one of the most beautiful and distinct Inns in the Southeast. The three-story Victorian Inn is quite roomy with thirteen guest rooms, yet the exquisite architectural detail gives it a doll house-like quality that lends charm and intimacy to its interior. A grand mahogany stairway gracefully curls up the fifty-foot atrium leading to rooms and porches on the upper floors. The guest rooms, which are named after Low Country Plantations, are all decorated in period furniture and photographs of their plantation namesake. Framed in beautiful wallcoverings, elaborate wood mouldings and golden heart pine floors, many rooms contain marble and slate fireplaces and large sunlit windows that open onto verandas. Two romantic guest rooms located in the Carriage House behind the Inn, overlook an enchanting brick courtyard area and fountain. All of the guest rooms have modern amenities. Twice a day, gourmet cuisine is served to guests and other visitors in the Inn's elegant restaurant. While the Inn's fourth generation chef, Peter DeJong, is originally from Amsterdam, Holland, and not the South, he adds a delightful regional accent to his creative breakfast and dinner menus. A full service bar is available. In just the Inn's first year after extensive renovation and opening, Innkeepers Debbie and Russell Fielden have been host to guests ranging from vacationers and business travelers to movie stars and celebrities. Both Julia Roberts and Paula Zahn have enjoyed weeklong stays at the Inn. Robert Duval, Lyle Lovett and Sharon Stone have all dined in the Inn's gourmet restaurant. Many guests return often for repeat visits. The wonderful cuisine, unsurpassed comfort and genuine southern hospitality you experience at the Beaufort Inn will keep you remembering the Low Country for a long time. **Airport:** Savannah-1 hr; Charleston-1-1/2 hr **Packages:** Group packages on an individual basis **Reservations:** Deposit required to guarantee reservation, 7 days (prior to 3pm of arrival day) cancel policy for full refund, including early departures; verify cancel policy for groups and corporate functions **Permitted:** Children 8+, smoking on outdoor porches only **Conference:** Conference room suitable for groups to eight; dining available for groups to forty five persons **Payment Terms:** Check AE/MC/V [U10HPSC1-22337] **COM YG ITC Member:** No

Rates: Pvt Bath 13
Single $ 110-185.00
Double $ 110-185.00

TwoSuns Inn B&B	1705 Bay St 29902	**Beaufort SC**
Carrol & Ron Kay	**Tel:** 800-532-4244 803-522-1122 **Fax:** 803-522-1122	
		Res Times 9am-9pm

Visit Historic Beaufort and stay in *"A Prince of an Inn in an Antebellum Brigadoon!"* Beaufort is one of the finest Nationally Landmarked small communities on the East Coast, rich with history and grand homes of another era. Stroll, take a carriage tour, boat tour or bicycle our historic district. Our quaint (three block long) downtown includes museum homes, antique shops, art galleries, boutiques and casual dining overlooking a scenic waterfront. Rest in a comfortable bayview guestroom individually designed with Victorian, American pastoral or oriental themes, and appointed with Carrol's custom window and bed treatment ensembles. In the morning, enjoy a special "menu of

National Edition *South Carolina*

the day" full breakfast - all homemade. *TwoSuns* has full personal and business amenities (room phones, fax, copier, computer, display material and meeting room), central a/c, handicap accessibility, guest bicycles, and warm, personal service by resident owners. Visit us soon! **Airport:** Savannah 45 mi; Charleston-65 mi **Discounts:** Corporate, AAA, AARP, Seniors **Seasonal:** No **Reservations:** One night's deposit, 48 hr cancel policy **Brochure:** Yes **Permitted:** Drinking **Conference:** Business seminar & meeting services (computer, copier, fax, display materials) for small workshops, meetings or seminars, 12-15 persons **Payment Terms:** Check AE/MC/V [I04HPSC1-12555] **COM** YG **ITC Member:** No **Quality Assurance:** Requested

Rates:	Pvt Bath 5
Single	$ 105.00
Double	$ 129.00

Hayne House 30 King St 29401 Charleston SC
Ben Chapman Tel: 800-948-1680 803-577-2633 **Fax:** 803-577-2633

The *Hayne House* is a historic Bed & Breakfast located in the Heart of Charleston, SC only one block from the beautiful Battery. The House was built in 1755 as a Charleston Single House. It was one room deep and perpendicular to the street for the beneficial Harbor breeze. In 1820 the Piazzas were replaced with what is now the foyer and a Regency-style living room was added along with the Master bedroom. The patios and garden were designed by the present owner and innkeeper, Ben Chapman. The *Hayne House* was in Mr. Chapman's family prior to its conversion to a B&B. The original home was built by General Robert Hayne and passed onto his son, who was a major political figure in Charleston and South Carolina after the Revolutionary War. This area which General Hayne chose for his home is now frequented by several types of tours including horse-drawn carriages. The area provides not only wonderful historic tours, but also marvelous restaurants, unique shopping. A continental plus breakfast is included. **Airport:** Charl-eston Intl-10 mi **Reservations:** 50% deposit in advance **Permitted:** Children, limited drinking **Payment Terms:** Check MC/V [I10GPSC-4772] **COM** Y **ITC Member:** No

Rates:	Pvt Bath 3	Shared Bath 2
Single	$ 100-110.00	$ 50-70.00
Double	$ 100-110.00	$ 50-70.00

John Rutledge House Inn 116 Broad St 29401 Charleston SC
Rick Widman, Owner Tel: 800-476-9741 803-723-7999
Res Times 24 Hrs

Fifty-five men signed the Constitution of the United States; prominent among them was John Rutledge of Charleston. His home, which was built here in 1763, is one of only fifteen belonging to those Signers that has survived the two intervening centuries - and the only one to accommodate lodging guests. Of such importance that it has been designated a *National Historic Landmark,* the *John Rutledge House Inn* graces Charleston's Broad Street in what is now the heart of its historic district. As a bed and breakfast inn, The *John Rutledge House Inn* offers the classic elegance of rooms in the main house and its three spacious Grand Suites, or the charm and seclusion of the rooms in the carriage house. Antiques and historically accurate reproductions give each room its own warmth and distinction. Every guest room has its own luxurious bath, the lat-

©*Inn & Travel Memphis, Tennessee*

est in climate controls, a color TV and a personal-size refrigerator. Guests enjoy World-class services. Each morning, guests enjoy fresh pastries, juices, coffee or tea, served in the comfort and privacy of their own room. Wine and sherries are offered in the opulent ballroom where patriots, statesmen and Presidents have met. Turndown service with chocolates is provided each evening. **Discounts:** AAA, AARP **Airport:** Charleston Intl-12 mi **Packages:** Discover Charleston **Seasonal:** No **Reservations:** First night deposit due 7 days before arrival, 48 hr cancel policy for full refund **Brochure:** Yes **Permitted:** Children, drinking, limited smoking **Conference:** Yes, for meetings, weddings and parties **Payment Terms:** Check AE/MC/V [K04HPSC1-6752] **COM** YG **ITC Member:** No **Quality Assurance** Requested

Rates: Pvt Bath 19
Single $ 120-220.00
Double $ 135-235.00

King George IV Inn	32 George St 29401	Charleston SC
BJ, Mike, Deb		Tel: 803-723-9339
		Res Times 9am-9pm

Stay in the Historic District of Charleston in a two-century old Federal Style House originally named the "Freneau House" after Peter Freneau, a prominent Charleston journalists and co-owner of the Charleston City Gazette, merchant, ship owner and Jeffersonian politician. Freneau was of Huguenot descent and his brother Philip Freneau was called *"the poet of the Revolution."* Peter Freneau served South Carolina as Secretary of State and as a State Legislator who was very prominent in local politics. Today, the Inn retains its Federal style home and Greek Revival parapet style roofline. There are four stories in all with three levels of lovely Charleston porches. All rooms include fireplaces, either Federal or Gothic revival, ten foot ceilings and six foot windows. Original lovely wide-planked hardwood floors and original six foot doors remain today. All of the guest rooms contain old furnishings with many antique pieces. A continental breakfast is included with each room. Conveniently located, guests are within one minute walking distance to King Street shopping, restaurants and historic sights. The Historic Market is a convenient five minute stroll through historic areas. Your hosts have maps and brochures on what to see and do while visiting their historic and beautiful Inn. **Discounts:** Available for stays of several nights **Airport:** 20 min drive to North Charleston airport **Seasonal:** No **Reservations:** Deposit required to guarantee reservation, 5 day cancel policy for refund. Check-in 10am-6pm or prepared package on door. Travel agent commissionable except 3/10-6/10 **Brochure:** Yes **Permitted:** Children, drinking, limited smoking (outdoor porches only), limited pets **Payment Terms:** Check MC/V [K01HPSC1-13072] **COM** Y **ITC Member:** No **Quality Assurance:** Requested

Rates: Pvt Bath 8
Single $ 70-125.00
Double $ 70-125.00

Rutledge Victorian Inn	114 Rutledge Ave 29401	Charleston SC
BJ, Mike, Lynn		Tel: 803-722-7551
		Res Times 9am-9pm

Enjoy this century old Victorian guest house located in the Historic District of Charleston. This charming Inn is just South of Calhoun St, across from the Old Museum Park and Roman Columns (the remains of the Confederate Soldiers Meeting House and Reunion Hall and the first Museum in the USA). This Inn is an elegant Charleston House of rare Italianate Architecture. Highlights include a unique 120 foot rounded decorative porch, splendid columns and gingerbread. This lovely porch beckons guests to "set a spell on an old rocker where time stands still and feel the history around you!" The interior is very elegant with 12-13 foot ceilings with plaster moldings, silk wallcoverings, decorative fireplaces, 8-10' oak doors and windows and furnished with beautiful antiques and heirlooms. Modern amenities include TV and modern baths (private or shared) and central heating and air conditioning. Your hosts provide a casual and relaxed atmosphere and are ready to help point-out the sights and wonderful dining places with maps, brochures and menus. A common lobby is open from 10am-6pm while guests can come and go 24 hrs a day. A continental plus breakfast of pastries, muffins, nutbreads and cereals and beverages is set out in the lovely dining room. Setting out each morning, you're just 5-20 mins walking distance from boat rides, shopping, dining, historic sights and the beautiful mansions of Charleston. Plantation tours and beaches are just a twenty minute ride from downtown. **Airport:** North Charleston airport-20 mins by car **Seasonal:** No **Reservations:** Deposit is required, 5 day cancel policy for refund, late arrival by prior arrangement, discount offered for multiple nights. Travel agent commissionable except 3/10-6/10 **Permitted:** Children, drinking, limited pets, limited smoking **Conference:** Lovely formal dining room and lobby area seating groups five to ten persons **Payment Terms:** Check MC/V [K01HPSC1-11155] **COM Y ITC Member:** No

Rates:	Pvt Bath 8	Shared Bath 3
Single	$ 75-125.00	$ 55-65.00
Double	$ 75-125.00	$ 55-65.00

Victoria House Inn 208 King St 29401 Charleston SC
Mary Kay Smith Tel: 800-933-5464 803-720-2944 **Fax:** 803-720-2930
Res Times 24 Hrs

Experience the intimacy of the Victorian Age at the *Victoria House Inn*. Completed in 1889, this Romanesque period style building houses eighteen elegantly renovated guest rooms. Large windows and exquisite appointments bring back the grandeur of the Victorian past. Petite Suites provide luxurious accommodations with whirlpool and fireplace. All modern amenities are provided in each room along with a stocked refrigerator. A Royal Breakfast is delivered to your room each morning for enjoying in bed. After touring Charleston, relax and enjoy wine or sherry served in the lobby or garden. Turndown service and chocolates complete your evening. Located on King Street just south of Market Street, the *Victoria House Inn* is convenient to the famous market area which is renowned for excellent shopping and dining. Enjoy the comfort, service and Southern Hospitality which are trademarks of the *Victoria House Inn*. **Discounts:** AAA, AARP **Airport:** Charleston Intl **Seasonal:** No **Reservations:** Deposit due 7 days prior to arrival date, noon of the day before arrival cancel policy for full refund **Brochure:** Yes **Permitted:** Children, limited smoking **Conference:** Yes; 700 sq ft area for various functions **Payment Terms:** Check MC/V [K04HPSC1-15674] **COM YG ITC Member:** No

Rates:	Pvt Bath 18
Single	$ 85-125.00
Double	$ 100-140.00

Claussens Inn 2003 Green St 29205 Columbia SC
Daniel Vance Tel: 800-622-3382 803-765-0440
Res Times 24 Hrs

Columbia's Landmark Inn. Just minutes away from the capitol building in downtown Columbia, Claussen's Inn is next to the University of South Carolina, within walking distance of the shops, restaurants and entertainment in exciting Five Points. You'll get the feel of our Bed & Breakfast Inn the moment you enter the lobby. We carefully preserved our historic architectural features and added amenities that make them even better, like an expansive vaulted sky light, terra cotta tile, lots of greenery and overstuffed seating. Each spacious guest room at *Claussen's Inn* has an individual character. With four-poster or iron and brass beds, rich colors and handsome traditional furnishings, every room is unique. Many of the rooms still have the original hardwood floors. The 29 luxurious guest rooms at *Claussen's Inn* feature all the amenities you expect - private baths, color TV with remote control, radio, a/c, phones and an outdoor jacuzzi. At *Claussen's Inn* you'll find plenty of convenient free parking and time-honored courtesies of a complimentary continental breakfast, nightly turn-down service. **Reservations:** Deposit at reservation time **Permitted:** Children, drinking, limited smoking **Payment Terms:** Check AE/MC/V [Z11CPSC-4789] **COM Y ITC Member:** No

Rates:	Pvt Bath 29
Single	$ 75-90.00
Double	$ 85-100.00

1790 House 630 Highmarket St 29440 Georgetown SC
John & Patricia Wiley
Tel: 800-890-7432 803-546-4821
Res Times 9am-9pm

Meticulously restored 200 year old West Indies Colonial plantation-style Inn is located in the heart of the Historic District of Georgetown providing spacious luxurious rooms, eleven foot ceilings, seven fireplaces with central a/c and heating. The spacious common rooms are reflective of an elegant Inn and reminiscent of great plantation homes of the past era. Guests can choose the "Slave Quarters" where servants once slept; the elegant "Rice Planters" and the "Indigo" rooms with four poster beds, lovely sitting areas and fireplaces; the "Prince George Suite", a perfect hideaway under the eaves with lots of charm. Relax in an original claw foot tub; "Gabrielle's Library", a bright and airy room in shades of mauve, accented by lovely built-in bookcases and fireplace; or the "Dependency Cottage", a private entrance enhanced by a lovely patio overlooking the gardens leading to a romantic hideaway -ideal for honeymooners. Amenities include queen size Windsor bed, charming sitting area, refrigerator and a spacious bath with jacuzzi tub and separate shower. Guests can enjoy their full gourmet breakfast served outdoors on the veranda or in the dining room. Walk to shops, restaurants and historic sites - while Myrtle Beach and the Grand Strand (a golfer's paradise) is just a short drive. Brookgreen Gardens, where art meets nature, Pawleys Island with beautiful beaches and Charleston's historic homes and cobblestone streets are convenient to the 1790 House. **Discounts:** Yes, inquire at res time **Airport:** Charleston SC-60 mi; Myrtle Beach-35 mi **Seasonal:** No **Reservations:** One night or 50% deposit (which ever is greater), late arrival only with prior notice, 7 day cancel policy: 1 suite available **Brochure:** Yes **Permitted:** Drinking, children **Conference:** Yes for groups up to 15 persons **Payment Terms:** Check AE/DISC/MC/V [I10IPSC1-4794] **COM YG ITC Member:** No

Rates:	Pvt Bath 6
Single	$ 75-125.00
Double	$ 75-125.00

Shaw House 613 Cypress Ct 29440 Georgetown SC
Mary & Joe Shaw
Tel: 803-546-9663

A spacious two-story colonial home in a serene natural setting, with a beautiful view overlooking miles of marshland formed by four rivers which converge and flow into the Intracoastal Waterway. Perfect for bird watchers; also within walking distance to downtown historic Georgetown. The wide front porch, extending the width of the home is outlined by tall white columns and features old-fashioned rockers ready to be used by guests who are welcomed as family. A nearby rose garden adds charm to the gracious retreat. All rooms are air conditioned, carpeted and beautifully furnished with family antiques - all have private baths. A full Southern breakfast is served at our guest's convenience - along with nighttime chocolates on pillows, turn

National Edition   *South Carolina*

backs and some loving extras. **Airport:** Charleston SC-60 mi **Discounts:** Yes, inquire at res time **Seasonal:** No **Brochure:** Yes **Permitted:** Children, smoking, drinking **Payment Terms:** Check [I03IPSC1-4795] **COM YG ITC Member:** No

Rates:	**Pvt Bath 3**
Single	$ 50-65.00
Double	$ 50-65.00

Rice Hope Plantation Inn   206 Rice Hope Dr 29461   **Moncks Corner SC**
Rick & Doris Kasprak   **Tel:** 800-569-4038 803-761-4832
    Res Times 7am-10pm

Rice Hope Plantation (c.1790) was once a working rice plantation. Today the remaining eleven acres are graced with live oak trees, Spanish moss, and over 200 year old terraced gardens of azaleas and camellias overlooking the Cooper River. Tir-Star Pictures filmed the movie "Consulting Adults" here, because it is the classic Southern Plantation setting. A friendly, relaxed atmosphere makes *Rice Hope* the perfect place to get away from everything, yet is located less than one hour from historic Charleston. The present home of 9000 sprawling feet, built in 1920's, is constructed of cypress with a slate roof. Antique and reproduction furniture are found throughout the home. Fresh fruit, just-baked muffins, orange juice and great coffee are standard breakfast fare and cooked breakfast are available on weekends, if requested. Complimentary refreshments are served from 4:00 to 5:00 in the afternoon, with iced tea, coffee, scones, shortbread, or cookies or wine and cheese, in the parlor or on the patio. A four course dinner served in the formal dining room will make you feel relaxed and pampered during your stay. A tennis court, bicycles and lawn games such as boccie ball, croquet and horse shoes will entertain you in the afternoons. Spectacular sunsets can be seen from the dock at the foot of the gardens, along with herons, egrets, osprey and eagles, fishing in the coastal marshes. Step back in time and experience the Old South that the plantation owners of long ago once enjoyed. **Discounts:** 20% discount for 5 room nights booked together **Airport:** Charleston SC-45 mi **Seasonal:** No **Reservations:** First night's deposit required at time of booking, 48 hour cancel policy **Brochure:** Yes **Permitted:** Children, drinking, limited pets **Conference:** Private parties, business meetings, garden weddings **Languages:** Spanish, German **Payment Terms:** Check MC/V [I11FPSC-17402] **COM Y ITC Member:** No

Rates:	**Pvt Bath 2**	**Shared Bath 3**
Single	$ 75.00	$ 60.00
Double	$ 75.00	$ 60.00

Brustman House B&B   400 25th Ave S 29577   **Myrtle Beach SC**
Dr & Mrs Wendell Brustman   **Tel:** 800-448-7699 803-448-7699
    Res Times 8am-10pm

Located 300 yards from the beach on almost two acres in a wooded setting, the *Brustman House B&B* is a large Colonial-style home offering a peaceful get away while still close to the sights and attractions. Golf courses (over eight), seafront restaurants, discount shopping and the Pavilion amusement complex are in the immediate area - with the beach 300 yards away! Nearby cultural attractions include the Brookgreen Gardens, historic Georgetown and the entertaining Carolina Opry. Of course, you might want to luxuriate until late hours in your room especially if you select one of the two guest rooms with a white onyx whirlpool tub for two. For larger groups or families, the fully equipped guest suite sleeps 3-8 persons and includes a full kitchen, washer/dryer, TV/VCR and private entry from the parking area. The European-furnished home is very quiet and is located on a quiet side street at the south end of

---

©*Inn & Travel Memphis, Tennessee*

the city, just five minutes from the airport. Guest rooms are furnished with Scandinavian classic furniture and the beds are fitted with down or Laura Ashely comforters. When you're ready, a complimentary breakfast can include the house healthful specialty - a ten-grain buttermilk pancakes. Afternoon tea is served at 4:00 pm and includes wine and cakes - usually fresh baked and served on exquisite Scandinavian dinnerware. This setting provides a peaceful setting to enjoy croquet, rose and herb gardens, badminton or bikes for touring the neighborhood. Guests can travel to lovely Charleston, just a two hour trip south on the King's Highway. AAA 3-Diamond Rated. **Discounts:** AAA, Seniors, Extended stays **Airport:** Myrtle Beach Jetport-2 mi **Seasonal:** No **Reservations:** First night's deposit or 1/3 which is greater, 14 day cancel policy (7 days in season), full payment upon arrival, check-in 2-4 pm, to 11pm with prior arrangements **Brochure:** Yes **Permitted:** Children 10-up, drinking, smoking outdoor veranda only **Conference:** Family gatherings and groups to fourteen **Languages:** Limited French **Payment Terms:** Check MC/V [I10HPSC1-17405] COM YG ITC **Member:** No

Rates:	Pvt Bath 4
Single	$ 42-80.00
Double	$ 46-85.00

Serendipity Inn 407 N 71st Ave 29572 **Myrtle Beach SC**
Terry & Sheila Johnson Tel: 800-762-3229 803-449-5268

An award-winning complex in Spanish-Mission style, this Inn is located on a quiet side street just three hundred yards from the lovely ocean beaches. Our friendly Garden Room provides a comfortable, cheery place for our complimentary full continental breakfast, or just old-fashioned socializing. All guest rooms are spacious, furnished individually in different periods, air-conditioned, private baths, color TV and small refrigerators and queen, double or twin beds. Studios are available with kitchenettes, suites include full bedrooms with dressing room, bath and a spacious living room with a sleeping couch and a kitchen/dining area. There is a large, heated pool, jacuzzi, shuffleboard, ping-pong and an outdoor grill for your enjoyment. Nearby are more than 75 golf courses, hundreds of fine dining places, tennis, theatres, nightclubs and the largest number of shopping outlets in the southeast! We're just a short drive to Calabsh NC, the seafood capital of the world; Brookgreen Gardens, a sculpture garden rivalling Europe's finest and less than 60 miles to historic Wilmington North Carolina and 90 miles to Charleston South Carolina, one of America's most beautiful and history-laden cities. **Airport:** Myrtle Beach Jet Port-15mi **Discounts:** 10% 5+ days, excluding July to Aug 15th **Seasonal:** Rates vary **Reservations:** One night's deposit with 7 day cancel policy for refund **Brochure:** Yes **Permitted:** Children, drinking, smoking **Payment Terms:** Check MC/V [I03HPSC1-4808] COM U ITC **Member:** No

Rates:	Pvt Bath 14
Single	$ 45-95.00
Double	$ 52-110.00

Nicholls-Crook Plantation 120 Plantation Rd 29388 **Woodruff SC**
Suzanne Brown Tel: 803-476-8820

A restored c1793 Georgian-style, up-country plantation home dating from the early days of the up-country and listed on the *National Register of Historic Places*. Step back into an earlier, more restful time. Warm and inviting; filled with period Southern antiques that convey the atmosphere of the early 1800's, but with modern amenities including air conditioning. Special features include original mantles and an unusual chimney - the widest in the upstate - that divides around second and third floor windows and serves three fireplaces on these floors. The bricks are handmade and laid in

Flemish bond. The grounds include extensive period gardens as well as a cutting garden and vegetable garden. There is a walled white rock courtyard and a pecan grove which features one of the largest pecan trees in South Carolina. Breakfast is brought in picnic baskets to guests' rooms and guests are tucked in at night with a bedtime snack. Located in a restful semi-rural setting with easy access from I-26 and I-85. Twenty minutes from Spartanburg and 30 mins from Greenville. Area points of interest include Cowpens National Military Park; Historic Walnut Grove Plantation; BMW visitor center; Carolina Panthers summer training camp. **Airport:** Greenville Spartanburg-12 mi **Packages:** Valentines Day, Honeymoon **Seasonal:** No **Reservations:** One night's deposit at res time **Brochure:** Yes **Permitted:** Limited drinking, children 12+ **Conference:** Yes for small groups **Languages:** French, Spanish **Payment Terms:** Check AE [I03HP-SC1-150] COM YG **ITC Member:** No

Rates:	Pvt Bath 2	Shared Bath 2
Single	$ 75.00	$ 75.00
Double	$ 85.00	$ 85.00

Majestic Mansion B&B 202 E Washington Ave 37303 **Athens TN**
Richard & Elaine Newman **Tel:** 423-476-9041
Res Times 6am-9pm

Nestled near the foothills of the Smokies, just off I-75 in southeast Tennessee, this 1909 gracious home adds to historic downtown Athens. Athens offers its guests white water rafting on the Ocoee, sight of the 1996 Summer Olympic competition. Stroll one block to the historic, quaint town square filled with shops from antiques to women's fashions. Relax in a rocking chair on the wooden porch with cool lemonade or play tennis on the nearby tennis courts. Awake to a power breakfast or a light fitness meal. French toast layers with pecans and syrup, apple pancakes with hot maple syrup, glazed bacon, spicy sausage and egg casserole are just some of the menus to delight your morning palette. You will be within walking distance to a banana split at the soda fountain, Tennessee Wesleyan College. The Living Heritage Museum, or a tour of our Mayfield's Dairy. Take a short drive to the Lost Sea, Cherokee National Forest, with hiking, trout fishing, deer and bear and beautiful scenery; or the Smoky Mountain National Park. In an hour you can be at the aquarium, shopping or Civil War historical battle grounds in Chattanooga or Knoxville. For fun you can drive to Dollywood, Gatlinburg, Pigeon Forge or Sevierville (the new country musical capital). As for either The Ambassador Room with its royal decor and clawfoot tub or The Empress Room with a sunken Jacuzzi and the feeling of the Orient. A rest stop or restful haven for some quite time, the *Majestic Mansion* will bring surprising treasures, a comfortable room, delicious breakfast, friendly hosts and the delightful downtown. **Airport:** Knoxville-60 mi; Chattanooga-50 mi **Discounts:** Military **Seasonal:** No **Reservations:** One night deposit, 48 hr cancellation policy for refund. Email Eden@cococo.net **Permitted:** Children **Languages:** Some Japanese, Spanish [I01JPTN1-27421] COM U **ITC Member** No **Payment Terms:** DISC/DC

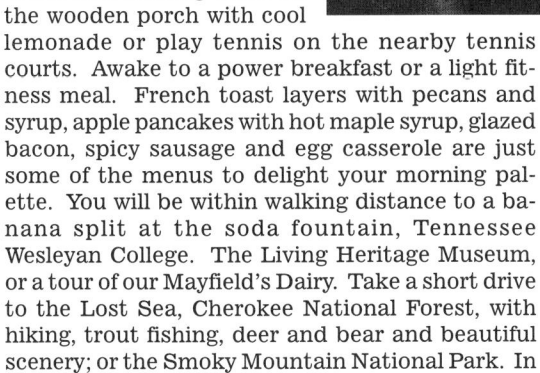

Rates:	Pvt Bath 2
Single	
Double	$ 65-75.00

New Hope B&B 822 Georgia Ave 37620 **Bristol TN**

Tennessee *National Edition*

Tom & Tonda Fluke **Tel:** 423-789-3343

New Hope has all the charm of a late Victorian home, yet comfort and convenience was high on the agenda while decorating and furnishing decisions were made. The guests often say *"I feel so at home."* That's the feeling *New Hope* has strived to achieve for everyone who enters her door. There are four guest rooms including the Andes Room, located on the first floor with a private entrance. Decorated with oak furniture and gas logs, the large bath is the feature that brings out the "ah" in each guest. The Reynolds Room with its beautiful large bath is very popular among our honeymooners and anniversary guests. Being a corner room, the Allen Room is dressed with mahogany furniture and is very light and charming. The Arnold Room, with it's unusual bath, is a cozy as a trip to grandmas. A delicious breakfast of casseroles, breads and fruits are served either in the lovely dining room, on the wrap around porch or by special request, in the bedroom. Guests are free to linger and enjoy the parlor with the ambience of a 1892 Victorian home, stroll through the beautiful neighborhood, or borrow *New Hope* bicycles. The town of Bristol is nestled in the foothills of the Blue Ridge Mountains. The area is known as the Tri-Cities of east Tennessee. Bristol is distinct in that it claims two states as home: one side Virginia - one side Tennessee. Bristol is only one hour from Boone, NC; 1-1/2 hours from Asheville, NC; 2 hours from Dollywood and is easily accessible to Interstate 81. **Airport:** Tri-Cities **Discounts:** Seniors, Travel Agents **Seasonal:** No **Reservations:** One night's deposit, 3 day cancel notice for refund **Brochure:** Yes **Permitted:** Children, drinking, limited smoking **Payment Terms:** Check MC/V [I04IPTN-26820] **COM** U **ITC Member:** No

Rates: Pvt Bath 4
Single $ 60-90.00
Double $ 60-90.00

Adams Hilborne	801 Vine St 37403	Chattanooga TN
Wendy & David Adams		**Tel:** 423-265-5000 **Fax:** 423-265-5555

Cornerstone to Chattanooga's Fort Wood Historic District is this rare Victorian Romanesque design with original coffered ceilings, handcarved oak stairway, beveled glass windows, Tiffany stained glass windows and ceramic tile embellishments. Old-world charm and hospitality in a tree-shaded setting rich with Civil War history and turn-of-the-century architecture. Guests are treated to small European-style hotel accommodations in nine tastefully restored, exquisitely decorated guest rooms. Private baths, fireplaces, complimentary breakfast for guests are included. A spacious ballroom, meeting and reception areas provide for private dining with catering and available to the public. Minutes from Chattanooga museums, fine shops and restaurants, the Aquarium, UTC arena and other cultural events and attractions. Private off-street parking provided. **Airport:** Chattanooga-7 mi **Packages:** Yes, inquire at res time **Seasonal:** No **Reservations:** Deposit required, check for cancellation policy when calling for reservation: E-mail AdamsInns@aol.com **Permitted:** Limited children, limited drinking, limited smoking **Conference:** Yes, four rooms and ballroom for that special occasion **Payment Terms:** Check AE/MC/V [I04HPTN1-21935] **COM** YG **ITC Member:** No

Rates: Pvt Bath 15
Single $ 125-295.00
Double $ 125-295.00

Browns Manor	215 Twentieth St NE 37311	Cleveland TN
Beverlee Brown		**Tel:** 615-479-5311

3-96   ©*Inn & Travel Memphis, Tennessee*

This contemporary residence provides a personal alternative to commercial lodging as your home away from home. Set on three acres of grounds, guests find a relaxful and peaceful atmosphere or any activity that includes swimming in the 20 x 40 pool, horseshoes, croquet, volleyball, softball or basketball. Nearby are tennis courts, park facilities, libraries, bike paths, white water rafting, glider flying, the beautiful Cherokee National Forest and Red Clay historical Indian grounds. Your hosts take pride in making guests feel at home in their intimate retreat. A full breakfast is included and can be enjoyed outdoors, in the patio area or in the bright sunroom. Complimentary high tea is offered daily. **Seasonal:** No **Reservations:** One night's deposit per room to confirm res; late arrival to 11 pm. **Brochure:** Yes **Permitted:** Children, limited drinking **Conference:** Yes, up to 8 persons. **Payment Terms:** [X06BCTN-8364] **COM** Y **ITC Member:** No

Rates:	Pvt Bath 1	Shared Bath 3
Single	$ 79.00	$ 65.00
Double	$ 89.00	$ 79.00

Bridgewater House	7015 Raleigh LaGrange 38018	Cordova TN
Katherine & Steve Mistilis		Tel: 901-384-0080
		Res Times 8am-10pm

A romantic stepback into history awaits you when you walk into this 100 year old Greek Revival home that has been magnificently renovated from a former school house, filled with remembrances of travels, antiques, family heirlooms and oriental rugs. You'll find the original hardwood floors, five different woods cut from trees on the property. There are leaded glass windows, fifteen foot ceilings, hand marbleized mouldings, enormous rooms, crown mouldings and twelve foot bookcases flanking a 200-250 year old Adam's Mantle with an ornate three-section mirror, reminiscent of a figurehead on a ship's bow, in the living room. The culinary background of the owners means you'll be awaking to an artfully prepared breakfast created from recipes collected from around the world. The Bridgewater House offers two spacious rooms with private baths, sitting and reading areas, tastefully furnished, overlooking gently sloping grounds and stately oak trees. Guests are just minutes from downtown Memphis and attractions such as the Mississippi River, the Pyramid, Beale Street, Mud Island, Memphis Zoo, Graceland and museums. Shelby Farm, the largest public city park in the USA, just a mile away, offers walking trails, buffalo herds, fishing, horseback riding, picnicking, sailing, canoeing and other outdoor activities. There are numerous colleges and universities in the area. Your innkeepers are glad to share their knowledge to help with recommendations on area attractions and restaurants. **Discounts:** Extended stays **Airport:** Memphis Intl-25 mi **Reservations:** One night deposit in advance with 7 day cancel policy for refund less 20% service fee, check-in 3-5pm, check out 11am **Brochure:** Yes **Permitted:** Children 13+, smoking on patio only **Conference:** Yes, for meetings and parties including catering to 100 persons **Payment Terms:** Check Tvlrs Ck [K07HPTN1-19325] **COM** YG **ITC Member:** No **Quality Assured:** Yes

Rates:	Pvt Bath 2
Single	$ 75-95.00
Double	$ 80-100.00

Havenhall	183 Houston Gordon Rd 38019	Covington TN
Houston & Debbie Gordon		Tel: 901-476-7226 Fax: 901-475-0773
		Res Times 8am-6pm

Best of both worlds! Secluded, peaceful country simplicity only thirty minutes outside of Memphis. Located near Covington Tennessee on Hwy 59E, 26 miles north of Memphis via Hwy 14N, or take I-40 Exit 66W. Just one hour from Graceland; 45 mins from University of Memphis, University of Tennessee, Memphis, downtown hospitals, Mud Island, The Pyramid or a steamboat ride; and only 20 mi south of historic Fort Pillow State Park. Reelfoot Lake is about 1-1/2 hrs north and guests are only five mins from local parks, tennis courts, golf and Community Theatre. Covington is the home of the

Tennessee — *National Edition*

World's Oldest Bar-be-que Festival. The finest barbecue in the south is right here in Tipton County. A rustic three bedroom barn apartment (full bath, large den, fully equipped kitchen, W/D) amidst 80 acres bearing forty kinds of trees, fox, squirrel, horses, rabbits and beautiful birds to offer peaceful comfort. Furnished with antiques and homemade quilts from another generation, feels like being at Grandma's. Enjoy a continental breakfast in your quarters, outdoors near a fountain, on a screen porch or under a beautiful wisteria arbor. For your leisure: bass/bream fishing pond, 1.8 mi all-terrain jogging trail, exercise room and pool. Experience the world's smoothest riding horse, the Peruvian Paso. Bred for stamina, truly natural 4-beat gait and gentleness, the Paso is a pleasant ride for even the inexperienced rider. Horseback riding extra. **Seasonal:** No **Reservations:** One night's deposit at res time. Special rates avail: 2 BR $95 nightly; 3 BR $125 nightly; Weekly family rate $650 for seven nights **Brochure:** Yes **Permitted:** Children, drinking, smoking, limited pets **Payment Terms:** Check MC/V [I03HPTN1-11191] COM YG **ITC Member:** No

Rates:	Pvt Bath 1	Shared Bath 2
Single	$ 65.00	$ 50.00
Double	$ 75.00	$ 60.00

Buckhorn Inn   2140 Tudor Mountain Rd 37738   Gatlinburg TN
John & Connie Burns   Tel: 615-436-4668

Buckhorn Inn today is exactly what the Bebb family meant it to be from it's very beginning in 1938, a comfortable retreat for the discriminating traveler, with a welcome blend of elegance and charm, style and grace, set in ideal natural surroundings of beauty, peace and solitude. Set on approximately thirty acres of walkways, meadows and woodland that offer guests spectacular views of the Great Smoky Mountains. The inn itself has a large common room with a massive stone fireplace with a sitting area and grand Steinway. Large picture-widows bring the beautiful year-round foliage into every corner of the room. Upstairs are five comfortable, intimate guest rooms beautifully furnished with antiques and art work collected by the owner, Rachel Young. In-addition, private cottages are scattered around the main house with porches for capturing cool evening breezes, living rooms, fireplaces, private bath and a/c. Each morning a full complimentary breakfast is served in the main house along with evening dinner (at additional cost) for guests and non-guests (space permitting). John Burns (Hubert Bebb's grandson) and his wife, Connie, along with their competent and friendly staff are happy to make reservations for you or provide additional information or assistance. **Discounts:** Inquire at res time **Airport:** McGee Tyson **Packages:** Stay seven days and the seventh day is "no charge" **Seasonal:** No **Reservations:** One night deposit, 14 day cancel policy for refund; call if arrival after 9pm **Brochure:** Yes **Permitted:** Drinking, children over 10, smoking permitted in some cottages and outdoors **Conference:** Bebb House, home of the original owner, accommodates private meetings and occasions for groups to 25 persons **Payment Terms:** Check MC/V [R12EPTN-4836] COM Y **ITC Member:** No

Rates:	Pvt Bath 12
Single	$ 85-250.00
Double	$ 95-250.00

Hilltop House   6 Sanford 37743   Greeneville TN
Denise Ashworth   Tel: 423-639-8202
    Res Times 8am-8pm

Hilltop House Bed & Breakfast Inn is a 1920's manor house on a hillside overlooking the Nolichucky River Valley with the Appalachian Mountains in the background. Since the owner is a landscape architect, the flower garden is beautiful, framing the mountain views and providing fresh flowers in all the rooms year round. There are three huge guest bedrooms, all with private bath, comfortably furnished and with mountain views. Two have their own verandah. Your innkeeper is English by birth and an English tea is served every afternoon. The furniture includes both English antiques and reproduction pieces. Breakfast is served family-style and consists of fruit, cereal, egg dishes and homemade biscuits or muffins. Guests may take advantage of local white-water rafting opportunities, mountain trail hiking, trout fishing, mountain biking, golf, antiquing, hunting on a private reserve or bird-watching. The Cherokee National Forest is within easy distance, as are the Great Smoky Mountains National Park and the Blue Ridge Parkway. **Airport:** Tri-Cities Airport-45 mi **Discounts:** Yes, business travelers & extended stays (one free night after staying five) **Packages:** Gardening Seminars (vary by season eg: April-Flower Arranging, June-Attracting butterflies, December-Christmas Decorations); Fly-fishing Seminar (basics to fishing for trout & bass); Mountain Biking, White Water Rafting. **Airport:** Tri-City-45 mi **Discounts:** Jan-Mar 10% **Seasonal:** No **Reservations:** One night's deposit, 7 day cancel policy full refund, check-in 3pm-later, late arrival with prior arrangement only **Brochure:** Yes **Permitted:** Children 3-up, limited drinking **Languages:** Some French, German **Payment Terms:** Check AE/MC/V [I04H-PTN1-13593] **COM YG ITC**

Member: No

Rates:	Pvt Bath 3
Single	$ 70.00
Double	$ 70-80.00

River Road Inn　　　　　PO Box 372 37774　　　　　**Loudon TN**
Pamela Foster　　　　　　　　　　　　　　　　　　　　**Tel:** 615-458-4861

Country atmosphere in this antebellum home on the *National Historic Register* with beautiful dogwoods on the grounds. Built c1857 by Albert Lenoir, the grounds served as the location for General Sherman's encampment during the Civil War. A full country breakfast is served by Kathy and features ham, biscuits with all the country trimmin's. **Seasonal:** No **Brochure:** Yes **Permitted:** Children, limited pets, limited smoking, limited drinking **Payment Terms:** Check [X11ACTN-3019] **COM Y ITC Member:** No

Rates:	Pvt Bath 2	Shared Bath 3
Single	$ 60.00	$ 55.00
Double	$ 60.00	$ 55.00

Lynchburg B&B　　　　　Mechanic St 37352　　　　　**Lynchburg TN**
Virginia & Mike Tipps　　　　　　　　　　　　　　　　**Tel:** 615-759-7158

Home of Jack Daniels "downhome" commercials and atmosphere offers one of the oldest residences in town to travelers. Furnished with plenty of country antiques, country collections and hospitality. Relax in this great small town! **Seasonal:** No **Reservations:** One night's deposit at res time, 5 day cancel notice for refund. **Brochure:** Yes **Permitted:** Children, smoking, drinking **Payment Terms:** Check [X11ACTN-2634] **COM Y ITC Member:** No

Rates:	Pvt Bath 3
Single	$ 50.00
Double	$ 60.00

Falcon Manor　　　　2645 Faulkner Springs Rd 37110　　　**McMinnville TN**
George & Charlien McGlothin　　　　　　　　　　　　　**Tel:** 615-668-4444

Retreat to the peaceful romance of the 1890's in one of the South's finest Victorian mansions. Huge gingerbread verandas are well-stocked with rocking chairs, and the three-acre lawn is shaded by century-old trees. Inside, twelve foot ceilings, a sweeping staircase, exquisite woodwork, rich colors, and museum-quality antiques add up to friendly elegance. Wealthy manufacturer Clay Faulkner (who produced Gorilla Jeans, "so strong, even a gorilla couldn't tear them apart") built the mansion in 1896 for his wife and five children. In the 1940's, it was converted into a beloved country hospital. Innkeeper George McGlothin left a career in retail management to work four years to restoring the house, while his wife Charline pitched in during time off from her job as a NASA public affairs writer. They love sharing stories about *Falcon Manor's* history and their adventures bringing it back to life, and a guided tour spiced with historic anecdotes is offered to every guest. A favorite for romantic getaways and anniversary celebrations, *Falcon Manor* is also the ideal base for a Tennessee vacation - halfway between Nashville and Chattanooga, with easy access to I-24 and I-40. Four of the state's most beautiful parks are nearby. McMinnville is the "nursery capital of the world" and the home of Cumberland Caverns, Tennessee's largest cave. *Falcon Manor's* country setting is just minutes from restaurants and shops in town. **Airport:** Nashville-72mi; Chattanooga-75mi **Seasonal:** No **Reservations:** First night's deposit to hold room, 7 day cancel policy for refund **Brochure:** Yes **Permitted:** Children 11+, limited smoking (outdoors) **Conference:** Yes, for special occasions such as weddings, receptions, luncheons **Payment Terms:** Check MC/V [I03HPTN1-18770] **COM YG ITC Member:** No

Rates:	Pvt Bath 2	Shared Bath 4
Single	$ 85.00	$ 75.00
Double	$ 85.00	$ 75.00

Bridgewater House — Memphis TN
Katherine & Steve Mistilis
Tel: 901-384-0080
Res Times 8am-10pm

Refer to the same listing name under Cordova, Tennessee for a complete description. **Seasonal:** No **Payment Terms:** Check Tvlrs Ck [M07HCTN1-21456] **COM YG ITC Member:** No

Rates:	Pvt Bath 2
Single	$ 75-95.00
Double	$ 80-100.00

Cottage Inn — Memphis TN
*Ruth Lindley
Tel: 800-363-2900 601-363-5997 Fax: 601-363-2985
Res Times 24 Hrs

Refer to the same listing name under Robinsonville, Mississippi for a complete description. **Seasonal:** No **Payment Terms:** AE/DISC/MC/V [M02HCTN1-22305] **COM YG ITC Member:** No

Rates:	Pvt Bath 20
Single	$ 59-up
Double	$ 59-up

Doler B&B — Memphis TN
Ray & Vera Marcum
Tel: 601-637-2695
Res Times 10am-10pm

Refer to the same listing name under Slate Springs, Mississippi for a complete description. **Seasonal:** No **Payment Terms:** Check MC/V [M01DPMS-12030] **COM Y ITC Member:** No

Rates:	Pvt Bath 5
Single	$ 75.00
Double	$ 125.00

Havenhall — Memphis TN
Houston & Debbie Gordon
Tel: 901-476-7226
Res Times 8am-6pm

Refer to the same listing name under Covington, Tennessee for a complete description. **Seasonal:** No **Payment Terms:** Check MC/V [M10CPTN-11584] **COM YG ITC Member:** No

Rates:	Pvt Bath 1	Shared Bath 2
Single	$ 65.00	$ 50.00
Double	$ 75.00	$ 60.00

National Edition *Tennessee*

Adams Edgeworth Inn	Monteagle Assembly 37356	**Monteagle TN**
Wendy & David Adams		**Tel:** ~~615~~-924-4000 **Fax:** 615-924-3236

931

This beautiful Queen Anne Carpenter Victorian was built as an Inn 100 years ago. It is furnished in the English Manor style with floral chintzes, antiques and a fine collection of original oil paintings. There are eleven rooms in the main house and three rooms in the attached "carriage House." A plantation bed and matching dresser set that was original to the Inn has been found, purchased and restored to its original surroundings. The Library with its burgundy colored walls is filled with interesting books and memorabilia. Curl up in front of the fire on a chilly evening, sip hot tea and feel the stress of city life melt away. Gourmet dinners are available by reservation in the intimate candlelit dining room. Should you wish to venture out of this charming setting, you can wander any of the 150 miles of hiking trails maintained by the South Cumberland State Recreation Area; drive to nearby Sewanee, University of the South and feel as if you have landed in jolly ole' England; sample baked goods from Tennessee's oldest bakery, call on the home of Jack Daniels' antique across the countryside; bike; swim; or find a partner for tennis or golf. Tired out? Find a "fourth" and return to the Inn for bridge, games or the wonderful art of southern conversation on the many verandahs. Rock the time away while sipping a cool drink of icy mountain water in the clear ever-fresh mountain air. Hurry up and hurry up! We can't wait to see you. Featured on PBS *"Inn Country USA."* **Airport:** 40 mins **Packages:** Yes, inquire at res time **Seasonal:** No **Reservations:** Deposit required, check cancellation policy at reservation time: E-mail: AdamsInns@aol.com **Brochure:** Yes **Permitted:** Limited children, limited drinking, limited smoking **Conference:** Yes **Payment Terms:** Check AE/MC/V [I04HPTN1-5849] **COM** Y **ITC Member:** No

Rates:	Pvt Bath 14
Single	$ 65-195.00
Double	$ 75-195.00

Fall Creek Falls B&B	Rt 3 Box 298B 37367	**Pikeville TN**
Doug & Rita Pruett		**Tel:** 423-881-5494 **Fax:** 423-881-5040
		Res Times 7am-10pm

Enjoy the relaxing atmosphere of a new country manor home located on forty acres of scenic rolling hills. The 6400 sq ft country manor is a "labor of love" for Rita and Doug Pruett. The elegant stenciled brick structure rests in a pastoral setting of meadow surrounded by woodland one mile from nationally acclaimed Fall Creek Falls State Park which boasts the highest waterfalls east of the Rockies. Within three miles is golfing, fishing, hiking, boating, tennis, swimming and horseback riding. Guest accommodations consist of seven air conditioned guest rooms and one suite, all with private baths and individually decorated in Victorian or Country furnishings. "Sweetheart Room" features a red heart-shaped whirlpool and "Wild Rose Suite" has a wild rose pink heart-shaped whirlpool and gas log fireplace. For guest enjoyment there are two sitting rooms for reading and relaxing in a sunny Florida room with a magnificent view. Breakfast is full gourmet, prepared by Doug and served in an elegant dining room or a cozy country kitchen. Bagged to go lunches available by reservation. A paved quiet and scenic country road for walking, jogging and picnic tables and benches on the five acre yard all invite guests enjoyment and solitude. AAA 3-Diamond Rated. Spa Services

©Inn & Travel Memphis, Tennessee 3-101

available by reservation. **Discounts:** Nurses 10% **Seasonal:** Clo: January **Reservations:** One night deposit required to guarantee reservation, 7 day cancel policy for refund *Suite available **Brochure:** Yes **Permitted:** Limited children, limited drinking, no smoking **Payment Terms:** Check MC/V [I02HP-TN1-15661] COM YG ITC **Member:** No Quality Assurance Requested

Rates:	Pvt Bath 8	Shared Bath 1
Single	$ 65-95.00	$ 130.00
Double	$ 75-105.00	

Blue Mountain Mist Country Inn 1811 Pullen Rd 37862 Sevierville TN
Sarah Ball
Tel: 800-497-2335 615-428-2335
Res Times 9am-9pm

The *Blue Mountain Mist Country Inn* is a beautiful, Victorian-style farmhouse filled with heirlooms, country charm and warm Southern hospitality. Year around innkeepers, Sarah and Norman Ball, work hard to make this the extra special place people come back to year after year. On cool evenings you can warm up by a cozy fireplace as you visit with the other guests and enjoy a delicious evening treat. The Inn features twelve individually decorated guest rooms, each with its own name and character. Each room has a private bath and special decorative touches such as old fashioned claw foot tubs, high antique headboards, vintage wardrobes, old photographs and heirloom quilts. Each morning in the sun-filled dining room, guests find tables heaping with a southern country breakfast. The menu changes daily and might include Sarah's special stuffed French toast or real Southern biscuits, gravy and all the fixin's. Nestled in the woods behind the Inn are five country cottages designed for romantic getaways. These each have their own two-person Jacuzzi, fireplace, kitchenette and romantic porch with porch swing. Setting among the rolling hills of the family's 60-acre farm, the Blue Mountain Mist offers superb views. A mix of valleys, hills and mountains with their ever-changing character from the mist rising early in the morning to the glow of the setting sun. Within a short drive, guests can enjoy: the natural beauty and tranquility of The Great Smoky Mountain National Park, shopping and entertainment of Pigeon Forge and Gatlinburg, the Crafts Community, golf, fishing and Dollywood. **Airport:** McGhee Tyson, Knoxville-30 mi **Packages:** Winter Weekend Special Event (call for details). **Reservations:** One night's deposit or credit card number; 10 day cancel notice for refund. **Brochure:** Yes **Permitted:** Children, smoking on porches **Conference:** Yes, inquire for details. **Payment Terms:** Check MC/V [I02FPTN-2645] COM Y ITC **Member:** No

Rates:	Pvt Bath 17
Single	$ 69.00
Double	$ 79-125.00

Calico Inn 757 Ranch Way 37862 Sevierville TN
Lill & Jim Katzbeck
Tel: 800-235-1054 423-428-3833
Res Times 10am-9pm

Located in the Great Smoky Mountain area, the *Calico Inn* offers guests true *Tennessee "log cabin"* accommodations and serenity on it's twenty-five acre setting. The Inn has a Country Charm, no matter which of the three guest rooms you may choose. It has many antiques and in someways, you feel a part of the past by allowing your mind to roam. The Wildflower Room is luxury and comfort at its best with a spectacular view and a large private bath. The Mountain Laurel Room offers a "shades of blue" decor with a queen iron bed and panoramic view of the mountains too. The Hemlock Room is finished with "shades of green" and includes a queen size bed and private bath. This room faces eight acres of woods, perfect for early morning hikes if you'd like. Activities abound with Dollywood minutes away and for shoppers - factory outlets offer great savings year round - while

National Edition   *Tennessee*

the Smoky Mountain National Forest is at your door step. Enjoy mountain streams, sightseeing, hiking, fishing, golfing, horseback riding, live entertainment shows, antique shops, flea markets and craft villages. A full country breakfast is served and includes juice, fresh seasonal fruits and a fresh made daily special of either eggs, waffles, homemade breads or muffins - sure to satisfy your hunger. Guests are served complimentary ice tea while enjoying the porch rockers in summer - while hot cider or homemade friendship tea is served fireside in winter. Come see, enjoy and share all of this with us and other guests. We will be waiting to greet you and help make your stay a fond cherished memory for years to come. **Discounts:** Off season rates **Airport:** Knoxville-30 mi **Seasonal:** No **Reservations:** 50% if one night, if longer one night's deposit by credit card to guarantee **Brochure:** Yes **Permitted:** Children (school age), smoking outdoors only **Payment Terms:** Check MC/V [I10IPTN1-27133] **COM** YG **ITC Member:** No **Quality Assured** Yes

Rates: Pvt Bath 3
Single $ 85-95.00
Double $ 85-95.00

Kero Mountain Resort	2319 Little Valley Rd 37862	Sevierville TN
Grace Roblee		**Tel:** 423-453-7514
		Res Times After 7 pm

Located in the foothills of the Smokys just minutes from fabulous Pigeon Forge and Gatlinburg but far enough away to avoid the hectic crush of traffic are four modern, fully equipped cabins and two beautiful Lodge connected suites. Fireplaces and whirlpool baths in some units. TV's. VCR's, a/c, dishes, linens - everything needed for a relaxing escape! Full stocked two acre pond - full of large mouth bass and Bluegill and row boats, no extra charge for either! And if you're inclined, its the perfect pond for daytime or evening dips to refresh yourself. Bring along the family - friends - or just relax with a favorite book. Beautiful mountain surroundings and totally non-commercial on 40 acres of solitude. Seventh day free when staying six! While not a B&B, *Kero Mountain Resort* is perfect for B&B'ers who want to be surrounded by nature in the beautiful Smokey Mountains. **Reservations:** Deposit required, @Cabins & suite rates. **Brochure:** Yes **Permitted:** Children, pets, drinking, smoking **Conference:** Yes in a large lodge with bar and fireplace **Payment Terms:** Check [R06BCTN-2646] **COM** U **ITC Member:** No

Rates: Pvt Bath 5
Single $ 55-105.00
Double $ 55-105.00

Taylor House B&B	300 East Lane 37160	Shelbyville TN
Kathy Taylor	**Tel:** 800-867-7326 615-684-3894	**Fax:** 615-684-7560

Feel at home and enjoy the warm southern hospitality that awaits you in the elegant yet comfortable surroundings of *Taylor House*. After a good night's sleep in our spacious bedrooms, we will start your day with a hearty, country-style breakfast served family style and help you plan an agenda from our many local surrounding attractions. Remodeled in 1995, our guest rooms have queen size beds and high quality bedding. The master of the house, Steve Taylor, aims for our guest *"to sleep like they do at home."* Large walk-in style closets, private baths with shower/tub combos, phones, cable TV and nice cherry and oak furniture can be found through out the house. While the main floor has beautiful hardwood floors, the guest areas are carpeted. A separate sitting area and entrance/exit has been provided for guest use. Conveniently located at the beginning of Shelbyville's historic walking tour and the Argie Cooper public

©*Inn & Travel Memphis, Tennessee*   3-103

library. We're within five (5) blocks of the Tennessee Walking Horse National Celebration Grounds and Museum, Calsonic Arena and many walking horse farms that you can visit daily. Only ten (10) minutes away from antique filled historic Bell Buckle and Wartrace. If you are a fisherman, Normandy Lake is nearby and golfers can enjoy Riverbend Country Club or Henry Horton State Park, each an 18 hole course. Murfreesboro's Civil War battlefield and Nashville's Opryland USA are less than and hour away, also Lynchburg's Jack Daniel Distillery is a hop, skip and jump away. We would be glad to send you a brochure or discuss any special needs you may have. Just call our toll free number or fax your request. Ya'll come! **Seasonal:** No **Reservations:** We take all major credit cards. Check-in from 2 until 6pm (CST), check out 11am or later with prior arrangements. **Permitted:** No smoking, no pets, limited drinking; just please treat our home as nice as you do yours. **Payment Terms:** AE/DC/DISC/MC/V [I09IPTN1-27147] **COM** YG **ITC Member:** No **Quality Assured** Yes

Rates:	Pvt Bath 5
Single	$ 65-100.00
Double	$ 65-100.00

Evins Mill Retreat	Evins Mill Rd 37166	Smithville TN
William Cochran, Jr		Tel: 615-597-2088 Fax: 615-597-2090

The area's oldest mill (Lockhart's Mill) was transformed by Tennessee State Senator Edgar Evins and Mrs Evins, who oversaw the construction of this 4,600 square foot lodge. Overlooking Fall Creek and the mill, it became a summer sanctuary for three generations of her politically prominent family. The homey environment still pervades the lodge, from immense stone fireplaces in both the large living and dining rooms to the cozy yet spacious bedrooms. Hardwood flooring, antiques and charming decor throughout, provides a warm welcome. Complementing the lodge are three newly constructed four-bedroom cottages, each accommodating up to ten persons. These cottages, surrounded by hemlock and oaks and situated on the bluff, provide guests with the calming sight and sound of Fall Creek. Your bed and breakfast stay at *Evins Mill* begins with a 4pm check in. It includes a hearty breakfast served from 8am to 9am. During your visit, you can do as little or as much as you like - and never leave *Evins Mill Retreat*. Relax on the banks of Evins Mill Pond. Enjoy the soothing sight and sound of Culcarmac Falls. You may choose to leisurely explore the beauty of the area. Browse through several local antique stores. If you're looking for physical activities, boating, fishing, skiing, golf and tennis are nearby. But you won't be the first guest to spend the entire day with a good book on one of the many breezy porches. Special arrangements can be made for dinner and lunch at the Millstone Restaurant. **Airport:** Nashville Intl-1 hr **Packages:** Groups, Holiday Theme Weekends, Fishing, Waterfalls, Bluegrass Music **Seasonal:** Yes, rates vary **Reservations:** Not more than one month in advance: 50% deposit, deposit refund only if re-booked for entire period **Permitted:** Children, drinking, limited smoking (outdoors) **Conference:** Four conference rooms **Languages:** Un peu francais **Payment Terms:** Check MC/V [I07H-PTN1-22224] **COM** YG **ITC Member:** No

Rates:	Pvt Bath 14
Single	$ 105-130.00
Double	$ 105-130.00

Bolins Prairie House	508 Mulberry 79601	Abilene TX
Sam & Ginny Bolin		Tel: 915-675-5855
		Res Times 9am-9pm

Nestled in the heart of Abilene, *Bolin's Prairie House B&B* is charming, cozy and comfortable. Antiques and modern luxuries are combined to create a warm home atmosphere. Built in 1902, the house was completely remodeled and enlarged in 1920. Virtually all evidence of Victorian architecture was obliterated in favor of the Frank Lloyd Wright "prairie style" design. Downstairs, guests enjoy high ceilings and hardwood floors with a cozy living room that invites warm conversation in front of the wood stove or while curling up with a good book. The den is great for stretching out and watching an old movie. Upstairs, there are four unique bedrooms - each offering a different mood. "Love" the largest, offers blue and beige floral striped wallpaper, antique maple dresser and wing back chairs. "Joy" features Mam-ma Bollins old bedroom furniture engulfed by riots of roses on the bed cover, curtains and pillows nestled in the rose-color rocking chairs. "Peace" brings a roomful of plants and "Patience" is a green, blue and rose-colored wallpaper - surrounded by dark green trim and priscilla curtains. One bath offers a huge seven foot clawfoot tub while the other offers two vanities and an oversized shower. Your hostess prepares a full complimentary breakfast of delicious egg dishes, homemade breads, fresh fruits and other scrumptious delights. **Reservations:** Deposit required to guarantee reservation, 24 Hr cancel policy for refund **Brochure:** Yes **Permitted:** Limited children, limited drinking **Conference:** Special gatherings for parties, bridesmaids brunches and office get-togethers, from 6 to 32 persons **Payment Terms:** Check AE/DC/MC/V [R08DPTX-12557] **COM** U **ITC Member:** No

Rates:	Shared Bath 4
Single	$ 30-50.00

Parkview House	1311 S Jefferson 79101	Amarillo TX
Carol & Nabil Dia		Tel: 806-373-9464
		Res Times 9am-9pm

Parkview House, Amarillo's first bed and breakfast, a 1908 Prairie Victorian, is owned and hosted by Carol and Nabil Dia (if you are wondering about the unusual name, Nabil is from Jordan). The house, once the home of a former Amarillo mayor, was moved to its present location in the 1920's, has been lovingly restored by your hosts and decorated throughout with antiques, lace and Victorian whatnots. Re-creating a warm and inviting ambiance for the indulgence of their guests. The Dia's continental "breakfast with a flourish" treats guests to warm homemade muffins topped with cinnamon or vanilla butter, custom blended American Aribic coffee and fruits served with Carol's own special toppings. Guests may savor these goodies in either the cozy eclectic kitchen or the formal dining room. Following breakfast, guests can relax on the wicker-furnished front porch, retreat to the shaded patio to enjoy complimentary minted iced tea and late evenings, take an evening soak in the hot tub under the stars! The Dias welcome guests with true friendly Texas hospitality. Head for Amarillo - there's plenty to do; tour Historic Rt 66, numerous museums, ballet, symphony, arts or Discovery Center and nearby Palo Duro Canyon to see "Texas" World famous outdoor Musical Romance. **Airport:** Amarillo Intl-8 mi **Seasonal:** No **Reservations:** Credit card for deposit to guarantee, late arrivals only with prior arrangement **Brochure:** Yes **Permitted:** Limited children, limited drinking **Languages:** Arabic **Payment Terms:** Check MC/V [Z03DPTX-5992] **COM** Y **ITC Member:** No

Rates:	Pvt Bath 3	Shared Bath 2
Single	$ 60.00	$ 50.00
Double	$ 60.00	$ 50.00

Austin's Wildflower Inn	1200 W 22-1/2 St 78705	Austin TX
Kay Jackson		Tel: 512-477-9639
		Res Times 7am-10pm

Austin's Wild Flower Inn is nestled in a quiet neighborhood of tree shaded streets. A beautiful large oak tree shades the front of the Wild Flower Inn. This lovely two-story home was built in 1936. There are four beautiful guest rooms furnished with antiques and windows filled with lace or embroidered curtains. There are beautiful hardwood floors throughout the home. In the spring, Texas wildflowers blossom through-out the grounds. Guests are awakened each morning with the aroma of freshly baked breakfast breads or muffins and fresh brewed coffee. Fresh fruit accompanies each

Texas *National Edition*

full complimentary breakfast - a *Wild Flower Inn* specialty - alternating between sweet and savory! The *Wild Flower Inn* is seven blocks from the University of Texas and just nine blocks to the State Capitol Complex. Caswell Tennis Courts are just two blocks from the Inn. We invite you to come and be pampered and experience true Texas hospitality. **Discounts:** Inquire at res time **Airport:** 9 minutes to Robert Mueller **Reservations:** One night's deposit **Brochure:** Yes **Permitted:** Drinking **Payment Terms:** Check AE/MC/V [Z04GPTX-123-41] **COM** Y **ITC Member:** No

Rates:	Pvt Bath 2	Shared Bath 2
Single	$ 60-65.00	$ 50.00
Double	$ 69-75.00	$ 59.99

Carringtons Bluff   1900 David St 78705   Austin TX
Lisa & Ed Mugford   **Tel:** 800-871-8908 512-479-0638 **Fax:** 512-479-0638
Res Times 7am-10pm

Carrington Bluff invites guests to enjoy the atmosphere of an English Country Bed & Breakfast where you'll find yourself surrounded by rooms filled with English and American antiques, handmade quilts and the sweet smell of potpourri. Situated in the heart of Austin on a tree-covered acre, this turn-of-the-century Texas classic home has been transformed into a "Country Inn in the City". The inviting front porch is lined with wooden rockers and blooming plants inviting guests to relax and enjoy the gentle breeze. They have combined Texas hospitality with English charm into a unique experience. Each guest room offers a unique experience including the Martha Hill Carrington Room offering English countryside decor. Handmade quilts adorn each guest bed and the decor ranges from shades of rose & blue to light and airy yellows. A full complimentary breakfast begins with gourmet coffee and fresh fruit served in fine English china. Homemade muffins or breads served with a House Specialty ensures you won't be hungry very long. Centrally located, guests will find they are close to all of the attractions and sights in Austin. **Airport:** 5 mi to Mueller Municipal **Discounts:** Extended stays **Seasonal:** No **Reservations:** 72 hr cancel policy, check-in 3pm, check-out 12 noon **Brochure:** Yes **Permitted:** Children, pets, drinking, smoking on outside porch **Conference:** Yes, for small groups **Languages:** Spanish **Payment Terms:** Check/AE/ CB/DC/DISC/MC/V [Z04IPTX1-11870] **COM** U **ITC Member:** No

Rates:	Pvt Bath 6	Shared Bath 2
Single	$ 69-99.00	$ 69-99.00
Double	$ 69-99.00	$ 69-99.00

Governors Inn   611 W 22nd St 78705   Austin TX
Gwen & David Fullbrook   **Tel:** 512-477-0711 **Fax:** 512-476-4769
Res Times 8am-10pm

Step back into Victorian elegance . . . in this 1897 neo-classical home, christened *Governor's Inn* in 1993. The *Governor's Inn* allows guests to step back into the Victorian Period while enjoying all of the necessities important to the discriminating traveler. Rooms are furnished with beautiful antiques but always with your comfort in mind. Each guest room is named for a famous Governor from Texas' colorful past. All rooms have private baths (many with clawfoot tubs). A full breakfast is served each morning. Located two blocks from the University of Texas campus and several blocks from the State Capitol grounds and downtown, the *Governor's Inn* is perfect whether you're visiting Austin for business or pleasure. **Airport:** 5 miles **Discounts:** Weekdays, Sun-Thursdays *Conferences:* Yes, small meetings **Seasonal:** No **Reservations:** One night's deposit required to guarantee reservation, 48 hr cancel policy for refund, less than 48 hrs notice, refund on if rebooked **Brochure:** Yes **Permitted:** Limited children, drinking, limited smoking **Payment Terms:** Check AE/DC/MC/V [I06GPTX-19741] **COM** U **ITC Member:** No

Rates:	Pvt Bath 8
Single	$ 55.00
Double	$ 99.00

©*Inn & Travel Memphis, Tennessee*

National Edition   *Texas*

Peaceful Hill B&B	6401 River Place Blvd 78730-1102	Austin TX
Mrs Peninnah Thurmond		Tel: 512-338-1817

Deer watch you come ... to this small, traditional country Bed & Breakfast located on ranch land high in the beautiful rolling hills just 15 minutes from the city - and five minutes to Lake Travis and The Oasis. Spring Time: South porch - rocking chairs, porch swing, sipping coffee or lemon tea punch, breakfast on big round table, view of city and countryside. Cold of Winter: grand stone fireplace, crackling fire; south glass wall bringing country-side view of city in to you. Lazy summer: hammock built for two in treed yard; hiking; bicycling; two miles to golf, swimming, tennis. All this and a home-cooked breakfast. Come and make Peaceful Hill your home away from home - warm and friendly and comfortable. Peaceful is its name and peaceful is the game. Deer watch you go ... **Airport:** Austin Mueller-40 mins **Discounts:** Extended stays over 7 days, $50.00. **Seasonal:** No **Reservations:** Deposit required to guarantee reservation, 48 hr cancel policy for refund, no drop-ins permitted. Add 7% state tax to room rate **Brochure:** Yes **Permitted:** Children-all ages, drinking, limited smoking (outdoors) **Conference:** Living room available for gatherings **Payment Terms:** Check MC/V [R09FPTX-15455] COM U ITC Member: No

Rates: **Pvt Bath 2**
Single $ 60.00
Double $ 60.00

Southard House	908 Blanco 78703	Austin TX
Jerry, Regina, Kara Southard		Tel: 512-474-4731

Elegant grand Texas tradition of entertaining in this grand house with cutwork linens, antique furnishings including clawfoot tubs with fireside dining during the cooler months. Downtown location. A continental breakfast is included. Guests can enjoy the garden with a gazebo, player piano, plenty of porches for rocking and a sitting room and library. **Seasonal:** No **Brochure:** Yes **Permitted:** Children and limited smoking and drinking **Payment Terms:** Check AE/MC/V [X11ACTX-2655] COM Y ITC Member: No

Rates: **Pvt Bath 5**
Single $ 55.00-up
Double $ 70-100.00

Trails End B&B		Austin TX
JoAnn & Tom Patty		Tel: 800-850-2901 512-267-2901
		Res Times 10am-10pm

Refer to the same listing name under Leander, Texas for a complete description. **Payment Terms:** Check AE/MC/V [M07GPTX-20114] COM Y ITC Member: No

Rates: **Pvt Bath 3**
Single $ 55-78.00
Double $ 65-95.00

Lains B&B	1118 Prarie St 78934	Columbus TX
Ernie & Dorothy Lain		Tel: 409-732-8373

Southern-style residence close to the historic area and furnished with antiques and family heirlooms. Just outside of Houston, guests are convenient to everything. Gracious hosts makes everyone feel at home. **Seasonal:** No **Reservations:** 50% deposit within 5 days of booking **Brochure:** Yes **Permitted:** Limited children and drinking **Payment Terms:** Check [X11ACTX-2667] COM Y ITC Member: No

Rates: **Pvt Bath 2**   **Shared Bath 1**
Single $ 55.00 $ 50.00
Double $ 60.00 $ 60.00

Anthonys By The Sea B&B		Corpus Christi TX

©*Inn & Travel Memphis, Tennessee*

Texas   *National Edition*

Denis - Tony   **Tel:** 800-460-2557 512-729-6100
                                                  Res Times 24 Hrs

Refer to the same listing name under Rockport, Texas for a complete description. **Seasonal:** No **Payment Terms:** MC/V [M04IPTX1-23815] **COM** YG **ITC Member:** No

Rates:	Pvt Bath 2	Shared Bath 2
Single	$ 65.00	$ 55.00
Double	$ 70.00	$ 65.00

Cayo del Oso B&B   6093 S Alameda 78412   **Corpus Christi TX**
Jerry Blake   **Tel:** 512-992-2711
                                                                Res Times 8am-8pm

A contemporary home nestled next to Oso Beach with a private balcony overlooking the fabulous Hans A Suter Wildlife Area that attracts birder and photo buffs year-round. Surrounded by plenty of land yet with just a few nearby residents, guest enjoy their privacy while being close to conveniences. Guests can enjoy the native vegetation with two fishpools, flowering gardens and a continuous fresh Gulf breeze that make the outdoors comfortable all day. The upstairs suite offers a queen bed, full bath, shared laundry facilities, security and smoke alarms, private entrance, off-street parking. Plenty to do with a public fishing pier just across the street, Padre Island beach, twenty minutes away, jogging and biking trails, wind-surfing, boating, golfing with fine shopping, antique shops and dining within strolling distance, along with picturesque fishing boats and Corpus Christi's harbor. Downtown attractions include a marina, the art and natural history museums and a collection of restored vintage homes. A full breakfast is included. Your hostess enjoys sharing her ideas and is always full of suggestions on what to do and see while visiting the Texas Riveria! **Seasonal:** Clo: Thank & Xmas **Reservations:** One night's deposit within 5 days, 24 hr cancel policy for refund, except on min stay periods; weekly winter rates available, may accept one-day guests, prefer long term guests with kitchen available **Brochure:** Yes **Permitted:** Drinking, limited smoking, children **Payment Terms:** Check [R06BCTX-8346] **COM** Y **ITC Member:** No

Rates:	Pvt Bath 1
Single	$ 70.00
Double	$ 70.00

Medrodd House   2344 Medford Ct East 76109   **Fort Worth TX**
Maribeth Ashley   **Tel:** 817-924-2765
                                                             Res Times 6pm-10pm

Historic area setting includes old-fashioned street lamps and lovely sidewalks. This charming home is an Empire Tudor design with oak woodwork, vaulted ceilings and antique furnishings. Guests are welcomed to use the pool, patio house and gas grill. Complimentary wine & cheese with cookies and milk for any children. A continental breakfast is included. **Seasonal:** No **Brochure:** Yes **Permitted:** Children, smoking and drinking **Payment Terms:** Check [X11ACTX-2681] **COM** Y **ITC Member:** No

Rates:	Pvt Bath 1
Single	$ 55.00
Double	$ 65.00

Gilded Thistle   1805 Broadway 77550   **Galveston TX**
Helen Hanemann   **Tel:** 800-654-9380 409-763-0194
                                                                  Res Times 24 hrs

Beautiful c1893 Victorian that remains in all its splendor and has been featured in *"Texas Monthly"*, *"PM Magazine"*, *"Houston Home & Garden Tour"* and *"Home Tours 1982"*. Fabulous antique furnishings, linens and wall coverings make this a perfect setting for accommodations or group meetings. Choose from one of the grand suites, all with period furnishings. Guests are pampered during their stay by the gracious hostess who offers guests evening appetizers and coffee and juice at your door in the morning. A hearty full breakfast lovingly prepared with homemade recipes is served indoors or outside on the veranda. Located in the East End, guests are convenient to all attractions and sights. **Seasonal:** No **Reservations:** Deposit required at res time, min stay on holidays **Brochure:** Yes **Permitted:** Children, limited smoking **Conference:** Yes for group luncheons and events to thirty persons **Payment Terms:** Check MC/V [Z03DPTX-2692] **COM** Y **ITC Member:** No

Rates:	Pvt Bath 1	Shared Bath 2
Single	$ 135.00	$ 125.00
Double		

Queen Anne B&B   1915 Sealy   77550   **Galveston TX**
Earl French/John McWilliams   Tel: 800-472-0930 409-763-7088

A visit to the Queen Anne is to experience the former splendor and true charm of historic Galveston Island. The late Victorian four-story Queen Anne-style home was built in 1905 by JJ Davis, a prominent banker and businessman. The house was sold to the First Methodist Episcopal Church in 1928 and became an elder house for eighteen years. In 1946, the Tucker family bought the home as their private residence. Forty-four years later (1990), it was purchased by the present owners and has undergone a total interior renovation. Beginning with the crystal-chandeliered and brightly-colored entry hall with its ten foot pocket doors, beautiful stairwell with stained glass windows - Victorian treasures abound. The spacious bedrooms are furnished with antiques and include king or queen size beds. The *Queen Anne B&B* is only six blocks from the Strand and 1/2 block from the East End Historic Home District. Guests are within easy walking distance of shopping, restaurants, entertainment and a host of other attractions. A short drive or bike ride takes you to the beach. Early morning juice and coffee is served in the upstairs morning room - while a full complimentary breakfast is prepared for serving in the dining room. **Airport:** Houston-35 mi **Seasonal:** No **Reservations:** One night's deposit or credit card number to guarantee reservation **Brochure:** Yes **Permitted:** Drinking **Payment Terms:** Check MC/V [K07FP-TX-14925] **COM** Y **ITC Member:** No

Rates:		Shared Bath 5
Single		$ 85-125.00
Double		$ 85-125.00

Trails End B&B   **Georgetown TX**
JoAnn & Tom Patty   Tel: 800-850-2901 512-267-2901
    Res Times 10am-10pm

Refer to the same listing name under Leander, Texas for a complete description. **Payment Terms:** Check AE/MC/V [M07GPTX-20115] **COM** Y **ITC Member:** No

Rates:	Pvt Bath 3
Single	$ 55-78.00
Double	$ 65-95.00

Durham House B&B   921 Heights Blvd   77008   **Houston TX**
Marguerite Swanson   Tel: 713-868-4654 **Fax:** 713-868-7965
    Res Times 8am-9pm

The *National Register of Historic Places* includes this Queen Anne Victorian. Located in the Historic Heights District, *Durham House* is within ten minutes of downtown Houston. Boasting upstairs bedrooms, a downstairs suite and a private carriage house, the lovely guest rooms are furnished in antiques, Victorian accessories, lace curtains and clawfoot bathtubs all reminiscent of another era. A full breakfast is served featuring home baked muffins or popovers and can be enjoyed in the dining room, on the back porch or another intimate location of your choosing. The Gazebo and garden setting is perfect for weddings and other special social or business functions. You'll love sit-

Texas   *National Edition*

ting on the Victorian porch with white wicker furnishings while listening to another guest in the parlor enjoying the player piano. And the complimentary bicycle built-for-two can be fun at any age. Come savor the splendor so many locals choose for their special affair or evening away from home! **Discounts:** Travel agents, stays over one week **Packages:** Honeymoon and Sweetheart **Airport:** 30 mins to Hobby, 45 mins to Inter-Continental **Seasonal:** No **Reservations:** Deposit required at res time, 72 hr cancel policy less $15 service fee. Booking fee if less than 72 hour cancellation. **Brochure:** Yes **Permitted:** Children, limited drinking **Conference:** Yes for groups to 40 persons. **Languages:** Limited Spanish & German **Payment Terms:** Check AE/MC/V [Z06DPTX-6761] **COM** Y **ITC Member:** No

Rates:	Pvt Bath 4	Shared Bath 1
Single	$ 50.00	$ 45.00
Double	$ 75.00	$ 55.00

Trails End B&B   12223 Trails End Rd 78641   Leander TX
Joan Patty   Tel: 800-850-2901 512-267-2901
Res Times 10am-10pm

The nicest words a Bed & Breakfast host would want to hear have got to be *"I love your B&B. I'm recommending your lovely B&B to all of my friends - old and new!" "Can't begin to tell you how great it was to stay here again. You both have a way of making those around you feel like part of the family".* Yes, as I read through my journals, the warm words of loving guests fill me with love in return. *Trail End Bed & Breakfast* is our home in the country, but it is much more than that. Our place can also be your home when you are visiting in this area. The area between Austin, Georgetown, Round Rock, Cedar Park, Leander, Jonestown and Lago Vista are just a few minutes away from *Trails End Bed & Breakfast*, of course, beautiful Lake Travis (two miles down the road). If you like large rooms, fireplaces, porches, gazebos, swimming pool, gardens, walking areas, bicycles, phones, decks with panoramic views of the hill country and Lake Travis, you will love Trails End Bed & Breakfast. If you like a room with a private bath with shower in the Main House, of if your taste runs to the privacy of a small guest house in the tree tops, we've got it. Monogrammed terry cloth robes furnished. A full breakfast is served to all guests. If your cup of tea is a quiet, peaceful, country setting in a home that looks old but feels now, give us a call. We hope there is always a room or cottage for you at *Trails End Bed & Breakfast*. **Discounts:** 10% after two days **Airport:** Austin Robert Mueller-45 mins **Seasonal:** No **Reservations:** One night's deposit, 48 hr cancel notice **Brochure:** Yes **Permitted:** Children, social drinking **Conference:** Small weddings, retreats, business meetings **Payment Terms:** Check MC/V [I07GPTX-18649] **COM** Y **ITC Member:** No

Rates:	Pvt Bath 3
Single	$ 55-78.00
Double	$ 55-78.00

Prince Solms Inn   295 E San Antonio 78130   New Braunfels TX
Ruth Wood   Tel: 800-625-9169 210-625-9196
Res Times 8am-10pm

Turn-of-the-century Inn c1898 on the main street furnished with antiques throughout. Full facility that offers guests comfort and a warm atmosphere. Visit the quaint towns' antique shops, tennis ranch, golf and rafting or tubing on the Guadalupe River. Amenities include refrigerators with fresh fruit and snacks. **Reservations:** Deposit required, 48 hr cancel policy for refund **Permitted:** Limited smoking **Payment Terms:** Check MC/V [X11ACTX-2737] **COM** Y **ITC Member:** No

Rates:	Pvt Bath 12
Single	$ 60.00
Double	$ 85-90.00

©*Inn & Travel Memphis, Tennessee*

Yacht Club Hotel	700 Yturra St 78578	**Port Isabel TX**
Lynn Speier		**Tel:** 512-943-1301
		Res Times 8am-10pm

A private yacht club c1926 converted into a hotel and restaurant overlooking a marina and boatyard just across the road. Nicely-furnished rooms create a peaceful and serene location for enjoying all the coastal water activities, including Mexico, just 30 mins away. You're in the heart of the Gulf Coast seafood country with a fine restaurant on the premises offering local specialties, steaks and prime rib. You're close to all activities including miles of beautiful beaches, bay or off-shore fishing charters and a cruise ship port (free transportation included from this location). Meals: Continental breakfast is included with other meals available on the premises. Heated pool and phones in rooms. **Seasonal:** No **Reservations:** Deposit required at res time with credit card number; 48 hr cancel policy for refund; 2pm check-in. Add 10% tax to room rates. **Brochure:** Yes **Permitted:** Children, drinking, smoking, limited pets **Conference:** Yes for groups to 100 persons **Languages:** Spanish **Payment Terms:** Check AE/DC/MC/V [Z06EPTX-2740] **COM** Y **ITC Member:** No

Rates:	Pvt Bath 24
Single	$ 45-59.00
Double	$ 45-69.00

Chism Trail Ranch	PO Box 649 76078	**Rhome TX**
Lee Ann Parker		**Tel:** 800-216-8865 817-638-2410 **Fax:** 817-636-2411
		Res Times 4pm-11am

The *Chisholm Trail Ranch* is a *"True & Authentic Working Cattle Ranch!"* This ranch is located on the original Chisholm Cattle Trail - and includes a historic native stone home built in 1883 which has withstood Indian attacks and stands as a tribute to the pioneer's struggle to tame the West. Actual Indian and pioneer confrontations have occurred on the ranch, many of which are documented and published in Wise County literature. Natural springs and Indian artifacts linger in the mystic rolling hills where deer, bobcats, raccoons and coyotes roam the 2,000 acres of wilderness. There are twelve stocked fishing lakes providing water for all of the wildlife. The ranch can host groups as well as individuals, providing a full range of amenities and activities including barn dances, hayrides, barbecue, sunrise breakfasts, campfire dances and western weddings. The ranch is perfect for company and private picnics, family reunions, corporate team building with complete meeting facilities. For individuals, the Bed & Breakfast Lodge provides a rustic, romantic and relaxing getaway with over 5,000 square feet of room. A two bedroom cottage, surrounded by beautiful oaks, rolling hills and a peaceful country atmosphere is available for those interested in complete seclusion. The ranch has two miles of paved road for walking, jogging and biking. Pool tables, basketball, horseshoes, volleyball, fishing and horseback riding are just a few of the activities. For a real western time, you'll get your fill of barbecue, sing western songs and rustle up all of the Old West with singing cowboys, wood-en dance floors and Wild West Times-just 30 minutes from downtown Fort Worth and DFW airport. **Airport:** DFW-30 mins **Packages:** Two nights and longer **Seasonal:** No **Reservations:** 20% deposit, 30 day cancel policy for refund less 10% service fee **Brochure:** Yes **Permitted:** Children, limited pets, drinking, limited smoking **Conference:** Perfect place for group events including indoor meeting space for small groups **Languages:** Spanish **Payment Terms:** Check AE/MC/V [I03HPTX1-21505] **COM** U **ITC Member:** No

Rates:	Pvt Bath 2	Shared Bath 5
Single	$ 95-125.00	$ 85-95.00
Double	$ 95-125.00	$ 85-95.00

Anthonys By The Sea B&B	732 S Pearl St 78382	**Rockport TX**
Denis - Tony		**Tel:** 800-460-2557 512-729-6100
		Res Times 24 Hrs

Featured in *"New York Times Travel Section"* November 11, 1995, *Anthony's By The Sea* is on two-thirds of an acre hidden by Live Oaks. This quiet retreat with many amenities is within walking distance of Rockport Beach Yacht Club and museums. Spacious Honeymoon Suite, master suite, full guest houses that include refrigerators, cable TV and VCR. The guest houses sleep six and has a fully equipped kitchen. It is ideal for families and small groups. Our Lanai is covered, carpeted with chandeliers, plants, BBQ and fountain. All add to the ambience of Anthony's. Casual, friendly and affordable. Your memory of *Anthony's* will make a return visit to the Texas Riveria a must. Your visit to *Anthony's* includes a gourmet breakfast served in the large open dining area or on the patio. While eating you might see hummingbirds, butterflies, squirrels or geckos playing in their natural environment. **Airport:** Corpus Christi-35 mi **Seasonal:** No **Reservations:** One night deposit, 72 hr cancel policy for refund **Brochure:** Yes **Permitted:** Children, pets, drinking, smoking **Conference:** Yes, specializing in weddings, receptions and conventions, dinner parties, and catered parties **Payment Terms:** MC/V [I03IPTX1-23768] **COM** U **ITC Member:** No

Rates:	Pvt Bath 2	Shared Bath 2
Single	$ 65.00	$ 65.00
Double	$ 70.00	$ 70.00

Trails End B&B — Round Rock TX
JoAnn & Tom Patty
Tel: 800-850-2901 512-267-2901
Res Times 10am-10pm

Refer to the same listing name under Leander, Texas for a complete description. **Payment Terms:** Check AE/MC/V [M07GPTX-20116] **COM** Y **ITC Member:** No

Rates:	Pvt Bath 3
Single	$ 55-78.00
Double	$ 65-95.00

Trails End B&B — Salado TX
JoAnn & Tom Patty
Tel: 800-850-2901 512-267-2901
Res Times 10am-10pm

Refer to the same listing name under Leander, Texas for a complete description. **Payment Terms:** Check AE/MC/V [M07GPTX-20117] **COM** Y **ITC Member:** No

Rates:	Pvt Bath 3
Single	$ 55-78.00
Double	$ 65-95.00

B&B On The River — 129 Woodward Place 78204 — San Antonio TX
AD Zucht
Tel: 210-225-6333

Set on the slopping banks of the San Antonio River, this romantic Victorian home has been recently fully restored. It is located in the block between the King William Historic District and the famous Riverwalk, and its shops and restaurants. All rooms have queen sized beds and large enclosed porches overlooking the river. Guests are within easy walking distance of the convention center, the Alamo, La Villita and other downtown tourist attractions. A continental breakfast is included. **Reservations:** 50% deposit at reservation time. **Permitted:** Limited children, limited smoking **Languages:** Spanish **Payment Terms:** Check DC/MC/V [R09CPTX-11501] **COM** Y **ITC Member:** No

Rates:	Pvt Bath 5
Single	$ 60.00
Double	$ 80.00

National Edition   *Texas*

Beckmann Inn & Carriage House   222 E Guenther St 78204   **San Antonio TX**
Betty Jo & Don Schwartz   **Tel:** 800-945-1449 210-229-1449 **Fax:** 210-229-1061
                                                                                              Res Times 8am-10pm

The perfect location to enjoy San Antonio at its best! An elegant and charming Victorian home built in 1886, located in the King William Historic District in the heart of San Antonio. The beautiful landscaped Riverwalk starts across the street and will take you leisurely to the Alamo, downtown shops and restaurants. Or, take the trolley, which stops at the corner, and within minutes you're there in style. A beautiful wrap-around porch warmly welcomes guests to the main house and wonderful Victorian hospitality - while white wicker furniture invites you to relax and enjoy your "welcome tea." The guest rooms feature antique Victorian queen size beds, private baths and colorfully decorated furnishings. Your complimentary gourmet breakfast with a breakfast dessert is served in the formal dining room on fine china with crystal and silver. A very special breakfast for our very special guests. The quiet and relaxed atmosphere offers a special respite after a full day of sightseeing - and a wonderful place to *"come home to."* AAA and Mobil approved **Airport:** San Antonio Intl-15 mins **Discounts:** Midweek on availability **Seasonal:** No **Reservations:** One night deposit to guarantee reservations, balance due upon arrival; 7 day cancel policy for refund, 2 night min weekends, check-in 4-6 pm, other times only by prior arrangement **Brochure:** Yes **Permitted:** Limited children, limited drinking **Payment Terms:** Check AE/DC/DISC/MC/V [I04HPTX1-16975] **COM** Y **ITC Member:** No

Rates: **Pvt Bath 5**
Single $ 80-120.00
Double $ 90-130.00

Bullis House   621 Pierce St 78208   **San Antonio TX**
Alma & Steve Cross   **Tel:** 210-223-9426 **Fax:** 210-299-1479
                                                                               Res Times 7:30am-11pm

Lovely historic Texas mansion built in 1909 for US Cavalry Gen John Bullis. Massive white columns frame the wide veranda and carriage-way. Within the neo-Classical-style home are geometrically patterned floors of fine woods, oak paneling and staircases, crystal chandeliers, decorative 14-ft plaster ceilings with large medallions, marble fireplaces and much more. All of the guest rooms are individually decorated in pastel colors and have quality antique reproductions. Within the spacious rooms are remote control TV, am/fm clock radios, heating/cooling units and beautiful chandeliers. Two guest rooms have phones and private baths; all the other rooms share three hall baths conveniently nearby. Fireplaces are located in most rooms along with French doors that open to bring in evening breezes. Other amenities include: large swimming pool, badminton, table tennis, volleyball and croquet. This Inn is available for weddings, receptions, business meetings and family reunions. Weekday and honeymoon packages are available. A continental-plus breakfast is included. **Seasonal:** No **Reservations:** Payment in full, 5 day cancel policy; no refund if less than 5 day cancellation notice **Brochure:** Yes **Permitted:** Children, smoking, drinking **Conference:** Yes, four parlors and landscaped garden area outdoors, catering available. **Payment Terms:** Check AE/DISC/MC/V [I10GPTX1-2745] **COM** YG **ITC Member:** No

Rates: **Pvt Bath 2**   **Shared Bath 6**
Single $ 65.00 $ 41-55.00
Double $ 69.00 $ 45-59.00

Riverwalk Inn   329 Old Guilbeau 78204   **San Antonio TX**

Texas *National Edition*

Jan & Tracy Hammer   **Tel:** 800-254-4440 210-212-8300 **Fax:** 210-229-9422

Five two-story log homes, relocated from Tennessee have been combined to form the two buildings of the *Riverwalk Inn*. The log homes were built from cottonwood trees which means "Alamo" in Spanish and date c.1842 (six years after the Battle of the Alamo). The homes were brought to San Antonio log by log and reconstructed to their original authenticity. It is the *Riverwalk Inn's* mission to have our guests relive the history of the old San Antonio, through the lifestyle of our Tennessee brothers, Davy Crockett and James Bowie ... who fought for Texas independence at the Battle of the Alamo. Our rooms have been named in honor of these historic people. The Riverwalk Inn, decorated in period antiques creates and ambience of *"country elegance." "Rock 'till you drop"* on our eighty foot porch lined with rocking chairs. Enjoy Aunt Martha's complimentary evening desserts and local story tellers that join us for our expanded complimentary breakfast. Amenities include fireplaces, refrigerators, private baths, phones, balconies, TV and Conference Room. A Texas tradition with a Tennessee flavor awaits you at the *Riverwalk Inn*. Exit Durango off IH-37, take a right, cross Alamo and St Mary streets, right on Aubrey. Call for brochure. **Discounts:** AAA, AARP **Airport:** San Antonio-15 mins **Reservations:** One night deposit, check-in 3-6pm **Brochure:** Yes **Permitted:** Limited children, limited drinking **Conference:** Accommodate groups to fifteen **Languages:** Spanish **Payment Terms:** Check AE/DISC/MC/V [I04I-PTX1-19703] **COM** YG **ITC Member:** No

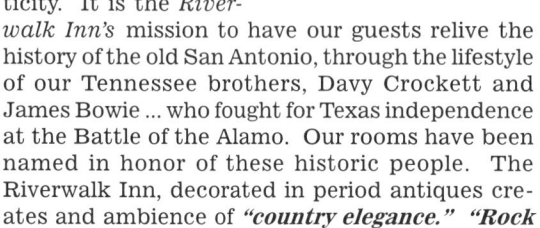

Rates: **Pvt Bath 11**
Single $ 89-145.00
Double $ 89-145.00

Crystal River Inn   326 W Hopkins 78666   San Marcos TX
Mike & Cathy Dillon   **Tel:** 512-396-3739 **Fax:** 512-353-3248

A romantic 1883 Victorian featuring fountain courtyard with topiaries and twinklelights, lots of wicker on the veranda and brandy and chocolates at bedtime. Close to antiquing, wineries, theme parks, whitewater sports, Austin, San Antonio, historical district and great shopping. All twelve guest rooms are designer furnished with tubs, fireplaces, canopied beds, private balconies, TV, phone and VCRs. A complimentary full gourmet breakfast often includes Bananas Foster, crepes or stuffed French toast with apricot sauce. Romantic interludes, murder mysteries and river trips are planned throughout the year. **Reservations:** Deposit required at res time. *Weekday rates; weekend rates are $60-100.00. **Brochure:** Yes **Permitted:** Smoking, drinking, children by prior arrangement. **Payment Terms:** Check AE/MC/V [X11ACTX-2752] **COM** Y **ITC Member:** No

Rates: **Pvt Bath 10**   **Shared Bath 2**
Single $ 55-60.00
Double $ 55-60.00

Brown Pelican Inn   207 W Aries 78597   South Padre Island TX
Vicky L Conway   **Tel:** 210-761-2722
                                              Res Times 10am-8pm

The *Brown Pelican Inn* is located at the southern tip of Texas, on the famed South Padre Island - near Harlingen and Brownsville, Texas. The region's subtropical climate make the renowned beaches and clear Gulf waters a year-round attraction. Texas' largest national wildlife refuge, Laguna Atascosa, is just twenty-five minutes away, offering some of the country's best birding opportunities. Other popular activities in the area include fly fishing or board sailing in the Bay or the Gulf, shopping in Old Mexico, and beachcombing on the nearby beach. Restaurants, shopping and attractions are within easy walking distance of the Inn. The Brown Pelican is a place to relax, make yourself at home and enjoy personalized service. The porches are a great spot to sit and watch the sun set over the Bay. The Inn is comfortably furnished with American and European antiques; all

National Edition *Texas*

guest rooms have private baths, and most rooms have spectacular views. Breakfast in the parlor includes fresh-baked breads, fresh fruit, cereal, juice and gourmet coffee or tea. We invite you to join us for a *"unique island experience."* **Airport:** Harlingen-45 mi; Brownsville-S Padre Isl-30 mi **Discounts:** Extended stays 3+ nights **Packages:** Guided birding, fly fishing and shopping excursions with prior arrangements to meet your needs and interests, packages can include dining at local restaurants **Seasonal:** Rates vary **Reservations:** One night's deposit to confirm reservation, 10 day cancel policy for refund **Brochure:** Yes **Permitted:** Limited children, limited drinking, limited smoking **Conference:** Entire inn can be reserved for small groups **Languages:** Spanish (Un poco) **Payment Terms:** Check MC/V [R12GPTX1-21425] **COM** U **ITC Member:** No

Rates: **Pvt Bath** 8
Single $ 70-150.00
Double $ 70-150.00

McLachian Farm B&B	24907 Hardy Rd 77383	Spring TX
Jim & Joyce Clairmonte		Tel: 800-382-3988 409-350-2400
		Res Times 8am-9pm

This Bed & Breakfast is one of Houston's Best Kept Secrets! Set back off the road among huge sycamore and pecan trees planted by family members in 1934, you feel like you are stepping back in time to an era of gracious lifestyles and down-home hospitality. Wrap-around porches with swings and winding forest trails invite you to relax and reminisce about trips to grandma's when life was simpler. Rooms are beautifully decorated with family antiques and collectibles picked up by the owners during their travels. Owned and operated by the fourth generation McLachlan family members, it is unique in Texas for the history that is here. A full country breakfast is served! Located just one mile from Old Towne Spring, with over 150 shops to enjoy. **Discounts:** 10% Mon-Thursday **Airport:** Houston Intercontinental-20 mins **Reservations:** $25 deposit per night within 7 days, 14 day cancel policy for refund less $20 service fee **Brochure:** Yes **Permitted:** Smoking outdoors only, children 12-up **Conference:** Yes, to ten persons **Languages:** English **Payment Terms:** Check [R11FPTX-17183] **COM** Y **ITC Member:** No

Rates: **Pvt Bath** 3   **Shared Bath** 2
Single $ 65-75.00 $ 55-65.00
Double $ 65-75.00 $ 55-65.00

Hubbard House B&B	621 Cedar 75860	Teague TX
John & Ruth Duke		Tel: 817-739-2629
		Res Times Before 5pm

Four large pillars highlight this large 1903 red brick and white frame Georgian home. Having served as the *Hubbard House Hotel* for railroad employees during part of its history, today guests can relax and enjoy this completely renovated home. Furnished mostly with 1900 early American antiques and thick burgundy carpeting in mauve decor, each guest room is large and includes king size beds, individual a/c and cable TV. Five guest rooms with shared baths (two baths floor include large free-standing claw foot tubs) on the second floor while one guest room is located in the first floor. A second floor balcony porch with swings offers guests an excellent opportunity to relax throughout the day and evening. A full country breakfast (flexible hours until 9 am) is served in the large formal dining room on an unusual glass-topped antique pool table for guests enjoyment. Located in Teague, Texas (3,200 population) in a rural area of east central Texas, guests have a good stopping point during their trip. Teague is just 10 miles west of I-45 on US 84 and Texas 179; 110 miles from Dallas, 140 miles from Houston; 130 miles from Fort Worth and 55 miles from Waco and Baylor University. Teague is home of a very good summer rodeo, the B&RI Railroad Museum, Bodine's large junk and antique shop and beautiful ranch and excellent free-stone peach orchard country is a quiet escape to leisure country living. The *Hubbard House B&B* is on the

©Inn & Travel Memphis, Tennessee

Annual Christmas Tour of Homes during the first week of December. **Airport:** Dallas-Ft Worth-120 mi; Houston Intercontinental-120 mi **Packages:** 15% discount on double room rates when using entire inn **Seasonal:** No **Reservations:** One night's deposit with credit card to guarantee reservation **Brochure:** Yes **Permitted:** Limited children, limited smoking (outside only) **Conference:** Yes, for groups of 16-20 featuring country banquet cooking with prior arrangements. **Payment Terms:** Check AE/DC/MC/V [I04IPTX1-14921] **COM** YG **ITC Member:** No

Rates:	Pvt Bath 2	Shared Bath 4
Single	$ 60.00	$ 40.00
Double	$ 100.00	$ 60.00

Marys Attic 413 S College at Hwy 31 75702 Tyler TX
Mary Mirsky Tel: 903-592-5181
Res Times 9am-9pm

Enjoy this charming 1926 bungalow which has been gracefully restored by the present owner/host. This home was originally built using rough-cut 2 x 12 floor and ceiling joists and roof rafters. The lentils above the entrance doors and windows were hand hewn from thick rough-cut oak and are still in place and excellent condition. Ceilings are all nine foot with seven foot doorways. All of the rooms are furnished with lovely English and American antiques with many to choose from at Mary's antique shop next door. An ideal location on a beautifully-kept brick street, guests can leisurely walk to the center of downtown Tyler's business district and the north-end Azalea Trails. Nearby is the Municipal Rose Garden, Goodman Museum, Tyler Museum of Art, Annual Azalea Trails, Tyler Medical Complex, UT at Tyler and annual events such as Eisenhower Sister Cities International Golf Pro/Am. A continental breakfast includes fresh home-baked rolls and breads, pastries, coffee, tea and juice. Complimentary soft drinks are in the fridge at all times. **Seasonal:** No **Reservations:** Deposit at reservation time to guarantee room, 10 day cancel policy for refund, check-in 2pm, check-out 11am **Brochure:** Yes **Permitted:** Limited drinking **Payment Terms:** Check DISC/MC/V [Z01DPTX-8762] **COM** Y **ITC Member:** No

Rates:	Pvt Bath 2
Single	$ 60.00
Double	$ 75.00

Rosevine Inn 415 S Vine 75702 Tyler TX
Bert & Rebecca Powell Tel: 903-592-2221
Res Times 7-11am, 7pm

Rosevine Inn is located on a historical brick street in beautiful Tyler. All the rooms are individually decorated and include private baths. The hosts enjoy entertaining and visiting with guests and will help guide you to the many sights and shops in this scenic town. Huge formal breakfast is served daily. Game room is available for all guests to use. Bring your swim suit - an outdoor hot tub offers soothing relaxation - day and night! **Reservations:** One night's deposit in advance **Permitted:** Drinking, limited children **Payment Terms:** Check AE/DC/DISC/MC/V [A04GPTX-2756] **COM** Y **ITC Member:** No

Rates:	Pvt Bath 4
Single	$ 65.00
Double	$ 75.00

Casa de Leona B&B 1149 Pearsall Rd Hwy 140 78802 Uvalde TX
Ben & Carolyn Durr Tel: 512-278-8550
Res Times 7-10am/3-10pm

Casa de Lona is a Spanish Hacienda with all accommodations surrounding a beautifully landscaped courtyard and bounded on the west by the Leona River and on the east by Ft Inge (Pilot Point) hill. Set on seventeen acres of wilderness on the Leona River, guests relax around the calming and flowing courtyard fountains or explore this park setting. Amenities include antique furnishings, a/c and heating, ceiling fans, sun decks, wood-burning fireplaces, cable TV, a rustic guest cottage, formal areas and a music room. There's plenty of fishing, hiking, camping, picnicking, wildlife and bird watching, BBQ pits and picnic tables and guided tours are available with prior reservation. A complimentary continental plus breakfast is included in the room rate. This location is convenient to Ft Inge Historical Site, Cactus Jack Festival, John Nance Garner Museum, Grand Opera House, Sea World, The Alamo, Markets in Mexico and fine antique shopping. The climate is terrific all year with plenty of sunshine and mild winters. **Airport:** San Antonio Intl-90 mi **Packages:** Yes, inquire when calling **Seasonal:** No **Reservations:** 50% deposit, late arrival by prior arrangement only. **Brochure:** Yes **Permitted:** Drinking, smoking outdoors only **Conference:** Yes, perfect for small art workshops and business meetings. **Payment Terms:** Check AE/MC/V [I05FPTX-11162] **COM** YG **ITC Member:** No

Rates:	Pvt Bath 4	Shared Bath 2
Single	$ 65-79.00	$ 55.00
Double	$ 65-79.00	$ 55.00

Judge Baylor House B&B 908 Speight St 76706 Waco TX
Bruce & Dorothy Dyer **Tel:** 888-JBAYLOR 817-756-0273 **Fax:** 817-756-0711

Judge REB Baylor was the founder of Baylor University which was chartered by the Republic of Texas in 1845. The residence is adjacent to the campus and is just a three minute drive to downtown Waco. This two story red brick home has four bedrooms and the Judge Baylor Suite, all with private bath and king, queen or double size beds. Each room is spacious and beautifully appointed. The rooms have been remodeled and arranged for privacy with no two rooms sharing an adjacent wall. With only five rooms, Bruce and Dorothy provide quality personal time to their guests - whenever needed. Whether you want a time away from your busy daily activities, are celebrating a birthday or anniversary, spending your wedding night, visiting a Baylor student, attending a function, athletic event or business in Waco or the University - we believe your stay with us will be rewarding. The world's largest collection of material relating to Robert and Elizabeth Barrett Browning is located in the Armstrong-Browning Library just 1-1/2 blocks away. As a guest, you are free to come and go at your leisure and have use of the common rooms. A full breakfast is served at 8am weekdays (8:30 weekends) while an earlier breakfasts can be arranged with prior notice. Other meals are available with prior notice and additional cost. Whether you sit in the swing that hangs from a large ash tree in the front lawn, play the grand piano in the living room or just enjoy reading a new book, you will feel relaxed and at home at the *Judge Baylor House B&B*. **Packages:** Browning Weekends **Airport:** Waco Regional **Discounts:** Weekday rates available **Reservations:** One night's deposit or 50%, which ever is greater Email: jbaylor@iamerica.net **Brochure:** Yes **Permitted:** Children, drinking **Conference:** Small groups [I12IPTX1-27264] **COM** N **ITC Member** No **Quality Assurance** Requestred **Payment Terms:** DISC/V

Rates:	Pvt Bath 4	
Single	$ 79.00	$ 89.00
Double	$ 79.00	$ 89.00

BonnyNook Inn 414 W Main St 75165 Waxahachie TX
Bonnie & Vaughn Franks **Tel:** 800-486-5936 214-938-7207 **Fax:** 214-923-0646
  Res Times 8am-8pm

A wonderful Victorian experience awaits travelers at the *BonnyNook Inn*, complete with gingerbread trim and a beautiful wide porch surrounded by a front yard full of flowers - just perfect for an afternoon of relaxation. *Listed on the National Register of Historic Places* and recognized by Historic Waxahachie, the Inn has appeared in numerous publications including *Bon Appetit,* March 1993.

The meticulously restored exterior includes details of the Sunbursts, Fish Scales, Bull'seyes, Brackets and framework so popular with Victorian artisans while the interior is pure Victorian. Antiques and family heirlooms furnish guest rooms with a variety of decor from a Pennsylvania Sleigh Bed set, French Country Belgium to a 150 year old English Suite. All rooms include large private bath facilities (some with Jacuzzis), bouquets of fresh flowers and plants everywhere and a tray of snacks - from cheese and crackers to cookies and brownies and plants everywhere! A full complimentary breakfast is a real treat since both Vaughn and Bonnie take turns preparing special recipes ranging from applesauce pancakes, ginger pears, special crepes to shoo-fly pie .... along with traditional fare. The largest concentration of Gingerbread Homes in Texas can be enjoy by walking or taking a riding tour along with an art museum, shops and many fine antique and boutique shops on the square. A coffee nook is stocked with complimentary beverages for guests. Seven course prix fixe $35.00 private dinners are available at the Inn by advance reservation only. **Discounts:** Midweek, extended stays, corporate **Airport:** DFW-40 min **Seasonal:** No **Reservations:** First night's deposit or credit card number to guarantee reservation, 24 hr cancel policy for refund, except holidays and special events which require 7 days cancel notice **Permitted:** Limited children, drinking, limited smoking **Conference:** Banquet facilities for groups to thirty, large meeting room with TV, VCR, and fax **Payment Terms:** Check AE/DC/MC/V [I02HPTX1-10873] COM YG **ITC Member:** No

Rates:	Pvt Bath 5
Single	$ 70-95.00
Double	$ 70-95.00

Old Oaks Ranch B&B   PO Box 912 78676   **Wimberley TX**
Bill & Susan Holt   **Tel:** 512-847-9374
Res Times 24 Hrs

Old Oaks features three cottages; the Barn, Storehouse and Chickenhouse which offer privacy, serenity and plenty of Texas Hill Country hospitality. Huge live oaks, cedar fences, stone walkways and rustic surroundings create an ideal atmosphere for rest and relaxation. All three cottages are decorated with antiques, have comfortable beds, plenty of towels and linens, clean electric a/c and heating, ceiling fans, color TV and outdoor patios or porches. The Barn and Storehouse have fireplaces and there are two bedrooms, a fully equipped kitchen and dining area with the Storehouse. A continental plus breakfast is served in the main house or on the adjacent patio featuring kolaches, pastries, muffins, juice, fruit and coffee. Wimberly is a small village for fun shops, interesting art galleries, fine restaurants and a first Saturday of the month Trades Day Market from April to December where people come from miles around to talk trades and sales. With mild winter, year-round golf and tennis can be enjoyed at the nearby Woodcreek Country Club along with whitewater rafting and tubing the nearby Guadalupe River. *Old Oaks* is conveniently located a few miles out H12 north of Wimberly, right on CR 221 and 3/4 mile to the entrances on the left. **Airport:** Austin-40 mi **Discounts:** 10% weekdays **Seasonal:** No **Reservations:** Full payment at reservation time to guarantee, 7 day cancel policy for refund less $5 service fee; less than 7 days notice, two night cancellation fee charged, *individual cottages available **Brochure:** Yes **Permitted:** Children 12-up, drinking, smoking outdoors **Payment Terms:** Check MC/V [R07FPTX-13603] COM Y **ITC Member:** No

Rates:	Pvt Bath 3
Single	$ 65-70.00
Double	$ 65-85.00

Rancho Cama B&B   2595 Flite Acres Rd 78676-9707   **Wimberley TX**
Nell & Curtis Cadenhead   **Tel:** 800-594-4501 512-847-2596
Res Times 8am-10pm

National Edition ***Texas - Virginia***

Peaceful, pastoral, enticing setting under a canopy of live oaks with abundant swings and rockers form which guests enjoy the panoramic beauty of Hill Country and adorable miniature horses, donkeys and dwarf goats frolicking at Piddy Paddocks. The Guest House is cozy, charmingly appointed honeymoon-type cottage with queen bed, sitting area, window seat with library and electric organ while the Bunk House has two rooms with a shared bath. One has extra long twin beds; the other, a double bed and bunks. Both rooms may be occupied by guests traveling together and willing to share the bath; otherwise, only one of the two rooms will be rented to allow guests to enjoy a private bath. Both houses have refrigerator, coffee maker, color cable TV and phone. A beautiful pool and hot tub, access to Blanco River and bicycles are available for guests. A delicious, generous full breakfast is served beside the pool. See Rancho Cama in June/July, 1992 *"Country"* magazine! Quaint village of Wimberley is only three miles away, with many shops, galleries and restaurants tucked into huge cypress trees nourished by the Blanco River and Cypress Creek. Each first Saturday, shop the famous Lion's Market Day for the latest fashions, crafts, antiques and bargains. An artist's haven, shopper's paradise - a beautiful escape. **Discounts:** One night free on fifth visit **Airport:** Austin-45 mi; San Antonio-60 mi **Seasonal:** No **Reservations:** One night's deposit, late arrival only with prior arrangements **Brochure:** Yes **Permitted:** Limited drinking **Payment Terms:** Check [Z03HPTX1-17187] **COM YG ITC Member:** No

Rates:	Pvt Bath 1	Shared Bath 2
Single	$ 75-85.00	$ 60-80.00
Double	$ 75-85.00	$ 60-80.00

Inn On Town Creek 445 E Valley St 24210 Abingdon VA
Dr & Mrs Roger Neal Tel: 703-628-4560 Fax: 703-628-9611
Res Times 8am-9pm

Meander Virginia roads in the Appalachian mountains and you'll soon encounter The *Inn On Town Creek*, on the banks of a creek itself which flows with the rains and snows of centuries past. Landscaped with rock gardens, tiered brick walls and patios, guests are surrounded with magnificent rhododendrons, dogwoods and pines while enjoying the outside brick covered patio where time becomes lost among the wildlife that flourishes in this rustic setting. Inside, there are two complete guest suites and two bedrooms. The first suite has two bedrooms with a shared bath and full kitchen and dining area inside, extending to an outside patio. A second suite has a bedroom-living room combination with bath, small kitchen and a small porch. Single bedroom offers a king size bed and private bath while the other single room contains a double bed with a private bath. All accommodations are furnished with antiques and one suite offers a beautiful stained glass window. A full complimentary breakfast might include pancakes, hand and sausage, muffins or diet conscious granola, yogurt and Florida orange juice. For those who desire privacy, the suites include a microwave and refrigerator for preparing your meals. Nearby is Hemlock Haven for the young-at-heart and hardy. The rustic cabin, built in 1923 is eleven miles from Abingdon and offers a large central room with kitchen and stone fireplace, great for socializing and dining. An unusual hot water shower and an uphill "outhouse" (for the hardy) as well as a regular bathroom and sink with shower provide the necessary amenities - perfect for those who like to fish, hike, tube down the river, picnic, cuddle-up with a good book before a roaring fire or just relax and meditate. Abingdon offers a wealth of art galleries and specialty shops, libraries of Southern history and pleasurable hikes along the Virginia Creeper Trail, a former track bed for steam locomotives that plied Virginia. **Airport:** Tri-City-40 mins **Seasonal:** No **Reservations:** Room payment in advance, 7 day cancel notice for refund; Hemlock Haven has a five day min and requires a two night deposit, available April through October **Brochure:** Yes **Permitted:** Drinking, smoking outside on covered porch **Payment Terms:** Check MC/V [I02HPVA1-18098] **COM YG ITC Member:** No

Rates:	Pvt Bath 4	Shared Bath 2
Single	$ 85-95.00	
Double	$ 85-95.00	$ 165.00

©*Inn & Travel Memphis, Tennessee*

Summerfield Inn	101 W Valley St 24210	Abingdon VA
Champe & Don Hyatt		Tel: 703-628-5905 703-628-5873
		Res Times 8am-10pm

Just off I-81 in Old Abingdon and half-way between Roanoke Virginia and Knoxville Tennessee, Summerfield sits at a 2200 foot altitude, surrounded by gorgeous mountain scenery, historic areas, world-renowned Barter Theater and an unusual selection of fine dining and shopping facilities. The Inn exudes an aura of another era; family portraits hand in the bedrooms and hallways, antique furniture is centered around a large portrait of the owner's children and occupies almost every corner while ceiling fans turn nearly as slowly as the pace enjoyed by the guests. The beautifully co-ordinated decor extends to the public living room, handsomely appointed morning room, sunroom-card facility and the outdoor porch with porch swings and wicker rockers for enjoying the cool evenings. Nearby are the Virginia Creeper Trail (27 mi of hiking and biking), the Appalachian Trail, Mt Rogers Natl Recreation Area, lakes, golf courses and tennis courts. The Annual Highlands Art and Crafts Festival & Antique Flea Market in August attracts thousands of tourists. Bater Theater is open from late April to November. A continental breakfast is included. **Seasonal:** No **Reservations:** One night's deposit at res time, 48 hr cancel policy less $10 service fee **Brochure:** Yes **Permitted:** Children 12-up, limited smoking **Payment Terms:** Check MC/V [R02BCVA-5052] **COM** Y **ITC Member:** No

Rates: Pvt Bath 4
Single $ 60-65.00
Double $ 70-87.00

Morrison House	116 S Alfred St 22314	Alexandria VA
Cari M Goodman		Tel: 800-367-0800 703-838-8000
		Res Times 24 Hrs

In the heart of Alexandria's historic Old Town, *Morrison House* features the charm of an 18th century-style manor house. Conveniently located just minutes from National Airport and public transportation, *Morrison House* is a comfortable base for exploring the monuments, museums and nightlife of Washington DC and the antique shops and waterfront of Alexandria. The 45 exquisitely appointed rooms are decorated with Federal period reproductions. Adding to the elegance are brass and crystal chandeliers, Italian marble baths, four-poster mahogany beds and decorative fireplaces. Afternoon tea is served each day in the Parlor and 24-hour concierge, butler and room service is available. Gourmet dining is available in the formal Dining Room or the pub-like Grill, with nightly entertainment. Regional American cuisine features fresh seasonal specialties. Voted 1990 *"Best Inn of The Year"*, Morrison House has also earned Four-Star and Four Diamond ratings from Mobil and AAA. **Seasonal:** No **Reservations:** Guarantee to a credit card, 24 hr cancel policy for refund. Corporate rates & weekend packages available. **Brochure:** Yes **Permitted:** Children, drinking, smoking **Conference:** Excellent capabilities for special business meetings, receptions, dinners, teas and etc. **Lang-uages:** French/Spanish/German/Russian **Payment Terms:** Check AE/DC/MC/V [Z11BPVA-5058] **COM** Y **ITC Member:** No

Rates: Pvt Bath 45
Single $ 135-200.00
Double $ 135-200.00

Newport House		Blacksburg VA
Harold & Pamela Kurst		Tel: 703-961-2480

Refer to the same listing name under Newport, Virginia for a complete description. **Seasonal:** No **Payment Terms:** Check MC/V [M02BCVA-6570] **COM** Y **ITC Member:** No

Rates: Pvt Bath 3
Single $ 80.00
Double $ 80.00

Oaks B&B Country Inn		Blacksburg VA

National Edition   *Virgina*

Tom & Margaret Ray   **Tel:** 800-336-OAKS 703-381-1500
Res Times 8am-10pm

Refer to the same listing name under Christ-iansburg, Virginia for a complete description. **Seasonal:** No **Payment Terms:** Check [M12BPVA-9808] **COM** Y **ITC Member:** No

Rates:	Pvt Bath 3	Shared Bath 2
Single	$ 75-95.00	$ 65-85.00
Double	$ 75-95.00	$ 65-85.00

Old Mansion   PO Box 845   22427   Bowling Green VA
Ruth Curlee & Peter Larson   **Tel:** 804-633-5781

A 1669 residence with a grand history that has been fully restored and furnished as original. George Washingtons' troops camped on the grounds on their way to Yorktown in 1781. Now guests play croquet on the beautiful grounds with ancient boxwoods, lovely gardens and cedars. The full breakfast includes specialties of farm-fresh eggs, country sausage and homemade breads. Historical sights abound. **Seasonal:** No **Brochure:** Yes **Permitted:** Children and limited pets, social drinking **Payment Terms:** Check [X11ACVA-5061] **COM** Y **ITC Member:** No

Rates:	Pvt Bath 2	Shared Bath 1
Single	$ 55.00	$ 65.00

Chesapeake Charm B&B   202 Madison Ave   23310   Cape Charles VA
Phyllis & Barry Tyndall   **Tel:** 800-546-9215 757-331-2676

Discover one of the last unspoiled treasures of Virginia . . . Cape Charles on the Eastern Shore. A perfect setting for the special birthday, anniversary or just to escape the pressures of today. *Chesapeake Charm B&B* offers all the modern conveniences of today in yesterday's setting, including period antiques, private baths and individually controlled heating and a/c. Stroll two blocks to enjoy sunning on the Chesapeake Bay beach and the Eastern Shore's spectacular sunsets. Bicycles are available to ride and enjoy the historic architecture of Cape Charles. For the sports minded, golf, tennis and chartered fishing are available. Venture out of town and nature lovers will find the unique ecosystem the Eastern Shore has to offer by hiking trails at the National Wildlife Refuge or Kiptopeke State Park. For a more restful trip, enjoy a book on our breezy front porch in one of our rockers or porch swing. Let us pamper you with our leisurely breakfast which includes homemade breads, muffins, or sweet rolls and our daily entree. Afternoon refreshments are made fresh daily that will remind guests of the treats from "grandma's kitchen." Special arrangements for flowers, candy or a picnic lunch can be arranged with advance notice. *Discover the Charm . . . Chesapeake Charm!* **Airport:** Norfolk Intl-45 mi **Reservations:** 50% deposit or credit card number to guarantee, 2 week cancellation notice for full refund **Brochure:** Yes **Permitted:** Children, drinking, limited smoking **Payment Terms:** Check MC/V [R10IPVA1-26930] **COM** YG **ITC Member:** No

Rates:	Pvt Bath 3
Single	$ 65-85.00
Double	$ 65-85.00

Picketts Harbor B&B   Box 97AA   23310   Cape Charles VA
Sara & Cooke Goffigon   **Tel:** 804-331-2212
Res Times 5pm-9pm

Featured in *"Mid-Atlantic Country"*, Feb 1990 is Pickett's Harbor nestled on twenty seven acres of Chesapeake Bay private beach at the southernmost tip of the Delmarva Peninsula (four miles north of the Chesapeake Bay Bridge Tunnel) - on Virginia's Historic Eastern Shore. Acres of beach are delightful for walking, shelling, fishing and swimming. Tennis courts, golf course and excellent seafood dining nearby. The land around the house was part of the original acreage Sara's English ancestors farmed in the 1600's arriving not long after Capt John Smith explored the peninsula in 1608. Pickett's Harbor, built in 1976, is traditional in style with high ceilings, fireplaces, tra-

©*Inn & Travel Memphis, Tennessee*   3-121

ditional furnishings, antiques and modern conveniences but with touches like floorboards and cupboards fashioned from 200 year-old barns along the James River. Sara serves a full country breakfast of homemade breads and jams, fruit in season, Virginia ham, quiche, eggs and casseroles. **Reservations:** Full deposit for one night stays; 50% deposit for longer periods **Permitted:** Children 6-up, social drinking, smoking outdoors, limited pets **Payment Terms:** Check [I05HPVA1-14076] **COM YG ITC Member:** No

Rates:	Pvt Bath 3	Shared Bath 3
Single	$ 75.00	$ 65.00
Double	$ 85-95.00	$ 75-85.00

Edgewood Plantaion   4800 John Tyler Hwy   Charles City VA
Dot & Julian Boulware   Tel: 800-296-EDGE 804-829-2962   Fax: 804-829-2962
Res Times 8am-11pm

Edgewood Plantation dating 1849 is just outside of Williamsburg in Plantation Country with lush green farm land on the oldest historical Virginia byway. *Edgewood* sits on a hill with huge oak trees, an English Garden and Benjamin Harrison's 1725 grist mill inviting you to the gothic mansion. Inside you will find true Virginia hostesses Julian and Dot Boulware. They are ready to share stories of Edgewood's history, their knowledge of antiques and a relaxing evening with their guests. Inside are six bedrooms; old canopy beds, antique linens, period clothing, oriental rugs, sitting areas in each room and ten fireplaces. Out back, in the servant's quarters, house two bedrooms, one used as a suite. Breakfast is enjoyed in a candle-lit dining room or outside in the gazebo by the pool. A new addition is the refurbished tavern that once served as a kitchen with warming ovens for breads made from grain in the grist mill. This tavern serves us well for corporate meetings and guest functions. Our new addition is the Victorian Tea Room used for High Tea for groups of eight or more. Call for reservations. This gothic mansion has been featured in *"Early American Life"* 1987; *"Southern Living"* 1988; *"Country Homes"* 1989; *"Traditional Country Christmas"* 1991 (the holidays are very special as we feature twenty Christmas trees); and the front cover of *"Country Victorian"* magazine 1992, *Country Inns*, Christmas 1993 featured Inn with eight page spread. A full complimentary breakfast, complimentary drink or dessert at nearby restaurants when dining there and refreshments upon arrival. *Edgewood* is a place where you collect memories. **Discounts:** Jan-March; booking entire property **Airport:** Byrd-28 mi **Packages:** Yes, inquire at res time **Seasonal:** No **Reservations:** Credit card number for one night's deposit, 15 day cancel policy; less than 15 days cancel notice refund only if room is re-booked. Arrival 3-6 pm, later only with prior arrangement *Suites available **Brochure:** Yes **Permitted:** Children 12-up, limited drinking **Conference:** Can seat groups to 35 persons **Payment Terms:** Check MC/V [Z08HPVA1-6882] **COM YG ITC Member:** No

Rates:	Pvt Bath 6	Shared Bath 2
Single	$ 105.00	$ 175.00
Double	$ 138.00	$ 175.00

North Bend Plantation B&B   12200 Weyanoke Rd 23030   Charles City VA
George & Ridgely Copeland   Tel: 800-841-1479 804-829-5176
Res Times 9am-3pm*

Enjoy old Virginia hospitality in this *National Register property* in Virginia Plantation Country. North Bend was built in 1819 using designs of noted architect/builder Asher Benjamin. It was the home of Sarah Harrison, sister of William Henry Harrison, ninth President of the US. During the Civil War, General Sheridan headquartered here and his desk remains in the Sheridan Room. The handsome two-story frame manor showcases the Federal Period with it's original mantels, staircarvings, wood graining and faux marble. It's 850 acres remain under cultivation by the owner who is the great great nephew of the ninth President and the great great grandson of Edmund Ruffin, the southerner who fired the first shot in the Civil War. Large rooms are beautifully appointed with antiques original to the house and family including magnificent tester, canopy and sleigh beds. Private bath

Virgina

facilities are included with three porches, a billiard room, pool and lawn games for guests to enjoy. A full complimentary breakfast and refreshments upon arrival are provided. Just 30 minutes west of Williamsburg. Your hosts will gladly arrange dinner reservations for you at two local taverns with 4-star ratings. Tour local historic plantations. ABBA Rated 3-Crown Excellent **Discounts:** Travel agents **Airport:** Richmond Intl-15 mi **Seasonal:** No **Reservations:** 50% deposit at res time, check-in 3pm, check-out 11am *Reservations after 6pm also **Brochure:** Yes **Permitted:** Children 6-up, drinking, limited smoking (not permitted in bedrooms) **Conference:** Perfect place for those special, intimate weddings and private parties for groups to fifteen **Payment Terms:** Check MC/V [I03HP-VA1-5066] **COM YG ITC Member:** No

Rates:	Pvt Bath 4
Single	$ 85-120.00
Double	$ 95-130.00

Clifton Country Inn   1296 Clifton Inn Dr 22901   Charlottesville VA
*Craig & Donna Hartman   Tel: 804-971-1800 Fax: 804-971-7098
                                                                     Res Times 8am-5pm

See why we were named *"One of America's 12 Best Inns"* February, 1993 issue of *"Country Inns"* magazine. Clifton - The Country Inn is an 18th Century manor house, rich in history and appeal, lovingly preserved and beautifully appointed in antiques. Our guests have 24-hour access to a cookie jar and a beverage refrigerator, stocked with sparkling water and soft drinks. Every room has a fireplace that will be stocked when you arrive to take the chill out of the winter mountain air. In the warmer months enjoy swimming, tennis, croquet and horseshoes on our 40-acre property. Even try your luck fishing, or just relax on an innertube on our private lake. In the spring and summer you will marvel at our Yesteryear Gardens, featuring many beautiful and exotic flowers and herbs. Tickle the ivory on our grand piano or curl up with a good book in our paneled library. Our gourmet restaurant has become known for exquisite dining, compliments of our expert chefs, both graduates of the Culinary Institute of America. Enjoy our full plantation breakfast, included with your rate. Also join us for our nightly prix-fixe dinner at extra charge through out the week. On Friday and Saturday, dinner consists of six courses and includes entertainment prior to seating. Our property is perfect for banquets, wedding receptions, retreats and meetings as well. Only four miles from Monticello, National Landmark and home of Thomas Jefferson. **Discounts:** Yes, corporate travelers **Airport:** Charlottesville Albemarle Airport-15 mi **Seasonal:** No **Reserva-tions:** $100 deposit per night per room; 14 day cancel policy for refund less 10% service fee, less than 14 days, deposit is non-refundable **Brochure:** Yes **Permitted:** Children, drinking **Conference:** Meetings to 24 persons including lodging, meals and meeting area **Payment Terms:** Check AE/MC/V [I03HPVA1-778-4] **COM YG ITC Member:** No

Rates:	Pvt Bath 14
Single	$ 165-225.00
Double	$ 165-226.00

Firmstone Manor B&B Inn   Charlottesville VA
Marko & Danica Diana Popin   Tel: 703-862-0892 Fax: 703-862-3554
                                                                     Res Times 9am-10pm

Refer to the same listing name located under Clifton Forge, Virginia for a complete description. **Seasonal:** No **Payment Terms:** Check MC/V [M05DPVA-12616] **COM Y ITC Member:** No

Rates:	Pvt Bath 4	Shared Bath 4
Single	$ 85-125.00	$ 65-75.00
Double	$ 85-125.00	$ 65-75.00

Virginia   *National Edition*

Frederick House   Charlottesville VA
Joe & Evy Harman   **Tel:** 800-334-5575 703-885-4220
                                                           Res Times 7am-10pm

Refer to the same listing name under Staunton, Virginia for a complete description. **Seasonal:** Rates vary **Payment Terms:** Check AE/DC/DISC/MC/V [M02EPVA-6561] **COM** Y **ITC Member:** No

Rates: Pvt Bath 14
Single $ 65-115.00
Double $ 65-115.00

Trillium House   Charlottesville VA
Dinwiddie Family   **Tel:** 800-325-9126 804-325-9126
                                                             Res Times 9am-9pm

Refer to the same listing name under Nellysford, Virginia for a complete description. **Seasonal:** No **Payment Terms:** Check MC/V [M11CPVA-11838] **COM** Y **ITC Member:** No

Rates: Pvt Bath 12
Single $ 65-70.00
Double $ 89-90.00

Upland Manor   Charlottesville VA
Stan & Karen Pugh   **Tel:** 804-361-1101
                                                             Res Times 9am-9pm

Refer to the same listing name under Nellysford, Virginia for a complete description. **Seasonal:** No **Payment Terms:** Check MC/V [M03EPVA-15286] **COM** U **ITC Member:** No

Rates: Pvt Bath 10
Single $ 85-115.00
Double $ 85-115.00

Sims Mitchell House   PO Box 846 24531   Chatham VA
Henry & Patricia Mitchell   **Tel:** 800-967-2867 804-432-0595

Italianate home of the 1870's with spacious comfortable guest rooms including private entrances and modern bath. Lovely setting and interesting hosts with Henry, a planetarium specialist and photographer/etcher and Patricia, a noted cookbook author. Full breakfast included. Evening meals available for $10.00/person. **Seasonal:** No

Brochure: Yes **Permitted:** Children **Payment Terms:** Check MC/V [X11ACVA-5077] **COM** Y **ITC Member:** No

Rates: Pvt Bath 1
Single $ 45.00
Double $ 55.00

Miss Mollys Inn   4141 Main St 23336   Chincoteague VA
David & Barbara Wiedenheft   **Tel:** 800-221-5620 804-336-6686

In 1886, Mr JT Rowley, then known as the *"Clam King of the World,"* built a charming Victorian home on Chincoteague Island and his daughter, *"Miss Molly"* was one of the island's most loved citizens, living in her home until the age of eighty-four. Today her home has been beautifully restored and offers accommodations and warm hospitality. Guests are assured of good conversation, interesting antiques, gentle evening ocean breezes on the porch for a most relaxing and memorable experience. While writing the book, "Misty", Marguerite Henry stayed in this grand old home and in fact the plot was worked out while rocking on the same front porch guests use today! Guest rooms are furnished with antiques and are a/c. As Islands go, there are few around as charming as *"that beautiful land across water called Chincoteague"* and as Rachel Field said so lyrically *..."If once you have slept on an island You'll never be quite the same..."* **Discounts:** Yes, extended stays **Airport:** Salisbury MD-45 mi **Seasonal:** Clo:1/1-2/15 **Reservations:** Full payment with reservation,

4 day cancel notice for full refund. **Brochure:** Yes **Permitted:** Children 10-up, drinking **Conference:** Yes for weddings and small corporate meetings. **Payment Terms:** Check [Z01EPVA-5080] **COM** U **ITC Member:** No

Rates:	**Pvt Bath** 5	**Shared Bath** 2
Single	$ 59-105.00	$ 59-89.00
Double	$ 69-115.00	$ 69-99.00

The Garden & The Sea Inn — Chincoteague VA
Tom & Sara Baker — Tel: 800-824-0672 804-824-0672

Refer to the same listing name under New Church, Virginia for a complete description. **Seasonal:** Open: 3/15-11/30 **Payment Terms:** Check AE/DISC/MC/V [M12HPVA1-22848] **COM** YG **ITC Member:** No

Rates: **Pvt Bath** 5
Single $ 60-150.00
Double $ 60-150.00

Watson House B&B — 4240 Main St 23336 — Chincoteague VA
T&J Derrickson/D&J Snead — Tel: 800-336-6787 757-336-1564 **Fax** 757-336-5776
Res Times 8am-10pm

Featured on The Learning Channels *"Romantic Escapes,"* The *Watson House* is a recently restored Victorian Country home built in the late 1800's by David Robert Watson. Nestled in the heart of Chincoteague, we are within walking distance from favorite shops and restaurants. Our guest rooms are tastefully and individually decorated with charming Victorian and Country antique furnishings, nostalgic pieces, wicker and many special touches. Each room includes a/c, ceiling fans and private bath for the guest's comfort. Mingle with other guests over a warm imaginative hardy full complimentary breakfast served at your leisure in the dining room or on the verandah. For those fun-minded adventurers, we offer complimentary use of bicycles to explore our beautiful island and free use of beach chairs and towels to enjoy the beautiful beach. Guests can enjoy Chincoteague Island, Virginia's only resort island, world famous for its wild ponies that roam Assateague's seashore. Chincoteague is the gateway to the Chincoteague National Wildlife Refuge and Assateague National Seashore. A visit to Chincoteague Island is sure to leave you with memories you'll cherish forever. So come join us, a warm and friendly atmosphere with gracious southern hospitality awaits. **Discounts:** 5% AAA, AARP **Airport:** Salisbury, MD-1 Hr; Norfolk-2 Hrs **Packages:** Midweek Specials: 3 Nights, 4th night 1/2 price; 6 nights, 7th night free **Seasonal:** Clo 12/1-3/1 **Reservations:** 50% deposit, 7 day cancel policy for refund **Brochure:** Yes **Permitted:** Limited children, drinking, limited smoking **Conference:** Yes, call for details **Payment Terms:** Check MC/V [I05GPVA-18759] **COM** YG **ITC Member:** No

Rates: **Pvt Bath** 6
Single $ 55-95.00
Double $ 65-105.00

Oaks B&B Country Inn — 311 E Main St 24073 — Christiansburg VA
Tom & Margaret Ray — Tel: 800-336-OAKS 703-381-1500
Res Times 8am-10pm

Experience a Classic Queen Anne Victorian built in 1889 with a private separate cottage and gazebo including a spa and sauna. The *Oaks* is the focal point of the East Main Historic District and offers guests quiet elegance and romance in a magnificently restored home. Step from the spacious wrap around front porch into the expansive entry hall with high ceilings, stained glass windows and a grand staircase and happily recapture the timeless spirit of gracious hospitality of a century ago. The *Oaks* delights and welcomes every guest with tall sunny windows, ornate fireplaces, turrets, queen-size or king-size canopy beds, window nooks and graceful mixes of modern and fine antique furnishings. Amenities: Lavish breakfasts, complimentary fresh fruit and refreshments, fluffy terry robes, toiletries and supper with advance reservations. Just 8 miles from Virginia Tech (26,000 students) and Radford University (10,000 students). The *Oaks* is conveniently located 3 miles from I-81, 24 miles from the Blue Ridge Parkway & 22 miles from the Roanoke Airport. Its an easy drive to the Southern Highlands. **Seasonal:** No **Reservations:** One night's deposit at res time (credit card ok). Refunded cheerfully with prior notice, without handling charge. **Brochure:** Yes **Permitted:** Limited children, drinking, smoking **Conference:** Perfect as a top management retreat for groups to 15 persons. **Social:** Ideal for wedding receptions and other social events. **Payment Terms:** Check [R12BPVA-9504] **COM** Y **ITC Member:** No

Rates:	Pvt Bath 3	Shared Bath 2
Single	$ 75-95.00	$ 65-85.00
Double	$ 75-95.00	$ 65-85.00

Kinderton Manor	Route #1 Box 19A 23927	Clarksville VA
Peter & Gail Eaton		Tel: 804-374-4439
		Res Times 8am-9pm

Kinderton Manor, a classic Georgian manor home dating from the 1830's, cordially invites you to experience the graciousness and serenity of Southern Virginia's antebellum past. The manor features 19th century French wood-block printed paper and large, elegantly proportioned bedrooms, each with a private bath. Located on a hill surrounded by the grounds of the Kinderton Country Club, this challenging 18-hole championship course covers a terrain of rolling hills and magnificent trees. The clubs facilities include a driving range, tennis courts and a swimming pool. (Separate arrangements may be made through the Country Club). Adjacent to Virginia's largest lake, Lake Kerr, also known as Buggs Island Lake, an angler's and boater's paradise, it features walleyes, large and small-mouth bass and striped bass. A marina is nearby for renting both fishing and pleasure boats while excellent public boat ramps for your boat are nearby. *Kinderton Manor* delights in accommodating its guests in the finest of bed and breakfast traditions along with touches of our own Southern Hospitality. Each morning, guests are treated to a full country breakfast in our sunny dining room. In-addition to the beauty of the manor and the lake, landmarks and historical sites of interest are found in the surrounding towns and countryside. **Discounts:** Yes, 10% for stays of 4 nights and longer **Airport:** Raleigh NC-50 min **Seasonal:** No **Reservations:** $50 per day deposit required per room to guarantee reservation, 7 day cancel policy for refund **Brochure:** Yes **Permitted:** Children 10-up, drinking, smoking **Payment Terms:** [R07FPVA-13668] **COM** Y **ITC Member:** No

Rates:	Pvt Bath 4
Single	$ 55.00
Double	$ 65.00

Firmstone Manor B&B Inn	Rt 1 PO Box 257 24422	Clifton Forge VA
Marko & Danica Diana Popin		Tel: 703-862-0892 Fax: 703-862-3544
		Res Times 9am-10pm

A beautifully restored 1873 rose-hued English Victorian manor house with gazebo porch is surrounded by breathtaking views of the Allegheny mountains, streams, gardenside with many songbirds. Select one of eight guest rooms furnished in Victorian, European or Southwestern decor. A romantic suite decorated with white wicker and muted peach and grey tones awaits newlyweds and second-honeymooners. Each room has an appealing decor and queen beds. Original furniture, art and chandeliers belonging to Harry Firmstone can be found throughout. Located in the historic iron industry of southwest Virginia's Allegheny Highlands where the stacks of the Lucy-Selina furnace quietly stand today. Excellent hiking, biking trails; river canoeing, golf nearby; boating; antiquing; theatres. Limited secretarial service and Fax is available. A full gourmet or continental breakfast is included with your room with dinners available by reservation on Fri/Sat nights. Gift certificates available. Directions: I-64, Exit #10, to Rt 60 East, to Longdale Furnace. Cottages (Motel-style) are available on the grounds and offer: five one-bedroom suites (2-4 persons) and seven single/double rooms, private showers, smoking permitted, $35-75/night. A AAA Triple Diamond award B&B facility. **Seasonal:** No **Reservations:** 50% deposit with reservation, 14 day cancel policy for full refund except special festival weekends, no refund and two day minimum. **Brochure:** Yes **Permitted:** Children **Conference:** Mid-week business or social breakfasts and luncheon meetings for groups to 20 persons. Advance reservations are required. **Languages:** Serbo-Croation **Payment Terms:** Check MC/V [R05DPVA-10710] **COM** Y **ITC Member:** No

Rates:	**Pvt Bath** 4	**Shared Bath** 4
Single	$ 85-125.00	$ 65-75.00
Double	$ 85-125.00	$ 65-75.00

Marys Country Inn 2185 S Main St 22824 Edinburg VA
Mary & Jim Clark
Tel: 703-984-8286
Res Times Evenings

c1850's home with beautiful Jeffersonian French doors and huge windows that open onto a wrap-around front porch, just perfect for rocking the evenings & afternoons away while sipping complimentary iced tea and sherry. Scenic views, skyline drive, caverns, battlefield, and antique shops are just a few of the attractions. Full country breakfast with homemade biscuits a specialty. **Seasonal:** No **Reservations:** Deposit required with a 10-day cancellation notice for refund, less handling charge. **Brochure:** Yes **Permitted:** Children, limited smoking, limited smoking **Payment Terms:** Check [X11ACVA-5084] **COM** Y **ITC Member:** No

Rates:	**Pvt Bath** 2	**Shared Bath** 3
Single	$ 55.00	$ 45.00
Double	$ 65.00	$ 55.00

Caledonia Farm - 1812 47 Dearing Rd 22627 Flint Hill VA
Phil Irwin
Tel: 800-BNB-1812 540-675-3693 **Fax:** 540-675-3693
Res Times 10am-6pm

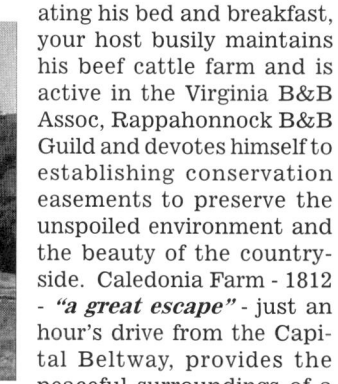

Caledonia, the mythological name for Scotland, honors the original immigrants to this magnificent area. The character of the English Irish countryside remains virtually unspoiled today - in Virginia's Rappahannock County. With Virginia's Blue Ridge Mountains in the background, *Caledonia Farm* offers guests a beautiful setting of scenic pasturelands surrounded by stone fences. The Federal-style house and companion summer kitchen were completed in 1812 and restored in 1965. The property is a Virginia Historic Landmark and is listed on the *National Register of Historic Places*. The guest rooms have working fireplaces, individual heat and a/c, views of the Skyline Drive and fine double beds. On the second floor of the main house are two private guestrooms and connected to the main house by a breezeway is the romantic 2-1/2 room guest house with the cooking fireplace of 1807. The winter kitchen's huge fireplace offers a delightful atmosphere. Enjoy an outstanding full breakfast menu choice which includes eggs benedict, smoked salmon, custom omelets and many unannounced extras, served at your preferred hour. In addition to operating his bed and breakfast, your host busily maintains his beef cattle farm and is active in the Virginia B&B Assoc, Rappahonnock B&B Guild and devotes himself to establishing conservation easements to preserve the unspoiled environment and the beauty of the countryside. Caledonia Farm - 1812 - *"a great escape"* - just an hour's drive from the Capital Beltway, provides the peaceful surroundings of a country estate making it a perfect location for business or governmental meetings, seminars and retreats. Top Rated AAA 3 Diamond, Top 5-Globe Award - A Treadway Inn Classic Inn designation, *Caledonia Farm* was recently selected *#1 in Virginia by INNovations for its hospitality, accommodations, scenery, history and recreation*. Adjacent to the Shenandoah National Park, farm activities include a spa, hayrides, bicycling, lawn games while nearby are caves, stables, climbing, canoeing, wineries, battlefields, golf, swimming, tennis and antiquing. **Airport:** Dulles Intl-1 hr **Packages:** Inquire at res time, (Weekdays, Jan-Sept) **Seasonal:** No **Reservations:** One nights deposit (full deposit if longer) deposit refunded only if re-rented less $20 service fee, two night min on 3-day holiday weekends and during October, 10am-6pm arrival **Permitted:** Children 12-up, drinking **Conference:** Groups to ten persons **Languages:** Danish, German **Payment Terms:** Check DISC/MC/V [I02HP-VA1-5166] **COM** YG **ITC Member:** No

Rates:	**Pvt Bath** 2	**Shared Bath** 2
Single	$ 140.00	$ 80.00
Double	$ 140.00	$ 80.00

Kenmore Inn/Fredericksburg	1200 Princess Anne St 22401	Fredericksburg VA
Alice Bannan		Tel: 800-437-7622 203-371-7622 **Fax:** 703-391-5480

The *Kenmore Inn* is a beautiful 18th century home converted into an elegant Country Inn and restaurant. Located in the heart of Fredericksburg, Virginia's historic district, guests are just steps from the home of our first president's mother, Mary Washington and many historical sites where our forefathers shaped the future of our then young Republic. Exquisitely appointed rooms offer private baths, eight working fireplaces (four located in guest rooms) and fine food are featured at the Kenmore Inn. A fine dining room serves lunch & dinner menus seven days a week, in which the chef places an emphasis on local produce. A wide choice of Virginia and domestic wines are available for dinner. Downstairs The Pub provides a relaxed, casual atmosphere for enjoying good company and fine spirits. Relax and be pampered in this wonderful & romantic old Inn. Enjoy the gracious ambience your hosts create for each guest through good food, fine wine, exquisite lodging and their own brand of Virginia Hospitality. High tea is served 3-4:30 daily. **Discounts:** AARP, Military **Packages:** MAP **Airport:** Washington National-50 mi; Dulles-60 mi; Richmond-50 mi **Seasonal:** No **Reservations:** Deposit or credit card to guarantee res, 72 hour cancel policy **Permitted:** Children, drinking, smoking **Conference:** Yes, private rooms available **Payment Terms:** Check AE/DC/MC/V [I06GPVA-2088] **COM** Y **ITC Member:** No

Rates:	**Pvt Bath** 12
Single	$ 85.00
Double	$ 95-150.00

Caledonia Farm - 1812		Front Royal VA
Phil Irwin		Tel: 800-BNB-1812 540-675-3693
		Res Times 9am-6pm

Refer to the same listing name under Flint Hill, Virginia for a complete description. **Payment Terms:** Check DISC/MC/V [M08GPVA-20166] **COM** Y **ITC Member:** No

Rates:	**Pvt Bath** 2	**Shared Bath** 2
Single	$ 140.00	$ 80.00
Double	$ 140.00	$ 80.00

Chester House B&B	43 Chester St 22630	Front Royal VA
Ann & Bill Wilson		Tel: 800-621-0441 703-635-3937

A stately Georgian mansion dating from the 1840s invites travelers to experience the warmth and hospitality of this historic residence and the charming hosts. Located in the heart of Front Royal's historic district, this former residence of Charles Samuels, a prominent international lawyer, remains much the same today with touches of antiques and contemporary pieces blended together for comfort. Guests can enjoy all the rooms including a library, a large living room with piano, fireplace and a writing desk and the beautiful patio with wrought iron furniture nestled into two acres of terraced gardens. The luxurious boxwoods, wisteria arbors, trees and shrubs, stone and

National Edition   *Virgina*

brick walls and seats with splashing fountains and statuary create your own *"Garden of Eden."* The Continental breakfast is served in the sunny dining room on bone china, silver, crystal and includes cold cereals, homemade bran muffins, huge homemade sticky buns with real cream, butter and homemade apricot preserves, and plenty of fresh squeezed orange juice and delicious coffee. Guests are within easy walking distance to the many historical sights and plenty of golfing, fishing, boating, tennis, canoeing, trail riding and hiking and camping along the Appalachian Trail. **Seasonal:** No

Reservations: One night's deposit at res time, 72 hr cancel policy for refund less 40% service fee **Brochure:** Yes **Permitted:** Drinking, limited children, limited smoking **Conference:** Yes for groups to 15 for business and social events, dining is also available **Payment Terms:** Check MC/V [X08BCVA-8538] **COM** Y **ITC Member:** No

Rates:	**Pvt Bath** 1	**Shared Bath** 5
Single		
Double	$ 110.00	$ 65-85.00

Killahevlin	1401 N Royal Ave 22630	Front Royal VA
Susan & John Lang	Tel: 800-847-6132 540-636-7335 **Fax:** 540-636-8694	
		Res Times 7am-9pm

Built at the turn-of-the-century and named to the *National Register* and *Historic Places* and the *Virginia Register*, *Killahevlin* is a stately Edwardian mansion situated on the highest spot in Front Royal, Virginia, which served as a Civil War encampment in 1864. Each of the property's professionally designed and restored guest rooms command spectacular views of the Blue Ridge or Shenandoah Mountains; all have working fireplaces adorned with antique mantels and luxurious private bathrooms - five with jacuzzi tubs, the one with an antique clawfoot tub original to the house. With a desire to reflect the strong Irish heritage common to the new owners as well as the original owner, on each floor of the three-story mansion, a wee bit of Ireland peaks out at guests. Complimentary beverages and snacks can be enjoyed in *Killahevlin's* private Irish Pub, at either of the two restored gazebos, on the spacious screened verandah or in winter, by the warmth of the parlor room's fireplace. Guests are welcomed to their room with a cozy evening turn-down service. A delicious full breakfast includes freshly brewed gourmet coffee and teas, fresh fruits and juices, specialty cereals, accompanied by home made muffins, breads and preserves. Your second course might include Belgian waffles and country sausage, french toast and crispy bacon, or a scrumptious omelette. Local attractions include: Skyline Drive and the Shenandoah National Park, George Washington National Forest, Bellegrove Plantation (National Trust), Cedar Creek and New Market battlefields, Skyline and Luray Caverns. Leisure activities include antiquing, canoeing, fine dining, golf, hiking, horseback riding, live theatre and wineries. Come to *Killahevlin* and prepare to be pampered! **Discounts:** Corporate midweek stays, National Trust **Airport:** Washington/Dulles-60 mi; Washington Natl-75 mi **Packages:** Yes, inquire at reservation time **Seasonal:** No **Reservations:** One night deposit or credit card number to guarantee reservation, 72 hr cancel policy for refund **Brochure:** Yes **Permitted:** Children 12+, drinking **Conference:** Great location for indoor and outdoor special occasions, private parties, business meetings for groups of 12 to 20 persons, weddings to 150 persons **Languages:** English (The Queen's) **Payment Terms:** Check AE/DISC/MC/V [I04IPVA1-16656] **COM** YG **ITC Member:** No

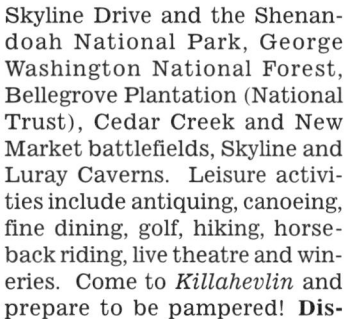

Rates:	**Pvt Bath** 6
Single	$ 105-170.00
Double	$ 105-170.00

Sleepy Hollow Farm B&B	Rt #3 Box 43 22942	Gordonsville VA
Beverly Allison		Tel: 703-832-5555
		Res Times 9am-10pm

Sleepy Hollow Farm lies on an historic country road near Montpelier, home of President James Madison. Colonial, Northern & Southern troops once trod over the countryside where cattle, sheep

---

©*Inn & Travel Memphis, Tennessee*   3-129

Virgina — National Edition

and horse farms now flourish. The farm is three miles north of Gordonsville, the charming historic railroad town where Union troops fought and failed to control. *Sleepy Hollow's* main brick house c1750, and chestnut cottage, once a slave cabin, are furnished with antiques and family heirlooms. Several sitting rooms, fireplaces, woodstoves, porches, terraces, gardens, and pond and a gazebo. Horseback riding, hiking, antiquing, and canoeing, historic sites and good restaurants are nearby. Horse stables are available. **Seasonal:** No **Reservations:** One night's deposit at booking; 7-day cancellation policy for refund; surcharge for credit card payments. **Brochure:** Yes **Permitted:** Children, pets, drinking, smoking **Languages:** French **Payment Terms:** Check MC/V [X02BCVA-5093] COM Y **ITC Member:** No

Rates: Pvt Bath 6
Single $ 55-60.00
Double $ 60-85.00

Tivoli 9171 Tivoli Dr 22942 Gordonsville VA
Phil & Sue Audibert Tel: 800-832-2225 703-832-2225

Tivoli is a unique three-story, twenty-four room hilltop Victorian mansion in the heart of Virginia's historic and scenic Piedmont Region. With its fourteen Corinthian columns, it commands views of the Blue Ridge Mountains in the distance and its own surrounding two hundred and thirty-five acre working cattle farm. *Tivoli* offers four carefully restored bedrooms, two with private baths, two with shared bath, and each with its own working fireplace. Included in the room rate is your choice of alcoholic and/or non-alcoholic beverages and a *"don't leave hungry" full American breakfast*, featuring big brown eggs from our chickens. With its ballroom, complete with Steinway grand piano, its twelve foot high ceilings, state-of-the-art kitchen and its antique-filled living and dining rooms, *Tivoli* offers ample space for wedding receptions, private parties, small conferences and seminars. Wineries, Civil War battlefields, Monticello, Montpelier, gourmet restaurants, Shenandoah National Park are all within easy driving distance. But best of all is the peace and quiet, the escape from the fast lane, and our easy-going hospitality, all of which we are eager to share with you. **Discounts:** 15% discount for booking all four guest rooms **Airport:** Charlottesville-22 mi **Reserva-tions:** One night's deposit required in advance, 7 day cancel policy for refund **Brochure:** Yes **Permitted:** Limited children, drinking, limited smoking **Conference:** Yes, for groups to thirty **Languages:** French, Spanish **Payment Terms:** Check MC/V [I02HPVA1-18709] COM YG **ITC Member:** No

Rates: Pvt Bath 2 Shared Bath 2
Single $ 75-100.00 $ 75.00
Double $ 100-125.00 $ 75-100.00

Hummingbird Inn Wood Lane 24439 Goshen VA
Diana & Jeremy Robinson Tel: 800-397-3214 540-997-9065 Fax: 540-997-0289
Res Times 8am-9pm

Accommodations in an early Victorian setting are offered by the *Hummingbird Inn* - in the beautiful Shenandoah Valley at the edge of the George Washington National forest. Dating from 1750, this unique Victorian Carpenter Gothic villa has operated as an Inn for many years and has been host to such celebrities as Eleanore Roosevelt. Architectural features include wraparound porch verandas on the first and second floor, original pine floors of varying widths, a rustic den and solarium. The guest rooms are comfortably furnished with antiques and combine old fashioned ambiance with modern conveniences. A more than full breakfast is served on lovely Meissen china and Early American Fostoria glassware. Breakfast specialties include fruit compote or fresh fruit in season, over-

National Edition *Virgina*

baked honey cinnamon french toast, omelettes, raisin-filled scones from a family recipe and rose geranium and lemon cakebreads. Elegant candlelight dining offers memorable four course continental meals such as chicken with wild porcini mushrooms, salmon with dill sauce and rabbit for two. Activities are endless and include golf, swimming, canoeing, tubing, fishing, hunting, hiking Goshen Pass, a spectacular rocky gorge and sampling the baths at Warm Springs and the Homestead. **Discounts:** 10% AARP **Packages:** Murder Weekend, Theater, Art Workshop **Reservations:** One night deposit required, 10 day cancel policy for refund **Brochure:** Yes **Permitted:** Well behaved children 12-up, drinking **Payment Terms:** Check AE/MC/V [I02HPVA1-13659] **COM** YG **ITC Member:** No **Quality Assurance:** Requested

Rates:	Pvt Bath 5
Single	$ 70-95.00
Double	$ 70-95.00

Vine Cottage Inn PO Box 918 Rt 220 24445 Hot Springs VA
Wendell Lucas Tel: 703-839-2422
Res Times 8am-11pm

Beautiful Virginia woodland setting at this guest house from the turn-of-the-century catering to guests' needs and offering antique furnishings and plenty of relaxation. Perfect setting for outdoor activities: championship golf courses, tennis, lake swimming, hunting, skiing, and the warm water hot springs at the Homestead. Continental breakfast included. **Seasonal:** No **Reservations:** Deposit required to hold res with 5-day notice for refund, less handling charge. **Brochure:** Yes **Permitted:** No pets, limited children, smoking, drinking **Payment Terms:** Check MC/V [X11ACVA-5097] **COM** Y **ITC Member:** No

Rates:	Pvt Bath 12	Shared Bath 2
Single	$ 50.00	$ 40.00
Double	$ 60.00	$ 50.00

Norris House Inn 108 Loudoun St SW 22075 Leesburg VA
Laura Walton/Libby Trevett Tel: 800-644-1806 703-777-1806 Fax: 703-771-8051

Historic district location for this fine example of 1806 architecture from the Virginias, that include beautiful antique furnishings throughout, plenty of atmosphere and history, and some guestrooms with fireplaces. Typical courtyard and English gardens for cool refreshing evenings. Full breakfast included. **Seasonal:** No **Reservations:** Deposit required to hold room; refunded if cancelled 5 days prior to arrival **Brochure:** Yes **Permitted:** Limited children, limited smoking **Payment Terms:** Check [X11ACVA-5102] **COM** Y **ITC Member:** No

Rates:	Pvt Bath 3	Shared Bath 4
Single	$ 65.00	$ 45.00
Double	$ 75.00	$ 55.00

Firmstone Manor B&B Inn Lexington VA
Marko & Danica Diana Popin Tel: 703-862-0892 Fax: 703-862-0892
Res Times 9am-10pm

Refer to the same listing name located under Clifton Forge, Virginia for a complete description. **Seasonal:** No **Payment Terms:** Check MC/V [M05-DPVA-12475] **COM** YG **ITC Member:** No

Rates:	Pvt Bath 4	Shared Bath 4
Single	$ 85-125.00	$ 65-75.00
Double	$ 85-125.00	$ 65-75.00

Jordan Hollow Farm Inn Luray VA
Marley & Jetze Beers Tel: 703-778-2285 Fax: 703-778-1759

©Inn & Travel Memphis, Tennessee

Virgina — National Edition

Refer to the same listing name under Stanley, Virginia for a complete description. **Seasonal:** No **Payment Terms:** Check DC/DISC/MC/V [M05FPV-A-16803] **COM** U **ITC Member:** No

Rates: Pvt Bath 21
Single $ 115.00
Double $ 140-180.00

Madison House	413 Madison St 24504	Lynchburg VA
Irene & Dale Smith		Tel: 800-828-6422 804-528-1503
		Res Times 9am-11pm

This beautiful circa 1880 Victorian, a fine example of Classic Italianate and Eastlake architecture (listed on the *National Register of Historic Places*) is located in Lynchburg's Historic Garland Hill District. The *Madison House* was selected for the *Historic Virginia Garden Club Tour* and has received the *Lynchburg Historical Foundation Merit Award*. Originally built for a tobacco baron, today the mansion features original woodwork, china bathroom fixtures, crystal chandeliers, a beautiful peacock stained glass widow, giant gold-leaf mirror, several original clawfoot tubs, seven fireplaces and a dining room with an exquisite antique 1850s English banquet table. The guest rooms are individually decorated in Victorian Period and are spacious, warm, comfortable and feature 100% cotton sheets, cozy bathrobes, plush linens, oversized bath towels and fireplaces in some. Your hosts enjoy sharing their private collection of antiques and their library with editions dating back to the 1700 & 1800s and numerous books on the Civil War. A full homemade breakfast featuring fresh fruit, homemade muffins, a hot daily entree, fresh perked coffee and the morning paper awaits guests at the breakfast table. Nestled in the foothills of the Blue Ridge Mountains, guests are centrally located to many Civil War battlefields, five colleges and universities, numerous antique shops, historic homes and churches, the Parkway and Skyline Drives, underground caverns, hiking and bike trails, weekend farmers' markets and fine restaurants. **Discounts:** Weekday, extended stays, travel agents **Airport:** Lynchburg Regional-5 miles **Seasonal:** No **Reservations:** 50% deposit (full payment in advance during May & October & two night min), 7 day cancel policy less $20 service fee. **Brochure:** Yes **Permitted:** Drinking, limited smoking **Conference:** Yes, for small intimate weddings and catered luncheon meetings and retreats. **Payment Terms:** Check MC/V [R06EPVA-14509] **COM** Y **ITC Member:** No

Rates: Pvt Bath 4
Single $ 60.00
Double $ 70-95.00

Riverfront House B&B & Cottage	Rt 14E 23109	Mathews VA
Mrs Annette Goldreyer		Tel: 804-725-9975
		Res Times 8am-10pm

This is a lovely nineteenth century farmhouse set right on the water! And among age-old shade trees on seven acres with plenty of tidal waterways and your own fishing dock for crabbing. A gracious entrance hall and staircase greets all guests, and handsome mantels and a wrap-around screened veranda for just relaxin'!! Plenty of activities nearby to explore that include all waterways, Williamsburg, plantations, and a quaint Virginia towns. Your lovely hostess will be glad to direct you to, all offering excellent antique shopping and fine dining, and plenty of craft shops. Private dock for your boat if you like, or you can take one of the boat tours to the Bay or Tangier Island and Rappahannock River. Full complimentary breakfast including a homemade specialty of the hostess, fresh baked muffins, and fresh garden fruits in season. Packed lunches are available for picnicking at nominal added cost. **Seasonal:** April-Nov **Reservations:** One night's lodging in advance, full payment on holidays. Late arrival notice. **Brochure:** Yes **Permitted:** Limited children, drinking, and smoking. **Languages:** Spanish **Payment Terms:** Check [A01DPVA-5112] **COM** Y **ITC Member:** No

Rates: Pvt Bath 6   Shared Bath 4
Single $ 52.00
Double $ 58-80.00

Wayside Inn	7783 Main St 22645	Middletown VA

Maggie Edwards

Tel: 703-869-1797 **Fax:** 703-869-6038

Welcome to the 18th Century where the past gently echoes throughout an elegantly restored Inn that also preserves the gracious service of a bygone era. Guests have been stopping by the Wayside since 1797 - to sample the local history, great outdoors, the mountain scenery and the gracious accommodations. Each of the twenty-four guest rooms and suites are uniquely decorated with rare antiques, fine art, object d'art and an interesting potpourri of memorabilia. Guests will find four-posters with canopies, cannonball and acorn carved detailings, French Provincial and Greek Revival period pieces all blended with modern comforts of private bath, special soaps, generous towels and individual climate control. You'll be glad to know some of the Inn's furnishings are available for purchase. Breakfast is not included in the room rate but breakfast and other meals are available in one of seven antique-filled dining rooms. You'll sample Regional American Cuisine such as peanut soup, spoon bread and country ham in the Lord Fairfax Room. A variety of game, seafood and homemade desserts are offered in the Old Slave Kitchen while the Portrait Dining Room provides a picturesque setting. The Shenandoah National Park and nearby ski resorts provide year-round activities with sightseeing at incredible nearby caves. Strasburg's museums, Wayside Antiques, Stonewall Jacksons Headquarters, Cedar Creek Battlefield and Belle Grove Plantation offer interesting trips. **Discounts:** Yes, 10% **Airport:** Dulles-60 mi; Wash Natl-75 mi. **Packages:** Romantic Escape, Dinner-Theatre **Seasonal:** No **Reservations:** Deposit required. **Brochure:** Yes **Permitted:** Children, drinking, smoking **Conference:** Excellent range of facilities for intimate business or social meetings to 25; evening dinners to 100 and gracious wedding or cocktail parties to 250 persons **Payment Terms:** Check AE/DC/MC/V [R01FPVA-5117] **COM** Y **ITC Member:** No

Rates: Pvt Bath 24
Single $ 65.00
Double $ 125.00

Guest Houses On The Water   Rt 354 PO Box 70   22517   Mollusk VA
Pam & Walt Smith

Tel: 804-462-5995 **Fax:** 804-462-5995
Res Times 7:30-10pm

The *Guest Houses On The Water* At Greenvale are two separate and very private houses on thirteen acres that overlook the Rappahannock River (-about two miles wide here) and the deep water of Greenvale Creek in historic Lancaster County. Greenvale Manor, now a private residence, circa 1840, is the centerpiece of these two dependencies. Enjoy the spacious lawns, 3400 feet of water frontage, and the atmosphere of yesteryear in your own private house with modern conveniences. Each house has a living room, kitchen two bedrooms, two baths, TV, phone and their own decks with sweeping views of the water. Each are furnished in antiques and reproductions. Unwind by swimming in the pool, sunning on the beach, crabbing or fishing from the dock, or just relaxing, listening to all the birds and watching beautiful sunsets. Bikes are available to explore the rural and peaceful countryside. Nearby are cruises on the Rappahannock or Chesapeake, championship golf, nature trails, antiquing, excellent seafood dining and historic sites. This is an ideal getaway for those who wish to be "far from the madding crowd." **Airport:** Richmond-1-1/2 hrs **Seasonal:** Rates vary **Reservations:** One night's deposit (full payment for weekly stays), 14 day cancel policy for refund less 10% service fee, 2 night min on summer weekends and year round for holiday weekends; weekly rates available **Brochure:** Yes **Permitted:** Children 16-up, drinking, limited smoking **Conference:** Yes **Payment Terms:** Check MC/V [Z07GCVA-6334] **COM** U **ITC Member:** No

Rates: Pvt Bath 2
Single $ 85-125.00
Double $ 85-125.00

Highland Inn   Main St 24465   Monterey VA
Michael Strand & Cynthia Peel

Tel: 703-468-2143
Res Times 9am-9pm

Classic Victorian Inn listed on the *National Register of Historic Places*. Tranquil, scenic location in the picturesque village of Monterey nestled in the foothills of the Allegheny Mountains. Seventeen

Virgina   *National Edition*

individually decorated rooms are furnished with antiques and collectibles, each with a private bath. Full-service dining room offers Continental Cuisine for dinner, Wednesday - Saturday and a Sunday Brunch. Nearby activities include antiquing, hiking, fishing, golf and mineral baths. **Seasonal:** Clo Xmas **Reservations:** Deposit or credit card for guarantee; 48-hr notice for cancellation with refund **Brochure:** Yes **Permitted:** Children, drinking, limited smoking **Conference:** Yes, with meeting rooms available. **Payment Terms:** Check MC/V [Z05FPVA-5119] **COM** Y **ITC Member:** No

Rates: Pvt Bath 17
Single $ 45-64.00
Double $ 45-64.00

Mark Eddy Manor	Rt 1 Box 375 22958	Nellysford VA
Joanne Maddox		Tel: 804-361-1101
		Res Times 9am-9pm

A quiet country escape conveniently located between the beautiful Blue Ridge Mountains and Thomas Jefferson's Charlottesville offers year-round relaxation. Perched on a knoll, *Mark Eddy Manor* was part of the huge Upland Estate until Dr JC Everett, a colorful physician acquired it in 1884 and expanded it in 1910. Beautifully restored to it's original grandeur, Upland Manor offers luxurious rooms and romantic suites. Guest rooms have a private bath with either a double whirlpool bath, double shower or an antique clawfoot tub with shower. For your comfort, each room is a/c, has a ceiling fan and features a feather comforter on an extra long bed. A continental plus breakfast is included and is served in the cheerful dining room. Activities abound from swinging in the hammock beneath the trees and rocking on the front porch to hot air ballooning, golf, skiing, swimming, horseback riding, hiking, fishing, antiquing and arts and crafts fairs. Driving distances include the Skyline Drive-15 mins, UVA-Charlotte-sville-30 mins, Richmond 1.5 hrs, Washington DC-3 hrs. Don't miss the nearby wineries and Wintergreen Resort which is open year-round. Fine dining is available at nearby restaurants. **Discounts:** Yes, AARP, AAA **Airport:** Charlottesville-35 mins **Packages:** Yes, Golf, Skiing, Weddings, Reunions **Seasonal:** No **Reservations:** One night or 50% of length of stay (which ever is greater), 10 day cancellation notice for refund. Check-in 3pm, check-out 11am, other times by prior arrangement. **Brochure:** Yes **Permitted:** Children over 12, drinks in privacy of your own room (no alcohol license for the Inn). A smoke-free inn. **Conference:** Yes for small executive retreats, private party, wedding or family reunions - 20 persons max, your hosts are prepared to handle all of your special needs. **Payment Terms:** Check MC/V [I03EPVA-14510] **COM** Y **ITC Member:** No

A beautifully restored historic home, now a Bed and Breakfast.

Rates: Pvt Bath 10
Single $ 85-115.00
Double $ 85-115.00

Trillium House	Wintergreen Dr 22958	Nellysford VA
Dinwiddie Family		Tel: 800-325-9126 804-325-9126 **Fax:** 804-25-1099
		Res Times 9am-8pm

A Country Inn built in 1983 which has been designed to meet today's standards while retaining the charm of yesterday is located in one of America's most beautiful year-round mountain resort Wintergreen. Located on 11,000 acres of natural settings, scenic views, great downhill skiing, a beautiful mountain-top golf course, tennis facilities which are listed in the Top 50 in the USA, 20 miles of marked hiking trails, health spa with indoor and two outdoor pools and English riding stables & trails all of which are available to *Trillium House* guests at standard fees while staying here. Other activities include historical sights such as Ash Lawn, Woodrow Wilson's birthplace and Monticello. Near-by colleges included; U Va, JMU, VMI, W&L, Sweetbriar, Mary Baldwin, R-MWC and Bridgewater. A full breakfast is included along with picturesque view of the golf course and the beautiful birds frolicking in the early morning. Family owned and operated. *Suites available $120-150.00. **Seasonal:** No **Reservations:** One night deposit or 50%, whichever is greater, to hold reservation

©Inn & Travel Memphis, Tennessee

within 7 days of booking; 14 day cancel policy for refund less $10 service fee. Full deposit during ski season. **Brochure:** Yes **Permitted:** Drinking, limited children, limited smoking **Conference:** Yes for small retreat type of functions. **Payment Terms:** Check MC/V [Z11DPVA-5126] **COM** Y **ITC Member:** No

Rates: Pvt Bath 12
Single $ 65-70.00
Double $ 85-90.00

The Garden & The Sea Inn 4188 Nelson Rd 23415 New Church VA
Tom & Sara Baker Tel: 800-824-0672 804-824-0672

This charming 1802 Victorian Inn with wonderful gingerbread trim, is just minutes from the islands of Chicoteague and Assateague. You will find a beautiful quiet beach and a wonderful wildlife refuge rich in waterfowl and the famous wild ponies. Also nearby you'll find fishing, golf, hiking, biking, canoeing and antiquing. The Inn offers large romantic air conditioned guest rooms with luxurious linens, antique furnishings, fresh flowers and complimentary robes, oriental rugs. Two guest rooms have beautiful stained glass bay windows. Each guest room has a private bath - three with whirlpools. Guests may enjoy an afternoon refreshment or their hearty extended continental breakfast on the garden patio or porch while listening to the splashing fountains. A perfect place for an engagement, anniversary, honeymoon or just an escape. Chef/owner Tom creates masterpiece meals to savor in the intimate candlelight dining room for casual and intimate gourmet dining. Elegant entrees are prepared from local produce and fresh seafood from the farm and waters of the Eastern Shore. House specialties include Sauteed Shrimp with Bourbon Cream Sauce and Fresh Sea Scallops, Shrimp and Oysters sauteed with chardonnay, tomatoes and mushrooms, served over spinach. Also featured are an array of scrumptious desserts and an extensive wine list to complement every dish. AAA 3-Diamond, Mobil 3-Star **Packages:** Off-season, Two nights and dinner **Discounts:** Off-season **Seasonal:** Open 3/15-11/30 **Reservations:** One night deposit, 10 day cancel policy less $10 service fee, 2 night min weekends, 3 night min holiday weekends and last week in July **Brochure:** Yes **Permitted:** Children, pets, drinking, limited smoking **Conference:** Groups to 60 for weddings, receptions, executive retreats **Payment Terms:** Check AE/DISC/MC/V [I12HPVA1-15821] **COM** YG **ITC Member:** No

Rates: Pvt Bath 5
Single $ 60-150.00
Double $ 60-165.00

Spinning Wheel B&B 31 North St 23417 Onancock VA
*David & Karen Tweedie Tel: 804-787-7311 703-684-0067

Innkeepers who know and love the Virginia Eastern Shore happily welcome you to their 1890's Folk Victorian Home. Located in the quiet waterfront village of Onancock, *The Spinning Wheel* offers guest a calm refuge near the beach, bay and ocean. The house is furnished with local antiques from plentiful country auctions. Each of the five guest rooms is comfortable, appointed with queen size brass or iron beds, quilts, antiques, a/c and a spinning wheel! All guest rooms have attached private baths complete with luxurious bathrobes. Each morning guests are served a full breakfast in the elegant dining room or lounge with a breakfast-in-bed picnic delivered to their door. Guests staying at *The Spinning Wheel* are able to arrange for golf, tennis and swimming at a private country club nearby. Bicycles are available for exploring Onancock, listed on the National Register of Historic Places. Kerr Place, a 1799 manor house museum and the Tangier Island cruise are a short walk from the house. Visitors to *The Spinning Wheel* enjoy the convenience of restaurants, shops - all within an easy walk. Onancock's deep water harbor wel-

Virgina   *National Edition*

comes visitors arriving by boat. Other activities include Chesapeake Bay and Atlantic Ocean fishing and scheduled tournaments, hunting, wildlife refuges, farm tours, summer festivals and carnivals, including Onancock's Harborfest in Chincoteague and Assateague Island National Seashore beaches. *The Spinning Wheel* has been inspected and approved by AAA and the BBAV. Gift certificates available. **Seasonal:** *Open 5/1-10/30 *Winter phone: 703-684-0067 **Airport:** Salisbury MD-1

Hrs **Seasonal:** *See below **Reservations:** One night's deposit required, 72 hr cancel policy, two night min on weekends **Brochure:** Yes **Permitted:** Limited children, drinking, limited smoking **Languages:** American Sign **Payment Terms:** Check MC/V [I03GPVA-18753] **COM** Y **ITC Member:** No

Rates: **Pvt Bath 5**
Single $ 70-80.00
Double $ 70-80.00

Hidden Inn   249 Caroline St 22960   Orange VA
Ray & Barbara Lonick   **Tel:** 800-841-1253 540-672-3625 **Fax:** 540-672-5029
        Res Times 9am-9pm

An intimate weekend in the country or simply a refreshing night's stay awaits guests in this beautifully restored Victorian filled with true Southern hospitality and the perfect retreat from hectic daily travel pressures. Nestled on eight acres in the historic town of Orange VA, this picture-postcard setting is reminiscent of a bygone era for travelers seeking fine lace, fresh-cut flowers, a wide wrap-around front porch filled with wicker furnishings. Uniquely furnished guest rooms are highlighted by a beautiful brass or canopy bed, antiques and cozy handmade quilts with jacuzzi baths and fireplaced rooms available. A hearty country breakfast is prepared by your hosts and served in a large sunlit dining room or guests can sip their fresh brewed morning coffee with home-baked muffins outdoors overlooking this tranquil setting. A romantic candlelight evening five course dinner with hors d'oeuvres is available by reservation, to top-off a relaxing and peaceful day. For daily outings into the rich local heritage, your hosts will be happy to prepare a picnic lunch for your enjoyment. Complimentary tea is offered each afternoon. **Packages:** Romantic, Candlelight Dinner, Candlelight Picnic **Airport:** Charlottesville-28mi; Richmond-77mi **Seasonal:** No **Reservations:** Deposit or credit card to confirm res, 7 day cancel policy for refund, late cancellations and early departures are subject to full charge. Check-in 3-8pm, later by arrangement **Brochure:** Yes **Permitted:** Children, drinking, (A No Smoking Inn) **Conference:** Yes for small group meetings & lodging; small weddings for 50-75 persons **Languages:** Spanish **Payment Terms:** Check MC/V [I03HPVA1-5133] **COM** YG **ITC Member:** No

Rates: **Pvt Bath 10**
Single $ 59-79.00
Double $ 79-159.00

Shadows B&B Inn   Rt 1 Box 535 22960   Orange VA
Barbara & Pat Loffredo   **Tel:** 703-672-5057
        Res Times 10am-10pm

Nestled on forty-four acres is this beautifully restored, c1913 stone home surrounded by old cedars on the historic "Constitution Route" just minutes from Montpelier and downtown Orange, Virginia. The Inn offers guests a choice of four tastefully decorated rooms with their own character and charm. The Blue Room is an elegantly decorated bed/sitting room with a pre-Civil War walnut bed, natural cedar bathroom and nostalgic clawfoot tub and pedestal sink. The Rose Room offers a Romantic feeling with frills and laces and a full size antique high-back oak bed, spectacular views of the Blue Ridge Mountains and rolling fields. The Peach Room is art deco all the way with burled walnut beds and unique armories with a private hall shower convenient to the room. The Victorian Room offers a nostalgic visit to the past with a full size iron/brass bed and ruffled bed and window dressings. Guests are invited to enjoy a good book from the extensive library while snuggling-up before the large stone fireplace and enjoying a cup of warm cider. Summer brings guests together onto the old-fashioned front porch swing! Nearby sights include Montpelier, Civil War battlefield & history and a local winery. A hearty full country breakfast is included in the room rate and is served in the Hunt Room. **Seasonal:** No **Reservations:** One night or 50% if longer, 14 day cancel policy with late arrival to midnight by prior arrangement **Brochure:** Yes **Permitted:** Drinking **Payment Terms:** Check [R06BCVA-6890] **COM** Y **ITC Member:** No

Rates:	Pvt Bath 4
Single	$ 75-90.00
Double	$ 80-95.00

Abbie Hill B&B	2206 Monument Ave 23220	Richmond VA
Barb & Bill Fleming		Tel: 804-355-5855 Fax: 804-353-4656
		Res Times 10-6pm M-S

Located within an urban Historic District, tree-lined streets highlighted by historic monuments, triangle parks, little neighborhood shopping areas, eateries; we are near museums and historic sites of cultural and architectural interest. Our 1909 Federal style three-story brick townhouse was built for a prominent broker of land and city buildings. The family lived in these gracious rooms for almost thirty years, which are now tastefully refurbished in period style, yet done with special attention to contemporary comfort. Your interior-designer host has furnished the rooms for your comfort and enjoyment. Relax in the plush double parlours or on the awning-shaded front porch. Breakfast is in the grand panelled dining room, highlighted by the lovely bay window filled with birds and plants. The room is lit by a giant crystal chandelier. Most guest rooms have fireplaces, ceiling fans, lavatories and a/c. You'll be pampered in decor of the period including down comforters for snuggling in winter in either the old family four-poster or sleigh bed. Bathrooms retain turn-of-the-century charm while providing luxurious space and all facilities. Come stay for a weekend or a month! You'll be delighted to find yourself "at home" in such a gracious manner. **Seasonal:** No **Reservations:** One night's fare deposit, 7 day cancel notice, late arrivals/early departures will be billed for unused period **Brochure:** Yes **Permitted:** Drinking, children, 12-up **Conference:** Small social or business meetings, 10-20 persons **Payment Terms:** Check MC/V [C06BCVA-5139] **COM** U **ITC Member:** No

Rates:	Pvt Bath 2	Shared Bath 2
Single	$ 65-85.00	$ 60-80.00
Double	$ 65-85.00	$ 70-90.00

North Bend Plantation B&B		Richmond VA
M&M George Copeland		Tel: 804-829-5176
		Res Times 9am-3pm

Refer to the same listing name under Charles City, Virginia for a complete description and address. **Seasonal:** No **Payment Terms:** Check MC/V [M03-HCVA-6830] **COM** YG **ITC Member:** No

Rates:	Pvt Bath 4
Single	$ 85-120.00
Double	$ 95-130.00

William Catlin House	2304 E Broad St 23223	Richmond VA
Robert & Josephine Martin		Tel: 804-780-3746
		Res Times 8am-10pm

Located in the Historic District of Church Hill, this home was one of the finest brick mansions in the country when it was built in 1845. Today it offers travelers an opportunity to experience a beautiful and richly appointed Inn which has been featured in national publications such as *"Southern Living"*, *"Colonial Homes"* and numerous travel magazines. Beautiful period furniture, canopied four-poster beds, large armoires, oriental rugs, crystal chandeliers and the Martin's hospitality will make your stay a most pleasant and memorable experience. The luxury of bedroom fireplaces, goose down pillows, a complimentary bedtime sherry and mints promises a restful night. Coffee or tea arrives at your room each morning and a delicious full breakfast featuring fresh fruit in season, sausage and pancakes or bacon and eggs, hot breads and endless pots of coffee or tea await you in the elegant

Virginia *National Edition*

dining room. Your comfort and consideration is of primary importance to the inn's skilled and pleasant staff. Richmond offers many historic sites and entertainment attractions including St John's Church, site of Patrick Henry's famous *"Liberty of Death"* speech, just one block away. Within a few blocks, Richmond swings in Shockoe Slip with its restaurants, shops and boutiques. **Airport:** Richmond Intl 15 mi **Seasonal:** No **Reservations:** One night's deposit (non-refundable unless extreme circumstances) to hold reservation. **Brochure:** Yes **Permitted:** Children, drinking, limited smoking **Payment Terms:** Check MC/V [R09DPVA-5137] **COM** Y **ITC Member:** No

Rates:	Pvt Bath 3	Shared Bath 2
Single	$ 72.50	$ 72.50
Double	$ 89.50	$ 70.00

Manor At Taylors Store		Roanoke VA
Lee & Mary Lynn Tucker		**Tel:** 800-248-6267 703-721-3951
		Res Times Anytime

Refer to the same listing name under Smith Mountain Lake, Virginia for a complete description. **Seasonal:** No **Payment Terms:** Check MC/V [M05DPVA-12130] **COM** YG **ITC Member:** No

Rates:	Pvt Bath 4	Shared Bath 2
Single	$ 80-125.00	$ 95.00
Double	$ 80-125.00	$ 95.00

Mary Bladon House	381 Washington Ave SW 24016	Roanoke VA
Bill & Sheir Bestpitch		**Tel:** 703-344-5361
		Res Times 24 Hrs

The *Mary Bladon House* is a lovely example of Victorian architecture in Roanoake's historic Old Southwest neighborhood, a National Register Historic District. The house, built in 1891, still has its original brass lighting fixtures as well as crown and bulls-eye mouldings. Spacious guest rooms feature period antiques as well as antique and handcrafted rockers and easy chairs. A complimentary hearty breakfast is served each morning in the dining room. Spacious porches and a hanging swing provide spots to relax. The bed and breakfast is just five minutes from the Blue Ridge Parkway, providing easy access to hiking and beautiful view of surrounding valley and mountains. It is also just ten blocks from the oldest continuously operating open air farmers' market in the Commonwealth of Virginia. The market is open every day except Sunday. Also, on the market, guests will find specialty shops, museums, art and antique galleries and excellent restaurants. Business travelers will find our location convenient too, and we are more than happy to serve breakfast as early as necessary for those travelers interested in keeping to a schedule. Complimentary airport shuttle service available with advance notice. **Discounts:** Corporate weekdays **Airport:** Roanoke Regional-5 mi **Seasonal:** No **Reservations:** One night deposit, 72 hr cancel notice for refund **Brochure:** Yes **Permitted:** Children, drinking, limited smoking **Conference:** For groups of 6-8 persons **Languages:** German **Payment Terms:** Check MC/V [K04GPVA-5140] **COM** Y **ITC Member:** No

Rates:	Pvt Bath 3
Single	$ 62.50
Double	$ 80-110.00

Manor At Taylors Store	Rt 1 Box 533 24184	Smith Mountain Lake VA
Lee & Mary Lynn Tucker		**Tel:** 800-248-6267 703-721-3951
		Res Times Anytime

A secluded historic 120 acre estate in the foothills of the Blue Ridge Mountains, minutes from Smith Mountain Lake and the Blue Ridge Parkway. Guest suites replete with antiques and special fea-

3-138   ©*Inn & Travel Memphis, Tennessee*

tures such as fireplaces and private porches. A separate cottage with three bedrooms and two baths is available for families with children. All guests enjoy a full, "heart-healthy" gourmet breakfast and the use of hot tub, billiard room, movies, exercise room, guest kitchen and six private spring-fed ponds for swimming, fishing and canoeing. There are numerous fine restaurants near the inn and in Roanoke for dinner. Antique shopping galore! This Is A Very Special Place! **Packages:** Hot Air Balloon **Airport:** Roanoke-45 min **Reservations:** One night's deposit, 7 day cancel policy or re-rented if less than 7 days **Permitted:** Drinking in main house; children and smoking permitted in cottages **Conference:** Yes for small groups **Languages:** German **Payment Terms:** Check MC/V [Z05GPVA-5143] **COM Y ITC Member:** No

Rates:	Pvt Bath 4	Shared Bath 2
Single	$ 80-125.00	$ 95.00
Double	$ 80-125.00	$ 95.00

Renaissance Manor & Art Gallery   2247 Courthouse Rd 22554   Stafford VA
D&J Brenard/J&T Houser   Tel: 800-720-3784 540-720-3785 **Fax:** 540-720-3785
                                                                      Res Times 9am-9pm

The *Renaissance Manor Bed & Breakfast and Art Gallery* was designed to resemble Mount Vernon, located twenty miles north. It is situated on a winding country road just north of the city of Fredericksburg on three rolling acres. Guests can relax in both front and rear gardens, and enjoy the gazebo, fountain, rose arbor and beautiful flowers. Inside guests will find ten foot ceilings, hardwood floors, fireplaces, four poster canopy and white iron beds, detailed decorating and attention to details creating a gracious southern home. Six bedrooms offer twins, double, queen and king beds, including a two bedroom suite with private sitting room and jacuzzi. Guests enjoy complimentary afternoon refreshments with sherry in the rooms and an expanded continental breakfast which includes homemade muffins, fresh fruit, gourmet coffee and teas, yogurt and cereals guaranteeing guests do not leave hungry. There is light classical music and wonderful books to browse through. Local artist's work is displayed and is for sale. Nearby sights include local battlefield tours, antique shops, wineries, craft fairs and a convenient train to all of the Washington DC sights. *Rooms can be arranged to share a bath at $55.00, double rate and going to $150.00. AAA 3 Diamond approved. **Reservations:** One night's deposit, refundable with one week notice of cancellation **Brochure:** Yes **Permitted:** Children **Conference:** Small groups, weddings and special events, can accommodate groups to twelve for lodging **Payment Terms:** Check AE/MC/V [I08H-PVA1-13664] **COM YG ITC Member:** No

Rates:	Pvt Bath 4
Single	$ 55-150.00
Double	$ 55-150.00

Frederick House   28 North New St 24401   Staunton VA
Joe & Evy Harman   Tel: 800-334-5575 703-885-4220
                                                                      Res Times 7am-10pm

Enjoy the relaxed atmosphere in these completely restored Greek Revival townhouses gracefully furnished with the hosts' personal collection of antiques and paintings by Virginia artists. The guest rooms are comfortably furnished and include oversized beds, a/c, phone, TV and full baths. Full breakfast is included and served in Chumleys Tea Room. There is plenty of sightseeing in this center-city locale and you can stroll to the many restaurants, quaint shops, antique and craft shops. Your hosts will direct you to any of the golf, tennis, swimming, nature trails, horseback riding, canoeing and fishing areas you might want to explore, including the Blue Ridge Mountains. Adjacent indoor pool and health club available for guests' use. Rated Mobil and AAA Triple Diamond. Excellent dining adjacent to Inn at McCormicks is available. Your hosts are native to Staunton and will make sure your visit is filled with things to do. Opening in 1996 is Cochran's Cottage, a five bedroom, three bath lodging with laundry room, kitchen, dining room and library and the Riddle House, offering six suites, each with its own kitchen. **Airport:** Shenandoah Valley-20 mins. **Seasonal:** *Rates vary **Reservations:** Deposit to secure reservation required within 5 days by credit card or check. *Rates lower in winter. **Brochure:** Yes **Permitted:** Children, drinking; no smoking or pets **Conference:** Yes **Payment Terms:** Check AE/DC/DISC/MC/V [I02HPVA1-5149] **COM** YG **ITC Member:** No

Rates:	Pvt Bath 14
Single	$ 65-115.00
Double	$ 65-115.00

Inn At Gristmill Square PO Box 359 24484 Warm Springs VA
Mc Williams Family Tel: 703-839-2231 Fax: 703-839-3058
Res Times 24 hours

Rustic Country Inn nestled onto a millsite complete with a splashing stream, antique furnishings and individual decor for each of the guest rooms. Fine gourmet dining. Continental breakfast included. Tennis, golf, swimming pool, and sauna are available. **Seasonal:** Clo 3/1-3/15 **Reservations:** Deposit required at res time with 48-hour cancellation. **Brochure:** Yes **Permitted:** Children, smoking, drinking **Payment Terms:** Check MC/V [X11ACVA-5163] **COM** Y **ITC Member:** No

Rates:	Pvt Bath 14
Single	$ 60.00
Double	$ 70.00

Caledonia Farm - 1812 Washington VA
Phil Irwin Tel: 800-BNB-1812 540-675-3693 Fax: 540-675-3693
Res Times 10am-6pm

Refer to the same listing name under Flint Hill, Virginia for a complete description. **Payment Terms:** Check DISC/MC/V [M02HPVA1-20165] **COM** YG **ITC Member:** No

Rates:	Pvt Bath 2	Shared Bath 2
Single	$ 140.00	$ 80.00
Double	$ 140.00	$ 80.00

L'Auberge Provencale PO Box 119 22663 White Post VA
Chef Alain & Celeste Borel Tel: 800-638-1702 703-837-1375 Fax: 703-837-2004
Res Times 10am-10pm

Set on ten acres in the heart of Virginia Hunt Country is the culinary treasure, *L'Auberge Provencale*. With the extensive flower, herb and vegetable gardens and orchard, this premier Country Inn offers the charm and sophistication of a true auberge of the south of France. We are proud we have been recognized nationally and internationally for our dedication to fine food, wine and service. Executive chef Alain Borel has been the chef at the Inn for fourteen years, and has earned the title of **"Great Country Inn Chef"** from the James Beard Foundation, and appeared on the television series, **"Great Chefs of the East."** Dining is a true Four-Diamond experience in our intimate and romantic restaurant, decorated with antiques, original art, and provencale ambiance. L'Auberge Provencale is a thoroughly country French experience From the magnificent menu to the lovely rooms. The guest rooms are individually decorated with French charm and gracious timelessness, some with fireplaces, and all rooms include a full gourmet breakfast "of one's dreams." Relax on our spacious porch and terrace with a glass of wine or enjoy one of our gourmet picnics as you tour the beautiful Blue Ridge countryside, or go horseback riding, canoeing, hiking, or wine tasting at our local vineyards. L'Auberge Provencale is the Inn where great expectations are quietly met. Articles & reviews have appeared in *"Bon Appetit", "Country Inns Bed & Breakfast", "Luxury Homes Washington", "Albemarle"* and *"Glamour Magazine."* **Airport:** Dulles Intl-45 mins **Seasonal:** No **Reservations:** One night deposit to guarantee, 7 day cancel policy for refund **Brochure:** Yes **Permitted:** Children 10-up on week nights only, drinking, limited smoking **Conference:** Yes, small groups for intimate meetings with gourmet dining available **Languages:** French, Spanish **Payment Terms:** Check AE/DC/DISC/MC/V [I04GHVA1-5170] **COM** YG **ITC Member:** No

Rates: **Pvt Bath 10**
Single $ 125.00
Double $ 195.00

Applewood Colonial B&B	605 Richmond 23185	**Williamsburg VA**
Marty Jones		**Tel:** 800-899-2753 804-229-0205
		Res Times 8am-10pm

This Flemish-bond brick home was one of the first homes built on Richmond Road after the restoration of Colonial Williamsburg, early in the 1920s. It is conveniently located four short blocks from Colonial Williamsburg and right across the street from the College of William & Mary. It was a guest house in years past and the new owners have restored it's elegant colonial decor. The parlor features 18th century style decor with dentil crown molding and fireplace where afternoon tea is served by your host. The dining room has a beautiful built-in corner cupboard and a crystal chandelier above the pedestal table where a complimentary full breakfast is served. Afternoon refreshments are enjoyed in the parlor. The owner's apple collection is evidenced throughout the house and inspired the names of the guest rooms. Your host wishes to make your stay in Williamsburg memorable whether it be a romantic getaway, honeymoon, anniversary, a family vacation (2 rooms accommodate extra children comfortably), shopping trip or a business trip to the Tidewater area (we pamper harried executives). The owner has beautifully furnished the rooms with antiques and family heirlooms. **Seasonal:** No **Reservations:** 50% deposit required within 7 days of booking; 14 day cancel policy for refund **Brochure:** Yes **Permitted:** Children, drinking **Conference:** Yes for groups to 10 persons **Payment Terms:** Check MC/V [Z05H-PVA1-8544] **COM** YG **ITC Member:** No

Rates: **Pvt Bath 4**
Single $ 75.00
Double $ 120.00

Edgewood Plantation		**Williamsburg VA**
Dot & Julian Boulware		**Tel:** 800-296-EDGE 804-829-2962 **Fax:** 804-829-2962
		Res Times 8am-11pm

Refer to the same listing name under Charles City, Virginia for a complete description. **Seasonal:** No **Reservations:** Suites available **Payment Terms:** Check MC/V [M08FPVA-16962] **COM** Y **ITC Member:** No

Rates: **Pvt Bath 6**   **Shared Bath 2**
Single $ 105.00 $ 175.00
Double $ 138.00 $ 175.00

Greenwoode Inn	104 Woodmont Place 23188	**Williamsburg VA**
Jim & Priscilla James Stam		**Tel:** 804-566-8800
		Res Times 8am-10pm

In a green wood in Williamsburg stands a three story Georgian home that is especially known for warm hospitality, good conversation, interesting art and antique furnishings, beautifully appointed accommodations, delicious breakfasts: in short, all the things one looks for in a Bed & Breakfast experience. There are four guest suites available; each with bedroom, comfortable sitting room and private bath. The rear porch and deck look out into a deep wood, a stream meanders through the ravine, squirrels chatter, hummingbirds flit and all cares and frustrations melt away. Hosts, Jim and Priscilla Stam, both retired from academia, love travel, antiques, art, architecture, history, music, poetry, hiking, skeet shooting and, of course, interesting people. **Airport:** Richmond-40 mi **Seasonal:** No **Reservations:** Payment in full, 4 day cancel notice for full refund **Permitted:** Drinking, limited children **Payment Terms:** Check [Z08GPVA-16871] **COM** U **ITC Member:** No

Rates: Pvt Bath 4
Single $ 95.00
Double $ 105.00

Legacy Of Williamsburg B&B   930 Jamestown Rd 23185   Williamsburg VA
Ed & Mary Ann Lucas   Tel: 800-WMBGS-BB 804-220-0524
                                                                  Res Times 7am-7pm

Step back in time to the 18th century here at the Legacy. With authentic 18th century furnishings throughout our lovely home its easy to let your mind wander to the early days of our forefathers. You'll love sleeping in the tall poster curtained beds. Before heading out each morning for Historic Williamsburg, Busch Gardens, possibly shopping at the Williamsburg Pottery - or visiting your son or daughter at the College of William & Mary - sit down to a breakfast fit for George himself! Just a ten minute walk to Historic Williamsburg. We are dealers in 18th century furnishings ranging from Fratues to Windsor Chairs. Your hosts are here twelve months a year and live on the premises and are looking forward to meeting travelers and making new friendships. Complimentary bikes are available. **Reservations:** One night's deposit, 50% for longer periods, 10 day cancel policy (14 days on holidays) for full refund **Permitted:** Drinking **Payment Terms:** Check MC/V [R06BCVA-6927] **COM** Y **ITC Member:** No

Rates: Pvt Bath 2
Single $ 80-120.00
Double $ 80-120.00

Newport House B&B   710 S Henry St 23185   Williamsburg VA
Cathy & John Millar   Tel: 804-229-1775

The *Newport House* was built to museum standards in 1988 from the 1756 design by famous colonial architect Peter Harrison for an important plantation house near Newport, Rhode Island, that was destroyed on its 200th birthday to make way for a car park. It is furnished totally in the period with English and American antiques and reproductions. We have only two large bedrooms (all the law permits here), each containing an extra-long queen four-poster bed plus another bed for additional guests in the room. Each room has a private bathroom. The house is fully air conditioned. A full breakfast often includes colonial period recipes, accompanied by interesting historical conversations with your host. The house is located only a five minute walk from Colonial Williamsburg's Historic area. Every Tuesday evening, *Newport House* hosts locals and visitors for colonial dancing in the ballroom - beginners and spectators welcomed. Your host is a former museum-director and captain of an historic full-rigged ship, and the author of many historical books. Inspected and approved BBAV & ABBA **Discounts:** Yes, extended stays **Airport:** Newport News VA-20 mi; Richmond-50 mi; Norfolk-60 mi **Seasonal:** No **Reservations:** Credit card number or deposit required to guarantee reservation, 14 day cancel notice for refund **Brochure:** Yes **Permitted:** Children, drinking **Conference:** Yes, ballroom (42' x 23') suitable for groups to forty **Languages:** French **Payment Terms:** Check [I03HPVA1-11777] **COM** YG **ITC Member:** No

Rates: Pvt Bath 2
Single $ 115-130.00
Double $ 115-130.00

National Edition *Virgina*

North Bend Plantation B&B — Williamsburg VA
George & Ridgely Copeland
Tel: 804-829-5176
Res Times 9am-3pm*

Refer to the same listing name under Charles City, Virginia for a complete description. **Seasonal:** No **Payment Terms:** Check MC/V [M03HCVA1-6804] **COM** YG **ITC Member:** No

Rates:	Pvt Bath 4
Single	$ 85-120.00
Double	$ 95-130.00

Primrose Cottage — 706 Richmond Rd 23185 — Williamsburg VA
Inge Curtis
Tel: 800-522-1901 757-229-6421 Fax: 757-259-0717
Res Times 7am-10pm

This cozy Country Cape Cod is within walking distance to the historic area of Williamsburg and to The William and Mary College. You'll experience all of these interesting sights with your helpful hosts who are anxious to help each guest with their plans. Guests will also experience an "at home feeling" with Pennsylvania Country antique furnishings, stenciled walls and queen-size canopy beds, all with private baths. Bernie & Mary owned their own bakery at one time so you'll awaken to the aroma of fresh-baked muffins, breads, biscuits and a full country breakfast including country ham - along with all the fresh-brewed coffee you might like. Himmel-Bed is just a few minutes away from Bush Gardens, Yorktown and Jamestown - and about 35 mins from Richmond. Guests are encouraged to use the complimentary bikes for leisurely seeing the surrounding countryside and historic sites. **Seasonal:** No **Reservations:** Two night's deposit to hold room, 14 day cancel policy for full refund **Brochure:** No **Languages:** German **Payment Terms:** Check [R12CPVA-8584] **COM** U **ITC Member:** No

Rates:	Pvt Bath 3
Single	$ 85.00
Double	$ 95-125.00

Spiggle Guest Home — 720 College Terrace 23185 — Williamsburg VA
Phil & Dottie Spiggle
Tel: 804-253-0202
Res Times 6pm-10pm

Spend the night with these gracious hosts in their cozy 6000 square foot brick colonial home on their beautiful quiet residential street next to the campus of The College of William & Mary and away from the city noise. You'll see all of Williamsburg from this convenient location - just a 10-15 minute walk to the restored area of Williamsburg and a ten minute drive to shopping centers, Busch Gardens, and the Pottery Factory. Guest rooms are comfortably furnished, some with family antiques and all include wall-to-wall carpeting, central a/c, inroom refrigerators, coffee and tea maker, phone jacks, TV, private baths and choice of king, queen, double or twin beds. A great location for seeing all the nearby sights of Jamestown and Yorktown. **Airport:** Newport News 20 mi; Richmond 40 mi; Norfolk 50 mi **Seasonal:** No **Reservations:** One night's deposit required with a 48 hr cancel policy; late arrival with prior notice. Two-night stay required certain periods during the year. **Brochure:** No **Permitted:** Drinking, limited children; no smoking **Payment Terms:** Check [Z05FPVA-14083] **COM** U **ITC Member:** No

Rates:	Pvt Bath 4	Shared Bath 2
Single	$ 30-35.00	$ 25.00
Double	$ 30-50.00	$ 30.00

Williamsburg Manor B&B — 600 Richmond Rd 23185 — Williamsburg VA
Laura Sisane
Tel: 800-422-8011 804-220-8011 Fax: 804-220-0245
Res Times 7am-10pm

Built during the reconstruction of Colonial Williamsburg, this 1927 Georgian brick Colonial has been restored to its original elegance. Guests return to an earlier era when hospitality was a matter of pride and fine living was an art practiced in restful surroundings. The *Williamsburg Manor*

Virgina *National Edition*

continues this tradition into the 20th Century, Interior details feature arched doorways, a grand staircase, brick study and living room fireplaces. Each guest room is uniquely furnished with fine antiques, Waverly fabrics, oriental rugs and hardwood floors. Private baths, central air conditioning, and color TV are provided for guest comfort. Laura, your hostess, is a hospitality professional who takes pride in making your stay a joyous and memorable experience. Guests arise to the aroma or freshly brewed coffee and homemade muffins. You will be treated to a culinary delight with a lavish presentation of regional Virginia foods. Conveniently located just three blocks to the historic area. Off-street parking. Full catering service. **Airport:** Richmond-40 mi; Norfolk-45 mi; Williamsburg Newport News-20 mi **Packages:** Yes, inquire at res time **Seasonal:** No **Reservations:** One night's deposit within 7 days of booking, 21 day cancel policy for refund **Permitted:** Children 10-up, drinking **Conference:** Special arrangements for meetings, dinners, social events **Payment Terms:** Check [I05HPVA1-16860] **COM** YG **ITC Member:** No

Rates: Pvt Bath 5
Single $ 85.00
Double $ 90.00

Williamsburg Sampler B&B   922 Jamestown Rd 23185   Williamsburg VA
Helen & Ike Sisane   **Tel:** 800-722-1169 804-253-0398 **Fax:** 804-253-2669
                                                                 Res Times 7am-10pm

Williamsburg's finest 18th Century plantation-style three-story brick colonial home, plus a replica of Colonial Williamsburg's 18th Century Coke-Garrett Carriage House which overlooks the beautiful grounds and wooded area. The task of architectural authenticity for this residence was given to William B Phillips, AIA, former architect for historic Colonial Williamsburg. AAA 3-Diamond and Mobil awards. Selected as the *1995 "Inn Of The Year"* of which Virginia's Governor said *"I call its significance to the attention of all our citizens."* The owner of Virginia's 1723 Shirley Plantation said *"I recommend it to anyone who wants something different and authentic in their Williamsburg accommodations."* Enter into the welcoming foyer and relax in elegance during your visit. Suites have wetbar, refrigerator, fireplace, TV and Roof Top Garden. Relax in the lovely Keeping Room or Tavern Library Reading Room. Have their famous *"Skip lunch"* breakfast with flickering candlelight and in view of a roaring fireplace. International guests help excite the morning conversation. This home is richly furnished throughout with antiques, pewter and samplers. The fine furniture and accessories were carefully collected through the years from auctions, estate sales or as gifts from treasured relatives and friends. Prominently located across from the College of William and Mary and at easy access to all points of interest. Personalized gift certificate letters are available for all occasions. **Airport:** Newport News-15 mi; Norfolk & Richmond, VA-50 mi **Seasonal:** No **Reservations:** 50% deposit required at res time with 14 day cancellation policy *Suites available **Brochure:** Yes **Permitted:** Children 12-up, social drinking, Smoking not permitted **Payment Terms:** Check [I10GPVA1-8896] **COM** Y **ITC Member:** No

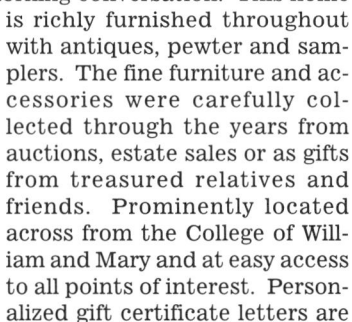

Rates: Pvt Bath 4   Suite
Single $ 90-130.00
Double $ 90-130.00 $ 130.00

3-144   ©*Inn & Travel Memphis, Tennessee*

Bold Name - Description appears in other section *Alabama - Arkansas*

ALABAMA

Anniston
Noble-MCCAA-Butler House
205-236-1791

Victoria
800-260-8781

Arab
Stamps Inn
205-586-7038

Ashville
Roses & Lace Country Inn
205-594-4366

Auburn
Crenshaw House
334-821-1131

Bear Creek Lakes
Little Bear B&B
205-331-0900

Boaz
Boaz B&B Inn
205-593-8031

Citronelle
Citronella
334-866-2849

Courtland
McMahon House B&B
205-637-2137

Decatur
Dancy Polk House
334-353-3579

Hearts & Treasures
205-353-9562

Elberta
Donrovan
334-986-7119

Eufaula
Kendall Manor
334-687-8847

St Marys B&B
334-687-7195

Eutaw
a Humble B&B
205-372-9297

Kirkwood 1806 B&B
205-372-9009

Fairhope
Away At The Bay
334-928-9725

Barrons On The Bay Inn
334-928-9725

Church Street Inn
334-928-8976

Don & Dawns Garden Cottage B&B
334-928-0253

Guest House
334-928-6226

Marcells Tea Room & Inn
334-928-9212

Mershon Court
334-928-7398

The Guest House
334-928-6226

Florence
River Park B&B
205-757-8667

Wood Avenue Inn
205-766-8441

Forest Home
Pine Flat Plantation
334-346-2739

Franklin
Rutherford Johnson House
334-282-4423-[Y--]

Geneva
Live Oaks B&B
334-684-2489

Greensboro
Blue Shadows B&B
205-766-8441

Huntsville
Dogwood Manor
205-859-3946

Wadlers Inn B&B
205-837-6694

Woodbine Guest House
205-536-3141

Jemison

Jemison Inn
205-688-2055

Lafayette
Hil-Ware-Dowdell Mansion
334-864-7861-[Y--]

Mentone
Blossom Hill B&B & Herb Farm
800-889-4200

Madaperca B&B
205-634-4792

Mentone Inn
205-634-4836

Mobile
Church Street Inn
334-438-3107

Malaga Inn
334-438-4701

Mallory Manor
334-432-6440

Portman House Inn
800-471-1701

Stickneys Hollow B&B
334-456-4556

Montgomery
Colonels Rest B&B
334-279-0380

Harbin Hotel
334-697-5652

Red Bluff Cottage
334-264-0056

Nauvoo
Old Harbin Hotel
205-697-5652

William Cook House B&B
205-697-5793

Opelika
Bluebonnet B&B

Heritage House
205-705-0485

Under The Oaks
334-745-2449

Orange Beach
Acadian Inn
334-981-6710

Romar House
800-487-6627

Prattville
Plantation House B&B
335-361-0442

Samson
Jola Bama Guest House
205-898-2478

Selma
Churchview
334-875-2144-[Y--]

Grace Hall
334-875-5744

Kelso Cottage
334-872-3047

Meriweather

Steele
Beeson House B&B
205-594-7878

Talladega
Governors House
205-763-7272

Historic Oakwood B&B
205-362-0662

Orangevale Plantation
205-362-3052

Troy
House of Dunns
334-566-9414

Valley Head
Woodhaven B&B
205-635-6438

Winfield
White Oaks Inn B&B
205-487-4115

ARKANSAS

Arkadelphia
Iron Mountain Lodge
501-246-4310

Augusta
Marys River B&B
501-347-2433

Arkansas   **Bold Name** - *Description appears in other section*

Brinkley
 Great Southern Hotel
 501-734-4955-[Y--]

Caddo Gap
 Rivers Edge B&B
 800-756-4864

Clarksville
 May House
 501-754-6851

Conway
 Olde Towne B&B
 501-329-6989-[G--]

 The Bruce House
 501-327-2947

Crossett
 Treischmann House B&B
 501-364-7592-[G--]

De Valls Bluff
 Palaver Place
 800-844-4425

Deer
 Piney Inn
 501-428-5878

Des Ark
 The 5 B's
 501-256-4789

Elkins
 McGuiretown B&B
 501-442-2122

Eureka Springs
 5 Ojo Inn
 800-656-6734
 [GQA-]

 Angels Rest
 501-253-7977

 Apple Annies B&B
 501-253-4918

 Applecore Cottage
 501-253-7358

 Arbour Glen B&B
 501-253-9010

 Arsenic & Old Lace
 800-243-LACE

 Basin Park Hotel

 Beaver Lake B&B
 501-253-9210

Bell Spring Cottage
501-253-8581

Benton Place
501-253-7602

Bon Repose

Bonnybrooke Farm
501-253-6903

Border House
501-253-7676

Brackenridge Lodge
501-253-6803

Bridgeford House B&B
501-253-7853

Brownstone Inn
501-253-7505

Brownstone Inn
501-253-7505

Cabin On The Boardwalk

Candlesticks Cottages
800-835-5184

Carriage House
501-253-8310

Cedarberry Cottage B&B
800-590-2424

Cliff Cottage, A B&B Inn
800-7-7409-[Y--]

Coach House Inn
501-253-80

Cobblestone Guest Cottage
501-253-8105

Cottage Inn
501-235-5282

Country House B&B
501-253-7586

Crescent Cottage Inn
501-253-6022-[G--]

Crescent Hotel

800-643-4972

Crescent Moon Townhouse
501-253-6022

Dairy Hollow House
800-562-8650

Dixie Cottage B&B
800-3-DIXIE2

Doll House Inn
501-253-8565

Dr RG Floyd House
501-253-7525

Edgewood Manor
501-253-6555

Ellis House At Trails End
800-243-8218

Elmwood House
501-253-7227

Enchanted Cottages
800-862-2788

Evening Shade Inn
501-253-6264

Fairwinds Mountain Cottages
501-253-9465

Flatiron Flats
800-421-9615

Floyd House
501-253-7525

Four WInds
501-253-9169

Fuller Cottage
501-751-7766

Garden of Eve Health Spa
501-253-7777

Garden Of Dreams
501-253-7841

Gardeners Cottage
800-833-3394-[G--]

Grand Central Hotel
800-344-6050

Greenwood Hollow

Ridge
501-253-5283

Harvest House
501-253-9363

Heart Of The Hills Inn
800-253-7468

Heartstone Inn
501-253-8916-[Y--]

Hidden Valley Guest Ranch
501-253-9777

Hillside Cottage B&B
501-253-8688

Inn At Rose Hall
800-828-HALL

Jordan Drive Hideaway B&B
800-245-5931-[Y--]

Lake Chalet Inn
501-523-9210

Lake Lucerne Resort
501-253-8085

Lazee Daze
501-253-7026

Lion Spring Inn
501-253-5410

Little Switzerland House
501-253-5916

Lookout Cottage
501-253-9545

Main Street Inn
501-253-6042-[Y--]

Maison DeVille
800-447-7242

Maple Leaf Inn
501-253-6876

Maple Ridge
501-253-5220

Mimosa Cottage
501-253-9344

Miss Priscillas
800-647-3268

3-146   ©*Inn & Travel Memphis, Tennessee*

Bold Name - Description appears in other section **Arkansas**

Morningstar Retreat
501-253-55

Mount Victoria
501-253-7979

New Orleans Hotel
800-243-8630

Oak Crest Cottages
501-253-9493

Old Homestead
501-253-7501-[Y--]

Paisley Rose
501-253-8251

Palace Hotel
501-253-7474

Peabody House B&B
501-253-5376

Petticoat Junction
501-253-7686

Pond Mountain Lodge
800-583-8043-[Y--]

Primrose Place
501-253-9818

Queen Anne Mansion
501-253-8825

Red Bud Valley Resort
501-253-9028

Redbud Manor
501-253-9649

Ridge Top Resort & Chapel
501-253-5163

Ridgeway House B&B
800-477-6618

Riverview Resort
501-253-8367

Roadrunner Inn
501-523-8166

Rock Cabins
501-253-8659

Rock Cottage Gardens
800-624-6646

Rosewood Guest Cottage
501-253-7674

Rustic Manor
501-253-8128

Sallys B&B
501-253-8916

Saras Cottage
501-253-5527

Scandia Inn & B&B Cottages
800-523-8922

Secret Garden B&B
501-253-5258

Shady Rest Cottages
501-253-8793

Singleton House B&B
800-833-3394-[G--]

Sleepy Hollow Guest Cottage
501-253-7448

Southern Rose Cottage
501-253-5800

Spider Creek resort
501-253-9241

Studio Guest House
501-253-8773

Sweet Seasons Guest Cottages
501-253-7603

Tatman-Garrett House
501-253-7617

Taylor Page Inn
501-253-7315

Tweedy House B&B
800-346-1735

Valais Hi
501-253-5140

Victorian Rose Inn
501-253-8537

White Dove Manor
800-261-6151-[G--]

White Flower Cottage
501-253-9636

White River Oaks B&B
501-253-9033

Willow Ridge Luxury Lodging
800-467-1737-[Y--]

Wisteria Lane Lodging
501-253-7544

Evening Shade
Turman House B&B
800-257-3405-[G--]

Everton
Corn Cobb Inn
501-429-6545

Fayetteville
Hill Avenue B&B
501-444-0865

Oaks Manor
501-443-5481

Shady Lane B&B
800-687-1659

Stay In Style
501-582-3590

Fordyce
Wynne Phillips House
501-352-7202

Fort Smith
Beland Manor B&B
501-782-3300

McCartney House
501-782-9057

Thomas Quinn Guest House
501-782-04

Gassville
Lithia Springs B&B Lodge
501-435-6100

Gilbert
Annas House
501-439-2888

Hardy
Hideaway Inn

501-966-4770

Olde Stonehouse B&B Inn
800-514-2983-[G-ITC]

Harrison
Hathaway House B&B
501-741-3321

Peaches 'n Cream
501-741-6527

Queen Anne House B&B
501-741-1304

Rock Candy Mountain B&B
501-743-1531

Heber Springs
Anderson House
800-264-5279

Essex Lodge B&B
800-892-0247

Oak Tree Inn
800-959-3857-[Y--]

Helena
Allin Inn
501-338-9155

Edwardian Inn
501-338-9155

Magnolia Hill B&B
501-338-6874

Hot Springs
Dogwood Manor
501-624-0896

Gables
501-623-7576

Stillmeadow Farm
501-525-94

Stitt House B&B Inn
501-623-2704-[GQA-]

Vintage Comfort B&B
501-623-3258

Wildwood 1884 B&B
501-624-4267

Williams House

©Inn & Travel Memphis, Tennessee

3-147

Arkansas - Florida
Bold Name - *Description appears in other section*

B&B Inn
501-624-4275-[Y--]

Woodbine Place
501-624-3646

Hot Springs Natl Park
Betty Robertson
B&B
501-624-6622

Hughes
Snowden House
501-339-3414

Huntsville
Fabus Mansion
800-737-2005

Jasper
Branbly Hedge
Cottage
800-BRA-MBLY

Carols Place
501-446-5144

Cliff House Inn
501-446-2292

Johnson
Johnson House
1882
501-756-1095

Stonefence Inn
501-582-1087

Kingston
Fools Cove Ranch
B&B
501-665-2986

Langley
Country School Inn
501-356-3091

Little Rock
Carriage House
501-374-7032

Hotze House
501-376-6563

Quapaw Inn
800-7325-559

Malvern
Gatewood House
B&B
501-332-6022

Mammoth Spring
Morris-Pace House
B&B
501-625-3378

McGhee
Magnolia House
501-222-6425

Monticello
Miss Rosalinds
B&B
501-367-2703

Morrilton
Mather Lodge
800-628-7936

Tanyard Springs
501-727-5200

Mountain View
Commercial Hotel
800-35 BANDB

Country Charm
B&B
800-756-8749

Country Oaks
800-455-2704

Inn At Mountain
View
800-535-1301

Murfreesboro
Queen Of
Diamonds Inn
501-285-3105

Norfolk
Schroder Haus
B&B
501-4-7775

Omaha
Aunt Shirleys
Sleeping Loft
501-426-5408

Ozark
1887 Inn
501-667-1121

Bunkhouse
501-292-3725

Lamplighter B&B
501-667-3889

Pine Bluff
Margladn II B&B
Inn
501-536-6000

Rogers
Arkansas Discovery
501-925-1744

Coppermine Lodge

Romance
Hammons Chapel
Farm
501-849-2819

Salem
Lespedeza B&B
501-895-3061

Siloam Springs
Washington Street
B&B
501-524-5669

Springdale
Magnolia Gardens
Inn
501-756-5744

Texarkana
Mansion On Main
903-792-1835

Van Buren
O'Malleys
501-474-4693

Old Van Buren Inn
501-474-4202

Warren
Burnett House
501-226-46

Washington
Old Country Jail
501-983-2461-[Y--]

Winslow
Sky-Vue Lodge
B&B
501-634-2003

Wooster
Patton House Inn
501-679-2975

Yellville
Red Raven Inn
501-449-5168

FLORIDA

Amelia Island
1735 House
800-872-8531-[G--]

Amelia Island
Williams House
904-277-2328

**Elizabeth Pointe
Lodge**

800-772-3359-[G--]

Fairbanks House
800-261-4838

Apalachicola
Coombs House Inn
904-653-91

Gibson Inn
904-653-2191

Pink Camellia
904-653-2107

Apollo Beach
B&B of Apollo
Beach
813-645-2471

Bartow
Stanford Inn
941-533-2393

Bay Harbor Islands
Bay Harbor Inn
305-868-4141

Belleair/Clearview
Bellview Biltmore

Big Pine
B&B On The Ocean
Casa Grande
305-872-2878

Barnacle
305-872-3298

Big Pine Key
B&B On The Ocean
305-872-2878

Canal Cottage B&B
305-872-3881

Deer Run
305-872-2015-[Y--]

Boca Grande
Gasparilla Inn
941-964-2201

Bradenton
Banyan House
941-746-8633

Nielsens
941-747-3541

Bradenton Beach
Duncan House B&B
941-778-6858-[Y--]

Brandon
Mary Lee B&B

3-148 ©Inn & Travel Memphis, Tennessee

Bold Name - *Description appears in other section*   *Florida*

813-653-3807

Bushnell
Cypress House B&B
904-568-0909

Cabbage Key
Cabbage Key Inn
904-283-2278

Cape Coral
Woodwards B&B
813-542-6207

Cedar Key
Cedar Key B&B
800-453-5051-[G--]

Historic Island Hotel
352-543-5111-[G--]

Island Hotel
352-543-5111

Cocoa
Coleman House B&B
305-632-8806

Colonial River House
305-632-8780

Cocoa Beach
Inn At Cocoa Beach
305-7-3460

Coleman
Sons Shady Brook B&B
352-PIT-STOP

Coral Gables
Hotel Place St Michel
305-444-1666

Hotel Ponce de Leon
305-444-34

Crescent City
Sprague House Inn
904-698-2430

Daytona Beach
Coquina Inn
800-727-0678

Higgins House B&B
904-324-9238-[Y--]

Live Oak Inn
800-253-4667-[Y--]

St Regis Hotel
904-252-8743

Daytona Beach Shores
Captains Quarters Inn
904-767-3119

DeFuniak Springs
Sunbright Manor
904-892-0656-[Y--]

Delray Beach
Hutchs Haven
407-276-7390

River Ranch Resort

DeLand
Deland Country Inn
904-736-4244

Destin
Henderson Park Inn
800-336-GULF

Eastlake Weir
Lakeside Inn B&B
904-288-1396

Edgewater
Colonial House
904-427-4570

Englewood
Lemon Bay B&B
941-474-7571

Manasota Beach Club
941-474-2614

Everglades
Rod & Gun Club
941-695-2101

Everglades City
Ivey House
941-683-32

Orange House
941-695-2343

Fernandina Beach
Addison House
904-277-1604

Bailey House
904-261-5390-[Y--]

Florida House Inn
800-258-3301

Greyfield Inn

904-261-6408

Hoyt House
904-277-4300

Posada San Carlos
904-277-8744

Seaside Inn
904-261-0954

Fernandnia Beach
1735 House
800-872-8531-[Y--]

Flagler Beach
Shire House
904-445-8877

Topaz Hotel
904-439-3301

Florida City
Grandma Newtons B&B
305-247-4413-[Y--]

Fort Lauderdale
Beauty Castle
954-565-5001

Casa Alhambra Inn
954-467-2262

Casa Glamaretta
800-327-7843

Deauville Inn
954-568-0869

Fort Myers
Davis Family
941-463-2843

Drum House Inn
941-332-5668

Embes Hobby House
941-936-6378

Mrs Campbells B&B
800-772-6207

Wind Song Garden
941-936-6378-[Y--]

Gainesville
Country Meadows
352-495-26

Magnolia Plantation B&B
352-375-6653-[G--]

Sweetwater Branch Inn
800-451-7111

Georgetown
Indigo Inn/Drayton Island
904-467-2446

Gulf Breeze
Summit Breeze
904-932-9697

Havana
Gaver B&B
904-539-5611

Hawthorne
Yearlings Cabins
904-466-3033

High Springs
Great Outdoors Inn
904-454-2900

Lacy Country Manor
904-454-1621

Spring House
904-454-8571

Hollywood
Maison Harrison Guest House
954-922-7319

Holmes Beach
Harrington House
941-778-5444-[Y--]

Homestead
Room At The Inn
305-246-0492

Indian Shores
B&B Cottages
813-595-6520

Indiantown
Seminole Country Inn
305-597-3777

Inverness
Crown Hotel
352-344-5555

Islamorada
B&B Of Islamorada
305-664-9321

Jacksonville
1217 On The Boulevard
904-354-6959

©*Inn & Travel Memphis, Tennessee*   3-149

Florida

Bold Name - *Description appears in other section*

1735 House
800-872-8531-[Y--]

Columns B&B
904-384-3429

House On Cherry Street
904-384-19-[Y--]

Judge Grays House
904-388-1248

Plantation Manor Inn
904-384-4630

Willows On St John River
904-389-6394

Jensen Beach
Hutchinson Inn
561-229-2000

Jupiter
Innisfall
561-744-5905

Key Biscayne
Hibiscus House
305-361-2456

Key Largo
Jules' Undersea Lodge
305-451-2353-[Y--]

Key West
Alexanders
305-294-19

Angela Guest House
305-294-4480

Artist House
305-296-3977-[Y--]

Authors
305-296-3977

Banyan Resort Of Key West
800-865-33-[G--]

Big Rubys Guesthouse
305-296-2323

Blue Parrot Inn
800-231-2473

Brass Key Guesthouse
305-296-4719

Casa Blanca Bogart
305-296-0815

Chelsea House
305-296-2211

Coconut Grove Guest House
305-296-5107

Colours Key West
305-294-6977

Conch House Heritage Inn
305-293-0020

Cottage
305-294-6003

Curry Mansion
800-253-3466-[Y--]

Cypress House
305-294-6969

Duval House
800-231-2473

Early House
305-296-0214

Eaton Lodge
305-294-3800

Eden House
800-533-KEYS

EH Gato Jr Guesthouse
305-294-0715

Ellies nest
954-296-5757

Enchanted B&B
305-294-9061

Garden House
305-296-5368

Gidson Lowe House
800-856-7444

Heron House
800-294-1644-[G--]

Hollinsed House
305-296-8031

Incentra Carriage House
305-296-5565

Island City House

800-634-8230-[Y--]

Key West B&B
305-296-7274

La Pensione Inn
305-292-23

Lightbourn Inn
800-352-6011

Marquesa Hotel
800-869-4631

Merlin Guesthouse
305-296-3336

Mermaid & The Alligator
305-294-1894

Nassau House
800-545-3907

Oasis Guest House
305-296-2131

Old Custom House Inn
305-294-8507

Old Town Garden Villas
305-294-4427

Orchid House
305-294-0102

Palms Of Key West
800-558-9374-[Y--]

Papas Hideaway Guesthouse
305-294-7709

Pilot House
800-648-3780-[Y--]

Pines of Key West
954-296-7464

Popular House
800-438-6155-[G--]

Rainbow House
305-292-1450

Red Rooster Inn
954-296-6558

Sea Isle Resort
305-294-5188

Seascape
305-296-7776

Simonton Court Guest House
305-294-6386

Southernmost Guest House
305-296-0641

Sunrise B&B
305-5-2706

Sweet Caroline B&B
305-296-5173

Tilton Hilton
305-294-8697

Treetop Inn
305-293-0712

Tropical Inn
305-294-77

Walden House
305-296-7161

Watson House
800-621-9405-[G--]

Westwinds
305-296-4440

Whispers B&B Inn
305-294-5969

Wicker Guesthouse
954-296-4275

Kissimmee
Beaumont House
407-846-7916

Unicorn Inn
407-846-1200

Lake Butler
Rolling Ridge Ranch
904-755-0211

Lake Helen
Clausers B&B
904-228-0310

Lake Park
B&B Of The Palm Beaches
407-848-6320

Lake Wales
Chalet Suzanne Country Inn
800-433-6011-[G--]

Noahs Ark
800-346-1613

Bold Name - *Description appears in other section* *Florida*

Lakeland
Lake Morton B&B
813-686-6788

Magnolias Inn The Park
813-686-7275

Lauderdale By The Sea
Breakaway Guest House
305-771-6600

Lighthouse Point
Posada Inn
800-330-HOME

Little Torch Key
Little Palm Island Resort
800-3GETLOST

Madeira Beach
Lighthouse B&B
813-391-0015

Maitland
Thurston House
407-539-1911

Marathon
B&B Of Florida Keys
305-743-4118

Hopp Inn Guest House
305-743-4118

Mayo
Jim Hollis River Rendevous
904-294-2510

Miami
Inn On The Bay
305-865-7100

Miami River Inn
800-468-3589
[G-ITC]

Roberts Ranch
305-598-3257

Miami Beach
Avalon Hotel
800-933-3306

Cadet Hotel B&B
305-672-6688

Cardozo Hotel
800-338-9076

Carlyle Hotel
800-338-9076

Cavalier Hotel
800-338-9076

Essex House
800-55 ESSEX

Jefferson House
305-534-5247

Leslie Hotel
800-338-9076

Penguin Hotel
305-534-9334

Micanopy
Herlong House
800-HERLONG
[G--]

Shady Oak B&B
904-466-3476

Milton
Exchange Hotel
904-626-1500

Minneola
Lake Minneola Inn
352-394-2232

Monticello
Peppermill B&B
904-7-4600

Mount Dora
Raintree House
904-383-5065

Seabrook B&B
904-383-4800

Naples
Inn By The Sea
941-649-4124-[Y--]

Netties B&B
941-643-5395

New Smyrna Beach
Indian River Inn
904-428-2491

Magnolia Inn
904-427-9120

Night Swan B&B
904-423-4940

Riverview Hotel
904-428-5858

North Bay Village

Inn On The Bay & Marina
305-865-7100

North Hutchson Island
Mellon Patch
407-461-5231

Ocala
Doll House B&B
352-351-1167

Nevas B&B
352-732-4607

Ritz Ocala Historic Inn
800-336-0066

Seven Sisters Inn
352-867-1170

Ocklawaha
Lake Weir Inn
904-288-3723

Orange Park
Club Continental
800-877-6070

Orange Springs
Orange Springs
904-546-2052

Orlando
Allens
407-896-16

Alpen Gast Haus
407-277-1811

Briercliff
407-894-0504

Browns B&B
407-423-8858-[Y--]

Buckets Bermuda Bay Hideaway
800-929-2428

Courtyard At Lake Lucerne
800-444-5289

Esthers B&B
407-896-16

Higgins House B&B
407-324-9238-[Y--]

Meadow Marsh
407-656-2064

Perrihouse B&B

800-780-4830

Rio Pinar House
407-277-4903

Spencer Home B&B
407-855-5603

Things Worth Remembering
407-291-2127

Ormond Beach
Dancing Palms
904-441-8800-[Y--]

Tea House Garden
904-672-5557

Palatka
Gaubert B&B

Palm Bay
Casa del Sol
407-728-4676

Palm Beach
Bradley House
561-832-7050

Open House B&B
561-842-5190

Palm Beach Historic Inn
561-832-4009-[G--]

Plaza Inn
561-832-8666

West Palm Beach B&B
800-736-4064-[G--]

Palm Beach Gardens
Heron Cay
561-744-6315

Palm Harbor
B&B Of Tampa Bay
561-785-2342

Florida Suncoast B&B
561-787-3500

Sunrise Guest House
813-934-7157

Palmetto
Five Oaks Inn
800-658-4167-[Y--]

Panama City Beach
Gulf View Inn

©Inn & Travel Memphis, Tennessee

3-151

Florida   **Bold Name** - *Description appears in other section*

904-234-6051

Pensacola
Homestead Inn
904-944-4816-[Y--]

New World Landing
800-258-1103

Sunshine
904-455-6781

Pineland
Cabbage Key Inn
941-283-2278

Pompano Beach
Waterside B&B
305-946-6784

Punta Gorda
Gilchrist B&B Inn
941-575-4129

Royal Palm Beach
LaBelle Francaise
407-793-3550

Ruskin
Ruskin House B&B
813-645-3842

Safety Harbor
Walters House
813-360-3372

Saint Augustine
Alexander Homestead B&B
904-826-4147-[Y--]

Carriage Way B&B
904-829-2467-[GQAR-]

Casa de La Paz
904-829-2915

Casa de Solana
800-771-3555-[Y--]

Casablanca Inn On The Bay
904-829-0928

Castle Garden B&B
904-829-3829-[G--]

Cedar House Inn
904-829-0079

Charlotte House
904-829-3819

Cordova House
904-825-0770

Flagler By The Sea
904-826-4266

Inn At Camachee Harbor
904-825-0003

Kenwood Inn
904-824-2116

Old City House Inn & Restaurant
904-826-0113

Old Mansion Inn
904-824-1975

Old Powder House
800-447-4149-[Y--]

Sailors Rest
904-824-3817

Secret Garden Inn
904-829-3678

Segui Inn
904-825-2811

Southern Wind Inn-East
904-825-3623

Southern Wind Inn-West
904-808-7384

St Francis Inn
800-824-6062-[G--]

Victorian House B&B
904-824-5214

Villas de Marin
904-829-1725

Westcott House
904-824-4301-[Y--]

Saint Cloud
Four Corners Manor
407-957-2328

Hunter Arms Inn
407-891-9855-[G--]

Saint Pete Beach Isl
Swanhome B&B Inn
813-360-1753

Saint Petersburg
Avalon Inn

813-822-7111
Bay Gables B&B
800-822-8803

Bayboro House Old Tampa Bay
813-823-4955-[G--]

Inn On The Beach
813-360-8844

Rose Marie Ray Mansion House B&B
800-274-7520

Saint Petersburg Beach
Bernards B&B

Harrington House
813-778-5444

Islands End
813-360-5023

San Mateo
Ferncourt B&B
904-329-9755

Sanford
Higgins House B&B
407-324-9238-[G--]

Sanibel Island
Song Of The Sea
800-231-1045-[Y--]

Santa Rosa Beach
Bay View House
904-267-1202

Crescent Cafe & Inn
904-267-3333

Highlands House
904-267-0110

Sarasota
B&B By The Sea
941-388-4039

Bay View Home
941-388-1772

Crescent House
941-346-0857

Hardisty Inn On The Bay
941-955-4683

Harrington House
813-778-5444-[Y--]

Phillippi Crest Inn
941-924-2396

Sarasota B&B

Seagrove Beach
Sugar Beach Inn
904-231-1577

Seaside
Dolphin Inn At Seaside
800-443-3146

Josephines B&B
800-848-1840

Sebastian
Davis House B&B
561-589-3108

Shalimar
B&B Emerald Coast
904-651-1567

Sparr
Tara Oaks
904-622-80

Stuart
Harborfront Inn
561-288-7289-[Y--]

Homeplace B&B
561-220-9148

Sugarloaf
Nancy Williams Street Inn
305-744-7207

Summerland
Knightswood
305-872-2246

Tallahassee
Governors Inn
904-681-6855

Riedel House
904-222-8569

Tampa
Country Inn
813-877-3649

Duncan House B&B
813-778-6858-[Y--]

Gram's Place B&B
813-221-0596-[Y--]

Hyde Park Inn
800-347-5834-[Y--]

Tarpon Springs

3-152   ©*Inn & Travel Memphis, Tennessee*

Bold Name - *Description appears in other section*   *Florida - Georgia*

Fioritos B&B
813-937-5487

Livery Stable

Spring Bay Bayou Inn
813-938-9333-[Y--]

Venice
Banyan House
941-484-1385

Wakulla
Wakulla Springs & Lodge
904-224-5950

West Palm Beach
Hibiscus House
561-683-5633

Morelands B&B
561-683-5372

West Palm Beach B&B
800-736-4064-[G--]

Winter Garden
Casa Abode
407-876-5432

Winter Haven
JD's Southern Oaks
407-293-2335

Winter Park
Fortnightly Inn
407-645-4440

Park Plaza Hotel
800-228-7220

Zolfo Springs
Double M Ranch B&B
813-735-0286

GEORGIA

Adairsvile
Old Home Place
706-625-3649

Albany
Beggars Bush-Cane Miller
912-432-9241

Americus
Cottage Inn
912-924-9316

Guerry House 1833
912-924-1009

Hideout B&B
912-924-9800

Lee Street 1884
912-928-3350

Merriwood Country Inn
912-924-42

Morgan Towne House B&B
912-649-3663

Morris Manor
912-924-4884

New Land B&B
912-928-9620

Pathway Inn
800-889-1466

Windsor Hotel
912-924-1555

Wise Old Pine Inn
912-846-5491

Andersonville
A Place Away
912-924-1044

Athens
Bed & Breakfast
706-546-9740

Bramlette B&B
706-546-9740

Hardeman/Hutchens House
706-353-1855

Magnolia Terrace
706-548-3860

Oakwood B&B
800-546-7886

Atlanta
Ansley Inn
800-446-5416

Bellaire House
404-237-5456

Beverly Hills Inn
800-331-8520-[Y--]

Halcyon B&B
404-688-4458

Inman Park-Woodruff Cottage B&B
404-688-9498-[G--]

King Keith House B&B
404-688-7330-[YQAR-]

Oakwood House B&B
404-521-9320 [GQA-]

Shellmont B&B Lodge
404-872-9290-[Y--]

Sixty Polk Street, A B&B
800-497-2075

Sugar Magnolia B&B
404-222-0226

Woodruff B&B
800-473-9449[G--]

Augusta
Oglethorpe Inn
706-724-9774

Partridge Inn
800-476-8888

Perrin Guest House Inn
706-736-3737

Telfair - Victorian Village
800-241-2407

West Bank Inn

Bainbridge
White House B&B
912-248-1703

Blairsville
Maple Bend Inn
706-745-6549

Southern Country Inn
800-297-1603

Blakely
Layside
912-723-8932-[Y--]

Blue Ridge
Merchants Hopes Inn
706-632-9000

Brunswick
Brunswick Manor-Maj Downing House
912-265-6889

Rose Manor Guest House
912-267-6369

Scarlett House
912-264-5902

Buena Vista
Jenny May & Sapps B&B
912-649-7307

Morgan Towne House B&B
912-649-3663

Yesteryears Inn
912-649-7307

Buford
Allen Mansion
770-945-1080

Cairo
B&B Widehall
912-377-6280

Calhoun
Stoneleigh
706-629-2093

Canton
Standifer Inn
770-345-5805

Cave Spring
Hearn Academy Inn
706-777-8865

Chickamauga
Gordon-Lee House
800-487-4728

Chula
Hummingbirds Perch B&B
912-382-5431-[Y--]

Clarkesville
Burns-Sutton House
706-754-5565

Charm House
706-754-9347

Glen-Ellen Springs Inn
800-552-3479

La Parades

Georgia **Bold Name** - *Description appears in other section*

706-947-3312

Le Pardes
706-947-3312

Spring Hill B&B
706-754-7094

Clarkston
Hensler House
404-296-9262

Clayton
Beechwood Inn
706-782-5485

English Manor Inn
800-782-5780

Green Shutters
706-782-3342

Lake Rabun Inn
800-782-5780

Old Clayton Inn
706-782-7722

Stoneybrook Inn

Cleveland
Cedar Hill B&B
706-865-2666

Lodge At Windy Acres
706-865-6635

Rusharon
706-865-5738

Schlemers B&B
706-865-5897

Towering Oaks B&B Lodge
706-865-6760-[Y--]

Tyson Homestead
706-865-6914

Vellum Valley Inn
706-865-6379

Colquitt
Country Inn
800-453-6581

Columbus
Mountain Top Inn & Resort
706-323-7331

Rothchild-Pound House
800-585-4075

Commerce
Pittman House
706-335-3823

Dahlonega
Cavender Castle
706-864-4895

Forrest Hills Mountain Resort
706-864-6465

Laurel Ridge
706-864-7817

Mountain Top Lodge
800-526-9754

Royal Guard Inn
706-864-1713-[Y--]

Smith House
800-852-9577

Stanton Storehouse B&B Inn
706-864-6114

Worley Homestead
706-864-7002-[Y--]

Dalton
Amy's Place
706-226-2481

Holly Tree House
706-278-6620

Danielsville
Honey Bear Hideaway Farm
706-789-2569

Danville
Danville Plantation
912-962-3988

Magnolia Plantation
912-962-3988

Darien
Open Gates
770-437-6985

Decatur
Oakwood House B&B
770-521-9320
[GQA-]

Dillard
Dillard Horse Farms

706-746-5349

Dillards House
706-746-5348

Gingerbread House
706-746-3234

White Hall Inn
706-746-5511

Dublin
VIP B&B
912-275-3739

Eastman
Dodge Hill Inn
800-628-3778

Eatonton
Crockett House
706-485-2248

Elberton
Sweet Georgia Suites
706-283-01-[Y--]

Ellijay
Elderberry Inn
706-635-2218

Fitzgerald
Dickson Farm Inn
912-423-9859

Forsyth
Country Place
912-4-2705

Fort Oglethorpe
Captain's Quarters B&B
706-858-0624-[Y--]

Fort Valley
Evans-Cantrell House
912-825-0611

Gainesville
Dunlap House
770-536-0200-[Y--]

Grantville
Bonnie Castle B&B
770-583-3090

Greensboro
Early Hill
706-453-7876

Greenville
Samples B&B
706-672-4765

Hamilton
Gray Oaks Inn
706-886-6496

Wedgwood B&B
706-628-5659

Hartwell
Hartwell Inn

Hawkinsville
Black Swan Inn
912-783-4466

Hawkinsville B&B
912-783-4001

Helen
Derdenhoff Inn

Dutch Cottage
706-878-3135

Greer Lodge B&B
706-878-3478

Habersham Hollow Inn
706-745-5147

Helendorf Inn
706-878-2271

Hilltop Haus
706-878-2388

Hepzibah
Into The Woods B&B
706-554-1400

Hiawassee
Mountain Memories Inn
706-896-1304

Hoboken
Blueberry Hill
912-458-2605

Hochston
Hillcrest Grove

Hogansville
Fair Oaks Inn
706-637-5100

Fernbrook B&B Inn
706-637-8828

Homerville
Helmstead
912-487-2222

Jasper
Woodbridge Inn

3-154 ©*Inn & Travel Memphis, Tennessee*

Bold Name - *Description appears in other section* *Georgia*

706-692-6293

Jesup
Trowell House
912-530-6611

Lakemont
Anapauo Farm
706-782-6442

Barn Inn
706-782-5094

Lake Rabun Inn
706-782-4946

Little Duck Inn
800-782-5780

Lavonia
Southern Trace
706-356-1033

Lookout Mountain
Chanticleer Inn
423-820-2015

Lyons
Robert Toombs Inn
912-526-4489

Macon
1842 Inn
800-336-1842-[Y--]

La Petite Maison
912-742-4674

Stone-Conner House
912-745-0258

Madison
Boat House B&B
706-342-3061

Brady Inn/Three Chimneys
706-342-4400

Burnett Place
706-342-4034

Turn Of The Century
706-342-1890

Marietta
Blue & Grey B&B
770-425-0392

Marlow House
770-426-1881

Sixty Polk Street, A B&B

800-497-2075-[Y--]

Stanley House
770-426-1881-[Y--]

Milledgeville
Plain Plantation Quarters
912-452-8350

Moultrie
Pinefields Plantation
912-985-2066

Mountain City
York House
800-231-YORK-[Y--]

Newnan
Parrott Camp Soucy House
770-253-4846

Southern Comfort B&B
770-254-9266

Norman Park
Quailridge B&B
912-769-3201

Palmetto
Serenbe B&B
770-463-2614

Parrott
217 Huckaby
912-623-5545

Perry
Swift Street Inn
912-987-3428

Pine Mountain
Davis Inn
800-346-2668

Mountain Top Inn & Resort
800-533-6376

Storms House
706-663-9100

Wedgwood B&B
706-628-5659

Plains
Plains B&B Inn
912-824-7252-[Y--]

Rabun Gap
Moon Valley Resort
706-746-2466

Valley Of Hidden Paths
706-746-2278

Ringgold
Buckleys Cedar House
706-935-2619

Roswell
Ten Fifty Canton Street
770-8-1050

Saint Marys
Goodbread House
912-882-7490-[Y--]

Hist Spencer House Inn
912-882-1872

Riverview Hotel
912-882-3242

Saint Simmons
Country Hearth Inn
912-638-7805

Saint Simons Island
Kings On The March
912-638-1426

Little St Simons Island
912-638-7472-[Y--]

Sautee
Glen-Kenimer-Tucker House
706-878-2364

Gramdpas Room B&B
706-878-2364

Lumsden Homeplace
706-878-2813

Nacochee Valley House
706-878-3830

Stovall House
706-878-3355

Woodhaven Chalet
706-878-2580

Savannah
"417" The Haslan Fort House
912-233-6380

118 West
912-234-8557

17 Hundred 90 Inn
912-236-7122

B&B Inn
912-238-0518

Ballastone Inn & Townhouse
800-822-4553-[G--]

Barrister House
912-234-0621

Bed & Breakfast Inn
912-238-0518

Camellias Tree Toad Inn
912-231-8811

Charlton Court
912-236-2895

Comer House
912-234-2923

East Bay Inn
800-500-1225

Eliza Thompson House
800-348-9378-[G--]

Foley House Inn
800-647-3708

Forsyth Park Inn
912-233-6800-[Y--]

Gastonian
800-322-6603

Guerard-McClelland House
912-236-1863

Haslam-Fort House
912-233-6380

Jesse Mount House
912-236-1774

Joan's On Jones
912-234-3863

Kehoe House
912-232-1020

Liberty Inn 1834
800-637-1007-[Y--]

Lions Head Inn
800-355-LION-[G--]

©*Inn & Travel Memphis, Tennessee* 3-155

Georgia - Louisiana **Bold Name** - *Description appears in other section*

Magnolia Place Inn
800-238-7674

Mary Lees House
912-232-0891

Morel House
912-234-4088

Mulberry Inn
800-554-5544

Olde Harbour Inn
800-553-6533

Planters Inn
800-554-1187

Presidents Quarters
800-227-0650

Pulaski Square Inn
800-227-0650

Remshart Brooks House
912-234-6928

River Street Place
800-A-LEGACY

Royal Colony Inn
912-232-5678

Stoddard Cooper House
912-233-6809

Timmons House
912-233-4456

Victoria Barie House
912-236-6446

Senoia
  Carriage House B&B
  770-5-6321

  Culpepper House
  770-5-8182

  Veranda
  770-5-3905-[Y--]

Statesboro
  Red's Trellis Garden Inn
  912-489-8781

  Statesboro Inn
  912-489-8628-[Y--]

Stone Mountain

Silver Hill B&B Inn
770-469-0432

The Village Inn B&B
800-214-8385

Swainsboro
  Coleman House B&B Inn
  912-237-2822

  Edenfield House Inn
  912-237-3007

Tate
  Tate House
  800-342-7515

Thomaston
  Gordon Street Inn
  770-647-5477

  Guest House
  706-647-1203

  Hightower Ironside House
  706-647-6440

  Whitfield Inn
  706-647-2482

  Woodall House
  770-647-7044

Thomasville
  1880 Paxton House B&B
  912-226-5197

  1884 Paxton House
  912-226-5197

  Deer Creek B&B
  912-226-7294-[Y--]

  Evans House B&B
  800-344-4717

  Grand Victoria Inn
  912-226-7460

  Our Cottage On The Park
  912-227-0404

  Quail Country B&B
  912-226-7218

  Susina Plantation Inn
  912-377-9644

  Victoria Grand

B&B Inn
912-226-7460

Willowlake
912-226-6372

Thomson
  1810 West Inn
  800-515-1810

  Four Chimneys B&B
  706-597-0220

  West Field B&B
  706-595-3156

Tifton
  Myron B&B
  912-382-0959

Toccoa
  Habersham Manor House
  706-886-6496

  Simmons-Bond Inn
  706-886-8411

Tybee Island
  Hunter House B&B
  912-786-7515

Valdosta
  Magnolia Plantation
  912-247-5318

Villa Rica
  Ahava Plantaion B&B
  770-459-4978

  Twin Oaks B&B & Farm Vacation
  770-459-4374

Warm Springs
  Burress B&B
  706-655-2168

  Hotel Warm Springs, A B&B
  706-655-2114

Washington
  Blackmon B&B
  404-678-2278

  Colley House B&B
  404-678-7752

  Holly Ridge Country Inn
  706-285-2594

Liberty B&B Inn
404-679-3107

Olmstead B&B
404-678-1050

Water Oak Cottage
404-678-3605

Watkinsville
  Rivendell B&B
  706-769-4522

Waverly Hall
  Raintree Farms
  706-582-3227

Waycross
  Caitlyns Courtyard Inn
  912-284-1755

Waynesboro
  Georgia's Guest B&B
  706-554-4863

West Point
  Nesting Place
  706-643-8164

Winterville
  Old Winterville Inn
  706-742-7340

LOUISIANA

Abbeville
  La Bonne Veillee
  318-937-5495

Amite
  Belle Amie
  504-748-9731

  Blythewood Plantation
  504-748-8183

  Elliott House
  504-748-8553

  Stewarts Cottage
  504-748-3700

  Sweethall
  504-748-8612

Armite
  Dr CS Stewarts Cottage
  504-748-3700

Bastrop
  Johnson House

Bold Name - *Description appears in other section* **Louisiana**

318-283-2200

Baton Rouge
Joys B&B
504-766-2291-[Y--]

Mount Hope
Plantation
504-766-8600

White Castle Inn
504-545-32-[G--]

Breaux Bridge
Bayor Boudin &
Cracklin
318-332-6158

Brittany
Rosewood Manor
504-675-5781

Broussard
Maison d'Andre Billeaud
800-960-REST-[G--]

Bunkie
Homeplace
318-826-7558

Carencro
La Maison de Campagne
800-368-3806-[Y--]

Chatham
Nostalgia Inn
318-323-3793

Clinton
Brame-Bennett
House
504-683-5241

Martin Hill
504-683-5594

Covington
Claiborne
Courthouse Inn
504-893-0119

Plantation Bell
Guest House
504-893-7693

Riverside Hills
Farm
504-892-1794

Darrow
Tezcuco Plantation B&B
504-562-3929-[Y--]

Folsom
Woods Hole Inn
504-796-9077

Gloster
Buena Vista
Plantation
318-925-2569

Greenwood
Lake At Lickskillte
318-938-7859

Houma
Cajun House Of
Hospitality
504-872-0465

Chez Maudrey B&B
504-879-3285

Peacock Inn
504-876-1810

Jackson
Asphodel Village
504-654-6868-[Y--]

Milbank Mansion
504-634-5901-[Y--]

Jeanerette
B&B On Bayou
Teche
318-276-5061

Patouts Guest
House
318-364-0644

Kenner
Seven Oaks
504-888-8649

Lafayette
A La Maison de
T'Frere
318-984-9347

Bois des Chenes
Plantation
318-233-7816

Mouton Manor Inn
318-237-66

Lafitte
Victoria Inn
504-689-4757-[Y--]

Lecompte
Hardy House B&B
318-776-5178

Leesville
Huckleberry Inn

B&B
318-238-4000

Madisonville
River Run B&B
504-845-4222

Martinville
La Place
d'Evangeline
318-394-4010

Metairie
Hedgewood
504-895-9708

Monroe
Boscobel Cottage
B&B
318-325-1550

Stratford House Inn
318-388-8868

Natchitoches
Breazeale House
318-352-5620

Cloutier Townhouse
318-352-5242

Fleur de Lis Inn
318-352-6621

Harling Lane B&B
318-357-8417

Jefferson House
318-352-3957

Laureate House
318-357-9594

Martins Roost B&B
318-352-9215

River Oaks B&B
318-352-9111

New Iberia
Estorge-Norton
House
318-365-7603

Inn At Le Rosier
318-367-5306

La Maision B&B
318-364-2970

Lerosier B&B
318-367-5306

Maison Marceline
318-364-5922-[Y--]

Perry House
318-365-1000

Pourtos House
800-336-7317

New Orleans
623 Ursulines
504-529-5489

Acadian House
504-891-4024

Andrew Jackson
Hotel
504-561-5881

Annabell's House
B&B
504-8-0701

Arlington House
504-596-6900

Beau Sejour B&B
504-897-3746

Bougainvillea House
504-525-3983

Casa Demarigny
Guesthouses
504-948-3875

Columns
504-8-9308

Cornstalk
504-523-1515-[Y--]

Creole House
504-524-8076

Dufour Baldwin
House
504-945-1503

Dusty Mansion
504-895-4576

Duvingneaud House
504-948-6730

Edgar Degas House
504-948-6730

Essems House B&B
504-947-3401

Fairchild House
800-256-8096

French Quarter
Maisons
504-524-18

Louisiana *Bold Name* - *Description appears in other section*

Garden District B&B
504-638-3890

Grenoble House Inn
504-522-1331

Hansel & Gretel House
504-524-0141

Hensens B&B
504-897-1895

Hotel Maison Deville
800-634-1600

Hotel Provincial
504-581-45

Hotel St Helene
800-348-3888

Hotel St Pierre
800-225-4040-[Y--]

Hotel The Frenchman
800-831-1781

Hotel Villa Covento
504-522-1793-[Y--]

House On Bayou Road
504-945-02

Jennys Guest House
504-482-9441

Josephine Guest House
504-524-6361

La Maison Marigny
800-729-2257

Lafayette Hotel
800-733-4754

Lafitte Guest House
800-331-7971-[Y--]

Lamothe House
800-367-5858

Longpre Gardens Guest House
504-561-0654-[Y--]

Macarthy Park Guest House

800-521-2790

Mardi Gras House
504-234-0192-[Y--]

Marigny Guest House
504-944-9700

Marquette House Ayh Hostel
504-523-3014

Mazant Street Guest House
504-944-2662

Mechlings 1860 Mansion
800-725-4131

Melrose
504-944-2255

New Orleans Guest House
504-566-1177

Nine-O-Five Royal Hotel
504-523-0129

Old World Inn
504-566-1330

Oliver House Hotel
504-525-8456

Park View Guest House
504-861-7564-[Y--]

Pegs Pad
504-861-7564

PJ Holbrooks Olde Victorian Inn
800-725-2446-[Y--]

Prince Conti Hotel
504-529-4172

Prytania Inn I
504-566-1515-[Y--]

Prytania Inn II
504-586-0858

Prytania Park Hotel
800-862-1984

Rathbone Inn
504-947-2100

Ruffled Pelican Guest Rooms

504-865-9869

Soniat House
800-544-8808

St Ann/Marie Antoinette
504-581-1881

St Charles Guest House
504-523-6556

St Peter House
800-535-7815-[Y--]

St Vincents Guesthouse
504-523-3411

Sully Mansion
504-891-0457

Terrell House
800-878-9859-[Y--]

Victoria Inn
504-689-4757-[Y--]

New Roads
Garden Gate Manor
800-487-3890

Mon Reve B&B
504-638-7848

Nondy House & Claiborne House

Pointe Coupee B&B
800-832-7412

River Blossom Inn
504-638-8650

Ponchatoula
Bedico Creek Inn
504-845-8057

Bella Rose Mansion
504-386-3857
[GQA-]

Port Sulphur
River Place B&B
504-564-2485

Prairieville
Tree House In The Park
800-LE-CABIN

Rayne
Ma Ti Reue
318-334-3489

River Ridge
Levee View
504-737-5471

Saint Francisville
Barrow House
504-635-4791

Butler Greenwood B&B
504-635-6312-[G--]

Cottage Plantation
504-635-3674

Green Springs Plantation
800-457-4978

Lake Rosemound Inn
504-635-3176

Myrtles Plantation
504-635-6277

Propinquity B&B
504-635-4116

Shadetree
504-635-6116

The Lodge At The Bluffs
504-634-3410

Wolf Schlesinger House
800-488-6502

Saint Martinsville
Evangeline Oak Inn
318-394-7675

La Place de Evangeline
318-394-4010

Shreveport
Columns On Jordan
318-222-5912

Fairfield Place
318-222-0048

Slattery House
318-222-6577-[G--]

Twenty Four Thirty Nine
318-424-2424-[Y--]

Silbey
Calloway Corner
800-851-1088

Bold Name - *Description appears in other section*   *Louisiana - Mississippi*

Slidell
 Salmen-Fritchie House
 800-235-4168

Sunset
 Chretien Point Plantation B&B
 318-233-7050

Thibodaux
 Robchiaux House
 504-447-4738

Vacherie
 Oak Alley Plantation
 504-265-2151

Vinton
 Old Lyons House
 318-389-2903

Wakefield
 Wakefield Plantation

Washington
 Camellia Cove
 318-826-7362

 Country House
 318-826-3052

 De La Morandiere
 318-826-3510

 La Chaumiere
 318-826-3976

White Castle
 Nottoway Plantation Inn
 504-545-2730
 [GQA-]

 White Castle Inn
 504-545-32-[G--]

Wilson
 Glencoe Plantation
 504-629-5387

Winnfield
 Southern Colonial B&B
 318-628-6087

MISSISSIPPI

Bay Saint Louis
 Bay View Inn
 601-352-6904

 Baytown Inn
 601-466-5870

Biloxi
 Red Creek Colonial Inn
 800-729-9670-[G--]

Brookhaven
 Edgewood
 601-833-2001

Chatham
 Mount Holly
 601-827-2652

Church Hill
 Cedars Plantation
 601-445-2203

Columbus
 Amzi Love B&B
 601-328-5413

 Cartney Hunt House
 601-327-4259

 Temple Heights

Corinth
 General's Quarters B&B & Restaurant
 601-286-3325-[Y--]

 Madison Inn
 601-287-7157

 Robbins Nest B&B
 601-286-3109

Dundee
 Uncle Henrys
 601-337-2757

Fayette
 Springfield Plantation
 601-786-3802

French Camp
 French Camp B&B
 601-547-6482

Greenville
 A Victorian B&B
 601-335-6000

Grenada
 Doler B&B
 601-637-2695-[Y--]

Gulfport
 Magnolia Plantation Hotel
 800-700-7858

Hernando
 Sassafras B&B
 800-882-1897

Houston
 Harmon Hall House
 601-456-2131

Jackson
 Fairview
 601-948-3429

 Millsaps Buie House
 601-352-0221-[Y--]

Kosciusko
 Redbud Inn
 601-289-5086-[G--]

Long Beach
 Red Creek Colonial Inn
 800-729-9670-[G--]

Louisville
 St Charles Place
 601-773-5786

Meadville
 Hancock House
 601-384-5080

Meridian
 Hamilton Hall
 601-483-8696

Natchez
 Anut Pitty-Pats
 601-446-5231

 Auburn
 601-442-5981

 Briars
 601-446-9654

 Burn
 800-654-8859

 Camellia Gardens
 601-446-7944

 Clifton House
 601-446-8047

 d'Evereux

 Dixie

 Dorsey House
 601-442-5845

 Dunleith
 800-443-2445

Elgin Plantation
601-446-6100

Gibson Gap
601-445-8788

Glen Auburn
601-442-40

Glenfield
800-553-8554

Governor Holmes House
601-442-2366

Guest House Of Natchez
601-442-1054

Harper House
601-445-5557

Highpoint
601-442-6963

Hope Farms
601-445-4848

Lansdowne
800-647-6742

Linden Place
601-445-5472

Lisle house
601-442-7680

Melrose
601-446-9408

Monmouth
601-442-5852

Mount Repose Plantation
601-442-0097-[Y--]

Oakland Plantation
800-824-0355
[GQA-]

Oakwood
601-445-5101

Perennials B&B
601-442-40

Pleasant Hill
601-442-7674

Presbyterian Manse
601-446-9735-[Y--]

Propinqity

Mississippi - North Carolina

Bold Name - *Description appears in other section*

Ravenna
601-446-73

Ravennaside
601-442-8015

Riverside B&B
601-446-5730

Shields Town House
601-442-7680

Sweet Olive Tree Manor
601-442-1401

T.A.S.S.
601-446-5231

Texada
601-445-4232

Trosclair House
601-442-2989

Twin Oaks

Wensel House
601-445-2105

Weymouth Hall
601-445-2304-[Y--]

Wigwam
601-446-8938

William Harris House
601-445-2003

Nesbit
Bonne Terre
601-781-5100

Olive Branch
Brigadoon Farm Retreat
800-895-3098

Oxford
Isom Place
601-234-3310

Oliver Britt House
601-234-8043

Pass Christian
Harbour Oaks Inn
800-452-93

Pontotoc
Nisbet House

Port Gibson
Oak Square

Plantation
800-729-0240
[YQA-]

Robinsonville
Cottage Inn
800-363-2900-[G--]

Satartia
No Mistake Plantation
601-746-6579

Senatobia
Spahn House
800-400-9853

Slate Springs
Doler B&B
601-637-2695-[Y--]

South Haven
Blue Bird Ridge
601-781-0173

Starkeville
Cotton District B&B
601-323-5132

Doler B&B
601-637-2695-[Y--]

Tunica
Tuncia Levee Inn
800-363-3008

Tupelo
Mocking Bird Inn B&B
601-844-5271-[Y--]

Vicksburg
Anchuca
800-262-4822

Annabelle
800-634-8564

Balfour House
601-638-3690

Belle Of The Bends
c1876
800-844-2308

Cedar Grove Mansion
800-862-1300-[Y--]

Ceres Plantation
c1820
800-259-0547

Cherry Street Cottage

601-636-7086

Corners
800-444-7421-[Y--]

Duff Green Mansion
800-2-0037

Flowerree (1870)
800-262-6315

Gray Oaks
601-638-4424

Manor House
601-638-0683

Old Feld Home

Tomil Manor
601-638-8893

West
Alexander House
601-967-2417-[G--]

Woodville
Square Ten Inn
601-888-33-[Y--]

NORTH CAROLINA

Aberdeen
Bryant House
919-944-3300

Almond
Euchella Sport Lodge
800-446-1603

Andrews
Cover House
704-321-5302-[G--]

Grant House B&B
704-321-6089

Howard Haus B&B
704-321-4103

Huntington Hall B&B
800-824-6189-[G--]

Walker Inn
704-321-5019

Arden
Blake House Inn
704-684-1847-[Y--]

Asheboro
Doctors Inn B&B

919-625-4916

Old Oak Guest House
919-672-2345

Asheville
Abbington Green
704-251-2454

Acorn Lodge
704-253-0609

Albemarle Inn
704-255-0027-[G--]

Applewood Manor
704-254-2244

Beaufort House Victorian B&B
704-254-8334

Black Walnut B&B
704-254-3878-[Y--]

Bois D Arc B&B
704-253-4345

Bridle Path Inn
704-252-0035

Carin Brae
704-252-9219

Carolina B&B
704-254-3608

Claddagh Inn
800-225-4700-[G--]

Corner Oak Manor
704-253-3525

Dogwood Cottage Inn
704-258-9725

Flint Street Inn
704-253-6723

Heritage Hill
704-254-9336-[Y--]

Inn On Montford
800-254-9569

Johnson Inn
704-258-2868

Lion & The Rose
704-255-ROSE

Millers Mountain Lodge
704-2-3542

3-160 ©Inn & Travel Memphis, Tennessee

Bold Name - Description appears in other section   **North Carolina**

Old Reynolds Mansion
704-254-0496

Ray House
704-252-0106

Reed House B&B
704-274-1604

Resting Place B&B
704-298-8500

Richmond Hill Inn
800-545-9238-[G--]

Waverly Inn
800-537-8195-[G--]

Windsong A Mountain Inn
704-627-6111-[Y--]

Wright Inn
704-251-0789

Atkinson
  Hawes House B&B
  910-283-5600

Bakersville
  Bakersville Inn B&B
  704-688-3064

Balsam
  Balsam Mountain Inn
  704-456-9498

Banner Elk
  Archers Inn
  704-898-9004-[Y--]

  Banner Elk Inn B&B
  800-547-8438

  Beech Alpen Inn
  704-387-2252

  Manning House
  704-898-9669

  Scammell Corner B&B
  704-963-7210

  Top Of The Beech Inn
  704-387-2252

Bat Cave
  Hickory Nut Gap Inn

704-625-9108

Old Mill Inn
704-625-4256-[Y--]

Original Hickory Nut Gap Inn
704-625-9108

Stonehearth Inn
800-535-6647

Bath
  Bath Guest House
  910-923-6811

Beaufort
  Beaufort Inn
  800-726-0321

  Captains Quarters
  910-728-7711-[Y--]

  Cedars Inn
  800-732-7036-[Y--]

  Delmar Inn
  910-728-4300

  Inlet Inn
  910-728-3600

  Langdon House
  910-728-54

  Pecan Tree Inn
  910-728-6733

  Shotgun House
  910-728-6248

Belhaven
  Pungo River Inn
  910-943-2117

  River Forest Manor
  800-346-2151

Black Mountain
  B&B Over Yonder
  704-669-6762-[Y--]

  Black Mountain Inn
  800-735-6128

  Blackberry Inn
  704-669-8303

  Engel House
  704-669-5960-[Y--]

  Red Rocker Inn
  704-669-51

Blowing Rock
  Gideon Ridge Inn

704-295-3644

Hound Ears Lodge & Club
704-963-4321

Maple Lodge
704-295-3331

Meadowbrook Inn
704-295-4300

Ragged Garden Inn
704-295-9703

Rocking Horse B&B
704-295-3311

Stone Pillar B&B
704-295-4141

Sunshine Inn
704-295-3487

Boone
  Grandma Jeans B&B
  704-262-3670

  Lions Dene
  704-963-5785-[Y--]

  Lovill House Inn
  800-849-0466

Brevard
  Inn Brevard
  704-884-2105-[Y--]

  Linden Tree Manor
  704-877-4735

  Red House Inn
  704-884-9349-[Y--]

  Womble Inn
  704-884-4770

Bryson
  West Oak B&B
  704-488-2438

Bryson City
  Calhoun House
  704-488-8757

  Fisher House B&B
  704-497-5921

  Folkestone Lodge
  704-488-2730

  Fryemont Inn
  800-845-4879

Hemlock Inn
704-488-2885

Nantahala Village
704-488-2826

Randolph House
704-488-3472-[Y--]

Settlers Mountain
800-327-1775

Watering Trough Inn
704-488-3796

Burlington
  Southern General Inn
  910-226-09

Burnsville
  A Little Bit Of Heaven
  704-675-5379

  Celo Inn
  704-675-5132

  Estes Mountain Retreat
  704-682-7264

  Hamrick Inn
  704-675-5251

  Little Bit Of Heaven B&B
  704-675-5379

  Nu Wray Inn
  800-368-9729

  Terrell House
  704-682-4505

Buxton
  Cape Hatteras B&B
  800-252-3316

Cape Careret
  Harbor Light Inn
  800-624-8439

Carolina Beach
  Bayberry B&B
  910-458-9663

  Harbor Lodge
  910-458-3644

Carthage
  Blacksmith Inn
  910-947-1692

Cashiers
  High Hampton Inn

©*Inn & Travel Memphis, Tennessee*   3-161

North Carolina **Bold Name** - *Description appears in other section*

Country Club
800-334-2551

Millstone Inn
704-743-2737

Cedar Mountain
Sassy Goose
704-966-9493

Chadbourn
Magnolia Manor
910-654-5138

Chapel Hill
Caroline Inn
919-933-2001

Fearrington House Country Inn
919-542-2121-[Y--]

Hillcrest House
919-942-2369

Inn At Bingham School
919-563-5583

Pineview Inn

Windy Oaks Farm
919-942-1001

Charlotte
Beckys B&B
704-541-0476

Elizabeth B&B
704-358-1368

Fourth Ward B&B
704-334-1485

Hampton Manor
704-542-62-[Y--]

Homeplace
704-365-1936-[Y--]

Inn On Providence
704-366-6700-[Y--]

Inn Uptown
800-959-10

McElhinney House
704-846-0783

Morehead A Country Inn
704-376-3357

New England Inn
704-362-0005

Overcarsh House
704-334-8477

Poplar Street B&B
704-358-1464

Rosewell Inn
704-3-62

Still Waters
704-3-62

The Elizabeth B&B
704-358-1368

Chimney Rock
Dogwood Inn
800-922-5557

Esmeralda Inn
704-625-9105

Gingerbread Inn
704-625-4038

Clemmons
Manor House
910-766-0594

Tanglewood Manor House
910-766-0591

Clinton
Shield House
800-462-9817-[Y--]

Clyde
Mountain Sunset B&B
704-627-1400

Windsong A Mountain Inn
704-627-6111-[G--]

Concord
HC Hahn House
704-784-1655

Crumpler
Enchanted Farm
910-982-9749

Cullowhee
Cullowhee B&B Inn
704-293-5447

Dillsboro
Applegate Inn
704-586-2397

Dillsboro Inn
704-586-3898

Jarrett House

800-972-5623-[Y--]

Olde Towne Inn
704-586-3461

Squire Watkins Inn
704-586-5244

Duck
Sanderling Inn
919-261-4111

Durham
Arrowhead Inn
800-528-2207-[Y--]

Blooming Garden Inn
919-687-0801

Old North Durham Inn
919-683-1885

Eagle Springs
Inn At Eagle Springs
910-673-2722

Edenton
Captains Quarters Inn
919-482-8945

Governor Eden Inn
919-482-2072

Granville Queen Inn
919-482-5296

Jason House
919-482-3400

Leigh House
919-482-3184

Lords Proprietor's Inn
919-482-3641-[Y--]

Mulberry Hill
800-348-1405

Trestle House Inn
919-482-2282-[Y--]

Elizabeth
Warwick House
910-862-4970

Elizabeth City
Arbor House At Fairlea
919-338-6516

Elizabeth City Inn

919-338-2177

Elizabeth House
919-335-2978

River City B&B
919-338-3337

Ellerbe
Ellerbe Springs Inn & Restaurant
800-248-6467-[Y--]

Emerald Isle
Emerald Isle Inn
919-354-3222

Everetts
B&B In Albermarle

Faison
Magnolia Hall
910-267-9241

Flat Rock
Highland Lake Inn
704-693-6812

Woodfield Inn
800-533-6016-[Y--]

Franklin
Buttonwood Inn
704-369-8985

Country Time B&B
704-369-3648

Franklin Terrace
800-633-2431-[Y--]

Hickory Knoll Lodge
704-524-9666

Lullwater Farmhouse Inn
704-524-6532

Olde Mill House B&B Inn
704-524-5226

Poor Richards Summit Inn
704-524-2006

Snow Hill Inn
800-598-8136

Fuquay Varina
Baileywick
919-552-4891

Gastonia
Falls Ridge B&B

©*Inn & Travel Memphis, Tennessee*

Bold Name - *Description appears in other section* **North Carolina**

704-865-4502

York Chester B&B
800-327-5067

Germanton
Meadowhaven B&B
910-593-36

Glendale Springs
Glendale Springs Inn
910-982-2102

Mountain View Lodge & Cabins
910-982-2233

Glenville
Innisfree Victorian Inn
800-782-1290

Graham
Leftwich House
910-226-5987

Grassy Creek
River House
910-982-2102

Greensboro
Greenwich Inn
910-272-3474

Greenwood B&B
800-535-9363-[Y--]

Plaza Manor
910-274-3074

Hatteras
Outer Banks B&B
919-986-2776

Hayesville
Broadax Inn
704-389-6987

Heather House
704-389-3343

Hazelwood
Belle Meade Inn
704-456-3234

Henderson
Henderson Manor
919-492-5064

La Grange Plantation
919-438-2421

Hendersonville
Claddagh Inn
800-225-4700-[Y--]

Echo Mountain Inn
704-693-9626-[Y--]

Ivy Terrace
800-749-9542-[Y--]

Stillwell House B&B
704-693-6475

Waverly Inn
800-537-8195-[GQAR-]

Westhaven B&B
704-693-8791

Hertford
1812 Inn
919-426-1812

Gingerbread Inn
919-426-5809

Hickory
Hickory B&B
800-654-2961

Hiddenite
Hidden Crystal Inn
704-632-0063

High Point
Premier B&B
919-889-8349

Highlands
4-1/2 Street Inn
704-526-4464

Chandler INn
704-526-52

Colonial Pines Inn
704-526-2060-[Y--]

Fredas B&B
704-526-2091

Highlands Inn
704-526-9380

Kalmia Of Highlands
704-526-2273

Lakeside B&B
704-526-4498

Long House B&B
800-833-0020

Mirror Lake Lodging

704-526-5941

Morningstar Inn
704-526-1009

Old Edwards Inn
704-526-5036

Phelps House
704-526-2590

The Guest House
704-526-4536

Ye Olde Stone House B&B
704-526-5911

Hillsborough
Colonial Inn
919-732-2461

Hillsborough House Inn
800-616-1660-[G--]

Inn At Teardrop
919-732-1120

Hot Springs
Duckett House Inn & Farm
704-622-7621

Hubert
Shell B&B
910-326-3667

Jefferson
Maple Hill B&B
910-246-4977

Rocking Chair B&B
910-246-3060

Kill Devil Hills
Cherokee Inn
800-554-2764-[G--]

Figurehead B&B
919-441-6929

Kitty Hawk
Three Seasons Guest House
919-261-4791

Lake Junaluska
Brookside Lodge
704-456-8897

Lagoalinda Lodge
704-456-3620

Lambuth Inn
800-222-4930

Providence Lodge
704-456-6486

Sunset Inn
704-456-6114

Lake Lure
Fairfield Mountains
704-625-9111

Lodge On Lake Lure
704-625-2789-[Y--]

Lake Norman
24 Spring Run B&B
704-664-6686

Lake Toxaway
Earthshine Mountain Lodge
704-862-4207

Greystone Inn
800-824-5766-[Y--]

Lake Waccamaw
B&B By The Lake
910-646-4744

Laurel Springs
Burgiss Farm
910-359-25

Doughton Hall B&B
910-359-2434

Lawsonville
Southwyck Farm
910-593-8006

Lenoir
R&R Hideaway
800-524-8904

Lewisville
Belford House B&B
919-728-6031

Lexington
Carefree Cottages
919-441-5340

Lillington
Waverleys Of Lillington
910-893-6760

Linville
Eseeola Lodge

Little Switzerland
Alpine Inn
704-765-5380

Big Lynn Lodge

©*Inn & Travel Memphis, Tennessee*

3-163

North Carolina

Bold Name - *Description appears in other section*

800-654-5232

Big Mill Lodge
919-792-3036

Switzerland Inn
704-765-2153

Louisburg
Hearthside Inn B&B
919-496-6776

Pond Meadows Inn
919-853-3555

Madison
Boxley B&B
910-427-0543

Maggie Valley
Cataloochee Ranch
704-976-1401

Maggie Valley Chalet
800-648-1210

Mountainbrook Inn
704-926-3962

Smoky Shawods Lodge
704-926-0001

Snuggle Inn
704-926-3782

Twinbrook Resort

Manteo
Scarborough Inn
919-473-3979

Tranquil House Inn
800-458-7069-[Y--]

Mars Hill
Barid House B&B Inn
704-689-5722

Marshall
Marshall House
800-759-9739

Mebane
Old Place B&B
919-563-1733

Milton
Woodside Inn
910-234-8646

Mocksville
Boxwood Lodge

704-284-2031

Monroe
Bunties B&B
704-289-1155

Mooresville
Oak Ridge Farm B&B
704-663-7085

Morehead City
Dill House B&B
919-726-4449

Morgantown
Burlesons House B&B
704-437-5356

Mount Airy
Mayberry B&B
919-786-2045

Merritt House
910-786-2174

Pine Ridge Inn
910-789-5034-[Y--]

Mountain Home
Courtland Manor
704-692-1133

Mountain Home Inn
800-397-0066

Murfreesboro
Windbourne House
919-398-5224

Murphy
Hill Street Guest House
704-837-8842

Hill Top House
704-837-8661

Hoover House
704-837-8734

Huntington Hall B&B
800-824-6189-[G--]

Nags Head
First Colony Inn
800-368-9390-[G--]

Ocean Inn
800-262-6082

Tranquil House Inn
800-458-7069-[G--]

Ye Olde Cherokee Inn
919-441-6127-[Y--]

New Bern
Airie
800-849-5553

Bradbury Inn
919-633-6122

Harmony House Inn
919-636-3810-[Y--]

Kings Arms Inn
800-872-9306-[Y--]

New Bern House
800-842-7688

Newland
Mortimer House
704-733-2114

Robbins Nest B&B
704-733-2702

Ocracoke
Beach House
919-928-6471

Berkley Country Inn
919-929-5911

Blackbeards Lodge
919-928-3421

Boyette House
919-928-4261

Crews Inn
919-928-7011

Eugenas B&B
919-928-1411

Island Inn
919-928-4351

Pamilco Lodges
919-928-1661

Pelican Lodge
919-928-1661

Ships Timbers B&B
919-928-4061

Ocracoke Island
Inn At Old Fort
910-668-9384

Oscars House
919-928-1311

Oriental
Cartwright House B&B
919-249-1337

Tar Heel Inn
919-249-1078-[Y--]

Outer Banks
Tranquil House Inn
800-458-7069-[Y--]

Oxford
Gen BS Royster B&B
919-690-1228

Penland
Chinquapin Inn
704-765-0064

Pilot Mountain
Pilot Know A-B&B Inn
910-325-2502

Pinehurst
Magnolia Inn
910-295-6900

Pine Crest Inn
910-295-6121

Pisgah Forest
Key Falls Inn
704-884-7559

Patton House
704-877-4000

Pines Country Inn
704-877-3131-[Y--]

Pittsboro
Fearrington House Country Inn
919-542-2121-[Y--]

Plymouth
Four Gables B&B
919-793-6696

Polkville
Pattersons Carriage Shop
704-538-3929

Raleigh
Acadian House B&B
919-975-3967

Oakwood Inn
919-832-9712-[Y--]

Bold Name - *Description appears in other section* **North Carolina**

Old Plough B&B
919-221-1212-[Y--]

The Shield House
800-462-9817-[Y--]

William Thomas Manor
919-755-9400

Ridgecrest
Abigails B&B
704-669-5196

Roaring Gap
Roaring Gap Inn
910-363-1234

Robbins
Delores Moores B&B

Robbinsville
Blue Boar Lodge
704-479-8126

Snowbird Mountain Lodge
704-479-3433

Rocky Mount
Sunset Inn
800-786-7386

Rosman
Red Lion Inn
704-884-6868

Rutherfordton
Carrier House
704-287-4222

Pinebrea Manor B&B
704-286-1543

Salisbury
1868 Stewart Marsh
704-633-6841

Rowan Oak House
800-786-0437-[Y--]

Stewart Marsh
704-633-6841

Saluda
Bear Creek Lodge
704-749-2272

Ivy Terrace
800-749-9542-[Y--]

Oaks
704-749-9613

Orchard Inn
800-581-3800

Saluda Inn
704-749-9842

The Oaks
704-749-9613

Woods House
704-749-9562

Shelby
Inn At Webbely
704-481-1403

Janus B&B
704-482-1262

Siler City
B&B At Laurel Ridge
800-742-6049-[SQAR-]

Sims
Strother House
919-237-5754

Smithfield
Eli Olives Inn
919-934-9823

Southern Pines
Inn The Pines
919-692-1632

Knollwood Inn
910-692-9390

Southport
Dosher Plantation House
910-457-5554

Lois Janes Riverview Inn
800-457-1152

Rivers End B&B
910-457-39

Sparta
Bella Columns B&B
910-372-2633

Mountain Hearth Lodge
910-372-8745

Red Roof Farm
910-372-8785

Turby-Villa
910-372-8490

Spruce Pine
Ashley Richmond Inn
704-765-63

Fairway Inn
704-765-4917

Richmond Inn
704-765-63-[Y--]

Still Hollow B&B
704-765-9380

Spruce Pint
Pinebridge Inn
704-765-5543

Statesville
Aunt Maes B&B
704-873-9525

Cedar Hill Farm
800-484-8457-[Y--]

Willos Oaks
704-878-8632

Sugar Grove
Bedside Manor
704-297-1120

Olde Cobblestone Chimney B&B
704-297-5111

Rivendell Lodge
704-297-1658

Supply
Doe Creek Inn
910-754-7736

Surf City
Gillies B&B
910-328-3087

Swan Quarter
Cutrell Inn
919-926-9711

Swansboro
Mount Pleasant B&B
919-326-7076

Scotts Keep
910-326-1257

Sylva
Mountain Brook
704-586-4329

Tabor City
Todd House
910-653-3778

Tarboro
Barrackes Inn
919-641-1614

Lady Ann Of Tarboro B&B
800-742-0427

Little Warren
919-823-1314

Main Street Inn
919-823-2560

Taylorsville
Barkley House B&B
704-632-9060

Tryon
Foxtrot Inn
704-859-9706

Melrose Inn
704-859-9419

Mill Farm Inn
800-545-62

Mimosa Inn
704-859-7688

Pine Crest Inn
800-633-3001

Stone Hedge Inn
704-859-9114

Tryon Old South B&B
704-859-6965

Union Grove
Madelyns Inn The Grove
800-948-4473

Valle Crucis
Bluestone Lodge
704-963-5177

Cat Pause Inn
704-963-7297

Manor At Green Hill
704-963-6831

Mast Farm Inn
704-963-5857

Mountainview Chateau
704-963-6593

Taylor House
704-963-5581-[Y--]

North Carolina - Oklahoma

Vilas
Chapel Brook B&B
704-297-4304

Wadesboro
Colleens B&B
704-694-6406

Wanchese
Pughs B&B
919-473-5466

Warrenton
Olde Christmas Inn
919-257-2727

Warsaw
Squires Vintage Inn
910-296-1831

Washington
Acadian House B&B
919-975-3967-[G--]

Belhaven Inn
919-943-6400

Pamilco House
919-946-7184

Waynesville
Forsyth Inn
704-456-3537

Grandview Lodge
800-255-7826-[G--]

Hallcrest Inn
800-334-6457

Hallcrest Inn
800-334-6457

Haywood Street House
704-456-9831-[Y--]

Heath Lodge
800-HEATH

Herren House
800-284-1932

Hyland Creek B&B
704-456-5509

Ketner Inn & Farm
800-545-5853

Mountain Creek B&B
704-456-5509

Old Stone Inn

800-432-84

Palmer House
704-456-7521

Piedmont Inn
704-456-3200

Pisgah Inn

Snuggery B&B
704-456-3660

Swag Country Inn
704-926-0430-[Y--]

Way Inn
704-456-3788

Waynes Creekside B&B
704-926-8300

Yellow House
800-563-1236

Weaverville
Dry Ridge Inn
704-658-38

Inn On Main Street
704-645-3442

Weldon
Weldon Place Inn
800-831-4470

West Jefferson
Ransoms Inn
919-246-5175

West Sapphire
Woodlands Inn Of Sapphire
704-966-4709

White Lake
White Lake Inn
910-862-2171

Whitesville
Coburn House B&B
910-642-2232

Whittier
Chalet Inn
704-586-0251

Stanley House
704-497-7329

Wilmington
Anderson Guest House
910-343-8128

Camellia Cottage
800-763-9171

Catherines Inn
800-476-0723

Dock Street Inn
910-763-7128

Five Star Guest House
800-382-82-[Y--]

Graystone Guest House
910-762-2000

Inn At St Thomas Ct
800-525-0909-[Y--]

Inn On Orange
800-476-0723

James Place B&B
910-251-09

Kingsley House Victorian B&B
800-763-6603-[G--]

Market Street B&B
800-242-5442

McKay Green Victorian
910-762-4863

Murchison House
910-343-8580

Rosehill Inn
910-815-0250

Stemmerman's 1855 Inn
910-763-7776

Taylor House Inn
800-382-82-[SQAR-]

Worth House
800-340-8559-[G--]

Wilson
Miss Betty's B&B Inn
800-258-2058

Winnabow
Funston Farm House
910-253-5643

Winston Salem
August T Zevely Inn

800-928-92

Brookstown Inn B&B
910-725-1120

Colonel Ludlow House
910-777-1887

Henry F Shaffner House
910-777-0052

Lady Annes Victorian
910-724-1074

Lowe-Alston House
910-727-1211

Mickle House B&B
910-722-9045

Thomas Welch House
910-723-3586

Wachovia B&B
910-777-0332

Wrightsville Beach
Edgewater Inn
910-256-2914

OKLAHOMA

Adair
Grand Lake Country Inn
918-257-8313

Aline
Heritage Manor
405-463-2563

Bartlesville
White Swan
918-336-3519

Bristow
Carolyn Inn
918-367-22

Broken Arrow
Stratford House Inn
918-258-7556

Broken Bow
Sojourners B&B
405-584-9324

Buffalo
Buffalo Trails
405-735-2301

3-166

©Inn & Travel Memphis, Tennessee

Bold Name - *Description appears in other section*

Oklahoma - South Carolina

Cheotah
　Sharp House B&B
　918-473-2832

Chickasha
　Campbell-Richison
　House B&B
　405-222-1754

Claremore
　Country Inn
　918-342-1894-[Y--]

Clayton
　Clayton Country
　Inn
　918-569-4165

Cleveland
　Victorian Inn
　918-358-3531

Coalgate
　Memories B&B
　405-927-3590

Davis
　Ceder & Green
　B&B
　405-369-2396

　Chigley Mansion
　405-369-3404

　Seven Springs
　405-369-3543

Disney
　Early Days
　918-435-8107

　Waters Edge
　918-435-4880

Edmond
　Arcadian Inn B&B
　800-299-6347-[Y--]

El Reno
　Goff House Inn
　405-262-9334

Guthrie
　Harrison House
　800-375-1001

　Stone Lion Inn
　B&B
　405-282-0012

　Victorian Rose
　405-282-3928

Guymon
　Prairie View B&B
　405-338-3760

Jenks
　Miss Lauries B&B
　918-298-1211

Keota
　Overstreet-Kerr
　Living Hist Farm
　918-966-3282

Ketchum
　Clarks B&B
　918-782-3851

Keyes
　Cattle Country
　B&B
　405-543-6458

Kingston
　Sur Ray Ranch
　B&B
　405-564-3602

Lawton
　Quinette House
　405-355-4012

Lexington
　Cranberry Hill B&B
　405-527-7251

Mannford
　Chateau In The
　Woods
　918-865-7979

Muskogee
　Graham-Caroll
　House
　918-683-0100

　Miss Addies B&B
　918-682-1506

　Queens House
　800-362-2321

Norman
　Cutting Garden
　B&B
　405-329-4522

　Holmberg House
　B&B
　405-321-6221

　Monfort Inn
　405-321-2200

　The Cutting Garden
　405-329-4522

Oklahoma City
　Arcadian Inn B&B
　800-299-6347-[Y--]

　Chisholm Springs
　405-942-5193

　Country House
　B&B
　405-794-4008

　Grandison B&B
　405-521-0011

　Willow Way
　405-427-2133

Park Hill
　The Lord & Taylors
　918-457-4756

Pawhuska
　Inn At Woodyard
　Farms
　918-287-26

Pawnee
　Denver House
　918-762-2444

Ponca City
　Davaranthey Inn
　405-765-22

　Rose Stone Inn
　800-763-22-[G--]

　Shepherds Rest
　405-762-0850

　Stratford House
　405-762-9133

　West End B&B
　800-954-8864

Poteau
　Edna Lees B&B
　918-647-9573

　Kerr Country
　Mansion
　918-647-5208

Purcell
　Horse Country Inn
　405-527-5582

Ramona
　Jarrett Farm
　Country Inn
　918-371-9868

Sallisaw
　Overstreet-Kerr
　Farm
　918-966-3282

Stillwater
　Thomasville B&B
　405-372-1203

Stroud
　Stroud House B&B
　800-259-2978

Sulphur
　Artesian B&B
　405-622-5254

Talihina
　Kiamichi Country
　Inn
　918-567-2243

Tulsa
　Lantern Inn Of
　Brookside
　918-743-8343

　Robins Nest
　918-446-8700

　Sunrise B&B
　918-743-4234-[Y--]

　The Lantern Inn
　918-747-5878

Watonga
　Kennedy Kottage
　405-623-4384

　Red Bud Manor
　405-623-8587

Woodward
　Anna Agusta Inn
　405-254-5400

SOUTH CAROLINA

Abbeville
　Abbewood B&B
　803-459-5822

　Belmont Inn
　803-459-9625

　Painted Lady
　803-459-8171

　Vintage Inn
　803-459-4784

Aiken
　Briar Patch
　803-649-2010

　Chancellor Carroll
　House
　803-649-5396

©*Inn & Travel Memphis, Tennessee*

South Carolina

Bold Name - *Description appears in other section*

Constantine House
803-642-8911

Hair Residence

Holley Inn
803-648-4365

Hollie Berries Inn
803-648-52

New-Berry Inn
803-649-2935

Pine Knoll Inn
803-649-5939

Wilcox Inn
800-368-1047-[Y--]

Anderson
  1109 South Main B&B
  864-225-1109

  Centennial Plantation B&B
  864-225-4448

  Evergreen Inn
  800-241-0034

  River Inn
  864-296-2203

Bamberg
  General Bamberg Inn
  803-245-5964

Batesburg
  Batchelors B&B
  803-532-2926

Beach Island
  Cedars B&B Inn
  803-827-0248

Beaufort
  Bay Street Inn
  803-522-2902-[Y--]

  Beaufort Inn
  803-521-9000-[G--]

  Cuthbert House
  800-327-9275

  Old Point Inn
  803-524-3177

  Rhett House Inn
  803-524-9030-[Y--]

  Trescot Inn
  803-522-8552

  Twelve Oaks Inn
  803-525-1371

  TwoSuns Inn B&B
  800-532-4244-[GQAR-]

Belton
  Belton Inn
  864-338-6020

Bennettsville
  Breeden House
  803-479-3665

Bishopville
  Fox Fire B&B
  803-484-5635

  Law Street Inn
  800-253-5474

Blacksburg
  White House Inn
  800-352-6077

Blackville
  Floyd Hall Inn
  803-284-3736

Bluffton
  Fripp House Inn
  803-757-2139

Branchville
  Branchville Country Inn
  803-274-8894

Calhoun Falls
  Latimer Inn
  864-391-2747

Camden
  Aberdeen
  803-432-2524

  Bloomsburg
  803-432-9714

  Candlelight Inn
  803-424-1057

  Carriage House
  803-432-2430

  Greenleaf Inn
  800-437-5874

  Inn On Broad
  803-425-1806

Central
  Hertiage House B&B
  864-639-1500

Charleston
  1837 B&B Inn
  803-723-7166

  27 State Street B&B
  803-722-4232

  36 Meeting Street B&B
  803-722-1034

  Anchorage Inn
  800-421-2952

  Ann Harpers B&B
  803-723-3947

  Ansonborough Inn
  800-522-2073

  Ashley Inn
  803-723-1848

  Barksdale House Inn
  803-577-4800

  Battery Carriage House
  800-755-5575

  Bed No Breakfast
  803-723-4450

  Belle Blanc
  803-853-3825

  Belvedere Guest House
  803-722-0973

  Brasington House B&B
  800-722-1274

  Cannonboro Inn
  803-723-8572

  Capers-Motte House
  803-722-2263

  Charleston Society B&B
  803-723-4948

  Church Street Inn
  800-552-3777

  Coach House
  803-722-8145

  Colonial Lake B&B
  803-722-6476

  Country Victorian B&B
  803-577-0682

  Elliott House Inn
  800-729-1855

  Fulton Lane Inn
  800-720-2688

  Hayne House
  800-948-1680-[Y--]

  Indigo Inn
  800-845-7639

  Jasmine House
  800-845-7639

  John Rutledge House Inn
  800-476-9741-[GQAR-]

  King George IV Inn
  803-723-9339-[YQAR-]

  Kings Courtyard Inn
  800-845-6119

  Kitchen House
  803-577-6362

  Lodge Alley Inn
  800-845-1004

  Loudes Grove Inn
  803-723-3530

  Maison Du Pre
  800-662-INNS

  Meeting Street Inn
  800-842-8022

  Middleton Inn Middleton Place
  800-543-4774

  Mills House Hotel
  800-577-2400

  Olde Towne Inn
  803-723-8572

  Opus 11 George
  803-772-1585

  Palmer House
  800-723-1574-[Y--]

  Planters Inn

Bold Name - *Description appears in other section* *South Carolina*

800-845-7082

Rutledge Victorian Inn
803-722-7551-[Y--]

Two Meeting Place
803-723-7322

Vendue Inn/Sweet Grass
800-845-7900

Victoria House Inn
800-933-5464-[G--]

Villa de la Fontaine
803-577-7709-[Y--]

Cheraw
505 Market Street B&B
803-537-9649

Spears B&B
803-537-7733

Clemson
James A Chisman House
864-639-2939

Clio
Henry Bennett House
803-586-2701

Columbia
Chestnut Cottage B&B
800-898-8555

Claussens Inn
800-622-3382-[Y--]

Richland Street B&B
800-779-7011

Dale
Coosaw Plantation
803-846-8225

Darlington
Croft Magnolia
803-393-1908

Dillon
Magnolia Inn
803-774-0679

Due West
Somewhere In Time B&B
864-379-8715

Edgefield
Adams House
803-637-5544

Carnoosie Inn
800-622-7124

Cedar Grove Plantation
803-637-3056

Inn On Main
803-637-3678

Village Inn
803-637-3789

Edisto Island
Cassina Point Plantation B&B
803-869-2535

Ehrhardt
Broxton Bridge Plantation
800-437-4868

Ehrhardt Hall
803-267-2020

Estill
John Lawton House
803-625-3240

Fairplay
Yoders Farm B&B
803-972-3133

Fort Mill
Victorian Manor
800-374-1234

Fountain Inn
Hollydale Farm
864-862-4077

Georgetown
1790 House
800-890-7432-[G--]

Ashfield Manor B&B
800-483-5002

Dozier Guest House B&B
803-527-1350

Du Pre House
803-546-0298

Five Thirty Prince Street
803-527-1114

Kings Inn At Georgetown
803-527-6937

Mansfield Plantation
800-355-3223

Shaw House
803-546-9663-[G--]

Shipwrights B&B
803-527-4475

Greenville
Nicholls-Crook Plantation
864-583-7337-[Y--]

Petigru Place B&B
864-242-4595

Greenwood
Grace Place B&B
864-229-0053

Inn On The Square
864-223-4488

Hartsville
Missouri Inn
803-383-9553

Hill City
Palmer Gulch Lodge
800-233-4331

Hilton Head
Ambiance B&B
803-671-4981

Halcyon
803-785-7912

Honea Path
Sugarfoot Castle B&B
864-369-6565

James Island
Almost Home B&B
803-795-8705

Johnston
Cox House Inn
803-275-2707

Lancaster
Wade Beckman House
803-285-1105

Landrum
Country Mouse Inn
864-457-4061

Holly Hill
864-457-4010

Latta
Bailie Hall B&B
803-752-7376

Manning House B&B
803-752-5090

Meeting House
803-752-5090

Leesville
Able House Inn
803-532-2763

Lexington
Lake Murray House
803-957-3701

Liberty
Liberty House
864-843-9696

Little River
Stellas Guest Home
803-249-1871

Long Creek
Chauga River Inn
864-647-9587

Marion
Cantey Residence
803-423-5578

Montgomerys Grove
803-423-5220

Rosewood Manor
803-423-5407

Maysville
Windsong
800-453-5004

McClellanville
Laurel Hill Plantation
803-887-3708

McClellans B&B
803-887-3371

Village B&B Inn
803-887-3266

Moncks Corner
Rice Hope Plantation Inn
800-569-4038-[Y--]

Montmorenci
Annies Inn

South Carolina - Tennessee

Bold Name - *Description appears in other section*

803-649-6836

Mount Pleasant
Guilds Inn
800-331-0510

Sailmasters House
803-884-8208

Tara Oaks B&B
803-884-7082

Mullins
Webster Manor
803-464-9632

Myrtle Beach
Brustman House B&B
800-448-76-[G--]

Cain House B&B
803-448-3063

Chesterfield Inn
803-448-3177

Serendipity Inn
800-762-3229

Newberry
Barklin House
803-321-9155

College Street Tourist B&B
803-321-9155

North Augusta
Bloom Hill
803-593-2573

Rosemary Hall
803-278-4840

Pamplico
Southern Belle B&B
803-493-1975

Pawleys Island
Litchfield Plantaion - Country Inn
800-869-1410

Manor House / Litchfield
803-237-9322

Pelican Inn
803-237-2298

Sea View Inn
803-237-4253

Tip Top Inn

Pendleton
One Ninety-Five East Main B&B
864-646-5732

Pickens
Schell Haus
864-878-0078

Ridge Spring
Southwood Manor B&B
803-685-5100

Ridgeland
Lakewood Plantation B&B
803-726-5141

Rock Hill
Book & Spindle B&B
803-328-1913

East Main Guest House
803-366-1161

Park Avenue Inn
803-325-1764

Saint Matthews
East Bridge Inn
803-874-4017

Salem
Sunrise Farm
864-944-0121

Sunrise Farm Corn Crib Cottage
864-944-0211

Simpsonville
Hunter House B&B
864-967-2827

Starr
Gray House
864-352-6782

Sullivans Island
Palmettos
803-883-3389

Summerville
B&B In Summerville
803-871-5275

Gadsen Manor
803-875-2602

Linwood
803-871-2620

Woodlands Resort & Inn

Sumter
B&B Of Sumter
803-773-2903

Calhoun Street B&B
803-775-7053

Magnolia House B&B
803-775-6694

Sumter B&B
803-773-2903

Sunset
Laurel Springs Country Inn
864-878-2252

Table Rock-Pickens
Laurel Mountain Inn
803-878-0078

Union
Forest Hill Manor
864-427-4525

Inn At Merridun
864-427-7025

Walhalla
Liberty Lodge
864-638-8639

Walhalla B&B
864-638-9320

Winnsboro
Brakefield B&B
803-635-4242

Carriage House B&B
803-635-9714

Popular Haven
803-635-7969

Woodruff
Nicholls-Crook Plantation
864-476-8820-[G--]

York
Brandon House

Kings Mountain Street Inn
803-684-7013

TENNESSEE

Allardt
Charlo
615-331-5244

Altamont
Manor 1885
615-692-3153

Woodlee House
615-692-2368

Athens
Majestic Mansion B&B
423-476-9041

Bell Buckle
Bell Buckle B&B
615-389-9371

Log Cabin Inn
615-389-6020

Spindle House
615-389-6766

Spindle House B&B
615-389-6766

Belvidere
Falls Mill Log Cabin
615-469-7161

Blountville
Woodland Place
423-323-2848

Bolivar
Magnolia Manor B&B
901-658-6700

Brentwood
English Manor
800-332-4640

Herberts B&B
615-373-9300

Sunny Hill Farm B&B
615-373-1514

Bristol
New Hope B&B
423-789-3343

Brownsville
Peach Tree Inn
901-772-5680

Chattanooga
Adams Hilborne

3-170

©Inn & Travel Memphis, Tennessee

Bold Name - *Description appears in other section*   Tennessee

423-265-5000-[G--]

Alford House
423-821-7625

Bluff View Inn
423-265-5033

Lookout Mountains
Guest House
423-821-8307

Milton House
423-265-2800

Christiana
　Cedar Thicket
　615-893-4015

Chuckey
　Harmony Hill Inn
　423-257-3893

Clarksville
　Hachland Hill Inn
　615-647-4084

Cleveland
　Browns Manor
　423-479-5311-[Y--]

Clifton
　Hidden Hollow
　Farm-Log Cabin BB
　615-676-5295

Cookeville
　"Dun Movin" B&B
　Log House
　615-526-1734

　Scarecrow Country
　Inn
　615-526-3431

Cordova
　Andy's B&B
　901-754-0420

　Bridgewater House
　901-384-0080
　[GQA-]

Cornersville
　Lairdland Farm
　B&B
　615-363-9080

Covington
　Havenhall
　901-476-7226-[G--]

Dandridge
　Debar Fork Lodge
　B&B
　423-397-7327

Milldale Farm B&B
800-767-3471

Sweet Basil &
Thyme B&B
423-397-7128

Duck River
　McEwen Farm Log
　Cabin B&B
　615-583-2378

Ducktown
　White House
　423-496-4166

Fayetteville
　Old Cowan
　Plantation B&B
　615-433-0225

Franklin
　Blueberry Hill B&B
　615-791-47

　Carothers House
　800-327-8492

　Dutch Treat B&B
　615-790-6861

　Franklin House
　615-794-0848

　Lyric Springs Inn
　800-621-7824

　Magnolia House
　615-794-8178

　Windsong Farm
　615-794-6162

Gallatin
　Hancock House
　800-242-6738

Gatlinburg
　7th Heaven Log
　Home Inn
　800-248-2923

　Brevard Inn
　423-436-7233

　Buckhorn Inn
　432-436-4668-[Y--]

　Butcher House
　423-436-9457

　Colonels Lady
　423-436-5432

　Eight Gables Inn

800-279-5716

Eight Gables Inn
800-279-5716

Highlander Inn
B&B
423-436-3447

Hippensteal Inn
800-527-8110

Leconte Lodge
432-436-4473

Old English Tudor
Inn
800-541-3798

Olde English Tudor
Inn
423-436-7760

Tennessee Ridge
Inn
423-436-4068

Tennessee Ridge
Inn B&B
800-737-7369

Goodlettsville
　Drake Farm
　Lumsley Creek
　800-586-7539

　Woodshire B&B
　615-859-7369

Gordonsville
　Pride Hollow B&B
　615-683-6396-[Y--]

Greeneville
　Hilltop House
　423-639-8202-[G--]

　Oak Tree Gallery
　B&B
　423-639-5253

　Timberfell Lodge
　423-234-9272

Hampshire
　Ridgetop B&B
　800-377-2770

Hendersonville
　Beryls B&B
　615-824-8549

　Mouthaven
　615-824-6319

Jackson

Moss Rose Inn &
Cafe
901-423-4777

Jefferson City
　Banner-Hicks House
　423-475-2302

　Campbells B&B
　423-475-9362

Johnson City
　A Touch Of Thyme
　B&B Inn
　423-926-7570

　Hart House B&B
　423-926-3147

Jonesborough
　Aiken-Brow House
　423-753-9440

　Bugaboo B&B
　423-753-9345

　Hawley House B&B
　423-753-8869

　Jonesborough B&B
　423-753-9223

　Sheppard Springs
　B&B
　423-753-6471

Knoxville
　Compton Manor
　423-523-1204

　Maple Grove Inn
　423-690-9565

　Middleton House
　615-524-8100

　Three Chimneys
　423-521-4970

　Windy Hill B&B
　423-690-1488

Kodak
　Grandmas House
　800-676-3512-[Y--]

La Follette
　Dogwood Acres
　B&B
　423-566-1207

Lawrenceburg
　Grandville House
　615-762-3129

Lebanon

©Inn & Travel Memphis, Tennessee   3-171

Tennessee

Bold Name - *Description appears in other section*

Campbell Country Inn
615-449-7713

Rockhaven House Inn
615-443-2327

Limestone
Snapp Inn
423-257-2482

Lookout Mountain
Chanticleer Inn
423-820-2015

Loudon
Mason Place
423-458-3921

River Road Inn
423-458-4861-[Y--]

Louisville
Mountain Vista
423-970-3771

Lyles
Silver Leaf 1815
615-670-3048

Lynchburg
Cottage Haus B&B
615-759-4273

Lynchburg B&B
615-759-7158-[Y--]

Martin
Wrens Nest
901-587-6563

Maryville
High Country Inn
423-981-2966

Mc Ewen
White Oak Creek B&B
615-582-3827

McMinnville
Falcon Manor
615-668-4444-[G--]

Memphis
B&B In A Castle
901-527-7174

Bridgewater House
901-384-0080
[GQA-]

Cedarwood Farms
901-794-7000

Cottage Inn
800-363-2900-[G--]

Doler B&B
601-637-2695-[Y--]

Havenhall
901-476-7226-[G--]

Lowenstein-Long House
901-527-7174

Talbot Heirs Guesthouse
901-527-9772

Monteagle
Adams Edgeworth Inn
615-924-4000-[Y--]

North Gate Lodge
615-924-27

Mountain City
Hidden Acres Farm
423-727-6564

Murfreesboro
Black Gnat House
615-890-0263

Clardys Guest House
615-893-6030-[Y--]

Nashville
Allison House
812-988-0814

Chateau Graeme B&B
615-883-1687

Commodore Inn
615-269-3840

End'O Bend Lodge
615-883-07

English Manor B&B
800-322-4640

Miss Annes B&B
615-885-18

Monthaven B&B
615-824-6319

Rose Garden B&B
615-356-8003

Savage House Inn
615-254-1277

Shepherd Inn
615-385-0540

Tanglewood Lodge
615-262-9859

Newport
Christopher Place
423-623-6333

Normandy
Cottage At The Cascade
615-455-0555

Parish Patch Inn
615-857-3441

Orinda
Aurora Inn B&B
615-654-4266

Pigeon Forge
Day Dreams Country Inn
423-428-0370

Evergreen Cottage Inn
800-264-3331

Hannahs House
423-428-2192

Hiltons Bluff B&B
423-428-9765

Mountain Home Inn & Cottages
423-453-6465

Pikeville
Colonial B&B
423-447-7183

Fall Creek Falls B&B
423-881-549
[GQAR-]

Pulaski
Milky Way Farms
615-363-9769

Red Boiling Springs
Armours Red Boiling Spring Hotel
615-6-2180

Donoho Hotel
615-6-2180

Rockford
Wayside Manor B&B
615-970-4823

Rogersville
Hale Springs Inn
423-272-5171

Rossville
Mebane-Nuckolls Perkins Home
901-465-5662

Rugby
Grey Gables B&B
423-628-5252

Newbury House/Hist Rugby
423-628-2430

Saltillo
Parker House
901-687-3456

Savannah
Ross House
901-925-3974

Ross House B&B
800-467-3174

Sevierville
Blue Mountain Mist Country Inn
800-497-2335-[Y--]

Calico Inn
800-235-1054
[GQA-]

Gallery House
423-428-6973

Huckleberry Inn
423-428-2475

Kero Mountain Resort
423-453-7514

Little Greenbrier Lodge
423-429-2500

Milk & Honey Country Hideway
615-428-4858

Mockingbird Country Inn
423-428-1398

Round D'Gap Inn
423-453-8714

Von Bryan Inn B&B

Bold Name - *Description appears in other section*   Tennessee - Texas

423-453-9832

Wonderland Hotel
423-436-5490

Seymour
 Country Inn
 423-573-7170

 Simpson Place
 423-453-8762

Shelbyville
 Bottle Hollow
 Lodge
 615-695-5253

 Cinnamon Ridge
 615-685-9200

 Gore House
 615-685-0636

 Taylor House B&B
 800-867-7326
 [GQA-]

Shiloh
 Leawood Williams
 Estate
 901-689-5106

Signal Mountain
 Charlet House
 423-886-4880

Smithville
 Evins Mill Retreat
 615-597-2088-[G--]

Sweetwater
 Flow Blue Inn
 423-442-2964

 Fox Trot Inn
 423-337-4236

Talbott
 Arrow Hill
 423-585-5777

Townsend
 Olympia Health
 Retreat
 800-727-7333

 Pioneer Cabins &
 Guest Farm
 423-448-6100

 Richmont Inn
 423-448-6751

 Tuckaleechee Inn
 800-487-6059

Triune
 Xanadu Farm
 615-395-4040

Tullahoma
 Jennys B&B
 615-455-9496

Vonore
 Edna's B&B
 423-295-2354

 Turkey Penn Resort
 423-295-2400

Walland
 Inn At Blackberry
 Farm
 800-862-7610

Wartrace
 Ledford Mill &
 Museum
 615-455-2546

 Log Cabin B&B
 615-389-6713

 Walking Horse
 Hotel & Restaurant
 615-389-6407

Watertown
 Watertown B&B

Waverly
 Nolan House Inn
 615-296-2511

White Pine
 Isabella Plantation
 423-674-0150

Winchester
 Antebellum Inn
 615-967-5550

 Green Pastures
 615-967-9509

TEXAS

Abilene
 B&B Abilene Style
 915-677-9677

 **Bolins Prairie
 House**
 915-675-5855

 Heritage Inn
 915-677-1461

Albany
 Old Nail House Inn

915-762-2928

Virginias B&B
915-762-2013

Alpine
 Cactus Rose
 915-837-7207

 Corner House
 915-837-7161

Alto
 Lincrest Lodge
 409-858-2222

Amarillo
 Galbraith House
 806-374-0237

 Parkview House
 806-373-9464-[Y--]

Austin
 Aunt Dollys Attic
 512-837-5320

 **Austin's Wildflower
 Inn**
 512-477-9639-[Y--]

 Bad Griesbach
 B&B
 512-452-1004

 Bremond House
 512-482-0411

 Brook House
 512-459-0534

 Carringtons Bluff
 800-871-8908

 Chequered Shade
 512-346-8318

 Cityview B&B
 512-441-2606

 Fairview B&B
 800-310-4746

 Governors Inn
 512-477-0711

 Lake Austin Spa
 Retreat
 800-847-5637

 Lake Travis B&B
 800-484-9095

 McCallum House
 512-451-6744

Medway Ranch
512-263-2347

Peaceful Hill B&B
512-338-1817

Shelby Retreat &
Confernece Center
409-865-9021

Southard House
512-474-4731-[Y--]

Stephen F Austin
Hotel

Trails End B&B
800-850-2901-[Y--]

Triple Creek Ranch
512-264-1371

Wildflower Inn
512-477-9639

Willow Spring Inn
512-445-2566

Woodburn House
512-458-4335

Ziller House B&B
800-949-5446

Avinger
 McKenzie Manor
 903-755-2240

Azle
 Where The Red
 Rooster Crows B&B
 817-444-4018

Bacliff
 Small Inn
 409-339-3489

Bandera
 Bandera Creek B&B
 210-796-3518

 Dixie Dude Ranch

 Mayan Dude Ranch

Bartlett
 Robbie Nells
 Country Manor
 817-527-4515

Bastrop
 Pfeiffer House
 512-321-2100

 The Colony
 512-321-7984

©*Inn & Travel Memphis, Tennessee*   3-173

Texas

Bold Name - *Description appears in other section*

Beaumont
Grand Duerr Manor
409-833-9600

Bellville
High Cotton Inn
800 321-9767

Townsquare Inn
409-865-9021

Belton
Belle Of Belton
817-939-6478

Ben Wheeler
Wild Briar
214-852-3975

Big Sandy
Annies B&B
214-636-4355

Blanco
My Little Guest House
210-833-5264

Boenre
Kendall Inn
210-249-8548

Boerne
B&B Hill Country Island
512-535-4050

Borgmans Sunday House
512-249-9563

Ye Kendall Inn
512-249-8548

Brenham
Breham House
409-830-0477

Captain Clays House
409-836-1916

Ingleside B&B

Secrets B&B
409-836-4117

Vernons B&B
409-836-6408

Broaddus
Cole House-Sam Rayburn Lake
409-872-3666

Brownwood
Troxler House
915-646-0889

Buchanan Dam
Knittel House
512-793-6408

Bulverde
Homestead B&B
800-2-4538

Burnet
Rocky Rest
512-756-2600

Williams Point
512-756-2074

Burton
Knittel Homestead
409-836-6525

La Bahia Prairie Inn
409-278-3881

Long Point Inn
409-289-3171

Calvert
Our House
409-364-2909

Camp Wood
Shady Acres B&B
210-597-2179

Canadian
Emerald House
806-323-5827

Canyon
Hudspeth House
806-655-9800

Canyon Lake
Aunt Noras B&B
210-905-3989

Castroville
Castrovilles B&B
210-538-9622

Landmark Inn State Historic Site
512-538-2133

Center
John C Rogers House
409-598-3971

Pine Colony Inn
409-598-7700

Center Point
Mariannes B&B
210-634-7489

Chappell Hill
Browning Plantation
409-836-6144

Mulberry Houes
409-830-1311

Stagecoach Inn
409-836-9515

Chireno
Gingerbread House
409-362-2365

Clarendon
Saints Roost Inn
806-874-2169

Cleburne
Anglin Queen anne
817-645-5555

Cleburne House
817-641-0085

Collins Manor
817-641-0085

Clifton
Courtney House B&B
817-675-3061

College Station
Twin Oaks B&B
409-846-3694

Columbus
Lains B&B
409-732-8373-[Y--]

Magnolia Oaks B&B
409-732-2726

Comfort
Comfort Common
201-5-3030

Gast Haus Lodge
512-5-2304

Idlewilde
512-5-3844

Corpus Christi
Anthonys By The Sea B&B
800-460-2557-[G--]

Cayo del Oso B&B
512-2-2711-[Y--]

Sand Dollar B&B
512-853-1222

Crockett
Arledge House
409-544-3955

Warfield House
409-544-4037

Crosbyton
Smith House
806-675-2178

Cuero
Clayton Street Guest House
512-275-3232

Reiffert Mugge Inn
512-275-2626

Daingerfield
Maberry Cottage
903-645-3227

Dallas
Inn On Fairmount
214-522-2800

Saint Germain
214-871-2516

Denison
Ivy Blue B&B
903-463-2479

Denton
Redbud Inn
817-565-6414

Dickinson
Desel House c1895
713-337-1397

Doss
Hill Top Cafe & Guest Home
210-7-8922

Jay Bar K Ranch B&B
210-669-2471

Eagle Lake
Farris 1912
409-234-2546

Veranda
409-234-5851

Edom
Red Rooster Square

©*Inn & Travel Memphis, Tennessee*

Bold Name - Description appears in other section   Texas

214-852-6774

El Campo
Crawfish Farm B&B

El Paso
Gardner Hotel
915-532-3661

Room With A View
915-534-4400

Sunset Heights B&B
915-544-1743

Elkhart
New Canaan Farm
214-764-2106

Emory
Sweet Seasons B&B
903-473-3706

Ennis
Raphel House
214-875-1555

Floydada
Lamplighter Inn
806-983-3035

Fort Davis
Boyton House
915-426-3123

Indian Lodge
915-426-3245

Old Texas Inn
915-426-3118

Prude Guest Ranch
800-458-6232

Sutler Limpia Hotel
800-662-5517

Wayside Inn
915-426-3535

Fort Worth
Colony B&B
817-624-1981

Medrodd House
817-924-2765-[Y--]

Miss Mollys Hotel
817-626-1522

Fredericksburg
Alleganis Sunday House

210-7-7448

Barons Creek Inn
210-7-9398

Birdsong B&B
210-7-0111

Commanders Place-Nevels Home
210-7-4712

Country Cottage Inn
210-7-8549

Countryside Escape B&B
210-7-7678

Delforge Place B&B
210-7-9047

Draches Haus B&B
210-7-7042

East of The Sun-West of The Moon
210-7-4981

Echte Gemuetlichkeit B&B
210-7-2262

Feather Your Nest
210-7-8343

Flagg Creek B&B
210-7-5363

Franklin Street Cottage
210-7-7678

Fredericksburg Herb Farm
210-7-8615

Fredericksburg Inn
210-7-0850

Fredericksburg Victorian House
210-7-0288

Grayson Summer House B&B
210-7-9375

Haus Wilhelmina
210-7-37

Heiraten Haus
210-7-5612

Herb Haus B&B
210-7-8615

Hotopp Haus
210-7-5612

Inn On Grap Creek
210-664-2710

Inn On The Creek
210-7-7434

Inn On The Creek
210-7-9585

J Bar K Ranch B&B
210-669-2471

JF Harris Haus
210-7-3860

Landhaus
210-7-4916

Magnolia House
210-7-0306

Main Street B&B
210-7-0153

Morning Star Ranch
210-7-0129

Pioneer House Inn
210-7-3566

Quinns Cottage
210-7-3340

River View Farm
210-7-7227

Rocky Top B&B
210-7-8145

Schmidt Barn B&B
210-7-5612

Settlers Crossing Hist Guest House
210-7-5612

Settlers Homestead
210-7-9620

Spring Creek Ranch
210-669-2715

Texas-Two-Step & A Little Waltz
210-7-5612

The Cottage
210-7-6906

Three Horse B&B
210-7-4461

Varneys Chemistlade

Victorian House
210-7-0288

Victorian Lace Gastehaus
210-7-0041

Walter John Haus
210-7-4347

Watkins Hill
210-7-6739

White House
512-479-0636

Gainesville
Honey Hush B&B
817-665-1010

Galveston
1890 Trube Castle
800-662-9647

Carousel Inn
409-762-2166

Gasthaus Kimmerie
409-765-6565

Gilded Thistle
800-654-9380-[Y--]

Golden Eagle Retreat
409-737-2112

Hazelwood House
409-762-1668

Inn On The Strand
409-762-4444

Key Largo
800-833-0120

Looking Glass Inn
409-762-1668

Mather-Root Home
409-439-6253

Michaels B&B
409-763-3760

Queen Anne B&B
800-472-0930-[G--]

San Luis Hotel

Texas **Bold Name** - *Description appears in other section*

Tremont House
800-874-2300

Victorian Inn
409-762-3235

Virginia Point Inn
409-673-2450

Galveston Island
Madame Dyers B&B
409-765-5692

Garland
Catnap Creek B&B
214-530-0819

George West
Casa Monte Lodge
512-449-2538

Georgetown
Page House
512-863-8979

Trails End B&B
800-850-2901-[Y--]

Gladewater
Honeycomb Suites B&B Bakery Inn
903-845-4430

Glen Rose
Fossil Rim WIldlife Refuge
817-897-2960

Inn On The River
817-897-2101

Old Maple Inn
817-897-3456

Ye Olde Maple Inn
817-897-3456

Goliad
Dial House B&B
512-645-3366

Madison Inn B&B
512-645-8693

The Madison
512-645-8693

Gonzales
St James Inn B&B
512-672-7066

Granbury
Dabney House B&B

817-579-1260

Doyle House
817-573-6492

Nutt House
817-573-5612

Pearl Street Inn
817-279-7465

Granite Shoals
La Casita B&B
512-598-6443

Harlingen
Ross Haus
210-425-1717

Helotes
Bunkhouse B&B
210-695-2670

Hillsboro
Tarlton House Of 1895 B&B
817-582-7216

Houston
Durham House B&B
713-868-4654-[Y--]

Highlander
713-861-6110

La Colombd d'Or
713-524-79

Lovett Inn
800-779-5224

Patrician Inn
713-523-1114

Robins Nest
800-622-8343

Saras B&B
800-593-1130-[Y--]

Webber House B&B
713-864-9472

Woodlake House

Hunt
Casa Bonita
210-238-4422

Joy Spring Ranch
512-238-4531

River Bend B&B
210-238-4681

Huntsville
Whistler B&B
409-295-2834

Ingram
Johnson Creek B&B
210-367-5312

Lazy Hills Guest House
800-880-0632

River Oaks Lodge B&B
210-367-4214

Jacksonville
English Manor
800-866-0946

Jasper
Belle-Jim Hotel B&B
800-373-3137

Jefferson
Austin Cottage
800-727-2204

Azalea Inn
903-665-2051

Bluebonnet Inn
903-665-8572

Captains Castle
903-665-2330

Claiborne House
903-665-8800

Cottonwood Inn
903-665-2080

Dixon House
903-665-8442

Duke Presbytery
903-665-2175

Excelsior House
903-665-2513

Faded Rose
903-665-2716

Falling Leaves
903-665-8803

Gingerbread House
800-794-84

Guset House
903-665-8774

Hale House
903-665-8877-[Y--]

Hodge Plantation
903-665-7442

Holcomb Lodge
903-665-3236

Home Sweet Home
903-665-2493

Horns Gingerbread
903-665-84

Hotel Jefferson
903-665-2631

Ice House
903-665-3321

Line Street Guest House
800-833-6758

Magnolias Inn
903-665-2754

Maison Bayou
903-665-7600

McKay House
903-665-7322-[Y--]

Pride House
800-894-3526

Roseville Manor
800-336-7736

Rowell House
903-665-2634

Seasons Guest House
903-665-1218

Secrets Of Lake Claborn
903-665-8518

Steamboat Inn
903-665-8946

Terry House
903-665-2644

Turner House
800-622-8616

Two Sisters Inn
903-665-8633

Urguhart House
Dixon Guest
903-665-8442

Bold Name - Description appears in other section *Texas*

William Clark House
903-665-8880

Wise Manor
903-665-2386

Johnson City
Hoppes Guest House
210-868-4548

Smiths Tin House On The Square
210-868-4548

Karnack
Mimosa Hall
214-679-3632

Kemah
Captains Quarters
713-334-4141

Kerrville
C.A.M.P. B&B
210-671-2598

Hill Country Inn
800-274-2111

Johnson Creek B&B
210-367-5312

Kerrville B&B
210-257-8759

La Reata Ranch B&B
210-896-5503

Old Ingram Studios B&B
210-367-4200

Prices Joy Spring B&B
210-238-4531

Kingsville
B Bar B Ranch Inn
512-296-3331

Knox City
Blue Goose Inn
817-658-3774

Lacoste
City Hotel

LaGrange
Ripple Creek B&B
800-657-1388

Lamesa
Waldrops Well
806-497-6421

Laredo
Hamilton Hotel
210-723-7421

La Posada

Susans B&B
210-725-7563

LaRue
Dunsavage Farm B&B
800-225-6982

Leander
Marshall Ranch
512-267-9642

Trails End B&B
800-850-2901-[Y--]

Ledbetter
Ledbetter B&B
409-249-3066

Livingston
Chateau Rouge B&B
409-327-8702

Llano
Badu Home
915-247-4304

Fraser House Inn
915-247-5183

Marathon
Gauge Hotel
915-386-4205

Marble Falls
Harlyn House
512-693-7651

Marshall
Cottens Patch
903-938-8756

Ginocchio Hotel
903-935-7635

La Maison Malfacon
903-935-6039

Meredith House
903-935-7147

Three Oaks B&B
903-938-6123

Weisman Hirsch

Biel Home
903-938-5504

Mason
Hasse House
915-347-6463

Mason Square B&B
915-347-6398

McAllen
La Posada
800-292-5659

McGregor
Lighthouse B&B
817-840-2683

McKinney
Dowell House c 1870
800-373-0551

Memphis
Memphis Hotel B&B
806-259-2198

Meridian
Rose Hill Terrace
817-435-6257

Mineola
Munzeshiener Manor
214-569-6634

Mount Vernon
Dutton Teague B&B
214-537-2603

Nacogdoches
Haden Edwards Inn

Hardeman House
409-569-1947

Hayden Edwards Inn

Mound Street B&B
409-569-2211

Tol Barret House
409-569-1249

Navasota
Castle Inn
409-825-8051

New Braunfels
Antik Haus Inn
210-625-6666

Bretzke Lane B&B

210-606-1049

Comfort Common
210-5-3030

Gruene Country Homestead
210-606-0216

Gruene Mansion Inn
210-264-2641

Hill Country Haven
210-629-6727

Historic Waldrip Haus B&B
800-2-8372

Hotel Faust
512-625-7791

Karbarh Haus
800-972-5941

Oak Hill Estate
210-625-3170

Prince Solms Inn
800-625-9169-[Y--]

River Haus B&B
210-625-6411

Riverside Haven
210-625-5823

Rose Garden
210-629-3296

T Bostin Bailey
800-566-3359

White House
210-629-9354

Painted Rock
Chaparral Ranch B&B
915-732-4225

Lipan Ranch B&B
915-468-2571

Palestine
Wiffletree Inn
903-723-6793

Paris
Magnolia House
903-785-5593

Pasadena
Oracle House
409-475-0309

©Inn & Travel Memphis, Tennessee   3-177

Texas   **Bold Name** - *Description appears in other section*

Pipe Creek
Lightning Ranch
210-535-4096

Pittsburg
Carson House Inn
903-856-2468

Plainview
Warrick Inn
806-293-4266

Plano
Hermitage
214-618-2000

Port Aransas
Port Aransas Inn
512-749-5937

Tarpon Inn
512-749-5555

Port Isabel
Yacht Club Hotel
512-943-1301-[Y--]

Post
Hotel Garza B&B
806-495-3962

Raymondville
Inn At El Canelo
210-689-5042

Rhome
Chism Trail Ranch
800-216-8865

Rio Frio
Rio Frio B&B Lodging
512-232-6633

Rio Grande
La Borde House
512-487-5101

Rockport
Anthonys By The Sea B&B
800-460-2557

Blue Heron Inn
512-729-7526

Round Rock
St Charles B&B
512-244-6850

Trails End B&B
800-850-2901-[Y--]

Round Top
Heart Of My Heart B&B

800-327-1242

Salado
Halley House B&B
817-947-1000

Inn At Salado
817-947-8200

Inn On The Creek
817-947-5554

Trails End B&B
800-850-2901-[Y--]

Tyler House

San Antonio
Adams House B&B
210-224-4791

B&B Falling Pines
800-880-4580

B&B On The River
210-225-6333-[Y--]

Beauregard House
210-222-1198

Beckmann Inn & Carriage House
800-945-1449-[Y--]

Belle Of Monte Vista
210-732-4006

Bonner Garden
800-676-2263

Bullis House
210-223-9426-[G--]

Cardinal Cliff
210-655-2939

Chabot-Reed Home
210-734-4243

Crockett Hotel

Edwin H Terrell Castle
210-271-9145

Falling Pines B&B
800-880-4580

Gatlin Guest House
210-223-6618

International House
210-647-3547

Linden House B&B
210-224-8902

Menger Hotel
210-233-4361

Nageglin B&B
800-373-3137

Norton Brackenridge House
800-221-1412

Oge House On The River Walk
800-242-2770

Riverwalk Inn
800-254-4440-[G--]

Royal Swan Guest House
210-223-3776

Sartor House B&B
210-227-5770

Summit Haus
210-736-6272

Terrell Castle B&B
210-271-9145

Victorian Lady Inn
800-879-7116

Yellow Rose B&B
800-950-03

San Augustine
Captain Downs B&B
409-275-2289

Wade House
409-275-5489

San Juan
San Juan Hotel
512-781-5339

San Marcos
Auqarena Springs Inn
512-396-8901

Crystal River Inn
512-396-3739-[Y--]

Finer Things B&B
512-353-2908

Lonesome Dove B&B
512-392-2921

Seguin
Lake Placid Guest House
512-379-7830

Weinert House B&B
210-372-0422

Shiner
Old Kasper House B&B
512-594-4336

South Padre Island
Brown Pelican Inn
210-761-2722

Spring
McLachian Farm B&B
800-382-3988-[Y--]

Spur
Spur Bunkhouse
805-271-3429

Stephenville
Oxford House
512-965-6885

Sunnyvale
Durant Star Inn
214-226-2412

Taylor
Century House
512-352-3278

Teague
Hubbard House B&B
817-739-2629-[G--]

Terlingua
Badlands Hotel

Lajitas On Rio Grande
915-424-3471

Texarkana
Main House
903-793-5027

Mansion On Main B&B
903-792-1835

Troup
Thomas House B&B
903-842-2466

Turkey
Hotel Turkey
800-657-7110

3-178   ©*Inn & Travel Memphis, Tennessee*

Bold Name - *Description appears in other section* *Texas - Virginia*

Tyler
 Charnwood Hill Inn
 903-587-3980

 Marys Attic
 903-592-5181-[Y--]

 Rosevine Inn
 903-592-2221-[Y--]

 Yellow Rose B&B
 903-592-7673

Utopia
 Indian Blanket Ranch B&B

Uvalde
 Casa de Leona B&B
 512-278-8550-[Y--]

Van
 Golden Pond B&B
 903-963-5128

Van Alstyne
 Durning House B&B
 903-482-5188

Vanderpool
 Tubbs Heritage House
 512-966-3510

Victoria
 Country Cousins B&B
 512-578-5336

 Santa Rose Oaks B&B
 512-578-1605

Village Mills
 Big Thicket Guest House
 409-834-2875

Volente
 Pickels Lake Travis B&B
 800-BED-REST

Waco
 Judge Baylor House B&B
 [UQAR-]
 800-888-JBAY

Waxahachie
 BonnyNook Inn
 800-486-5936-[G--]

 Chaska House B&B

 214-937-3390
 Millies Victorian B&B
 214-938-7211

 Rose Of Sharon B&B
 214-938-8833

 Seven Gables
 214-938-7500

 Yellow House
 214-938-9800

Weatherford
 Victoria House B&B
 800-687-1660

Weslaco
 Rio Grande B&B
 512-968-9646

West
 Zachary Davis B&B
 817-826-3953

Wharton
 Canry Creek Lodge
 409-532-5856

Whitney
 Collins Manor
 817-694-5746

Wichita Falls
 Harrison House B&B
 817-322-22

Wimberley
 Blair House Country Inn
 512-847-8828

 Dancing Waters Inn
 512-847-9391

 Eagles Nest B&B
 800-725-3909

 Inn Above Onion Creek
 512-268-1617

 JR Doble House
 800-725-3909

 Old Oaks Ranch B&B
 512-847-9374-[Y--]

 Rancho Cama B&B
 800-594-4501-[G--]

 Singing Cypress Gardens
 512-847-9344

 Southwind B&B
 800-508-5277-[Y--]

Winnsboro
 Hubbell House
 800-227-0639

 Yesteryear B&B
 903-342-3024

Woodville
 Antiquerose B&B
 409-283-8926

Yoakum
 Our Guest House
 512-293-3482

 Sandelwood B&B
 512-293-7706

Yorktown
 Hygenia Health Retreat
 512-564-3670

VIRGINIA

Abingdon
 Cabin On The River
 540-623-1267

 Inn On Town Creek
 540-628-4560-[G--]

 Litchfield Hall B&B
 540-676-2971

 Maplewood Farm
 703-628-2640

 River Garden B&B
 800-952-4296

 Silversmith Inn
 540-676-3924

 Summerfield Inn
 540-628-5905-[Y--]

 Victoria & Albert Inn
 540-676-2797

 White Birches
 540-676-2140

Accomac
 Drummondtown Inn

 804-787-3679

Afton
 Looking Glass House
 540-456-6844

Alberta
 Englewood
 804-949-0111

Aldie
 Little River Inn
 703-327-6742

Alexandria
 Alexandria Lodgings
 703-836-5575

 Little House
 703-548-9654

 Morrison House
 800-367-0800-[Y--]

Altavista
 Altivista B&B
 804-369-7891

 Castle To Country House
 804-369-4911

Amherst
 Dulwich Manor
 804-946-7207-[Y--]

 Fairview B&B
 804-277-8500

Amissville
 Bunree
 540-937-4133

Appomattox
 Appomattox Court House Inn
 804-352-5001

Arlington
 Brick House

 Memory House
 703-534-4607-[Y--]

 Swedish Inn
 703-524-4682

Ashland
 Henry CLay Inn
 800-343-4565

 Wisteria Inn
 804-798-9494

Banco Madison

©*Inn & Travel Memphis, Tennessee* 3-179

Virginia *Bold Name - Description appears in other section*

County
Olive Mill- A B&B
703-923-4664

Bedford
Bedford House
540-586-5050

Elmos Rest
540-586-3707

Otters Den B&B
540-586-2204

Peaks Of Otter Lodge
540-586-1081

Belle Haven
Bay View Waterfront B&B
800-422-6966

Bentonville
Statewood
540-635-9070

Berryville
Battletown Inn
540-955-4100

Berryville B&B
540-955-2200

Blacksburg
Bush Mountain Inn
540-951-7530

L'Arche Farm B&B
540-951-1808

Newport House
540-961-2480-[G--]

Oaks B&B Country Inn
800-336-OAKS-[Y--]

Per Diem B&B
800-272-4707

Sycamore Tree B&B
540-381-1597

Twin Porches B&B
540-552-0930

Blackstone
Grey Sway B&B
804-292-31

Bland
Willow Bend Farm B&B
540-688-3719

Boston
Thistle Hill B&B
540-987-9142

Bowling Green
Old Mansion
804-633-5781-[Y--]

Willoughby B&B
804-633-9268

Boyce
River House
540-837-1476

Bridgewater
Bear & Dragon B&B
540-828-2807

Jeans B&B

Brodnax
Sherwood Manor Inn
804-848-0361

Buchanan
Wattstull Inn
540-254-1551

Bumpass
Rockland Farm Retreat
540-895-5098-[Y--]

Burkeville
Hyde Park Farm
804-645-8431

Cape Charles
Cape Charles House
804-331-4920

Chesapeake Charm B&B
800-546-9215-[G--]

Nottingham Ridge
804-331-1010

Picketts Harbor B&B
804-331-2212-[G--]

Sea Gate B&B
804-331-2206

Stratton Manor

Sunset Inn
804-331-2424

Capron
Sandy Hill Farm

Castleton
Blue Knoll Farm B&B
540-937-5234

Champlain
Linden House
800-622-1202

Charles City
Country Antiques & B&B
804-829-5234

Edgewood Plantation
800-296-EDGE [G--]

Evelynton Plantation
800-473-5075

North Bend Plantation B&B
800-841-1479-[G--]

Piney Grove B&B
804-829-2480

Charlottesville
1817 Antique Inn
800-730-7443

200 South Street Inn
800-964-7008-[Y--]

Clifton Country Inn
804-971-1800-[G--]

English Inn of Charlottesville
804-971-00

Firmstone Manor B&B Inn
703-862-0892-[G--]

Frederick House
800-334-5575-[G--]

Guesthouses B&B
804-979-7264

Inn At Monticello
804-973-3593

Silver Thatch Inn
804-978-4686

Slave Quarters
804-979-7264

Trillium House
800-325-9126-[G--]

Upland Manor
804-361-1101

Woodstock Hall, Historic B&B Inn
804-293-8977

Chatham
Eldon - Inn At Chathan
804-432-0935

House Of Laird
804-432-2523

Sims Mitchell House
800-967-2867-[Y--]

Chilhowie
Clark Crest B&B
540-646-3737

Clarkcrest B&B
540-646-3707

Pendleton House Inn
540-646-2047

Chincoteague
Channel Bass Inn
804-336-6148

Duck Haven Cottages
804-336-6290

Island Manor House
804-336-5436

Little Traveler Inn
804-336-5436

Main Street House
800-491-2027

Miss Mollys Inn
800-221-5620

The Garden & The Sea Inn
800-824-0672-[G--]

Watson House B&B
800-336-6787-[Y--]

Year Of The Horses Inn
804-336-3321

Christiansburg
Evergreen Bell-Capozzi House

3-180

©Inn & Travel Memphis, Tennessee

Bold Name - Description appears in other section **Virginia**

800-905-7372

Oaks B&B Country Inn
800-336-OAKS-[Y--]

Churchville
Buckhorn Inn
540-337-6900

Clarksville
Kinderton Manor
804-374-4439-[Y--]

Needmoor Inn
804-374-2866

Noreens Nest
804-374-0603

Simply Southern
804-374-9040

Clifton Forge
Firmstone Manor B&B Inn
540-862-0892-[Y--]

Cluster Springs
Oak Grove Plantation
804-575-7137

Colonial Beach
Quiet Water Cove
804-224-7410

Columbia
Upper Byrd Farm
804-842-2240

Copper Hill
Bent Mountain Inn
540-929-4979

Covington
Milton Hall B&B
540-965-0196

Culpeper
Fountain Hall B&B
800-476-2944

Dabneys
Bare Castle Farm B&B
804-749-3950

Dalveville
Baileywick Farm B&B
540-2-2022

Danville
Broadstreet Manor
804-792-0324

Deltaville
River Place
804-776-9153

Dillwyn
Buckingham Springs Plantation
800-759-5957

Tranquility Farm B&B
804-392-4456

Draper
Clayton Lake Homestead Inn
800-676-LAKE

Dublin
Bells B&B
800-437-0575

East Amherst
Buffalo River B&B & Stables
703-263-8652

Edinburg
Edinburg Inn B&B
540-984-8286

Marys Country Inn
540-984-8286-[Y--]

Elkton
Jo AnnesB&B
540-298-9723

Emporia
Little Guest House
804-634-2590

Etlan
Dulaney Hollow B&B
540-923-4470

Exmore
Gladstone House
800-BNBGUEST

Marthas Inn
804-442-4641

Fairfax
Bailiwick Inn
800-366-7666

Falls Church
Military B&B

Flint Hill
Caledonia Farm - 1812
800-BNB-1812-[G--]

School House Inn

Stone House Hollow
703-675-3279

Floyd
Brookfield Inn
540-763-3363

Franktown
Stillmeadow Inn
800-772-8379

Fredericksburg
Fredericksburg Inn
540-371-5666

Kenmore Inn Fredericksburg
800-437-7622-[Y--]

La Vista Plantation
540-898-8444-[Y--]

Richard Johnston Inn
540-8-7606

Shelby House B&B
540-373-7037

Spooner House B&B
540-371-1267

Front Royal
Caledonia Farm - 1812
800-BNB-1812-[G--]

Chester House B&B
800-621-0441-[Y--]

Constant Spring Inn
540-635-7010

Killahevlin
800-847-6132-[G--]

Glasgow
Balcony Downs Plantation
800-359-3616

Gloucester
Willows B&B
804-693-4066

Gordonsville
Norfields Farm B&B
540-832-2952

Ridge Top Country Cottage
540-832-2946

Rocklands
540-832-7176

Sleepy Hollow Farm B&B
540-832-5555-[Y--]

Tivoli
800-832-2225-[G--]

Gore
Rainbows End B&B
540-858-2888

Goshen
Hummingbird Inn
800-397-3214
[GQAR-]

Hampton
Squirrel Hotel
804-723-7462

Hardyville
Rivers Rise B&B
804-776-7521

Harrisonburg
Joshua Wilton House
540-434-4464

Kingsway B&B
540-867-9696

Haywood
Shenandoah Springs Inn
540-923-4300

Hillsville
Brays Manor B&B
800-753-BRAY

Hot Springs
Homestead

Kings Victorian Inn
540-839-3134

Vine Cottage Inn
540-839-2422-[Y--]

Independence
Riverview B&B
800-841-6628

Irish Gap
Irish Gap Inn
804-922-7701

©Inn & Travel Memphis, Tennessee

Virginia *Bold Name* - Description appears in other section

Irvington
Irvington House
804-438-6705

Kendall Hall Inn

King Carter Inn
804-438-6053

Tides Inn

Lancaster
Inn At Levelfields
804-435-6887

Leesburg
Fleetwood Farm B&B
703-327-4325

Hillcrest Inn

Laurel Brigade Inn
703-777-1010

Leesburg Colonial Inn
703-777-5000

Norris House Inn
800-644-1806-[Y--]

Lexington
Alexander Withrow House
540-463-2044

Brierley Hill
800-422-4925

Fassifern B&B
540-463-1013

Firmstone Manor B&B Inn
540-862-0892-[G--]

Inn At Union Run
540-463-9715

Lavender Hill Farm
800-446-4240

Llewellyn Lodge
800-882-1145

Maple Hall
540-463-2044

McCampbell Inn
540-463-2044

Seven Hills Inn
540-463-4715

Lincoln

Springdale Country Inn
800-388-1832

Locust Dale
Inn At Meander Plantation
540-672-4912

Louisa
Ginger Hill B&B
540-967-0589

Luray
Boxwood Place
540-743-9484

Jordan Hollow Farm Inn
540-778-2285

Lion and The Crow Lodge
540-743-6605

Momslyn
540-743-5105

Ruffner House
540-743-7855

Shenandoah Countryside
540-743-6434

Spring Farm B&B
540-743-4701

Lynchburg
Langhorne Manor B&B
800-851-1466

Lynchburg Mansion Inn
800-352-11

Madison House
800-828-6422-[Y--]

Lyndhurst
Mountain Place B&B
540-943-7203

Madison
Shenahdoah Springs
540-923-4300

Madison Heights
Winridge
540-384-7220

Manassas
Doves CoVe B&B

703-361-5637

Sunrise Hill Farm
703-754-8309

Mathews
Ravenswood Inn
804-725-7272

Riverfront House B&B & Cottage
804-725-75-[G--]

Welbourne
804-687-3201-[Y--]

Maurertown
Good Intent
540-459-2985

McGaheysville
Shenandoah Valley Farm
540-289-5402

Meadows of Dan
Spangler B&B
703-952-2454

Woodbury Inn

Middleburg
Middleburg Country Inn
800-262-6082

Middleburg Inn
800-432-6125

Red Fox Inn & Tavern
800-223-1728

Middletown
Wayside Inn
540-869-1797-[Y--]

Millboro
Fort Lewis Lodge
540-925-2314

Millwood
Black Penny B&B
540-837-2150

Clark House
540-837-3021

Red Schoolhouse
540-837-3033

Mineral
Littlepage Inn
800-248-1803

Mitchells

Stuartfield Hearth
540-825-8132

Mollusk
Greenvale Manor Waterfront
804-462-55

Guest Houses On The Water
804-462-55

Moneta
Holland Duncan House
540-721-8510

Monroe
St Moor House
804-929-8228

Monterey
Highland Inn
540-468-2143-[Y--]

Montross
Inn At Montross
800-321-0979-[Y--]

Morattico
Holley Point
804-462-7759

Mount Crawford
Pumpkin House Ltd
703-434-6963

Mount Holly
Mount Holly House

Mount Holly Steamboat Inn
804-472-3336

Mount Jackson
Sky Chalet
540-856-2147

Widow Kips Country Inn
540-477-2400

Mount Sidney
Spiff Inn
540-248-7307

Narrernton
Blackhorse Inn
540-347-5422

Natural Bridge
Burgers Country Inn
540-291-2464

Nellysford
Acorn Inn At

3-182 ©Inn & Travel Memphis, Tennessee

Bold Name - *Description appears in other section* **Virginia**

Wintergreen
804-361-9357

Mark Addy
800-278-2154

Mark Eddy Manor
804-361-1101-[Y--]

Meander Inn
804-361-1121

Trillium House
800-325-9126-[Y--]

New Church
The Garden & The Sea Inn
800-824-0672-[G--]

New Market
A Touch Of Country
540-740-8030

Cross Roads Inn
540-740-4157

Red Shutter Farmhouse
540-740-4281

Newport
Newport House
540-961-2480-[Y--]

Norfolk
Cameron Residence
804-587-0673

Erikas B&B
804-583-5725

Page House Inn
804-625-5033

North Garden
Inn At The Crossroads
804-976-6452

Occoquan
Rockledge 1758
703-690-3377

Swift Run Gap Inn
804-985-2740

Old Town Alexandria
Mallard Guest House
703-548-5618

Onancock
Colonial Manor Inn
804-787-3521

Market Street B&B
804-787-7600

Spinning Wheel B&B
804-787-7311-[Y--]

Orange
Five Oaks Farm B&B

Hidden Inn
800-841-1253-[G--]

Holladay House
800-358-4422

Shadows B&B Inn
540-672-5057-[Y--]

Willow Grove Inn
800-949-1778

Oroville
Montgomery Inn
916-532-1400

Paconian Springs
Cornerstone B&B
703-882-3722

Palmyra
Danscot House
804-589-1977

Palmer Country Manor
800-253-4306

Paris
Ashby Inn
540-592-3900

Parkersburg
Harmony House
804-485-1458

Petersburg
Folly Castle Inn
804-733-6463

The Owl & The Pussycat B&B
804-733-0505

Mayfield Inn
804-733-0866

Port Haywood
Inn At Tabbs Creek Landing
804-725-5136

Port Republic
Busy Bee B&B
540-289-5480

Pratts
Colvin Hall B&B
540-948-6211

Providence Forge
Jasmine Plantation B&B
804-966-9836

Pulaski
Count Pulaski B&B
800-980-1163

Pungoteague
Evergreen
804-442-3375

Pungoteague Junction B&B
804-442-3581

Raphine
Oak Spring Farm & Vineyard
540-377-2398

Rapidan
Eastern View Plantation
540-854-6705

Reedville
Cedar Grove
804-453-3915

Elizabeth House
804-453-7016

Magnolia Tree B&B
804-453-4720

Richmond
Abbie Hill B&B
804-355-5855

Be My Guest B&B
804-358-01

Bensonhouse, Emmanuel Hutzler
804-353-6900

Carrington Row Inn
804-343-7005

Leonine Experience

Linden Row
804-783-7000

Lions Inn
804-355-7265

Mr Patrick Henrys Inn

800-932-2654

North Bend Plantation B&B
804-829-5176-[G--]

Patrick Henrys Inn
800-932-2654

West-Bocock House B&B
804-358-6174

William Catlin House
804-780-3746-[Y--]

Roanoke
Lone Oaks B&B
540-989-95

Manor At Taylors Store
800-248-6267-[Y--]

Mary Bladon House
540-344-5361-[Y--]

Rochelle
Dawsons Country Place
540-948-7013

Rocky Mount
Amber Inn
540-483-9560

Claiborne House
540-483-4616

Rosedale
Rosedale Country Inn
540-880-1268

Round Hill
Poor House Farm B&B
703-554-2511

Salem
Inn At Burwell Place
703-387-0250

Scottsburg
Falkland Farms
804-575-1400

Scottsville
Chester B&B
804-286-3960-[Y--]

High Meadows Vineyard Inn
800-232-1832-[Y--]

©Inn & Travel Memphis, Tennessee

Virginia

Smith Mountain Lake
Manor At Taylors Store
800-248-6267-[Y--]

Smithfield
Isle Of Wright Inn
800-357-3245

Smithfield Station
804-357-7700

Sperryville
Apple Hill Farm B&B
540-987-9454

Conyers House
540-987-8025

Spotsylvania
Roxbury Mill B&B
540-582-6611

Stafford
Renaissance Manor & Art Gallery
800-720-3784-[G--]

Stanardsville
Edgewood Farm B&B
804-985-3782

Stanley
Milton House
540-778-3451

Staunton
Ashton Country House
800-296-7819

Belle Grae Inn
540-886-5151

Frederick House
800-334-5575-[G--]

Hilltop House
540-886-0042

Kenwood
540-886-0524

Lambsgate B&B
540-885-8798

Sampson Eagon Inn
800-597-9722

Thornrose House At Gypsy Hill
540-885-7026

Steeles Tavern
Osceola Mill Inn
800-242RELAX

Sugar Tree Inn
703-377-2197

Stephens City
The Inn At Vaucluse Spring
800-869-0525

Sterling
Round Hill Manor
703-338-9221

Strasburg
Hotel Strasburg
540-465-9191

Suffolk
Chateau
804-253-2323

Surry
Seward House Inn
804-294-3810

Surrey House
804-294-3191

Syria
Graves Mountain Lodge Inn
540-923-4231

Tangier
Browns Boarding House

Toano
Bluebird Haven
804-566-0177

Trevilians
Prospect Hill
800-277-0844

Troutdale
Fox Hill Inn
800-874-3313

Troutville
Woods Edge Guest Cottage
703-473-22

Upperville
1763 Inn
800-669-1763

Chases Inn
540-592-3680

Urbanna
Atherston Hall

804-758-2809

Duck Farm Inn
804-758-5685

Hewick Plantation
804-758-4214

Vesuvius
Irish Gap Inns
540-922-7701

Sugar Tree Inn
540-377-2197

Virginia Beach
Angies Guest Cottage
804-428-4690

Barclay Cottage B&B
804-422-1956

Beach B&B
804-481-4353

Wachapreague
Burton House B&B
804-787-4560-[Y--]

Harts Harbor House
804-787-4848

Warm Springs
Anderson Cottage
540-839-2975

Hidden Valley B&B
540-839-3178

Inn At Gristmill Square
540-839-2231-[Y--]

Meadow Lane Lodge
540-839-5959

Three Hills Inn
540-839-5381

Warm Springs Inn
540-839-5351

Warsaw
Greenwood
804-333-4353

Washington
Caledonia Farm - 1812
800-BNB-1812-[G--]

Fairlea Farm B&B

540-675-3679

Foster Harris House
800-666-0153

Gay Street Inn
540-675-3288

Heritage House
540-675-3207

Inn At Little Washington
540-675-3800

Sunset Hills Farm
800-980-2580

Sycamore Hill House & Gardens
540-675-3046

Waterford
Pink House
540-882-3453

Waterford Inn
540-882-3465

Waynesboro
Iris Inn
540-943-11

Weyers Cave
Inn At Keezletown Road
800-358-2298

White Post
L'Auberge Provencale
800-638-1702-[G--]

Williamsburg
Alice Person House
804-220-9263

Applewood Colonial B&B
800-8-2753-[G--]

Brass Lantern Lodge
804-229-9089

Candlewick B&B
804-253-8693

Carters Guest House
804-229-1117

Cedars
800-296-3591

Chantilly

Bold Name - Description appears in other section *Virginia*

804-229-3434-[Y--]

Colonial Capital
B&B
800-776-0570

Colonial
Williamsburg Inn

**Edgewood
Plantation**
800-296-EDGE-[Y--]

Forest Hill Guest
Home
804-229-1444

Four Cant Hill
Guest House
804-229-6623

Fox Grape Of
Williamsburg
800-292-3669

Governors Trace
804-229-7552

Greenwoode Inn
804-566-8800

Hites Guest House
804-229-4814

Hollands Lodge
804-253-6474

Homestay B&B
800-836-7468

Hughes Guest
House
804-229-3493

Indian Spring B&B
800-262-9165

Johnsons Guest
House
804-229-3909-[Y--]

**Legacy Of
Williamsburg B&B**
800-WMBGS-BB
[Y--]

Liberty Rose
Colonial B&B
800-545-1825

Magnolia Manor
800-462-6667

**Newport House
B&B**
804-229-1775-[G--]

**North Bend
Plantation B&B**
804-829-5176-[G--]

Piney Grove
Southalls
Plantation
804-829-2480

Primrose Cottage
800-522-1901

Riverfront House
B&B & Cottage
804-725-75-[Y--]

**Spiggle Guest
Home**
804-253-0202

Thompson Guest
House
804-229-3455

War Hill Inn
800-743-0248

**Williamsburg
Manor B&B**
800-422-8011-[G--]

**Williamsburg
Sampler B&B**
800-722-1169-[G--]

Woods Guest House
804-229-3376

Willis Wharf
Ballard House
Homestay
804-442-2206

Winchester
Boxwood Inn
540-662-2521

Wintergreen
Upland Manor
804-361-1101-[Y--]

Woodstock
Azalea House B&B
540-459-3500

Candlewick Inn
540-459-8008-[Y--]

Country Fare
540-459-4828

Inn At Narrow
Passage
540-459-8000-[Y--]

River'd Inn
800-637-4561

Shenandoah Valley
B&B
540-459-8241

Woolwine
**Mountain Rose
B&B**
540-930-1057-[Y--]

Wytheville
Boxwood Inn
540-228-8911

West Coast

The Southwest

The Southwest is wide open spaces

> *with multi-hued red rock formations*
> *snow-capped mountains*
> *with pine, spruce and shimmering aspen*
> *the first mesa, second mesa*
> *and the plateau with endless desert.*

We are isolated ranches, small villages, reservations, towns and large cities. Wherever you travel, the scenic beauty and complexity of the Southwest changes faster than the shadows of the clouds, but we have one thing in common - *The Hoo Hoo Kam - "The people who have gone before"*. That is how the Pima-Maricopa Indians of Arizona describe their ancestors.

Yes, this is Indian Country. It is home to the largest number of Native Americans in North America. On their reservations they are sovereign nations .... a very private, independent people. But the *Hoo Hoo Kam* knew of no barriers nor borders. This land belonged to no man, no tribe, no nation. The land, the mountain, the tree, the stream, the river, the rock .... like the wind, the thunder and the rain; like the bird, the deer and the snake, belong to all people .... are one with the people.

The *Hoo Hoo Kam* marked this land; and there is no appreciation of its wonder, its beauty or its awesome danger other than as they knew it and have loved it. It is a sacred land, an enchanted land. When you travel the Southwest, travel in this spirit.

Paul Kelley, Innkeeper
Maricopa Manor
Phoenix, Arizona

Mendocino County

As I grew up in Ukiah, California, Mendocino County, I never realized the beauty and unique experiences this valley had to offer for the body and soul. It was not until I returned home from my first year at college that I realized what drew so many people here to live and an increasing number to play. This valley holds some of the finest wineries in the world, home to the largest supplier of environmentally aware products, a museum full of paintings and artifacts from the Pomo Indians, and of course, The Redwood Forests on the way to Mendocino Coast. It was not until I returned home from the traditions and heritage of my east coast college and surroundings did I see the traditions and heritage that make Mendocino County what it is today.

The thirty-five wineries to which I refer are sprinkled throughout Mendocino County, with Ukiah being home to eight of them. Some of these wineries are world-renown, with others being hidden jewels, nestled in their vineyards awaiting discovery. Mendocino County is also home to two of the world's best brandy distilleries, Jepson Vineyards and Germaine-Robin, whose brandies have won awards and both have been served in the White House. Ukiah, the county seat, is home to the innovative company *Real Goods*, an environmentally-centered mail order catalog with its showroom open to the public. A visitor can learn about solar power and hydro power while shopping for energy saving products for their home and office. The store also offers alternatives to the run of the mill toys with is educational toys and books.

The Sun House Museum is another one of Ukiah's unique experiences because of the Pomo Indians who live here. The museum consists of the original redwood house built by Dr. and Mrs. Hudson. Mrs. Hudson was well known internationally as an artist who painted incredible oil paintings of these Native Americans before they changed to modern clothing. The portraits of babies and families glow with the beauty of these people, their culture and her appreciation of their way of life. These paintings are displayed in the new art museum located behind the original house and is filled with her paintings, artifacts from the tribe and touring exhibits related to the Native Americans in this region.

The city of Ukiah is also a perfect starting point from which to explore the nearby California Redwoods either by car or via the town of Willit's famous *Skunk Train* that winds its way over to the coast. The Mendocino Coast, one of the most popular stops in Northern California, is a scenic drive and a perfect day trip or weekend getaway. This quaint town is featured on *CBS* every Sunday night on *Murder She Wrote* as Angelia Lansbury's hometown in Maine, Cabbot Cove. The town itself offers a host of incredible art galleries, shops and restaurants. It is also home to Cafe Beaujolais, owned and operated by gourmet chef Margaret Fox.

For those who would like outdoor recreation, there are several lakes, including Mendocino County's own Lake Mendocino, and the appropriately named Lake County with Blue Lakes and Clear Lake, California's largest natural lake, for water skiing, fishing, canoeing andboating. The Russian River runs through Mendocino County, offering fishing and tubing, while the Eel River is known for its steelhead and salmon fishing. Ukiah is located in a long valley 600 feet above sea level and is surrounded by mountains that are up to 4,500 feet in elevation with trails for mountain biking, motorcycling and hiking.

Mendocino County and its surrounding areas offer guests the opportunity to explore Northern California to the fullest. Located only two hours north of San Francisco, this area offers the classic beauty of the world famous Mendocino Coast, the traditions of the wine country, and the timeless beauty of the outdoors. I invite you to come and see why people want to save the old growth forests, stop offshore oil drilling and preserve the beauty that draws people, like myself, back to Mendocino County.

Annelies Ashoff, Innkeeper
Vichy Springs Resort
Ukiah, California

Destination: Durango

Durango has come a long way since 1846, when Daniel Webster described this mountain outpost as

"a vast, worthless area, a region of savages and wild beasts, of deserts, of shifting sands and endless mountain ranges impenetrable, and covered with eternal snow."

Even after Durango was established as a railroad town in 1880 -- servicing the many local gold, silver, and coal mines in the vicinity -- it was far from *"civilized."* Saloons and brothels dominated the downtown area; hangings and shoot-outs were not uncommon.

Although, today, Durango has settled down some, it still retains much of its frontier flavor. Moreover, Durango is one of the few funky cowboy towns with a functioning, self-supporting downtown area still intact.

Friendly folks here, now, and a good mix -- cowboys and Indians (of course), but also professionals and working-class folks, and a lot of young outdoor types -- hikers, bikers, and skiers. In fact, Durango is one of the most engaging towns left in the Old West - - kind of a throwback to the gentle 60's -- no doubt due to the influence of Ft. Lewis College, founded here in 1956. Good book stores (Maria's on Main), music stores (Southwest Sound, right next to Maria's), even poetry -- the most unique event being the annual Cowboy Poetry Festival in the fall.

What To Do

There is so much to do in and around Durango you really need to stay more than just a couple of days. Durango is truly a *"destination"* resort. Here are just a few suggestions:

©Inn & Travel Memphis, Tennessee

Have a great time power-shopping downtown Durango. Hit all the shops and galleries -- including many new factory outlets.

Take a walk along the Animas River (cross the footbridge at the base of Twelfth Street). Or take a hike up to the top of the mesa on "The Nature Trail" (east end of Tenth Street) to Ft. Lewis College -- great views of Durango and the surrounding La Plata Mountains. Also check out the Victorian homes on historic Third Avenue.

Go rafting, kayaking and fishing on the Animas River. During the summer, the local rafting and kayaking companies have their booths set up on both sides of Main.

Although the downtown stretch of the Animas River is pretty gentle, there are a couple of good Class II rapids downstream. The kayak course north and south of town has been the site of Olympic trials. Fly fishing is also good right downtown (some catch and release) and elsewhere in La Plata County, rivers, alpine lakes and streams abound.

World-class fly fishing for trophy-size trout can be found here all-year-round. Fishing, boating, water-skiing and swimming are available at nearby Vallecito and Navajo reservoirs. Or if it's warmer waters you seek, go for a soak in the pools at Trimble Hot Springs just north of town (the site of the summer jazz festival).

Attend the bi-weekly P.R.C.A. Rodeo at the County Fairgrounds. Picture this:

Ext. Rodeo Arena - - Night

CAMERA focuses on dust of rodeo in progress.

Then, as dust clears, CAMERA sees bronc rider mounted on wild-looking bronc.

Roar of crowd momentarily rises to deafening level on AUDIO.

DISSOLVE TO shot off bronc rider being violently bucked off bronc and sent head over heels to dusty floor of arena.

Crowd becomes suddenly hushed.

Voice of announcer comes up in AUDIO background.

ANNOUNCER

Boy, that'll jerk the puddin' out of ya'.

CUT TO ANGLE ON head of snorting bronc.

CUT TO shot of bronc rider on all fours - dazed, struggling to get up.

Have you seen this movie yet? Just another night at the Durango P.R.C.A. Rodeo.

Take the Durango-Silverton Narrow Gauge Railroad. Without a doubt, the centerpiece of Durango's thriving tourist industry is this classic narrow gauge train ride through the rugged Animas Canyon. This old coal-fired train has become highly recognizable as a result of being used as a famous prop in the many Western movies filmed in and around the Durango area -- *Viva Zapata*, *How The West Was Won*, *Butch Cassidy And The Sundance Kid*, to name a few. The ride itself is well worth the cinders and smoke. Tickets are available at the train station at the south end of Main.

Vist Mesa Verde National Park. One of the most magical places in the Four Corners area is the Mesa Verde National Park -- one hour west of Durango on Route 160. Established in 1906 (the second oldest park in the National Park system), Mesa Verde was the home of the ancient Anasazi Indians, who inhabited this site for five hundred years before mysteriously disappearing in the early 1300's. Spend some time at the Chapin Mesa Museum and be sure to walk to Spruce Tree House -- probably the most well-known cliff dwelling in North America. If you have time, drive the rim trail -- where you can view some of the hundreds of other cliff dwellings in this magnificent natural setting. Although the park is open year-round, lodging and camping facilities are seasonal.

Ski at Purgatory. In the wintertime, of course, the most popular attraction is the Durango-Purgatory Ski Resort -- twenty minutes north of Durango on Highway 550. Especially suited for families, the resort offers over 600 acres of maintained ski terrain, 150 acres of it groomed, and nine chair lifts. Regular shuttle service is provided from Durango. While there, dine at The Sow's Ear down the hill or at The Cascades down the highway -- one of the finest gourmet restaurants in the Four Corners area. After skiing, relax at Farquharts; the bar faces the slopes. Across the road, you can also cross-country ski at the Nordic Center (lessons available).

One of my favorite things to do is to take a drive through the surrounding countryside -- north, south, east or west -- some of the most spectacular drives in the Southwest.

There are many fine restaurants downtown. These are some of my favorites:

For Sunday brunch, try The Red Lion (they have a patio right over the river) or Francisco's (the best place to catch the game on weekends -- four TV screens in the lounge). The best brunch by far, though, is served at The Palace Grill -- right next to the train station.

During weekdays, get your basic breakfast at the local greasy spoon, The Durango Diner on Main.

For lunch, go to Lola's Place, just one block up from Main on Second Avenue. This unique restaurant -- located in the newly-restored Victorian "painted Lady" just two doors north of The Leland House -- offers a gourmet menu featuring delicious and healthy daily specials, including soups and salads. Bright, colorful atmosphere!

Back on Main Street, you might try Carver's Bakery and Brew Pub Cafe -- your minimum daily required foodstuffs here -- fresh-baked bread and home-made beer.

My favorite entrees: the veggie ruben and the grilled veggie sandwiches, the garden Swiss burger (the veggie burger), and the chicken stew in a bread bowl (reminds me of Mom's chicken-and-dumplings). Eat at the pub in the back -- or order at the counter and eat by the windows in front.

Another good place is the Olde Tymer's Cafe. Formerly the 100-year-old Wall Drugstore, Olde Tymer's still retains the original ornate Victorian mouldings and ceiling. Artifacts, sundries from the period line the walls. Books, bottles, vintage vending machines, packaged medicines and potions fill the upstairs balconies. These days, Olde Tymer's is the unofficial headquarters of the local mountain bikers. Old Tymer's is known for its American cuisine (especially the burgers) and the inexpensive menu. Full bar. Patio out back.

One of my favorite places for the atmosphere is Father Murphy's -- which has all the ambience of an Irish pub. I always get the club sandwich or the BLT here, though their specialty is beer-battered cod. Father Murhpy's also has a patio out back. Friendly waitresses here (*"Go and sin no more,"* inscribed on their T-shirts).

For genuine Northern New Mexico cuisine, go to Gazpacho. Try the veggie combo plates. The tamales are especially good.

After lunch (or earlier if you like) visit the Durango Coffee Company -- simply the best cappuccino place in Durango -- friendly service, a number of well-lighted tables, jazz on the stereo.

For evening hors d'oeuvres, the fresh oysters at The Red Snapper are excellent -- delivered fresh on Tuesdays and Fridays. The hot oyster appetizers are only $3.95 during "Oyster Hour" -- 5:00 to 6:00 p.m., seven days a week.

For dinner I would recommend Ariano's, Randy's, or the Ore House -- all corners of a triangle in the middle of Sixth Street, between Main and Second Avenues. Ariano's features northern Italian specialties. I like the chicken in parchment paper, the linguine in clam sauce (red or white), the beef, the fish -- everything is good (though sometimes a bit rich). Pasta comes on the side with every dish. Randy's, same side of the street, is known for veal chops, chicken, and escular -- when available (a delicate, white fish from Mexico). Randy's serves food at the bar -- making it another good place to watch the game. The Ore House, directly across the street, is a great steak and lobster place -- with salad bar. The fresh Colorado mountain trout is always excellent -- pan-fried, grilled, almandine, or Sonora style.

Another consistently good restaurant is The Palace Grill (next to the train station). I remember the baby-back pork ribs, the honey duck and the goulash (simmered with mushrooms and onions in a red wine sauce).

After dinner entertainment might include rock and roll at Farquahrts, honky-tonk piano at The Diamond Belle, or jazz at The Pelican. Do the two-step at The Sundance, where all the cowboys hang out. Or tour the local saloons.

The Old Muldoon, up from The Palace on Main Avenue, is my regular hangout: Victorian setting -- flower print wallpaper, wainscotted walls, lots of mirrors, paintings of reclining nudes, velveteen-covered love seats, high-backed chairs, marble-topped coffee tables -- two barber chairs in the back (where the dart boards are located) -- Tiffany lamps, stained-glass everywhere, brass rails, ornate, hand-carved wood-back bar. Older group here, but a good mix -- local businessmen, hat-maker who owns the shop across the street (O'Farrel's), owner of the leather shop next door (The Apaloosa Trading Company) -- assorted cowboys -- construction crews -- occasional Indians (Lone Eagle, a Sioux from South Dakota who was mixing it up with a Navajo last time I was here). Local character, calls himself Little Beaver, comes in looking for cigarettes -- loose change in cracks of the overstuffed couches. Little Beaver wearing headband and feather, or bandanna wrapped around his head, or one time a Mexican sombrero -- serape -- pants too short -- hair cut in spiky short butch, or mohawk, or shaved bald -- Little Beaver carrying on long discussion with himself.

The Diamond Belle (next block up Main) is another interesting place -- Victorian decor -- part of the Strater Hotel (the oldest hotel in town). At the Diamond Belle, I run into a young guy from back east who has quit his office job and set out to conquer the highest peaks in every state in the west -- just did Wheeler Peak in New Mexico -- now headed for Humphrey's Peak in Arizona. After a few beers, though, I find out that there is also a lost love behind this enterprise.

And further up the street is Farquharts -- typical, low key college dance place -- your usual poster-flecked falls -- brick and wood decor -- main floor crammed with tables -- full bar and pretty good pizza -- and your usual young lovelies drifting in -- college coeds. But in Durango, there's always a good mix -- working class guys in for the happy-hour pitcher specials -- young professionals -- but no cowboys ("Bouncer ushers them right out of here", one of the locals tells me -- "they just don't mix with the hippie-types, I guess -- don't like the music maybe.") "Leftover Salmon" is playing tonight.

The most colorful saloon in town is The El Rancho at the Central Hotel -- local dive and pool hall (seven tables) -- also known at "Ol' Rauncho." I am sitting at the bar the El Rancho when I am tapped on the shoulder -- and turn around to greet Larry Harjo, Medicine Man from Oklahoma -- Seminole, he tells me. Larry apologizes, thinking I'm someone else, chats with me about a spirit gathering in Kansas that he's about to attend -- tells me he's in town to exorcise bad medicine from house of local Ute man -- says he hears spirits, but none he can identify -- but he'll try once more tonight -- says he does bad medicine too. We shake left hands (Indian style) and he blesses me -- gives me good medicine -- for me and my family. I wish him luck and apologize for having to leave -- not sure what to make of all this medicine, his holy words, his generous incantation.

But you might just say it's just another day in Durango -
a true vacation destination.

Fred Wildfang
Leland House B&B Suites
Durango, Colorado

The Valley of the Sun - Arizona

We offer the rugged excitement and natural beauty of the Old Southwest blended with all the sophistication of the *New* Southwest. We also offer wonderful experiences you'll remember for a lifetime. Because when it comes to the things you want most in a destination, the Valley has all of them. No matter how long you plan on staying, you'll find our Bed and Breakfast accommodations and Southwestern hospitality will make you want to stay longer. You can pamper yourself. Phoenix and the Valley of the Sun will make you feel right at home, no matter how far from home.

Our name, Valley of the Sun, just about says it all. Phoenix has over 300 days of sunshine a year, very low humidity and an average yearly temperature of 72 degrees. To go along with our comfortable weather, we also have a very comfortable dress code. Other than several restaurants which require jacket and tie for dinner, the dress is casual year round. Shorts in summer are perfect. Be sure to pack swim suits anytime of the year. Jeans and western wear are always in style. And when the rest of the country is wrapped in parkas, a sweater or jacket is all you'll need.

Fresh Atlantic lobster grilled over Southwestern mesquite. Savory cowboy steaks charbroiled under a Southwestern sunset. From unforgettable down-home cooking to sophisticated continental cuisine to a traditional Mexican fiesta, memorable dining experiences await you in the Valley of the Sun. Comedy clubs, jazz, rock, big band music... there are so many things to do in the Valley.

Life may not be all fun and games but in the Valley it certainly comes close. We're home of the NFL Phoenix Cardinals, NBA Phoenix Suns, Arizona State Sun Devils and the Arizona Rattlers. We're the annual site of the Fiesta Bowl, PGA Phoenix Open, LPGA Standard Register Turquoise Classic, PGA Seniors Tradition Tournament, Checker 500 NASCAR Winston Cup and CART Indy Car races. We also host polo matches, Arabian horse shows, dog racing, thoroughbred racing - even authentic western rodeos. And, as much as there is to see, there's even more to do. Water skiing, swimming, tubing down the Salt River, glider flying, hot-air ballooning, horseback riding, mountain climbing, jeep touring, trail hiking and endless hours of camera clicking. Sports fans are sure to become devoted fans of the Valley of the Sun.

If variety is the spice of life, wait until you get a taste of our golf and tennis. In the Valley of the Sun, golfers can tee-off on over one hundred courses. Choose a desert course, stadium course, traditional course - even a choice of challenging designs by Jack Nicklaus and Tom Weiskopf... and that's just half of it! For tennis, the Valley offers a thousand courts of clay, laykoid, grass and stadium play. Obviously, if you love golf or tennis, don't miss Phoenix and the Valley of the Sun.

For visitors who love the arts, Phoenix can easily become a first love. You can see the culture of the American Indian come to life at the world-renown Heard Museum. See the acclaimed permanent collection, the national and international traveling exhibits at the Phoenix Art Museum. Enjoy the sights and sounds of symphonies, ballets, opera and live theatre. You can walk into the past at an Old West town, walk

©Inn & Travel Memphis, Tennessee

through the timeless architecture of Frank Lloyd Wright, take in the natural beauty of the Desert Botanical Garden and naturally, don't miss the Phoenix Zoo.

Shop hop ... mall crawl ... seek a boutique ... if you're serious about shopping, we've got fun for you! The art galleries, Western shops and international boutiques in the Valley of the Sun are legendary ... Italian leather, French lingerie, dusty antique, sparkling diamonds, American Indian sculpture and good-old American bargains abound. Even if you have the energy, you're bound to wear-out your credit card before the day is over.

Centrally located in Arizona and the heart of the Sonora Desert, Phoenix is the perfect getaway to the beauty of one of the nation's most diverse states. Towering pines, a forest of majestic cactus, the red rock country of Sedona, the man-made wonder of Lake Powell, nature's greatest wonder ... the Grand Canyon - even the experimental world of Biosphere II are within easy reach! Whether your plans allow you the opportunity of just a few days or an extended stay, you'll discover for yourself why we're the number one visitor destination of the Southwest USA! Arizona, **One Grand Adventure After Another!**

Darrell Trapp,
Keeper of the Inn
Phoenix, Arizona

The Mendocino Coast

Do you dream about serene coutryside, azure blue seas, dramatic cliffs, endless beaches, billowy clouds, misty mornings, redwood forests?

It's real and you will find it all on the Mendocino Coast. Driving scenic Pacific Coast Highway One, you will discover the villages and towns of Gualala, Anchor Bay, Point Arena, Manchester, Irish Beach, Elk, Albion, Little River, Mendocino, Caspar, Fort Bragg, Cleone, Westport and Rockport.

The Mendocino Coast is a mecca for multi-talented people. Old-timers and newcomers pool their experiences to share with the community. Whether it's a pancake breakfast at the Grange, symphony concert, musical theater at Cotton Auditorium, or benefit art show and wine tasting, you can count on the folks from all walks of life to Be There. Our celebrations include: **Whale Festivals**, Mendocino, Fort Bragg and Gualala - last three weekends in March; **Heritage Days**, Mendocino - First week of May; **World's Largest Salmon BBQ**, Noyo Harbor - July 4th weekend; **Paul Bunyan Days**, honoring the Logging Industry, Fort Bragg - Labor Day Weekend; **Great Day in Elk**, Parade, BBQ, dancing - mid-July; **Hometown Christmas**, Fort Bragg - First weekend in December. Romance ... music ... theatre ... fine arts ... crafts ... great food ... towering Pacific breakers ... deep secret forests ... meandering peaceful rivers ... All on the Mendocino Coast!

Colette M Bailey, Innkeeper
The Grey Whale Inn
Fort Bragg, California

©Inn & Travel Memphis, Tennessee

Central Coast of California

The Central Coast of California welcomes you with the distinct Pacific breeze that freshens the hillsides golden with poppies, tempers the heat of the summer sun and warms the sands during afternoon strolls on winter beaches. Sounds unique to the region will entice you at each stop along your travel route -- the bark of seals and otters in Monterey Bay, the clatter of the *Giant Dipper* on the Santa Cruz Beach Boardwalk, the cable car clang on San Francisco hills and the gull cries over Point Reyes. The silent redwood giants harbor peaceful glens. Complementing the serenity of these natural wonders, the large cities and small towns offer informative museums, enriching art centers and lively theatre faire. The richness of the ethnic diversity of this area is reflected in an array of food palaces offering the finest cuisines of the world. At each destination you innkeeper-host will help you fully experience the gifts of the region whether you are the vigorous hiker looking for spectacular views from coastal peaks, the determined shopper seeking treasure or trinket of local beauty or the wine connoisseur pursuing a great chardonnay. Like the first discoverers of California, when you reach the Central Coast you'll exclaim **"Eureka! I've found it".**

Patricia O'Brien, Innkeeper
Blue Spruce Inn
Soquel California

Grandview Gardens B&B	4424 Campus St #2 99507-1578	Anchorage AK
		Tel: 907-277-REST

Enjoy the *Northern "Frontier"* in this elegant log cabin lodge setting that includes all the "creature comforts" you'd find anywhere much less here! Three different theme rooms are available along with elegant guest services to assure romantic evenings during your stay. There's a hot tub, flowers, complimentary wine, bikes and car rentals available along with a continental breakfast included with your room. **Seasonal:** No **Brochure:** Yes **Permitted:** Smoking, drinking **Payment Terms:** Check [X11ACAK-20] **COM** Y **ITC Member:** No

Rates:	**Pvt Bath** 2	**Shared Bath** 2
Single	$ 75.00	$ 55.00
Double	$ 85.00	$ 65.00

Lilac House	950 P St 99501	Anchorage AK
Cathy Kerr		Tel: 907-272-3553

Built in 1989, this second story addition to a lovely old Anchorage home is perfectly located in a quiet tree-filled neighborhood for the vacationer and business traveler. The guest rooms are light and airy and include original artwork, stimulating books and tasteful furnishings selected by the owner, an interior decorator. Choose from among the three guest rooms, each with its own name. Sleeping Lady is named for the beautiful view of Cook Inlet and includes a queen size bed, two comfortable lounge chairs, dining table, chairs and a private bath. Tree-shaded Denali View features lovely vistas of Mount Denali and the Chugach Mountains, two single beds, dining table and chairs and writing desk. Facing west, the Sun Room fills with glorious Alaska sun light when the insulated shades are lifted. Laura Ashley linens grace the two single beds with a writing desk, chairs and a chest complete the comfortable decor. Each room has a private phone for free local calls and the Denali View and Sun Room have a deck with a beautiful view of the Chugach Mountains. Tempting, fresh-baked breakfasts are served in each guest room and are included in the room rate. Located adjacent to Delaney Park, guests are just a ten minute walk to downtown Anchorage shops, restaurants, offices and courthouses and the Coastal Trail, a walking, bicycling and skiing trail is just a few minutes walk away. Ample on-street parking and short-term storage is available along with fishing gear for everyone interested in trying their luck. **Airport:** Anchorage is a 15 min direct drive. Alaska Railroad Depot is just a 3 min drive. **Seasonal:** Rates vary **Reservations:** One night's deposit, 48 hr cancel policy in season, 7 day policy low season (Oct-Apr). $10 up-charge for one night's stay. 11am check-out. **Brochure:** Yes **Permitted:** Children, drinking, smoking outdoors only **Languages:** Some French **Payment Terms:** Check MC/V [R05DPAK-12222] **COM** Y **ITC Member:** No

Rates:	**Pvt Bath** 1	**Shared Bath** 2
Single	$ 65.00	$ 55.00
Double	$ 85.00	$ 65.00

McCarthy B&B	PO Box 111241 99511	Anchorage AK
Babbie Jacobs		Tel: 907-277-6867
		Res Times 24 Hrs

In the heart of the Wrangell and Saint Elias National Park, McCarthy has changed little since the early 1900s. Mail is delivered by bush plane weekly - no phones, electricity, running water. Water is hauled from a crystal clear spring, bathing is done in a wood fired log sauna bath house, reading by kerosene lamps and plumbing is outdoors! The cabins were once the Territorial Commissioner's Cabin and the other was the Mother Lode Powerhouse (on the *National Historic Register*). Groups can occupy the Commissioner's Cabin while there are three bedrooms in the Powerhouse. Both cabins offer a perfect and intimate retreat from the "fast life" and a unique opportunity to sample the frontier life of Alaska. Your host offers guided tours and trips to Historic Kennicott, White Water Rafting, Exploring Root Glacier along with a multi-day venture which includes mountaineering, glacial skiing, backpacking and rafting. A hearty full breakfast is included to begin each daily adventure. **Seasonal:** No **Reservations:** Deposit of 50% of length of stay required. **Brochure:** Yes **Permitted:** Children, drinking **Payment Terms:** Check [X07BCAK-24] **COM** Y **ITC Member:** No

Alaska

National Edition

Rates: **Shared Bath 4**
Single $ 50.00
Double $ 70.00

Favorite Bay Inn   On Favorite Bay 99820   **Angoon AK**
Roberta & Dick Powers   **Tel: 907-788-3123**

Located on Admiralty Island overlooking the Angoon Boat Harbor, you're in the heart of wildlife with whales, bald eagles, sea lions and drumming grouse that frequently serenade guests. The rambling home was built in 1937 and enlarged to serve as a general store. Your hosts are familiar with all the points of interest and where to go, depending on your interests. The island is accessible by daily ferry and sea plane service from Juneau and Sitka. A continental breakfast is included, with other meals available at added cost. **Seasonal:** No **Reservations:** Deposit of $25 per days stay required at booking time. **Brochure:** Yes **Permitted:** Children, drinking (BYOB, the island is dry) **Payment Terms:** Check [X02BCAK-25] **COM Y ITC Member:** No

Rates: **Shared Bath 4**
Single $ 65.00
Double $ 75.00

Porter House B&B   624 First Ave 99559   **Bethel AK**
Rose Porter   **Tel: 907-543-3552**

Over look the Kuskokwim River in this comfortable combination of country and contemporary living accommodations while exploring Alaska. All the comforts of home away from home but with the frontier atmosphere. Breakfast is a real treat served on china and silver that includes imported jams, homemade croissants, omelettes and reindeer sausage. Airport pick-ups available. **Seasonal:** No **Brochure:** Yes **Permitted:** Children, limited, pets limited **Payment Terms:** Check MC/V [X11ACK-26] **COM Y ITC Member:** No

Rates: **Shared Bath 4**
Single $ 60.00
Double $ 80.00

---

7 Gables Inn   4312 Birch Lane 99708   **Fairbanks AK**
Paul & Leicha Welton   **Tel: 907-479-0751 Fax: 907-479-2229**
                                                    Res Times 8am-10pm

Historically, *7 Gables Inn* was a fraternity house within walking distance to the UAF campus, yet across the road from the Chena River. Our spacious Tudor home offers 10,000 square foot of unique custom-energy efficient design. Guests enter through the floral solarium into the antique stained-glass decorated foyer with an indoor waterfall - just part of the unique architecture. Other features include cathedral ceilings, a wedding chapel, wine cellar and rooms with dormers, giving a quiet elegance to the premises. A gourmet breakfast is served daily, ranging from a variety of crepes, quiches and specialty egg dishes, as well as fresh fruit, muffins, sweetbreads, coffee cakes, fruit juices, coffee and tea. The area offers: Univ of Alaska Fairbanks campus and Museum, Riverboat Discovery, Alaskaland, Pumphouse Restaurant, Cripple Creek Resort, Alaska Pipeline "permafrost house", Gold Dredge #8, Public Lands Info Center, fishing, skiing, dog mushing and the Santa Claus House. Laundry facilities are available, eight private Jacuzzi bath rooms, bikes, luggage and a library collection. Each room includes cable TV, VCR and phone. Complimentary canoes are available for river rides down to the historic Pumphouse Restaurant. **Discounts:** Fall, Winter, Spring **Airport:** Fairbanks Intl-2 mi **Seasonal:** Rates vary

Reservations: One night deposit (4-nights special deposit arrangement), 48 hr cancel notice for refund **Brochure:** Yes **Permitted:** Children, drinking, limited pets, limited smoking **Conference:** Wedding chapel is available for dancing, business meetings and rehearsal dinners, groups to 100 persons **Languages:** Spanish **Payment Terms:** Check AE/DC/ DISC/MC/V [K02HPAK1-11978] **COM YG ITC Member:** No

Rates:	Pvt Bath 12
Single	$ 50-120.00
Double	$ 50-120.00

Magic Canyon Ranch
Carrie Reed
HCR 40015 Waterman Rd 99603
Homer AK
Tel: 907-235-6077
Res Times 8-5pm

Just outside of town you'll enjoy this *"Raw Country Setting"* with all the comforts of home though! Deluxe rooms with all modern amenities but furnished with frontier Alaska antiques offering tremendous views of Kachemak Bay and Glaciers. Full breakfast plus and other meals available. **Seasonal:** No **Brochure:** Yes **Permitted:** Children limited, drinking limited **Payment Terms:** Check [C11AC-AK-50] **COM Y ITC Member:** No

Rates:	Pvt Bath 1	Shared Bath 2
Single	$ 58-65.00	$ 52-58.00
Double	$ 65-75.00	$ 57-67.00

B&B Inn Juneau
Ronda Flores
1801 Old Glacier Hwy 99801
Juneau AK
Tel: 907-463-5855 **Fax:** 907-463-5259
Res Times 7am-10pm

Located on the outskirts of town, *Bed & Breakfast Inn Juneau* offers six rooms with shared baths and one room with a private bath, along with an apartment for family groups or large parties. There is a large comfortable lounge area with cable TV and laundry facilities. The whole Inn is decorated with artwork by some of Alaska's most popular artists and may be purchased if desired. The grounds are landscaped and picnic tables and barbecues are available. Bicycles are also available for those wishing to see the area in a relaxed fashion. Bus service to town is readily available or assistance with rental cars can be provided if needed. The full breakfast includes specialties of crepes, Alaskan sourdough hotcakes, fresh fruit, syrups and jams from berries grown on the grounds and occasionally fresh salmon. Assistance with sight-seeing activities, fishing charters or other travel arrangements can be provided. We look forward to providing further information on our accommodations. **Seasonal:** No **Reservations:** Deposit required **Brochure:** Yes **Permitted:** Children, no handicap facilities **Payment Terms:** Check AE/MC/V [Z11DPAK-6306] **COM Y ITC Member:** No

Rates:	Pvt Bath 1	Shared Bath 6
Single	$ 65.00	$ 48.00
Double		$ 55.00

Wintels B&B
Willie & Betty Heinrich
PO Box 2812 99615
Kodiak AK
Tel: 907-486-6935
Res Times 8am-10pm

Whether you're traveling for business or pleasure, *Wintels* has everything needed to make your stay in Kodiak more enjoyable and relaxing. You're located within walking distance of shops, beaches, jogging paths, hiking trails and the boat harbor, home of the world-famous fishing fleet. Guests can choose a pleasant and comfortably furnished single or double guest room, each with a complimentary fruit basket. You can enjoy one of the many books and videos your hosts have available for guests to use in the separate den area or enjoy the soothing jacuzzi. You'll be treated to a delicious full Alaskan breakfast each morning - with your hosts ready to prepare box lunches and evening dinners upon request. This great location offers spectacular views from the Inn of eagles, sea birds, sea lions or a beautiful channel view. Nearby you can browse the many specialty shops or even shop at the gift shop in the Inn and choose from the many Alaskan gift items, jewelry, basketry and artwork created by some of Alaska's famous artists. Fishing is spoken here! Try your favorite rod and reel in some of Kodiak's legend fishing scenic rivers or your hosts can help with arrangements for ocean and air charters. **Discounts:** Yes, off season **Airport:** Kodiak State-5 mi **Packages:** Yes, Individually planned and money-saving for interested activities **Seasonal:** No **Reservations:** $50 deposit to hold reservation **Brochure:** Yes **Permitted:** Limited children, smoking outdoors only **Languages:** Spanish, some German **Payment Terms:** Check [I05IPAK1-12173] **COM Y ITC Member:** No

Rates:	Pvt Bath 1	Shared Bath 4
Single	$ 90.00	$ 55-80.00
Double	$ 90.00	$ 55-80.00

Managers House Inn   #1 Greenway Dr 85321   Ajo AZ
Jean & Micheline Fournier   Tel: 520-387-6505 Fax: 520-387-6508
Res Times 7am-10pm

Situated atop the highest hill in Ajo and built in 1919, the *Manager's House* was the former residence of the New Cornilia Company Mine manager. Today, much remains the same with each room offering a different decor with comfortable furnishings. There are spacious common rooms suitable for business and social events along with beautifully maintained grounds which provide a quiet and serene setting. Ajo and the surrounding area offer natural sights such as Organ Pipe Cactus National Park with over 300,000 acres of nature trails, rare organ pipe and senita cacti, Kitt Peak Observatory and Cabez Prieta Natl Wildlife Refuge. While relaxing at the Inn, guests can enjoy the Library/Sunroom, Spa, TV and VCR and a small gift shop. A lavish country breakfast is included along with a decanter of brandy on your nightstand for guests desiring a nightcap before retiring in this peaceful desert setting. **Seasonal:** No **Reservations:** Credit card to hold reservation, same as AAA. A pet B&B is available off-site to board your pet during your stay **Brochure:** Yes **Permitted:** Drinking, limited smoking **Conference:** Yes for groups to 16 persons, including patio area **Payment Terms:** Check MC/V [X08BCAZ-8370] **COM Y ITC Member:** No

Rates:	Pvt Bath 5
Single	$ 69.00
Double	$ 69.00

Inn At Castle Rock   112 Tombstone Canyon 85603   Bisbee AZ
Jim Babcock   Tel: 800-566-4449 602-432-4449 Fax: 602-432-7868

Driving into Bisbee through Mule Pass Tunnel brings travelers to another era - a unique setting of an early Western mining town set in the Mule Mountains. The Inn, built in 1890 as a miner's boarding house, is centrally located on the Main Street of Old Bisbee at the edge of the business district and across from Castle Rock. The Inn was built over a mine shaft that later filled with water (guests will find goldfish swimming in the well) which is now a centerpiece of the dining area, with natural rock walls, Mexican tiles and antique furniture. Each of the sixteen guest rooms and suites has a private bath and its own unique decor and furnishings, including Victorian antiques and original art. The one acre hillside garden at the back of the Inn has fruit trees, wildflowers and ramadas and many little trails to explore. A glass-walled upper sitting room has a fireplace, books and lovely views of the town. A ground floor parlor features Mexican tile and a sacred Indian springs while an art gallery is located in the top floor parlor. A full breakfast is included along with complimentary evening wine served around the fireplace. Local sights include Lavender Open Pit Mine, Mining Museum, historic houses, art galleries and shops, an underground mine tour and excellent restaurants. If we were to describe ourselves, we might say "personable, a bit off-beat, and a fine alternative to impersonal hotels". **Discounts:** June **Seasonal:** No **Reservations:** One night deposit to guarantee, cancel by noon, day of arrival for full refund **Brochure:** Yes **Permitted:** Children, drinking **Conference:** Yes, two meetings rooms plus garden sitting area for groups to 30 persons **Languages:** Spanish **Payment Terms:** Check MC/V [I08HPAZ1-69] **COM** U **ITC Member:** No

Rates:	Pvt Bath 16
Single	$ 40.00
Double	$ 50-60.00

DesertFarren Private Hacienda Inn   PO Box 5550   85377   Carefree AZ
Darrell Trapp   Tel: 602-488-1110 **Fax:** 602-488-1500
    Res Times 8am-5:30pm

Where the air is clear. And the sky is blue. Saguaro cactus dot the landscape below as you stand looking from the courtyard. Distant ranges reflect the pastel color of the sky. At your back, a mountain rises. Within arms length, deer approach to drink and feed on the property. A pool is nestled in the natural hollow of the rock behind the house. Behind the pool, another mountain rises. You are surrounded by the grace and charm of an old, rambling, recently restored hacienda that sits at the summit of a hill. An adobe-encircled spa, and secluded spots to savor interludes of tranquility awaked the simple pleasures in all of us. This is *DesertFarren.* Located a scenic 45 minute drive from Phoenix Sky Harbor Airport, the heart of Scottsdale, and only minutes away from the famous Boulders Resort. The pristine desert, views, solitude, wildlife, privacy and more views await. As our valued guest, we look forward to your arrival and the opportunity to serve you at the stressless getaway you deserve. **Airport:** Sky Harbor-25 mi **Packages:** Golf, Tennis, Health Week **Reservations:** Credit card guarantee to confirm room reservation **Brochure:** Yes **Permitted:** Limited drinking, limited smoking, children discouraged **Conference:** Yes **Languages:** Spanish, German, Italian, French **Payment Terms:** Check AE/MC/V [K02HPAZ1-21518] **COM** YG **ITC Member:** No

Rates:	Pvt Bath 6
Single	$ 69-149.00
Double	$ 69-149.00

Cochise Stronghold Lodge   RD #1 Box 51   85606   Cochise AZ
Rita Wilburn & Al Okemah   Tel: 602-862-3442
    Res Times 8-5pm

Snuggled in the Dragoon Mountains at 4500 feet is this complete guest cottage providing spectacular views surrounding the entire home. All amenities including a wood-burning fireplace for chilly evenings plus a/c for any humid nights that might occur. This is just the place for those travelers wanting to experience the Wild West! Ghost towns, Ft Huachuca, Wonderland of Rocks along the Cochise Train and plenty of Indian settlements are just part of the sights. **Seasonal:** No **Reservations:** A $5.00 surcharge for just one night's stay. **Brochure:** Yes **Permitted:** Smoking, drinking, children 4-up **Payment Terms:** Check [C11ACAZ-72] **COM** Y **ITC Member:** No

Rates:	Pvt Bath 1	Shared Bath 2
Single	$ 50.00	$ 32.00
Double		$ 41.00

Arizona   *National Edition*

Inn At Four Ten   410 N Leroux 86001   **Flagstaff AZ**
Sally & Howard Krueger   **Tel:** 800-774-2008 520-774-0088
Res Times 8am-8pm

The Place with the Personal Touch, The Inn at 410 offers four seasons of hospitality in a charming Craftsman home. Curl up in front of the living room fireplace with a mug of hot cider and a book from the Inn's library. Relax with a glass of iced tea and enjoy summer sunsets from the garden gazebo. A scrumptious gourmet breakfast is served in our dining room each morning. Eight spacious guest rooms, all with private bath and some with fireplace and oversized jacuzzi tubs are uniquely decorated. Immerse yourself in the ambiance of "The Southwest" or pamper yourself in the luxurious "Tea Room." "Monte's Garden", which opens onto the patio garden, is wheelchair accessible. *The Inn at 410 is a perfect **"home base"** for your Northern Arizona getaway.* It's an easy jaunt to the Grand Canyon and other attractions. The innkeepers are happy to recommend their favorite hiking, biking and skiing trails in the San Francisco Peaks. Walk two blocks to shops, galleries and restaurants in historic downtown Flagstaff. Plan to make your reservations early - we're a popular place to stay, no matter what the season. **Airport:** Pulliam-5 mi; Phoenix Sky Harbor-145 mi **Reservations:** One night's stay, full deposit, more than one night 50% deposit, 7 day cancel notice **Brochure:** Yes **Permitted:** Children, limited drinking **Conference:** Yes, for limited group size **Payment Terms:** Check MC/V [K04HPAZ1-1-8988] **COM YG ITC Member:** No

Rates:	Pvt Bath 8
Single	$ 90-150.00
Double	$ 90-150.00

Heart Seed B&B Retreat Center & Spa   **Phoenix AZ**
Judith Polich   **Tel:** 505-471-7026 **Fax:** 505-471-7026
Res Times 9am-9pm

Refer to the same listing name under Santa Fe, New Mexico for a complete description. **Payment Terms:** Check MC/V [M02HPNM1-22299] **COM YG ITC Member:** No

Rates:	Pvt Bath 4
Single	$ 89.00
Double	$ 89.00

Maricopa Manor   15 W Pasadena Ave 85013   **Phoenix AZ**
Mary Ellen & Paul Kelley   **Tel:** 800-292-6403 602-274-6302 **Fax:** 602-266-3904
Res Times 7am-10pm

Imagine yourself a privileged guest, among good friends, in the sumptuous atmosphere of a fine home ... enjoying all of the comforts of home while being catered to with the most attentive service ... and a home that reflects your finest sensibilities while fulfilling your personal and professional needs. Experience the *Maricopa Manor ... in the very heart of North Central Phoenix, a few minutes Central and Camelback, Uptown Plaza Shopping Center and restaurants.* This beautiful Spanish-styled manor house was built in 1928 on what was then a quiet country road, five miles from downtown Phoenix. Today *Maricopa Manor* is at the crossroads of the Valley of the Sun, offering travelers and intimate am-

4-16   ©*Inn & Travel Memphis, Tennessee*

bience and an elegant suburban lifestyle. The main house provides three unique guest rooms with various amenities such as canopied king beds, outside private entrances, beautiful antiques, a Franklin Stove while The Guest House offers two luxurious suites, Reflections Past and Reflections Future - each a spectacular experience. Surrounded by a forest of palms - evenings bring guests outdoors to relax and enjoy a patio fire with the hosts and other guests. A continental plus breakfast is served each morning. AAA 3-Diamond and Mobil 3-Star Award; member of Arizona Association of B&B Inns **Airport:** Sky Harbor Intl-3 mi **Discounts:** Summer **Seasonal:** Rates vary **Reservations:** One night deposit, 7 day cancel notice for refund less $15 fee **Brochure:** Yes **Permitted:** Children, drinking, limited smoking **Conference:** Yes, small groups **Payment Terms:** Check AE/DISC-/MC/V [I06HPAZ1-12115] COM YG **ITC Member:** No

Rates:	Pvt Bath 5
Single	$ 79-129.99
Double	$ 79-159.00

Mount Vernon Inn   204 N Mount Vernon 86301   Prescott AZ
Michele & Jerry Neumann   Tel: 520-778-0886 **Fax:** 520-778-7305

Built in 1900, the *Mount Vernon Inn* is nestled among the shade trees in the center of the Mount Vernon Historical District, Arizona's largest Victorian neighborhood. The grand house with its candle snuffer turret, gables, pediments and Greek Revival porch, proudly recalls a time when imagination and frontier self-confidence expressed itself in an architecture best described as whimsical. Today, the *Mount Vernon Inn*, which is listed on the *National Register of Historic Places*, offers a glimpse of a past era that seems simpler, slower and completely charming. Each main house guest room has a private bath and a queen bed. All are tastefully decorated and furnished with period furniture. As guests, you are invited to enjoy the comfortable hospitality of our Victorian home. Our parlor and sitting room can be yours for the evening. Whether you choose a book, a movie or some interesting conversation, our Inn will always make you feel at home. The guest cottages, originally the carriage and tack houses and the studio house are separate from the main house. Completely private, cottage guests can prepare breakfast in the convenient kitchen or stroll to any of the wonderful restaurants within easy walking distance. **Airport:** Phoenix-93mi **Discounts:** Nov 1 to April 30 **Seasonal:** Yes **Reservations:** Full deposit by credit card or check within 7 days of booking, 7 day cancel notice for refund for most reservations; Internet: http:// prescott-link.com/mtvrnon/index.htm **Brochure:** Yes **Permitted:** Limited smoking **Conference:** Three country cottages available for groups **Payment Terms:** Check DC/MC/V [KI10IP-AZ1-18200] COM YG **ITC Member:** No

Rates:	Pvt Bath 7
Single	$ 90.00
Double	$ 90-120.00

Inn At The Citadel   8700 E Pinnacle Peak Rd 85255   Scottsdale AZ
Jane DeBeer   Tel: 800-927-8367 602-585-6133

Let the splendor of the Sonoran Desert enchant you at the Inn. Eleven private, intimate suites are all appointed with antiques and original art work. Fireplaces, terraces and spectacular views are woven together into a tapestry of unequalled ambiance. Fine dining, shopping and salons await you at the Citadel. A deluxe continental breakfast is included with your stay, which is served in the Market or delivered to your room. Room service is available from 7:00am to 10:00pm, Complimentary robes are in each suite, cable TV with HBO and a Service Bar is located inside the armoire. Massages, facials and manicures are also available in rooms. For business, our Board Room is available; VIP Lounge, complete with up-to-the-minute stock quotes and national newspapers; computer and fax facilities; full-service banking services and conference room capacity of thirty with banquet and catering service.

Arizona   *National Edition*

Airport: Phoenix Sky Harbor Airport-30 mi **Packages:** Yes, inquire at reservation time **Seasonal:** Rates vary **Reservations:** Deposit required to guarantee reservation, 7 day cancel policy for refund **Brochure:** Yes **Permitted:** Children **Conference:** Yes **Payment Terms:** Check AE/DC/MC/V [Z07GPAZ-14801] **COM Y ITC Member:** No **Quality Assurance**: Requested

Rates: Pvt Bath 11
Single $ 150-265.00
Double $ 150-265.00

Briar Patch Inn	Star Rt 3 Box 1002 86336	Sedona AZ
Jo Ann & Ike Olson		Tel: 520-282-2342

As your hosts, we look forward to sharing with you our love of the Red Rock Country of Sedona. The *Briar Patch* is not a resort of typical amenities but a Bed and Breakfast Inn whose desire is to create a quiet, soothing atmosphere that will give you the opportunity to create your own discovery experience. Private cottages are furnished in an Arizona Indian and Mexican decor - designed for those whose sensitivities ask for rustic ambiance with comfort. Fireplaces, shaded patios and privacy lead to the reading of a good book or the pure enjoyment of a private moment. Nestled at the base of the Mogollon Rim, the mountains invite guests to nurture a relationship with nature. Noted as one of five major centers for experiencing the *"Vortex Energy"* in this area, guests from around the world are drawn to Oak Creek Canyon. Activities at selected times throughout the year include small workshops in creative arts of painting, Navajo weaving, Indian arts, photography and music appreciation. Also available are Astrology, Philosophy and Self-Healing through spiritual, emotional and physical awareness. We welcome you to experience the sparkling music of the cool and refreshing Oak Creek - whiling your time as your private moment. Complimentary breakfast is included. **Airport:** Phoenix Sky Harbor-115 mi **Seasonal:** No **Reservations:** One night deposit within one week of booking, 10 day cancel policy less $10 service fee. **Brochure:** Yes **Permitted:** Children, drinking **Conference:** Yes, groups to sixteen. **Languages:** Spanish, French **Payment Terms:** Check MC/V [I12EPAZ-89] **COM Y ITC Member:** No

Rates: Pvt Bath 15
Single $ 110-165.00
Double $ 110-165.00

Cactus Paradise Inn	PO Box 38722 86359	Sedona AZ
Ralph & June Merchenson		Tel: 520-282-2677 Fax: 520-282-2677
		Res Times 10am-6pm

Join us in Red Rock Country where nature calls twenty-four hours each day. Beginning with wonderous sunrises and ending with quite evenings, guests are lulled to sleep by the stillness. This adobe structure has been rebuilt over the past 100 years and includes primitve as well as modern suites and decor. Western artifacts and touches abound through out the common areas both indoors and outdoors. All guest rooms have kivas to take off evening chills while great for snuggling into late mornings. Each guest room is individually decorated by your hostess who is also an interior decorator. If you see something you like, don't hesitate to ask if you can take it since most of the furnishings are for sale. An inground pool and tennis court on the premises provides a country club atmosphere to this private Inn. A full breakfast is morning features your choice of western or traditional meals. The menu includes delicious western omlettes, eggs benedict, Belgium waffles and home baked breads. Plenty of hot beverages and fresh fruit is included. Activities feature back pack trips through the heart of the moutain passes. **Seasonal:** No **Reservations:** One night's deposit, 48 hour cancel policy less $15 service fee **Permitted:** Children 12-up, drinking, smoking outdoors **Brochure:** Yes **Languages:** Spanish, French **Payment Terms:** Check, AE/MC/V [R01IGAZ1-8766] **COM Y ITC Member:** No

4-18   ©*Inn & Travel Memphis, Tennessee*

Rates:	Pvt Bath 8	Shared Bath 4
Single	$ 105.00	$ 85.00
Double	$ 125.00	$ 95.00

Cozy Cactus B&B   80 Canyon Circle Dr 86351-8673   Sedona AZ
Bob & Lynne Gillman   Tel: 800-788-2082 520-284-0082
Res Times 9am-9pm

Cozy Cactus weaves magical red rock vistas and breath-taking sunsets playing across the nearby red cliffs with healthy doses of old-fashioned hospitality into a memorable experience. Located at the foot of Castle Rock and overlooking the valley between Sedona's red rock cliffs and Wild Horse Mesa, one of John Wayne's favorite movie locations, is this ranch-style home, comfortably furnished with family heirlooms and theatrical memorabilia from Lynne and Bob's diverse professional careers. All of the cozy bedrooms are uniquely furnished and include the Wyeth Room (Andrew Wyeth's simple style is reflected in the decor), the Country French Room, and the Nutcracker Room, (showcasing Bob's extensive collection of nutcrackers from around the world) and the American Room (featuring a queen-size bed with handmade quilt) and Music Box Room. Each room has large windows and private baths; each pair of bedrooms share a sitting room featuring a fireplace and small kitchen. Full breakfasts are served in the great room where guests can watch the morning sun begin to warm the face of Bell Rock. Relaxing afternoon sunsets are enjoyed with complimentary beverages on the patio while the sun slips behind Castle Rock. Nearby sights include Coconino National Forest for hiking, bird watching and photography, Jerome, an historic old copper mining town, Montezuma's Castle, Walnut Canyon and Sunset Crater. Your hosts are delighted to help arrange golf at two excellent courses, jeep and horseback trips in the back-country, tours, or dinner in nearby Sedona. **Discounts:** Yes for weekly stays **Airport:** Phoenix Sky Harbor-120 mi **Seasonal:** No **Reservations:** One night's deposit with 7 day cancel policy; check-in 4-6pm, later by prior arrangement. Two night min weekends; three night min holiday weekends **Brochure:** Yes **Permitted:** Children, drinking, smoking on outdoor patio only **Languages:** Italian **Payment Terms:** Check AE/DISC/MC/V [K05HPAZ1-14572] **COM YG ITC Member:** No **Quality Assurance** Requested

Rates:	Pvt Bath 5
Single	$ 80-100.00
Double	$ 90-110.00

Greyfire Farm   1240 Jacks Canyon Rd 86336   Sedona AZ
David Payne/Elaine Ross   Tel: 520-284-2340

You are welcome to join us at *Greyfire Farm*, a 2-1/3 acre farm nestled amidst pine trees in the rural valley between Sedona's red rocks and Wild Horse Mesa, one of John Wayne's favorite Western movie sites. The views of both are exceptional. The nearby National Forest Service land has beautiful bridle paths suitable for horseback riding or hiking - offering heavily-wooded areas by the dry creek beds and panoramic views from the higher ridges. The comfortable ranch home, furnished mainly with antiques and quilts, provides just two guest rooms: The Canyon Suite (a spacious room with private full bath attached) which offers spectacular sunrise views of Jacks Canyon with Lee Mountain on one side and Wild Horse Mesa on the other; and Red Rock Vista with a large picture-window framing Courthouse Butte, a well-known Sedona landmark. It has a private, full bath with skylight directly across the hall. Both rooms have queen size beds. A full hearty breakfast is served which features waffles, homemade muffins, or buttermilk blueberry pancakes with fresh seasonal fruits. A quiet peaceful setting, just 1.8 miles from the shopping and restaurants in the Village of Oak Creek and 8 miles from downtown Sedona, guests can easily visit the many art galleries and shops, including Tlaquepaque, the beautiful and famous replica of an old Mexican village. **Packages:** Seven nights for the price of six **Airport:** Phoenix Sky Harbor - 2 hrs **Seasonal:** No **Reservations:** One night or 50% deposit (which ever is greater), 14 day cancel policy (less $10 fee) check-in 4-6 pm or other with prior arrangement. Two night min weekends, 3 night min holiday weekends. **Brochure:** Yes **Permitted:** Children, drinking, limited pets and smoking. Horses boarded, $6.00 night extra. **Payment Terms:** Check MC/V [R11DPAZ-1-4338] **COM** U **ITC Member:** No

Rates:	Pvt Bath 2
Single	$ 75.00
Double	$ 80.00

Rose Tree Inn   376 Cedar St   86336   Sedona AZ
Gail & Stephen Hayter   Tel: 520-282-2065   Fax: 520-282-0083
Res Times 7am-7pm

"Best Kept Secret in Sedona," The *Rose Tree Inn* is located in the heart of "Old Town", one block off the highway 89A. Guests are within easy walking distance to shops, restaurants, art galleries and tour companies. The Rose Tree Inn is a charming property situated in a lovely English Garden environment. Inviting patios, whirlpool, gas BBQ grill allows our guests to enjoy the beauty of Sedona. Four of our five units have kitchenettes and two have fireplaces. Complimentary coffee and tea are provided in an attractive setting in each room. A great location, guests are, just two hours north of Phoenix and 2-1/2 hours south of the Grand Canyon - there is golf, tennis, hiking, horseback riding and numerous activities to enjoy nearby. **Airport:** Phoenix-100 mi **Package:** Five night rate (Sun-Thurs) available **Seasonal:** Yes, rates vary **Reservations:** One night's deposit, 50% for longer stays, 48 hr cancel policy for one to six nights; seven night cancellations require 14 days cancel notice Check-in 2 pm, check out 11am **Brochure:** Yes **Permitted:** Children **Payment Terms:** Check MC/V [I05HPAZ1-94] **COM** YG **ITC Member:** No

Rates:	Pvt Bath 5
Single	$ 85.00
Double	$ 115.00

Copper Bell B&B   25 N Westmoreland Ave   85745   Tucson AZ
Hans Herbert/Gertrude Kraus   Tel: 520-629-9229
Res Times 7am-10pm

Copper Bell is a unique turn-of-the-century lava stone home which was built from 1902 to 1920 providing a unique blend of architectural styles, including art-nouveau. The current owners relocated here from their native border town between Germany, France and Luxembourg. They brought heirloom furnishings from Germany along with German doors, windows and building materials not normally seen in the USA and created an Inn that combines the old world with the new. A lovely arched porch on the house front provides great shade for relaxing with an afternoon tea and socializing with your charming hosts and guests. The beautiful copper bell hung in a place of honor is another treasure brought from a German church. Guests can choose from among five unique guest rooms all individually decorated including stained glass windows. Try the Arizona Room with a private balcony offering a magnificent view of the city lights. A lovely honeymoon suite including a waterbed is available too. You'll enjoy the homemade full breakfasts, included in your room rate, where Gertrude creates either a German, French or American-style meal - including homemade marmalade and jam! Conveniently located, your hosts will help you find the sights of Tucson including downtown, shops and restaurants, Old Tucson, Sabino Canyon, A-Mountain, Sonora Desert Museum, San Xavier Mission, Titan Missile Museum, Pima Air Museum and local colleges. While you're staying here, you can learn about gem carving and sculpting from their son or goldsmithing from their daughter, a well-known gold craftsperson. Hans and Gertrude provide pleasant European hospitality and are interested in introducing their guests to all of the excitement in South Arizona. **Airport:** 10 mi to Tucson Intl Meals: Homemade European luncheon and dinners are available with prior arrangement **Seasonal:** Rates vary **Reservations:** Deposit required to guarantee reservation; 4-6pm check-in (late arrival upon arrangement) check-out 11am.

Long stay discounts. Low season 5/1 to 8/30. **Brochure:** Yes **Permitted:** Limited smoking, children 10-up **Conference:** Yes, two rooms for 10-12 persons **Languages:** Fluent German, French **Payment Terms:** Check [J05FPAZ-12116] **COM** Y **ITC Member:** No

Rates:	Pvt Bath 6	Shared Bath 2
Single	$ 65.00	$ 60.00
Double	$ 75.00	$ 70.00

El Presidio Inn B&B 297 N Main Ave 85701 Tucson AZ
Patti Toci Tel: 800-349-6151 520-623-6151
Res Times 7am-9pm

A luxury Inn in an award-winning Victorian Adobe mansion situated in *"El Presideo Historic District"* close to downtown Tucson. Listed in the *National Register*, circa 1879. Romantic, lush garden courtyards filled with old Mexico ambience, fountains and cobblestone surround the richly-appointed guest house and suites. Gourmet full breakfast, complimentary beverages and fruit, private baths and entrances, TV, phones, his and her robes, individual designer-decor with antiques. Walk two blocks to fine dining, Southwestern cuisine, Mexican or Continental, museums, shopping and the Arts District. "Carriage House Suite", a guest house, has a living room, kitchenette, bath w/shower, bedroom with one queen size bed - $110.00. "Gate House Suite" offers a combined bed and sitting room, kitchenette, full bath (one queen size bed) - $85.00. "Victorian Suite" has one bedroom (queen size), full bath, parlor - $100.00. "Territorial Room" offers a queen bed with bath and shower - $75.00. Featured in numerous national magazines: *"Gourmet, Travel & Leisure, Glamor, Innsider"* and the book *"The Desert Southwest,"* Mobil 3-star rated. Excellent location for pleasure and business travelers alike. **Discounts:** Yes, business and extended stays **Airport:** Tucson Intl-18 mi **Packages:** Honeymoon, Family Reunions, Weddings **Seasonal:** No **Reservations:** One night deposit; 50% for extended stays with 2 week cancel policy for refund, late arrival only with prior arrangements **Brochure:** Yes **Permitted:** Children 12-up, drinking **Conference:** Yes, for groups six to twelve persons **Payment Terms:** Check [I10HPAZ1-67] **COM** YG **ITC Member:** No

Rates:	Pvt Bath 4
Single	$ 65.00
Double	$ 95-110.00

La Posada del Valle B&B 1640 N Campbell Ave 85719 Tucson AZ
Tom & Karin Dennen Tel: 520-795-3840 **Fax:** 520-795-3840
Res Times 9am-7pm

An elegant Southwest adobe home built in 1929 that greets guests through a courtyard surrounded by gardens and orange trees that perfume the air each spring. The guest rooms, each with private bath and outside entrance, are tastefully decorated with antique furnishings and pieces from the 1920's and 30's. Each room is named after women from that same period: for example Sophie's Room is named after Sophie Tucker, Pola's Room after Pola Negri and Claudette's Room after Claudette Colbert. A large book-lined living room offers guests a warm retreat as they end their busy days and gather for tea each afternoon. A basket of menus from some of Tucson's finest restaurants is waiting for their perusal. Breakfast is always a sumptuous array of freshly-baked breads and pastries, homemade granola, fresh fruit juices, and on weekends, surprises like cream cheese blintzes with fresh raspberry sauce or banana buckwheat pancakes and mesquite-smoked bacon. Meals ailable on request

Discounts: Yes, inquire at res time **Airport:** Tucson - 20 minutes **Seasonal:** Rates vary **Reservations:** 50% of stay required as deposit by check or credit card within 5 days of booking. **Brochure:** Yes **Permitted:** Children 12-up, drinking **Conference:** Great setting for business retreats for groups to 15-20 **Languages:** German **Payment Terms:** MC/V [I04HPAZ1-101] **COM YG ITC Member:** No

Rates:	Pvt Bath 5
Single	$ 90-100.00
Double	$ 94-120.00

Lodge On The Desert — 306 N Alvernon 85711 — Tucson AZ
Schuyler Lininger — Tel: 800-456-5634 520-325-3366

A rare example of a vanishing tradition of personal hospitality and individual service - *Lodge On The Desert* is one of the few remaining owner-operated resorts in the country and is one of the select few resorts in Arizona listed in the prestigious *"Country Inns and Back Roads."* For more than fifty years this unique garden resort has been a haven of quiet and seclusion for knowledgeable travelers from around the world. Here they find the old-world charm of a Spanish hacienda with adobe-styled casitas and ocotillo-shaded verandas overlooking spacious lawns and colorful, flower-filled gardens. The *Lodge* provides a tranquil retreat for vacationers and small business and professional groups. Most of the spacious guestrooms are on the ground floor, many offering mesquite log-burning fireplaces - one even includes an indoor heated pool! Room decor is enhanced with beamed ceilings, hand-painted Mexican tile accents and authentic Monterey furniture. Semi-private patios, surrounded with the fragrant scent of fresh flowers and blossoming fruit trees, overlook vistas of distant mountains. The tradition of fine dining, which made famed restaurant critic Duncan Hines a frequent visitor, still continues at the *Lodge* today. All of Tucson's cultural and recreational activities are available while trips can be arranged to Mexico and Tombstone. Nature areas of Southern Arizona - includes some of the best bird watching locations in the nation. **Packages:** The 12 Days of Christmas (Dec 22-Jan 2), American and European Plans available **Discounts:** Yes, inquire at res time **Airport:** Tucson Intl-8 mi **Seasonal:** No **Reservations:** Cash deposit or credit card number to guarantee reservation, 10 day or 48 hr cancellation **Brochure:** Yes **Permitted:** Children, pets, drinking, smoking **Conference:** Yes, for groups to 25 persons **Languages:** Spanish, some French **Payment Terms:** Check AE/DC/MC/V [R05FPAZ-102] **COM Y ITC Member:** No

Rates:	Pvt Bath 40
Single	$ 50.00-up
Double	$ 54.00-up

Peppertrees B&B — 724 E University Blvd 85719 — Tucson AZ
Marjorie G Martin CTC — Tel: 800-348-5763 520-622-7167 **Fax:** 520-622-5959
Res Times 7am-7pm*

Your charming English hostess greets guests to a warm and charming Victorian home built at the turn-of-the-century. The old house, filled with wonderful antique furniture is complimented by guest houses having a modern western decor, making for a house-full of surprises. Marjorie, a travel agent and CTC for twenty years, knows what guests look for when traveling and she makes sure they are spoilt while here. The location is absolutely unique since it's within walking distance of the U of Arizona campus with it's museums, theaters and entertainment. A full choice of restaurants and shopping areas are within an easy stroll or else guests can hop aboard the old trolley that passes the door and go to the 4th Avenue shopping district with boutiques, antique shops, thrift stores or else continue onto downtown to the convention center, historic and art districts and

National Edition   *Arizona - California*

city offices. Or else they can explore the Arizona Sonora Desert Museum, Tucson Valley or the attractions in southern Arizona by car. A full gourmet breakfast with homemade breads, scones, a variety of entrees, jams, jellies and fresh fruit. The professional chefs in the family, trade their expertise and secret recipes in preparing the likes of Scottish Shortbread for high tea. Picnic lunch/private dinners are available by special arrangement. Meals are served family-style in the dining room or outdoors in the cool, quiet, fountain-dominated patio. Complimentary non-alcoholic beverage upon arrival. **Discounts:** 15% June-Sept **Airport:** Tucson Intl-20 min **Seasonal:** No **Reservations:** 1 night's deposit, 7 day cancel policy for refund. *Winter PST (Summer). *Guest house available, includes two beds, four persons at $150.00/night **Brochure:** Yes **Permitted:** Children, limited smoking **Conference:** Yes for groups to 8 persons. **Languages:** French, Spanish. **Payment Terms:** Check DISC/MC/V [I04-GPAZ-8347] **COM** Y **ITC Member:** No

Rates:	Pvt Bath 3	Shared Bath 4
Single	$ 78.00	
Double	$ 88.00	$150.00*

SunCatcher	105 N Avenida Javalina 85748	Tucson AZ
Dave Williams		Tel: 800-835-8012 520-885-0883
		Res Times 24 Hrs

Guest rooms at *The SunCatcher* bear homage to four of the world's great hotels - The Connaught in London; The Regent in Hong Kong; The Oriental in Bangkok; and The Four Seasons in Chicago. Each of these four rooms is furnished in the style of its namesake. All the desired amenities are provided - from luxurious bath soaps and fine linens, to the convenience of a video player in every room. Days begin with unhurried conversations over a complimentary full breakfast. After using our pool, guests can hike in the adjacent Sahuaro National Monument East, use our pass to a nearby tennis or athletic club, or simply sit in our large outdoor jacuzzi. At the eastern edge of Tucson, *The SunCatcher* offers uncompromising views of both the Catalina and Rincon Mountains. Our four acres of rolling hills and cactus will provide the greatest degree of privacy and "quiet". **Discounts:** Travel agents **Airport:** Tucson Intl-20 mi **Seasonal:** No **Reservations:** Two night minimum stay, two night deposit required **Brochure:** Yes **Permitted:** Children, drinking, limited smoking **Conference:** Yes for small groups **Languages:** Spanish **Payment Terms:** Check AE/MC/V [R09EPAZ-15783] **COM** Y **ITC Member:** No

Rates:	Pvt Bath 4
Single	$ 110-130.00
Double	$ 110-130.00

Fensalden Inn	33810 Navarro Ridge Rd 95410	Albion CA
Scott & Francis Brazil		Tel: 800-959-3850 707-937-4042
		Res Times 8am-8pm

The panoramic view of the ocean, cypress trees, deer feeding in the meadow - the symphony of frogs after the rain - the whales spouting and playfully tending their calves - the quietness gently accented by the buoys bobbing in the ocean - the cozy crackle and warmth of the fireplace as the day fades into evening. Overlooking the Pacific Ocean from twenty tree-lined pastoral acres, *Fensalden Inn* offers a quiet respite for the perfect get-away. A Stagecoach Way Station during the 1860's, the Inn has been completely restored and now offers a restful, yet interesting stay for the traveler. There are eight guest quarters, some are suites with fireplaces and kitchens, most have beautiful ocean views and all are furnished with antiques and have private baths with tiled showers or tubs. Come and whale watch, glimpse the deer during a stroll through our meadow, or just relax and enjoy! **Discounts:** Yes, weekly rates **Airport:** San Francisco or Oakland-100 mi **Packages:** Yes, inquire at res time **Seasonal:** No **Reservations:** 50% deposit of entire stay with check or credit card. **Brochure:** Yes **Permitted:** Drinking, limited children **Conference:** Full meeting rooms and catering are available. **Payment Terms:** Check MC/V [R03FPCA-168] **COM** Y **ITC Member:** No

Rates:	Pvt Bath 8
Single	$ 80-135.00
Double	$ 80-135.00

Forest Manor	415 Cold Spring Rd 94508	Angwin CA

©*Inn & Travel Memphis, Tennessee*

California   *National Edition*

Dr Harold & Corlene Lambeth   **Tel:** 800-788-0364 707-965-3538
                                                              Res Times 8am-10pm

Forest Manor, steeped in splendid solitude, is nestled in a vast hillside glade of evergreens and vineyards in the renowned Napa Wine Valley. This twenty acre English Tudor estate has been described by travel writers as ***"one of the most romantic country Inns ... a peaceful wooded sanctuary ... a small exclusive resort."*** In roaming the picturesque forest trails past vineyards, redwood groves, springs and a waterfall, one often catches glimpses of deer and other delightful forest creatures. The majestic three-story manor is tastefully furnished with English antiques, Persian carpets and treasures from travels around the world. The romantic ambiance is enhanced with fireplaces, verandahs, massive hand hewn beams and high vaulted ceilings. Large windows overlook lawns surrounded by profuse flowers, ferns, shrubbery and forest creating a delightful setting for total relaxation. Further enjoyment is provided with the fifty-three foot swimming pool, spas, library, games, croquet, billiards, exercise room, roving TV/VCR and nearby tennis courts. Each of the spacious air conditioned suites is uniquely decorated and include top of the line queen or king beds with down comforters and pillows, private baths, in-room refrigerators, coffee makers with an assortment of hot drinks, robes and fruit baskets. Some guest rooms have fireplaces, private verandahs, sitting rooms, private entrances and private spas. A full lavish breakfast may be served in the suite, on the verandah among the trees or in the dining room. Nearby attractions include 200+ wineries, vineyards, forests, superb restaurants, ballooning, gliding, mud baths, spas, golf, bicycling, antiques, boutiques, museums, historical landmarks, boating and fishing at Lake Berryessa. **Discounts:** Mon-Thru 2+ nights **Airport:** San Francisco-70 mi **Seasonal:** No **Reservations:** One night deposit, 7 day cancel policy for refund **Brochure:** Yes **Permitted:** Limited children, drinking, smoking outdoors **Payment Terms:** Check AE/MC/V [I05HP-CA1-6252] **COM YG ITC Member:** No

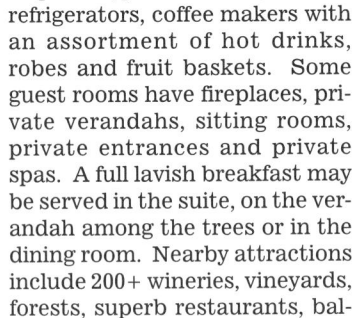

Rates: Pvt Bath 4
Single $ 110-239.00
Double $ 110-239.00

Apple Lane Inn   6265 Soquel Drive 95003   Aptos CA
Doug & Diana Groom   **Tel:** 800-649-8988 408-475-6868 **Fax:** 408-475-6868
                                                                   Res Times 8am-8pm

Minutes south of Santa Cruz, this fully restored historic Victorian farmhouse offers charm and tranquility of another era. Nestled on four acres of vineyards and apple orchards, its a peaceful oasis for weekend guests to get-away and a great location for mid-week travelers. Guests enjoy the afternoon sun on the brick patio with blooming wisteria, roses and trailing vines. A Victorian gazebo perched amid trim lawns and flowering gardens - where weddings are frequently held - is another favorite spot for guests. Your hosts have decorated each guest room in different themes ranging from the Blossom Room with mauve and white decor, lace queen canopy bed, to the Pineapple Room in blue and white, antique pine furniture with a four-poster queen bed. The old Wine Cellar with large wicker casks of wine, exposed floor joists and redwood plank floor finds guests enjoying a spacious suite. An elegant full complimentary breakfast includes a platter-full of fresh fruit, coffee, fresh-squeezed juices, hot spicy apple and a trayful of warm Danish coffee-cakes - followed by a fluffy omelette-souffle, Eggs Christy or Morning Monte Cristo. Activities range from visiting the horses and chickens, picking apples or vegetables, playing horseshoes and croquet, to borrowing a novel from the library. Nearby is Cabrillo College with a Saturday farmer's market, New Brighton State Beach, Nisene Marks State Park, golf, antiquing, wine tasting , sailing and deep sea fishing and all of Santa Cruz sights within 10 miles. Guests are welcome at the full-service health club and pool across the street. **Airport:** 35 miles to San Jose **Discounts:** $15 off weekdays, Sun-Thursday **Seasonal:** No **Reservations:** One night's deposit in advance with 5 day cancel policy less $15 service fee. Check-in 3-6pm, check-out by 11am **Brochure:** Yes **Permitted:** Limited children, limited pets, limited drinking, smoking outdoors. Bring your horse! **Conference:** Outdoor garden receptions and weddings to 100 persons **Languages:** Spanish **Payment**

National Edition *California*

Terms: Check DISC/MC/V [Z05HPCA1-175] COM YG ITC Member: No

Rates:	Pvt Bath 5	Shared Bath 1
Single	$ 80-145.00	
Double	$ 95-175.00	

Bayview Hotel B&B	8041 Soquel Drive 95003	Aptos CA
Barry & Sue Hooper		Tel: 408-688-8654
		Res Times 10am-6pm

This Santa Cruz County vintage California Victorian was built in 1878 and soon became famous for its warmth, hospitality and culinary excellence. It also functioned as a community center, housing the area's first post office and general store. The village of Aptos was alive with activity during the late 1800s. Next door to the hotel, trains left daily from the Aptos Station, loaded with lumber and produce from the surrounding area and returned with thousands of tourists from around the world. The guest list the *Bayview's* Golden Era included Lillian Russell, King Kalakaua of Hawaii and many distinguished European visitors. Today, the Bayview remains the focal point of the modern-day Aptos, an affluent residential community 90 miles south of San Francisco and 35 miles from San Jose. Our comfortable accommodations are in a convenient location near golf, tennis, fishing, state beaches, antique shops and restaurants, only a block from the entrance to the 10,000 acre Nisene Marks State Park.

All rooms have private baths and are furnished with antiques. Our buffet-style breakfast includes fresh squeezed orange juice, seasonal fruit, pastries, muesli, savory egg dish and gourmet coffee. If you wish, guests may also enjoy lunch or dinner in the fine restaurant. **Discounts:** Mid-week business and extended stays **Airport:** San Jose-35 mi **Packages:** Dinner packages at Veranda, a fine restaurant on the premises **Seasonal:** No **Reservations:** One night's deposit or 50% if longer must be received within 7 days of booking to hold room; 7 day cancel policy, less $10 service fee. Check-in 3-6pm, later by prior notice. **Brochure:** Yes **Permitted:** Children 5-up **Languages:** French, Italian. **Payment Terms:** Check MC/V [Z11DPCA-176] COM Y ITC Member: No

Rates:	Pvt Bath 8
Single	$ 80-100.00
Double	$ 85-125.00

Elegant Victorian Mansion		Arcata CA
Doug & Lily Vieyra		Tel: 800-EVM-1888 707-444-3144
		Res Times 10am-6pm

Refer to the same listing name under Eureka, California for a complete description. **Seasonal:** No **Payment Terms:** Check MC/V [M04FPCA-16980] COM Y ITC Member: No

Rates:	Pvt Bath 2	Shared Bath 2
Single	$ 85-115.00	$ 75.00
Double	$ 95-125.00	$ 85-95.00

Arroyo Village Inn	407 El Camino Real 93420	Arroyo Grande CA
Gina Glass		Tel: 800-563-7762 805-489-5926
		Res Times 8am-10pm

This award-winning, country Victorian Inn offers a delightful blend of yesterday's charm and hospitality with today's comforts and conveniences. Featuring seven unique garden-theme suites decorated in Laura Ashley prints with antique furnishings and special touches of window seats, skylights and balconies. A full gourmet breakfast is served in the parlor and teas and cordials are served in the late afternoon. Located half-way between Los Angeles and San Francisco in the heart of California's beautiful Central Coast, you're near Hearst Castle, San Luis Obispo, Pismo Beach, mineral spas, beaches and horseback riding on the beach and wineries. **Airport:** San Luis Obispo-15 mi **Discounts:** Midweek-first night at regular price, 2nd night free on

©Inn & Travel Memphis, Tennessee

California *National Edition*

$145 suites and up, excluding holidays; 20% seniors **Seasonal:** No **Reservations:** Full payment prior to arrival, late arrival okay, 14 day cancel notice for refund less $25 service fee, unless room is rerented **Brochure:** Yes **Permitted:** Children, limited drinking, smoking outdoors only **Conference:** Yes for groups to 20 persons **Languages:** Italian, Spanish

Payment Terms: Check AE/DISC/MC/V [I05IP-CA1-182] **COM YG ITC Member:** No

Rates:	Pvt Bath 7
Single	$ 75.00
Double	$ 95.00

Baywood B&B Inn	1370 2nd St 93402	**Baywood Park CA**
Tricia Chasse		**Tel:** 805-528-8888 **Fax:** 805-528-8887
		Res Times 9am-6pm

Nestled in a tranquil neighborhood overlooking beautiful south Morro Bay, this charming Inn offers travelers fifteen different reasons to return because each of the fifteen rooms is unique - - each with its own personality. Whether you're planning a romantic or an adventurous vacation, *Baywood B&B Inn* has a room that's just right for you that will bring you back again. While each room has a distinctive theme, all rooms provide a beautiful view of the bay, private bath with tub and shower, phone, outside entrance, sitting area, kitchenette with microwave and queen beds. In-addition, suites have

Cover Featured B&B Inn

separate sleeping areas and some include sleeper sofas and dining areas. Two bedroom suites and a handicapped fitted suite are available. From Americana to Santa Fe, Williamsburg, Queen Victoria, California Beach, Manhattan, Granny's Attic, Emerald Bay, Kensington, Avonlea to Appalachian - choose the one you want to suit your mood! During your stay, you'll be treated to a tour of all of the rooms not occupied so you can choose the one you want to try on your next trip. Unlike many bed and breakfasts, *Baywood B&B Inn* allows for the privacy and convenience of a larger Inn. Your stay at the Inn includes evening wine and hors d'oeuvres on the mezzanine overlooking the bay. A full breakfast is served in your room each morning. Breakfast varies but typically includes an egg dish, rolls, fresh-squeezed juice and a selection of fine coffees or teas. Conveniently located near shops, restaurants, boating, golf, hiking, biking and picnicking - beautiful Montano De Oro State Park, San Luis Obispo and Hearst Castle are just minutes away. *Suites available $100-150.00 **Airport:** Los Angeles-200 mi; San Luis Obispo-12 mi **Seasonal:** No **Reservations:** One night's deposit required, two night minimum on holidays, five day cancel policy. Check-in 2-6pm, please call to arrange arrivals after 8pm, e-mail: jabenson@ix.netcom.com **Brochure:** Yes **Permitted:** Limited children, drinking **Conference:** Yes, for groups to 12 persons **Payment Terms:** Check MC/V [I04IPCA1-12483] **COM YG ITC Member:** No

Rates:	Pvt Bath 15
Single	$ 80-130.00
Double	$ 80-150.00

Gold Mountain Manor	1117 Anita 92314	**Big Bear CA**
John & Conny Ridgway		**Tel:** 909-585-6997
		Res Times 8am-8pm

Breath-taking experience in this lavish and historic Gold Mining log mansion used as a commercial location for "*Ralph Lauren*", "*Vogue*", "*Eddie Bauer*" magazines. Recommended in "The Best Places To Kiss" and "Fifty Most Romantic Places In Southern California. History abounds everywhere in this Inn where the wealthy original owner planned to make this manor the "wealthiest and most beautiful resort in all of the West!!" Antique furnished, gorgeous verandas, beamed ceilings, handhewn staircase and wait until you see the guestrooms, each named for a different event and with individual decor. Three-star and AAA rated you can journey back in time to the days of extravagant Wild West!! State Historic Monument on prestigious North Shore. **Airport:** Ontario-50 mi; Los Angeles LAX-100 **Seasonal:** Rates vary **Reservations:** Deposit required, 7 day cancel policy, check-in 2-9pm, later by arrangement, two night min weekends **Brochure:** Yes **Permitted:** Limited children, drinking, smoking outdoors only **Conference:** Perfect spot for seclusion and privacy with luxury for groups of 40 persons. **Languages:** French, German, Dutch **Payment Terms:** Check MC/V [A05GPCA-202] **COM Y ITC Member:** No

Rates:	Pvt Bath 3
Single	$ 75-180.00
Double	$ 75-180.00

Matlick House 1313 Rowan Lane 93514 Bishop CA
Ray & Barbara Snowalter
Tel: 619-873-3133
Res Times 7am-9pm

Nestled at the base of the Eastern Sierra Nevada Mountains, Bishop, California is close to year-round fishing, hiking, backpacking, skiing, trail-riding and just plain relaxing. Completely renovated, this 1906 ranch home once housed the Alan Matlick Family, pioneers to Owens Valley. All rooms are individually decorated and complete with handmade quilts and curtains with authentic antique furnishings throughout. Wine and hors d'oeuvres are served nightly in the parlor and a full gourmet breakfast of ranch fresh eggs, mahogany smoked bacon and sausage, country fries, fresh squeezed orange juice, homemade biscuits and bread starts your day right. Located mid-way between Los Angeles and Reno-Tahoe, you have the perfect stopping-off place for spending an enjoyable and restful night. Other meals available with prior notice including picnic lunches. **Seasonal:** No **Reservations:** Full payment within 7 days of booking, two night min on weekends, 7 day cancel policy **Brochure:** Yes **Permitted:** Limited children, limited smoking, limited drinking **Conference:** For business and social meetings up to 14 persons including dining **Payment Terms:** AE/MC/V [Z07GPCA-206] **COM Y ITC Member:** No

Rates:	Pvt Bath 5
Single	$ 59-69.00
Double	$ 79-89.00

Cain House 340 Main St 93517 Bridgeport CA
Chris & Marachal Gohlich
Tel: 800-433-CAIN 619-932-7040 Fax: 619-932-7419
Res Times 10am-9pm

The *Cain House*, a successful blend of European elegance with a relaxing Western atmosphere is nestled in a country setting where mornings bring the beauty of crystallized trees set against the deep blue sky while the air sparkles with the morning frost. At a 6500 foot elevation - summer evenings cool perfectly, spring valleys become alive with green meadows, meandering streams and wildflowers while aspens turn fiery red, gold and orange with the beginning of fall's crisp air. The culmination of years of experience and travel throughout Europe where your hosts gathered ideas for interior design and food preparation - the *Cain House* is **"the perfect place to spend a few nights or a few weeks,"** reports Meta Cheryl Coffey, *"The Review-Herald."* Guest rooms are furnished with antiques and include queen size beds, quilts, down comforters, TV discretely tucked away in armoires, thick towels, plush comforters and feature their own unique decor. A gourmet/country full breakfast is served at your convenience between 8-10 am offering a daily changing menu that makes it tempting enough to stay another day just for breakfast! In the middle of a valley with the rugged beauty of the Eastern Sierra Mountain range as a backdrop - valleys, streams and lakes await you for hiking, boating, fishing, hunting and cross country skiing. Nearby is a ghost town, Bodie; Yosemite Valley, a two hour drive and downhill skiing and Nevada gaming. *Cain House* is rated AAA 3-Diamond, Mobil 3-Star, ABBA 3 Crown approved. *Closed 10/431-4/26 **Airport:** Reno/Cannon-113 mi **Seasonal:** Yes **Reservations:** One night deposit or credit card number, 48 hr cancel policy **Brochure:** Yes **Permitted:** Children, drinking **Payment Terms:** Check AE [Z04IPCA1-10050] **COM YG ITC Member:** No

Rates:	Pvt Bath 7
Single	$ 80-135.00
Double	$ 80-135.00

©*Inn & Travel Memphis, Tennessee*

California *National Edition*

Brannan Cottage Inn 109 Wapoo Ave 94515 **Calistoga CA**
Jack & Pamela Osborn **Tel:** 707-942-4200
Res Times 8am-10pm

Perfect setting for this Victorian cottage from the turn-of-the-century in the wine country nestled on lovely grounds; and furnished in period antiques and details. You'll be close to the wineries, world-famous spas, restaurants, shops, antique stalls, and all the Valley sights. Full breakfast included with complimentary bikes and beverages. **Seasonal:** No **Reservations:** Deposit at res time and refund for cancellation if prior to 10 days of res date. **Brochure:** Yes

Permitted: Children, pets, smoking, drinking, handicap access available **Languages:** French, Spanish **Payment Terms:** Check [X11ACCA-221] **COM** Y **ITC Member:** No

Rates: Pvt Bath 6
Single $ 80-95.00
Double $ 100-110.00

Christophers Inn 1010 Foothill Blvd 94515 **Calistoga CA**
Christopher & Adele Layton **Tel:** 707-942-5755
Res Times 8am-8pm

Christopher's Inn is a recent arrival to the Napa Valley offering guests elegance, intimacy, and located in Calistoga, close proximity to all the wine country has to offer. The owner, Christopher Layton, a San Francisco architect and landscape designer, turned three buildings, built fifty years ago as a summer visitor's hideaway into a traditional English Country Inn with Georgian elegance. The ten gracious rooms include private bath. Each room inspires its own mood from the Chinois Suite - the largest room, featuring a sleigh bed, fireplace, and antiques with an exotic Far Eastern flavor -- to the cozy Blue Room which features delicate Wedgewood Blue figurines and it's own small jasmine-covered porch. There is also a two room suite with fireplace and private patio, and the Secret Garden Room which provides a spacious, gated garden patio with an umbrella shaded table for enjoying a glass of Napa Valley wine or a morning coffee alfresco. Breakfast is a country basket filled with fresh-baked croissants, muffins, fresh fruit and yogurt or hot fruit cobbler, coffee and juice - delivered to your door each morning. *Christopher's Inn* offers a complete concierge service to help you plan a perfect stay in the wine country. Calistoga is the home of the world-famous hot springs and more than a dozen spas offering a multitude of treatments - from mud baths and massages to aromatherapy and seaweed wraps - are within walking distance from the Inn. The newly opened Lavender Hill Spa, which specializes in a spa experience for couples is just across the street. When you call, ask about our special Spa Packages. **Discounts:** Midweek Nov 1-May 1 (excluding holidays and special Valley events) **Airport:** San Francisco Intl-2 hrs, Santa Rose-45 mins **Packages:** Spa, Bicycle, Balloon, Wine Train **Seasonal:** No **Reservations:** Full payment 2 days or less, 50% if longer within 5 days of booking, 7 day cancel policy less $15 service fee, commissionable only weekdays; two night min weekends and holidays **Permitted:** Limited children, drinking **Conference:** Yes, groups to ten persons **Payment Terms:** Check AE/MC/V [J02HPCA1-17608] **COM** Y **ITC Member:** No

Rates: Pvt Bath 10
Single $ 120-170.00
Double $ 120-170.00

Quail Mountain B&B 4455 N St Helena Hwy 94515 **Calistoga CA**
Alma & Don Swiers **Tel:** 707-942-0316
Res Times 10am-9pm

4-28 ©*Inn & Travel Memphis, Tennessee*

National Edition   *California*

Quail Mountain is our home offering luxurious guest accommodations while visiting the beautiful Napa Valley. Located on twenty six acres and 300 feet above Napa Valley, this secluded hide-away is on a heavily forested mountain range. Traveling along Hwy 29, guests drive into Quail Mountain Lane, our private road, alongside our vineyard and orchard. A delicious full breakfast is served in the sunny solarium, outdoors on one of the many decks or before a blazing fire in the formal dining room. Breakfast consists of fruit juices, fresh bread and/or pastries, a hot entree and beverage which varies each day. Guests can begin or end their day with a refreshing dip in the pool or hot tub. Your hosts will help plan a memorable trip to Napa Valley by providing directions and information on the activities ranging from winery visits to an afternoon at a nearby spa. Upon request, they will also help with reservations at one of the fine Napa Valley restaurants. **Discounts:** Yes, to travel agents **Airport:** Oakland and San Francisco-75 mi; Santa Rosa -20 mi; Calistoga-1-1/2 mi **Seasonal:** No **Reservations:** Deposit to hold reservation at time of reservation, 5 day cancellation policy for refund, less 10% handling fee. Check-in 4-6pm, 11:30 am check-out. Two night min weekends and holidays. **Brochure:** Yes **Payment Terms:** Check MC/V [I02FPCA-236] **COM** Y **ITC Member:** No

Rates:	Pvt Bath 3
Single	$ 90-115.00
Double	$ 100-120.00

The Elms B&B Inn   1300 Cedar St 94515   Calistoga CA
Steve Wyle   Tel: 800-235-4316 707-942-9476

The last of Calistoga's Great Eight Homes and the only example of the Second Empire style still standing today, it is listed in the *National Register of Historic Places*. A tribute to preservation commemorating the finest chapter of the last century's heritage, the Elms was completed in 1871 when the first European Elm seedlings were planted, which stand today as the largest elm trees in the Napa Valley. Guests receive royal treatment beginning with immaculate rooms many with personal touches, antique furnishings, private baths, robes, coffee and tea in your room plus a decanter of port for your nightcap, queen or king size feather beds, down comforters, lots of pillows and reading lights. Your thoughtful hostess hasn't overlooked anything - from the full multi-course gourmet breakfast served in the dining room or outside on the patio to nighttime chocolates ... guests find intimacy, romance and step into the past where life was quieter and the pace relaxed. Located on the Napa River, you'll relax outdoors among gardens, huge elm trees, brick patios and comfortable lawn chairs. The city park next door has a gazebo that's perfect for afternoon picnics - and the gentle, lovable, laid-back German Shepherd "Boomer" is available for petting and walks. Located just a half-block off Calistoga's Main Street, you are within easy walking distance to shops, fine restaurants, spas, tennis, golf, bike rentals, glider rides and hot air ballooning. Fifteen of Napa Valley's wineries are within biking distance. Your hostess is delighted to assist in making all of your reservations. **Discounts:** Off-season, midweek **Airport:** San Francisco-1-1/2 hr **Reservations:** Full payment for length of stay at reservation time, 7 day cancel policy for refund. Gift certificates available **Brochure:** Yes **Permitted:** Drinking **Conference:** Yes, for groups to 14 persons **Payment Terms:** Check AE/MC/V [K05FPCA-6257] **COM** Y **ITC Member:** No

Rates:	Pvt Bath 7
Single	$ 100-165.00
Double	$ 110-175.00

The Pink Mansion   1415 Foothill Blvd 94515   Calistoga CA
Jeff Seyfried   Tel: 800-238-7465 707-942-0558
    Res Times 24 Hrs

©*Inn & Travel Memphis, Tennessee*

Turn-of-the-century elegance with modern amenities are combined in *The Pink Mansion* - offering wine-country travellers *"old fashioned comfort."* Built in Calistoga's heyday, the crystal-chandeliered grand parlor treated numerous visiting dignitaries and townspeople to enjoyable evenings. Built in the 1870s on land given by Calistoga's founder Sam Brannan, William F Fisher cleared the steep mountainside for vineyards and dug the wine caves for the Schramsberg and Beringer operations. A pioneer and adventurer, Fisher also established Calistoga's first stage line, linking the town with mining sites on Mount St Helena. Today guests are treated to individually decorated guest rooms in keeping with your innkeepers aunt, Alma Simic, the Pink Mansion's last and longest owner. An ardent collector, many of the rooms are adorned with her angels, cherubs, Victorian and Oriental treasures. Each guest room includes queen size beds, valley or forest view and private bath. Guests are invited to share the large Victorian parlour, drawing room, dining room and to enjoy the lavish full breakfast in the breakfast room. Less than a 1/4 mile from downtown, all of Calistoga's shops, restaurants, spas and much more. Calistoga is ideally situated among the famous wine districts of Napa and Sonoma, a little more than one hour to the Pacific Ocean, the magnificent Redwoods and the city of San Francisco. **Airport:** Santa Rosa-15 mi **Seasonal:** No **Reservations:** One night's deposit required within 7 days of booking to confirm reservation; 72 hr cancel policy for refund less $10 service fee. **Permitted:** Limited children, limited pets, no smoking **Languages:** Spanish **Payment Terms:** Check MC/V [I01FPCA-235] **COM Y ITC Member:** No

Rates: **Pvt Bath 5**
Single $ 105.00
Double $ 115.00

Wishing Well Inn	2653 Foothill Blvd (Hwy 128) 94515	Calistoga CA
Marina & Keith Dinsmoor		Tel: 707-942-5534

A long chapter of California's history was written at the *Wishing Well Inn*, formerly known as the Cyrus Ranch and dating from the 1840s. Many of Calistoga's early travelers were welcomed at the Cyrus Ranch, and the original Bear Flag, the forerunner of the current California state flag, was sewn here. Today the white three-story home is reminiscent of visiting your grandmother - the grounds are filled with grape vines, fig, mulberry and walnut trees along with a friendly poodle named Misha who frequently is the first to greet guests. There are two guest rooms in the main house, or guests can choose the private carriage house, furnished in an old fashioned country style including a clawfoot tub with a fireplace in the sitting room that offers extra space for family travelers. A full country breakfast is standard fare and varies from Marina's delicious baked pears, breads and egg frittati or Keith's special banana blintzes accompanied with homemade plum syrup and preserves. The *Wishing Well Inn* provides a quiet rural setting for enjoying all that the Valley and Calistoga has to offer. **Airport:** San Francisco or Oakland-90 mi **Seasonal:** No **Reservations:** Deposit required, 5 day cancel policy less $10 service fee for any cancellations. **Permitted:** Children, drinking **Payment Terms:** Check AE/MC/V [R11EPCA-241] **COM Y ITC Member:** No

Rates: **Pvt Bath 3**
Single $ 100.00
Double $ 120-150.00

Holiday House	Camino Real At 7th 93921	Carmel CA
Dieter & Ruth Back		Tel: 408-624-6267
		Res Times 7am-9pm

This comfortable wood shingled home is located on a hillside amidst a colorful, well maintained garden. Built in 1905 as a summer retreat, it still reflects the congenial and slightly Bohemian side of Carmel, that attracted so many artists to this part of the coast. All bedrooms look out to the ocean or onto the beautiful garden. The sloping roof with its protruding dormer-windows adds charm that is irresistible. Sunset can be observed from the sunporch while enjoying a glass of sherry. It is ideally located three blocks from the beach and one block from the main street. Pebble Beach and Monterey's proximity as well as the rugged Big Sur coast make it a perfect area to explore. A full breakfast is offered, buffet style. **Seasonal:** No **Reservations:** One night's deposit to hold reservation, two night minimum on weekends, 5 day notice of cancellation for refund less $10.00 handling fee **Permitted:** Drinking **Languages:** German **Payment Terms:** Check [A05FPCA-257] COM Y ITC **Member:** No

Rates:	Pvt Bath 4	Shared Bath 2
Single	$ 95.00	$ 90.00
Double	$ 100.00	$ 95.00

Sandpiper B&B Inn At The Beach   2408 Bay View Ave 93923   Carmel CA
The MacKenzies   **Tel:** 800-633-6433 408-624-6433 **Fax:** 408-624-5964
Res Times 9am-9pm

An intimate European-style Country Inn since 1929 in a quiet and beautiful residential area just sixty yards from Carmel Beach. Sixteen charmingly furnished rooms and cottages filled with antiques and fresh flowers, all with private bathrooms and queen or king size beds. Some rooms have glorious ocean views along one mile of the beach, others have fireplaces. Complimentary continental breakfast is served beside the fireplace in the comfortable lounge and library. The atmosphere is informal and relaxed and there are lots of paths along the beach for walking or jogging. Ample parking is provided. **Discounts:** Value Season Rates: 11/15-4/15, midweek periods (Sun-Thur), excluding holidays and special events **Air-port:** San Francisco-90 mi; San Jose-60 mi; Monterey Peninsula-3 mi **Packages:** Honeymoon, Monterey Aquarium **Seasonal:** No **Reservations:** Advance deposit required, minimum stay on weekends and special events, 7 day notice prior to 2pm cancel policy for refund **Brochure:** Yes **Permitted:** Children 13-up, drinking, limited smoking **Conference:** Sunday-Thursday, groups to twenty **Languages:** German, French **Payment Terms:** AE/MC/V [K02H-PCA1-264] COM YG ITC **Member:** No

Rates:	Pvt Bath 16
Single	$ 92-185.00
Double	$ 92-185.00

Robles del Rio Lodge   200 Punta del Monte 93924   Carmel Valley CA
Glen Gurries   **Tel:** 800-883-0843 408-659-3705
Res Times 8am-10pm

Built in the 1920's, the oldest operating lodge in Carmel Valley, this rustic Inn is perched on top of a mountain with spectacular views and nestled into the mountainside forests. Completely refurbished, you can choose guest rooms from a board-and-battened countryside look to a Laura Ashley motif, with color TV's hidden in armories, or you can choose from among the guest cottages that include private fireplace and kitchenettes. Continental plus breakfast is enjoyed in the Lodge living room offering guests a warm fireplace setting from which to enjoy the panoramic views of the mountain scenery. You're close to world-class golf courses, just 12 1/2 miles to Carmel by the Sea and the Pacific Ocean or you can enjoy trail-riding nearby. There is an olympic-sized pool, hot tub, sauna and tennis courts on the premises. **Seasonal:** No **Reservations:** One night's deposit or credit card guarantee; 48 hr cancel policy. **Brochure:** Yes **Permitted:** Children, drinking, smoking **Conference:** Yes, groups to 40 persons **Languages:** Spanish, French **Payment Terms:** Check MC/V [Z11C-PCA-271] COM Y ITC **Member:** No

Rates:	Pvt Bath 31
Single	$ 69-149.00
Double	$ 69-149.00

Inn On Mount Ada   398 Wrigley Rd 90704   Catalina Island CA
Marlene McAdam/Susie Griffin   **Tel:** 310-510-2030
Res Times 8-10pm

California *National Edition*

Georgian colonial mansion built c1921 for William Wrigley Jr, chewing gum multi-millionaire with nothing spared. Completely restored by the island residents at a cost of over one million, this is the perfect spot for a special occasion. Spectacular views of the ocean town and bay with antique furnishings throughout. Full breakfast included and evening wine and hors d'oeuvres. Free pick-up at ferry or airport and complimentary shuttle for riding around the island. Make your reservations early - this Inn is booked one year in advance! **Seasonal:** Closed 12/24and25 **Reservations:** Make them early, six months or more!! **Brochure:** Yes **Permitted:** Children 13-up, limited smoking **Payment Terms:** Check AE/MC/V [C11ACCA-188] **COM Y ITC Member:** No

Rates:	Pvt Bath 6
Single	$ 150.00
Double	$ 250-350

Ye Olde Shelford House   29955 River Rd 95425   **Cloverdale CA**
Al Sauder   **Tel:** 800-833-6479 707-894-5956

Ye Olde' Shelford House, c1885, is a stately Victorian charmer built on property given to Eurastus M Shelford which was formerly part of Rancho Musalacon. Completely restored with beautifully decorated rooms - guests are reminded of the pleasures of the Victorian days. There are three cozy bedrooms with lots of windows and window seats for viewing the surrounding vineyards. Each room has authentic family antiques, home made quilts, plants and fresh flowers from our own flower gardens. A Carriage House offers three beautiful rooms of antique furnishings. A game room offers fun and entertainment while the wrap-around porch provides a relaxing swing where you can enjoy a glass of wine or reading a book. Since Ye Olde' Shelford House borders acres of vineyard - the view is exceptional. You'll relax and enjoy the detail and the crisp, clean - light and airy atmosphere of our Inn. Three additional beautiful guest rooms full of antique furnishings are located in the Carriage House. Each morning you'll awaken to the aroma of fresh oven baked goods wafting through the hallowed halls. In-addition, you'll find fresh squeezed orange juice, fresh fruit, jams, jellies, quiches, coffee, tea or milk. Complimentary beverages and homemade cookies are always ready in our homey kitchen. Complimentary ten-speed bikes or a bike built-for-two take guests on vineyard tours - while a hot tub offers a romantic dip under the clear and star-filled evening. There's also a pool for the guests to enjoy. Guests shouldn't miss the *"Surrey & Sip"* Tour in an authentic *"surrey with a fringe on top"* and a sip of wine in a barrel gazebo. **Discounts:** Yes, travel agents **Airport:** San Francisco-90 mi **Packages:** Surrey & Sip; Antique Car Tour with 1929 Model A, five local winery stops and an afternoon picnic lunch **Seasonal:** No **Reservations:** One night deposit to guarantee reservation; 14 day cancel policy for refund. Check-in 3-6pm; Check-out 11am. **Brochure:** Yes **Permitted:** Limited children, drinking, smoking outdoors only **Conference:** Yes, for groups to twenty persons. **Payment Terms:** Check DC/MC/V [I03FP-CA-282] **COM Y ITC Member:** No

Rates:	Pvt Bath 6
Single	$ 85-110.00
Double	$ 85-110.00

Columbia City Hotel   Main Street 95310   **Columbia CA**
Tom Bender   **Tel:** 209-532-1479 **Fax:** 209-532-7027
                                                 Res Times 8am-10pm

Footsteps on the boardwalk ... Live Theater ... Panning for gold ... Fine Dining ... Tall Tales ... Catching the next stage - some things haven't changed in Columbia for over 130 years. Relive the frontier days in a small, intimate hotel which remains much the same as when the gold miners strolled the streets. Each room is individually appointed with antiques to convey a genuine feeling of the gold-rush era but with modern plumbing, heating and a/c. Balcony rooms overlook the tree-lined main street while Parlor Rooms open onto the main sitting parlor. The tradition of a fine Country Inn begins with a generous continental breakfast of quiche, fresh baked breads, muffins, cereal, orange juice and our own houseblend of coffee. Dining is unforgettable, offering California Cuisine incorporating the fundamentals of French cooking with the influence of contemporary flavors. A seasonally changing menu is based exclusively upon the availability of fresh ingredients - with emphasis on locally grown and produced items. The hotel's wine list is regarded as one of the finest in California. Located in Columbia State Historic Park, activities include Fallon House Theater, built in 1875 and home of Columbia Actors Repertory, Hidden Treasures offer gold mining tours and gold panning, visiting the 1855 Columbia Gazette and enjoying a thirst-quenching sasparilla at the Douglass Saloon before boarding the stage coach for a ride around town. Nearby attractions include Yosemite National Park, caverns, wine tasting and tours and winter skiing. **Airport:** Columbia Airport-1 mi; Stockton-50 mi **Packages:** Dinner, Theater, Lodging **Seasonal:** No **Reservations:** Advance deposit, 72hr cancel policy for refund **Brochure:** Yes **Permitted:** Children, drinking **Conference:** Inn has two meetings rooms (25 & 50 person capacity) and next door hall for 150-200 **Payment Terms:** Check AE/MC/V [I03HPCA1-288] COM YG ITC **Member:** No

Rates:	Pvt Bath 10
Single	$ 90.00
Double	$ 90.00

Victorian House 1894-Dance Studio
Bonnie Marie Kinosian
1000 Eighth St 92118

Coronado CA
Tel: 619-435-2200
Res Times 7am-9pm

A truly unique accommodation and experience is waiting guests in beautiful Coronado, California, sister city to San Diego. This charming 1894 Victorian home welcomes guests to a fascinating getaway with an added bonus: a vacation and dance package! Owner/host/dance teacher, Bonnie Marie, showers her guests with personal attention. You are treated to a full menu of Armenian and Lebanese hospitality and health foods including fresh fruits, juices, rolls, and baklava pastry served on the outdoor patio. Guest rooms are furnished with period antiques and family heirlooms, oriental rugs, brass beds or pre-Civil War Sleigh beds and stained glass doors and windows throughout. This three-story home is located in the very center of Coronado's activities: one block from the central business district for great shopping, galleries, restaurants, theater, parks and entertainment. With great weather year-round, you can fill your days with walks on miles of Pacific beaches, biking tennis, golf, trolley rides and ferry boat trips into San Diego to find the largest zoo in the world, Sea World, Wild Animal Park and Old Town. Add to all this, your choice of dance lessons. Choose social, ballroom, ballet, jazz, tap, Hawaiian, belly dancing or low-impact aerobics and stretching! Enjoy meeting this pleasant hostess and her warm and welcoming Victorian which has been featured in many articles in "San Diego and "Bridge & Bay" magazines and the "San Diego Union" newspaper. **Seasonal:** No **Reservations:** Full payment in advance for entire stay, two week cancellation policy less 15% service fee. 2-day min on weekends and 3-day min for holidays. *Two Bedroom Suite **Brochure:** Yes **Permitted:** Children, limited drinking, smoking outdoors **Conference:** Yes, groups to 35 **Payment Terms:** Travelers Check [R02BCCA-6554] COM Y ITC **Member:** No

Rates:	Pvt Bath 4	Shared Bath 2
Single	$ 200-250.00	
Double	$ 200-250.00	$ 200-250.00

Garden Gate B&B
Donna & Frank Riddle
3646 Schaffer St 90232

Culver City CA
Tel: 310-204-1218
Res Times 9am-12am

Your charming hostess, Donna, designed and built a porch-over-porch Victorian in the old section of interesting Culver City. Yesteryear it was the Keystone Cops and Tarzan and more recently Chips and the A-Team - filming on the streets and sometimes even in the front yard of this lovely home. Drive by Tara of "Gone With The Wind", now Lorimar TV studios nearby. Or take the bus or drive to the convenient beaches or the many attractions of Southern California and Los Angeles area. There is a shuttle or LAX fifteen minutes away. For relaxing with Donna and Frank, there is a spa available and

California — National Edition

complimentary wines and cheese in the parlor. Stay the weekend and feel free to come and go or just relax in the wonderful California sunshine and read in the laid-back style of California. **Seasonal:** No **Reservations:** Check-in 2-6 pm, one week cancellation policy with 50% refund of deposit **Brochure:** Yes **Permitted:** Drinking, limited smoking, limited children **Payment Terms:** Check [R01BPCA-290] **COM Y ITC Member:** No

Rates:	Pvt Bath 1
Single	$ 75.00
Double	$ 75.00

A Weavers Inn — 1440 B St 95501 — Eureka CA
Dorothy & Bob Swendeman
Tel: 707-443-8119

A *Weaver's Inn*, home and studio of a fiber artist and her husband, is a stately Queen Anne/Colonial Revival home built in 1883 and remodeled in 1907. Placed in a spacious fenced garden, it is airy and light but cozy and warm when veiled by wisps of fog. Arriving early, you might visit the studio, try the spinning wheel before the fire or weave on the antique loom, before having refreshments. Each guest room is uniquely furnished with special names like the Pamela Suite which offers two romantic rooms with sliding door, fireplace, bath with tiled shower, queen bed and sofa bed in sitting room and the Cynthia Room with a sunny bay window and wicker furnishings, fireplace, king bed and a shared bath with clawfoot tub. A complimentary delectable full breakfast may include treats from the garden and is served in the gracious dining room or from trays on the sunlit porch. After breakfast, play croquet surrounded by colorful flowers or contemplate the Japanese garden before exploring the ambience of the Victorian Era in Old Town, playing golf, fishing or combing a beach. Elegant relaxing is always in style in the Victorian Parlor with its piano. Your hosts will pamper you, the weather will refresh you and the visit delight you. Come visit us soon. **Discounts:** Weekly rate **Airport:** Eureka-Arcata-10 mi **Packages:** Weaving Instruction and Lodging **Seasonal:** No **Reservations:** One night's deposit or credit card number to guarantee within 7 days of booking, 72 hr cancel policy for refund **Brochure:** Yes **Permitted:** Children, pets, drinking, smoking outdoor porches only **Payment Terms:** Check AE/DC/DISC/MC/V [Z12GPCA1-12280] **COM Y ITC Member:** No

Rates:	Pvt Bath 2	Shared Bath 2
Single	$ 75.00	$ 55.00
Double	$ 110.00	$ 80.00

Elegant Victorian Mansion — 1406 "C" Street 95501 — Eureka CA
Lily & Doug Vieyra
Tel: 800 EVM 1888 707-444-3144
Res Times 10am-6pm

This elegantly restored *National Historic Landmark* is Eureka's most prestigious and luxurious accommodation. Spectacular Victorian architecture outside - authentically restored and furnished opulence inside. Both AAA and Mobil recommended (3-Star), the Inn is exclusively for the non-smoker. Spirited and eclectic Innkeepers serve lavish hospitality in the regal splendor of a meticulously restored 1888 Victorian masterpiece; complete with original family antique furnishings. The inviting guest rooms offer both graceful refinement and modern-day comfort. Each room is individually decorated with elegance and comfort in mind. Guests enjoy gourmet breakfasts and a heavenly night's sleep on world-famous custom-made mattresses. Tranquil setting on a park-like estate with colourful Victorian flower gardens, croquet field with bicycles, sauna and tennis. Secured garage parking, complimentary laundry service. Butler, fireplaces, cable TV, VCR with a library of silent film classics. Impeccable style, grace, charm and unrivaled quality lead to an unforgettable Bed and Breakfast Experience. Located in a quiet, historic residential neighborhood overlooking the city and Humboldt Bay. Near "Old Town", carriage rides, Bay Cruises, museums, antique shops, theatre, dining. Just minutes from Giant Redwood National Park, coastal beaches, ocean charters, horseback riding, golf and fishing. The Inn has been featured in the *"New York Times"*, *"LA Times"*, *"San Francisco Chronicle"*, *"Focus"*,

National Edition

California

"Sunset" and *"Country"* magazines, among others. **Discounts:** 10% for cash **Airport:** San Francisco-300 mi; Arcata Commuter Airport-25 mi **Packages:** Dinner, Bay Cruise, Carriage Ride and lodging $160.00; Museums, Art Gallery Tour, Theatre, Bay Cruise, Dinner & lodging $160.00 **Seasonal:** No **Reservations:** Full payment at time of reservation, 3-6pm check-in, 11am check-out, 7 day cancel notice required for refund **Brochure:** Yes **Permitted:** Drinking **Conference:** Yes, for groups to 15 persons **Languages:** French, Dutch **Payment Terms:** Check MC/V [I04GPCA-12481] **COM** Y **ITC Member:** No

Rates:	Pvt Bath 2	Shared Bath 2
Single	$ 85-115.00	$ 75.00
Double	$ 95-125.00	$ 85-95.00

Gingerbread Mansion Inn   400 Berding St   95536-0040   **Ferndale CA**
Ken Torbert   **Tel:** 800-952-4136   707-786-4000 **Fax:** 805-564-4811
Res Times 8:30am-9pm

Nestled between the giant redwoods and the rugged Pacific Coast of northern California is one of the state's best-kept secrets: the Victorian village of Ferndale. A *State Historic Landmark*, and listed on the *National Historic Register*, Ferndale is a community frozen in time, with Victorian homes and shops relatively unchanged since their construction in the mid-to-late 1800's. Originally settled by Scandinavians, followed by Portuguese and various Europeans, the principle industry is dairy farming, followed by tourism. Ferndale boasts a population of 1450, and offers art galleries, live theater, museums, old cemeteries, many fairs and festivals throughout the year, as well as the tallest living Christmas tree, which is the focal point of the holiday activities. Well known as one of Northern California's most photographed Inns, and recently awarded Four Diamonds from AAA, the *Gingerbread Mansion Inn* is a spectacular example of Victorian splendor, both inside and out. The exterior boasts spindlework, turrets and gables, as well as a formal English garden. The Inn offers four parlors and ten romantic guestrooms, all decorated with antiques. Guests are pampered with luxuriously appointed baths (some with his-and-her clawfoot tubs and/or fireplaces, bathrobes, turndown service, morning coffee and a delicious full breakfast. The new-est room, the Empire Suite, offers all of this and more: king size bed, a large bathing area with a marble and glass shower and clawfoot tub in front of a fireplace; a sitting area with fireplace and dining area (for breakfast ensuite) complete the other side of the suite. **Discounts:** 10% travel agents **Airport:** Arcata-Eureka Airport-35 mi **Packages:** Honeymoon, call for details **Seasonal:** No **Reservations:** Full payment at time of reservation, 3-6pm check in, 14 day cancel policy less $10 service fee **Brochure:** Yes **Permitted:** Children 10-up, drinking **Payment Terms:** Check AE/MC/V [K0-7HPC-A1-315] **COM** YG **ITC Member:** No

Quality Assured: Yes

Rates:	Pvt Bath 9
Single	$ 100-170.00
Double	$ 125-195.00

Karen's Yosemite Inn   PO Box 8   93623   **Fish Camp CA**
Karen Bergh & Lee Morse   **Tel:** 800-346-1443   209-683-4550
Res Times 7am-10pm

Towering pines and whispering cedars welcome guests to the quiet and warmth of this contemporary country home nestled high in the Sierras (5000 ft). The quiet of the front porch brings scurrying squirrels - scolding jays and wind sighs of the forest while evening produces millions of sequins splashed across a velvet sky. Indoors, your hosts have individually decorated and named each room. Choose the Rose Room (light and airy with wicker furniture and twin day beds), Blue Room with a queen bed (its intimate coziness is a favorite for romantic getaways) or the Peach Room (cheery charm of soft

©*Inn & Travel Memphis, Tennessee*

4-35

curtains and brass appointments with a queen bed). Evening offers the warmth of an upstairs fireplace and a library or a crackling fire in the woodstove or a good movie or TV show in the living room. A bountiful full country breakfast in a romantic dining room setting begins each day. Tempting tidbits from Karen's kitchen and seasonal beverages are offered each afternoon (4-6pm). Regardless of the season, guests will enjoy the pristine beauty of winter or the challenge of summer. Winter brings crystal silence of a cross-country ski trail or the delightful sounds of music from the outdoor skating rink. Summer offers rock climbing, back woods exploring by horseback or train through beautiful lush mountain meadows. Sights include Yosemite Park (3 mins), Mariposa Grove of Giant Sequoias (5 mins), Wawona Village (15 mins), Bass Lake, Badger Pass Ski area and Glacier Point. **Airport:** Fresno CA, 65 mi **Discounts:** 10% for 7 day stays or longer, $5 for multiple room bookings **Seasonal:** No **Reserva-tions:** 50% deposit (one night's min), 7 day cancel policy except holidays (14 days) group bookings (2-3 rooms) 21 days. No refund for early departures. Late arrival (after 8pm) requires prior notice. **Brochure:** Yes **Permitted:** Children, NO radios, TV, music or sound equipment is permitted in the upstairs guest areas unless booking all three guest rooms. *Quite time 10pm to 6am.* **Payment Terms:** Check [I05FPCA-6261] **COM** Y **ITC Member:** No

Rates:	Pvt Bath 3
Single	$ 80.00
Double	$ 85.00

Narrow Gauge Inn   48571 Hwy 41   93623   Fish Camp CA
Carol Donnell, GM   Tel: 209-683-7720

A cozy mountain lodge at the Southern Gateway to Yosemite National Park - relive the turn-of-the-century wild west! The buildings (including the inn), offer a unique blend of Victorian and Western-style architecture with rich panelling, massive fireplaces and stain glass. The Dining Hall is lit with kerosene lamps and charmed by an oak fire - creating an intimate setting for your evening dinner. There's a swimming pool, hot bubbling pool, garden courtyard and miles of hiking trails to enjoy. The twenty-eight cozy rooms with patios provide guests with splendid views of the forest and mountains beyond and unrivaled sunrises. Fine food and spirits and comfortable lodgings combine for a tradition of gracious hospitality. Breakfast and other meals are available at added cost from a full selection menu. The adjoining buildings include The Bull Moose Saloon for the high-spirited guest; the General Store, a den of delights offering books, handmade gifts and necessities for the mountain hiker and traveler. Next door to the Inn is the Logger, a narrow gauge steam powered railroad that relives old fashioned sights and sounds of a steam powered train while riding open logging cars through the forest to Lewis Creek Canyon. **Airport:** Fresno-65 mi **Discounts:** Travel agents **Seasonal:** No **Reservations:** One night's deposit by check or money order. Four day cancel notice for full refund. **Brochure:** Yes **Permitted:** Children, drinking, smoking **Payment Terms:** Check AE/DC/MC/V [R02FPCA-317] **COM** Y **ITC Member:** No

Rates:	Pvt Bath 27
Single	$ 80-120.00
Double	$ 80-120.00

Grey Whale Inn   615 N Main St   95437   Fort Bragg CA
Colette & John Bailey   Tel: 800-382-7244   707-964-0640
    Res Times 8am-8pm

A Mendocino Coast landmark since 1915, the *Grey Whale Inn* is Fort Bragg's first Bed and Breakfast Inn. Stately, romantic, serene, the *Grey Whale Inn* is the perfect place to celebrate that special occasion, or to just bask in anonymous solitude. The Grey Whale Inn is exceptionally conducive to group parties - family reunions, weddings and birthdays. Whales can be seen from the Inn during their migration. And the Inn is conveniently located, in strolling distance of the ocean, fine restaurants, unique gift shops, art galleries, antique stores, theatre and music performance houses. Beaches, hiking trails, dramatic coastal headlands are only minutes away by automobile. Each room has a special feeling, and provides spacious surroundings and the utmost in privacy. All rooms have baths and telephones. Some rooms feature TV's, fireplaces, kitchenettes. Sunrise suite has a jacuzzi for two and private sun deck; Point Cabrillo is wheelchair accessible. Views vary: ocean, town and hillside, or garden. The recreation area has a pool table room, TV/VCR theater, fireplace lounge; an immense selection of books and board games is available. The buffet breakfast is lavish and includes a hot entree, prize-winning coffee cakes, fresh fruit, juices, cereal, special blend *Grey Whale Inn* coffee, teas and cocoa. We're happy to assist you with dining, fishing, theatre and Skunk Train reservations. The *Grey Whale Inn*, gracious accommodations on the Mendocino Coast ..... a world away. **Discounts:** Yes, seasonal **Airport:** San Francisco Intl-160 mi **Packages:** Special promotions available, inquire at reservation time. [Photo of Sunrise Suite, courtesy Leona Walden, Mendocino CA] **Seasonal:** Rates vary **Reservations:** One or more night's prepayment upon booking, 2-3 nite min on week-ends and holidays with full prepayment. 800 for reservations only. **Brochure:** Yes **Permitted:** Children 12-up; No Smoking within the building **Conference:** Yes, for groups to 16 persons. **Languages:** Spanish, German **Payment Terms:** Check AE/DISC/MC/V [K01IPCA1-324] **COM YG ITC Member:** No **Quality Assurance** Request-ed

Rates: Pvt Bath 14
Single $ 66-145.00
Double $ 88-165.00

Pudding Creek Inn	700 N Main St 95437	Fort Bragg CA
Carol Anloff/Jacque Woltman	**Tel:** 800-227-9529 707-964-9529 **Fax:** 707-961-0282	
	Res Times 8am-9pm	

Intrigue, romance and adventure were the criteria for owners Gary and Carole Anloff in their search for a Bed & Breakfast Inn. At *Pudding Creek* they found it all. Built in 1894 by a Russian Count, who, according to legend, buried his mysteriously-acquired riches on the property. The Inn is a triumph of renovation. New features have been added but the historic past of the structures and property have been retained and cherished. Each room is romantically named and decorated in its own style and filled with antique furnishings. Travelers and romantics who choose to stay close to home will find much to occupy themselves at the Inn. A stroll through the garden full of award-winning flowers; a picnic with a basket of goodies, prepared upon request; snuggling before the fire with a good book or game in the parlor or in the new TV and recreation room. A full complimentary breakfast begins each day. Phone, fax and laundry facilities are available. For those venturing out, the delights of the Mendocino Coast and Ft Bragg are close-by. The overall experience of *Pudding Creek Inn* is nostalgic, founded on a tradition of fine innkeeping. **Reservations:** Deposit required, 5 day cancel policy for refund, check-in noon to 9pm **Permitted:** Children, drinking, **Payment Terms:** Check AE/DC/MC/V [I04FPCA-328] **COM Y ITC Member:** No

Rates: Pvt Bath 10
Single $ 50.00
Double $ 125.00

Campbell Ranch Inn	1475 Canyon Rd 95441	Geyserville CA
Mary Jane & Jerry Campbell	**Tel:** 800-959-3878 707-857-3476 **Fax:** 707-857-3239	
	Res Times 8am-10pm	

Spectacular views highlight a stay at this 35 acre ranch located in the heart of Sonoma County Wine Country. Surrounded by beautiful rolling vineyards and Mary Jane's abundant flower garden creates a perfect setting for summer breakfast - while enjoying the wonderful view. A full complement of amenities for guests include a professional tennis court, 20x40 swimming pool, hot tub spa, bikes, horseshoes and ping pong. The Inn has four spacious guestrooms in the house and a separate cottage, all with king size beds. Most rooms have a balcony and there's a fireplace in the Cottage. Fresh flowers and fruit greet guests along with bathrobes, pool towels and back rests for reading in bed. A masseuse is available for an hour massage in your room. Guests gather in a lovely room with a large fireplace or in the comfortable family room offering music, TV with satellite dish and a VCR. A full breakfast selected from a menu offers choices of fruits, cereals, hot dishes, homemade breads, muffins and coffee cakes. Homemade pie or cake welcome guests upon their return from evening dinner while daytime ice tea or lemonade are readily served. All of Sonoma County wineries and sights are nearby along with water recreation, hiking, fishing, canoeing with short trips to visit historical sights, Redwood parks, Russian River area and the Mendocino Coast and Napa Valley. Come to the *Campbell Ranch* and enjoy the peaceful and serene 35 acre country estate. **Airport:** Santa Rosa Sonoma Airport-15 mi **Reservations:** Credit card number for deposit guarantee; 72 hr cancel policy for refund. Check-in after 1:00pm, check-out 12 noon. Two day min on weekends, 3 day min on holidays. **Permitted:** Drinking, limited children **Conference:** Yes, for groups to 10-12 **Payment Terms:** Check AE/MC/V [I04HPCA1-337] **COM YG ITC Member:** No **Quality Assured:** Yes

Rates: Pvt Bath 5
Single $ 90-155.00
Double $ 100-165.00

Country Rose Inn	PO Box 2500 95021-2500	Gilroy CA
Rose Hernandez		Tel: 408-842-0441
		Res Times 6-8am/8-10pm

Featured in *"Country Inns,"* the Country Rose Inn is nestled in a grove of ancient trees at the base of Santa Clara Valley. This manor is of the Dutch Colonial-style from the 1920s offering comfort and relaxation in rural grandeur. Surrounded by farmland - guests get a sense of Old California - in this natural and beautiful setting. Virgin rolling hills are feathered in grass and oak - while an immense Magnolia and pines tower above the fertile valley floor. The spacious guest rooms include private baths - with a special bridal suite including a bathtub with jets and a steam shower. Each room is infused by this peaceful and serene rural setting and furnished in warm understated tones. A full breakfast of freshly-squeezed juice, coffee and granola is followed by a specially prepared California entree, served with fruit and dessert. Nearby activities include: wineries, hiking, hot air ballooning, outlet shopping, Hecker Pass Theme Park, Henry Coe State Park. A perfect locale for traveling to San Juan Bautista, the ocean, San Francisco and Silicon Valley. **Reservations:** First night's deposit required with 7 day cancel policy for refund less $10 service fee. Late arrival by prior arrangement; add state and hotel taxes to above rates **Permitted:** Limited drinking **Conference:** Yes for groups to twenty persons **Languages:** Spanish **Payment Terms:** Check AE/MC/V [Z06FPCA-6211] **COM Y ITC Member:** No

Rates: Pvt Bath 5
Single $ 79-169.00
Double $ 79-169.00

Groveland Hotel	18767 Main St 90321	Groveland CA
Peggy Mosley		Tel: 800-273-3314 209-962-4000 **Fax:** 209-962-6674
		Res Times 24 Hrs

The recently restored 1849 Monterey Colonial Adobe and 1914 Queen Anne buildings are of major historical significance to the area. Listed on the *National Register of Historic Places,* the *Groveland Hotel* was built to support the hundreds of miners from the Gold Rush Era. It provided lodging, food and pleasure - gambling and ladies of the evening, and acquired recognition as the *"best house on the hill."* The fourteen rooms and three suites are furnished in European antiques, with terry robes, down comforters, upscale linens and private baths. Some have private entrances to the verandas where white wicker abounds. Suites have separate sitting rooms, fireplaces and jacuzzi tubs. The parlour has books, games, a fireplace and television. A European continental breakfast and afternoon wine and cheese hour are included in room rate. The gourmet restaurant on the premises presents California seasonal, fresh cuisine in a most exciting manner. Your dining experience is enhanced by great music and an outstanding wine list. A conference facility and courtyard dining create a magnificent setting for meetings, parties, receptions and weddings. The *Groveland Hotel* presents an outstanding calendar of events throughout the year. These include a Luau, Winemaker Dinners, Halloween Party, The Twelve Days of Christmas and Valentine's Day, New Year's Puttin' On The Ritz Bash, Murder Mystery Weekends, Monte Carlo Carnival Night, '50s Night, art shows and others. Call for a schedule. Nearby attractions include Yosemite National Park, golf, tennis, hiking, world-class white water rafting, swimming, horseback riding and gold panning. The concierge will gladly assist in making all your arrangements for sightseeing, weddings, special occasions, meeting planning and reservations. **Airport:** Sacramento-2 Hrs; San Francisco-3 Hrs **Packages:** Mid-week Winter Special $280.00 includes three nights lodging, one evening dinner with wine for two, Sun-Thursday; Executive Stress Relief Fly Fishing - novice or expert **Seasonal:** No **Reservations:** One night deposit or credit card number to guarantee reservation: E-mail: Groveland@yosemitegold.com; Internet-htpp://www.-yosemite-gold.com/grovcland **Brochure:** Yes **Permitted:** Children, limited pets **Conference:** Groups to twenty five, private entrance, complete audio visual equipment **Languages:** Some Spanish **Payment Terms:** Check AE/DC/DISC/MC/V [I08HPCA1-12488] COM YG ITC **Member:** No

Rates:	Pvt Bath 17
Single	$ 85-165.00
Double	$ 85-165.00

North Coast Country Inn 34591 S Hwy 1 95445 Gualala CA
Loren & Nancy Flanagan Tel: 800-959-4537 707-884-4537
Res Times 8am-10pm

Nestled in the forest with the sound of barking sea lions in the distance is the *North Coast Country Inn*, an enchanting and rustic array of buildings on the coast of Northern California. The Inn is unique in many ways, with its foliaged privacy and ocean views. From the masses of flowering shrubs and bushes to the open beamed ceilings and wood-burning fireplaces, the owners have sought a romantic and private feeling throughout the complex. With a delicate balance of exquisite antiques, art treasures, potted greenery and authentic collectibles and memorabilia, this is country elegance at its very best. The four guest rooms each have a fireplace, spacious bathroom, kitchenette, a sitting area and private deck. All have antiques and a queen size, four poster bed. On the shelves are books and games. A flower, candy and juice, plus a tray set with the makings for coffee/tea are but a few of the amenities. After a day of sightseeing or beach combing an outdoor hot tub is ideal for relaxing and in the upper garden, the gazebo is perfect of lounging on a quiet afternoon. A full breakfast is served in the room, along with a hot entree and fresh bakery from the oven is a fruit dish and pot of special blend fresh ground coffee. The Inn's office boasts an antique shop with many unique country pieces for sale. The North Coast Country Inn is a perfect place for a vacation getaway, with great hospitality and comfort, all in an elegant country environment. **Airport:** San Francisco-135 mi **Reservations:** One night's deposit, 5 day cancel policy for refund, call to arrange for late arrival **Brochure:** Yes **Permitted:** Drinking, limited children **Languages:** Spanish **Payment Terms:** Check AE/MC/V [I04HPCA1-6187] COM YG ITC **Member:** No

Rates:	Pvt Bath 4
Single	$ 135.00
Double	$ 135.00

California National Edition

Cypress Inn	407 Miranda Rd 94019	**Half Moon Bay CA**
Jude Wright		**Tel:** 800-83-BEACH 415-726-6002
		Res Times 7am-9pm

Cypress Inn is located 5 miles north of Half-Moon Bay and 26 miles south of San Francisco and offers guests the essence of California beach-side living. The Inn is on a five-mile stretch of pristine white sand beach and each of the eight luxury rooms offers a private deck overlooking the ocean. The interior decor is Mexican Indian folk art with wonderful bright colors, carved animals and terra cotta tile floors. Each guest room includes a private bath and a fireplace for romantic evenings. Our in-house masseuse was a pioneer of the healing art of therapeutic massage since 1981 and was featured in a well-known pictorial book *"A Day in the Life of California."* Breakfast is a specialty - with unexpected superb fare. Jazz and classical music are just steps away each weekend along with fine restaurants and nightclubs. Your host is ready to make your stay unforgettable - all you have to do is ask! **Discounts:** Yes, inquire at res time **Package:** Yes, inquire **Airport:** San Francisco Intl-25mi **Seasonal:** No **Reservations:** Deposit required within 10 days of booking **Brochure:** Yes **Permitted:** Drinking, limited children, limited smoking **Conference:** Yes for all special occasions **Payment Terms:** Check AE/MC/V [R01EPCA-10039] **COM** Y **ITC Member:** No

Rates: **Pvt Bath 8**
Single $ 135-250.00
Double $ 135-250.00

Old Thyme Inn	779 Main St 94019	**Half Moon Bay CA**
George & Marcia Dempsey		**Tel:** 415-726-1616 **Fax:** 415-712-0805
		Res Times 7am-10pm

Snuggled into a fragrant English herb and flower garden - *Old Thyme Inn* is a beautifully-restored 1899 Queen Anne Victorian offering guest rooms appropriately named for familiar herbs. All of the rooms are unique with lovely antiques, whimsical stuffed animals, fresh-cut flowers and private baths. Cozy fireplaces and whirlpool tubs are available in four of the guest rooms while clawfoot tubs are featured in the others. The Inn provides a friendly informal atmosphere - where the center of daily activity begins with a delicious breakfast in the dining room and ends with complimentary beverages served around the wood-burning stove each evening. Breakfast specialties may include homemade banana bread, quiche, cinnamon-raisin scones with raspberry jam, Swedish egg cake with fresh fruit, blueberry muffins, frittata and baked croissants with cheeses and turkey. After breakfast and within a short walking distance are beaches, quaint shops, art galleries and restaurants in this historic seaside village. Be our guest at the *Old Thyme Inn* for a wonderful experience from a bygone era. **Airport:** San Francisco Intl-22 mi; San Jose Intl-29 mi **Seasonal:** No **Reservations:** One night's deposit or credit card number to guarantee reservation, 7 day cancel policy for refund less $10 service fee, check-in 3-7pm **Brochure:** Yes **Permitted:** Children, drinking, limited smoking **Conference:** Yes, for groups to 14 persons **Languages:** Spanish, French **Payment Terms:** Check MC/V [I04HPCA1-366] **COM** YG **ITC Member:** No **Quality Assurance:** Requested

Rates: **Pvt Bath 7**
Single $ 75.00
Double $ 210.00

Irwin Street Inn	522 N Irwin St 93230	**Hanford CA**
Michael Bates		**Tel:** 209-583-8791 **Fax:** 209-583-8793
		Res Times 24 Hrs

Four impeccably restored, turn-of-the-century Victorian homes and surrounding tree-shaded lawns form a one acre sanctuary in the downtown Hanford Historic District. The *Irwin Street Inn* offers a step back in time to a period of grace and gentility with its leaded glass windows, preserved wood detailing, period artifacts and close attention to historic accuracy - all combined to recreate the late nineteenth century ambiance at its best. Thirty delightfully appointed rooms and suites, each with its own bath, offer Victorian charm with contemporary convenience. Each room is different - each with is own character. Rooms with lavish four-poster beds, antique armoires and period furniture are made even more comfortable with cable TV, radios and phones. In the morning, guests are treated to a continental breakfast featuring, among other offerings, the Inn's own Morning Glory Muffins. Our elegant restaurant occupies the lower floor of one of the four Victorian homes. Breakfast, lunch and dinner are served, depending upon the season, in high-style in the interior dining room area or outdoors on the gracious awning-covered verandah with its sweeping view of the grounds. Within easy strolling distance is the Hanford Historic District with elegant Court House Square, numerous restaurants and shops, all enthusiastically embracing a turn-of-the-century spirit. Guests may also enjoy the use of the pool on the grounds. **Discounts:** Corporate rates, AARP, AAA **Airport:** Fresno Airport-35 mi **Packages:** Romance, Weddings are a specialty **Seasonal:** No **Reservations:** Credit card number for deposit to guarantee reservation, 73 hr cancel policy for deposit refund **Brochure:** Yes **Permitted:** Children, pets, drinking, limited smoking **Conference:** Three meeting rooms for business meetings and banquets to 75 persons. Spacious grounds for perfect weddings, receptions and private parties **Languages:** Spanish **Payment Terms:** Check AE/DC/DISC/MC/V [K03IPCA1-368] **COM YG ITC Member:** No

Rates: Pvt Bath 31
Single $ 69.99-89.99
Double $ 69.99-89.99

Healdsburg Inn On Plaza 110 Matheson 95448 Healdsburg CA
Genny Jenkins/LeRoy Steck Tel: 800-431-8663 707-433-6991 **Fax:** 707-433-9516
Res Times 8am-10pm

A quiet place in the center of town where history and hospitality meet. This historic Wells Fargo Building of 1890 now accommodates bed and breakfast guests who enjoy browsing through our art gallery and gift shop on the main floor. A grand staircase in the gallery takes you to the guest rooms, most with fireplaces and clawfooted tubs for two. All ten rooms include queen or king size beds, private bathrooms, fluffy towels, central a/c, even a rubber ducky. Each room has telephone, television with VCR. A library of video tapes are available. Front room bay windows look over the park and catch the afternoon sun and sunsets. Back rooms have open balconies shaded by large trees, a great place for that first cup of coffee in the morning sun with birds singing. Our newly remodeled solarium with windows and skylights, provides a bright, cheerful setting for a scrumptious country breakfast including a hot entree, orange juice, fresh fruit, assorted breads and muffins, assorted teas and our special blend coffee: Champagne Brunch on weekends. Afternoon guests gather for wine tasting, table games and friendly conversation. Coffee, assorted teas, soft drinks and chocolate chip cookies available 24 hours. Convenient to wine tasting, restaurants, antiques, galleries, shopping, hot air balloon rides, canoeing and hiking. **Airport:** San Francisco-80 mi **Discounts:** Midweeks **Seasonal:** No **Reservations:** Credit card number for deposit to guarantee reservation, 3 day cancel policy for refund with $15 service fee **Permitted:** Children by arrangement, limited drinking, smoking outdoors only, no pets **Payment Terms:** Check MC/V [I10IPCA1-374] **COM U ITC Member:** No

Rates: Pvt Bath 10
Single $ 155-210.00
Double $ 155-210.00

California
National Edition

Rockwood Lodge	5295 W Lake Blvd 96141-0266	Homewood CA
Louis Reinkens/Constance Stevens	**Tel:** 800-LE TAHOE 916-525-5273 **Fax:** 916-525-5949	

This Thirties-style chalet beckons guests with a warm, friendly atmosphere of Lake Tahoe's magical west shore, just down the road from Fleur Du Lac, a lakeside villa where *Godfather Part II* was filmed. Originally built as a second home in the mid-thirties, your hosts completely renovated this *"Old Tahoe-Style"* home of stone, knotty pine and hand-hewn beams into the perfect mountain chalet for romantics. Guest suites are named for actual places around Lake Tahoe and offer a range of furnishings and decor from a queen size feather bed with a puffy down comforter, Laura Ashley curtains and fabrics to Early American and European furnishings, private bath with brass fixtures, pedestal wash basin and a welcomed 20th century convenience - a seven foot long Roman tub with double showers. Added a full complement of body lotions, shampoos, cozy terry cloth bathrobes and bedtime chocolates discretely placed on the nightstand. A full complimentary breakfast in the dining room offers a selection of homemade fruit crepes, Lou's special "Dutch Baby" - a breakfast souffle, all complemented by fresh-squeezed orange juice, yogurt and granola begins each days' events. Conveniently located for skiers, its a short drive to Squaw Valley and Alpine Meadows and within easy walking distance to Homewood Ski Area. Apres-ski amenities are close by with one of Lake Tahoe's most celebrated European-style restaurants - Swiss Lakewood within walking distance. Staying at *Rockwood* means leaving your car parked because you're within walking distance of great dining, sights and activities. **Airport:** Reno Cannn-55 mi **Discounts:** Upgrade room at no charge when available **Seasonal:** No **Reservations:** Payment in full within ten days of booking **Brochure:** Yes **Permitted:** Drinking **Payment Terms:** [Z04GPCA-380] **COM** Y **ITC Member:** No

Rates:	Pvt Bath 3	Shared Bath 2
Single	$ 135.00	$ 100.00
Double	$ 250.00	$ 125.00

Fairwinds Farm B&B Cottage	PO Box 581 94937	Inverness CA
Joyce Goldfield		**Tel:** 415-663-9454
		Res Times 24 Hrs

The ultimate secluded getaway! High atop Inverness Ridge, amidst towering bishop pines and bays, with direct access to 75,000 acre Point Reyes National Seashore. One large (1000 sq ft) cottage, living room, central heat plus a large fireplace with wood, fully-equipped kitchen, full bath, private garden with pond and swing, deck-top hot tub with ocean view! Amenities include barnyard animals, library, TV, stereo, VCR (movies) typewriter, guitar, binoculars, beach chairs and umbrella, robes and beach towels. Quaint, rustic and cozy. A very special hideaway, secluded and private, the only light visible from the farm is the lighthouse on Farallon Islands. There's a queen size bed and futon couch in the living room with a double bed in the loft bedroom and a crib is available. A generous country breakfast is provided with baked goodies and fresh fruit, gourmet coffee and tea and homemade jam. For evenings movies by the fire, special cookies, cheese cakes, popcorn and chocolate bars are provided. Ocean and bay beaches, meadows of wildflowers, forested mountain tops - to explore and photograph. Whale watching in winter, bird-watching year-round - you'll find wild deer, elk, fox, bobcat and raccoons as well. Horseback riding and biking available in the National Park outside your front door! **Airport:** San Francisco and Oakland-1 hr **Packages:** Stay 7 nights, pay for 6 **Seasonal:** No **Reservations:** Full payment required, 14 day cancel policy for refund. Check-in 3pm, late arrival only with prior arrangements. Add 10% county tax to room rates. *$25 for each additional person **Brochure:** Yes **Permitted:** Children, smoking outdoors, social drinking **Languages:** Sign language **Payment Terms:** Check [Z02HPCA1-12697] **COM** U **ITC Member:** No

Rates:	Pvt Bath 1
Single	$ 125.00*
Double	$ 125.00

Columbia City Hotel		Jamestown CA
Tom Bender		**Tel:** 209-532-1479 **Fax:** 209-532-7027
		Res Times 8am-10pm

©*Inn & Travel Memphis, Tennessee*

National Edition   *California*

Refer to the same listing name under Columbia, California for a complete description. **Seasonal:** No **Payment Terms:** Check AE/MC/V [M03HPCA1-16690] **COM** YG **ITC Member:** No

Rates:	Pvt Bath 10
Single	$ 90.00
Double	$ 90.00

National Hotel   Main St 95327   Jamestown CA
Steve Willey
Tel: 800-894-3446 209-984-3446
Res Times 8am-10pm

1859 restored and gateway setting to the **Mother-Lode Country! The Wild West lives again!** One of the oldest continuously operating hotels in California, you can stand at the original redwood bar while listening to the ghosts that surround this place. Guest rooms include pull-chain toilets, and antique furnishings but also modern amenities such as showers! Full breakfast included. **Seasonal:** No **Reservations:** Deposit required to hold room, cancellation notice of 5 days for full refund. **Brochure:** Yes **Permitted:** Children 8-up, limited drinking, limited smoking **Conference:** Yes, for groups to 15 persons including gourmet dining. **Payment Terms:** Check MC/V [X02BCCA-6216] **COM** Y **ITC Member:** No

Rates:	Pvt Bath 5	Shared Bath 7
Single	$ 55-65.00	$ 45-55.00
Double	$ 65-75.00	$ 55-65.00

Murphys Jenner Inn   10400 Hwy One 95450-0069   Jenner CA
Sheldon & Richard Murphy
Tel: 800-732-2377 707-865-2377
Res Times 10am-8pm

Fifteen miles of sandy beaches, hundreds of acres of state parks with hiking trails through magnificent redwoods, pines and cypress, an ocean that continuously washes away the earth's impurities . . . all of nature's gifts are abundant just seventy scenic miles north of the Golden Gate Bridge on Coastal Highway One. Spend time on the beach just sitting, walking or meditating! Pick fresh herbs and wild mushrooms, catch a steelhead or seabass for dinner, whale-watch in winter or canoe the Russian River! Choose one of the ten guest rooms which are furnished in varying decor including some with river and ocean views, hot tub, open-fire woodstoves, antique and wicker furnishings, quilts, books, houseplants, personal loving touches and without TV or phones! Several beach-side vacation rental homes are also available. A restaurant on the grounds offer Continental Cuisine featuring local seafoods, meats, vegetarian dishes and fine wines from the local Russian River Valley wineries. A continental breakfast is included. Nearby activities include surfing, hang gliding, golf, tennis, deep sea fishing, sailing, beachcombing, Ft Ross, sunset boat cruising and horseback riding on the beach. **Seasonal:** No **Reservations:** One night's deposit in advance, 7 day cancel policy less $10 service fee. Full payment at check-in. **Brochure:** Yes **Permitted:** Children, limited pets, smoking outdoors on decks only **Conference:** Yes, the Terra Nova Institute at Salmon Creek Beach, just 8 miles S of the Inn. Weddings by the Sea are directed by Mrs. Sheldon Murphy. **Payment Terms:** Check MC/V [Z01EPCA-399] **COM** Y **ITC Member:** No

Rates:	Pvt Bath 11
Single	$ 50-110.00
Double	$ 70-150.00

Kern River Inn B&B   *PO Box 1725 93238   Kernville CA
Marti Andrews/Mike Meeham
Tel: 619-376-6750
Res Times 8am-10pm

The new *Kern River Inn Bed & Breakfast* is truly a home away from home for people who enjoy personal service and western hospitality. Located on the Kern River in the quaint western town of Kernville, California in the southern Sierras within Sequoia National Forest. Only three driving hours north of Los Angeles. The Inn features six tastefully, individually decorated country bedrooms, all with private baths and river views. Some rooms include fireplaces, whirlpool tubs, sitting areas, queen and king size beds, and wheelchair access. Relax with new friends in our country traditional

California   *National Edition*

parlor or enjoy refreshments on the front porch while you enjoy the view of the park and river. An expanded continental breakfast features home-baked giant cinnamon rolls, special cereals, fresh fruit, juices, coffee and teas. Complimentary afternoon refreshments are served daily. Year-round activities include fishing, golf, white-water rafting, kayaking, mountain biking, hiking, Lake Isabella, water sports and downhill skiing at Shirley Meadows ski area. Restaurants, parks, museums and antique shops are within walking distance, and it's just a short drive to the high country and the beautiful giant redwoods. Come and visit Mike and Marti for that special occasion or for just a relaxing getaway. **Discounts:** Special group and others, inquire at res time **Airport:** Bakersfield CA-45 mi **Packages:** Honeymoon, birthday, anniversary and that special occasion. *Street address: 119 Kern River Dr, same city. **Seasonal:** No **Reservations:** One night's or 50% of length of stay (which ever is greater), late arrival by prior arrangement. 7 day cancel policy; two or more room require 14 day notice for refund; Arrival 3-6pm, checkout 11 am. **Brochure:** Yes **Permitted:** Drinking, children 12-up, smoking on porches only - outside **Conference:** Yes, small retreat for 10-12 persons. **Payment Terms:** Check* MC/V [R10D-PCA-14351] **COM** Y **ITC Member:** No

Rates:	Pvt Bath 6
Single	$ 65-75.00
Double	$ 75-85.00

Knights Ferry Hotel   11713 Main St 95381   Knights Ferry CA
Rich & Chris Coleman Ehmig   Tel: 209-881-3271
                                                                     Res Times 7am-9pm

Situated on the Stanislaus River is this c1854 hotel still serving the weary guests traveling the Great Western Route, including Ulysses S. Grant when he was an army captain!! Privacy and beautiful natural surroundings keep guests coming back yearly. **Seasonal:** No **Reservations:** One night's deposit required to hold room and if cancelled, refunded with 5 days notice **Permitted:** Limited children, smoking, drinking **Payment Terms:** Check [C11ACCA-407] **COM** Y **ITC Member:** No

Rates:	Pvt Bath 14	Shared Bath 3
Single	$ 50-65.00	$ 45-50.00
Double	$ 60-75.00	$ 55-60.00

Carriage House   1322 Catalina St 92651   Laguna Beach CA
Dee & Thom Taylor   Tel: 714-494-8945

One of Laguna's designated *Historical Landmarks*, this New Orleans-style Inn is located in the heart of the Village and just a few houses away from the beautiful beaches of the Pacific Ocean! Each guest room is individually decorated from the Springtime freshness of the Lilac Time Suite to the tropical coolness of Green Palms with emerald greens and white touches in wicker! All guest rooms are suites with sitting rooms and most have a fully-equipped kitchen. A spectacular courtyard is surrounded by the guest rooms and is the focal point for relaxation among the tropical plants and the splashing fountains. You'll never know who you might meet here because a number of celebrities (Linda Lavin, Jane Withers and Lauren Hutton) have already discovered the charm of this wonderful inn. Your hosts are committed to service and you'll start each morning with a Complimentary continental plus breakfast served outdoors in the courtyard beneath a carrotwood tree covered with moss while the fresh ocean breeze reminds you the ocean is just a few steps away. In their usual California-custom, Dee and Vern treat each guest upon arrival, to a complimentary bottle of California wine, fresh fruit and flowers in their rooms. **Airport:** LA and San Diego are 75 minutes away (Laguna is midway) **Discounts:** Yes, inquire at res time **Seasonal:** No **Reservations:** One night's deposit at res time, 7 day cancel policy for refund, two night min on weekends **Brochure:** Yes **Permitted:** Children, limited drinking and smoking **Payment Terms:** Check [Z07GPCA-409] **COM** Y **ITC Member:** No

Rates:	Pvt Bath 6
Single	$ 95-150.00
Double	$ 95-150.00

Channel Road Inn   Los Angeles CA
Kathy Jensen   Tel: 310-459-1920 Fax: 310-454-9920
                                                                     Res Times 7:30am-10pm

4-44   ©Inn & Travel Memphis, Tennessee

Refer to the same listing name under Santa Monica, California for a compete description. **Seasonal:** No **Payment Terms:** Check MC/V [M04BPCA-9495] **COM** Y **ITC Member:** No

Rates: Pvt Bath 14
Single $ 95-200.00
Double $ 95-200.00

Terrace Manor	1353 Alvarado Terrace 90006	Los Angeles CA
Jim & Josie Jones		**Tel:** 213-381-1478

A *National Registered Landmark* built c1902, this residence is an excellent example of hardwood flooring, stained and leaded glass windows, and ornate hardwood carvings. Antique furnishings and host collectibles complete the excellent decor of all rooms. Full Complimentary breakfast included with room. Complimentary wine upon arrival. Close to Chinatown, Little Tokyo, Magic Castle and Dodger's stadium. **Seasonal:** No **Brochure:** Yes **Permitted:** Limited children, drinking **Payment Terms:** Check AE/MC/V [X11ACCA-425] **COM** Y **ITC Member:** No

Rates: Pvt Bath 5
Single $ 70-100.00
Double $ 70-100.00

Big Canyon Inn	11750 Big Canyon Rd 95457	Lower Lake CA
John & Helen Wiegand		**Tel:** 707-928-5631

A secluded and peaceful home on a hilly twelve acres of pines and oaks beneath Cobb Mountain provides guests an opportunity to relax with nature's beauty surrounding them. Enjoy the many outdoor recreational activities: hike the mountains and search for Lake Country diamonds, enjoy the wildflowers blooming each Spring or the changing colors in the Fall, go fishing, or enjoy the wine tasting at nearby wineries. You'll have a separate suite with a private entrance, kitchenette and bath. You'll enjoy the wood-burning stove during the cooler months. Private airport pick-ups arranged at Hoberg Airport. **Seasonal:** No **Reservations:** One night's deposit to hold room; arrival by 6:30pm unless other arrangements have been made. **Permitted:** Children, drinking **Payment Terms:** Check [C11ACCA-435] **COM** Y **ITC Member:** No

Rates: Pvt Bath 1
Single $ 65.00
Double $ 65.00

Casa Larronde	PO Box 86 90265-0086	Malibu CA
Jim & Charlou Larronde		**Tel:** 310-456-9333

Walk among the stars in Malibu near surfer's beach with over 4,000 square feet of luxury including full glass windows, fireplace, outdoor wood deck for sunbathing. World traveled hosts also enjoy entertaining if you desire. Full complimentary breakfast included. With beach activities close at hand and star watching with movie stars for neighbors. **Seasonal:** No **Pay-ment Terms:** Check [C11ACCA-437] **COM** Y **ITC Member:** No

Rates: Pvt Bath 2
Single $ 70.00
Double $ 85.00

Oak Meadows, too	5263 Hwy 140N 95338	Mariposa CA
Don & Francie Starchman		**Tel:** 209-742-6161 **Fax:** 209-966-2320
		Res Times 4pm-9pm

Just a short drive to Yosemite National Park. *Oak Meadows, too* is located in the Historic Gold Rush town of Mariposa, at the intersection of Hwy 49 and Hwy 140N. *Oak Meadows, too* was built in 1985 with New England architecture and turn-of-the-century charm. A stone fireplace greets your arrival in the guest parlor, where a continental plus breakfast is served each morning. Take a walking tour of Mariposa, see the California State Mining and Mineral Museum or just relax in your comfortably furnished

California National Edition

room. All rooms have private baths and are furnished with handmade quilts, brass headboards, and charming wallpapers. **Seasonal:** Clo Christmas **Reservations:** First night's deposit, 3 day cancel policy for refund, add 10% bed tax **Brochure:** Yes **Permitted:** Limited children, drinking **Languages:** French, German **Payment Terms:** Check MC/V [Z10HPCA1-2916] **COM** YG **ITC Member:** No

Rates: Pvt Bath 6
Single $ 59.00
Double $ 59-89.00

Grey Whale Inn   Mendocino CA
Colette & John Baily   Tel: 800-382-7244 707-964-0640
    Res Times 8am-8pm

Refer to the same listing name under Fort Bragg, California for a complete description. **Seasonal:** Rates vary **Payment Terms:** Check AE/DISC/MC/V [M04FPCA-16854] **COM** Y **ITC Member:** No

Rates: Pvt Bath 14
Single $ 66-145.00
Double $ 88-165.00

John Dougherty House   571 Ukiah St 95460   Mendocino CA
David & Marion Wells   Tel: 707-937-5266
    Res Times 8am-8pm

Stop a while .... and enjoy California as it was one hundred and twenty-five years ago. Built in 1867, the *Historic John Dougherty House* offers some of the best ocean and bay views in the historic village of Mendocino - while just steps away from great restaurants and shopping. The Main House is furnished with period country antiques reminiscent of the 1860's and provides a quiet peaceful night's sleep seldom experienced in today's urban lifestyles. All of the guest rooms include a private bath, queen size bed and are furnished with antiques and individually decorated, accented with dried flower wreaths and arrangements gathered from our garden. Most of the rooms feature color cable TV, a small refrigerator and a woodburning fireplace. Breakfast is served by a crackling fire in the historic New England-style keeping room where guests are surrounded by period country antiques, handstenciled walls and a view of Mendocino Bay and the Pacific Ocean. The expansive full complimentary breakfast includes homemade scones and breads, a large selection of locally grown fresh fruit - decorated with edible flowers from our English garden. In-addition, you'll sample natural honey, Almond Granola with yogurt, a hot entree and a large selection of natural cereals. Breakfast is also a pleasant time to share your daily plans with the other guests and your hosts .... where you'll learn there's canoeing up the Big River, hiking the headlands, beaches and tidepools along the rugged coast. Mendocino, a National Historic Preservation Area, is near nine state parks where you can enjoy whale watching, green fern canyons, lush botanical gardens and majestic redwoods. The arts thrive with numerous craft shops and galleries offer items unique to the area. **Discounts:** Special mid-week rates, Special winter rates **Airport:** San Francisco-175 mi; Santa Rosa-90 mi **Packages:** Inquire at res time **Seasonal:** No **Reservations:** One night's deposit within 5 days of making reservation; 7 day cancel policy for refund less $15 service fee, two night min of weekends, late arrival with prior notice **Brochure:** Yes **Permitted:** Drinking, limited children, limited smoking **Payment Terms:** Check DISC/MC/V [I04HPCA1-12703] **COM** YG **ITC Member:** No

Rates: Pvt Bath 6
Single $ 95-175.00
Double $ 95-175.00

Goose & Turrets   835 George St 94037-0937   Montara CA
Raymond & Emily Hoche-Mong   Tel: 415-728-5451
    Res Times 8am-10pm

©*Inn & Travel Memphis, Tennessee*

At the *Goose & Turrets* you'll find geese on the pond ... hummingbirds in the fuschias ... Mozart on the tape deck ... bread baking in the oven ... a wood fire in the living room ... down comforters to cuddle under ... and surf and foghorns in the distance. The *Goose & Turrets* has helped folks unwind for a long time. In the early 1900's, San Francisco Bohemians rode the Ocean Shore Railroad to Montara Beach and Art Colony. During Prohibition, the adventurous indulged in the forbidden along the sparsely patrolled coast. The cannon flanking the front door date from a time as the Spanish American War Veterans Country Club. Today Montara is a peaceful seaside village of horse ranches and straw flower farms. This 1908 Italian villa is a family-run bed and breakfast where you are pampered with tea and tasty things in the afternoon and a full four-course breakfast in the morning. Menus change daily. Only 20 minutes from San Francisco Airport, the *Goose & Turrets Bed and Breakfast* is also only 1/2 mile from a clean, uncrowded Pacific beach. Nearby are restaurants, galleries, tidepools, golf, hiking, horseback riding, and remnants of the area's lurid past during Prohibition. Montara is a small village 25 miles south of San Francisco and 8 miles north of historic Half Moon Bay. It's a convenient headquarters for excursions to Silicon Valley or Berkeley to the east, Monterey Aquarium and Carmel to the south, and San Francisco and Muir Woods and Sausalito to the north. Hosts Raymond and Emily Hoche-Mong are pilots and have traveled the world. Living in Nashville, Key West, Beirut and Cairo has acquainted them with the customs and cuisines of those places famous for food and hospitality. Their personal art and artifact collections enliven the guest and common rooms. **Discounts:** 15% Mon-Thursday, AARP & ASU; 10% any stay of five nights **Airport:** San Francisco Intl-20 mins; Half Moon Bay-2mi (pick-up for GA pilots and Sailors at HMB and Pillar Point by prior arrangement **Seasonal:** No **Reservations:** Credit card guarantee or check for full amount; 72-hour cancellation policy **Brochure:** Yes **Permitted:** Drinking, children **Conference:** Yes, maximum 15 people for day events; reunions and meetings not requiring more than five bedrooms **Languages:** Nous parlons francais **Payment Terms:** Check AE/DISC/MC/V [I02HPCA1-6205] **COM YG ITC Member:** No **Quality Assured:** Yes

Rates: Pvt Bath 5
Single $ 85-110.00
Double $ 85-110.00

Babbling Brook Inn   Monterey CA
Helen King   Tel: 800-866-1131 408-427-2437 **Fax:** 408-427-2457
                                                    Res Times 7am-11pm

Refer to the same listing name under Santa Cruz, California for a complete description. **Seasonal:** No **Payment Terms:** Check AE/DC/DISC/MC/V [M10H-CCA1-4604] **COM YG ITC Member:** No

Rates: Pvt Bath 12
Single $ 85-150.00
Double $ 85-150.00

Monterey Hotel (1904)   406 Alvarado St 93940   Monterey CA
Vera Houston   Tel: 800-727-0960 408-375-3184
                                                    Res Times 24 Hrs

Established in 1904 and lovingly restored to its original elegance, The *Monterey Hotel* was reopened in 1987. Located in the center of downtown Monterey, only two blocks from Fisherman's Wharf, The Center and State Historic Park. It is surrounded by shops, restaurants and boutiques. All rooms are filled with custom period furnishings plus antique style beds with down comforters. The Master Suites offer jacuzzi-spa tubs, fireplaces and wet-bars. The four-story structure has the oldest operating elevator in the area. Mornings begin with a complimentary Continental breakfast buffet served in the lobby courtyard garden area. Freshly brewed coffee and teas, a variety of muffins, breads and pastries, cereals, seasonal fruits, plus the latest edition of the newspaper help start your day. Afternoon wine and

California National Edition

cheese is provided around the cozy fireplace in the lobby. Meals available. **Seasonal:** No **Reservations:** Deposit or credit card for one night's stay at res time, 72 hr cancel policy. Group and corporate rates available. **Brochure:** Yes **Permitted:** Children, non-smoking inn **Conference:** Yes, 900 sq ft total space with two conference rooms, suitable for 5 to 50 persons   **Payment Terms:** Check AE/DC/MC/V [Z11BPCA-6523] **COM** Y **ITC Member:** No

Rates: **Pvt Bath 44**
Single $ 95.00-up
Double $ 95.00-up

Mount Shasta Ranch B&B   1008 W A Barr Rd 96067   Mount Shasta CA
Bill & Mary Larsen   Tel: 916-926-3870 **Fax:** 916-926-6882

This Northern California, two-story ranch home offers affordable elegance in a historical setting. Built in 1923 by HD "Curley" Brown as a thoroughbred horse ranch, the original guest accommodations include the main house and several cottages and bungalows. Today, guests still enjoy the unique atmosphere and mood of those early years. The magnificent home has four spacious guestrooms, a separate carriage house with five bedrooms and a two-bedroom cottage. Guestrooms are furnished with antiques, queen size beds, most offer mountain views and the rooms in the main house offer enormous baths. Amenities include drinks, snacks, piano, game room with ping pong and pool table, a large hot spring spa and beautiful sunsets enjoyed on the outdoor veranda. A full complimentary breakfast begins your day - awakening to the aroma of imported coffee. Mount Shasta provides more than a spectacular backdrop for the *Mount Shasta Ranch* - there's downhill and cross country skiing, fishing, sailing, swimming, three golf courses, fish hatchery, museums and an enthusiastic climb of 14,162 feet to the top. **Discounts:** 7th night free **Airport:** Redding-60 mi; Sacramento-200 mi **Reservations:** Credit card number or one night's deposit, check-in 3-9pm or other time with prior arrangement, two night min holiday summer weekends and stays in the cottage **Brochure:** Yes **Permitted:** Children, limited drinking, limited smoking **Conference:** Yes, limited   **Payment Terms:** Check AE/MC/V [Z05HPCA1-6198] **COM** YG **ITC Member:** No

Rates: **Pvt Bath 4**   **Shared Bath 5**
Single $ 70.00 $ 55.00
Double $ 85.00 $ 65.00

Arbor Guest House   1436 G St 94559   Napa CA
Bruce & Rosemary Logan   Tel: 707-252-8144
 Res Times 7am-10pm

After an eventful day touring, shopping and exploring the Napa and/or Sonoma wine country, Arbor Guest House is an inviting setting in which to relax and unwind. Enjoy refreshments at a garden patio table or before the glowing embers of the fireplace and the peaceful hospitality will envelop you. Each of the five guest accommodations is uniquely designed with comfortable queen beds, charming period furnishings, and private baths with clawfoot tubs/showers and pedestal sinks. The lovingly restored 1906 home is centrally heated and cooled while the carriage house rooms are individually heated and cooled. Extra beds are available for two rooms for a party of four or those desiring separate beds. The Colonial transition home and carriage houses are attractively surrounded by a vine-covered arbor, a stately sequoia, rose bushes, fruit and walnut trees and flowering shrubs. The interior features the garden motif throughout the Inn with the wallpaper, window coverings, and a medley of antique furniture in brass, iron, oak, mahogany, wicker and etched glass. The full breakfast includes freshly-baked breads, two selections of scones, croissants, coffee cakes, banana bread or nut breads with fresh juice and choice of hot beverages. **Seasonal:** No **Reservations:** One night's deposit at res time, 72-hr cancel policy for refund, check-in 4-6pm **Brochure:** Yes **Conference:** Yes **Payment Terms:** Check MC/V [Z08GPCA-479] **COM** Y **ITC Member:** No

Rates: **Pvt Bath 5**
Single $ 80-110.00
Double $ 85-165.00

Blue Violet Mansion   443 Brown St 94559   Napa CA

4-48   ©*Inn & Travel Memphis, Tennessee*

National Edition *California*

Bob & Kathy Morris　　　　　　　　　　　　　　　　　　　　　　　　　　　　Tel: 800-799-2583 707-253-2583

The *Blue Violet Mansion* has been lovingly restored by your hosts over the past four years and offers guests a blend of country living and Victorian elegance in the historic district of Napa. This elegant 1886 Queen Anne home was built for Emanuel Manasse, an executive at the Sawyer Tannery who developed innovative leather tanning techniques which remain in the leather wainscotting adorning the main foyer. Awarded the Napa Country Landmark Award of Excellence for historic preservation, your innkeepers pride themselves on catering to the romantic at heart and their Inn was chosen by Bill Gleeson to be included in his book, 50 Most Romantic Places in Northern California, referring to the Blue Violet Mansion as the "... *Cabernet of Napa Valley Inns*". Guests may choose from rooms with names such as Queen Victoria, His Majesty, Garden Bower, Rose Room or The French Boudoir. All rooms are spacious, sun-filled, peaceful and include complete guest services, amenities, with fireplaces and jacuzzi spas in many rooms. Special amenities such as private candlelight champagne dinners served ensuite, massage packages including two tables and two massage professionals, gift baskets, wine and food trays, flowers, picnic baskets - or whatever would make your stay complete and perfect can be arranged ahead of arrival. Napa is situated at the top of San Francisco Bay and is the gateway to the Napa and Sonoma Valleys and the Carneros Wine Region. In addition to the wineries, there are hot springs (one of the world's three Old Faithful Geysers), a natural petrified forest, Lake Hennessey and Lake Berryessa and beautiful mountain ranges. When not sightseeing, guests relax in the Victorian parlors or outside in the garden gazebo, verandah or shaded deck. A full complimentary breakfast is included. This comfortable Victorian home awaits your arrival. **Airport:** San Francisco-65 mi; Oakland-50 mi **Packages:** Golf, Hot Air Ballooning, Massage **Seasonal:** No **Reservations:** Deposit required to guarantee reservations, 10 day cancel policy with 10% cancellation fee (less than 10 day cancel notice, refund only if rebooked), two day minimum stay **Brochure:** Yes **Permitted:** Children, drinking, limited smoking **Conference:** Small groups **Payment Terms:** Check AE/DC/MC/V [J07HPCA1-14355] **COM YG ITC Member:** No

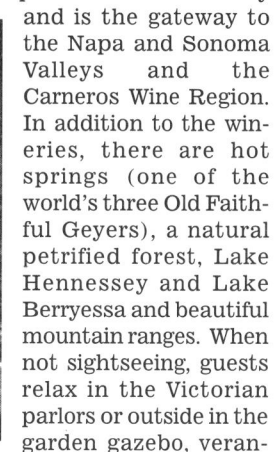

Rates:　　Pvt Bath　7
Single　　$ 125.00
Double　$ 195.00

Cedar Gables Inn　　　　　　　　486 Coombs St　94559　　　　　　　　　　　　　　Napa CA
Margaret & Craig Snasdell　　　　　　　　　　　Tel: 800-309-7969 707-224-7969 **Fax:** 707-224-4838

Located in *"Old Town Napa,"* Cedar Gables is a unique home with an exciting history. Built in 1892 as a wedding gift for Edward W Churchill, it was designed by English architect Ernest Coxhead and it is Old English in design. Fashioned after the days of Shakespeare, it is entirely different from any other residence in the state. Winding staircases lead to six beautifully appointed guest rooms furnished with antiques with modern amenities such as whirlpool tubs and fireplaces. Uniquely furnished, each guest room provides another experience. For example, Count Bonzi's Room is decorated in shades of green and is named after Count Bonzi who lived at *Cedar Gables* in the 1920s. This large room is Victorian in decor featuring an eight-foot high headboard queen size bed, sunny window seat area and a two-person whirlpool tub and shower. There is a large family room with a huge fireplace in this 10,000 square foot home, with a big screen TV, VCR and which serves nicely for those special occasions and meetings. Each evening, you may join other guests and

©*Inn & Travel Memphis, Tennessee*

California — National Edition

chat with Innkeepers Margaret and Craig Snasdell, as they welcome you with a spread of fruit, cheese and wine. A bountiful breakfast is served each morning in either the elegant dining room or the cheerful sunroom. Take that well-deserved vacation or long awaited romantic getaway. Come and enjoy the past and the present. From the old-time Cedar Gables to all the pleasures the renowned Napa Valley has to offer - your visit is sure to be memorable. **Airport:** SF, Oakland Sacra-mento -75 mins **Packages:** Napa Valley Wine Train, Hot Air Ballooning, Golf **Seasonal:** Yes, rates vary **Reservations:** One night deposit within 7 days, 7 day cancel policy for refund **Brochure:** Yes **Permitted:** Limited children, drinking **Conference:** Yes, for groups to twelve persons **Payment Terms:** AE/MC/V [I04HPCA1-9899] **COM** YG **ITC Member:** No

Rates:	Pvt Bath 6
Single	$ 99-159.00
Double	$ 99-159.00

Churchill Manor   485 Brown St 94559   **Napa CA**
Brian Jensen/Joanna Guidotti   Tel: 707-253-7733 **Fax:** 707-253-8836
Res Times 9am-9pm

Built in 1889 for local banker Edward Churchill, *Churchill Manor* is reputed to be the largest historic home built in Napa Valley. The magnificent three-story mansion has been placed on the *National Register of Historic Places*. Churchill Manor rests on an acre of beautifully landscaped grounds and is surrounded by a sweeping veranda supported by large white columns. Entering through the original lead glass doors, one discovers four grand parlors, each with an elegant fireplace, carved redwood ceiling, mouldings and columns, a gorgeous sunroom with an original marble-tiled floor, and one guestroom. On the upper floors are nine more guest bedrooms, each with a private bathroom, several with fireplaces, one with jacuzzi spas and each decorated with an individual theme. The entire home is furnished with lovely antiques, oriental rugs, brass and crystal chandeliers and a grand piano in the music room. Guests at the Manor enjoy coffee and tea along with fresh-baked cookies every afternoon, evening varietal wines with cheese and crackers, a full gourmet breakfast including omelettes and french toast, complimentary tandem bicycles for viewing Old Town Napa and nearby wineries, and croquet on the expansive lawns. **Airport:** San Francisco-1 hr **Packages:** Wine Train, Balloon Rides **Seasonal:** No **Reservations:** Deposit required, 5 day cancel policy for refund; call if arriving late. Saturday nights require a two-night booking. **Permitted:** Children 12-up, limited drinking, limited smoking **Conference:** Groups to 50 during daytime periods, evening groups only if reserving all 10 guest rooms. **Languages:** Spanish **Payment Terms:** Check AE/DISC/MC/V [I05GP-CA1-482] **COM** Y **ITC Member:** No

Rates:	Pvt Bath 10
Single	$ 75-145.00
Double	$ 145.00

Coombs/Inn The Park B&B   720 Seminary St 94559   **Napa CA**
Tel: 707-257-0789
Res Times 9am-6pm

One of the oldest and most beautiful residences in Napa Valley is this two-story Victorian home built in 1852, it is completely restored and elegantly furnished with beautiful European and American antiques. Located in the lovely town of Napa and across the street from a small neighborhood park, guests can enjoy strolling the peaceful and tranquil setting or relaxing in the parlor while enjoying complimentary refreshments in front of a cozy fire. Guest rooms are furnished in various themes and include down comforters and pillows and luxurious terry robes and bath sheets. Continental breakfast is included and offers special house-blend coffees, croissants, homemade muffins and nutbread, juices, and seasonal fruits. You can relax in the pool, jacuzzi, or use one of the complimentary bikes for a leisure trip around town. The charming hosts will help arrange hot air balloon rides, champagne gourmet picnics, glider rides, mud baths or if you need help in choosing from all the excellent dining spots, you just need to ask. Menus of local restaurants, winery and local events information are available.

Seasonal: No **Reservations:** One night's deposit at res time to hold room, 48 hour cancel notice for full refund **Brochure:** Yes **Permitted:** Drinking **Payment Terms:** Check MC/V [A09APCA-489] **COM** Y **ITC Member:** No

Rates:	Pvt Bath 1	Shared Bath 3
Single	$ 110.00	$ 85-95.00
Double	$ 110.00	$ 85-95.00

Elm House   800 California Blvd 94559   Napa CA
David & Betsy McCracken   **Tel:** 800-788-4356 707-255-1831
Res Times 7:30am-10pm

The Elm House, Napa Valley's most gracious new Inn, invites you to your home away from home. We wish to share the charm of The Valley with you by providing courteous and knowledgeable service. Sheltered by three magnificent historic elms, The *Elm House* is located at the gateway to the world-famous Napa Valley wine region. Our comfortable living room with its elegant furnishings and large Italian marble fireplace, provides and engaging setting for conversation, reading or relaxation. In the adjoining courtyard, a spa and fountain invites guests to enjoy its soothing waters. Each morning guests are served a complimentary expanded continental breakfast of coffee, tea, fresh fruit, juices and assorted pastries and muffins. Modern construction provides sixteen sound-insulated guest rooms decorated in pine and attractive fabrics. The guest rooms have queen size beds, private baths, separate dressing vanities, individual temperature controls, remote TV, radios, phones and stocked refrigerators. Several rooms offer Italian marble fireplaces. For that special celebration, reserve our largest room with high ceilings, fireplace and chandelier. Our staff is experienced in anticipating your every need, including the need for privacy. We are able to assist with restaurant reservations, winery tours, balloon rides, wine train packages and golf at some of Wine Country's most beautiful courses. About an hour's drive from San Francisco, *The Elm House* is an elegant and ideal departure point to Napa Valley's numerous wineries and to historic Napa. **Airport:** 1-1/2 hrs to San Francisco **Discounts:** Business, some midweeks, inquire when calling **Reservations:** One night's deposit to guarantee, 72 hr cancel policy for refund **Brochure:** Yes **Permitted:** Children, drinking, limited smoking **Conference:** Conference room for groups to twenty **Languages:** English **Payment Terms:** Check AE/MC/V [R01IPCA1-26892] **COM** YG **ITC Member:** No

Rates:	Pvt Bath 16
Single	$ 79-130.00
Double	$ 79-130.00

Napa Inn   1137 Warren St 94559   Napa CA
Dennis & Ann Mahoney   **Tel:** 800-435-1444 707-257-1444
Res Times 6am-9pm

The *Napa Inn* is a beautiful three-story Queen Anne Victorian built in 1899 and is located on a quiet residential street in the old historical section of Napa. The Inn has been recently redecorated in keeping with the Victorian Era including primarily Victorian furnishings, phonographs, books, musical instruments, china, and much more! A perfect Victorian hideaway! Complimentary afternoon refreshments are served in a large parlor and a full breakfast is served each morning in the formal dining room. Guest rooms are located on the second floor, each with a private bath, fireplace, queen-size bed and a sitting area. The entire third floor is devoted to one large suite which includes a king-size bed, private bath and a private balcony. The town of Napa is in the south end of Napa Valley, home to over 200 wineries. In-addition, guests can experience hot air ballooning, glider plane rides, lakes, bik-

California *National Edition*

ing, hiking, horse back riding, excellent restaurants, Napa Valley Wine Train and many historical landmarks. **Airport:** San Francisco-60mi, Sacramento-50mi, Oakland-50mi **Seasonal:** Clo: Christmas **Reservations:** Credit card number for authorization. Special arrangements made for late check-ins. **Brochure:** Yes **Permitted:** Drinking **Payment Terms:** Check AE/DC/DISC-/MC/V [I03HPCA1-492] **COM YG ITC Member:** No **Quality Assurance** Requested

Rates:	Pvt Bath 6
Single	$ 120-170.00
Double	$ 120-170.00

Oleander House		Napa CA
John & Louise Packard		Tel: 800-788-3057 707-944-8315

Refer to the same listing name under Yountville, California for a complete description. **Seasonal:** No **Payment Terms:** Check MC/V [M05FCCA-8757] **COM** Y **ITC Member:** No

Rates:	Pvt Bath 5
Single	$ 115-150.00
Double	$ 115-150.00

Grandmeres Inn	449 Broad St 95959	Nevada City CA
Doug & Geri Boka		Tel: 916-265-4660

Traditional French Country architecture residence is nestled in perfect setting in center Nevada City. National Register of Historic Places listing, relax in comfort and experience the ambience of turn-of-the-century France. Perfect place for social or business affairs. Hosts prepare gourmet breakfast for guests daily and served in the country kitchen or outdoors in the garden/patio area. **Seasonal:** No **Brochure:** Yes **Permitted:** Children **Conference:** Dinner/catering by arrangement with space for seating 12-15 at dining and conferences **Payment Terms:** Check MC/V [C11ACCA-502] **COM** Y **ITC Member:** No

Rates:	Pvt Bath 6
Single	$ 90.00-up
Double	$ 120.00-up

Red Castle Inn, Historic B&B	109 Prospect St 95959	Nevada City CA
Conley & Mary Louise Weaver		Tel: 916-265-5135
		Res Times 9am-9pm

High on a forested hillside where breezes linger on wide verandas, strains of Mozart echo through lofty hallways, chandeliers sparkle, the aura of another time prevails. Overlooking the *"Queen City"* of the Gold Country since before the Civil War, this imposing 1867 Gothic Revival Inn has welcomed travelers since 1964. *"Gourmet Magazine"* writes *"The Red Castle Inn would top my list of places to stay. Nothing else quite compares with it."* Every guest room is memorable in the four-story mansion located within the historic district steps away from antique shops, fine dining, dancing, performing arts, museums, art galleries, carriage rides, tennis courts and picnic areas. The landmark "Icicle" draped brick Inn is surrounded by terraced gardens and furnished comfortably in antiques. White-water rafting, swimming, hiking, fishing in lakes and rivers, alpine and nordic skiing, golfing and gold panning are nearby. The bountiful buffet breakfast and sumptuous afternoon tea receives rave reviews from every guest. *Sunset Magazine* writes *"attention to detail in this charming hostelry keeps rooms booked well in advance."* 8% tax applicable to room rate. **Seasonal:** No **Reservations:** One nite's deposit within 10 days of res or credit card plus 5% for deposit; two night min on Sat nights (4/1-12/31) with 7 day cancel policy and 21 days for holidays or multiple rooms for full refund. **Brochure:** Yes **Permitted:** Drinking, limited children **Conference:** Yes up to 10 for informal business or social meetings. **Payment Terms:** Check MC/V [Z11CPCA-6833] **COM** Y **ITC Member:** No

Rates:	Pvt Bath 6	Shared Bath 2
Single	$ 80-105.00	$ 65.00
Double	$ 85-110.00	$ 70.00

National Edition   *California*

Dahl House	2025 E Ocean Blvd 92661	Newport Beach CA
Ron & Anne Dahl		**Tel:** 714-673-3479
		Res Times 8am-10pm

Situated near the tip of the Balboa Peninsula in Newport Beach, the *Dahl House* is forty miles south of Los Angeles Airport and ten miles from the Orange County Airport and is perfectly located for beach and bay activities along California's "Gold Coast". This charming home creates a cozy, intimate atmosphere with stained-glass, used brick, natural wood, and a raised-hearth fireplace. The downstairs Brass Bedroom is filled with antiques and has a recently-renovated bathroom. The upstairs Loft Bedroom has access to a large sun deck and upper "Crows Nest" for spectacular ocean, beach, and city views. Disneyland and other local theme parks are only minutes away, as are first-class shopping malls at South Coast Plaza and Fashion Island. Daily ferry service runs from Balboa to Catalina Island. Beach chair and bicycles are provided and complimentary beverages, hors d'oeuvres and a delicious full breakfast are served. With only two guest rooms, guests may be assured of complete privacy and full personal attention to their needs. Business people and tourists alike will enjoy this relaxing location in this nearly crime-free residential neighborhood. Every effort will be made so their stay in Southern California will be an enjoyable and memorable one. **Airport:** LAX-40 mi; Orange County-10 mi **Packages:** Inquire at reservation time **Seasonal:** No **Reservations:** 50% deposit of length of stay, 14 day cancel policy for full refund **Brochure:** No **Permitted:** Children 6-up, drinking **Payment Terms:** Check [Z04HPCA1-193] **COM** YG **ITC Member:** No **Quality Assurance:** Requested

Rates: **Pvt Bath** 2
Single $ 50-75.00
Double $ 50-75.00

Feather Bed Raidroad Co	2870 Lakeshore Blvd 95864	Nice CA
		Tel: 707-274-4434

Nine cabooses from the Santa Fe and SP Railroad on five acres offer a theme vacation trip with bunk "feather beds", TV, swimming pool, jacuzzi and all on a lake front setting. **Seasonal:** No [X02CXCA-10036] **COM** U **ITC Member:** No

Rates: **Pvt Bath** 9
Single $ 92-142.00
Double $ 92-142.00

Boat & Breakfast USA	40 Jack London Square 94607	Oakland CA
Rob Harris/Andrew Roettger		**Tel:** 510-444-5858 415-291-8411
		Res Times 10am-6pm

Spend the night on a yacht! We've arranged for a select few private yachts to be available dockside for overnight guests. Take your choice! Choose from luxury power and sailing yachts ranging in length from 35' to 75' - all perfect for a Special Evening! All of the yachts are comfortably furnished with a main salon, separate sleeping quarters, head with shower, a galley with refrigerator, coffee maker and other appliances. A continental breakfast is included in the rate. Each yacht has is own unique amenities and include TV and stereo sound systems. To further enhance your stay, we can arrange private charters on the Bay, catered dinners, massage, limo service and more. *Boat & Breakfast USA* accommodations in San Francisco and San Diego as well. **Seasonal:** No **Reservations:** 50% deposit upon booking, discounts for 3 nights and longer. Best check-in 2-6pm. $25 added charge for more than two guests. **Brochure:** Yes **Permitted:** Children, drinking **Conference:** Yes on the larger yachts. **Languages:** English and Hebrew **Payment Terms:** Check AE/MC/V [R04DPCA-11617] **COM** Y **ITC Member:** No

Rates: **Pvt Bath** 22
Single $ 95-250.00
Double $ 95-250.00

Bear Valley Inn	88 Bear Valley Rd 94950	Olema CA
Jo Ann & Ron Nowell		**Tel:** 415-663-1777

©*Inn & Travel Memphis, Tennessee*

California

c1899 classic Victorian farmhouse still retains its character and is furnished with period decor and family heirlooms. Each room is furnished with period pieces and include either queen or king-size beds. Point Reyes National Park and Seashore offers visitors a spectacular year round treat of nature's artistry. Full country breakfast included.

Seasonal: No **Brochure:** Yes **Payment Terms:** Check [C11ACCA-519] **COM** Y **ITC Member:** No

Rates:	Pvt Bath 3
Single	$ 70.00
Double	$ 85.00

Centrella B&B Inn — 612 Central Ave 93950 — Pacific Grove CA
Maureen Diaz
Tel: 800-233-3372 408-372-3372 **Fax:** 408-372-2036
Res Times 7am-11pm

This 19th century Victorian received the Gold Key Award, an international award for design excellence for poetically combining the old with the new. You find large open parlor rooms, lofty corridors, arched beams surrounding the attic suites - all combined with touches of Laura Ashley decor of contrasting colors of banana yellow, canary blue and rose-colored interiors. Nostalgic touches include clawfoot tubs with brass fixtures in some rooms, bedside candles, large beveled-glass windows along the north side of the Inn's parlor with an evening fire dancing across the glass. Evening relaxation brings complimentary hors d'oeuvres, sherry, wine or tea. Beautiful gardens of camellia and gardenia beds aflame in brilliant color and brick walkways surround the main house and lead to the Inn's private cottage suites. Pacific Grove is home to the Monarch butterflies that flock in droves each November only to depart during February and March - a sight travelers should experience. Monterey Peninsula provides breath-taking views while California sea otters play in the kelp beds just off shore - except for the occasional cracking sound of an abalone shell being opened for lunch. There's Fisherman's Wharf, Cannery Row and historic abodes and shops to visit along the wharf. A full sumptuous breakfast of fresh California fruit and pastries, fresh ground coffee and perhaps a waffle or egg entree is prepared to perfection. **Discounts:** Off-season and weekdays **Packages:** Romance, includes champagne and dinner **Seasonal:** No **Reservations:** One night's deposit required; 2 night min on weekends and special holidays. **Brochure:** Yes **Permitted:** Limited children, drinking **Conference:** Small groups to ten persons for meetings; up to thirty five persons for weddings. **Languages:** Spanish, Italian, Portuguese **Payment Terms:** Check AE/MC/V [Z08GPCA-527] **COM** U **ITC Member:** No

Rates:	Pvt Bath 24	Shared Bath 2
Single	$ 125-185.00	$ 90.00
Double	$ 125-185.00	$ 90.00

Gatehouse Inn — 225 Central Ave 93950 — Pacific Grove CA
Doug & Kristi Aslin
Tel: 800-753-1881 408-649-1881 **Fax:** 408-375-2539
Res Times 8am-10pm

A light and airy Victorian home of Senator Benjamin F Langford was constructed in 1884 as a vacation home for his family. Situated in the quaint town of Pacific Grove, it is within easy walking distance of John Steinbeck's Cannery Row, home of Monterey Bay Aquarium and Fisherman's Wharf. With stunning views of the beautiful bay, this lovely Victorian has been fully restored to capture the essence of warmth of a graceful bygone era. The eight unique guest rooms are furnished with Victorian and 20th Century antiques and touches of Art Deco. There are fireplaces, private baths with claw-foot tubs, Queen-size beds with down comforters - no guest comforts have been overlooked here! This residence greets you with the warmth and hospitality of the turn-of-the-century, complete with an expanded continental breakfast to be enjoyed before a roaring fire with the other guests or else in the privacy of your room. Tea, sherry and hors d'oeuvres are served in the afternoon. Local sights and activities abound with famous museums, three world-renowned golf courses at Pebble Beach, elegant dining in numerous restaurants and in January, the annual migration of the Grey Whale can be watched with stunning views from the breakfast table. **Seasonal:** No **Reservations:** One night deposit, cancel notice of 7 days prior to reservation date, except on holidays or for multiple rooms, when 20 day cancel notice is required, $10 service fee for cancellations. **Brochure:** Yes **Permitted:** Drinking, limited children, limited smoking **Conference:** Yes **Payment Terms:** Check AE/MC/V [R02CPCA-9948] **COM** Y **ITC Member:** No

Rates: Pvt Bath 8
Single $ 95-145.00
Double $ 95-145.00

Gosby House Inn 643 Lighthouse Ave 93950 Pacific Grove CA
*Suzanne Russo Tel: 408-375-1287 Fax: 408-655-9621
Res Times 7am-11pm

This classic Victorian Inn was built in 1887 with additions over the following years to accommodate seasonal visitors to Pacific Grove. Listed on the *National Historic Register*, this Inn is featured in Pacific Grove's annual Victorian Home Tour each spring. A two-story wooden structure, the unique rounded tower/entrance porch and large bay windows provide a special character. The common rooms are furnished with period antiques, floral print wallpaper, comfortable English style seating with a wood-burning fireplace in the beautiful parlor. The guest rooms are inspired by the comfort and luxury of fine European Country inns. There are soft-colored wallpapers and wall-to-wall carpeting, off-white heirloom spreads, ruffled curtains, lace pillows, quilts, fresh fruit, plenty of green plantings and antique beds and furniture. Twelve guest rooms include fireplaces with small kitchens available in some. An old-fashioned garden including a winding brick path is a peaceful retreat for enjoying your full complimentary breakfast or just relaxing or talking over a cup of coffee. Breakfast in bed is available upon request. Welcoming guests for over a century, *The Gosby House* is one of nature's magnificent meetings of land and sea-the Monterey Peninsula. Treat yourself to a visit soon. **Airport:** Monterey-20 mins **Packages:** Dining Package through 3-92, includes one night's stay and dinner, shared or private bath $125.00, fireplace room $140.00 **Seasonal:** No **Reservations:** Credit card to guarantee room, 48 hr cancel policy. Less than 48 hr cancel notice, refund only if room is re-rented. **Brochure:** Yes **Permitted:** Children, drinking, limited smoking **Conference:** Yes, business and social meetings for groups to 20, including dining. **Payment Terms:** Check AE/MC/V [Z01EPCA-528] **COM** Y **ITC Member:** No

Rates:	Pvt Bath 20	Shared Bath 5
Single	$ 85-130.00	$ 100-105.00
Double	$ 85-130.00	$ 100-105.00

Green Gables Inn 104 5th St 93950 Pacific Grove CA
Kim Post Waston Tel: 800-722-1774 408-375-2095
Res Times 7am-11pm

A stately c1888 Victorian built by William Lucy which has been offering accommodations as a bed & breakfast since 1958. This two-story Queen Anne Victorian mansion and carriage house is painted white with green trim and offers a spectacular view of Monterey Bay. The Inn is listed on the *National Historic Register*. Features inside include high ceilings, large bay window alcoves facing the sea, a unique fireplace framed with stained-glass panels. All the rooms are furnished with antiques and heirlooms reminiscent of the Victorian period. The guest rooms are varied in decor and include soft pastel colors, garden-fresh flowers in each room, fresh fruit, cozy quilts for chilly evenings, bathrobes, large towels and a basket of amenities. Fireplaces are available in some rooms. A full complimentary breakfast buffet with afternoon wine and hors d'oeuvres are included. Nearby is a great shore line for jogging and strolling, a public beach that's perfect for scuba diving and picnicking. Within a short walk is Cannery Row with a myriad of shops, restaurants and the Monterey Bay Aquarium. Experience romance, elegance and comfort in this ultimate Bed and Breakfast Inn while visiting Pacific Grove. **Seasonal:** No **Reservations:** One night's deposit at res time. 48 Hr cancel policy for refund; less than 48 hrs, refund only if room is re-rented. **Brochure:** Yes **Permitted:** Children **Conference:** Yes for small groups for business and social events. **Payment Terms:** Check AE/MC/V [C09BCCA-529] **COM** Y **ITC Member:** No

Rates:	Pvt Bath 7	Shared Bath 4
Single	$ 120-180.00	$ 110-170.00
Double	$ 120-180.00	$ 110-170.00

Maison Bleue Inn PO Box 51371 93950 Pacific Grove CA

California *National Edition*

Jeanne E Coles

Tel: 408-373-2993 408-373-1358

A lovely and romantic Country French *"Home away from Home"* completely restored to reflect the grace and hospitality of a stay in the French countryside and the finest of its kind on the beautiful Monterey Peninsula. Each room is individually furnished with Country French antiques and has its own unique flavor including queen and king canopied beds. A lavish full breakfast is served in the "Morning Room" or in bed if you like and includes fresh fruits, continental beverages and a gourmet entree to start your day. You're just minutes from world-renowned diving locations (picture perfect picnic spots too), Steinbeck's Cannery Row, the fabulous Monterey Bay Aquarium, beaches, world famous golf courses, shore-side recreation trails, theaters, seafood restaurants and plenty of shopping.. all minutes away and within walking distance. This quaint inn is listed on the *"Heritage Society Register"* and is shown on the *"Victorian Home Tour"* and *"Christmas At The Inns"* during the year. Located between Carmel and Monterey, you'll be able to enjoy the *"Home of the Monarch Butterfly"* year-round. **Seasonal:** No **Reservations:** Full payment within 7 days, 7-day cancel policy (10 days on holidays and special events) for full refund, check in 2-6:00pm, checkout 11am, late cancel and no show charge one night's lodging plus 10%. **Brochure:** Yes **Permitted:** Limited children, limited smoking, limited drinking **Conference:** Yes for groups to 10 persons. **Payment Terms:** Check AE/DC/MC/V [A09APCA-530] **COM Y ITC Member:** No

Rates:	Pvt Bath 1	Shared Bath 2
Single	$ 125.00	$ 100.00
Double	$ 125.00	$ 110.00

Martine Inn 255 Oceanview Blvd 93950 **Pacific Grove CA**
Marion & Don Martine **Tel:** 800-852-5588 408-373-3388 **Fax:** 408-373-3896
Res Times 8am-9:30pm

"One of America's top twelve B&Bs" Country Inns, Feb 1992, indicates what guests experience in this 12,000 square feet gracious mansion resting high atop the cliffs of Pacific Grove - overlooking the rocky coastline of Monterey Bay. Your hosts have prepared an experience not to be missed, beginning with guest rooms furnished with authentic museum quality antiques (including an incredible Mahogany suite from the Malaren Estates that was exhibited in the 1893 Chicago Worlds Fair), private bath, a fresh rose, a silver Victorian bridal basket filled with fresh fruit and spectacular views of the waves crashing against the rocks and/or a wood-burning fireplace (wood included). Evening brings hors d'oeuvres in the parlor while enjoying the 1923 Knabe Reproducing Baby Grand and camaraderie of new friends. Within four blocks, you'll find the Monterey Bay Aquarium and Cannery Row. A seven mile recreational trail offers walking, jogging or biking along the scenic coastline while within a five minute drive, you'll reach 17 Mile Drive, Carmel and Pebble Beach. Day trips will take you to Monterey Wine Country, Big Sur and Hearst Castle. Each eventful day can finish with a relaxing bath or soaking in the clawfoot tub. Special requests for wine or chilled champagne, gifts or flowers, homemade picnic lunches and reservations are graciously provided. **Airport:** Mont-erey-10 mi. **Packages:** Yes, inquire at res time **Seasonal:** No **Reservations:** Deposit in full, in advance; 72 hr cancellation policy; prior arrangements preferred to late arrivals. **Brochure:** Yes **Permitted:** Children, drinking, limited smoking **Languages:** AT&T language line. **Payment Terms:** Check AE/MC/V [I11EPCA-531] **COM Y ITC Member:** No

Rates:	Pvt Bath 19
Single	$ 115-225.00
Double	$ 115-225.00

Seven Gables Inn 555 Oceanview Blvd 93950 **Pacific Grove CA**
Susan Flatley **Tel:** 408-372-4341 408-375-6641

4-56 ©*Inn & Travel Memphis, Tennessee*

"Lavish and Opulent" can only describe the details of this Victorian Gem nestled at the ocean's edge, dressed in the finest exterior Victorian yellow and sparkling white trim! There are spectacular views of the ocean and coastal mountains from every guest room; guests are lulled to sleep by the romantic surf outside. Museum-quality antiques and furnishings gives everyone an opportunity to live like a **Queen For One Day.** Outside you'll find a gorgeous profusion of flowers year-round, while inside you'll be treated to complimentary English-style *"high tea and delicious homemade treats and imported cakes"*. Just outside of your doorway, you'll find a world-renowned ocean drive (17 miles) to Pebble Beach and Carmel. **Reservations:** Full payment upon reservation; 7-day cancellation policy for refund. **Brochure:** Yes **Languages:** Spanish, French, Arabic **Payment Terms:** Check [X02BCCA-534] **COM** Y **ITC Member:** No

Rates:	Pvt Bath 14
Single	$ 95-155.00
Double	$ 95-155.00

Casa Cody	175 S Cahuilla 92262	**Palm Springs CA**
Frank Tysen/Therese Hayes	Tel: 800-231-CODY 619-320-9346 **Fax:** 619-325-8610	

This romantic, historic hideaway was founded by Buffalo Bill's niece, Harriet Cody in the 1920s. Nestled against the spectacular San Jacinto Mountains in the heart of Palm Springs Village, the Inn was recently restored in a Santa Fe motif with Saltillo tile floors, Southwestern pine furnishings and handwoven Dhurri rugs. *Casa Cody* consists of three single-story buildings featuring seventeen rooms, studios and one and two bedroom suites with private patios, fireplaces and kitchens. There are two heated pools and a secluded, tree-shaded whirlpool spa. *Casa Cody* has been highlighted in numerous travel articles. A delightful continental breakfast is served daily. If you're seeking relaxation, you've picked the right place. *Casa Cody* is a friendly, quiet hotel - fondly reminiscent of the original Palm Springs. **Discounts:** Weekdays and summer **Airport:** Palm Springs-3 mi **Seasonal:** Rates vary **Reservations:** Credit card number or deposit required, 72 Hr cancellation notice for stays of less than 3 days, longer stays require 7 days notice for refund, summer rates $45-105.00 **Brochure:** Yes **Permitted:** Well-behaved children, pets, drinking, smoking **Conference:** Yes, for small weddings and groups **Languages:** French, Dutch **Payment Terms:** Check AE/MC/V [K04GPCA-9924] **COM** Y **ITC Member:** No

Rates:	Pvt Bath 17
Single	$ 65-160.00
Double	$ 65-160.00

Villa Royale	1620 Indian Trail 92264	**Palm Springs CA**
Bob Lee	Tel: 800-245-2314 619-327-2314 **Fax:** 619-322-3794	
		Res Times 8am-11pm

An international Country Inn on a 3-1/2 acre tropical setting in beautiful Palm Springs offers guests an experience they won't forget. All thirty-three rooms are individually decorated with treasures from around the world creating an "old world charm" and ambience. The resort is a series of interior courtyards framed with statuesque pillars, cascading bougainvillea and hovering shade trees with pots of flowers and asymmetrical gardens with a musical fountain courtyard where classical music can frequently be overheard. Guests can relax around the pool/patio area or visit the wonderful Palm Canyon shops and night life. There are bikes for guests to use along with picnic lunches for a day's outing. A continental breakfast is served in the poolside dining room. **Airport:** Palm Springs-5 mi **Seasonal:** No **Reservations:** One night deposit with 10 day cancel policy for refund **Brochure:** Yes **Permitted:** Limited children, drinking, smoking **Lan-**

California *National Edition*

guages: Spanish **Payment Terms:** Check AE/DISC/DC/MC/V [Z08HPCA1-537] **COM YG ITC Member:** No

Rates: **Pvt Bath 33**
Single $ 75-295.00
Double $ 75-295.00

Victorian On Lytton   555 Lytton Ave 94301   Palo Alto CA
Susan & Maxwell Hall   **Tel:** 415-322-8555 **Fax:** 415-322-7141
                                                                    Res Times 7am-closing

This lovely Victorian home c1895 was the first B&B in Palo Alto and has been completely renovated in what Architectural Digest comments of *"Understated Elegance."* Each suite has been tastefully decorated with the charm and quietness of yesteryear and offers sitting parlors, private bath, and canopy or poster king, queen and twin beds. Just refresh yourself in the charming English Garden area outside. Continental breakfast is even served in your room each morning too! Close to center Palo Alto with all fine restaurants, cafes, theaters, and shops within walking distance. Enjoy that special occasion or business trip here! **Seasonal:** No **Reservations:** Credit card to hold a room, 10% cancellation charge with 10 day minimum notice. T/A commissions on selected rates; leave voice mail message if innkeeper is out **Brochure:** Yes **Payment Terms:** Check AE/MC/V [K06HPCA1-538] **COM Y ITC Member:** No

Rates: **Pvt Bath 10**
Single $ 112.00-up
Double $ 112.00-up

Inn At Playa del Rey   425 Culver Blvd 90293   Playa del Rey CA
Susan Zolla   **Tel:** 310-574-1920 **Fax:** 310-574-9920
                                                                    Res Times 7am-9pm

The *Inn At Playa del Rey* is an all new luxury Bed and Breakfast Inn located a few blocks from the beach and overlooking the main boat channel of Marina del Rey. Situated on several hundred acres of national bird preserve, the Inn offers peace, solitude, and magnificent views of the sailboats, the mountains and the birds. The rooms are just as magnificent with fireplaces, four poster beds, porches and jacuzzi tubs. Two rooms have a fireplace in the bathroom. A full breakfast and afternoon wine and cheese are included in the room rates as is the use of bicycles for exploring the 30 mile ocean side bike path. The village of Playa de Rey - beside offering some of the finest beaches in Los Angeles, also offers a variety of restaurants, shops, nature walks, fishing and boating. Los Angeles International Airport is just four minutes away, making the *Inn At Playa del Rey* the only airport area hotel in Los Angeles that is walking distance to the beach. Finally, the *Inn at Playa del Rey* is most proud of its staff. Their ability to serve their guests efficiently, gracefully and with full knowledge of the area is the best feature of the Inn. **Airport:** LAX-4 mi **Seasonal:** No **Reservations:** Deposit required, 72 hr cancellation policy for refund **Brochure:** Yes **Permitted:** Children, drinking, limited smoking **Conference:** Yes **Languages:** Spanish, French **Payment Terms:** Check AE/MC/V [I08HPCA1-22332] **COM YG ITC Member:** No

Rates: **Pvt Bath 22**
Single $ 85-200.00
Double $ 85-200.00

INN AT PLAYA DEL REY

Carriage House	325 Mesa Rd 94956	**Point Reyes Station CA**
Felicity Kirsch		**Tel:** 415-663-8627
		Res Times 7am-10pm

The *Carriage House Bed & Breakfast Inn* is in coastal Marin, adjacent to Point Reyes National Seashore and Tomales Bay State Park; one hour north of San Francisco and one hour south of the Wine Country. Built in the 1920's, it has recently been remodeled into two spacious suites that are furnished with lovely antiques and folk art. Each suite has a comfortable queen size bed, living room with fireplace, full bath and complete kitchen. Quiet, privacy and warm hospitality abide here and a warm breakfast is brought to your suite. Wonderful old trees, flowers, beautiful sunrises and sunsets along with views of the countryside, soothe your senses. From this serene setting you can hike to Tomales Bay or to local village restaurants, galleries and shops. There are more than 100 miles of riding, hiking and bicycling trails in the Seashore Park as well as an 18 hole golf course nearby. Whales migrate along the miles of beaches during the winter - while wildflowers bloom profusely in the spring. This comfortable Bed & Breakfast is ideal for a private retreat, a romantic getaway or a vacation with family and friends. It can accommodate 10 comfortably. Childcare is available with prior notice. **Discounts:** Yes, mid-week from Sept thru April **Seasonal:** No **Reservations:** 50% deposit required. *Two suites are available and include BR, LR, kitchen, wet bar **Brochure:** Yes **Permitted:** Smoking outside **Payment Terms:** Check [Z06GPCA-14357] COM Y **ITC Member:** No

Rates: Pvt Bath 2
Single $ 110.00
Double $ 120.00

Ferrandos Hideway	12010 Hwy 1 94956	**Point Reyes Station CA**
Greg & Doris Ferrando		**Tel:** 415-663-1966

A lovely contemporary-style home built in 1972 by your hosts offers two guest rooms along with a separate Cottage offering complete privacy. Great attention to detail in building and decorating brings a warm and harmonious atmosphere throughout the main house. The guest rooms are comfortably equipped with private baths and king size beds for luxurious resting. Rooms have a separate entrance and patio for privacy. There is a cozy sitting room which is shared by all guests who care to gather and warm up around the wood stove each evening. The Cottage is separated from the main house by a hot tub and a spacious vegetable garden and includes a fully equipped kitchen where guests can prepare breakfast at their leisure. Your hosts have thoughtfully filled the fridge with eggs fresh from their chickens, homemade bread, muffins, fresh fruit, cheese or yogurt, jam, coffee, herb teas and juice. Guests staying in the Cottage retire in a king size bed located in the loft and can relax on the sunny deck outdoors offering beautiful views of the rolling hills of West Marin. A full bath, wood stove and stereo insure a relaxful stay. A plentiful continental breakfast is served in the sunny breakfast room for guests staying in the main house. Guests are assured of complete relaxation by enjoying the hot tub along with taking advantage of a certified massage therapist who is available by appointment. Close to Point Reyes National Seashore, there's plenty of outdoor activities such as hiking, biking, birding, horseback riding, whale watching and miles of beautiful sand beaches. Sights include Tide Pools at Agate Beach, Tule Elk at Pierce Pt Ranch, enjoying oysters at the Johnson Oyster Company, Audubon Canyon Ranch featuring unique egret and herons, Rouge et Noir (French cheese factory) and various galleries in Point Reyes and Inverness. **Airport:** San Francisco Intl **Seasonal:** No **Reservations:** Deposit required prior to arrival, 7 day cancel policy for refund less $15 service charge per night cancelled. Less than 7 days, refund less service fee only if rebooked, two night weekends **Brochure:** Yes **Permitted:** Children **Conference:** Yes, for groups to six **Languages:** German   **Payment Terms:** Check [K04GPCA-15684] COM U **ITC Member:** No

Rates: Pvt Bath 3
Single $ 105.00
Double $ 120.00

California *National Edition*

Jasmine Cottage — 11561 Coast Rt #1 94956 — **Point Reyes Station CA**
Karen Gray
Tel: 415-663-1166
Res Times 8am-9pm

The secluded privacy of these country cottages is the ideal arrangement in a B&B: all amenities of a bed and breakfast with the seclusion of a vacation home. Set in its own charming garden behind the owner's schoolhouse home, Jasmine Cottage is a complete home-away-from-home with a fully equipped kitchen, woodstove, garden room, naturalist's library, oak desk, queen beds, two twin beds, a romantic alcove, and beautiful views of sunsets. Only one hour north of San Francisco, one hour to Wine Country and just 5 minutes from the magnificent Point Reyes National Seashore on the California Coast! Last year's guests included four business executives on a weekend retreat, a caterer who wrote a cookbook, honeymooners starting an annual tradition, and dozens of families, who made the cottage their base exploring the national park. A secluded hot tub is set in the garden for relaxation. A full breakfast is included. Weekly rate of $650.00 plus tax. Can sleep 10 persons between both cottages. **Airport:** San Francisco-40 mi **Seasonal:** No **Reservations:** 50% deposit at reservation time, bal upon arrival, 7 day cancel policy for refund. **Permitted:** Children, drinking, limited pets, limited smoking (on patio) (Inquire about pet restrictions) **Payment Terms:** Check [Z06FPCA-2917] **COM** Y **ITC Member:** No

Rates:	Pvt Bath	1
Single	$ 115.00	
Double	$ 115.00	

Palisades Paradise B&B — 1200 Palisades Ave 96003 — **Redding CA**
Gail Goetz
Tel: 800-382-4649 916-223-5305
Res Times 10am-10pm

You feel you are in Paradise when you watch the magnificent sunsets from a lovely contemporary home overlooking the Sacramento River. Enjoy a spectacular view of the city, Shasta Bally and the surrounding mountains, sleep to the sound of the flowing river, and awake to the music of singing birds. An excellent place for bird watching. You are always made to feel "special" here. Travelers and business people alike seek out the comfort and relaxed atmosphere of Palisades Paradise, in a quiet, residential neighborhood. You will be offered complimentary refreshments upon arrival, turn down services, and chocolates. All rooms are centrally heated and air conditioned. After dinner at one of the many fine restaurants in the area, you may choose to sit by the fire in the large living room with a wide-screen TV, relax in the old-fashioned porch swing under the oak tree, or soak your cares away in the garden spa before retiring to the "Sunset Suite" or the "Cozy Retreat" for a restful night of sleep. Your hostess, Gail Goetz, has enjoyed a career in education. She is gracious and knowledgeable in directing you to local restaurants, entertainment and attractions. You will find *Palisades Paradise* a serene setting for a quiet hideaway, yet conveniently located one mile from the Hilltop business/shopping area and Interstate 5. Redding is the center of a naturally beautiful area. Come and enjoy fishing, rafting, swimming and boating on Whiskeytown Lake, Shasta Lake and the Sacramento River. For those who love hiking, Lassen National Park, Mount Shasta, Castle Crags, Lake Shasta Caverns, Trinity Alps, Burney Falls State Park are all within driving distance. Rates quoted for two persons, including an expanded continental breakfast. If you can find a place to stay with a better view of the River, your money will be refunded! **Discounts:** Travel agents, corporate **Airport:** Redding Municipal **Packages:** Wedding **Seasonal:** No **Reservations:** Deposit required to guarantee, 5 day cancel (except corporate accounts) policy for refund less $10 service charge. Less than 5 day notice, refund only if rebooked for the same night. **Brochure:** Yes **Permitted:** Children when renting both rooms, limited drinking, smoking outdoor patio only **Payment Terms:** Check AE/MC/V [I10HPCA1-6201] **COM** YG **ITC Member:** No

Rates:	Shared Bath	2
Single	$ 55.00	
Double	$ 85.00	

National Edition   *California*

| *Amber House B&B* | 1315 22nd St 95816 | Sacramento CA |

Mike Richardson & Jane Ramey   **Tel:** 800-755-6526 916-444-8085 **Fax:** 916-552-6529

The *Amber House* offers deluxe accommodations in two meticulously restored vintage structures. The Poet's Refuge, a 1905 Craftsman-style home touched with period elegance offers nine guest rooms, all with private bath and two with jacuzzi tubs for two, one of which includes a fireplace. The Artist's Retreat is a fully restored 1913 Mediterranean-style home which offers four luxurious guest rooms with marble-tiled baths and large jacuzzi bathtubs for two. The Van Gogh room in this home features a spectacular solarium bathroom with a heart-shaped jacuzzi tub and waterfall. All rooms have cable TV, private phones (modem ready with voice mail) and central air conditioning. A full gourmet breakfast is served in the guest room, the dining room or on the outside patio. Compliment-ary bikes (and a bike for two) are available for guests use. Whatever your mood, you'll find the warm hospitality and personal attention you deserve. The Inn is located just eight blocks east of the state capitol and near other historical sights, shops and restaurants. **Airport:** Sacramento Metro-12 mi **Seasonal:** No **Reservations:** One night deposit or credit card number to guarantee reservation **Permitted:** Drinking, limited children **Conference:** Yes, for groups to twenty persons **Payment Terms:** Check AE/DC-MC/V [K10HPCA1-566] **COM** Y **ITC Member:** No

Rates: **Pvt Bath 9**
Single $ 89-155.00
Double $ 99-219.00

| *Red Castle Inn, Historic B&B* | Sacramento CA |

Conley & Mary Louise Weaver   **Tel:** 916-265-5135
                                                                                  Res Times 9am-9pm

Refer to the same listing name under Nevada City, California for complete description. **Seasonal:** No **Payment Terms:** Check MC/V [M11BCCA-6865] **COM** Y **ITC Member:** No

Rates: **Pvt Bath 6**   **Shared Bath 2**
Single $ 80-105.00 $ 65.00
Double $ 85-110.00 $ 70.00

| *Cinnamon Bear B&B* | 1407 Kearney St 94574 | Saint Helena CA |

Cathye Raneri   **Tel:** 707-963-4653 **Fax:** 707-963-0251
                                                                                   Res Times 9am-9pm

A classic Craftsman Bungalow with spacious front porch and gabled dormer, this charming estate was built in 1904 for Susan Smith and her groom, Walter Metzner, who would serve as mayor of St Helena for twenty years. Later owned by Genny Jenkins, she founded the Cinnamon Bear in 1980. She began renting rooms to overnight guests visiting the wineries. Located in the heart of the Napa Valley, we are just a two block walk to St Helena's Main Street shops and restaurants. In it's glorious original condition, the home is filled with antiques, elegant light fixtures, quilts, teddy bears, oriental carpets and gleaming hardwood floors. The guest rooms are quaint and cozy with queen beds and private baths, air conditioning and central heat. A full gourmet breakfast is served in the dining room or on the spacious front porch. Guests

©Inn & Travel Memphis, Tennessee   4-61

California

National Edition

relax by the common fireplace, TV/VCR available. We offer friendly personal attention, afternoon refreshments and evening sweets to insure a pleasurable stay. The home is now owned by Cathye Raneri and her husband, a local chef. After many years in the restaurant business, their goal is to provide a home away from home where guests can enjoy the beautiful Napa Valley again and again. Nearby: golf, cycling, spas, hot air balloons, winery tours, great restaurants. **Airport:** San Francisco-60 mi **Discounts:** Extended stays, midweek, winter season **Reservations:** Credit card deposit holidays/weekends or to guarantee reservation, 7 day cancel policy, $10 service fee **Brochure:** Yes **Permitted:** Drinking, limited smoking (outdoors only) **Conference:** Entire Inn can be booked for business and social functions and can include cooking classes and wine makers' dinners **Languages:** English **Payment Terms:** Check AE/MC/V [I10HPCA1-16875] **COM YG ITC Member:** No

Rates: Pvt Bath 3
Single $ 85-160.00
Double $ 85-160.00

Deer Run Inn 3995 Spring Mountain Rd 94574 Saint Helena CA
Thomas & Carol Wilson Tel: 800-843-3408 707-963-3794
Res Times 8am-8pm

Old World hospitality awaits you at this "lodge" nestled in a forest on four acres with an enchanting atmosphere. In the tradition of inns of early days, there is one guest room in the main residence and one in a separate building. Also, a complete self-sufficient cottage - with breakfast delivered each morning. Each unit has a private bath and entrance with a fireplace in one room. Rooms are decorated with antique furnishings and fully carpeted. All possible amenities have been included by your hosts to insure your total comfort. Delicious full breakfast is included with home-grown fresh raspberries and freshly ground coffee in the morning. Your location is just minutes from wineries, fine restaurants, spas, balloon rides, and all of famous Napa Valley. And you are situated on Spring Mountain, close to the winery used for "Falcon Crest" series. Inground pool for refreshing swimming. **Airport:** San Francisco-1-3/4 Hrs **Seasonal:** No **Reservations:** One night's deposit within 7 days of reservation. 72 hour cancellation notice for refund less $10.00 service fee. **Brochure:** Yes **Payment Terms:** Check AE [A04EPCA-583] **COM Y ITC Member:** No

Rates: Pvt Bath 3
Single $ 95-125.00
Double $ 95-125.00

Ink House B&B 1575 St Helena Way 94574 Saint Helena CA
Jim Annis/Ernie Veniegas Tel: 707-963-3890
Res Times 8-10pm

Classic Italianate Victorian Farmhouse built by Theron H. Ink in 1884 situated in the heart of the famous Napa Valley Wine Country. Guests may relax in the parlor or the observatory situated on top of the house offering a 360 degree view of the vineyards. The four bedrooms with private baths are complete with period antique furnishings including beds, dressers, and finished with beautiful handmade quilts and lace curtains. Twelve foot ceilings on the first floor bring back the nostalgic 1880's including the 1870 pump organ and other antiques throughout the residence that is listed on the *National Register of Historic Places*. A homemade complimentary breakfast includes special recipe muffins and nutbread with juices, coffee/tea, and seasonal fruits. Enjoy your stay while visiting the mud baths, wineries, or try ballooning and tennis. **Seasonal:** No **Reservations:** Full amount required at time of reservation. **Brochure:** Yes **Permitted:** Drinking **Payment Terms:** Check [A05APCA-588] **COM Y ITC Member:** No

Rates: Pvt Bath 4
Single
Double $ 90-110.00

Oleander House Saint Helena CA
John & Louise Packard Tel: 800-788-3057 707-944-8315

©Inn & Travel Memphis, Tennessee

National Edition   *California*

Refer to the same listing name under Yountville, California for a complete description. **Seasonal:** No **Payment Terms:** Check MC/V [M05BPCA-8758] **COM** Y **ITC Member:** No

Rates: **Pvt Bath** 5
Single $ 115-150.00
Double $ 115-150.00

Quail Mountain B&B   Saint Helena CA
Alma & Don Swiers   **Tel:** 707-942-0316
Res Times 10am-9pm

Refer to the sane listing name under Calistoga, California for a complete description. **Seasonal:** No **Payment Terms:** Check MC/V [M02FPCA-15262] **COM** U **ITC Member:** No

Rates: **Pvt Bath** 3
Single $ 90-115.00
Double $ 100-125.00

Caroles B&B Inn   3227 Grim Ave 92104   San Diego CA
Carole Dugdale/Mike O'Brien   **Tel:** 619-280-5258
Res Times 7am-10pm

Built in 1904 by Mayor Frary, this historic site has the handsome style and craftsmanship of its time. It has been restored by the present owners, who live on site, giving it constant loving care. The decor is of its period, with antiques and comfort as the focus. Amenities include a black bottom pool, spa and rose garden. Location is within walking distance (three blocks) of world-famous Balboa Park a mile to the San Diego Zoo, fifteen minutes to Sea World, Old Town and the Convention Center and two miles from downtown and the Gas Lamp District. A continental plus breakfast includes homemade bread, muffins, cereal, fruit, yogurt, fresh ground coffee and fresh squeezed orange juice. **Discounts:** Extended stays **Airport:** San Diego Lindburg-14 mins **Seasonal:** No **Reservations:** 50% advance deposit (can be by check), 7 day cancellation notice for refund *2 Suites available $95.00 **Brochure:** Yes **Permitted:** Children, limited drinking, limited smoking **Languages:** Spanish **Payment Terms:** Check AE/DISC/MC/V [I10IPCA-1-604] **COM** YG **ITC Member:** No

Rates: **Pvt Bath** 2   **Shared Bath** 2
Single $ 75.00 $ 60.00
Double $ 85.00* $ 65.00

Harbor Hill Guest House   2330 Albatross St 92101   San Diego CA
Dorothy Milbourn   **Tel:** 619-233-0638
Res Times 24 hours

Overlooking San Diego Harbor, this charming tri-level residence full of character, craftsmanship, and comfort is located in the famous "Bankers Hill" area. Each level has private entrance, and private kitchen or kitchenette. Choose from rooms, with outstanding harbor view, sundeck, or overlooking the garden area, complete with gazebo. You'll be close to all points of interest including downtown, Balboa Park, Zoo, Old Town, Seaport Village, Sea World, Coronado Ferry. Half hour trolley ride to Mexico border. Ideal area for walkers, joggers, hikers. House is most convenient and comfortable for special occasions such as family reunions and special functions for up to 18 persons. Complimentary continental breakfast included. *$10 extra adult, children under 12, free. **Discounts:** Yes, 4 days or longer stay **Airport:** Lindberg-10 mins **Seasonal:** No **Reservations:** Deposit required, one week cancellation policy for refund. **Brochure:** Yes **Permitted:** Children, drinking **Conference:** Can accommodate large group (to 16 persons) for social events. **Payment Terms:** Traveler Check MC/V [A04EPCA-607] **COM** Y **ITC Member:** No

Rates: **Pvt Bath** 5
Single $ 65-85.00
Double $ 65-85.00

©*Inn & Travel Memphis, Tennessee*

California   *National Edition*

Heritage Park B&B Inn	2470 Heritage Park Row 92110	**San Diego CA**
Nancy Helsper	Tel: 800-995-2470 619-299-6832 **Fax:** 619-299-9465	
		Res Times 8am-9pm

Heritage Park Bed & Breakfast Inn's unique location in a quiet 7.8 acre Victorian Park in the heart of San Diego's Old Town can fit the needs of any traveler. Guest accommodations include your choice from nine distinctive guest chambers furnished with authentic period antiques and documented Victorian wall coverings. A tantalizing homemade complimentary breakfast will be brought to you in your room or on the large front veranda. Enjoy a social hour each evening in the parlor with refreshments and stay to watch one of the nightly vintage film classics. At bedtime find your antique filled room with covers turned back and fancy pillow chocolates waiting for you. Romantic in-room candlelight dinners or Victorian suppers are available along with special occasion packages with 24 hour advance notice. Within a short walk, all of Old Town's excitement is at your feet and six minutes away is Balboa Park with the famous San Diego Zoo. The International Airport, Amtrack and Mission Valley, filled with restaurants and nightclubs are equally close. At your request the staff will make dinner reservations for you at one of San Diego's finest dining establishments. **Discounts:** Corp on weekdays **Airport:** Lindberg-5 mi **Seasonal:** No **Reservations:** Full payment in advance. Travel agent's commissions on weekday (Sun-Thur nites) bookings only. Two night min on weekends. **Brochure:** Yes **Permitted:** Drinking, children over 12 and smoking outdoors **Languages:** Spanish, Italian **Payment Terms:** Check MC/V [R07DXCA-608] **COM** Y **ITC Member:** No

Rates:	**Pvt Bath 5**	**Shared Bath 4**
Single	$ 100-115.00	$ 75-110.00
Double	$ 105-120.00	$ 80-115.00

Amsterdam Hotel	749 Taylor St 94108	**San Francisco CA**
Kenny	Tel: 800-637-3444 415-673-3277 **Fax:** 415-673-0453	
		Res Times 24 Hrs

A little bit of Europe in America with a great location in San Francisco just two blocks from Nob Hill and just a short cable car ride to all the exciting sights of Chinatown, Fisherman's Wharf, art galleries, Sausali-to, legitimate theatre and fine restaurants. Built originally in 1909, the *Amsterdam Hotel* reflects the charm of a small European hotel with quality accommodations, friendly service at very modest rates. The clean and spacious rooms include color TV, cable, AM/FM radio, phones and totally renovated in 1993. A continental breakfast is served daily from 8-10:00 am is included with your room. **Airport:** San Francisco Intl-14 mi **Seasonal:** Rates vary **Reservations:** One night's deposit or credit card at res time **Brochure:** Yes **Permitted:** Children, drinking, limited smoking **Languages:** German **Payment Terms:** Check AE/MC/V [K10HPCA1-614] **COM** YG **ITC Member:** No

Rates:	**Pvt Bath 28**	**Shared Bath 6**
Single	$ 60-69.00	$ 45.00
Double	$ 69-89.00	$ 50.00

Art Center B&B	1902 Filbert St 94123	**San Francisco CA**
Helvi Wamsley	Tel: 800-927-8236 415-567-1526	
		Res Times 8am-9pm

Leave your heart in San Francisco!! This lovely 1857 Country Inn is fully restored into four Queen Suites with unusual period decor recalling the 1800's, with fireplaces in each suite, canopy beds in some, all with modern amenities. Relax in the garden patio or the artists/hosts art gallery and workshop, if classes aren't in session or you can join the class. Close to everything, you can walk everywhere in Old San Francisco: Golden Gate Bridge, China Town, Fisherman's Wharf, Nobb Hill, Fort Mason, or see the Art Circuit with help from your hosts. Sign-up for the three day art class before arriving to improve your skills! Private kitchen provisioned for your continental breakfast plus or full, self-prepared and

4-64   ©*Inn & Travel Memphis, Tennessee*

other meals too if you want. **Seasonal:** No **Reservations:** One week advance, one night's deposit at res time, refundable if cancelled 10 days prior to arrival. Arrive after 2pm, late arrival by arrangement **Brochure:** Yes **Permitted:** Children, limited drinking, small pets, smoking in garden area only **Conference:** Enclosed rear deck and artist studio accommodating groups to 13 persons. **Languages:** Finnish **Payment Terms:** Check AE/DC/MC/V [K01HPCA1-617] **COM YG ITC Member:** No

Rates:	Pvt Bath 5
Single	$ 85-95.00
Double	$ 125.00

Babbling Brook Inn San Francisco CA
Helen King Tel: 800-866-1131 408-427-2437 Fax: 408-427-2457
Res Times 7am-11pm

Refer to the same listing name under Santa Cruz, California for a complete description. **Seasonal:** No **Payment Terms:** Check AE/DC/DISC/MC/V [M10H-CCA1-4352] **COM YG ITC Member:** No

Rates:	Pvt Bath 12
Single	$ 85-150.00
Double	$ 85-150.00

Boat & Breakfast USA San Francisco CA
Rob Harris/Andrew Roettger Tel: 510-444-5858 415-291-8411
Res Times 10am-6pm

Refer to the same listing name under Oakland, California for a complete description. **Seasonal:** No **Payment Terms:** Check AE/MC/V [M04DSCA-12474] **COM Y ITC Member:** No

Rates:	Pvt Bath 22
Single	$ 95-250.00
Double	$ 95-250.00

Chateau Tivoli 1057 Steiner St 94115 San Francisco CA
Rodney Karr/Willard Gersbach Tel: 800-227-1647 415-776-5462 Fax: 415-776-0505
Res Times 9am-10pm

A landmark mansion c1892 located in the center of Historic Alamo Square - the greatest of "The Famous Painted Ladies" of San Francisco's Victorian Period! Over five years and $750,000 in restorations has returned this famous landmark to her former glory. Filled with museum-quality antiques from the estates of Vanderbilts, Chas deGaulle, J Paul Getty and madame Sally Stanford - guests can experience the lavish lifestyle of the countless celebrities who stayed here. Resplendent with hardwood floors, grand oak staircase, stately columns, double parlors and restored 23k gold leaf trim. Guest rooms feature canopy beds, marble baths, balconies, views, fireplaces, stained glass, towers and turrets! The movie *"Earthquake"* from the '30s starring Clark Gable and Jeanette McDonald is based on Ernestine Kreling, a former owner and proprietress of San Francisco's world famous Tivoli Opera, life story and the Tivoli. Guests are just eight blocks from the San Francisco

Opera House and Civic Center; six blocks to the Japan Center; seven minute drive to upper Fillmore Street with its restaurants and shops; ten minutes to Golden Gate Park and less than twenty minutes to Fisherman's Wharf, downtown and Chinatown. *Suites available from $200-up. **Discounts:** Available, inquire at res time **Meals:** Complimentary breakfast included, continental weekdays, full weekends, other meals with prior arrangement **Seasonal:** No **Reservations:** One night's deposit; 7 day cancel policy for refund less 10% fee based on entire length of stay. 14 day notice for holiday periods. Less than 7 day notice, no refund. *Checks require pre-approval. **Brochure:** Yes **Permitted:** Children, drinking **Conference:** The "perfect locale" for all "special occasions"- weddings, receptions, social events and business meetings for groups to 100 persons available. Catering can be arranged. **Languages:** Spanish, German **Payment Terms:** Check* AE/MC/V [I08HPCA1-10936] COM YG ITC **Member:** No

Rates:	Pvt Bath 4	Shared Bath 4
Single	$ 100-200.00	$ 80-125.00
Double	$ 100-200.00	$ 80-125.00

Grove Inn	890 Grove St 94117	San Francisco CA
Klaus & Rosetta Zimmerman	Tel: 800-829-0780 415-929-0780 **Fax:** 415-929-1037	
		Res Times 9am-10pm

The Grove Inn, a Bed & Breakfast place in the true European tradition, is surprisingly affordable, charming and intimate. It is part of the Alamo Square Historic District, noted for its picture-postcard row of Victorian houses. The Grove Inn is located six blocks from the Opera House, Davies Symphonie Hall and the War Memorial with the Museum of Modern Art and the Herbst Theatre, Place of the signing of the United Nations Charter. The Inn was built during the Gold Rush Era as a residence and became a boarding house after the San Francisco Earthquake. The present owners renovated and refurbished The Grove Inn in 1983 and opened it to the public the same year. The guest rooms are individually furnished in the Victorian style. Most of the rooms have large bay windows and include a shower or tub-/shower. A complimentary continental breakfast is included in the room rate. Your hosts will gladly answer any questions and will help in the planning of daily itineraries to make your stay most enjoyable. Group and family rates are available. **Airport:** San Francisco Intl-15 mi **Seasonal:** No **Reservations:** One night deposit at res time; 7-day cancel policy for refund, rates do include 12% hotel tax. Arrival only to 10pm. **Brochure:** Yes **Permitted:** Children **Languages:** Italian, German **Payment Terms:** AE/MC/V [Z01HPCA1-631] COM U ITC **Member:** No

Rates:	Pvt Bath 14	Shared Bath 4
Single	$ 65.00	$ 55.00
Double	$ 75.00	$ 65.00

Haus Kleebauer	225 Clipper St 94114	San Francisco CA
Don Kern/Howard Johnson	Tel: 415-821-3866 **Fax:** 415-821-1417	
		Res Times 24 Hrs

Haus Kleebauer is in a storybook-like Victorian home with all the charm of San Francisco. Built in 1892 by Frederick Kleebauer and his son, the house retains all of its original beauty. Stained and etched glass windows, elaborate exterior trim and manicured gardens transport you an earlier era of refined elegance and charm. *Haus Kleebauer* offers a three room suite with private entrance and bath accommodating up to five people with one queen-size bed in the bedroom and a full size sofa bed in the parlor, a Pullman kitchen (refrigerator, microwave) TV, VCR and stereo. *Haus Kleebauer* is conveniently located in one of San Francisco's premier neighborhoods, Noe Valley. As one of the city's first suburbs, "the valley" offers a splendid display of original Victorian architecture. Within walking distance, you will find many interesting shops, galleries, restaurants and coffee houses. Just minutes away by street car or bus, you will find all the major tourist attractions that have made San Francisco America's Favorite City. Brochure and discounted airport transportation available upon request. A complimentary full breakfast includes fresh fruit with yogurt, juices, cold cereals, hot beverages, homemade jams and fresh bread and your entree choice of Belgium Waffles with fresh fruit and cream, pancakes or French Toast and garnish. **Discounts:** Yes, extended stays over 14 days **Airport:** San Francisco-12 mi; Oakland14; San Jose-40 mi Discount coupon available for Super Shuttle at San Francisco Intl **Packages:** Tour Packages with front door pick-up **Seasonal:** No **Reservations:** 50% deposit of total amount, $85 cancellation fee, late arrivals only with prior arrangement. Additional guests $25 per person/per night, children (under 12 years of age) $10.00 per child/per night **Brochure:** Yes **Permitted:** Children, drinking, limited pets **Conference:** Facilities for groups to ten **Payment Terms:** Traveler Check AE/MC/V [K04HCCA1-15610] **COM YG ITC Member:** No **Quality Assured:** Yes

Rates:	Pvt Bath 1
Single	$ 85.00
Double	$ 85.00

Inn At Union Square	440 Post St 94102	San Francisco CA
*Brooks Bayly		Tel: 800-288-4346 415-397-3501 **Fax:** 415-989-0529
		Res Times 24 Hrs

The *Inn At Union Square* is an elegant small hotel located in the heart of downtown San Francisco. The financial and theater districts are a short walk from the hotel's front door. The City's fabled car is half a block away and can make raveling to view the City's historical sites both convenient and fun for anyone. The Inn provides a complimentary breakfast of flaky croissants, muffins, fresh juice and fruit and coffee served in bed or in the intimate lobbies located on each floor. Enjoy our afternoon tea service with fresh cakes and crisp cucumber sandwiches or hors d'oeuvres and wine served every day. Each of our rooms has been decorated with Georgian furniture in warm colorful fabrics by noted San Francisco, Nan Rosenblatt. Nightly rates for rooms and suites range from $130 to $300. Guests can choose the Penthouse Suite with whirlpool bath, sauna, fireplace and refrigerator stocked with wine, beer and soft drinks. Services include fax and photo copying, dual line phones with modem port, overnight courier services, auto rental, airport shuttle service, theatre, sports and special event tickets, restaurant and airline reservations. Tipping is not accepted from guests. *The Inn At Union Square* provides guests to San Francisco with intimate charm and impeccable service. **Airport:** San Francisco-30 mins **Seasonal:** No **Reservations:** Credit card to guarantee reservation, cancel by 2pm the day prior to arrival for refund **Brochure:** Yes **Permitted:** Children, drinking **Payment Terms:** AE/DC/DISC/MC/V [K08HPCA1-633] **COM YG ITC Member:** No

Rates:	Pvt Bath 30
Single	$ 130-300.00
Double	$ 130-300.00

Jasmine Cottage	San Francisco CA
Karen Gray	Tel: 415-663-1166

Refer to the same listing name under Point Reyes Station, California for a complete description. **Seasonal:** No **Payment Terms:** Check [M06B-PCA-2920] **COM Y ITC Member:** No

Rates:	Pvt Bath 1
Single	$ 115.00
Double	$ 115.00

Marina Inn	3110 Octavia 94123	San Francisco CA
Suzie Baum		Tel: 415-928-1000
		Res Times 24 Hrs

This four-story Victorian hotel, c1922, was completely redone in 1987 in the style of an English Country Inn, complete with large bay windows, intricate detailing, fresh light colors. An oasis in the midst of the city. The gracious pink and white marble lobby with high ceilings and country furnishings greet each guest and offers the amenities of a large hotel such as an elevator and barber shop. The second level offers a cozy sitting room with country furnishings and hardwood floors. A complimentary continental breakfast is served here each morning and a decanter of sherry is served each evening. Each guest room offers pine furnishings, two-poster beds, a soft comforter, fresh flowers reminiscent of an English Inn. Evening turn-down service and a chocolate on your pillow completes each day. The *Marina Inn* is conveniently locate near Union Street, the Marina Green, the Golden Gate Bridge and a 15 min stroll to Ghiradelli Square. The Marina Inn is a charming inn with a friendly staff that's ready to help you enjoy your stay in San Francisco while offering reasonably priced accommodations. A great find in San Francisco! **Seasonal:** No **Reservations:** One night's deposit or credit card guarantee at res time with 24 hr cancel policy for refund. If less than 24 hrs and room is re-rented, refund will be made. **Permitted:** Children, limited drinking **Payment Terms:** Check AE/MC/V [R09BCCA-6209] **COM Y ITC Member:** No

Rates: Pvt Bath 40
Single $ 55-75.00
Double $ 55-75.00

The Mansions Hotel   2220 Sacramento St 94115   San Francisco CA
*Robert Pritikin   Tel: 800-826-9398 415-567-9444 **Fax:** 415-567-9391
                                                                        Res Times 8am-10pm

The Mansions Hotel is two historic mansions interconnected by an interior corridor. The rates include a sumptuous breakfast, flowers in your room, nightly magic concerts, a performing ghost, a billiard/game room, sculpture gardens, the magic parlor and so much more. The *Mansions* also houses one of San Francisco's most important restaurants. The Mansions is minutes from all of San Francisco's famed attractions -- but really a million miles away. *"Lovely, marvelous hospitality"* says former guest Barbara Streisand. ***"You jump back a century, slow down a bit and breath an atmosphere of forgotten elegance"***, says the *Christian Monitor*. *"Elegance to the Nth degree"*, says the *San Francisco Examiner*. The public rooms and private guest rooms feature a five million dollar collection of sculpture, antiques and treasures of art. The historic document museum in one of the parlors displays handwritten letters and documents of Lincoln, Thomas Edison, Houdini, John Hancock and more. The private guest rooms and suites are richly appointed and all have private baths. Your guest room may have a fireplace, a grand piano, a jacuzzi bath spa or any number of surprise amenities. Should you engage the Presidential Suite you will be surrounded by a library of more than 2000 books. Recent overnight guests include Robin Williams, Eddie Fisher, Susanne Sommers, Joe Montana, the late Andre Sakharov and countless luminaries from the world of theater, the arts and business. But the omnipresent motif is magic which includes live performance of world-class magic every evening before dinner and the haunting but rather marvelous presence of documented ghost Claudia. Two blocks from

National Edition *California*

Filmore Street with its elegant boutiques and restaurants, the Mansions is in the middle of San Francisco's most prestigious neighborhood, Pacific Heights. **Discounts:** Yes, inquire at res time **Airport:** San Francisco Intl-20 mins car trip **Packages:** Tailored to your specific needs and interests **Seasonal:** No **Reservations:** Credit card commitment, three day cancellation notice required **Brochure:** Yes **Permitted:** Children 10-up, limited smoking, drinking **Conference:** Full conference facilities available **Languages:** Spanish, French **Payment Terms:** Check MC/V [J07HPCA1-632] **COM** YG **ITC Member:** No

Rates:	Pvt Bath 21
Single	$ 129-350.00
Double	$ 129-350.00

Washington Square Inn	1660 Stockton St 94133	San Francisco CA
*Brooks Bayly		Tel: 800-388-0220 415-981-4220 **Fax:** 415-397-7242
		Res Times 24 Hrs

The *Washington Square Inn* offers the charm and hospitality of a country inn - one block from Telegraph Hill in the heart of San Francisco's North Beach area. It is a special hotel for those who care about quiet and comfort with liberal tastes of elegance. The Inn provides a complimentary breakfast of flaky croissants, muffins, fresh fruit and our famous "Graffeo" coffee served in bed or at the table by the hearth. Tea includes an array of cakes and cookies, cucumber sandwiches, complimentary wine and hors d'oeuvres. Friday evenings the Inn provides an informal wine tasting, giving visitors a chance to sample some of California's best. Each of our rooms has been decorated and individually furnished with English and French antiques by San Francisco designer Nan Rosenblatt. Nan has created a European-style Inn which sits inside the Italian district, North Beach. For the vacationing visitor, the *Washington Square Inn* is the essence of San Francisco. The *Washington Square Inn* is located midway between downtown San Francisco and Fisherman's Wharf. The Inn overlooks Washington Square Park, views Coit Tower and is a stroll to Chinatown. The location provides easy access to buses and cable car lines.

For those on business, we offer every convenience plus a pleasant change from the ordinary. Nightly rates range from $85-180.00. Most rooms have a private bath, all have phones and beautiful fresh flowers. Our staff has time to concentrate on guests' individual needs and wants and guests will be spoiled with individual terry cloth robes, thick thirsty towels, down pillows and comforters, handmilled soaps, a morning Wall Street Journal, local paper and polished shoes at your door - all complimentary of course! **Discounts:** Seniors 20% **Airport:** San Francisco Intl-15 mi. **Packages:** Washington Square Sensation; North Beach Holiday; Little Italy Getaway **Seasonal:** No **Reservations:** Credit card to guarantee or one night paid in advance; 24 Hr cancel policy for refund or forfeit first night's deposit. **Brochure:** Yes **Permitted:** Children, drinking. The Inn is entirely a *non-smoking* establishment. **Languages:** French **Payment Terms:** Check AE/DC/MC/V [U03FPCA-657] **COM** Y **ITC Member:** No

Rates:	Pvt Bath 10	Shared Bath 5
Single	$ 95-180.00	$ 85-95.00
Double	$ 95-180.00	$ 85-95.00

White Swan Inn	845 Bush St 94108	San Francisco CA
Kim Post Watson		Tel: 800-999-9570 415-775-1755 **Fax:** 415-775-5717
		Res Times 24 Hrs

Built in 1908, just after the Great San Francisco earthquake, guests are ideally located in the heart of the city in this fully renovated four-story hotel in the English tradition. Reminiscent of a bit of London, guests experience formal English decor which includes an English garden setting, curved bay windows, warm woods and handsome antique furnishings. Fireplaces welcome guests in all of the guest rooms and common rooms, including the living room, furnished with rich colors and the library done in the style of an English gentleman's club. A full breakfast is served in the dining room, just off the

©Inn & Travel Memphis, Tennessee

tiny secluded English garden and includes warm homemade baked goods, cereals, fresh fruit and juices and a hot dish with a fine selection of coffee and tea. The English theme continues to each guest room where warm polished woods, softly colored English wallpapers and prints, comfortable beds, a separate sitting area, fresh flowers, fruit, wet bar and frige, TV and bedside phones meet every guest's wish. Nightly turndown service and towel change with a morning newspaper are provided. The perfect setting for the traveler who wants the intimacy of an Inn and the service of a larger hotel. A place where guests return again and again. **Seasonal:** No

Reservations: Credit card guarantee or one night's deposit at res time, 24 hr cancel policy. **Brochure:** Yes **Permitted:** Children, limited smoking and drinking **Conference:** Yes, seated groups to 30 persons and larger areas for receptions. A full-time staff member handles all group activities. **Payment Terms:** Check AE/MC/V [R09BCCA-658] **COM** Y **ITC Member:** No

Rates:	Pvt Bath 26
Single	$ 145-160.00
Double	$ 145-160.00

Apple Lane Inn
Doug & Diana Groom

San Jose CA
Tel: 800-649-8988 408-475-6868 Fax: 408-475-6868
Res Times 8am-8pm

Refer to the same listing name under Aptos, California for a complete description. **Seasonal:** No **Payment Terms:** Check DISC/MC/V [M05F-PCA-13073] **COM** U **ITC Member:** No

Rates:	Pvt Bath 5	Shared Bath 1
Single	$ 80-145.00	
Double	$ 95-175.00	

Country Rose Inn
Rose Hernandez

San Jose CA
Tel: 408-842-0441
Res Times 6-8am/8-10pm

For a complete description refer to the same listing name under Gilroy, California. **Seasonal:** No **Payment Terms:** Check AE/MC/V [M06FPCA -11279] **COM** Y **ITC Member:** No

Rates:	Pvt Bath 5
Single	$ 79-169.00
Double	$ 79-169.00

Hensley House
Sharon Layne

456 N 3rd St 95112

San Jose CA
Tel: 800-298-3537 408-298-3537 Fax: 408-298-4676
Res Times 7am-10pm

Step into Victorian comfort and elegance reminiscent of great inns but with an intimate setting of just five guest rooms. From the moment you step inside the Inn, you will find a world of tranquility providing warm caring service to satisfy all guests - from weekend getawayers to business executives needing phones, TV, VCR and fax services. Guests discover a lavish-style of decor represented by fine French and English crafted antiques, crystal chandeliers and ancient stained glass windows capturing sparkles of sunlight and unique guest rooms like the Judge's Chambers featuring the comfort of a feather bed, wet bar, fireplace, whirlpool for two, English antiques and hand painted gilded ceilings and walls. Each room is unique, but each includes a queen feather bed, down comforters, TV, phone and VCR. Mornings bring a full complimentary breakfast of fresh ground coffee, espresso and cappuccino, fresh juices, fruits, muffins, croissants and a delicious entree. Wine, tea, hors d'oeuvres are served afternoons with high tea served Thursdays and Saturdays - where guests can relax beside the wood-burning fireplace with a good book. Located within walking distance of all downtown offices, courts, convention center and major restaurants - with light rail transport available for easy access to airport, Santa Clara and Silicon Valley. Prestigious private

National Edition *California*

athletic club (pool, full gym, racketball, spa, restaurant, bar) available to guest. Full concierge at your service. **Airport:** San Jose Intl-5 mi **Seasonal:** No **Reservations:** One night's deposit, 4 day cancel policy for refund; complimentary San Jose Airport pick-ups with prior arrangements **Permitted:** Drinking, limited children; a non-smoking inn **Conference:** Relaxed meetings, retreats, banquets, Victorian weddings and private parties - catering, private luncheons, dinners - let us know your needs, for groups to 75 persons. **Payment Terms:** Check AE/DC/MC/V [I05FPCA-9958] **COM** Y **ITC Member:** No

Rates:	Pvt Bath 5
Single	$ 75.00
Double	$ 125.00

Casa Soldavini   531 C St 94901   San Rafael CA
Linda Soldavini-Cassidy   **Tel:** 415-454-3140
Res Times 8-10pm

Built in the 1930's by grandfather Joseph Soldavini - your hostess shares her lovely home built in a quaint Italian neighborhood. While grandpa was a winemaker by trade, his lush gardens were his pride and joy and still flourish today. Located in Historic Mission San Rafael, guests can take a bike ride or picnic at a nearby park or museum - or relax on the front porch swing. Three lovely guest rooms are private, comfortable and furnished with original antiques and family heirlooms. Guests can relax in the large sitting room with piano, TV, VCR or they can enjoy the outdoor patio with a large built-in BBQ and fresh fruit and vegetables from the back garden. A complimentary continental breakfast includes fresh brewed hot beverages, juices and plenty of homebaked goods with special treats to tuck you in at night. Guests are within easy walking distance of many fine restaurants and just a short drive to San Francisco, Redwoods, beaches and much more. Your hosts can even provide a private massage therapist upon request! Kitchen privileges; phone available. **Seasonal:** No **Reservations:** One night's deposit required; late arrivals okay with prior arrangement. 5 day cancel notice for refund. **Brochure:** Yes **Permitted:** Pets with prior arrangements **Payment Terms:** Check [Z05FPCA-8157] **COM** Y **ITC Member:** No

Rates:	Pvt Bath 1	Shared Bath 2
Single	$ 65.00	$ 60.00
Double	$ 80.00	$ 70.00

Casa del Mar Inn   18 Bath St 93101   Santa Barbara CA
Mike & Becky Montgomery   **Tel:** 800-433-3097 805-963-4418 **Fax:** 805-966-4240
Res Times 7am-10pm

A charming Mediterranean-style bed and breakfast Inn with a special home-like atmosphere, just steps away from the beach, harbor and Stewart's Wharf, that combines the intimacy of a Bed and Breakfast Inn and the privacy of a small hotel. Walk to elegant restaurants and fine shops. A wide variety of room types are available ranging from bungalow-style family suites with kitchens and fireplaces to cozy queens surrounding a private courtyard with lush gardens year-round, meandering pathways and relaxing spa. Business travelers will appreciate fax, in-room modem hook-ups and comfortable work areas. Non-smoking and handicap accessible rooms available; CATV, phones and private bath in all rooms. Amenities include a very generous continental breakfast with fruit and cereals and a two hour evening wine and cheese buffet. **Discounts:** Seniors, business, travel agents, weekly and monthly rates **Airport:** Santa Barbara-10 mi **Seasonal:** Rates vary **Reservations:** One night credit card or check deposit, 48 hr cancel policy **Brochure:** Yes **Permitted:** Children, drinking, limited smoking, limited pets **Languages:** German **Payment Terms:** Check AE/DC/DISC/MC/V [K04HPCA1-11028] **COM** YG **ITC Member:** No

Rates:	Pvt Bath 20
Single	$ 59-169.00
Double	$ 59-209.00

©*Inn & Travel Memphis, Tennessee*

California   *National Edition*

Cheshire Cat Inn B&B   36 W Valerio 93101   **SANTA BARBARA CA**
*Margaret Goeden   **Tel:** 805-569-1610   **Fax:** 805-682-1876
Res Times 10am-9pm

Victorian elegance for the romantic at heart and travelers seeking a relaxed family environment while traveling. Two of Santa Barbara's oldest homes have been magically restored to their former elegance with modern conveniences. High ceilings and pagoda-like bay windows create extraordinary atmosphere of comfort and charming public rooms where guests find large sitting areas with private nooks and corners for friendly conversation and a wood-burning fireplace. The guest rooms are uniquely decorated with either a queen or king brass bed, enhanced by beautiful Laura Ashley wallpapers and fabrics. English antiques grace charming sitting areas with gorgeous views and some with added extras such as a fireplace, patio or spa. Guest amenities include fresh flowers, private phones, chocolates and liqueurs in each guest room and complimentary guest bikes for touring Santa Barbara in the traditional style. A full gourmet breakfast of fresh-ground European coffees, pastries, fresh fruits and assorted juices are included. Complimentary regional wines are served Saturday evening guests. An outdoor brick patio courtyard joining the two stately homes is perfect for relaxing in comfortable seating, spa or within a beautiful gazebo. The *Cheshire Cat* is conveniently located four blocks from theatres, restaurants and shops. **Discounts:** Travel agents weekday FAM trips, call for details **Airport:** Los Angeles LAX-2 hrs; Santa Barbara-10 mi **Seasonal:** No **Reservations:** One night's deposit required within 7 days of booking, one week cancel policy for refund less $15 service fee. **Brochure:** Yes **Permitted:** Drinking, limited children, limited smoking **Conference:** Yes, meeting room for groups to ten persons. **Languages:** Limited Spanish, French **Payment Terms:** Check MC/V [I11EPCA-677] **COM** Y **ITC Member:** No

Rates:	Pvt Bath 14
Single	$ 79-249.00
Double	$ 89-249.00

Old Yacht Club Inn   431 Corona Del Mar Dr 93103   **Santa Barbara CA**
S Hunt/L Caruso/N Donaldson   **Tel:** 800-676-1676   805-962-1277   **Fax:** 805-962-3989
Res Times 8am-9pm

Dating from the roaring '20s as Santa Barbara's temporary Yacht Club when their club washed out to sea, this gracious location was fully restored in 1980 and furnished with period pieces, classic European and Early American antiques while oriental rugs cover the hardwood floors creating the warm and "homey" feeling of another era. There are large light-filled rooms, a massive fireplace, and large covered porches surrounded with colorful hanging baskets of flowers. Guest rooms are individually decorated with an "old-fashioned touch" and include details such as flowers and sherry decanters with some including cozy sitting areas and balconies. The Hitchcock House next door includes four private-entry rooms exquisitely furnished with antique treasures and family heirlooms. The full breakfast is a memorable experience with fresh-brewed coffee, orange juice, fruit, baked breads and omelettes. The five-course dinner is available only to guests on Saturday evening and is selected from the gourmet palate of your hostess/ "Chefess" Nancy! All year-round activities are nearby: golf, tennis, fish-

National Edition   *California*

ing, horseback riding and quaint seaside shopping. Complimentary bikes, beach chairs and towels. **Discounts:** Midweek during off-season **Airport:** Los Angeles Intl-90 mi; Santa Barbara-12 mi **Reservations:** Deposit within 7 days, 7-day cancellation policy for refund, two night min on weekends **Permitted:** Children **Conference:** Yes, if entire Inn is reserved with conferences in common areas **Languages:** Spanish **Payment Terms:** Check AE/DISC/MC/V [K03HPCA1-685] **COM YG ITC Member:** No

Rates: Pvt Bath 9
Single $ 85-145.00
Double $ 90-150.00

Parsonage   1600 Olive St 93101   Santa Barbara CA
Jussie Peacock   **Tel:** 800-775-0352 805-962-9336

Built in 1892 as a parsonage for the Trinity Episcopal Church, the *Parsonage*, one of Santa Barbara's most notable Queen Anne Victorians, has operated as a unique and memorable Bed and Breakfast Inn for over a decade. Lovingly restored to recapture the openess and grandeur of its distinctive light and cheerful rooms, the *Parsonage* has maintained the touches of rare bird'seye redwood throughout this historic structure. The Inn is within walking distance of the mission and just a few short blocks from theatre going, dining and shopping in Historic Santa Barbara. Guests begin each morning with a generous full breakfast. **Airport:** Santa Barbara-10 mi; Los Angeles Intl-90 mi **Reservations:** First night's deposit or credit card number to guarantee, bal upon arrival **Permitted:** Limited children, drinking **Payment Terms:** Check AE/MC/V [R04FPCA-687] **COM Y ITC Member:** No

Rates: Pvt Bath 6
Single $ 105-185.00
Double $ 105-185.00

Simpson House   121 E Arrellaga 93101   Santa Barbara CA
Glyn & Linda Davies   **Tel:** 800-676-1280 805-963-7067 **Fax:** 805-564-4811
                                                                         Res Times 8am-9pm

A beautiful Italianate-style Victorian home c1874 secluded in an acre of English gardens yet just a five minute walk to Santa Barbaras' restaurants, theatres, museums and shops. Lovingly restored by the host/owners, you can relax in the spacious sitting room with its fireplace and book-lined walls or in the gardens. Cottages, suites and rooms are elegantly appointed with oriental carpets, antiques, goose-down beds and fresh flowers. Some feature private patios, woodburning fireplaces, stereos, jacuzzi tubs, VCRs and wet bars. Enjoy your full gourmet breakfast of fresh California organic orange juice and fruits, the finest of coffees and teas, homemade scones and hot entrees on the veranda overlooking the spectacular gardens! Complimentary afternoon tea and local wine served with hors d'oeuvres in a variety of gracious settings. Complimentary bikes for your use too! AAA 4-Diamond, ABBA 4 Crowns Rated, *Grand Hotels Award-**Best Bed & Breakfast, Southern California* **Airport:** LA Intl-90 mi; Santa Barbara-15 mi **Packages:** Inquire at res time **Seasonal:** No **Reservations:** Deposit at res time, 7 day cancel policy for refund, late arrival with prior arrangement only **Brochure:** Yes **Permitted:** Children, drinking, limited smoking **Conference:** Yes, groups to 25 person **Languages:** Spanish **Payment Terms:** Check AE/DISC/MC/V [K02HPCA1-689] **COM YG ITC Member:** No

Rates: Pvt Bath 14
Single $ 145-350.00
Double $ 145-350.00

Upham Hotel/Garden Cottages   1404 De La Vina St 93101   Santa Barbara CA
Jan Martin Winn   **Tel:** 800-727-0876 805-962-0058 **Fax:** 805-963-2825
                                                                          Res Times 24 hours

Established in 1871, making it the oldest continuously operating hostelry in Southern California, this beautifully restored Victorian is situated on an acre of gardens in downtown Santa Barbara. Walk to museums, galleries, historical attractions, shops and restaurants. Accommodations are located in the Main House and Cottages. All rooms are individually decorated with period furnishings, antiques and beds with cozy comforters. Most cottages have fireplaces and most have private porches or patios. The Master Suite beckons with Jacuzzi-spa, fireplace, wet-bar and private yard including a relaxing hammock! Complimentary Continental breakfast is served in the lobby and garden veranda. Freshly brewed coffee and tea, juices, a variety of muffins, breads and pastries, cereals, seasonal fruits plus the latest edition of the newspaper help start your day. Wine and cheese is provided around the lobby fireplace in late afternoon. Enjoy Louie's restaurant serving excellent California Cuisine for lunch and dinner. Special group and corporate rates are available. For that romantic weekend or mid-week retreat, the Upham is the answer! **Discounts:** Yes, inquire at res time **Airport:** Santa Barbara Municipal; LA Intl-2 hrs **Seasonal:** No **Reservations:** Deposit or credit card for first night's stay to guarantee res, 72 hr cancel policy, check-in 3:00pm, check-out 12:00pm **Brochure:** Yes **Permitted:** Children, drinking, limited smoking **Conference:** Yes **Languages:** Spanish **Payment Terms:** AE/DC/DISC/MC/V [I10I-PCA1-692] COM YG ITC **Member:** No

Rates:	Pvt Bath 50
Single	$ 125-150.00
Double	$ 125-150.00

Villa d'Italia   780 Mission Canyon Rd 93105   Santa Barbara CA
Florence Van Tuyl   Tel: 805-687-6933
                                                                 Res Times AM

Hide-away of the Hollywood Stars!! Romantic and enchanting Italianate Villa setting for just two rooms that include: full three course breakfast served in your room, hot tub, sauna, tennis, grand piano, VCR, library, and luxurious surroundings for that special night out! Make your reservations early to make sure you stay here. **Seasonal:** No **Permitted:** Drinking, limited smoking **Payment Terms:** Check [C11ACCA-693] COM Y ITC **Member:** No

Rates:	Pvt Bath 2
Single	
Double	$ 115-155.00

Madison Street Inn   1390 Madison St 95050   Santa Clara CA
Ralph & Teresa Wigginton   Tel: 800-491-5541 408-249-5541 Fax: 408-249-6676
                                                                 Res Times 24 Hrs

An ideal location for all visitors to the Bay Area, travelers are assured of a restful night's stay after trips to nearby San Francisco and the Napa Valley, south to the Carmel/Monterey area or business trips to Bay Area firms. The *Madison Street Inn* is the culmination of an award winning restoration offering a gracious perspective of a different era. An ideal place for work or relaxation, there are five individually decorated rooms, all with phones, a sunny breakfast room overlooking flower filled gardens; a parlor decorated with authentic Victorian wall papers and museum-quality furnishings; and by special request, laundry, dry cleaning and fax services. The half-acre of landscaped gardens, highlighted with an arbor of fushia-colored Bougainvillea, makes a perfect setting for spring and summer weddings or parties. The grounds around the pool and spa can easily accommodate 20-75 guests. The *Madison Inn* offers superb dining - whether its breakfast, luncheons, dinners or catered parties. The day begins with a complimentary full breakfast of juices, fresh fruit, baked muffins and breads and entrees of Eggs Benedict or Belgian Waffles. Dinners, by prior arrangement only, brings Ralph's delicious entrees, such as Poached Salmon with Basil and Olive Butter or In-

National Edition   *California*

dividual Beef Wellington - all prepared with fresh herbs grown outside the kitchen door. Nearby sights include Winchester Mystery House, Great American Park, Rosicruician and Triton Museums. **Discounts:** Yes, inquire at res time **Airport:** San Jose-10 mins **Seasonal:** No **Reservations:** One night's deposit with 4-day cancellation policy for full refund; e-mail: Madstinn @eworld.com **Brochure:** Yes **Permitted:** Children, drinking **Conference:** Meeting space for private groups of 10-15 persons **Languages:** French **Payment Terms:** Check AE/DC/DISC/MC/V [K02HPCA1-695] **COM YG ITC Member:** No

Rates:	Pvt Bath 4	Shared Bath 2
Single	$ 75-85.00	$ 60.00
Double	$ 75-85.00	$ 60.00

Apple Lane Inn   Santa Cruz CA
Doug & Diana Groom   **Tel:** 800-649-8988 408-475-6868 **Fax:** 408-475-6868
                                                          Res Times 8am-8pm

Refer to the same listing name under Aptos, California for a complete description. **Seasonal:** No **Payment Terms:** Check DISC/MC/V [M05FPCA-13074] **COM U ITC Member:** No

Rates:	Pvt Bath 5	Shared Bath 1
Single	$ 80-145.00	
Double	$ 95-175.00	

Babbling Brook Inn   1025 Laurel St 95060   Santa Cruz CA
Helen King   **Tel:** 800-866-1131 408-427-2437 **Fax:** 408-427-2457
                                                      Res Times 7am-11pm

Cascading waterfall, historic waterwheel and meandering brooks grace an acre of terraced gardens, fruit trees and redwoods surrounding this secluded Inn built in 1909 on the foundation of an 1870 tannery, a 1790 flour mill and the site of a 2,000 year-old Indian fishing village. Choose from twelve rooms in Country French decor located in four buildings beside the brook. All have private bath, telephone, TV, and most have cozy fireplaces, private decks and an outside entrance. Four rooms offer deep-soaking jet bathtubs. The Inn has off-street parking. Included in your stay is a full country breakfast featuring memorable egg casseroles served buffet-style in the large living room parlor between 8-10 am, so guests may arrive at their leisure. Afternoon tea and Mrs. King's famous cookies, followed by evening wine and cheese served during the social hour with the other guests complimentary. The unusual Country Inn location is within walking distance of ocean beaches, wharf, boardwalk, shopping, tennis and historic homes. Three golf courses, 200 restaurants and seven wineries are within twenty minutes! The narrow gauge railroad trip over old logging trails, elephant seals at Ano Nuevo Reserve, whale-watching, the annual winter haven of Monarch butterflies, deep-sea fishing, evening sails and antiquing are some of the "seeing/doing" ideas for this city on the North end of Monterey Bay. The weather is comparatively mild in winter and cool in the summer. AAA-Approved, Mobil Travel Guide's 3-Star Rated **Airport:** San Francisco Intl-90 mins; 40 mins to Monterey and its aquarium and 30 mins from San Jose and its airport. Comp Wine and Sherry 5:30-8:00 pm. **Packages:** Get-Away Special, 2 nights/3 days for $175.00 for rooms up to $125.00, includes champagne and flower in room, Sun-Thurs, Oct 1 - May 1, except holidays **Discounts:** Off-season midweek with some restrictions, inquire at res time **Seasonal:** No **Reservations:** 50% deposit to confirm reservation, check-in 3-10:30pm **Brochure:** Yes **Permitted:** Drinking, limited children **Languages:** Spanish and French, AT&T language service available **Payment Terms:** Check AE/DC/DISC/MC/V [I10HPCA1-696] **COM YG ITC Member:** No

Rates:	Pvt Bath 12
Single	$ 85-150.00
Double	$ 85-150.00

California   National Edition

Bayview Hotel B&B   Santa Cruz CA
Barry & Sue Hooper   Tel: 408-688-8654
Res Times 10am-6pm

Refer to the same name listed under Aptos, California for a complete description. **Seasonal:** No **Payment Terms:** Check MC/V [M11BCCA-8534] **COM** Y **ITC Member:** No

Rates:	Pvt Bath 8
Single	$ 80-100.00
Double	$ 85-125.00

Blue Spruce Inn   Santa Cruz CA
Pat & Tom O'Brien   Tel: 800-559-1137 408-464-1137
Res Times 7am-10pm

Refer to the same listing name under Soquel, California for a complete description. **Seasonal:** No **Payment Terms:** Check AE/MC/V [M04GPA-20118] **COM** Y **ITC Member:** No

Rates:	Pvt Bath 5
Single	$ 85-135.00
Double	$ 85-135.00

Darling House   314 W Cliff Drive 95060   Santa Cruz CA
Karen & Darrell Darling   Tel: 408-458-1958

Ocean side mansion c1910 by architect William Weeks, revival styling. Unsurpassed ocean views, beveled stained glass, intricate inlaid woodwork, original hardware (sinks, tubs, light fixtures, fireplaces). Superb antique furnishing include Tiffany, Chippendale and other period furnishings. Continental breakfast included with fresh fruits, yogurts, homemade jams and jellys, and granola made by Karen. **Seasonal:** No **Brochure:** Yes **Permitted:** Children, smoking in cottage only **Payment Terms:** Check AE/MC/V/DC [X11ACCA-700] **COM** Y **ITC Member:** No

Rates:	Pvt Bath 3	Shared Bath 6
Single	$ 75.00-up	$ 65.00-up
Double	$ 85.00-up	$ 75.00-up

Channel Road Inn   219 W Channel Rd 90402   Santa Monica CA
Kathy Jensen   Tel: 310-459-1920 Fax: 310-454-9920
Res Times 7:30am-10pm

Sitting on the back deck overlooking the sea and flowering hillside, it is difficult to believe one is in the hectic city of Los Angeles! But the *Channel Road Inn*, a 1910 colonial revival has been lovingly restored and graciously furnished to become one of the few Bed and Breakfasts in Los Angeles. In-addition to the fine antique furnishings in each of the fourteen guest rooms, every guest will also find fresh fruit or flowers, embroidered linens, down pillows, cozy comforters or antique quilts, extra firm mattresses and thick bath robes. After a healthful breakfast of homebaked berry muffins, bread pudding and a variety of fresh California fruits, guests may bicycle (complimentary bikes available) along the beach bike path, or walk along the hillside nature trails. The John Paul Getty Museum is five minutes up the coast; the Santa Monica Pier, just one mile south. Horseback riding and tennis nearby. A seafood restaurant, Italian cafe and a fun Tex-Mex restaurant are within a block. Other fine restaurants, museums, and shops are located in nearby Santa Monica or in the Pacific Palisades. The Inn is only twenty minutes from the airport or downtown Los Angeles. But with the gracious staff and the restful atmosphere of the Inn, many guests never wander far from the front porch. **Airport:** LAX-20 min **Seasonal:** No **Reservations:** One night's deposit required at res time with 72 hr cancel policy for refund. Wheelchair accessible. *Corporate and weekly discounts available. **Brochure:** Yes **Permitted:** Children, drinking **Conference:** Excellent facilities for social or business meetings and conferences **Languages:** Spanish, French **Payment Terms:** Check MC/V [I04HP-CA1-8421] **COM** YG **ITC Member:** No

Rates:	Pvt Bath 14
Single	$ 95-200.00
Double	$ 95-200.00

Melitta Station Inn	5850 Melitta Rd 95409	Santa Rosa CA
V Amstadter/D Crandon		**Tel:** 707-538-7712
		Res Times 8am-9pm

The *Melitta Station* is a turn-of-the-century railroad station which has been caringly and lovingly turned into a rustic American Country B&B Inn and family home with 6 guest rooms, a large sitting area which is warmed by a wood-burning stove, and a balcony that overlooks the surrounding pepperwood trees. Located in the middle of the Valley of the Moon, guests have their choice of activities, including biking, horseback riding, hiking or sailing in the several parks, located within minutes of the Inn. Guests may wish to visit some of the many wineries in the area or this historic towns of Sonoma and Calistoga, where they can enjoy mud baths, massages, hot air ballooning and glider rides. A full breakfast is included along with complimentary wine and cheese service in the early evening. Many fine restaurants are within a short drive for your dining experiences. **Seasonal:** No **Reservations:** One night's deposit within 7 days of booking; 7 day cancellation policy for refund; check-in after 3pm, check-out 11am **Brochure:** Yes **Permitted:** Limited children **Payment Terms:** Check MC/V [Z05GPCA-2927] **COM** Y **ITC Member:** No

Rates:	Pvt Bath 4	Shared Bath 2
Single	$ 85.00	$ 75.00
Double	$ 90.00	$ 80.00

Pygmalion House B&B	331 Orange St 95407	Santa Rosa CA
Caroline Berry		**Tel:** 707-526-3407
		Res Times 24 Hrs

One of Santa Rosa's historical landmarks, this Grand Lady survived the great earthquake and fire of 1906 and has been transformed into a fine examples of Victorian Queen Anne architecture. Ideally located in a secluded residential street in Santa Rosa's "Old Town", it is within walking distance of Railroad Square, popular for its specialty shops and fine restaurants. The interior is an eclectic combination of unique colorful rooms each with a vintage claw foot tub and or shower, central a/c and heat. Each morning a bountiful (full) breakfast is served in the country kitchen including fresh squeezed orange juice! Throughout the day guests are treated to complimentary soft drinks, bottled spring water and in the evening, there's coffee, snacks and tea while socializing around the fireplace in the double parlor or relaxing in their room. Your helpful hostess is anxious to help guests choose from the many activities, including: Napa Valley and Sonoma County wineries, hot air ballooning, golfing, bike trails, the Northern California Coast, Muir Woods, Sausalito and much more. **Seasonal:** No **Reservations:** One night's deposit with 7 day cancel policy for refund less $10 service fee. Late cancellation or no-show forfeits deposit unless re-rented. **Brochure:** Yes **Permitted:** Children with special arrangements, smoking outside **Payment Terms:** Check MC/V [Z0-4DPCA-711] **COM** Y **ITC Member:** No

Rates:	Pvt Bath 5
Single	$ 45-65.00
Double	$ 50-70.00

Storybook Inn	Lake Arrowhead 92385	Skyforest CA
Kathleen & John Wooley		**Tel:** 800-554-9208 909-336-1483
		Res Times 8am-9pm

An excitingly different experience is offered in this classical hideaway offering romance and magical experiences in all of the ten different theme guest rooms. Snuggled atop San Bernardino Mountains, enjoy the spectacular 100 mile view of the snow-capped mountains and the Pacific Ocean or relax

California National Edition

in the glassed-in solarium and porches that bring in all the abundant wildlife. Furnishings include antiques and contemporary pieces throughout the guest and common rooms with fresh flowers sprinkled everywhere. This peaceful and serene setting includes a gorgeous stone fireplace and a three-story main lobby, hot tub, hors d'oeuvres, complimentary wine, outdoor activities at Lake Arrowhead, breath-taking nature trails for hiking, old-fashioned picnics with prepared lunches, and wonderful skiing in winter. A picturesque cabin *"Call of the Wild"* is available and offers privacy and a hunting lodge setting with open beam ceilings, stone fireplace and John's hunting and fishing trophies. A full gourmet breakfast is included daily along with the morning paper. Lunch and Dinner available. **Discounts:** Mid-week 20 and 25%, seminars and other special events **Airport:** Ontario CA, 40 mins **Packages:** Swiss Alps Getaway; Honeymoon; Ski Trips; Wedding which includes a romantic wedding gazebo and reception facilities **Seasonal:** No **Reservations:** One night deposit, 7 day cancel policy, late arrival notice. **Brochure:** Yes **Permitted:** Children, drinking, smoking outdoors on patio **Conference:** Yes, excellent meeting and dining location for seclusion and privacy for social or business up to 20 persons. **Languages:** French, Italian, Spanish. **Payment Terms:** Check AE/DISC/MC/V [I05FPCA-722] **COM** Y **ITC Member:** No

Rates: Pvt Bath 10
Single $ 98.00
Double $ 200.00

Victorian Garden Inn   316 E Napa St 95476   Sonoma CA
Ms Donna Lewis   **Tel:** 800-543-5339 707-996-5339 **Fax:** 707-996-1689
Res Times 8am-5pm

1870 Greek Revival residence and Woodcutter's Cottage are nestled within this wooded setting and lush garden area including private patio, and romantic atmosphere and a therapeutic spa. Choose from three rooms and suites all with individual decor from a Merrimekko-styled blue and white room with wicker accents at the top of the "old water tower", to the Garden Room, with a queen size iron framed bed, classic Laura Ashley Rose wallcoverings and fabrics, gas fireplace, wicker furnishings and gardenside with its own babbling brook. The Woodcutters Cottage offers guests a Hunter Green and redwood decor, complete with clawfoot tub/shower, queen size brass bed, your own fireplace, and sitting area. Gourmet breakfast is included and is served in the dining room, the Garden or in your room. Country massage, tour and excursions are available. **Airport:** San Francisco-Oakland-65 mi **Seasonal:** No **Reservations:** Full deposit required in advance, 7 day cancel notice required for refund less $10.00 service fee http:www.victorian-arden-inn.com **Brochure:** Yes **Permitted:** Limited children, limited smoking **Conference:** Flexible for midweek social or business style meetings, to 10 persons **Payment Terms:** Check AE/JCB/-MC/V [I04HPCA1-736] **COM** YG **ITC Member:** No

Rates: Pvt Bath 3   Shared Bath 1
Single
Double $ 109-149.00 $ 85.00

Blue Spruce Inn   2815 S Main St 95073   Soquel CA
Pat & Tom O'Brien   **Tel:** 800-559-1137 408-464-1137 **Fax:** 408-475-0608
Res Times 7am-10pm

At the *Blue Spruce Inn*, guests enjoy the flavor of yesterday blended with the luxury of today in a friendly 1875 Victorian farm house. Each room derives its own mood from the handmade quilt on the queen-size bed which complements the representative work of a local artist displayed in the room. Accommodations offer gas fireplaces, some spa tubs or full body showers, private entrances and deck

4-78   ©*Inn & Travel Memphis, Tennessee*

areas. The window seat parlor is a place to read, play a game or watch the flowers grow. Just down the street, guests can enjoy fine dining, browse through antique shops or visit premier wineries. The day begins in the parlor or out in the garden with a bounteous complimentary breakfast of just-squeezed juice, fresh fruits, and baked breads, perhaps hearty blueberry pancakes or a baked ham strata accompanied by steaming cups of coffee or tea. Beyond the neighborhood lies the entire Monterey Bay - the redwood groves in the mountains to the north; the blue Pacific shore to the south. Three State Parks in the area have extensive hiking, bicycle and horse trails, historic displays and beautiful beaches. When guests retire, pillows will be fluffed, robes laid out and a nightcap waiting to assure a perfect ending to a wonderful day. **Discount:** 10% Nov through Feb **Airport:** 30 mi to San Jose **Seasonal:** No **Reservations:** One night's deposit, three day cancel notice. A gift certificate in the amount of the first night's stay for use at another time will be given for cancellations within the 3 day period **Brochure:** Yes **Permitted:** Limited children, limited drinking, limited smoking **Languages:** Spanish **Payment Terms:** Check AE/MC/V [I04GPCA1-13226] **COM** Y **ITC Member:** No **Quality Assured:** Yes

Rates:	Pvt Bath 5
Single	$ 85-135.00
Double	$ 85-135.00

Whites House　　　17122 Farsmith Ave 90504　　　Torrance CA
Rusell & Margaret White　　　　　　　　　　Tel: 310-324-6164

Quiet suburban locale for this charming contemporary home with sunbathing deck, patio, fireplaces, and convenient to all sights within 30 mins to Disneyland, Marineland, and Knott's Berry Farm. You'll feel right at home with these hospitable hosts. Continental breakfast included. **Reservations:** Airport and bus station pick-ups available at nominal charge. **Permitted:** Children, pets with advance notice, smoking, social drinking **Payment Terms:** Check [X11ACCA-771] **COM** Y **ITC Member:** No

Rates:	Pvt Bath 2
Single	$ 40.00
Double	$ 45.00

Vichy Hot Springs Resort　　　2605 Vichy Springs Rd 95482　　　Ukiah CA
Gilbert & Marjorie Ashoff　　　　Tel: 707-462-9515　**Fax:** 707-462-9516
　　　　　　　　　　　　　　　　　　　　Res Times 7:30am-10pm

Vichy Hot Springs Resort, a two hour drive north on Hwy 101 from San Francisco, is one of California's oldest continuously operating hot springs resorts. Opened in 1854 the original buildings have been completely renovated and individually decorated. Bed & Breakfast is offered for our guests in twelve rooms and two self-contained cottages. A few feet from your room await the fourteen natural tubs built in 1860 and used by the rich and famous in California's history including Jack and Charmaigne London, Mark Twain, Teddy Roosevelt and his daughter Alice, Ulysses Grant and pugilists Jim Corbett and John L Sullivan. *Vichy* features naturally sparkling 90 degree mineral baths, a communal hot tub and olympic size pool that will gently caress your cares and stress away. The baths are backdropped by a five million year old travertine/onyx grotto, formed from the Spring. *Vichy* has seven hundred acres for your hiking, jogging, picnicking and mountain bicycling pleasure. Vichy offers Swedish massage, reflexology and herbal facials. A quiet healing environment is what a stay at a

*Ukiah Goodwill Ambassador
See travel article at the beginning of the West Coast Section*

mineral springs resort should be. *Vichy's* idyllic setting amidst native oak, madrone, manzanita, bay, fir, pine and buckeye will leave you refreshed, renewed and invigorated. An expanded complimentary breakfast is included in your room rate. **Airport:** Santa Rosa-60 mi **Package:** One week stay, seventh nite free. Massage therapy available on-site. **Seasonal:** No **Reservations:** Deposit at res time, 4 day cancel policy for refund; late arrivals accommodated **Brochure:** Yes **Permitted:** Children, drinking and smoking (outside only), bathing suits required in mineral baths and pools **Conference:** Yes with space from 400 to 4400 square feet **Languages:** Spanish **Payment Terms:** Check AE/DC/DISC/MC/V [Z04GPCA-10038] **COM** Y **ITC Member:** No **Quality Assured:** Yes

Rates:	Pvt Bath 14
Single	$ 85.00
Double	$ 125-160.00

B&B of Ventura   PO Box 87732 93032   Ventura CA
Madeline Jameson   Tel: 805-652-2201
   Res Times 9am-9pm

Begin each day close to town in this turn-of-the century charmer. Restored by your hosts during the past six years - guests will find a "real treat" stepping back in time. Furnished with period furnishings including all of the details, the common rooms and guest rooms include antiques and family heirlooms. Guest rooms have been updated with modern amenities including a choice of either whirlpool tubs or clawfoot tubs. Canopy or brass beds beckon guests to bed. A full breakfast is served *ensuite* or outdoors if you like. **Reservations:** First night's deposit, 72 hr cancel policy **Permitted:** Drinking, children **Brochure:** Yes **Payment Terms:** Check, AE/MC/V **COM** U **ITC Member:** No

Rates:	Pvt Bath 4
Single	$ 90.00
Double	$110.00

Clocktower Inn   181 E Santa Clara St 93001   Ventura CA
Dale Sedgemeyer   Tel: 800-727-1027 805-652-0141
   Res Times 24-hr

In 1985, interior designer Tom Brooks was commissioned to create an inn from the existing structure of 1940 California Spanish firehouse and clocktower! Southwestern style fiber wall hangings, original art, beamed ceilings, handsome wood furnishings and a large fireplace have transformed the firehouse into the easy grace and simplicity of the *Clocktower Inn*. Located in the heart of historic downtown Ventura, it is surrounded by a park and adjacent to the Mission and Historical downtown Ventura, it is surrounded by a park and adjacent to the Mission and Historical Museum. The State Beach, restaurants, antique shops, boutiques and County Fairgrounds are all within easy walking distance. The two-story guest wings are accessed by elevator and Spanish tiled stairs. Most rooms have private balconies or patios and several include fireplaces. Mornings begin in the glass-covered Atrium with a Complimentary continental breakfast buffet. Freshly-brewed coffee and teas, juices, a variety of muffins, breads and pastries, cereal, seasonal fruits plus the latest edition of the newspaper help start your day. In late afternoon enjoy complimentary wine and cheese around the lobby fireplace. **Discounts:** Special corporate and group rates available **Seasonal:** No **Reservations:** Deposit for first night's stay to guarantee res. 72-hr cancel policy **Brochure:** Yes **Permitted:** Children allowed, no smoking **Conference:** Yes, three conference rooms for groups to 125 persons, 1900 square feet total in comfortable Santa Fe style **Languages:** Spanish **Payment Terms:** Check AE/D/DC/MC/V [Z11BPCA-785] **COM** Y **ITC Member:** No

Rates:	Pvt Bath 50
Single	$ 85.00-up
Double	$ 95.00-up

La Mer   411 Poli St 93001   Ventura CA
Gisela & Michael Baida   Tel: 805-643-3600 Fax: 805-485-5430

Authentic c1890 Victorian with hillside locale offering splendid ocean views and a historic landmark now. Just three blocks from the beach, you'll relive history in the restored guest rooms decorated with family touches and handicrafts or lounge in the pleasant yard and gardens. Sumptuous Bavarian breakfast is included with fresh fruits, Black Forest ham, homemade sweet rolls or other fresh pastries. **Seasonal:** No **Reservations:** Two night stay on weekends **Brochure:** Yes **Permitted:** Children 14-up **Languages:** German, Spanish. **Payment Terms:** Check AE/MC/V [X11ACCA-787] **COM** Y **ITC Member:** No

Rates:	Pvt Bath 5
Single	$ 80.00
Double	$ 110.00

Gasthaus Zum Baren	2114 Blackstone Dr 94598-3721	Walnut Creek CA
		Tel: 415-934-8119
		Res Times 3pm-8pm

Gasthaus Zum Baren is a rambling ranch home in a quiet neighborhood near the foot of Mount Diablo. It is 27 miles from downtown San Francisco with Oakland and Berkeley enroute. Relaxed country decor and an international collection of handcrafted bears and antiques create Old World charm in a suburban setting! Hearty country breakfast is served poolside in summer and by the fireplace in winter. Our own pool, jacuzzi, barbeque grill, bicycles, and laundry facilities are available to guests. Hiking and bike trails, restaurants, golf, tennis, and public transportation are within walking distance. **Seasonal:** No **Reservations:** One night's deposit with two night minimum stay **Brochure:** Yes **Permitted:** Children 6-up who can swim **Languages:** Spanish, German, Italian. **Payment Terms:** Check [A05-ACCA-791] **COM** Y **ITC Member:** No

Rates:	Pvt Bath 1	Shared Bath 2
Single	$ 65.00	
Double	$ 75.00	

Coleens California Casa	PO Box 9302 90608	Whittier CA
Coleen Davis		**Tel:** 310-699-8427
		Res Times 7an-7pm

Come to the top of the hill and find your own quiet paradise. This home is located less than five minutes from #605 Freeway and is near #5 and #60 highways, yet seems to be in a rural area. The quiet peacefulness is enhanced by the luxuriant patio where you may enjoy the sunshine along with a full breakfast prepared by you home economist hostess. Other meals available with prior arrangements and nominal fee. She will direct you to the nearby Disneyland, Knott's Berry Farm and other Los Angeles attractions. Accommodations include: (a) large king size bed with electric adjustment and extra large PB, with private entrance and (b) two extra long twin beds with PB, (c) double bed with private entrance and SB and (d) extra long twin bed with PB. After your sightseeing, enjoy wine and cheese as the sun sets and the lights of the city flicker from below. The view from the deck is enchanting. You may dine here with previous arrangements. Well-behaved children over 12 are welcome. This home is near tennis, is excellent for jogging and it's five minutes to Whittier College. Excellent hiking is found in the canyon nearby. *"Home is thirty minutes east of Los Angeles in a quiet, uncongested and historic Quaker Town."* **Airport:** LAX, Ontario, Long Beach **Reservations:** Payment by check in advance to guarantee reservation **Brochure:** Yes **Permitted:** Drinking, limited children, smoking outdoors only **Languages:** Spanish **Payment Terms:** Check [R08GPCA-2929] **COM** Y **ITC Member:** No

Rates:	Pvt Bath 3	Shared Bath 1
Single	$ 60.00	$ 55.00
Double	$ 65.00	$ 60.00

Karen's Yosemite Inn		Yosemite CA
Karen Bergh & Lee Morse		**Tel:** 800-346-1443 209-683-4550
		Res Times 7am-10pm

Refer to the same listing name under Fish Camp, California for a complete description. **Payment Terms:** Check [M05FPCA-16891] **COM** U **ITC Member:** No

Rates:	Pvt Bath 3
Single	$ 80.00
Double	$ 85.00

California - Colorado   *National Edition*

Oak Meadows, too	Yosemite CA
Don & Francie Starchman	Tel: 209-742-6161
	Res Times 4pm-9pm

Refer to the same listing name under Mariposa, California for a complete description. **Seasonal:** Clo Xmas **Payment Terms:** Check MC/V [M05-BCCA-9461] **COM** Y **ITC Member:** No

Rates: Pvt Bath 6
Single $ 59.00
Double $ 58-89.00

Burgundy House	6711 Washington St 94599	Yountville CA
Denna Roque		Tel: 707-944-0899
		Res Times 7am-9pm

Originally a brandy distillery, this c1870 structure is solidly built with 22" thick walls of local fieldstone and river-rock well combined in harmonious manner to bring comfort and warmth to guests. You are in a choice location of the famous Napa Valley, ideally located for exploring the magnificent wine growing region. Terraced mountains with Reisling and Chardonnay grapes are close by and closer yet, you'll find shade and privacy in our sheltered garden where roses bloom profusely. The rustic character of the residence is complimented by antique country furniture, comfortable beds, and colorful quilts. Fresh flowers and a decanter of local wine greet all guests. Full breakfast is included buffet-style and includes cereals, juice, coffee, tea, pastries and muffins, fresh fruits as-well-as egg dishes or casseroles enjoyed indoors or in the outdoor garden area for the perfect beginning of your day. Local activities include: wine tasting, bicycling, ballooning and plenty of sight-seeing. **Seasonal:** No **Reservations:** First night's deposit to hold reservation, 2 night min on weekends, 5-day cancellation notice for refund less a $15.00 handling charge, check-in 2:00pm. **Brochure:** Yes **Permitted:** Drinking **Languages:** German **Payment Terms:** Check [A05GPCA-801] **COM** Y **ITC Member:** No

Rates: Pvt Bath 5
Single $ 105.00
Double $ 120.00

Oleander House	7433 St Helena Way 94599	Yountville CA
John & Louise Packard		Tel: 800-788-3057 707-944-8315

Country French two-story home recently featured in the *"New York Times"*, combines the best of old world design with modern amenities and is located at the entrance to the spectacular and unique Napa Valley, midway between the champagne cellars of Domaine Chandon and the Robt Mondavi Winery! Guests enjoy the spacious high-ceiling rooms with private balconies offering beautiful valley views, full private baths with gleaming solid brass fixtures and pedestal sinks, cozy wood-burning fireplaces, comfortable queen-size beds, antiques and Laura Ashley wallcoverings and fabrics. Fresh-brewed coffee beckons guests to the large dining room furnished with antiques and fine art each morning to enjoy a full complimentary breakfast. Daily activities could include soaring over the valley in hot air balloons, gliders or helicopters; luxuriating in the mineral spas with mudbaths and massages, golf, tennis, horseback riding, cycling; delightful shopping and fine dining at the numerous excellent restaurants. Upon your return, you can relax on the patio and sample a complimentary soft drink or brandy, while the sun set dances over the distant mountain tops . . . enjoying the delightful fragrance of star jasmine blending into the cool evening breeze. **Airport:** San Francisco or Oakland-70 mi **Seasonal:** No **Reservations:** One night's deposit by credit card required, 7 day cancel policy. Two night min on weekends and holidays. **Brochure:** Yes **Permitted:** Drinking **Conference:** Small meetings for 10-12 persons. **Languages:** Some Japanese **Payment Terms:** Check MC/V [Z05FPCA-804] **COM** Y **ITC Member:** No

Rates: Pvt Bath 5
Single $ 115-150.00
Double $ 115-150.00

Cottonwood Inn	123 San Juan 81101	Alamosa CO

National Edition *Colorado*

Julie & George Mordecai-Sellman

Tel: 800-955-BNBE 719-589-3882
Res Times 8am-9pm

A lovely turn-of-the-century home where hospitality is a way of life with your charming hosts. This elegant and very affordable lodging is in the heart of the San Luis Valley and offers beautiful scenic nature trails for hiking, biking and picnicking. Each guest room is uniquely decorated with comfortable antique furnishings and art work from area artists. Your hosts will be glad to help plan your visit to local sights of: Wolf Creek, Monarch, Taos, Rio Costilla and Cuuchara ski areas, Cumbres and Toltec Railroad, The Great Sand Dunes, Monte Vista and Alamosa National Wildlife Refuge and the Creede Repertory Theatre. A hearty family-styled full breakfast is included in the rate and is served in the comfortable dining room. **Seasonal:** No **Reservations:** One night's deposit at res time or credit card, 7 day cancel policy less $10 service fee **Brochure:** Yes **Permitted:** Limited children, limited drinking **Conference:** Small groups to nine persons **Languages:** Spanish **Payment Terms:** Check MC/V [X08BCCO-6079] **COM** Y **ITC Member:** No

Rates:	Pvt Bath 3	Shared Bath 2
Single	$ 56.00	$ 46-48.00
Double	$ 60.00	$ 50-52.00

Cottonwood Inn 123 San Juan 81101 Alamosa CO
Julie & George Mordecai-Sellman

Tel: 800-955-BNBE 719-589-3882
Res Times 8am-9pm

A lovely turn-of-the-century home where hospitality is a way of life with your charming hosts. This elegant and very affordable lodging is in the heart of the San Luis Valley and offers beautiful scenic nature trails for hiking, biking and picnicking. Each guest room is uniquely decorated with comfortable antique furnishings and art work from area artists. Your hosts will be glad to help plan your visit to local sights of: Wolf Creek, Monarch, Taos, Rio Costilla and Cuuchara ski areas, Cumbres and Toltec Railroad, The Great Sand Dunes, Monte Vista and Alamosa National Wildlife Refuge and the Creede Repertory Theatre. A hearty family-styled full breakfast is included in the rate and is served in the comfortable dining room. **Seasonal:** No **Reservations:** One night's deposit at res time or credit card, 7 day cancel policy less $10 service fee **Brochure:** Yes **Permitted:** Limited children, limited drinking **Conference:** Small groups to nine persons **Languages:** Spanish **Payment Terms:** Check MC/V [X08BCCO-6079] **COM** Y **ITC Member:** No

Rates:	Pvt Bath 3	Shared Bath 2
Single	$ 56.00	$ 46-48.00
Double	$ 60.00	$ 50-52.00

On Golden Pond B&B 7831 Eldridge 80005 Arvada CO
Katy Kula

Tel: 303-424-2296
Res Times 8am-9pm

"European hospitality and relaxing country comfort" is assured in this custom-built two story home located on ten acres with dramatic views of the mountains, prairies and downtown Denver from the wrap around verandahs - and in a secluded Rocky Mountain foothill setting, just fifteen miles west of Denver. Choose from five uniquely decorated guest rooms including Italian Provincial with king bed and large jacuzzi, African motif including a hanging bed, fireplace and large jacuzzi; a romantic Victorian room and an Oriental furnished setting with brass bed where you'll awake to the beauty of the natural pond and native birds. Each room has a large sliding glass door framing the gorgeous views and which opens onto your private deck. The great room offers a crackling fire, TV, VCR, games and books in a very comfortable setting. Your German hostess provides an extensive breakfast served on the deck or indoors and a late afternoon *"kaffeklatsch"* with fresh brewed coffee and pastries. A gazebo on a natural fishing pond on the grounds provide exciting wildlife viewing while soaking in the hot tub or swimming laps in the pool will keep you fit. Nearby foothills offer excellent hiking, biking, country roads and horseback riding trails. Of course, all of Denvers' activities and sights are just minutes away. Your host Katy, is a German native who enjoys an active lifestyle and looks forward to sharing her home with you. **Seasonal:** No **Reservations:** 50% deposit required, 7 day cancel notice for refund less

Colorado

National Edition

$15 service fee **Brochure:** Yes **Permitted:** Smoking outdoors **Languages:** German **Payment Terms:** Check [R04GPCO-13241] **COM** U **ITC Member:** No

Rates: Pvt Bath 5
Single $ 60-100.00
Double $ 60-100.00

Snow Queen Victorian Inn	124 E Cooper Ave 81611	Aspen CO
Norma Dolle/Larry Leduigham		Tel: 970-925-8455 Fax: 970-925-8455

Within easy walking distance to the center of town and local activities, the *Snow Queen Lodge* is just minutes away from the Gondola and shuttle busses to the surrounding ski areas too. The *Snow Queen Lodge* is a romantic and charming Victorian home built in 1886 with modern amenities and Victorian furnishings. This family-operated lodge specializes in a friendly and congenial atmosphere with western hospitality. There are a variety of rooms all named after famous silver mines with most offering private baths and two units include kitchen facilities. Reasonable year-round rates vary between off-season (summer, spring, fall) and four winter rate schedules. Off-season rates listed in heading; Seasonal rates are: Low 11/24-12/18, Holiday 12/19-1/2, Mid 1/2-2/6 and High 2/6-3/27. The woodburning fireplace in the lounge is a favorite gathering place for relaxing, watching TV or visiting with others. Smoking is allowed in rooms. A lovely outdoor hot tub is available for guests to relax in while enjoying the beautiful view of Aspen Mountain. A continental breakfast is included in your room rate and there are afternoon parties/get-togethers from tine to time. Studio loft apartments next door are available. **Discounts:** More than one week **Packages:** Ski **Airport:** Aspen Airport-3 mi **Seasonal:** Rates vary **Reservations:** 50% deposit within 7 days, bal 30 days before arrival/45 days-holidays, cancel policy; refund if 30/45 days before arrival less $20 per person; less than 30/45 days, only if rebooked **Brochure:** Yes **Permitted:** Children, drinking, smoking **Languages:** Some German, Spanish **Payment Terms:** Check MC/V [I02HPCO1-2939] **COM** Y **ITC Member:** No

Rates:	Pvt Bath 5	Shared Bath 2
Single	$ 50-85.00	$ 45-75.00
Double	$ 50-85.00	$ 55-75.00

Boulder Victoria Historic Inn	1305 Pine St 80302	Boulder CO
Jacki or Kirsten Peterson		Tel: 303-938-1300

The *Boulder Historic Bed & Breakfast* is a showcase of classic elegance in the heart of downtown Boulder, Colorado. Just two blocks from the famous Pearl Street Pedestrian Mall, this distinctive inn is within easy walking distance to shops, restaurants and nightspots, as well as year-round mountain activities and the University of Colorado campus. Originally built in the 1870's, The Boulder Victoria has recently been renovated to reflect its original Victorian grandeur. Guests experience the charm and personal service of a bed and breakfast, and the amenities and modern conveniences of a fine hotel. The seven beautifully appointed guest rooms, each with a private bath and telephone, are furnished with period antiques, queen size brass beds and down comforters. Many rooms also feature steam showers and/or private balconies or patios. A European-style continental breakfast buffet is served on the flagstone terrace or in the bay-windowed dining room. The elegant parlour provides and inviting atmosphere for afternoon tea and cookies, and a glass of port wine in the evening. Above the north wing of the inn, a spacious canopied patio is an ideal setting for catered receptions and meetings. **Discounts:** Corporate **Airport:** Stapelton, Denver-35 mi **Reservations:** Credit card number to guarantee reservation, 7 day cancel policy for refund. **Permitted:** Drinking **Conference:** Meeting space in parlour and canopied patio **Languages:** Spanish, German **Payment Terms:** Check AE/MC/V [R09EPCO-14847] **COM** Y **ITC Member:** No

Rates: Pvt Bath 7
Single $ 88.00
Double $ 153.00

National Edition   ***Colorado***

Allaire Timbers Inn	9511 Hwy #9/S Main St 80424	Breckenridge CO
Jack & Kathy Gumph	**Tel:** 800-624-4904 303-453-7530 **Fax:** 303-453-8699	
		Res Times 10am-8pm

The *Allaire Timbers Inn* is the intimate way to experience Breckenridge Colorado. Nestled in the trees at the south end of historic Main Street, this new log and stone B&B was designed and built in 1991 with every comfort of its guests in mind. Eight lodge rooms are named for historic Colorado mountain passes and each is uniquely decorated according to its name history. Each has a private bath and deck. Two elegant suites, the Summit and Breckenridge, boast a private fireplace and hot tub, as well as a private bath and deck. Join friends by a crackling fire in the log and beam Great Room. Relax in the Sunroom, or read in the Loft, all designed for you to share quiet times together. After a full day of activities, unwind in the large rejuvenating spa located on the main deck which offers spectacular views of the Ten Mile Range. The *Allaire Timbers* is located in the heart of Summit County, home of four major ski resorts and four championship golf courses. The *Allaire Timbers Inn* is wheelchair accessible. Gourmet breakfasts, afternoon treats and personalized hospitality makes the *Allaire Timbers* the perfect getaway in Colorado. Check with innkeeper for cancel policy for less than 30 days. Check-in 3-7pm, late arrivals only with prior arrangements, check-out 11am **Airport:** Denver Stapleton-100 mi **Seasonal:** No **Reservations:** 50% deposit within 10 day of booking, balance due 30 days prior to arrival; reservations within 30 days of arrival, bal due at res time; 30 day cancel policy for full refund **Brochure:** Yes **Permitted:** Children 13-up, drinking, maximum 2 persons a guest room **Conference:** Yes, perfect setting for small retreats and groups to 20 persons **Payment Terms:** Check AE/DC/MC/V [I07GPCO-153-17] **COM** Y **ITC Member:** No

Rates: Pvt Bath 10
Single $ 115-230.00
Double $ 115-230.00

Cotten House	102 S French St 80424	Breckenridge CO
Peter & Georgette Contos		**Tel:** 303-453-5509

In the heart of beautiful Breckenridge is this exciting 1886 Victorian home which is listed on the *National Historic Register* that has been fully restored in the theme of the mining era of the Gold Rush of the 1860's. The guest rooms are furnished in individual themes with names of "Colorado Room" with a four-poster queen bed and down bedding; "Victorian Room", turn-of-the-century furnishings, hardwood floors in a romantic setting; "Room With A View" overlooks the ski slopes and town and offers a relaxing Southeast American decor. The private and shared baths include antique clawfoot tubs. The common room has a beautiful view of the Breckenridge ski area and includes TV, VCR, books, games and a comfortable atmosphere. Phone service, ski and bike storage are available along with on-site parking and laundry facilities. A seven day, full menu complimentary breakfast and afternoon refreshments are offered. Conveniently located, winter skiing is available right at your door-step via a free shuttle bus, nightlife, restaurants, shopping and many other activities are within walking distance including summer music festivals which shouldn't be missed. Members of Innkeepers of Colorado, American B&B Assoc and AAA approved. **Airport:** Denver Stapleton-1.5-2 Hrs **Packages:** Honeymoon, Anniversary Roses, Champagne Gift Certificates available **Seasonal:** Rates vary **Reservations:** Non-refundable deposit by check within 5 days of reservation, arrival only 4-6pm, unless prior arrangements have been made, *credit card accepted only for deposit guarantee **Brochure:** Yes **Permitted:** Children, limited drinking **Languages:** French, Greek **Payment Terms:** Check Yes* [Z04GPCO-16397] **COM** U **ITC Member:** No

Rates:	Pvt Bath 1	Shared Bath 2
Single	$ 60.00	$ 50-55.00
Double	$ 60.00	$ 50-55.00

©*Inn & Travel Memphis, Tennessee*

Colorado *National Edition*

Cottonwood Hot Springs Inn aka Cottonwood Pass Rd 81211 Buena Vista CO
Cathy Manning Tel: 800-241-4119 719-395-6434
Res Times 8am-10pm

We would like to invite you to our ole-west style Country Inn, nestled in a high mountain area of the majestic collegiate Peaks. We are bordered by Cottonwood Creek and surrounded by San Isabel National Forest. Located 5.5 miles out of the picturesque town of Buena Vista. This Inn revolved around our pure and natural stone soaking pools, three private clothing optional spas. Also, a wet/dry sauna and cold plunge. Massage therapists on site. Our accommodations include four rustic creekside cabins with private hot tubs, twelve spacious guest rooms, unique camping tepees and a dormitory. Unlimited recreational activities are available in the area, including white water rafting, golfing, fishing, nature walks, hiking, back packing, rock and mountain climbing, cross country and downhill skiing. We offer skiing, rafting and group packages with or without meals at reasonable rates for family reunions, meetings, workshops and seminars. At this ancient site we come together for the purpose of creating a holistic/spiritual retreat and a intentional community - a haven for the healing and rejuvenation of the body/mind/spirit. Supportive of individual and group retreats, one another and mother earth. A relaxing Country Inn, a healing place and a unique lodging experience. **Airport:** Denver-Stapleton 110-mi; Colorado Spring-90mi **Packages:** Skiing, Rafting, including meals **Seasonal:** Yes, rates vary **Reservations:** 25% deposit or credit card guarantee, 72 hr cancellation policy *Creekside cabin available **Brochure:** Yes **Permitted:** Limited pets, limited children, limited smoking **Conference:** Can accommodate up to 200 persons in single or divided rooms for smaller groups for workshops, seminars. **Payment Terms:** Check AE/DC/DISC/MC/V [Z02HPCO1-13243] **COM YG ITC Member:** No

Rates: Pvt Bath 12   Shared Bath 4
Single $ 47-52.00
Double $ 52-57.00

Cheyenne Canon Inn 2030 W Cheyenne Blvd 80906 Colorado Springs CO
John & Barbara Starr Tel: 719-633-0625 Fax: 719-633-8826

Opened in 1994, this exceptionally spacious 1920's Mission-style mansion of over 13,000 square feet is situated at the mouth of two canyons in one of Colorado's most spectacular locations. Features of the Inn include the Great Room (with its seven foot tall windows overlooking the mountains and canyons) and seven unique, private bath guestrooms, each decorated for a different region of the world. The Hacienda has a king carved Santa Fe style bed, private sitting room with views of Cheyenne Canon. The king size bed in the Tea House (Oriental) yields to some of the most beautiful sunrises anywhere. Rounding out the tour are the Villa (Italy), Chalet (Switzerland), Cabana (Caribbean), and the Hut (Africa). The French Chateau, a luxury cottage just opened and offers a private hot tub, mountain view, marble bath with shower for two and a rock fireplace. Numerous hiking and mountain biking trails start at the doorstep. The Inn is minutes from the famous 5-star Broadmoor Hotel and all Pikes Peak area attractions. There is also a private Hot Tub Room available for use by reservation (no additional charge). A full breakfast features quiches, specialty fruit dishes and more is served each morning. **Airport:** Denver-65 mi; Colorado Springs-7 mi **Reservations:** 50% of length of stay or one night's full rate, which ever is greater, 5 day cancel policy **Brochure:** Yes **Permitted:** Children 13+, drinking **Conference:** Yes, groups to thirty-five **Languages:** French **Payment Terms:** Check AE/DISC/MC/V [I10HPCO1-18993] **COM YG ITC Member:** No

Rates: Pvt Bath 8
Single $ 65-165.00
Double $ 75-175.00

Hearthstone Inn 506 N Cascade 80903 Colorado Springs CO
Dot Williams Tel: 719-473-4413
Res Times 7am-11pm

4-86 ©*Inn & Travel Memphis, Tennessee*

Elegantly restored 1885 Queen Anne mansion on a beautiful tree-lined residential boulevard furnished with antiques from the period but with modern conveniences like full private baths, comfortable firm mattresses with king beds and fireplaces available in some of the guest rooms. Featured in *"Country Inn & Back Roads."* You can relax in the warmth and grace of a bygone era. Charming hostess includes a full gourmet breakfast to start your day with unique egg dishes, homemade breads and fresh fruit and all beverages. In this Pike's Peak region, you're close to many sights including the Air Force Academy, Pike's Peak, Garden of the Gods, Cave of the Winds and the gorgeous mountains themselves. Located on a large lot, you're just three blocks from Colorado College and within blocks of many parks, churches and restaurants offering fine dining experiences. And your hostess will provide maps, reservations and directions to all areas you might like to visit. **Seasonal:** No **Reservations:** One night's deposit required at res time to hold room with 24 hour cancel notice for refund less $10.00 handling charge. **Brochure:** Yes **Permitted:** Children, drinking, limited smoking **Conference:** Yes, for groups to 30 persons for accommodations and dining. **Payment Terms:** Check AE/MC/V [I10APCO-826] **COM** Y **ITC Member:** No

Rates:	Pvt Bath 23	Shared Bath 2
Single	$ 70-100.00	$ 55.00
Double	$ 75-120.00	$ 60.00

Holden House-1902 B&B Inn   1102 W Pikes Peak Ave 80904   Colorado Springs CO
Sallie & Welling Clark   Tel: 719-471-3980
    Res Times 9am-9pm

Built by Isabel Holden, the widow of a wealthy Colorado Springs businessman, this 1902 storybook Victorian and 1906 carriage house are centrally located near historic "Old Colorado City", in a residential area. The Inn was lovingly restored by the Clarks in 1985 and is furnished with antiques, family treasures and heirloom quilts. Named for Colorado mining towns, the six individually decorated guest rooms are furnished with queen beds, period furnishings and down pillows. The Inn also boasts four romantic suites with "tubs for two", fireplaces, mountain views and more! Gourmet breakfasts - served in the formal dining room, might include blueberry-corn muffins, Sallie's famous Eggs Fiesta, fresh fruit, gourmet coffee, tea and juice. Complimentary refreshments, 24-hour coffee and tea, homemade cookies and turn-down service and in room phones are just a few of the *Holden House's* special touches. Sallie and Welling will be happy to help in planning your itinerary. Colorado Springs is nestled at the base of 14,100 ft Pikes Peak and offers a variety of activities from scenic beauty to cultural attractions. Spend a few days, a week or more. You'll find plenty to keep you busy. AAA & Mobil Approved. Friendly cats "Mingtoy" and "Muffin" in residence. Aspiring Innkeeper Seminars and Gift Certificates are available. **Packages:** Romance, stay 2 or more nights in the Aspen/Independence Suite and have breakfast in bed for $10 additional to room rate **Airport:** Colorado Springs-10 mi; Denver Stapleton-83 mi **Seasonal:** No **Reservations:** One night or 50% deposit (which ever is more) 8 day cancel policy $15 service fee, 30 day cancel notice for special events, minimum stay holidays/weekends and High Season, disabled access room **Brochure:** Yes **Permitted:** Drinking, no Smoking **Payment Terms:** Check AE/DC/DISC/MC/V [I03-HPCO1-6081] **COM** YG **ITC Member:** No

Rates:	Pvt Bath 6
Single	$ 75-110.00
Double	$ 75-110.00

Room At The Inn B&B   618 N Nevada Ave 80903   Colorado Springs CO

©*Inn & Travel Memphis, Tennessee*   4-87

Colorado *National Edition*

Jan, Chick & Kelly McCormick

Tel: 719-442-1896 Fax: 719-442-6802
Res Times 10am-8pm

The recently opened *Room At The Inn* features the romance, charm and hospitality of the Victorian Era, while pampering guests with in room whirlpool tubs for two, fireplaces, outdoor hot tub, fresh cut flowers and evening turn-down service. A short stroll takes you to the many unique restaurants, coffee houses, ice creameries and shops of a vibrant downtown or through the beautiful campus of Colorado College. The Fine Arts Center, United States Olympic Training Center and several museums are all within close proximity. The Inn, which won an award for it's careful restoration, is a classic Queen Anne Victorian with a three-story turret, wraparound porch and seven styles of fish scale siding. The interior boasts nine foot ceilings, waiting bench, an oak staircase, four original fireplaces as well as hand painted murals dating from 1896. The guest rooms feature queen sized beds, designer linens, period antiques, oriental rugs, private baths, new original wall paintings and air-conditioning. One guest room is wheel chair accessible. The smell of fresh ground coffee and homemade muffins invite you to a delicious breakfast served in the dining room or on the porch. Banana Foster French toast or Raspberry Cheese Blintz accompanied with fresh squeezed orange juice and seasonal fresh fruit are just a sample of the breakfast fare. Afternoon refreshments greet guests upon their arrival. The Inn is a perfect haven to retreat to after a busy day at work or a day of enjoying the numerous attractions of the Pikes Peak Region. **Airport:** Colorado Springs Municipal-11 mi **Discounts:** Extended stays (3 days-longer) **Reservations:** One night or 50% of length of stay (which ever is greater) deposit required within 7 days of booking, 14 day cancel policy for refund **Permitted:** Limited children, limited drinking **Conference:** Yes, groups to fourteen **Payment Terms:** Check AE/DISC/MC/V [K03HPCO1-18835] **COM YG ITC Member:** No **Quality Assurance** Requested:

Rates: **Pvt Bath 7**
Single $ 80-115.00
Double $ 80-115.00

Castle Marne   1572 Race St 80206   Denver CO
Jim & Diane Peiker   Tel: 800-821-2976 303-331-0621

Come fall under the spell of one of Denver's grandest historic mansions. Built in 1889, Castle Marne is considered by many to the be finest example of *"America's most eclectic architect",* William Lang. Your stay at Castle Marne combines old world elegance and Victorian charm with modern convenience and comfort. Each room is a unique experience in pampered luxury. Carefully chosen furnishings combine period antiques, family heirlooms and exacting reproductions to create a mood of long ago elegance. Whether your stay is for business, vacation or a honeymoon, it will be unforgettable in one of our luxury suites. Two rooms have jetted whirlpool tubs, three rooms have the original clawfooted tubs with shower rings and all have showers and pedestal sinks. Gourmet full breakfast of fresh fruits, homebaked breads, muffins and hot entree is included; afternoon tea is served daily. Castle Marne is located in the heart of one of Denver's most historic neighborhoods, minutes from the finest cultural, shopping, dining and sightseeing attractions. Castle Marne is near City Park, running paths, tennis courts, a public golf course, Denver Zoo, Imax Theatre, Gates Planetarium, Botanic Gardens, Denver Art Museum, Museum of Natural History, downtown Denver, US Mint, State Capitol and the State History Museum. **Seasonal:** No **Reservations:** One night's deposit within 7 days of booking, cancel policy of $25 service fee if cancelled less than 5 days prior to arrival date. **Brochure:** Yes **Permitted:** Drinking **Conference:** Yes **Payment Terms:** Check AE/DC/MC/V [Z11CPCO-8371] **COM Y ITC Member:** No

Rates: **Pvt Bath 9**
Single $ 65-145.00
Double $ 75-145.00

Cheyenne Canyon Inn
John & Barbara Starr

Denver CO
Tel: 719-633-0625

Refer to the same listing name under Colorado Springs, Colorado for a complete description. **Payment Terms:** Check AE/DISC/MC/V [M08GPCO-20109] COM Y **ITC Member:** No

Rates:	Pvt Bath 7
Single	$ 65-165.00
Double	$ 75-175.00

Haus Berlin B&B
Christiana & Dennis Brown

1651 Emerson 80218

Denver CO
Tel: 303-837-9527
Res Times 7am-10pm

Haus Berlin, a recently renovated Victorian townhouse, has three guest rooms and one suite offering private bath, shower, inroom phones and special touches such as king or queen size beds dressed in luxurious, all-cotton linens and down comforters. Located on a quiet tree-lined street where the architecture reflects the charm of the turn-of-the-century, business and leisure travelers appreciate the closeness of Denver's central business district. *Listed on The National Register of Historic Places*, all rooms reflect urban elegance while providing the warmth and feeling of European tradition. The main floor offers a cozy Country French theme. The furnishings are eclectic as are the original paintings and pieces of art. This is truly a different Bed and Breakfast! A continental plus breakfast includes hot beverages, juices, jam, cereals and fresh baked goods or guests may choose traditional German bread, cold cuts and cheese. Come and discover us and Denver - at the foothills of the Rocky Mountains! Cable TV, fax and complimentary beverages are available **Airport:** New Denver Airport Intl-30 mi **Seasonal:** No **Reservations:** One night deposit, 7 day cancel policy **Permitted:** Limited children, drinking **Languages:** German **Payment Terms:** Check AE/MC/V [R05GPCO-18840] COM Y **ITC Member:** No

Rates:	Pvt Bath 4
Single	$ 80-120.00
Double	$ 80-120.00

Queen Anne B&B Inn
Tom & Chris King

2147 Tremont Place 80205

Denver CO
Tel: 800-432-INNS 303-296-6666 Fax: 303-296-2151
Res Times 7am-11pm

Facing quiet Benedict Fountain Park in the Clement Historic District of Downtown Denver are the Inn's two side-by-side *National Register* Victorians (1879/1886). They are within easy walking distance of the Capitol, US Mint, 16th Street Mall, Convention Center, most offices, Larimer Square, museums and many fine restaurants. Because of the Inn's downtown location, and the Inn's quiet, friendly atmosphere, business men and women are half of the Inn's guests. There are fourteen guest rooms including four gallery suites dedicated to famous artists: Audubon, Calder, Remington and Rockwell. Fresh flowers, chamber music, period antiques, direct dial phones and private baths are in all rooms. Six guest rooms offer special deep tubs and one room features a fireplace. The Inn is air conditioned. There is plenty of free parking and a no-tipping policy is in effect. Complimentary full breakfast (ensuite if you wish) and evening beverages are included. Your knowledgeable innkeepers will suggest seeing-doing-shopping in and around Denver, arrange dinner reservations at nearby restaurants, tours and sport activities (perhaps see a working gold mine or take a horse-drawn carriage ride to dinner downtown), or advise you about other B&Bs in Colorado. The Inn's thirty-two awards include: *Best Ten B&Bs In The USA, Twelve Most Romantic B&Bs in the Nation, Best of Denver, Seven Most Romantic Destinations in Colorado,* AAA and Mobil inspected and approved. **Reservations:** Full payment within two weeks of booking reservation, 50% if more than 4 mos in advance, with bal due 30 days

Colorado

prior to arrival; cancel policy: 3 day cancel notice for full refund, except holidays (two weeks notice) or groups of 3 rooms or more (30 day notice) **Discounts:** AAA, Corporate, Groups **Packages:** Midweek (11/1-5/31), Three Day Holiday Weekends **Airport:** Denver Intl **Seasonal:** No **Brochure:** Yes **Permitted:** Children, limited drinking **Conference:** Groups to 15 indoors, to 75 outdoors **Payment Terms:** Check/Eurocard AE/DC/DISC/MC/V [I04HPCO1-840] **COM** YG **ITC Member:** No

Rates:	Pvt Bath 14	Suites
Single	$ 75-135.00	
Double	$ 75-138.00	$ 135-155.00

Room At The Inn B&B — Denver CO
Jan, Chick & Kelly McCormick
Tel: 719-442-1896 Fax: 719-442-6802
Res Times 10am-8pm

Refer to the same listing name under Colorado Springs, Colorado for a complete description. **Payment Terms:** Check AE/DISC/MC/V [M08GPCO-20108] **COM** Y **ITC Member:** No

Rates:	Pvt Bath 7
Single	$ 80-115.00
Double	$ 80-115.00

Victoria Oaks Inn — 1575 Race St 80206 — Denver CO
Clyde Stephens & Ric
Tel: 800-662-6257 303-355-1818

Victoria Oaks Inn; a Bed and Breakfast in Capitol Hill in the Wyman's Historic District. Conveniently located one mile east of downtown Denver and central to clubs, restaurants, museums, shopping, the zoo and parks. The mountains are only fifteen minutes from our front door. The Victoria Oaks Inn was built in 1879 and greets guests with the same warmth and ambiance of a period long ago, with modern convenience of todays' standards. Each room has detailed antique furnishings, phones, comfortable beds; some rooms include fireplaces, plaster decorated ceilings, leaded glass and bay windows. Each room boasts its own warmth and character certain to please the most weary travelers. Guests begin each morning with an inspiring continental breakfast including freshly squeezed orange juice, blended coffee and teas, and a choice of fresh pastries, croissants, bagels and fresh fruits with the early morning paper. For groups and long term stays, you will be happy to know discounts are available. There is another three bedroom fully furnished townhouse for rent. Fully appointed with kitchen, utensil, phone and TV. Victoria Oaks Inn, a home you'll be glad to come back to. Nearby Tourist attractions such as the Historic Capitol Hill District, the "Unsinkable" Molly Brown House, Botanic Gardens and within walking distance is Denver's City Park and 72 acre zoo, Museum of Natural History, Laserium and Imax Theatre. **Airport:** Denver's newest-20 min **Discounts:** Extended stays, inquire at reservation time **Seasonal:** No **Reservations:** One night's deposit required, 48 hr cancel policy for refund **Brochure:** Yes **Conference:** From meetings to dining - the Victoria Oaks Inn provides full service designed to meet your needs. **Payment Terms:** Check AE/DC/DISC/MC/V [I11HPCO1-842] **COM** YG **ITC Member:** No

Rates:	Pvt Bath 7	Shared Bath 2
Single	$ 65.00	$ 50.00
Double	$ 85.00	$ 60.00

Apple Orchard Inn — 7758 County Rd 203 81301 — Durango CO
John & Celeste Gardiner
Tel: 800-426-0751 970-247-0751
Res Times 24 Hrs

The Apple Orchard Inn is set in the beautiful Animas Valley, eight miles north of Durango at Hermosa. Lined with fruit orchards and historic farms, Country Road 203 leads you to the Inn. The newly constructed farmhouse main house and six private cottages are situated on four and a half acre apple orchard. The main house offers four guest rooms on the second floor, each uniquely trimmed with exquisite hardwoods and features elegant country furnishings, including queen-size featherbeds to sink into. A master bedroom features a river rock fireplace, Jacuzzi tub and a king size featherbed for romantic evenings. All of the guest rooms are spacious and have views of the orchard and mountains. A hearty full breakfast that changes daily, is served each morning, overlooking the surrounding cliffs, mountains and the steaming Durango and Silverton Narrow Gauge Train as it passes. Celeste practices her many culinary skills honed while living in Europe with John. An accomplished chef, she attended the Ritz-Escoffier Cooking School in Paris as well as schools in Florence, Italy. Gourmet dinners are available with advance notice and added cost. Nearby sights include downtown Durango, Puragory Ski Area, Trimble Hot Springs, Mesa Verde National Park, prime fly fishing waters and river rafting on the Animas River, golf and hiking. AAA 3-Diamond rated. Internet http://www.databahn.net/apple/ **Seasonal:** Rates vary **Reservations:** 50% deposit or one night's stay due within 7 days of booking reservation, 14 day cancel policy for refund less $20 service fee per room cancelled **Brochure:** Yes **Permitted:** Drinking, limited children, limited smoking **Conference:** Special events, parties, retreat, wedding groups **Languages:** Portuguese, Italian **Payment Terms:** Check DISC/MC/V [I03IPCO1-22948] **COM YG ITC Member:** No

Rates:	Pvt Bath 10
Single	$ 70-135.00
Double	$ 85-150.00

Leland House B&B — 721 E Second Ave 81301 — **Durango CO**
The Komick Family — **Tel:** 800-664-1920 970-385-1920
Res Times 7am-7pm

The *Leland House Bed & Breakfast Suites* offer distinctive overnight lodging in historic downtown Durango. The property is a lovingly restored historic Inn built in 1927, steps away from Durango's Main Avenue and a variety of charming shops and excellent restaurants. There are six one bedroom suites with private bath, fully equipped kitchens, full or queen size beds, queen size sofa sleepers and living rooms, and four studios with a combined bedroom/living area, partially equipped kitchenette, private bath and either queen or full size beds. There's cable TV, daily maid service, private on-site parking and cribs for small children. Guests awake to freshly baked breads and muffins served with the complimentary full gourmet breakfast each morning. Complimentary refreshments are offered at an afternoon social hour. Sights include Durango-Silverton train, Mesa Verde National Park, PRCA Rodeo with excellent skiing at Purgatory, hiking, biking and rafting, kayaking and fishing the Animas River. Full concierge services include information, reservation service, guided tours, train tickets and picnic arrangements. As you settle in for the night, chocolates on your pillow bid you sweet dreams at the *Leland House*. **Discounts:** Yes, inquire at res time **Airport:** La Plata-16 mi **Packages:** Yes, inquire at res time **Seasonal:** Rates vary **Reservations:** One night deposit or credit card number to guarantee reservation, 7 day cancel policy for refund **Brochure:** Yes **Permitted:** Children, drinking **Payment Terms:** Check MC/V [K11GPCO1-17793] **COM Y ITC Member:** No **Quality Assurance** Requested

Rates:	Pvt Bath 16	Shared Bath
Single	$ 112.50	$ 75.50
Double	$ 125.00	$ 85.00

Pennys Place — 1041 County Rd 307 81301 — **Durango CO**
Penny O'Keefe — **Tel:** 970-247-8928

Colorado *National Edition*

Penny's Place is eleven picturesque, paved miles from downtown Durango, located on 26 acres in quiet, rolling countryside overlooking the spectacular La Plata Mountains. There are deer and meadowlarks visiting most days. There is a gabled ceiling room with a king-size bed that has a private entrance, deck, bath, kitchenette and washer and dryer. The room has a marvelous view of the mountains from the deck. A spiral staircase joins this room to the common room with a hot tub, satellite TV and woodburning stove. Also available is another gabled-ceiling room with a queen-size brass bed that shares a bath with a room with a four-poster double bed. A full breakfast is served including homemade bread, jams and syrup. Dietary restrictions upon request and flexible breakfast time.

A visit of several days is recommended to see the wonderful sites of the Durango area, including Narrow Gauge Train, Mesa Verde, hiking, horseback riding, fishing and skiing at Purgatory Ski Area. **Airport:** LaPlata Field, Durango-5 mi **Seasonal:** Rates vary **Reservations:** One night's deposit, 7 day cancel policy for refund. Check-in 4-6pm, other by prior arrangement. Two night minimum stay required during summer. **Brochure:** Yes **Permitted:** Drinking, limited children **Payment Terms:** Check MC/V [R11DPCO-12489] **COM** Y **ITC Member:** No

Rates:	Pvt Bath 1	Shared Bath 2
Single	$ 60-70.00	$ 40-50.00
Double	$ 65-75.00	$ 44-55.00

River House B&B   495 Animas View Dr 81301   Durango CO
Crystal, Kate, Lars   **Tel:** 800-254-4775 970-247-4775 **Fax:** 970-259-1465

The elegant simplicity of southwest living is enjoyed by guests at the *River House Bed & Breakfast*. Just on the north edge of Durango you'll enjoy vacation living at its best, on the river with a view of the Animas Valley and in a true European B&B manner but with American style. Each guest room is uniquely furnished and named after some of the enchanting rivers of the San Juan Mountains such as the Rio Grande River Room or the Gunnison River Room which has a king size bed, a large library and a clawfoot tub for soaking while enjoying your favorite passages. Each day begins with a full complimentary breakfast in the early-morning sunfilled Atrium with astonishing proportions. Common rooms include living room with fireplace, wet bar, game room and large screen cable TV, snooker table and an outdoor therapeutic hot tub dubbed "Rainbow Hot Spring", after one of our favorite spots in the Rockies, or spoil yourself with our inhouse masseuse. Added amenities available at added cost include massage therapy and hypnotherapy. We invite you to experience our lifestyle and hospitality in the Colorado tradition. **Airport:** Durango-20 mi **Discounts:** Yes, inquire at res time **Packages:** Yes, inquire at res time **Seasonal:** No **Reservations:** One night's deposit, 14 day cancel policy for refund; 50% deposit on 3 nights or more. Late cancel refund only if room is rebooked. **Brochure:** Yes **Permitted:** Children, limited drinking **Conference:** Yes; weddings, receptions, meetings for 16-100 persons **Payment Terms:** Check AE/DISC/MC/V [Z11GPCO1-849] **COM** Y **ITC Member:** No **Quality Assurance** Requested

Rates:	Pvt Bath 7
Single	$ 50-70.00
Double	$ 65-95.00

Scrubby Oaks B&B   1901 Florida Rd 81302   Durango CO
Mary Ann Craig   **Tel:** 970-247-2176
    Res Times 8am-5pm

Lovely two story home nestled upon ten acres of country overlooking Animals Valley and enclosed by mountain peaks. Enjoy the outdoors among the trees and gardens surrounding the patio while enjoying breakfast where strawberry waffles are a specialty of the hostess. Relax around the warm fireplace in the kitchen in winter and the year-round sauna. **Seasonal:** No **Brochure:** Yes **Permitted:** Children, social drinking **Payment Terms:** Check [X11ACCO-2944] **COM** Y **ITC Member:** No

Rates:	Shared Bath 3
Single	$ 40.00
Double	$ 50.00

Vagabond Inn B&B   2180 Main Ave 81301   Durango CO
Ace & Mary Lou Hall   **Tel:** 970-259-5901

©*Inn & Travel Memphis, Tennessee*

National Edition   ***Colorado***

Enjoy the down-home comfort of the *Vagabond Inn*. This unique and charming Bed & Breakfast has eight rooms, each different from the other. The Bridal Suite has a hand-carved four-poster bed and a heart-shaped hot tub in the room. All rooms have color TV, very comfortable beds, and some have waterbeds and/or fireplaces. Guests receive a continental breakfast and a complimentary glass of wine each day of their stay. Message and wake-up service, reasonable rates and an outdoor hot tub are some of the other amenities that await you at the Vagabond Inn. Visit us and see the splendor of southwest Colorado in any season. Ride the Durango and Silverton Narrow Gauge Train. See the ancient Anazasi Indian Ruins. Ski Purgatory. Sample food from over seventy restaurants, and experience Durango while you stay at our *"turn-of-the-century"* roadhouse. Durango has plenty of nightlife and old-fashioned fun if you've got the notion. It's a perfect match for some of the best skiing Colorado has to offer. We accept most major credit cards. Sorry no pets permitted. Call or write for more information. We're looking forward to your stay with us! **Airport:** La Plata County Airport 17 mi **Discounts:** Yes, inquire at res time **Seasonal:** Rates vary **Reservations:** One night's deposit at res time, 24 hr cancel policy for full refund, except Holiday seasons when 2 wk notice required. **Brochure:** Yes **Permitted:** Children, smoking, drinking **Conference:** Yes **Payment Terms:** AE/DC/MC/V [Z11DPCO-8460] **COM Y ITC Member:** No

Rates:	Pvt Bath 8
Single	$ 36-125.00
Double	$ 36-125.00

Blue Lake Ranch   16919 Hwy 140   81326   Durango (Hesperus) CO
David Alford   **Tel:** 303-385-4537 **Fax:** 303-385-4088
                                                                                                   Res Times 8am-8pm

Homesteaded in the early 1900s by Swedish immigrants, *Blue Lake Ranch* has evolved from a simple homestead to a luxurious, European-style estate. The main house with antique and flower-filled rooms, is surrounded by gardens that supply *Blue Lake Ranch's* various businesses with lavender for jelly, heirloom seeds and everlasting flowers. From every room there is a view of the magnificent mountains that form a backdrop to the lake and the grazing herds of sheep. There is absolute privacy and quiet without another house in sight. At the cabin, overlooking a lake, window boxes of geraniums cascade to the outside deck. Furnished in Southwestern-style, there are three rooms equally comfortable for a couple or a group. Dramatic shifts of clouds pass over the lake; deer graze below in open meadows; and star-gazing is unparalled. A full European-style buffet breakfast and afternoon tea are included in the room rate. *Blue Lake Ranch* is 20 minutes from Durango and close to Mesa Verde with hiking in the San Juan Mountains. The lake on the grounds is stocked with trout to be fished or guests can simply relax in the hot tub or in the Adirondack chairs strategically placed on the 90 acres to take in the beautiful sunsets. **Seasonal:** No **Reservations:** 50% deposit of total stay within 7 days of booking, bal due 30 days prior to arrival, 30 day cancel policy for full refund; less than 30 days total amount forfeited unless re-rented for the same time. **Brochure:** Yes **Permitted:** Children, drinking **Languages:** French **Payment Terms:** Check [Z11DPCO-847] **COM Y ITC Member:** No

Rates:	Pvt Bath 2	Shared Bath 2
Single	$ 95-125.00	$ 70.00
Double	$ 95-125.00	$ 70.00

Mad Creek B&B   167 Park Ave (US 40)   80438   Empire CO
Heather & Mike Lopez   **Tel:** 303-569-2003

1881 Victorian Cottage with old mountain charm! Antiques, family heirlooms, original artwork and unique artifacts of the past adorn this house. The common area includes a snowshoe style loveseat in a bay window. Relax in front of the rock fireplace while watching a movie, pursue the library filled with local lore, or plan your next adventure with our guides and maps. Your rooms are furnished with antiques, down comforters, knotty pine floors and other pleasantries. Complimentary cross-country skis, snowshoes and numerous mountain bikes are available for guests, including the outdoor hot tub. A full complimentary breakfast is included. On the continental divide at over 8600 foot altitude, Empire's picturesque star-shaped mountain valley is conveniently located within minutes of some of the best Colorado has to offer. Located just 42 miles west of Denver, Empire and its surrounding Historic Communities are living visions of a colorful mining past. Six major ski areas and wonderful back-coun-

Colorado *National Edition*

try trails are 15-45 minutes away. Summer fun includes rafting, hiking, mountain biking, horseback rides, fishing and train rides. Scenic drives, Mine Tours, unique shopping and gourmet dining all year-round. Come - join us! **Airport:** Denver Stapleton-45 mins **Packages:** Downhill Mountain Bike Tours, Raft Trips **Seasonal:** No **Reservations:** Credit card number for one night's deposit, 7 day cancel policy for refund **Brochure:** Yes **Permitted:** Children 10-up; No smoking or pets **Languages:** Some Spanish **Payment Terms:** Check MC/V [R03GPCO-16667] **COM** U **ITC Member:** No

Rates:	Pvt Bath 1	Shared Bath 2
Single	$ 59.00	$ 39.00
Double	$ 69.00	$ 49.00

Eagle Cliff House	PO Box 4312 80517	Estes Park CO
Nancy & Mike Conrin		Tel: 970-586-5425

Eagle Cliff House is a warm and friendly bed and breakfast nestled in ponderosa pines at the base of Eagle Cliff Mountain in Estes Park. We invite you to relax in the comfort of soft colors native to Southwestern decor combined with the beautiful woods used in American antiques. We invite you to enjoy the enticing aromas of a hearty country breakfast served in our bright and sunny breakfast nook. Tender homemade breads and rolls and fresh fruit greet you each morning. With our abundant full breakfast and an "ever-ready" cookie jar of delicacies - you'll be ready for a full day of activities. The guest rooms and a separate cottage are variously furnished in turn-of-the-century country antiques, American Southwest decor and a Victorian theme. The Victorian Cottage is a private, romantic retreat featuring a queen size bed, fully stocked kitchenette and a sunny deck for enjoying the natural setting. Within walking distance of Rocky Mountain National Park, your hosts are expert backpacking and hiking enthusiasts and are happy to share their knowledge of the local areas. Summers offer a full complement of golf, hiking, tennis, swimming and horseback riding while winters feature excellent cross country skiing, snowshoeing - with spectacular views year-round! The quaint village of Estes Park offers an abundance of Western history, unique shops and restaurants. Your hosts can help with special touches such as flowers, champagne, fruit, cheese, balloons - just let them know. **Airport:** Denver Stapleton-2 hrs **Seasonal:** No **Reservations:** Credit card number accepted only for one night deposit (or cash, check), two week cancel policy for refund less $10 service fee, two night stay weekends requested **Brochure:** Yes **Permitted:** Children, drinking **Languages:** Some Spanish **Payment Terms:** Check [I08HPCO1-16785] **COM** U **ITC Member:** No

Rates:	Pvt Bath 3
Single	$ 70-95.00
Double	$ 80-95.00

Hardy House	605 Brownell 80444	Georgetown CO
Carla & Mike Wagner		Tel: 303-569-3388
		Res Times 8am-9pm

Quaint ten room red Victorian home which began life in 1877, invites guests to a special experience relaxing by the pot-belly stove or resting beneath feather comforters, in this charming home. Period furnishings throughout, guests can choose one of the four rooms/suites: Victoria Suite, Ruby Room or Under The Eaves. All with period decor, private baths, fireplaces and an outdoor hot tub. A gourmet candlelight breakfast is included in summer and winter. You're just ten minutes from the "best skiing" in Colorado. Plenty of hiking at 14,000 foot altitude including picnics along mountain streams or in the meadowlands. Flowers, carriage drives by request, complimentary bikes for guests to use. **Airport:** Denver Intl-45 min **Packages:** Anniversary, Honeymoon **Seasonal:** No **Reservations:** Full payment required 7-10 days after booking, 7 day cancel policy for refund, 30 day cancel notice for special events, holiday or ski groups *MC/V accepted only to hold, cash/check payment required **Brochure:** Yes **Permitted:** Children limited **Payment Terms:** Check MC/V* [R08GPCO-862] **COM** Y **ITC Member:** No

Rates:	Pvt Bath 4
Single	$ 63-67.00
Double	$ 73-77.00

©*Inn & Travel Memphis, Tennessee*

Dove Inn	711 14th St 80401-1906	Golden CO
Sue & Guy Beals		Tel: 303-278-2209 Fax: 303-278-4029
		Res Times 8am-8pm

Charming 1878-1886 country Victorian residence on beautifully landscaped grounds and mature plantings is nestled in the foothills of West Denver, offering some of the best scenery Colorado has to offer. This residence offers all the Victorian features with dormers, angled ceilings, large bay windows, and other points of interest. Each guest room offers a unique decor. A spacious second floor room is furnished with a writing table and a spectacular view overlooking Golden and the foothills. An exciting room includes an antique 7-foot bathtub. All rooms include phone, TV, a/c with beds and cribs available. A full or continental breakfast is included. Nearby attractions included: Coors Brewery tour, Colorado School of Mines and Railroad Museum, Golden Gate Canyon State Park, Rocky Mountain National Park with plenty of skiing within an easy drive. Denver is just a twenty minute drive. **Discounts:** 10% stays 7 days or longer **Airport:** Stapleton Intl-20 mi **Seasonal:** Clo Xmas **Reservations:** Deposit or credit card number to hold room; notify if arriving after 9 pm, 48 hr cancel policy. Airport shuttle is available. *Shower facility. **Brochure:** Yes **Permitted:** Limited children, limited drinking, limited smoking **Payment Terms:** Check AE/DC/MC/V [Z03FPCO-867] **COM** Y **ITC Member:** No

Rates:	Pvt Bath 4	Shared Bath 2
Single	$ 44.00	$ 44.00
Double	$ 66.00	$ 51.00

Mary Lawrence Inn	601 N Taylor 81230	Gunnison CO
Pat & Jim Kennedy		Tel: 970-641-3343
		Res Times 10am-10pm

Built in 1885 and named for its long-time owner, *The Mary Lawrence Inn* was restored as a B&B in 1988. Rooms are furnished with Victorian antiques, hand-stenciled walls, home-made quilts, colorful art work, desks, fans and radios. A complimentary breakfast is imaginative and creative and served around an expandable table and differs each day. Menus take into account whether children are among the guests, and there's always a choice of juices and a wide range of hot beverages. Guests will find a sitting room filled with books, games and maps of the area. There's a fenced yard with deck and picnic area. Summer offers nearby lakes for fishing and boating while cross country skiing begins right outside of your door and downhill skiing at Crested Butte is just 30 mins away. **Airport:** Gunnison-2 mi **Packages:** Ski Packages start at $47/person including B&B and lift ticket; Valentine Special February, Fishing Weekends **Discounts:** Cycling and fishing **Seasonal:** No **Reservations:** Credit card number to guarantee one night's deposit, late arrival only with prior arrangements, airport pick-up available with prior arrangements **Brochure:** Yes **Permitted:** Children 6-up, drinking **Payment Terms:** Check MC/V [Z03HPCO1-9028] **COM** YG **ITC Member:** No

Rates:	Pvt Bath 5
Single	$ 69-85.00
Double	$ 69-85.00

Apple Blossom Inn	120 W Fourth St 80461	Leadville CO
Maggie Senn		Tel: 800-982-9279 719-486-2141
		Res Times 8am-8pm

You are invited to enjoy an authentic slice of Colorado's rich past in this lovingly restored and tastefully decorated home. Built in 1879 by a prominent Leadville banker and business man whose holdings included interests in various lucrative mines such as The Little Pittsburg and Little Johnny. His wife Estelle, earned the reputation of a gracious hostess because of the numerous parties and events they hosted. This lovely home retains many of their Victorian touches such as the beautiful crystal and brass lights, fireplaces adorned with Florentine tile, beveled mirrors, stained glass windows and maple and mahogany inlaid floors. The six guest rooms are uniquely furnished ranging from warm and cozy to large and sunny. Guests are welcomed into both of the charming living rooms, to enjoy the piano or the many board games or to choose a book from among the many selections on our shelves. A full complimentary breakfast is included and can be served in the dining room or your guest room. Packed lunches and delicious home-cooked dinners are available with prior arrangements. Complimentary hot and cold beverages are always available along with a full cookie jar of homemade goodies! Your hostess is ready to help plan your stay from finding the best fishing spot to locating baby sitters - just let her know. **Airport:** Denver-110 mi **Discounts:** 10% for seniors (over 64) and business **Packages:** Ski Packages from $59 /person including lift ticket; Summer Package from $49/person with museum passes **Seasonal:** No **Reservations:** One night or 50% due within 7 days after reservation, 14 day cancel policy for refund, less than 14 days, refund only if rebooked. Late arrival and check out only with prior arrangements **Brochure:** Yes **Permitted:** Children, drinking, limited smoking **Conference:** Ideal for groups with sleeping facilities for 13-22 persons **Payment Terms:** Check AE/MC/V [R10HPCO1-16407] **COM** YG **ITC Member:** No

Rates:	Pvt Bath 3	Shared Bath 5
Single	$ 69.00	$ 54.00
Double	$ 79.00	$ 59.00

Grays Avenue Hotel	711 Manitou Ave 80829	Manitou Springs CO
Tom & Lee Gray		Tel: 719-685-1277

Queen Anne shingle Victorian which was built c1880's and in the center of the historic district and is the oldest continuously used hotel in Colorado. Guest rooms are furnished with antiques and spacious. You're close to all Colorado's major attractions here; Pike's Peak, Cog Railroad, Seven Falls, Air Force Academy, and Mount Manitou incline. Full country breakfast included daily. **Seasonal:** No **Permitted:** Children 9-up **Conference:** Yes, for social and business needs, groups to 15 persons. **Payment Terms:** Check [C11ACCO-880] **COM** Y **ITC Member:** No

Rates:	Pvt Bath 6	Shared Bath 4
Single		
Double	$ 70.00	$ 50.00

Inn At Chalk Cliffs	16557 County Rd #162 81236	Nathrop CO
Phyllis Terry		Tel: 719-395-6068
		Res Times 7am-Noon

The *Inn at Chalk Cliffs* is nestled beneath breathtaking Mount Princeton (14,197 ft) and looks out onto Mount Antero (14,269 ft). It is located near the geographic center of Colorado and within 20 miles of the Continental Divide between the towns of Salida and Buena Vista. This is the ideal getaway for people who enjoy the outdoors, photography and geothermal mineral hot springs. Spectacular sunrises greet guests from our patios each morning while birds sing and wildlife makes regular appearances. The *Inn at Chalk Cliffs* is located in the Heart of the Rockies and enjoys 300 days (average) of sunshine making our locale the ideal spot for vacations year-round. Hike, bike, fish, golf, hunt (in season), snowmobile, raft the Arkansas River, ski the local slopes or visit a historic mining town - all within minutes of our cozy retreat. At night, view the setting sun going behind the Rockies and warm up to a snug fire in the crisp mountain summer night air. We have three spacious rooms and one smaller one for our guests sleeping comfort. A full breakfast including many specialties awaits guests in the mornings. Let us make your vacation a memorable one - - join us for a vacation you won't forget. **Airport:** Colorado Springs-115 mi; Denver-130 mi **Discounts:** Yes, inquire at res time **Seasonal:** No **Reservations:** Full deposit required, 50% for extended stays **Brochure:** Yes **Permitted:** Children 6-up, limited smoking, limited drinking **Payment Terms:** Check MC/V [Z04FPCO-15172] **COM** U **ITC Member:** No

Rates:	Pvt Bath 2	Shared Bath 2
Single	$ 50.00	$ 50.00
Double	$ 60.00	$ 60.00

St Elmo Hotel	426 Main St 81427	Ouray CO
The Lingenfelters		Tel: 970-325-4951 Fax: 970-325-0348
		Res Times 8am-10pm

The *St Elmo Hotel* was built in 1898 as a miner's hotel in the booming mining era of the day, in the San Juan Mountains of southwestern Colorado. Today the *St Elmo* is a beautifully restored nine room, Victorian Bed and Breakfast Inn with antiques (many thought to be original pieces) in the guest rooms and common areas. A breakfast buffet of juice, homemade muffins and breads, cold cereal and a special entree of the day, awaits overnight guests each morning in the sunny breakfast room with its magnificent view of the surrounding mountains. The very popular Bon Ton Restaurant is located in the hotel, serving dinner nightly and a Sunday champagne brunch. Ouray sits in one of the most picturesque mountain settings that one will ever see, and has been known as "The Switzerland of America" for over a hundred years. **Airport:** Denver Stapleton-325 mi **Packages:** Two night special including dinner **Seasonal:** Rates vary **Reservations:** Credit card number for deposit required to guarantee reservation, 7 day cancel policy for refund **Brochure:** Yes **Permitted:** Children, drinking, a non-smoking property **Payment Terms:** AE/DISC-/MC/V [Z08GPCO1-889] **COM** Y **ITC Member:** No

Rates:	Pvt Bath 9
Single	$ 88.00
Double	$ 88.00

Orchard House 3573 E 1/2 Rd 81526   Palisade CO
William & Stephanie Schmid   Tel: 303-464-0529
   Res Times Anytime

Enjoy the spectacular views of Mount Garfield, Lincoln and Grand Mesa from this 4000 square foot charming home set on its own peach orchard. Offers guests a large king-size room along with twin beds downstairs in this separate guest house complete with its own private entrance and full kitchen. A full country breakfast is included where you can sample your host's talents for preparing Eggs Benedict, French toast, omelets with all the extras. Dinners are also available at added cost. Plenty of things to see and do here and your knowledgeable hosts are most anxious to help you with any plans. **Seasonal:** No **Reservations:** Pre-payment with reservation, 72-hr cancellation policy for refund. **Brochure:** Yes **Permitted:** Children, pets, smoking, drinking **Payment Terms:** Check MC/V [X02BXCO-6069] **COM** Y **ITC Member:** No

Rates:	Pvt Bath 2
Single	$ 60.00
Double	

Castillo de Caballeros PO Box 89 81201   Salida CO
Cheri Rost   Tel: 719-539-2002
   Res Times 5-9pm

"Castle of Horsemen" is the ideal name for this mountain hide-away, a true paradise at the top of paradise road! This large tudor-style home is situated next to public lands and trails - perfect for year round outdoor activities. Cheri, your hostess, enjoys cooking, handicrafts, photography, piano, fishing, skiing, mountain camping - and most of all, raising, training and competing her Arabian horses. Nestled high on a pinon hill, one mile from Salida with access to BLM and San Isabel National Forest Trails - a perfect location for 4 wheel, motocross, horse and bike riders. Cheri provides transportation to trail heads and pick-up later, down trail. Guests can relax in the outdoor hot tub which offers spectacular panoramic mountain views, play the piano or chess, relax by the cozy woodstove, browse in the library, watch a favorite movie on the VCR, warm-up in down comforters and enjoy the bottomless pot of coffee, tea or cider at the end of the day. A full breakfast with a variety of tempting and filling choices served country-style from heaping platters is served each morning. Special requests for breakfast are honored if requested in advance and subject to availability. Year-round activities include whitewater rafting, skiing, fishing and hunting, rockhounding, ghost towns, golf and special events ranging from winter torchlight parades to summer chili cook-offs. Member of B&B Colorado, Salida CC and ETA (Equine Travelers America). **Airport:** Denver Staplcton-150 mi; Colorado Springs-90 mi **Reservations:** 50% deposit at res time, 14 day cancel policy for refund unless re-rented, check-in 6-9pm. Two day min on weekends. **Permitted:** Children 7-up, limited pets and drinking. No smoking in house or barn. Pets must stay outside in pens. Horses: $7/night in paddock, must have negative coggins and current health permit. **Payment Terms:** Cert Check [R02EPCO-15284] **COM** Y **ITC Member:** No

Rates:	Shared Bath 4
Single	$ 37-45.00
Double	$ 37-45.00

Colorado *National Edition*

Alpine Inn B&B	PO Box 2398 81435	**Telluride CO**
Denise & John Weaver		**Tel:** 800-707-3344 970-728-6282 **Fax:** 970-728-3424
		Res Times 10am-9pm

We invite you to experience the *"magic of Telluride"* in one of it's original landmark hotels - now restored to a charming Bed & Breakfast. Each of the eight guest rooms transport you back to a Victorian Era filled with handmade quilts, arm-oires, soft colors and a touch of elegance. King, queen and single bed accommodations with private baths create a comfortable atmosphere suited for a variety of guest needs. Our honeymoon suite has a private terrace looking out to Ingram Falls and the ski mountain. Each morning enjoy a full breakfast served in our sunroom or on the veranda. After a day of activity, relax in the hot tub while soaking-up the "best hot tub views in town". During the summer, Telluride hosts a variety of festivals which include Bluegrass, Wine, Film and Jazz and a few other eclectic treats like the Mushroom and Talking Gourds festivals. All are within walking distance of the Inn. During winter, Telluride is a skier's paradise. Within two blocks of the Inn, the ski lifts take you to the *"most beautiful place you will ever ski."* Over 1000 acres of skiing terrain will excite skiers of all levels. Lift lines are virtually non-existent. Your hosts invite you to *"views that will take your breath away"* and a town that retains very much of its historical ambiance. Both Telluride and the *Alpine Inn* have strong environmental objectives and hope you will share in our commitment. **Discounts:** Yes, inquire at res time **Airport:** Telluride, Montrose, Grand Junction **Packages:** Skiing **Seasonal:** No **Reservations:** One night's deposit (50% winter and festival periods), within 7 days of booking, bal due on arrival, deposit required 30 days prior to arrival during winter and festivals **Permitted:** Children over 11-up, drinking **Payment Terms:** Check MC/V [I10HPCO1-15743] **COM** YG **ITC Member:** No

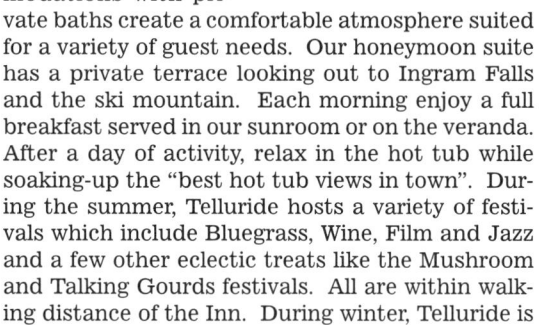

Rates:	**Pvt Bath** 6	**Shared Bath** 2
Single	$ 70-220.00	$ 55-130.00
Double	$ 70-220.00	$ 55-130.00

Penningtons Mountain Village Inn	PO Box 2428 81435	**Telluride CO**
Judy & Michale MacLean		**Tel:** 800-543-1437 970-728-5337
		Res Times 24 Hrs

A B&B resort that's more like everyone's dream home surrounded by the unrivaled scenic beauty of the Rocky Mountains while nestled along side the 12th fairway on Telluride's Championship 18 hole course. The inn is reminiscent of a picture-perfect postcard and features warm and comfortable French country decor, spacious rooms with queen and king beds all with panoramic views of Colorado's most beautiful mountains. Each guest room includes a private refrigerator stocked with refreshments and snacks - all included in the room rate. There's more too; a full breakfast with specialties of blueberry pancakes, eggs Benedict, fresh ground coffee and tea served in your room or dining room - a complimentary Happy Hour (4-6 daily) with wine, brandy, champagne, hot tea and hors d'oeuvres. A library, indoor jacuzzi and steam room, game room, ski lockers, laundry facilities, kitchen for preparing snacks and mountain bikes for your use. Outdoors is world class alpine skiing, x-country Nordic trails, snowmobiling, ice skating, sleigh rides and in spring and summer there's golf, tennis, hiking, fishing, white-water rafting and plenty of sightseeing in Telluride. Courtesy airport pick-up and free ski shuttle. **Reservations:** First night's deposit 21 days from res date incl 8.29% tax; 30 day cancel policy for refund, bal due on arrival. *Rates higher during seasonal peaks. **Permitted:** Children, drinking, limited smoking **Conference:** Yes for groups to 25 persons including special room rates and packages. **Payment Terms:** Check AE/DC/MC/V [R07BCCO-8458] **COM** Y **ITC Member:** No

Rates:	**Pvt Bath** 12
Single	$ 95-155.00
Double	$ 95-155.00

National Edition **Colorado**

San Sophia	330 W Pacific Ave 81435	**Telluride CO**
Dianne & Gary Eschman	**Tel:** 800-537-4781 970-728-3001 **Fax:** 970-728-6226	
		Res Times 7am-10pm

Elegant and luxurious sixteen room Inn located in Telluride, the most scenic of Colorado's five historically designated towns. The Inn is superbly located to afford spectacular views of the surrounding 13,000 foot mountains, waterfalls and box canyon. The San Miguel River is located right out the back door, running under one of the major ski lifts of the Telluride Ski Area. Additionally, most all the local hiking, biking and cross-country ski trails emanate from here. The San Sophia Observatory provides a 360 degree panoramic vista of the town and valley. The outdoor Jacuzzi is located in the garden, underneath the gazebo. Views from this area look up toward the ski mountain. Enjoy sunrise as it appears over Ingram Falls - Colorado's tallest waterfall - during an exquisite, mountain breakfast. Watch the sunset off the West Dock during daily Happy Hour. Bright, pristine rooms, all with contemporary amenities including sparkling private "tubs for two." The decor consists of brass beds, handmade quilts, TV's in armoires, stained glass, resplendent plush carpeting and bright print wallpapers. The library, with fireplace, provides a pleasant location to relax, both Winter and Summer. Guests can enjoy books on local history, original artwork, local restaurant menus, current magazines and daily newspapers. Ski lockers, boot dryers, bike storage and underground parking provide extra convenience for the discriminating traveler. *"... One of the most deluxe and romantic Inns in America"*, Inside America, 1991. *" ...the epitome of everything an elegant small inn in a ski resort should be"*, Elegant Small Hotels, 1993. **Airport:** Telluride-5mi **Discount:** Travel agents, World Ski Card **Reservations:** 50% deposit of total within 10 days. Less than 45 days prior to arrival, entire amount due at res time, 45 day cancel policy less $20 service fee, less than 30 days notice, refund only if rebooked **Permitted:** Children 10-up, drinking, smoking outdoors only, no pets **Conference:** Excellent for groups to 25 including multimedia and AV: 6x8 ft projection screen, large screen TV, VCR, slide projectors **Languages:** English **Payment Terms:** Check AE/MC/V [I04H-PCO1-8459] **COM YG ITC Member:** No

Rates: Pvt Bath 16
Single $ 95-195.00
Double $ 95-195.00

Woodland Inn B&B	159 Trull Rd 80863	**Woodland Park CO**
Frank & Nancy O'Neil	**Tel:** 800-226-9565 719-687-8209 **Fax:** 719-687-3112	
		Res Times 8am-9pm

Enjoy the home-like atmosphere of this cozy Country Inn nestled in the Colorado Rocky Mountains. Relax with a book or work on a puzzle in the parlor with huge bay windows that look out to peaceful woodlands. A hearty breakfast will be served fireside in the dining room or on the sunny patio. Guests may also use the grill on the covered patio or walk down the lane to a fine restaurant for lunch or dinner. Snuggle up in one of six romantic and comfortable guest rooms with private baths and wonderful views of Pikes Peak and the surrounding woodlands. Each room is uniquely decorated with aspen or pine log furnishings, white wicker, or a green iron canopy bed. One room has a king size or two twin beds and all others are queen size. Woodland Inn is peacefully secluded on twelve private acres of aspen and fir trees where guests may wander and enjoy breath-taking views. There are play areas for children with swings, tetherball, badminton and volley ball, plus an ice skating rink. From the corner of their pasture, guests are greeted by *Cinnamon* the llama and *Nutmeg*, the miniature donkey, and at the door by *Ginger* the dog. Waiting inside is *Sam*, a flame point Siamese cat. For a day of hiking, biking, trail riding or cross country skiing, your hosts will prepare a picnic lunch and assist with the arrangements prior to your arrival. Guests may also join the hosts for an exciting morning of hot air ballooning! **Airport:** Denver-90 mins; Colorado Springs-40 mins **Discounts:** Extended stays (7 days+), 10% corporate **Packages:** Hot Air Ballooning Crew Package **Seasonal:** Rates vary **Reservations:** One night deposit, 7 day cancel policy for refund **Brochure:** Yes **Permitted:** Children, drinking, limited smoking **[Payment Terms:** Check AE/DISC/MC/V [R03JPCO1-22071] **COMG ITC Member** No

Rates: **Pvt Bath 6**
Single $ 60-80.00
Double $ 60-80.00

Aston Waikiki Beach Side Hotel   2452 Kalakaua Ave   96815   Honolulu HI
Donna Wheeler   **Tel:** 800-922-7866   808-931-2100   **Fax:** 808-931-2129
Res Times 24 Hours

Unique to Waikiki sits *a charming little hotel that most certainly is Waikiki's most secret find*! Built on the grounds of the former estate of Prince Jonah Kuhio Kalanianaole, the hotel contains 17th and 18th century artwork and antiques collected from around the world. The European inspired Chinoiserie is prevalent throughout the lobby and rooms contain a myriad of European and Asian furnishings and flavors that complement the attractive peach, coral and black decor. A complimentary continental breakfast is served on the mezzanine level where hot coffee is served from silver baroque-style samovars, a selection of fine teas and juices from beautiful crystal pitchers are also offered. The petite guestrooms are comfortable for a single or couple, and each room is decorated with hand painted Oriental screens and has a custom designed armoire that conceals the appliances including a remote controlled color television, video cassette player (video library with the Receptionist) and a mini refrigerator. The beds have a tailored appearance and pillows are imported from England of the finest goose down. Twice daily maid service is provided by Housekeepers in charming peach outfits with white ruffled aprons and collars. An evening turndown is completed before 8 pm and on the first night, guests receive a seashell in a silk pouch with a welcome note. Handsome wooden skirt and coat hangers are provided as well as comfortable yukata kimono robes. Each room has it's own private bath and showers are encased in Italian travertine marble and glass with dramatic black and brass European fixtures. French milled toiletries are imported from England and are attractive bath amenities. Blow dryer, a concealed private safe and second phone are provided in the bath area. What has to be the most enthusiastic and friendly staff team up to provide attentive and gracious service - where employees remember guests by name. Concierge services are provided for dining and sight-seeing tours. Nearby activities include a Gold's Gym for a complete work out, beach vendors offering everything from rubber rafts to surfing lessons, tennis courts, jogging paths, the zoo, aquarium and the Waikiki Shell for concerts. The quaintness of a Country Inn, the personalized and warm service of a bed and breakfast and the sophistication and elegance of a fine hotel - cannot be found in Waikiki - except at the *Aston Waikiki Beachside Hotel*! **We don't just sell a hotel room, we provide an experience!** **Discounts:** *Inn & Travel Club* member guests request spcial rate at reservation time **Packages:** Seniors, Romance **Seasonal:** Rates vary **Reservations:** Credit card to confirm reservations **Brochure:** Yes **Permitted:** Drinking, smoking **Languages:** German, Spanish, French, Hawaiian, Tagalog, Ilocano, Visayan **Payment**

National Edition *Hawaii*

Terms: Checks/AE/DC/DISC/JCB/MC/V [I11IPHI1-27174] **COM** YG **ITC Member:** Yes **Quality Assurance:** Requested

Rates: **Pvt Bath 79**
Single $ 180-310.00
Double $ 180-310.00

Suites 2
$295-375.00

Oceanfront, Doris Epp — Honolulu HI
Doris Epp
Tel: 800-999-6026 808-263-4848
Res Times 24 Hrs

Refer to the same listing name under Kailu, Oahu, Hawaii for a complete description. **Sea-onal:** No **Payment Terms:** Check [M05CPHI-423] **COM** Y **ITC Member:** No

Rates: **Pvt Bath 2**
Single $ 75.00
Double $ 75.00

Papaya Paradise B&B   395 Auwinala Rd 96734   Kailua, Oahau HI
Bob & Jeanette Martz
Tel: 808-261-0316
Res Times 6am-9pm

Papaya Paradise is located in Kailua on the windward side of Oahu approximately 20 miles from the Honolulu Airport and Waikiki. It's private, quiet, tropical and removed from the hectic activity of Waikiki but still only 20 mins away for those who want an evening's entertainment. All major attractions on the island can be reached within 90 mins from Papaya Paradise .. Kailua Beach, a beautiful uncrowded four miles of white sandy beach, offering all of the water sports is just a short walk ... there are two bedrooms each with two beds, ceiling fans, a/c, cable color TV and private bath and private entrances. A full breakfast which includes fresh Papaya (when available) from our own grove is served on the lanai overlooking a 20 x 40 pool and jacuzzi which is surrounded by tropical plants, trees and Hawaiian flowers. Mount Olomana is in the background. A 17 cu ft refrigerator is available for our guests use, along with beach towels, mats, hats, chairs and coolers. Bob is a full-time host who enjoys cooking, baking and sharing his Hawaiian experience with his guests. **Seasonal:** No **Reservations:** 20% deposit at time of reservation **Brochure:** Yes **Permitted:** Drinking, smoking; limited children **Payment Terms:** Travelers Check [R11CPHI-11834] **COM** Y **ITC Member:** No

Rates: **Pvt Bath 2**
Single $ 60.00
Double $ 60.00

Kailua Plantation   75-5948 Alii Dr 96740   Kona HI
Danielle Berger
Tel: 808-329-3727
Res Times 24 Hrs

A tropical paradise awaits you at the *Kailua Plantation House* in Kona on the Big Island of Hawaii. This newly constructed inn is perched on a promontory of black lava rocks with an unobstructed view of the Pacific Ocean. Each guest room in this oceanfront inn boasts a private bath as well as a private lanai. Awaken to the aroma of freshly ground and brewed Kona coffee and a continental breakfast featuring fresh tropical fruits, breads and muffins. Enjoy a leisurely breakfast in the living area - elegantly designed with high ceilings, exposed dropped beams, crown moldings and fan lights - or outside by the dipping pool and jacuzzi. Watch migrating whales while you sunbathe on the lanai in soft ocean breezes. Savor a glass of wine as the sun gently slips into the water. Within walking distance are tennis facilities, fine restaurants and shops. The *Kailua Plantation House* retains its secluded beauty. For the traveler who seeks the niceties of an oceanfront resort yet desires the cozi-

©*Inn & Travel Memphis, Tennessee*

ness and charm of a bed and breakfast, the *Kailua Plantation House* offers the best of both worlds. **Discounts:** 10% to Hawaiian residents **Airport:** Keahole Airport 10 mi **Seasonal:** No **Reservations:** 50% of full length of stay. **Brochure:** Yes **Permitted:** Children 12-up, drinking, limited smoking (outside) **Languages:** French **Payment Terms:** Check AE/MC/V

[I10DPHI-14586] **COM** Y **ITC Member:** No

Rates:	Pvt Bath 5
Single	$ 120-175.00
Double	$ 120-175.00

Kilauea Lodge	PO Box 116 96785	Volcano Village HI
Lorna & Albert Jeyte		Tel: 808-967-7366 Fax: 808-967-7367

Kileaua Lodge is located in peaceful, secluded Volcano Village only a mile from the entrance to Hawaii Volcanoes National park. Owners Lorna and Albert Jeyte take pride and care of their Country Inn. A former YMCA camp, today *Kilauea Lodge* offers spacious rooms with private baths and central heating systems. All are beautifully appointed with country furnishings, Hawaiian art and other inviting items providing personal comfort. Seven of the rooms and cottages have private fireplaces. Guests may gather around a lovely common room with fireplace enjoying a large selection of Hawaiian books and games. A full breakfast is included in the room rate. The restaurant provides excellent continental cuisine. European trained owner-chef Albert, offers a tantalizing variety of dishes. Seafood Mauna Kea - a blend of pasta, herbs, and seafood or the Lamb Provencal with papaya-apple-mint sauce are a few of the house specials. Homemade soups and desserts as well as intriguing locally made wines augment an already excellent wine list. *Kilauea Lodge* is perfectly located as a homebase for exploring the island of Hawaii. The Volcano area provides miles and miles of hiking trails, an active volcano and the splendor of Pele herself. For further recreation there is a golf course and a local winery. The Big Island includes misty rain forests to sunny beaches, quaint villages, macadamia nut grove and flower farms to the old plantation town of Hilo, where one finds the unexpected splendor of Rainbow Falls and turn-of-the-century storefronts. The genuine welcome awaiting guests at *Kilauea Lodge* is a fine preparation for an unforgettable visit. **Airport:** Hilo-26mi, Kona-100mi **Seasonal:** No **Reservations:** One night deposit by cash or money order; 3 day cancel notice for refund, 2 night min on holidays **Brochure:** Yes **Permitted:** Children, drinking, limited smoking **Languages:** German, English **Payment Terms:** Check MC/V [I05HPHI1-8182] **COM** U **ITC Member:** No

Rates:	Pvt Bath 12
Single	$ 90-130.00
Double	$ 95-135.00

Pension Hermine	937 W 200 South 83221	Blackfoot ID
Hermine Balbi		Tel: 208-684-3857
		Res Times 8am-8pm

Your hostess (a French, German and Latin high school teacher at Blackfoot High School) shares her modern ranch home located on twenty eight acres of countryside pleasure. Guests find horses, cows, sheep, one goat and dogs and cats in this relaxing, natural setting. The clean air, beautiful landscape and relative solitude offers guests a peaceful setting for visiting Idaho. A full breakfast is included and lunch and dinner are available upon request. Nearby Blackfoot (10,000 pop) is in the lower extension of the Teton Mountains and is an agricultural town (potatoes, wheat, cattle) without industry. There is an indoor pool, two movie theaters, good restaurants and a picturesque lake with picnic areas. Sightseeing includes Yellowstone National Park, Teton National Park, Salt Lake City, Jackson Hole Wyoming, Sun Valley Idaho and Craters of the Moon, Lava Hot Springs, Ice Caves with year-round events which include rodeos, horse races, chariot races, Wild West Days. Guests can enjoy swimming, skiing, water-skiing, canoeing and rafting, horseback riding, fishing, hiking and hand gliding. **Seasonal:** No **Reservations:** Deposit requested to hold reservation **Brochure:** Yes **Permit-

National Edition   *Idaho*

ted: Children, pets, drinking, smoking **Languages:** German/French **Payment Terms:** Check [X08BCID-1205] **COM Y ITC Member:** No

Rates: **Pvt Bath 2**
Single $ 35.00
Double $ 45.00

Sleeping Place Of The Wheels   PO Box 5723 Lodgepole Rd 83814   Coeur D'Alene ID
Donna & Wallace Bedord   Tel: 208-765-3435

Pleasant residence that invites children and adults to stop and visit. Wagon wheels line the entrance to this location along with flower gardens and tall pine trees. Spring and summer offer guests the chance to pick fresh fruit from trees on the premises. The home decor includes handmade quilts and wood furnishings. **Seasonal:** No **Brochure:** Yes **Per**mitted: Children and pets. **Payment Terms:** Check [C11ACID-1212] **COM Y ITC Member:** No

Rates: **Shared Bath 3**
Single $ 38.00
Double $ 45.00

Idaho City Hotel   215 Montgomery St 83631   Idaho City ID
Don and Pat Campbell   Tel: 208-392-4290

A true Western hotel from the 1930's located near hot springs and includes a backyard creek that splashes past the guests' rooms, and furnished with authentic antiques in a town that's listed as a National Historic Site. Just 45 minutes from Boise, you'll enjoy the freshness and natural setting here. Full country breakfast included in room rate. **Seasonal:** No **Reservations:** Deposit required at res time with refund if cancelled. **Brochure:** Yes **Permitted:** Children, pets, smoking, drinking **Payment Terms:** Check AE/MC/V [C11ACID-1221] **COM Y ITC Member:** No

Rates: **Pvt Bath 5**
Single $ 38-50.00
Double $ 45-55.00

Northwest Passage B&B   201 Rio Vista Blvd 83638   McCall ID
Tel: 208-634-5349

Built in 1938 to house the stars in filming of *"Northwest Passage."* You can relive this era and be close to excellent skiing areas and you'll find fine country dining nearby. Continental breakfast included **Seasonal:** No **Reservations:** Require a deposit for first night's stay, refunded if cancelled. **Brochure:** Yes **Permitted:** Limited children, limited smoking, limited drinking **Payment Terms:** Check [C11AXID-1228] **COM Y ITC Member:** No

Rates: **Pvt Bath 3**   **Shared Bath 2**
Single $ 50.00 $ 45.00
Double $ 55.00 $ 50.00

Angel Of The Lake   410 Railroad Ave 83864   Sandpoint ID
Tel: 208-263-0816

Right next to the lakeshore is this centrally located inn offering guests convenience and great hospitality. Year-round outdoor sporting activities available including hiking, swimming and all water sports, skiing. Full complimentary breakfast starts off your day. **Seasonal:** No **Brochure:** Yes **Permitted:** Children **Payment Terms:** Check AE/MC/V [C11ACID-1232] **COM Y ITC Member:** No

Rates: **Pvt Bath 3**   **Shared Bath 6**
Single $ 52.00 $ 44.00
Double $ 66.00 $ 52.00

Pine Street Inn   177 King St 83873   Wallace ID
Jean McCorkle   Tel: 208-752-4391

©*Inn & Travel Memphis, Tennessee*

Idaho - Montana *National Edition*

Quaint country Inn snuggled in a hillside pine setting overlooking a historic silver mining town with Placer Creek running through the backyard. Plenty of outdoor activities including mining for your own silver. Continental breakfast included. **Seasonal:** No **Brochure:** Yes **Permitted:** Children, smoking, drinking **Payment Terms:** Check MC/V [C05ACID-1238] **COM** Y **ITC Member:** No

Rates:	Pvt Bath 2	Shared Bath 4
Single	$ 43.00	$ 45.00
Double	$ 48.00	$ 50.00

Bad Rock Country B&B — Bigfork MT
Jon & Sue Alper — **Tel:** 800-422-3666 406-892-2829

Refer to the same listing name under Columbia Falls, Montana for a complete description. **Seasonal:** No **Payment Terms:** Check AE/DC/DISC-/MC/V [M07FPMT-17787] **COM** Y **ITC Member:** No

Rates:	Pvt Bath 3
Single	$ 85-125.00
Double	$ 95-135.00

Odauchain Country Inn 675 Ferndale Dr 59911 — Bigfork MT
Mrs Margot Doohan — **Tel:** 406-837-6851

Genuine log cabin, furnished with frontier antiques and art works, set on five acres of wilderness. Picture perfect locale for enjoying glorious views, wildlife, nature trails, and waterfowl. Full country breakfast included. **Seasonal:** No **Brochure:** Yes **Permitted:** Children limited **Payment Terms:** Check MC [C11ACMT-2203] **COM** Y **ITC Member:** No

Rates:	Pvt Bath 2	Shared Bath 2
Single	$ 75.00	$ 65.00
Double	$ 85.00	$ 75.00

Sacajawea Inn — Bozeman MT
Jane & Smith Rodel — **Tel:** 800-821-7326 406-285-6515
Res Times 24 Hrs

Refer to the same listing name under Three Forks, Montana for a complete description. **Seasonal:** No **Payment Terms:** Check AE/DC/MC/V [M10EPMT-16116] **COM** U **ITC Member:** No

Rates:	Pvt Bath 30
Single	$ 49.00
Double	$ 49-99.00

Torch & Toes B&B 309 S Third Ave 59715 — Bozeman MT
Ron & Judy Hess — **Tel:** 406-586-7285
Res Times 8am-10pm

Set back from the street, this Colonial Revival house is centrally located in one of Bozeman's historic districts. Lace curtains, leaded glass windows and period pieces remind one that this is a house with a past. While trying to decide what to call their bed and breakfast enterprise, Ron and Judy happened upon an old photo of the first pieces of the Statue of Liberty to arrive in the United States: the torch and her foot. Taken by the whimsy, they dubbed their home the *Torch and Toes*, hanging the framed photo in the entry-way as much to amuse guests as to explain the off-beat name. Ron is a professor of architecture and Judy is a weaver. Their home is furnished in a charming blend of nostalgic antiques, humorous collectibles and fine furnishings. A full complimentary breakfast includes a special egg dish, fresh fruit and muffins or coffee cake. There are three guest rooms on the second floor all with private baths. In-addition, there is a converted carriage house that can sleep up to six persons complete with a private bath and kitchenette. Nearby attractions include blue-ribbon trout streams, hiking, skiing, the Museum of the Rockies and Yellowstone National Park. **Discounts:** Yes, inquire at res time **Airport:** Gallatin Field-8 mi **Reservations:** One night's deposit or credit card number to guarantee reservation **Brochure:** Yes **Permitted:** Children **Languages:** French **Payment Terms:**

Check MC/V [R05FPMT-9033] **COM** Y **ITC Member:** No

Rates: **Pvt Bath 4**
Single $ 55.00
Double $ 65-70.00

Bad Rock Country B&B	480 Bad Rock Dr 59912	Columbia Falls MT
Jon & Sue Alper		Tel: 800-422-3666 406-892-2829 **Fax:** 406-892-2930

For the visitor to Glacier National Park. Nestled on thirty rolling acres in a gorgeous farming valley; enjoy the spectacular views of the nearby 7200 foot high Swan Mountains, the magic of the quiet countryside, the wild geese flying overhead, the coyotes howling at night. Your hosts, Jon and Sue Apler, have recreated in their home (built 18 years ago by the local banker), the style of elegant Montana country living, with circa 1870 to 1910 antiques. There are three beautiful guest rooms in the house and four in two new, exquisite log buildings, built the way settlers did over 100 years ago. The unusual hand-hewn square logs are peeled down to bare wood and lightly stained and oiled to preserve their natural warmth and light pine color. Step into a romantic guest room complete with gas-log fireplace and beautiful lodgepole pine furniture. Breakfast is served in the Montana style, hearty and plentiful, with such dishes as: Belgium Waffles heaped with wild huckleberries; Montana potato pie; Grizzly Big Bite; Sundance eggs. A luxurious hot tub sits off in its own secluded corner, looking out at the Big Mountain ski resort and the Rockies. Guests reserve the hot tub for their own private thirty minutes of wonderful soaking time. Reserved for non-smokers only. Inspected and approved by: ABBA with a A+ rating, given only to forty-seven other B&B's in the entire nation; AAA and the Montana B&B Assoc. Kalispell Intl-15 min **Packages:** Custom designed to meet your interest, upon request **Seasonal:** No **Reservations:** One night's deposit to guarantee reservation **Brochure:** Yes **Permitted:** Children 10-up, drinking; Smoking is not permitted **Payment Terms:** Check AE/DC/DISC/MC/V [I02HPMT1-16782] **COM** YG **ITC Member:** No

Rates: **Pvt Bath 7**
Single $ 85-125.00
Double $ 95-135.00

Huckleberry Hannah's B&B	3100 Sophie Lake Rd 59917	Eureka MT
Jack & Deanna Doying		Tel: 406-889-3381
		Res Times Evenings

All wrapped up in over 5,000 square feet of old-fashioned, country-sweet charm, *Huckleberry Hannah's Montana Bed and Breakfast* is the answer to vacationing in Northwestern Montana. Sitting on fifty wooded acres, and bordering a fabulous trout-filled lake with glorious views of the Rockies, this bed and breakfast depicts a quieter time in our history .... a time when the true pleasures of life represented a walk in the woods or a moonlight swim. Or maybe just a little early morning relaxation in a porch swing, sipping a fresh cup of coffee, and watching a colorful sunrise. A complimentary continental breakfast is included with stay. Deanna Hansen-Doying is a retired tourism marketing specialist. Her hobby is collecting and developing wonderful recipes, cooking, baking and taking the research for this book off her waistline. She now lives on a lake near Eureka Montana with four horses, three cats, two dogs and one husband (not necessarily in that order), where she is currently writing the next book in the Huckleberry Hannah Series **Discounts:** 10% Senior citizen **Airport:** Kalispell Intl-60 mi; County Private airport-4 mi **Seasonal:** No **Reservations:** 50% on long term stays, walk-ins welcomed as vacancies are available. Lake cottage available. **Brochure:** Yes **Permitted:** Children 13-up, limited pets, smoking outdoors only **Payment Terms:** Check DC/MC/V [R07FPMT-17204] **COM** Y **ITC Member:** No

Rates: **Pvt Bath 5**
Single $ 40.00
Double $ 65.00

Montana *National Edition*

Bad Rock Country B&B — Kalispell MT
Jon & Sue Alper
Tel: 800-422-3666 406-892-2829

Refer to the same listing name under Columbia Falls, Montana for a complete description. **Seasonal:** No **Payment Terms:** Check AE/DC/DISC/MC/V [M07F-PMT-17785] COM Y **ITC Member:** No

Rates: Pvt Bath 3
Single $ 85-125.00
Double $ 95-135.00

Huckleberry Hannah's B&B — Kalispell MT
Jack & Deanna Doying
Tel: 406-889-3381
Res Times Evenings

Refer to the same listing name under Eureka, Montana for a complete description. **Seasonal:** No **Payment Terms:** Check DC/MC/V [M07FPMT-17790] **COM** U **ITC Member:** No

Rates: Pvt Bath 5
Single $ 40.00
Double $ 65.00

Sacajawea Inn PO Box 648 59752 Three Forks MT
Jane & Smith Rodel
Tel: 800-821-7326 406-285-6515 **Fax:** 406-285-6515
Res Times 24 Hrs

Since William Howard Taft was President, people have enjoyed the gracious hospitality of the *Sacajawea Inn* a National Landmark which is listed on the *National Historic Register*. The Inn, named after Sacajawea, a guide of the Lewis and Clark Expedition, was built in 1910 and today the original lofty wood beams and polished hardwood floors form the main lobby. The ambience is casual elegance - from the rocking chairs and large veranda to comfortable nostalgic guest rooms all with private baths. A perfect location from which to explore the Gallatin Valley, including the Lewis and Clark Caverns, Madison Buffalo Jump state Monument, Three Forks Museum and the Museum of the Rockies - the area is renowned for Blue Ribbon trout fishing on the Jefferson, Madison and Gallatin Rivers. Excellent hunting for deer, elk, geese, ducks. Yellowstone National Park is just a two hour drive from the front door. Excellent skiing, biking, hiking are nearby and a public golf course is within walking distance of the Inn. Dinner is served nightly with breakfast and lunch served during the summer. AAA 3-Diamond Rated **Discounts:** AAA, AARP **Airport:** Bozeman-25 mins. **Packages:** Hunting; Fly fishing **Seasonal:** No **Reservations:** Deposit or credit card to guarantee reservations; 24 hr cancel policy **Brochure:** Yes **Permitted:** Children, drinking, limited pets **Conference:** Yes, meetings room for groups to seventy **Languages:** Some Spanish **Payment Terms:** Check AE/DC/MC/V [I10EPMT-14208] COM Y **ITC Member:** No

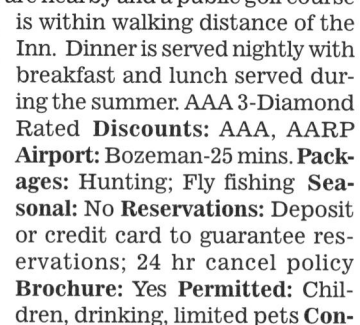

Rates: Pvt Bath 30
Single $ 49.00
Double $ 49-99.00

Foxwood Inn 1 Sportsman Lane 59645 White Sulphur Springs MT
Shane & Shelly Dempsey
Tel: 406-547-3918

A renovated 1890's *"poor farm"* featuring sixteen individually decorated guest rooms. The Inn is located in the middle of the mountains in west central Montana. Guests can enjoy guided fishing tours, floating trips, horseback riding, downhill and cross country skiing. Guided tours can be arranged for historical and photographic outings. Enjoy great outdoors and western hospitality. Located midway between Yellowstone and Glacier Park areas; customized vacation packages and trips can be arranged. **Seasonal:** No **Reservations:** 50% deposit at res time, late arrivals must notify 5 days in advance

©*Inn & Travel Memphis, Tennessee*

to obtain refund. **Brochure:** Yes **Permitted:** Children, pets, drinking, limited smoking **Conference:** Yes for groups to 30 persons. **Payment Terms:** Check MC/V [X06BCMT-2225] **COM** Y **ITC Member:** No

Rates:
Single
Double

Shared Bath 16
$ 35.00
$ 45-50.00

Bad Rock Country B&B — Whitefish MT
Jon & Sue Alper
Tel: 800-422-3666 406-892-2829

Refer to the same listing name under Columbia Falls, Montana for a complete description. **Seasonal:** No **Payment Terms:** Check AE/DC/DISC/MC/V [M07FPMT-17786] **COM** Y **ITC Member:** No

Rates: Pvt Bath 3
Single $ 85-125.00
Double $ 95-135.00

Duck Inn 1305 Columbia Ave 59937 — Whitefish MT
Ken & Phyllis Adler
Tel: 406-862-DUCK

Relaxing views of Big Mountain and Whitefish River make this ideal spot for both indoor and outdoor activities. Guest rooms include iron or brass beds, cozy fireplace, deep soak tubs, and a balcony. Outdoors you have fishing, hunting, canoeing, nature trails, swimming, and boating. Close to Glacier National Park. Jacuzzi available too. Continental breakfast included. **Seasonal:** Rates vary **Brochure:** Yes **Permitted:** Children, smoking, drinking **Payment Terms:** Check AE/MC/V [X11ACMT-2223] **COM** YITC **Mem-ber:** No

Rates: Pvt Bath 10
Single
Double $ 59.00

Huckleberry Hannah's B&B — Whitefish MT
Jack & Denna Doying
Tel: 406-889-3381
Res Times Evenings

Refer to the same listing name under Eureka, Montana for a complete description. **Seasonal:** No **Payment Terms:** Check DC/MC/V [M07FPMT-17791] **COM** U **ITC Member:** No

Rates: Pvt Bath 5
Single $ 40.00
Double $ 65.00

Deer Run Ranch B&B 5440 Eastlake Blvd 89704 — Carson City NV
David & Muffy Vhay
Tel: 702-882-3643
Res Times 8am-8pm

Relax and unwind on two hundred of the most beautiful acres in Western Nevada. Our working alfalfa ranch is located just eight miles north of Carson City, and twenty two miles south of Reno, Nevada. Watch the deer in the fields, enjoy the smell of western sage and listen for the cry of the coyotes at night. Our unique architect-designed-and-built western ranch house, shaded by tall cottonwood trees, over-looks our pond, Washoe Valley and the Sierra Nevada Mountains to the West. Two comfortable guest rooms (queen size beds) have private baths, window seats, spectacular views and lots of privacy. Both guest rooms share the sitting room with woodburning wood stove, dining area, guest refrigerator, TV/VCR and other amenities. The owner's pottery studio and woodshop are on the premises. Full ranch breakfasts include house specialties and fresh fruits and vegetables from our garden. Recreation at the ranch includes swimming in our above ground pool, horseshoes, hiking, biking, ice skating on the pond in winter. (We supply the skates and hot chocolate!) We are conveniently close to golf, skiing, casinos and showrooms and many excellent restaurants. **Discounts:** Check for specials **Airport:** Reno-22 mi **Seasonal:** Clo Thanksgiving and Christmas **Reservations:** 50% deposit required at res time, 7 day cancel policy for full refund, maximum stay one week (a county restriction) **Brochure:** Yes **Permit-

Nevada   *National Edition*

ted: Children (10-up), drinking, smoking outdoors only **Payment Terms:** Check MC/V [R09EPNV-156-63] **COM** U **ITC Member:** No

Rates:	Pvt Bath 2
Single	$ 75-85.00
Double	$ 75-85.00

Winters Creek Ranch   1201 Hwy 395 N 89701   **Carson City NV**
Mike & Pat Stockwell   **Tel:** 702-849-1020

Historic horse ranch c1865 on fifty acres of ponderosa pines with theme guest rooms of Oliver's Nook, Nevada Room, or Colonial Room. Spectacular views of Sierra Nevadas, hot tub, and complimentary wine and hors d'oeuvres in evening. Virginia City, Lake Tahoe, Carson City and Reno nearby. **Seasonal:** No **Brochure:** Yes **Permitted:** Children, drinking, limited pets. Full Western breakfast served outdoors, weather permitting. **Payment Terms:** Check MC/V [X11ACNV-2240] **COM** Y **ITC Member:** No

Rates:	Pvt Bath 2
Single	
Double	$ 85.00

Old Pioneer Garden   Star Rt 89418   **Imlay NV**
Mitzi & Lew Jones   **Tel:** 702-538-7585

c1861 frontier ranch set in a Nevada mining town along canyon walls, perfect for solitude and experiencing the western outdoors. Picturesque setting with babbling brook, deer, rabbits, and other fauna and flora. Fourteen acres for fishing, swimming in creeks, water sports. Family style meals prepared from the home garden! **Seasonal:** No **Brochure:** Yes

Permitted: Children, pets, drinking. **Payment Terms:** Check [X11ACNV-2245] **COM** Y **ITC Member:** No

Rates:	Pvt Bath 4	Shared Bath 12
Single	$ 45.00	$ 35.00
Double	$ 50.00	$ 40.00

Hotel Lamoille   PO Box 1208 89828   **Lamoille NV**
Ron & Pam Druck   **Tel:** 702-753-6363
                                                                                  Res Times 9am-11pm

Located just twenty miles from Elko, the tiny town of Lamoille, a picturesque agricultural community offers a quiet peaceful setting for those who like out-of-the-way places. Visitors find stunning mountain scenery in the lush glacier-carved Lamoille Canyon. High alpine lakes provide exceptional fishing opportunities along with numerous hiking trails, streams and ponds. Snowmobiling, cross country skiing and helicopter skiing are available, inquire at time of reservation. Home of the Annual Cowboy Poetry in late January. National Basque Festival every 4th of July. An eighteen hole golf course is within twenty minutes. Gambling in large casinos. Our restaurant, the Pine Lodge, offers excellent night-time dining and a saloon for those who enjoy spirits and fun times. The guest rooms are comfortable with queen size beds and one room offers a king size bed and hot tub. A full breakfast is included and dinner is available. **Discounts:** Yes, inquire at res time **Airport:** Elko Regional-20 mi **Seasonal:** No **Reservations:** Full deposit in advance, 5 day cancel policy for full refund less $5 handling fee; 50% refund if less than 5 days notice **Brochure:** Yes **Permitted:** Drinking, smoking, limited children, limited pets **Conference:** Yes for small groups **Payment Terms:** Check MC/V [Z04FPNV-15061] **COM** U **ITC Member:** No

Rates:	Pvt Bath 3
Single	$ 65.00
Double	$ 65.00

Deer Run Ranch B&B   **Reno NV**
David & Muffy Vhay   **Tel:** 702-882-3643
                                                                        Res Times 8am-8pm

Refer to the same listing name under Washoe Valley, Nevada for a complete description. **Seasonal:** Clo Thanksgibing and Christmas **Payment Terms:** Check MC/V [M09EPNV-16108] **COM** U **ITC Member:** No

Rates:	Pvt Bath 2
Single	$ 75-85.00
Double	$ 75-85.00

Edith Palmers Country Inn — South B St 89440 — Virginia City NV
Erlene & Norm Brown
Tel: 702-847-0707
Res Times 8am-6pm

c1862 country home of Nevada's first wine merchant in Victorian design, and today offering a gourmet restaurant in the former stone wine cellar. Walking distance from historic sights of Virginia City and close to Lake Tahoe and Reno. Country full breakfast of freshly ground coffee, eggs and homemade breads and pastries. Meals available on premises.

Seasonal: No **Permitted:** Social drinking **Payment Terms:** Check MC/V [X11ACNV-2997] **COM** Y **ITC Member:** No

Rates:	Pvt Bath 1	Shared Bath 4
Single	$ 75.00	$ 70.00
Double	$ 80.00	$ 80.00

Casita Chamisa B&B — 850 Cahmisal Rd NW 87107 — Albuquerque NM
Kit & Arnold Sargeant
Tel: 505-897-4644

A lovely country guest house and main adobe home with indoor pool, just 15 minutes to downtown Albuquerque with an archaeologist host who delights in showing guests around local excavations. Close to ski area plus all homemade breads and cakes for breakfast. Bikes, hot tub, and hearty Southwestern breakfast are included. **Seasonal:** No **Brochure:** Yes **Permitted:** Children, smoking, drinking, and limited pets. **Payment Terms:** Check MC/V [C11ACNM-3957] **COM** Y **ITC Member:** No

Rates:	Pvt Bath 2	Shared Bath 1
Single	$ 75.00	$ 70.00
Double		

Hacienda Vargas B&B — Albuquerque NM
Paul & Jule DeVargas
Tel: 505-867-9115 Fax: 505-867-1902
Res Times 8:30-6pm

Refer to the same listing name under Algodones, New Mexico for a complete description. **Seasonal:** Rates vary **Payment Terms:** Check MC/V [M07GPNM-20119] **COM** Y **ITC Member:** No

Rates:	Pvt Bath 4
Single	$ 69-89.00
Double	$ 69-109.00

Heart Seed B&B Retreat Center & Spa — Albuquerque NM
Judith Polich
Tel: 505-471-7026 Fax: 505-471-7026
Res Times 9am-9pm

Refer to the same listing name under Santa Fe, New Mexico for a complete description. **Payment Terms:** Check MC/V [M02HPNM1-22298] **COM** YG **ITC Member:** No

Rates:	Pvt Bath 4
Single	$ 89.00
Double	$ 89.00

The Inn At Paradise — 10035 Country Club Lane NW 87114 — Albuquerque NM
Lefty, Christena
Tel: 505-898-6161
Res Times 24 Hrs

©*Inn & Travel Memphis, Tennessee*

New Mexico   National Edition

Located on the first tee of the lush Paradise Hills Golf Club, you can experience golf course living at its finest! Whether you are spending an executive retreat with your company, having a competitive tournament with family and friends, or taking a romantic holiday with that special someone, the Inn is a great get-away. Each of our newly remodeled rooms features original art work on consignment from local artists and craftsmen, so bring your eye for style. We also have suites available with fireplaces and kitchens. Start your morning with fresh juice, coffee and fresh pastries. Relax and enjoy the sunrise or head out for an early round of golf. Bring your family and friends and plan your next fiesta at the Full Moon Saloon. While in Albuquerque, ride the world's longest tram up the Sandia Mountains, air balloon ride while here in the ballooning capital of the west. You'll find a complete pro shop, restaurant and lounge, Caring Hands Massage, award-winning Rede to Cater and Sun Country Amateur Golf Assoc. **Discounts:** Corporate, groups **Airport:** Albuquerque-20 mi **Packages:** Skiing, Golf **Seasonal:** No **Reservations:** Credit card deposit required to guarantee, contact property for cancellation policy **Brochure:** Yes **Conference:** Yes **Languages:** German, some French **Payment Terms:** Check AE/MC/V [I02HPNM1-18202] **COM** YG **ITC Member:** No

Rates:	Pvt Bath 15
Single	$ 50.00
Double	$ 60-110.00

Hacienda Vargas B&B   PO Box 307 87001   Algodones NM
Paul & Jule Vargas   Tel: 505-867-9115 Fax: 505-867-9115
                                                                              Res Times 8:3--6pm

This historic stagecoach stop and Indian trading post, Adobe Hacienda dates back to the 1700's, and has been completely restored and elegantly decorated with antiques. A charming courtyard is home to a two-hundred year old tree and a historic chapel. The four beautiful guest rooms offer fireplaces, private baths and private entrances. One room includes a two person jacuzzi tub while a hot tub and barbecue are available for guests to use. Situated on two acres by the Rio Grande and thirty minutes south of Santa Fe and north of Albuquerque on the historic El Camino Real, guests enjoy the majestic views of the Mexico Mesas and Sandia Mountains, golf, fishing, snow skiing and horseback riding nearby. A full country breakfast, prepared by New Mexican chef. Member New Mexico B&B Association, AAA Rated **Discounts:** 10% seniors **Airport:** Albuquerque-20 mi **Packages:** Romance, includes champagne and breakfast in room **Seasonal:** Rates vary **Reservations:** One night's deposit or 50% of length of stay, which ever is greater **Brochure:** Yes **Permitted:** Children 13-up, drinking, smoking outside only **Languages:** Spanish, German **Payment Terms:** Check MC/V [R07GPNM-19206] **COM** Y **ITC Member:** No **Quality Assurance:** Requested

Rates:	Pvt Bath 4
Single	$ 69-89.00
Double	$ 69-109.00

Sierra Mesa Lodge   Ft Stanton Rd 88312   Alto NM
Harry & Lila Goodman   Tel: 505-336-4515
                                                                          Res Times 8am-10pm

Nestled into a two-and-a-half acre hillside overlooking the magnificent Captain Mountains. Bountiful woods and meadows surround this elegant inn designed for relaxation and privacy. Enjoy thoughtful service, quiet charm and the warm hospitality of New Mexico's friendliest Inn. We offer five charming guest rooms with private baths, each individually decorated (Victorian, French Country, Oriental, Country Western and Queen Anne). Comforters and goose down pillows, graceful period furniture, brass and four poster beds, rockers and chaise lounges - tasteful elegance blended with modern comforts. Start your day with a generous gourmet breakfast of waffles, quiches or omelettes, fruits and freshly baked breads. Join us in the late afternoon for coffee, tea and pastries and in the evening for wine, cheese and conversation, or relax in the Inn's indoor hot tub spa! The Inn, located near Ruidoso

New Mexico is close to restaurants, shops, "Ski Apache" ski basin, Ruidoso Down racetrack, Lincoln National Forest and day trips to Carlsbad Caverns, White Sands, National Monument and the historical town of Lincoln - home of Billy-the-Kid. Hiking, picnicking, horseback riding, golf, tennis, swimming, hunting, fishing, skiing, sledding, or just plain loafing - all within reach of this *"Inn For All Seasons!"* **Seasonal:** No **Reservations:** One night's deposit within 7 days of booking or credit card to hold room with 7-day cancellation policy for full refund. **Brochure:** Yes **Permitted:** Children 15-up, drinking **Payment Terms:** Check MC/V [R02BCNM-6321] **COM** Y **ITC Member:** No

Rates: Pvt Bath 5
Single $ 65.00
Double $ 75.00

Jones House Inn	Terrace & Third 87520	Chama NM
Sara Jayne Cole		Tel: 505-756-2908

Enjoy the friendly, comfortable atmosphere of this lovely historic home. Across from the Cumbres-Toltec Scenic Railroad, this Inn is *a Rail Fans Dream Come True!* Our library is full of railroad books and train videos. We offer a train package that includes meals and the train ticket. Within walking distance to the Sargent Wildlife Preserve and the Chama River. **Airport:** Albuquerque Intl-3 hr drive **Seasonal:** No **Reservations:** Deposit or credit card number for one night's stay, 7 day cancel policy for refund **Brochure:** Yes **Permitted:** Limited children, drinking **Payment Terms:** Check AE/MC/V [R05FPNM-1110-9] **COM** Y **ITC Member:** No

Rates:	Pvt Bath 4	Shared Bath 2
Single	$ 65.00	$ 50.00
Double	$ 85.00	$ 60.00

Lodge At Cloudcroft	Corona Place 88317	Cloudcroft NM
Mike Coy		Tel: 800-842-4216 505-682-2566
		Res Times 24 Hrs

Perched atop New Mexico's Southern Rockies at 9000 ft, guests are treated to fiery sunsets and starbright nights in a unique natural setting and wilderness offering wild bears and grazing elk among the verdant pine, blue spruce and golden aspen. Constructed in 1899 as a haven to escape the heat and relax, The Lodge has been meticulously restored inside and out; dressed with rich wood moldings, turn-of-the-century furnishings, antique fixtures, mounted game and lazy paddle fans. Each guest room has been restored and individually decorated including cozy high beds filled with down quilts for cool evenings. Dining is excellent with New Mexico's most award-wining chef blending continental cuisine and exquisite sunsets for a marvelous evening. A year-round resort, all the outdoor activities (including equipment rentals) are offered with over 22 different ski runs on the grounds alone! There are ghost towns, horse racing, state parks, observatories, trout fishing, over 500 prehistoric cave drawings, Billy the Kid's stomping grounds and much more. Don't miss this historic mountain railroad resort where Victorian tradition, majestic scenery and generous service join to form a singular world of charm, elegance and romance. **Seasonal:** No **Reservations:** Credit card to guarantee, 7 day cancel policy for refund less $10 service fee; one night's lodging if cancel notice is less than 72 hrs. *Ski and golf package rates available. *American Plan Rates **Brochure:** Yes **Permitted:** Children, smoking, drinking **Conference:** Yes with five meeting rooms offering complete A/V facilities. Excellent capability for handling corporate retreats. **Languages:** Spanish **Payment Terms:** Check AE/DC/DISC/MC/V [R10BCNM-3962] **COM** Y **ITC Member:** No

Rates: Pvt Bath 59
Single
Double $ 55-155.00

Sandhill Crane B&B	389 Camino Hermosa 87048	Corrales NM
Phil Thorpe/Carol Hogan		Tel: 800-375-2445 505-898-2445 **Fax:** 505-898-2445
		Res Times 8am-7pm

©*Inn & Travel Memphis, Tennessee*

Follow the brick path through the old turquoise gate and you step back to a time of walled homes and rambling adobe haciendas. Three southwestern style guest rooms, each with bath offer a choice of accommodations. Amenities include a hot-tub, cable TV, nearby horseback riding and therapeutic massages by appointment. In warm weather enjoy one of Phil's memorable breakfasts on the patio while being entertained by a dazzling display of hummingbirds or an occasional feisty Roadrunner. Wisteria draped walls surrounding peaceful patios contribute to the feeling of privacy and solitude. Enjoy unusual furniture and a contemporary collection of art, American Indian wall hangings and rugs. When asked why people choose their B&B, the couple refers to comments left by guests who have stayed at the *Sandhill Crane B&B* - *"warm, unique, creative, restful"* - A short walk to the small village of Corrales is to return to a time where not much has changed since the 1770's. The historic old church is the gathering place for social activities, political meetings and art shows. Ancient cottonwood trees line the roads and irrigation canals lined with dirt roads offer miles of walking paths. **Discounts:** Extended stays, business travelers, some midweek periods **Airport:** Albuquerque Intl-25 mi **Packages:** Yes, inquire at res time. Inspected and approved by Albuquerque B&B Assoc. **Reservations:** Full payment for one night, 50% if longer, 14 day cancel policy for refund **Brochure:** Yes **Permitted:** Limited children, drinking **Conference:** Groups of 6-8 persons **Payment Terms:** Check AE/MC/V [I07HPNM1-18764] **COM YG ITC Member:** No

Rates:	Pvt Bath 3
Single	$ 65-85.00
Double	$ 85-135.00

The Cottonwoods B&B   PO Box 3028 87048   Corrales NM
Jan McConnell   Tel: 505-897-5086 Fax: 505-898-9725
                                                              Res Times 7am-10pm

A completely adobe-built passive solar design, *The Cottonwoods* combines modern comforts with the rustic charm, beauty and relaxation of old New Mexico. Enjoy beautiful views of the Sandia Mountains from our rural setting among cottonwoods by the Rio Grande. Relax by the pool, or in the guest rooms featuring exposed adobe walls, wooden viga ceilings, antique furnishings, Sealy Posturepedic mattresses, and in-room cable television. One room features a large jacuzzi tub. The other is available either as one room or as a two-room suite. Indulge in our gourmet continental breakfasts with freshly-baked pastries, seasonal fruits and fresh-squeezed orange juice. We have bicycles available for exploring the adjacent Bosque nature preserve and the extensive network of acequias, or irrigation canals. Our location in the historic village of Corrales is within 25 minutes of Albuquerque airport and provides convenient access to the city's museums, shopping and cultural activities. The village of Corrales contains several excellent restaurants, as well as galleries and shops. The site of the famous Hot Air Balloon Fiesta is nearby, and quick access to interstate highways 25 and 40, places all north-central New Mexico attractions within easy reach. You are within an hour's drive of Santa Fe, the Turquoise Trail, Jemez Springs, numerous Pueblos, the Cibola National Forest, the Sandia National Wilderness and the Petroglyph National Monument. The Sandia Peak and Santa Fe ski resorts are an easy drive away and numerous excellent golf courses are nearby. Member, Albuquerque B&B Association. **Discounts:** Extended stays **Airport:** Albuquerque-12 mi **Packages:** Restaurant Dining **Seasonal:** No **Reservations:** 50% deposit by check within 5 days of booking **Brochure:** Yes **Permitted:** Children 13+, limited drinking **Payment Terms:** Check MC/V [I09HPNM1-22318] **COM YG ITC Member:** No

Rates:	Pvt Bath 2
Single	$ 65-130.00
Double	$ 65-130.00

National Edition   ***New Mexico***

Casa del Rio	PO Box 92 87532	Espanola NM
Eileen & Mel Vigil		**Tel:** 800-333-2267 505-753-2035

Casa del Rio, a totally modern bed and breakfast, reflects the peace, beauty and charm of New Mexico without compromising high standards for service and authenticity. This private guesthouse is appointed with local handmade crafts, rugs, bed coverings and furniture. A traditionally designed viga and latilla ceiling reflects the soft light of a kiva fireplace. The guest beds can be arranged as one king or two twin beds. A modern bath finished in handmade Mexican tile completes this comfortable, yet traditional New Mexico accommodation. A patio and window brings magnificent views of wild life which include eagles and whooping cranes. Occasionally guests are treated to the vocalizations of the local coyotes enjoying the crisp night air. Your hosts invite guests to enjoy their ranch on which they breed Arabian horses and fine wool sheep. A full breakfast, including special dietary needs, is included with your room and is served in the main house each morning. Nearby sights/activities include: Ghost Ranch Living Museum, Rio Grande Gorge, skiing, bicycling, hiking and fishing. Located equi-distance from Santa Fe or Taos, both towns offer guests an interesting day trip. **Seasonal:** No **Reservations:** 50% deposit of total amount at res time, 14 day cancel policy less 10% service fee. **Brochure:** Yes **Permitted:** Limited drinking, limited smoking **Languages:** Spanish **Payment Terms:** Check MC/V [R09BCNM-3968] **COM** Y **ITC Member:** No

Rates: Pvt Bath   1
Single $ 70.00
Double $ 70.00

Llewellyn House	618 S Alameda 88005	Las Cruces NM
Linda & Jerry Lundeen		**Tel:** 505-526-3327

Fourteen room adobe home furnished in western decor with large living and dining room and art gallery. Perfect spot for business or social meetings, including dining. Continental breakfast included. **Seasonal:** No **Brochure:** Yes **Permitted:** Children 12-up, limited smoking, drinking **Languages:** Spanish

Payment Terms: Check AE/MC/V [X11ACNM-3971] **COM** Y **ITC Member:** No

Rates: Pvt Bath   14
Single $ 55-70.00
Double $ 65-85.00

Sierra Mesa Lodge		Ruidoso NM
Harry & Lila Goodman		**Tel:** 505-336-4515
		Res Times 8am-10pm

Refer to the sane listing name under Alto, New Mexico for a complete description. **Seasonal:** No **Payment Terms:** Check MC/V [M02BXNM-6587] **COM** Y **ITC Member:** No

Rates: Pvt Bath   5
Single $ 65.00
Double $ 75.00

Adobe Abode	202 Chapelle 87501	Santa Fe NM
Pat Harbour, Innkeeper		**Tel:** 505-983-3133 **Fax:** 505-983-3133
		Res Times 8am-9pm

The spectacular landscape of New Mexico will welcome you like an old friend and so will this inviting and intimate European-styled B&B, just three blocks from the Plaza and a minute's walk to the best restaurants, museums and shopping. In an important Santa Fe historic district, this 84-year-old adobe home maintains its old world feeling despite extensive renovation to add every modern convenience. Decorated with sophistication and flair, there's authentic Southwest charm in vigas, native New Mexican furniture and Indian art, rugs and unusual artifacts. There are two delightful guest rooms in the main house, both with private baths featuring oversized art-tiled showers and sharing a large living room with fireplace. Newly opened are three rooms with private bath in a Courtyard Compound, all with private entrances off a flower-filled patio and all in pure Santa Fe Style. All five rooms offer the amenities of a fine Country Inn, including custom terry cloth robes, bath accessories, designer linens, private phones, writing desks and TV. The full gourmet breakfast with fresh-squeezed juice, fresh fruit an assortment of homemade pastries and daily changing entrees. **Airport:** Albuquerque-60 mi **Seasonal:** No **Reservations:** One night deposit on all reservations, 10 day cancel policy for refund less 10% service fee, 4-6pm check-in **Brochure:** Yes **Permitted:** Children 11+, drinking, limited smoking **Languages:** Some Spanish, French **Payment Terms:** Check DC/MC/V [Z04GPNM-11107] COM Y ITC **Member:** No **Quality Assurance:** Requested

Rates:	Pvt Bath 5
Single	$ 90-135.00
Double	$ 95-140.00

Alexanders Inn	529 E Palace 87501	Santa Fe NM
Carolyn Lee		Tel: 505-986-1431
		Res Times 7:30am-10pm

***Featuring the best of American Country Charm** - Alexanders* is located in a lovely residential neighborhood on the town's historic east side. Built in 1903, the Inn has been newly renovated to offer modern comfort and convenience along with the romance and charm of earlier, simpler times. The Inn is lovingly decorated with stenciling, plants, antiques and collectibles creating a warm, relaxing and nurturing ambiance. Each delightfully different guest room is spacious, sun-filled and charming, furnished with your personal comfort in mind, including luxurious down comforters and fluffy bathrobes. A complimentary continental breakfast is served ensuite or on the veranda overlooking a grassy lawn lined with fragrant lilacs and shade trees and includes homemade breads or muffins, homemade granola, yogurt, freshly ground coffee and tea. Homemade cookies and chips and salsa are served in the warm homey kitchen each afternoon. A world of warmth and hospitality awaits travelers at Alexander's Inn in Santa Fe. **Airport:** Albuquerque Intl-1 hr **Seasonal:** No **Reservations:** One night's deposit (50% if longer than 2 nights) within 7 days of booking; 7 day cancel policy for refund less $10 service fee. Two night min on weekends **Permitted:** Children 6-up, quiet dogs, drinking **Languages:** French **Payment Terms:** Check MC/V [R07FPNM-11108] COM Y ITC **Member:** No

Rates:	Pvt Bath 5	Shared Bath 1
Single	$ 85-150.00	$ 75.00
Double	$ 85-150.00	$ 75.00

Canyon Road Casitas	652 Canyon Rd 87501	Santa Fe NM
Trisha Ambrose		Tel: 800-279-0755 505-988-5888
		Res Times *10am-5pm

Located on Santa Fe's famous Canyon Road within walking distance to distinctive art galleries, numerous museums, unique shops and historic landmarks. Luxury accommodations are featured in this 100-year-old Historic Territorial adobe. The large suite offers southwestern designer furnishings including a separate dining room, kiva fireplace, queen and double beds, separate rooms, original art work and private bath with shower and tub. Both guest rooms have kitchenettes, down quilts and pillows, feather beds, queen and double beds, separate entrances, with completely quiet, private patio full of local flowers. Truly a four-season retreat. Knowledgeable hostess will make dinner reservations and will help with local sightseeing in the most picturesque 100-square-miles of Amer-ica, offering mountains, valleys, deserts, and plenty of dramatic contrasts. A continental breakfast is included. A complimentary bottle of wine greets all guests upon their arrival. **Seasonal:** No **Reservations:** One night's fee or 50% of stay with 10-day cancellation policy for refund. *24-hr answering machine. $15 per extra person. **Brochure:** Yes **Permitted:** Children and drinking, smoking outdoors, local kennel available for pet boarding. **Languages:** Spanish **Payment Terms:** Check AE/DC/MC/V

Canyon Road Casitas

4-114 ©*Inn & Travel Memphis, Tennessee*

National Edition New Mexico

[K05HPNM1-6586] **COM YG ITC Member:** No

Rates: Pvt Bath 2
Single $ 85-145.00
Double $ 95-145.00

Dos Casas Viejas	610 Agua Fria St 87501	Santa Fe NM
Jois & Irving Belfield		Tel: 505-983-1636
		Res Times 8am-8pm

A special Inn . . . in a special city. Within the heart of picturesque Santa Fe is a small special Inn, *Dos Casas Viejas* (Two Old Houses). The two historical buildings have recently been restored to their 1860's architecture representing the three cultures of Santa Fe; Anglo, Indian and Hispanic. A spacious brick patio surrounded by six foot high adobe walls leads to each guest room (all with private entrance), furnished with French doors opening into rooms containing original vigas, Mexican tiled floors and wood-burning kiva fireplaces. The rooms are furnished with authentic Southwest antiques and original art; all rooms have phones, TV and private baths. Cozy down comforters and pillows, fresh linens and canopy beds (in some rooms) insure a comfortable night's rest. The main building houses the lobby/library and dining area where guests can relax on an overstuffed sofa next to the fire with a novel - or outdoors on sunny days, next to the forty foot lap pool with a cascading fountain. A complimentary continental European breakfast is available indoors or out. Centrally located, Dos Casa Viejas enables you to discover Santa Fe's renowned galleries, shops, museums and the finest restaurants. **Airport:** Albuquerque-65 mi **Reservations:** One night tariff due within 7 days of booking; arrival time 3-6pm, late arrival only by special arrangement, 14 day cancel policy for refund **Permitted:** Drinking, limited children **Payment Terms:** Check MC/V [Z04-GPNM-15805] **COM Y ITC Member:** No

Rates: Pvt Bath 5
Single $ 135-185.00
Double $ 135-185.00

Grant Corner Inn	122 Grant Ave 87501	Santa Fe NM
Louise Stewart		Tel: 505-983-6678
		Res Times 8am-8pm

A charming country setting complete with a white picket fence and gazebo is offered in this large residence c1900's of a former wealthy New Mexican ranching family. Completely restored and furnished by Pat, a designer-builder and Louise, an interior designer, with antique furnishings that provide a warm and charming atmosphere. You'll find each guest room uniquely furnished with brass and four-poster beds, armories, works of art, and treasures from around the world. Continuing the European tradition of *"Bed & Breakfast"*, Pat creates culinary delights for a full morning meal before either a crackling fire in the dining room or on the veranda in summer. The varied menu includes treats such as banana waffles, eggs Florentine, New Mexican souffle and accompanied by freshly ground European coffee, fresh squeezed orange juice, fresh fruit and homemade rolls and jellies. Complimentary wine is offered guests in the evening and You're just two blocks' strolling distance from Santa Fe's historic plaza. Other gourmet meals including picnics, catered dinners available with prior arrangements. AI and additional cost **Airport:** Albuquerque-1 Hr **Discounts:** 10%, 8 days or longer **Reservations:** One night's full rate or 1/2 of full length of stay within 10 days of reservation, 10 day cancel policy less 15% service charge **Brochure:** Yes **Permitted:** Children 9+, drinking **Conference:** Yes, groups to 20 persons **Languages:** Spanish, German **Payment Terms:** Check MC/V [I10HPNM1-3988] **COM YG ITC Member:** No

Rates:	Pvt Bath 10	Shared Bath 2
Single	$ 70-85.00	$ 80-95.00
Double	$ 85-155.00	$ 85-95.00

Heart Seed B&B Retreat Center & Spa
Judith Polich

PO Box 6019 87502

Santa Fe NM
Tel: 505-471-7026 Fax: 505-471-7026
Res Times 9am-9pm

The *Heart Seed B&B Retreat Center and Spa* offers some of the most spectacular mountain views in all of Santa Fe County and also the most breathtaking sunsets. Located on 100 acres only 25 miles south of Santa Fe on the famous Turquoise Trail and one hour from the Albuquerque airport, the *Heart Seed* provides a relaxing setting for exploring the attractions in this part of the Southwest. The *Heart Seed* is near the historic village of Los Cerrillos and the popular artist's colony, Madrid. The simple but elegant Southwest decor complements the rich high desert mountain views available from every window. Gourmet-style breakfasts are served each morning in the main house while guests bird watch from the kitchen windows. The *Heart Seed's* main quarters include two bedroom suites, the upstairs Mountain-Sky room, with a private deck opening to stunning 360 degree views and the Desert Hearts room, which has two queen sized beds and is decorated in a cowgirl-cowboy motif. The secluded Pinon and Juniper rooms in the retreat house are small studio apartments which each have fully equipped kitchenettes. All Heart Seed rooms have private baths and queen size beds. The 100 acre high desert grounds include a shaded deck, outdoor hot tub, meditation garden, labyrinth, common room/library and hiking and biking trails. Also available is a telescope for stargazing. The Common room contains a library and comfortable chairs and sofas as well as a tea and coffee station with fresh baked goodies and snacks and a guest refrigerator. A spacious shaded deck with hot tub provides the ideal setting for enjoying the morning sunrise with a cup of tea, resting after a spa treatment, or submerging in soothing waters under the stars. Discount packages are available for weeklong, weekend and weekday stays. These packages include massage or spa treatments as well as breakfast and the use of all facilities. Additional body work sessions may be scheduled. The Spa offers an outdoor hot, nurturing Swedish and deep tissue massage, and spa treatments, including salt glows, herbal wraps, aromatherapy and foot baths. All body work sessions are provided by licensed practitioners skilled in the latest techniques for reducing stress, relieving pain and relaxing and rejuvenating the mind, body and spirit. **Discounts:** Yes, special weekend, weekday and weeklong packages available **Airport:** Albuquerque-1 hr **Packages:** Yes **Reservations:** Minimum 50% payment, 15 day cancellation policy less 10% **Permitted:** Limited children, limited outdoor smoking **Conference:** Available for private workshops and group retreats **Payment Terms:** Check MC/V [J01HPNM1-21452] **COM YG ITC Member:** No

Rates:	Pvt Bath 4
Single	$ 89.00
Double	$ 89.00

Inn Of The Animal Tracks
Daun Martin

707 Paseo de Peralta 87501

Santa Fe NM
Tel: 505-988-1546

Your charming hostess relocated to Santa Fe from San Diego to begin this special Inn offering a harmonious, peaceful, fun-loving environment for travelers. Guest rooms are named after different animal (and their spirit) offering unique decor. Choose from the "Soaring Eagle", an airy room with six large windows, a fireplace that invites lofty, contemplative thoughts to the "Gentle Deer" which offers pale pastels, oatmeal and cream colors with a queen-size platform bed, hardwood floors and vigas. The other rooms are the "Playful Otter" and the "Loyal Wolf". With names such as these, guests may put aside all that robs them of their joy of life. Full homemade breakfasts are offered in the "Sign of the Buffalo" room with special recipe yeast breads, fresh juices, fruits and innovative egg entrees. Summer brings breakfast outdoors onto the patio area. Picnic baskets are available with two-day notice. Plenty of sights with galleries, restaurants, museums, parks, festivals, theatres, opera and recreational activities.

Seasonal: No **Brochure:** Yes **Payment Terms:** Check [X09BCNM-8947] **COM** Y **ITC Member:** No

Rates:	Pvt Bath 4
Single	$ 95-105.00
Double	$ 95-105.00

Inn Of The Turquoise Bear   342 E Buena Vista St 87501-4423   **Santa Fe NM**
Ralph Bolton/Robert Frost   **Tel:** 800-396-4104   505-983-0798   **Fax:** 505-988-4225
Res Times 7am-11pm

The *Inn of the Turquoise Bear*, Santa Fe's newest bed and breakfast, is located six blocks from the Plaza, within walking distance of museums, galleries, fine restaurants and nightlife. Nearby attractions include the Santa Fe Opera, Indian pueblos, Bandelier National Monument, the regional flea market, and hot springs, and such outdoor activities as hiking, skiing, river rafting and horseback riding. On the estate of one of Santa Fe's leading citizens for several decades, the poet Witter Bynner, this rambling adobe villa, built over a period of more than 100 years, is considered one of the City Different's most significant historical buildings. Among the celebrities entertained by Bynner in this house were DH Lawrence, Willa Cather, Errol Flynn, Rita Hayworth, Stephen Spender, WH Auden, Christopher Isherwood, Igor Stravinsky, Edna St Vincent Millay, Robert Oppenheimer, Aldous Huxley, Clara Bow, Ansel Adams, Martha Graham, Georgia O'Keeffe, Thornton Wilder, Robert Frost and many others.

The Inn has ten delightful guest rooms, most of which have queen-size beds, kiva fireplaces, viga beam ceilings, and private baths and entrances. The superior amenities of the *Turquoise Bear* include TV/VCRs, phones, robes, off-street parking, sunset refreshments, and an expanded continental breakfast that includes fresh fruit, berries and juice, a selection of breads, pastries and cereals, yogurt, and gourmet coffee. Set on a walled and secluded acre of gardens, terraces and meandering flagstone paths under a canopy of tall pines, the *Inn of the Turquoise Bear* offers guests the experience of a unique, authentic ambiance that captures the essence of traditional Santa Fe. **Dis-counts:** AAA, AARP **Airport:** Albuquerque-55mi **Packages:** Entire house available for special occasions. Web address: www.travelbase.com/destina-tions/santa-fe/turquoise-bear **Seasonal:** Rates vary **Reservations:** One night deposit or 50% of stay, 14 day cancel policy for refund, less 20% processing fee *Two suites available $115-210.00 Email: blue-bear@roadrunner.com **Permitted:** Limited children, drinking, limited pets, smoking outdoors **Conference:** Yes, meeting room available **Languages:** Spanish, French, German, Norwegian [K11IPNM1-27214] **Payment Terms:** Check AE/DISC/MC/V **ITC Member** No

Rates:	Pvt Bath 6	Shared Bath 2	Suite 2
Single	$ 80-160.00	$ 80-110.00	$ 115-210
Double	$ 80-160.00	$ 80-110.00	$ 115-210

Preston House   106 Faithway St 87501   **Santa Fe NM**
Singe Bergaman   **Tel:** 505-982-3465

Listed on the *National Register of Historic Places*, this fine example of Queen Anne includes fine antique furnishings and decor, family heirlooms, plenty of quilts and handicrafts. Continental plus breakfast included. Complimentary wine or sherry. **Seasonal:** No **Brochure:** Yes **Permitted:** Limited children, limited smoking **Payment Terms:** Check MC/V [X11ACNM-3994] **COM** Y **ITC Member:** No

Rates:	Pvt Bath 4	Shared Bath 2
Single	$ 65.00-up	$ 55.00-up
Double	$ 75-105.00	$ 65.00-up

El Rincon B&B   114 Kit Carson 87571   **Taos NM**
Nina Meyers   **Tel:** 505-758-4874
Res Times 24 Hrs

©*Inn & Travel Memphis, Tennessee*

Described in Frank Waters classic book of the Southwest *"The Man Who Killed The Deer"*; once the home of La Dona Luz Lucero De Martinez, the sister-in-law of the famous (or infamous) Padre Martinez; the former world-renown restaurant La Donna Luz - guests are truly living in Taos history. Located in the heart of historic Taos, you're across the street from Kit Carson's home - just 1/2 block from Old Town Plaza and within walking distance of museums, art galleries and shops. Each room is unique with its own surprises; a large collection of fine art, both contemporary and from the early days is distributed throughout the large adobe. All rooms have private baths, most have a small refrigerator, TV, VCR and stereos. During warm months breakfast is served in a colorful outdoor patio or before a warming fire in an ancient fireplace during the cooler periods. Your hostess, Nina Meyers (an artist in her own right), is the daughter of Ralph Meyers, a well-known Indian trader, writer and craftsman of early Taos. Fifty feet away is the oldest trading post in Taos (also named El Rincon) which is still operated by Rowene Martinez, Ralph's widow. Your host, Paul "Paco" Castillo, is Nina's son and shares his family's rich background and knowledge of New Mexico. **Airport:** Albuquerque NM-130 mi **Reservations:** One nights deposit or credit card number**Brochure:** Yes **Permitted:** Children, pets, smoking, drinking **Languages:** Spanish, English **Payment Terms:** Check AE/MC/V [Z07GPNM-139-61] **COM** Y **ITC Member:** No

Rates: Pvt Bath 12
Single $ 49-129.00
Double $ 49-129.00

Hacienda del Sol B&B   109 Mabel Dodge Lane 87571   Taos NM
Marcine & John Landon
Tel: 505-758-0287
Res Times 7am-9pm

Once part of Art Patroness Mabel Dodge Luhan's estate, *Hacienda del Sol* is a 180 year old adobe adjoining the 95,000 acre Taos Pueblo Indian Lands. With 1.2 acres of tree-shaded grounds, the nine room Inn offers country ambiance just 1-1/2 miles north of the Taos Plaza. With viga ceilings, arched pueblo-styled doorways, and large, quiet rooms, the Inn takes visitors back to the days when famous author Frank Waters wrote *"People of the Valley"* in what is now one of the B&B's larger guest rooms. Handcrafted Southwest furnishings, original works of art (many for sale), fireplaces and down comforters add to the warm feeling of this special place. One room features its own huge jacuzzi tub with a large skylight above and another has its own steam room. Outdoors, just steps from the Reservation, and with an unobstructed view of Taos Mountain is a large Hot-Tub and deck. Complimentary snacks are served in the evening. Breakfast includes home-baked specialties, hot entrees, fresh fruit and a secret blend of coffee. **Airport:** Albuquerque-120 mi **Seasonal:** No **Reservations:** 50% deposit or one night's rate (whichever is greater); 10-day cancellation policy for refund, less $15, deposit forfeited if less than 10 days **Brochure:** Yes **Permitted:** Children, drinking, smoking permitted outdoors only **Languages:** Spanish **Payment Terms:** Check [Z01H-PNM1-4004] **COM** YG **ITC Member:** No **Quality Assurance** Requested

Rates: Pvt Bath 9
Single $ 62-122.00
Double $ 72-132.00

Heart Seed B&B Retreat Center & Spa   Taos NM
Judith Polich
Tel: 505-471-7026 Fax: 505-471-7026
Res Times 9am-9pm

Refer to the same listing name under Sante Fe, New Mexico for a complete description. **Seasonal:** No **Payment Terms:** Check MC/V [M02HPNM1-22297] **COM** YG **ITC Member:** No

Rates: Pvt Bath 4
Single $ 89.00
Double $ 89.00

La Posada de Taos   309 Juanita Lane 87571   Taos NM
Nancy & Bill Swan
Tel: 800-645-4803 505-758-8164 Fax: 505-751-3294
Res Times 9am-9pm

National Edition ***New Mexico - Oregon***

Bask in the warm and friendly hospitality. The Inn offers six charming guest rooms, (each with its own bathroom), tastefully decorated with country antiques, handmade quilts, local arts and attention to detail. At 8:00 am, we all sit down together for a delicious breakfast. Romantic moments abound **. . . from dramatic sunrises to sunset walks and stargazing nights.** Intimate evenings by your fireplace . . relaxing on your veranda surrounded by gardens that capture the spirit of New Mexico and our century-old home. Capture the enchantment . . . the quiet and calm . . . the slower and simpler world of Southwest Elegance and charm. A place to get away, a time to relax, a retreat to a beautiful hacienda, under a northern New Mexico sky. Discover the magic that is Taos. The historic world-renowned Art Colony. Eighty galleries, museums, shops and wonderful restaurants are just a few blocks away. Visit the Taos Pueblo, ride the whitewater down the Rio Grande, horseback or hike through the Sangre de Cristo Mountains, ski down world class Taos Ski Valley slopes or enjoy nearby cross country ski areas. Escape to a romantic secluded adobe Inn, 2-1/2 blocks from Plaza - in historic district - first B&B in Taos. Walk to galleries, museums, restaurants, shops. Return to casual elegance-country pine antiques, private baths, fireplaces. Private courtyards and patios. Savor a delicious full breakfast. Six rooms to choose from, each different. All decorated with country pine and southwest flavor. Separated honeymoon house. Inspected and rated AAA 3 star, ABBA 3 crown. Members PAII, New Mexico B&B Assoc, Taos B&B Assoc. **Airport:** Albuquerque **Seasonal:** No **Reservations:** 50% deposit within two weeks of booking, 10 day cancel policy for full refund **Brochure:** Yes **Permitted:** Children 11+, drinking **Conference:** Yes, meeting room for groups to 15 **Languages:** Spanish **Payment Terms:** Check Trvlr Check [I03IPNM1-4008] **COM YG ITC Member:** No

Rates: Pvt Bath 6
Single $ 70-107.00
Double $ 80-117.00

Mabel Dodge B&B 240 Morada Lane 87571 Taos NM
Robin Davis Tel: 800-84-MABEL 505-758-9465 Fax: 505-751-0431

Historic home of Mabel Dodge Luhan offers historical setting for guests today. Stay where DH Lawrence, Georgia O'keefe and other famous guests collected their thoughts in this pleasant setting. Full breakfast included. **Seasonal:** No **Brochure:** Yes **Permitted:** Children, smoking, limited drinking **Payment Terms:** Check [X11ACNM-4007] **COM Y ITC Member:** No

Rates: Pvt Bath 5   Shared Bath 4
Single $ 65.00 $ 55.00
Double $ 75.00 $ 65.00

Mountain Light B&B PO Box 241 87571 Taos NM
Gail Russell Tel: 505-776-8474

Enjoy gorgeous views from this adobe-style residence of a well-known photographer who will introduce you to all that's here and help with camera tips if you need. Full breakfast is included. **Seasonal:** No **Reservations:** Deposit required at res time **Brochure:** Yes **Permitted:** Children, limited smoking **Languages:** Photography and the West! **Payment Terms:** Check [X11ACNM-4009] **COM Y ITC Member:** No

Rates: Pvt Bath 2   Shared Bath 1
Single $ 45.00 $ 40.00
Double $ 55.00 $ 45.00

Chanticleer Inn 120 Gresham St 97520 Ashland OR

©*Inn & Travel Memphis, Tennessee*

Oregon   *National Edition*

Peggy Kuan   Tel: 503-482-1919

Charm and warmth in this country residence offering antique furnishings, patio garden, and fluffy comforters for all guests. Close to ski lifts, including discounts. Full breakfast included. **Seasonal:** No **Brochure:** Yes **Permitted:** Children, drinking **Payment Terms:** Check [X11ACOR-4272] **COM** Y

ITC Member: No

Rates: Pvt Bath 7
Single $ 75.00
Double $ 85-100.00

Cowslips Belle   159 N Main St 97520   **Ashland OR**
Jon & Carmen Reinhardt   Tel: 503-488-2901

This darling Craftsman home of 1913 remains essentially as then with the original woodwork and bevel glass throughout the residence. Vintage furnishings include canopy, brass and iron beds, stained glass windows, antique quilts and tiffany-style lamps and beautiful garden views from each guest room in the main house. Your hosts have tended to everything for your comfort including fresh flowers to brighten each room! A scrumptious full breakfast includes roasted Italian coffee and espresso. Guests are conveniently located within three blocks for leisurely walking to shops, restaurants, Lithia Park and the Shakespearean Theatres. **Seasonal:** No **Reservations:** One night's deposit within 7 days of booking, 14 day cancel policy, check-in 3pm, check-out 11am. **Brochure:** Yes **Permitted:** Drinking, smoking outdoors only **Payment Terms:** Check MC/V [X10BCOR-4277] **COM** Y **ITC Member:** No

Rates: Pvt Bath 4
Single $ 57-87.00
Double $ 62-92.00

Hersey House B&B   451 N Main St 97520   **Ashland OR**
Gail Orell   Tel: 503-482-4563   Fax: 503-482-2839
     Res Times 8am-8pm

c1900's saltbox Victorian that has been restored and furnished with period decor and family heirlooms, nestled among lovely garden areas. Furnished with antiques, queen beds and plenty of love and charm to satisfy even the most discriminating guest. **Seasonal:** 4/1-10/15 **Reservations:** Deposit required at res time with refund if cancelled **Brochure:** Yes **Permitted:** Children 13-up **Payment Terms:** Check\V [X11ACOR-4279] **COM** Y **ITC Member:** No

Rates: Pvt Bath 4
Single $ 65.00
Double $ 65.00

Iris Inn   59 Manzanita St 97520   **Ashland OR**
Vicki Lamb   Tel: 800-460-7650 541-488-2286 **Fax:** 541-488-3709
     Res Times 8am-9pm

The *Iris Inn* is situated in a quiet neighborhood with views of the Valley and the Mountains surrounding this Rogue Valley setting. Guests often spend time relaxing on the deck overlooking the Rose Garden, when not at the award-winning Oregon Shakespeare Festival, Historic Jacksonville, The Britt Music Festival, Crater Lake and local wineries. The peaceful ambiance of this 1905 Victorian Inn is enhanced with antique furnishings and custom amenities making it a great place not only when traveling but for those special occasions, birthdays and anniversaries. Each guest room reflects the innkeeper's thoughtfulness in making your stay enjoyable with special touches of hospitality - such as the guest robes. Elegant and creative breakfast start your day - specialties such as Peaches 'n Cream French Toast, Crepes, Apple Pancakes and fresh baked Buttermilk Scones bring guests back again and again. Following breakfast, nearby activities might include fishing, rafting, downhill and cross country skiing - all nearby, or a day full of wonderful sightseeing. **Airport:** Medford-12 mi **Reservations:** Deposit or credit card number required within 7 days of booking with 20 day cancel policy for refund less $10 service fee

National Edition   **Oregon**

Brochure: Yes **Permitted:** Limited children, limited drinking, smoking outdoors **Languages:** Spanish, French, Greek, English, Italian **Payment Terms:** Check MC/V [Z07HPOR1-4281] COM U **ITC Member:** No

Rates:	Pvt Bath 5
Single	$ 71-81.00
Double	$ 85-95.00

Franklin Street Station   1140 Franklin St 97103   **Astoria OR**
Renee Caldwell   **Tel:** 800-448-1098 503-325-4314
Res Times 24 Hrs

Featured in the *"Los Angeles Times"* Travel Section and excellent ratings in many B&B guide books, this Victorian home is decorated beautifully and reflects the early years of Astoria with its ornate craftsmanship, built by Shipbuilder Ferdinand Fisher. We are the closest of all Bed and Breakfasts in Astoria, to the downtown area. Within walking distance to museums and restaurants. Our accommodations include six rooms, three of which have views of the Columbia River and three are two-room suites, with all rooms offering private baths. Try our Captain's Quarters which features a beautiful view of the Columbia River and downtown, queen size bed, fireplace, TV, VCR, stereo plus a luxurious bath with clawfoot tub, brass shower and fixtures. Very private! Our full complimentary breakfast is served either at 8:30 or 9:30 and includes our speciality of Belgium Waffles, sausage, fresh fruit, juice and coffee. We will make your stay a memorable one and know you'll return again. **Airport:** Portland Intl-90 mi **Discounts:** Yes, winter rates lower **Seasonal:** No **Brochure:** Yes **Permitted:** Children, drinking **Payment Terms:** Check MC/V [I04HPOR1-16874] COM YG **ITC Member:** No

Rates:	Pvt Bath 6
Single	$ 58-110.00
Double	$ 63-115.00

Grandview B&B   1574 Grand 97103   **Astoria OR**
Charleen Maxwell   **Tel:** 800-488-3250 503-325-5555
Res Times 9am-9pm

Wonderful Columbia River view in a light, cheerful 3-story Victorian, located on *Historical Homes Walking Tour*. Rooms and suites have queen beds, country decor, hardwood floors, books, and fluffy comforters. Walk to superb Maritime Museum, Columbia Lightship, Heritage Museum and 100-year-old churches. Ships from many nations dock here, and some allow tours. Golf, clam-digging, beach-combing, surfing, boating, and tennis are close-by. Hike to "Astoria Column" or stroll on the college campus; boat watch or bird watch. Two hours from Portland on the Northwest tip of Oregon. Continental-plus breakfast includes tea-coffee, hot cocoa, cider, milk, fruit and juices and two or more kinds of fresh muffins. *Reservations for large groups or for exclusive use of the Inn need to be arranged well in advance. **Airport:** Portland-87 mi **Seasonal:** No **Reservations:** Full amount due at time of res or credit card guarantee to hold room, 24-hr cancellation policy for full refund; add 7% room tax; check-in by 6 pm **Brochure:** Yes **Permitted:** Children 10-up **Conference:** Yes, groups of ten to fifteen persons **Payment Terms:** DISC/MC/V [K05HPOR1-6337] COM Y **ITC Member:** No

Rates:	Pvt Bath 6
Single	$ 39-87.00
Double	$ 39-92.00

©*Inn & Travel Memphis, Tennessee*

Oregon *National Edition*

Yankee Tinker B&B	5480 SW 183rd Ave 97007	**Beaverton OR**
Jan & Ralph Wadleigh		**Tel:** 800-TINKER2 503-649-0932
		Res Times 9am-5pm

"A handcrafted New England experience in the heart of Washington County." Located ten miles west of Portland in a peaceful residential neighborhood. From here, visit wineries, farmers' markets, historical sights as well as the dramatic Columbia River Gorge and grand Oregon beaches. Three distinctive guest rooms with comfortable beds are graced by handmade quilts, antiques and family heirlooms. Guest sitting room features a fireplace and TV, private yard has spacious deck and gardens. Memorable breakfasts, served alfresco weather permitting, are designed to accommodate special dietary needs and your schedule. The mouth watering choices might be blueberry pancakes or muffins, peaches'n cream french toast or herbed omelettes. The traditional Yankee offering of pie for breakfast is available for the hearty eater. Benefit from "all the extras" that make your business or leisure travel successful. The *Yankee Tinker's* warmth and hospitality will convince you to linger an extra day or two as well as planning your return visit. **Discounts:** Yes, for extended stays **Airport:** Portland Intl-20 mi **Seasonal:** No **Reservations:** One night deposit /credit card number with 72 hr cancel policy for refund **Brochure:** Yes **Permitted:** Drinking, limited children **Payment Terms:** Check AE/DC/MC/V [Z06GPOR-8918] **COM** Y **ITC Member:** No

Rates:	**Pvt Bath 1**	**Shared Bath 2**
Single	$ 65.00	$ 50-55.00
Double	$ 70.00	$ 60.00

Mirror Pond House	1054 NW Harmon Blvd 97701	**Bend OR**
Beryl Kellum		**Tel:** 503-389-1680

Relax and reflect while staying at this charming Cape Cod on the water and next to a wildlife refuge for enjoying nature at its best. Year round retreat with interesting host that will give directions to all sights, including excellent snow skiing in winter. Full breakfast included. **Seasonal:** No **Reservations:** Deposit is necessary to hold room. **Brochure:** Yes **Permitted:** Children 12-up, smoking, drinking **Payment Terms:** Check [X11ACOR-4301] **COM** Y **ITC Member:** No

Rates:	**Pvt Bath 2**
Single	$ 70.00
Double	$ 80.00

Campbell House, A City Inn	252 Pearl St 97401	**Eugene OR**
Myra Plant		**Tel:** 800-264-2519 503-343-1119 **Fax:** 503-343-2258
		Res Times 8am-11pm

"Classic elegance, exquisite decor and impeccable service"... Old world elegance and charm nestled on the East side of Skinner's Butte, overlooking the city of Eugene, in the National Historic District. The *Campbell House*, A City Inn, built in 1892 and fully restored as an elegant fourteen room Inn. You will sense the hospitality as you stroll up the curved walk, surrounded by acres of lawn, flowers and a hillside of natural landscaping. You feel at-once welcome the moment you enter through the French doors into the charming and elegant lobby with marble floor, open staircase and gracious innkeeper. Just beyond the lobby is the parlor, dining room and library, each with majestic views of the city, offering several sitting areas with wing back chairs and an extensive selection of fine leather bound books and videos (mysteries and classics). Each of the beautiful fourteen guest rooms have private bath, TV with VCR, telephone and all the amenities one would find in a small European hotel. Selected rooms feature: gas fireplaces, four-poster bed and jetted or claw footed bath tub. Ideally located just three blocks away from downtown, the performing arts Hult Center, the Fifth Street public market with several unique shops, fine restaurants and charming antique stores.

4-122 ©*Inn & Travel Memphis, Tennessee*

Leisure adventures include: hiking, rock climbing, bicycling (two blocks away is the river with miles of bike paths), golf, jogging and we also make arrangements for fishing or white-water rafting trips down one of the most scenic rivers in the nation. **Discounts:** Corporate and frequent traveler rates) **Airport:** Eugene-15 mi **Packages:** Business Retreats, Weddings, Theater, Romance Getaway **Brochure:** Yes **Permitted:** Children, limited drinking, smoking in outside courtyard **Conference:** Three separate meeting rooms for groups **Payment Terms:** AE/MC/V [K07HPOR1-20014] **COM YG ITC Member:** No

Rates:	Pvt Bath 14
Single	$ 70-220.00
Double	$ 75-225.00

Kjaers House In The Woods B&B 814 Lorane Hwy 97405 Eugene OR
Eunice & George Kjaer Tel: 541-343-3234
Res Times 8am-8pm

Urban convenience and suburban tranquility describe this 1910 Craftsman-Style home in a park-like setting with covered porches and swing from which to enjoy the deer, birds and wildflowers. Even though a shopping center is just six blocks away - deer and raccoon are almost daily visitors. Your hosts gladly share their interest and knowledge of wildflowers with their guests along with giving wildflower seeds and plants to guests to start in their home gardens. This lovely home is located within walking distance to hiking, biking, jogging trails and parks. Many museums, art galleries, theaters, the U of Oregon and fine restaurants are within four miles. The House In The Woods has been in operation since 1984 and is furnished with antiques, Oriental carpets and an unusual square rosewood grand piano as well as a wonderful music and record library which guests enjoy browsing through to hear their favorite songs. A full complimentary breakfast is planned for the guest's convenience and includes specialties of the house featuring local cheeses, nuts and fruits. Inspected by the Eugene Area B&B Assoc & Oregon B&B Guild. Members of PAII. **Airport:** 15 mi to Mahlon Sweet Airport **Discounts:** Travel agents, seniors, extended stays-7th night free **Seasonal:** No **Reservations:** One night's deposit, 72 hr cancel policy for full refund. Check-in 4-6pm, other by prior arrangement. Checkout by 11am. Add 9.5% room tax to above rates. **Brochure:** Yes **Permitted:** Limited drinking, children by prior arrangement **Conference:** Meeting room available for up to 15 persons **Languages:** German **Payment Terms:** Check [Z08HPOR1-4323] **COM YG ITC Member:** No

Rates:	Pvt Bath 1
Single	$ 40-45.00
Double	$ 65-75.00

Lorane Valley B&B 86621 Lorane Hwy 97405 Eugene OR
Esther & George Ralph Tel: 503-686-0241

Four and one-half miles from the hustle and bustle of downtown Eugene is a haven of tranquility. The Lorane Valley Bed & Breakfast is a beautiful, new two level cedar home set on twenty-two acres of wooded hillside overlooking the picturesque Lorane Valley and presided over by a small herd of Angus cattle. Guests can enjoy the luxurious combination of rich antique furnishings and the convenience of a thoroughly modern home. Catering to one party at a time, secluded accommodations include a bedroom with a king-size bed, window seat and plant window; a living room with two day beds; a kitchen that included a microwave, stove, oven, dishwasher, and an instant hot water tap. The private bath contains a shower, tub and Jacuzzi. Additional amenities are a full English breakfast, fresh-cut flowers, a split of French champagne and a wide assortment of reading materials. Come and relax in the sedate beauty of the Oregon countryside. The Lorane Valley Bed & Breakfast is an excellent choice for families or individuals who want to retreat to country comforts. **Seasonal:** No **Reservations:** Deposit required by credit card number **Brochure:** Yes **Permitted:** Limited children **Payment Terms:** Check MC/V [R09BCOR-6356] **COM Y ITC Member:** No

Rates:	Pvt Bath 1
Single	$ 55.00
Double	$ 69.00

Pine Meadow Inn 1000 Crow Rd 97527 Grants Pass OR

©Inn & Travel Memphis, Tennessee

Oregon *National Edition*

Nancy & Maloy Murdock **Tel:** 800-554-0806 541-471-6277 **Fax:** 541-471-6277
Res Times 8am-9pm

Pine Meadow is a distinctive country retreat on nine acres of secluded meadow and woods, near the gateway to the wild and scenic Rogue River. Our home is styled after Midwestern farmhouses, with a wrap around porch and wicker furniture, a sitting room with fireplace and a dining room with bay windows to capture the morning sun. The French doors open out to the English cutting and herb gardens and a deck with a hot tub under the towering pines. The sitting area near the Koi pond is a favorite place to enjoy the natural beauty surrounding the area. Upstairs are four large bedrooms, well-lit for reading, each with window seat and/or sitting area. The Inn is filled with elegant, yet comfortable, turn-of-the-century antiques. Come play on the Rogue River - whitewater rafting, fishing or jet boat trips. Enjoy the nearby Shakespeare Festival, Britt Festival, Historic Jacksonville, the California Redwoods and Crater Lake. Ski Mount Ashland, visit the Oregon Caves or hunt for antiques. If you come just to relax or renew, our country roads are ideal for long walks, jogging and for biking, in a beautiful country setting. *Pine Meadow* is fully air conditioned and we are open year round. We feature healthy breakfasts with seasonal fruits and vegetables from our garden. We invite you to come and enjoy the magnificent Rogue Valley with us. **Airport:** Medford-40 min **Reservations:** One night's deposit per room required within 7 days of booking, 7 day cancel policy for full return **Brochure:** Yes **Permitted:** Children 8-up **Payment Terms:** Check [I08HPOR1-20046] **COM** YG **ITC Member:** No

Rates: Pvt Bath 4
Single $ 80-110.00
Double $ 80-110.00

McCully House Inn 240 E California 97530 **Jacksonville OR**
Pat Groth/Phil Accetta **Tel:** 503-899-1942

Classical 1861 Revival home in the center of historic Jacksonville and close to Shakespeare Festival, and Rogue River. Full breakfast included. **Seasonal:** No **Brochure:** Yes **Permitted:** Children, limited smoking **Payment Terms:** Check [X11ACOR-4349] **COM**

Y **ITC Member:** No

Rates: Pvt Bath 4
Single $ 65.00
Double $ 75.00

Touvelle House 455 N Oregon St 97530-9098 **Jacksonville OR**
Carolee Casey **Tel:** 800-846-8422 503-899-8938
Res Times 8am-10pm

A grand picturesque home just a few blocks off the famous Main Street of the old Gold Rush town of Jacksonville - guests feel like pioneers after checking into this 1916 Craftsman-style home, to be pampered and spoiled like hotel guests were at the turn-of-the-century. Jacksonville has experienced a rebirth beginning in the 1950's when a few people began restoring the buildings and their homes. Today, over eighty restored buildings are on the National Historic Register and the town has been designated a National Historic Landmark District. Streets are bustling again with horse-drawn carriages and trolley cars taking travelers past craft and antique shops and the sights. Your hosts have restored

4-124 ©*Inn & Travel Memphis, Tennessee*

National Edition   *Oregon*

their home in keeping with the period and style of the 1900s - and welcome all guests to make themselves feel at home. The common areas include The Great Room, featuring a large-stoned fireplace; The Library, featuring TV and VCR; The Sunroom which consists of almost all windows and the Dining Room, featuring an intricate built-in buffet. Outdoors there are two spacious covered verandas and by the carriage house, there's swimming in the pool and a spa for soaking (complimentary robes and beach towels are provided). The guest rooms are uniquely furnished and range from The Garden Suite, a floral fantasy in pinks, blues, greens and whites with a queen bed and an antique iron day bed to Granny's Attic, where childhood memories are rekindled with cozy hideaways and angular rooflines. A full breakfast and afternoon appetizers are included. **Airport:** Medford-5 mi **Discounts:** Corporate Sun-Thursday **Seasonal:** Rates vary **Reservations:** Deposit within 7 days of when reservation is made, 10 day cancel policy for refund less $10 service fee **Brochure:** Yes **Permitted:** Social drinking **Conference:** Only when booking entire home, space for groups to twenty **Payment Terms:** Check [I05-FPOR-4347] **COM** Y **ITC Member:** No

Rates:	Pvt Bath 6
Single	$ 90-95.00
Double	$ 90-95.00

Brey House "Oceanview" B&B	3725 NW Keel Ave 97367	Lincoln City OR
Milt & Shirley Brey		**Tel:** 503-994-7123
		Res Times 9am-7pm

The ocean awaits you just across the street! The never-ending beach, whale watching, beachcombing is just starters for guests staying at the Brey House. Famous restaurants abound, along with factory stores and antiquing and famous kite shops. Guests enjoy one of the four bedrooms, all offering private baths. This three-story Cape Cod-style home built in 1941 is in the heart of Lincoln City. You'll enjoy one of Milt's and Shirley's hearty breakfasts with the ocean looking at you while conversing with the other guests. All rooms have queen size beds, electric blankets, flannel sheets and are beautifully decorated. **Airport:** Portland-90 mi **Discounts:** Yes, off season **Packages:** Yes, inquire at res time **Seasonal:** No **Reservations:** Deposit or credit card number required, 72 hr cancel policy for refund **Brochure:** Yes **Permitted:** Drinking, smoking restricted to certain areas **Payment Terms:** Check DC/MC/V [Z04GPOR-6342] **COM** Y **ITC Member:** No

Rates:	Pvt Bath 4
Single	$ 60-80.00
Double	$ 65-85.00

Pine Meadow Inn	1000 Crow Rd 97532	Merlin OR
Maloy & Nancy Murdock		**Tel:** 800-554-0806 541-471-6277
		Res Times 8am-9pm

Refer to the same listing name under Grants Pass, Oregon for a complete description. **Seasonal:** No **Payment Terms:** Check [M08GPOR1-20144] **COM** Y **ITC Member:** No

Rates:	Pvt Bath 4
Single	$ 80-110.00
Double	$ 80-110.00

Three Capes B&B	1685 Maxwell Mtn Rd 97134	Oceanside OR
Ross & Kathy Holloway		**Tel:** 503-842-6126

Darling contemporary home nestled in secluded coastal community hillside. You'll enjoy the sandy beaches, sightseeing or watching shore birds and wildlife in the sanctuary. In early Spring, wales will be close enough to see. Continental breakfast weekdays. **Seasonal:** No **Brochure:** Yes **Permitted:** Children, limited smoking and drinking. **Payment Terms:** Check [X11ACOR-4369] **COM** Y **ITC Member:** No

Rates:	Pvt Bath 2	Shared Bath 1
Single	$ 50.00	$ 45.00
Double	$ 60.00	$ 55.00

©*Inn & Travel Memphis, Tennessee*

Oregon *National Edition*

Home By The Sea 444 Jackson St 97465 **Port Orford OR**
Brenda & Alan Mitchell **Tel:** 503-332-2855
Res Times 9am-9pm

Home by the Sea is a contemporary owner-built home with beach access and spectacular ocean views from its two guest bedrooms that overlook Historic Battle Rock and it's uncrowded beach in the background. Located away from highway noise, guests are within an easy stroll to fine restaurants, sand beaches and Oregon's only fishing fleet that has to be launched by a crane! A full breakfast is included with your room rate. **Seasonal:** No **Reservations:** One night's deposit to confirm reservation, 72 hour cancel policy **Brochure:** Yes **Permitted:** Limited children, limited drinking **Payment Terms:** Check DC/MC/V [X06BCOR-4383] **COM** Y **ITC Member:** No

Rates:	Pvt Bath 2
Single	$ 60-70.00
Double	$ 60-70.00

J Palmer House 4314 N Mississippi Ave 97217 **Portland OR**
Mary & Richard Sauter **Tel:** 503-284-5893

The *John Palmer House* has been recognized by National TV, Newspapers and Magazines as being one of the most complete authentic Victorian restorations in the country. Located in Portland Oregon, it offers the convenience of many day trips to mountains, wine country and the Pacific Coast as-well-as the attractions that are part of any big city. The Inn is operated by three generations: Granny at ninety-six is the oldest; David, the CCA trained chef is twenty-nine. With a need to be creative and inventive, the Innkeepers offer multiple ways to enjoy the home that goes well beyond the B&B. High Tea and Dinners for two are served by advance reservation. Whether you are planning a relaxing vacation or a once-in-a-lifetime experience, the Inn wants to be there helping serve you. Two suites with private bath and kitchen available for long term stays. **Seasonal:** No **Reservations:** Credit card to guarantee all reservations with a 7 day cancel policy for refund. Two-day minimum stay for travel agent reservations. **Brochure:** Yes **Permitted:** Drinking, limited children, limited pets **Languages:** Sign **Payment Terms:** Check AE/DISC/MC/V [Z07GPOR-4377] **COM** Y **ITC Member:** No

Rates:	Pvt Bath 4	Shared Bath 8
Single	$ 80-120.00	$ 35-70.00
Double	$ 85-122.00	$ 40-75.00

Yankee Tinker B&B **Portland OR**
Jan & Ralph Wadleigh **Tel:** 800-TINKER2 503-649-0932
Res Times 9am-5pm

Refer to the same listing name under Beaverton, Oregon for a complete description. **Seasonal:** No **Payment Terms:** Check AE/DC/MC/V [M06GP-OR-8919] **COM** Y **ITC Member:** No

Rates:	Pvt Bath 1	Shared Bath 2
Single	$ 65.00	$ 50-55.00
Double	$ 70.00	$ 60.00

State House B&B 2146 State St 97301 **Salem OR**
Mike Winsett & Judy Uselman **Tel:** 503-588-1340

Snuggled in a natural setting of lawns and mature plantings and on the bank of Mill Creek you'll find animals walking everywhere you turn, including ducks and geese. Originally the 1920's residence of a state politician, it's still filled with the atmosphere of another era. **Seasonal:** No **Reservations:** Deposit required at res time with refund if cancelled 10 days prior to arrival. **Brochure:** Yes **Permitted:** Limited children, smoking, drinking **Payment Terms:** Check MC/V [X11ACOR-4385] **COM** Y **ITC Member:** No

Rates:	Pvt Bath 5	Shared Bath 2
Single	$ 65.00	$ 50.00
Double	$ 75.00	$ 60.00

National Edition   *Oregon - Utah*

Williams House Inn	608 W 6th St 97058	The Dalles OR
Don & Barbara Williams		Tel: 503-296-2889

At the end of the Oregon Trail is this large Victorian home, registered as a *National Historic Place*. Offers guests hospitality and exciting antique furnishings throughout; clawfoot tubs, four-poster beds, and balconies off each guest room. Continental breakfast included. **Seasonal:** No **Brochure:** Yes **Permitted:** Limited children, limited drinking **Payment Terms:** Check [X11ACOR-4316] **COM** Y **ITC Member:** No

Rates:	Pvt Bath 2	Shared Bath 3
Single	$ 55.00	$ 45.00
Double	$ 65.00	$ 55.00

Blue Haven Inn	3025 Gienger Rd 97141	Tillamook OR
Joy & Ray Still		Tel: 503-842-2265
		Res Times 24 Hrs

Located on a two acre parklike setting surrounded by tall evergreens, *Blue Haven Inn* provides guests a peaceful and quiet place to *"relax and unwind"* and assures a restful night's sleep. Built in 1916, your hosts, Joy and Ray, have lovingly restored and individually decorated each guest room with antiques, limited edition collectibles and modern amenities for a comfortable stay. The Inn has extensive grounds and gardens for the guests to enjoy along with croquet, lawn tennis, a country porch swing, library/game room with a variety of games, books, music provided by an old radio or antique gramaphone and a VCR for enjoying a movie. Complimentary gourmet breakfasts are served in the formal dining room in a style reminiscent of a more gracious way of dining. Adjacent to the Inn is an "over-flow shop" containing antique furnishings, glassware, old sewing machines and claw foot tubs - all for sale. The land of *"cheese, trees and ocean breeze"*, guests can visit the famous Tillamook Cheese Factory, try the excellent fishing, crabbing and clamming at one of the eight rivers and the beautiful ocean nearby. Other activities include antiquing, hand gliding, hiking, kite flying, train rides through picturesque settings and winery tours. **Discounts:** Yes, inquire at res time **Airport:** Portland-75 mi **Packages:** Yes; long term stays and groups. Dinner available at added cost. **Seasonal:** No **Reservations:** One night's deposit to guarantee reservation, 48 hr cancel notice for refund. Unless by prior arrangements, check-in time is 4-6 pm, check-out by 11 am. **Brochure:** Yes **Permitted:** Drinking, limited children, limited smoking **Payment Terms:** Check [R09EPOR-11136] **COM** Y **ITC Member:** No

Rates:	Pvt Bath 1	Shared Bath 2
Single	$ 75.00	$ 50.00
Double	$ 75.00	$ 60.00

Sea Quest	95354 Hwy 101 97498	Yachats OR
George & Elaine Rozsa		Tel: 800-341-4878 541-547-3782

Modern two-story home on the beach! Spectacular views, queen-size beds, and a pleasant beach for strolling and enjoying the natural things in life. Host has pets. Full breakfast included. **Seasonal:** No **Brochure:** Yes **Permitted:** No pets **Payment Terms:** Check [X06DXOR-4397] **COM** Y **ITC Member:** No

Rates:	Pvt Bath 2
Single	$ 35.00
Double	$ 50.00

Center Street B&B	169 E Center St 84321	Logan UT
Clyne & Ann Long		Tel: 801-752-3443

Elegant turn-of-the-century Victorian in the heart of town furnished with period antiques and family heirlooms. Amenities include a canopy water bed, marble jacuzzi with a crystal chandelier that extends from a vaulted ceiling. Continental breakfast is included. **Seasonal:** No **Brochure:** Yes **Permitted:** Children 8-up **Payment Terms:** Check [X11ACUT-2769] **COM** Y **ITC Member:** No

Rates:	Pvt Bath 8	Shared Bath 2
Single	$ 35-65.00	$ 35-65.00
Double	$ 35-65.00	$ 35-65.00

©Inn & Travel Memphis, Tennessee

Utah   National Edition

Castle Valley Inn   CVSR Box 2602 Moab 84532   Moab UT
Robert Ryan/Hertha Wakesfield   Tel: 801-259-6012
                                                                                                Res Times 7am-9pm

Secluded nature's haven for artists and naturalists in a beautiful location close to Colorado Canyon River and Matni-La Sal Range. For everyone seeking a tranquil and peaceful setting. Continental plus breakfast is included. Sauna, Roman jet bath, bikes and sitting room. **Seasonal:** No **Brochure:** Yes **Permitted:** Children, limited smoking, drinking, pets

Payment Terms: Check AE/MC/V [X11ACUT-2765] **COM** Y **ITC Member:** No

Rates:	Pvt Bath 2	Shared Bath 4
Single	$ 50.00	$ 45.00
Double	$ 65.00	$ 55.00

505 Woodside B&B Inn   505 Woodside 84060   Park City UT
                                                                                                Tel: 801-649-4841

Center of historic district offers this restored miner's cabin complete and exact. Antique furnishings and gourmet dining at breakfast. Hot tub, complimentary wine or tea and a full breakfast. **Seasonal:** No **Brochure:** Yes **Permitted:** Limited children **Payment Terms:** Check AE/V [X11ACUT-2774] **COM** Y **ITC**

Member: No

Rates:	Pvt Bath 2
Single	$ 55.00
Double	$ 55.00

Old Miners' Lodge   615 Woodside Ave 84060-2639   Park City UT
Hugh Daniels/Susan Wynne   Tel: 800-648-8068 801-645-8068 **Fax:** 801-645-7420
                                                                                                Res Times 9am-9pm

A lovingly restored 1889 lodge for miners beckons guests who feel more like staying with friends than at a hotel! Each guest room is named for a Park City's historic personality and they are restored to the period fullness including down pillows and comforters. A large fireplace-focused living room becomes the gathering place in the evening for guests to enjoy complimentary refreshments. There's a hot tub for revitalizing after a day of skiing or hiking. The Historic Main Street offers guests restaurants, shops and galleries. A hearty country breakfast greets each guest in the morning, including fresh hot coffee, tea and nectars. Skiers will find The Lodge within easy walking distance of the Town Lift servicing Park City Ski Area along with the ability to "ski home" at the end of the day! There's plenty of activities including snowmobiling, hot air ballooning, golf, tennis, hiking and horseback riding. Share the warmth of yesteryear at The Old Miners' Lodge. **Packages:** Winter Ski **Airport:** Salt Lake Intl-35 mi **Seasonal:** Rates Vary **Reservations:** Seasonal deposit and cancel policies, inquire at time of booking, check in 2-6pm, other only by prior arrangement **Brochure:** Yes **Permitted:** Children, drinking, no smoking **Conference:** Yes for social and business events **Payment Terms:** Check AE/DISC/MC/V [Z03HPUT1-2777] **COM** YG **ITC Member:** No

Rates:	Pvt Bath 10
Single	$ 55-205.00
Double	$ 55-205.00

Old Town Guest House   1011 Empire Ave 84060   Park City UT
John & Debbie Lovci   Tel: 801-649-2642
                                                                                                Res Times 24 Hrs

This beautifully historical registered home is the perfect place for active skiers, hikers and bikers or anyone wishing to escape to the beautiful mountains of Utah. Guests may enjoy all the conveniences of Park City such as Utah's largest ski area and the well-preserved Main Street district which includes over eighty-five shops, boutiques, galleries and restaurants. This small and charming Inn has three rooms, each furnished country-style with lodge-pole pine furniture and genuine hospitality making it a nice place to come home to after your active day. Guests may enjoy all of the comforts of

4-128   ©*Inn & Travel Memphis, Tennessee*

the family room which has beautiful hardwood floors and the original fireplace. A complimentary full hearty mountain breakfast is served each morning. Your innkeepers, John and Debbie are very active skiers and bikers and are always able to offer suggestions to help you make the most of your stay. Their love for the mountains of Utah is overflowing and will definitely rub off on you. Back country ski tours and Mountain biking tours are available as well as additional meals upon request. To complete your active day, apres ski snacks are served and you're welcomed to sooth any aching muscles in the hot tub under the stars. **Airport:** SLC Airport-30 mi **Seasonal:** No **Reservations:** 50% deposit required prior to arrival. *Winter rates; Summer rates are $60.00 and $45.00 **Brochure:** Yes **Permitted:** Children, drinking, limited smoking **Payment Terms:** Check [Z06GPUT-15277] **COM** Y **ITC Member:** No

Rates:	Pvt Bath 2	Shared Bath 2
Single	$ 125.00	$ 95.00
Double	$ 125.00	$ 95.00

Old Miners' Lodge — Salt Lake City UT
Hugh Daniels/Susan Wynne
Tel: 800-648-8068 801-645-8068 **Fax:** 801-645-7420
Res Times 8am-10pm

Refer to the same listing name under Park City, Utah for a complete description. **Seasonal:** Rates vary **Payment Terms:** Check AE/DISC/MC/V [M03EPU-T-8713] **COM** Y **ITC Member:** No

Rates:	Pvt Bath 10
Single	$ 55-205.00
Double	$ 55-205.00

Saltair B&B   164 S 900 East 84102   Salt Lake City UT
Jan Bartlett/Nancy Saxton
Tel: 800-533-8184 801-268-8184 **Fax:** 801-328-2060

A lovely 1903 Victorian home restored to its former elegance and filled with antique furnishings and family heirlooms. Listed on the Utah Historical Register. Family-style homemade breakfast included with room. **Seasonal:** No **Reservations:** Station pick-up available with prior arrangement **Brochure:** Yes **Permitted:** Children **Payment Terms:** Check [X11ACUT-2786] **COM** Y **ITC Member:** No

Rates:	Shared Bath 5
Single	$ 49.00
Double	$ 49.00

Mountain Hollow B&B   10209 S Dimple Dell Rd 84092   Sandy UT
Doug & Kathy Larson
Tel: 801-942-3428
Res Times 8am-6pm

Mountain Hollow is located on a wooded secluded two-acre estate close to the base of Little Cottonwood Canyon. This puts the world-class resorts of Alta, Brighton, Snowbird and Solitude at our doorstep. In the summer there is hiking and mountain biking as well as golf, tennis, swimming and horseback riding nearby. Our rooms are decorated with antique country and Victorian furniture, making each comfortable and romantic. After a day of exercise, shopping in metropolitan Salt Lake City, or business, our ten person hot tub will be welcomed. Located outside under the trees, you can count the stars or catch a snowflake while encircled by luxurious warm water. A waterfall and stream on the property provides relaxation while enjoying the ever-present hummingbirds. Our breakfast buffet can be eaten in the dining room or the patio. We feature muffins, croissants, fruits, juices, yogurts and cereals. Complimentary beverages and snacks are always available. After an evening out, our video library will provide entertainment in the upstairs lounge with a cozy fireplace. *Mountain Hollow* is a peaceful, relaxing way to spend your vacation, honeymoon or getaway! **Airport:** SL Intl-25 mi **Seasonal:** No **Reservations:** 50% deposit within 7 days of booking, full payment before arrival - 30 days in-season with 30 day cancel notice (11/20-4/15) 15 days other period with 15 day cancel notice, refunds less $30 fee **Brochure:** Yes **Permitted:** Children 5-up, limited drinking **Payment Terms:** Check AE/DISC/MC/V [I03HPUT1-6331] **COM YG ITC Member:** No

Rates:	Pvt Bath 2	Shared Bath 8
Single	$ 125.00	$ 65.00
Double	$ 150.00	$ 75.00

Albatross B&B	5708 Kingsway W 98221	Anacortes WA
Barbie & Ken Arasim		Tel: 800-622-8864 360-293-0677
		Res Times 7:30am-10pm

The *Albatross* is a charming Cape Cod style home located adjacent to Skyline Marina in Anacortes. The seascape view to the south includes several islands, beaches and mountains. Hiking trails, bicycle paths lead from our driveway to sand beaches, backroad avenues to Deception Pass, Washington Park or the San Juan ferry boat terminal to the islands. Our Seasonal Package Special offers a romantic getaway that appeals to the adventurous and features a taste of the beautiful Pacific Northwest by land, sea and air. The adjacent waterfront harbors of Washington Park, Skyline Marina, Mount Erie and Deception Pass are minutes away and invite exploration by car, bicycle or foot. Later that day, these familiar scenes will be viewed by sea from the 46-foot sailboat "Charisma" during a sightseeing cruise or sunset sail that will delight your romantic soul. After dark, the night lights of our town include the outdoor sparkle of our old town, the indoor excitement of our local casino or the quiet serenity of our starlight beaches. In the evening, unwind with a cup of tea and sample homebaked desserts under the light of the crystal chandelier in the dining room or enjoy the warmth of the living room fireplace. Morning holds the promise of a full home-cooked breakfast, featuring special family recipes and served with a smile.

The second day, discover the beauty of the San Juan Islands during a flight to Friday Harbor on San Juan Island. You will be able to explore the waterfront town, enjoy the harbor scenery, tour the coastline or go whale watching with the many available services. At day's end, board the Washington State Ferry for a sunset voyage returning to Anacortes. The *Albatross Bed & Breakfast* is open all year and provides the comforts of country living with hometown hospitality. We welcome you, your families and friends for romantic adventure, an enjoyable visit and a delightful meal. **Airport:** Anacortes-1 mi; Seattle SeaTac-95 mi **Packages:** Seasonal Specials, call for details **Seasonal:** Rates vary **Reservations:** One night's deposit at res time, 72 hr cancel notice, arrival 4pm-6pm, 800 Number code #5840 **Brochure:** Yes **Permitted:** Children 5+, drinking; kitchen privileges for your "catch of the day" **Conference:** Nearby facilities available **Payment Terms:** Check AE/MC/V [I10HPWA1-11836] **COM YG ITC Member:** No

Rates:	Pvt Bath 4
Single	$ 85.00
Double	$ 90.00

Outlook Inn On Orcas Island	Main St 98245	Eastsound WA
Jeannine & Jamie		Tel: 800-767-9506 360-376-2200 **Fax:** 206-376-2256
		Res Times 8am-10pm

At the sea's edge on Orcas Island, the Gem of the American San Juan Islands, the *Outlook Inn* carries the look of a Nantucket inn from years past. Originally a homesteader's cabin, the Inn was expanded in 1888 to include the local general store, barber shop, jail and guest rooms. Since the turn-of-the-century. when Orcas Island became popular with travelers from Bellingham and Seattle, the *Outlook Inn* has enjoyed a reputation as the travelers "home away from home". Today, forty one tastefully decorated guest rooms offer the vacationer "old" style comfort blended with "new" amenities. Rooms in the Victorian style have private baths, those in the Old style, share baths conveniently located nearby in the hall. Recently completed Luxury Suites have sunken living areas, broad views of Eastsound bay and whirlpool tubs. All rooms have phones, rooms with private baths have televisions. The restaurant at the *Outlook Inn* is open for all meals during the summer season and for breakfast and dinner off-season. Thai, seafood and vegetarian entrees are featured. Drinks are available in a turn-of-the-century brass-railed bar. Off-season rates: Private Bath; $64.00, Suites $120.00, Shared Bath $34.000. **Airport:** Seatac-80 mi; commuter airline 1-mi **Discounts:** Seniors, AAA, Corporate, Government **Reservations:** One night deposit to guarantee, 7 day cancel policy for refund **Permitted:** Children, smoking, drinking **Conference:** Yes, for groups to 75 with full kitchen and bar **Payment Terms:** AE/MC/V [K07GPWA-3196] **COM** Y **ITC Member:** No

Rates:	Pvt Bath 16	Shared Bath 15
Single	$ 110-210.00	$ 69.00
Double	$ 110-210.00	$ 69.00

Hillside House B&B	365 Carter Ave 98250	Friday Harbor WA
Cathy & Dick Robinson		Tel: 800-232-4730 360-378-4730

This contemporary home is nestled on an acre of woodlands offering a quiet adult and ideal B&B atmosphere. Beautiful views abound with open pastures to the north, a panoramic view of the harbor entrance with its ferries and Mount Baker to the east. The home is newly remodeled and offers three guest rooms upstairs, the largest is called "Captains Quarters" with its spacious king size bed, private bath and dramatic views. Two other rooms with queen beds share the upstairs setting. Downstairs, the "Ventana" has a king size bed, view, private bath and its own private entrance. Two other rooms, one with a queen size bed and one with two twin beds, share one bath. All of the rooms have cozy window seats for enjoying the beautiful woodland setting.

A complimentary country breakfast includes homemade specialties, eggs right from the hen house, coffee, tea, juices all served in the living room or on the front deck. Telephones are available from guest use - but don't look for a TV here! **Seasonal:** No **Reservations:** Deposit for one night due 7 days before res date, full refund if cancelled 7 days prior to res date or if the rooms are re-rented. *$25.00 per extra person **Permitted:** Children over 10, smoking outside and no pets**Payment Terms:** Check MC/V [R11CPWA-11632] **COM** Y **ITC Member:** No

Rates:	Pvt Bath 2	Shared Bath 4
Single	$ 95.00	$ 65.00*
Double	$ 95.00	$ 65.00

Shumway Mansion	11410 99 Pl NE 98033	Kirkland WA
Richard & Salli Harris		Tel: 206-823-2303 Fax: 206-822-0421
		Res Times 8am-10pm

Overlook Lake Washington from this twenty four room mansion built c1909-10 that has been completely renovated and restored, using antique period furnishings and including oriental carpeting. Guest rooms are individually decorated, five of which have water views and one with a veranda. Just twenty five minutes from downtown Seattle, Kirkland is the place for good restaurants as well as antique and small shop browsing. Water and snow sports are close at hand. There are two major waterfront parks within two blocks which offer swimming, tennis, bicycling, jogging and nature trails. Three major Washington State wineries are just fifteen minutes away by car

©*Inn & Travel Memphis, Tennessee*

and provide tours and tasting experiences. Complimentary use of Juanita Bay Athletic Club. Full breakfast and evening snacks included. **Seasonal:** No **Reservations:** One night's deposit at res time; 7-day cancellation notice for refund; check-in 3-8:00pm-later with advanced notice; check-out 11:00am **Brochure:** Yes **Permitted:** Children 12-up, smoking outdoors on covered patio **Conference:** Excellent facilities for business and social events up to 175 persons, including two full floors, large ballroom, outdoor area, gazeboand patios, with catering available **Payment Terms:** AE/MC/V [J04HP-WA1-3226] **COM YG ITC Member:** No

Rates:	Pvt Bath 8
Single	$ 65-95.00
Double	$ 65-95.00

Log Castle	3273 E Saratoga Rd 98260	Langley WA
Senator Jack & Norma Metcalf		Tel: 360-221-5483
		Res Times 8am-9pm

"One of the seven most unusual B&Bs in the USA ..." says "USA Week-End"!
Now you can step into this beautiful waterfront log lodge on Whidbey Island near the historic villages of Langley and Coupeville - with your own private and secluded beach with beautiful views of Mount Baker and the snow-topped Cascade Mountains. This lovely home has now become *The Log Castle B&B*, a charming country Inn providing gracious accommodations for travelers and those wishing to experience the quiet, peaceful island life. This exciting residence features leaded glass windows, wormwood stairways, turret bedrooms, charming wood-burning stoves, a large grand stone fireplace and fantastic views of Puget Sound and the surrounding mountains. Our guest rooms are named after our four grown daughters. Choose from the Gayle Room with cozy French doors opening to a porch facing the beach, mountains and morning sun; The Marta Suite, complete with porch and hanging swing overlooking the water to the Cascade Mountains; The Lea Room with two large windows overlooking Saratoga Passage to Camano Island and beyond; and perhaps the favorite - The Ann Room with a panoramic view through five large windows. You'll find the lodge warm and inviting and nature inviting you to relax to the sound of gulls while watching for the bald eagles and sea lions who reside here. A complimentary canoe or row boat is available for guests wanting to enjoy the scenery or try their fishing skills. Don't miss the opportunity to stay at this rare Inn when visiting Seattle - Tacoma. A full complimentary breakfast includes Norma's legendary homemade bread and hot cinnamon rolls, direct from her oven and is served daily on a large round log table. **Airport:** Seattle-Tacoma Intl 50 mi **Reservations:** Deposit required at res time refunded if cancelled with 7 day notice **Permitted:** Children over 10, limited drinking **Conference:** Yes, only when renting the entire lodge **Payment Terms:** Check MC/V [K05GPWA-3232] **COM Y ITC Member:** No

Rates:	Pvt Bath 4
Single	$ 80-105.00
Double	$ 80-105.00

Pine River Ranch	19668 Hwy 207 98826	Leavenworth WA
Mary Ann & Mike Zenk		Tel: 509-763-3959
		Res Times 8am-10pm

Imagine yourself relaxing on an open wrap-around porch looking out at an immense serene valley with breath-taking Cascade Mountain views. It is so easy to get lost in the magic of the Pine River Ranch. This historic Ranch was built in the 40's as a state-of-the-art dairy farm; now it is an exceptional Inn. The rooms are spacious and beautifully decorated, some with woodstoves, decks and sunny sitting areas. Two deluxe suites pamper you with romantic seclusion. Enjoy the hosts warm hospitality and attention to every detail during your stay. Fabulous food and soothing hot tubs help top-off any occasion. The Ranch offers hiking, stream fishing, biking and picnicking in the warmer months. Golf, windsurfing, swimming, boating, water skiing, horseback riding and rock climbing are all close-by. When the snow flakes begin to fall, the Pine River Ranch becomes a winter wonderland. Strap on your x-country skis and indulge yourself on the Ranch's private groomed trails. Perfectly located in the beautiful Lake Wenatchee Recreational Area, just two hours from Seattle and minutes from the Bavarian Village of Levenworth. Listed in Northwest Best Places, member of AAA and Washington B&B Guild. **Discounts:** Extended stays, inquire at res time **Airport:** Seattle Seatac-2 hrs **Seasonal:** No **Reservations:** One night's deposit required **Brochure:** Yes **Permitted:** Children, drinking **Conference:** Small groups and family gatherings **Payment Terms:** Check MC/V [R12EPWA-16172] **COM** U **ITC Member:** No

Rates:	Pvt Bath 6	Shared Bath 2
Single	$ 75-125.00	$ 65.00
Double	$ 75-125.00	$ 65.00

West Shore Farm B&B   2781 W Shore Dr 98262   **Lummi Island WA**
Carl & Polly Hanson   **Tel:** 360-758-2600
Res Times 8:30am-9:30pm

Guests looking for a quiet and peaceful setting will find this unique octagonal home on an island a fine choice. Polly (librarian) and Carl (an engineer) built their home in 1977 from native materials such as the Alaskan yellow cedar driftwood log center pole and completed the all-wood interior with the help of their artist/craftsman son, Eric. Built into a slope overlooking the northern tip of island, scenic views abound. Privacy is assured by having the guest rooms on a separate level. One guest room, with an eagle motif, features a reading corner with a leather recliner and the other bedroom, with a blue heron motif, offers its own sink/vanity. Furnishings in each room include a table, chairs and a king-size bed. A full breakfast is included with other meals available at added cost. Meals are served family-style, next to the viewing windows and a twelve-sided freestanding fireplace. Food preparation is natural (mostly home grown and preserved) and gourmet enough to be interesting. Quiet beaches, seabirds, eagles, seals, eighteen miles of country roads, spectacular views of the Canadian Mountains will please any nature-lover. For entertainment, Carl, a member of the Bellingham Pipe Band, gladly awaits all requests, with his bagpipe. Everyone will enjoy their warm and charming hosts who have been doing their own version of English Bed and Breakfasts that inspired them while in England. **Airport:** Bellingham-12 mi; Seattle-100 mi **Seasonal:** No **Reservations:** $40 deposit per room or first night's amount if longer than one night stay. Seventh night free! Deposit refunded only if room is rebooked, less a $5 service fee, 11am check-out, 3pm check-in **Brochure:** Yes **Permitted:** Children, drinking **Payment Terms:** Check MC/V [Z06GPWA-3250] **COM** Y **ITC Member:** No

Rates:	Pvt Bath 2
Single	$ 75.00
Double	$ 85.00

Ann Starrett Mansion   **Oak Harbor WA**
Edel & Bob Sokol   **Tel:** 800-321-0644 206-385-3205
Res Times 8am-10pm

Refer to the same listing name under Port Townsend, Washington for a complete description. **Seasonal:** No **Payment Terms:** Check AE/DC/MC/V [M02EPWA-15268] **COM** Y **ITC Member:** No

Rates:	Pvt Bath 8	Shared Bath 2
Single	$ 79-145.00	$ 69.00
Double	$ 79-145.00	$ 69.00

Ann Starrett Mansion   **Port Angeles WA**
Edel & Bob Sokol   **Tel:** 800-321-0644 206-385-3205
Res Times 8am-10pm

Washington

National Edition

Refer to the same listing name under Port Townsend, Washington for a complete description. **Seasonal:** No **Payment Terms:** Check AE/DC/MC/V [M02EPWA-15267] **COM** Y **ITC Member:** No

Rates:	Pvt Bath 8	Shared Bath 2
Single	$ 79-145.00	$ 69.00
Double	$ 79-145.00	$ 69.00

Ann Starrett Mansion	744 Clay St 98368	Port Townsend WA
Edel & Bob Sokol		Tel: 800-321-0644 360-385-3205
		Res Times 8am-10pm

Situated on the bluff overlooking mountains and Puget Sound sits the lovingly restored *Ann Starrett Mansion Victorian B&B*. It epitomized the heart and soul of historic Port Townsend. Built by George Starrett in 1889 as a wedding present for his wife Ann, the Inn is internationally renown for its classic Victorian architecture, frescoed ceilings and free-hung spiral staircase which leads to a glorified celestial calendar with frescoes depicting the four seasons. On the first day of each season, the sun shines on a ruby-red glass, causing a read beam to point to the appropriate season. The second floor rooms are furnished with period antiques and offer water and mountain views. The Gable Suite commands a view second to none and includes a hot tub. The Carriage House Level features charming rooms with antique brick walls and garden views. Breakfasts at the Inn are truly memorable with a menu only a European pastry chef could dream up. The Inn has been featured in numerous publications including *"The New York Times"*, *"Vancouver Canada Sun"*, *"London England Times"*, *"Elle Magazine"*, *"Conde Naste Traveler"* and *"Northwest Best Places."* Come - stay in this *National Historic Landmark* - ***the most photographed house in the Northwest.*** **Airport:** Sea-Tac-1-1/2 hrs **Seasonal:** No **Reservations:** Full advance deposit at res time, 5 day cancel notice less $10 service fee **Brochure:** Yes **Permitted:** Children 13-up, limited drinking **Conference:** Yes, for dining and meetings **Languages:** German **Payment Terms:** Check AE/DC/MC/V [R02EPWA-3288] **COM** Y **ITC Member:** No

Rates:	Pvt Bath 8	Shared Bath 2
Single	$ 79-145.00	$ 69.00
Double	$ 79-145.00	$ 69.00

Bishop Victorian Suites	714 Washington St 98368	Port Townsend WA
Lloyd & Marlene Cahoon		Tel: 800-824-4738 360-385-6122
		Res Times 8am-10pm

Built by William Bishop in 1890, the three-story Bishop Block Building is a fine example of the award-winning downtown restoration for which Port Townsend is famous. Located in the heart of the National Historic District, the Bishop houses business and professional offices at street level with two stories of exceptional accommodations above. A short climb upstairs and the unsuspecting visitor is transported into Victorian grace and comfort. Spacious apartments have been renovated into guest suites. Each is furnished with vintage pieces reflecting the grandeur and charm of a bygone era. A home away from home, guests enjoy the comfort and luxury of a complete kitchen, living room, one or two bedrooms and a private bath. Views range from Mount Baker, the Cascade Mountains and rugged peaks of the Olympics to the waters or Port Townsend. The downtown location means convenient access to the town's shops and the Whidbey Island ferry. Port Townsend one of the top attractions in the Northwest. **Airport:** Sea Tac Intl-70 mi **Discounts:** Yes, extended stays **Seasonal:** No **Reservations:** Deposit required to guarantee reservation. **Brochure:** Yes **Permitted:** Children, pets (with prior approval, drinking, limited smoking **Conference:** Yes, conference room to 25 persons **Payment Terms:** Check AE/MC/V [R04FPWA-3278] **COM** Y **ITC Member:** No

Rates:	Pvt Bath 13
Single	$ 68.00
Double	$ 78-98.00

Lilac Lea Christian B&B	21008 NE 117th St 98052	Redmond WA
Chandler & Ruthanne Haight		Tel: 206-861-1898

Welcome to Redmond Washington, the Bicycle Capital of the Great Northwest. Many miles of fine trails are available to the biker as well as hiker or horseback rider. We welcome you to your large (700 square feet), self-contained, antique furnished suite in your own private, squeaky-clean woodland cottage. Your suite features private bath, private entrance, queen bed, large desk and study area, TV and phone. An extra room with twin beds is available to those in the same party. A large outside deck and wooded picnic area are available. Your continental breakfast is ready when ever you want and features locally grown farm fresh fruits, berries, gourmet coffee, herbal teas, fresh juice, muffins and cereal. Our home is located seventeen miles east of Seattle Center on a secluded private dead-end country road of forested acreage shared with birds, squirrels, chipmunks and deer - in a smoke free and alcohol free environment. Your hosts have widely traveled the local area and will provide assistance in planning your activities. Unsuitable for children or pets. **Discounts:** AARP, Corporate, Off-season **Airport:** Sea-Tac, Seattle **Seasonal:** Rates vary **Reservations:** One night deposit, 7 day cancel policy less $20 service fee **Brochure:** Yes **Payment Terms:** Check [R04GPWA-8658] **COM U ITC Member:** No

Rates:	Pvt Bath 1
Single	$ 65.00
Double	$ 75.00

Lilac Lea Christian B&B
Chandler & Ruthanne Haight

Seattle WA
Tel: 206-861-1898

Refer to the same listing name under Redmond, Washington for a complete description. **Seasonal:** Rates vary **Payment Terms:** Check [M04GPWA-18845] **COM U ITC Member:** No

Rates:	Pvt Bath 1
Single	$ 65.00
Double	$ 75.00

BD Williams House B&B
Williams Family

1505 4th Ave N 98109

Seattle WA
Tel: 800-880-0810 360-285-0810 Fax: 206-285-8526

A restful sleep in the city is what the *Williams House* is known for. The 1905 home offers stunning mountain, lake, sound and city views. Renovations uncovered and retained the original woodwork, including the coffered ceiling and lincrusta walls. Parlor and guest rooms are furnished with comfortable antiques. Glassed and open porches overlook gardens on this quiet residential street, yet the Seattle center attractions and the busy waterfront are nearby. Breakfast is served family-style in the light filled dining room which reflects the owners own comfortable approach to the daily gathering of guests and is sure to please. Featured in many publications, including *"Seattle & Northwest Best Places,"* AAA Rated, Member of PAII, Washington B&B Guild, Washington State Hotel & Motel Association. **Airport:** Sea Tac-30 mins **Discounts:** 10% off-season, extended stays of seven days or longer **Seasonal:** No **Reser-vations:** Deposit with credit card number for first night rate, check-in 4-6pm **Brochure:** Yes **Permitted:** Drinking **Conference:** Yes, groups to fifteen persons **Payment Terms:** Check AE/DC/MC/V [I04HPWA1-3088] **COM U ITC Member:** No

Rates:	Pvt Bath 2	Shared Bath 3
Single	$ 89.00	$ 79.00
Double	$ 125.00	$ 99.00

Chambered Nautilus B-B Inn
Innkeeper

5005 22nd Ave NE 98105

Seattle WA
Tel: 206-522-2536 Fax: 206-522-0404
Res Times 7am-10pm

A Classic 1915 Georgian Colonial, *Chambered Nautilus Bed & Breakfast* combines the warmth of a spacious Country Inn with excellent access to the city's theatres, restaurants and shopping. This gracious Inn is perched on a green and peaceful hill in Seattle's University district, with a fine view of the Cascade Mountains. Downtown Seattle is ten minutes away by car or bus and the Univ of Wash campus is within walking distance. The area is a haven of nature trails and cherished site for walkers, joggers and bicyclists. Featured in many publications, such as *"Innsider"*, *"Historic American Inns & Guest Houses," "Seattle Best Places"* and *"Northwest Best Places", Chambered Nautilus* is Seattle's grandest B&B. Four of the comfortable guest rooms have private porches, a thirty foot living room includes a grand piano, and there is a fine mixture of American and English antiques throughout. The Inn has two fireplaces and there are fully stocked bookcases in every room. Breakfasts are a diner's delight, featuring specialties of the hosts such as our national award winning *Chambered Nautilus* Apple Quiche, homemade biscuits and muffins, fresh fruits and juices, cheese-baked eggs, French toast with homemade syrups and freshly ground coffee. **Airport:** Sea Tac Intl Airport-25 mins by car **Seasonal:** Rates vary **Reservations:** One night's deposit or credit card; one week cancellation notice for refund less $10 bank processing fee for credit issuance, check-in 4-6 pm; other hours by arrangement **Brochure:** Yes **Permitted:** Children 10-up (only one in same room), limited drinking, limited smoking **Conference:** Yes, up to 25 persons; living room, dining room and porch, with catering available **Languages:** German, English **Payment Terms:** Check AE/CB/DC/MC/V [I08GPWA-3072] **COM Y ITC Member:** No **Quality Assurance:** Requested

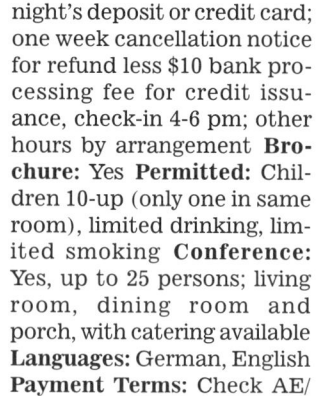

Rates:	Pvt Bath 4	Shared Bath 2
Single	$ 75-97.50	$ 69.00
Double	$ 82.50-105.00	$ 79.00

Chelsea Station B&B Inn   4915 Linden Ave N 98103-6542   Seattle WA
John Griffin/Karen Carbonneau   **Tel:** 800-400-6077 206-547-6077 **Fax:** 206-632-5107
Res Times 10am-9pm

Chelsea Station on the Park, a 1929 Federal Colonial home, nestles between the Fremont Neighborhood and Woodland Park, minutes north of downtown Seattle. Since 1984, *Chelsea Station* has provided guests a relaxing retreat within the city. Largely decorated in mission-style, the house features antiques throughout. Our king and queen size beds invite you with soft down comforters. Peek-a-boo views of the Cascade Mountains can be seen from our second floor. Awake to the aroma of fresh-brewed coffee followed by a hearty breakfast including plenty of fresh fruit and delicious selections such as orange french toast or ginger pancakes with lemon sauce. Throughout the day, help yourself to a cup of hot tea and freshly baked cookies. Our neighborhood offers wonderful places to stroll; perhaps the Seattle Rose Garden, the zoo, Greenlake or the famous Fremont Troll. Enjoy the warm and casual mood of *Chelsea Station*. Relax and put your feet up. Truly a place to refresh your spirit. **Airport:** Sea-Tac-30 min **Discounts:** Weekly stays and off-season rates available **Seasonal:** No **Reservations:** Deposit required to guarantee reservation, cancellation policy as applicable **Brochure:** Yes **Permitted:** Children 12+; limited drinking and no smoking or animals of any kind permitted **Payment Terms:** Check AE/DC/DISC/MC/V [I04HPWA1-3073] **COM YG ITC Member:** No

Rates:	Pvt Bath 6
Single	$ 64-104.00
Double	$ 69-109.00

Lilac Lea Christian B&B   Seattle WA
Chandler & Ruthanne Haight   **Tel:** 206-861-1898

Refer to the same listing name under Redmond, Washington for a complete description. **Seasonal:**

National Edition   **Washington**

Rates vary **Payment Terms:** Check [M04GPWA-18845] **COM** U **ITC Member:** No

Rates: **Pvt Bath 1**
Single $ 65.00
Double $ 75.00

Swallow's Nest Guest Cottages   Seattle WA
Bob Keller/Robin Hughes   **Tel:** 206-463-2646 **Fax:** 206-463-2646
                                                                                           Res Times 7am-10pm

Refer to the same listing name under Vashon Island, Washington for a complete description. **Seasonal:** Rates vary **Payment Terms:** Check AE/DISC/MC/V [M07GPWA-17776] **COM** Y **ITC Member:** No

Rates: **Pvt Bath 5**
Single $ 50-165.00
Double $ 50-165.00

Tugboat Challenger   1001 Fairview Ave N 98109   Seattle WA
Jerry & Buff Brown   **Tel:** 206-340-1201 **Fax:** 206-621-9208
                                                                                           Res Times 8am-9pm

"Bunk & Breakfast" in downtown Seattle while listening to the sound of lapping water outside of your porthole window! This authentic West Coast tug boat offers a one of a kind floating B&B experience from the solarium and granite fireplace to a sunken conversation pit lavishly furnished in mahogany, pine, oak and polished brass. Guests can relax before the fireplace and chart imaginary courses around the world! A variety of "quarters" are available, including the Tug Master's Cabin, complete with private bath, extra long queen size beds and a private entrance. Amenities include private and shared bath guest rooms, carpeting, a working bar with complimentary mixers, VCR and film library, room stereos, phones and fresh cut flowers. Of eight cabins, no two are alike and though the tug is especially popular with newlyweds, many guests are business travelers who find the *Challenger* a home-like retreat in downtown Seattle. For joggers - jogging is permitted (22 laps around the deck is one mile). Sunrise brings freshly brewed coffee and you'll find your captain ready to serve a full complimentary breakfast featuring mouth-watering crab omelettes, sausage, fresh fruit compotes, waffles, pancakes or french toast and hot muffins all served on the original white Armorlite china that came with the boat. While surrounded by sleek yachts, sloops and houseboats, guests will find all of downtown Seattle nearby with numerous waterside restaurants, great shops, parks, Seattle Center, the Space Needle, the Center for Wooden Boats and other sights within a short walking distance. The *MV Challenger* has been featured by newspapers, magazines and TV programs across the USA - so don't miss this unique adventure during your trip to the northwest. **Discounts:** Yes, inquire at res time **Airport:** Seattle/Tacoma-10 mi **Seasonal:** No **Reservations:** Full deposit at res time with 14 day cancellation notice for refund. Less than 14, deposit is not refunded but may be applied within one year for another date **Brochure:** Yes **Permitted:** Drinking, limited children **Conference:** Unforgettable setting for business and social meetings, parties, dinners and weddings for groups to ten persons **Payment Terms:** Check AE/DC/DISC/MC/V [K07HPWA1-3082] **COM** YG **ITC Member:** No

Rates: **Pvt Bath 9**   **Shared Bath 3**
Single $ 90-165.00 $ 55-75.00
Double $ 90-165.00 $ 75.00

Greywolf Inn   177 Keeler Rd 98382   Sequim WA
Bill & Peggy Melang   **Tel:** 360-683-5889 360-683-1487

©*Inn & Travel Memphis, Tennessee*   4-137

Northwest hospitality with a southern flair welcomes the traveler to *Greywolf Inn*, a quiet, country retreat. Tucked between meadow and forest on a hilltop overlooking Sequim, Greywolf provides peaceful seclusion with easy access to the myriad attractions of the Olympic Peninsula: exploring, camping, hiking, bird-watching, fishing, boating and golf. Six comfortable guest rooms are available, each with private bath. The Pamela, with its huge pine canopy bed and family memorabilia, reflects the owner's German heritage. Visions of the Orient surround those who sleep in Nancy's queen canopy bed, while Kimberleigh's room exudes the warmth and comfort of the Old South. Glass doors opening onto a broad deck contribute to the French feeling of the Edith Kirk Room. Miss Lillian's cozy hideaway has twin beds and a private entrance from the south deck. The Marguerite, with it's hand-painted king size sleigh bed, is Greywolf's premier accommodation. Together with Miss Lillian, it becomes a two-bedroom, two-bath suite with private entrance and decks. The full breakfast served from 8-9:30 in the French country dining room features random gourmet specialties such as country ham with red-eye gravy or a delicious salmon tart accompanied by fresh fruit, assorted hot rolls and muffins. Greywolf Inn has a walking trail winding through five acres of trees, field and stream; broad decks and patios; a library/game room; a sitting/living room with huge fireplace and interesting hosts who appreciate travel, music and good company. Make Greywolf Inn your seat of adventure on the north Olympic Peninsula, America's mythic land. **Airport:** Sea Tac 80 mi; Port Angeles 20 mi **Reservations:** One night's deposit with 7 day cancel policy for refund. Check in 3-6pm, other by prior arrangement. **Brochure:** Yes **Permitted:** Children 12-up, drinking **Conference:** Limited facilities for meetings. **Payment Terms:** Check AE/MC/V [R10DPWA-12576] **COM Y ITC Member:** No

Rates:	Pvt Bath 6
Single	$ 50-95.00
Double	$ 50-95.00

Moore House 526 Marie 98943-0629 South Cle Elum WA
Eric & Cindy Sherwood
Tel: 800 22 TWAIN 509-674-5939
Res Times 8am-10pm

All aboard! Destination: The Moore House. Relive the grand era of railroading at this unique Inn, formerly a hotel for train crewmen. Built in 1909 and now listed on the *National Register of Historic Places, The Moore House* offers ten guest rooms, plus two genuine cabooses. Antiques, historic photographs, and authentic railroad memorabilia lend a museum-like atmosphere to this comfortable inn. Bring your family and stay in one of the charming cabooses adjacent to the Inn. Each caboose features a queen size bed plus three twin bunks, private bath, color TV, and sun deck. Or bring your loved one and enjoy the intimacy of the elegant bridal suite with private jacuzzi. A hearty full breakfast is served each morning in the dining room. The *Moore House* is adjacent to Iron Horse State Park, a non-motorized recreation trail, formerly the railroad right-of-way. Located in the foothills of the Cascade Mountains in Central Washington, this beautiful area offers a wonderful variety of outdoor recreation: biking, hiking, golf, horseback riding, river rafting, fishing, snowmobiling, cross country and down hill skiing. Visit historic Cle Elum and Roslyn (known as Cicely, Alaska, in the popular TV series "Northern Exposure." **Airport:** Seattle-Tacoma Intl 90 mins **Seasonal:** Clo Xmas **Reservations:** One night deposit to confirm res, 7 day cancel policy for refund. Check-in after 10:30 pm by prior arrangement only **Brochure:** Yes **Permitted:** Children, limited drinking, smoking **Conference:** Yes for business, social meetings, seminars and family get-togethers. Luncheon and dinners available for groups. **Payment Terms:** Check AE/MC/V [Z05FP-WA-3094] **COM Y ITC Member:** No

Rates:	Pvt Bath 6	Shared Bath 6
Single	$ 59-95.00	$ 30-59.00
Double	$ 59-95.00	$ 30-59.00

Swallow's Nest Guest Cottages Tacoma WA
Bob Keller/Robin Hughes
Tel: 206-463-2646 Fax: 206-463-2646
Res Times 7am-10pm

Refer to the same listing name under Vashon Island, Washington for a complete description. **Seasonal:** Rates vary **Payment Terms:** Check AE/DISC/MC/V [M07GPWA-17777] **COM Y ITC Member:** No

Rates:	Pvt Bath 5
Single	$ 50-165.00
Double	$ 50-165.00

National Edition **Washington**

Swallow's Nest Guest Cottages
Bob Keller/Robin Hughes

6030 SW 248th St 98070

Vashon Island WA
Tel: 800-ANY-NEST 206-463-2646 Fax: 206-463-2646
Res Times 7am-10pm

An idyllic island retreat -- just a short boat ride from Seattle, Tacoma or the Olympic Peninsula. Our private cottages vary from studios to a two story house that sleeps eight. Each is furnished with plants, books, rocking chairs and has cooking facilities and TV. Three of the cottages, The Nest (one bedroom), The Robins Nest (two bedrooms and The Bird Blind (studio), are on a bluff with *"spectacular views"* of Puget Sound, Mount Rainier and the Cascades. They are one mile from the Vashon Golf & Country Club where guests may play on one of Puget Sound's *"premier golf courses."* It is a quiet spot with mature landscaping surrounded by several hundred acres of field and forest. Guests are soothed by soaking in our "outdoor hot tub" before a *"luxurious massage"* by our professional masseuse. The deer and birds (49 species in a week) come to visit. Fruits and berries are abundant. *"It would be hard to imagine a more delightful get-away-from-it-all spot than the Nest".* Edson House, our two story Victorian restoration in the Village of Burton, has views of Quartermaster Harbor. Only *"one block to the beach"* and a good restaurant, it is *"perfect for a small group retreat or a family reunion."* It is furnished with antique oak furniture and colorful oriental carpets and has a full kitchen. One of it's bathrooms is graced with a 5-1/2 foot clawfooted tub. **Discounts:** Off-season rates (Oct to May) **Airport:** Seattle-Tacoma, one hour by car including ferryboat; Wax Orchards or Vashon Municipal are 2-8 mi, grass strips on Island **Packages:** Professional Masseuse, golf, hot tub, sailing **Seasonal:** Rates vary **Reservations:** Full deposit in advance is required, 21 day cancel policy for refund; less than 21 day notice, refund only if rebooked. Credit card payment requires additional 5% for service fees **Brochure:** Yes **Permitted:** Children, drinking, smoking on porches, pets with prior arrangement only **Conference:** Seminars and retreats in Victorian Living Room, sleeping space for six couples-plus in several cottages **Payment Terms:** Check AE/DISC/MC/V [I08GCWA1-3103] **COM** Y **ITC Member:** No

Rates:	Pvt Bath 5
Single	$ 50-165.00
Double	$ 50-165.00

'37 House
Mike Taylor

4002 Englewood Ave 98908

Yakima WA
Tel: 509-965-5537
Res Times 8am-10pm

Welcome to the *'37 House*, an Inn of extraordinary elegance completed in 1937 - a Yakima landmark gracing a scenic 9.5 acre knoll just northwest of the heart of the city. When it became an Inn, great care was taken to preserve its physical grandeur, warmth and gracious hospitality. From the sweeping hardwood staircase, the formal dining room still furnished with many of the original family's possessions, including cherry dining room chairs with hand-woven cushions to the impressive living room with its massive wood-burning fireplace ... guests are truly at home. With a total of 7500 square foot, a variety of accommodations offer king and queen size beds, a suite with two spacious bedrooms and sitting area - each room has its own unique charm - special touches from '37; built-in desks, window seats tucked under sloping eaves, shutter window panes and full-tile baths. Every overnight stay includes a full gourmet breakfast, artfully prepared and served - and of course, arrangements can be made for additional meals and refreshments to be served in your favorite part of the home - or outside in a sun-splashed corner of the English Garden or the Inn's adjoining grounds and tennis court. Individual attention is the hallmark of *The '37 House*. When you return, you're greeted by a staff who remembers your preferences in accommodations and food. We purposely keep our own schedule flexible enough to meet the time tables and needs of our guests. Inspected and approved by AAA, ABBA **Discounts:** Yes, corporate **Airport:** 7-mi **Seasonal:** No **Reservations:** Verifiable credit card for first night's lodging, 24 hour cancel policy for refund **Brochure:** Yes **Permitted:** Limited children, limited drinking **Conference:** Perfect for memorable retreats, dinner parties, meetings and other special events hosted by you and carefully orchestrated by *The '37 House* staff **Payment Terms:** Check AE/MC/V [K07FPWA-14648] **COM Y ITC Member:** No

Rates: Pvt Bath 6
Single $ 65-120.00
Double $ 65-120.00

Lockhart B&B Inn	109 W Yellowstone Ave 82414	Cody WY
Mark & Cindy Baldwin		Tel: 307-587-6074

Residence of western author Caroline Lockhart still offering antique furnishings, western hospitality, and hearty country breakfasts. Close to spectacular flora and fauna. **Seasonal:** No **Brochure:** Yes **Permitted:** Children 4-up, limited smoking **Payment Terms:** Check MC/V [X11ACWY-5018] **COM Y ITC**

Member: No

Rates: Pvt Bath 6
Single $ 45-65.00
Double

Parson's Pillow B&B	1202 14th St 82414	Cody WY
Lee & Elly Larabee		Tel: 800-377-2348 307-587-2382
		Res Times 24 Hrs

Comfort, elegance and the sense of coming home are yours to enjoy as a guest of the *Parson's Pillow* B&B. Antiques and turn-of-the-century lace surround you. Our 1902 former church has been caringly restored so that you might experience home-style hospitality. Choose from four individually decorated rooms with many personal touches. Enjoy a delectable full breakfast with fellow guests in the dining room. The parlour is always available for socializing, reading (peruse the library), a game or two, piano, TV, take a snooze on the front porch, or croquet anyone? We are *"Just Boot Steps from Everything"*- Buffalo Bill Historical Center with the Plains Indian Museum, Whitney Gallery of Western Art, and Winchester Arms Museum. Browse unique shops and galleries. Experience white-water rafting on the Shoshone, golf, tennis, or go western at Cody Night Rodeo. Just of Hwys 14, 16, 20 and 120, Parson's Pillow Bed & Breakfast is the natural starting point while touring northwest Wyoming - *"Cody Country"*. Just minutes from Buffalo Bill Dam Visitor Center and Reservoir, Sunlight Basin, spectacular Wapiti Valley and Shoshone National Forest on the way to Yellowstone National Park. Always remember, *"It's Alright to Sleep in Our Church."* **Discounts:** Week stays, less $10 per day **Airport:** Yellowstone Regional Airport-2 mi **Seasonal:** No **Reservations:** Full payment in advance of reservation date, 10 day cancel policy for refund; less than 10 days notice credit or refund only if rebooked, less $15 service fee **Brochure:** Yes **Permitted:** Limited children, drinking **Payment Terms:** Check MC/V [R07FPWY-12580] **COM Y ITC Member:** No

Rates:	Pvt Bath 2	Shared Bath 2
Single	$ 70.00	$ 60.00
Double	$ 75.00	$ 65.00

Wolf Hotel	101 E Bridge 82331	Saratoga WY
Doug & Kathleen Campbell		Tel: 307-326-5663

Built as a stage coach stop in c1893, everything is still the same. All the rooms are in the same original condition and without TV and phones during your stay. Lunch and dinner available at added cost. **Seasonal:** No **Brochure:** Yes **Permitted:** Children, smoking, drinking **Payment Terms:** Check AE/MC/

National Edition **Wyoming**

V [X11ACWY-5037] **COM Y ITC Member:** No

Rates:	Pvt Bath 6	Shared Bath 12
Single	$ 32.00	$ 32.00
Double		

Savery Creek Thoroughbred Ranch   PO Box 24   82332   Savery WY
Joyce B Saer   **Tel:** 307-383-7840
Res Times 24 Hrs

Pristine countryside and abundant wildlife at this small and quaint Inn and YL Ranch lodge offers guests a unique and interesting western experience which includes a taste of the "original west" but with modern amenities such as a tennis court for keeping fit. A photographer's and wildlife enthusiast's paradise, trips to the Red Desert offer interesting formations, antelope and wild horses. Horseback riding is featured with fly-fishing, creek swimming, cookouts, rodeos and buggy rides at this oasis with its own private landing field for guests who want to fly in! Guests' quarters are furnished with antiques and fireplaces in some suites with an extensive library to choose for your reading pleasure. Individual luxurious bedrooms offer queen size beds and oversized beds in converted sheep wagons. All meals are available on the premises which include home grown vegetables, salads, fruits, fish, beef, lamb and poultry all lovingly prepared by your hostess. Your opportunity to unwind in a serene and spectacular setting. **Seasonal:** No **Reservations:** 25% deposit of entire stay within 10 days of booking; will meet planes at Steamboat Springs CO ($40 additional charge) **Brochure:** Yes **Permitted:** Limited children, limited pets, limited drinking **Conference:** Yes with advance notice **Languages:** Spanish, French **Payment Terms:** Check [X11ACWY-5038] **COM Y ITC Member:** No

Rates:	Pvt Bath 1	Shared Bath 2
Single	$ 65-250.00	$ 65-250.00
Double	$ 65-250.00	$ 65-250.00

Teton View B&B   2136 Coyote Loop   83014   Wilson WY
Jane & Tom Neil   **Tel:** 307-733-7954
Res Times 8am-10pm

Enjoy the personal touches your hosts offer during your stay in their charming home with spectacular mountain views, large comfortable beds fitted with flannel sheets and comforters just perfect for snuggling in winter and a cozy country decor. Each guest room offers a second-story deck overlooking the Teton Mountain Range where you can enjoy watching soaring hawks, geese in formation or the resident hummingbirds feeding nearby. Conveniently located just five miles from Jackson and the ski resort offering year-round activities including sleigh rides in the National Elk Refuge or around town, excellent hunting (elk, deer, antelope, geese), western museums, performing arts, Snake River raft trips, and nightly *"shoot-outs" on the town square!* The continental breakfast brings homemade pastries and breads, fresh fruit, juices, teas and famous freshly ground coffee served family-style around a large table in the family dining room. A common lounge for guests includes a small fridge, coffee maker, indoor games, books and brochures on the sights around town and even a telescope for viewing the peaks. A washer dryer are available along with a storage area for hanging your skis and warming your boots. Relax in the hammock, toss a few horseshoes while your children can enjoy the swing set. **Seasonal:** No **Reservations:** 1-2 nights deposit (depending on length of stay) balance due 30 days prior to arrival. Two week cancel policy for refund. **Brochure:** Yes **Permitted:** Children, drinking, limited pets, smoking outdoors only **Payment Terms:** Check AE/MC/V [R11BPWY-9501] **COM Y ITC Member:** No

Rates:	Pvt Bath 1	Shared Bath 2
Single	$ 75.00	$ 55.00
Double	$ 80.00	$ 60.00

©*Inn & Travel Memphis, Tennessee*

Alaska   **Bold Name** - *Description appears in other section*

ALASKA

Anchor Point
Wallins Hilltop B&B
907-235-8354

Anchorage
42nd Avenue Annex B&B
907-561-8895

6th B B&B
907-279-5293

Alaska Aunties B&B
907-562-7626

Alaska Frontier Gardens
907-345-6556

Alaska House B&B
907-248-3484

Alaska Sourdough B&B
907-563-6244

Alaska Wildberry B&B
907-248-0447

All The Comforts Of Home
907-345-4279

Anchorage B&B
907-333-1425

Anchorage Eagle Nest Hotel
907-243-3433

Annas B&B
907-338-5331

Arctic Fox Inn
907-272-4818

Arctic Loon
907-345-4935

Arctic Poppy B&B
907-258-7795

B&B At Raspberry Meadows
907-278-9275

Bed & Breakfast Inn
907-276-1902

Beech Lane B&B
907-272-6228

Beeson B&B
907-235-3757

Big Bear B&B Inn
907-277-8189

Big Lake B&B
907-272-6228

Camai B&B
907-333-2219

Cape Blossom South
907-276-0976

Caribou Express Inn
907-278-5776

Chelsea Inn
907-276-5002

Coastal Trail B&B
907-243-5809

Copper Whale Inn
907-258-7999

Country Garden
907-344-0636

Country Style B&B
907-243-6746

Crossroads B&B Inn
907-528-7378

Darbyshire House B&B
907-279-0703

De Vauxs B&B
907-349-8910

Down Home B&B
907-243-4443

Fairbanks B&B

Fays B&B
907-243-0139

Fernbrook B&B
907-345-6443

Forget-Me-Not B&B
907-243-1638

Gallery B&B
907-274-2567

Gingham House B&B
907-276-0407

Glacier Bear B&B
907-243-8818

Grandview Gardens B&B
907-277-REST-[Y--]

Heart Of Anchorage B&B
907-243-6814

Heavenly View B&B
907-346-1130

Heidis B&B
907-563-8517

Hillcrest Haven B&B
907-276-8411

Hospitality Plus
907-333-8504

Lakeside B&B
907-334-1662

Lilac House
907-272-3553-[Y--]

Log Home
907-276-8527

Lynns Pine Point B&B
907-333-3244

McCarthy B&B
907-277-6867-[Y--]

Mt McKinley Alaska
907-274-8539

North Country Castle
907-345-7296

Northwoods Guesthouse
907-243-3249

Oscar Gill House
907-274-1344

Pilots Row B&B
907-274-3305

Qupqugaig B&B
907-562-5681

Rest Assured B&B
907-344-3583

Siegfrieds B&B
907-346-3152

Six-Bar-E Ranch B&B

907-279-9907

Sixth & B B&B
907-279-5293

Snowline B&B
907-346-1631

Snowshoe Inn
907-258-7463

Snug Harbor Inn
907-272-6249

Valley Of The Moon B&B
907-279-7755

Walkabout Town B&B
907-279-2918

Wrights B&B
907-561-1990

Wrights B&B
907-561-1990

Angoon
Favorite Bay Inn
907-788-3123-[Y--]

Whalers Cove B&B
907-788-3123

Bethel
Bell House B&B
907-543-3552

Bentleys Porterhouse B&B
907-543-3552

Porter House B&B
907-543-3552-[Y--]

Big Lake
Blodgett Lake Inn
907-892-6877

Jeanies On Big Lake

Cantwell
Adventures Unlimited Lodge

Central
Arctic Circle Hot Springs
907-520-5113

Chugiak
Peters Creek Inn
907-688-2776

Coffman Cove

4-142   ©*Inn & Travel Memphis, Tennessee*

Bold Name - *Description appears in other section*   *Alaska*

Bayview Bed & Meals
907-747-3111

Cooper Landing
Coopers Landing
907-595-1281

Cordova
Harbor View B&B
907-424-5356

Midnight Sun B&B
907-424-3492

Oystercatcher B&B
907-424-5154

Queens Chair B&B
907-424-3000

Reluctant Fisherman Inn
907-474-3272

Craig
Inn Of The Blue Heron
907-826-3606

Delta Junction
Peggys Cabbage Patch
907-895-4200

Denali National Park
McKinley-Denali Cabins
907-683-2258

Denali Natl Park
Camp Denali
907-683-2290

Denali Crows Nest
907-683-2321

Kantishna Roadhouse
907-345-1160

Douglas
Windsock Inn
907-364-2431

Eagle River
Alaska Chalet B&B
907-694-1528

Andys Eagle Park B&B
907-694-2833

Three Bs Inn
907-694-4041

Fairbanks
1940's Age Old B&B
907-451-7526

7 Gables Inn
907-479-0751-[G--]

Aba Bettys B&B
907-479-5035

Ah Rose Marie B&B
907-456-2040

Alasaka Heritage B&B
907-451-6587

Alaska Golden Heart
907-474-3438

Alaska House Inn
907-451-0435

Beaver Bend B&B
907-452-3240

Bell House B&B
907-452-3278

Betty's B&B
907-479-5016

Birch Haven Inn
907-457-2451

Blue Goose B&B
800-478-6973

Bonnies Abode
907-452-7386

Borealis Hotel

Chena River B&B
907-479-2532

College B&B
907-452-1014

Cowles Street B&B
907-452-5252

Daybreak B&B
907-479-2753

Eleanore Northern Lights B&B
907-452-2598

Evergreen Lodge
907-822-3250

Fairbanks B&B
907-452-4967

Fairbanks Downtown B&B
907-452-7700

Fox Creek B&B
907-457-5494

Geiger Haus B&B
907-474-2131

Goldstream B&B
907-455-6550

Hillside B&B
907-457-2664

Iniakeek Lake Lodge
907-479-6354

Joans B&B
907-479-6918

Karen's B&B
907-456-3146

Michaels B&B
907-452-3505

Midnight Sun B&B
907-479-2564

North Woods Lodge
907-479-5300

Pioneer B&B
907-452-5393

Poolside B&B
907-452-4119

Richards House B&B
907-474-8448

Shady Rest B&B
907-451-7378

Sophie Station Hotel
907-479-3650

Sourdough B&B
907-457-7784

Summit Lake Lodge
907-822-3969

This Old B&B
907-452-6343

Tolovan B&B
907-479-6004

Vivians Viewpoint B&B
907-479-3577

Wild Iris Inn
907-474-IRIS

Gakona
Chistochina Trading Post Lodge
907-822-3366

Girdwood
Alyeska View B&B
907-783-2747

Footloose Alaska B&B
907-783-2637

Glennallen
Poplars B&B
907-822-3755

Gustavus
Annie May Lodge
907-697-2346

Glacier Bay Country Inn
907-697-2288-[Y--]

Good River B&B
907-697-2241

Gustavus Inn
907-698-2254

Puffin B&B
907-679-2260

Haines
Cache Inn Lodge
907-697-2254

Chilkat Valley Inn
907-766-3331

Fort William Seward B&B
907-766-2856

Hotel Halsingland
907-766-2000

Officers B&B
800-542-6363

Riverhouse B&B
907-766-2060

Summer Inn B&B
907-766-2970

Halibut Cove
Quiet Place Lodge
907-296-2212

Healey
Dome Home

©*Inn & Travel Memphis, Tennessee*   4-143

Alaska   ***Bold Name*** - Description appears in other section

907-683-1239

Healy
La Hacienda B&B
907-683-2340

Pat & Wendells B&B
907-683-2824

Homer
Alaskas PioneerB&B
907-235-5670

B&B/Seekins
907-235-8996

Beach House
907-235-5945

Brass Ring B&B
907-235-5450

Buffalo & Boar B&B
907-235-7591

Driftwood Inn
907-235-8019

Halcyon Heights B&B
907-235-2148

Halibut Cove Cabins
907-296-2214

Island Watch B&B
907-235-2265

Kachemak Bay Wilderness Lodge
907-235-8910

Lakewood Inn
907-235-6144

Lily Pad
907-235-6630

Magic Canyon Ranch
907-235-6077-[Y--]

Pioneer BnB
907-235-5670

Ridgetop B&B
907-235-7590

Sadie Cove Wilderness Lodge
907-235-7766

Seaside Farm
907-235-7850

Snuggles Harbor
907-235-3632

Spit Road Lodge
907-235-6764

Stardust Retreat B&B
907-235-6820

Tutka Bay Lodge
907-235-3905

Wandering Star B&B
907-235-6788

Wild Rose B&B
907-235-8780

Willards Moose Lodge
907-235-8830

Iliamna
Roadhouse Inn
907-571-1272

Juneau
Admiralty Inn
907-789-3263

Alaskan Hotel
800-327-9347

Annies Dragon Lair
907-789-7901

B&B Inn Juneau
907-463-5855-[Y--]

Blueberry Lodge
907-463-5886

Cashen Corner B&B
907-586-9863

Channelview With Room
907-586-1754

Cozy Log B&B
907-279-5293

Dannerhouse B&B
907-586-1936

Dawsons B&B
907-586-9708

Eagles Nest B&B
907-586-6378

Grandmas Feather Bed-Country Inn
907-789-5005

Inn At The Waterfront
907-586-3800

Jans View B&B
907-463-5897

Larsons Landing B&B
907-789-7871

Lost Chord B&B
907-789-7296

Louies Place Elfin Cove
907-586-2032

Mullins House
907-586-2959

Pearsons Pond
907-789-3772

Pot Belly B&B
907-586-1279

Sepel Hollow B&B
907-789-5220

Silverbow Inn
907-586-4146

Sutton Place B&B
907-463-3232

Tenakee Inn
907-586-1000

Kasilof
Deals Den
907-262-2643

Kenai
Chinulna Point Lodge
907-283-7799

Daniels Lake Lodge
907-776-5578

Drifters Landing Inn
907-283-9328

Kantnu B&B
907-283-7152

Lyns Inn
907-283-8090

Silver Pines B&B
907-283-3352

Ketchikan
Alaskas First City B&B
907-225-7378

Great Alaska Cedar Works
907-247-8287

Hidden Inlet Lodge
907-225-4656

Ketchikan B&B
907-225-8484

Main Street B&B
907-225-8484

North Tongass B&B
907-247-2467

Waterfall Resort
907-544-5125

Klawock
Fireweed Lodge
800-544-5125

Klawock Bay Inn
907-755-2929

Kodiak
Baranof Museum / Erskine House
907-486-5920

Baranov Bluff B&B
907-486-5407

Inlet B&B
907-486-4004

Kodiak B&B
907-486-5367

Wintels B&B
907-486-6935-[Y--]

Kotzebue
Drakes Camp
907-442-2736

Lake Louise
Evergreen Lodge
907-822-3250

Manley Hot Springs
Manley Lodge
907-672-3161

Matanuska
Yukon Dans B&B
907-376-7472

McGrath
Rosas Riverside Inn
907-524-3666

Moose Pass

4-144   ©*Inn & Travel Memphis, Tennessee*

Bold Name - *Description appears in other section*   *Alaska*

Alaska Nellies Inn
907-288-3124

Ninilchik
Bluff House B&B
907-567-3605

Deep Creek B&B
907-567-3567

Gentle Breeze B&B
907-567-1008

Nome
Big Bear B&B
907-443-2419

Junes B&B
907-443-5984

Oceanview Manor B&B
907-443-2133

Palmer
North Country B&B
907-822-3670

Oceanview Manor B&B
907-443-2133

Pollens B&B
907-745-8920

Russells Bed & Board
907-376-7662

Sheep Mountain Lodge
907-745-5121

Tern Inn By The Lake B&B
907-745-1984

Wagon Wheel B&B
907-745-1020

Paxson
Paxson Lodge
907-822-3330

Petersburg
Beachcomber Inn
907-772-3888

Brackens Waters Edge
907-772-3736

Broom Haus
907-772-3459

Gypsy B&B
907-772-4531

Jewels By The Sea B&B
907-772-3620

Little Norway Inn

Scandia Haus
907-772-4281

Port Graham
Fedora's BnBnSkiffs
907-284-2239

Seldovia
Annie McKenzies
907-234-7816

Crow Hill B&B
907-234-7410

McKenzie Boardwalk Hotel
907-234-7816

Seldovia Rowing Club Inn
907-234-7614

Seward
Mon CLocks B&B
907-224-5563

Seward Waterfront Lodging
907-224-5563

Stoney Creek Inn
907-224-3940

Swiss Chalet B&B
907-224-3939

Van Gilder Hotel
907-224-3079

White House B&B
907-224-3614

Sitka
Abners B&B
907-747-8779

Alaska Ocean View B&B
907-747-8310

B&B Inn 518
907-747-3305

Biorka B&B
907-747-3111

Brownies B&B
907-747-5402

Creeks Edge B&B
907-747-6484

Hannah's B&B Fishing Charter
907-747-8309

Helga's B&B
907-747-5479

Karras B&B
907-747-3978

Mountain View B&B
907-747-8966

Ottor Cove B&B
907-747-8160

Puffin B&B
907-747-3912

Rockwell Lighthouse
907-747-3056

Sitka House B&B
907-747-4935

Skagway
Golden North Hotel
907-983-2294

Grammas B&B
907-983-2312

Irenes Inn
907-983-2520

Sgt Prestons Lodge

Skagway Inn
907-983-2294

Skagway
Wind Valley Lodge
907-983-2236

Skwentna
Skwentna Roadhouse

Soldotna
Arctic Tern B&B
907-262-5720

Brumleys B&B
907-262-6252

Bunk House Inn
907-262-4584

Eagles Nest B&B
907-262-5396

Eagles Roost Inn
907-262-9797

Honeymoon Cove B&B
907-262-4286

Kenai Penninsula B&B
907-262-1002

Knight Manor B&B
907-262-2438

Poseys Kenai River Hideaway
907-262-7430

Riverside Inn
907-262-4451

Soldotna B&B
907-262-4779

Sterling
Sunrise B&B
907-262-4951

Talkeetna
Bays B&B Inn
907-733-1342

Fairview Inn
907-733-2423

Paradise Lodge
907-733-1471

River Beauty B&B
907-733-2741

Sunshine Creek Inn
907-733-1485

Talkeetna Roadhouse
907-733-1351

Trapper Johns B&B
907-733-2354

Twister Creek Union
907-258-1717

Whistlestop B&B
907-733-1515

Tallkeetna
Alaska Log Cabin
907-733-2668

Tok
Cleft Of The Rock
907-883-4219

©*Inn & Travel Memphis, Tennessee*   4-145

Alaska- Arizona   **Bold Name** - *Description appears in other section*

Stage Stop
907-883-5338

Trapper Creek
Reflection Pond
907-733-2457

Trapper Creek B&B
907-733-2220

Unalaska
Jackis B&B House
907-581-2964

Valdez
Alpine Mountain Inn B&B
907-835-2624

Always Inn
907-835-4634

Angies Downhome B&B
907-835-2832

Artic Tern B&B
907-835-5290

B&B Of Valdez
907-835-4211

Baileys B&B
907-835-2690

Best Of All B&B
907-835-4524

Blueberry Marys B&B
907-835-5015

Boathouse B&B
907-835-4407

Casa de La Bellezza
907-835-4489

Chalet Alpine View B&B
907-835-5223

Christian B&B
907-835-2609

Colonial Inn B&B
907-835-4929

Comfort & Joy B&B
907-835-4929

Coopers Cottage B&B
907-835-4810

Downtown Inn B&B

907-835-2791

Fishermans Inn
907-835-2073

Forget-Me-Not B&B
907-835-2717

France Inn B&B
907-835-4295

Frostys B&B
907-835-4679

Gussies Lowe Street Inn
907-835-4448

Hickory Stick B&B
907-835-5218

Johnson House B&B
907-835-5289

Lake House B&B
907-835-4752

Milles B&B
907-835-4388

Mineral Creek B&B
907-835-4205

Mountain View B&B
907-835-5438

Pats Place B&B
907835-5078

Rainbow Lodge

Ravens Nest B&B
907-346-2377

Starrs Country Inn
907-835-2917

Totem Inn
907-835-4443-[Y--]

Two Bucks B&B
907-835-2577

Wendys B&B
907-835-4770

Ward Cove
North Tongass B&B
907-247-0879

Wasilla
Broken Horseshoe Ranch
907-376-5478

Cottonwood Lake Inn
907-373-0300

Country Lakes B&B Inn
907-373-6934

Ede Den B&B
907-376-2162

Mat-Su Resort
907-376-3228

Wasilla Lake B&B
907-375-5985

Yukon Dons B&B
800-848-7472

Whittier
Sportmans Inn

Willow
Clines B&B On Caswell Lake
907-495-1014

Ruth Lake Lodge
907-495-9000

Wrangell
Clarke B&B
907-874-2125

Yakutat
Blue Heron B&B
907-784-3287

Yes Bay
Yes Bay Lodge
907-247-1575

ARIZONA

Ajo
Guest House Inn
520-387-6133-[Y--]

Managers House Inn
520-387-6505-[Y--]

Bisbee
Bisbee Inn
800-421-1909-[Y--]

Copper Queen Hotel
602-432-2216

Curry Home B&B
602-432-4815

Greenway House
800-253-3325

Inn At Castle Rock
800-566-4449

Judge Ross House
520-432-4100

Mile High Court B&B
520-432-4636

Oliver House
602-432-4286

Park Place B&B
800-388-4388

School House Inn
800-537-4333

Whitehouse B&B
602-432-7215

Carefree
DesertFarren Private Hacienda Inn
602-488-1110-[G--]

Cave Creek
Debra Anns B&B
602-488-2644

Gortlands Inn Cave Creek
602-488-9636

Chandler
Cones Tourist Home
602-839-0369

Clarkdale
Flying Eagle Country B&B
602-634-0663

Cochise
Cochise Hotel
520-384-3156

Cochise Stronghold Lodge
602-862-3442-[Y--]

Cornville
Pumpkinshell Ranch
520-634-4797

Cottonwood
Creekside Inn At Sedona
602-634-2029

Douglas
Family Crest B&B
602-364-3998

4-146   ©*Inn & Travel Memphis, Tennessee*

Bold Name - Description appears in other section **Arizona**

Flagstaff
Arizona Mountain Inn
520-774-8959

Birch Tree Inn
800-645-5811-[Y--]

Cedar B&B
520-774-1636

Comfi Cottages
520-779-2236

Dierker House
520-774-3249-[Y--]

Inn At Four Ten
800-774-2008-[G--]

Walking L Ranch
520-779-2219-[Y--]

Florence
Inn At Rancho Sonora
800-205-6817

Forest Lakes
Forest Lakes Lodge
520-535-4727

Fountain Hills
Fountain Hills B&B
800-484-9746

Villa Galleria B&B
602-837-1400

Fredonia
Jackson House B&B
602-635-2178

Globe
Noftsger Hill Inn
602-425-2260

Gold Canyon
Sinells B&B
602-983-3650

Grand Canyon
Phantom Ranch

Grand Canyon Village
El Tovar Hotel

Greer
Greer Lodge
520-735-7217

Molly Butler Lodge
520-735-7226

White Mountain Lodge
520-735-7568

Hereford
Ramsey Canyon Inn
520-378-3010

Jerome
Ghost City Inn
520-63GHOST

Miners Roost

Kingman
Arcadia Lodge
520-753-1925

Lake Havasu City
Havasu Dunes Resort
520-855-6626

Lake Montezuma
Beaver Creek Inn
520-567-4475

Lakeside
Bartrams B&B
520-367-1408-[Y--]

Lake Of The Woods
520-368-5353

Litchfield Park
Wigwam Resort
602-935-3811

Oracle
Triangle L Ranch
800-266-2804-[Y--]

Villa Cardinale
800-266-2660-[Y--]

Page
Lake Powell B&B
602-645-2525

Patagonia
Little House
602-394-2493

Patagonia Patio B&B
602-394-2671

Payson
Kohls Ranch Lodge
602-271-9731

Pearce
Grapevine Canyon Ranch
520-826-3185

Phoenix
Gerrys B&B
602-973-2542

Heart Seed B&B Retreat Center & Spa
505-471-7026-[G--]

Hillside B&B
602-997-8826

Hotel San Carlos

Maricopa Manor
800-292-6403-[G--]

Talbots Stop Over
602-840-3254

Pinetop
Coldstream B&B
520-369-0115

Pinetop-Lakeside
The Meadows
520-367-8200

Prescott
1900 Pleasant Street B&B

Cottages At Prescott Country Inn
520-445-7991

Drake House B&B
520-445-7747

Hassayampa Inn
520-778-9434

Juniper Well Ranch
520-442-3415

Lynx Creek Farm
520-778-9573

Marks House Inn
520-778-4632-[Y--]

Mount Vernon Inn
520-778-0886-[G--]

Pleasant Street Inn
520-445-4774

Prescott Country Inn
800-362-4759-[Y--]

Prescott Pines Inn
800-541-5374-[Y--]

Victorian Inn Of Prescott
800-704-2642

Prescott Valley
Bensons B&B
520-772-8358

Safford
Onley House B&B
520-428-5118

Sasabe
Rancho de La Ossa
520-823-4257

Scottsdale
Azura East
602-945-3298

Casa de Mariposa
602-947-9704

Inn At The Citadel
800-927-8367-[Y--]

Valley O'The Sun B&B
602-941-1281

Sedona
B&B At Saddle Rock Ranch
520-282-7640

Briar Patch Inn
520-282-2342-[Y--]

Cactus Paradise Inn
520-282-2677

Canyon Villa Inn
800-453-1166

Casa Sedona
800-525-3756

Cathedral Rock Lodge
520-282-7608

Country Elegance
800-432-3529

Country Gardens B&B
800-570-0102

Cozy Cactus B&B
800-788-2082-[GQA]

Creekside Inn At Sedona
520-282-4992

Garlands Oak Creek

©*Inn & Travel Memphis, Tennessee*

Arizona - California **Bold Name** - *Description appears in other section*

Lodge
520-282-3343

Grahams B&B Inn
520-284-1425

Greyfire Farm
520-284-2340

Inn On Oak Creek
800-499-7896

Keyes B&B
520-282-6008

L'Augerge de Sedona Resort
800-272-6777

Lantern Light Inn
520-282-3419

Leduc's B&B
520-282-6241

Lodge At Sedona
800-619-4467

Rose Tree Inn
520-282-2065-[G--]

Saddle Rock Ranch
520-282-7640-[Y--]

Slide Rock Lodge
520-282-3531

Territorial House
800-802-2737

Touch Of Sedona
520-282-6462-[Y--]

Wishing Well
800-728-WISH

Sierra Vista
Brown Family
520-458-6678

Springerville
Paisley Corner
520-327-4447

Tempe
Fiesta Inn
602-976-1441

Tombstone
Buford House
602-457-3168

Priscillas B&B
602-457-3844

Tombstone

Boarding House
602-457-3716

Tubac
Tubac Country Inn
520-398-3178

Valle Cerde Ranch
520-398-2246

Tucson
Adobe Rose Inn
800-328-4122

Arizona Inn
800-933-1093

Bird In Hand B&B
520-622-5428

Birdsalls

Brimstone Butterfly
800-323-9157

Car Mar's Southwest B&B
602-578-1730

Casa Alegre
520-628-1800

Casa Suecia B&B

Casa Tierra
520-578-3058

Catalina Park Inn
800-792-4885

Congenial Quail
520-887-9487

Copper Bell B&B
520-629-9229-[Y--]

Desert Dream
520-297-1220

Desert Needlework Ranch

Desert Yankee
800-845-6792

El Presidio Inn B&B
800-349-6151-[G--]

Ford's Eastside B&B
520-885-1202

Gable House
800-756-4846

Hacienda del Desierto
800-982-1795

Horizons B&B
602-749-2955

Junes Home
520-578-0857

La Madera Ranch & Resort
520-749-2773

La Posada del Valle B&B
520-795-3840-[G--]

Lodge On The Desert
800-456-5634-[Y--]

Mariposas Inn
602-322-9157

Mesquite Tree
800-317-9670

Myers Blue Corn House
520-327-4663

Peppertrees B&B
800-348-5763-[Y--]

Rancho Quieto
602-883-3300

Redbud House B&B
520-721-0218

Springview
520-790-0664

SunCatcher
800-835-8012-[Y--]

Tanque Verde Ranch
520-296-6275

White Stallion Ranch
520-297-0252

Wickenburg
Flying E Ranch

J BAR J Ranch
520-684-9142

Kay El Bar Ranch
520-684-7593-[Y--]

Rancho de Los Caballeros
520-684-5484

Wickenburg Inn

Wilcox
Horsehead Lodge
520-828-3593

Williams
Canyon Country Inn
520-635-2349

Johnstonian B&B
520-635-2178

Red Garter B&B
800-328-1484

Terry Ranch B&B
800-210-5908

Yuma
Casa de Osgood B&B
602-342-0471

CALIFORNIA

Ahwahnee
Apple Blossom B&B
209-642-2001

Ol-Nil Gold Town
209-683-2155

Silver Spur B&B
209-683-2896

Alameda
Garrett Mansion
415-521-4779-[Y--]

Webster House
415-523-9697-[Y--]

Albion
Albion River Inn
707-937-1919

Fensalden Inn
800-959-3850-[Y--]

Wool Loft
707-937-0377

Allegheny
Kenton Mine Lodge
916-287-3212-[Y--]

Alpine
Cedar Creek Inn
619-445-9605

Alta
Crystal Springs Inn
916-389-2355

4-148 ©Inn & Travel Memphis, Tennessee

Bold Name - *Description appears in other section*   California

Alturas
Dorris House B&B
916-233-3786

Amador City
Culberth House
209-267-0440-[Y--]

Imperial Hotel
800-242-5594

Mine House Inn
800-646-3673-[Y--]

Anaheim
Anaheim B&B
714-533-1884

Anderson
Plantation House
800-950-2827

Angels Camp
Cooper House B&B
209-736-2145

Utica Mansion Inn
209-736-4209

Angelus Oaks
Whispering Pines B&B
909-794-2962

Angwin
Angwin Linda Falls B&B
707-965-2440

Big Yellow Sunflower B&B
707-965-3885

Forest Manor
800-788-0364-[G--]

Aptos
Apple Lane Inn
800-649-8988-[G--]

Bayview Hotel B&B
408-688-8654-[Y--]

Mangels House
408-688-7982-[Y--]

Arcata
Elegant Victorian Mansion
800-EVM-1888-[Y--]

Lady Anne Victorian Inn
707-822-2797

Plough And The Stars
707-822-8236

Arnold
Lodge At Manuel Mill B&B
209-795-2622

Arroyo Grande
Arroyo Village Inn
800-563-7762-[G--]

Crystal Rose Inn
805-481-1854-[Y--]

Guest House
805-481-9304

Rose Victorian Inn
805-481-5566

Auburn
Dry Creek Inn
916-878-0885-[Y--]

Lincoln House
916-885-8880-[Y--]

Powers Mansion Inn
916-885-1166

Victorian Hill House
916-885-5879

Avalon
Banning House Lodge
310-510-0303

Garden House
310-510-0356-[Y--]

Glenmore Plaza Hotel
800-4-CATALA

Gull House
310-510-2547-[Y--]

Hotel Monterey
310-510-0264

Hotel St Lauren
310-510-2299

Hotel Villa Portofino
310-510-0555

Island Inn

Mavilla Inn
310-510-1651

Old Turner Inn
310-510-2236

Seacrest Inn
310-510-0196

Zane Grey Pueblo Hotel
310-510-0966

Avila Beach
San Luis Bay Inn
805-595-2333

Bakersfield
Helen K B&B
805-325-5451-[Y--]

Ballard
Ballard Inn
805-688-7770

Bass Lake
Bass Lake B&B
209-642-3618

Bushnells Mountain Lodge B&B
209-877-2755

Ducys On The Lake
805-528-3098

Lakehouse B&B
209-683-8220

Baywood Park
Baywood B&B Inn
805-528-8888-[G--]

Ben Lomond
Chateau des Fleurs
408-336-8943-[Y--]

Fairview Manor
408-336-3355-[Y--]

Benica
Painted Lady
707-746-1646

Benicia
Capt Dillinghams Inn
800-544-2278-[Y--]

Capt Walsh Home B&B
707-747-5653

Union Hotel
707-746-0100-[Y--]

Berkeley
Bancroft Club Hotel
800-549-1002

Flower Garden B&B
510-644-9530

French Hotel
510-548-9930

Gramma's Rose Garden Inn
510-549-2145

Hillegass House
510-548-5517

Victorian Hotel
510-540-0700

Big Bear
Gold Mountain Manor
909-585-6997-[Y--]

Big Bear Lake
Apples B&B Inn
909-866-0903

Cathys Country Cottage
800-544-7454

Eagles Nest
909-866-6465-[Y--]

Knickerbocker Mansion
909-866-8221

Moonridge Manor
909-585-0457

Wainwright Inn
909-585-6914

Big Bend
Royal Gorges Rainbow Lodge
916-426-3661

Big Sur
Deetjens Big Sur Inn
408-667-2377

Lucia Lodge
408-667-2391

Post Ranch Inn
800-527-2200

River Inn
408-625-5255

Ventana Inn
800-628-6500

Bishop
Chalfant House
619-872-1790

California   **Bold Name** - *Description appears in other section*

Matlick House
619-873-3133-[Y--]

Blairsden
  Elwell Lakes Lodge
  916-836-2347

  Graeagle Lodge
  916-836-2511

Blue Jay
  Eagles Landing
  909-336-2642-[Y--]

Bodega
  School House Inn
  707-876-3257-[Y--]

  Taylors Estero Vista Inn
  707-876-3300-[Y--]

Bodega Bay
  Bay Hill Mansion
  707-875-3577

  Bodega Harbor Inn
  707-875-3594

  Chanslor Guest Ranch
  707-875-2721

  Sea Horse Guest Ranch
  707-875-2721

  Studio "1140" Room With A View
  707-875-3018

Bolinas
  Blue Heron Inn
  415-868-1102

  Bolinas Villa
  415-868-1650

  Garden Pump House
  415-868-0243

  Ritas B&B
  415-868-0113

  Rose Garden Cottage
  415-868-2209

  Star Route Inn
  415-868-2502

  Thomas White House Inn
  415-868-0279

Wharf Road B&B
415-868-1430

Bonita
  Burley Ranch
  619-479-9838-[Y--]

Boonville
  Anderson Creek Inn
  800-LLAMA-02

  Bear Wallow Resort
  707-895-3335-[Y--]

  Boonville Hotel
  707-895-2210

  Colfaxs Guest House
  707-895-3241

  Furtados Hideaway
  707-895-3630

  Toll House Inn
  707-895-3630-[Y--]

Brentwood
  Diablo Vista B&B
  415-634-2396

Bridgeport
  Bridgeport Hotel
  619-932-7380

Cain House
800-433-CAIN-[G--]

Brownsville
  Mountain Seasons Inn
  916-675-2180

Burbank
  Belair
  818-848-9227

Burlingame
  Burlingame B&B
  415-344-5815

  Sister Moon Inn

Burnt Ranch
  Madrone Lane B&B
  916-629-3642

Calistoga
  Brannan Cottage Inn
  707-942-4200-[Y--]

  Brannans Loft
  707-963-2181

Calistoga Country Lodge
707-942-5555

Calistoga Inn
800-845-3632

Calistoga Wayside Inn
800-845-3632

Calistoga Wishing Well Inn
707-942-5534

Christophers Inn
707-942-5755-[Y--]

Culvers, A Country Inn
707-942-4535-[Y--]

Falcons Nest
707-942-0758

Fannys
707-942-9491

Foothill House
800-942-6933-[Y--]

Golden Haven Hot Springs
707-942-6793

Hideaway Cottages
707-942-4108

Hillcrest B&B
707-942-6334

La Chaumiere
707-942-5139

Larkmead Country Inn
707-942-5360

Le Spa Francais
707-942-4636

Meadowlark Country House
707-942-5651

Mount View Hotel
707-942-6877

Mountain Home Ranch
707-942-6616

Old Toll Road Inn

Pine Street Inn
707-942-6829

Quail Mountain B&B
707-942-0316-[Y--]

Rebecca's Shadow Of Calistoga
707-942-9463

Scarletts Country Inn
707-942-6669-[Y--]

Silver Rose Inn
800-995-9381-[Y--]

Sleepy Hollow B&B
707-942-4760

The Elms B&B Inn
800-235-4316-[Y--]

The Pink Mansion
800-238-7465-[Y--]

Trailside Inn
707-942-4106-[Y--]

Village Inn & Spa
707-942-0991

Washington Street Lodging
707-942-6968

Wine Way Inn
707-942-0680-[Y--]

Wishing Well Inn
707-942-5534-[Y--]

Zinfandel House
707-942-0733

Cambria
  Beach House
  800-549-6789-[Y--]

  Blue Whale Inn
  805-927-4647

  Cambria Landing Inn
  800-549-6789

  Cambria Pines By The Seas
  805-927-4200

  Homestay

  J Patrick House
  800-341-5258-[Y--]

  Kraemers Kozy Kastle
  805-927-8270

4-150   ©*Inn & Travel Memphis, Tennessee*

Bold Name - *Description appears in other section*   *California*

Olalliberry Inn
805-927-3222-[Y--]

Pickford House
805-927-8619-[Y--]

Squibb House
805-927-9600

Sylvias Rigdon Hall Inn
805-927-5125

Windrush
805-927-8844

Camino
Seven Mile House-Camino Hotel
916-644-7740

Capistrano Beach
Capistrano Edgewater Inn
714-240-0150

Capitola
Inn At Depot Hill
408-462-3376

Monarch Cove Inn
408-464-1295

Capitola Valley
Summer House B&B
408-475-8474

Cardiff By The Sea
Cardiff By The Sea B&B

Whale House
619-942-1503

Carlsbad
Pelican Cove Inn
619-434-5995

Carmel
Candle Light Inn
408-624-6451

Carriage House Inn
800-433-4732-[Y--]

Coachmans Inn
800-336-6421

Cobblestone Inn
800-833-8836-[Y--]

Colonial Terrace Inn
408-624-2741

Cypress Inn
408-624-3871

Dolphin Inn
408-624-5356

Forest Lodge
408-624-7023

Grosnevors Garden Inn
408-624-3190

Happy Landing Inn
408-624-7917

Highlands Inn
408-624-3801

Hofsas House
800-421-0000

Holiday House
408-624-6267-[Y--]

Homestead
408-624-4119

House Of England
408-624-3004

Lincoln Green Inn
800-262-1262

Martin House B&B
408-624-2232

Mission Ranch
800-538-8821

Monte Verde Inn
800-328-7707-[Y--]

Normandy Inn

San Antonio House
408-624-4334

Sandpiper B&B Inn At The Beach
800-633-6433-[G--]

Sea View Inn
408-624-8778

Stonehouse Inn
800-544-9183-[Y--]

Stonepine Estate Resort
408-659-2245-[Y--]

Sundial Lodge
408-624-8578

Sunset House

408-624-4884

Svendsgaards Inn
408-624-1511

Tally Ho Inn
408-624-2232

Tickle Pink Inn
408-624-1244

Vagabonds House
800-262-1262

Wayfarer Inn
408-624-2711

Wayside Inn
408-624-5336

Carmel By The Sea
Green Lantern Inn
408-624-4392-[Y--]

Pine Inn
800-228-3851

San Carlos Lodge
800-831-3008

Carmel Valley
Los Laureles Lodge
408-659-2233

Robles del Rio Lodge
800-883-0843-[Y--]

Valley Lodge
800-641-4646

Capinteria
D&B Schroeder Ranch
805-684-1579-[Y--]

Castella
Castlestone Cottage Inn
916-235-0012

Castro Valley
Lores Haus
415-781-1553

Catalina Island
Inn On Mount Ada
310-510-2030-[Y--]

Sand Castle B&B
310-510-0682

Catheys Valley
Chibchas Inn
310-966-2940

Cayucos
Beachwalker Inn
805-995-2133

Cazadero
Cazanoma Lodge
707-632-5225

Timberhill Ranch
707-847-3258

Cedarville
Cressler-Hill House
916-279-2650

Chester
Bidwell House
916-258-3338

Bullard House
916-342-5912

Cinnamon Teal B&B
916-258-3993

Chico
Canyon Shadows B&B
916-345-5461

Esplenade B&B
916-345-8084

Johnsons Country Inn
916-345-STAY

Music Express Inn
916-345-8376

O Flaherty House
916-893-5494

Palms of Chico
916-343-6868

Chula Vista
Brookside Farm
619-421-8698

Clayton
Farmhouse At Clayton
510-672-8404

Clearlake
Muktip Manor
707-994-9571-[Y--]

Clearlake Park
Inn Oz
707-995-0853

Clio
White Sulphur Springs Ranch

©Inn & Travel Memphis, Tennessee

California   **Bold Name** - *Description appears in other section*

916-836-2387-[Y--]

Cloverdale
Abrams House Inn
800-764-4466

Vintage Towers
888-V TOWER

Ye Olde Shelford House
800-833-6479-[Y--]

Cobb
Forest Lake Inn
707-928-1991

Colfax
Bear River Mountain Farm
916-878-8314

Coloma
Coloma Country Inn
916-622-6919-[Y--]

Columbia
City Hotel & Restaurant
209-532-1479

Columbia City Hotel
209-532-1479-[G--]

Fallon Hotel
209-532-1470

Harlan House
209-533-4862

Colusa
O Rourke Mansion
619-458-5625-[Y--]

Coronado
Coronado Victorian House
619-435-2200

Coronado Village Inn
619-435-9318

Victorian House 1894-Dance Studio
619-435-2200-[Y--]

Coto De Caza
Strattons Inn On The Creek
714-858-0503

Coulterville
Jeffrey Hotel
209-878-3417

Sherlock Holmes B&B
800-354-5679

Crescent
Fernbrook Inn B&B
707-458-3202

Crescent City
Pebble Beach B&B
707-464-9086

Crescent Mills
Crescent Hotel
916-284-9905

Crest Park
Bracken Fern Manor
909-337-2055

Crowley Lake
Rainbow Farms
619-935-4556

Culver City
Garden Gate B&B
310-204-1218-[Y--]

Dana Point
Blue Lantern Inn
800-234-1425

Davenport
New Davenport B&B
408-425-1818

Davis
Aggie Inn
916-756-0352

Davis BNB
916-753-9611

University Inn
916-756-UNIV

Death Valley
Furnace Creek Resort
619-786-2345

Del Mar
Blue Door
619-755-3819

Gulls Nest
619-259-4863-[Y--]

Rock Haus
619-481-3764-[Y--]

Desert Hot Springs
Royal Palms Inn
619-329-7975

Travelers Repose
619-329-9584

Dinsmore
Dinsmore Lodge
707-574-6466

Dinuba
Country Living
310-591-6617

Dorrington
Dorrington
209-795-5800

Dorris
Hospitality Inn
916-397-2097

Downieville
Sierra Shangri La
916-289-3455

Dulzura
Brookside Farm
619-468-3043-[Y--]

Duncan Mills
Dunan Mills Lodge
707-865-1855

Superintendents House
707-865-1572

Dunsmuir
Abbotts River Walk Inn B&B
916-235-4300

Dunsmuir Inn
916-235-4534

El Cajon
Lions Head Guest House
619-463-4271

El Cerrito
Dolphin B&B
510-527-9622

Elk
Elk Cove Inn
707-877-3321

Elk Guest House
707-877-3308

Green Dolphin Inn
707-877-3342

Greenwood Pier Inn
707-877-9997

Griffin House
707-877-3422

Harbor House
707-877-3203

Sandpiper House Inn
707-877-3587

Elkcreek
Stony Creek Retreat B&B
800-643-7183

Encinitas
Sea Breeze B&B
619-944-0318

Escondido
Castle Creek Inn
619-751-8800

De Bolton B&B
619-741-5578

Halbigs Hacienda
619-745-1296-[Y--]

Oakmeadow
619-749-9426

Eureka
A Weavers Inn
707-443-8119-[G--]

Camellia Cottage
707-445-1089

Campton House
707-443-1601

Carter House
707-445-1390-[Y--]

Daly Inn
800-321-9656

Eagle House Inn
707-442-2334-[Y--]

Elegant Victorian Mansion
800 EVM 1888-[Y--]

Heurs Victorian Inn
707-445-7334

Hollander House
707-443-2419

Hotel Carter
707-444-8062-[Y--]

Iris Inn
707-445-0307

4-152   ©*Inn & Travel Memphis, Tennessee*

Bold Name - *Description appears in other section*   *California*

Old Town B&B Inn
800-331-5098-[Y--]

Shannon House
707-443-8130

Upstairs At The Waterfront
707-443-0179

Fairfield
Freitas House Inn
707-425-1366

Fall River Mills
Lava Creek Lodge
916-336-6288

Fallbrook
La Estancia Inn
619-723-2888

Fawnskin
Inn At Fawnskin
909-866-3200

Windy Point Inn
909-866-2746

Felton
Felton Crest Hannas B&B
408-335-4011

Ferndale
Ferndale Inn
707-786-4307-[Y--]

Freitas House Inn
707-786-4000

Gingerbread Mansion Inn
800-952-4136
[GQA-]

Grandmothers House
707-786-9704

Shaw House Inn
707-786-9958

Victorian Inn
707-786-4949

Fish Camp
Apple Tree Inn
209-683-5111

Karen's Yosemite Inn
800-346-1443-[Y--]

Narrow Gauge Inn
209-683-7720-[Y--]

Scottys B&B
209-683-6936

Folsom
Plum Tree Inn
916-351-1541

Sturms Hotel
916-985-2530

Forestville
Farmhouse Inn
800-464-6642

Fort Bidwell
Fort Bidwell Hotel
916-279-6199-[Y--]

Fort Bragg
Avalon House
707-964-5555

Cleone Lodge
707-964-2788

Colonial Inn
707-964-9979

Country Inn
707-964-3737-[Y--]

Glass Beach B&B Inn
707-964-6774

Grannys Village & Resort
707-961-9600

Grey Whale Inn
800-382-7244
[GQA-]

Jug Handle Inn
707-964-1415

Noyo River Lodge
800-628-1126

Old Stewart House
707-961-0775

Orca Inn
707-964-5585

Pudding Creek Inn
800-227-9529-[G--]

Ricochet Ridge Ranch
707-964-7669

Riverivew House
707-964-5236

Roundhedge Inn
707-964-9605

Freestone
Green Apple Inn
707-874-2526

Fremont
Lord Bradley's Inn
415-490-0520-[Y--]

Margot's Continental Lodge
415-657-8862

Fresno
Victorian
209-233-1988

Garberville
Benbow Inn
707-923-2124

Ranch House
707-923-3441

Ranch House Inn
707-923-3441

Garden Grove
Hidden Valley B&B
714-636-8312

Hidden Village B&B
714-636-8312

Gasquet
Patrick Creek Lodge
707-457-3323

Georgetown
American River Inn
800-245-6566

Geyserville
Campbell Ranch Inn
800-959-3878
[GQA-]

Hope Bosworth House
800-825-4BED-[Y--]

Isis Oasis Lodge
707-857-3524-[Y--]

Gilroy
Country Rose Inn
408-842-0441-[Y--]

Glen Ellen
Beltane Ranch B&B
707-996-6301

Deerfield Ranch
707-833-5214

Gaige House
707-935-0237-[Y--]

Glenelly Inn
707-966-6720-[Y--]

Jack London Lodge
707-938-8501

JVB Vineyard
707-966-4533

Stone Tree Ranch
707-996-8173

Tanglewood House
707-996-5021

Top O'The World Lodge
707-938-4671

Glendale
Shroff B&B Home
818-507-0774

Glenhaven
Kristalberg B&B
707-274-8009

Goleta
Circle Bar B Ranch
805-968-1113

Grass Valley
Annie Horans
916-272-2418-[Y--]

Domikes Inn
916-273-9010-[Y--]

Golden Ore House B&B
916-272-6870

Holbrooke & Purcell House
916-273-1353-[Y--]

Murphys Inn
916-273-6873-[Y--]

Swan Levine House
916-272-1873-[Y--]

Green Valley Lake
Serenity Summit
909-867-4109

Gridley
McCracken's Inn
916-846-2108

Thresher Mansion
916-846-0530

©*Inn & Travel Memphis, Tennessee*

California *Bold Name* - Description appears in other section

Groveland
Berkshire Inn
209-962-6744

Groveland Hotel
800-273-3314-[G--]

Hotel Charlotte
209-962-6455

Sheets n'Eggs B&B
209-984-0915

Gualala
Gail York Rodgers
707-785-2124

Gualala Hotel
707-884-3441

North Coast Country Inn
800-959-4537-[G--]

Old Milano Hotel
707-884-3256

Saint Orres
707-884-3303

Whale Watch By The Sea
800-942-5342

Guerneville
Applewood
800-555-8509

Camelot Resort
707-869-2538

Charming Country Inn, Grey Cottages
707-869-3623

Creekside Inn
800-776-6586-[Y--]

Estate
707-869-9093-[Y--]

Fern Grove Inn
800-347-9083

Fifes
800-FIFES-1

Jim & Rodneys Guest Cottage
707-869-1146

River Lane Resort
707-869-2323

Rodenhour Ranch

House
707-887-1033-[Y--]

Santa Nella House
707-869-9488-[Y--]

Willows
707-869-3279

Half Moon Bay
Cypress Inn
800-83-BEACH-[Y--]

Half Moon Bay B&B

Little Creek Mansion
415-747-0810

Mill Rose
800-829-1794-[Y--]

Old Thyme Inn
415-726-1616
[GQA-]

San Benito House
415-726-3425

Zaballa House B&B
800-77B NB4U

Hanford
Irwin Street Inn
209-583-8791-[G--]

Happy Camp
Culvers Lodge
916-493-2473

Healdsburg
Belle de Jour Inn
707-431-9777-[Y--]

Calistoga Silver Rose Inn
707-942-9581

Camellia Inn
800-727-8182-[Y--]

Frampton House
707-433-5084

George Alexander House
800-310-1358

Grape Leaf Inn
707-433-8140-[Y--]

Haydon House
707-433-5228-[Y--]

Healdsburg Inn On Plaza

800-431-8663

L'Auberge du San Souci
707-431-1110

Lions Lair
707-431-1211

Lytton Springs Inn
707-431-1109

Madrona Manor
800-258-4003-[Y--]

Raford House
707-887-9573-[Y--]

Villa Messina
707-433-6655

Helena
Meadowood Resort
707-963-3646

Helmet
Gracious English Manor
909-625-0555

Hollywood
Chateau Marmont
213-656-1010

Hollywood Hills
Black Rabbit Chateaus
213-851-8470

Homeland
Rancho Kareu B&B
909-926-5133

Homewood
Rockwood Lodge
800-LE TAHOE-[Y-]

Hope Valley
Sorensens Resort
800-423-9949

Hopland
Hopland House
707-744-1404

Idyllwild
Cedar Street Inn
909-659-4789

Silver Pines Lodge
909-659-4335

Strawberry Creek Inn
800-262-8969

That Special Place
909-659-5033

Wilkum Inn B&B
909-659-4087

Independence
Winnedumah Country Inn
619-878-2040

Inverness
Alder House B&B
415-669-7218

Ark
415-663-9338-[Y--]

Blackthorne Inn
415-663-8621-[Y--]

Dancing Coyote Beach
415-669-7200

Duck Lodge Cottage
415-669-1520

Dunrobin Cottage
415-669-7170

Fairwinds Farm B&B Cottage
415-663-9454

Gray Whale Upstairs
415-669-1330

Hotel Inverness
415-669-7393

Inverness Valley Inn
415-669-7250

Maclean House
415-669-7392

Mankas Inverness Lodge
415-669-1034

Moorings
415-669-1464

Rosemary Cottage
415-663-9338

Sandy Cove Inn
415-669-1233

Ten Inverness Way
415-669-1648-[Y--]

Tree House
415-663-8720

4-154

©Inn & Travel Memphis, Tennessee

Bold Name - *Description appears in other section* *California*

Ione
Heirloom
209-274-4468-[Y--]

Isleton
Delta Daze Inn
916-777-7777

Jackson
Ann Maries Country Inn
800-729-4287

Broadway Hotel
209-223-3503

Court Street Inn
209-223-0416

Gate House Inn
209-223-3500-[Y--]

Wedgewood Inn
800-933-4393-[Y--]

Windrose Inn
209-223-3650

Jamestown
Columbia City Hotel
209-532-1479-[G--]

Jamestown Hotel
209-984-3902

National Hotel
800-894-3446-[Y--]

Palm Hotel
209-984-3429

Royal Hotel
209-984-5271

Jamul
Lions Head Inn
619-463-4271

Mon Petite Chateau

Jenner
Fort Ross Lodge
707-847-3333

Murphys Jenner Inn
800-732-2377-[Y--]

Salt Point Lodge
707-847-3234

Sea Coast Hideaways
707-847-3278

Stillwater Cove Ranch

707-847-3277
Timber Cove Inn

Joshua Tree
Joshua Tree Inn
619-366-1188

Julian
Butterfield B&B
619-765-2179

Carole's Place
619-765-0251

Fair Oaks B&B
619-765-0704

Julian Gold Rush Hotel
800-734-5854-[Y--]

Julian Lodge
800-542-1420

Julian White House
619-765-1764

Pine Hills Lodge
619-765-1100

Pinecroft Manor B&B
619-765-1611

Shadow Mountain Lodge
619-765-0323

Villa Idaleen
619-765-1252

Kelsey
Mountainside B&B
800-237-0832

Kelseyville
Ely State Stop
707-279-0352

Kenwood
Kenwood Inn & Spa
707-833-1293

Little House
707-833-2536

Kernville
Kern River Inn B&B
619-376-6750-[Y--]

Neill House
619-376-2771

Wispering Pines Lodge B&B

619-376-3733

Kings Canyon Natl Pk
Montectio Sequoia Lodge
209-565-3388

Kingsburg
Kingsburg Swedish Inn
209-897-1022

Klamath
Requa Inn
707-482-8205

Knights Ferry
Knights Ferry Hotel
209-881-3271-[Y--]

Kyburz
Strawberry Lodge
916-659-7200

La Jolla
B&B Inn At La Jolla
619-456-2066-[Y--]

Irish Cottage
619-454-6075

Prospect Park Inn
800-433-1609

Scripps Inn
619-454-3391

La Porte
Lost Sierra Country Inn
916-675-2525

Lafayette
Donner Country Inn
916-547-5574

Laguna Beach
Carriage House
714-494-8945-[Y--]

Casa Laguna Inn
800-233-0449-[Y--]

Eilers Inn
714-494-3004-[Y--]

Hotel California
714-497-1457

Hotel Firenze
714-497-2446

Hotel San Maarten
714-494-9436

Inn At Laguna Beach

714-494-7535
Laguna House
714-497-9061

Spray Cliff
714-499-4022

Lake Arrowhead
Bluebelle House B&B
909-336-3292

Brocken Fern Manor
909-337-8557

Carriage House B&B
909-336-1400

Chateau due Lac
909-337-6488

Lakeview Lodge
909-337-6633

Prophets Paradise B&B
909-336-1969

Saddleback Inn
909-336-3571-[Y--]

Willow Creek Inn
909-336-2008

Lake Elsinore
Deborahs B&B

Lakeport
Forbestown Inn
707-263-7858

Wooden Bridge B&B
707-263-9125

Leggett
Bell Glen Resort
707-925-6425

Mad Creek Inn
707-984-6206

Sky Canyon Ranch
707-925-6415

Lemon Cove
Lemon Cove B&B
209-597-2555

Lewiston
Lewiston Inn
916-778-3385

Little River
Fools Rush Inn
707-937-5339

©Inn & Travel Memphis, Tennessee

4-155

California

Bold Name - Description appears in other section

Glendeven
800-822-4536

Heritage House
707-937-5885

Little River Inn
707-937-5942

Victorian Farmhouse
707-937-0679-[Y--]

Lodi
  Golden Era Hotel
  209-333-8866

  Wine & Roses Country Inn
  209-334-6988-[Y--]

Long Beach
  Appleton Place B&B Inn
  310-432-2312

  Cranes Nest
  310-435-4084

  Lord Mayor's Inn
  310-436-0324

Los Alamos
  Union Hotel
  805-344-2744

Los Angeles
  California Home Hospitality
  213-390-1526

  Casablanca Villa
  213-398-4794

  Century City Inn
  310-553-1000

  Channel Road Inn
  213-459-1920-[Y--]

  Eastlake Victorian Inn
  213-250-1620-[Y--]

  Herb Garden B&B
  213-465-0827

  Inn At 657
  213-741-2200

  Norja B&B Inn
  213-933-3652

  Salisbury House
  800-373-1778

  San Vicente Inn
  213-854-6915

  Secret Garden B&B

  Terrace Manor
  213-381-1478-[Y--]

  Town & Country Guest House
  213-464-8166

  West Adams B&B
  213-737-5041

  West Hollywood B&B
  213-650-8376

Los Banos
  Mercy Hot Springs

Los Gatos
  Courtside
  408-395-7111

  La Hacienda Inn
  408-354-9230

Los Olivos
  Country Cottage
  805-688-1395

  Los Olivos Grand Hotel
  800-446-2455

  Red Rooster Ranch
  805-688-8050

  Zaca Lake
  805-688-4891

Los Osos
  Bayview House
  805-528-3098

  Geraldas B&B
  805-528-3973

Lotus
  Golden Lotus
  916-621-4562

Lower Lake
  Big Canyon Inn
  707-928-5631-[Y--]

  Swiss Chalet
  707-994-7313

Loyalton
  Clover Valley Mill House
  916-993-4819-[Y--]

Lucerne
  Kristalberg B&B
  707-274-8009

Lytle Creek
  Mount Streams B&B
  909-887-2993

Magalia
  J&Js B&B
  916-873-4782

Malibu
  Casa Larronde
  310-456-9333-[Y--]

  Malibu Beach Inn
  213-456-6444

  Malibu Country Club
  310-457-9622

Malibu Hills
  Stallup House
  800-383-3513-[Y--]

Mammoth Lakes
  Jagerhof Lodge
  619-934-6162

  Snow Goose Inn
  800-874-7368-[Y--]

  Tamarack Lodge
  619-934-2442

  White Horse Inn
  619-924-3656

Manchester
  Blueroses
  707-882-2240

Marina del Ray
  Mansion Inn
  800-828-0688

Marina del Rey
  Marina B&B
  310-821-9862

Mariposa
  Boulder Creek B&B
  209-742-7729

  Canyon View B&B
  209-742-6268

  Chalet On The Mount
  209-966-5115

  Dick & Shirls B&B
  209-966-2514

  Dubords Restful Nest
  209-742-7127

  Eagles Nest
  209-966-3737

  Fitch Haven
  209-966-4738

  Grannys Garden
  209-377-8342-[Y--]

  Little Valley Inn
  800-889-5444

  Mariposa Inn
  209-966-4676

  Meadow Creek Ranch & B&B
  800-955-8843-[Y--]

  Oak Meadows, too
  209-742-6161-[G--]

  Pelennor B&B At Bootjack
  209-966-2832-[Y--]

  Poppy Hill B&B
  209-742-6273

  Restful Nest B&B
  209-742-7127

  Rock & Rill B&B
  209-742-4494

  Rockwood Gardens
  209-742-6817

  Schlageter House
  209-966-2471

  Shangri-La B&B
  209-966-2653

  Shiloh B&B
  209-742-7200

  Vista Grande B&B
  209-742-6206

  Winsor Farms B&B
  209-966-5592

  Yosemite Mariposa B&B
  209-742-7666

McCloud
  Francois' Grey Squirrel Inn

Bold Name - Description appears in other section California

916-964-3105

Hogin House B&B
916-964-2882

Joanies B&B
916-964-3160

McCloud B&B Hotel
916-964-2822

McCloud Guest House
916-964-3160

Stoney Brook Inn
800-369-6118

Mendocino
1021 Maine Street Guest House
707-937-5150

Agate Cove Inn
800-527-3111-[Y--]

Ames Lodge
707-937-0811

Big Ranch Inn
707-937-5322

Big River Lodge
707-937-5615

Blackberry Inn
707-937-5281

Blair House
707-937-1800

Blue Heron Inn
707-937-4323

Brewery Gluch Inn
707-937-4752

Cypress House
707-937-1456

Grey Whale Inn
800-382-7244-[Y--]

Headlands Inn
707-937-4431

Hill House
707-937-0554

John Dougherty House
707-937-5266-[G--]

Joshua Grindle Inn
707-937-4143

Kelly Attic
707-937-5588

MacCallum House
707-937-0289-[Y--]

Mama Moon Gardens
707-937-4234

McElroys Inn
707-937-1734

Mendocino Bay Trading Co
707-937-5266

Mendocino Farm House
707-937-0241-[Y--]

Mendocino Hotel
707-937-0511

Mendocino Village Inn
707-937-0246-[Y--]

Rachel's Inn
707-937-0088

Reeds Manor
707-937-5446

Sea Gull Inn
707-937-5204

Sea Rock
707-937-5517

Sears House Inn
707-937-4076

SS Seafoam Lodge
707-937-1827

Stanford Inn By The Sea
800-331-8884-[Y--]

Stevenswood Lodge
800-421-2810

Whitegate Inn
800-531-7282

Middletown
Brookhill Inn
707-928-5029

Harbin Hot Springs
707-987-2477-[Y--]

Nethercott Inn
707-987-3362

Midpines
Happy Medium
209-742-6366

Homestead Guest Ranch
209-966-2820

Lions Den Guest Ranch
209-966-5254

Sierra B&B
209-966-5478

Mill Creek
St Bernard Lodge

Mill Valley
A'Top Valley B&B
415-388-0372

All Marin B&B
415-388-8927

Mill Valley B&B
415-389-4040

Mountain Home Inn
415-381-9000

Sycamore House
415-383-0612

Modesto
Vineyard View
209-523-9009

Mokelumne Hill
Hotel Leger
209-286-1401

Montara
Farallone Hotel
415-728-7817

Goose & Turrets
415-728-5451
[GQA-]

Montara B&B
415-728-3946

Monte Rio
Highland Dell Inn
800-767-1759

Huckleberry Springs
800-822-2683-[Y--]

Rio Villa Beach Resort
707-865-1143

Village Inn
800-303-2303

Montecito
San Ysidro Ranch
805-969-5046

Monterey
Babbling Brook Inn
800-866-1131-[G--]

Carter Art Galleries B&B
408-655-0177

Jabberwock
408-372-4777

Merritt House
408-646-9686

Monterey Hotel (1904)
800-727-0960-[Y--]

Old Monterey Inn
800-350-2344

Spindrift Inn
408-646-8900

Victorian Inn
800-225-2902

Monterio
House Of 1000 Flowers
707-632-5511

Morgana
Hallmans
415-376-4318

Morro Bay
Marina Street Inn
805-772-4016

Moss Beach
Seal Cove Inn
415-728-7325

Mount Shasta
Carylyn's Inn Town
916-926-6078

Mount Shasta Ranch B&B
916-926-3870-[G--]

Wagon Creek Inn
916-926-0838

Ward's Bigfoot Ranch
916-926-5170-[Y--]

Muir Beach
Pelican Inn

©Inn & Travel Memphis, Tennessee

4-157

California	**Bold Name** - *Description appears in other section*

415-383-6000

Murphys
Dunbar House B&B 1880
800-225-3764-[Y--]

Murphys Hotel
209-728-3444-[Y--]

Napa
Arbor Guest House
707-252-8144-[Y--]

Beazley House
800-559-1649-[Y--]

Blue Violet Mansion
800-799-2583-[G--]

Bowen Manor

Brookside Vineyard B&B
707-944-1661

Candlelight Inn
707-257-3717

Cedar Gables Inn
800-309-7969-[G--]

Chateau
707-253-9300

Churchill Manor
707-253-7733-[G--]

Clarion Inn
707-253-7433

Coombs/Inn The Park B&B
707-257-0789-[Y--]

Country Garden Inn
707-255-1197

Cross Roads Inn
707-944-0646

Crystal Rose Victorian Inn
707-944-8185

Elm House
800-788-4356-[G--]

Gallery Osgood B&B Inn
707-224-0100-[Y--]

Goodman House
707-257-1166-[Y--]

Hennessey House

B&B
707-226-3774-[Y--]

John Muir Inn
707-257-7220

La Bella Epoque
707-257-2161

La Residencia Inn
707-253-0337

Magnolia Hotel
707-944-2056

Napa Inn
800-435-1444
[GQA-]

Oak Knoll Inn
707-255-2200

Oakville Ranch
707-944-8612

Old World Inn
800-966-6624-[Y--]

Oleander House
800-788-3057-[Y--]

Rockhaven
707-944-2041

Stahlecker House B&B
707-257-1588

Tall Timber Chalets
707-252-7810

Village Inn
707-257-2089

Yesterhouse Inn
707-257-0550

Napa Valley
Rancho Caymus Inn
707-963-1777-[Y--]

Villa Saint Helena
707-963-2514-[Y--]

National City
Dickinson/Boal Mansion
619-477-5363

Needles
Old Trails Inn B&B
619-326-3523

Nevada City
Deer Creek Inn
916-265-0363

Downey House
800-258-2815

Flumes End
916-265-9665

Grandmeres Inn
916-265-4660-[Y--]

Kendall House
916-265-0405

National Hotel
916-263-4551

Pally Place
916-265-5427

Parsonage
916-265-9478-[Y--]

Piety Hill Inn
916-265-2245-[Y--]

Red Castle Inn, Historic B&B
916-265-5135-[Y--]

US Hotel
916-265-7999

Newcastle
Victorian Manor
916-663-3009

Newport Beach
Dahl House
714-673-3479
[GQA-]

Dorymans Inn
714-675-7300

Little Inn On The Bay
800-538-4466-[Y--]

Portiofino Hotel
714-673-7030-[Y--]

Nice
Feather Bed Raidroad Co
707-274-4434

Nipomo
Kaleidoscope Inn
805-929-5444

Nipton
Hotel Nipton
619-856-2335

Norden
Norden House

916-426-3326

North Fork
Ye Olde South Fork Inn
209-877-7025

North Hollywood
La Maida House
818-769-3857

Northridge
Hideaway House
818-349-5421-[Y--]

Oak Glen
St Anley Inn
909-797-7920

Oakhurst
Chateau de Sureau
209-683-6860

Pine Rose Inn
209-642-2800

Sierra Sky Ranch
209-683-4433

Oakland
Bedside Manor
510-452-4550

Boat & Breakfast USA
510-444-5858-[Y--]

Rockridge B&B
510-655-1223

Washington Inn
510-452-1776

Occidental
Heart's Desire Inn
707-874-1311

Occidnetal
Inn At Occidental
800-522-6324

Ojai
Casa de La Luna
805-646-4528

Ojai B&B
800-422-OJAI

Ojai Manor Hotel
805-646-0961

Salubrium
805-649-4577

Theodore Woolsey House

4-158	©Inn & Travel Memphis, Tennessee

Bold Name - Description appears in other section   *California*

805-646-9779

Wheeler Hot Springs

Olema
Bear Valley Inn
415-663-1777-[Y--]

Inn At Point Reyes Ranch
415-663-8888

Olema Inn
415-663-9559-[Y--]

Point Reyes Seashore Lodge
415-663-9000-[Y--]

Roundstone Farm
415-663-1020

Olympic Valley
Christy Hill Inn
916-583-8551

Dolphins Home
916-581-0501

Ondio
Palm Shadow Inn
619-347-3476

Ontario
Red Lion Inn
909-983-0909

Orange
Country Comfort B&B
714-532-2802

Culver House
714-774-1888

French Inn
714-997-5038

Orinda
Heidi Haus
503-388-0850

Orland
Inn At Shallow Creek Farm
916-865-4093

Shallow Creek Farm Inn
916-865-4093

Stearman House

Orosi
Valley View Citrus Ranch

209-528-2275-[Y--]

Oroville
Jeans Riverside B&B
916-533-1413

Montgomery Hotel
916-532-1400

River Haven Hideaway
916-534-3344

Oroville/Berry Creek
Lake Oroville B&B
916-589-0700

Pacific Grove
Adnril Fireplace Cottages
408-375-0994

Centrella B&B Inn
800-233-3372

Down Under Inn
408-373-2993

Gatehouse Inn
800-753-1881-[Y--]

Gosby House Inn
408-375-1287-[Y--]

Green Gables Inn
800-722-1774-[Y--]

Lighthouse Lodge
408-655-2111

Maison Bleue Inn
408-373-2993-[Y--]

Martine Inn
800-852-5588-[Y--]

Old St Angela Inn
800-873-6523-[Y--]

Pacific Gardens Inn
408-646-9414

Ross Cottage
800-729-7677

Seven Gables Inn
408-372-4341-[Y--]

Palm Springs
Casa Cody
800-231-CODY-[G--]

Garbo Inn
619-325-6737

Hacienda las Palmas
619-325-6374

Ingleside Inn
619-325-0046-[Y--]

Korakia Pensione Historic
619-320-0708

Le Petit Chateau
619-325-2686

Orchid Tree Inn
800-733-335

Pepper Tree Inn
619-325-9124-[Y--]

Raffles Palm Springs
619-320-3949

Sakura, Japanese B&B Inn
619-327-0705

Sunbeam Inn

Villa Royale
800-245-2314-[G--]

Palo Alto
Adelia Villa
415-321-5195

Cowper Inn
415-327-4475

Hotel California
415-322-7666

Victorian On Lytton
415-322-8555-[Y--]

Pasadena
Donnymac Irish Inn
818-440-0066

Paso Robles
Almond View Inn
805-238-4220

Roseleith B&B
805-238-5848

Pescadero
Hidden Forest Cottage
415-879-1046

Petaluma
7th Street Inn
707-769-0480

Cavanagh Inn B&B
707-765-4657

Philo
Philo Pottery Inn
707-895-3069

Philo Ranch Country Inn
707-895-2550

Piercy
Hartsook Inn
707-247-3305

Pine Grove
Druid Guest House B&B
209-296-4156

Pismo Beach
Pismo Landmark B&B
805-773-5566-[Y--]

Placerville
Chichester House B&B
800-831-4008

Combellack Blair House
916-622-3764

Fleming Jones Homestead
916-626-5840

James Blair House
916-626-6136

River Rock Inn
916-622-7640-[Y--]

Rupley House Inn
916-626-0630

Playa del Rey
Inn At Playa del Rey
310-574-1920-[G--]

Pleasanton
Evergreen
510-426-0901

Plum Tree Inn
510-426-9588

Plymouth
Amador Harvest Inn
209-245-5512

Indian Creek
800-24-CREEK

Shenandoah Inn
209-245-4491

©*Inn & Travel Memphis, Tennessee*   4-159

California *Bold Name - Description appears in other section*

Point Arena
Coast Guard House
800-524-9320

Point Arena Lighthouse
707-882-2777

Wagners Windhaven
707-884-4617

Wharf Masters Inn
707-882-3171

Point Reyes
Berry Patch Cottage
415-663-1942

Burgers Beds
415-663-1410

Casa Mexicana
415-663-8313

Drakes Cottage
415-663-9373

Holly Tree Inn
415-663-1554

Inverness Park Place
415-663-9515

Neon Rose
415-663-9143

Thirty Nine Cypress Way
415-663-1709-[Y--]

Tradewinds
415-663-9326

Point Reyes Station
Carriage House
415-663-8627-[Y--]

Country House
415-663-1627

Eureka House

Ferrandos Hideway
415-663-1966

Gallery Cottage

Horseshoe Farm Cottage
415-663-9401

Jasmine Cottage
415-663-1166-[Y--]

Knob Hill

415-663-1784

London House
415-388-2487

Marsh Cottage
415-669-7168

Terris Homestay

Windsong Cottage
415-663-9695

Point Richmond
East Brother Light Station
415-233-2385-[Y--]

Pope Valley
James Creek Ranch B&B

Port Costa
Burlington Hotel

Porterville
Rosebed Inn
209-782-5675

Portola
Tullman House B&B
916-832-0107

Upper Feather B&B
916-832-0107

Posey
Roads End
805-536-8668

Princeton by the Sea
Pillar Point Inn
415-728-7377-[Y--]

Qunicy
Feather Bed
916-283-0102-[Y--]

New England Ranch
916-283-2223

Ranch Palos Verdes
By The Sea
310-377-2113

Rancho Cucamonga
Christmas House B&B Inn
909-980-6450-[Y--]

Rancho Santa Fe
Huntington Hotel
619-756-1131

Red Bluff
Buttons & Bows

916-527-6405

Drakesbad Guest Ranch

Falukners House
916-529-0520-[Y--]

Jarvis Mansion
916-527-6901

Jefferson Houes
916-527-4133

Jeter Victorian Inn
916-527-7574

Redding
Cabral House On Chestnut
916-244-3766

Palisades Paradise B&B
800-382-4649-[G--]

Reddings B&B
916-223-2494

Tiffany House B&B
916-244-3225

Redlands
Georgianna Manor
909-793-0423

Magnolia House
909-798-6631

Morey Mansion B&B
909-793-7970

Wissahickon Inn
909-793-7319

Redondo Beach
Ocean Breeze Inn
310-316-6631

Sea Breeze B&B
310-316-5123

Redwood City
Virginia City Rail Co
415-369-5405

Redwood Valley
Olson Farmhouse B&B
707-485-7523

Reedley
Fairweather Inn
209-638-1918

Hotel Burgess
209-638-6315

Reedley Country Inn
209-638-6333

Ridgecrest
BevLen Haus
800-375-1989

Jerrys B&B
916-446-3138-[Y--]

Running Springs
Spring Oaks B&B
909-867-9636

Rutherford
Auberge du Soleil
707-963-1211

Sacramento
Abigails B&B
800-848-1568-[Y--]

Amber House B&B
800-755-6526-[G--]

Briggs House
916-441-3214-[Y--]

Driver Mansion Inn
916-455-5243-[Y--]

Hartley House
916-447-STAY-[Y--]

Inn At Parkside
800-995-7275

Red Castle Inn, Historic B&B
916-265-5135-[G--]

River Rose, A Country Inn
916-443-4248

Riverboat Delta King
916-444-KING

Savoyard
916-442-6709

Sterling Hotel
800-365-7660

Vizcaya
916-455-5243

Saint Helena
Ambrose Bierce House
707-963-3003-[Y--]

Asplund Country Inn

Bold Name - Description appears in other section *California*

707-963-4614

Auberge Brisebois
707-963-4658

Bale Mill Inn
707-963-4545

Barro Station B&B
707-963-5169

Bell Creek B&B
707-963-2383

Bertels Ranch
800-932-4002-[Y--]

Bylund House B&B
707-963-9073-[Y--]

Chestleson House
800-959-4505-[Y--]

Cinnamon Bear B&B
707-963-4653-[G--]

Creekside Inn
707-963-7244

Creekwood
707-963-8590

Deer Run Inn
800-843-3408-[G--]

Elsies Conn Valley Inn
707-963-4614

Erikas Hillside
707-963-2887

Farmhouse
707-963-3431

Glass Mountain Inn
707-963-5373

Harvest Inn
800-950-8466

Hotel St Helena
707-963-4388

Ink House B&B
707-963-3890-[Y--]

Judy Ranch House
707-963-3081

La Fleur B&B
707-963-0233

Milat B&B
707-963-2612

Oleander House
800-788-3057-[Y--]

Oliver House B&B Inn
707-963-4089-[Y--]

Prager Winery B&B
707-963-3713

Quail Mountain B&B
707-942-0316

Rose Garden Inn
707-963-4417

Rustridge Ranch
707-965-9353

Shady Oaks Country Inn
707-963-1190

Spanish Villa
707-963-7483-[Y--]

Tollers Guest Cottage

Trubody Ranch B&B
707-255-5907

Villa Saint Helena
707-963-2514-[Y--]

Vineyard Country Inn
707-963-1000

White Ranch
707-693-4635-[Y--]

Wine Country Inn
800-473-3463-[Y--]

Wine Country Victorian
709-963-0852

Zinfandel Inn
707-963-3512

San Andreas
 Black Bart Inn

Courtyard B&B
209-754-1518

Robins Nest
209-754-1076

Thorn Mansion
209-754-1027

San Clemente
 Casa de Flores B&B
 714-498-1344

Casa Tropicana
714-492-1234

Jeans Retreat
714-492-1216

San Diego
 Abigail
 619-583-4738

Bettys B&B
619-692-1385

Blom House B&B
619-467-0890

Caroles B&B Inn
619-280-5258-[G--]

Castaway Inn
619-298-5432

Cottage
619-299-1564

Dmitris
619-238-5547

Dockside Inn
619-296-8940

Erenes B&B
619-295-5622

Harbor Hill Guest House
619-233-0638-[G--]

Heritage Park B&B Inn
800-995-2470-[Y--]

Hill House B&B
619-239-4738

Horton Grand Hotel
800-999-1886

Inn By The Park
619-232-1253

Keating House Inn
619-239-8585-[Y--]

La Jolla Oasis B&B
619-456-1776

Monets Garden
619-464-8296

Quince Street Trolley

619-422-7009

Shepards
619-582-3972

Skyview II
619-584-1548

Surf Manor & Cottages
619-225-9765-[Y--]

Veras Cozy Corner
619-296-1938

San Francisco
 1818 California
 415-885-1818

Abigail Hotel
800-243-6510

Adelaide Inn
415-441-2261

Alamo Square Inn
800-345-9888-[Y--]

Albion House
415-621-0896

Alexander Inn
415-928-6800

Amsterdam Hotel
800-637-3444-[G--]

Andrews Hotel
800-926-3739

Annas Three Bears
800-428-8559

Ansonia B&B
415-672-2670

Archbishops Mansion
800-543-5820

Art Center B&B
800-927-8236-[G--]

Aurora Manor
415-564-2400

B&B Inn
415-921-9784

B&B Near The Park
415-753-3574

Babbling Brook Inn
800-866-1131-[G--]

Black Stallion Inn

©*Inn & Travel Memphis, Tennessee*

4-161

California

Bold Name - Description appears in other section

415-863-0131

Boat & Breakfast USA
510-444-5858-[Y--]

Bocks B&B
415-664-6842

Brady Acres
415-929-8033

Casa Arguello
415-752-9482

Casita Blanca
415-564-9339

Chateau Tivoli
800-227-1647-[G--]

Clementinas Bay Brick
415-431-8334

Commodore Intl
415-885-2464

Dolores Park Inn
415-621-0482

Ed & Monica Widburg

Edward II Inn
800-GREATINN [Y--]

Fay Mansion Inn
415-921-1816

Fords B&B
415-776-1564

Four Sisters Inn
415-775-6698

Glenwood Hotel
888-442-2020

Golden Gate Hotel
800-835-1118-[Y--]

Grove Inn
800-829-0780

Haus Kleebauer
415-821-3866
[GQA-]

Hill Pointe Guest House
415-753-0393

Hotel David B&B
415-771-1600

Hotel Louise
415-775-1755

Hotel Sheehan
415-775-6500

Hyde Park Suites
415-771-0200-[Y--]

Inn - San Francisco
800-359-0913-[Y--]

Inn At The Opera
415-753-3574

Inn At Union Square
800-288-4346-[G--]

Inn On Castro
415-861-0321-[Y--]

Jackson Court
415-929-7670

Jasmine Cottage
415-663-1166-[Y--]

Kensington Park

Le Petit Manior
415-864-7232

Majestic
415-441-1100

Marina Inn
415-928-1000-[Y--]

Millefiori Inn
415-433-9111

Moffatt House
415-661-6210

Monte Cristo
415-931-1875-[Y--]

Nob Hill Inn
415-673-6080

Nob Hill Lambourne
415-433-2287

Nolan House
800-736-6526

Obrero Hotel
415-989-3960

Pacific Bay Inn
800-445-2631

Pacific Heights Inn
415-776-3310

Pensione San Francisco
415-864-1271

Petite Auberge
800-365-3004-[Y--]

Queen Ann Inn
800-227-3970

Red Castle Inn, Historic B&B
916-265-5135-[Y--]

Red Victorian B&B Inn
800-GO BANDB [Y--]

Redwood Inn
800-221-6621

San Remo Hotel
415-776-8688

Sherman House
415-563-3600

Spencer House
415-626-9205

Spreckles Mansion
415-861-3008-[Y--]

Stanyan Park Hotel
415-751-1000-[Y--]

Subtleties/Carols Cow Hollow Inn
415-775-8295

The Mansions Hotel
800-826-9398-[G--]

Union Street Inn
415-346-0424

UN Plaza Hotel

Victorian Inn On The Park
800-435-1967

Washington Square Inn
800-388-0220-[Y--]

White Swan Inn
800-999-9570-[Y--]

Willows B&B Inn
415-431-4770

San Gregorio
Rancho San Gregorio

415-747-0810-[Y--]

San Jose
Apple Lane Inn
800-649-8988

Briar Rose
408-279-5999-[Y--]

Country Rose Inn
408-842-0441-[G--]

Hensley House
800-298-3537-[G--]

Mrs K'S Retreat
408-371-0539

O Neils
408-996-1231

San Juan Bautista
B&B San Juan
408-623-4101

Country Rose Inn
408-842-0441-[G--]

San Juan Capistrano
Hotel California
714-496-9444

San Leandro
Best House B&B
415-351-0911

San Luis Obispo
Adobe Inn
800-676-1588

Apple Farm Inn
800-374-3705

Garden Street Inn
805-545-9802

Heritage Inn
805-544-7440-[Y--]

Madona Inn
805-543-3000

Megans Friends B&B
805-544-4406

San Miguel
Darken Downs Equestre Inn
805-467-3589

Ranch B&B
805-463-2320

Victorian Manor
805-467-3306

4-162 ©Inn & Travel Memphis, Tennessee

Bold Name - *Description appears in other section* California

San Paula
Fern Oaks Inn
805-525-7747

San Rafael
Casa Soldavini
415-454-3140-[Y--]

Gerstle Park Inn
800-726-7611

Ole Rafael B&B
415-453-0414

Panama Hotel
800-899-3993

San Ramon
Gold Quarte Inn
209-267-0747

San Ysidro
Tringhams B&B

Santa Ana
Old Oak Table
714-639-7798

Santa Barbara
Arlington Inn
805-965-6532

B&B At Vallis View
805-969-1272

Bath Street Inn
800-788-BATH-[Y--]

Bayberry Inn
805-682-3199-[Y--]

Blue Quail Inn
800-549-1622-[Y--]

Brinkerhoff B&B Inn
805-963-7844

Casa del Mar Inn
800-433-3097-[G--]

Cheshire Cat Inn B&B
805-569-1610-[G--]

Coast Village Inn
805-969-3266

Cottage
805-682-4997

Eagle Inn
800-767-0030

Glenborough Inn

800-962-0589-[Y--]

Ivanhoe Inn
805-963-8832

Longs Seaview B&B
805-687-2947

Ocean View Guest House
805-966-6659

Old Mission House
805-569-1914

Old Yacht Club Inn
800-676-1676-[G--]

Olive House
800-786-6422-[Y--]

Parsonage
800-775-0352-[Y--]

Santa Barbara B&B
805-963-8191

Simpson House
800-676-1280-[G--]

Tiffany Inn
805-963-2283-[Y--]

Upham Hotel Garden Cottages
800-727-0876-[G--]

Vallis View
805-969-1272

Villa d'Italia
805-687-6933-[Y--]

Villa Rose Inn
805-966-0851-[Y--]

Santa Clara
Madison Street Inn
800-491-5541-[G--]

Santa Cruz
Apple Lane Inn
800-649-8988

Babbling Brook Inn
800-866-1131-[G--]

Bangerts
408-476-1906

Bayview Hotel B&B
408-688-8654-[G--]

Blue Spruce Inn
800-559-1137-[Y--]

Chateau Victorian
408-458-9458

Cliff Crest Inn
408-427-2609-[Y--]

Darling House
408-458-1958-[Y--]

Heron House
408-429-8963

Inn Laguna Creek
408-425-0692

Pleasure Point Inn
408-475-4657

Sea & Sand Inn
408-427-3400

Victorian House
800-421-6662

Wayfarer Station
408-425-5949

Santa Maria
Santa Maria Inn
805-928-7777

Santa Monica
Channel Road Inn
310-459-1920-[G--]

Shutters On The Beach
800-334-9000

Sovereign At Santa Monica
800-331-0163

Victorian Inn
310-396-7456

Santa Paula
Glen Tavern Inn
805-525-6658

Lemon Tree Inn
805-525-7747

White Gables Inn
805-933-3041

Santa Rosa
Belvedere Inn
707-575-1857

Coopers Grove Ranch
707-526-3135

Gables Inn
707-585-7777

Gee-Gee's B&B Home
707-833-6667-[Y--]

Hilltop House
707-944-0880-[Y--]

Hotel La Rose
800-LAROSE 8

Melitta Station Inn
707-538-7712-[Y--]

Pygmalion House B&B
707-526-3407-[Y--]

Vinters Inn
800-421-2584-[Y--]

Saratoga
Eden Valley Place
408-867-1785

Inn At Saratoga
408-867-5020

Sausalito
Alta Mira Hotel
415-332-1309

Butterfly Tree
415-383-8447

Casa Madrona Hotel
800-288-0502

Sausalito Hotel
415-332-4155

Scotia
Scotia Inn
707-764-5683

Sea Ranch
Sea Ranch Lodge
707-785-2371

Seal Beach
Seal Beach Inn & Gardens
310-493-2416-[Y--]

Villa Pacifica
310-594-0397

Sebastopol
Gravenstein Inn
707-829-0493

O Hagans Guest House
707-823-4771

Shelter Cove

California   **Bold Name** - *Description appears in other section*

Shelter Cove B&B
707-986-7161

Sherman Oaks
Scott Valley Inn
916-467-3229

Sierra City
Busch/Heringlake Country Inn

High Country Inn B&B
916-862-1530

Sierraville
Consciousness Village
916-994-8984

Skyforest
Storybook Inn
800-554-9208-[G--]

Smith River
Casa Rubio
707-487-4313

Soda Springs
Rainbow Lodge
916-426-3661

Serene Lakes Lodge
916-426-9001

Traverse Inn
916-426-3010

Solvang
Chimney Sweep Inn
800-824-6444

Danish Country Inn
805-688-2018

El Ranchito
805-688-9517

Kronborg Inn
805-688-2383

Solvang Castle Inn
805-688-9338

Solvang Inn
805-688-3248

Storybrook Inn B&B
805-688-1703

Sunflower House
805-688-4492

Tivoli Inn
805-688-0559

Somerset
7-Up Bar Branch
209-245-5450

Fitzpatrick Winery & Lodge
209-245-3248

Somis
Ranch de Somis
805-987-8455

Sonoma
Au Relais Inn
707-996-1031

Chalet B&B
707-938-3129

Country Cottage
707-938-2479

El Dorado Inn
707-996-3030

Hidden Oak
707-996-9863-[Y--]

Katy Murphy Cottage
707-996-4359

Magliulo's Pensione
707-996-1031

Sonoma Chalet B&B
707-938-3129

Sonoma Hotel
800-468-6016

Starwae Inn
800-793-4792

The Barn
707-938-9335

Thistle Dew Inn
707-938-2909-[Y--]

Trojan Horse Inn
800-899-1925-[Y--]

Victorian Garden Inn
800-543-5339-[G--]

Vineyard Inn
707-938-2350

Sonora
Baretta Gardens Inn
209-532-6039-[Y--]

Gunn House
209-532-3421

Hammons House Inn
209-532-7921

La Casa Inglesa
209-532-5822

Lavender Hill Inn
209-532-9024

Llamahall Guest Ranch
209-532-7264-[Y-]

Lulu Belles
800-538-3455-[Y--]

Ryan House B&B Inn
800-831-4897-[Y--]

Serenity - A B&B
800-426-1441

Sonora Inn
209-532-7468

Via Serena Ranch
209-532-5307

Soquel
Blue Spruce Inn
800-559-1137
[GQA-]

Devlin Wine Cellars
408-476-7288

Soulsbyville
Willow Springs Country Inn
209-533-2030

South Lake Tahoe
Christiana Inn
916-544-7337-[Y--]

Les Geraniums
916-544-6450

Richardsons Resort
800-544-1801

South Pasadena
Artists Inn
818-799-5668

South San Francisco
Oyster Point Marina Inn
415-737-7633

Springville

Annies B&B
209-539-3827

Stinson Beach
Casa del Mar
415-868-2124

Shorelane House
415-868-1062

Stirling City
Stirling City Hotel
916-873-0858

Stockton
Old Victorian Inn
209-462-1613

Studio City
Figs Cottage
818-769-2662

Summerland
Inn On Summer Hill
800-845-5566

Sunset Beach
Harbour Inn
310-592-3547

Sunset B&B Inn
310-592-1666

Susanville
Roseberry House
916-257-5675

Sutter Creek
Foxes In Sutter Creek
209-267-5882-[Y--]

Gold Quarte Inn
800-752-8738

Hanford House
209-267-0747

Nancy/Bobs 9 Eureka Street Inn
209-267-0342

Sutter Creek Inn
209-267-5606

Tahoe City
Chaney House
916-525-7333

Chateau Place
800-773-0313

Cottage Inn
916-581-4073

Lakeside House

Bold Name - *Description appears in other section*   *California*

916-588-8796

Mayfield House
916-583-1001-[G--]

River Ranch
916-583-4264

Tahoe Vista
Shore House
800-207-5160

Tahoma
Alpenhaus
916-525-5000

Captains Alpenhaus
916-525-5000

Temecula
Loma Vista B&B
909-676-7047-[Y--]

Templeton
Country House Inn
800-362-6032

Thomasville
Quail Country B&B
912-226-7218

Three Rivers
Cort Cottage
209-561-4671

Redwood Manor
209-561-4145

Sequoia Village
209-561-3652

Tomales
Tomales Country Inn
800-547-1463

US Hotel
707-878-2742

Torrance
Doris Mae Richey
310-534-2298

Noone Guest House
310-328-1837

Whites House
310-324-6164-[Y--]

Wild Goose
310-325-3578

Trinidad
Lost Whale Inn
800-677-7859

Trinidad B&B
707-677-0840

Trinity Center
Carrville Inn
916-266-3511

Truckee
Alta Hotel
916-587-6668

Bradley House

Hilltop Lodge
916-587-2545

Mountain View Inn
916-587-5388

Star Hotel
916-587-3007

Truckee Hotel B&B
916-587-4444

Tuolumne
Oak Hill Ranch
209-928-4717

Twain Harte
Twain Hartes B&B
209-586-3311-[Y--]

Twentynine Palms
Circle C
619-367-7615

Homestead B&B
619-367-0030

Homestead Inn
619-367-0030

Ukiah
Oak Knoll B&B
707-468-5646-[Y--]

Sanford House
707-462-1653

Vichy Hot Springs Resort
707-462-9515
[YQA-]

Upper Lake
Narrows Lodge
707-275-2718

Valley Center
Lake Wohlford B&B
800-831-8238

Valley Ford
Inn At Valley Ford
707-876-3182

Valley Ford Hotel
800-696-6679

Venice
Rose Inn
310-301-7073

Venice Beach House
310-823-1966

Ventura
B&B of Ventura
805-652-2201

Baker Inn
805-652-0143

Bella Maggiore Inn
800-523-8479-[Y--]

Clocktower Inn
800-727-1027-[Y--]

La Mer
805-643-3600-[Y--]

Roseholm
805-649-4014

Visalia
Spalding House
209-739-7877

Volcano
St George Hotel
209-296-4458

Volcano Inn
209-296-4959

Walnut Creek
Diablo Mountain Inn
415-937-5050

Gasthaus Zum Baren
415-934-8119-[Y--]

Mansion At Lakewood
800-477-7898

Warner Springs
Warner Springs Ranch
619-782-4219

Watsonville
Dunmovin B&B
408-722-2810

Rancho de La Mazana
408-763-1420

West Covina
Hendrick Inn
818-919-2125

Westport
Blue Victoria Inn
707-964-6310

Bowens Pelican Inn
707-964-5588

DeHaven Valley Farm Inn
707-961-1660

Howard Creek Ranch
707-964-6725

Whittier
Benell Inn

Coleens California Casa
310-699-8427-[Y--]

Williams
Wicketts Side Door Inn
916-473-2306

Wilbur Hot Springs
916-473-2306

Willits
Doll House
707-459-4055

Windsor
Country Meadow Inn
707-431-1276-[Y--]

Yosemite
Karen's Yosemite Inn
800-346-1443

Oak Meadows, too
209-742-6161-[Y--]

Telaros Wawona B&B
209-375-6582

Yosemite National Park
Waldschloss
209-372-4958

Yosemite Peregrine B&B
800-396-3639

Yountville
Bordeaux House
707-944-2855

©*Inn & Travel Memphis, Tennessee*   4-165

California - Colorado

Bold Name - *Description appears in other section*

Burgundy House
707-944-0899-[Y--]

Magnolia Hotel
707-944-2056

Napa Valley Railway Inn
707-944-2000

Oleander House
800-788-3057-[Y--]

Sybron House
707-944-2785-[Y--]

Vintage Inn
707-944-1112

Webber Place
707-944-8384

Yreka
3rd Street Inn
916-842-7058

McFaddens Inn
916-842-7712

Yuba City
Harkey House B&B
916-674-1942-[Y--]

Moore Mansion B&B
916-674-8559

COLORADO

Alamosa
Cottonwood Inn
800-955-BNBE-[Y--]

Allenspark
Allenspark Lodge
303-747-2552

Lazy H Ranch
303-747-2532

Wild Basin Lodge
303-747-2454

Antonito
Conejos Ranch
719-376-2464

Arriba
Tarado Mansion
719-768-3468

Arvada
On Golden Pond B&B

303-424-2296

Tree House
303-431-8352

Aspen
Aplina Haus
800-24-ASPEN

Aspen B&B
800-36A SPEN

Aspen Country Inn
970-925-2700

Aspen Manor
800-344-3853

Aspen Ski Lodge
970-925-3434

Brass Bed Inn
970-925-3622

Buckhorn Lodge
970-925-7630

Christiana Lodge
970-925-3014

Christmas Inn
970-925-3822

Cresthaus Lodge
800-925-7081

Featherbed Lodge
970-925-7077

Fireside Inn
970-772-7678

Hearthstone House
970-925-7632

Hotel Lendao
800-321-3457

Independence Square Hotel
970-920-2313

Inn At Aspen

Innsbruck Inn
970-925-2980

Inverness B&B
970-925-8500

Lazy 7 Guest Ranch

Little Red Ski Haus
970-925-3333

Mountain Chalet

Aspen
800-321-7813

Mountain House B&B
970-920-2550

Pomegranate Inn
970-525-4012

Sardy House
800-321-3457-[Y--]

Snow Queen Victorian Inn
970-925-8455-[Y--]

St Moritz Lodge
970-925-3220

Tipple Inn
800-321-7025

Ullr Lodge
970-925-7696

Ault
Eastridge Farms
970-834-2617

Avon
Beaver Creek Lodge
800-732-6777

Inn At Beaver Creek
970-845-7800

Poste Montane Lodge
970-845-7500

Bailey
Glen-Isle On The Platte

Basalt
Altamira Ranch Inn
970-927-3309

Double Diamond Ranch
970-927-3404

Shenandoah Inn
970-927-4991

Bayfield
Deer Valley Resorts
970-884-2600

Bellvue
Mountain Meadow Inn
970-482-3769

Raindrop Inn

970-493-0799

Scorched Tree B&B
970-881-2817

Berthoud
Parrish Country Squire
970-772-7678

Beulah
Ravens Roost B&B
719-485-3227

Black Hawk
Gaslight Inn
303-582-5266

Gilpin Hotel
303-582-5012

Shamrock Inn B&B
303-582-5513

Boulder
Alps Boulder Canyon Inn
303-444-5445

Bluebird Lodge
303-443-6475

Boulder Victoria Historic Inn
303-938-1300-[Y--]

Briar Rose B&B
303-442-3007-[Y--]

Hotel Boulderado

Magpie Inn
303-449-6528

Pearl Street Inn
800-232-5949

Room With A View
303-440-8075

Salina House
303-442-1494

Sandy Point Inn
303-530-2939

University Inn
303-442-3830

Breckenridge
Allaire Timbers Inn
800-624-4904-[Y--]

Brown Hotel
970-453-0084

4-166

©*Inn & Travel Memphis, Tennessee*

Bold Name - Description appears in other section   **Colorado**

Cotten House
970-453-5509

Daytons Nordic Inn
970-453-6617

Fireside Inn
970-453-6456-[Y--]

Hunt Placer Inn
800-472-1430

Muggins Gulch Inn
970-453-7414

Ridge Street Inn
970-453-4680

Swiss Inn
970-453-6489

Williams House B&B
800-795-2975

Broomfield
Broomfield Guest House
303-469-3900

Buena Vista
Adobe Inn
719-395-6340

Blue Sky Inn
719-395-8865

Bluebird Ridge B&B
719-395-2336

Cottonwood Hot Springs Inn
800-241-4119-[G--]

Rainbow Lake Resort
719-395-2509

Trout City Inn
719-495-0348

Carbondale
Ambiance Inn
719-963-3597

Aspen Valley B&B
719-963-2628

Avalanche Ranch
970-963-2846

Biggerstaff House
719-963-3605

Carbondale Country Inn & Suites
719-963-8880

Cleveholm Manor
800-643-4887-[Y--]

Crystal River Inn
719-963-3902

Harmony House B&B
719-963-3369

Historic Redstone Inn
970-963-2526

McClure House
719-963-1020

Mount Sopris Inn
800-437-8675

Van Horn House On Lions Ridge
719-963-3605

Cascade
Eastholme
719-684-9901

Sue's Guest House
719-684-2111

Top Of Timpa B&B
719-684-2296

Cedaridge
Cedars Edge
970-856-6836

Melinda Meadows B&B
970-856-6384

Timberline B&B
970-856-7379

Central City
High Steet B&B Inn
303-582-0622

Hillside House
303-582-0622

Primrose Inn B&B
303-582-5808

Cimarron
Inn At Arrowhead
719-249-5634

Clark
Home Ranch
970-879-1780

Inn At Hahns Pean

Inn At Steamboat Springs
970-879-3906

Colorado Springs
Aware Nest Victorian
719-630-8241-[--]

Black Forest B&B
719-495-4208

Cheyenne Canon Inn
719-633-0625-[G--]

Griffins Hospitality House
719-599-3035-[Y--]

Hearthstone Inn
719-473-4413-[Y--]

Holden House- 1902 B&B Inn
719-471-3980-[G--]

Our Hearts Inn
719-473-8684

Painted Lady B&B
719-473-3165

Room At The Inn B&B
719-442-1896
[GQAR-]

Cortez
Kellys Place
719-565-3125

Crawford
Becher Ranch B&B
970-921-6877

Van Egen House
970-921-6177

Creede
Creede Hotel
719-658-2608

Crested Butte
Alpine Lace B&B
970-349-9857

Brumder Hearth
970-349-6253

Claim Jumper
970-349-6471

Crested Beauty
970-349-1201

Cristiana Guest

Haus B&B
970-349-5326

Elizabeth Anne B&B
970-349-0147

Forest Queen Hotel
970-349-5336

Gophic Inn
970-349-7215

Nordic Inn
970-349-5542

Purple Mountain Lodge
970-349-5888

Tudor Rose B&B
970-349-6253

Wedgewood Cottage B&B
719-636-1829

Crestone
Rendezvous Cottage Inn
719-256-4821

Cripple Creek
Imperial Hotel
719-689-2713

Pheonix House B&B
719-689-2030

Strawberry House
719-689-2427

Del Norte
Golden Fleece Antiques & Inn
719-657-2850

Wild Iris Inn
719-754-2533

Delores
Mountain View B&B
800-228-4592

Delta
Delta-Escalante Ranch
303-874-4121

Denver
901 Penn House
303-831-8060

Cambridge Club
800-877-1252

Capitol Hill Mansion

©*Inn & Travel Memphis, Tennessee*   4-167

Colorado   **Bold Name -** *Description appears in other section*

800-839-9329

Castle Marne
800-821-2976-[Y--]

Cheyenne Canyon Inn
719-633-0625-[G--]

Franklin House B&B
719-331-9106

Haus Berlin B&B
303-837-9527-[Y--]

Merritt House B&B
303-861-5230

Mountain Mansion
303-486-0655

Oxford
303-228-5838

Queen Anne B&B Inn
800-432-INNS-[G--]

Room At The Inn B&B
719-442-1896-[G--]

Victoria Oaks Inn
800-662-6257-[G--]

Dillon
  Annabelles B&B
  970-468-8667

  Blue Valley Guest House
  800-530-3866

  Grannys Inn
  970-468-9297

  Ptarmigan Mountain B&B
  970-468-5289

  Swan Mountain Inn
  970-453-7903

Divide
  Silverwood B&B At Divide
  719-687-6784

Dolores
  Little Southfork Ranch B&B
  970-882-4259

  Rio Grande Southern Hotel
  970-882-7527

  Simon Draw Guest House
  970-565-8721

Drake
  Dripping Springs B&B
  970-586-3406

Durango
  Apple Orchard Inn
  800-426-0751-[G--]

  Country Sunshine B&B
  800-383-2853

  Edgemont Ranch
  970-247-2713

  Elk Meadows Inn
  970-247-4559

  General Palmer Hotel
  800-523-3358

  Hermosa House
  970-385-5298

  Jarvis Suite Hotel
  800-824-1024-[Y--]

  Leland House B&B
  800-664-1920 [GQAR-]

  Lightner Creek Inn
  970-259-1226

  Logwood B&B
  800-369-4082

  Pennys Place
  970-247-8928-[Y--]

  River House B&B
  800-254-4775 [GQAR-]

  Scrubby Oaks B&B
  970-247-2176-[Y--]

  Starter Hotel
  800-247-4431

  Tall Timber
  970-259-4813

  Vagabond Inn B&B
  970-259-5901-[Y--]

  Victorian Inn
  970-247-2223

Durango (Hesperus)
  Blue Lake Ranch
  303-385-4537-[Y--]

Duray
  Historic Western B&B
  970-325-4645

Eaton
  Victorian Veranda B&B
  970-454-3890

Edwards
  Lodge At Cordillera
  800-548-2721

Eldora
  Goldminer Hotel
  800-422-4629

Empire
  Mad Creek B&B
  303-569-2003

  Peck House
  303-569-9870

Estes Park
  Anniversary Inn
  970-586-6200

  Aspen Lodge & Guest Ranch
  970-586-8133

  Baldpate Inn
  970-586-6151

  Big Horn Guest House
  800-734-0473

  Black Dog Inn
  970-586-0374

  Cottenwood House
  970-586-5104

  Eagle Cliff House
  970-586-5425

  Emerald Manor
  970-586-8050

  Inn At Rock'n River
  800-448-4611

  Riversong, A B&B Inn
  970-586-4666-[Y--]

  Sapphire Rose Inn
  970-586-6607

  Stanley Hotel
  800-ROCKIES-[Y--]

  Terraces
  970-586-9411

  Waneks Lodge At Estes
  970-586-5851-[Y--]

  Wind River Ranch
  970-586-4212

Evergreen
  Highland Haven
  800-459-2406

  Inn At Soda Creek
  303-670-3798

  Marshdale Lodge
  303-670-1205

Fairplay
  Hand Hotel B&B
  719-836-3595

Florissant
  Pinecrest Lodge
  719-687-3425

Fort Collins
  Edwards House B&B Inn
  970-493-9191

  Elizabeth Street Guest House
  970-493-BEDS-[Y--]

  Emerald Manor
  970-223-1396

  Helmshire Inn
  970-493-4683

  Shining Mountains Inn
  970-586-5886

  West Mulberry Street B&B
  970-221-1917

Fraser
  Karens B&B
  970-726-9398

Frisco
  Creekside Inn

  Frisco Lodge
  800-279-6000

  Galena Street

Bold Name - *Description appears in other section* **Colorado**

Mountain Inn
800-248-9138

Glena St Mountain Inn
970-668-3224

Lark B&B
970-668-5237

Mar Deis Mountain Retreat
970-668-5337

Twlight Inn
800-262-1002

Woods Inn Intl Lte
970-668-3389

Fruita
Valleyview B&B
970-858-9503

Garnby
Drowsey Water Ranch
303-725-3456

Georgetown
Hardy House
303-569-3388-[Y--]

Hillside House
303-569-0912

Glen Haven
Inn At Glen Haven
970-586-3897

Inn Of Glen Haven
970-586-3897

Glenwood Springs
Adduccis Inn
970-945-9341

Back In Time B&B
970-945-6183

Hideout
970-945-5621

Hotel Colorado
970-945-6511

Hotel Denver
970-945-6565

Kaiser House B&B
970-945-8827

Talbott House
970-945-1039

Gold Hill

Gold Hill Inn
303-443-6461

Golden
Antique Rose B&B
303-277-1893

Dove Inn
303-278-2209-[Y--]

Jameson Inn
303-278-2209

Royal Scot B&B Inn
303-526-2411

Table Mountain Inn
303-277-9898

Granby
Shadow Mountain Ranch
970-887-9524

Grand Junction
Cider House B&B
970-242-9087

Gatehouse
970-242-6105

Junction Country Inn
970-241-2817

Grand Lake
Hummingbird B&B
970-627-3417

Spirit Mountain Ranch
970-887-3551

Terrace Inn
970-627-3079

Winding River Resort
970-627-3215

Grandy
Circle H Lodge
303-887-3955

Grant
Tumbling River Ranch
303-838-5981

Green Mountain Falls
Columbine Inn
719-684-9062

Columbine Lodge
719-684-9062

Outlook Lodge
719-684-2303

Gunnison
Mary Lawrence Inn
970-641-3343-[G--]

Waunita Hot Springs Ranch
970-641-1266

Gypsum
7-W Guest Ranch
970-524-9328

Sweetwater Creek Ranch
970-524-9301

Hot Sulphur Springs
Riverside Hotel
970-725-9996

Hotchkiss
Ye Olde Oasis
970-872-3794

Hugo
Lincoln Manor
719-743-2173

Idaho Springs
Hansons Lodge At Idaho
303-567-9391

St Marys Glacier B&B
303-567-4084

Van Eden Ranch Inn
303-567-2566

Ignacio
Kelsalls Ute Creek Ranch
970-563-4464

Keystone
Keystone Resort Village
303-468-5251

Ski Tip Lodge
303-468-4202-[Y--]

La Veta
1899 Inn
719-742-3576

Lake City
Abobe B&B
970-944-2642

Cinnamon Inn
970-944-2641

Crystal Lodge
970-944-2201

Moncrief Mountain Ranch
970-944-2796

Moss Rose B&B
970-366-4069

Old Carson Inn
970-944-2511

Ryans Roost
970-944-2339

Leadville
Apple Blossom Inn
800-982-9279-[G--]

Delaware Hotel
800-748-2004

Ice Palace Inn & Antiques
719-486-8272

Leadville Country Inn
800-748-2354

Mountain Mansion Inn
719-486-0655

Wood Haven Manor B&B
800-748-2570

Limon
Midwest Country Inn
719-775-2373

Littleton
Huckleberry Inn

Loveland
Apple Avenue B&B
970-667-2665

Dale Sylvan Ranch
970-667-3915

Derby Hill Inn
970-667-3193-[--]

Lovelander B&B
970-669-0800

Sylvan Dale Ranch

The Lovelander
800-866-0621-[Y--]

Wild Lane B&B

©Inn & Travel Memphis, Tennessee

4-169

Colorado | **Bold Name** - *Description appears in other section*

970-669-0303

Lyons
  Peaceful Valley Lodge

  Rock n' River B&B
  800-448-4611

Mancos
  Lost Canyon Lake Lodge
  800-992-1098

Manitou Springs
  Billys Cottage
  719-685-1828

  Grays Avenue Hotel
  719-685-1277-[Y--]

  On A Ledge
  800-530-8253

  Peaceful Place B&B
  719-685-1248

  Prickly Pear Cottage
  719-685-5899

  Red Crags B&B
  719-685-1920

  Red Eagle Mountain B&B
  719-685-4541

  Red Stone Castle
  719-685-5070

  Spring Creek Inn
  719-685-0852

  Sunnymede B&B
  719-685-4619

  Two Sisters Inn
  719-685-9684

  Victorias Keep A B&B Inn
  800-905-KEEP

Marble
  Inn At Raspberry Ridge
  303-963-3025

Meeker
  Snow Goose B&B
  970-878-4532

Meredith
  Diamond J Guest Ranch
  970-927-3222

  Fryingpan River Ranch
  970-927-3570

Minturn
  Eagle River Inn
  800-344-1750-[Y--]

Monte Vista
  Monte Ville Inn

  Windmill
  719-852-0438

Montrose
  Fifth Street B&B
  970-249-4702

Morrison
  Cliff House Lodge
  303-697-9732-[Y--]

Mosca
  Dunes Country Inn
  719-378-2356

  Great Sand Dunes Inn
  719-378-2356

Nathrop
  Cleaveus Streamside B&B
  719-395-2553

  Inn At Chalk Cliffs
  719-395-6068

  Stream Side B&B
  719-395-2553

Northrup
  Centerville Inn
  970-539-4786

  Deer Valley Ranch
  970-395-2353

Norwood
  Back Narrows Inn
  303-327-4417

  Mug & Muffin B&B
  303-327-4707

Ohio City
  Gold Creek Inn

Olathe
  Uncompahgre Cabin
  970-323-6789

Ouray
  Bakers Manor
  970-325-4574

  Damn Yankee B&B
  800-845-7512

  House Of Yesterday
  970-325-4277

  Kunz House
  970-325-4220

  Manor B&B
  970-325-4574

  Ouray 1898 House
  970-838-4167

  Ouray Victorian Inn
  800-443-7361

  St Elmo Hotel
  970-325-4951-[G--]

  The Manor B&B
  970-325-4574

  Weisbaden Spa & Lodge
  970-325-4347

  Western Hotel
  970-325-4645

  Yellow Rose
  970-325-4175

Pagosa Springs
  Davidsons Country Inn
  970-264-5863

  Echo Manor
  970-264-5646

  Royal Pine Inn
  800-955-0274

Palisade
  Orchard House
  970-464-0529-[Y--]

Parshall
  Bar Lazy J Guest Ranch
  970-725-3437

Pine
  Meadow Creek B&B
  303-838-4167

Poncha Springs
  Jackson Hotel
  719-539-4861

Pueblo
  Abriendo Inn
  719-544-2703

  Park Royal B&B
  719-543-4414

  Storyteller Inn & Restaurant
  719-544-1025

Pueblo West
  Swallows Inn
  719-547-0439

Red Cliff
  Pilgrims Inn
  800-827-5333

Ridgway
  Chipeta Sun Lodge B&B
  800-633-5868

  San Juan Guest Ranch
  970-626-5360

Rifle
  Coulter Lake Guest Ranch
  970-625-1473

Salida
  Castillo de Caballeros
  719-539-2002-[Y--]

  Century House B&B
  719-539-7064

  Gazebo Country Inn
  719-539-7806

  Mount Elbert Lodge
  719-486-0594

  Ponderosa Lodge
  719-539-2730

  Poor Farm Country Inn
  800-373-4995

  Robins Nest B&B
  719-942-4176

  Thomas House Inn
  719-539-7104

  Victorian Manor
  719-539-4112

San Acacio
  Depot Inn
  719-672-3943

San Luis
  El Covento B&B

Bold Name - Description appears in other section **Colorado - Hawaii**

719-672-4223

Shawnee
North Fork Ranch
303-838-9873

Silver Plume
Brewery Inn
303-571-1151

Silverthorne
Alpen Hutte Lodge
970-468-6336

Mountain Vista B&B
970-468-7700

Silverton
Alma House
970-387-5336

Alpine House
970-387-5628

Christopher House B&B
970-387-5857

Fools Gold Inn
970-387-5879-[Y--]

Grand Imperial Hotel
970-387-5527

Smedleys B&B
970-387-5423

Teller Guest House
800-342-4338-[Y--]

Wingate House B&B
970-387-5423

Wyman Hotel
970-387-5372

Snowmass
Mountain Chalet
800-843-1579

Starry Pines
970-927-4202

Steamboat Springs
Bear Pole Ranch
970-879-0576

Country Inn Steamboat Springs
970-879-5767

Crawford House
970-879-1859

Harbor Hotel

970-543-8888

Inn At Steamboat
970-879-2600

Mariposa B&B Inn
970-879-1467

Ski Valley Lodge
970-879-7749-[Y--]

Steamboat B&B
970-879-5724

Steamboat Springs B&B
800-530-3866

Vista Verde Guest Ranch
800-526 RIDE

Steamboat Village
Scandinavian Lodge
303-879-0517

Sterling
Crest House
970-522-3753

Stoneham
Elk Echo Ranch Country B&B
970-753-2426

Stratton
Claremont Inn
719-348-5948

Telluride
Alpine Inn B&B
800-707-3344-[Y--]

Bear Creek B&B
800-338-7064

Cimarron Lodge
970-728-3803

Dahl Haus
970-728-4158-[Y--]

Johnstone Inn
800-628-4750

Manitou House
800-237-0753

New Sheridan Hotel
970-728-4351

Oak Street Inn
970-728-3383

Penningtons Mountain Village Inn
800-543-1437-[Y--]

San Sophia
800-537-4781-[G--]

Skyline Guest Ranch
970-728-3757

Victorian Inn
970-728-3684

Twin Lake
Twin Lakes Mountain Retreat
719-486-2593

Twin Lakes
Twin Lakes Accommodations
719-486-0228

Twin Lakes Nordic Lodge
719-486-1830

Vail
Black Bear Inn
970-478-1304

Christiana At Vail
800-476-5641

Columbine Chalet B&B
970-476-1122

Gasthor Gramshammer
970-476-5626

Mountain Weavery
970-476-5539

Sitzmark Lodge
970-476-5001

Wild Ridge Inn
970-949-6064

Vallecito Lake
Wit's End
303-884-4113

Victor
Kessey House
719-689-2235

Portland House
800-669-2102

Virginia Dale
Two Bars Seven Ranch
719-742-6072-[Y--]

Westcliffe
Purnells Rainbow B&B
719-783-2313

Rainbow Inn
719-689-2102

Westminster
Looking Glass Chalet
303-420-4123

Winter Park
Alpen Rose B&B
970-726-5039

Baeu West B&B
800-473-5145

Chalet Zirbisegger
970-726-5416

Englemann Pines B&B
800-992-9512

Gasthaus Eichier Hotel
970-726-5133

Gelmark B&B
800-424-2158

Millers Inn

Outpost Inn
970-726-5346

Quilted Bear B&B
970-726-5084

Something Special: A B&B
970-726-5360

Temples Anglemark B&B
970-726-5354

Woodspur Lodge
970-726-8417

Wolcott
Wolcott Inn
970-926-5463

Woodland Park
Hackman House B&B
719-687-9851

Inn At Trull Road
719-687-8209

Lofthouse

©*Inn & Travel Memphis, Tennessee* 4-171

719-687-9187

Pikes Peak Paradise
800-728-8282

Woodland Hills
Lodge
719-621-8386

Woodland Inn B&B
800-226-9565 [G--]

Yellow Jacket
Wilsons Pinto Bean
Farm
970-562-4476

HAWAII

Aiea, Oahu
Doris Epp-Reichert
800-999-6026

Oceanfront, Doris
Epp
800-999-6026-[Y--]

Pearl Harbor View
B&B
808-487-1228

Alea
Alohaland Guest
House
808-487-0482

Anahola
Anahola Beach Club
808-822-6966

Anahola, Kauai
Mahina Kai
808-822-9451

Big Island
Volocano Heart
Chalet
808-248-7725

Captain Cook
Adrienne B&B
800-328-9726

Manago Hotel
808-323-2642

Rainbow Plantation
800-494-2829

Samurai House
808-328-9210

South Point B&B
808-929-7466

Haiku Heulo Maui
Halfway To Hana
House
808-572-1176

Haiku Maui
Pilialoha B&B
Cottage
808-572-1440

Haiku, Maui
Haikuleana B&B
Inn Plantation
808-575-2890

Hamakualoa Tea
House

Hana, Maui
Hana Plantation
Houses
800-657-7723

Heavenly Hana Inn
808-248-8442

Hotel Hana-Maui
808-248-8211

Kaia Ranch & Co
808-248-7725

Hanalei, Kauai
B&B and Beach
808-826-6111

Hana Hideaway
808-826-9522

Orchid Hut
808-826-7298

Hawi
Aha Hui Hawaiian
808-889-5523

Hilo
Amy Lannas Liki
Kai
808-935-7865

Arnotts Lodge
808-969-7097

Hal Kai B&B
808-935-6330

Holmes Sweet
Holmes
808-961-9089

Maureens B&B
808-935-9018

Wild Ginger Inn
808-935-5556

Holualoa
Holualoa Inn
808-324-1121

Rosys Rest
800-988-2246

Honaunau
Dragonfly Ranch
800-487-2159

Lions Gate B&B
808-328-2335

Honokaa
Luana Ola B&B
Cottages
800-357-7727

Paauhau Plantation
B&B
808-775-7222

Waipio Treehouse
808-775-7160

Waipio Wayside
B&B
800-833-8849

Honolulu
**Aston Waikiki
Beach Side Hotel**
800-922-7866
[GQARITC]

B&B Manoa
808-988-6333

B&B Waikiki Beach
808-923-5459

Hale O Kahala
808-732-5889

John Guild Inn
800-634-5115

Kahala Hibiscus Inn
808-732-5889

Mango House
808-595-6682

Oceanfront, Doris
Epp
800-999-6026-[G--]

Honolulu, Oahu
Bevs & Monteys
B&B
808-422-9873

Hale Plumeria B&B
808-732-7719

Manoa Valley Inn
808-947-6019

Kailua, Kona
Adrienees Casa Del
Sol B&B
800-395-2272

Affordable Paradise
B&B
808-261-1693

Akamai B&B
800-642-5366

Hale Maluhia B&B
808-239-7248

Hale Pau Kala
808-261-3098

Pateys Place In
Paradise
808-326-7018

Sharons Serenity

Sheffield House
808-262-0721

Three Bears B&B
800-765-0480

Wild Orchid B&B
808-262-5015

Kailua, Oahau
**Papaya Paradise
B&B**
808-261-0316-[Y--]

Kailua, Oahu
Allis B&B
800-262-9545

Kalaheo
Black Bamboo Guest
House
808-332-7518

South Shore Vista
B&B
808-332-9339

Kalapana
Kaiani House Bt The
Sea
808-965-7828

Kalapana Shores
Hailua Plantation
House
808-965-8661

Hale Kipa O Kiana

Bold Name - *Description appears in other section*   Hawaii

808-965-8661

Kamuela
Kamuelas Mauna Kea View
808-885-8425

Mountain Meadow Ranch
800-535-9376

Walmer Gardens Cottage
800-262-9912

Kaneohe
5 Star B&B
808-235-8235

Kaneohe, Oahu
Emma's Guest Rooms
808-239-7248

Kapaa
Aleva House
808-822-4606

Alohilani B&B
808-823-0128

Hale O Wailele
800-775-2824

Keapana B&B
800-822-7968

Lampys B&B
808-822-0478

Mountain View Manor
808-822-0406

Paradise Inn
808-822-4104

Rosewood B&B
808-822-5216

Waonahele Kupono Farm
808-822-1515

Winters McNut Farm & Inn
808-822-3470

Kapaa, Kauai
Kauai Calls B&B
800-522-9699

Orchid Hut
800-578-2194

Kauai

Hale Aha Hospitality House
800-826-6733

Kay Barkers B&B
808-822-3073

Poipu Plantation
808-742-6757

Victoria Place
808-332-9300

Kaunakakai, Molokai
Kamalo Plantation
808-558-8236

Pau Hana Inn
808-966-4600

Keaau
Paradise Place
808-966-4600

Rainforest Retreat
808-966-7712

Kealakekua
Merrymans
800-545-4390

Reggies Tropical Hideaway
800-988-2246

Kihei, Maui
Ambrosia Inn
800-550-7212

Whale Watch House
808-879-0570

Whalers Way B&B
808-879-7984

What A Wonderful World B&B
808-879-9103

Kilauea
Mahi Ko Inn
800-458-3444

Kilavea, Kauai
Hale Ho'o Maha
800-851-0291

Kohala Coast
Bungalows Of Mauna Lani Bary
800-367-2323

Kola Kaui
Popipu Plantation
808-742-7038

Koloa
Kona Oceanfront Inn
800-552-0095

Kona
Kailua Plantation
808-329-3727-[G--]

Kukuihaele
Hamakua Hideaway
808-775-7425

Kula
Country Garden Cottage
808-878-2858

Kula Lodge
808-878-2517

Silver Cloud Ranch
808-878-6101

Kula Maui
Kula Cottage
808-871-6230

Kurtistown
B&B Mountain View
808-968-6868

Lahaina, Maui
Lahaina Hotel
800-669-3444-[Y--]

Old La Haina House
800-847-0761

Plantation Inn
800-433-6815

Lawai, Kauai
Victoria Place B&B
808-332-9300

Maui
Bloom Cottage
808-878-1425

Chaunce & Bettys B&B
808-572-2347

Maui Hana
Hala Ranch Tropical Garden
808-248-7725

Naalehu
Beckys B&B
800-235-1233

Nutt House
808-929-9940

Napli, Maui
Coconut Inn
800-367-8006

Ocean View
Bougainvillea B&B
800-688-1763

Paauilo
Suds Acres
800-735-3262

Pahala
Wood Valley B&B
800-854-6754

Pahoa
Ohia Inn
808-965-6212

Oloha B&B
808-965-9898

Pearls Shell B&B
808-965-7015

Village Inn Pahoa
808-965-6444

Pahoa, Kalapana
Kalani Honua By The Sea
808-965-7828

Papikou
Our Place Papaihouse
800-245-5250

Poipu, Kauai
Glorias Spouting Horn B&B
800-742-6995

Princeville Kauai
Hale 'Aha
800-826-6733

Volcano
Carsons Volcano Cottage
800-845-5282

Chalet Kilauea At Volcano
800-937-7786

Country Goose
800-238-7101

Edies Victorian Rose B&B
808-967-8026

Guest Houes At

©Inn & Travel Memphis, Tennessee   4-173

Hawaii - Idaho   **Bold Name -** *Description appears in other section*

Volcano
808-967-7775

Hale Kiauea
808-967-7216

Holo Holo Inn
808-967-8025

Lokahi Lodge B&B
800-457-6924

My Island B&B
808-967-7216

Volcano B&B
808-967-7779

Volcano Comfort B&B
808-967-7448

Volcano Village
Kilauea Lodge
808-967-7366

Waialua, Kauai
B&B Plantation House
808-637-4988

Fern Grotto Inn
808-822-2560

Wailuku
Banana Bungalo
808-244-6880

IDAHO

Ahsahka
Ahsahka Inn
208-476-9980

Albion
Mountain Manor
208-673-6642

Ashton
Jessens B&B
208-652-3356-[Y--]

Blackfoot
Pension Hermine
208-684-3857-[Y--]

Boise
Idaho Heritage Inn
208-342-8066-[Y--]

Idanha
208-334-6764

Mackay Bar Ranch

208-344-1881

Mendels Inn
208-344-7971

Robins Nest B&B
208-336-9551

Sunrise
208-345-5260

Victorias White House
208-362-0507

Bonners Ferry
Old Rose Inn
208-267-2117

Caldwell
Manning House B&B
208-459-7899

Cascade
Alpine Village

Wapiti Meadow Ranch
208-382-4336

Yellow Pine Lodge
208-382-4336

Coeur D'Alene
Andersons Country Cabin
208-667-2988

Baragar House B&B
208-664-9125

Berry Patch
208-765-4994

Blackwell House
208-664-0656

Coeur d'Alene B&B
208-667-7527

Cricket On The Hearth B&B
208-664-6926

Crystal Willow B&B
208-765-0891

Gables
208-664-5121

Greenbriar B&B Inn

208-667-9660

Gregory Mc Farland House
208-667-1232

Inn The First Place
208-667-3346

Katies Wild Rose Inn
208-756-9474

McFarland B&B
208-667-1232

Roosevelt Inn
208-765-5200

Sleeping Place Of The Wheels
208-765-3435-[Y--]

Warwick Inn
208-765-6565

Coolin
Old Northern Inn
208-443-2426

Council
Heartland Inn
208-253-6423

Driggs
High Country B&B
307-353-8560

Fairfield
Manard Hall B&B
208-764-2807

Fish Haven
Bear Lake B&B Inn
208-945-2688

Gooding
Gooding Hotel B&B
208-934-4374

Grangerville
Tulip House
208-983-1034

Hagerman
Cary House
208-837-4848

Haley
Comfort Inn
208-788-2477

Harrison

Maryannes On O'Gara Bay
208-689-3630

Pegs B&B Place
208-689-3525

Hayden Lake
Clark House
800-765-4593

Horseshoe Bend
Riverside B&B
208-793-2408

Idaho City
Idaho City Hotel
208-392-4290-[Y-]

Idaho Falls
Littletree Inn
208-523-5993

Indian Valley
Indian Valley Inn
208-256-4423

Irwin
McBrides B&B
208-483-4221

Swan Valley B&B
208-483-4663

Kamiah
Whitewater Ranch
208-935-2568

Kellogg
Montgomery Inn
800-SNOW FUN

Patricks Inn & Steakhouse
208-786-2311

Scotts Inn
208-786-8581

Silver Mountain Inn
208-786-2311

Sterling Silver B&B
208-783-4551

Ketchum
Aspen Inn

Busterback Ranch
208-774-2217

Heidleberg Inn
208-726-5361

Idaho Country Inn
208-726-1019

4-174   ©*Inn & Travel Memphis, Tennessee*

Bold Name - *Description appears in other section*   **Idaho - Montana**

Lift Haven Inn
208-726-5601

Pinncale Club
800-521-2515

Powderhorn Lodge
208-726-3107

River Street Inn
208-726-3611

Kooskia
Looking Glass Guest Ranch
208-926-0855

Three Rivers Resort
208-926-4430

Laclede
Mountain View B&B
208-265-5768

River Birch Farm
208-263-3705

Lava Hot Springs
Lava Hot Springs Inn
208-776-5830

Riverside Inn
800-733-5504

Royal Hotel B&B
208-776-5216

Lenore
Harpers Bend River Inn
208-486-6666

Lewiston
Carriage House B&B
208-746-4506

Dahmen Guest House
208-799-9020

Shiloh Rose B&B
208-743-2482

Snake River Getaway
208-746-2589

Lowman
Haven Lodge
208-259-3344

McCall
1920 House
208-634-4661

Hotel McCall Mountain Inn
208-634-8105

Northwest Passage B&B
208-634-5349-[Y--]

Meridian
Home Place
208-888-3857

Moscow
Beaus Butte
208-882-4061

Cottage House
208-882-0788

Peacock Hill
208-882-1423

The Cottage
208-882-0778

Twin Peaks Inn
208-882-3898

Van Buren House
208-882-8531

Mountain Home
Rosestone Inn
208-587-8866

Nampa
Marshall House
208-466-8884

Naples
Deep Creek Inn
208-267-2373

Norman
Grandview Lodge

Northfork
Cummings Lake Lodge
208-865-2424

Indian Creek Ranch
208-394-2126

Pinehurst
Hillcrest House
208-682-3911

Plummer
Bonnies B&B
208-686-1165

Owl Chalet
208-686-1597

Pocatello
Holmes Retreat
208-232-5518

Liberty B&B
208-232-3825

Mountain Retreat B&B
208-234-7114

Post Falls
Corbin Inn B&B
208-773-8225

Potlach
Rolling Hills B&B
208-668-1126

Riggins
The Lodge B&B
208-628-3863

Sagle
Pinewoods B&B
208-263-5851

Saint Anthony
Riverview B&B
208-624-4323

Saint Maries
Knoll Haus
208-245-4137

Salmon
Heritage Inn
208-756-3174

Salmon River Inn
208-756-3033

Sandpoint
Angel Of The Lake
208-263-0816-[Y--]

Osprey Cover B&B
208-265-4200

Page House B&B
208-263-6584

Priest Lake B&B

Whitaker House
208-263-0816

Shoshone
Governors Mansion
208-886-2858

Shoup
Smith House B&B
800-238-5915

Spirit Lake
Fireside Lodge
208-623-2871

Stanley
Idaho Rocky Mountain Ranch
208-774-3544

Redfish Lake Lodge
208-774-3536

Sawtooth Hotel
208-774-9947

Tensed
Seven Springs B&B
208-274-2470

Wallace
Beal House
208-752-7151

Jameson B&B
208-556-1554

Pine Street Inn
208-752-4391-[Y--]

Pine Tree Inn
208-354-2774

Weiser
Galloway Manison
208-549-2659

MONTANA

Absarokee
Magpies Net

Alberton
Hole In The Wall Lodge
406-523-6145

Petty Creek Inn
406-864-2111

Anaconda
Mountain View B&B
406-563-2618

Babb
Thornsons
406-732-5530

Two Sisters
406-732-5535

Wagners B&B
406-338-5770

Belfrade
Heart Mountain

©Inn & Travel Memphis, Tennessee

Montana *Bold Name* - Description appears in other section

B&B
406-587-2004

Big Fork
Gustin Orchard Farm
406-982-3329

Big Sandy
SkyView Ranch Resort B&B
406-378-2549

Big Sky
Lone Mountain Ranch
406-995-4644

Big Timber
Big Timber Inn
406-932-4080

Java Inn B&B
406-932-6595

Lazy K Bar Ranch
406-537-4404

The Grand
406-932-4459

The Grand
406-932-4459

Yellowstone River Ranch
406-932-6525

Bigfork
Averills Flathead Ranch

Bad Rock Country B&B
800-422-3666-[Y--]

Bigford Inn

Burgrafts Countrylane B&B
406-837-4608

Echo Lake Resort
406-837-5414

Odauchain Country Inn
406-837-6851-[Y--]

Our Point Of View
406-837-4742

Rainbows Inn
406-837-6665

Schwartz Family

406-837-5463

Swan Lake B&B
406-837-3600

The Harbor
406-837-5550

Billings
Feather Cove Inn
800-735-1695

Josephines B&B
406-248-5898

Sanderson Inn
406-656-3388

Blegrade
Rainbow Ranch Lodge B&B
406-995-4132

Boulder
Boulder Hot Springs
406-225-4339

Bozeman
Bear Canyon B&B
406-587-5482

Bergfeld B&B Home
406-586-7778

Crosscut Ranch

Fox Hollow B&B
800-431-5010

Lehrkind Mansion
406-586-1214

Sacajawea Inn
800-821-7326

Silver Forest Inn
406-586-1882

Sun House B&B
406-587-3651

Torch & Toes B&B
406-586-7285-[Y--]

Voss Inn B&B
406-587-0982

Bridger
Circle Of Friends B&B
406-662-3264

Butte
Copper King Mansion
406-782-7580

Raven Crest
406-782-1055

Cameron
Cliff Lake Lodge
406-682-4982

Cardwell
Hood Park Riverview Inn
406-287-3281

Choteau
Country Lane B&B
406-466-2816

Clyde Park
Gibson-Cassidy House
406-686-4743

Columbia Falls
Bad Rock Country B&B
800-422-3666-[Y--]

Canyon Bar, Cafe & Hotel
406-892-2131

Mountain Timbers Lodge
406-387-5830-[Y--]

Ol River Bridge Inn
406-892-2181

Plum Creek House
800-682-1429

Turn In The River
800-892-2472

Condon
Holland Lake Lodge
800-648-8859

Cooke City
Big Bear Lodge
406-838-2267

Coram
Glacier River Ranch B&B
406-387-4151

Coran
Heartwood
406-387-5541

Darby
Triple Creek Ranch
406-821-4664

DeBorgia

Hotel Albert
800-678-4303

Dillon
Hildreth Livestock Ranch
406-681-3111

Lansingburg Inn
406-683-5315

Dodson
Stage Road Inn
406-383-4410

Emigrant
Paradise Gateway
406-333-4063

Ennis
979 Ranch
406-682-7659

Essex
Izaak Walton Inn
406-888-5700

Eureka
Creek Side
406-296-2361

Grave Creek B&B
406-882-4658

Huckleberry Hannah's B&B
406-889-3381-[Y--]

Trails End B&B
406-889-3486

Fortine
Laughing Water Ranch
406-882-4680

Gallatin Gateway
Gallatin Gateway
800-626-4886

Gardiner
Yellowstone Country Inn
406-848-7000

Gold Creek
Lingenfelter Hansen Ranch B&B
406-288-3436

Great Falls
Chalet B&B Inn
406-452-9001

Gentrys Cozy House
800-786-9002

Bold Name - Description appears in other section   *Montana*

Murphys B&B
406-452-3598

Old Oak Inn
406-452-3598

Park Garden B&B
406-727-8127

Sarah B&B Inn
800-575-5906

Sovekammer Inn B&B
406-453-6620

Three Feathers Inn
406-453-5257

Three Pheasant Inn
406-453-0519

Hamilton
Bavarian Farm B&B
406-363-4063

Deer Crossing B&B
800-763-2232

Havre
House On The Prairie
406-394-2263

Helena
Barrister B&B
800-823-1148

Sanders-Helenas B&B
406-442-3309

Upcountry Inn
406-442-1909

Helmville
Sunset Guest Ranch
800-757-5574

Hilger
Van Haur Ranch

Hobson
Meadow Brook Farm B&B
406-423-5537

Hudson
Schoolhouse & Teacherage B&B
406-626-4879

Kalispell
Bad Rock Country B&B

800-422-3666-[G--]

Blaine Creek B&B
800-752-2519

Bonnies B&B
800-755-3778

Creston Country Willows B&B
800-257-7517

Huckleberry Hannah's B&B
406-889-3381-[Y--]

River Rock
800-477-0699

Stillwater Inn
800-398-7024

Switzer House Inn
800-257-5837

Lakeside
Shoreline Inn B&B
800-645-0255

Laurel
Riverside B&B
406-628-8185

Lewiston
Symes-Wicks House
406-259-7993

Libby
Bobtail B&B
406-293-3926

Livingston
Davis Creek B&B
406-333-4353

Greystone Inn
406-222-8319

Montana Ranch B&B
406-686-4946

Remember When B&B
406-222-8367

Marion
Rocky Meadow Ranch
406-854-2505

Missoula
Country Gallery B&B
406-728-1303

Goldsmith B&B
406-721-6732

Gracenote Garden
406-543-3480

Greenough B&B
406-728-3626

Nevada City
Nevada City Hotel
406-843-5377

Noxon
Bighorn Lodge
406-847-5597

Pary
Chico Hot Springs
800-HOT-WADA

Polaris
Grasshopper Inn
406-834-3456

Polson
Bayview B&B
406-883-6744

Borchers Of Finley Point
406-887-2500-[Y--]

Hammonds B&B
406-887-2766

Hawthorne House B&B
800-290-1345

Ruths B&B
406-883-2460

Swan Hill B&B
800-537-9489

Pompys Pillar
Byxbe Ranch

Red Lodge
Maxwells Mountain B&B
406-446-3052

Pitcher Guest House
406-446-2859

Warren James Inn
406-446-1431

Willows Inn
406-446-3913-[Y--]

Reedpoint
Fraser Ranch
406-932-4451

Rexford
Yoders B&B
406-889-3466

Ronan
Timbers B&B
800-775-4373

Saco
Big Dome Hotel B&B
406-527-3498

Saint Igantius
Mandorla Ranch B&B
800-TLC-MONT

Mission Mountains B&B
406-745-4331

Seeley Lake
Double Arrow Lodge
800-468-0777

Emily B&B
406-677-3474

The Emily, A B&B
406-677-3474

Sheridan
Kings Rest
406-842-5185-[Y--]

Somers
Osprey Inn
800-258-2042

Stevensville
Country Caboose
406-777-3145

Schoolhouse B&B
407-777-3904

Sula
Camp Creek Inn B&B
406-821-3508

Swan Lake
Stoney Creek Ranch Inn
406-886-2002

Three Forks
Madison River Inn
406-285-3914

Perren Park Inn
406-446-2859

Sacajawea Inn

Montana - Nevada **Bold Name** - *Description appears in other section*

800-821-7326-[Y--]

Townsend
Bedford Inn
406-266-3629

Hidden Hollow Hideaway
406-266-2322

Troy
Bull Lake Guest Ranch
406-295-4228

Turah
Colonial House, A B&B
800-251-6787

Valier
Pine Terrace B&B
800-446-6924

Vandalia
Double J B&B
406-385-2508

Victor
Duck Creek B&B
406-642-3073

Wildlife Outfitter Guest Ranch

Virginia City
Fairweather Inn

Just An Experience B&B
406-843-5402

Stonehouse Inn
406-843-5504

Virginia City Country Inn
406-843-5515

West Glacier
Glacier West Chalet
406-888-5507

Mountain Timbers Wilderness Lodge
800-841-3835

West Yellowstone
Rainbow Point Inn
406-646-7848

Sportsman's High
800-272-4227

Westby
Hilltop House

406-385-2508

White Sulpher Springs
The Columns
406-547-3666

White Sulphur Springs
Foxwood Inn
406-547-3918-[Y--]

Gillettes Elkhorn Lodge
405-547-2260

Montana Mountain Lodge
406-547-3773

Whitefish
Bad Rock Country B&B
800-422-3666-[Y--]

Castle B&B
406-862-1257

Crenshaw House
800-453-2863

Dancing Waters B&B

Duck Inn
406-862-DUCK-[Y--]

Eagles Roost B&B
406-862-5198

Edgewood B&B
406-862-9663

Garden Wall B&B
406-862-3440

Good Medicine Lodge
406-862-5488

Hampton House
406-862-0738

Hibernaton House
406-862-3511

Huckleberry Hannah's B&B-[Y-]
406-889-3381

LaVilla Montana
406-892-0689

Maples B&B
800-775-2862

Wise River
Sundance Lodge Montana

Wolf Creek
Bungalow B&B
406-235-4276

Wolf Point
Forsness Farm B&B
406-653-2492

NEVADA

Carson City
Deer Run Ranch B&B
702-882-3643

Elliot Chartz House
702-882-5323

Savage Mansion
702-847-0574

Winters Creek Ranch
702-849-1020-[Y--]

East Ely
Steptoe Valley Inn
702-289-8687

Eureka
Parsonage House
702-237-5756

Gardnerville
Nenzel Mansion B&B
702-782-7644

Reid Mansion
702-782-7644

Sierra Spirit Ranch
702-782-7011

Genoa
Genoa House Inn
702-782-7075

Orchard House
702-782-2640

Walleys Hot Springs
702-782-8255

Wildrose Inn
702-782-5697

Goldfield
Sundog B&B
702-485-3438

Imlay
Old Pioneer Garden
702-538-7585-[Y--]

Incline Village
Haus Bavaria
800-GO TAHOE

Lamoille
Breitenstein House
702-753-6351

Hotel Lamoille
702-753-6363

Michaels Ranch House
702-753-6356

Lamorlle
Pine Lodge
702-753-6363

Paradise Valley
Stone House Country Inn
702-578-3530

Reno
Deer Run Ranch B&B
702-882-3643

Lace & Linen
702-826-3547

Silver City
Hardwicke House
702-847-0215

Smith
Windybruch Ranch
702-465-2481

Sparks
Blue Fountain B&B
702-359-0359

McCarran House Inn
800-548-5798

Tahoe City
Cottage Inn At Lake Tahoe
916-581-4073-[Y--]

Tonopah
Mizapah Hotel

Truckee
Richardson House
916-587-7585

Virginia City
Chollar Mansion

4-178

©Inn & Travel Memphis, Tennessee

Bold Name - *Description appears in other section*   *Nevada - New Mexico*

702-847-9777

Edith Palmers Country Inn
702-847-0707-[Y--]

Gold Hill Hotel
702-847-0111

House On The Hill
702-847-0193

Winnemucca
Robins Nest
702-623-2410

Stauffer House
702-623-2350

Yerington
Harbor House
702-463-2991

Robric Ranch
702-463-3515

NEW MEXICO

Alamogordo
Cottonwood Inn
505-437-6761

Albuquerque
Adobe & Roses
505-898-0654

Adobe Garden Inn
505-345-1954

Bottger Mansion B&B
505-243-3639

Casa del Granjero
505-897-4144

Casas de Suenos
800-CHATW/US

Casita Chamisa B&B
505-897-4644-[Y--]

Corner House
505-295-5000

Enchanted Vista
505-823-1301

Hacienda Vargas B&B
505-867-9115-[Y--]

Heart Seed B&B Retreat Center &

Spa[G--]
505-471-7026-[G--]

Las Palomas Valley B&B
505-345-7228

Lightening Field
505-898-5602

My Ranchette
505-877-5140

Old Town B&B
505-764-9144

Sandcastle B&B
505-256-9462

Sarabande B&B
505-345-4923

The Inn At Paradise
505-898-6161-[G--]

We Mauger Inn
505-242-8755

Windmill Ranch
505-898-6864

WJ Marsh House
505-247-1001

Algodones
Hacienda Vargas B&B
505-867-9115
[YQAR-]

Alto
La Junta

Sierra Mesa Lodge
505-336-4515-[Y--]

Angel Fire
Monte Verde Ranch B&B
505-377-6928

Arroyo Hondo
New Buffalo B&B
505-776-2015

Arroyo Seco
Casa Colibri
505-776-2814

Aztec
Miss Gails Inn
505-334-3452

Bernalillo
La Hacienda Grande
505-867-1887

Carlsbad
La Casa Muneca B&B
505-887-1891

Cedar Crest
Elaines, A B&B
800-821-3092

Norma Gremore
505-281-3092

Chama
Jones House Inn
505-756-2908-[Y--]

Oso Ranch & Lodge Inn

Chimayo
Casa Escondida
800-643-7201

Hacienda Rancho de Chimayo
505-351-2222

La Posads de Chimayo
505-351-4605

Rancho de Chimayo
505-351-4444

Cimarron
Casa del Gavilan
800-445-5251

Cimarron House
505-376-2616

St James Hotel
505-376-2664

Cloudcroft
All Seasons B&B
505-682-2380

Lodge At Cloudcroft
800-842-4216-[Y--]

Columbus
Marthas Place
505-531-2467

Coolidge
Sauders Navajo Lodge

Corrales
Albuquerque-Yours Truly
505-898-7027

Casa la Resolana

800-884-0203

Chocolate Turtle B&B
800-898-1842

Corrales Inn B&B
505-897-4422

Sandhill Crane B&B
800-375-2445-[G--]

The Cottonwoods B&B
505-897-5086-[G--]

Costilla
Costilla B&B
505-586-1683

Deming
Spanish Stirrup Guest House
505-546-3165

Dixon
La Casita Guesthouse
505-579-4297

Eagles Nest
Laguna Vista Lodge
505-377-6522

El Prado
Blue Star Retreat
505-758-4634

Little Tree
800-334-8467

Salsa de Salto
800-530-3097

Elephant Butte
Elephant Butte Inn

Espanola
Casa del Rio
800-333-2267-[Y--]

La Pueblo House
505-753-3981

Farmington
Silver River Inn
505-325-8219

Galisteo
Galisteo Inn
505-982-1506

Glenwood
La Casita

Los Olmos Guest

©*Inn & Travel Memphis, Tennessee*   4-179

New Mexico *Bold Name - Description appears in other section*

Ranch
505-539-2311

Hillsboro
Enchanted Villa
505-895-5686

Jemez Springs
Dancing Bear B&B
505-829-3336

Jemez River Inn
505-829-3262

Kingston
Black Range Lodge
505-895-5652

Las Cruces
Elms
505-524-1513

Hilltop Hacienda
505-382-3556

Llewellyn House
505-526-3327-[Y--]

Lundeen Inn Of The Arts
505-526-3326

Las Vegas
Carriage House B&B
505-454-1784

Plaza Hotel
505-425-3591

Lincoln
Casa de Parton
505-653-4676

Wortley Hotel
505-653-4500

Los Alamos
Casa del Rey
505-672-9401

Los Alamos B&B
505-662-6041

Orange Street B&B
505-662-2651

Wilson House B&B
505-662-7490

Los Ojos
Casa de Martinez

Mescalero
Inn Of The Mountain Gods

Mesilla
Meson de Mesilla
505-525-9212

Nageezi
Chaco Inn At The Post
505-632-3646

Ojo Caliente
Inn At Ojo
505-583-2428

Portales
Harpers
505-356-3773

Morning Star Inn
505-356-2994

Ranchos De Taos
Adobe & Pines Inn
800-723-8267

Don Pascual Martinez B&B
505-758-7364

Ranchos Ritz B&B
505-758-2640

Two Pipe B&B
505-758-4770

Raton
Red Violet Inn
505-445-9778

Red River
Lodge At Red River

Ruidoso
Shadow Mountain Lodge
505-257-4886

Sierra Mesa Lodge
505-336-4515-[Y--]

Ruidoso Downs
La Prelle Place B&B
512-441-2204

San Antonio
Casa Blanca B&B
505-835-3027

San Juan Pueblo
Chinguague Compound
505-852-2194

Sandia Peak
Pine Cone Inn
505-281-1384

Santa Cruz
Santa Cruz Inn
505-753-8306

Santa Fe
Adobe Abode
505-983-3133-[YQAR-]

Adobe Guest House
505-983-9481

Alexanders Inn
505-986-1431-[Y--]

Arius Compound
800-735-8453

Camas de Santa Fe
505-984-1337

Canyon Road Casitas
800-279-0755-[G--]

Canyon Road Compound
505-982-8859

Casa de la Cuma B&B
505-983-1717

Dancing Ground Of The Sun
800-645-5673

Don Gaspar Lodge
505-986-8664

Dos Casas Viejas
505-983-1636-[Y--]

Dunshees
505-982-0988

El Farolito B&B
505-988-1631

El Paradero
505-988-1177

Four Kachinas Inn
800-397-2564

Grant Corner Inn
505-983-6678-[G--]

Guadalupe Inn
505-989-7422

Heart Seed B&B Retreat Center & Spa
505-471-7026-[G--]

Hotel St Francis
505-983-5700

Inn Of The Animal Tracks
505-988-1546-[Y--]

Inn Of The Turquoise Bear
800-396-4104-[--]

Inn Of The Victorian Bird
505-455-3375

Inn On The Alameda
505-984-2121-[Y--]

La Posada de Santa Fe
800-727-5276

Manzano House
505-983-2045

Pollys Guest House
505-983-9781

Preston House
505-982-3465-[Y--]

Pueblo Bonito
505-984-8001-[Y--]

Rancho Encantado
800-722-9339

Spencer House B&B Inn
505-988-3024

Sunset House
505-983-3523

Territorial Inn
505-989-7737

Water Street Inn
505-984-1193

Silver City
Bear Mountain Guest Ranch
505-538-2538

Carter House
505-388-5485

Hummingbird Inn
505-388-3606

Socorro
Eaton House
505-835-1067

4-180 ©Inn & Travel Memphis, Tennessee

Springer
  Brown B&B
  505-483-2269

Taos
  Adobe & Stars B&B
  800-211-7076

  American Artists
  Gallery House
  800-532-2041

  Amizette Inn
  505-776-2451

  Blue Door B&B
  505-758-8360

  Brooks Street Inn
  800-758-1489

  Casa Benavides
  505-758-1772

  Casa de las
  Chimeneas
  505-758-4777

  Casa de Milagros
  505-758-8001

  Casa Encantada
  505-758-7477

  Casa Europa
  505-758-9798

  Casa Feliz B&B
  505-758-9790

  Cassa Encantada
  800-223-TAOS

  El Monte Lodge

  El Rincon B&B
  505-758-4874-[Y--]

  **Hacienda del Sol
  B&B**
  505-758-0287
  [GQAR-]

  **Heart Seed B&B
  Retreat Center &
  Spa**
  505-471-7026-[G--]

  Historic Taos Inn
  800-TAOS INN

  Hotel La Fonda de
  Taos
  505-758-2211

  Inn On La Loma
  Place
  800-530-3040

  La Posada de Taos
  800-645-4803-[G--]

  Laughing Horse Inn
  505-758-8350

  Mabel Dodge B&B
  800-84-MABEL-[Y--]

  **Mountain Light
  B&B**
  505-776-8474-[Y--]

  Old Taos
  Guesthouse
  800-758-4448

  Orinda
  800-847-1837

  Ruby Slipper
  505-758-0613

  Sagebrush Inn
  800-428-3626

  San Geronimo
  Lodge
  800-828-TAOS

  Silvertree Inn
  505-758-3071

  Stagebrush Inn
  505-758-2254

  Stewart House B&B
  505-776-2913

  Taos Country Inn
  505-758-4900

  Taos Hacienda Inn
  505-758-1717

  Willows Inn-Taos
  505-758-2558

  Zia House
  505-751-0697

Taos Ski Valley
  Hotel Edelweiss
  505-776-2301

  Taos Mountain
  Lodge
  505-776-2229

Tome
  Pas Pamonas B&B
  505-864-0464

Truchas
  Rancho Arriba B&B
  505-689-2374

OREGON

Albany
  Brier Rose Inn
  503-926-0345

  Farm Mini Barn
  503-928-9089

Arch Cape
  St Bernards B&B
  503-436-2800

Ashland
  Adams Cottage
  800-345-2570

  Arden Forest Inn
  541-488-1496

  Ashberry Inn
  541-488-8000

  Ashland Colony Inn
  541-482-2668

  Ashland Guest Inn
  541-488-1508

  Ashland Knights Inn
  541-482-5111

  Ashland Valley Inn
  541-482-2641

  Ashland Victory
  House
  541-488-4428

  Ashlands Main
  Street Inn
  541-488-0969

  Auburn Street
  Cottage
  541-482-3004

  Bayberry Inn
  541-488-1252

  Buckhorn Springs
  541-488-2200

  Cadburys Cottage
  541-488-5970

  Cedarwood Inn
  541-488-2000

  Chanticleer Inn
  541-482-1919-[Y--]

  Coach House Inn
  541-482-2257

  Colonel Silsbys B&B
  541-488-3070

  Columbia Hotel
  541-482-3726

  Coolidge House
  541-482-4721

  Country Willows Inn
  800-945-5697

  Cowslips Belle
  541-488-2901-[Y--]

  Daniels Roost
  541-482-0121

  Drovers Inn
  541-482-6280

  Eagle Mill B&B
  541-488-4482

  Edinburg Lodge
  541-488-1050

  Faddens Inn
  541-488-0025

  Fox House Inn
  541-488-1055

  Hersey House B&B
  541-482-4563-[Y--]

  Highland Acres
  541-482-2170

  Hillside Inn
  541-482-2626

  Iris Inn
  800-460-7650

  Laurel Street Inn
  800-541-5485

  Lithia Rose Lodging
  541-482-1882

  Lithia Springs Inn
  800-482-7128

  Mainstreet Inn
  541-488-0696

  McCall House
  541-482-9296

  Morical House

Oregon *Bold Name* - *Description appears in other section*

541-482-2254

Mount Ashland B&B
800-830-8707-[--]

Mount Ashland Inn
541-482-8707

Neil Creek House
541-482-6443-[Y--]

Oak Hill Country B&B
541-482-1554

Oak Street Station B&B
541-482-1726

Parkside
541-482-2320

Pinehurst Inn At Jenny Creek
541-488-1002

Queen Anne
541-482-0220

Redwing B&B
541-482-1807

Romeo Inn
541-488-0884

Royal Carter House
541-482-5623

Shrews House
800-482-9214

Stone House
541-482-9233

Treons Country Homestay
541-482-0746

Waterside Inn
541-482-3315

Wimer Street Inn
541-488-2319

Winchester Country Inn
800-972-4991

Woods House
800-435-8260

Astoria
Astoria Inn
503-325-8153

Clementines B&B
503-325-2005

Franklin Street Station B&B
800-448-1098-[G--]

Grandview B&B
800-488-3250-[Y--]

Inn-Chanted B&B
503-325-5223

KCs Mansion By The Sea
503-325-6172

Rosebriar Inn B&B
503-375-7427

Baker City
Powder River B&B
541-523-7143

Bandon
Cliff Harbor Guest House
541-347-3956

Floras Lake House
541-347-9205

Lighthouse B&B
541-347-9316

Riverboat B&B
541-347-1922

Beaverton
Yankee Tinker B&B
800-TINKER2-[Y--]

Bend
Farewell Bend B&B
541-382-4374

Gazebo B&B
541-389-7202

Guest Cottage
541-382-9451

Heidi Haus
541-388-0850

House At Waters Edge
541-382-1266

Lara House B&B
541-388-4064

Mill Inn
541-389-9198

Mirror Pond House

541-389-1680-[Y--]

Three Sisters B&B
541-382-5884

Boring
Lariat Gardens B&B
503-663-1967

Brookings
Chetco River Inn
800-327-2688-[Y--]

Holmes Sea Cove B&B
541-469-3025

Oceancrest
541-469-9200

Sea Dreamer Inn
541-469-6629

Ward House B&B
541-469-5557

Brownsville
Kirks Ferry B&B
541-466-3214

Camp Sherman
House On The Metolius
541-595-6620

Metolius Inn
541-595-6445

Metolius River Lodges
541-595-6290

Cannon Beach
Stephanie Inn
503-436-2221

Tern Inn B&B
503-436-1528

Cascade Locks
Inn At The Locks
541-374-8222

Cave Junction
Oregon Caves Chateau
541-592-3400

Clackamas
Kippling Rock Farm
503-658-5056

Cloverdale
Hudson House
503-392-3533

Sandlake Country Inn
503-965-6745

Coburg
Wheelers B&B
503-344-1366-[Y--]

Coos Bay
Captains Quarters B&B
541-888-6895

Coos Bay Manor
541-269-1224

Old Tower House
541-888-6058

Talavar Inn
541-888-5280

This Olde House B&B
541-267-5224

Upper Room Chalet
541-269-5385

Coquille
Coquille B&B
541-396-5272

Corbett
Chamberlain House
503-695-2200

Corvallis
A Bed & Breakfast
541-757-7321

Bed & Breakfast At Sparks
541-757-7321

Chapman House B&B
541-758-3323

Hanson Country Inn
541-752-2919

Harrison House
541-752-6248

Hungtinton Manor
541-753-3735

Madison Inn B&B
541-757-1274

Cottage Grove
Ivanoffs Inn
541-942-3171

Bold Name - *Description appears in other section*   *Oregon*

Lea House Inn
541-942-0933

River Country Inn
541-942-9334

Crescent Lake
Odell Lake Lodge
541-433-2540

Creswell
Country House
541-895-3924

Dallas
Woodridge Haven
503-623-6924

Depoe
Gracies Landing Inn
800-228-0448

Depoe Bay
Channel House
800-447-2140-[Y--]

Pirates Cove B&B
541-765-2477

Elkton
Elkqua Lodge
541-584-2161

Elmira
Dome B&B
541-485-4495

McGillivrays Log Home B&B
541-935-3564

Enterprise
Loziers Country Loft
541-426-3271

Eugene
Aristeas Guest House
541-683-2062

Atherton Place
800-507-1354

B&Gs B&B
541-343-5739

Backroads B&B
541-485-0464

Campbell House, A City Inn
800-264-2519-[G--]

Campus Cottage B&B Inn
541-342-5346

Chambers House
541-686-4242

Country Lane
541-686-1967

Duckworth B&B
800-713-2451

Gables View Cottage
541-686-8422

Gettys Emerald Garden B&B
541-688-6344

House In The Woods
541-686-2026

Kjaers House In The Woods B&B
541-343-3234-[G--]

Lorane Valley B&B
541-686-0241-[Y--]

Lyon & The Lambe Inn
541-683-3160

Maryellens Guest House
541-342-7375

Morning Rose B&B
541-683-0605

Shellys Guest House
541-683-2062

Van Buren House
541-687-1074

Florence
Blue Heron Inn
541-997-4091

Johnson House
541-997-8000

Forest Grove
Main Street B&B
402-357-9812

Frenchglen
Frenchglen Hotel
541-493-2565

Gardiner
Guest House At Gardiner
541-271-4005

House At Gardiner By The Sea
541-271-4005

Garibaldi
Hilltop B&B
503-322-3221

Gates
Dragovich House
503-897-2157

Glide
Sportsmans Chalet
541-496-3978

Steelhead Run B&B
541-496-0562

Gold Beach
Bein Venue B&B
541-247-2335

Endicott Gardens
541-247-6513

Fair Winds B&B
541-247-6753-[Y--]

Heather House B&B
541-247-2074

Irelands Rustic Lodge
541-247-7718

Nesika Beach Inn
541-247-6434

Tu Tu Tun Lodge
541-247-6664

Grants Pass
Ahlf House B&B
541-474-1381

Chriswood Inn
541-474-9733

Clemens House B&B
800-344-2820

Handmaidens Inn
541-476-2932

Lawnridge House
541-476-8518-[Y--]

Marthas Inn
541-476-4330

Paradise Ranch Inn
541-479-4333

Pine Meadow Inn
800-554-0806-[Y--]

Sky Ranch Inn B&B
541-476-9038

Washington Inn
541-476-1131

Wilson House Inn
541-479-4754

Halfway
Birch Leaf Lodge
541-742-2990-[Y--]

Clear Creek Farm B&B
541-742-2238-[Y--]

Hammond
Hammond House
503-861-3454

Hood River
Barkheiner House & Estate
541-386-5918

Casa Baja
541-386-5462

Cascade Ave B&B
541-387-2377

Columbia Gorge Hotel
800-826-4027

Cottage
541-386-7747

Cottonwood B&B
541-386-1310

Datnoff Copple House
541-386-3686

Gorge View B&B
541-403-1199

Hackett House
541-386-1014

Inn At Gorge B&B
541-386-4429

Lakecliff Estate
541-386-7000

Nackett House
541-386-1014

PanoramaLodge
541-387-2687

State Street Inn
541-386-1899

©*Inn & Travel Memphis, Tennessee*

Oregon **Bold Name** - *Description appears in other section*

Stewarts Farm Inn
541-386-6343

Idleyld Park
Idlewyld Park Lodge
541-496-0132

Independence
Out Of The Blue
'B&B
503-838-3636

Ione
Woolery House B&B
541-422-7218

Jacksonville
Colonial House B&B
541-770-2783

Farmhouse B&B

Jacksonville Inn
800-321-9344

Livingston Mansion Inn
541-899-7107

McCully House Inn
541-899-1942-[Y--]

Meadow Lark B&B
541-899-8963

Old Stage Inn
800-US STAGE

Orth House B&B
541-899-8665

Reames House
541-899-8963

Touvelle House
800-846-8422-[Y--]

Joseph
Changlers Bed & Trail Inn
541-432-9765

Tamarack Pines Inn
541-432-2920

Wallowa Lake Lodge
541-432-4982

Junction City
Black Bart B&B
541-998-1904

Kerby
Kerby Ville Inn
541-592-4689

Kimberly
Lands End B&B
541-934-2333

Klamath Falls
Klamath Manor B&B
541-883-5459

Thompsons B&B By The Lake
541-882-7938

La Grande
Pitcher Inn
541-963-9152

La Grange
Stange Manor
541-963-2400

Lake Oswego
Gran-Mothers House
503-244-4361

LaPine
Big Blue House B&B
541-536-3879

Lebanon
Booth House B&B
541-256-2954

Lincoln City
Brey House Inn
503-994-7123

Enchanted Cottage
541-996-4101

Inlet Garden Oceanview B&B
541-994-7932

Rustic Inn
800-293-0414

Spyglass Inn B&B
541-994-2785

Youngs B&B
541-994-6575

Madras
Madras
541-475-2345

Manzanita
Arbors At Manzanita
503-368-7566

Manzanita Inn
503-368-6754

Maupin
Desert Rose B&B
503-395-2662

McMinnville
Baker Street B&B
503-472-5575

Mattey House B&B
503-434-5058

Orchard View Inn
503-472-0165

Steiger Haus B&B
503-472-0821

Youngberg Hill Farm B&B
503-472-2727

Medford
Nendels Inn
541-779-3141

Under The Greenwood Tree
541-776-0000

Waverly Cottage B&B
541-779-4716

Merlin
Morrisons Lodge
800-126-1953

Pine Meadow Inn
800-554-0806-[G--]

Milton-Freewater
Birch Tree Manor
541-938-6455

Monmouth
Hovey Manor
503-838-2085

Monroe
Valley Grand House
541-847-5523

Mosier
Cherry Hill Farm
541-478-4455

Mount Hood Parkdale
Falcons Crest Inn
800-624-7384

Pear Ridge B&B
503-352-6637

Myrtle Creek

Sonkas Sheep Station Inn
541-863-5168

Neskowin
Chelan
503-392-3270

Newberg
Hannahs House
503-538-4050

Littlefield House
503-538-9868

Owls View B&B
503-538-6498

Partridge Farm
503-538-2050

Secluded B&B
503-538-2635

Smith House
503-538-1995

Springbrook Hazelnut Farm
503-538-4606

Newport
Oar House
541-265-0571

Ocean House B&B
541-265-6158

Sea Cliff B&B
541-265-6664

Sylvia Beach Hotel
541-265-5428

North Bend
Baywood B&B
541-756-6348

Sherman House B&B
541-756-3496-[Y--]

Oakland
Pringle House
541-459-5038

Tollys Beckley House
541-459-9320

Oceanside
Sea Haven Inn
503-842-3151-[Y--]

Three Capes B&B
503-842-6126-[Y--]

4-184

©*Inn & Travel Memphis, Tennessee*

Bold Name - Description appears in other section **Oregon**

Oregon City
Fellows House
503-656-2089

Hydrangea B&B
503-650-4421

Inn Of The Oregon Trail
503-656-2089

Jagger House
503-657-7820

Tolle House
503-655-4325

Otis
Salmon River Lodge
541-994-2639

Oxbow
Hells Canyon B&B
541-785-3352

Pacific City
Pacific View B&B
541-965-6498-[Y--]

Pendleton
Grahams B&B
541-278-1743

Parker House BNB
800-700-8581

Swift Station Inn
541-276-3739

Port Orford
Gwendolyns B&B
541-332-4373

Home By The Sea
541-332-2855-[Y--]

Portland
Ainsworth B&B
503-227-6841

Bed & Rosees
503-254-3206

Cape Cod B&B
503-246-1839

Clinkerbrick House
503-281-2533

Eastmoreland B&B
503-775-7023

Garden House Inn
503-236-0794

Gedney Garden B&B
503-226-6514

General Hookers B&B
503-222-4435

Georgian House
503-281-2250

Gray Gables Inn
503-654-0470

Green Gables Guest House
503-287-1221

Hartmans Hearth B&B
503-281-2182

Heron House
503-274-1846

Historic Broetje House
503-659-8860

Holladay House
503-282-3172

Hostess House
503-284-7892

Irvington House
503-282-6409

J Palmer House
503-284-5893-[Y--]

John Palmer Inn
503-284-5893

Lion and The Rose
503-287-9245

Mac Master House
503-223-7362

Mumford Manor
503-243-2443

Old Portland Estate
503-236-6533

Peninsula Guest House
503-289-9141

Portland Guest House
503-282-1402

Portlands White House B&B
503-287-7131

Terwilliger Vista B&B
503-244-0602

Tudor House
503-287-9476

Victorian Rose
503-223-7673

Yankee Tinker B&B
800-TINKER2-[Y--]

Prairie City
Riverside School House
541-820-4731

Prineville
Baldwin Inn B&B
541-447-5758

Elliott House
541-447-7442

Prospect
Prospect Historical Hotel
541-560-3664

Redmond
Dolliver House B&B
541-548-1606

Last Camp Llamas
541-548-6828

Roseburg
Hokansons Guest House
541-672-2632

House Of Hunter
541-672-2335

Umpqua House
541-459-4700

Woods B&B
541-672-2927

Saint Helens
Hopkins House
503-397-4676

Salem
Cottonwood Cottage B&B
503-362-3979

Cumberland Cottage
503-585-5201

Hampshire House
503-370-7181

Harbison House
503-581-8818

Marquee House
503-391-0837

State House B&B
503-588-1340-[Y--]

Sandy
Augerge des Fleurs
503-663-9449

Fernwood At Alder Creek
503-622-3570

Whispering Firs
503-668-4283

Scappoose
Marlarkey Ranch Inn
503-543-5244

Scio
Wesley House B&B
503-394-3210

Seal Rock
Blackberry Inn B&B
541-563-2259-[Y--]

Seaside
Baileys Bide A Wee Bed
503-738-3711

Beachwood B&B
503-738-9585

Boarding House
503-738-9055

Castons Beachside B&B
503-738-8320

Chocolates For Breakfast
503-738-3622

Custer House B&B
503-738-7825

Gilbert House
503-738-9770

Riverside Inn B&B
503-738-8254

Sand Dollar B&B
503-738-3491

Seaside Inn

©*Inn & Travel Memphis, Tennessee* 4-185

Oregon - Utah   **Bold Name** - *Description appears in other section*

503-738-3238

Summer House
800-745-2378

Tita Mase Great B&B
503-738-8800

Victoria B&B
503-738-8449

Walker House
503-738-5520

Shaniko
  Shaniko Historic Hotel
  541-489-3441

Sheridan
  Sheridan Country Inn
  503-843-3226

Silverton
  Silverton B&B
  503-873-7824

Sisters
  Cascade Country Inn
  800-316-0089

  Conklin Guest House
  541-549-0123

  Lake Creek Lodge
  541-595-6331

Sixes
  Sixes River Hotel
  503-332-3900

Spray
  Pioneer B&B
  541-462-3934

Stayton
  Gardner House
  503-769-5478

  Horncroft
  503-769-6287

Steamboat
  Steamboat Inn
  541-496-3495

The Dalles
  Bigelow
  541-298-8239

  Boarding House Inn
  541-296-5299

  Captain Grays House
  541-298-8222

  Columbia Windrider Inn
  541-296-2607

  Heimrich-Seufert House
  541-296-1012

  Williams House Inn
  541-296-2889-[Y--]

Tillamook
  Blue Haven Inn
  503-842-2265-[Y--]

  Whiskey Creek B&B
  503-842-2408

Troutdale
  McMenamins Edgefield
  503-669-8610

Tualatin
  Stafford Road Country Inn
  503-638-0402

Vida
  McKenzie River Inn
  541-822-6260

Waldport
  Cliff House
  541-563-2506

  Colleens Country B&B
  541-563-2301

Walterville
  Marion B&B
  541-896-3145

Welches
  Mountain Shadows B&B
  503-622-4746

  Old Welches Inn
  503-622-3754

West Linn
  Walden House B&B
  503-655-4960

Westfir
  Westfir Lodge
  541-782-3103

Westport

  King Salmon Lodge

Wheeler
  View Of West Country B&B
  503-368-5766

Wilsonville
  Willows B&B
  503-638-3722

Wolf Creek
  Wolf Creek Tavern
  541-866-2474

Woodburn
  Carriage House
  503-982-1543

Yachats
  Adobe
  541-547-3141

  Amaroo Inn
  541-547-3639

  Birds Nest Inn
  541-547-3683

  Kittiwake B&B
  541-547-4470

  Old Haggerty House
  541-547-4444

  Oregon House
  541-547-3329

  Sanderling B&B
  541-563-4752

  Sea Quest
  800-341-4878-[Y--]

  Serenity B&B
  541-547-3813

  Ziggurat
  541-547-3925

Yamhill
  Flying M Ranch
  503-662-3222

UTAH

Blanding
  Old Hotel B&B
  801-678-2388

Bluff
  Bluff B&B
  801-672-2220

  Calabre B&B
  801-672-2252

  Recapture Lodge
  801-672-2281

Boulder
  Boulder Pines
  801-335-7375

Cedar City
  Bards Inn
  801-586-6612

  Meadau View Lodge
  801-682-2495

  Paxmans Summer House
  801-586-3755

  Willow Glen Inn
  801-586-3275

  Woodbury Guest House
  801-586-6696

Duck Creek Village
  Meadeu View Lodge
  801-682-2495

Eden
  Snowberry Inn
  801-745-2634

Ephraim
  Ephraim Homestead B&B
  801-283-6367

  Pherson House B&B
  801-283-4197

Escalante
  Rainbow Country Tours & B&B
  800-252-UTAH

Fillmore
  Suite Dreams
  801-743-6622

Garden City
  Inn Of The Three Bears
  801-946-8590

Glendale
  Homeplace
  801-648-2194

  Smith Hotel
  801-648-2156

Hatch

Bold Name - Description appears in other section **Utah**

Calico House B&B
801-735-4382

Heber City
Cottage B&B
801-654-2236

Helper
Kenilworth Inn
801-472-3221

Henefer
Deardon B&B
801-336-5698

Huntsville
Jackson Fork Inn
800-255-0672

Trappers Inn

Hurricane
Pah Tempe Hot Springs B&B
801-635-2879

Kamas
Patricia's Country Manor
800-658-0643

Kanab
Judd House B&B
801-644-2936

Miss Sophies B&B
801-644-5952

Nine Gables Inn
801-644-5079

La Verkin
Zion Overlook B&B
801-877-1061

Liberty
Vue de Valhalla B&B
801-745-2558

Loa
Road Creek Inn B&B
800-38-TROUT

Logan
Birch Trees B&B Inn
801-753-1331

Boulevard B&B
801-753-6663

Center Street B&B
801-752-3443-[Y--]

Logan House Inn
801-752-7727

Manti
Brigham House Inn
801-835-8381

Heritage House
801-825-5050

Manti House Inn
801-835-0161

Manti Old Grist Mill Inn
801-835-6455

Yardley B&B Inn
800-858-6634

Midway
Inn On The Creek
801-654-0892

Luke House At Mountain Spa Resort
801-654-0807

Schneitter Hotel B&B
800-327-7220

Moab
Canyon Country B&B
800-635-1792

Castle Valley Inn
801-259-6012-[Y--]

Desert Chalet
801-259-5793

Moab Guest House
801-259-4457

Pack Creek Ranch
801-259-5505

Ron Tez Guest House
800-232-7247

Rose Tree B&B
801-259-6015

Sandis B&B
801-259-6359

Slickrock Inn
801-259-2266

Sunflower Hill B&B Inn
801-259-2974

Westwood

Guesthouse
800-526-5690

Monroe
Petersons B&B
801-527-4830

Monticello
Grist Mill Inn
800-645-3762

Mount Pleasant
Mansion House B&B
801-462-3031

Nephi
Whitemore Mansion
801-623-2047

Oakley
Graystone Lodge & Guest House
800-675-9379

Ogden
25th & Jefferson B&B
801-381-3545

Rogers Rest B&B
801-393-5824

Park City
1904 Imperial Hotel
800-669-8824

505 Woodside B&B Inn
801-649-4841-[Y--]

Alpine Prospectors Lodge
801-649-9975

Blue Church Lodge
801-649-8009

Goldener HirschInn
801-649-7770

Imperial Hotel
801-649-1904

Old Miners' Lodge
800-648-8068-[G--]

Old Town Guest House
801-649-2642-[Y--]

Owls Roost
801-649-6983

Snowed Inn
800-545-SNOW-[Y--]

Washington School Inn
800-824-1672-[Y--]

Providence
Providence Inn
801-752-3432

Provo
Sundance
801-225-4100

Rockville
Blue House B&B
801-772-3867

Handcart House
801-772-3867

Saint George
An Olde Penny Farthing Inn
800-673-7522

Aunt Annies Inn
801-673-5504

Diamond Valley Guest Ranch
801-574-2281

Greene Gate Village
800-350-6999

Morris Mulberry Inn
800-915-7070

Penny Farthing Inn
801-673-7755

Seven Wives Inn
800-484-1084

Salina
Victorian Inn
801-529-7342

Salt Lake City
Anniversary Inn
801-363-4900

Anton Boxrud B&B
800-524-5511

Armstrong Mansion Inn
801-631-1333

Brigham Street Inn
801-364-4461

Daves Cozy Cabin B&B
801-278-6136

©Inn & Travel Memphis, Tennessee

Utah - Washington   **Bold Name** - *Description appears in other section*

Grandmothers House
801-943-0909

Log Cabin On The Hill
801-942-1435

National Historic B&B
801-485-3535

Old Miners' Lodge
800-648-8068-[Y--]

Pinecrest B&B Inn
800-359-6663

Saltair B&B
800-533-8184-[Y--]

Spruces B&B
800-820-8762

Tea Pot Inn
801-362-4211

Westminster B&B
801-467-4114

Wildflowers
800-569-0009

Sandy
 Mountain Hollow B&B
 801-942-3428-[Y--]

 Quail Hills B&B
 801-942-2858

Spanish Fork
 Escalante B&B
 801-798-6652

Spring City
 Horseshoe Mountain Inn
 801-462-2871

Springdale
 Bumbleberry Inn
 801-772-3224

 Harvest House
 801-772-3880

 O Tooles Under The Eaves
 801-772-3457

 Under The Eaves Guest House
 801-772-3457

 Zion House B&B

 801-772-3281-[Y--]

Sterling
 Cedar Crest B&B
 801-835-6352

Teasdale
 Cockscomb Inn
 801-425-3511

Toquerville
 Your Inn Toquerville
 801-635-9964

Torrey
 Sky Ridge
 801-425-3223

Tropic
 Bryce Point B&B
 801-679-8629

 Francisco B&B
 801-679-8721

Vernal
 Seeleys B&B
 801-789-0933

Virgin
 Zions Blue Star B&B
 801-635-3830

WASHINGTON

Acme
 River Valley B&B
 360-595-2686

Anacortes
 Admirals Hideaway B&B Inn
 360-293-0106

 Albatross B&B
 800-622-8864-[G--]

 Blue Rose B&B
 360-293-5175

 Burrows Bay B&B
 360-293-4792

 Campbell House
 360-293-4910

 Channel House
 800-238-4353-[Y--]

 Dutch Treat House
 360-293-8154

 Hasty Pudding House

 800-368-5588

 Lowman House B&B
 360-293-0590

 Nantucket Inn
 360-293-6007

 Old Brook Inn
 360-293-4768

 Outlook B&B
 360-293-3505

 Sunset Beach B&B
 360-293-5428

Anderson Island
 Inn At Burgs Landing
 206-884-9185

Ashford
 Alexanders Country Inn
 800-654-7615

 Ashford Mansion
 360-569-2739

 Growly Bear
 360-569-2339

 Jasmers Guest House & Cabins
 360-569-2682

 Lodge Near Mount Ranier
 360-569-2312

 Mountain Meadows Inn
 360-569-2788

 Mountain Village Inn
 360-569-2312

 Paradise Inn
 360-569-2275

 Wild Berry Inn

Auburn
 Blomeen House B&B
 206-939-3088

Bainbridge
 Agate Pass Waterfront B&B
 206-842-1632

 Mariths Place B&B

 206-842-1427

 Our Country Haus
 206-842-4941

 Waterfront B&B
 206-842-2431

 Woodsman
 206-842-7026

Bainbridge Island
 Bainbridge House B&B
 206-842-1599

 Bainbridge Inn
 800-347-7564

 Beach Cottage
 206-842-6081

 Bombay House
 800-598-3926

 Captains House
 206-842-3926

 Marys Farmhouse B&B
 206-842-4952

 Our Guest House
 206-842-4941

 Rose Cottage
 206-842-6248

 West Blakely Inn
 206-842-1427

Beaver
 Eagle Point Inn
 360-327-3236

Bellevue
 Bellevue B&B
 206-453-1048

 Bridle Trails B&B
 206-861-0700

 Lions B&B
 206-455-1018

 Petersen B&B
 206-454-9334

Bellingham
 Anderson Creek Lodge
 360-966-2126

 Big Trees B&B
 206-547-2850

4-188   ©*Inn & Travel Memphis, Tennessee*

Bold Name - Description appears in other section   **Washington**

Castle B&B
800-922-6414

Circle F B&B
360-733-2509

De Cann House B&B
360-734-9172

North Garden Inn
800-922-6414

Schnauzer Crossing
360-733-0055

Secret Garden
360-671-5327

Springcrest Farm B&B
360-966-7272

Sunrise Bay B&B
360-647-0376

Benton City
  Palmer Farm B&B
  509-588-3701

Bingen
  Grand Old House
  509-493-2838

Bow
  Alice Bay B&B
  360-766-6396

  Benson Farmstead
  360-757-0578

  Chuckanut Manor B&B
  360-766-6191

Bremerton
  Wilcox House
  360-830-4492

Camano Island
  Salal Hill B&B
  360-387-3763

  Wilcon House B&B
  360-629-4746

Carnation
  Idyl Inn On The River
  206-333-4262

Carson
  Carson Hot Springs
  509-427-8292

Cashmere
  Cashmere Country Inn
  509-782-4212

  Grandview Orchard Inn
  509-782-2340

  Warm Hearth B&B
  509-782-1553

Cathlamet
  Cathlamet Hotel
  800-446-0454

  Country Keeper B&B
  800-551-1691

  Gallery B&B At Little Cape Horn
  360-425-7395

  Redfern Farm
  360-849-4108

Centralia
  Candalite Mansion
  360-736-4749

Chehalis
  Whispering River B&B
  360-262-9859

Chelan
  Brick House Inn
  509-682-4791

  EM B&B Inn
  509-682-4149

  Highland Guest House
  509-682-2892

  Mary Kays Whaley Mansion
  800-729-2408

  North Cascades Lodge
  509-682-4711

Chimacum
  Summer House
  360-732-4017

Clarkston
  Highland House
  509-758-3126

Clinton
  Beach House
  360-321-4335

  Bs Getaway
  360-321-4721

  Home By The Sea B&B
  360-221-2964-[Y--]

  Kittleson Cove
  360-221-2734

  Lovely Cottage
  360-321-6592

  Room With A View
  360-321-6264

Colfax
  Tulin House
  509-397-3312

Concrete Birdsview
  800-826-0015

Conway
  South Fork Moorage
  360-445-4803

Cougar
  Montforts B&B
  360-238-5229

Coulee City
  Main Stay
  509-632-5687

Coulee Dam
  Four Windows Guest House
  800-786-3146

Coupeville
  Anchorage Inn
  360-678-5581

  Captain Whidbey Inn
  800-366-4097

  Col Crockett Farm B&B
  360-466-3207

  Compass Rose B&B
  800-237-3881

  Coupeville Inn
  360-678-6668

  Fort Casey Inn
  360-678-8792

  Inn At Penn Cove
  800-688-COVE-[Y--]

  Victorian House
  360-678-5305

Cusich
  River Bend Inn
  509-445-1476

Darrington
  Hemlock Hills B&B
  360-436-1274

  Sauk River Farm B&B
  360-436-1794

Davenport
  Victorian Christman House
  509-725-0308

Dayton
  Baker House B&B
  509-382-4764

  Carriage House
  509-382-4568

  Chez Nous
  509-382-2711

  Purple House
  509-382-3159

Deer Harbor
  Palmers Chart House
  360-376-4231

Deer Park
  Loves B&B
  509-276-6939

Deming
  Guest House B&B
  360-592-2343

Eastsound
  Blue Heron
  360-376-2954

  Gibsons North Beach Inn
  360-376-2660

  Kangaroo House
  360-376-2175

  Outlook Inn On Orcas Island
  800-767-9506-[Y--]

  Rosario Resort Hotel
  360-376-2222

  Turtleback Farm Inn
  360-376-4914

  Whale Watch House
  360-376-4793

©Inn & Travel Memphis, Tennessee

Washington

Bold Name - Description appears in other section

Eatonville
Old Mill House B&B
360-832-6506

Edmonds
Aardvark House
206-778-7868

Dayton B&B
206-778-3611

Driftwood Lane B&B
206-776-2686

Harrison House
206-776-4748

Heather House
206-778-7233

Hudgens Haven
206-776-2202

Maple Tree
206-774-8420

Ellensburg
Murhphs Country B&B
509-925-7986

Surrey House B&B
509-962-5425

Enumclaw
Homestead B&B
360-825-6381

Stillmeadow B&B
360-825-6381

Everett
Katmai Lodge
206-337-0326

Ridgeway House B&B

Everson
Applewood Farm B&B
360-966-5183

Wilkins Farm B&B
360-966-7616

Ferndale
Anderson House B&B
360-384-3450

Hill Top B&B
360-384-3619-[Y--]

Larson Dairy
360-733-8642

Mountain View B&B
360-384-3693

Sager B&B
360-733-8642

Slater Heritage House B&B
360-384-4273

Forks
Manitou Lodge B&B
800-374-0483

Miller Tree Inn
360-374-6806

Misty Valley Inn
360-374-9389

River Inn
360-374-6526

Shadynook Cottage
360-374-5497

Shirleys Rain Country Inn
360-374-5073

Freeland
Bush Point Wharf B&B
360-321-0405

Cliff House
360-321-1566

Pillars By The Sea
360-221-7738

Uncle Johns Cottage
360-321-5623

Whidbey Westside Lodgings
800-772-7055

Friday Harbor
Blair House B&B
360-378-5907

Duffy House
360-378-5604

Farmhouse
360-378-3463

Fridays
360-378-5848

Hillside House B&B
800-232-4730-[Y--]

Mariella Inn & Cottages
360-378-6868

Meadows
360-378-4004

Moon & Six Pence
360-378-4138

Olympic Lights
360-378-3186

San Juan Inn
360-378-2070

States Inn
360-378-6240

Tower House
360-378-5464

Trumpeter Inn
360-378-3884

Tucker House B&B
360-378-2783

Westwinds B&B
360-378-5283

Wharfside B&B-Aboard Jacquelyn
360-378-5661

Gig Harbor
Davenport Hotel B&B
206-851-8527

Hillside Gardens B&B
206-851-3965

Johnsons Scandinavian B&B
206-265-2247

No Cabbages B&B

Olaila Orchard B&B
206-857-5915

Olde Glencove Hotel
206-884-2835

Parsonage
206-851-8654

Pillars B&B
206-851-6644

Tall Ship Krestine
206-858-9359

Glenwood
Flying L Guest Ranch
509-364-3488

Gold Bar
Bush House
206-363-1244

Goldendale
Three Creeks Lodge
509-773-4026

Goose Prairie
Hopkinson House B&B
509-454-9431

Granger
Rinehold Cannery Homestead
509-854-2508

Greenbank
Guest House B&B
360-678-3115

Smugglers Cove Haven
360-678-7100

Hamilton
Smith House B&B
360-826-4214

Harrington
Harrington Inn
509-253-4728

Hoquaim
Lytle House B&B
360-533-2320

Ilwacoq
Inn At Ilwaco
360-642-8686

Kola House B&B
360-642-2819

Index
Bush House
360-466-3366

Indianola
Indianiola B&B
360-297-2382

Issaquah
Mountains & Planes B&B
206-557-9335

Wildflower
206-392-1196

Bold Name - *Description appears in other section*   Washington

Kalaloch
Kalaloch Lodge
503-489-3441

Kalama
Blackberry Hill B&B
360-673-2159

Kettle Falls
My Parents Estate B&B
509-738-6220

Kirkland
Shumway Mansion
206-823-2303-[G--]

La Conner
Country Cottage Inn
509-548-4591

Downey House
360-466-3207

Heather House
360-466-4675

Heron Inn La Conner
360-466-4626

Hotel Planter
360-466-4710

Kathys Inn
360-466-3366

La Conner Country Inn
360-466-3101

Rainbow Inn
360-466-4578

Ridgeway B&B
360-428-8068

Wild Iris
360-466-1400

Lake Stevens
Lake Shores Peony House
206-334-1046

Landley
Inn At Langley
360-221-3033

Langley
Blue House Inn
360-221-8392

Carolines Country Cottage
360-221-8709

Chirstys Country Inn
360-321-1815

Eagles Nest Inn
360-321-5331

Edgecliff Cottage
360-221-8857

Gallery Suite
360-221-2978

Garden Path Inn
360-221-5121

Grampa Arts Place
360-321-1838

Log Castle
360-221-5483-[Y--]

Lone Lake Cottage
360-321-5325

Maple Tree Guest House
360-221-2434

Orchard
360-221-7880

Primrose Path Cottage
360-221-3722

Saratoga Inn
360-221-7526

Strawbridge Inn
360-221-7115

The Courtyard
360-321-5331

The Pine Cottage
360-321-1376

Thickenham House
800-874-5009

Whidbey House
360-221-7115

Leavenworth
All Seasons River Inn
800-254-0555

Bavarian Meadows B&B
509-548-4449

Bosch Garden
509-548-6900

Browns Farm
509-548-7863

Canyons Inn
509-548-7130

Der Sportsman Pension
509-763-5623

Edle Haus Pension
509-548-4412

Haus Lorelei Inn
509-548-5726

Haus Rohrbach Pension
509-549-7024

Heaven Cant Wait Lodge
206-881-5350

Hotel Europa
509-548-5221

Hotel Pension Anna
509-548-6273

Leavenworth Village Inn
800-253-8900

Leirvangen B&B
509-548-5165

Morgans Serendipity
509-548-7722

Mountain Home Lodge
509-548-7077

Mrs Andersons Lodging House
800-253-8990

Old Brick Silo B&B
509-548-4772

Pension Diane
509-548-9382

Phippens B&B
800-666-9806

Pine River Ranch
509-763-3959

Run Of The River B&B
800-288-6491

Tabak B&B
509-548-4390

Wards Haus
509-548-7853

Long Beach
Edgewood Inn
800-460-7196-[--]

Lands End B&B
360-642-8268

Our Place At The Beach
360-642-3793

Scandinavian Gardens Inn
360-642-8877

Longmire
National Park Inn
360-569-2565

Longview
The Mansion
360-636-5611

Lopez Island
Aleck Bay Inn
360-468-3535

Edenwild Inn
360-468-3238

Inn At Swifts Bay
360-468-3636

Mackaye Harbor
360-468-2253

Mareans Blue Fjord Cabins
360-468-2749

Village Guest House
360-468-2191

Lummi Island
Deer Creek Farm
360-758-2678

Loganita, A Villa By The Sea
360-758-2651

Otters Nest B&B
360-758-2667

Shorebird House
360-758-2177

West Shore Farm B&B
360-758-2600-[Y--]

Willows Inn

©Inn & Travel Memphis, Tennessee

4-191

Washington *Bold Name - Description appears in other section*

360-758-2620

Lynden
Century House
360-354-2439

Le Cocq House
360-354-3032

Staps B&B
360-354-2609

Manson
Hubbard House B&B
509-687-3058

Maple Falls
Country Hill B&B
206-599-2407

Thurston House B&B
206-599-2261

Yoedler Inn
800-642-9033

Maple Valley
Maple Valley B&B
206-432-1409

Mazawa
Mazawa Country Inn
509-996-2681

Mercer Island
Duck-in B&B
206-232-2554

Fayes B&B
206-232-2345

Mercer Island Hideaway
206-232-1092

Montesano
Abel House B&B
800-235-ABEL

Sylvan House
360-249-3453

Mount Vernon
Hill Crest House
206-336-6810

Whispering Firs
360-428-1990

White Swan Guest House
360-445-6805

Moxee
Desert Rose B&B
509-452-2237

Naches
Hopkinson House
509-575-0417

Nahcotta
Anatalias On The Bay
360-665-6838

Moby Dick Hotel B&B
360-665-4543

Our House In Nahcotta
360-665-6667

Newport
Burroughs House B&B
509-447-2590

Nordland
Ecologic Place
360-385-3077

North Bend
Apple Tree Inn
360-888-3572

Inn New England
360-888-3879

Oak Harbor
Ann Starrett Mansion
800-321-0644-Y--]

Earth Shelter
360-398-2030

Elfreedas Place
360-675-3379

Harbor Pointe B&B
360-675-3379

John Quincy Adams Country B&B
360-675-7108

Maratatha Sea Horse B&B
360-679-2075

Ocean Park
Coast Watch B&B
360-665-6774

Ocean Shores
Ocean Front Lodge
360-289-3036

Olalla
Olalla Orchard B&B
206-857-5915

Olgal
Sand Dollar Inn
360-376-5696

Spring Bay Inn
360-376-5531

Olympia
Britts Place
360-264-2764

Cinnamon Rabbit
360-357-5520

Harbinger Inn
360-754-0389

Puget View Guesthouse
360-459-1676

Orcas
Orcas Hotel
360-376-4300

Windsong B&B
360-376-2380

Orcas Island
Annwn B&B
360-376-4779

Island Farm House
360-468-2864

Liberty Call B&B
360-376-4231

Orting
Sierra Ranier
360-893-6422

Pacific Beach
Sandpiper Beach Resort
360-276-4580

Packwood
Packwood Hotel
360-494-5431

Pateros
Amys Manor B&B
509-923-2334

Peshastin
Lietz B&B
509-548-7504

Mount Valley Vista B&B
509-548-4475

Point Roberts
Old House
360-945-5210

Port Angeles
Ann Starrett Mansion
800-321-0644-[Y--]

Annikens B&B
360-457-6177

Bararian Inn
360-457-4098

Bemis House B&B
360-457-0870

Daytons On The Buff B&B
360-457-5569

Domaine Madeleine
360-457-4174

Glen Mar B&B
360-457-6110

Kennedys B&B
360-457-3628

Nice Touch B&B
800-598-3007

Our House B&B
800-882-9051

Tudor Inn
800-522-5174

Port Hadlock
Port Hadlock Inn
800-395-1595

Port Orchard
"Reflections" A B&B
360-871-5582

Burley Cottage Naturals
206-857-4372

Northwest Interlude
360-871-4676

Ogles B&B
360-876-9170

Port Townsend
Ann Starrett Mansion
800-321-0644-[Y--]

Bold Name - *Description appears in other section* **Washington**

Annapurna Inn
360-385-2909

Arcadia Country Inn
360-385-5245

Baker House
360-385-6673

Bay Cottage
360-385-2035

Bishop Victorian Suites
800-824-4738-[Y--]

Bolands Landing
360-385-6280

Heritage House Inn
360-385-6800

Holly Hill House
800-435-1454-[Y--]

James House
360-385-1238

Lincoln Inn
800-477-4667

Lizzies Victorian B&B
360-385-4168

Manresa Castle
800-732-1281

Old Consulate Inn
360-385-6753

Parakeet Bills Guest House
360-385-3205

Quimper Inn
360-385-1060

Ramage House
360-385-1086

Ravenscroft Inn
360-385-2784

Salmon Berry Farm
360-385-1517

Summer Room
360-385-1267

The Cabin
360-385-5571

Trenholm House
360-385-6059

Poulsbo
Bonnies Beach House
360-697-1891

Foxbridge B&B
360-598-5599

Manor Farm Inn
360-779-4628

Solliden Guest House
360-779-3969

Poulsboro
Edgewater Beach B&B
800-641-0955

Murphy House
800-779-1606

Prescott
Country Living B&B
509-849-2819

Pullman
Ash Street House B&B
509-332-3638

Puyallup
Harts Tayberry B&B
206-848-4594

Quinault
Lake Quinault Lodge
206-288-2571

Randle
Hampton House B&B
360-497-2907

Redmond
Cottage Creek Manor B&B
206-881-5606

Lilac Lea Christian B&B
206-861-1898

Renton
B&B Afloat
206-940-7245

Holly Hedge House
206-226-2555

Ritzville
Portico B&B
206-659-0800

Yorkshire Victorian B&B
509-659-0800

Roche Harbor
Roche Harbor Resort
360-378-2155

Roslyn
Roslyn Inns
509-649-2936

Salkum
Shepherds Inn
206-985-2434

San Juan Island
Hotel de Haro

States Inn
360-378-6240

Seabeck
Summer Song
360-830-5089

Tides Inn Cottage
360-692-8109

Walton House
360-830-4498

Seattle
Alexis Hotel Seattle
206-624-4844

BD Williams House B&B
800-880-0810

Beech Tree Manor
206-281-7037

Bellevue Place B&B
206-325-9253

Broadway Guest House
206-329-1864

Capital Hill Inn
206-323-1955

Capitol Hill House
206-322-1752

Chambered Nautilus B-B Inn
206-522-2536
[YQAR-]

Chelsea Station B&B Inn
800-400-6077-[G--]

College Inn Guest House
206-633-4441

Gaslight Inn
206-325-3654

Green Gables Guest House
206-282-6863

Hainsworth House
206-938-1020

Hill House B&B
206-720-7161

Inn At The Market
800-446-4484

Lake Union B&B
206-547-9965

Lilac Lea Christian B&B
206-861-1898

Lofas B&B
206-454-8551

Marits B&B
206-782-7900

Mildreds B&B
206-325-6072-[Y--]

Pensione Nichols
206-441-7125

Prince of Whales
800-327-9692

Queen Anne Hill B&B
206-284-9779

Robertas B&B
206-329-3326

Sailsbury House
206-328-8682

Seattle B&B
206-784-0539

Swallow's Nest Guest Cottages
206-463-2646-[G--]

Three Tree Point B&B
206-669-7646

Tugboat Challenger
206-340-1201-[G--]

©*Inn & Travel Memphis, Tennessee*

Washington

Bold Name - Description appears in other section

Villa Heidelberg
206-938-3658

Seaview
Enchanted Blue Wave
360-642-4900

Gumms B&B Inn
360-642-8887

Shelburne Inn
360-642-2442

Sou' Wester Ldoge
360-642-2542

Sequim
Brigadoon B&B
360-683-2255

Diamond Point Inn, A B&B
800-551-2615

Gagnons Vacation Cottage
360-683-4373

Granny Sandys Orchard B&B
800-841-3347

Greywolf Inn
360-683-5889-[Y--]

Groveland Cottage
360-683-3565

M&M B&B
360-683-9805

Margies B&B
360-683-7011

Rancho Lambo B&B
360-683-8133

Shelton
Abbeys Angel Inn B&B
360-426-9307

Twin River Ranch B&B
360-426-1023

Silverdale
Heavens Edge B&B
800-413-5680

Seabreeze Beach Cottage
360-692-4648

Snohomish
Cabbage Patch Inn
360-568-9091

Country Manor B&B
360-568-8254

Countryman B&B
360-568-9622

Eddys B&B
360-568-7081

Iverson
360-568-3825

Victorian Rose
360-568-9472

Snoqualmie
Old Honey Farm
800-826-9077

Snoqualmie Pass
Wardholm West B&B
206-434-6540

Soap Lake
Noraras Lodge
509-246-0462

Roxies Inn
509-246-1132

Tumwata Lodge
509-246-1416

South Cle Elum
Moore House
800 22 TWAIN-[Y--]

Spokane
Blakely Estate B&B
509-926-9426

Durocher House B&B
509-328-2971

Forheringham House B&B
509-838-4363

Hillside House
509-534-1426

Loves Victorian B&B
509-276-6939

Luckeys Residence
509-624-3627

Marianna Stoltz House

509-483-4316

Shakespeare Inn
509-534-0935

Spokane Room B&B
509-467-9804

Town & Country B&B
509-466-7559

Waverly Place B&B
509-328-1856

Stehekin
Silver Bay Lodging
509-682-2212

Stevenson
Evergreen Inn
509-427-4158

Home Valley B&B
509-427-7070

Snug Harbor Lodge
509-427-4287

Sumas
BB Border Inn
360-988-5800

Sumner
Carlesns
206-863-4557

Sunnyside
Sunnyside Inn
509-839-5557

Tacoma
Blounts Guest Home
206-759-4534

Chinaberry Hill-A Victorian B&B
206-272-1282

Inges Place
206-584-4514

Keenan House
206-751-0702

Sallys Bear Tree Cottage
206-475-3144

Swallow's Nest Guest Cottages
206-463-2646-[Y--]

Traudels Haus

206-535-4422

Tekoa
Touch O'Country B&B
509-284-5183

Tokeland
Tokeland Hotel
360-267-7006

Tonasket
Orchard Country Inn
509-486-1923

Trout Lake
Mio Amore Pensione
509-395-2264

The Farm
509-395-2488

Twisp
Riverview Retreat
509-997-2477

Twisp B&B
509-997-6562

Usk
Inn At Usk
509-445-1526

Vashon
All Seasons Lodging
206-463-3498

Artists Studio Loft
206-463-2583

Crown & Secptre B&B
206-463-2697

Peabodys B&B
206-463-3506

Rock Ranch Inn
206-463-5058

Shepherds Loft
206-463-2116

Smyth Beach House
206-567-4049

Wee Bit O'Ireland
206-463-3881

Vashon Island
Goosies B&B
206-463-2059

Old Tjomsland House
206-463-5275

4-194

©Inn & Travel Memphis, Tennessee

Bold Name - Description appears in other section   **Washington - Wyoming**

Purple Finch Haven
206-463-5631

**Swallow's Nest
Guest Cottages**
800-ANY-NEST-[Y--]

Walla Walla
Green Gables Inn
509-525-5501

Rees Mansion
509-529-7845

Sicyon Garden B&B
509-525-2964

Stone Creek Inn
509-529-8120

Washtucna
Grays Country B&B
509-646-3482

Waterville
Tower House B&B
509-745-8320

Wenatchee
Apple Blossom Lodge
509-664-1090

Forget-Me-Not B&B
800-843-7552

Pink House
509-663-1911

Stonehouse B&B
509-663-8409

Westport
Glenacres B&B
360-268-9391

Wheeling
Yesterdays Ltd B&B

White Salmon
Inn Of The White Salmon
509-493-2335

Llama Ranch B&B
509-395-2786

Orchard Hill Inn
509-493-3024

Winlock
Greenbrier Colonial Inn
360-262-3381

Winthrop
Dammann B&B
509-996-2484

Farmhouse Inn
509-996-2191

Mountainview B&B
509-996-3234

River Run Inn & Resort
509-996-2173

Sunny Meadows
509-996-3103

Woodinville
Bear Creek Inn
206-881-2978

Woodland
Grammas House
360-225-7002

Yakima
'37 House
509-965-5537-[Y--]

Birchfield Manor
509-452-1960

Irish House B&B
509-453-5474

Meadowbrook B&B
509-248-2387

Tudor Guest House
509-452-8112

Yelm
Log House B&B
306-458-4385

WYOMING

Big Horn
Spahns Big Horn Lodge
307-674-8150

Buffalo
Cloud Peak Inn
307-684-5794

Paradise Guest Ranch
307-684-7876

South Fork Inn
307-684-9609

V Bar F Cattle Ranch
307-758-4382

Casper
Bessemer Bend B&B
307-265-6819

Durbin Street Inn
307-577-5774

Cheyenne
Adventures Country B&B
307-632-4087

Bit-O-Wyo Ranch B&B
307-638-8340

Drummonds Ranch
307-634-6042

Howdy Partner B&B
307-634-6493

Porch Swing B&B
307-778-7182

Rainsford Inn
307-638-BEDS

Cody
Bill Codys Ranch Inn

Goff Creek Lodge
307-587-3753

Hidden Valley Ranch
307-587-5090

Hunter Peak Ranch
307-587-3711

Lockhart B&B Inn
307-587-6074-[Y--]

Parson's Pillow B&B
800-377-2348-[Y--]

Rimrock Dude Ranch
307-587-3970

Shoshone Lodge Resort
307-587-4044

Siggins Triangle X Ranch
307-587-1031

The Irma
800-626-4886

Trout Creek Inn
307-587-6288

Valley Ranch
307-587-4661

Wind Chimes Cottage B&B
307-527-5310

Devils Tower
R Place
307-467-5938

Douglas
Akers Ranch
307-358-3741

Deer Forks Ranch
307-358-2033-[Y--]

Pellatz Ranch
307-358-2380

Two Creek Ranch
307-358-3467

Dubois
Geyser Creek B&B
307-455-2702

Jakeys Fork B&B
307-455-2769

Lazy L&B Ranch
307-455-2839

Sunshine & Shadows B&B
800-472-6241

Encampment
Lorraines B&B Homestay
307-327-5200-[Y--]

Platts B&B
307-327-5539

Evansville
Miskimins Ranch
307-265-5725

Gillette
Pettersen Haus
307-686-1030

Glenrock
Hotel Higgins
800-458-0144

Opals B&B
307-436-2626

Guernsey
Annettes White House

©*Inn & Travel Memphis, Tennessee*   4-195

Wyoming *Bold Name - Description appears in other section*

307-836-2148

Jackson
  Davy Jackson Inn
  800-584-0532

  Moose Meadows B&B
  307-733-9510

  Rusty Parrot Lodge
  307-733-2000

  Spring Creek Ranch
  307-733-8833

  Sundance Inn
  307-733-3444

  Twin Mountain River Ranch B&B

  Wildflower Inn
  307-733-4710

Jackson Hole
  Alpine House
  800-753-1421

  Buckrail Lodge
  307-733-2079

  Nowlin Creek Inn
  307-733-0882

  Powderhorn Ranch
  307-733-3845

Lander
  Country Fare B&B
  307-332-5906

  Empty Nest B&B
  307-332-7516

  Enda's B&B
  307-332-3175

  McDougall B&B
  307-332-3392

  Miners Delight Inn
  307-332-3513

Laramie
  Annie Morres Guest House
  307-721-4177

  Inn On Ivinson
  307-745-8939

  V-Bar Guest Ranch
  800-788-4630

Lusk

  Wyoming Whale Ranch
  307-334-3598

Medicine Bow
  Hist Virginian Hotel

Moose
  Bunkhouse
  307-733-7283

Moran
  Box K Ranch
  800-729-1410

  Fir Creek Ranch
  307-543-2416

  Jenny Lake Lodge
  307-543-2811

Newcastle
  4W Ranch
  307-746-2815

  Horton House B&B
  800-845-2717

Pinedale
  Window On The Winds B&B
  307-367-2600

Powell
  Bar X Ranch
  307-645-3231

Ranchester
  Masters Ranch
  307-655-2386

Rawlins
  Ferris Mansion
  307-324-3961

  Lamont Inn
  307-324-7602

Recluse
  TR Ranch
  307-736-2250

Riverton
  Blue Spruce Lodge

  Cottonwood Ranch
  307-856-3064

  Hillcrest Manor Inn
  307-856-6309

Rock River
  Dodge Creek Ranch
  307-322-2345

Rock Springs
  Sha Hol Dee B&B
  307-362-7131

Saratoga
  Brooksong Home
  307-326-8744

  Hood House
  307-326-5624

  Saratoga Inn

  Saratoga Safaris B&B

  Wolf Hotel
  307-326-5663-[Y--]

Savery
  Savery Creek Thoroughbred Ranch
  307-383-7840-[Y--]

Shell
  Clucas Ranch B&B
  307-765-2946

Sheridan
  Kilbourne Kastle B&B
  307-674-8716

Sundance
  Canfield Ranch
  307-283-2062

  Hawken Guest Ranch
  800-544-4309

Wapiti
  Elephant Head Lodge
  307-587-3980

  Mountain Shadows Ranch
  307-587-2143

Wheatland
  Blackbird Inn
  307-332-4540

  Edwards B&B
  307-322-3921

  Mill Iron Spear Ranch
  307-322-5940

Wilson
  Fish Creek B&B
  307-733-2586

  Heck Of A Hill Homestead
  307-733-8023-[Y--]

  Heidelberg B&B
  307-733-7820

  Teton Tree House
  307-733-3233

  Teton View B&B
  307-733-7954-[Y--]

- E N D -

Canada

Halliburton House Inn	5184 Morris St B3J...	Halifax NS CANADA
Dr Bruce Pretty		Tel: 902-420-0658 Fax: 902-423-2334

Take a memory home with you - *Halliburton House Inn*! Experience the pleasure of stepping into the past by visiting this heritage property, for an overnight stay or gourmet meal. *Halliburton House* was build in 1816 as the home of Sir Brenton Halliburton, Chief Justice of the Nova Scotia Supreme Court. From 1885 to 1887, the building served as Dalhousie University Law School. Today, this registered heritage property is Halifax's finest Inn. All of the Inn's thirty comfortable guest rooms are tastefully furnished with period antiques. Each has a private bath, as well as the modern amenities expected by today's guests. Several suites are available, some with fireplaces. Sit in front of a warm crackling fire and relax before dinner in the library. Our restaurant offers a relaxed elegant setting for both lunch and dinner. The *Halliburton* menu specializes in wild game and fresh Atlantic seafood. During the summer months, relax over lunch in the outdoor garden cafe. With its central location and free parking, the Inn is ideally located in the heart of downtown Halifax. *Halliburton House Inn* is known for its high standards, relaxed ambience and excellent service. **Discounts:** Yes, inquire at res time **Seasonal:** Rates vary **Reservations:** One night's deposit, 24 hr cancel policy *Suites available **Brochure:** Yes **Permitted:** Children, drinking, limited smoking **Conference:** Yes, our boardroom seats 35 persons **Languages:** English, French **Payment Terms:** MC/V [I07GPCN-11793] **COM** Y **ITC Member:** No

Rates:	Pvt Bath 30	Suite
Single	$ 100.00	
Double	$ 100.00	$ 160.00

Albert House	478 Albert St K1R...	Ottawa ON CANADA
John & Cathy Delroy		Tel: 800-267-1982 613-236-4479
		Res Times 8am-11pm

Albert House is a charming Victorian mansion built in 1875 by and for noted Canadian architect, Thomas Seaton Scott who was the Chief Architect for the Ministry of Public Works at that time. Scott oversaw many government projects including the original Customs House and Post Office in downtown Ottawa and part of the Parliament Buildings. Our seventeen guest rooms are individually decorated and all have ensuite facilities, colour cable TV, direct dial phones and air conditioning/individual heat control. Guests can enjoy our famous *Albert House* full, hot breakfast in the dining room or continental service is available for those who wish to breakfast in their room. A cozy lounge with fireplace provides a pleasant place to chat with other guests or read one of the many periodicals from our large selection. We have two very large but friendly dogs who have become quite well-known and welcome presence at *Albert House*. **Discounts:** Seasonal weekends **Airport:** Ottawa Intl-7 mi **Seasonal:** No **Reservations:** One night's deposit or credit card number to guarantee, arrival before 11pm unless prior arrangements have been made **Brochure:** Yes **Permitted:** Limited children, limited pets, drinking, smoking **Languages:** English, some French **Payment Terms:** TravelerCheck AE/DC/MC/V [I06GPCN-9185] **COM** Y **ITC Member:** No

Rates:	Pvt Bath 17
Single	$ 60-85.00
Double	$ 70-95.00

©*Inn & Travel Memphis, Tennessee*

5-1

Canada   National Edition

Australis Guest House   35 Marlborough Ave K1N...   Ottawa ON CANADA
Brian & Carol Waters   **Tel:** 613-235-8461
                                                                    Res Times 8am-10pm

We are the oldest established and still operating Bed & Breakfast in the Ottawa area. Located on a quiet, tree-lined street one block from the Rideau River, with its ducks and swans and Strathcona Park ... but just a twenty minute walk from the Parliament Buildings. This period, architecturally designed house boasts leaded windows, fireplaces, oak floors and unique eight foot high stained glass windows overlooking the hall. Our spacious rooms, including a suite and private bathroom, feature many of our collectibles from our time living in different parts of the world. The hearty, home-cooked, delicious breakfast, with homebaked breads, pastries, ensure you will start the day in just the right way. Our Australian and English heritage combined with our time in Canada provide a truly international flavour with a relaxed atmosphere. We are located downtown and have off-street parking. In-addition we provide free pick-up and delivery from/to the bus and train stations for our guests. We speak both English and French. Multiple winner of the Ottawa Hospitality Award and recommended by *"Newsweek."* We are a full member of the Ottawa Tourism and Convention Authority. **Discounts:** 10% 11/1 to 3/1 **Packages:** Yes, with local restaurants **Seasonal:** No **Reservations:** One night's deposit required **Brochure:** Yes **Permitted:** Children, limited smoking **Languages:** English, French **Payment Terms:** Check [R04FP-CN-9186] **COM** Y **ITC Member:** No

Rates:	Pvt Bath 1	Shared Bath 2
Single	$ 48.00	$ 35-Up
Double	$ 58.00	$ 45-Up

Palmerston Inn   322 Palmerston Blvd M6G...   Toronto ON CANADA
Judy & Wayne Carr   **Tel:** 416-920-7842 **Fax:** 416-960-9529
                                                             Res Times 10am-7pm

Palmerston Inn is located in a beautiful residential downtown Toronto neighborhood next to public transportation and where most attractions can be reached within 30 minutes. Our home is well-kept, quiet and accommodates only non-smokers. Four guest rooms on each floor are wonderfully furnished with antiques with European-style bath facilities (washbasins in each room) while sharing the full bath with three others on the same floor. Each room is equipped with a telephone and includes maid service. A continental breakfast is served in the breakfast room or on the outdoor deck in summer. A TV lounge provides relaxation with a generous supply of newspapers and books. Limited free parking is available on the premises. Their friendly and capable service will make your visit to Toronto most enjoyable. **Discounts:** Weekly rates Nov to April **Airport:** Toronto Pearson Intl-15 km **Seasonal:** No **Reservations:** Deposit required to guarantee reservation, 48 hr cancellation policy **Brochure:** Yes **Permitted:** Children, drinking **Languages:** English, German, French **Payment Terms:** MC/V [K05GPCN-9199] **COM** Y **ITC Member:** No

Rates:	Shared Bath 8
Single	$ 45-55.00
Double	$ 60-65.00

Albion Guest House   592 W Ninteenth Ave V5Z...   Vancouver BC CANADA
Bill Browning   **Tel:** 604-873-2287

On a quiet tree-lined residential street near city hall is the turn-of-the-century character home with five restful rooms and whose restful beds are covered with thick feather mattresses, fine cotton linens and down filled duvets. Imagine yourself sitting in the beautiful sitting room with freshly cut flowers, while relaxing in front of the fireplace, sipping complimentary wine or sherry. At the Albion Guest House, we serve a sumptuous breakfast in the formal dining room overlooking the flower garden. Later, you may use one of the complimentary bikes to explore Vancouver on your own. Because we're located near city hall, Chinatown and Gastown are just a few minutes away and the Expo Skytrain, and just a three minute walk to gambling casinos, restaurants, specialty coffee shops, delicatessens, theatre and Queen Elizabeth Park. A myriad of attractions and activities are available, including boating, parasailing, windsurfing, and health clubs. It's just a 30 minute drive to the famous Capilano Suspension Bridge or to Grouse Mountain, a major ski area with panoramic views of Vancouver. **Discounts:** Off season **Airport:** Vancouver-20 min **Packages:** Romantic (Bubble bath, Champagne, Candles and fresh cut flowers) **Seasonal:** No **Reservations:** Deposit is required to guarantee reservation, one week cancel policy for refund. **Brochure:** Yes **Permitted:** Drinking **Languages:** French **Payment Terms:** MC/V [R09FPCN-17199] **COM** Y **ITC Member:** No

Rates:	Pvt Bath 2	Shared Bath 2
Single	$ 110.00	$ 66.00
Double	$ 110.00	$ 99.00

Abigails Hotel   906 Mc Clure St V8V...   Victoria BC CANADA
Frauke & Daniel Behune   **Tel:** 800-561-6565 250-388-5363 **Fax:** 250-388-7787
    Res Times 8am-10pm

Following in the tradition of European-style Inns, *Abigail's* has been marvelously transformed into a small luxurious hotel. Decorated with soft colours, comfortable furnishings, crystal chandeliers and fresh flowers, you will want to guiltlessly pamper yourself in this romantic ambience . . . All guest rooms have private baths and fluffy goosedown comforters. Dream before your crackling fire or relax in a jacuzzi or soaking tub before retiring. Join us in the library each late afternoon for a platter of cheese, fresh fruit and a glass of port before you sample some of the best restaurants in Victoria. In the morning you'll awake to the aroma of fresh coffee and our famous Innkeepers full breakfast. Located just three blocks east of the city centre, we are within strolling distance of Victoria's specialty shops, floral parks and oceanside delights. Ours is a world of intimate charm and pleasure . . . **Seasonal:** No **Reservations:** One night's credit card deposit, 48 hr cancel policy for refund, no check-in after 10pm **Brochure:** Yes **Permitted:** Children 10+, limited drinking **Payment Terms:** AE/MC/V [K04IPCN1-6620] **COM** Y **ITC Member:** No

Rates:	Pvt Bath 16
Single	$ 127-249.00
Double	$ 127-249.00

Beaconsfield Inn   998 Humboldt St V8V...   Victoria BC CANADA
Con & Judi Sollid   **Tel:** 604-384-4044
    Res Times 8am-8pm

In 1905, during the Edwardian Era, *"the height of the British Empire"*, famous architect Samuel McClure was commissioned by RP Rithet to built the Beaconsfield for his daughter, Gertrude, as a wedding gift. A gleaming sun room, rich mahogany panelling, period antiques, oil paintings, a book-lined library and an elegant dining room complete the main floor. The three suites, Emily Carr, Gatekeeper's and Garden Suite; six guest rooms and one oceanfront Beach Cottage. Each guest room has a private bathroom, goosedown comforter, flowers and is luxuriously decorated. The guest rooms include wood-burning fireplaces and jacuzzi baths. Each afternoon join us in the library for a sherry hour where we serve an assortment of cheese, crackers and fresh fruit. The following morning guests awake to the aroma of our special blend coffee and the Innkeeper's famous full breakfast. Located only a few minutes walk from our specialty shops, Beacon Hill Park and the Inner Harbor. The Beaconsfield Inn, an experience that will linger in your memory . . . **Seasonal:** No **Reservations:** Credit card prepayment, 7 day cancel policy for refund, check-in 3-6pm. **Brochure:** Yes **Permitted:** Limited drinking **Payment Terms:** MC/V [Z04IPCN1-6619] **COM** Y **ITC Member:** No

Rates:	Pvt Bath 60
Single	$ 200-450.00
Double	$ 200-450.00

Rose Cottage B&B	3059 Washington Ave V9A...	**Victoria BC CANADA**
Robert & Shelley Bishop		**Tel:** 604-381-5985

Victoria's oldest Bed and Breakfast, *Rose Cottage* is a 1912 traditional Victorian home carefully restored to retain all of the Heritage features of turn-of-the-century Victoria. Rose Cottage has high ceillinged rooms, period furniture, guest parlor in a nautical theme, a large dining room with library and quiet, well-appointed bedrooms. Your hosts, Robert and Shelley, are part of the character of Rose Cottage. We have travelled extensively before settling in Victoria and know the value of a warm welcome for our visitors. Located on a quiet street close to downtown, guests are just a few blocks from the beautiful Gorge Park Waterway. A full course compli-mentary breakfast includes fresh fruits and muffins. We have lots of inside info about Victoria to make your visit as adventuresome or as relaxing as you wish. **Discounts:** Yes **Airport:** Victoria Intl-10 mi **Reservations:** First night's deposit or credit card number to guarantee reservation **Permitted:** Children, drinking **Languages:** Canadian and American **Payment Terms:** Check MC/V [R07FPCN-9114] **COM Y ITC Member:** No

Rates:		**Shared Bath**	4
Single		$ 70-80.00	
Double		$ 70-80.00	

Blomindon Inn	127 Main St B0P...	**Wolfville NS CANADA**
*Jim Laceby		**Tel:** 902-542-2291 **Fax:** 902-542-7461

Situated only an hour's drive from Halifax Intl Airport is this elegant mansion built in the 1870s by Capt Rufus Burgess. Capt Burgess made his fortune in the glorious days of sailing as a shipbuilder and sea captain. Today his home has been beautifully restored offering twenty seven elegant rooms (many with handmade quilts and four-poster beds) and two dining rooms and parlours, complete with fireplaces. Nestled near the world's highest tides in a micro-climate that enables the Valley to have a worldwide recognition for its apples and grape harvests! Nearby guests find Grande Pre National Park, the setting for Longfellow's *"Evangeline"*. A continental break-fast is included with other gourmet entrees offered in the restaurant on the premises. **Seasonal:** No **Reservations:** Deposit required within 14 days of booking, with 48 hr cancel policy for refund **Brochure:** Yes **Permitted:** Children, drinking, smoking **Payment Terms:** AE/MC/V [X11BCCN-8785] **COM Y ITC Member:** No

Rates:	**Pvt Bath** 25	**Shared Bath** 2
Single	$ 61-88.00	$ 39.00

Bold Name - *Description appears in other section*   **Canada**

CANADA

Alberta NB
Florentine Manor
506-882-2271

Allen SK
Moldenhauers B&B
306-257-3578

Alma NB
Captain's Inn
506-887-2017

Alton ON
Horseshoe Inn
519-927-5779

Amherst NS
Amherst Shore Inn
902-667-4800

Annapolis Royal NS
Bread & Roses
902-532-5727

Cheshire Cat
902-532-2100

Garrison House
902-532-5750

Milford House
902-532-2617

Poplar B&B
902-532-7936

Queen Anne Inn
902-532-7850

Antigohsih NS
Old Manse Inn
902-863-5696

Augustine Cover PE
Shore Farm B&B
902-855-2871

Baie St Paul QE
La Maison Otis
418-435-2255

Bamfield BC
Aguilar House
604-728-3323

Bayfield ON
Little Inn Of Bayfield
519-565-2611

Belfast PE
Linden Ldoge
902-659-2716

Beresford NB
Les Peupliers
506-546-5271

Blackstock ON
Landfall Farm
416-986-5588

Blaine Lake SK
Vereshagins Country B&B
306-497-2782

Bonshaw PE
Churchill Farm
902-675-2481

Boyle AL
Donatberry Inn
403-689-3639

Bracebridge ON
Holiday House Inn
705-645-2245

Brackley Beach PE
Shaws Cottage
902-672-2022

Bradford ON
Country Guest Home
416-775-3576

Braeside ON
Glenroy Farm
613-432-6248

Brentwood Bay BC
Brentwood Bay B&B
604-652-2012

Brooks AL
Douglas Country Inn
403-362-2873

Bulyea SK
Hillcrest Hotel
306-725-4874

Caledon East ON
Caldeon Inn
416-584-2891

Campbell River BC
April Point Lodge
604-285-2222

Campbell River Lodge
800-663-7212

Dogwoods
604-287-4213

Camrose AL
Nordbye House
403-672-8131

Canmore AL
Georgetown Inn
403-678-3439

Canning
1850 House
902-582-3052

Cap-a-l'Aigle QE
Auberge la Pinsonniere
418-665-4431

Cape Breton NS
Riverside Inn
902-235-2002

Carleton Place ON
Ottawa Valley B&B
613-257-7720

Centreville NB
Reids Farm Home B&B
506-276-4787

Charlevoix QE
La Pinsonniere
418-665-4431

Charlottetown PE
Just Folks B&B
902-569-2089

Chemainns BC
Grants
604-246-3768

Chester NS
McNeil Manor B&B
902-275-4638

CH Trudel QE
Otter Lake Haus
819-687-2767

Cobourg ON
Northunberland Hts Inn
416-372-7500

Coin duBacn-Perce QE
Auberge le Coin du Banc
418-645-2907

Collingwood NS
Cobequid Hills Country Inn
902-686-3381

Como QE
Willow Inn
514-458-7006

Comte de Mantane QE
Auberge la Martre
418-288-5533

Cookstown ON
Chestnut Inn
705-458-9751

Cornwall PR
Obanlea Tourist Home
902-566-3067

Corwan PE
Chez Hous B&B
902-566-2779

Cranmore AL
Cougar Creek Inn
403-678-4751

Cte Matapedia QE
Gite du Passant
418-775-5237

Darthmouth NS
Martin House B&B
902-469-1896

Denman Island BC
Denman Island Inn
604-335-2688

Digby County NS
Harbour View Inn
902-245-5686

Downsview ON
Schweizer Lodge
514-538-2123

Duncan BC
North Pacific Springs
604-748-3189

Duncan Island BC
Fairburn Farm
604-746-4637

Dunham QE
Maplewood
514-295-2519

Eagle Creek BC
Bradshaw's Lodge

©*Inn & Travel Memphis, Tennessee*   5-5

Canada   ***Bold Name*** - *Description appears in other section*

604-397-2416

Elora ON
Penstock Inns Ltd
519-846-5356

Fanny Bay BC
Ships Point Beach House
800-925-1595

Fenelon Falls ON
Eganridge Inn & CC
705-738-5111

Fergus ON
Breadelbane Inn
519-843-4770

Fort Steele BC
Wild Horse Farm
604-426-6000

Frederickton AL
Backporch B&B
506-454-6875

Gabriola Island BC
Surf Lodge
604-247-9231

Galiano Island BC
Hummingbirg Inn
604-539-5472

La Berengerie
609-539-5392

Gaspe Peninsula QE
Hotel La Normandie
418-782-2112

Gaspesie QE
Henry House
418-534-2115

Georgeville QE
Georgeville Country Inn
819-843-8683

Gores Landing ON
Victoria Inn
416-342-3261

Grand Manan Isl NB
Shorecrest Lodge
506-662-3216

Grand Manan NB
Cross Tree Guest House
506-662-8663

Ferry Wharf Inn
506-662-8588

Grand Harbour Inn
506-662-8681

Granville Ferry NS
Bayberry House
902-532-2272

Shining Tides B&B
902-532-2770

Guysborough NS
Limbscombe Ldoge
902-779-2307

Halfmoon Bay BC
Lord Jim's Hotel
604-885-7038

Halifax NS
Apple Basket B&B
902-429-3019

Halliburton House Inn
902-420-0658-[Y--]

Queen Street Inn
902-422-9828

Hampstead NB
Eveleigh Hotel
506-425-9993

Hartland NB
Woodsview II B&B
506-375-4637

Hebron NS
Manor Inn
902-742-2487

Hopewell Cape NB
Dutch Treat B&B
506-882-2552

Hornby Island BC
Sea Brreeze Inn
604-335-2321

Howick QE
Hazelbrae Farm
514-825-2390

Huntington St Anicet
Leduc
514-264-6533

Iona NS
Highland Heights Inn

Iroquois ON

Cedarlane Farm B&B
613-652-4267

Jackson Point ON
Briars Inn & Country Club
800-465-2376

Kamourasha QE
Gite du Passant B&B
418-492-2921

Kelowna BC
Blair House
604-762-5090

Gables Country Inn
604-768-4468

Kensington PE
Beach Point View Inn
902-836-5260

Blakeneys B&B
902-836-3254

Murphys Sea View Inn
902-836-5456

Sherwood Acres B&B
902-836-5430

Woodingtons Country Inn
902-836-5518

Kingston ON
Prince George Hotel
613-549-5440

Kleena Kleene BC
Chilanko Resort
604-553-3625

Knowlton QE
Auberge Laketree
514-243-6604

Ladysmith BC
Manana Lodge
604-245-2312

Yellow Point Lodge
604-245-7422

Lansdowne ON
Ivylea Inn
613-659-2329

Little York PE
Dalvay By The Sea
902 672-2048

Lle d Orleans QE
Chez les Dumas
418-828-9442

Manor de L'Anse
418-828-2248

London ON
Rose B&B
519-433-9978

Lousibourg NS
Greta Cross B&B
902-733-2833

Lower Bedeque PE
Waughs B&B
902-887-2320

Mabou NS
Cape Breton Island Farm
902-945-2077

Mactaquac NB
Mactaquac B&B
506-363-3630

Marshfield PE
Rosevale Farm
902-894-7821

May River AL
Harbor House
403-874-2233

Mayne Island BC
Fernhill Lodge
604-539-2544

Gingerbread House
604-539-3133

Oceanwood Country Inn
604-539-5074

Maynooth ON
Bea's B&B House
613-338-2239

McKeller ON
Inn & Tennis Club/ Manitou
416-967-3466

Merrickville ON
Sam James Inn
613-269-3711

Mill Bay BC

Bold Name - *Description appears in other section*　　　　　　　　　　　　　　　　　　　　　　　　　　　　　　　　**Canada**

Pine Lodge B&B
604-743-4083

Millarville AL
  Mesa Creek Ranch
  403-931-3573

Millet AL
  Broadview Farm
  403-387-4963

Minden ON
  Minden House
  705-286-3263

Mont Tremblant QE
  Auberge Sauvignon
  819-425-2658

  Chateau Beauvallon
  819-425-7275

Montague PE
  Brydons B&B
  902-838-4717

Montreal East QE
  Le Breton
  514-52-7273

Montreal QE
  Armor Inn
  514-285-0894

Montreal QE
  Downtown B&B
  514-289-9794

  Manoir Ambrose

Morris BC
  Deerbank Farm
  204-746-8395

Murray Harbor PE
  Harbourview B&B
  902-962-2565

Murray River PE
  Bayberry Cliff Inn
  902-962-3395

Musquodoboit Harbor NS
  Camelot
  902-889-2198

Nanoose Bay BC
  The Lookout
  604-468-9796

Nanton AL
  Timberridge Homestead
  403-646-5683

Nelson BC
  Heritage Inn
  604-352-5331

Nelson NB
  Governor's Mansion
  506-622-3036

New Brunswick NB
  Happy Apple Acers

New Hanburg ON
  Waterlot Inn
  519-662-2020

Newboro ON
  Sterling Lodge
  613-272-2435

Niagara On Lake ON
  Angel Inn
  416-468-3411

  Kiely House
  Heritage Inn
  416-468-4588

  Moffat Inn
  416-468-4116

  Oban Inn
  416-468-2165

  Old Bank House

Nine Mile Creek PE
  Laine Acres B&B
  902-675-2402

Nobel ON
  Paiens B&B
  705-342-9266

Normandale ON
  Union Hotel
  519-426-5568

North Sydney NS
  Annfield Tourist Manor
  902-736-8770

North Vancouver BC
  Grouse Mountain B&B
  604-986-9630

  Helens B&B
  604-985-4869

  Laburnum Cottage
  604-988-4877

  Platts B&B

604-987-4100

  Victorian B&B
  604-985-1523

Norwich ON
  Willi-Joy Farm B&B
  519-424-2113

Okotoks AL
  Wildflower Country

Ottawa ON
  Albert House
  800-267-1982-[Y--]

  Australis Guest House
  613-235-8461-[Y--]

  Beatrice Lyon House
  613-236-3904

  Blue Spruce B&B
  613-236-8521

  Cartier House Inn
  613-236-INNS

  Constance House
  613-235-8888

  Doral Inn Hotel
  613-230-8055

  Flora House
  613-230-2152

  Gasthaus Switzerland
  613-237-0335

  Gwens Guest House
  613-737-4129

  Haydon House
  613-230-2697

  McGees Inn

  Rideau View Inn
  613-236-9309

  Westminster Guest House
  613-729-2707

Owen Sound ON
  Moses Sunset B&B
  519-371-4559

Parson BC
  Talisin Guest House

604-348-2247

Pender Island BC
  Corbett House
  604-629-6305

Pentifcton BC
  Rose Cottage B&B
  604-492-3462

  Tina's Tuc INn
  604-492-3366

Perth ON
  Perth Manor
  519-271-7129

Pictou NS
  L'Auberge
  902-485-6900

Plaster Rock NB
  Northern Wilderness Lodge
  506-356-8327

Plympton NS
  Westway Inn
  902-837-4097

Pointe-Au-Oic QE
  Augerge Donohue
  418-665-4377

Port Carling ON
  Sherwood Inn
  705-765-3131

Port Dufferin NS
  Marquie Dufferin Seaside Inn

Port Renfrerw BC
  Feathered Paddle B&B
  604-647-5433

Port Severn ON
  Arrowwood Lodge
  705-538-2354

Port Stanley ON
  Kettle Creek Inn
  519-782-3388

Port Williams NS
  Planter's Barracks Inn
  902-542-7879

Portneuf QE

  Edale Place
  418-286-3168

  France Beaulieu

©*Inn & Travel Memphis, Tennessee*　　　　　　　　　　　　　　　　　　　　　　　　　　　　　　　　5-7

Canada   **Bold Name** - *Description appears in other section*

House
418-336-2724

Pugwash NS
Blue Heron Inn
902-243-2900

Quathiaski Cove BC
Tsa-Kwa-Luten Lodge
800-665-7745

Quebec City QE
Au Chateau Fleur de Lis
418-694-1884

Au Manoir Ste Genevieve
418-694-1666

Auberge de la Choutte
418-694-0232

Chateau de la Terrasse
418-694-9472

Le Chateau de Pierre
418-694-0429

Maison Marie-Rollet
418-694-9271

Quebec QE
Chateau Bellevue
800-463-2617

Chateau Laurier
800-463-4453

Manoir Lafayette
800-363-8203

Quyon QE
Memorylane Farm
819-458-2479

Regina SK
Turgeon Intl B&B
306-522-4200

Riverside NB
Cailswick Babbling Brook
506-882-2079

Rockport ON
Amaryllis Houseboat B&B
613-659-3513

Rossland BC
Rams Head Inn
604-362-9577

Rothesay NB
Shadow Lawn Country Inn
506-847-7539

Sackville NB
Marshlands Inn
506-536-0170

Salmon Arm BC
Cindosa B&B Inn
604-832-3342

Silver Creek Guest House
604-832-8870

Salt Spring Isl BC
Hastings House
800-661-9255

Seebe AL
Bresters Kananaskis Ranch
403-673-3737

Sooke BC
Harbour House
800-665-7745

Souix Narrows ON
Yellowbird Lodge
807-226-5279

St Andrews NB
Pansy Patch B&B
506-529-3834

Puff Inn
506-529-4191

Shiretown Inn
506-529-8877

St Anne De Mont
Giet du Mont Albert
800-463-0860

St Antoine Tilly QE
Auberge Manoir de Tilly
418-886-2407

St Jacobs ON
Jacobstettel Guest House
519-664-2208

St Laurent QE
Maison Sous Le Arbres
418-828-9442

St Marc Richelieu QE
Handfield Inn
514-584-2226

St Roch Aulnaies QE
Pelletier House
418-354-2450

St Sauveur des Monts QE
Auberge St-Denis
514-227-4766

Stanley Bridge PE
Creekside Farm B&B
902-886-2713

Gulf Breeze B&B
902-886-2678

Ste Petronille QE
Auberee la Goeliche
418-828-2248

Stratford ON
Burnsdie Guest Home
519-271-7076

Shrewsbury Manor
519-271-8520

Stone Maiden Inn
519-271-7129

Summerland BC
Three Pines Lodge
604-494-1661

Summerside PE
Silver Fox Inn
902-436-4033

Sussex NB
Andersons Holiday Farm
506-433-3786

Sutton QE
Auberge Schweizer
514-538-2129

Tantallon NS
Seabright B&B
902-823-2987

Tingish PE
Harbour Lights
902-882-2479

Tisdale SK
Prairie Acres B&B
306-873-2272

Tofino BC
Clayoquot Lodge
604-725-3284

Toronto ON
Ashleigh Heritage Inn
416-535-4000

Palmerston Inn
416-920-7842-[Y--]

Treherne MA
Beulah Land Inn
204-723-2828

Tyne Valley PE
West Island Inn
902-831-2495

Ucluelet BC
Burleys Lodge
604-726-4444

Upper Stewiacke NS
Landsdown Inn
902-671-2749

Val David QE
Auberge du Vieus Foyer
819-322-2686

Parkers Lodge
819-322-2026

Vancouver BC
Albion Guest House
604-873-2287-[Y--]

Beautiful B&B
604-327-1102

Diana's B&B
604-321-2855

Penny Farthing Inn
604-739-9002

Pillow'n Porridge Guest House

Prior House B&BInn
604-592-8447

Rose Garden Guest Inn
604-435-7129

Vincents Guest House

5-8   ©Inn & Travel Memphis, Tennessee

Bold Name - Description appears in other section | **Canada**

604-254-7462

West End Guest Inn
604-681-2889

Vernon BC
  Five Junipers B&B
  604-549-3615

  Schroth Farm B&B
  604-545-0010

  Twin Willows
  604-542-8293

  Windmill House B&B
  604-549-2804

Victoria BC
  Abigails Hotel
  800-561-6565-[G--]

  Battery Street B&B
  604-385-4623

  Beaconsfield Inn
  604-384-4044-[G--]

  Captains Palace Inn
  604-388-9191

  Cherry Bank Hotel

  Craigmyle B&B
  604-595-5411

  Elk Lake Lodge
  604-658-8879

  Hibernia B&B
  604-658-5519

  Holland House
  604-384-6644

  Oak Bay Beach Hotel
  604-598-4556

  Oxford Castle Inn
  604-388-6431

  Portage Inlet B&B
  604-479-4594

  Prior House B&B

  Rose Cottage B&B
  604-381-5985-[Y--]

  Sunnymead House Inn
  604-658-1414

  Top O' Triangle Mountain
  604-478-7853

  Tucherk's B&B
  604-658-5531

Victoria By Sea PE
  Victoria Village Inn
  902-658-2288

Vieux-Quebec QE
  Au Petie Hotel
  418-694-0965

W Vancouver BC
  Bramblewyck By The Sea
  604-926-3827

Wallace NS
  Senator Guest House
  902-257-2417

Waterloo QE
  Perras
  514-539-2983

Wawota SK
  Pleasant Vista Angus Farm
  306-739-2915

West Vancouver BC
  Park Royal Hotel
  604-926-5511

Weymouth NS
  Gilberts Clover Farm
  902-837-4505

Whistler BC
  Durlacher Hof
  604-932-1924

  Sabey House B&B
  604-932-3498

Windermere ON
  Windermere House
  705-769-3611

Winnipeg MA
  Chestnut B&B
  204-772-9788

Winnipeg NS
  Ray Antymis
  204-786-3105

Wolfville NS
  Blomindon Inn
  902-542-2291-[Y--]

  Tattingstone Inn
  902-542-7696

  Victoria Historic Inn
  902-542-5744

York PE
  Amber Lights B&B
  902-894-5868

Youngs Point ON
  Old Bridge Inn
  705-652-8507

©*Inn & Travel Memphis, Tennessee*

Caribbean

BERMUDA

Hamilton HM
Rosedon
800-225-5567

Royal Palms Club
800-441-7087

Hamilton HM AX
Quq Sear
809-236-1998

Hamilton HM BX
Oxford House
800-546-7758

Hamilton HM CX
Fordham Hall
800-537-4163

Hamilton HM DX
Woodbourne Guest House
809-295-3737

Hamilton HM EX
Edgehill Manor
809-295-7124

Hamilton HM HX
Pleasant View
809-292-4520

Paget PG 01
Salt Kettle House
809-236-0407

Paget PG 03
Loughlands Guest House
809-236-1253

Paget PG BX
Dawinks Manor
809-236-7419

Pembroke HM 04
Hi-Roy
809-292-0808

Southampton SN BX
Greenes Guest House
809-238-0834

Royal Heights
800-247-2447

St George's GE BX
Hillcredt Guest House
809-297-1630

Warwick WK BX
Granaway Guest House & Cottage
809-236-1805

PUERTO RICO

Cabo Rojo
Parador Boquemar
800-443-0266

Parador Perichis
800-443-0266

Coamo
Parador Banos de Coamo
800-443-0266

Jayuya
Parador Hacienda Gripinas
800-443-0266

Lajas
Parador Villa Arguera
800-443-0266

Luquillo
Parador Martorell
800-443-0266

Maricao
Parador Hacienda Juantia
800-443-0266

Quebradillas
Parador El Guajataca
800-443-0266

Paradou Vistamar
800-443-0266

San German
Parador Oasis
800-443-0266

Utuado
Parador Casa Grande
800-443-0266

US VIRGIN ISLANDS

Danish Chalet Inn
800-635-1531

NOTE PAGE

Tell the innkeeper you found them in Inn & Travel, a publication of Bed & Breakfast Guest Houses & Inns of America, the largest B&B Inn association with over 15,000 members - founded over ten years ago. They are interested in knowing what guide books are used by guests

If your favorite B&B Inn is not included in this edition, send information to us or better yet, give the innkeeper our address and so they become a member and be listed in the next edition.

NOTE PAGE

Join the Inn & Travel Club - it's free if you purchased a book, CD-Rom or membership on the Inn & Travel Web Site. Begin earning points while staying at your favorite B&B Inn or Boutique Hotel and your favorite restaurants!

Let the innkeepers and restaurants you frequent know about the Inn & Travel Club - they can call   800-431-8258

No Other Market Begs For More Specialized Information As Does The Bed & Breakfast Industry

Introducing

B&B MANAGEMENT

Whether you're a seasoned innkeeper or an aspiring innkeeper, this new and innovative magazine will provide you with the kinds of information you need to stay competitive and profitable in this rapidly expanding industry.

Beth Hillis
Editor

"B&B/Inn hosts have not been shy to tell us about the kinds of information they really need to stay on top of industry issues. Our goal is to make B&B MANAGEMENT the first resource you turn to for help in achieving your goals."

B&B MANAGEMENT covers a wide range of topics including:

- ☑ **marketing ideas for all budgets**
- ☑ **accounting, insurance and legal issues**
- ☑ **money-saving ideas on supplies, materials**
- ☑ **advice from industry professionals**

For a one year subscription to B&B Management, send a check - payable to US Publications for $25.50 to:

B&B MANAGEMENT
c/o U.S. Publications
2670 Union Ave. Ext. #1132
Memphis, TN 38112

The Bed & Breakfast Collection™
Innkeeper Shopping Service

TOP QUALITY NATIONAL BRAND NAMES
FURNISHING - DECORATING - BUILDING
REMODELING - RENOVATING

40-60% Savings!

VIKING PROFESSIONAL

The World of Bob Timberlake™

Wicker by Henry Link™

Lexington®

Welcome to Cal Spas!

Opening in 1997 Online Shopping Mall

Furnish with the best names - the best quality - all at affordable prices - 40-60% savings! Now innkeepers can buy direct from over 300 top quality - top name manufacturers - and save just like large chain hotels. From bath to kitchen to patio to guest rooms - savings everywhere. Inn & Travel Club members save too - many of the products are available to members as well.

http://www.innandtravel.com

Tel: 800-431-8258   901-755-9613   Fax 901-758-0816

Bed & Breakfast
COLLECTION™

furniture & accessories for every . . .

period . . .

room . . .

Boothbay Harbor

style & taste . . .

Lexington

and price range . . . all with 40-60% savings!

SHARP®

The entire product line of Sharp, the largest manufacturer of fax machines and copiers is available to all members - innkeepers, subscribers and Inn & Travel Club members. When you're in the market for a copier or fax machine don't overlook Sharp and The Bed & Breakfast Collection for 40-60% savings on equipment, supplies and service contracts.

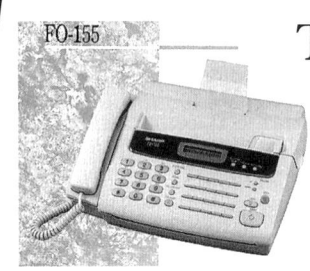

The right product for every office and need - from the smallest . . .

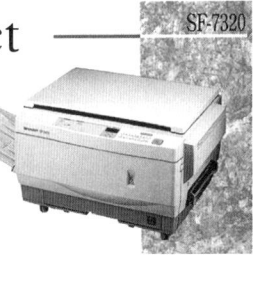

. . .to the largest

The best products - the best prices - the best value and . . . local installation set-up, training and service. Call 800-431-8258 before buying - you'll save hundreds and thousands.

Because you care about your guests -
.... we care too!

After **10 years of searching** . . . we've finally found a company with the "*best-made mattress sets*" just for your guests . . . and we're so proud - it carries the name *The Bed & Breakfast Collection*

Doctor Approved

Chiropractic are the only mattresses endorsed and recommended by the American Chiropractic Association. Over 22,000 Doctors of Chiropractic endorse and recommend Chiropractic Mattresses and Box Springs.

Chiropractic®

The only mattress endorsed and recommended by the American Chiropractic Association!

Multilastic-Plus Coils maintain their correct alignment

Conventional Springs "sag" under weight and "hammock.

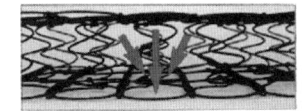

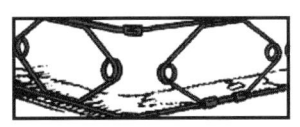

One third more sleeping surface with side support design. Guests sleep right to the edge without sag

Airlet border allows the airflow inside - allowing the mattress to "breathe"

Heavy duty upholstery materials are the best available, using double garnetted cotton batting and modern space age foam. Covered in attractive, luxurious fabric, multineedled quilted layer of polyurethane.

Air ventilation system

Double pillow top mattress

Stain resistant and flame retardant treated to pass all Federal, state and local standards.

Before ordering your next mattress set *buy the best* - call for the great innkeeper savings on this premier mattress set. And . . . special savings for Inn & Travel Club Members too!

Correct Postural Alignment

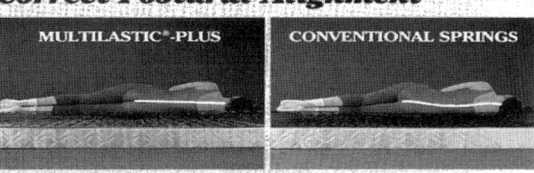

MULTILASTIC®-PLUS

CONVENTIONAL SPRINGS

Call: 800-431-8258 or 901-755-9613

THE BED & BREAKFAST COLLECTION

Inn & Travel™
BED & BREAKFAST GUEST HOUSES & INNS OF AMERICA
N E T W O R K

The first Internet site dedicated to keepers of the Inn, their guests and travel professionals. A major site providing innkeepers and travelers with the most extensive collection of services and best value. A fee-based site - for members only

Opening in 1997

Opening with the programs listed below. Other major programs are planned to further enhance the site and will be announced during the year.

http://www.innandtravel.com

Interactive B&B Search 
- 15,000 Listings
- 1500 Descriptions
- 1000+ color photos
- Multimedia
- Unlimited Searches
- Print Out

Frequent Travel Club 
- Member Travel Files
- Member Discounts
- Member Shopping

Signature Recipes 
- Interactive search Recipes from chefs at B&B Inns, Boutique Hotels and leading restaurants

e-mail service for members

Interactive Shopping Mall
- Open 24 Hours 
- Shop at home
- Major Names
- Top Quality
- High-end and import furniture, tapestries, antique reproductions, unusual and hard-to-find items for home and garden

Properties For Sale 
- Forum for sellers and buyers
- B&Bs - Inns
- Boutique Hotels
- Restaurants

Links
Links to furniture manufacturers for shopping, B&B Inns and associations

Bed & Breakfast Guest Houses & Inns of America®
THE LARGEST ASSOCIATION OF B&B INNS 15,000 MEMBERS STRONG

1986 Eleventh Year 1997

PO Box 38939 Memphis TN 38183-0929
Tel: 800-431-8258   901-755-9613   Fax 901-758-0816

Inn & Travel
FREQUENT TRAVEL CLUB

Bed & Breakfast Inns are more enjoyable now because you earn free gifts as a member of the Inn & Travel Club™ - a frequent travel club just for B&B guests!

Free Travel

Redeem points for thousands of gifts including car rentals, lodging, dining, airline trips to Europe and Caribbean cruises.

York Harbor Inn, York Harbor, ME

As a member, you earn ten points for each dollar you spend at member B&B Inns and restaurants. Points add up fast because Inn & Travel is the only frequent travel club where you earn points for meals too!

The "Fun Ships" of **Carnival**
THE MOST POPULAR CRUISE LINE IN THE WORLD!

AVIS We try harder.

Free Gifts

Home Furnishings
Oriental Rugs
Furniture
Jacuzzi

Electronics
Notebook Computers
Projection TVs
Fax Machines

Walkabout Inn, Lancaster, PA

Complete the application on the other side of this page and mail it with the annual $25.00 membership fee. Your membership card and all of the details will be mailed. Each stay and meal at your favorite member Bed & Breakfast or restaurant has just become more valuable!

Free Membership

If you are an individual (not a travel agency) and purchased this book, you will receive a one year free membership in Inn & Travel Club.™ Remove this page from your book, complete and mail the application with your receipt. Do not send a copy, the original is required for a free membership.

Inn & Travel
FREQUENT TRAVEL CLUB

Inn & Travel
FREQUENT TRAVEL CLUB

Free membership in the Inn & Travel Club -
a $25.00 value when purchasing a guidebook.
Receive free travel and gifts for home with each
stay and meal at member B&B Inns and restaurants.

Inn & Travel™ — TRAVELER MEMBER APPLICATION
FREQUENT TRAVEL CLUB

☐ Yes, I want to become a member in the Inn & Travel Club and I agree to all of the Terms and Conditions and all future changes that occur.

Type of Membership   ☐ Paid   ☐ Free (Attach original book payment receipt)

Title: Mr. ☐   Mrs. ☐   Ms. ☐   Other _____   ☐ Male   ☐ Female

First Name _____ Middle Initial ___ Last Name _____
Street Address _____
City/State/Zip Code _____
Home Phone _____   Business Phone _____

Signature _____   Date _____

Send this page or a copy with the original payment receipt or $25.00 and mail to:
Inn & Travel PO Box 38929 Memphis Tennessee 38183-0929.

We would like to know more about you! Please tell us about your travel needs so Inn & Travel can better serve you!

Percent of travel arrangements: Travel Agent _____ Self _____ ?
How many: Trips do you take a month _____ year _____ ?
           Lodging stays per month _____ year _____ ?
Percent of yearly travel for: Business _____ Leisure _____
Percent of yearly travel by:
Personal Car _____ Rental Car _____ Plane _____ Train _____ Other _____
Preferred Airlines: (1) _____ (2) _____ (3) _____
Preferred Car Rental (1) _____ (2) _____ (3) _____
Preferred Credit Card (1) _____ (2) _____ (3) _____
Lodging Choices: What percent of your lodging is spent at:
Commercial Hotels _____ Bed & Breakfast _____ Country Inns _____
Preferred Commercial Hotels: (1) _____ (2) _____ (3) _____
Desired Amenities at lodging:
  (1) _____ (2) _____ (3) _____ (4) _____ (5) _____
Most annoying aspect of lodgings:
  (1) _____ (2) _____ (3) _____ (4) _____ (5) _____

How many times do you dine out weekly _____ monthly _____ yearly _____ ?
What percent of meals do you dine out: Breakfast _____ Lunch _____ Dinner _____
What period of the week do you dine out (percent of time)
Weekday _____ Saturday _____ Sunday _____

The "Fun Ships"® of
Carnival®
THE MOST POPULAR CRUISE LINE IN THE WORLD!®

An Inn & Travel Club Partner

Choose Your Free Cruise Where Ever Carnival Sails!

Join the Inn & Travel Club Today

Mountain top to ocean front — they are all in

Inn & Travel
Publications
Still the largest reference - published since 1986

Over 15,000 B&B Inns are indexed with detailed information on over 1500 B&B Inns - in full color and sound in the electronic editions.

$29.95 *

Lights - Camera
Action - Music
Full Color

$45.00 *

CD-Rom technology means you can find any B&B Inn with any amenity or feature in 10-15 seconds . . . in color & multimedia!

To order your personal copy, or to give a copy as a gift, send your payment to
Bed & Breakfast Guest Houses & Inns of America
PO Box 38929
Memphis, Tennessee 38183-0929

For the most current listings and other travel information, visit our Web Site
http://www.innandtravel.com opening 1997.

* Retail edition, travel agent version slightly higher, add $3.00 S&H for each book.